ISBN 978-1-5285-0599-4
PIBN 10915409

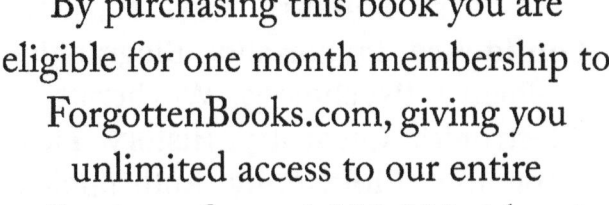

Ward 1—Precinct 1

CITY OF BOSTON

LIST OF RESIDENTS
20 YEARS OF AGE AND OVER

(NON-CITIZENS INDICATED BY ASTERISK)
(FEMALES INDICATED BY DAGGER)

AS OF

JANUARY 1, 1938

JOSEPH F. TIMILTY, } *Listing*
FREDERIC E. DOWLING, } *Board.*

CITY OF BOSTON PRINTING DEPARTMENT

Border Street

B *Peters Leon	4	seaman	65	here
C *Pandellos James	4A	shoeworker	56	“
E Bard Thomas	5	clerk	22	Chelsea
F Perez Manuel	5	longshoreman	45	here
K Vecchione Marie—†	7	housewife	23	“
L Vecchione William	7	clerk	30	“
O McCormack Hugh	10	retired	68	
P McCormack Winifred—†	10	housewife	66	“
R McKay Mary—†	10	at home	40	
S *Morrison Patrick	10	fisherman	48	“
T Flynn Helen—†	10	at home	34	
X *Amore Angelina—†	18	housekeeper	35	“
Y *Amore Theresa—†	18	at home	75	“
2				
C Calafatis Demitrius	22	seaman	49	24 Border
D Santossuosso Benjamin	22	“	30	here
E *Santossuosso Louise—†	22	housewife	55	“
F Ahearn Alfred	23	laborer	53	“
G Ahearn Rose—†	23	housewife	48	“
H Lentini Louise—†	23	“	31	“
K Lentini Samuel	23	laborer	37	“
L Rizzo Catherne—†	23	inspector	20	“
M *Rizzo Diego	23	tailor	45	
N *Rizzo Marie—†	23	housewife	45	“
O Rizzo Pauline—†	23	seamstress	22	“
P Cenoules Alexander	24	fireman	48	
R *Cenoules Peter	24	“	41	“
S *Moratis Anthony	24	“	41	“
T Salamone Angelina—†	24	housewife	41	“
U Salamone Benedetto	24	laborer	51	
V Sylvester Antonio	24	“	22	“
W Sylvester Concetta—†	24	housewife	53	“
X Sylvester Fiori	24	laborer	20	
Y Sylvester Mary—†	24	operator	36	
Z Sylvester Vincenzo	24	tailor	54	
3				
A *Pistoni Annie—†	rear 25	at home	80	
B *Tedesco Angelo	“ 25	laborer	53	
C Tedesco Margaret—†	“ 25	seamstress	20	“
D *Tedesco Nellie—†	“ 25	housewife	54	“

Page.	Letter.	Full Name.	Residence, Jan. 1, 1938.	Occupation.	Supposed Age.	Reported Residence, Jan. 1, 1937. Street and Number.

Border Street—Continued

Page.	Letter.	Full Name.	Residence, Jan. 1, 1938.	Occupation.	Supposed Age.	Reported Residence, Jan. 1, 1937. Street and Number.
	E	Carabinos Constance—†	26	housewife	29	52 Border
	F	Carabinos George	26	engineer	49	52 "
	G	Petrakes Bessie—†	26	seamstress	21	here
	H	*Petrakes Mary—†	26	housewife	55	"
	K	Petrakes Nicholas	26	cutter	23	"
	L	Petrakes Sotero	26	longshoreman	24	"
	M	*Theophiles Bessie—†	26	housewife	48	"
	N	Theophiles Georgia—†	26	stitcher	22	
	O	Theophiles James	26	laborer	53	
	P	Pullo Annie—†	27	housewife	58	"
	R	Pullo Benedict	27	retired	64	
	S	Pullo Frank	27	clerk	25	"
	T	Gobez Ronald	27	"	23	150 Gold
	U	Gobez Sarafina—†	27	housewife	25	here
	V	Magri Catherine—†	rear 27	"	24	30 London
	W	Magri Salvatore	" 27	laborer	27	30 "
	Y	Giambarresi Emelia—†	29	operator	28	here
	Z	Grugnale Ma —†	29	housewife	50	"
		4ry				
	A	Grugnale Palma—†	29	social worker	20	"
	B	*Demetrio Margaret—†	29	housewife	44	"
	C	*Demetrio Salvatore	29	laborer	52	
	D	*Teixeira Mary—†	31	housewife	46	"
	E	*Teixeira William	31	laborer	38	
	F	Cabral Joseph	31	barber	34	
	G	Cabral Loretta—†	31	housewife	28	"
	H	Napoleon Nicholas	31	fireman	45	2 Cross
	K	*Camerlengo Ralph	32	retired	82	here
	L	Masiello Rose—†	32	housekeeper	40	"
	M	Camerlengo Alberto	32	painter	39	"
	N	*Camerlengo Anna—†	32	housewife	63	"
	O	Camerlengo Anna—†	32	at home	26	
	P	Camerlengo Anthony	32	clerk	29	
	R	Camerlengo Ernesto	32	chairmaker	31	"
	S	Camerlengo Julia—†	32	at home	21	
	T	Camerlengo Mary—†	32	"	35	
	U	Camerlengo Michael	32	painter	25	
	V	Camerlengo Ella—†	32	housewife	28	"
	W	Camerlengo Henry	32	clerk	34	
	Y	Senna Adelaide—†	33A	housewife	26	"
	Z	Senna John	33A	counterman	30	"

Border Street—Continued

Page.	Letter.	Full Name.	Residence, Jan. 1, 1938.	Occupation.	Supposed Age.	Reported Residence, Jan. 1, 1937. Street and Number.
5	A	Mendosa Mary—†	33A	housewife	34	here
	B	*Mendosa Peter	33A	longshoreman	50	"
	C	Rosenthal Marcus	33A	broker	33	"
	D	Rosenthal Michael	33A	"	75	
	E	*Sacramone Daniel	35	laborer	33	
	F	*Sacramone Josephine—†	35	housewife	24	"
	G	*Saldi Alphonse	35	laborer	53	
	H	*Saldi Angelina—†	35	housewife	46	"
	K	*DeGerolamo Adelina—†	35	"	30	
	L	DeGerolamo Antonio	35	barber	37	
	M	Miller Anna—†	35	housewife	63	"
	N	Miller Arnold	35	salesman	24	"
	O	Miller Benjamin	35	"	30	
	P	Miller Hyman D	35	retired	64	
	R	Ryder Esther—†	37	housewife	32	"
	S	Ryder Leo	37	fisherman	38	"
	T	Decker Bernard	37	mechanic	33	"
	U	Decker Mary—†	37	housewife	35	"
	V	Ryder Margaret—†	37	at home	71	
	W	*Lucci John	38	bootblack	47	"
	X	Vernacchio John	38	chauffeur	23	"
	Y	*Vernacchio Sarah—†	38	housewife	23	"
	Z	Scenna Antonio	38	laborer	33	
6	A	Scenna Linda—†	38	housewife	25	"
	B	*Scenna Domenica—†	38	"	57	
	C	*Scenna Salvatore	38	laborer	58	
	D	Forrey Catherine—†	39	housewife	58	"
	E	Forrey John	39	laborer	68	
	F	Burke Helen—†	39	at home	24	
	G	*Burke John	39	longshoreman	68	"
	H	Burke John P	39	clerk	31	
	K	*Burke Sabine—†	39	housewife	60	"
	L	Burke Thomas J	39	clerk	29	
	M	Columbo Ernest	40	storekeeper	55	"
	N	*Columbo Philomena—†	40	housewife	50	"
	S	Giuliano Mary—†	43	tailoress	38	
	T	Vella Luciano	43	printer	25	
	U	*Vella Marie—†	43	housewife	59	"
	V	Bue Frank	43	cutter	23	22 London

Page.	Letter.	FULL NAME.	Residence, Jan. 1, 1938.	Occupation.	Supposed Age.	Reported Residence, Jan. 1, 1937. Street and Number.

Border Street—Continued

	W	Bue Lena—†	43	housewife	20	22 London
	X	Vella Louis	43	shoemaker	35	here
	Y	Vella Mary—†	43	housewife	24	"
7						
	A	Rizzo Michael	45	packer	37	
	B	Rizzo Rita—†	45	housewife	24	"
	C	Cataldo Harry	45	laborer	43	
	D	Cataldo Tina—†	45	housewife	33	"
	E	Rizzo Emma—†	45	at home	27	
	F	*Rizzo Genaro	45	laborer	66	
	G	Rizzo Louise—†	45	packer	28	
	H	Rizzo Mary—†	45	clerk	25	
	K	Sanchez Manuel	46	engineer	30	
	L	Sanchez Rose—†	46	housewife	39	"
	M	Sanchez Charles	46	repairman	23	"
	N	Sanchez Frank	46	mechanic	22	"
	O	Sanchez Joseph	46	shoeworker	20	"
	T	*Triantafilakis Christopher	50	cook	38	"
	U	Triantafilakis Helen—†	50	housewife	20	26 Border
	V	*Triantafilakis Nicholas	50	fireman	33	4 "
	W	*DeCicco Dionigia—†	50	housewife	40	here
	X	*DeCicco Joseph	50	plasterer	40	"
	Y	*Sacramone Antonetta—†	52	housewife	33	Italy
	Z	Sacramone Luca	52	laborer	45	40 Border
8						
	A	Cefaiolo Francesco	52	baker	25	here
	B	*Foschi Annie—†	52	at home	55	"
	C	*Molfresses Constantino	52	seaman	42	"
	D	*Arnone Guiseppe	52	barber	55	
	E	Arnone Josephine—†	52	clerk	23	
	F	*Arnone Litizia—†	52	housewife	53	"
	G	*Rispoli Angelina—†	52	at home	57	"
	M	*Hill John J	65	laborer	50	335 Maverick
	N	*Hill Olga—†	65	housewife	58	335 "
	O	Matson Alex	65	laborer	26	335 "
	P	Matson Fred	65	"	30	335 "
	R	*Wolinsky Fannie—†	65	housewife	55	here
	S	*Wolinsky Henry	65	tailor	62	"
	T	Wolinsky Ida—†	65	stitcher	29	"
	V	DeGregorio Isabella A—†	67	at home	48	150 Princeton
	W	Martin Frank	67	machinist	47	here

Page.	Letter.	Full Name.	Residence, Jan. 1, 1938.	Occupation.	Supposed Age.	Reported Residence, Jan. 1, 1937. Street and Number.

Border Street—Continued

Page.	Letter.	Full Name.	Residence, Jan. 1, 1938.	Occupation.	Supposed Age.	Reported Residence, Jan. 1, 1937. Street and Number.
	X	Martin Frank, jr	67	operator	21	here
	Y	*Martin Rose—†	67	housewife	41	"
	Z	*Amerault Edward	67	laborer	37	"
9						
	A	*Amerault Madeline—†	67	housewife	35	"
	B	Eleftherion Miltiades	69	bartender	41	"
	C	*Orfanos George	69	seaman	40	
	D	Leao Albertina—†	69	at home	22	
	E	*Leao Docelina—†	69	housewife	50	"
	F	*Leao Louis M	69	longshoreman	57	"
	G	Leao Orlando	69	cutter	21	
	H	Remer Edward	71	merchant	64	"
	K	Ventrescci Anthony	75	laborer	32	"
	L	Ventrescci Beatrice—†	75	housewife	26	"
	M	Rodriguez Anthony	75	laborer	20	
	N	Rodriguez Manuel	75	"	32	
	O	*Rodriguez Mary—†	75	housewife	55	"
	P	Livramento Carolino	75	cook	50	176 Everett
	R	*Brown Mary E—†	77	at home	65	here
	S	*Rodrigues Antonio	77	operator	36	26 Decatur
	T	*Rodrigues Mary—†	77	housewife	37	here
	U	*O'Reilly Bridget—†	77	at home	62	"
	W	Curto Antonio	79	laborer	30	"
	X	Curto Francis	79	bartender	22	"
	Y	Curto Joseph	79	retired	65	
	Z	Curto Rose—†	79	housewife	51	"
10						
	A	Curto Rose—†	79	at home	41	"
	B	Berardi Joseph	79	porter	54	141 Everett
	X	Willis Andrew	rear 148	laborer	48	here
11						
	L	Pendleton Alice E—†	172	student	20	
	M	Pendleton Clarissa—†	172	housewife	46	"
	N	Pendleton Helen E—†	172	waitress	23	
	O	Pendleton Hollis	172	longshoreman	48	"
	P	Morrison Herbert	172	laborer	21	372 Border
	R	Preble Allen	172	"	57	372 "
	S	Preble Elizabeth—†	172	housewife	44	372 "

Page.	Letter.	FULL NAME.	Residence, Jan. 1, 1938.	Occupation.	Supposed Age.	Reported Residence, Jan. 1, 1937. Street and Number.
12						

Cross Street

	X	Angelidis Peter	2	seaman	48	here
	Y	*Francesco Christopher	2	retired	66	"
	Z	*Francesco Lena—†	2	housewife	38	"
13						
	A	*Papafoti Giacomo	2	seaman	30	
	B	*Raymandes John	2	"	58	"
	C	*Holland Abigail—†	4	housewife	65	"
	D	Holland Martin	4	laborer	63	
	F	*Pasqualetto Alfred	5	chauffeur	30	"
	G	Pasqualetto Viola—†	5	housewife	23	"
	H	*Pasqualetto Gilbert	5	clerk	28	"
	K	Pasqualetto Mary—†	5	housewife	22	215 Princeton
	L	*Landry Daniel	6	fisherman	49	here
	M	*McNiel James	6	laborer	60	"
	N	Poirier Edward	6	fisherman	59	Rhode Island
	O	*DePola Joseph	6	rigger	44	here
	P	Gaeta Anthony M	6	carpenter	53	"
	R	Gaeta Lucy—†	6	housewife	44	"
	S	*Samarco Antonio	7	retired	70	
	T	Pilcher Theresa—†	7	housekeeper	36	"
	U	Pistone Gaetano	8	laborer	35	"
	V	*Pistone Leboria—†	8	housewife	44	"
	W	Pistone Vincenzo	8	pedler	54	
	X	*Cameron Charles	9	clerk	40	
	Y	*Cameron Rose—†	9	housewife	36	"
	Z	*Incrovato Anna—†	9	"	64	
14						
	A	*Kanali Sylvester	9	operator	40	"
	B	Aliguo Anna—†	10	stitcher	22	
	C	Aliguo Anthony	10	laborer	24	
	D	*Aliguo Concheta—†	10	housewife	36	"
	E	Aliguo Richard	10	laborer	25	
	F	*Aliguo Salvatore	10	foreman	55	
	G	Beck Josephine—†	11	housewife	47	"
	H	Beck William P	11	salesman	48	"
	K	Bradley Annette—†	11	housewife	24	"
	L	Bradley Walter	11	mechanic	23	"
	N	Alabiso Anthony	12	barber	52	
	O	*Alabiso Sarah—†	12	housewife	43	"

Decatur Street

P	White Bernice—†	20	housewife	26 here
R	White James V	20	painter	29 "
S	Sbordoni Madeline—†	20	housewife	29 "
T	Sbordoni Ralph	20	laborer	29
U*	Sbordoni Camella—†	20	housewife	58 "
V	Sbordoni Giuseppe	20	laborer	64
W*	Zagarella Liboria—†	22	housewife	35 "
X	Zagarella Rocco	22	laborer	46
Y	Matterazzo Emilio	22	"	25 "
Z*	Matterazzo Lenzi—†	22	housewife	54 "
	15			
A*	Matterazzo Pasquale	22	laborer	57
B	Greco Esther—†	22	operator	23
C	Greco Joseph	22	rubberworker	25 "
D	Marianos John	24	painter	43
E	Perry Clara—†	24	housekeeper	44 "
F	Dell'Orfano Michael	24	laborer	61 "
G	Dell'Orfano Anthony	24	serviceman	27 "
H	Dell'Orfano Mary—†	24	housewife	26 "
K	Mannetta Filomena—†	25	"	30
L	Mannetta Thomas	25	painter	42
M*	Fabiano Antonio	25	candyworker	38 "
N	Fabiano Mary—†	25	housewife	39 "
O	Filippone Leo	25	laborer	39
P	Filippone Mary—†	25	housewife	29 "
R	Palermo Concetta—†	26	"	22 141 Havre
S	Palermo Domenic	26	baker	24 141 "
T*	LaConte Filamena—†	26	housewife	24 12 Cottage
U	LaConte Joseph	26	laborer	26 12 "
V	Indelicato George	26	"	28 242 Paris
W	Indelicato Olympia—†	26	housewife	26 242 "
X*	Ingale Michelina—†	27	"	30 here
Y*	Ingale Philip	27	laborer	40 "
Z	Cimmino Louis	27	tailor	38 "
	16			
A	Cimmino Rose—†	27	housewife	30 "
B*	Tirone Angelina—†	27	"	48
C*	Tirone Paul	27	laborer	53 "
D*	DiClerico Cesira—†	28	housewife	40 47 Maverick sq
E	DiClerico Felice	28	woodcarver	64 47 "
F	Joseph Francis	28	rigger	28 here

Page.	Letter.	Full Name.	Residence, Jan. 1, 1938.	Occupation.	Supposed Age.	Reported Residence, Jan. 1, 1937. Street and Number.

Decatur Street—Continued

Page.	Letter.	Full Name.	Residence, Jan. 1, 1938.	Occupation.	Supposed Age.	Reported Residence, Jan. 1, 1937. Street and Number.
	G	Joseph Lillian—†	28	housewife	26	here
	H	*Rossano Catherine—†	28	"	47	"
	K	*Rossano Thomas	28	laborer	47	"
	L	Penta George	29	"	25	
	M	Penta John	29	retired	72	
	N	Penta Joseph	29	machinist	32	"
	O	Penta Edward	29	lithographer	20	"
	P	Penta Margaret—†	29	housekeeper	22	"
	R	Jannini Ella—†	29	operator	22	"
	S	Jannini Joseph	29	laborer	50	
	T	Jannini Nellie—†	29	housewife	45	"
	V	*Papandria Camella—†	30	"	32	
	W	*Papandria John	30	laborer	62	
	X	*Amato Phyllis—†	30	housekeeper	33	"
	Y	*Camuso Jennie—†	30	"	63	79 Everett
	Z	Esposito Anna—†	30	housewife	26	79 "
17						
	A	Esposito Nicolas	30	laborer	26	79 "
	B	Nash Lillian—.†	32	housewife	46	233 London
	C	Nash Walter	32	laborer	52	233 "
	D	*Pedro Manuel	32	seaman	32	233 "
	E	*Allescia Angela—†	32	housewife	48	here
	F	*Allescia Peter	32	operator	56	"
	G	O'Donnell Arthur J	32	polisher	52	"
	H	O'Donnell Mary—†	32	housewife	42	"
	K	Marley Annie—†	34	"	73	
	L	Marley Frederick	34	B F D	33	
	M	Marley Harry J	34	policeman	44	"
	N	Marley Walter	34	clerk	30	
	O	Marley Agnes—†	34	typist	27	
	P	Marley Albert	34	salesman	35	"
	T	Bogmanno Frank	36	storekeeper	52	"
	U	Bogmanno Rose—†	36	housewife	46	"
	V	Saporito Fannie—†	36	"	23	
	W	Saporito Rocco	36	mechanic	26	"
	X	*Pizzuro Frances—†	36	housewife	46	"
	Y	*Pizzuro Vito	36	laborer	60	
	Z	*Venuti Josephine—†	37	housewife	24	"
18						
	A	*Venuti Vito	37	carpenter	26	"
	B	*DiDeo Angelo	37	laborer	69	

Decatur Street—Continued

C	*DiDeo Josephine—†	37	housewife	58	here
D	Indelicato Rosario—†	37	"	21	84 Prince
E	Indelicato Salvatore	37	butcher	21	304 North
F	Gallucci Phyllis—†	37	housewife	23	174 Havre
G	Gallucci Victor	37	machinist	23	174 "
H	*Basillio Concetta—†	37	housewife	21	15 "
K	Basillio Gregory	37	painter	21	90 Chelsea
L	Marciello Mary—†	37	housewife	30	here
M	Marciello Philip	37	salesman	34	"
O	*Fernandez Adolph	38	fireman	31	"
P	Fernandez Anita—†	38	housewife	22	"
R	Smith Laurence	38	laborer	21	34 Paris
S	*Turco Rose—†	38	housewife	35	here
T	Turco Salvatore	38	laborer	44	"
V	*Falzone Filippa—†	39	housewife	39	"
W	*Falzone Michael	39	laborer	40	"
X	*Cammarata Catherine—†	39	housewife	41	57 Chelsea
Y	*Cammarata Michael	39	laborer	53	57 "
	19				
A	DeGloria Joseph	40	"	27	here
B	DeGloria Mildred—†	40	housewife	28	"
C	Silla Carmine	40	tailor	38	"
D	Silla Julia—†	40	housewife	33	"
E	Sbraccia Grace—†	40	"	21	
F	Sbraccia Louis	40	painter	25	
G	Mauricci Salvatore	41	tailor	34	
H	Mauricci Vincenza—†	41	housewife	29	"
K	Correnti Joseph	41	barber	44	
L	Correnti Mary—†	41	housewife	35	"
M	Zuffante Jennie—†	41	"	53	
N	Zuffante Saverio	41	laborer	26	
P	Cavaretta Mary—†	43	housewife	43	"
R	Cavaretta Vincent	43	storekeeper	44	"
S	Cardosi Edith—†	43	housewife	45	"
T	Cardosi Joseph	43	roofer	46	
W	*Casparone Daniel	45	laborer	35	
X	*Casperone Louise—†	45	housewife	27	"
Y	*Gutro Elizabeth—†	45	"	53	

Page.	Letter.	Full Name.	Residence, Jan. 1, 1938.	Occupation.	Supposed Age.	Reported Residence, Jan. 1, 1937. Street and Number.

Havre Court

	z	Lima Manuel R	8	cook	37	New Bedford
20						
	A	*Santos Frank F	8	fireman	38	here
	B	*Vicenti Amarisia L	8	laborer	49	"
	C	Doherty Edward J	10	retired	69	"
	D	Garvey Joseph	10	laborer	35	134 Sumner
	E	Garvey Margaret—†	10	housewife	35	134 "
	F	*Venniro Alfonsa—†	10	"	70	here

Havre Street

	G	Katrimadas Vasielos	2	fireman	38	4 Border
	H	McClellan Rosanna—†	2	housekeeper	35	82 Brooks
	K	Tsolakis Loukas	2	fisherman	59	82 "
	L	Merner John	2	laborer	41	here
	M	*Merner Josephine—†	2	housewife	34	"
	N	Bergin Daniel J	3	salesman	70	"
	O	Hill Edna—†	3	housekeeper	26	"
	P	Riley John J	3	fisherman	20	95 Maverick
	R	Donovan Cornelius J	3	contractor	51	here
	S	Donovan Cornelius J, jr	3	clerk	30	"
	T	Donovan John J	3	proprietor	53	"
	U	Donovan Margaret C—†	3	housewife	84	"
	V	McCarthy Patrick H	3	retired	73	
	W	Taylor Philomena—†	4	housewife	75	"
	X	*Cook Harry I	4	watchman	63	"
	Y	Cook Helen—†	4	housewife	60	"
	Z	Talieri Anna—†	4	"	59	Revere
21						
	A	Talieri Anthony	4	laborer	29	
	B	Talieri Josephine—†	4	clerk	21	"
	C	DeZenzo Anthony	5	carpenter	25	69 Frankfort
	D	DeZenzo Mary—†	5	housewife	20	69 "
	E	Coutinho Emily—†	5	"	55	here
	F	Coutinho Manuel	5	seaman	54	"
	G	Coutinho Manuel N	5	clerk	24	"
	H	Silva Alice—†	5	housewife	38	"
	K	Silva Anselino	5	engineer	36	
	L	Foster Marie—†	6	waitress	24	
	M	Monroe Effie—†	6	housewife	44	"
	N	*Monroe Harry	6	laborer	48	

Havre Street—Continued

O	Hassen Joseph	6	fireman	45	here
P	Hassen Mary—†	6	housewife	54	“
R	Farrell Mary—†	7	housekeeper	37	4 Havre
S*	Marotta Salvatore	7	shoemaker	52	4 “
T*	Telespro Carmine	7	retired	59	here
U	Telespro Michael	7	plumber	24	“
V	Fernandes Ethel—†	8	housewife	33	“
W*	Fernandes Joseph	8	fireman	45	“
X*	Moe Einer	9	tinsmith	32	Canada
Y*	Moe Ellen—†	9	housewife	25	“
Z	McArdle Albert H	9	policeman	41	here
	22				
A	McArdle Margaret A—†	9	housewife	38	“
B*	Costello Joseph	10	longshoreman	65	“
C*	Hagen Louis	10	chauffeur	49	“
D	Holmberg Emma—†	10	housekeeper	64	“
E*	Matterson Oscar	10	plasterer	37	“
F*	Nelson Arman	10	longshoreman	63	“
G*	Sanderson Paul	10	fisherman	45	“
H	DeFreitas John J	11	janitor	50	
K	DeFreitas Julia—†	11	housewife	40	“
L	Furlong James P	11	longshoreman	56	“
M*	Villa Joseph	11	fireman	52	
N*	Villa Mary—†	11	housewife	53	“
O	Villa Raymond	11	fishhandler	22	“
P	Austin Francis	12	retired	75	
S	Matthews George	12	laborer	50	
T	McCarthy Florence	12	retired	75	
U	Minon Mary—†	12	housekeeper	65	“
V	Rice John J	12	retired	73	“
W	Roach Edward J	12	fisherman	40	“
X	Salfiros Nicholas	12	fireman	65	“
Y*	Sforza Christina—†	13	housewife	57	“
Z*	Sforza John	13	retired	65	
	23				
A	Lembo Adeline—†	13	housewife	29	“
B	Lembo Camella—†	13	seamstress	24	“
C*	Lembo Filomena—†	13	housewife	56	“
D*	Lembo Genaro	13	shipper	28	
E	Lembo Michael	13	dairyman	57	“
F	Lembo Nancy—†	13	dressmaker	21	“

Page.	Letter.	FULL NAME.	Residence, Jan. 1, 1938.	Occupation.	Supposed Age.	Reported Residence, Jan. 1, 1937. Street and Number.

Havre Street—Continued

	G	Lozine Naomi—†	13	housekeeper	62	here
	H	Mauriello Helen—†	14	"	21	3 Maverick
	K	*Russo Joseph	14	painter	30	59A Fifth
	L	Russo Minnie—†	14	housewife	29	59A "
	M	Mazzola Charles	14	laborer	47	here
	N	Mazzola Lillian—†	14	housewife	36	"
	O	Scandura John	14	laborer	54	"
	P	*Scandura Mary—†	14	housewife	44	"
	R	*Costanza John	15	laborer	54	
	S	*Costanza Vincenzia—†	15	housewife	54	"
	T	*Siciliano Filippa—†	15	"	49	
	U	*Siciliano Rocco	15	laborer	58	
	V	Carnevale Joseph	15	"	40	
	W	Carnevale Madeline—†	15	housewife	30	"
	X	*Mazzolla Philemena—†	16	housekeeper	69	"
	Y	*Vardaro Angelina—†	16	housewife	44	192 Bremen
	Z	Vardaro Liberato	16	laborer	46	192 "
24						
	A	*Miccichi Jennie—†	16	housewife	54	here
	B	*Miccichi Joseph	16	laborer	54	"
	C	Horn Arthur F	17	longshoreman	32	"
	D	Horn Isabel—†	17	housewife	31	"
	E	*Mauriello Angelina—†	17	"	50	
	F	Mauriello Concetta—†	17	stitcher	21	
	G	*Mauriello Joseph	17	laborer	48	"
	H	Mauriello Nicolas	17	operator	50	Billerica
	K	Belmonte Alexander	17	packer	21	here
	L	*Belmonte Mary—†	17	housewife	52	"
	M	Belmonte Phyllis—†	17	housekeeper	28	"
	N	Belmonte Richard	17	lithographer	32	"
	O	Iacono Frank	17	machinist	21	"
	P	*Iacono Josephine—†	17	housekeeper	56	"
	R	Iacono Pia E—†	17	stenographer	23	"
	S	*Olivolo Alphonso	18	laborer	45	"
	T	Olivolo Antoinette—†	18	operator	20	
	U	*Olivolo Carmella—†	18	housewife	50	"
	V	Galante Guy	18	laborer	47	
	W	*Galante Josephine—†	18	housewife	48	"
	X	Anderson Edith—†	18	"	35	
	Y	Anderson Sidney	18	longshoreman	37	"
	Z	Montesano Josephine—†	19	housekeeper	25	"

Page.	Letter.	Full Name.	Residence, Jan. 1, 1938.	Occupation.	Supposed Age.	Reported Residence, Jan. 1, 1937. Street and Number.
25		**Havre Street**—Continued				
	A	Candello Alphonso	19	operator	28	162 F
	B	*Candello Luigi	19	retired	67	162 "
	C	Belmonte Angeline—†	19	housewife	28	here
	D	Belmonte John	19	pressman	32	"
	E	*Constantino Angelina—†	19	housekeeper	56	42 Frankfort
	F	Constantino Antoinetta—†	19	stenographer	20	42 "
	G	Constantino Mary—†	19	housekeeper	22	42 "
	H	*Rose Domingo—†	20	housewife	55	here
	K	*Rose Manuel	20	laborer	66	"
	L	Pirrello Joseph	20	"	45	16 Havre
	M	*Pirrello Josephine—†	20	housewife	36	16 "
	N	*Pirrello Mary—†	20	"	83	16 "
	O	Rodrigues George P	20	machinist	20	132 Sumner
	P	*Rodrigues Joseph	20	laborer	55	132 "
	R	Rodrigues Joseph	20	machinist	27	132 "
	S	*Rodrigues Mary—†	20	housewife	53	132 "
	T	Meaney Edward	21	laborer	43	here
	V	*Ward William	23	longshoreman	65	"
	W	Anderson Anton	23	rigger	62	"
	X	Anderson Edith—†	23	at home	24	
	Y	*Anderson Olga—†	23	housewife	51	"
	Z	*Walker John	23	chef	63	
26						
	A	Romano Anthony	24	chauffeur	33	"
	B	Romano Mary—†	24	housewife	29	"
	C	Miana Louis	24	laborer	41	
	D	Miana Mary—†	24	housewife	39	"
	E	Rosata John	24	machinist	29	"
	F	Rosata Rose—†	24	housewife	28	"
	G	*Maffei Maria—†	26	"	63	
	H	*Maffei Michael	26	retired	75	
	K	Martorano Sylvia—†	26	at home	22	
	L	Alferi Anna—†	26	housewife	33	"
	M	Alferi Guy	26	laborer	45	"
	N	McKinnon Catherine—†	27	housewife	52	41 Liverpool
	O	McKinnon Lena—†	27	housekeeper	28	41 "
	P	McKinnon Stephen	27	fisherman	51	41 "
	R	Pina Camella—†	27	housekeeper	51	here
	S	Pina Jennie—†	27	"	21	"
	T	Silva John	27	seaman	31	"

Page.	Letter.	Full Name.	Residence, Jan. 1, 1938.	Occupation.	Supposed Age.	Reported Residence, Jan. 1, 1937. Street and Number.

Havre Street—Continued

Page.	Letter.	Full Name.	Residence, Jan. 1, 1938.	Occupation.	Supposed Age.	Reported Residence, Jan. 1, 1937. Street and Number.
	U	*Duarte Mary—†	27	housekeeper	42	Wareham
	V	*Lemba Catherine—†	28	housewife	58	here
	W	*Lemba Michael	28	laborer	24	"
	X	Lemba Pietro	28	"	58	"
	Y	Melanson Marie—†	28	housewife	31	34 Paris
	Z	Melanson Wallace D	28	laborer	22	34 "
27						
	A	Pettella Joseph	28	machinist	42	here
	B	*Pettella Marion—†	28	housewife	37	"
	C	*Gouthro Ellen—†	29	housekeeper	72	"
	D	*Barros Antone	29	operator	37	"
	E	Barros Linda—†	29	housewife	27	"
	F	D'Ortona Mary—†	30	"	25	27 Havre
	G	D'Ortona Nicholas	30	operator	28	27 "
	H	*Chiodi Anthony	30	fisherman	35	here
	K	*Chiodi Rose—†	30	housewife	32	"
	L	Canciamelo John	30	retired	69	"
	M	Brogna Albert	31	laborer	25	
	N	Brogna Angela—†	31	housewife	22	"
	O	Spattaro Filomena—†	31	"	23	160 Maverick
	P	Spattaro Salvatore	31	cutter	23	160 "
	R	Giangregorio Angelo	31	chauffeur	26	here
	S	*Giangregorio Antoinetta–†	31	housewife	56	"
	T	*Giangregorio Antonio	31	retired	77	"
	U	Giangregorio Edith—†	31	operator	20	
	V	Giangregorio Joseph	31	laborer	25	
	W	Giangregorio Louis	31	mechanic	35	"
	X	*Scoffio Alfonzo	32	retired	74	
	Y	*Scoffio Angelina—†	32	housewife	68	"
	Z	*Dastole Carman	32	shoemaker	37	"
28						
	A	Dastole Carrie—†	32	housewife	37	"
	B	Amico Catherine—†	32	stitcher	28	
	C	*Amico Grace—†	32	housewife	50	"
	D	Amico Peter	32	operator	23	"
	F	Meola Anthony	33	pedler	23	
	G	Meola John	33	laborer	65	
	H	*Meola Lucy—†	33	housewife	53	"
	K	Giaimo John	33	cutter	23	261 North
	L	Giaimo Phyllis—†	33	housewife	21	261 "
	M	*Mollica Antonio	33	laborer	67	here

Page.	Letter.	Full Name.	Residence, Jan. 1, 1938.	Occupation.	Supposed Age.	Reported Residence, Jan. 1, 1937. Street and Number.

Havre Street—Continued

	N	Coffey Thomas F, jr	34	investigator	43	here
	O	Locke William J	34	salesman	41	"
	P	Coffey Edna A—†	34	housewife	27	"
	R	Coffey Joseph L	34	chauffeur	27	"
	S	Coffey Mary A—†	34	housewife	65	"
	T	Coffey Thomas F	34	agent	67	
	U	*Ardagna Gandolfa—†	35	housewife	32	"
	V	*Ardagna William	35	laborer	37	
	W	Ferrario Aldo	35	operator	23	
	X	Ferrario Rose M—†	35	housewife	22	"
	Y	Frasca Charles	35	merchant	31	"
	Z	*Frasca Grace—†	35	housekeeper	54	"
29						
	A	Frasca Joseph	35	laborer	20	
	B	Frasca Patrick	35	"	24	
	C	Rotunda Blanche—†	36	housewife	48	"
	D	Rotunda Carmine	36	chauffeur	46	"
	E	*Rotunda Rose—†	36	housekeeper	74	"
	F	Verphosky Albert	36	laborer	24	"
	G	Verphosky John	36	clerk	22	
	H	Verphosky Michael	36	"	22	
	K	*Verphosky Victor	36	tailor	54	
	L	Bellone Gaetano	37	operator	23	
	M	Bellone Ida—†	37	housewife	23	"
	N	DiNatale Jennie—†	37	stitcher	26	
	O	*DiNatale Josephine—†	37	housewife	55	"
	P	DiNatale Salvatore	37	barber	21	
	R	*DiNatale Vincenzo	37	"	61	
	S	*Maceiras Felicia—†	37	housewife	43	"
	T	Maceiras Juan	37	engineer	42	
	U	*Noguerol Joseph	37	carpenter	44	"
	V	*DiNatale Phyllis—†	38	housekeeper	62	"
	W	Labriola Mary—†	38	housewife	32	"
	X	Labriola Ralph	38	hairdresser	38	"
	Y	Amico Albert	38	tailor	27	33 London
	Z	Amico Rose—†	38	housewife	24	33 "
30						
	A	Trocchio Gilda—†	38	packer	29	here
	B	Trocchio Lydia—†	38	"	31	"
	C	Trocchio Nicholas	38	tailor	58	"
	D	Merchand Peter	38	retired	75	84 Paris

Page.	Letter.	Full Name.	Residence, Jan. 1, 1938.	Occupation.	Supposed Age.	Reported Residence, Jan. 1, 1937. Street and Number.

Havre Street—Continued

Page.	Letter.	Full Name.	Residence, Jan. 1, 1938.	Occupation.	Supposed Age.	Reported Residence, Jan. 1, 1937. Street and Number.
	E	Moscillo Joseph	51	laborer	30	here
	F	Moscillo Mary—†	51	housewife	55	"
	G	Maloney James	51	fisherman	45	"
	H	Maloney Sadie—†	51	housewife	48	"
	K	Powers James A	51	laborer	52	65 Havre
	L	Powers James J	51	"	22	65 "
	M	Powers Loretta E—†	51	operator	26	65 "
	N	Powers Willam E	51	chauffeur	27	65 "
	O	Brogna Camella—†	53	housewife	22	Revere
	P	Brogna Domenic	53	laborer	26	"
	R	Chieppo Angelo	53	plumber	20	here
	S	Chieppo Pasquale	53	shoemaker	50	"
	T	*Chieppo Raffiolo—†	53	housewife	43	"
	U	Chieppo Anthony	53	laborer	24	"
	V	Chieppo Catherine—†	53	operator	23	"
	Y	Barry Helen M—†	56	teacher	28	Beverly
	Z	Brawley Catherine—†	56	"	43	Worcester
31						
	A	Caron Anna—†	56	houseworker	54	"
	B	Collins Gertrude—†	56	teacher	50	207 E
	C	Connelly Margaret—†	56	"	52	here
	D	Devlin Margaret—†	56	"	54	"
	E	Donovan Mary—†	56	"	29	Worcester
	F	Feeney Elizabeth—†	56	houseworker	46	"
	G	Garlow Sarah F—†	56	teacher	34	"
	H	Hanrahan Mary—†	56	supervisor	76	here
	K	Harney Evelyn—†	56	houseworker	78	"
	L	Hayes Kathleen—†	56	teacher	33	Worcester
	M	Heukamp Edith—†	56	"	37	"
	N	Martikke Agnes—†	56	"	26	"
	O	Mawn M Gertrude—†	56	"	47	here
	P	McDonald Florence—†	56	"	27	"
	R	McGrath Teresa M—†	56	"	22	2214 Dor av
	S	O'Brien Teresa—†	56	"	31	here
	T	*O'Donnell Catherine—†	56	houseworker	40	Worcester
	U	O'Donnell Ellen G—†	56	teacher	39	Peabody
	V	Quigley Mary C—†	56	"	23	Andover
	W	Quinn Helen—†	56	"	28	Worcester
	X	Reilly Mary R—†	56		28	"
	Y	Timiny Mary—†	56		54	"
	Z	Walsh Mary M—†	56	"	37	here

Page.	Letter.	Full Name.	Residence, Jan. 1, 1938.	Occupation.	Supposed Age.	Reported Residence, Jan. 1, 1937. Street and Number.
32		**Havre Street**—Continued				
	A	Webb Catherine—†	56	teacher	23	Worcester
	B	Zielinger Louise—†	56	houseworker	70	"
	C	Brown Alice—†	57	operator	29	here
	D	Brown Catherine—†	57	forewoman	41	"
	E	Brown Nonie—†	57	at home	32	"
	F	DeSpirito Edward	57	laborer	21	
	G	DeSpirito Mary—†	57	housewife	40	"
	H	Powers Grace—†	57	stenographer	34	"
	K	Powers John	57	policeman	43	"
	L	Powers Margaret—†	57	housewife	74	"
	M	Powers Patrick	57	salesman	39	"
	N	*O'Brien Catherine—†	57	housewife	49	370 Sumner
	O	O'Brien Mary—†	57	cutter	21	370 "
	P	*O'Brien Patrick	57	laborer	51	370 "
	R	Dooley Helen M—†	59	operator	35	here
	S	Dooley John J	59	retired	68	"
	T	Dooley John J, jr	59	laborer	38	"
	U	Dooley Mary—†	59	housewife	67	"
	V	Dooley Michael F	59	laborer	22	
	W	Giordano Charles	61	"	47	
	X	Giordano Fannie—†	61	housewife	38	"
	Y	Giordano Joseph	61	laborer	20	
	Z	Giordano Patrick	61	"	21	
33						
	A	Giordano Theresa—†	61	at home	21	
	B	DiGregorio Andrew	61	operator	26	"
	C	DiGregorio Angelo	61	"	30	
	D	DiGregorio Josephine—†	61	stenographer	20	"
	E	DiGregorio Paul	61	operator	57	"
	F	DiGregorio Pauline—†	61	at home	26	
	G	*Murphy Anna—†	63	operator	45	"
	H	*Murphy Bridget—†	63	"	47	
	K	Murphy Elizabeth—†	63	cutter	50	
	L	*Petrillo Henry	63	tailor	33	
	M	Petrillo Mary—†	63	housewife	36	"
	N	Rapa Joseph	63	operator	55	
	O	Ring Lillian—†	65	teacher	40	
	P	Ring Margaret—†	65	clerk	50	
	R	Ring Thomas	65	laborer	35	
	T	DiNubla Mary—†	65	housewife	51	"

Page.	Letter.	Full Name.	Residence, Jan. 1, 1938.	Occupation.	Supposed Age.	Reported Residence, Jan. 1, 1937. Street and Number.

Havre Street—Continued

	U	DiNubla Rocco	65	baker	50	here
	V	*Hayes Mary A—†	67	housewife	45	"
	W	*Hayes William	67	fisherman	60	"
	X	Roccia Josephine—†	67	housewife	34	"
	Y	Roccia Louis	67	laborer	46	
	Z	Gregory Anthony	67	operator	39	
34						
	A	Gregory Rose—†	67	housewife	32	"
	B	Capone Carman	69	laborer	31	
	C	Capone Frances—†	69	housewife	32	"
	D	Paone Alexander	69	jeweler	41	
	E	Paone Ella—†	69	housewife	40	"
	F	Vecchio Constanzo	69	cutter	48	
	G	Vecchio Filomena—†	69	housewife	36	"
	H	Chianca Rose—†	76	"	20	1 Hooten ct
	K	Chianca Vincent	76	laborer	24	1 "
	L	*Luiso Angelina—†	76	housewife	47	52 Cooper
	M	Luiso Angelo	76	laborer	56	52 "
	N	Canzana Joseph	76	printer	23	here
	O	*Pisano Anna—†	76	housewife	57	"
	P	Volta Joseph	78	operator	30	"
	R	Volta Rose—†	78	housewife	27	"
	S	Mellio Carman	78	baker	26	
	T	Mellio Merrennia—†	78	housewife	28	"
	U	Volta Anna—†	78	operator	21	"
	V	Volta Anthony	78	chauffeur	34	"
	W	Volta Carman	78	operator	35	"
	X	Volta Cosmo	78	laborer	26	
	Y	Volta Jennie—†	78	operator	24	"
	Z	Volta Minnie—†	78	housewife	34	"
35						
	A	Amarosi Lucy—†	80	"	27	129 Chelsea
	B	Amarosi Pasquale	80	barber	28	129 "
	C	Casaletto Frank	80	chauffeur	32	here
	D	Casaletto Lena—†	80	housewife	28	"
	E	*Amarosi Angelo	80	tailor	49	"
	F	Amarosi Rose—†	80	housewife	49	"
	G	*Reynolds Catherine—†	82	"	25	108 Brooks
	H	*Reynolds Thomas	82	fisherman	31	108 "
	K	*DePado Frances—†	82	housewife	53	here
	L	DePaolo Joseph	82	laborer	22	"

Page.	Letter.	Full Name.	Residence, Jan. 1, 1938.	Occupation.	Supposed Age.	Reported Residence, Jan. 1, 1937. Street and Number.

Havre Street—Continued

Page.	Letter.	Full Name.	Residence, Jan. 1, 1938.	Occupation.	Supposed Age.	Reported Residence, Jan. 1, 1937. Street and Number.
	M	DePaolo Michael	82	laborer	55	here
	N	Ardagna Bartholomew	82	packer	40	"
	O	Ardagna Camilla—†	82	housewife	24	"
	P	Spagnolo Rosara	84	laborer	45	
	R	*Spagnolo Theresa—†	84	housewife	33	"
	S	*Terilli Dora—†	84	"	55	
	U	Terilli Frances—†	84	stenographer	23	"
	T	Terilli Raymond	84	chauffeur	52	"
	V	Terilli John	84	"	22	
	W	Faretra Pasquale	86	carpenter	55	"
	X	Rotonda Rose—†	86	housewife	37	"
	Y	Rotonda Roy	86	baker	38	"
	Z	Stella Frances—†	86	dressmaker	23	"
36						
	A	Stella Grace—†	86	clerk	28	"
	B	*Stella Joseph	86	retired	70	197 Salem
	C	*Stella Josephine—†	86	housewife	58	197 "
	D	Faretra Caroline—†	88	seamstress	23	here
	E	Faretra Joseph	88	laborer	26	"
	F	*Faretra Mary—†	88	housewife	50	"
	G	DiDonata Joseph	88	laborer	40	
	H	*DiDonata Mary—†	88	housewife	31	"
	K	Tennero Daniel	88	operator	27	
	L	*Tennero Lena—†	88	housewife	23	"
	M	Cimino Carmella—†	90	"	25	
	N	Cimino Carmine	90	packer	25	
	O	LaMonica Frances—†	90	operator	27	
	P	LaMonica James	90	clerk	32	
	R	LaMonica Josephine—†	90	operator	27	
	S	LaMonica Lucy—†	90	clerk	21	
	T	LaMonica Micalena—†	90	operator	23	
	U	*LaMonica Philip	90	retired	70	"
	V	*LaMonica Rose—†	90	housewife	50	"
	W	*LaMonica Gaetano	90	laborer	64	
	X	LaMonica Jennie—†	90	at home	20	
	Y	LaMonica Lena—†	90	operator	24	
	Z	LaMonica Vincent	90	bellboy	22	
37						
	A	*Marciello Emilia—†	94	housewife	52	"
	B	*Marciello Thomas	94	laborer	57	

Page.	Letter.	Full Name.	Residence, Jan. 1, 1938.	Occupation.	Supposed Age.	Reported Residence, Jan. 1, 1937. Street and Number.

Liverpool Avenue

	D	*Farriezo Pasquale	2	laborer	48	here
	E	*Moreira Louis	2	longshoreman	40	"
	F	*Moreira Mary—†	2	housewife	43	"
	G	*McCormack William H	2	laborer	76	"
	H	Souza John	2	student	25	Lowell
	K	Souza Joseph	2	operator	30	here
	L	*Arinico Mary—†	3	housewife	71	404 Walk Hill
	M	*Coranado Frances—†	3	"	59	here
	N	*Farona Josephine—†	3	at home	70	60 Liverpool
	O	*Giovanniello Amelio	4	student	22	here
	P	*Giovanniello Mary—†	4	housewife	43	"
	R	*Giovanniello Rocco	4	laborer	49	"
	S	*Ciulla Philip	4	"	46	6 Wilbur ct
	T	*Caputa John	4	"	40	New York
	U	Stearns Benjamin	6	"	70	here
	V	Robinson Catherine—†	6	housewife	24	"
	W	Robinson John H	6	operator	31	"

Liverpool Street

	X	Holt Marie—†	6	waitress	25	134 Sumner
	Y	Meola Helen—†	6	housekeeper	21	25 Morton
	Z	Cook Florence—†	6	houseworker	22	here
38						
	A	Worth Gladys—†	6	trimmer	22	"
	B	*Montori Mathilda—†	6	housewife	49	7 Cottage
	C	*Montori Joseph	6	baker	62	7 "
	D	*Arpino Antonio	7	plumber	49	15 New
	E	*Arpino Lucy—†	7	housewife	42	15 "
	F	Russo Adello	8	florist	27	58 Bremen
	G	Russo Genevieve—†	8	housewife	26	236 Princeton
	H	Morley Nancy—†	8	"	22	6 Havre
	K	Morley Nicolas	8	laborer	27	6 "
	L	Dimino Lillian—†	8	housewife	36	8 Moon
	M	*Dimino Salvatore	8	fisherman	47	8 "
	N	*Crosby Gertrude—†	9	housewife	39	262 Lexington
	O	*Crosby Harold W	9	cutter	41	262 "
	P	Repucci Adeline—†	10	housewife	37	here
	R	Repucci Anna—†	10	"	32	"
	S	Repucci Anthony	10	salesman	25	"
	T	Repucci Carutta—†	10	housewife	70	"

Page.	Letter.	Full Name.	Residence, Jan. 1, 1938.	Occupation.	Supposed Age.	Reported Residence, Jan. 1, 1937. Street and Number.

Liverpool Street—Continued

	U	Repucci George	10	salesman	37	here
	V	Repucci Pasquale	10	retired	72	"
	W	Bua Angelo	10	cutter	24	"
	X	Bua Jennie—†	10	houseworker	21	"
	Y	Bua Micheline—†	10	housewife	54	"
	Z	Giglio Frances—†	10	"	44	
39						
	A	Giglio Joseph, jr	10	cutter	20	"
	B	*Pagnotti John	rear 10	tailor	62	220 Havre
	C	*Cappozzoli Dominico	" 10	laborer	68	here
	D	Giglio Joseph	" 10	"	48	"
	E	DeMarco May—†	11	housewife	32	"
	F	*DeMarco Angelina—†	11	"	65	
	G	*DeMarco Frank	11	salesman	66	"
	H	DeMarco John	11	roofer	35	
	K	Gatta Emilio	11	finisher	41	
	L	Gatta Mary—†	11	housewife	34	"
	M	Marabella Joseph	13	laborer	50	
	N	*Marabella Santa—†	13	housewife	47	"
	O	Testa George	13	operator	25	"
	P	Testa Josephine—†	13	housewife	23	"
	R	Testa Anna—†	13	wrapper	20	"
	S	Testa Carmen	13	printer	24	"
	T	Testa Felix	13	laborer	63	
	U	*Testa Susie—†	13	housewife	61	"
	W	*Cardone Amelia—†	15	"	39	"
	X	Cardone Gabriel	15	laborer	40	"
	Y	*Frances Joseph	16	longshoreman	42	"
	Z	*Frances Rosa—†	16	housewife	35	"
40						
	A	Fici Nicolas	17	fisherman	23	"
	B	Fiei Phyllis—†	17	housewife	24	"
	C	*Dulcetta Joseph	18	laborer	55	
	D	*Dulcetta Santa—†	18	housewife	53	"
	F	*Abanese Bruno	18	carpenter	55	"
	G	*Emma Emmalata—†	18	housewife	53	Italy
	H	*Emma George	18	carpenter	60	18 Cooper
	K	*Maggotto Rosarie—†	18	housewife	66	here
	L	Aiesi Frank S	18	laborer	50	"
	M	*Aiesi Rose—†	18	housewife	46	"
	N	Salvagio Josephine—†	18	stitcher	20	"

Page.	Letter.	Full Name.	Residence, Jan. 1, 1938.	Occupation.	Supposed Age.	Reported Residence, Jan. 1, 1937. Street and Number.
		Liverpool Street—Continued				
	S	Sordillo Angelo	19	operator	24	here
	T	Sordillo Arthur	19	laborer	21	"
	U	Sordillo Julia—†	19	housewife	40	"
	V	Sordillo Ralph	19	operator	48	
	W	Terlino Constantino	20	laborer	24	
	X	Terlino Mary—†	20	housewife	22	"
	Y	*Morello Ida—†	20	"	29	
	Z	Morello Salvatore	20	hairdresser	34	"
41						
	A	*Lauria Frances—†	20	housewife	53	"
	B	Lauria Nellie—†	20	houseworker	20	"
	C	Lauria Peter	20	operator	63	"
	D	Romano Anna—†	20	housewife	27	"
	E	Romano Benjamin	20	fisherman	30	"
	F	*Demitrelis Despena—†	21	housewife	40	85 Orleans
	G	Demitrelis Themistocles	21	laborer	50	85 "
	H	*Cardinale Andrew	21	fisherman	22	here
	K	*Cardinale Annie—†	21	housewife	38	"
	L	*Cardinale Francisco	21	fisherman	47	"
	M	Maloney Margaret—†	21	housewife	36	S Carolina
	N	Maloney Thomas H	21	carpenter	46	"
	O	Arnone Catherine T—†	22	housewife	21	52 Border
	P	Arnone Paul V	22	laborer	24	52 "
	R	*Squardito Jerome	22	fisherman	45	here
	S	*Squardito Martha—†	22	housewife	31	"
	T	*Vaiarella Joseph	22	fisherman	56	"
	U	Vaiarella Rose—†	22	housewife	20	"
	V	DiMartino Catherine—†	22	"	29	
	W	DiMartino Joseph	22	laborer	34	
	X	Viarella Joseph	23	fisherman	29	"
	Y	Viarella Vita—†	23	housewife	24	"
	Z	*Bertolino Andrew	23	fisherman	55	"
42						
	A	Bertolino Anthony	23	"	24	
	B	*Bertolino Vita—†	23	housewife	49	"
	C	*Costa Frances—†	23	"	35	
	D	*Costa John	23	painter	31	
	E	Precopio Conchetta—†	24	operator	28	
	F	Precopio Frank	24	salesman	34	"
	G	Precopio John	24	operator	26	
	H	*Precopio Leo	24	retired	65	

Page.	Letter.	Full Name.	Residence, Jan. 1, 1938.	Occupation.	Supposed Age.	Reported Residence, Jan. 1, 1937. Street and Number.

Liverpool Street—Continued

Page.	Letter.	Full Name.	Residence, Jan. 1, 1938.	Occupation.	Supposed Age.	Reported Residence, Jan. 1, 1937. Street and Number.
	K	Precopio Mario	24	foreman	29	here
	L	Precopio Natalie	24	shipper	21	"
	M	Precopio Philomena—†	24	operator	33	"
	N	*Guarino Anna—†	25	housewife	37	"
	O	Guarino Giuseppe	25	packer	41	"
	P	Wirth Agnes V—†	26	housewife	32	"
	R	Wirth Harold F	26	longshoreman	36	"
	S	Wirth Mary—†	26	housewife	78	"
	T	*Belletti Charles	27	laborer	53	
	U	*Belletti Crocaefissa—†	27	housewife	42	"
	V	Belletti John	27	operator	21	
	W	Belletti Lena—†	27	"	20	
	X	*Miner Olive—†	28	housewife	66	"
	Y	Miner Robert	28	laborer	25	
	Z	Peacock Emily—†	28	at home	91	
43						
	A	*Gallo Mary—†	28	housewife	28	Cambridge
	B	Marino Angelina—†	28	tailoress	25	here
	C	*Marino Gaetano	28	retired	75	"
	D	Galante Ovidio	29	instructor	28	"
	E	Galante Rosalie—†	29	housewife	26	"
	F	*Alimonti Joseph	29	salesman	37	25 North sq
	G	Alimonti Mary—†	29	housewife	35	25 "
	H	*Galante Josephine—†	29	"	54	here
	K	Galante Michael	29	operator	23	"
	L	Galante Tito	29	blacksmith	52	"
	M	Celona Mary—†	30	clerk	25	
	N	Celona Nunzio	30	laborer	53	
	O	Celona Stephen	30	printer	23	
	P	DiMuro Joseph	30	barber	31	
	R	DiMuro Santa—†	30	housewife	27	"
	S	Christianson Carl	31	laborer	36	
	T	Christianson Harold	31	seaman	33	
	U	Christianson Sophie—†	31	housewife	69	"
	V	Driscoll Lawrence	31	longshoreman	22	"
	W	Lamb Charles	31	salesman	56	15 Cambridge
	X	Pizano Albert	32	laborer	24	here
	Y	Pizano Anna—†	32	at home	21	"
	Z	Pizano Carmen	32	laborer	52	"
44						
	A	Pizano Christina—†	32	housewife	50	"

Page.	Letter.	FULL NAME.	Residence, Jan. 1, 1938.	Occupation.	Supposed Age.	Reported Residence, Jan. 1, 1937. Street and Number.

Liverpool Street—Continued

	B	Cacciatore Concetta—†	32	housewife	34	here
	C	Cacciatore Giuseppe	32	laborer	38	"
	D	Defino Josephine—†	32	housewife	46	22 Havana
	E	Defino Salvatore	32	laborer	22	22 "
	F	Defino Stephen	32	"	47	22 "
	G	*Monaro Antonio	33	"	42	127 Saratoga
	H	Voci Elizabeth—†	33	stitcher	21	here
	K	*Voci George	33	laborer	59	"
	L	Voci George, jr	33	clerk	20	"
	M	*Voci Mary—†	33	housewife	55	"
	P	Chiccarelli Joseph B	33	carpenter	53	"
	N	*Schipani Angeline—†	33	housewife	29	"
	O	Schipani Anthony	33	laborer	38	
	R	Loverme Felicia—†	34	housewife	53	"
	S	Loverme Mary—†	34	tailoress	25	
	T	Loverme Phyllis—†	34	"	30	
	U	Capizzi Anthony	34	operator	40	"
	V	Capizzi Mary—†	34	housewife	33	"
	W	Lucifora Mary—†	34	"	34	35 London
	X	Lucifora Paul	34	laborer	42	35 "
	Y	Anzalone Edward	35	"	28	here
	Z	*Anzalone Filomena—†	35	housewife	52	"
45						
	A	Anzalone Rose—†	35	"	26	
	B	Choquette Lenwood	35	clerk	20	
	C	Durant Francis D	35	laborer	31	
	D	Durant Gladys—†	35	housewife	28	"
	E	Chillemi Alfred	36	operator	28	"
	F	Chillemi Anthony	36	jeweler	32	
	G	Chillemi Conchetta—†	36	housewife	58	"
	H	Chillemi Grace—†	36	operator	24	"
	K	Mayo Emma—†	36	housewife	29	"
	L	Mayo Frank	36	jeweler	30	"
	R	Rizzotto Guy J	37	attorney	30	Hingham
	M	Sanfilippo Charles	37	clerk	30	here
	N	*Sanfilippo Ercole	37	retired	72	"
	O	*Sanfilippo Jennie—†	37	housewife	61	"
	P	Sanfilippo Mary A—†	37	packer	32	
	S	*Cappa Josephine—†	39	housewife	41	"
	T	*Cappa Pasquale	39	plasterer	48	"
	U	Risti Ernest	41	laborer	43	

Page.	Letter.	Full Name.	Residence, Jan. 1, 1938.	Occupation.	Supposed Age.	Reported Residence, Jan. 1, 1937. Street and Number.

Liverpool Street—Continued

Page.	Letter.	Full Name.	Residence, Jan. 1, 1938.	Occupation.	Supposed Age.	Reported Residence, Jan. 1, 1937. Street and Number.
	v	*Risti Jennie—†	41	housewife	42	here
	w	*Vultaggio Jack	41	operator	47	Arlington
	x	*Vultaggio Sarah—†	41	housewife	37	"
	y	Riccobene Angelo	42	laborer	55	here
	z	Riccobene Concetta—†	42	housewife	53	"
46						
	A	Sanfilippo Salvatore	42	laborer	48	
	B	Sanfilippo Tina—†	42	housewife	34	"
	C	Riccobini Antoinetta—†	42	"	23	
	D	Riccobini Peter	42	laborer	25	
	E	*Berinato Anna—†	44	housewife	44	"
	F	Berinato Anthony	44	printer	24	"
	G	*Berinato Antonio	44	polisher	53	"
	H	Lucifora Lucy—†	44	housewife	35	89 Maverick
	K	Lucifora Salvatore	44	plasterer	45	89 "
	L	Sardella Angelo	44	retired	68	147 Chelsea
	M	Sardella Conchetta—†	44	housewife	64	147 "
	O	DiMartino Giovanna—†	46	"	67	here
	P	DiMartino Margaret—†	46	operator	27	"
	R	Tontodnato Antonia—†	46	housewife	24	"
	S	Tontodnato John	46	laborer	24	"
	T	Curcio Carmella—†	46	housewife	43	"
	U	Curcio Emilio	46	repairman	51	"
	V	Cappello Anna—†	48	housewife	45	"
	W	Cappello Gaspar	48	baker	50	
	Y	Cappello Joseph	48	"	26	
	X	Cappello Helen—†	48	housewife	24	"
	Z	Cappello William	48	operator	24	"
47						
	C	Penta Michael	52	glazier	36	
	D	Palladino Anna—†	52	housewife	39	"
	E	Palladino Edward	52	salesman	22	"
	F	Bradley Mary—†	53	housewife	42	18 Paris
	G	*Rosario Eugenio	53	operator	40	42 Porter
	H	*Rosario Marie—†	53	housewife	34	42 "
	K	*Newell Blanchard	54	laborer	26	here
	L	Newell Yolanda—†	54	housewife	21	"
	M	Calzada Susan—†	54	housekeeper	48	"
	N	Sardina Marcelino	54	fireman	48	"
	P	Repetto Anna—†	58	housewife	25	137 Havre
	R	Repetto Nicolas	58	laborer	30	137 "

Page.	Letter.	FULL NAME.	Residence, Jan. 1, 1938.	Occupation.	Supposed Age.	Reported Residence, Jan. 1, 1937. Street and Number.

Liverpool Street—Continued

	S	Catalanotto Leo	58	laborer	41	here
	T	Catalanotto Vincenza—†	58	housewife	36	"
	U	*Morello Angelo	58	retired	66	50 Border
	V	*Morello Conchetta—†	58	housewife	54	50 "
	W	Cuddi Josephine—†	60	"	58	here
	X	Cuddi Edith—†	60	at home	21	"
	Y	Cuddi Clementina—†	60	housewife	21	"
	Z	Cuddi Louis	60	laborer	25	
48						
	A	*Falzarano Stephen	62	"	50	
	B	*Falzarano Susan—†	62	housewife	44	"
	C	Falzarano Victoria—†	62	decorator	21	"
	D	Saetti Albert	62	machinist	43	"
	E	Saetti Mary—†	62	housewife	40	"
	F	*Miraglia Nancy—†	62	"	51	
	G	*Miraglia Salvatore	62	laborer	59	
	H	Rizzo Carmella—†	62	clerk	30	
	K	Rizzo Ernest	62	laborer	26	
	N	Rizzo Grace—†	62	housewife	60	"
	L	Rizzo John	62	chauffeur	36	"
	M	Rizzo Philomina—†	62	operator	26	"
	O	Rizzo William	62	laborer	60	
	P	Lamarco Ida—†	71	housewife	26	"
	R	Lamarco Orlando	71	operator	29	"
	S	Fatello Anthony	71	laborer	22	29 Liverpool
	T	Fatello Grace—†	71	housewife	53	29 "
	U	Fatello Jennie—†	71	saleswoman	23	29 "
	V	*Brogna Angeline—†	71	housewife	60	here
	W	Brogna Guy	71	chauffeur	34	3 Jay
	X	Brogna Lena—†	71	housewife	30	3 "
	Y	*Brogna Pasquale	71	fireman	60	here
	Z	Chiampa Caroline—†	72	housewife	28	"
49						
	A	Chiampa Frank	72	mechanic	30	"
	B	Paglucco Marion—†	72	housewife	43	"
	C	*Paglucco Michael	72	laborer	43	
	D	Sala Geraldine—†	72	housewife	59	"
	E	Sala Jerome	72	laborer	60	
	F	Sala Josephine—†	72	operator	23	"
	G	Sala Mary—†	72	stitcher	28	
	H	Sala Rose—†	72	"	26	

Page.	Letter.	FULL NAME.	Residence, Jan. 1, 1938.	Occupation.	Supposed Age.	Reported Residence, Jan. 1, 1937. Street and Number.

Liverpool Street—Continued

Page.	Letter.	FULL NAME.	Residence, Jan. 1, 1938.	Occupation.	Supposed Age.	Reported Residence, Jan. 1, 1937. Street and Number.
	K	Cusimano Casimire	73	barber	56	here
	L	*Cusimano Josephine—†	73	housewife	55	"
	M	*Cusimano Theresa—†	73	"	77	"
	N	Cusimano Theresa—†	73	"	26	
	O	Guarini Anthony	73	engineer	26	
	P	*Guarini Lillian—†	73	housewife	48	"
	R	Guarini Richard	73	engineer	50	
	S	Tollis Angelo	73	clerk	44	
	T	Tollis Flora—†	73	housewife	42	"
	U	Ciampa Felix	74	laborer	58	
	V	Ciampa Louise—†	74	housewife	56	"
	W	Ciampa Anthony	74	chauffeur	25	"
	X	Ciampa Mary—†	74	housewife	23	"
	Y	Correia Jordan	74	laborer	37	
	Z	Correia Josephine—†	74	housewife	40	"
50						
	B	Dorso Adelaide—†	75		25	
	C	*Dorso Angeline—†	75	"	57	
	D	Dorso Frank	75	fisherman	27	"
	E	Doros John	75	"	30	
	F	Dorso Michael	75	"	29	"
	K	Imbrescia Carmella—†	85	housewife	26	Chelsea
	L	Imbrescia Philip	85	laborer	28	"
	M	Aleo Alexander	85	"	59	here
	N	*Aleo Dorothy—†	85	housewife	47	"
	O	Aleo Philip	85	laborer	22	"
	P	Barker Frank	85	"	22	
	R	Barker Mary—†	85	housewife	20	"
51						
	A	*Ferreira Antonio	93	janitor	45	
	B	*Ferreira Antonio	93	seaman	21	
	C	*Ferreira Canida—†	93	housewife	47	"
	D	Insalacco Ida—†	93	"	26	
	E	Insalacco Joseph	93	retired	62	
	F	*Insalacco Josephine—†	93	housewife	45	"
	G	Hickey Daniel J	93	laborer	60	
	H	Hickey John J	93	"	63	
	K	Morgardo John	93	"	20	
	L	*Morgardo Josephine—†	93	housewife	55	"
	N	Blake Fred	95	laborer	54	
	R	Burke Helen L—†	97	housewife	37	"

Liverpool Street—Continued

Page.	Letter.	Full Name.	Residence, Jan. 1, 1938.	Occupation.	Supposed Age.	Reported Residence, Jan. 1, 1937. Street and Number.
	S	Burke Thomas J	97	superintendent	46	here
	Z	*Feulo Julia—†	103	housewife	29	"
52						
	A	Feulo Samuel	103	laborer	42	
	B	*Caggiano Marciano	103	salesman	52	"
	C	*Caggiano Mary—†	103	housewife	53	"
	D	Desimone Josephine—†	103	"	22	54 London
	E	Desimone Melaino	103	salesman	23	54 "
	F	Latorella Annie—†	105	housewife	65	here
	G	Latorella Carmilla	105	retired	69	"
	H	Celestino Contina	105	laborer	54	"
	K	Celestino Josephine—†	105	stitcher	20	
	L	*Celestino Rose—†	105	housewife	48	"
	M	Caggiano Fiore	105	chauffeur	25	103 Liverpool
	N	Caggiano Grace—†	105	stitcher	23	here
	O	Cosmos George	107	merchant	50	"
	P	*DeAngelus Antonio	107	laborer	53	"
	R	*DeAngelus Elvira—†	107	housewife	48	"
	S	DeAngelus William	107	laborer	20	
	U	*Caponigro Angelina—†	109	housewife	48	"
	V	Caponigro George	109	operator	22	"
	W	Caponigro James	109	bootblack	20	"
	X	*Caponigro Serafino	109	salesman	51	"
	Y	Caponigro Angelo	109	operator	27	"
	Z	Caponigro Rose—†	109	housewife	23	"

London Street

Page.	Letter.	Full Name.	Residence, Jan. 1, 1938.	Occupation.	Supposed Age.	Reported Residence, Jan. 1, 1937. Street and Number.
53						
	G	Bogan James	6	laborer	50	here
	H	Feggar Emma—†		housekeeper	40	"
	K	Pratt Monson		retired	70	Provincetown
	L	Blake Herbret		"	60	here
	M	Cleary John		"	70	9 Winthrop
	N	Cleary John		longshoreman	40	9 "
	O	Geogione Roy		chauffeur	22	149 Cottage
	P	*Palewick Albert		laborer	38	477 Meridian
	R	*Pulico Ricco	6	"	40	106 Sumner
	S	Smallcomb Stephen	6	fisherman	55	here
	T	*Wall William	6	longshoreman	54	"
	V	Monroe Leander W	7	machinist	54	"
	W	Monroe Margaret—†	7	housewife	53	"

Page.	Letter.	Full Name.	Residence, Jan. 1, 1938.	Occupation.	Supposed Age.	Reported Residence, Jan. 1, 1937. Street and Number.
		London Street—Continued				
	x	*Pecilio Basilio	8	cutter	50	here
	y	*Pecilio Rose—†	8	housewife	55	“
	z	*Nazzaro Raffaele—†	8	housekeeper	41	“
54						
	A	Baglio Joseph	8	baker	23	55 Webster
	B	Baglio Mary—†	8	housewife	21	55 “
	C	Ferrelli Sarfino	9	chauffeur	25	here
	D	*Antuori Andriana—†	9	housewife	48	“
	E	Antuori Carmella—†	9	dressmaker	21	“
	F	Antuori Dominic	9	fisherman	23	“
	G	Antuori Frank	9	“	50	
	H	Capone Conchetta—†	9	housewife	29	“
	K	Capone John L	9	laborer	30	
	L	Pisello Elizabeth—†	11	housewife	40	“
	M	Pisello Joseph	11	roofer	40	
	N	Corvotta Angelo	11	laborer	35	
	O	Corvotta Josephine—†	11	housewife	72	“
	P	Perrone Antonetta—†	11	“	29	“
	R	Perrone Frank	11	carpenter	34	“
	S	Thornton Henry	12	laborer	41	
	T	*Thornton Mary—†	12	housewife	36	“
	U	*Lopes Jean—†	12	“	44	“
	V	*Lopes Manuel	12	operator	44	“
	W	*Anzalone Joseph	13	laborer	38	
	X	Anzalone Rose—†	13	housewife	31	“
	Y	Dello Russo Amarto	13	laborer	40	
	Z	Dello Russo Ralph	13	retired	78	
55						
	A	Dello Russo Sylvia—†	13	at home	27	“
	B	Dello Russo Margaret—†	13	housewife	37	“
	C	Dello Russo Marino	13	clerk	43	
	D	Beaupre Alfred J	14	cutter	31	
	E	Beaupre Caroline—†	14	housewife	24	“
	F	*Tortora Anna—†	14	“	38	
	G	*Tortora Francesco	14	painter	50	
	H	Bringolla Frank	15	fisherman	72	“
	K	Bringolla James	15	“	29	“
	L	Bringolla Lucy—†	15	housewife	68	“
	M	Bringolla Thomas	15	fisherman	35	“
	N	*Imperato Cero	15	laborer	42	“
	O	*Imperato Mary—†	15	housewife	36	“

Page.	Letter.	Full Name.	Residence, Jan. 1, 1938.	Occupation.	Supposed Age.	Reported Residence, Jan. 1, 1937. Street and Number.

London Street—Continued

Page.	Letter.	Full Name.	Residence, Jan. 1, 1938.	Occupation.	Supposed Age.	Reported Residence, Jan. 1, 1937. Street and Number.
	P	Walsh Margaret—†	15	housewife	40	here
	R	Walsh Patrick	15	fisherman	22	"
	S	*Napolitano Assunta—†	16	housewife	48	"
	T	Napolitano Brigida—†	16	stitcher	20	
	U	*Napolitano Ferardo	16	pedler	44	
	V	Napolitano Ralph	16	laborer	22	
	W	*Guida Annie—†	16	housewife	55	"
	X	Guida Giacomo	16	laborer	56	
	Y	*Guida Leone	16	shoemaker	62	"
	Z	*Vernaglia John	16	retired	72	
56						
	A	Incarroto Frank	17	laborer	24	185 Everett
	B	Incarroto Mary—†	17	housewife	21	185 "
	C	DiFillippo Anthony	17	laborer	21	here
	D	*DeFillippo Louis	17	"	49	"
	E	*DeFillippo Rose—†	17	housewife	43	"
	F	DiFillippo Theresa—†	17	clerk	22	
	G	Lentini Michael	17	barber	42	
	H	*Lentini Teresa—†	17	housewife	35	"
	L	*Melanson Fannie—†	18	housekeeper	44	104 Morris
	M	Melanson Frank	18	cutter	21	Chelsea
	N	Poirier Wilford	18	laborer	37	24 Princeton
	O	*Otolo Joseph	20	merchant	25	33 Havre
	P	Otolo Tina—†	20	housewife	24	33 "
	R	Testa Amodeo	20	printer	27	here
	S	Testa Jennie—†	20	housewife	23	"
	T	Pericolo Eve—†	20	"	22	200 Marion
	U	Pericolo Virginio	20	florist	20	200 "
	V	Marsomo Adeline—†	21	housewife	24	448 Hanover
	W	Marsomo Dominic	21	counterman	26	448 "
	X	Fanale Biagga—†	21	housewife	66	here
	Y	Fanale Giuseppe	21	retired	69	"
	Z	Gubitosi Joseph	21	bookbinder	28	"
57						
	A	Gubitosi Philomina—†	21	housewife	27	"
	B	Belsito Jerry	21	chauffeur	42	"
	C	Toscano Joseph	21	laborer	30	"
	D	Toscano Petrina—†	21	housewife	25	"
	E	LaPlace Caroline—†	21	"	25	
	F	LaPlace Mario	21	laborer	26	"
	G	DeBonis Frank	22	valet	25	12 Chelsea

Page.	Letter.	Full Name.	Residence, Jan. 1, 1938.	Occupation.	Supposed Age.	Reported Residence, Jan. 1, 1937. Street and Number.
		London Street—Continued				
	H	DeBonis Mary—†	22	operator	21	130 Chelsea
	K	Fatalo Americo	22	laborer	26	here
	L	Fatalo Ann—†	22	housewife	24	"
	M	Polito Devigio—†	22	"	33	"
	N	Polito Joseph	22	inspector	36	"
	O	Sbordoni Phyllis—†	23	housewife	30	"
	P	Sbordoni Saverio	23	seaman	30	
	R*	Dellaria Jack	23	retired	67	
	S*	Dellaria Rose—†	23	housewife	61	"
	T	Dellaria Victor	23	laborer	36	
	U	Toscano Josephine—†	23	at home	32	
	W*	Moretti Joseph	24	retired	69	
	X*	Moretti Mary—†	24	housewife	68	"
	Y	Mahoney Agnes—†	24	"	66	
	Z	Mahoney Michael F	24	laborer	63	
58						
	A	Nuccio Rose—†	26	housewife	22	48 Lowell
	B	Buccio Salvatore	26	clerk	22	16 Liverpool
	C	Marcella James	26	laborer	30	here
	D	Marcella Theresa—†	26	housewife	30	"
	E	Bertucelli Joseph	26	laborer	28	96 Everett
	F	Bertucelli Louise—†	26	housewife	23	96 "
	G	Uva Anna—†	27	"	53	here
	H	Uva Carmella—†	27	stitcher	22	"
	K	Uva Mary—†	27	"	26	"
	L	Uva Michael	27	laborer	52	"
	M	Currier Tina—†	27	at home	21	62 Greene
	N	Roma Anna—†	27	clerk	22	52 Allen
	O*	Roma Joseph	27	laborer	48	52 "
	P	Roma Rose—†	27	housewife	44	52 "
	R	Vincini Anthony	28	mechanic	22	here
	S*	Vincini Frances—†	28	housewife	63	"
	T	Vincini Gaetano	28	painter	24	"
	U*	Vincini Henry	28	retired	64	
	V	Indingaro Anthony	28	porter	25	
	W	Indingaro Eleanor—†	28	at home	22	
	X*	Indingaro Mary—†	28	housewife	53	"
	Y	Indingaro Michael	28	salesman	24	"
	Z*	Indingaro Samuel	28	bootblack	53	"
59						
	B	Scarpelli Mary—†	29	at home	37	

Page.	Letter.	FULL NAME.	Residence, Jan. 1, 1938.	Occupation.	Supposed Age.	Reported Residence, Jan. 1, 1937. Street and Number.

London Street—Continued

Page.	Letter.	FULL NAME.	Residence, Jan. 1, 1938.	Occupation.	Supposed Age.	Reported Residence, Jan. 1, 1937. Street and Number.
	C	Vitale James	29	chauffeur	29	here
	D	Vitale Sarah—†	29	housewife	29	"
	E	Naso Joseph	30	chauffeur	21	58 Maverick
	F	Vanella Catrina—†	30	housewife	23	here
	G	Vanella Joseph	30	barber	31	"
	H	Cammarata Baldassore	30	laborer	66	"
	K	*Cammarata Josephine—†	30	housewife	57	"
	L	Rossetti Primo	31	laborer	52	545 E Third
	M	Junta Louis	31	"	20	29 Moulton
	N	Vitale Frank	31	"	64	here
	O	Virale Vincenza—†	31	housewife	59	"
	P	*Iacamino Antonetta—†	31	"	30	"
	R	*Iacamino John	31	laborer	41	
	S	Cirone Margaret—†	31	housewife	50	"
	T	Cirone Mario	31	laborer	51	
	U	Salerno Rose—†	31	housewife	43	"
	V	Salerno Salvatore	31	laborer	43	
	W	Castrini Josephine—†	32	housewife	40	"
	X	Castrini Sylvia—†	32	operator	20	"
	Y	Castrini William	32	laborer	47	
	Z	Cangiano Pasquale	32	electrotyper	26	"
60						
	A	*DiBenedetto Angelo	33	retired	67	
	B	DiBenedetto Helen—†	33	typist	21	
	C	*DiBenedetto Mary—†	33	housewife	57	"
	D	Celona Mary—†	33	"	28	
	E	Celona Nicolas	33	laborer	27	"
	F	Santagate Guy	33	"	24	Belmont
	G	Santagate Marion—†	33	housewife	25	"
	H	Tibaudo Antonetta—†	33	"	53	80 Porter
	K	Tibaudo Frank	33	laborer	38	80 "
	L	Russo Rose—†	33	housewife	27	180 Marion
	M	DeFrancesco Charles	33	painter	33	31 Havre
	N	DeFrancesco Emily—†	33	housewife	29	31 "
	O	*Campanaro Florence—†	34	housekeeper	68	here
	P	Scorporto Leon	34	salesman	47	"
	R	Scorporto Michael	34	laborer	48	"
	S	Menkello Albert	35	operator	23	18 Hull
	T	Menkello Angelina—†	35	housewife	22	18 "
	U	Buonopane Nicolas	35	laborer	38	here
	V	Buonpoane Philomina—†	35	housewife	31	"

Page.	Letter.	Full Name.	Residence, Jan. 1, 1938.	Occupation.	Supposed Age.	Reported Residence, Jan. 1, 1937. Street and Number.

London Street—Continued

	W	Bickford Leslie	36	chauffeur	39	here
	X	Moscatelli Olga—†	36	housewife	32	"
	Y	Moscatelli Sabino	36	laborer	35	"
	Z	Buonopane Dolores—†	37	housewife	33	"
61						
	A	Buonopane Ralph	37	clerk	36	
	B	Buonopane John	37	"	29	
	C	Buonopane Mary—†	37	housewife	28	"
	D	Buonopane Pasqualina—†	37	"	65	
	E	Buonopane Phyllis—†	37	operator	26	"
	F	*Scifano Frank	38	merchant	54	"
	G	Scifano Grace—†	38	dressmaker	23	"
	H	Scifao Joseph	38	laborer	22	
	K	*Scifano Rose—†	38	housewife	40	"
	L	*Guerrero Jennie—†	38	"	42	20 Havre
	M	Guerrero Ralph	38	chauffeur	44	20 "
	N	Keene Frances—†	38	housewife	25	here
	O	Keene George F, jr	38	clerk	25	"
	P	DiLorenzo Grover	39	operator	27	"
	R	DiLorenzo Michelina—†	39	housewife	22	"
	S	*Luise Michael	39	operator	57	
	T	*Luise Sarah—†	39	housewife	51	"
	U	Verrazzani Josephine—†	41	"	35	
	V	Verrazzani Lawrence	41	operator	40	
	W	*Gandino Anna—†	41	housewife	43	"
	X	*Gandino Nicolas	41	laborer	54	
	Y	Gandino Rose—†	41	at home	23	
	Z	*Mancuso Madeline—†	50	housewife	75	"
62						
	A	*Mancuso Phamia	50	retired	72	"
	B	Fraser Margaret—†	50	operator	30	25 London
	C	Alabiso Angelo	50	laborer	55	here
	D	*Alabiso Maria—†	50	housewife	45	"
	E	Melino Francesco	52	laborer	35	85 Liverpool
	F	*Melino Maria—†	52	housewife	48	85 "
	G	Colombo Anthony	52	operator	59	here
	H	Colombo Gaetano	52	"	21	"
	K	*Colombo Marion—†	52	housewife	53	"
	L	Colombo Mary—†	52	operator	28	"
	M	Colombo Rose—†	52	"	24	
	N	Petrella Gaetano	52	clerk	20	

Page.	Letter.	FULL NAME.	Residence, Jan. 1, 1938.	Occupation.	Supposed Age.	Reported Residence, Jan. 1, 1937. Street and Number.

London Street—Continued

	o	*Petrella Saverio	52	operator	56	here
	P	Petrella Saverio, jr	52	"	25	"
	S	Cavaretto Antonio	54	"	44	Revere
	T	Cavaretto Louisa—†	54	housewife	34	"
	V	Vitale Amelia—†	54	clerk	25	"
	W	*Vitale Amelo	54	shoemaker	69	"
	U	Vitale Anna—†	54	clerk	23	here
	X	*Vitale Liza—†	54	housewife	60	"
	Y	Lyons Patrick	56	retired	60	"
	Z	Amico Joseph A	56	laborer	35	
63						
	A	Amico Mary C—†	56	housewife	29	"
	B	*Caggino Mary—†	56	"	26	
	C	*Caggino Michael	56	laborer	36	"
	D	Amico Mary—†	58	housewife	25	Somerville
	E	Amico Peter	58	operator	30	here
	F	Amico Catrina—†	58	housewife	25	"
	G	*Amico Santa—†	58	"	62	"
	H	Vella Joseph	58	laborer	40	43 Border
	K	Vella Tina—†	58	housewife	32	43 "
	L	Buonopane Anthony	60	laborer	25	37 London
	M	Buonopane Margaret—†	60	housewife	22	37 "
	N	Chillemi Frances—†	60	operator	28	here
	O	Miano Frank	60	"	32	"
	P	Miano Mary—†	60	housewife	63	"
	R	*Sanim Cecelia—†	62	"	47	195 Lexington
	S	*Sanim James	62	cutter	44	195 "
	T	Martello Helen—†	62	housekeeper	21	29 Eutaw
	U	Martello Peter	62	salesman	45	29 "
	V	Martello Phyllis—†	62	housewife	30	29 "
	W	Meli Flora—†	62	"	32	Medford
	X	Meli Joseph	62	salesman	37	"
	Y	Campbell Albert	64	janitor	32	88 W Newton
	Z	Fleming Hannah J—†	64	housewife	59	70 London
64						
	A	Fleming William	64	retired	73	70 "
	B	Jeffers John	64	clerk	63	here
	C	Bayers Sidney H	65	clergyman	30	"
	D	Foley Cornelius A	65	"	48	"
	E	Londrigan James T	65	"	59	
	F	Murphy Emma J—†	65	cook	56	

Page.	Letter.	FULL NAME.	Residence, Jan. 1, 1938.	Occupation.	Supposed Age.	Reported Residence, Jan. 1, 1937. Street and Number.

London Street—Continued

	G	McDonald John A	66	carpenter	69	here
	H	McDonald Margaret—†	66	housewife	67	"
	K	Coughlin Catherine—†	66	attendant	45	"
	L	Goodwin Beatrice—†	66	housewife	50	20 Princeton
	M	Goodwin Ernest F	66	cutter	56	20 "
	N	*Goodwin Sarah—†	66	housewife	80	113 Eutaw
	O	Bannon Sarah G—†	68	housekeeper	60	here
	P	Cannon Charles H	68	retired	82	"
	R	Cannon Julia—†	68	housewife	60	"
	S	Gallagher Margaret—†	68	"	51	"
	T	McDonald Edward	70	laborer	23	44 Saratoga
	U	McDonald Margaret Z—†	70	housewife	68	44 "
	V	McDonald Victor	70	retired	72	44 "
	W	Gillispie Dorothy—†	70	operator	35	here
	X	Parziale Lysander	70	laborer	32	"
	Y	Murphy Frances—†	70	housewife	61	"
	Z	Incorvato James	72	cutter	27	"
65						
	A	Incrovato Vivian—†	72	housewife	27	"
	B	*Martello Ida—†	72	operator	21	"
	C	Martello Vincenzo	72	laborer	55	
	D	*Scanapico Amelia—†	72	housewife	48	"
	E	*Scanapico John	72	finisher	63	
	F	*Tiano Anthony	72	"	40	
	G	*Tiano Nicholas	72	counterman	46	"
	H	Santarpio Arnold	74	operator	25	"
	K	Santarpio Theresa—†	74	housewife	23	"
	L	*Milito Anna—†	74	"	34	
	M	*Milito Joseph	74	mason	38	"
	N	Falzone Michael	74	laborer	44	33 London
	O	Falzone Santa—†	74	housewife	36	33 "
	P	Cordan Catherine—†	75	"	52	here
	R	Cordan Walter J	75	carpenter	54	"
	S	Giordano Anna—†	75	housewife	34	"
	T	Giordano Arthur	75	mechanic	41	"
	U	Papia Josephine—†	75	housewife	45	"
	V	*Papia Rosario	75	laborer	46	
	W	Caristo Carl	76	operator	22	"
	X	Caristo John	76	"	26	"
	Y	Caristo Rose—†	76	housewife	49	"
	Z	*Lopez Elvira—†	76	"	38	

Page.	Letter.	Full Name.	Residence, Jan. 1, 1938.	Occupation.	Supposed Age.	Reported Residence, Jan. 1, 1937. Street and Number.

66

London Street—Continued

Page.	Letter.	Full Name.	Residence, Jan. 1, 1938.	Occupation.	Supposed Age.	Reported Residence, Jan. 1, 1937. Street and Number.
66	A	Lopez Frank	76	baker	41	here
	B	Martori Edith—†	76	housewife	29	"
	C	Martori Joseph	76	cutter	30	"
	D	Anastas Nicholas	76	merchant	54	"
	E	Brown Patrick	77	laborer	57	
	F	Cavaleri Joseph	77	"	48	
	G	Cavaleri Mary—†	77	housewife	36	"
	H	*Micciche Guiseppe	77	laborer	57	
	K	*Micciche Stella—†	77	housewife	55	"
	L	Orchard Florence G—†	78	"	38	
	M	Orchard Richard J	78	longshoreman	37	"
	N	Kanelakos Arthur	78	storekeeper	50	"
	O	Kanelakos George	78	"	48	"
	P	Poto Ettore	78	clerk	23	148 Webster
		Poto Ida—†	78	housewife	22	72 London
		Gibbons Helen L—†	79	at home	26	here
		Gibbons John C	79	clerk	60	"
		Gibbons John F	79	"	23	"
	[illegible]	Gibbons Susan L—†	79	housewife	66	"
	W	Gibbons William H	79	electrician	58	"
	X	Gibbons William H	79	laborer	41	
	Y	Pistone Joseph	80	"	44	
	Z	*Pistone Mary—†	80	housewife	31	"
67						
	A	*Prizio Anthony	80	laborer	43	57 Maverick
	B	*Prizio Filomena—†	80	housewife	47	57 "
	C	DeSantis John	80	carpenter	34	137 Paris
	D	*DeSantis Michelena—†	80	housewife	33	137 "
	E	*Bevilaqua Joseph	81	laborer	40	here
	F	*Bevilaqua Virginia—†	81	housewife	36	"
	G	Tortorice Angelo	81	shoemaker	54	"
	H	Tortorice Michael	81	laborer	23	
	K	Tortorice Rosaria—†	81	housewife	43	"
	L	*Novella Catrina—†	82	housekeeper	58	"
	M	Della Iacono Agnes—†	82	decorator	26	84 London
	R	Della Iacono Pasquale	82	chairmaker	52	84 "
	N	Della Iacono Ralph	82	operator	23	84 "
	O	Della Iacono Virginia—†	82	housewife	47	84 "
	P	Della Iaclno Virginia—†	82	stitcher	22	84 "
	T	*Stucco Concetta—†	83	housewife	66	here

Page.	Letter.	Full Name.	Residence, Jan. 1, 1938.	Occupation.	Supposed Age.	Reported Residence, Jan. 1, 1937. Street and Number.

London Street—Continued

Page.	Letter.	Full Name.	Residence, Jan. 1, 1938.	Occupation.	Supposed Age.	Reported Residence, Jan. 1, 1937. Street and Number.
	U	Stucco Frank	83	laborer	37	here
	V	*Stucco Gaetano	83	retired	71	“
	W	Sclafani Mary—†	83	at home	33	“
	X	Trippe Jack	83	operator	38	“
	Y	Trippe Virginia—†	83	housewife	33	“
68						
	B	Breslin Flora—†	85	housekeeper	75	“
	C	McLean Neil	85	laborer	55	“
	D	Quinn John F	85	“	53	
	E	DePerri John	85	“	24	
	F	Lanavaro Rose—†	85	housewife	22	“
	G	Lanavaro Stephen	85	cutter	22	“
	H	*DiMarco Antonetta—†	85	housewife	54	“
	K	DiMarco Phyllis—†	85	operator	36	“
	L	*DiMarco Salvatore	85	retired	65	
	M	*Salerno Carmella—†	87	housewife	50	“
	N	*Salerno Michael	87	laborer	65	
	O	DeBenedictis Edward	87	salesman	24	“
	P	DeBenedictis Marie—†	87	housewife	28	“
	R	Salerno Elizabeth—†	87	“	24	
	S	Salerno Joseph	87	laborer	27	
	T	Colacchio Anthony	89	“	33	
	U	Colacchio Josephine—†	89	housewife	27	“
	V	Ferrara Frances—†	89	“	48	
	W	Ferrara Grace—†	89	dressmaker	26	“
	X	Ferrara Joseph	89	laborer	21	
	Y	Pasqualetto Catrina—†	89	housewife	39	“
	Z	Pasqualetto Gasper	89	operator	48	“
69						
	A	Cardinale Joseph	91	laborer	26	20 London
	B	Cardinale Lillian—†	91	housewife	22	20 “
	C	Schifano Antonetta—†	91	“	20	here
	D	Schifano Charles	91	operator	24	“
	E	*Schifano Antonio	91	laborer	57	“
	F	*Schifano Marie—†	91	housekeeper	51	“
	H	*Longobardi Luigi	93	baker	52	“
	K	*Levesque Clara—†	93	housewife	31	N Cambridge
	L	*Levesque Joseph R	93	chauffeur	33	“
	M	*DeSimone Anna—†	93	housewife	47	here
	P	*Corraro Natale	99	cook	35	135 Chelsea
	R	Corraro Tina—†	99	housewife	27	51 Morris

Page.	Letter.	Full Name.	Residence, Jan. 1, 1938.	Occupation.	Supposed Age.	Reported Residence, Jan. 1, 1937. Street and Number.

London Street—Continued

Page.	Letter.	Full Name.	Residence, Jan. 1, 1938.	Occupation.	Supposed Age.	Reported Residence, Jan. 1, 1937. Street and Number.
	S	Miano Albert L	99	mechanic	30	here
	T	Miano Elizabeth—†	99	housewife	28	"
	U	Franco Carmella—†	99	housekeeper	20	93 London
	V	*Franco Sabina—†	99	housewife	48	93 "
	W	Franco Vincenzo	99	laborer	48	93 "
	X	*Vitale Jennie—†	101	housewife	50	here
	Y	Vitale Michael	101	laborer	53	"
	Z	Zagarella Frances—†	101	clerk	23	"
70						
	A	Zagarella Lawrence	101	"	22	
	B	*Zagarella Marie—†	101	housewife	60	"
	C	*Zagarella Peter	101	laborer	63	
	F	Lanza Irene—†	102	housewife	29	"
	G	Lanza James	102	manufacturer	29	"
	H	*Lanza Angelina—†	102	housewife	54	"
	K	Lanza Anna—†	102	stitcher	24	
	L	*Lanza Frank	102	storekeeper	58	"
	M	Lanza Richard	102	clerk	22	"
	N	Ardagna Bartolo	102	repairman	40	"
	O	*Ardagna Josephine—†	102	housewife	70	"
	P	*Ardagna Josephine—†	102	"	35	
	U	*Kelley Mary J—†	104	"	76	
	V	*Kelley Thomas B	104	laborer	33	
	W	*Kelley Thomas P	104	retired	82	
	X	Sasso Amelia—†	104	housewife	24	"
	Y	Sasso Anthony	104	laborer	27	
	Z	Camarata Gaspare	104	"	52	
71						
	A	Camarata Mary—†	104	housewife	56	"
	B	Giacobbo Carmello	106	engineer	30	
	C	*Giacobbo Joseph	106	operator	68	
	D	Giacobbo Margaret—†	106	stitcher	28	
	E	Mini Anthony	106	counterman	20	"
	F	Mini Lawrence	106	clerk	24	
	G	*Mini Pasquale	106	retired	61	
	H	*Mini Rose—†	106	housewife	51	"
	K	*Amengual Bartholomew	106	fireman	42	"
	L	*Amengual Maria—†	106	housewife	45	"
	N	Falzone Louis G	108	cabinetmaker	40	202 Havre
	O	*Falzone Mary—†	108	housewife	31	202 "
	P	*Soldi Antoinetta—†	108	"	40	here

Page.	Letter.	Full Name.	Residence, Jan. 1, 1938.	Occupation.	Supposed Age.	Reported Residence, Jan. 1, 1937. Street and Number.

London Street—Continued

Page.	Letter.	Full Name.	Residence, Jan. 1, 1938.	Occupation.	Supposed Age.	Reported Residence, Jan. 1, 1937. Street and Number.
	R	Soldi Frank	108	laborer	46	here
	S	Pucillo Albert	108	butcher	23	“
	T	*Pucillo Nicholas	108	“	58	“
	U	*Pucillo Rose—†	108	housewife	58	“
	V	Pucillo Samuel	108	shipper	21	“
	W	DeLavoro Felice	110	laborer	66	
	X	*DeLavoro Rose—†	110	housewife	65	“
	Y	Halperin Ethel—†	110	“	57	
	Z	Halperin Phillip	110	storekeeper	59	“
72						
	A	Halperin Theodore	110	clerk	26	
	B	Anastasio Anthony	110	machinist	20	“
	C	*Anastasio Teresa—†	110	housewife	39	“
	D	Anastasio Vincent	110	machinist	40	“
	E	Lamie David J	112	engineer	49	“
	F	Lamie William	112	laborer	44	
	G	LaCascia Gasper	112	baker	43	
	H	LaCascia Mary—†	112	clerk	37	“
	K	*Fiore Louis	112	retired	75	
	L	*Fiore Pasqualena—†	112	housewife	75	“
	M	Stocco Charles	114	electrician	35	“
	N	*Stocco Concetta—†	114	housewife	30	“
	O	DeSantis Anthony	114	musician	35	“
	P	DeSantis Mary—†	114	housewife	52	“
	R	DeSantis Rose—†	114	“	28	“
	S	Drakoulas Elefthereos	114	counterman	41	“
	T	DiGiovanni John	114	salesman	31	“
	U	DiGiovanni Rose—†	114	packer	26	
	V	DiMare Esther—†	114	housewife	28	“
	W	DiMare Santo	114	operator	28	“
	X	*Balcom Susan—†	116	housewife	40	“
	Y	Balcom Thomas	116	cook	67	
	Z	Grant Frederick	116	fireman	52	
73						
	A	Grant William	116	painter	45	
	B	Reagan Bernard	116	foreman	30	
	C	*Reagan Lillian—†	116	housewife	30	“
	D	*Scanlon Elizabeth—†	116	cook	65	
	E	Dixon Anna T—†	118	housekeeper	54	“
	F	Dodd Richard	118	fisherman	29	“
	G	Flaherty Thomas J	118	U S A	34	New York

Page.	Letter.	Full Name.	Residence, Jan. 1, 1938.	Occupation.	Supposed Age.	Reported Residence, Jan. 1, 1937. Street and Number.

London Street—Continued

Page.	Letter.	Full Name.	Residence, Jan. 1, 1938.	Occupation.	Supposed Age.	Reported Residence, Jan. 1, 1937. Street and Number.
	H	Galloway Dorothea—†	118	housewife	27	here
	K	Goss William	118	fisherman	30	"
	L	Keith Fred	118	clerk	24	62 Saratoga
	M	Murphy John	118	fisherman	32	here
	N	Corderio Peter M	120	laborer	65	"
	O	Hanlon Stephen	120	fisherman	30	"
	P	McCarthy Thomas	120	"	45	
	R	Oliver Anthony	120	clerk	35	
	S	Rock Mary M—†	120	housekeeper	55	"
	T	Rock Timothy J	120	retired	60	"
	U	Surette Eugene	120	cutter	45	139 Saratoga
	V	Titus Herman	120	yardmaster	55	107 Meridian
	W	Dunn John J	122	fisherman	46	here
	X	*Finn William	122	"	38	"
	Y	Hoffman Elizabeth—†	122	housekeeper	48	"
	Z	Insana Giuseppe	122	barber	41	"
74						
	A	Keenan Joseph P	122	carpenter	54	38 Woodville
	B	Mitts Joseph	122	janitor	38	here
	C	Norris George	122	fisherman	35	"
	D	*Ryan Laurence	122	"	43	"
	E	Ryan Richard A	122	"	37	
	F	Sampson Patrick	122	"	42	
	G	Brady Dorothy—†	124	stenographer	30	"
	H	Brady Edward	124	laborer	59	"
	K	Brady Margaret—†	124	housewife	59	"
	L	Davie Luigi	124	chauffeur	25	122 London
	M	*Dinnan William	124	laborer	55	37 Maverick sq
	N	Druken Mogue	124	fisherman	32	here
	O	Druken Richard	124	"	35	"
	P	Fothergill John L	124	operator	35	"
	R	Larkin Everett	124	seaman	35	
	S	Lyons Horace	124	foreman	70	
	T	McArdle Michael T	124	machinist	80	"
	U	*Murphy James	124	fisherman	30	118 London
	V	Troy John	124	laborer	55	here
	W	Walsh Michael J	124	cutter	50	"
	X	*Yee Lee	128	laundryman	45	"
	Y	*Massa Anthony	128	physician	49	"
75						
	A	Fabiano Teresa G—†	128	social worker	34	124 London

Page.	Letter.	FULL NAME.	Residence, Jan. 1, 1938.	Occupation.	Supposed Age.	Reported Residence, Jan. 1, 1937. Street and Number.

Maverick Street

Page.	Letter.	FULL NAME.	Residence, Jan. 1, 1938.	Occupation.	Supposed Age.	Reported Residence, Jan. 1, 1937.
	B	Martignippi Anthony	1	laborer	42	here
	C	*Martignippi Olympia—†	1	housewife	39	"
	D	Ciampa Carmine	1	plasterer	48	"
	E	*Ciampa Maria—†	1	housewife	34	"
	F	Cicero Bartolo	1	laborer	42	"
	G	*Cicero Emma—†	1	housewife	35	"
	H	Incravato Anthony	3	laborer	33	
	K	Incravato Mary—†	3	housewife	27	"
	L	Barletto Grace—†	3	"	21	
	M	Barletto James	3	shipper	24	
	N	Nicholas Anastatius	3	fireman	42	
	T	*Dias Joseph	9	"	50	
	U	*Dias Josephine—†	9	housewife	41	"
	V	Vacaro Angelo	9	chauffeur	24	"
	W	*Vacaro Anthony	9	laborer	62	
	X	Cardinale Dominic	9	"	22	
	Y	Cardinale Joseph	9	operator	37	"
	Z	Cardinale Nicola	9	laborer	62	
76						
	C	Ambrosino Alphonse	11	operator	31	
	D	Ambrosino Carmella—†	11	housewife	25	"
	M	McKenna Anna—†	22	"	55	
	N	McKenna Edward	22	laborer	48	
	O	McKenna John	22	seaman	20	"
	P	Hain Margaret—†	24	at home	80	
	R	Hart Catherine—†	24	"	50	
	S	Mack James	24	sorter	63	
	T	Mack Mary—†	24	housewife	60	"
	U	Putwain Margaret—†	25	"	62	"
	V	Flaherty John	25A	laborer	29	80 Havre
	W	Flaherty Rose—†	25A	housewife	64	80 "
	X	*Caruso Josephine—†	26	"	34	here
	Y	*Caruso Matteo	26	baker	49	"
	Z	*Calandra Dominick	26	fisherman	32	297 Sumner
77						
	A	Calandra Rita—†	26	housewife	31	297 "
	B	Meledy Alzono	27	operator	45	here
	C	Willneff Annie—†	27	housewife	57	"
	D	Carlson Martha—†	27A	"	70	"
	E	Bibbey Lillian J—†	28	typist	27	28 Monument
	F	Gagnon Stephen	28	electrician	44	here

Page.	Letter.	Full Name.	Residence, Jan. 1, 1938.	Occupation.	Supposed Age.	Reported Residence, Jan. 1, 1937. Street and Number.

Maverick Street—Continued

	G	Shannon Anna—†	28	packer	45	here
	H	Shannon Catherine L—†	28	housewife	54	"
	K	Shannon Michael J	28	retired	74	"
	L	Delisio Clementine—†	30	packer	23	
	M	Penta Anthony	30	glazier	45	
	N	Penta Ernest	30	packer	24	
	O	Penta John C	30	clerk	22	
	P	Penta Mary L—†	30	housewife	43	"
	R	Simpson Edith B—†	31	"	59	
	S	Simpson Walter E	31	shipper	23	
	T	Simpson Wilfred R	31	porter	29	
	U	Simpson William A	31	watchman	61	"
	V	Whitten Elizabeth E—†	31	housewife	63	"
	X	*Rollo Nettie—†	33	"	27	
	Y	*Rollo Vito	33	fisherman	38	"
	Z	Bertolino Anthony	33	"	23	
78						
	A	*Bertolino Antonetta—†	33	housewife	50	"
	B	*Bertolino Baldasare	33	fisherman	56	"
	C	*Bertolino Rose—†	33	stitcher	24	
	D	Ardagna Giovanni	33	laborer	45	
	E	*Ardagna Rose—†	33	housewife	40	"
	F	*DeSouza Adretto	42	laborer	38	
	G	*DeSouza Mary—†	42	housewife	46	"
	K	Weeks Elmer	44	laborer	40	
	L	*Pettipas Jerome	44	carpenter	65	"
	M	*Pettipas Marion—†	44	housewife	63	"
	N	Leary Norbert	45	garageman	21	"
	O	Nugent Eleanor—†	45	housewife	63	"
	P	Nugent John	45	clergyman	65	"
	R	Recchia Helen—†	45	housewife	39	"
	S	Recchia Lovairio	45	laborer	47	
	T	*Bonguano Joseph	46	"	51	
	U	*Bonguano Nunzita—†	46	housewife	44	"
	V	Bordonaro Innocenzo	46	laborer	56	84 Chelsea
	W	*Bordonaro Josephine—†	46	housewife	49	84 "
	X	Lombardo Anna—†	46	"	34	here
	Y	Lombardo Joseph	46	laborer	43	"
	Z	Smallcomb John P	47	"	47	"
79						
	A	Mason Pearl—†	47	housewife	39	"

E	Piazza Rose—†	48	housewife	31	"
F	Hayden Sophia—†	48	"	20	"
G	*Hayden Stephen	48	laborer	25	
H	Valade Nellie—†	49	housewife	27	"
K	Valade Omer	49	operator	31	
L	*Labbati Francesca—†	49	housewife	47	"
M	*Lamarca Pasqualina—†	49	"	77	
N	*Marotta Concetta—†	49	at home	61	
O	Marotta Joseph	49	barber	24	
R	*Cali Antonio	50	shoemaker	58	"
S	Cali Frank	50	cleaner	28	
T	*Cali Mary—†	50	housewife	48	"
U	Cali Theresa—†	50	"	26	"
V	*Fiore Fortunato	50	fisherman	35	46 Maverick
W	Fiore Lillian—†	50	housewife	25	46 "
X	McKinnon Eleanor M—†	53	"	23	here
Y	McKinnon Melvin F	53	fisherman	23	"
Z	Hunt Mary—†	53	housewife	45	"
	80				
A	Hunt Vere	53	laborer	40	
B	Caporale Joseph	53	"	35	
C	Caporale Julia—†	53	housewife	27	"
D	Guiltre Bruno	54	barber	22	
E	Guiltre Carmella—†	54	dressmaker	20	"
F	Guiltre Dominic	54	laborer	46	
G	*Guiltre Louise—†	54	housewife	42	"
H	*Andreadis Stamatia—†	54	"	40	
K	*Andreadis Theodore	54	fisherman	46	"
L	*Angell Duncan J	54	retired	71	
M	Angell Edward	54	laborer	32	
N	Angell Harold	54	"	22	"
O	*Angell Helen—†	54	housewife	55	"
P	Ravagna Angelo	55	operator	23	5 Wilbur ct
R	Ravagna Thomasina—†	55	"	23	5 "
S	Powers Mary F—†	55	"	31	here
T	Powers Thomas F	55	laborer	49	"
U	Waterman Ethel—†	55	housewife	41	"
V	Fernandez Ferando	57	canvasmaker	20	370 Commerc'l

Maverick Street---Continued

Page.	Letter.	Full Name.	Residence, Jan. 1, 1938.	Occupation.	Supposed Age.	Reported Residence, Jan. 1, 1937. Street and Number.
	X	*Campanella Rocco	57	laborer	47	82 London
	Y	*Campanella Rose—†	57	housewife	42	82 “
81						
	A	*Naso Maria—†	58A	“	42	here
	B	Naso Nicholas	58A	storekeeper	43	“
	C	*Martino Alfonsina—†	59	housewife	46	“
	D	Martino Eliseo	59	storekeeper	48	“
	E	*Patturelli Mary—†	59	housewife	50	“
	F	Delisio Louisa—†	59	operator	25	“
	G	*Delisio Margaret—†	59	housewife	51	“
	K	Zichella Amedeo	60	operator	29	50 London
	L	Zichella Rose—†	60	housewife	23	50 “
	M	*Loguidice Rocco	60	carpenter	46	here
	N	Loguidice Rose—†	60	housewife	34	“
	P	Denning June—†	67	“	41	19 Eutaw
	R	Denning Thomas	67	laborer	56	19 “
	T	Jeffers Mary—†	69	housewife	70	56 Bennington
	U	Walsh William A	69	salesman	45	56 “
	V	Lawlor Ellen M—†	69	housewife	57	here
	W	Lawlor Peter P	69	cooper	54	“
	X	Manning Josephine—†	71	housewife	64	“
	Y	Murphy Esther—†	71	clerk	40	“
	Z	Calbanano Annie—†	73	housewife	52	137 Chelsea
82						
	A	*Calbano Joseph	73	operator	52	137 “
	B	*Terranova Felita—†	73	housewife	27	here
	C	Terranova Frank	73	laborer	42	“
	D	DiDomenico Concezio	79	“	46	“
	E	*DiDomenico Louise—†	79	housewife	41	“
	F	*Trippi Joseph	79	laborer	41	
	G	Trippi Phyllis—†	79	housekeeper	33	“
	H	*DiCarolis Amato	79	laborer	56	“
	K	*DiCarolis Concetta—†	79	housewife	46	“
	L	Hartigan Marion—†	81	clerk	35	
	M	Hartigan Richard H	81	custodian	66	“
	N	Sloan Margaret—†	81	milliner	52	
	O	Fountain Helen—†	81	housewife	38	“
	P	Fountain Robert	81	salesman	50	“
	R	Thompson Susan—†	81	cook	52	
	S	Comosa James	83	chauffeur	44	“
	T	Comosa John	83	laborer	21	

Page.	Letter.	Full Name.	Residence, Jan. 1, 1938.	Occupation.	Supposed Age.	Reported Residence, Jan. 1, 1937. Street and Number.

Maverick Street—Continued

Page.	Letter.	Full Name.	Residence, Jan. 1, 1938.	Occupation.	Supposed Age.	Reported Residence, Jan. 1, 1937. Street and Number.
	U	Comosa Mary—†	83	housewife	38	here
	W	Paolillo Carmine	85	laborer	41	“
	X	*Paolillo Jennie—†	85	housewife	41	“
	Y	*Benevento Anna—†	85	“	44	
	Z	*Benevento Nunzio	85	fisherman	44	“
83						
	A	*Bertolino Carmella—†	85	housewife	41	“
	B	*Bertolino Peter	85	fisherman	42	“
	C	*Ruggiero Maria—†	86	at home	59	“
	D	Scopa Angelina—†	86	housewife	20	“
	E	Scopa Pasquale	86	counterman	23	“
	F	Gallo Baldassare	86	operator	43	“
	G	*Gallo Benedetta—†	86	housewife	28	“
	H	Bushee Peter	88	retired	73	2 Havre
	K	*Flynn Benjamin F	88	seaman	56	here
	L	Jeffrey Alice M—†	88	at home	55	“
	M	*Mahoney Richard	88	seaman	64	“
	N	McDonald Walter	88	carpenter	55	Chelsea
	O	Moran John F	88	laborer	60	here
	P	Smith Lena—†	88	housewife	28	143 Webster
	R	Fouhy Charles	89	longshoreman	53	here
	S	McGinn Charles	89	“	22	“
	T	McGinn Harold	89	“	45	“
	U	McGinn Rose—†	89	housewife	32	“
	X	*Fatalo Joseph	91	laborer	70	
	Y	*Fatalo Rose—†	91	housewife	64	“
	Z	Ruggiero Angelina—†	91	“	30	
84						
	A	Ruggiero Anthony	91	bookbinder	30	“
	B	Carrozza Maria—†	91	housewife	22	“
	C	Carrozza Mario	91	assembler	28	“
	D	*Indresano Thomasina—†	92	at home	55	
	E	Indresano Albert	92	chauffeur	30	“
	F	Indresano Lena—†	92	housewife	28	“
	G	Indresano Joseph	92	repairman	34	“
	H	Indresano Lena—†	92	housewife	26	“
	K	Riley John J	95	teamster	55	“
	L	Riley Lillian—†	95	housewife	52	“
	M	Bernardo Connie—†	95	“	24	Revere
	N	Bernardo Guy	95	barber	25	“
	O	*Mangiafico Lena—†	95	housewife	33	here

Page.	Letter.	Full Name.	Residence, Jan. 1, 1938.	Occupation.	Supposed Age.	Reported Residence, Jan. 1, 1937. Street and Number.

Maverick Street—Continued

Page.	Letter.	Full Name.	Residence, Jan. 1, 1938.	Occupation.	Supposed Age.	Reported Residence, Jan. 1, 1937. Street and Number.
	P	*Mangiafico Paul	95	laborer	38	here
	S	*Ippolito Anthony	97	"	62	"
	T	*Ippolito Frances—†	97	housekeeper	60	"
	U	Ippolito Rocco	97	laborer	28	"
	V	*Tribuna Antonette—†	97	housewife	67	"
	W	Tribuna Joseph	97	fisherman	29	"
	X	Bonta Carnello	97	laborer	35	
	Y	Bonta Sarah—†	97	housewife	31	"
	Z	Goldberg Bertha—†	98	"	45	
85						
	A	Goldberg Joseph	98	physician	47	"
	B	Goldberg Ruth—†	98	technician	23	"
	C	DeLario Eva—†	98	housewife	29	"
	D	DeLario Vito	98	shipper	30	
	F	*Goldenberg Nellie—†	100	housewife	67	"
	G	Goldenberg Sarah—†	100	"	43	
	H	Goldenberg William	100	storekeeper	41	"
	K	Rubenstein Esther—†	100	clerk	23	"
	L	Finklestein Annie—†	100	housewife	49	"
	M	Finklestein Morris	100	storekeeper	50	"
	N	Ginsberg Sarah—†	100	at home	90	"
	O	Lipner Mary—†	100	teacher	25	
	P	Latorer Nellie—†	101	housewife	56	"
	R	Latorer William	101	laborer	63	
	S	*Gomes Joseph	101	"	32	
	T	*Silva Domenica—†	101	housewife	47	"
	V	Brandano Celestino	103	baker	43	
	W	Brandano Emma—†	103	housewife	34	"
	Y	*Bellino Robert	106	laborer	41	
	Z	Bellino Ruth—†	106	housewife	39	"
86						
	A	Rall Arthur	106	laborer	35	
	B	Ruden John	106	"	46	
	C	Zirk Carol	106	"	56	
	D	Chin Ching Shaw	108	laundryman	55	"
	E	*Chin Quan Shee—†	108	housewife	45	"
	F	Hafey Edward	108	caretaker	24	"
	G	Hafey James U	108	laborer	54	
	H	Hafey James U	108	clerk	28	
	K	Hafey Joseph	108	laborer	26	
	L	Hafey Paul	108	"	21	

Maverick Street—Continued

Page.	Letter.	Full Name.	Residence, Jan. 1, 1938.	Occupation.	Supposed Age.	Reported Residence, Jan. 1, 1937. Street and Number.
	M	Hafey Thomas	108	cook	22	here
	N	Bickford Melvin	109	gatetender	43	“
	O	Colburn Andrew	109	laborer	54	“
	P	Garvin Isabella—†	109	housewife	67	“
	R	Riley Alice—†	111	“	31	27 Princeton
	S	Riley Frederick	111	glazier	34	27 “
	T	Cecere Edith—†	111	housewife	28	123 Orleans
	U	Cecere William	111	chauffeur	27	123 “
	V	Dockery Bernard	111	retired	77	123 “
	W	Miller Bernard J	111	salesman	39	123 “
	X	Miller Bridget—†	111	housewife	71	123 “

Meridian Street

Page.	Letter.	Full Name.	Residence, Jan. 1, 1938.	Occupation.	Supposed Age.	Reported Residence, Jan. 1, 1937. Street and Number.
87						
	E	Thompson Charles	62	retired	89	here
	F	Thompson Alfred	62	“	75	“
	G	*Fleming Sadie—†	62	at home	68	“
	H	Leckie Mary—†	62	housewife	78	“
	K	Leckie William	62	retired	76	“
	T	Buccheri Mary—†	74	housewife	27	221 Border
	U	Buccheri Paul	74	chauffeur	26	221 “
	W	DeBenedictis Alfred	78	salesman	20	here
	X	DeBenedictis Elvira—†	78	housewife	54	“
	Y	DeBenedictis Richard	78	laborer	22	“
88						
	B	Ward Marie—†	86	housewife	29	“
	C	Avallone Nunziante	86	barber	49	“
	F	Monihan Hannah—†	92	at home	75	“
	G	Runney Sarah—†	92	“	75	“
	H	Tyler John P	92	painter	59	“
	O	Eicholz Jessie M—†	102A	clerk	32	17 Yarmouth
	P	Eicholz Maurice T	102A	clergyman	31	17 “
	R	Sheehan Elizabeth—†	102A	housewife	49	here
	S	Sheehan James W	102A	laborer	49	“
	T	Cohen Eva—†	108	secretary	30	17 Central
	U	Cohen Helen—†	108	at home	29	17 “
	V	Cohen Louis	108	physician	37	17 “
	W	Cowan Maurice I	108	optometrist	26	220 Paris
	X	Novakoff Goldie—†	108	housewife	35	17 Central sq
	Y	Novakoff Joseph	108	retired	45	17 “
89						
	C	Hickey Frederick	122	clerk	23	66 London

Page.	Letter.	Full Name.	Residence, Jan. 1, 1938.	Occupation.	Supposed Age.	Reported Residence, Jan. 1, 1937. Street and Number.
		Meridian Street—Continued				
	D	Hickey Mary—†	122	clerk	40	66 London
	E	Hickey Richard	122	"	21	66 "
	F	*Gillis Alexander	122	painter	47	here
	G	Gillis Laura—†	122	housewife	38	"
	K	*Buck Patrick	126	laborer	66	"
	L	Callahan Patrick	126	"	59	
	M	Furlong William T	126	"	58	
	N	Jones Frederick	126	retired	66	
	O	Mullen Mary E—†	126	housekeeper	54	"
	P	Ryley Horace	126	laborer	28	"
	R	Ryley Melvin	126	"	23	
	S	Thibeau Paul	126	"	65	
	U	*Nigro Angelina—†	130	housewife	40	"
	V	Nigro Joseph	130	laborer	48	
	W	*Centofanti Clorinda—†	130	at home	35	
	X	*Testa Christina—†	130	housewife	43	"
	Y	Testa Joseph	130	operator	47	"
90						
	A	Intraversato Joseph	134	laborer	60	
	B	*Intraversato Maria—†	134	housewife	50	"
	C	Intraversato Savino	134	laborer	32	
	D	*Ligiero Michelena—†	134	at home	49	"
	E	Melarno Carlo	134	laborer	23	149 Chelsea
	F	Melarno Mary—†	134	housewife	21	149 "
	G	Nigro Dante	134	cook	21	here
	H	*Nigro Eupremio	134	laborer	45	"
	K	*Nigro Philomena—†	134	housewife	46	"
	M	Fingerman Annie—†	138	clerk	22	
	N	Fingerman Fannie—†	138	at home	65	
	O	*Fingerman Joseph	138	tailor	40	
	P	*Fingerman Mary—†	138	housewife	39	"
		New Street				
	T	Incagnoli Mary—†	11	housewife	23	289 Sumner
	U	Incagnoli Nunzio	11	operator	23	289 "
	V	*Intingaro Mary—†	11	housewife	45	here
	W	Intingaro Salvatore	11	laborer	41	"
	Y	Poli Christine—†	13	housewife	26	44 Liverpool
	Z	Poli Raymond	13	mechanic	26	44 "
91						
	D	Drago Anthony	15	laborer	40	here

Page.	Letter.	Full Name.	Residence, Jan. 1, 1938.	Occupation.	Supposed Age.	Reported Residence, Jan. 1, 1937. Street and Number.

New Street—Continued

	E	Landry Josephine—†	15	housekeeper	64	here
	F	Gardina Frances—†	17	housewife	32	"
	G	Gardina Joseph	17	laborer	39	"
	H	*Riggo Lena—†	17	housekeeper	42	"
	K	Franco John	17	laborer	41	"
	M	Cummings Nicholas	21	"	60	
	N	Costa Antonio	21	"	40	
	O	*Costa Georgina—†	21	housewife	37	"
	R	*Pappas Constantine—†	23	"	30	
	S	Pappas Manuel	23	laborer	40	"
	T	Catalano Angelo	23	"	47	
	U	Catalano Manuel	23	student	20	
	V	Catalano Philomena—†	23	housewife	37	"
	Z	Sullivan Annie—†	27	at home	56	
92						
	C	Carraco Amelia—†	33	housewife	35	"
	D	Carraco John	33	laborer	41	
	E	Ruggiero Inez—†	33	inspector	20	"
	F	Ruggiero Joseph	33	laborer	24	
	G	Ruggiero Mary—†	33	housewife	50	"
	H	Ruggiero Nicholas	33	laborer	46	
	K	Geogalos Eggale	33	engineer	57	
	L	Geogalos Mary—†	33	housewife	47	"
	M	Geogalos Thomas	33	engineer	20	"
	N	Luti Anna—†	35	housewife	30	"
	O	*Luti John	35	laborer	31	
	P	*Corranti Angelo	35	tailor	37	
	R	Corranti Maria—†	35	housewife	34	"
	S	Barletta Anthony	35	operator	23	"
	T	Barletta Felix	35	"	34	
	U	Barletta George	35	"	27	
	V	*Barletta William	35	retired	64	
	X	Aragio Frank	37	laborer	48	
	Y	*Aragio Nancy—†	37	housewife	43	"

Paris Street

	Z	McArdle Grace—†	6	housewife	52	here
93						
	A	McArdle Thomas	6	machinist	56	"
	B	Dorso Anthony	6	barber	28	

Page.	Letter.	Full Name.	Residence, Jan. 1, 1938.	Occupation.	Supposed Age.	Reported Residence, Jan. 1, 1937. Street and Number.

Paris Street—Continued

	C	Dorso Frank	6	shoemaker	65	here
	D	Dorso Margaret—†	6	housewife	57	“
	E	Antico Domenic	6	laborer	43	“
	F	Sweeney Anne J—†	8	housewife	66	13 Meridian
	G	Sweeney William J	8	watchman	64	13 “
	H	DeSousa Manuel	8	fireman	66	here
	K	DeSousa Rose—†	8	housewife	50	“
	L	Lima Anaset B	8	laborer	30	“
	M	Russell Abraham	8	retired	70	“
	N	Zarbo Richard	8	laborer	23	180 Marion
	O	Zarbo William	8	artist	21	180 “
	P	Sidebotham Samuel C	10	glazier	61	here
	R	*Brogna Anthony	12	laborer	60	“
	S	Brogna Mary—†	12	operator	21	“
	T	*Brogna Vincenza—†	12	housewife	62	“
	U	*DiPerri Charles	12	laborer	50	
	V	DiPerri John	12	“	21	
	W	DiPerri Phyllis—†	12	stitcher	20	
	X	*DiPerri Vincenza—†	12	housewife	40	“
	Y	*Trippi Rosaria—†	12	housekeeper	68	“
	Z	*DiPerri Filippa—†	12	housewife	49	“
94						
	A	DiPerri Jennie—†	12	stitcher	24	
	B	*DiPerri Joseph	12	laborer	55	
	C	Cibello Edith—†	14	housewife	27	“
	D	Cibello Louis	14	operator	31	
	E	Cibello Anthony	14	“	32	
	F	*Cibello Maria—†	14	housewife	59	“
	G	Cibello Mary—†	14	operator	34	“
	H	Perillo Elizabeth—†	14	housewife	34	“
	K	Perillo Gustave	14	operator	39	“
	L	*Secatore Adele—†	16	housewife	65	“
	M	Secatore Dominic	16	tailor	68	
	N	Secatore Edmund	16	technician	25	“
	O	*Secatore Enis—†	16	housewife	35	“
	P	*Secatore Hamlet	16	tailor	38	“
	R	Lewis Alfred	18	proprietor	32	72 Eutaw
	S	Lewis Anna—†	18	housewife	26	72 “
	T	Twomey Andrew J	18	letter carrier	57	here
	U	Twomey Catherine A—†	18	teacher	25	“
	V	Twomey Eleanor G—†	18	“	23	“

Page.	Letter.	Full Name.	Residence, Jan. 1, 1938.	Occupation.	Supposed Age.	Reported Residence, Jan. 1, 1937. Street and Number.

Paris Street—Continued

	W	Twomey Raymond A	18	clerk	21	here
	X	*Bright Joseph	20	fisherman	58	"
	Y	*Bussey James	20	longshoreman	70	"
	Z	Callahan Timothy	20	laborer	71	
95						
	A	*Conway Philip	20	longshoreman	62	"
	B	Doyle Martha A—†	20	housekeeper	85	"
	C	Lynch John J	20	plumber	65	"
	D	Lynch William P	20	janitor	61	
	E	*O'Brien James	20	fisherman	61	"
	F	Stanton John F	20	cooper	66	
	G	Anderson Catherine—†	22	housewife	54	"
	H	Anderson Hans P	22	longshoreman	52	"
	K	Anderson Mary—†	22	clerk	23	
	L	Anderson William	22	laborer	21	
	M	Foydenlund Vilderma	22	fisherman	53	"
	N	*Haas Max	24	seaman	55	
	O	Lanning Cornelius M	24	clerk	27	"
	P	Lanning Ellen—†	24	housewife	56	"
	R	Lanning Ellen—†	24	clerk	20	
	S	Lanning John M	24	attorney	24	"
	T	Lanning Julia—†	24	clerk	25	
	U	Lanning Michael C	24	foreman	66	"
	V	Obit Anton	24	seaman	45	
	X	Coolin Rita J—†	32	housekeeper	43	"
	Y	Betts Edward	32	clerk	56	"
	Z	Betts Emma—†	32	housewife	56	"
96						
	A	Betts George	32	laundryman	51	"
	B	Doucette Laura—†	34	housewife	28	Gloucester
	C	Doucette Lester	34	laborer	38	"
	D	*Careau Richard	34	"	58	191 Sumner
	E	Clark Margaret—†	34	clerk	60	6 London
	F	Cronin William	34	retired	56	here
	G	French Cyrus	34	laborer	73	9 Winthrop
	H	*Lindstrom John	34	"	40	Chelsea
	K	Mease John	34	"	40	here
	L	Patterson Harry J	34	"	52	"
	M	Penta Ernest	36	glazier	31	"
	N	Penta Margaret—†	36	housewife	29	"
	O	Macrones Mary—†	36	"	31	"

Page.	Letter.	Full Name.	Residence, Jan. 1, 1938.	Occupation.	Supposed Age.	Reported Residence, Jan. 1, 1937. Street and Number.
Paris Street—Continued						
	P	Macrones Spiro	36	chef	38	here
	R	Frusciante Anthony	36	laborer	30	"
	S	Frusciante Carmella—†	36	housewife	25	"
	T	Buckley Jeremiah	38	clerk	34	171 Lexington
	U	Buckley Marie—†	38	housewife	28	333 Paris
	V	Crandall Harold F	38	longshoreman	40	here
	W	Goode Lemuel	38	fireman	66	N Hampshire
	X	Greene Edward P	38	janitor	63	here
	Y	Kavanaugh George W	38	retired	66	Chelsea
	Z	Morgan Joseph	38	laborer	57	here
97						
	A	Rogers James	38	longshoreman	32	160 Sumner
	B	Cone Birthday	46	retired	79	38 Paris
	C	Boutchia Albert	46	clerk	27	20 Havre
	D	Boutchia Estella—†	46	housewife	47	20 "
	E	Boutchia Robert W	46	laborer	58	20 "
	F	Boutchia William	46	"	28	20 "
	G	Lopilato Louis	48	clerk	31	here
	H	Lopilato Mary—†	48	housewife	30	"
	K	Rosato Anthony	48	chauffeur	25	"
	L	*Rosato Rachael—†	48	housewife	53	"
	M	*Rosato Thomas	48	plasterer	51	"
	P	Megna Frank	64	chauffeur	27	"
	R	Megna Grace—†	64	housewife	30	"
	S	Dioguardi George	64	chauffeur	21	"
	T	Dioguardi Nicholas	64	attendant	29	"
	U	Tubin Bessie—†	66	housewife	41	"
	V	Tubin Emanuel	66	merchant	43	"
	W	Miller Eunice E—†	66	nurse	24	143 Kilsyth rd
	X	Wood Elizabeth E—†	66	"	23	1 Autumn
	Y	Marafino Antonio	66	barber	55	here
	Z	Marafino Mary—†	66	housewife	51	"
98		**Sumner Street**				
	B	*Sorrento Fred	34	laborer	53	95 London
	C	*Sorrento Gaetana—†	34	housewife	41	95 "
	D	Arciero Angelina—†	34	"	41	here
	E	Arciero Christoforo	34	chauffeur	42	"
	F	*Bellitti Joseph	34	laborer	52	"
	G	*Bellitti Katherine—†	34	housewife	38	"

Page.	Letter.	Full Name.	Residence, Jan. 1, 1938.	Occupation.	Supposed Age.	Reported Residence, Jan. 1, 1937. Street and Number.

Sumner Street—Continued

	H	Bellitti Mario	34	laborer	22	here
	K	D'India Adaline—†	38	housekeeper	50	"
	L	D'India Albert	38	laborer	21	"
	T	Ingaciola Beatrice—†	66	at home	20	
	U	Ingaciola Jennie—†	66	houseworker	22	"
	V	Ingaciola Maria—†	66	housewife	54	"
	W	Ingaciola Pasquale	66	laborer	62	
	X	Piazza Angelo	66	"	49	
	Y	Piazza Stella—†	66	housewife	37	"
	Z	Lombardo Anthony	66	fisherman	55	"
99						
	A	*Lombard Sebastina—†	66	housewife	46	"
	B	*Italiano Benidito	66	plumber	53	"
	C	*Italiano Maria—†	66	housewife	50	"
	D	Italiano Peter	66	laborer	20	
	E	Italiano Salvatore	66	plumber	22	"
	H	Dunbar Milan	76	cutter	39	82 Sumner
	K	Dunbar Thelma—†	76	housewife	35	82 "
	L	Cavalaro Alexander	76	laborer	20	here
	M	*Cavalaro Angelena—†	76	housewife	54	"
	N	Cavalaro Calogero	76	laborer	57	"
	O	Rindone Diana—†	76	stitcher	22	
	P	*Rindone Josephine—†	76	housewife	58	"
	R	*Rindone Michael	76	laborer	31	"
	S	Spatarro Joseph	76	"	57	
	T	Spatarro Maria—†	76	operator	21	"
	U	*Spatarro Stella—†	76	housewife	57	"
	V	DeBlaisi Antonio	76	storekeeper	48	"
	W	*DeBlaisi Maria—†	76	housewife	45	"
	X	Evans Augusta—†	76	"	44	163A Falcon
	Y	Evans Robert	76	laborer	53	163A "
	Z	Cavalaro Carmella—†	76	housewife	22	here
100						
	A	Cavalaro Raymond	76	barber	24	
	B	*Piermattei Panfilio	76	laborer	59	
	C	Lovermo Charles	76	"	45	
	D	*Lovermo Lucia—†	76	housewife	36	"
	E	Guerreri Mary—†	76	"	33	6 Liverpool
	F	Guerreri Salvatore	76	"	42	6 "
	K	Moran Frank	82	watchman	44	90 Sumner
	L	Moran Margaret—†	82	housewife	47	90 "

Page.	Letter.	FULL NAME.	Residence, Jan. 1, 1938.	Occupation.	Supposed Age.	Reported Residence, Jan. 1, 1937. Street and Number.

Sumner Street—Continued

	M	Powers Tohmas	82	laborer	20	90 Sumner
	N	Santos John	82	seaman	33	53 Liverpool
	O	Santos Mary—†	82	housewife	23	53 "
	P	Hrono James	84	chef	39	here
	R	Hrono Mary—†	84	housewife	24	"
	S	Cantara Homer	84	fisherman	27	"
	T	Cantara Margaret—†	84	housewife	27	"
	U	Lazzerino Frank	84	storekeeper	75	"
	X	*Faragi Fillipa—†	88A	housewife	47	"
	Y	*Faragi Joseph	88A	laborer	68	
	Z	*Faragi Joseph	88A	"	22	
101						
	A	Faragi Lewis	88A	"	27	
	B	Gonsalas Mamie—†	90	housekeeper	40	"
	C	Merchant Catherine—†	90	"	45	"
	D	Chase Margaret—†	92	housewife	45	"
	E	*Chase Roy	92	plumber	51	
	F	Hagerty Catherine—†	92	housekeeper	50	"
	G	*Golisano Gaetano	94	laborer	43	"
	H	*Golisano Grace—†	94	housewife	38	"
	K	D'Andrea Carmello	94	laborer	36	
	L	*D'Andrea Mary—†	94	housewife	28	"
	M	Costa Angela—†	94	at home	20	6 Liverpool
	N	Costa Carmillo	94	laborer	48	6 "
	O	*Costa Rosario—†	94	housewife	37	6 "
	P	*Catalano Francesca—†	96	"	48	here
	R	Catalano Joseph	96	laborer	57	"
	S	Catalano Manuel	96	"	28	"
	T	Santos George	96	longshoreman	50	"
	U	*Santos John	96	oiler	27	
	V	*Santos Josephine—†	96	housewife	46	"
	X	*Pitsano Julietta—†	98	"	49	
	Y	Pitsano Louis	98	laborer	48	"
	Z	*Mazzola Catherine—†	100	housewife	42	118 Sumner
102						
	A	Mazzola Philip	100	laborer	52	118 "
	B	*Marino Maria—†	100	housewife	63	here
	C	Marino Michael	100	laborer	23	"
	D	Marino Nicola	100	"	60	"
	E	Marino William	100	electrician	31	"
	F	*Gomez Manuel	100	cook	65	118 Sumner

Page.	Letter.	Full Name.	Residence, Jan. 1, 1938.	Occupation.	Supposed Age.	Reported Residence, Jan. 1, 1937. Street and Number.

Sumner Street—Continued

Page.	Letter.	Full Name.	Residence, Jan. 1, 1938.	Occupation.	Supposed Age.	Reported Residence, Jan. 1, 1937. Street and Number.
	G	*Lava Antonio	100	laborer	51	118 Sumner
	H	*Mercie Joseph	100	cook	62	118 "
	M	Bennett Harold L	106	fisherman	53	50 Howard
	N	Bennett Minnie—†	106	housewife	49	50 "
	O	*Anthony John	106	painter	39	here
	P	Bowes Nicholas	106	laborer	61	"
	R	Ellis Edward	106	"	60	"
	S	Murphy Joseph	106	chauffeur	57	6 London
	T	Olisky Louis	106	dealer	45	here
	U	Riley Maurice	106	longshoreman	35	191 Sumner
	V	*Rodney Joseph	106	laborer	38	21 Havre
	W	*Wrejcibidi John	106	fireman	35	4 Border
	X	Anderson Christopher	108	longshoreman	46	6 London
	Y	Anderson Vernon	108	rigger	36	here
	Z	Bertucelli Charles	108	longshoreman	36	"
103						
	A	Bertucelli Jessie—†	108	housewife	29	"
	B	Cunningham Joseph	108	retired	55	21 Havre
	C	Gleason George	108	laborer	38	106 Sumner
	D	Gomez Jesse	108	painter	67	here
	E	*Grasso Raffello	108	laborer	60	"
	F	*Lund Gustaf A	108	"	60	11 Henry
	G	Morton Samuel	108	retired	70	here
	H	*Nardo Anthony	108	laborer	63	"
	K	Quimby Benjamin	108	"	57	"
	L	*Riley William	108	"	47	
	M	Woodger Fred	108	"	45	"
	O	*Romano Assunta—†	120	housewife	29	22 Fleet
	P	*Romano Giacomo	120	laborer	33	22 "
	R	*Oliva Vincenza—†	120	housewife	47	here
	S	DiPerri John	122	chauffeur	28	"
	T	*DiPerri Mary—†	122	housewife	24	35 London
	U	*DePerri Anthony	122	operator	22	here
	V	*DePerri Cologero	122	retired	69	"
	W	*DePerri Mary—†	122	housewife	56	"
	X	Salvaggio Michael	122	operator	48	"
	Y	*Salvaggio Rose—†	122	housewife	36	"
	Z	Roche Henry	128	retired	72	"
104						
	A	Roche Stella—†	128	housekeeper	40	"
	G	Ciccorelli Mary—†	134	housewife	52	"

Page.	Letter.	Full Name.	Residence, Jan. 1, 1938.	Occupation.	Supposed Age.	Reported Residence, Jan. 1, 1937. Street and Number.

Sumner Street—Continued

	H	Ciccorelli Sarafino	134	storekeeper	54	here
	L	Lombardo John	134	fisherman	24	66 Sumner
	N	Salvasta Carmella—†	134	seamstress	22	here
	O	Salvasta Crucificia—†	134	housewife	52	"
	P	Salvasta Orazio	134	laborer	58	"
	R	Salvasta Phyllis—†	134	at home	21	
	S	Maurici Angelena—†	134	housewife	46	"
	T	Maurici Plazito	134	laborer	60	
	Y	Setu Joseph	154	laundryman	43	"
	Z	Bowe Mary—†	154½	seamstress	40	"
105						
	A	McCarthy John J	154½	musician	33	"
	B	Price Emily—†	154½	forewoman	32	713A Tremont
	D*	George Axel	158	longshoreman	63	here
	E	Gorgan Patrick	158	"	62	"
	F	Hart George	158	retired	67	"
	G	Lema Joseph	158	longshoreman	67	"
	H	McDonough Edward	158	retired	67	
	K*	Milrick John	158	"	58	
	L	Riley Matthew	158	laborer	49	
	M	Silvia Frank	158	"	48	
	N	Camera John	160	"	49	
	O	Frazer Clarence	160		54	"
	P	Furlough Frank	160	"	65	10 Paris
	R	Orchard Alfred	160	longshoreman	32	here
	S	Orchard Elsie—†	160	housewife	31	"
	T	Schwaster Frank	160	longshoreman	40	"
	Y	Chacos George	172	cook	61	
	Z	Cornetta John	172	bartender	26	"
106						
	A	Cornetta Mary—†	172	housewife	42	"
	B	Cornetta Vivian—†	172	at home	23	
	C	Dyer Elmer	172	engineer	45	"
	D	Pastore James	172	bartender	26	34 Shelby

William J. Kelly Square

	F	Stanley Charles A	64	floorwalker	20	here
	G	Stanley Jane E—†	64	housewife	46	"
	H	Stanley Martin K	64	electrician	46	"
	K	Stanley Martin K, jr	64	cook	23	

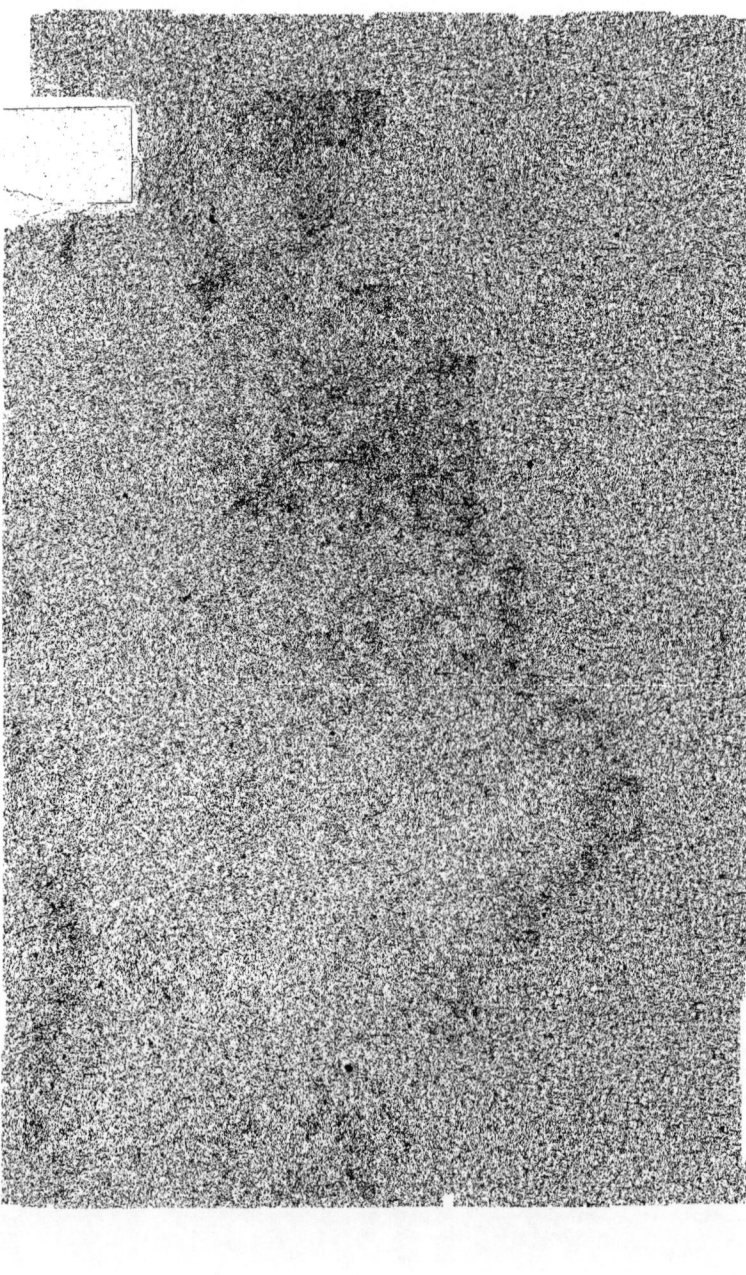

Ward 1—Precinct 2

CITY OF BOSTON

LIST OF RESIDENTS
20 YEARS OF AGE AND OVER

(NON-CITIZENS INDICATED BY ASTERISK)
(FEMALES INDICATED BY DAGGER)

AS OF

JANUARY 1, 1938

JOSEPH F. TIMILTY, } *Listing*
FREDERIC E. DOWLING, } *Board.*

CITY OF BOSTON PRINTING DEPARTMENT

Page.	Letter.	FULL NAME.	Residence, Jan. 1, 1938.	Occupation.	Supposed Age.	Reported Residence, Jan. 1, 1937. Street and Number.
117						
		Alna Place				
	A	Hanlon Bernard T	1	longshoreman	33	here
	B	Hanlon Charles J	1	electrician	39	"
	C	Hanlon John J	1	longshoreman	66	"
	D	Hanlon John J	1	"	37	
	E	Hanlon Thomas T	1	laborer	25	
	F	Hanlon William J	1	electrician	41	"
	G	*Snow Elizabeth V—†	1	housekeeper	21	"
		Brigham Street				
	H	Morrissey John	1	painter	24	here
	K	Morrissey Sylvester	1	laborer	26	"
	L	Wood Mary—†	1	housewife	42	"
	M	Morton Helen—†	1	"	27	Somerville
	N	Morton Lawrence	1	fireman	26	"
	O	Trainor Alice—†	1	housewife	28	here
	P	Trainor John T	1	longshoreman	30	"
	S	Shioshetti Maria—†	2	housekeeper	48	1 Brigham
	T	*Publicover Howard	2	laborer	46	here
	U	Publicover Nellie—†	2	housewife	45	"
	V	Soderlund Alice—†	3	"	27	"
	W	Soderlun Herbert	3	painter	28	
	X	Marotta Jenny—†	3	student	20	
	Y	Marotta John	3	operator	47	"
	Z	Marotta Mary—†	3	housewife	41	"
118						
	A	DeCoste Charles H	4	laborer	31	
	B	*Kavanagh Virginia—†	4	housekeeper	60	"
	C	Frasca Anthony	4	shoecutter	21	"
	D	Frasca Nicholas	4	laborer	27	
	E	*Frasca Pasquale	4	"	53	
	F	Frasca Susie—†	4	teacher	20	
	H	DeSisto Generoso	5	buffer	31	
	K	DeSisto Lena—†	5	housewife	26	"
	L	Grappi James	5	laborer	24	
	M	Grappi Louise—†	5	factoryhand	35	"
	P	Ferrera John	6	clerk	21	
	R	*Ferrera Joseph	6	laborer	61	"
	S	Ferrera Joseph, jr	6	longshoreman	27	"
	T	Ferrera Louise—†	6	clerk	30	

Page.	Letter.	FULL NAME.	Residence, Jan. 1, 1938.	Occupation.	Supposed Age.	Reported Residence, Jan. 1, 1937. Street and Number.

Brigham Street—Continued

Page.	Letter.	FULL NAME.	Residence, Jan. 1, 1938.	Occupation.	Supposed Age.	Reported Residence, Jan. 1, 1937.
	U	*Ferrera Rose—†	6	housewife	55	here
	V	*Barkhouse Beatrice—†	6	housekeeper	51	"
	W	Hamilton Ralph P	6	conductor	44	"
119						
	K	*Santorio Julius	9	laborer	63	
	M	Leonard John	10	clerk	21	
	N	*Leonard Mary—†	10	housewife	51	"
	O	Leonard Michael	10	longshoreman	48	"
	P	Johnson Catherine—†	10	clerk	25	
	R	*Johnson Nellie—†	10	housewife	54	"
	S	Johnson Thomas	10	painter	25	
	T	*Johnson William	10	longshoreman	54	"
	U	Johnson William, jr	10	laborer	23	
	V	Rocco Anthony	10	"	40	
	W	Rocco Mary—†	10	housewife	33	"
	X	*Sirianni Michael	10	laborer	70	
	Y	*Sirianni Rose—†	10	housewife	55	"
120						
	B	Morrissey John G	20	laborer	77	
	C	*Morrissey Katherine—†	20	housewife	52	"
	D	McCarthy Alice—†	21	"	32	"
	E	McCarthy Daniel	21	fisherman	24	18 Brigham
	F	McCarthy Joseph	21	fireman	35	here
	G	Fagin John	22	retired	83	"
	H	Hahn Elizabeth—†	22	housekeeper	67	"
	K	Jones Thomas	22	bricklayer	65	"

Cheever Court

Page.	Letter.	FULL NAME.	Residence, Jan. 1, 1938.	Occupation.	Supposed Age.	Reported Residence, Jan. 1, 1937.
	M	Repici Anna—†	5	housewife	30	83 Webster
	N	Repici Pasquale C	5	papercutter	36	83 "
	P	*Caccaviello Filomena—†	8	housewife	53	here
	R	*Caccaviello Vincenzo	8	laborer	60	"
	S	*Giardini Charles	8	clerk	29	185 Marion
	T	Giardini Sebastina—†	8	housewife	24	185 "
	U	*Ruggiero Dora—†	9	"	63	here
	V	Ruggiero Frank	9	laborer	20	"
	W	Ruggiero Giuseppe	9	"	64	"
	X	Ruggiero Mary—†	9	stitcher	23	
	Y	DeStefano Josephine—†	10	"	50	
	Z	*Vigorita Josephine—†	10	"	33	

Page.	Letter.	Full Name.	Residence, Jan. 1, 1938.	Occupation.	Supposed Age.	Reported Residence, Jan. 1, 1937. Street and Number.
		121				
		Cheever Court—Continued				
	A	*Paci Angelina—†	10	housewife	42	here
	B	Paci Vincenzo	10	laborer	49	"
	C	*Pirello Charles	11	"	50	"
	D	*Pirello Josephine—†	11	housewife	41	"
	F	Castellano Mary—†	12	at home	24	
	G	Castellano Rose—†	12	seamstress	26	"
	H	Indelicato Catherine—†	12	"	21	
	K	Indelicato Charles	12	clerk	24	
	L	Indelicato Mary—†	12	seamstress	23	"
	M	*Indelicato Michael	12	laborer	57	
	N	*Indelicato Serafina—†	12	housewife	52	"
	O	Castellano Camella—†	12	"	31	
	P	Castellano Joseph	12	millwright	35	"
		Cottage Street				
	T	*Cocchi Ezolina—†	10	housewife	49	here
	U	*Cocchi Paul	10	laborer	52	"
	V	Donovan Dorothy—†	10	packer	27	"
	W	Donovan Francis	10	longshoreman	40	"
	X	Donovan Margaret—†	10	operator	24	"
	Y	Donovan Mary—†	10	at home	60	
	Z	Donovan William	10	chauffeur	36	"
		122				
	A	Giuditta Adeline—†	12	housewife	27	294 Meridian
	B	*Giuditta Frank	12	shoeworker	27	294 "
	C	*DeSimone Mary—†	12	housewife	46	here
	E	Palermo Anthony	14	timekeeper	35	"
	F	*Palermo Mary—†	14	housewife	33	"
	H	Mosca Alfred	14	longshoreman	21	27 Border
	G	*Mosca Leonard	14	laborer	52	27 "
	K	LaMarco Anna—†	14	housewife	24	here
	L	LaMarco Carlo	14	painter	28	"
	M	Ciavola Richard	15	operator	23	64 Bremen
	N	Ciavola Sadie—†	15	housewife	22	64 "
	O	Conti Carlo	15	laborer	48	here
	P	Conti Peter	15	electrician	21	"
	R	*Conti Rose—†	15	housewife	41	"
	S	Salvo Joseph A	15	tailor	24	
	T	Salvo Theresa—†	15	housewife	24	"

Page.	Letter.	FULL NAME.	Residence, Jan. 1, 1938.	Occupation.	Supposed Age.	Reported Residence, Jan. 1, 1937. Street and Number.

Cottage Street—Continued

	U	Ponzo Joseph, jr	16	fisherman	30	here
	V	Ponzo Josephine—†	16	housewife	33	"
	W	Menbrino Giacomo	16	candyworker	46	"
	X	*Menbrino Rosina—†	16	housewife	36	"
	Y	Gravellese Michael	16	mechanic	24	"
	Z	Gravellese Pasquale	16	shoeworker	38	"
123						
	A	Vaccari Andrew	17	milkman	39	"
	B	Vaccari Margaret—†	17	housewife	24	"
	C	Humphrey Mary—†	17	"	40	
	D	Humphrey Oliver	17	longshoreman	44	"
	E	Mahoney Frances—†	17	packer	20	
	F	*McKenna Nora—†	17	housewife	53	"
	G	*McKenna William	17	longshoreman	54	"
	H	*Benelli Columbia—†	18	housewife	44	"
	K	Benelli Mary—†	18	at home	24	
	L	Benelli Ubaldo	18	barber	47	"
	M	Terrizzi Frank	18	carpenter	23	57 Saratoga
	P	LoCalzo Raffaele	18	operator	44	here
	N	Salis Gina—†	18	housewife	48	"
	O	Salis Giovanni	18	fireman	55	"
	R	Goodwin Eva M—†	31	at home	53	"
	S	Kennedy Martin	31	laborer	28	112 Webster
	T	Filomina Louis	31	"	45	3 Murray ct
	U	Barone Amelia—†	31	housewife	35	13 New
	V	*Barone Louis	31	spinner	45	13 "
	X	Ragusa Dorothy—†	32	housewife	23	69 Webster
	Y	Ragusa James	32	laborer	28	69 "
124						
	A	*Ferrera John	33	grocer	44	here
	B	*Ferrera Modesta—†	33	housewife	40	"
	D	Lombardi Ida—†	34	"	30	"
	E	Lombardi Jennie—†	34	at home	35	
	F	Lombardi Michael	34	machinist	32	"
	G	Stasio Amelia—†	34	housewife	34	"
	H	Stasio John B	34	installer	38	
	K	*Pecci Luigi	34	retired	69	
	L	Stasio Emilio	34	technician	34	"
	M	Stasio Rose—†	34	housewife	31	"
	O	*Ravagno Rosa—†	36	at home	60	"
	P	DiFilippo Antonio	36	laborer	50	81 Lubec

Page.	Letter.	Full Name.	Residence, Jan. 1, 1938.	Occupation.	Supposed Age.	Reported Residence, Jan. 1, 1937. Street and Number.

Cottage Street—Continued

	R	*DiFilippo Marie—†	36	housewife	49	81 Lubec
	S	DiFilippo Marie—†	36	stitcher	23	81 "
	T	*Renna Angelina—†	36	housewife	54	here
	U	Renna Clemento	36	laborer	55	"
	V	Renna Santa—†	36	candy packer	24	"
	W	DiChiara Antonetta—†	36	housewife	45	"
	X	DiChiara Joseph	36	longshoreman	50	"
	Y	DiChiara Maria—†	36	at home	20	
125						
	A	Varone Fred	37	mechanic	21	99 Everett
	B	*Varone Margaret—†	37	housewife	48	99 "
	C	Varone Pasquale	37	woodworker	26	99 "
	D	Varone Severo	37	laborer	53	99 "
	E	Natalucci Rose—†	38	housewife	30	here
	F	*Natalucci Vincent	38	bricklayer	33	"
	G	*Sica Anthony	38	mattressmaker	35	"
	H	*Sica Immaculata—†	38	housewife	23	"
	K	Lomano Frank	38	shoeworker	35	"
	L	Mazzotta Gregorio	38	janitor	50	
	M	Mazzotta Maria—†	38	housewife	43	"
	N	Bulger Mary—†	39	housekeeper	51	"
	O	Curtin John W	39	longshoreman	47	"
	P	Moreno Antonio	41	laborer	43	55 Maverick
	R	Moreno Carmena—†	41	housewife	30	55 "
	S	Cunningham Nora—†	41	at home	52	here
	T	Cunningham Nora M—†	41	floorwoman	20	"
	U	*Tripari Alfonzina—†	41	housewife	40	"
	V	*Tripari Simoni	41	laborer	47	
	W	*LoPorto Ignazio	42	"	52	
	X	LoPorto Joseph	42	"	21	"
	Y	Franks Ellena—†	42	housewife	22	Virginia
	Z	Franks Robert	42	seaman	31	"
126						
	A	DiChiaro Angelo	42	laborer	22	here
	B	*Presterone Joseph	42	candymaker	33	"
	C	*Presterone Rita—†	42	housewife	27	"
	D	*Turrilli Antonetta—†	42	at home	20	"
	E	*Turrilli Concetta—†	42	housewife	49	129 Webster
	F	*Turrilli Mario	42	chauffeur	27	here
	G	*Turrilli Raymond	42	painter	22	"
	H	*Turrilli Remo	42	laborer	54	129 Webster

Page.	Letter.	Full Name.	Residence, Jan. 1, 1938.	Occupation.	Supposed Age.	Reported Residence, Jan. 1, 1937. Street and Number.

Cottage Street—Continued

	K	*Turrilli Vincent	42	fishcutter	25	here
	N	*DiChiara Olga—†	43	housewife	38	"
	O	DiChiara Raffaele	43	laborer	41	"
	P	Micciche Giuseppe	43	"	40	"
	R	Guanciali Anthony	43	shoemaker	26	"
	S	Guanciali Mary—†	43	housewife	24	"
	T	*Ciamarra Matilda—†	44	stitcher	26	28 Princeton
	U	*Francalancia Anthony	44	clerk	36	28 "
	V	*Francalancia Emelie—†	44	housewife	36	28 "
	X	DeBonis Catherine—†	49	"	29	278 Marginal
	Y	DeBonis Vincent	49	shipper	27	278 "
	Z	Carbon Elmer	49	rigger	25	365 Sumner
127						
	A	Carbon Mary—†	49	housewife	21	365 "
	B	*Almeida Passidonio	49	longshoreman	40	269 "
	C	*Martins Frank	49	millworker	36	269 "
	D	Spencer August	49	longshoreman	52	269 "
	F	Ostrom Mary—†	54	at home	56	here
	G	Venezia Antonio	54	laborer	32	"
	H	Guarino Concetta—†	54	housewife	31	21 Unity
	K	Guarino Pasquale	54	laborer	45	21 "
	L	Terrazano Giovanni	54	"	43	31 Snow Hill
	M	Terrazano Maria—†	54	housewife	35	31 "

Cottage Street Place

	N	Runney Arline—†	2	floorwoman	45	here
	O	Runney Georgiana—†	2	at home	83	"
	P	Chiarella Mildred—†	2	housewife	23	30 Orleans
	R	Chiarella Vincent	2	laborer	22	30 "
	S	Emma Catherine—†	2	housewife	33	here
	T	Emma Frank	2	laborer	43	"
	U	Amico Jennie—†	2	housewife	48	"
	V	Amico Luciano	2	mason	55	
	W	*Polignone Antonio	4	lather	51	
	X	*Polignone Michelina—†	4	housewife	46	"

Haynes Street

128						
	C	Lemire William	2	laborer	48	here
	D	Harnish Lottie—†	2	houseworker	44	34 Haynes

Page.	Letter.	Full Name.	Residence, Jan. 1, 1938.	Occupation.	Supposed Age.	Reported Residence, Jan. 1, 1937. Street and Number.

Haynes Street—Continued

	E	McCashion Joseph	2	laborer	51	34 Haynes
	F	McCashion Sarah A—†	2	housewife	51	34 "
	G	Lombardo Joseph	4	retired	77	here
	H	Lombardo Rose—†	4	housewife	67	"
	L	Hanson Angela—†	6	"	21	"
	M	Hanson James	6	laborer	24	
	N	*Bardi Concetta—†	6	housewife	41	"
	O	Bardi Louis	6	retired	41	
	P	*Cormacchio Palma—†	6	housewife	47	"
	R	Cormacchio Tullio	6	laborer	44	"
	S	Monttalto John	7	"	23	36 Haynes
	T	Spano Salvatore	7	chauffeur	22	Vermont
	U	Kootz Herbert E	7	florist	27	here
	V	Kootz Rose—†	7	housewife	27	"
	W	*Pettrivelli Etta—†	7	"	33	"
	X	Pettrivelli Joseph	7	laborer	41	
	Y	Doyle Alice T—†	8	housewife	21	"
	Z	Doyle John J	8	ironworker	31	"
129						
	A	Cioffi Enrico	8	tailor	47	
	B	*Cioffi Jennie—†	8	housewife	47	"
	C	Cioffi Joseph	8	tailor	22	
	E	*Sogliero Florence—†	9	housewife	49	"
	F	*Sogliero Ginaro	9	retired	60	
	G	Sogliero Joseph	9	laborer	22	
	H	Sorrentino Louis	9	"	41	
	K	Sorrentino Virginia—†	9	housewife	31	"
	L	Marrone Philip	10	manufacturer	44	"
	M	DiGregorio Felicia—†	10	housewife	53	"
	N	DiGregorio Joseph	10	manufacturer	28	"
	O	DiGregorio Michael	10	retired	63	
	P	DiGregorio Sadie—†	10	operator	32	
	R	Jameson Helen F—†	11	packer	36	
	S	Jameson John E	11	laborer	34	
	T	Jameson John F	11	retired	65	
	U	Staffiero Frank P	11	laborer	57	"
	V	*Staffiero Philomena—†	11	housewife	53	"
	W	Ranese Antoinette—†	11	"	28	"
	X	Ranese Joseph	11	laborer	47	"
	Z	*Rongo Gaetano	12	retired	76	

Page.	Letter.	Full Name.	Residence, Jan. 1, 1938.	Occupation.	Supposed Age.	Reported Residence, Jan. 1, 1937. Street and Number.

130

Haynes Street—Continued

	A	*Rongo Josephine—†	12	housewife	74	here
	C	O'Leary Daniel	13	longshoreman	61	"
	D	O'Leary Daniel P	13	"	31	"
	E	O'Leary Ellen—†	13	seamstress	21	"
	F	O'Leary Harold F	13	laborer	25	
	G	O'Leary Margaret—†	13	millworker	27	"
	H	O'Leary Mary M—†	13	housewife	64	"
	K	O'Leary William F	13	typesetter	23	"
	L	*Gallue Michael	14	laborer	47	187 Brooks
	M	*Forgione Joseph	14	"	46	here
	N	*Forgione Mary—†	14	housewife	43	"
	O	*Montalto Josephine—†	14	"	55	"
	P	Montalto Mary—†	14	candyworker	21	"
	R	Hanson Catherine A—†	15	housewife	57	"
	S	Hanson John E	15	clerk	64	
	T	Hanson John J	15	longshoreman	28	"
	U	Hanson Rose C—†	15	housewife	26	"
	V	Coviello Erminia—†	16	"	60	
	W	Bellino Erica—†	16	clerk	20	
	X	*Bellino James	16	laborer	32	
	Y	*Bellino Joseph	16	retired	65	
	Z	*Montello Grace—†	16	housewife	59	"
131						
	A	*Driscoll Mary—†	16	housekeeper	84	"
	B	*Indorato Anna—†	16	"	44	"
	C	Indorato Louis	16	salesman	49	"
	D	Sheehan Mary—†	16	operator	22	"
	E	Malagrifa Theresa—†	17	housekeeper	40	"
	F	*Barbetta George	18	retired	63	"
	G	Barbetta Michael	18	laborer	28	23 Haynes
	H	Barbetta Rose—†	18	housewife	32	here
	K	Barbetta Santo	18	laborer	21	"
	L	*Bucci Anthony	18	retired	75	"
	M	Sweeney Elinor—†	18	housewife	26	2 Haynes
	N	Sweeney William F	18	seaman	30	2 "
	O	Barbetta Philomena—†	18	housewife	24	here
	P	Barbetta Ralph	18	laborer	29	"
	R	*Kirby Catherine—†	19	housewife	56	"
	S	*Kirby James	19	retired	61	

Page.	Letter.	Full Name.	Residence, Jan. 1, 1938.	Occupation.	Supposed Age.	Reported Residence, Jan. 1, 1937. Street and Number.

Haynes Street—Continued

Page.	Letter.	Full Name.	Residence, Jan. 1, 1938.	Occupation.	Supposed Age.	Reported Residence, Jan. 1, 1937. Street and Number.
	T	Kirby Paul	19	laborer	22	here
	U	*Malerba Mary—†	20	housewife	55	14 Haynes
	V	*Malerba Michael	20	laborer	60	14 “
	W	*Corlito Mary—†	20	housewife	33	here
	X	Limoli Joseph	20	laborer	29	“
	Y	Limoli Saveria—†	20	housewife	20	“
	Z	*Siracusa Annie—†	21	“	48	
132						
	A	Siracuso Ethel—†	21	operator	21	“
	C	*DeBonis Mary—†	22	housewife	50	16 Everett
	D	Bickford Charles L	22	deckhand	40	here
	E	Bickford Victoria M—†	22	housewife	33	“
	F	Fiorillo Arthur	22	painter	33	“
	G	*Fiorillo Lucy—†	22	housekeeper	67	“
	H	*Stasia Anthony	22	retired	74	Fall River
	K	Barbetta Anthony	23	welder	31	here
	L	Barbetta Charlotte—†	23	housewife	27	“
	M	Modica Michael	24	timekeeper	26	“
	N	Modica Antonio	24	foreman	53	“
	O	Modica Joseph	24	mattressmaker	28	“
	P	Modica Josephine—†	24	housewife	48	“
	R	Modica Nunzio	24	longshoreman	24	“
	S	Modica Peter	24	instructor	20	“
	T	*Olivieri John	24	laborer	45	
	U	*Olivieri Mary—†	24	housewife	40	“
	V	Sullivan Catherine—†	26	teacher	48	
	W	Cappucci Antonio	28	chauffeur	20	“
	X	Cappucci Constantino	28	salesman	30	“
	Y	Cappucci Daniel	28	storekeeper	58	“
	Z	Cappucci Dionisio	28	marblesetter	28	“
133						
	A	Cappucci Enrico	28	student	26	
	B	Cappucci Louis	28	longshoreman	22	“
	C	Cappucci Mary—†	28	housewife	49	“
	D	Cappucci Robert	28	fishcutter	24	“
	H	Roto Concetta—†	30	housewife	21	“
	K	*Roto Joseph	30	laborer	23	Malden
	L	Pagliuca Felix	30	“	62	here
	M	*Pagliuca Louise—†	30	housewife	58	“
	N	*Angelo Rose—†	30	“	57	20 Haynes
	O	Angelo Sebastiano	30	laborer	56	20 “

Page.	Letter.	Full Name.	Residence, Jan. 1, 1938.	Occupation.	Supposed Age.	Reported Residence, Jan. 1, 1937. Street and Number.

Haynes Street—Continued

Page.	Letter.	Full Name.	Residence, Jan. 1, 1938.	Occupation.	Supposed Age.	Reported Residence, Jan. 1, 1937. Street and Number.
	P	Fiorillo Mary C—†	31	housewife	33	here
	R	Fiorillo Paul	31	carpenter	37	"
	S	Cintolo Alexander	31	laborer	22	"
	T	Cintolo Esther—†	31	dressmaker	24	"
	U	Cintolo Frank	31	salesman	31	"
	V	Cintolo Margaret—†	31	stitcher	20	
	W	Cintolo Michael	31	retired	65	"
	X	*Cintolo Susan—†	31	housewife	54	"
	Y	Matterazzo Armand	31	chauffeur	24	"
	Z	Matterazzo Jennie—†	31	housekeeper	21	"
134						
	A	Matterazzo Letitia—†	31	stitcher	22	"
	B	Matterazzo Margaret—†	31	bookbinder	26	"
	F	Ciampa Feliciano	33	cook	30	
	G	*Ciampa Antonio	33	laborer	60	
	H	Ciampa Antonio, jr	33	"	27	
	K	Ciampa Carmella—†	33	candyworker	21	"
	L	*Ciampa Olympia—†	33	housewife	56	"
	M	Ciampa Salvatore	33	laborer	32	
	N	*Siracusa Anna—†	34	housewife	52	"
	O	*Siracusa Joseph	34	laborer	59	
	P	Siracusa Josephine—†	34	laundress	26	"
	S	Matanza Santa—†	34	housewife	28	"
	T	*Matanza Sebastian	34	laborer	29	
	U	*Palucca Elinor—†	35	housewife	64	"
	V	*Palucca Michael	35	laborer	56	
	X	Venuti Antonio	35	"	42	
	Y	*Venuti Concetta—†	35	housewife	42	"
	Z	*Montalto Agrippina—†	36	"	63	
135						
	A	*Montalto Peter	36	retired	69	"
	B	*Russo Jerolamo	36	laborer	45	132 Marginal
	C	*Russo Mary—†	36	housewife	42	here
	D	Olivieri Luigi	36	mason	46	"
	E	Olivieri Mario	36	chauffeur	22	"
	F	*Olivieri Nancy—†	36	housewife	43	"
	G	*Sega Romeo	37	laborer	48	
	H	*Pagliuca Maria—†	37	housewife	40	"
	K	Pagliuca Nicola	37	laborer	40	"
	M	Picardi Pasquale	39	shoeworker	27	33 Haynes
	N	*Voto Antonetta—†	39	housewife	53	here

Page.	Letter.	FULL NAME.	Residence, Jan. 1, 1938.	Occupation.	Supposed Age.	Reported Residence, Jan. 1, 1937. Street and Number.

Haynes Street—Continued

	O	Voto Antonio	39	painter	54	here
	P	*LaRosa Jennie—†	39	housewife	28	"
	R	LaRosa Philip	39	laborer	32	"
	S	Gigliello John	41	"	27	
	T	Gigliello Theresa—†	41	housewife	26	"
	U	DiFelice Helen—†	41	"	42	"
	V	Lemire Sedulie—†	41	"	74	2 Haynes
	W	*Brogione Ernest	43	porter	50	here
	Y	Zinna Agrippino	44	laborer	43	192 Cottage
	Z	*Zinna Santa—†	44	housewife	32	here
136						
	A	*Guarracino Frank	45	laborer	66	
	D	McKenna Isabella—†	47	housewife	23	"
	E	McKenna Thomas	47	longshoreman	23	"
	F	Casey Hugh	47	"	54	
	G	Costello Beatrice—†	47	inspector	21	"
	H	Costello Harold	47	freighthandler	28	"
	K	*Costello Nellie—†	47	housewife	52	"
	L	Cammarano Anthony	48	chauffeur	25	"
	M	Cammarano Ernestine—†	48	housewife	25	"
	N	Cammarano Dominic	48	foreman	54	
	O	*Cammarano Mary—†	48	housewife	52	"
	P	Cammarano Pasquale	48	longshoreman	20	"
	R	*Landrigan Edward	49	"	58	
	S	*Landrigan Nora—†	49	housewife	59	"
	T	Callahan Charles L	49	clerk	27	"
	U	Callahan Eileen A—†	49	"	25	
	V	Callahan Florence M—†	49	saleswoman	24	"
	W	Callahan John B	49	clerk	28	
	X	Callahan John J	49	laborer	56	
	Y	Callahan Mary—†	49	housewife	55	"
	Z	Dennehy Helen—†	49	cook	50	
137						
	A	Shine Anna—†	49	"	54	
	B	Shine Mary P—†	49	nurse	22	
	C	Driscoll Julia—†	52	housekeeper	65	"
	D	McCarthy Dennis	52	freighthandler	56	"
	E	*Damore Anna—†	62	housewife	45	"
	F	Damore Gennaro	62	wool grader	43	"
	G	Gauthier Albert C	62	longshoreman	33	"
	H	Gauthier Camille	62	"	61	

Page.	Letter.	Full Name.	Residence, Jan. 1, 1938.	Occupation.	Supposed Age.	Reported Residence, Jan. 1, 1937. Street and Number.

Haynes Street—Continued

Page.	Letter.	Full Name.	Residence, Jan. 1, 1938.	Occupation.	Supposed Age.	Reported Residence, Jan. 1, 1937. Street and Number.
	K	Gauthier Homer F	62	seaman	28	here
	L	Gauthier John J	62	longshoreman	27	"
	M	Gauthier Nellie A—†	62	housewife	61	"
	N	Voto Alma—†	62	"	28	
	O	Voto Ralph	62	musician	30	"

Marginal Street

Page.	Letter.	Full Name.	Residence, Jan. 1, 1938.	Occupation.	Supposed Age.	Reported Residence, Jan. 1, 1937. Street and Number.
	S	Anderson Effie—†	72	housewife	33	here
	T	Anderson Irene N—†	72	social worker	31	"
	U	Anderson Victor	72	letter carrier	34	"
	V	Perry Elizabeth—†	72	social worker	24	"
	W	Spaulding Rosco	72	janitor	29	211 Longwood av
138						
	B	Lanza Biagio	90	laborer	27	here
	C	Lanza Frank	90	"	22	"
	D	*Lanza Venera—†	90	housekeeper	57	"
	F	*St Maria Pasqualena—†	91	"	57	"
	G	Waters Antoinette—†	91	housewife	25	"
	H	Waters Edmund	91	chauffeur	28	"
	K	*Capone Joseph	92	laborer	43	
	L	*Capone Mary—†	92	housewife	36	"
	M	Bondanza Joseph	92	laborer	31	
	N	Bondanza Laura—†	92	housewife	27	"
	O	Capone Julia—†	92	housekeeper	36	"
	U	*Furello Antonio	96	retired	74	"
	X	Gigliello Francis A	100	laborer	24	
	Y	*Gigliello Michael	100	"	52	
	Z	Gigliello Florence—†	100	housewife	21	"
139						
	A	Gigliello Nicholas	100	painter	26	
	B	*Mascis Frank	102	retired	70	
	C	*Mascis Michelina—†	102	housewife	54	"
	E	*DeSisto Maria—†	104	"	75	
	D	*DeSisto Raffaele	104	retired	87	
	H	Dolan Charles H	106	"	73	
	K	Dolan Mary—†	106	housekeeper	53	"
	L	Manganelli Charles	110	student	25	"
	M	Manganelli Frank	110	salesman	57	"
	N	Manganelli Madaline—†	110	cashier	26	
	O	Manganelli Mary—†	110	at home	21	

Page.	Letter.	Full Name.	Residence, Jan. 1, 1938.	Occupation.	Supposed Age.	Reported Residence, Jan. 1, 1937. Street and Number.

Marginal Street—Continued

	P	Manganelli Rose—†	110	housewife	48	here
	R	Smith Nathaniel	112	longshoreman	47	"
	S	Fahey Bridget F—†	112	housewife	59	"
	T	Fahey Catherine J—†	112	operator	28	"
	U	Fahey David	112	longshoreman	65	"
	V	Fahey David F	112	laborer	33	
	W	Fahey John M	112	longshoreman	35	"
	X	Fahey Leo	112	clerk	22	
	Y	Fahey Mary M—†	112	operator	30	"
	Z	O'Brien John T	112	longshoreman	43	"
140						
	B	Goodwin Beatrice—†	116	housewife	25	"
	C	Goodwin James	116	shipfitter	32	"
	D	Quilty Jessie—†	116	housekeeper	40	"
	E	Hanlon John J	116	longshoreman	37	"
	F	Hanlon Rita—†	116	housewife	30	"
	G	Costello Mary J—†	118	housekeeper	65	"
	H	Regan Margaret—†	118	housewife	34	"
	K	Regan Martin J	118	chauffeur	34	"
	L	Dalton Margaret A—†	118	housekeeper	32	"
	M	Reidy John E	118	laborer	22	"
	N	Reidy Michael L	118	"	24	
	P	Aceto Antonio	126	"	24	"
	R	Aceto Lena—†	126	housewife	20	"
	S	*Aceto Beatrice—†	126	"	60	
	T	Aceto Louis	126	tailor	25	
	U	*Aceto Simon	126	retired	69	
	V	Aceto Vincenzo	126	laborer	29	
	W	Crowley Catherine C—†	126	housewife	42	"
	X	Crowley Daniel J	126	longshoreman	43	"
	Y	Crowley Daniel J, jr	126	freighthandler	20	"
	Z	Crowley Mary A—†	126	operator	22	"
141						
	C	Visconte Vito	128	laborer	25	
	D	Broussard Charles	128	"	37	
	E	Broussard Dorothy—†	128	housewife	35	"
	F	Diaz Anna—†	128	"	21	"
	G	Diaz Richard	128	machinist	24	"
	H	*Rossi Girolamo	rear 128	laborer	48	"
	K	Ashley Alice M—†	" 128	housewife	63	"
	L	Ashley George E	" 128	laborer	64	

Page.	Letter.	Full Name.	Residence, Jan. 1, 1938.	Occupation.	Supposed Age.	Reported Residence, Jan. 1, 1937. Street and Number.

Marginal Street—Continued

Page.	Letter.	Full Name.	Residence, Jan. 1, 1938.	Occupation.	Supposed Age.	Reported Residence, Jan. 1, 1937. Street and Number.
	M	*Cimelli Domenic	132	laborer	50	41 Cottage
	N	*Stella Salvatore	132	reamer	47	here
	O	*Terenzi Amelia—†	132	housewife	44	"
	P	*Terenzi Osvaldo	132	tailor	50	"
	R	Terenzi Thomas	132	laborer	22	
	S	Mascis Frank	136	"	24	
	T	Mascis Ruby—†	136	housewife	23	"
	U	McDonough George	136	laborer	23	128 Marginal
	V	McDonough Thomas	136	"	26	here
	W	Vallen John	136	"	47	"
	X	Vallen Lillian—†	136	housewife	49	"
	Y	Goggin Edward	136	longshoreman	31	"
	Z	Goggin Mary—†	136	housekeeper	37	"
142						
	A	Goggin Thomas	136	longshoreman	27	"
	B	*Tedesco Anthony	138	laborer	65	37 Chelsea
	C	*Zichella Anthony	138	"	42	248 Maverick
	D	Cinelli Domenic	138	shoeworker	21	here
	E	*Cinelli Frank	138	laborer	52	"
	F	*Cinelli Nancy—†	138	housewife	53	"
	G	*Morcaldi Ralph	138	teacher	69	
	K	Ratta Celia—†	140	housewife	34	"
	L	Ratta Onofrio	140	laborer	38	"
	N	Lomanno Joseph	140	packer	31	125 Webster
	O	*Lomanno Maria—†	140	housekeeper	72	125 "
	P	Lomanno Mary—†	140	housewife	26	125 "
	R	Siciliano Anthony	142	bartender	46	here
	S	Siciliano Leo	142	longshoreman	21	"
	T	Siciliano Mary—†	142	housewife	43	"
	U	Gill Helen—†	142	"	48	
	V	Gill Henry	142	longshoreman	50	"
	X	Barr Frederick W	180	retired	72	135 Webster
	Y	Cadden Bernard	180	laborer	57	141 "
	Z	Cadden Bridget—†	180	housewife	37	141 "
143						
	A	Mastrangelo Angelo	184	laborer	44	here
	B	*Mastrangelo Maria—†	184	housewife	59	"
	C	*Russo Anello	184	laborer	39	"
	D	Russo Charlotte—†	184	housewife	21	Lowell
	G	Grifoni Joseph	188	laborer	44	here
	H	*Grifoni Vincenza—†	188	housewife	39	"

Page.	Letter.	Full Name.	Residence, Jan. 1, 1938.	Occupation.	Supposed Age.	Reported Residence, Jan. 1, 1937. Street and Number.

Marginal Street—Continued

Page.	Letter.	Full Name.	Residence, Jan. 1, 1938.	Occupation.	Supposed Age.	Reported Residence, Jan. 1, 1937. Street and Number.
	K	LeGallo James F	188	retired	68	here
	L	Richardson Julia—†	188	housewife	30	“
	M	Richardson Paul S	188	shoeworker	40	“
	N	Richardson William L	188	carpenter	37	“
	O	Lowry Ernest	194	painter	32	
	P	Twitchell Frank	194	“	33	
	R	Twitchell Gladys—†	194	housewife	31	“
	S	*Gaudet Charles	198	retired	69	
	T	*Gaudet Monique—†	198	housewife	67	“
	U	Hagen Elizabeth M—†	198	housekeeper	65	“
	V	Hagen Henry J	198	janitor	34	“
	Y	Downey John	204	plasterer	74	“
	Z	Downey Mary A—†	204	housekeeper	71	“
144						
	B	*DeFiore Michelena—†	210	“	42	
	C	DeFiore Nicholas	210	storekeeper	23	“
	D	*DeBuzzio Angie—†	210	housewife	54	19 Murray ct
	E	*DeBuzzio Nicola	210	tailor	55	19 “
	F	*Maze Josephine—†	210	housekeeper	38	here
	K	Cavignano Angelina–†	rear 216	housewife	28	“
	L	Cavignano Genaro	“ 216	printer	29	“
	M	Cavignano Carmella–†	“ 216	at home	23	
	N	*Cavignano Frank	“ 216	watchman	56	“
	O	*Cavignano Josephine	“ 216	housewife	53	“

Murray Court

Page.	Letter.	Full Name.	Residence, Jan. 1, 1938.	Occupation.	Supposed Age.	Reported Residence, Jan. 1, 1937. Street and Number.
	Z	Coviello Anthony	1	agent	33	here
145						
	A	Coviello Antoinette—†	1	housewife	38	“
	B	*Garofalo Raffaela—†	1	“	50	
	C	*Garofalo Francisco	1	laborer	57	
	D	DeRocco Dominic	1	investigator	39	“
	E	DeRocco Grace—†	1	housewife	30	“
	F	*Bozzo Arthur	2	barber	41	
	G	*Bozzo Chester	2	painter	46	
	H	Bozzo Helen—†	2	housewife	35	“
	K	*Indorato Annie—†	2	“	40	
	L	Indorato Joseph	2	shipper	20	
	M	Indorato Salvatore	2	laborer	46	“
	N	Lavalle George	2	“	31	42 Phillips
	O	Lavalle Mildred—†	2	housewife	29	42 “

Page.	Letter.	Full Name.	Residence, Jan. 1, 1938.	Occupation.	Supposed Age.	Reported Residence, Jan. 1, 1937. Street and Number.

Murray Court—Continued

Page.	Letter.	Full Name.	Residence, Jan. 1, 1938.	Occupation.	Supposed Age.	Reported Residence, Jan. 1, 1937. Street and Number.
	R	*McDonnell Alice—†	3	housewife	50	39 Everett
	S	McDonnell John	3	freighthandler	30	39 "
	T	*McDonnell Richard	3	longshoreman	58	39 "
	U	McDonnell Richard	3	laborer	26	39 '
	V	McDonnell William	3	cutter	29	39 "
	W	Campagnoni Frank	3	shipper	41	here
	X	*Campagnoni Jennie—†	3	housewife	37	"
	Y	*Ciano Michael	4	laborer	55	2 Murray ct
	Z	Ciano Theresa—†	4	housekeeper	21	2 "
146						
	A	DeMarco Manuel	4	retired	60	here
	B	Pedalino Charles J	4	chauffeur	43	"
	C	Pedalino Jennie—†	4	examiner	23	"
	D	Pedalino Rose—†	4	millworker	22	"
	E	Pedalino Theresa—†	4	housewife	43	"
	F	DeAngelis Ernest	4	laborer	24	
	G	DeAngelis Mildred—†	4	housewife	25	"
	H	*Gentilotti Patrick J	5	laborer	50	
	K	Gigliello Albert	5	mechanic	26	"
	L	Gigliello John	5	laborer	41	
	M	Gigliello Michael	5	"	34	
	N	*Gigliello Ralph	5	retired	80	
	O	*Gigliello Rose—†	5	housewife	70	"
	P	Desario Celestine—†	9	operator	28	
	R	Desario Marie—†	9	housewife	70	"
	S	*Landi Ercoli	9	operator	27	Cambridge
	T	Landi Jennie—†	9	housewife	26	here
	U	Limongiello Gabriel	9	machinist	36	"
	V	Limongiello Mary—†	9	housewife	33	"
	W	*Simole Agrippino	9	laborer	53	
	X	*Simole Mary—†	9	housewife	44	"
	Y	Simole Mary—†	9	operator	25	"
147						
	B	*McDonnell Leo	15	painter	35	389 Sumner
	C	McDonnell Ruth—†	15	housewife	24	389 "
	D	Fagone Agrippino	15	factoryhand	46	here
	E	Fagone Helen—†	15	"	21	"
	F	Fagone Joseph	15	barber	40	"
	G	*Fagone Josephine—†	15	housewife	45	"
	K	*Marsilia John	16	pressman	49	"
	L	*Marsilia Mary—†	16	housewife	48	"
	M	*Marsilia Yolanda—†	16	tailoress	20	

Page.	Letter.	Full Name.	Residence, Jan. 1, 1938.	Occupation.	Supposed Age.	Reported Residence, Jan. 1, 1937. Street and Number.

Murray Court—Continued

	N	Ciano Carmella—†	17	housewife	22	here
	O	Ciano Pasquale	17	plumber	25	“
	P	Buono Emma—†	17	housewife	28	“
	R	Buono Leopold	17	bartender	27	“
	S	Chiampa Albert	17	chauffeur	32	“
	T	Chiampa Mary—†	17	housewife	25	“
	U	*Grieco Nancy—†	19	“	27	352 Sumner
	V	Grieco Peter	19	mason	30	352 “
	W	Triulzi Edith—†	19	secretary	20	here
	X	Triulzi Edward	19	storekeeper	53	“
	Y	Triulzi Frank	19	jeweler	26	“
	Z	Triulzi James	19	“	30	
148						
	A	*Triulzi Rose—†	19	housewife	53	“
	B	*Renna Anna—†	22	“	27	
	C	Renna Paul	22	foreman	32	
	D	Repucci Blanche—†	22	dressmaker	23	“
	E	Repucci George	22	laborer	26	
	F	*Repucci Mary—†	22	housewife	60	“
	G	Repucci Pelegrino	22	laborer	58	
	H	Repucci Philomena—†	22	factoryhand	28	“

Noble Court

	K	Walter Anna—†	4	housewife	28	here
	L	Walter Charles, jr	4	retired	68	“
	M	Naumann Aloysius	6	“	67	“
	N	Naumann Mary—†	6	inspector	38	“
	O	Politano John	7	laborer	67	“
	P	*Politano Josephine—†	7	housewife	59	“
	S	Leto Josephine—†	9	“	49	
	T	Leto Salvatore	9	machinist	23	“
	U	Leto Joseph	9	engineer	26	
	V	Leto Lucy—†	9	dressmaker	31	“
	W	Laracy Mary J—†	10	housekeeper	42	“

Orleans Street

	Y	Scaramella Albert	39	undertaker	35	here
	Z	*Scaramella Madeline—†	39	housekeeper	78	“
149						
	A	Scaramella Rose—†	39	housewife	25	“

Page.	Letter.	Full Name.	Residence, Jan. 1, 1938.	Occupation.	Supposed Age.	Reported Residence, Jan. 1, 1937. Street and Number.

Orleans Street—Continued

Page.	Letter.	Full Name.	Residence, Jan. 1, 1938.	Occupation.	Supposed Age.	Reported Residence, Jan. 1, 1937. Street and Number.
	B	Scaramella Flora—†	39	housewife	40	here
	C	Scaramella Madeline—†	39	secretary	22	“
	D	Scaramella Vincent	39	clerk	48	“
	F	Castucci Julio	41	chef	28	8 Everett
	G	Castucci Rose—†	41	housewife	26	8 “
	H	Giacalone Frances—†	41	“	27	46 “
	K	Giacalone Vito	41	barber	31	46 “
	L	*Venezia Margaret—†	43	housewife	53	here
	M	Venezia Michael A	43	finisher	63	“
	N	DeMasellis James	43	tailor	47	“
	O	DeMasellis Josephine—†	43	housewife	45	“
	P	Vitale Joseph	43A	laborer	22	227 Everett
	R	Katz Molly—†	45	housewife	51	here
	S	Katz Rose—†	45	clerk	23	“
	T	Katz Samuel	45	storekeeper	55	“
	U	Larsen Edith—†	45	at home	21	335 Maverick
	V	Larsen James P	45	seaman	50	335 “
	W	Larsen Mary A—†	45	housewife	45	335 “

Seaver Street

Page.	Letter.	Full Name.	Residence, Jan. 1, 1938.	Occupation.	Supposed Age.	Reported Residence, Jan. 1, 1937. Street and Number.
	Y	*Fagin Delia—†	3	housewife	27	Brookline
	Z	Fagin John	3	longshoreman	32	here
150						
	A	Fagin Philip	3	clerk	35	
	B	Curl Ellen M—†	3	at home	72	
	C	McLaughlin Elizabeth A–†	3	“	60	
	D	McLaughlin James A	3	laborer	63	“
	E	McLaughlin Michael F	3	retired	74	
	F	Brady Mary G—†	5	saleswoman	24	“
	G	Brady Robert T	5	longshoreman	24	“
	H	Brady Mary E—†	5	housewife	49	“
	K	Brady Robert M	5	machinist	49	“
	L	*McGowan James G	5	“	34	
	M	*McGowan Margaret—†	5	housewife	56	“
	N	McGowan Peter	5	janitor	61	

Sumner Place

Page.	Letter.	Full Name.	Residence, Jan. 1, 1938.	Occupation.	Supposed Age.	Reported Residence, Jan. 1, 1937. Street and Number.
	R	DeBole Fannie—†	3	hairdresser	21	here
	S	DeBole Joseph	3	laborer	23	“

Page.	Letter.	Full Name.	Residence, Jan. 1, 1938.	Occupation.	Supposed Age.	Reported Residence, Jan. 1, 1937. Street and Number.

Sumner Place—Continued

	T	DeBole Leo	3	laborer	50	here
	U	DeBole Leo, jr	3	steward	22	“
	V	*DeBole Mary—†	3	housewife	46	“
	X	Vocino Imbriano	3	shoeworker	42	“
	Z	DiCenzo Ernest	5	laborer	34	
151						
	A	DiCenzo Mary—†	5	housewife	28	“
	B	Faiella Arcangelo	5	laborer	62	“
	C	Faiella Christina—†	5	housewife	56	“
	D	Faiella Felix	5	laborer	20	
	E	Faiella Orlando	5	carpenter	29	“
	F	Faiella Pasquale	5	plasterer	26	“
	G	*DeGregorio Michael	6	laborer	44	10 Haynes
	H	Patti Andrew	6	“	41	here
	K	*Patti Grace—†	6	housewife	37	“
	L	Zirpolo Anthony	6	chauffeur	36	“
	M	Zirpolo Sophie—†	6	housewife	34	“
	N	Massa Caroline—†	6	at home	74	“
	O	Massa Marciano	6	longshoreman	47	“
	P	Chiuchiolo Angelina—†	7	at home	20	
	R	Chiuchiolo John	7	cabinetmaker	22	“
	S	*Chiuchiolo Joseph	7	candymaker	52	“
	T	*Bernazzani Delia E—†	7	housewife	44	“
	U	Bernazzani George	7	printer	22	
	V	*Bernazzani Louis A	7	“	47	
	W	Bernazzani Mary—†	7	stenographer	20	“
	X	DiRocco Domenic	7	laborer	41	“
	Y	DiRocco Ida—†	7	housewife	31	“
	Z	*Tucciariello Donati	8	retired	73	90 Everett
152						
	A	Buccella Angelina—†	8	trimmer	20	here
	B	Buccella Anna—†	8	inspector	21	“
	C	Buccella Josephine—†	8	stitcher	23	“
	D	*Buccella Louise—†	8	housewife	49	“
	E	Buccella Rosario	8	laborer	46	“
	F	*Donnaruma Anna—†	8	housewife	37	“
	G	*Donnaruma Samuel	8	laborer	36	
	H	Sylvester Ernest	8	longshoreman	49	“
	K	Sylvester Mary—†	8	housewife	33	“
	L	Thornton Mary J—†	9	dressmaker	49	“
	M	Thornton Mary J—†	9	bookkeeper	29	“

Page.	Letter.	Full Name.	Residence, Jan. 1, 1938.	Occupation.	Supposed Age.	Reported Residence, Jan. 1, 1937. Street and Number.

Sumner Place—Continued

	o	Reid Louise—†	9	teacher	28	here
	p	Reid Mary A—†	9	at home	59	"

Sumner Street

	r	*Picardi Carmela—†	265	housewife	43	here
	s	Picardi Michael	265	storekeeper	43	"
	t	Vitagliano Catherine—†	265	housewife	28	"
	u	Vitagliano Mario	265	laborer	32	
	w	*Miano Carmella—†	269	housewife	55	"
	x	*Miano Louis	269	barber	58	
	y	Miano Olga—†	269	typist	22	"
	z	*Caserta Anna—†	269	housewife	42	305 Sumner
153						
	a	Caserta Carmen	269	tinsmith	54	305 "
	b	Caserta Jennie—†	269	at home	20	305 "
	c	Caserta Vincent	269	laborer	24	305 "
	d	*Infantino Joseph	269	"	52	here
	e	*Infantino Rose—†	269	housewife	54	"
	f	Marannano Angela—†	269	dressmaker	27	"
	g	Marannano Mario	269	laborer	28	"
	l	Addivinola Carmella—†	271	at home	22	107 Everett
	m	*Addivinola John	271	laborer	54	107 "
	n	Addivinola Joseph	271	knitter	20	107 "
	o	*Addivinola Philomena—†	271	housewife	42	107 "
	p	McDonald Walter J	273	laborer	24	39 "
	r	*Lupoli Nicolo	273	"	53	here
	s	*Lupoli Selvina—†	273	housewife	56	"
	t	*Saia Rita—†	273	"	54	"
	u	*Saia Valerio	273	pressman	65	"
	v	Lombardi Joseph, jr	275	laborer	21	264 Sumner
	w	Lombardi Josephine—†	275	housewife	20	264 "
	x	Tentindo Antonio	275	laborer	43	here
	y	*Tentindo Arcangelo	275	carpenter	75	"
	z	*Tentindo Nunzio	275	"	48	"
154						
	a	*Tentindo Teresa—†	275	housewife	39	"
	b	*Giugicello Esther—†	279	"	67	
	c	*Giugicello Vito	279	retired	71	
	d	Cornetta John	279	laborer	42	
	e	Cornetta Mary R—†	279	housewife	33	"

Page.	Letter.	Full Name.	Residence, Jan. 1, 1938.	Occupation.	Supposed Age.	Reported Residence, Jan. 1, 1937. Street and Number.

Sumner Street—Continued

	F	*Cornetta Raffaela—†	279	at home	77	here
	G	*Cornetta Phyllis—†	279	housewife	28	"
	H	Cornetta Rosario	279	cobbler	37	"
	L	Panzini Dominic	281	laborer	38	
	M	*Panzini Mary—†	281	housewife	33	"
	N	*Valestrino Luigi	281	storekeeper	59	"
	O	*Valestrino Sophie—†	281	housewife	55	"
	P	Caliendo Anna—†	281	"	39	
	R	Caliendo Raymond	281	barber	42	
	S	*Matarese Concetta—†	283	at home	73	
	T	*Matarese Gesumino	283	presser	35	
	U	*Gulinallo Josephine—†	283	packer	24	
	V	*Gulinallo Mary—†	283	housewife	42	"
	W	*Matarese Clara—†	283	"	35	
	X	*Matarese Vito	283	barber	39	
	Y	Fothergill John J	285	clerk	47	
	Z	Fothergill Teresa M—†	285	housewife	42	"
155						
	A	McLaughlin Louise J—†	285	bookkeeper	36	"
	B	*DiSpirito Cora—†	287	housewife	55	"
	C	*DiSpirito Generoso	287	woodworker	45	"
	D	Campanaro Dominic	287	musician	40	"
	E	Campanaro Florence—†	287	housewife	38	"
	F	Granna John	287	electrician	23	"
	G	Granna Matilda—†	287	housewife	21	"
	H	Incagnoli Mary—†	289	marker	22	
	K	Barressi Anthony	289	messenger	20	"
	L	Barressi Frank	289	shoeworker	35	"
	M	Barressi Joseph	289	salesman	24	"
	N	Barressi Josephine—†	289	shoeworker	33	"
	O	Barressi Salvatore	289	seaman	26	
	P	Barressi Virginia—†	289	housewife	53	"
	R	Barressi Virginia—†	289	shoeworker	21	"
	S	Pace Albert	289	agent	23	
	T	Pace Edmund	289	hat cleaner	22	"
	U	Pace Helen—†	289	at home	20	
	V	*Pace Nicola	289	retired	78	
	W	Pace Pacifico	289	shoeworker	49	"
	X	Pace Theresa—†	289	housewife	47	"
	Y	Delelio Josephine—†	rear 289	"	22	15 Murray ct
	Z	Russo Adeline—†	" 289	"	29	288 Sumner

Page.	Letter.	Full Name.	Residence, Jan. 1, 1938.	Occupation.	Supposed Age.	Reported Residence, Jan. 1, 1937. Street and Number.
156						

Sumner Street—Continued

Page.	Letter.	Full Name.	Residence, Jan. 1, 1938.	Occupation.	Supposed Age.	Reported Residence, Jan. 1, 1937. Street and Number.
	A	Russo Anthony	rear 289	busboy	30	288 Sumner
	B	Modica Angelina—†	291	housewife	32	5 Chelsea
	C	*Modica Jack	291	shoemaker	33	5 "
	D	*Rella Angelina—†	291	housewife	34	here
	E	Rella Sabino	291	laborer	46	"
	F	Gaeta Albert	291	milkman	24	"
	G	*Gaeta Margaret—†	291	housewife	44	"
	H	*Gaeta Matteo	291	laborer	57	
	K	Gaeta Thomas	291	carpenter	22	"
	L	DeLelio Dominic	rear 291	laborer	34	
	M	*DeLelio James	" 291	"	62	
	N	DeLelio Michael	" 291	"	24	
	O	Cappellatti Lucy—†	293	stitcher	33	
	P	Cappellatti Toaldo	293	hairdresser	33	"
	R	Gravalese Michael	293	butcher	48	
	S	Iavicoli Nina—†	293	seamstress	21	"
	T	Tarquinio Sabatino	293	barber	45	
	U	*Amirault James	293	engineer	43	
	V	Belliveau Marie G—†	293	operator	23	
	W	*Belliveau Mary M—†	293	housewife	56	"
	X	*Belliveau William N	293	laborer	66	
	Z	Petrella Antoinetta–†	rear 293	housewife	30	"
157						
	A	Petrella Alexander	" 293	laborer	32	
	B	Jorgensen Esther—†	295	housewife	42	"
	C	Jorgensen George	295	fireman	20	
	D	Jorgensen Jorgen P	295	steward	47	
	E	Twitchell Charles	295	oiler	24	
	F	Celia Joseph	295	merchant	46	"
	G	*Celia Josephine—†	295	housewife	43	"
	H	Celia Rose—†	295	waitress	21	
	K	Grugnale Antonio	295	chauffeur	26	"
	L	Grugnale Florence—†	295	housewife	27	"
	M	Constantino Joseph	297	electrician	32	130 Webster
	N	Constantino Rose—†	297	housewife	26	130 "
	O	Jenkins Julia—†	297	matron	57	here
	P	Yocum Ernest L	297	engineer	67	"
	R	Constantino Angelina—†	297	housewife	62	"
	S	Constantino Anthony	297	operator	23	"
	T	Constantino Eleanor—†	297	"	22	

Page.	Letter.	Full Name.	Residence, Jan. 1, 1938.	Occupation.	Supposed Age.	Reported Residence, Jan. 1, 1937. Street and Number.

Sumner Street—Continued

Page.	Letter.	Full Name.	Residence, Jan. 1, 1938.	Occupation.	Supposed Age.	Reported Residence, Jan. 1, 1937. Street and Number.
	U	Constantino George	297	laborer	61	here
	V	Falanga Joseph	299	"	24	147 Cottage
	W	Falanga Rose—†	299	housewife	23	147 "
	X	Doria Anna—†	299	"	23	here
	Y	Doria Vito	299	shoeworker	27	"
	Z	*Manzo Marie—†	299	housewife	61	"
158						
	A	*Manzo Ralph	299	laborer	63	
	B	Giambrome Joseph	299	shoeworker	22	"
	C	*Marino Anthony	299	laborer	53	
	D	*Marino Frances—†	299	housewife	46	"
	F	Todisco Edith—†	305	packer	23	
	G	Todisco Emma—†	305	"	25	
	H	Todisco Louise—†	305	at home	26	"
	K	*Todisco Mildred—†	305	housewife	47	"
	L	*Todisco Vincent	305	shoeworker	57	"
	M	Grana Leonard	305	millworker	28	241 Webster
	N	Grana Mary—†	305	housewife	28	241 "
	O	Cicoria Nicholas	305	laborer	42	here
	P	Cicoria Rachelina—†	305	housewife	36	"
	R	Gualtiere Catherine—†	307	"	33	"
	S	Gualtiere Salvatore	307	shoeworker	40	"
	T	*DelTergo Emilia—†	307	housewife	41	"
	U	DelTergo Michael	307	laborer	47	
	W	Milazzo Luigi	rear 309	pedler	54	
	X	*Cesarini Oswaldo	" 309	laborer	46	
	Y	Morano Vincenzo	" 309	tailor	39	
	Z	Mirabile Benjamin	" 309	laborer	58	
159						
	A	*Mirabile Pasquale	" 309	"	59	108 Sumner
	B	Interrante Carmella-†	" 309	housewife	22	here
	C	*Interrante Charles	" 309	laborer	38	"
	D	Walsh John	" 309	clerk	22	282 Lexington
	E	Walsh Mary—†	" 309	housewife	20	282 "
	F	Buschetti Hannah—†	" 309	"	66	here
	G	Buschetti Pasquale	" 309	retired	74	"
	H	Robinson Joseph F	" 309	waiter	24	"
	K	*Rossello Dominic	315	retired	73	
	L	Giaquinto Andrew	315	laborer	30	
	M	Giaquinto Teresa—†	315	housewife	29	"
	O	*Graziano Sarah—†	315	"	39	96 Cottage

Page.	Letter.	FULL NAME.	Residence, Jan. 1, 1938.	Occupation.	Supposed Age.	Reported Residence, Jan. 1, 1937. Street and Number.

Sumner Street—Continued

	P	*Rizzo Carmella—†	315	housewife	53	here
	R	*Rizzo Thomas	315	laborer	66	"
	S	Deliago Frank	315	"	26	"
	T	Deliago Teresa—†	315	packer	22	
	U	*Spaziani Sista—†	315	housewife	60	"
	V	*Spaziani Thomas	315	shoeworker	60	"
	Z	Scavo Antonio	317	baker	44	
	Y	*Scavo Josephine—†	317	housewife	39	"
160						
	A	Sciarrillo Antonio	317	storekeeper	39	"
	B	*Sciarrillo Gabriella—†	317	housewife	42	"
	C	*Fabello Enrico	rear 317	operator	55	"
	D	Fabello Frank	" 317	chauffeur	21	"
	E	*Fabello Palma—†	" 317	housewife	48	"
	F	Iannino Joseph	" 317	painter	38	
	G	Iannino Philomena–†	" 317	housewife	26	"
	H	Ventola Dominic	" 317	candymaker	27	"
	L	*Campo Angelina—†	319	housewife	42	"
	M	Campo Paul	319	storekeeper	48	"
	N	Munofo Ida—†	319	housewife	29	"
	O	Munofo Nazio	319	mason	39	
	P	Masullo Madalena–†	rear 319	at home	66	
	R	Zecchino Antonio	" 319	laborer	40	
	S	*Zecchino Raffaela—†	" 319	housewife	39	"
	U	Lanzello Giuseppe	325	operator	60	"
	V	*Lanzello Lucia—†	325	housewife	64	"
	X	DePasquale Anthony	329	baker	23	
	Y	DePasquale Teresa—†	329	housewife	21	"
161						
	D	Sharkey James W	343	watchman	53	520 Sumner
	E	*Sharkey Margaret—†	343	housewife	50	520 "
	G	*Albano Anna—†	345	"	52	here
	H	Albano Anna—†	345	at home	21	"
	K	Albano Fred	345	baker	33	"
	L	Albano Gennaro	345	"	23	
	M	Connell John J	347	waiter	54	
	N	Connell Mary E—†	347	at home	54	
	O	Murphy Margaret J—†	347	housewife	57	"
	R	Constantino Nicholas	349	bricklayer	29	83 Webster
	S	*Giglio Carmella—†	349	housewife	54	15 Murray ct
	T	*Giglio Frank	349	retired	64	15 "

Page.	Letter.	Full Name.	Residence, Jan. 1, 1938.	Occupation.	Supposed Age.	Reported Residence, Jan. 1, 1937. Street and Number.

Sumner Street—Continued

	U	Giglio Maria—†	349	seamstress	20	15 Murray ct
	V	Giglio Pasquale	349	laborer	21	15 "
	W	*Caccamesi Mary—†	349	packer	21	here
	X	*Caccamesi Teresa—†	349	housewife	51	"
	Y	O'Dea Margaret—†	351	"	73	"
	Z	Aiken Catherine H—†	351	"	45	
162						
	A	Aiken Edward F	351	shipper	25	
	B	Aiken George E	351	painter	47	
	C	Aiken Mary L—†	351	saleswoman	23	"
	D	Rotondo Angelo	353	laborer	39	
	E	Rotondo Mary—†	353	housewife	33	"
	F	Cuozzo Adele—†	353	stamper	21	
	G	*Cuozzo Antonetta—†	353	housewife	50	"
	H	Cuozzo Antonio	353	laborer	59	
	K	Cuozzo John	353	shoeworker	26	"
	L	Cuozzo Louis	353	electrician	28	"
	M	*Johnson Beda—†	357	housewife	60	"
	N	Johnson Elizabeth—†	357	saleswoman	25	"
	O	Johnson Henry	357	laborer	24	
	P	Redmond Catherine—†	357	housewife	38	"
	R	Redmond Joseph	357	clerk	42	
	S	Lynch Edward	357	longshoreman	42	"
	T	Lynch Mary E—†	357	bowmaker	34	"
	U	*Caccanisi Charles	361	shoeworker	26	28 Bremen
	V	*Caccanisi Josephine—†	361	housewife	22	28 "
	W	O'Connell Ellen—†	361	"	74	here
	X	O'Connell John J	361	laborer	39	"
	Y	*Locatelli Alexandra—†	361	housewife	60	"
163						
	A	Locatelli Frank	361	clerk	64	
	B	Locatelli Frank G	361	mechanic	23	"
	C	Locatelli Joseph	361	bookbinder	31	"
	D	Constantine Elizabeth—†	363	housewife	32	"
	E	Constantine William	363	longshoreman	32	"
	F	Galvin John	363	laborer	34	
	G	Galvin Julia—†	363	housewife	28	"
	H	*Goglia Frank	363	laborer	74	
	K	Goglia John	363	"	24	
	L	*Goglia Louise—†	363	housewife	58	"
	M	Goglia Silvio	363	laborer	22	"

Page.	Letter.	Full Name.	Residence, Jan. 1, 1938.	Occupation.	Supposed Age.	Reported Residence, Jan. 1, 1937. Street and Number.

Sumner Street—Continued

	N	*Bruno Louise—†	363	housewife	36	here
	O	*Bruno Michael	363	laborer	41	"
	R	Gagliardi Lillian—†	365	housewife	28	158 Webster
	S	*Gagliardi Paul	365	molder	31	158 "
	T	Rapolla Angelo	365	mechanic	24	here
	U	Rapolla Dominic	365	barber	46	"
	V	Rapolla Mary—†	365	housewife	45	"
	W	Rapolla Ralph	365	barber	23	
	X	Rapolla Theresa—†	365	clerk	20	
	Y	Gioioso Dominic	1st r 365	laborer	52	
	Z	Gioioso Mary—†	1st " 365	housewife	45	"
164						
	A	DelGrosso Henry	2d " 365	laborer	22	
	B	*DelGrosso Michael	2d " 365	"	66	
	D	Colbert Thomas	3d " 365	"	68	
	E	Norman Henry	3d " 365	painter	36	
	F	Norman Lillian—†	3d " 365	housewife	30	"
	G	Frazier Mary—†	3d " 365	"	38	
	H	Paquin Joseph	367	laborer	43	
	K	*Paquin Myrtle—†	367	housewife	28	"
	L	Martinello Alexander	367	laborer	57	
	M	Martinello Anna—†	367	clerk	27	
	N	Martinello Jennie—†	367	housewife	52	"
	O	Martinello Michael	367	laborer	28	
	P	DeMarco Albert	367	"	32	
	R	DeMarco Silvia—†	367	housewife	28	"
	T	Reppucci Ethel—†	371	"	34	
	U	Reppucci Michael	371	electrician	42	"
	V	Lupoli Dominic	371	baker	57	
	W	Lupoli Theresa—†	371	housewife	48	"
	X	Landolfi Dewey	371	roofer	31	"
	Y	*Landolfi Lucy—†	371	housewife	28	"
165						
	A	Lupoli Joseph	371	baker	33	
	B	Lupoli Nicholas	371	"	20	
	C	Giorgio Edith—†	371	clerk	21	
	D	*Giorgio Emelia—†	371	housewife	44	"
	E	*Giorgio Michael	371	shoemaker	49	"
	F	*Rinna Joseph	371	laborer	56	
	G	Rinna Joseph	371	"	23	
	H	*Rinna Mary—†	371	housewife	53	"

Page.	Letter.	Full Name.	Residence, Jan. 1, 1938.	Occupation.	Supposed Age.	Reported Residence, Jan. 1, 1937. Street and Number.

Sumner Street—Continued

	L	Petruccelli Anthony	381	manager	21	146 Everett
	M	Petruccelli Rose—†	381	housewife	21	5 Sumner pl
	N	Graziano John	381	laborer	45	here
	O	*Graziano Mary—†	381	housewife	36	"
	P	Riccio Angelina—†	381	"	21	138 Webster
	R	Riccio Antonio	381	barber	26	130 Lubec
	T	*DiForte Joseph	383	laborer	62	185 Chelsea
	U	*DiForte Mary—†	383	housewife	57	185 "
	V	DiNoto Andrew	383	laborer	42	here
	W	*DiNoto Mary—†	383	housewife	41	"
	X	*Corraggi Ida—†	383	"	51	"
	Y	Corraggi Joseph	383	laborer	51	
	Z	*Colangelo Carmela—†	387	housewife	42	"
166						
	A	Colangelo Joseph	387	mechanic	41	"
	B	*Buono Fortuna—†	387	housewife	45	"
	C	*Buono Nickolas	387	laborer	42	"
	D	DiCicco John	389	barber	39	10 Lamson ct
	E	DiCicco Margaret—†	389	housewife	37	10 "
	F	Little Delia—†	391	"	56	here
	G	Little Valentine	391	laborer	55	"
	H	Little Valentine	391	"	24	"

Webster Avenue

	K	*Petroccione Francesco	1½	retired	73	here
	L	Costello James	1½	laborer	26	"
	M	Costello Mafalda—†	1½	housewife	21	"
	N	Goddard Albert E	1½	laborer	42	315 Sumner
	O	Goddard Jennie—†	1½	housewife	34	315 "
	P	Grosso Louise—†	2	"	55	here
	R	Grosso Rosario	2	retired	69	"
	S	Grosso Angelo	2	laborer	22	"
	T	Grosso Antonio	2	"	29	
	U	Grosso Peter	2	"	33	
	V	*Battista Felicia—†	3	housewife	33	"
	W	Battista Samuel	3	laborer	33	
	X	DiTomasso Nicholas	3	"	41	
	Y	DiTomasso Sylvia—†	3	housewife	41	"
	Z	Rozzi Petronella—†	4	housekeeper	73	"
167						
	A	*Rozzi Vincenzo	4	laborer	73	"

Page.	Letter.	Full Name.	Residence, Jan. 1, 1938.	Occupation.	Supposed Age.	Reported Residence, Jan. 1, 1937. Street and Number.

Webster Avenue—Continued

	E	Perito Paul	5	laborer	75	here
	B	Lopilato Elizabeth—†	5	housewife	26	“
	C	Lopilato Samuel	5	painter	33	“
	G	Venuti Angela—†	6	at home	27	
	H	*Venuti John	6	laborer	53	
	K	Venuti Virgilio	6	candymaker	22	“
	L	*DiSpirito Antonio	7	laborer	63	
	M	*DiSpirito Robina—†	7	housewife	64	“
	N	Dalimonte George	7	electrician	26	“
	O	Dalimonte Rachel—†	7	housewife	25	“
	P	DiSpirito Mary—†	7	candymaker	20	“
	R	DiGregorio Antonio	8	laborer	65	
	S	DiGregorio Christoforo	8	“	34	
	T	DiGregorio Michael	8	“	26	
	U	DiGregorio Tilly—†	8	housekeeper	25	“
	V	Ferullo Lucy—†	9	housewife	45	284 Sumner
	W	Ferullo Marion—†	9	dressmaker	20	284 “
	X	Ferullo William	9	shoeworker	50	284 “
	Y	Morro Lorenzo	10	laborer	59	23 Monmouth
	Z	*Pasquale Michael	10	“	39	here
168						
	A	Pasquale Rose C—†	10	housewife	32	“
	B	Buonopane Angelo	10	laborer	40	
	C	*Buonopane Nancy—†	10	housewife	35	“
	D	Contestabile Arthur A	11	laborer	24	
	E	Contestabile Margaret—†	11	housewife	23	“
	F	Selvitella John	11	electrician	26	“
	G	Selvitella Lucy—†	11	housewife	27	“
	H	Orsini Angelina—†	12	“	49	“
	K	Orsini Henry	12	shoeworker	49	“
	L	Orsini Albert	12	“	24	“
	M	Orsini Dante	12	“	26	
	N	Collins Antoinette—†	15	housewife	29	“
	O	Collins James	15	cabinetmaker	29	“
	P	*Colarusso Joseph	15	retired	70	

Webster Street

	R	*Romano Luigi	55	tailor	56	here
	S	*Romano Mary—†	55	housewife	56	“
	T	Romano Rose—†	55	tailoress	21	“
	U	*Baglio Carmella—†	55	housewife	42	“

Page.	Letter.	Full Name.	Residence, Jan. 1, 1938.	Occupation.	Supposed Age.	Reported Residence, Jan. 1, 1937. Street and Number.
		Webster Street—Continued				
	v	*Baglio John	55	laborer	48	here
	w	Campbell Edward	57	longshoreman	55	"
	x	Farley Alice—†	57	inspector	48	"
	y	*DeFlorio Gaetano	57	retired	84	
	z	*DeFlorio Maria—†	57	housewife	73	"
169						
	A	DeFlorio Sarah—†	57	tailoress	36	"
	B	Iarossi Hazel—†	57	housewife	25	94 Webster
	C	Iarossi Louis	57	plumber	28	94 "
	D	DiGirolamo Ernest	59	mechanic	29	here
	E	DiGirolamo Jennie—†	59	housewife	27	"
	F	Mogardo Barbara—†	59	"	31	"
	G	*Mogardo Joseph	59	cook	33	
	H	Frances George	59	laborer	21	
	K	Frances James	59	"	40	
	L	Mirra Joseph	59	shoemaker	41	"
	M	Montalto Jennie—†	60	housewife	25	"
	N	Montalto Joseph	60	factoryhand	30	"
	O	Pizzano Andrew	60	laborer	34	
	P	Pizzano Mildred—†	60	housewife	34	"
	R	*Liberatore Anna—†	60	"	39	
	S	*Liberatore Mary—†	60	"	37	
	T	Liberatore Peter	60	candymaker	38	"
	U	Liberatore Stanley	60	"	40	
	V	Belmont Anthony	61	laborer	24	
	W	Belmont Lillian—†	61	housewife	24	"
	X	Masiello Carmen	61	laborer	79	
	Y	*LaGambina Drago—†	61	housewife	41	"
	Z	*LaGambina Sebastina	61	laborer	40	
170						
	A	Prezioso Edward	61		24	
	B	Prezioso Olindo	61	"	64	
	C	Masillo Clara—†	61	housewife	30	"
	D	Masillo Joseph	61	foreman	36	
	E	*Munro Alba—†	62	housewife	40	"
	F	*DiSavino Frances—†	62	"	35	
	G	DiSavino Michael	62	laborer	45	"
	H	Gallo Caesar	62	salesman	42	New York
	K	Johns Edward	62	painter	36	460 Sumner
	L	Johns Theresa—†	62	housewife	34	460 "
	M	*Cavagnaro Filomena—†	63	"	48	here

Page.	Letter.	FULL NAME.	Residence, Jan. 1, 1938.	Occupation.	Supposed Age.	Reported Residence, Jan. 1, 1937. Street and Number.

Webster Street—Continued

Page.	Letter.	FULL NAME.	Residence, Jan. 1, 1938.	Occupation.	Supposed Age.	Reported Residence, Jan. 1, 1937. Street and Number.
	N	Cavagnaro Gennaro	63	laborer	50	here
	O	Cavagnaro Louis	63	"	25	"
	P	Cavagnaro Michael	63	"	22	"
	R	Dagostino Anthony	63	"	58	
	S	*Dagostino Pasqualina—†	63	housewife	56	"
	T	Moscillo Joseph	63	laborer	33	
	U	Moscillo Sebastina—†	63	housewife	31	"
	W	*Mendolia Mary—†	64	"	35	
171						
	A	*Grana Maria—†	66	"	54	
	B	Grana Vincent	66	carpenter	62	"
	C	Canto Guy	67	laborer	25	78 Everett
	D	Canto Rose—†	67	housewife	23	78 "
	E	Ciardulli Orazio	67	laborer	48	here
	F	Vocino Helen—†	67	dressmaker	23	"
	G	Vocino Joseph	67	laborer	20	"
	H	Vocino Matteo	67	storekeeper	52	"
	K	Vocino Teresa—†	67	housewife	50	"
	L	Tedesco Jennie—†	68	"	40	
	M	*Nostro Frank	68	salesman	35	"
	N	Nostro Josephine—†	68	housewife	30	"
	O	*Santilli Louise—†	68	"	55	74 Everett
	P	Santilli Michael	68	laborer	63	74 "
	R	Capuana James	69	"	26	88 Bremen
	S	Capuana Lena—†	69	housewife	25	88 "
	T	*Olympio Anthony D	69	laborer	37	here
	U	*Romano Constantino	69	"	59	"
	V	Romano Fannie—†	69	factoryhand	25	"
	W	*Romano Mary—†	69	housewife	58	"
	X	DeNietolis Edith—†	69	"	21	1211 Bennington
	Y	DeNietolis Emelio	69	laborer	27	1211 "
	Z	Bruno Ralph	70	mechanic	25	10 Haynes
172						
	A	Bruno Virginia—†	70	housewife	21	10 "
	B	Porrozzo Luigi	70	laborer	48	here
	C	Porrozzo Mary—†	70	housewife	46	"
	D	Porrozzo Michael	70	printer	24	"
	E	*Mattei Erminia—†	70	housewife	37	"
	F	*Mattei Mario	70	mechanic	44	"
	G	*DiBello Elizabeth—†	71	housewife	73	"
	H	DiBello John	71	laborer	42	

Page.	Letter.	FULL NAME.	Residence, Jan. 1, 1938.	Occupation.	Supposed Age.	Reported Residence, Jan. 1, 1937. Street and Number.

Webster Street—Continued

	K	*Siracusa Frances—†	71	housewife	57	here
	L	*Siracusa Nicholas	71	laborer	45	"
	M	Formicola Frank	71	barber	48	"
	N	*Formicola Margaret—†	71	housewife	42	"
	P	Menard Alfred	73	longshoreman	31	22 Saratoga
	O	Menard Amelia—†	73	housewife	28	22 "
	R	*Greco Isabella—†	73	"	28	here
	S	Greco Pasquale	73	bricklayer	32	"
	T	Sorentino Frances—†	73	housewife	28	"
	U	Sorentino Frank	73	laborer	30	
	V	*Mottola Margaret—†	74	housewife	30	"
	W	*Mottola Michael	74	printer	31	
	X	Tranfaglia Anthony	74	laborer	42	
	Y	Tranfaglia Raffaela—†	74	housewife	34	"
	Z	Mottola Amato	74	factoryhand	32	"
173						
	A	Mottola Michelina—†	74	housewife	32	"
	B	*Parcelli Mary—†	75	"	45	
	C	*Parcelli Nicholas	75	laborer	43	
	D	*D'Abene Antonio	75	"	55	
	E	*D'Abene Mary—†	75	housewife	45	"
	F	DiGirolamo Elvira—†	75	clerk	28	"
	G	DiGirolamo Frank	75	laborer	62	
	H	*DiGirolamo Michelina—†	75	housewife	60	"
	K	DiGirolamo Minnie—†	75	clerk	25	"
	L	Mottola Adolph	76	longshoreman	28	79 Webster
	M	Mottola Frances—†	76	housewife	25	79 "
	N	Mottola Fioro	76	orderly	24	here
	O	*Mottola Stephanie—†	76	housewife	61	"
	P	*Mottola Vincent	76	laborer	62	"
	R	Bozza Alberico	76	mechanic	48	"
	S	*Bozza Amelia—†	76	housewife	30	"
	T	*Mazzola Michelina—†	77	"	37	
	U	Mazzola Sebastiano	77	laborer	41	
	V	*Infussi Anthony	77	cook	57	"
	W	*Infussi Margaret—†	77	housewife	42	"
	X	Luongo Alfred A	77	bartender	36	"
	Y	DiTomasso Dominic	77	laborer	35	36 Frankfort
	Z	DiTomasso Dora—†	77	housewife	27	36 "
174						
	A	*Ryan Mary—†	79	"	74	here

Page.	Letter.	FULL NAME.	Residence, Jan. 1, 1938.	Occupation.	Supposed Age.	Reported Residence, Jan. 1, 1937. Street and Number.

Webster Street—Continued

Page.	Letter.	FULL NAME.	Residence, Jan. 1, 1938.	Occupation.	Supposed Age.	Reported Residence, Jan. 1, 1937. Street and Number.
	B	Ryan Thomas	79	longshoreman	57	here
	C	Giardone Christine—†	79	housewife	23	64 Webster
	D	*Giardone William	79	laborer	25	64 "
	E	*Giardone Louise—†	79	housewife	48	77 "
	F	*Giardone Philip	79	laborer	53	77 "
	G	*Bozza Sarah—†	80	housewife	65	here
	H	Bozza Zachario	80	retired	76	"
	K	Bozza Aurora—†	80	teacher	26	"
	L	Bozza Filomena—†	80	housewife	52	"
	M	Bozza Mary—†	80	factoryhand	23	"
	N	Bozza Setimo	80	barber	55	
	O	Voto Lydia—†	80	housewife	24	"
	P	Voto Salvatore	80	mechanic	25	"
	R	Cardarelli Nicholas	81	laborer	45	
	S	*Cardarelli Phyllis—†	81	housewife	43	"
	T	DiCicco Louise—†	81	clerk	28	
	U	*DiCicco Mary—†	81	housewife	63	"
	V	*Vassallo Angelina—†	81	"	31	
	W	Vassallo James	81	meatcutter	35	"
	X	Nocito Joseph	82	painter	21	73 Webster
	Z	Nocito Michael	82	shoemaker	35	here
	Y	*Nocito Elizabeth—†	82	housewife	43	"
175						
	A	*Nocito Orazio	82	barber	50	"
	B	*Corrado Concetta—†	83	housewife	79	75 Webster
	C	*Stellabotta Lucy—†	83	"	42	here
	D	*Corrado Lucy—†	83	"	38	75 Webster
	E	Corrado Ralph	83	carpenter	42	75 "
	F	Napolitania Dominic	84	laborer	29	here
	G	Napolitania Mary—†	84	housewife	30	"
	H	*Vaccaro Cornelia—†	84	"	34	"
	K	Vaccaro John	84	laborer	46	
	L	Ferrara Girolamo	84	"	65	
	M	*Ferrara Victoria—†	84	housewife	57	"
	N	Rauseo James	85	laborer	53	
	O	*Rauseo Phyllis—†	85	housewife	40	"
	P	Giangrande Louis	85	laborer	41	
	R	*Giangrande Rose—†	85	housewife	31	"
	S	*Rossi Antonio	85	laborer	55	
	T	Rossi Fannie—†	85	clerk	20	
	U	Rossi Luigi	87	stonecutter	73	"

V Rossi Olympia—†	87	clerk	31	here
W*Cotte Adeline—†	87	housewife	59	"
X*Cotte Ralph	87	janitor	58	"
Y Cotte Nunzio	87	laborer	25	"
Z Cotte Olga—†	87	housewife	22	58 Webster
176				
A Pisiello Carmen	88	laborer	24	Malden
B Pisiello George	88	mattressmaker	30	here
C Pisiello Mary—†	88	housewife	30	"
D DeAngelis Maria—†	88	"	62	"
E*DeAngelis Michael	88	laborer	56	"
F Scire Theresa—†	88	housewife	31	Medford
G Marmorale Anthony	88	laborer	42	here
H Marmorale Caroline—†	88	housewife	34	"
K Snow Lauretta—†	89	"	27	"
L*Zeoli Ernest	89	shoemaker	44	"
M*Zeoli Josephine—†	89	housewife	42	"
O*Haggstrom Emelia—†	90	"	55	"
P Haggstrom Olga—†	90	factoryhand	32	"
R*Haggstrom Otto	90	laborer	64	
S Forti John	90	candymaker	39	"
T Forti Margaret—†	90	housewife	36	"
U Kevin John	90	shipper	65	
V Kevin Margaret—†	90	housewife	65	"
W Cleary Helen C—†	91	domestic	46	
X Moore Joseph	91	laborer	23	
Y O'Hare John F	91	deckhand	38	"
Z O'Hare Sarah A—†	91	housewife	73	"
177				
A Christopher Dominic	91A	carpenter	57	"
B*Christopher Palma—†	91A	housewife	58	"
C*Pessia Elvira—†	91A	"	50	
D Pessia Loreto	91A	mechanic	21	"
E Pessia Michael	91A	tailor	54	
G*Acquaviva Carolina—†	92	housewife	45	"
H Esposito Gaetano	92	shoemaker	47	"
K Esposito Josephine—†	92	housewife	41	"
L McMullen Ida—†	93	"	52	"
M McMullen John	93	stevedore	49	"
N Ciliberto Antonio	93A	laborer	26	79 Webster
O Ciliberto Frances—†	93A	saleswoman	22	79 "

Page.	Letter.	Full Name.	Residence, Jan. 1, 1938.	Occupation.	Supposed Age.	Reported Residence, Jan. 1, 1937. Street and Number.

Webster Street—Continued

Page.	Letter.	Full Name.	Residence, Jan. 1, 1938.	Occupation.	Supposed Age.	Reported Residence, Jan. 1, 1937. Street and Number.
	P	Ciliberto Henrietta—†	93A	factoryhand	32	79 Webster
	R	*DiGiacomo Isadore	93A	laborer	68	here
	S	*Taylor Antonetta—†	93A	housewife	38	"
	T	Taylor Francis	93A	tinsmith	49	"
	U	Taylor Frederick	93A	laborer	24	
	V	Iarossi Eleanor—†	94	domestic	22	"
	W	*Iarossi Lawrence	94	carpenter	56	"
	X	Iarossi Pasquale	94	plumber	25	
	Y	*Iarossi Vincenza—†	94	housewife	76	"
	Z	Vicirca Joseph	94	laborer	22	
178						
	A	*Vacirca Josephine—†	94	housewife	43	"
	B	*Vacirca Philip	94	laborer	47	
	C	*Pearson Anna—†	94	housewife	56	"
	D	Pearson Peter	94	longshoreman	63	"
	E	Christoforo Maurice	95	shoeworker	25	97 Webster
	F	Christoforo Minnie—†	95	housewife	22	130 Bremen
	G	McCarthy Hugo	96	laborer	45	here
	H	McCarthy Theresa—†	96	housewife	40	"
	K	Auciello Dominic	96	laborer	42	"
	L	Auciello Mary—†	96	housewife	29	"
	M	*Rausco Carmela—†	96	"	48	
	N	Rausco Rocco	96	laborer	53	
	O	Christoforo Charles	97	chauffeur	41	"
	P	*Christoforo John	97	retired	69	
	R	Christoforo Mary—†	97	candyworker	26	"
	S	*Christoforo Rachel—†	97	housekeeper	67	"
	T	DelGaizo Anacleto	97	tailor	36	"
	U	DelGaizo Rose—†	97	housewife	37	"
	V	DeAngelis Julius	98	chauffeur	24	"
	W	*DeAngelis Lucy—†	98	housewife	25	"
	X	Grallo Martin	98	laborer	49	
	Y	*Grallo Mary—†	98	housewife	50	"
	Z	*Ferrario John	98	baker	58	
179						
	A	*Ferrario Louise—†	98	housewife	52	"
	B	Pascale Eli	98	teacher	54	
	C	Leone Guy	99	clerk	33	
	D	Rongone Alfred	99	engineer	33	
	E	Rongone Susan—†	99	housewife	30	"
	F	Roach Allan	100	chauffeur	38	"

Page.	Letter.	Full Name.	Residence, Jan. 1, 1938.	Occupation.	Supposed Age.	Reported Residence, Jan. 1, 1937. Street and Number.

Webster Street—Continued

	G	Roach Margaret—†	100	housewife	38	here
	H	DiBello James	100	fireman	32	"
	K	DiBello Jennie—†	100	housewife	31	"
	L	DiBello Adeline—†	100	clerk	28	
	M	DiBello Anna—†	100	"	21	
	N	*DiBello Josephine—†	100	housewife	67	"
	O	Costello Arthur	101	freighthandler	24	"
	P	*Costello Bridget—†	101	housewife	57	"
	R	Costello Evelyn—†	101	stitcher	20	
	S	Costello Michael	101	longshoreman	31	"
	T	Forgione Mildred—†	101	at home	28	
	U	Kennedy David J	101	retired	65	
	V	Kennedy David R	101	longshoreman	31	"
	W	Kennedy Elizabeth A—†	101	at home	33	
	X	Kennedy Ernest E	101	laborer	20	
	Y	Kennedy Mary M—†	101	housekeeper	29	"
	Z	Kennedy Robert R	101	weigher	21	"
180						
	A	DiBello Joseph	102	musician	46	"
	B	DiBello Josephine—†	102	housewife	35	"
	C	Simione Joseph	102	chauffeur	33	"
	D	Simione Mary—†	102	housewife	38	"
	E	DelGaizo Gerald	102	mechanic	53	"
	F	DelGaizo Mary—†	102	housewife	42	"
	G	Ragusa Josephine—†	102	factoryhand	20	"
	H	DiRago Pasquale	rear 102	laborer	53	
	K	Giello Florence—†	103	typist	30	
	L	Giello Joseph	103	shoemaker	70	"
	M	Giello Rose—†	103	housewife	59	"
	N	Greco Anna—†	106	factoryhand	31	"
	O	Greco Margaret—†	106	"	28	
	P	*Greco Marianna—†	106	housewife	59	"
	R	*Greco Salvatore	106	contractor	62	"
	S	Greco Thomas	106	laborer	25	
	T	Magliano Antonetta—†	108	housewife	22	"
	U	Magliano John	108	laborer	22	"
	V	Rotigliano Joseph	108	clerk	23	62 Frankfort
	W	Rotigliano Mary—†	108	housewife	21	62 "
	Y	Karovas May—†	110	"	39	here
	Z	Karovas Nicholas	110	seaman	52	"

Page.	Letter.	FULL NAME.	Residence, Jan. 1, 1938.	Occupation.	Supposed Age.	Reported Residence, Jan. 1, 1937. Street and Number.
181		**Webster Street**—Continued				
	A	Sistiolio John	110	laborer	23	2 Wilbur ct
	B	Sistiolio Josephine—†	110	housewife	22	2 "
	C	Carroll Agatha—†	112	"	20	363 Sumner
	D	Carroll Robert	112	painter	21	254 Webster
	E	Emmett Mary—†	112	housewife	20	365 Meridian
	F	Emmett Oliver	112	laborer	25	40 Jeffries
	G	*Lettien Rosaria—†	112	housewife	50	here
	H	Tosiello Joseph	112	laborer	25	"
	K	*Sordello Eleanor—†	112	housewife	42	"
	L	Sordello Ralph	112	mechanic	47	"
	M	Goggin Helen E—†	115	housewife	24	"
	N	Goggin Joseph	115	chauffeur	29	"
	O	Goggin James	115	guard	32	
	P	Goggin John	115	laborer	65	
	R	Goggin Josephine—†	115	housewife	68	"
	S	Goggin Richard	115	freighthandler	33	"
	T	Gillen Catherine—†	116	housewife	69	"
	U	Gillen Catherine A—†	116	inspector	34	"
	V	Gillen James	116	longshoreman	40	"
	W	Gillen Margaret—†	116	clerk	25	
	X	Gillen Mary—†	116	"	38	
	Y	Jacobs Helen—†	116	housewife	26	"
	Z	Jacobs John	116	seaman	26	23 Jeffries
182						
	A	Pezzella Angelina—†	116	clerk	24	here
	B	Pezzella Antonio	116	laborer	50	"
	C	Faretra Mary—†	116	housewife	39	"
	D	Faretra Virgilio	116	bartender	50	"
	E	Bergquist Hjalmar	117	porter	40	
	F	Dinolfo Vincenzo	117	salesman	52	"
	G	Dragan John	117	"	50	
	H	Johnson Andrew B	117	porter	61	
	K	Johnson Gerda—†	117	housewife	62	"
	L	Salami Domenick	117	salesman	51	"
	M	Sheehan Mary—†	117	factoryhand	50	"
	N	Albano Carmen	118	baker	26	
	O	Albano Mary—†	118	housewife	23	"
	P	Tancredi John	118	laborer	29	
	R	Tancredi Pasquale	118	shoemaker	54	"

Page.	Letter.	Full Name.	Residence, Jan. 1, 1938.	Occupation.	Supposed Age.	Reported Residence, Jan. 1, 1937. Street and Number.

Webster Street—Continued

	S	*Tancredi Rose—†	118	housewife	56	here
	T	Albano James	118	baker	29	"
	U	Albano Theresa—†	118	housewife	27	"
	V	Fulziniti Joseph	118	seaman	25	
	W	Cappucci John	119	longshoreman	32	"
	X	Cappucci Mary—†	119	housewife	25	"
	Y	Ciampa Filomena—†	119	"	27	
	Z	Ciampa Joseph F	119	operator	28	"
183						
	A	Bagnera Anthony	119	shoeworker	29	"
	B	Bagnera Viola—†	119	housewife	22	"
	D	*Molea Filomena—†	120	"	28	
	E	Molea Nathaniel	120	laborer	29	
	F	Covolucci Amando	120	"	21	
	G	Covolucci Joseph	120	"	55	
	H	Covolucci Joseph	120		24	
	K	DeAngelis Anthony	120	"	44	"
	L	*DeAngelis Margaret—†	120	housewife	47	"
	M	*Marratto Anthony	122	barber	54	
	N	Marratto Dora—†	122	clerk	22	
	O	Marratto Edward	122	hairdresser	24	"
	P	Marratto Helen—†	122	stitcher	25	
	R	Marratto Ida—†	122	"	21	
	S	*Marratto Mary—†	122	housewife	54	"
	T	DiBenedetto Mark	122	laborer	40	
	U	*DiBenedetto Rose—†	122	housewife	42	"
	V	Marciano Anthony	123	factoryhand	24	"
	W	Marciano Camilla—†	123	"	21	
	X	*Marciano Grace—†	123	housewife	49	"
	Y	*Marciano Joseph	123	storekeeper	48	"
	Z	Faria Anna—†	123	housewife	53	"
184						
	A	Faria Mary A—†	123	stenographer	24	"
	B	Faria Raffaele	123	janitor	63	"
	C	Faria Stephen A	123	engineer	27	
	D	Long Margaret A—†	123	operator	37	"
	E	Long William	123	laborer	41	
	G	*DeMarino Pasquilina—†	125	housekeeper	53	"
	H	Fulgione Gregory	125	accountant	40	"
	K	Fulgione Mary—†	125	housewife	31	"
	L	Walsh Mary J—†	125	at home	60	

Page.	Letter.	FULL NAME.	Residence, Jan. 1, 1938.	Occupation.	Supposed Age.	Reported Residence, Jan. 1, 1937. Street and Number.

Webster Street—Continued

	M	Walsh William J	125	retired	60	here
	N	Walsh William J, jr	125	laborer	33	"
	O	*Piccardi Esta—†	126	housewife	38	"
	P	Piccardi Ralph	126	laborer	41	
	R	*Ambrasino Mary—†	126	housewife	65	"
	S	*Ambrasino Michael	126	laborer	60	
	T	Ambrasino Rose—†	126	candymaker	26	"
	U	Ardagna Antonio	126	laborer	48	
	V	*Ardagna Frances—†	126	housewife	38	"
	W	Bowman Jane A—†	127	clerk	40	
	X	Bowman Jennie A—†	127	housekeeper	69	"
	Y	Garadozzi Albert	127	janitor	24	"
	Z	*Garadozzi Josephine—†	127	housewife	58	"
185						
	A	Garadozzi Robert	127	mechanic	22	"
	B	Crocetti Domenic	127	storekeeper	52	"
	C	Crocetti Jennie—†	127	housekeeper	43	"
	D	Zirpolo Angelina—†	128	housewife	34	"
	E	Zirpolo Michael	128	longshoreman	42	"
	F	Vacca Michael	128	laborer	25	4 Foster
	G	*Vacca Rose—†	128	housewife	38	Italy
	H	Iacobacci Peter	128	laborer	42	here
	K	*Iacobacci Winifred—†	128	housewife	41	"
	L	Racana John	129	bricklayer	58	"
	M	Racana Louise—†	129	housewife	50	"
	N	Racana Rocco	129	laborer	24	
	O	Mirabile Pasquale	129	machinist	23	"
	P	Mirabile Rocco	129	clerk	33	
	R	Mirabile Rose—†	129	cigarmaker	26	"
	S	Maragiolgio Anthony	129	baker	36	
	T	Maragiolgio Eleanor—†	129	housewife	30	"
	U	Cirolli Albert	130	laborer	41	
	V	Curzi Giovanni	130	"	34	
	W	*Mazzarini John	130	"	39	
	X	*Mazzarini Urlianna—†	130	housewife	26	"
	Y	DiViasio Angelina—†	130	"	29	Somerville
	Z	DiViasio Emilio	130	cigarmaker	29	"
186						
	A	Rigano Caroline—†	130	typist	28	"
	B	Rigano Margaret—†	130	cigarmaker	43	here
	C	Liberti Ettore	131	guard	51	"

Page.	Letter.	Full Name.	Residence, Jan. 1, 1938.	Occupation.	Supposed Age.	Reported Residence, Jan. 1, 1937. Street and Number.
	D	Liberti Ferminia—†	131	teacher	26	here
	E	*Liberti Prassede—†	131	housewife	50	"
	F	Liberti Sabatino	131	chauffeur	24	"
	G	Devlin Annie A—†	135	housewife	50	"
	H	Devlin John J	135	painter	53	
	K	Bruno Josephine E—†	136	nurse	27	
	L	Shoemaker Clementina—†	136	housewife	23	"
	M	Shoemaker William	136	counterman	25	"
	N	*DiGiovanni Joseph	136	laborer	36	
	O	DiGiovanni Raffaella—†	136	housewife	32	"
	P	*Elia Anthony	136	laborer	70	"
	R	*Ippolito Mary—†	136	housewife	55	"
	S	Ippolito Pasquale	136	laborer	21	
	T	*Ippolito Thomas	136	"	60	
	U	Tosi Alice—†	136	packer	23	
	V	Tosi Helen—†	136	housewife	43	"
	W	Digan Anna W—†	137	operator	50	"
	X	Digan Arthur E	137	attorney	42	"
	Y	Digan Carrie L—†	137	saleswoman	47	"
	Z	Digan Lucy E—†	137	housekeeper	44	"
187						
	B	*Marotto Amelia—†	138	housewife	48	"
	C	Marotto Henry	138	laborer	43	
	D	Marotto Melinda—†	138	factoryhand	23	"
	E	Giusti Dante	138	chauffeur	21	"
	F	Giusti Muriel—†	138	housewife	21	"
	G	*DiSimone Catherine—†	138	"	25	
	H	*DiSimone Louis	138	factoryhand	26	"
	K	Young Anna T—†	141	housewife	45	"
	L	Costello Mary M—†	141	"	30	14 Cottage
	M	Costello Michael F	141	longshoreman	32	14 "
	N	DiSario Angelina—†	141	housewife	47	here
	O	DiSario Emilio F	141	sculptor	49	"
	P	DiSario Frederick P	141	laborer	22	"
	R	DePasquale Parisi	143	"	60	
	T	Gill Mary F—†	143	housewife	26	"
	U	Gill William H	143	longshoreman	27	"
	V	Sarnie Eugene	146	salesman	40	"
	W	Sarnie Jennie—†	146	housewife	37	"
	X	Albano Fred	146	laborer	28	189 Cottage
	Y	Albano Marion—†	146	housewife	25	189 "

Page.	Letter.	Full Name.	Residence, Jan. 1, 1938.	Occupation.	Supposed Age.	Reported Residence, Jan. 1, 1937. Street and Number.

Webster Street—Continued

Page.	Letter.	Full Name.	Residence, Jan. 1, 1938.	Occupation.	Supposed Age.	Reported Residence, Jan. 1, 1937. Street and Number.
	Z	Salvaggio Joseph	146	baker	21	114 Everett
188						
	A	Venuti Frank	146	plumber	28	40 Webster
	B	Venuti Lillian—†	146	housewife	23	40 “
	C	Pinta Guy	146	laborer	76	here
	D	Pinta Joseph	146	“	28	“
	E	Pinta Mabel—†	146	housewife	26	“
	G	Petrillo Anthony	147	laborer	48	
	F	*Petrillo Carmella—†	147	housewife	49	“
	H	Keohane Timothy J	147	blacksmith	63	“
	K	Vitale Domenic A	147	milkman	23	“
	L	Vitale Mary S—†	147	housewife	20	“
	M	Rossi Francis	147	mechanic	30	“
	N	Rossi Louise M—†	147	housewife	24	“
	O	Gigliello Gerald	148	guard	47	
	P	Gigliello Katherine—†	148	housewife	44	“
	R	Gigliello Rosaria—†	148	“	65	
	S	*Balzotti Maria—†	148	“	56	
	T	*Balzotti Paul	148	laborer	56	“
	U	Balzotti Arthur	148	“	21	
	V	Balzotti Domenic	148	“	25	
	W	*Spinazola Jennie—†	148	housewife	41	“
	X	Spinazola Joseph	148	laborer	41	
	Y	Spinazola Maria—†	148	clerk	20	“
	Z	*Andriotti Mary—†	149	housewife	57	“
189						
	A	Andriotti Yolanda—†	149	clerk	20	
	B	Barry James J	149	timekeeper	26	“
	C	Barry Susan—†	149	housewife	53	“
	D	Flynn John J	149	longshoreman	65	“
	E	Muse Evelyn—†	149	housewife	34	“
	F	Muse Michael J	149	engineer	33	“
	G	*Barbato Anthony	150	tailor	36	Italy
	H	*Barbato Louise—†	150	housewife	29	“
	K	Gigliello Alfred	150	laborer	23	here
	L	Gigliello Elsie—†	150	housewife	24	“
	M	Gigliello Gervasio	150	laborer	24	“
	N	*Gigliello Victoria—†	150	housewife	27	“
	O	Ciampa Generoso	150	laborer	22	148 Webster
	P	Yecchetti Amelia—†	150	housewife	24	here
	R	Yecchetti Louis	150	barber	25	“

Page.	Letter.	Full Name.	Residence, Jan. 1, 1938.	Occupation.	Supposed Age.	Reported Residence, Jan. 1, 1937. Street and Number.

Webster Street—Continued

	s	*Contestabile Antonio	150	gardener	55	here
	T	Contestabile Louis	150	laborer	28	"
	U	Contestabile Peter	150	milkman	27	"
	V	Salamanco Mary—†	154	housewife	22	"
	W	*Salamanco Paul	154	laborer	53	
	X	Salamanco Peter	154	"	21	
	Y	Abate Alfred	154	shoemaker	20	"
	Z	*Abate Amodio	154	"	53	
190						
	A	*Abate Mary—†	154	housewife	25	"
	B	Occhipinti Anthony	154	carpenter	48	"
	C	Occhipinti Mary—†	154	housewife	39	"
	D	Rotigliano Mary—†	155	"	61	
	E	Rotigliano Michael	155	shoemaker	61	"
	F	Aronson Aaron	155	storekeeper	38	30 Wentworth ter
	G	Aronson Goldie—†	155	housewife	37	30 "
	H	Lopilato Arthur	155	painter	21	here
	K	Lopilato George	155	"	28	"
	L	Lopilato Lucy—†	155	housewife	61	"
	M	Lopilato Massey	155	chauffeur	35	"
	N	Lopilato Rose—†	155	candyworker	33	"
	O	Lopilato Vincenzo	155	laborer	65	
	P	Cashman Charlotte—†	156	housewife	40	"
	R	Agnew Margaret M—†	156	"	48	"
	S	Mealey Louise—†	156	"	59	221 Webster
	T	Iorio Anthony	158	salesman	37	188 "
	U	Iorio Evelyn—†	158	housewife	35	here
	V	O'Neil Elizabeth—†	158	bowmaker	31	"
	W	O'Neil Emily—†	158	housewife	62	"
	X	O'Neil Evelyn—†	158	packer	27	"
	Y	O'Neil Gertrude—†	158	operator	28	
	Z	O'Neil Helen—†	158	clerk	20	
191						
	A	O'Neil John J	158	laborer	30	
	B	O'Neil Patrick J	158	bricklayer	63	"
	C	*Ciampa Aurora—†	160	housewife	31	"
	D	Ciampa Nicholas	160	shipper	31	
	E	Pesella Charles J	160	laborer	34	
	F	Pesella Frank A	160	salesman	29	"
	G	Pesella Joseph	160	clerk	27	
	H	Pesella Rose—†	160	"	25	

Page.	Letter.	FULL NAME.	Residence, Jan. 1, 1938.	Occupation.	Supposed Age.	Reported Residence, Jan. 1, 1937. Street and Number.

Webster Street—Continued

Page.	Letter.	FULL NAME.	Residence, Jan. 1, 1938.	Occupation.	Supposed Age.	Reported Residence, Jan. 1, 1937. Street and Number.
	K	Pesella Assunta—†	160	housewife	53	here
	L	Pesella Margaret—†	160	clerk	24	"
	M	Pesella Pasquale	160	engineer	60	"
	N	Nigro Anna—†	162	housewife	31	"
	O	Nigro Dominic	162	chauffeur	32	"
	P	Brennan Francis E	162	shipper	39	
	R	Brennan George C	162	retired	84	
	S	Brennan Margaret E—†	162	bookkeeper	49	"
	T	Brennan Sarah B—†	162	teacher	45	"
	U	Brennan William G	162	engineer	47	"
	V	Cacici Arthur	166	barber	51	"
	W	*Cacici Concetta—†	166	housewife	44	"
	X	Benvenuto Frances—†	166	"	23	
	Y	Benvenuto Louis	166	laborer	25	"
	Z	Puccio Rose—†	166	housewife	31	155 Webster
192						
	A	Puccio Vincent	166	tailor	31	155 "
	B	Lombardo Beatrice—†	168	housewife	27	here
	C	Lombardo Margheritino	168	shoeworker	36	"
	D	Mastralio Liberato	168	restaurateur	55	"
	E	Mastralio Rose—†	168	housewife	54	"
	F	Mastralio Vito	168	bartender	25	"
	G	Mastralio William	168	"	22	
	H	Martinello Anna—†	172	housewife	46	"
	K	Martinello Jennie—†	172	stenographer	23	"
	L	Martinello Joseph A	172	retired	58	"
	M	Belgiorno Florence—†	172	housewife	26	"
	N	Belgiorno John A	172	manager	29	"
	O	Pepe Antonio	174	candymaker	67	"
	P	Pepe Louise—†	174	housewife	26	"
	R	Pepe Ralph	174	boxmaker	30	"
	S	*Stallone Mary—†	174	housewife	46	166 Webster
	T	*Stallone Nicholas	174	tailor	46	166 "
	U	*Scherma Ciro	176	barber	43	here
	V	*Scherma Katherine—†	176	housewife	40	"
	W	DeModena John	176	physician	51	"
	X	DeModena Mary—†	176	housewife	51	"
	Y	DeModena Silvio	176	electrician	21	"
	Z	*Cutrone Teresa—†	176	housewife	67	"
193						
	A	Cutrone Vito	176	retired	69	

Page.	Letter.	Full Name.	Residence, Jan. 1, 1938.	Occupation.	Supposed Age.	Reported Residence, Jan. 1, 1937. Street and Number.

Webster Street—Continued

	B	Simms Myrtle—†	177	housewife	44	here
	C	Simms Stockwell	177	social worker	48	"
	D	Vellante Guistino	178	laborer	44	"
	E	*Vellante Teresa—†	178	housewife	40	"
	F	*Torti Louise—†	178	"	37	
	G	*Torti Zeno	178	tailor	39	
	H	*Schifino Angelina—†	178	housewife	53	"
	K	Schifino Irene—†	178	inspector	25	"
	L	*Schifino Michael	178	packer	58	
	M	Schifino Millie—†	178	stitcher	23	"
	N	Dowse Margaret—†	179	teacher	24	Sherborn
	O	Kennedy Ellen—†	179	"	25	Connecticut
	P	Staples Edith—†	179	"	28	Alabama
	R	*Serino Angelina—†	181	housewife	43	here
	S	*Serino Domenic	181	shoemaker	45	"
	U	Pastore Amando	181	barber	30	"
	V	*Pastore Anna—†	181	housewife	22	"
	W	*Faugno Carmella—†	181	"	36	
	X	Faugno Michael	181	shoeworker	45	"
	Y	Vardaro Anthony	181	musician	29	"
	Z	*Vardaro Mary—†	181	housekeeper	65	"
194						
	A	Donegan Anna—†	182	housewife	42	"
	B	Donegan James	182	retired	54	
	C	Manganiello Joseph	182	printer	47	
	D	Pollini Domenick	182	stonecutter	52	"
	E	Pollini Frances—†	182	housewife	49	"
	F	Indelicato Alphonso	182	longshoreman	28	"
	G	*Indelicato Carmela—†	182	housewife	50	"
	H	Indelicato Joseph	182	cook	20	
	K	Indelicato Vincenzo	182	watchman	62	"
	L	Lafuente Nicholas	182	chef	49	
	N	Vardaro Julia—†	183	housekeeper	29	"
	O	Vardaro Louis	183	laborer	34	"
	P	Mariano Louis	183	shoeworker	45	"
	R	Mariano Olympia—†	183	housewife	45	"
	S	Lightbody Carmella—†	183	"	22	85 Webster
	T	Lightbody William	183	clerk	21	3 Lexington pl
	U	Vardaro Domenic	183	painter	39	here
	V	Vardaro Jennie—†	183	housewife	37	"
	W	Masale Antonetta—†	184	"	35	"

Page.	Letter.	Full Name.	Residence, Jan. 1, 1938.	Occupation.	Supposed Age.	Reported Residence, Jan. 1, 1937. Street and Number.

Webster Street—Continued

	X	Masale John	184	mason	39	here
	Y	*Cicero Jennie—†	184	housewife	41	"
	Z	Cicero Josephine—†	184	stitcher	21	"
195						
	A	Cicero Salvatore	184	tailor	48	
	B	*Zucco Elizabeth—†	184	housewife	58	"
	C	*Zucco Salvatore	184	retired	60	
	D	*LaMarca Catherine—†	185	housewife	51	"
	E	LaMarca Catherine—†	185	tailoress	31	
	F	*LaMarca Joseph	185	storekeeper	62	"
	G	LaMarca Josephine—†	185	tailoress	22	"
	H	Panzone John	185	operator	28	
	K	*Panzone Pompilio	185	chauffeur	41	"
	L	Panzone Theresa—†	185	housekeeper	25	"
	M	Manzo Marie—†	185	housewife	24	"
	N	Manzo Peter	185	candymaker	33	"
	O	*Giangregorio Assunta—†	186	housewife	38	"
	P	Giangregorio John	186	laborer	50	
	R	Roccia Elizabeth—†	186	telegrapher	26	"
	S	Roccia Mary—†	186	housekeeper	65	"
	T	Roccia Michael	186	timekeeper	24	"
	U	Cirone Guerino	186	bricklayer	39	"
	V	*Cirone Settimia—†	186	housewife	32	"
	W	Brogan Mary A—†	187	at home	65	
	X	Pierce James T	187	janitor	56	
	Y	Pierce Mary A—†	187	housewife	55	"
	Z	Pierce Mary G—†	187	clerk	21	
196						
	A	Pierce William J	187	printer	30	
	B	Danes Elizabeth D—†	187	bookkeeper	34	"
	C	Danes Joseph F	187	salesman	37	42 Woodford
	D	Acone Agatha—†	188	housewife	49	here
	E	Acone Benjamin	188	druggist	48	336 Sumner
	F	McIsaac Hilary C	188	longshoreman	43	95 Webster
	G	McIsaac John G	188	"	33	1977 Dor av
	H	McIsaac Sylvester J	188	clerk	47	95 Webster
	K	D'Ambrozio Christos	188	laborer	38	here
	L	D'Ambrozio John	188	engineer	44	"
	M	*D'Ambrozio Pauline—†	188	housewife	45	"
	N	Iorio Jennie—†	188	"	28	
	O	Iorio John	188	barber	30	

Page.	Letter.	Full Name.	Residence, Jan. 1, 1938.	Occupation.	Supposed Age.	Reported Residence, Jan. 1, 1937. Street and Number.

Webster Street—Continued

	P	Anderson Alice A—†	189	teacher	52	here
	R	Watt Helen E—†	189	at home	62	"
	S	MacLean Arthur B	189	painter	55	"
	T	MacLean Arthur F	189	clerk	27	
	U	MacLean Grace E—†	189	housewife	43	"
	V	*Costanza Mary M—†	191	dressmaker	34	"
	W	Santangelo Guy	191	clerk	41	
	X	*Santangelo Rose—†	191	housewife	40	"
	Y	Dioguardi Elvira—†	191	"	49	
	Z	Dioguardi Joseph	191	mechanic	22	"
197						
	A	Dioguardi Mary A—†	191	candyworker	20	"
	B	Dioguardi Vincent	191	shoeworker	52	"
	C	Healey William C	193	commissioner	63	"
	D	Leonard Elizabeth F—†	193	housekeeper	54	"
	E	Leonard William L	193	clerk	53	"
	F	O'Connor Helen R—†	193	stenographer	33	"
	G	Marotto Louise A—†	195	housewife	28	8 Cheever ct
	H	Marotto Philip	195	barber	28	8 "
	K	Ulwick Alma E—†	195	housewife	54	here
	L	Ulwick Ole N	195	longshoreman	55	"
	M	Ulwick Walter N	195	painter	25	"
	O	*Capone Anthony	rear 195	laborer	44	
	P	*Capone Josephine—†	" 195	housewife	40	"
	R	Gigli Leonilde—†	" 195	"	56	
	S	Gigli Lydia—†	" 195	stitcher	27	
	T	Gigli Nicholas	" 195	painter	59	
	V	Barry William	199	clergyman	64	"
	W	Burke Nellie T—†	199	housekeeper	58	"
	X	Hamilton James F	199	clergyman	38	1 Monum'nt sq
	Y	*Hassett Mary—†	199	housekeeper	26	here
	Z	*Pelosi Teresa A—†	201	housewife	34	"
198						
	A	Pelosi Torindo	201	tailor	38	
	B	*Tringali Carmelo	201	boat builder	71	"
	C	Tringali Domenic	201	"	23	
	D	Tringali Domenica—†	201	housekeeper	26	"
	E	*Sirianni Jennie H—†	201	housewife	34	"
	F	Sirianni Paul L	201	salesman	35	"
	G	Brady James J	205	brewer	30	Somerville
	H	Brady Marie A—†	205	housewife	27	here

Page.	Letter.	Full Name.	Residence, Jan. 1, 1938.	Occupation.	Supposed Age.	Reported Residence, Jan. 1, 1937. Street and Number.

Webster Street—Continued

	K	Jeffers Helen C—†	205	housewife	34	here
	L	Jeffers Jasper J	205	welder	37	"
	M	Jeffers Jennie F—†	205	candyworker	36	"
	N	Jeffers Robert T	205	clerk	32	
	O	McGee Frank N	205	retired	67	
	P	McGee Minnie—†	205	housewife	60	"
	R	Dowd Mary A—†	207	housekeeper	69	"
	S	Dowd Mary C—†	207	secretary	33	"
	T	Finn Sarah G—†	207	clerk	50	
	U	Usseglio Aurelia—†	211	at home	63	
	V	Usseglio Mary—†	211	housekeeper	40	"
	W	Ryan Cecilia C—†	211	housewife	40	"
	X	Ryan George E	211	superintendent	36	"
	Y	Usseglio Charles	213	pipefitter	32	"
	Z	Usseglio Helen J—†	213	housewife	28	"
199						
	A	Walter Emma A—†	213	"	73	
	B	Walter Mary R—†	213	at home	49	
	C	Walter Otto F	213	retired	74	
	D	Faiello Annette—†	215	housewife	25	"
	E	Faiello Rugerio	215	transitman	27	"
	F	Ventresea Adelia—†	215	nurse	21	"
	G	*Ventresea Mary—†	215	housewife	44	"
	H	Amore Ciriaco	215	laborer	26	67 Frankfort
	K	Amore Lucy—†	215	housewife	24	67 "
	L	Ciambelli Elsie—†	217	"	28	5 Stillman
	M	Ciambelli Jeremiah	217	laborer	30	5 "
	N	Schetino Annette—†	217	housewife	42	here
	O	Schetino Michael	217	shoemaker	49	"
	R	Mealey Louise—†	221	at home	54	"
	S	Murphy Elizabeth—†	221	housekeeper	75	"
	T	Hall Margaret J—†	221	housewife	36	153 Everett
	U	Hall Thomas J	221	rigger	39	153 "
	W	Crowley Mary—†	223	at home	75	here
	X	Knowles Catherine M—†	223	housewife	47	"
	Y	Knowles Catherine M—†	223	factoryhand	20	"
	Z	Knowles James E	223	builder	49	
200						
	A	Yarrow Charles J	223	longshoreman	23	"
	B	Yarrow Ellen—†	223	housewife	53	"
	C	Yarrow Helen C—†	223	clerk	21	"

3 14

4 15

5 16

17

18

2

11

Wa

LIST

Ward 1—Precinct 3

CITY OF BOSTON

LIST OF RESIDENTS
20 YEARS OF AGE AND OVER

(NON-CITIZENS INDICATED BY ASTERISK)
(FEMALES INDICATED BY DAGGER)

AS OF

JANUARY 1, 1938

JOSEPH F. TIMILTY, }
FREDERIC E. DOWLING, } *Listing Board.*

CITY OF BOSTON PRINTING DEPARTMENT

Page.	Letter.	FULL NAME.	Residence, Jan. 1, 1938.	Occupation.	Supposed Age.	Reported Residence, Jan. 1, 1937. Street and Number.
212						
		Airport Road North				
	L	Dow Helga—†	65	stenographer	31	here
	M	Rouillard Paul R	65	armorer	31	"
		Airport Street				
	N	Malerba Anthony	3	laborer	26	here
	O	Malerba Rose—†	3	housewife	21	"
	P	Donahue Ellen M—†	3	"	49	"
	R	Donahue Hugh	3	clerk	28	"
	S	Donahue John J	3	shipper	24	
	T	Donahue Walter L	3	longshoreman	30	"
	U	Sansone Anthony G	5	chauffeur	28	"
	V	Sansone Sarah—†	5	housewife	26	"
	W	Sallimi Joseph	5	laborer	45	"
	X	Sallimi Mary—†	5	housewife	45	"
		Deer Island				
	Z	Black Frank		engineer	54	here
213						
	A	Black Marie F—†		housewife	53	"
	B	Borden Cora E—†		"	46	
	B	Borden Cora N—†		operator	23	
	D	Borden George E		engineer	51	
	E	Borden George H		"	25	
	F	Borden Hazel F—†		accountant	20	"
	G	Borden Helen—†		nurse	24	1153 Centre
	H	Cloran Francis M		officer	34	here
	K	Connelly Joseph T		"	46	"
	L	Delaney Thomas J		instructor	50	"
	M	Devine Joseph A		officer	44	
	N	Ford Daniel F		"	43	
	O	Gallagher Francis W		"	44	
	P	Gilmore John P		clerk	36	
	R	Grappi Louis		officer	39	
	S	Hutchins Walter A		"	66	
	T	Jacques William E		"	37	
	U	Keefe Frank P			45	"
	V	Kerivan John C		"	31	11 Taft
	W	King Charles E		engineer	62	here

Page.	Letter.	Full Name.	Residence, Jan. 1, 1938.	Occupation.	Supposed Age.	Reported Residence, Jan. 1, 1937. Street and Number.

Deer Island—Continued

Page.	Letter.	Full Name.	Residence, Jan. 1, 1938.	Occupation.	Supposed Age.	Reported Residence, Jan. 1, 1937. Street and Number.
	X	Luciano Frank J		officer	38	here
	Y	Lynch Justin B		"	59	"
	Z	Mackie Robert F		deputy	46	"
214						
	A	Martin Coleman F		officer	54	
	B	McCarthy Andrew H		deputy	48	
	C	McCarthy Margaret A—†		housewife	46	"
	D	McCuskef William J		officer	33	
	E	McDonough George M		"	36	
	F	McKenna Edson L		"	43	
	G	McMullan Peter A		clerk	35	
	H	Mills Benjamin B		engineer	60	
	K	Mills Minnie—†		housewife	68	"
	L	Moylette William J		officer	49	
	M	Mulcahy George F		master	45	
	N	Mulcahy Hazel D—†		housewife	44	"
	O	O'Brien John J		officer	52	
	P	O'Neil John P		"	61	
	R	Parziale James		"	41	
	S	Pearce Arthur G		engineer	52	
	T	Pearce Arthur G, jr		"	27	
	U	Pearce Margaret—†		maid	26	
	V	Pearce Nellie—†		housewife	50	"
	W	Smith Gordon A		officer	43	
	X	Teevens Patrick H		"	52	
	Y	Tobin David		fireman	61	
	Z	Walters Stephen J		officer	38	
215						
	A	Yirrell Frederick W		storekeeper	37	"

Everett Court

Page.	Letter.	Full Name.	Residence, Jan. 1, 1938.	Occupation.	Supposed Age.	Reported Residence, Jan. 1, 1937. Street and Number.
	B	Sheridan Bridget—†	1	at home	82	here
	C	Crowley Edward A	1	clerk	53	"
	D	Crowley Elsie—†	1	housewife	48	"
	E	Bradshaw Catherine—†	2	"	62	
	F	Bradshaw George T	2	broker	27	
	H	Famaletto Philomena—†	4	operator	31	"
	K	LaPia Antonnette—†	4	stitcher	23	
	L	LaPia Gennaro	4	carpenter	49	"
	M	*LaPia Jennie—†	4	housewife	43	"

Page.	Letter.	Full Name.	Residence, Jan. 1, 1938.	Occupation.	Supposed Age.	Reported Residence, Jan. 1, 1937. Street and Number.

Everett Court—Continued

Page.	Letter.	Full Name.	Residence, Jan. 1, 1938.	Occupation.	Supposed Age.	Reported Residence, Jan. 1, 1937. Street and Number.
	N	LaPia Michael A	4	carpenter	22	here
	O	*Costopoulos John	5	laborer	45	"
	P	*Costopoulos Olga—†	5	housewife	37	"
	R	D'Eramo Andrew	6	laborer	35	
	S	D'Eramo Rose—†	6	housewife	30	"
	T	*Ventresca Domenic	6	laborer	58	
	U	*Ventresca Dora—†	6	housewife	53	"
	V	Ventresca Helen—†	6	at home	20	
	W	Ventresca Lucy—†	6	clerk	23	

Everett Place

Page.	Letter.	Full Name.	Residence, Jan. 1, 1938.	Occupation.	Supposed Age.	Reported Residence, Jan. 1, 1937. Street and Number.
	X	Clericuzio Angelina—†	2	housewife	45	here
	Y	Clericuzio Charles	2	laborer	45	"
	Z	Mucci Anna—†	4	housewife	25	"
216						
	A	Mucci Anthony	4	mechanic	22	"
	B	Mucci Camillo	4	laborer	27	"
	C	Mucci Frank D	4	clergyman	30	Italy
	D	Mucci Irene—†	4	milliner	20	here
	E	*Mucci John	4	laborer	62	"
	F	Visca Carlo	6	"	47	"
	G	*Visca Valentino	6	"	51	"
	H	*Paolini Edith—†	6	housewife	33	175 Cottage
	K	*Paolini Nicholas	6	laborer	44	175 "
	L	Todisco Albert	7	carpenter	22	here
	M	Todisco Anna—†	7	stitcher	24	"
	N	Todisco Rocco	7	laborer	31	"
	O	Todisco Violet—†	7	shoeworker	23	"
	P	Carbone Jennie—†	7	housewife	29	"
	R	Carbone Ralph	7	painter	31	Somerville

Everett Street

Page.	Letter.	Full Name.	Residence, Jan. 1, 1938.	Occupation.	Supposed Age.	Reported Residence, Jan. 1, 1937. Street and Number.
	T	*Patti Mary—†	185	housewife	35	here
	U	Sefuni Charles	187	laborer	26	"
	V	*Sefuni Genaro	187	"	56	"
	W	*Sefuni Mary—†	187	housewife	52	"
	X	Sefuni Nellie—†	187	clerk	20	
	Y	*Screnci Saverio—†	189	housewife	49	"
	Z	Screnci Thomas	189	laborer	47	

Page.	Letter.	Full Name.	Residence, Jan. 1, 1938.	Occupation.	Supposed Age.	Reported Residence, Jan. 1, 1937. Street and Number.
217						
		Everett Street—Continued				
	A	Rizzo Joseph	189	laborer	25	here
	B	*Rizzo Rose—†	189	housewife	24	"
	C	Ferullo Florence—†	191	"	27	967 Saratoga
	D	Ferullo Michael	191	wrapper	25	967 "
	E	*Sereno John	191	carpenter	49	here
	F	Sereno Joseph	191	laborer	21	"
	G	*Sereno Lucy—†	191	housewife	48	"
	H	Albanese Michael	191	laborer	66	"
	K	Albanese Santa—†	191	bookbinder	21	"
	L	Patterson Alice—†	192	housekeeper	43	"
	M	*Patterson Suzan—†	192	housewife	75	"
	N	Cetrullo Frank	192	laborer	46	
	O	Cetrullo Lillian—†	192	housewife	38	"
	P	*Luguri Frank	192	salesman	57	"
	R	*Luguri Josephine—†	192	housewife	52	"
	S	Grilli Louis	193	operator	34	"
	T	Grilli Mary—†	193	housewife	31	"
	U	Murphy Dennis W	193	letter carrier	45	"
	V	Hogan Anastasia—†	193	housewife	48	"
	W	*Hogan Thomas	193	operator	47	"
	X	Fay Edward C	195	boilermaker	35	"
	T	Fay Mabel E—†	195	housewife	33	"
	Z	*Lauletta Angelina—†	195	"	39	
218						
	A	*Lauletta Antonio	195	merchant	43	"
	B	Cifuni Mary—†	195	housewife	22	Everett
	C	Cifuni Salvatore	195	cutter	23	187 Everett
	D	Lacy Alice—†	196	stenographer	20	here
	E	Stenman Elias	196	laborer	55	"
	F	Sullivan Nora—†	196	housekeeper	48	"
	G	Knowles James	198	clerk	24	"
	H	Knowles Mary—†	198	housewife	24	"
	K	Clark James	198	cook	38	
	L	Clark Margaret A—†	198	housewife	33	"
	N	Downing Catherine M–†	200	housekeeper	45	"
	O	*Greenald Annie M—†	200	"	63	"
	P	Festa Anglina—†	206	housewife	23	"
	R	Festa Nicolas	206	laborer	29	
	S	*Bonimano Augustus	206	butcher	51	
	T	*Bonimano Lillian—†	206	housewife	46	"

Page.	Letter.	Full Name.	Residence, Jan. 1, 1938.	Occupation.	Supposed Age.	Reported Residence, Jan. 1, 1937. Street and Number.

Everett Street—Continued

Page.	Letter.	Full Name.	Residence, Jan. 1, 1938.	Occupation.	Supposed Age.	Reported Residence, Jan. 1, 1937. Street and Number.
	U	Melchione Anthony	206	shoeworker	27	here
	V	Melchione Marie—†	206	housewife	27	"
	W	Consalvi Frances—†	206	"	30	"
	X	Consalvi James	206	cobbler	32	
	Y	Pasco Margaret—†	210	housewife	32	"
	Z	Pasco Nicholas	210	carpenter	38	"
219						
	A	Sullivan Ethel E—†	210	housewife	24	"
	B	Sullivan John M	210	chauffeur	26	462 Sumner
	C	*Cifelli Genaro	210	polisher	46	here
	D	*Cifelli Rosa—†	210	housewife	55	"
	E	*Licciardi Antoinnette—†	210	"	24	"
	F	Licciardi Paul	210	machinist	29	5 Airport
	G	Todisco John J	214	baker	41	here
	H	Todisco Margaret—†	214	housewife	35	"
	K	Almatto Fred	216	laborer	40	206 Everett
	L	*Pugliere Antonio	216	blacksmith	49	here
	M	*Pugliere Concetta—†	216	housewife	42	"
	N	*Ferrante Anthony	216	laborer	52	"
	O	*Ferrante Carmella—†	216	housewife	49	"
	P	McCarthy Patrick T	218	wrapper	26	18 Brigham
	R	McCarthy Phyllis L—†	218	housewife	22	256 Sumner
	S	Agesppino Marie—†	218	"	70	here
	T	Agesppino Salemi	218	porter	75	"
	U	Marinelli Carmella—†	218	housewife	30	"
	V	Marinelli John	218	laborer	41	
	W	Cozzy Isabella—†	221	housewife	23	"
	X	Cozzy Louis	221	laborer	22	540 Sumner
	Y	Mascuili Eleanor—†	221	at home	21	here
	Z	Mascuili Luciano	221	retired	67	"
220						
	A	Mascuili Lucy—†	221	housewife	54	"
	B	Mascuili Nuncio	221	laborer	26	
	C	*Fulchino Antonio	221	shoeworker	44	"
	D	*Fulchino Margaret—†	221	housewife	36	"
	E	*Aiello Jasper	222	laborer	45	
	F	Pasquariello James	222	bricklayer	39	"
	G	Pasquariello Theresa—†	222	housewife	31	"
	H	Sarro Anthony	222	laborer	50	
	K	Sarro Catherine—†	222	packer	24	
	L	Sarro Feliciona—†	222	housewife	45	"

Page.	Letter.	Full Name.	Residence, Jan. 1, 1938.	Occupation.	Supposed Age.	Reported Residence, Jan. 1, 1937. Street and Number.

Everett Street—Continued

Page.	Letter.	Full Name.	Residence, Jan. 1, 1938.	Occupation.	Supposed Age.	Reported Residence, Jan. 1, 1937. Street and Number.
	M	Sarro Josephine—†	222	packer	22	here
	N	Prezioso Antoinette—†	223	housewife	27	26 London
	O	Prezioso Edward	223	painter	27	26 "
	P	Perosino Genara	223	tailor	45	here
	R	Perosino Joseph	223	laborer	21	"
	S	Perosino Raffina—†	223	housewife	43	"
	T	Squillacioti Alfonse	223	tinsmith	46	
	U	Squillacioti Victoria—†	223	housewife	37	"
	V	*Pagliuca Michael	224	laborer	39	249 Maverick
	W	*Pagliuca Philomena—†	224	housewife	25	249 "
	X	*Delsette Anna—†	224	"	55	20 Bremen
	Y	Delsette Peter	224	laborer	55	20 "
	Z	Porcaro Alfred	224	painter	30	378 Sumner
221	A	Porcaro Florence—†	224	housewife	28	378 "
	C	Ascolillo Amerigo	225	laborer	34	221 Everett
	D	Ascolillo Rose—†	225	housewife	28	221 "
	E	Thompson George	225	teamster	42	here
	F	Thompson Josephine—†	225	housewife	36	"
	G	*Consalvi Constance—†	226	"	65	"
	H	Consalvi Joseph	226	laborer	20	
	K	Curran Evelyn—†	226	housewife	20	"
	L	Curran Thomas	226	clerk	27	1 Staniford
	M	Macchia Alfonse	226	"	22	here
	N	*Macchia Leopold	226	shoeworker	56	"
	O	*Macchia Mary—†	226	housewife	52	"
	P	Macchia Peter	226	clerk	25	
	V	Tringale Antonio J	228	boatbuilder	43	"
	W	Tringale Mary G—†	228	housewife	35	"
	X	Gravallese Joseph	228	laborer	68	"
	Y	Gravallese Lucy—†	228	housewife	68	"
222	C	*Luciano Ida—†	229	"	54	
	B	Luciano Peter	229	laborer	54	"
	D	*Lafferty Edith—†	229	housewife	71	"
	E	Lafferty Margaret—†	229	stenographer	33	"
	F	*Lafferty Robert C	229	carpenter	76	"
	G	Wallace Edith—†	229	stenographer	31	43 Bennington
	H	*Gizzi Angelina—†	230	housewife	50	here
	K	Gizzi Helen—†	230	clerk	23	"
	L	Gizzi Theresa—†	230	operator	21	"

Page.	Letter.	FULL NAME.	Residence, Jan. 1, 1938.	Occupation.	Supposed Age.	Reported Residence, Jan. 1, 1937. Street and Number.

Everett Street—Continued

Page.	Letter.	FULL NAME.	Residence, Jan. 1, 1938.	Occupation.	Supposed Age.	Reported Residence, Jan. 1, 1937. Street and Number.
	M	Gizzi Thomas	230	plasterer	63	here
	N	*Vitale Antonetta—†	233	housewife	36	237 Everett
	O	*Vitale Rocco	233	laborer	40	237 "
	P	*Todisco Aurilla—†	234	housewife	43	here
	R	Todisco Carmen	234	tailor	47	"
	S	Anderson Agnes—†	235	housewife	45	"
	T	Anderson Augusta M—†	235	"	75	
	U	Anderson Ruben A	235	steamfitter	45	"
	V	Heil Margaret—†	237	housewife	27	"
	W	Heil William	237	laborer	29	"
	X	*Zichello Michael	237	"	51	
	Y	*Zichello Vincenza	237	housewife	40	"
223						
	B	Todisco Albert	238	candymaker	21	"
	C	Todisco Anthony	238	"	50	"
	D	Todisco Joseph	238	clerk	25	
	E	Cassidy William	239	retired	71	
	F	Enos Bessie—†	239	housewife	72	"
	G	*Draniere Donato	239	laborer	44	
	H	*Draniere Elvira—†	239	housewife	37	"
	K	Driscoll Daniel J	239	clerk	40	
	L	Driscoll Marie A—†	239	"	38	
	M	Coviello Anthony	241	laborer	25	
	N	Coviello Grace—†	241	housewife	24	"
	O	Corrao Charles	241	wrapper	46	87 Webster
	P	Corrao Frances—†	241	housewife	35	here
	R	*Baldassaro Carmella—†	241	"	48	"
	S	Baldassaro Joseph	241	laborer	54	"
	T	Baldassaro Louis	241	"	23	
	U	Baldassaro Pasquale	241	clerk	22	
	V	DiSessa Charles R	242	laborer	24	
	W	DiSessa Samuel	242	barber	65	
	X	DiSessa Sarah—†	242	housewife	58	"
	Y	Bona Elizabeth—†	243	"	42	
	Z	Bona Helen—†	243	typist	21	"
224						
	A	*Boivin Eliza—†	243	housewife	75	"
	B	Boivin John H	243	painter	42	"
	D	Larsen Dagny—†	244	housewife	59	442 Sumner
	E	Larsen Henry B	244	laborer	28	442 "
	F	Larsen Herbert N	244	"	24	442 "

Page.	Letter.	Full Name.	Residence, Jan. 1, 1938.	Occupation.	Supposed Age.	Reported Residence, Jan. 1, 1937. Street and Number.

Everett Street—Continued

	G	Flanagan Andrew	245	student	22	260 Everett
	H	Flanagan Eleanor—†	245	housewife	52	260 "
	K	Flanagan William	245	laborer	55	260 "
	L	LeGallo Francis	245	electrician	25	80 Carruth
	M	LeGallo Mary—†	245	housewife	22	80 "
	N	Smith Thomas	245	carpenter	61	80 Brooks
	O	*Brogna Anthony	246	laborer	56	here
	P	*Brogna Antoinnetta—†	246	housewife	57	"
	R	Brogna Lena—†	246	packer	28	"
	S	Brogna Michael	246	painter	21	
	T	Brogna Mildred—†	246	stitcher	22	
	U	*Cinelli Bridget—†	247	housewife	38	"
	V	*Cinelli Rocco	247	laborer	46	
	W	*Caruso Anna—†	247	housewife	42	"
	X	*Caruso Anthony	247	operator	44	"
	Y	DiFiore Frederick	247	"	45	"
	Z	DiFiore Pauline—†	247	housewife	31	"
225						
	A	Alberto Jennie—†	249	"	40	315 Maverick
	B	Alberto Matteo	249	laborer	47	315 "
	C	Amerena Anthony	249	machinist	30	here
	D	Amerena Frances—†	249	housewife	27	"
	E	*Manfra Alfred	249	cabinetmaker	36	"
	F	Manfra Philomena—†	249	housewife	28	"
	G	Laglio Giuseppi	250	laborer	48	
	H	*Rindone Lena—†	250	housewife	48	"
	K	*Rindone Vincent	250	laborer	57	
	L	Cataldo Fiori	254	"	28	
	M	Cataldo Marion—†	254	housewife	28	"
	N	Cataldo James	254	instructor	35	"
	O	Cataldo Madeline—†	254	housewife	33	"
	P	Guarente Elizabeth—†	254	"	24	Revere
	R	Perone Adeline—†	254	"	26	here
	S	Perone Constantino	254	agent	29	"
	T	Nardone Giuseppi	255–257	laborer	57	"
	U	Nardone Joseph F	255–257	salesman	33	"
	V	Nardone Lena—†	255–257	housewife	56	"
	W	*Coviello Geraldine—†	256	"	27	
	X	Coviello John	256	mechanic	23	"
	Y	Bickford Arthur	256	shipper	27	
	Z	*Bickford Elvira T—†	256	housewife	73	"

Page.	Letter.	Full Name.	Residence, Jan. 1, 1938.	Occupation.	Supposed Age.	Reported Residence, Jan. 1, 1937. Street and Number.
226		**Everett Street**—Continued				
	A	*Bickford Herbert	256	retired	69	here
	B	*Foster Anna—†	258	housewife	26	227 Everett
	C	Foster John	258	laborer	36	227 "
	D	Haseman Anna E—†	258	housewife	40	here
	E	Haseman Philip	258	clerk	41	"
	F	Walker Daniel P	258	rigger	39	"
	G	Walker Esther H—†	258	housewife	36	"
	H	Walker William J	258	carpenter	42	"
	K	Nardone Emilio	259	chauffeur	46	"
	L	Nardone Charles	259	fireman	25	
	M	Nardone Mary—†	259	housewife	25	"
	N	Fay Herbert C	259	laborer	32	"
	O	Fay Josephine M—†	259	housewife	32	"
	P	Gray Catherine J—†	260	"	42	"
	R	*Jensen Arni	260	seaman	40	11 Hendry
	S	Nelsen Magda—†	260	housewife	46	here
	T	O'Brien James W	260	ironworker	47	258 Everett
	U	O'Brien Lillian S—†	260	housewife	41	here
	V	Mucci Dominick	261	laborer	20	253 Lexington
	W	Mucci Michelina—†	261	housewife	21	257 Everett
	X	Ellis Arthur	261	chef	43	here
	Y	Ellis Mary—†	261	housewife	37	"
	Z	Cinalli Flora—†	261	"	31	"
227						
	A	*Cinalli Joseph	261	laborer	43	
	C	Bruno John	263	foreman	49	
	D	*Bruno Lillian—†	263	housewife	42	"
	E	Arena Frank	263	laborer	30	
	F	Arena Jennie—†	263	housewife	28	"
		Ipswich Place				
	H	Malerba Anna—†	1	housewife	20	381 Maverick
	K	Malerba Dominic	1	chauffeur	23	381 "
	L	Volta Helen Z—†	1	housewife	28	here
	M	Volta Salvatore	1	painter	30	"
	N	Taromino Joseph	1	packer	35	"
	O	Taromino Louise—†	1	housewife	28	"
	P	*Hennessy Bridget—†	3	housekeeper	80	"
	R	Morgan Mary—†	3	"	70	"

Page.	Letter.	Full Name.	Residence, Jan. 1, 1938.	Occupation.	Supposed Age.	Reported Residence, Jan. 1, 1937. Street and Number.

Jeffries Street

	W	*Burrows Elizabeth—†	4	housekeeper	37	here
	X	Muise John D	4	fishcutter	32	"
	Y	*Muise Loran	4	"	40	"
	Z	*Muise Mary—†	4	housewife	69	"
228						
	A	*Muise William H	4	cutter	67	
	B	Larsen Charles J	4	painter	45	
	C	Larsen Charles J, jr	4	"	20	
	D	Larsen Mary B—†	4	housewife	45	"
	H	Trainor Dorothy—†	7	"	24	
	K	Trainor Edward J	7	cutter	24	
	L	*DiPasquale Irene—†	7	housewife	31	"
	M	DiPasquale Michael	7	musician	31	"
	R	Gregorio Agnes—†	9	housewife	38	"
	S	*Gregorio Cecil	9	laborer	47	
	T	*Gonsalves Anthony	9	fireman	51	
	U	*Gonsalves Mary—†	9	housewife	47	"
	V	Rock Gilbert	9	electrician	37	New York
	W	Rock Rose—†	9	housewife	21	here
229						
	A	St John Marie—†	12	"	38	
	B	St John Patrick	12	longshoreman	40	"
	C	Eisenberg Mary—†	12	seamstress	28	"
	D	Costa Laura—†	12	saleswoman	26	"
	E	*Costa Manuel	12	retired	68	
	F	Costa Margaret—†	12	at home	30	
	G	*Costa Virginia—†	12	housewife	57	"
	H	Jacobs Aajot—†	23	"	58	
	K	Jacobs John	23	machinist	61	"
	L	Anderson George	25	wrapper	20	6 London
	M	Vitale Joseph	25	bricklayer	46	here
	N	Vitale Rose—†	25	operator	21	"
	O	Morrissey Helen E—†	27	housewife	40	2 Brigham
	P	Morrissey Joseph P	27	blacksmith	39	2 "
	R	Clark Carrie—†	27	housewife	38	here
	S	Clark Thomas	27	longshoreman	39	"
	T	Fay Gerald T	27	painter	38	"
	U	Fay John B	27	chauffeur	71	"
	V	Fay Mary A—†	27	housewife	68	"
	W	Fay Richard N	27	laborer	26	
	X	Fay William M	27	painter	28	"

Page.	Letter.	FULL NAME.	Residence, Jan. 1, 1938.	Occupation.	Supposed Age.	Reported Residence, Jan. 1, 1937. Street and Number.

Jeffries Street—Continued

	Y	Spinney Harold	29	porter	35	here
	Z	Spinney Helen—†	29	housewife	32	"
230						
	A	Call Blanche—†	29	housekeeper	28	"
	B	Spinney Charles	29	wrapper	33	"
	C	Spinney Jane—†	29	housewife	58	"
	D	Coleman Johanna—†	29	housekeeper	54	"
	E	Willis Andrew	29	longshoreman	53	"
	G	Sassa Isabelle—†	40	housewife	47	"
	H	Sassa Joseph	40	laborer	21	
	K	Sassa Vincent	40	shoemaker	48	"
	M	Schraffa John	42	laborer	26	249 Maverick
	N	Schraffa Josephine—†	42	housewife	24	15 Webster av
	O	Frazier Helen—†	42	"	40	here
	P	Frazier Joseph	42	cutter	54	"
	R	Distasio Anna—†	42	housewife	31	"
	S	Distasio Joseph	42	watchman	33	"
	T	Frevold Elizabeth—†	44	housewife	20	92 Eutaw
	U	Frevold William	44	leatherworker	25	92 "
	V	Jackson Gilbert C	44	painter	39	here
	W	Jackson Margaret—†	44	housewife	34	"
	X	Lindergreen Elizabeth—†	44	"	58	"
	Y	Lindergreen Rudolph	44	longshoreman	53	"
231						
	A	Shaughnessy John F	45	clerk	25	
	B	Shaughnessy Mary—†	45	stenographer	23	"
	C	Copeman Estelle—†	45	housewife	29	408 Sumner
	D	Copeman John	45	packer	31	408 "
	E	Swenson Emil R	46	timekeeper	35	here
	F	Swenson Genevieve—†	46	housewife	36	"
	G	Hankard Esther E—†	46	"	51	"
	H	Hankard Ruth C—†	46	typist	25	
	K	Campbell Anna C—†	46	housewife	55	"
	L	Campbell Archibald F	46	electrician	60	"
	M	Campbell Francis N	46	compositor	34	"
	N	Campbell Hazel M—†	46	stenographer	24	"
	O	MacDonald George A	46	aviator	34	"
	P	Moran Clara B—†	47	housewife	61	"
	R	Moran Michael L	47	retired	67	
	S	Moran Ethel B—†	47	clerk	32	
	T	Moran Agnes F—†	47	housewife	25	"

Page.	Letter.	Full Name.	Residence, Jan. 1, 1938.	Occupation.	Supposed Age.	Reported Residence, Jan. 1, 1937. Street and Number.

Jeffries Street—Continued

	U	Moran Francis W	47	engineer	27	here
	V	Ulwick Celia—†	48	housewife	20	48 Maverick sq
	W	Ulwick Donald	48	painter	21	195 Webster
	X	Judge Christine L—†	48	housewife	36	here
	Y	Judge Peter F	48	splicer	38	"
	Z	Rigano Letterio	48	cigarworker	37	Medford
232						
	A	Rigano Margaret—†	48	housewife	33	"
	B	Porcaro Frank	49	laborer	64	here
	C	*Porcaro Rose—†	49	housewife	59	"
	D	Porcaro Fiorello	49	painter	27	"
	E	Porcaro Josephine—†	49	operator	24	
	F	Pepe Mary—†	49	housewife	34	"
	G	*Pepe Samuel	49	laborer	42	
	K	Hanton George	50	chauffeur	38	"
	L	Hanton Julia—†	50	housewife	35	"
	M	Gallagher Mary E—†	50	operator	29	
	N	Sheehan Catherine	50	housewife	67	"
	P	Salamone Jennie—†	51	"	41	245 Webster
	R	Salamone Joseph	51	bricklayer	42	245 "
	S	Barron Leo	51	painter	35	here
	T	Barron Violet—†	51	housewife	32	"
	U	*Milano Antoinetta—†	52	"	52	"
	V	Milano Luigi	52	carpenter	64	"
	W	Milano Luigi, jr	52	laborer	25	
	X	Milano Michael	52	"	27	
	Y	Milano Richard	52	"	20	
	Z	Milano Samuel	52		24	
233						
	A	Petrucelli Lucille—†	52	operator	29	285 Webster
	B	Trail Angela—†	52	housewife	27	here
	C	Trail James	52	counterman	30	"
	D	Grasso Phyllis—†	53	housewife	24	492 Commerc'l
	E	Grasso Silvio	53	operator	24	412 Sumner
	F	Tulipani Rose—†	53	housewife	53	here
	G	Tulipani Salvatore	53	musician	29	"
	K	*Giampietro Filomena—†	54	housewife	43	"
	L	Giampietro John	54	laborer	46	
	M	Ventresca Angelina—†	54	packer	21	
	N	Gianfelice Gaetano	54	laborer	43	
	O	*Gianfelice Therese—†	54	housewife	30	"

Page.	Letter.	Full Name.	Residence, Jan. 1, 1938.	Occupation.	Supposed Age.	Reported Residence, Jan. 1, 1937. Street and Number.
		Jeffries Street—Continued				
	P	Sirianni Dominico	56	laborer	36	here
	R	Sirianni Mary—†	56	housewife	31	"
	S	DelBene Giulo	56	laborer	45	"
	T	*DelBene Nicolina—†	56	housewife	50	"
	U	Belmonte Agostino	56	laborer	44	
	V	*Belmonte Clarinda—†	56	housewife	41	"
		Lamson Street				
	W	Powell Elizabeth R—†	1	housewife	49	here
	X	Powell Joseph M	1	retired	59	"
	Y	Powell Sarah A—†	1	housewife	51	"
	Z	Delorey Frances—†	1	"	66	
234						
	A	Delorey Henry	1	cutter	65	
	B	Riley Harriet—†	2	housekeeper	68	"
	C	Riley Margaret—†	2	operator	26	"
	R	Riley Regina M—†	2	clerk	35	"
	E	Douglas Alice—†	2	operator	50	Everett
	F	McDonald Gertrude—†	2	housewife	44	here
	G	McDonald Warren	2	clerk	44	"
	H	Donahue Francis	3	machinist	26	"
	K	Storlazzi Alfred	3	cleanser	24	
	L	Storlazzi Gertrude—†	3	housewife	24	"
	M	Telles Arthur W	3	salesman	27	Medford
	N	Telles Geraldine—†	3	housewife	22	"
	O	*Storlazzi Adolf	3	tailor	49	here
	P	Storlazzi Anthony	3	"	23	"
	R	*Storlazzi Cesira—†	3	housewife	50	"
	S	Storlazzi Enos	3	clerk	28	
	T	Storlazzi Ernoni	3	"	25	
	U	*Brown Charles	3	longshoreman	59	"
	V	*Brown Rose—†	3	housewife	69	"
	W	*D'Olympia Lawrence	4	boxmaker	68	"
	X	*Dolympia Mary—†	4	housewife	64	"
	Y	Taft Joseph	4	lonsghoreman	32	"
	Z	Taft Patrick	4	"	68	"
235						
	A	Taft Rose E—†	4	housewife	58	"
	B	Pompeo Domenica—†	4	"	40	368 Sumner
	C	Pompeo John	4	bricklayer	46	368 "

Lamson Street—Continued

Page.	Letter.	Full Name.	Residence, Jan. 1, 1938.	Occupation.	Supposed Age.	Reported Residence, Jan. 1, 1937. Street and Number.
	D	*Greco Alphonse	5	laborer	45	here
	E	Greco Philomena—†	5	housewife	50	“
	F	Marino Frank	5	laborer	35	“
	G	Marino James	5	“	32	
	H	Marino Christino—†	5	housewife	30	“
	K	Marino Louis	5	agent	36	
	L	Donahue Catherine—†	5	housewife	35	“
	M	Donahue Helen—†	5	packer	33	
	N	Donahue John	5	clerk	23	
	O	Donahue Mary—†	5	boxmaker	37	“

Long Island

Page.	Letter.	Full Name.	Residence, Jan. 1, 1938.	Occupation.	Supposed Age.	Reported Residence, Jan. 1, 1937. Street and Number.
	P	Anderson Mary C—†		nurse	48	here
	R	Beaudin Leontine—†		attendant	32	“
	S	Berry Katherine—†		nurse	35	“
	T	Blinkoff John		physician	24	Newton
	U	Brady Christopher G		clerk	50	here
	V	Breslin Frances M—†		stenographer	31	“
	W	Brown Mary A—†		nurse	51	“
	X	Browne Ethel C—†		teacher	31	
	Y	Burm Elvina—†		attendant	36	“
	Z	Cahill Nora M—†		nurse	46	
236						
	A	Capelotte Angela M—†		“	37	425 Harvard
	B	Carey Marion H—†		clerk	33	here
	C	Carion Suzanne—†		dietitian	26	“
	D	Carrow Helen M—†		laundress	58	“
	E	Cashman Eleanor K—†		clerk	41	64 Chalesgate East
	F	Clay Charles L		director	40	here
	G	Clay Helen L—†		housewife	40	“
	H	Cochran Lillian—†		nurse	38	Somerville
	K	Connors Elizabeth A—†		dietitian	31	here
	L	Curran James W		watchman	55	“
	M	Dalton Margaret M—†		operator	31	“
	N	Davies Annie—†		attendant	65	“
	O	Dodd Anna J—†		“	59	
	P	Dodd Katherine—†		“	61	
	R	Donnelly Frances M—†		hygienist	29	“
	S	Egan Mary G—†		nurse	56	
	T	Falvey Eleanore—†		clerk	40	“

Page.	Letter.	Full Name.	Residence, Jan. 1, 1938.	Occupation.	Supposed Age.	Reported Residence, Jan. 1, 1937. Street and Number.

Long Island—Continued

Page.	Letter.	Full Name.	Residence, Jan. 1, 1938.	Occupation.	Supposed Age.	Reported Residence, Jan. 1, 1937. Street and Number.
	U	Farrow Bernice J—†		attendant	24	here
	V	Fawcitt Alice—†		nurse	49	1607 Tremont
	W	Fraser Daniel A		cook	34	here
	X	Goldstein Louis		physician	25	Newton
	Y	Gray Annie T—†		laundress	63	here
	Z	Greene Mabel B—†		nurse	37	"
237						
	A	Hackett Mary J—†		maid	43	119 Mass av
	B	Hagerty Sarah L—†		matron	56	here
	C	Harrington Marion H—†		laundress	48	"
	D	Hayes Helen M—†		"	35	"
	E	Heels George E		physician	33	"
	F	Heels Vera—†		housewife	31	"
	G	Hickey Annie M—†		nurse	35	
	H	Kelleher Dorothy H—†		"	30	
	K	Knightly Josephine—†		cook	63	"
	L	Knox Agnes M—†		organist	32	
	M	Kulik Camilla B—†		nurse	25	
	N	Kuntz John J		chauffeur	22	"
	O	Lynch Hannah—†		attendant	32	"
	P	Maguire Frederick		porter	40	123 Pembroke
	R	McCarthy Mary A—†		attendant	37	here
	S	McCavith Alice A—†		nurse	35	"
	T	McClintock William		attendant	23	"
	U	McGillivary Florence—†		"	45	
	V	McGrail Bartholomew		watchman	61	"
	W	McGrath Mary A—†		maid	40	
	X	McNamara Catherine—†		matron	53	
	Y	Morrison Mary T—†		supervisor	61	"
	Z	Neville Anna M—†		nurse	54	
238						
	A	O'Brien James W		porter	62	
	B	O'Neil Theresa B—†		seamstress	53	"
	C	Powers Helen A—†		nurse	37	
	D	Reagan Josephine J—†		"	27	
	E	Robinson Agnes—†		matron	57	
	F	Strain Florence A—†		technician	29	"
	G	Strain Margaret—†		attendant	22	"
	H	Sullivan Marjorie J—†		"	21	
	K	Tero Florence B—†		nurse	31	

Page.	Letter.	Full Name.	Residence, Jan. 1, 1938.	Occupation.	Supposed Age.	Reported Residence, Jan. 1, 1937. Street and Number.
		Long Island—Continued				
	L	Wallace Margaret—†		nurse	54	here
	M	Welch Mary A—†		matron	49	"
		Marginal Street				
	U	Ashcroft Jean—†	278	cook	45	48 Jeffries
	V	Riley John	278	clerk	44	here
	W	Riley Mildred P—†	278	housewife	43	"
	X	Tulipani Louis	278	musician	34	"
	Y	Tulipani Nellie—†	278	housewife	32	"
	Z	Botting William	280	freighthandler	52	"
239						
	A	Gifford Frederick	280	painter	43	"
	B	Gifford Theresa—†	280	housewife	38	365 Sumner
	D	Moore Josephine—†	286	"	37	here
	E	Moore Raymond	286	leatherworker	33	"
	F	Rolfe Alice M—†	286	clerk	24	"
	G	Rolfe Fenwick	286	longshoreman	52	"
	H	Rolfe James	286	fireman	28	
	K	Rolfe Mary A—†	286	housewife	47	"
	L	Rolfe William J	286	mechanic	22	"
	M	Rolfe Arthur	286	chemist	29	
	N	Rolfe Josephine—†	286	housewife	22	"
	O	McCormick Charles A	288	clerk	34	
	P	McCormick Sarah A—†	288	housewife	35	"
	R	Kirwan Mary—†	288	"	40	
	S	Kirwan Thomas J	288	plumber	42	"
	T	McInnes Daniel B	288	clerk	65	
	U	McInnes Edith—†	288	stenographer	30	"
	V	McInnes Ellen—†	288	housewife	50	"
	W	Talbot Harry	290	operator	30	
	X	*Talbot Hilda—†	290	housewife	29	"
	Y	Hyde Letitia C—†	290	"	57	498 Sumner
	Z	Hyde Thomas J	290	seaman	30	498 "
240						
	A	Viveiros Manual	290	electrician	31	Rhode Island
	B	Viveiros Margaret E—†	290	housewife	28	498 Sumner
	C	McDonough Catherine–†	290	"	31	498 "
	D	McDonough Myles W	290	fireman	31	498 "
	E	Sullivan Rose M—†	292	operator	31	here

Page.	Letter.	Full Name.	Residence, Jan. 1, 1938.	Occupation.	Supposed Age.	Reported Residence, Jan. 1, 1937. Street and Number.

Marginal Street—Continued

	F	Sullivan Timothy A	292	watchman	67	here
	G	Guay Germaine—†	292	clerk	27	"
	H	Guay Joseph	292	fireman	67	"
	K	Guay Dorothy M—†	292	housewife	23	"
	L	Guay Roy M	292	chauffeur	29	"
	M	DiFelice Cisidio	294	retired	78	
	N	DiFelice Rose—†	294	housewife	75	"
	O	Newbury Leroy	294	machinist	38	"
	P	*Newbury Mary S—†	294	housewife	32	"
	R	*Scolastico Angelina—†	294	"	66	
	S	*Scolastico Gena—†	294	"	30	
	T	Scolastico Michael	294	laborer	39	
	U	Hansjon Henry W	300	decorator	43	"
	V	Hansjon Nora C—†	300	housewife	39	"
	W	*Ottelson Anna—†	300	"	63	
	X	Ottelson Harry	300	longshoreman	65	"
	Y	Buckley Beda O—†	300	housewife	53	"
	Z	Buckley Edward L	300	printer	48	
241						
	A	Buckley Thelma O—†	300	typist	21	

Maverick Street

	B	Annese Domenic	333	laborer	40	here
	C	*Annese Mary—†	333	housewife	37	"
	D	Costanzo Lucy—†	333	"	38	"
	E	Costanzo Nicholas	333	chauffeur	40	"
	F	Cino Anna—†	333	housewife	58	"
	G	Cino Josephine—†	333	assembler	26	"
	H	Colarusso Anna—†	335	seamstress	23	108 Orleans
	K	Colarusso Fioranto	335	chauffeur	27	108 "
	L	Salamone Evelyn—†	335	housewife	38	483 Sumner
	M	Salamone James	335	chauffeur	38	483 "
	N	Morioni Angelina—†	335	at home	20	here
	O	Morioni Leonardo	335	laborer	22	"
	P	*Morioni Lorenzo	335	retired	65	"
	R	Morioni Margaret—†	335	beautician	23	"
	S	Morioni Michele	335	machinist	35	"
	T	Gay Ernest W	337	chauffeur	49	"
	U	Gay Veronica E—†	337	housewife	42	"
	V	Scandone Alfonso	337	mechanic	20	"

Maverick Street—Continued

Page.	Letter.	Full Name.	Residence, Jan. 1, 1938.	Occupation.	Supposed Age.	Reported Residence, Jan. 1, 1937. Street and Number.
	W	Scandone Eleanor—†	337	at home	22	here
	X	Scandone Madeline—†	337	clerk	24	"
	Y	Scandone Nellie—†	337	housewife	46	"
	Z	Scandone Peter A	337	teacher	51	
242						
	A	Manzo Annie—†	337	housewife	35	"
	B	Manzo Louis R	337	craftsman	38	"
	C	Durante Catherine—†	343	housewife	23	"
	D	Durante John	343	mechanic	29	"
	E	Bonavita Angelina—†	343	housewife	47	"
	F	Bonavita Frank	343	laborer	50	
	G	Bonavita Mildred—†	343	shoeworker	21	"
	H	Bonavita Nicholas	343	operator	22	
	K	Caruana Alfonso	343	salesman	36	"
	L	Caruana Gladys—†	343	housewife	35	"
	M	Jones John P	345	roofer	38	
	N	Jones Margaret—†	345	housewife	30	"
	O	DiRienzo Carmela—†	345	seamstress	23	"
	P	*DiRienzo Felix	345	plasterer	69	"
	T	DiRienzo Frank	345	laborer	34	
	R	*DiRienzo Rose—†	345	housewife	55	"
	S	DiRienzo Susie—†	345	shoeworker	21	"
	U	Bognore Alfonso	345	chauffeur	35	"
	V	*Bognore Jennie—†	345	housewife	35	"
	W	Rizzo Edith—†	347	stenographer	25	"
	X	Rizzo John	347	printer	26	"
	Y	Rizzo Alfred	347	operator	23	"
	Z	*Rizzo Catherine—†	347	housewife	55	"
243						
	A	Rizzo Michael	347	clerk	55	
	B	Rizzo Marviano	347	upholsterer	33	"
	C	Rizzo Mary—†	347	housewife	31	"
	D	*Lauletta Carmela—†	363	"	60	
	E	Lauletta Grace—†	363	"	32	
	F	*Lauletta Vincent	363	operator	37	
	G	*Dellacroce Vincenzo	363	laborer	63	
	H	*Tozzi Josephine—†	363	cook	27	
	K	Farren James J	367	boilermaker	42	"
	L	Farren John A	367	clerk	36	
	M	Annese Domenic	367	laborer	55	"
	N	Annese Lucy—†	367	at home	24	

Page.	Letter.	FULL NAME.	Residence, Jan. 1, 1938.	Occupation.	Supposed Age.	Reported Residence, Jan. 1, 1937. Street and Number.

Maverick Street—Continued

	o	*Annese Teresa—†	367	housewife	50	here
	P	Capizza Anthony	367	operator	24	"
	R	Capizza Demostene	367	chauffeur	25	"
	s	*Capizza Vincenzo	367	salesman	67	"
	T	Ardito Anna—†	369	housewife	49	"
	U	Ardito Carmen	369	bootblack	51	"
	V	Wardell Joseph F	369	supervisor	29	"
	W	*DeNisco Giuseppi	369	laborer	62	"
	X	*DeNisco Henrietta—†	369	housewife	62	"
	Y	*Popeo Esther—†	369	"	35	
	Z	Popeo Vincent	369	agent	41	
244						
	A	Lombardy Anthony	371	cutter	25	
	B	Lombardy Joseph	371	laborer	60	
	C	*Lombardy Maria—†	371	housewife	61	"
	D	Lombardy Michael	371	mechanic	28	"
	F	Famigletti John	375	attendant	40	"
	G	Famigletti Mary—†	375	housewife	32	"
	H	*Tuttesanti Genoveffa—†	377	"	51	
	L	Tuttesanti Louis	377	bricklayer	54	"
	T	Tuttesanti Carmen	377	presser	32	
	M	Tuttesanti Fannie—†	377	housewife	29	"
	N	Beneditto James	377	carpenter	34	"
	O	*Beneditto Rachel—†	377	housewife	29	"
	P	Zaccaro Anthony	377	baker	24	
	R	Zaccaro Nicholas	377	manager	30	"
	S	Ladorella Anthony	379	laborer	46	
	T	Ladorella Susan—†	379	housewife	37	"
	U	*Loriso Giuseppi	381	plasterer	54	144 Havre
	V	*Loriso Sabina—†	381	housewife	52	144 "
	W	*Cilibrosi Charles	381	laborer	47	135 Orleans
	X	*Cilibrosi Josephine—†	381	housewife	42	135 "
	Y	*Gaito Teresa—†	381	"	39	here
	Z	*Gaito Vincenzo	381	laborer	39	"
245						
	A	Goglia Amedeo	383	chauffeur	40	"
	B	*Goglia Mary—†	383	housewife	33	"
	C	*Tiso Antonette—†	383	"	48	Connecticut
	D	*Tiso Domenic	383	fireman	47	"
	E	Tiso Michael	383	clerk	22	"
	F	Tiso Pasquale	383	laborer	21	

Page.	Letter.	FULL NAME.	Residence, Jan. 1, 1938.	Occupation.	Supposed Age.	Reported Residence, Jan. 1, 1937. Street and Number.

Maverick Street—Continued

	G	*Triolo Antonette—†	383	housewife	35	here
	H	Triolo Phillip N	383	clerk	30	"

McCormick Square

	K	Tranfaglia George P	1	shoecutter	34	here
	L	Tranfaglia Jennie—†	1	housewife	23	"
	M	Tranfaglia Michael	1	gilder	64	"
	N	Tranfaglia Orlando	1	shoeworker	30	"
	O	*Tranfaglia Orsola—†	1	housewife	53	"
	P	Tranfaglia Pasquale	1	laborer	32	
	R	Angrisano George	1	barber	32	
	S	*Angrisano Josephine—†	1	stitcher	31	
	T	Rubano Alfred	3	counterman	21	"
	U	Rubano Angelo	3	merchant	60	"
	V	Rubano Frank	3	counterman	26	"
	W	Rubano Lois—†	3	at home	22	
	X	Rubano Rose—†	3	housewife	60	"
	Y	Naumann Delia—†	3	"	33	35 Faywood av
	Z	Naumann Frederick	3	surveyor	33	35 "
246						
	A	Sharp Allan M	3	clerk	55	here
	B	Sharp Mary—†	3	housewife	53	"

Short Street

	D	Ciulla Joan—†	1	housewife	30	here
	E	Ciulla Vincent	1	fisherman	34	"
	F	Lee Mary—†	2	housewife	49	"
	G	*Juliano Rosaria	3	laborer	27	
	H	Juliano Rose—†	3	housewife	24	"
	K	*Bonabest Catherine—†	3	"	53	
	L	*Bonabest Vincent	3	laborer	54	
	M	*Bruno Concetta—†	4	housewife	50	"
	N	Bruno John	4	fisherman	56	"
	O	*Brogna Joseph	5	cutter	27	246 Everett
	P	Brogna Rose—†	5	housewife	21	246 "
	R	Trobicco Jennie—†	5	"	30	here
	S	Trobicco Joseph	5	foreman	33	"
	T	*Pagnani Hugo	5	laborer	46	"
	U	*Salerni Josephine—†	5	housewife	48	"

Short Street—Continued

Page.	Letter.	Full Name.	Residence, Jan. 1, 1938.	Occupation.	Supposed Age.	Reported Residence, Jan. 1, 1937. Street and Number.
	v	Salerni Sebastina	5	laborer	46	here
	w	Salerni Theresa—†	5	clerk	22	"

Spectacle Island

Page.	Letter.	Full Name.	Residence, Jan. 1, 1938.	Occupation.	Supposed Age.	Reported Residence, Jan. 1, 1937. Street and Number.
	x	*Gannof Jessie M—†		housekeeper	55	here
	y	Haskins Nellie—†		housewife	28	"
	z	*Haskins William		mechanic	51	"
247						
	A	*Kalinski Karol		laborer	65	"
	B	*Leskewicz Michael		"	49	"
	C	*Leskewicz Stella—†		housewife	59	10 Hill
	D	Lowther George		watchman	57	here
	E	Rudnicki Martin		laborer	63	"
	F	*Strominski John		"	53	"
	G	Timmons Annie A—†		housewife	49	"
	H	Timmons Warren F		mechanic	48	"
	K	Wyatt Elsie M—†		housewife	46	"
	L	Wyatt Mary F—†		at home	21	
	M	Wyatt Roy E		electrician	47	"

Sumner Street

Page.	Letter.	Full Name.	Residence, Jan. 1, 1938.	Occupation.	Supposed Age.	Reported Residence, Jan. 1, 1937. Street and Number.
	P	Kelly Annie—†	461	housewife	32	here
	R	Kelly Jerome	461	manager	36	"
	S	*Natalė Columba—†	461	housewife	49	"
	T	*Natale Gerard	461	shoeworker	60	"
	U	Natale Mary—†	461	operator	21	"
	V	Natale William	461	attendant	24	"
	W	McHugh Edith—†	461	housewife	28	"
	X	McHugh John A	461	laborer	30	"
	Y	Rowan Catherine—†	462	housewife	48	195 Everett
	Z	Rowan Edward J	462	shifter	45	195 "
248						
	A	Woods Bella—†	462	at home	75	here
	B	Woods Harry	462	laborer	45	"
	D	Carbon Christine—†	463	housewife	40	"
	E	Carbon Francis	463	rigger	32	
	F	DeLuca Eleanor—†	463	stenographer	25	"
	G	*DeLuca Lucia—†	463	housewife	55	"
	H	DeLuca Romeo	463	mechanic	27	"

Page.	Letter.	Full Name.	Residence, Jan. 1, 1938.	Occupation.	Supposed Age.	Reported Residence, Jan. 1, 1937. Street and Number.

Sumner Street—Continued

	K	Natale Nicholas	463	machinist	54	here
	L	*Natale Stella—†	463	housewife	40	"
	M	Ferren John	464	retired	80	"
	N	*McLaughlin Charles	464	mechanic	24	"
	O	McLaughlin Edward	464	proprietor	37	"
	P	McLaughlin Elizabeth–†	464	housewife	30	"
	R	Pendleton Jennie M—†	464	housekeeper	62	49 Hooker
	S	Antonelli James	464	longshoreman	50	here
	T	Cioffi Joseph	464	laborer	35	"
	U	Cioffi Louise—†	464	housewife	28	"
	V	Avellino Constance—†	464	"	29	
	W	Avellino Michael	464	surveyor	27	"
	Y	Manza Alfonse	465	chauffeur	30	"
	X	Manza Angelina—†	465	housewife	30	"
	Z	Duffy Emma—†	465	operator	32	"
249						
	A	Duffy Sarah—†	465	"	30	
	C	Smith Margaret A—†	466	housewife	60	"
	D	Smith Sarah C—†	466	teacher	50	"
	E	McColgan John C	467	janitor	53	
	F	McColgan Julia T—†	467	housewife	52	"
	G	Moran John C	467	clerk	30	15 Cottage
	H	Clark John	468	"	22	here
	K	Clark Sarah—†	468	operator	40	"
	L	Phelan Ella—†	468	"	24	"
	M	Phelan James	468	photographer	26	"
	N	Phelan Mary A—†	468	housewife	52	"
	O	Phelan Michael	468	towerman	50	"
	P	*Zambella Bruna—†	469	housewife	34	"
	R	Zambella Vincent	469	barber	44	
	S	Zambella Andrew	469	machinist	52	"
	T	Zambella Celia—†	469	clerk	23	
	U	Zambella Emma—†	469	dressmaker	22	"
	V	Zambella Lucy—†	469	housewife	45	"
	W	Bussey Frederick W	470	engineer	35	Beachmont
	X	Bussey Mercy B—†	470	custodian	56	"
	Y	Hyland Annie J—†	470	at home	84	here
	Z	Whalen Elizabeth—†	470	stitcher	55	"
250						
	A	Whalen Helen—†	470	housewife	58	"
	B	Whalen William J	470	glassworker	53	"

Page.	Letter.	Full Name.	Residence, Jan. 1, 1938.	Occupation.	Supposed Age.	Reported Residence, Jan. 1, 1937. Street and Number.
		Sumner Street—Continued				
	c	Flood Carolina—†	472	housewife	42	here
	D	Flood Henry	472	laborer	44	"
	E	Hankard Mary T—†	472	shoeworker	52	"
	F	LaPlato Annie—†	472	housewife	60	"
	G	LaPlato Edith—†	472	clerk	25	
	H	LaPlato James	472	proprietor	60	"
	K	Clark Annette—†	472	housewife	26	"
	L	Clark William	472	gateman	30	
	M	DeLuca Eulanda—†	473	operator	20	
	N	DeLuca Fred	473	laborer	52	
	O	DeLuca Gemma—†	473	clerk	23	
	P	*DeLuca Incoronata—†	473	housewife	42	"
	R	DeLuca Mary—†	473	clerk	22	
	S	Muldoon Ellen—†	473	operator	23	
	T	Muldoon Joseph J	473	installer	48	
	U	Muldoon Joseph J, jr	473	laborer	21	
	V	Muldoon Mary A—†	473	housewife	42	"
	W	Sherwin Catherine—†	474	"	50	
	X	Sherwin Francis C	474	machinist	21	"
	Y	Sherwin James J	474	laborer	52	
	Z	Sherwin James P	474	waiter	24	
251						
	A	Sherwin John F	474	clerk	22	
	B	Sherwin Joseph	474	machinist	25	"
	C	Sherwin Rose M—†	474	waitress	23	
	D	Griffin Mary A—†	474	housewife	48	"
	E	Griffin Patrick J	474	longshoreman	49	"
	F	O'Keefe John F	474	chauffeur	28	"
	G	Bussey John J	475	retired	76	
	H	Bussey Mary L—†	475	housewife	64	"
	K	Iannarone Agnes—†	475	"	26	
	L	Iannarone Leonard	475	engineer	26	
	M	*Grasso Millie—†	477	housewife	38	"
	N	*Grasso Ralph	477	shoemaker	47	"
	O	Rocha Clara—†	477	housewife	28	"
	P	Rocha John	477	salesman	28	"
	R	Lee Christina—†	477	at home	46	
	S	Peterson Hedley	477	seaman	39	"
	T	Siciliano Joseph	477	clerk	22	142 Marginal
	U	Siciliano Rose—†	477	housewife	24	54 Eutaw
	V	Dermody Anna T—†	479	"	34	here

Page.	Letter.	FULL NAME.	Residence, Jan. 1, 1938.	Occupation.	Supposed Age.	Reported Residence, Jan. 1, 1937. Street and Number.

Sumner Street—Continued

	W	Dermody George	479	steamfitter	38	here
	X	*Pettinicchio Luigi	479	merchant	45	524 Sumner
	Y	*Pettinicchio Mary—†	479	housewife	44	524 "
	Z	Cacamo Antonio	479	laborer	21	61 Maverick sq
252						
	A	*Corrinti Angelo	479	tailor	41	here
	B	*Corrinti Jennie—†	479	housewife	36	"
	C	Accomando Angie—†	481	"	22	90 Everett
	D	Accomando Louis	481	mechanic	27	130 Porter
	E	LaRosa Fred	481	carpenter	49	here
	F	*LaRosa Gaetana—†	481	housewife	51	"
	G	LaRosa John	481	carpenter	25	"
	H	*Zecchino Mary—†	481	housewife	42	"
	K	Zecchino Ralph	481	showworker	42	"
	L	Natale Mario	483	carpenter	30	"
	M	Natale Mary—†	483	housewife	27	"
	N	Barbere Frank	483	laborer	43	210 Everett
	O	Barbere Theresa—†	483	housewife	40	210 "
	P	*Ruggiero Fanny—†	483	"	40	here
	R	Ruggiero Michael	483	laborer	40	"
	S	Kenney Alice U—†	488	leatherworker	52	"
	T	Melanson Priscilla—†	488	operator	54	"
	U	Murphy Charles J	488	clerk	22	
	V	Murphy Margaret—†	488	housewife	51	"
	W	Murphy Patrick J	488	longshoreman	52	"
	X	Harkins Mary E—†	490	housekeeper	42	"
	Y	Sharkey Edward D	490	attorney	38	"
	Z	Sharkey Marie B—†	490	housewife	34	"
253						
	A	Kilduff Helen—†	490	housekeeper	35	"
	B	Chiochetti Edmund	492	laborer	42	"
	C	Chiochetti Theresa—†	492	housewife	37	"
	D	Penta Mary—†	492	"	38	
	E	Penta Michael C	492	agent	38	
	F	Guida Martin	492	builder	44	
	G	Mercandante Joseph	492	laborer	27	
	H	*Mercandante Raphaela–†	492	housewife	60	"
	K	*Mercandante Vincent	492	laborer	63	"
	L	Buchanan Mildred M—†	494	housewife	30	215 Webster
	M	Buchanan William	494	chauffeur	31	215 "
	N	Bartolo Andrew	494	nickelplater	22	here

Page.	Letter.	Full Name.	Residence, Jan. 1, 1938.	Occupation.	Supposed Age.	Reported Residence, Jan. 1, 1937. Street and Number.

Sumner Street—Continued

Page.	Letter.	Full Name.	Residence, Jan. 1, 1938.	Occupation.	Supposed Age.	Reported Residence, Jan. 1, 1937. Street and Number.
	O	*Bartolo Biagio	494	mechanic	49	here
	P	*Bartolo Mary C—†	494	housewife	54	"
	R	Bartolo Phyllis—†	494	factoryhand	21	"
	S	Bartolo Romeo	494	painter	28	"
	T	Carlucci Carmella—†	494	housewife	20	381 Sumner
	U	*Carlucci Joseph	494	retired	67	381 "
	V	Carlucci Joseph, jr	494	bartender	29	381 "
	W	Martin Ada—†	496	housewife	62	here
	X	Martin Moses	496	carpenter	58	"
	Y	Grillo Agnes—†	496	housewife	22	284 Chelsea
	Z	Grillo Peter T	496	printer	21	284 "
254						
	A	DeAngelis Frances A—†	496	housewife	20	134 Sumner
	B	DeAngelis Joseph A	496	attendant	24	107 Liverpool
	C	Hilton Catherine—†	497	at home	65	here
	D	Frizzell Helen—†	497	housekeeper	47	"
	E	Sweeney Walter	497	laborer	25	"
	F	Russo Joseph	498	"	56	496 Sumner
	G	Russo Mary—†	498	housewife	41	496 "
	H	Scarpaci Daniel	498	operator	27	494 "
	K	Scarpaci Stella—†	498	housewife	23	494 "
	L	Musto Anna—†	498	"	28	here
	M	Musto John	498	cabinetmaker	37	494 Sumner
	N	Emmett Helen—†	499	stitcher	48	40 Jeffries
	O	Hancock John H	499	welder	47	40 "
	P	Stoddard Anna—†	499	housewife	22	here
	R	Stoddard John	499	fisherman	24	"
	S	Masello Carmeno M	500	laborer	31	8 London
	T	Masello Christina—†	500	housewife	28	8 "
	U	Colelle Peligrino	500	machinist	43	here
	V	Colelle Philomena—†	500	housewife	39	"
	W	Valentine Lude	500	machinist	29	"
	X	Valentine Theresa—†	500	housewife	24	"
	Y	Capone Alfred	502	laborer	22	
	Z	*Capone Annette—†	502	housewife	50	"
255						
	A	Capone Gerardo	502	laborer	54	
	B	Capone Grace—†	502	operator	26	"
	C	Usseglio Edward	502	butcher	30	
	D	Usseglio Mary—†	502	housewife	27	"
	E	*Barrasso Augustino	502	painter	31	

Page.	Letter.	Full Name.	Residence, Jan. 1, 1938.	Occupation.	Supposed Age.	Reported Residence, Jan. 1, 1937. Street and Number.

Sumner Street—Continued

	F	Barrasso Rose—†	502	housewife	24	here
	G	Woodside Viola—†	504	"	24	"
	H	Woodside William	504	machinist	33	"
	K	Crocker George C	504	longshoreman	34	"
	L	Crocker Nellie—†	504	housewife	59	"
	M	Payne Emma—†	504	housekeeper	67	"
	N	Penio Stephen	504	laborer	45	"
	O	Woodside Alfred A	504	painter	56	
	P	Woodside Gordon	504	"	27	
	R	*Mirasolo Joseph	506	laborer	51	
	S	*DiPietro Mary—†	506	housewife	60	"
	T	Volpini Angelo	506	bookbinder	49	"
	U	*Volpini Josephine—†	506	housewife	45	"
	V	Casiello Elvira—†	508	"	25	"
	W	Casiello Joseph	508	cutter	30	215 Havre
	X	LeGallo Helen—†	508	housewife	31	here
	Y	LeGallo Joseph	508	painter	31	"
	Z	Rideout Jennie—†	508	clerk	52	228 Webster
256						
	A	Vernucci Anthony	508	mechanic	21	here
	B	Vernucci Carmella—†	508	tailoress	23	"
	C	*Vernucci Josephine—†	508	housewife	54	"
	D	Vernucci Lena—†	508	stitcher	22	
	E	Vernucci Nicholas	508	tailor	53	
	F	*Terenzio Concetta—†	510	housewife	71	"
	G	*Terenzio Ralph	510	retired	74	
	H	Terenzio Antoinette—†	510	seamstress	32	"
	K	Terenzio Vincent	510	plasterer	34	"
	N	Capone Annie—†	512	housewife	40	"
	O	Capone Anthony	512	laborer	21	
	P	*Carangelo Angelina—†	512	housewife	48	"
	R	Carangelo Cosmo	512	laborer	47	"
	T	Fay Helen G—†	514	housekeeper	41	31 Cottage
	U	Parrelli Benjamin	514	shoeworker	22	36 Monmouth
	V	Parrelli Helen—†	514	housewife	22	here
	W	Saponaro Anna—†	514	"	40	"
	X	Saponaro Joseph	514	barber	21	"
	Z	Boudreau Eva—†	516	housewife	35	"
257						
	A	Boudreau Wilfred	516	cutter	35	
	B	Hanton Bernadette F—†	516	clerk	29	"

Page.	Letter.	Full Name.	Residence, Jan. 1, 1938.	Occupation.	Supposed Age.	Reported Residence, Jan. 1, 1937. Street and Number.

Sumner Street—Continued

Page.	Letter.	Full Name.	Residence, Jan. 1, 1938.	Occupation.	Supposed Age.	Reported Residence, Jan. 1, 1937. Street and Number.
	C	Hanton Elizabeth F—†	516	housewife	67	here
	D	Hanton Genevieve V—†	516	operator	35	"
	E	Hanton John R	516	clerk	23	"
	F	Hanton Ralph J	516	painter	32	"
	G	*Pingiaro Mary—†	516	housewife	40	256 Webster
	H	*Pingiaro Savario	516	barber	49	256 "
	K	Heil Joseph	518	B F D	37	here
	L	Heil Otto	518	painter	43	"
	M	Heil Rita—†	518	housewife	37	"
	N	Trieber Frederick	518	laborer	21	
	O	Trieber Rose A—†	518	housewife	49	"
	P	Trieber William H	518	repairman	24	"
	R	Halliday Anna—†	518	housewife	52	"
	S	Halliday George J	518	constable	54	"
	T	Halliday Wilbur	518	machinist	35	"
	U	Platt Ernest C	520	longshoreman	31	78 Lexington
	V	Platt Helen M—†	520	housewife	27	78 "
	W	Heil Elizabeth M—†	520	"	34	here
	X	Heil John F	520	painter	38	"
	Y	Jameson Isabella—†	520	factoryhand	44	"
	Z	Jameson Robert	520	cutter	67	
258						
	A	McCormack Anna—†	522	housewife	64	"
	B	McCormack Anna F—†	522	stenographer	26	"
	C	McCormack Francis J	522	retired	64	"
	E	Harkins Celia—†	522	housewife	50	"
	F	Harkins Charles J	522	manager	24	"
	G	Harkins John P	522	clerk	23	"
	H	Harkins Mary—†	522	stenographer	26	"
	L	White Josephine—†	524	proprietor	48	462 Sumner
	M	Mealey Leo	524	checker	39	here
	N	Mealey Martin J	524	pipecutter	30	"
	O	Mealey Mary—†	524	housewife	65	"
	P	Platt John C	524	clerk	35	
	R	Platt Marion—†	524	housewife	34	"
	S	Smith Robert J	535	operator	45	"
	T	Higgenbotham Alice—†	535	housewife	69	"
	U	Higgenbotham John	535	plumber	47	
	V	Smith Albert	535	machinist	37	"

Page.	Letter.	Full Name.	Residence, Jan. 1, 1938.	Occupation.	Supposed Age.	Reported Residence, Jan. 1, 1937. Street and Number.

Sumner Street—Continued

Page.	Letter.	Full Name.	Residence, Jan. 1, 1938.	Occupation.	Supposed Age.	Reported Residence, Jan. 1, 1937. Street and Number.
	W	Smith Mildred—†	535	housewife	27	here
	X	*Parla Carmello	537	laborer	31	"
	Y	Parla Marion—†	537	housewife	26	"
	Z	Tagariello Lenardo	537	finisher	47	
259						
	A	Tagariello Mary—†	537	housewife	41	"
	B	Tagariello Joseph	537	finisher	50	
	C	Tagariello Maria—†	537	housewife	44	"
	D	Powers Catherine—†	539	at home	78	
	E	Fraser Albert	539	watchman	65	"
	F	Fraser Theresa—†	539	housewife	69	"
	G	Smith Annie L—†	539	"	62	
	H	Smith Arthur J	539	chauffeur	30	"
	K	Smith James	539	seaman	52	
	M	Boy Catherine C—†	541	housewife	23	"
	N	Boy Domenic L	541	laborer	26	
	O	DePalma Giuseppe	541	carpenter	50	"
	P	DePalma Olympia—†	541	housewife	44	"
	R	Woodside Edward	541	painter	32	
	S	Woodside Josephine—†	541	housewife	29	"
	T	Burke Edward J	545	retired	73	
	U	Burke Elizabeth J—†	545	at home	82	
	V	Burke Rita—†	545	housewife	44	"
	W	Burke Thomas J	545	operator	45	"
	X	*Correale Minerale—†	549	housewife	72	"
	Y	*Correale Vincenzo	549	retired	75	
260						
	A	Fay Charles J	549	painter	25	
	B	Fay Herbert	549	"	20	
	C	Fay Isabella E—†	549	housewife	46	"
	D	Fay Joseph J	549	operator	47	"
	E	Fay Joseph T	549	painter	23	
	F	*Ciavolo Alexander	551	laborer	60	"
	G	Ciavolo John	551	"	22	
	H	*Cuzzi Carman	551	retired	64	
	K	Cuzzi Giulio	551	gardener	22	"
	L	*Cuzzi Mary—†	551	housewife	59	"
	M	*Pelusi Eleanor—†	551	"	36	
	N	Pelusi Luigi	551	laborer	45	

Page.	Letter.	Full Name.	Residence, Jan. 1, 1938.	Occupation.	Supposed Age.	Reported Residence, Jan. 1, 1937. Street and Number.
		Thompson's Island				
	P	Albee Clifton E		director	31	here
	R	Baird Mark C		instructor	38	"
	S	Baird Zella M—†		housewife	34	"
	T	Belcher Margaret J—†		"	62	E Saugus
	U	Christiansen Etta—†		teacher	28	Rhode Island
	V	Coffill Henrietta—†		maid	51	here
	W	Fisher Laura L—†		"	58	Brookline
	X	Haynes Edward S		engineer	64	here
	Y	*Jardine James H		seaman	28	"
	Z	Jones Mary C—†		maid	54	"
261						
	A	Jones R Carroll		teacher	24	Maine
	B	Kihlstrom Bror Y		instructor	54	here
	C	Kitching Robert R		"	54	"
	D	MacDonald John R		supervisor	20	Weston
	E	Mathewson Mary F—†		maid	50	here
	F	Meacham Rena M—†		housewife	42	"
	G	Meacham William M		headmaster	42	"
	H	Mitchell May—†		instructor	53	"
	K	Nichols Marion L—†		maid	53	
	L	Pickard Arthur H		instructor	21	"
	M	Ronka George R		teacher	28	"
	N	Ronka Marjorie F—†		"	26	Maine
	O	Stiles Carlton W		instructor	24	here
	P	Stiles Isabel L—†		bookkeeper	26	"
	R	Thomas Raymond		supervisor	27	"
	S	Thomas Wilhelmina B—†		secretary	25	"
	T	Varney May B—†		instructor	60	"
	U	Webb Benjamin A		painter	45	Maine
	V	Williams Grace F—†		teacher	57	here
		Webster Place				
	W	*Catalano Antoinetta—†	1	housewife	40	here
	X	Catalano Pasquale	1	storekeeper	47	"
	Y	Hopp Alfred	1	chauffeur	32	120 Marginal
	Z	Hopp Edith—†	1	typist	35	120 "

Page.	Letter.	Full Name.	Residence, Jan. 1, 1938.	Occupation.	Supposed Age.	Reported Residence, Jan. 1, 1937. Street and Number.
262						
		Webster Street				
	A	DiTroia Mary—†	208	housewife	35	Attleboro
	B	*DiTroia Peter	208	foreman	37	"
	C	*Borrelli Antoinetta—†	208	housewife	49	here
	D	Borrelli Michael	208	blacksmith	52	"
	E	Borrelli Vincent	208	salesman	26	"
	F	Hennessy Ellen F—†	210	at home	84	
	G	Hennessy James L	210	student	23	
	H	Hennessy Mary—†	210	bookkeeper	55	"
	K	Hennessy Mary A—†	210	"	57	"
	L	Stafford Charles A	212	retired	73	
	M	Satfford Ellen K—†	212	teacher	27	
	N	Stafford Mary E—†	212	housewife	62	"
	O	Swenson Corinne—†	216	stenographer	25	"
	P	Sullivan Delia A—†	216	housewife	74	"
	R	Sullivan John A	216	retired	75	
	S	*Catrone Jeanette—†	218	at home	67	
	T	Russo Margaret—†	218	housewife	42	"
	U	Russo Modestino	218	lather	48	
	V	Maioli Anthony	218	pressman	45	"
	W	Maioli Irene—†	218	housewife	39	"
	Z	*Licciardi Mary—†	228	"	59	
263						
	A	Licciardi Vincenzo	228	carpenter	58	"
	B	Millerick George E	228	chauffeur	36	"
	C	Millerick Isabelle—†	228	housewife	27	"
	D	Marino Anthony	228	rigger	23	Quincy
	E	*Marino Georgiana—†	228	housewife	20	"
	F	Younie Beatrice J—†	233	"	36	here
	G	Younie Edward T	233	mechanic	40	"
	H	Younie William	233	retired	83	"
	K	Murphy Anna A—†	233	at home	58	
	L	Murphy Jeremiah F	233	boatman	66	"
	M	Murphy John R	233	salesman	53	"
	N	Roan Daniel F	234	painter	50	4 Lamson
	O	Roan John F	234	"	21	4 "
	P	Roan Rose—†	234	housewife	50	4 "
	R	Coughlin Joseph J	234	agent	40	Revere
	S	Leary Daniel A	234	salesman	42	here
	T	Leary Frances M—†	234	housewife	39	"
	U	Nelson Claire L—†	234	"	28	"

Page.	Letter.	Full Name.	Residence, Jan. 1, 1938.	Occupation.	Supposed Age.	Reported Residence, Jan. 1, 1937. Street and Number.

Webster Street—Continued

Page.	Letter.	Full Name.	Residence, Jan. 1, 1938.	Occupation.	Supposed Age.	Reported Residence, Jan. 1, 1937. Street and Number.
	v	Nelson Horatio J	234	manager	32	here
	w	Sullivan Joseph C	234	engineer	54	"
	x	Thornton Thomas J	234	salesman	29	912 Saratoga
	y	Seaward Harold A	235	mechanic	34	here
	z	Seaward Mabel K—†	235	housewife	32	"
264						
	A	Goodwin Caroline—†	235	"	45	
	B	Goodwin Mary A—†	235	clerk	23	"
	C	Domegan James P	235	laborer	26	
	D	Donegan Mary C—†	235	housewife	23	"
	E	Soldani Josephine—†	235	clerk	29	
	F	Murphy Dennis	236	retired	77	
	G	Murphy Lucy—†	236	housewife	55	"
	H	Pope Ernest F	236	clerk	21	
	K	Pope George H	236	usher	20	
	L	Pope Mary E—†	236	housewife	57	"
	M	Pope Thomas F	236	fireman	23	
	N	*Vallen Catherine—†	236	housewife	32	"
	O	Vallen Daniel	236	longshoreman	39	"
	P	Brogna Achilles	237	boilermaker	53	"
	R	Brogna Antonetta—†	237	housewife	44	"
	S	Brogna Carmela—†	237	saleswoman	21	"
	T	*Capone Josephine	237	at home	80	"
	U	Guarino Mary—†	237	housewife	26	258 Webster
	V	Guarino Michael	237	shoeworker	28	258 "
	W	*Bosco Antoinetta—†	238	housewife	74	15 Chelsea
	X	Bosco Christina—†	238	seamstress	37	15 "
	Y	Bosco Ralph	238	laborer	40	15 "
	Z	DeLuca John	238	salesman	66	here
265						
	A	*Marotta Charles	238	musician	50	"
	B	*Marotta Gemma—†	238	housewife	39	"
	C	Granna James	238	salesman	27	"
	D	Granna Marion—†	238	housewife	24	"
	E	Sweeney Gertrude M—†	239	stenographer	27	"
	F	Sweeney Mary E—†	239	housewife	52	"
	G	Blasetti Angelo	239	trackman	30	Everett
	H	*Blasetti Viola—†	239	housewife	25	here
	L	Napier Charles J	241	shipper	27	381 Sumner
	M	Napier Elvira A—†	241	housewife	25	381 "

Page.	Letter.	Full Name.	Residence, Jan. 1, 1938.	Occupation.	Supposed Age.	Reported Residence, Jan. 1, 1937. Street and Number.

Webster Street—Continued

Page.	Letter.	Full Name.	Residence, Jan. 1, 1938.	Occupation.	Supposed Age.	Reported Residence, Jan. 1, 1937. Street and Number.
	N	DiSalvo Anthony N	241	cutter	31	here
	O	*DiSalvo Carmela—†	241	housewife	60	"
	P	DiSalvo Frances—†	241	"	27	"
	R	DiSalvo Joseph	241	retired	68	
	S	DiSalvo Matilda—†	241	seamstress	20	"
	T	DiBenedetto Agostino	242	springmaker	32	"
	U	*DiBenedetto Mary—†	242	housewife	30	"
	V	*Carini Adeline—†	242	"	52	
	W	Carini Clara—†	242	seamstress	26	"
	X	*Carini Joseph	242	laborer	62	
	Y	Carini Joseph, jr	242	painter	24	
	Z	Carini Louise—†	242	seamstress	21	"
266						
	A	Sinagra Joseph	242	laborer	28	
	B	*Sinagra Louis	242	retired	56	
	C	*Sinagra Nancy—†	242	housewife	27	"
	D	Sacco Antoinetta—†	244	packer	24	
	E	Sacco Antonio	244	operator	21	"
	F	*Sacco Jeremiah	244	laborer	52	
	G	*Sacco Josephine—†	244	housewife	55	"
	H	Garofolo Mary—†	245	housekeeper	46	"
	K	Puccia Natalie—†	245	housewife	32	Somerville
	L	Puccia Philip	245	salesman	38	"
	M	DeLeonardis Umberto	245	pressman	57	here
	N	*DeLeonardis Vincenza-†	245	housewife	48	"
	O	Genzale Rose—†	245	"	21	"
	P	Angrisano Angelina—†	246	clerk	23	
	R	Angrisano Emilio	246	laborer	37	
	S	Angrisano Joseph	246	"	44	
	T	Angrisano Margaret—†	246	clerk	47	
	U	*Angrisano Pasquale	246	retired	71	
	V	*Fagone Joseph	246	laborer	52	
	W	Fagone Josephine—†	246	cutter	21	
	X	*Fagone Rose—†	246	housewife	50	"
	Y	Costello Albert M	247	plumber	30	
	Z	Costello Isabel A—†	247	housewife	27	"
267						
	A	Millerick Elizabeth—†	247	housewife	60	"
	B	Millerick Elizabeth A—†	247	teacher	40	
	D	Sheridan Charlotte—†	248	housewife	49	"

Page.	Letter.	Full Name.	Residence, Jan. 1, 1938.	Occupation.	Supposed Age.	Reported Residence, Jan. 1, 1937. Street and Number.

Webster Street—Continued

	E	Sheridan Edward J	248	machinist	24	here
	F	Sheridan Mary E—†	248	typist	21	"
	G	*DeAngelis Gaetana—†	249	housekeeper	64	"
	H	Mastrangelo Frank	249	laborer	40	"
	K	Mastrangelo Michelina-†	249	housewife	32	"
	L	Fagioli Amerasa—†	249	"	31	
	M	Fagioli Amerino	249	laborer	34	
	N	Coscia Caroline—†	249	housewife	46	"
	O	Coscia Jennie—†	249	stenographer	25	"
	P	Coscia Michael	249	shoeworker	49	"
	R	Coscia Anne—†	250	housewife	21	"
	S	Coscia Anthony	250	barber	25	"
	T	Coscia Jennie—†	250	operator	23	183 Webster
	U	*Cirone Elisa—†	250	housewife	43	here
	V	Cirone Ricardo	250	bricklayer	51	"
	W	Paulicelli Cosmo	250	cook	23	"
	X	Paulicelli Marion—†	250	housewife	23	"
	Y	Johnson Adolph	251	ironworker	28	"
	Z	Johnson Florence—†	251	housewife	22	"
268						
	A	Stibolt Eugene	251	retired	64	
	B	Stibolt Frank	251	woodworker	30	"
	C	Stibolt Mina—†	251	housewife	63	"
	D	Sharkey Frank S	252	carpenter	30	"
	E	Sharkey James J	252	checker	32	
	F	Sharkey James P	252	"	60	
	G	Sharkey Julia F—†	252	housewife	33	"
	H	Cappelluzzo Ida—†	252	"	39	
	K	Cappelluzzo Liberato	252	chauffeur	43	"
	L	Buccella Carl	254	engineer	26	
	M	Buccella Louise—†	254	housewife	25	"
	N	Landolfi Domenic	254	tailor	44	
	O	Landolfi Virginia—†	254	housewife	37	"
	P	Carroll Alice—†	254	"	46	
	R	Carroll Robert	254	blacksmith	46	"
	S	Carroll Ruth E—†	254	seamstress	22	"
	V	*Tipping Charles	255	longshoreman	51	"
	W	Tipping Joseph E	255	freighthandler	23	"
	X	*Tipping Nettie—†	255	housewife	51	"
	Y	Ranieri Frederico	256	blacksmith	47	"

Page.	Letter.	FULL NAME.	Residence, Jan. 1, 1938.	Occupation.	Supposed Age.	Reported Residence, Jan. 1, 1937. Street and Number.

Webster Street—Continued

	z	*Ranieri Natalina—†	256	housewife	47	here
269						
	A	Annese Celia—†	256	"	23	
	B	Annese Joseph	256	shoeworker	26	"
	C	Palmari Edward	256	barber	30	268 Maverick
	D	Palmari Josephine—†	256	housewife	25	192 Benningt'n
	E	Eskedahl Herbert	257	painter	25	here
	F	Eskedahl Marie—†	257	housewife	54	"
	G	Porzio Alfonzo	257	barber	45	"
	H	Porzio Raffaela—†	257	housewife	37	"
	K	Brophy Veronica—†	257	housekeeper	52	"
	L	Sirianni John	258	chauffeur	29	"
	M	*Sirianni Rose—†	258	housewife	21	"
	N	*Coscia Nancy—†	258	"	36	261 Webster
	O	Coscia Pasquale	258	shoeworker	47	261 "
	P	Tringali Clara—†	258	housewife	37	here
	R	Tringali Sebastian	258	builder	42	"
	S	*Discenza Carmine—†	259	tailor	61	"
	T	Discenza Louis	259	laborer	36	
	U	Discenza Nicolas	259	painter	27	
	V	*Discenza Rosina—†	259	housewife	56	"
	W	Broussard Charles	259	carpenter	67	"
	X	Broussard Georginna—†	259	housewife	53	"
	Y	Jaynes Madeline J—†	259	"	21	
	Z	Gleason Elizabeth—†	259	"	40	
270						
	A	Gleason Joseph	259	chauffeur	42	"
	B	Andriotti Anna—†	261	housewife	25	"
	C	Andriotti Michael	261	engineer	26	
	D	DiMaio Concetta—†	261	housewife	41	"
	E	DiMaio William	261	clerk	21	"
	F	Paolini Salvatore	261	shoeworker	57	251 Webster
	G	Paolini Virginia—†	261	housewife	50	251 "
	H	Galvin Estelle A—†	263	"	48	here
	K	Galvin Ruth E—†	263	clerk	22	"
	L	Galvin William F	263	printer	54	"
	M	Morelli Margaret—†	263	housewife	31	"
	N	*Morelli Nicolas	263	shoeworker	33	"
	O	Ferrara Alfred	263	laborer	23	
	P	*Ferrara Anna—†	263	housewife	62	"

Page.	Letter.	Full Name.	Residence, Jan. 1, 1938.	Occupation.	Supposed Age.	Reported Residence, Jan. 1, 1937. Street and Number.

Webster Street—Continued

Page.	Letter.	Full Name.	Residence, Jan. 1, 1938.	Occupation.	Supposed Age.	Reported Residence, Jan. 1, 1937. Street and Number.
	R	Ferrara George	263	retired	68	here
	S	Ferrara Joseph	263	buffer	25	"
	T	Pizzi Benjamin	264	laborer	21	"
	U	*Pizzi Daniel	264	shoeworker	28	"
	V	Pizzi Edward	264	attendant	65	"
	W	Pizzi Minnie—†	264	operator	23	"
	X	*Pizzi Raffaela—†	264	housewife	55	"
	Y	Iannarone Dominic	264	shoeworker	28	"
	Z	Iannarone Lillian—†	264	seamstress	31	"
271						
	A	Iannarone Olga—†	264	operator	29	
	B	Laconia John B	264	laborer	43	
	C	*Laconia Louise—†	264	housewife	36	"
	D	*Gallo Elizabeth—†	265	"	42	
	E	Gallo Frank	265	laborer	20	
	F	Gallo Helen—†	265	seamstress	22	"
	G	*Marino Louise—†	265	housewife	33	"
	H	DeMarco Frank	265	bootblack	41	"
	K	*DeMarco Jennie—†	265	housewife	41	"
	M	Aliprandi Dominic	269	storekeeper	60	"
	N	Aliprandi Frances—†	269	housewife	42	"
	O	Bellio Mary—†	269	"	29	
	P	Bellio Silvio	269	painter	41	
	R	Frances Elizabeth—†	271	housekeeper	59	"
	S	*Gore John	271	longshoreman	33	"
	T	*Belliveau Alice—†	271	housewife	62	"
	U	Belliveau Andrew	271	chauffeur	36	"
	V	Belliveau Margaret—†	271	laundress	29	"
	W	*Belliveau Moses	271	retired	65	"
	X	Belliveau Peter	271	laborer	32	
	Y	O'Neil Celina—†	271	housewife	30	"
	Z	O'Neil James J	271	mariner	30	
272						
	A	McLaughlin Alice—†	273	clerk	41	
	B	McLaughlin Pauline—†	273	"	22	
	C	Kirwin Margaret—†	273	"	48	
	D	Kirwin Mary—†	273	housewife	35	"
	E	Kirwin Philip	273	longshoreman	66	"
	F	McLaughlin Elizabeth—†	273	clerk	46	"
	G	McLaughlin Mary—†	273	saleswoman	48	"
	H	Murphy Edward L	275	proprietor	41	"

Page.	Letter.	Full Name.	Residence, Jan. 1, 1938.	Occupation.	Supposed Age.	Reported Residence, Jan. 1, 1937. Street and Number.

Webster Street—Continued

	K	Downing Catherine M–†	275	clerk	25	here
	L	Downing George D	275	laborer	24	"
	M	Downing John F	275	clerk	20	"
	N	Downing Sanford M	275	retired	54	
	O	Murphy Margaret M—†	275	clerk	30	
	P	Gallagher Edward A	275	"	22	
	R	Gallagher Ellen J—†	275	housewife	53	"
	S	Gallagher Hugh B	275	boilermaker	52	"
	T	Gallagher Mary M—†	275	operator	25	"
	U	Donahue Agnes F—†	277	housewife	58	"
	V	Donahue Arthur J	277	clerk	30	
	W	Donahue Jeremiah F	277	"	64	"
	X	Donahue Margaret M—†	277	housewife	26	39 Cottage
	Y	Barry Florence—†	277	clerk	40	here
	Z	Barry Mary—†	277	candyworker	42	"
273						
	A	Travaglino Dominick	277	coremaker	51	"
	B	Travaglino Dominick, jr	277	"	21	
	C	*Travaglino Giovanna—†	277	at home	74	
	D	Travaglino Horace	277	bookkeeper	22	"
	E	Travaglino Matilda—†	277	housewife	48	"
	F	Millerick Edward C	279	chauffeur	34	"
	G	Millerick Imelda M—†	279	housewife	28	"
	H	Cullen Elizabeth A—†	279	"	41	
	K	Cullen James H	279	watchman	43	"
	L	*Matera Dominic	279	barber	47	
	M	Matera Eugene	279	laborer	40	
	N	*Matera Giuseppe	279	retired	79	
	O	*Matera Margaret—†	279	housewife	36	"
	P	Long Annie T—†	281	at home	75	
	R	Connell James H	281	clerk	28	
	S	Connell John F	281	"	25	
	T	Connell Margaret—†	281	housewife	64	"
	U	Connell Mary L—†	281	at home	32	
	V	Flanagan Rose M—†	281	housewife	24	"
	W	Flanagan William J	281	shipper	26	
	X	DiNatalis Anna—†	283	housewife	26	"
	Y	DiNatalis Vincent	283	salesman	30	"
	Z	Moran Charles L	283	clerk	37	
274						
	A	Moran Margaret I—†	283	housewife	23	"

Page.	Letter.	Full Name.	Residence, Jan. 1, 1938.	Occupation.	Supposed Age.	Reported Residence, Jan. 1, 1937. Street and Number.

Webster Street—Continued

	B	*Giammatteo Anthony	283	laborer	57	here
	C	Giammatteo Irma—†	283	stitcher	23	"
	D	*Giammatteo Maria—†	283	housewife	44	"
	E	Laiacona Joseph	285	tailor	32	
	F	Laiacona Rose—†	285	housewife	28	"
	G	Cundari Joseph	285	laborer	20	
	H	Cundari Lillian O—†	285	operator	23	"
	K	*Cundari Maria—†	285	housewife	54	"
	L	McLaughlin Dorothy—†	285	packer	20	
	M	McLaughlin Elizabeth T–†	285	housewife	43	"
	N	McLaughlin Harry J	285	laborer	22	
	O	Howland Catherine—†	291	at home	27	
	P	Howland James M	291	freighthandler	65	"
	R	Howland Margaret—†	291	operator	29	"
	S	Warner Josephine—†	291	housewife	51	42 Jeffries
	T	Warner Leonard F	291	laborer	21	42 "
	U	Lloyd Bertha A—†	291	housewife	46	here
	V	Lloyd Curtis K	291	foreman	52	"
	W	Lloyd William H	291	cutter	22	"
	X	Wingard Carrie—†	293	housewife	54	"
	Y	Wingard Olaf	293	longshoreman	52	"
	Z	Kerrigan Hugh	293	"	71	
275						
	A	Kerrigan Nora—†	293	housewife	60	"
	B	O'Brien Mary J—†	293	"	58	
	C	O'Brien Patrick J	293	teamster	51	"

Wood Island Station

	F	DuWors Julia C—†		housewife	28	here
	G	DuWors William J		carpenter	27	"

1

1

14

4

51

7

8

9

2

2

1

11

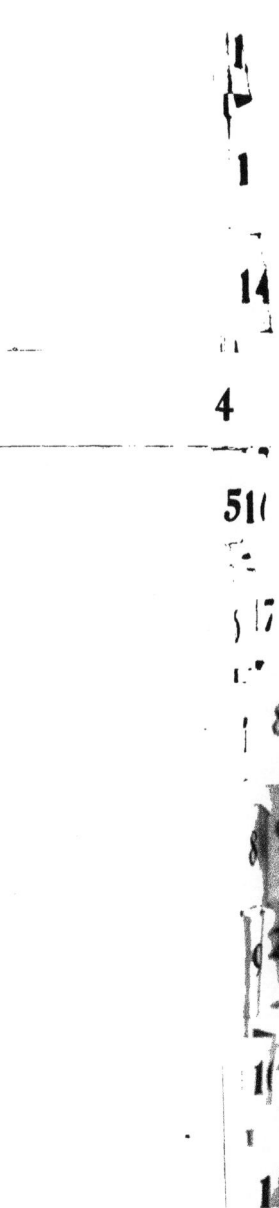

Ward 1—Precinct 4

CITY OF BOSTON

LIST OF RESIDENTS
20 YEARS OF AGE AND OVER

(NON-CITIZENS INDICATED BY ASTERISK)
(FEMALES INDICATED BY DAGGER)

AS OF

JANUARY 1, 1938

JOSEPH F. TIMILTY, } *Listing*
FREDERIC E. DOWLING, } *Board.*

CITY OF BOSTON PRINTING DEPARTMENT

Page.	Letter.	Full Name.	Residence, Jan. 1, 1938.	Occupation.	Supposed Age.	Reported Residence, Jan. 1, 1937. Street and Number.
284		**Bremen Place**				
	A	Wilson Mary—†	4	at home	65	349 Sumner
	B	*Serafino John	4	laborer	47	2 Airport
	C	*Vasques Anna—†	4	housewife	38	here
	D	Vasques Sabestiano	4	mason	41	"
		Bremen Street				
	E	*Luke Frederick	6	laborer	42	here
	F	*Luke Olive—†	6	housewife	43	"
	G	Bucci Anna—†	8	"	26	"
	H	*Bucci Ovidio	8	actor	39	
	K	Messina Frank A	8	longshoreman	51	"
	L	Messina Marie—†	8	housewife	49	"
	M	Amoroso Anthony	8	timekeeper	24	154 Cottage
	N	Amoroso Phyllis—†	8	housewife	22	154 "
	P	Minichiello Angelo	12	polisher	71	289 Sumner
	R	Minichiello Antonette—†	12	housewife	66	289 "
	S	Minichiello Frank	12	musician	34	289 "
	T	Minichiello Josephine—†	12	housewife	31	289 "
	U	*Todisco Antonetta—†	14	"	37	12 Bremen
	V	Todisco Antonio	14	laborer	43	12 "
	W	DeSimone Amedeo	14	"	28	here
	X	DeSimone Angelina—†	14	housewife	36	"
	Y	D'Argenio Angelina—†	16	"	42	"
	Z	D'Argenio Antonio	16	operator	44	"
285						
	A	D'Argenio Faustino	16½	"	22	16 Bremen
	B	*D'Argenio Maria—†	16½	housekeeper	80	here
	C	Carrozza Lena—†	16½	hairdresser	24	Lawrence
	D	*Schifano Antonio	16½	operator	56	here
	E	*Schifano Gaetanina—†	16½	housewife	44	"
	F	Tufo Albert	16½	laborer	42	"
	G	Tufo Josephine—†	16½	housewife	41	"
	H	Antonelli Frank	rear 16½	cutter	55	"
	K	Petrillo Frank	18	operator	22	Malden
	L	Rizzuti Dorothy—†	18	housewife	31	here
	M	*Rizzuti John	18	merchant	31	"
	N	Loverro John	18	operator	47	"
	O	Loverro Mary J—†	18	housewife	38	"
	P	*Arcinoli Elvira—†	20	"	55	

Page.	Letter.	Full Name.	Residence, Jan. 1, 1938.	Occupation.	Supposed Age.	Reported Residence, Jan. 1, 1937. Street and Number.
		Bremen Street—Continued				
	R	Arcinoli John	20	laborer	58	here
	S	Trainor Catherine—†	20	housewife	23	Everett
	T	Trainor William	20	cutter	26	Peabody
	V	*Costa Nuncia—†	20	housewife	61	here
	U	Costa Philip	20	laborer	62	"
	W	Farulla Vincent	22	"	40	"
	X	Fucarino Antonio	22	operator	46	
	Y	Mogauro Grace—†	22	housewife	33	"
	Z	Mogauro Michael	22	laborer	33	
286						
	A	DeFronzo Anthony	22		22	
	B	*DeFronzo Carmen	22		62	
	C	DeFronzo John	22	"	24	
	D	*DeFronzo Maria—†	22	housewife	54	"
	E	Bordamo Antonio	24	laborer	38	147 Cottage
	F	*Bordamo Josephine—†	24	housewife	34	147 "
	G	Fradestefano Albert	24	plumber	32	here
	H	*Fradestefano Domenic	24	laborer	68	"
	K	Fradestefano Henry	24	orderly	22	"
	L	Fradestefano Joseph	24	painter	37	
	M	Giglio Agrippina—†	24	packer	24	
	N	*Giglio Giuseppina—†	24	housewife	46	"
	O	*Giglio Mario	24	laborer	47	
	P	Deveau David L	26	retired	73	
	R	Deveau Emily—†	26	housewife	67	"
	S	*Teta Antonetta—†	26	"	35	44 Haynes
	T	Teta Stefano	26	laborer	42	44 "
	U	Caporrello Carmen	26	"	46	here
	V	*Ciani Annie—†	26	housewife	48	"
	W	*Ciani James	26	laborer	55	"
	X	Ciani Tillio	26	machinist	20	"
	Y	DeCicco Angelo	26	operator	50	
	Z	DeCicco Nicholas	26	laborer	38	
287						
	A	*Ciampa Angelo	28	retired	60	"
	B	Dascoli Anthony	28	foreman	30	Everett
	C	Dascoli Parmie—†	28	housewife	27	"
	D	*Maratta Jennie—†	28	"	48	here
	E	Maratta Pino	28	operator	33	"
	F	*Furtado Antonio	30	seaman	44	"
	G	*Pimental Mary—†	30	housekeeper	59	"

Page.	Letter.	Full Name.	Residence, Jan. 1, 1938.	Occupation.	Supposed Age.	Reported Residence, Jan. 1, 1937. Street and Number.

Bremen Street—Continued

	H	Montiero Anthony	30	steward	24	27 Havre
	K	Montiero George	30	busboy	21	27 "
	L	Montiero Louise—†	30	housewife	23	27 "
	M	*Ruliera Candido	30	oiler	47	151 Marion
	N	Ruliera Mary—†	30	housewife	39	151 "
	O	O'Neil Olive—†	32	"	36	here
	P	Bruno Jennie—†	32	"	21	"
	R	Bruno Vincent	32	manager	24	"
	S	*Gentile Maria—†	32	housewife	53	"
	T	Gentile Mildred—†	32	stitcher	20	
	U	Murphy Francis J	34	teamster	53	"
	V	Murphy Helen E—†	34	housewife	50	"
	W	*D'Errico Concetta—†	34	"	25	376 Sumner
	X	D'Errico Michael	34	laborer	24	376 "
	Y	Coleman John	34	teamster	61	here
	Z	Coleman Patrick	34	laborer	63	"
288						
	A	Cooper Catherine—†	34	housekeeper	65	"
	B	Cucia John	36	mason	59	"
	C	Antillio Albert	36	operator	24	"
	D	*Antillio Frederick	36	"	56	
	E	Antillio Joseph	36	cook	28	
	G	Antillio Raimondi	36	clerk	20	
	F	Antillio Ralph	36	"	21	
	H	*Profenna Emilio	36	tailor	51	
	K	Oliva Gaetano	38	retired	73	
	L	Oliva Rose—†	38	housewife	72	"
	M	*Anello Joseph	38	shoemaker	67	"
	N	*Anello Maria—†	38	housewife	50	"
	O	*D'Isola Maria G—†	38	housekeeper	38	"
	P	Laurano Gaetano	38	laborer	70	"
	R	Cardinale Joseph	54	waiter	45	
	S	*Cardinale Maria—†	54	housewife	65	"
	T	*Pescetti Nunci—†	56	"	56	
	U	Pescetti Rosario	56	laborer	54	"
	V	*Kennedy Mary W—†	56	housekeeper	57	58 London
	W	Woodford William	56	laborer	26	58 "
	Y	DellaRusso Arthur	58	clerk	25	here
	Z	DellaRusso Carlo	58	florist	62	"
289						
	A	DellaRusso James	58	clerk	21	

Page.	Letter.	Full Name.	Residence, Jan. 1, 1938.	Occupation.	Supposed Age.	Reported Residence, Jan. 1, 1937. Street and Number.

Bremen Street—Continued

Page.	Letter.	Full Name.	Residence, Jan. 1, 1938.	Occupation.	Supposed Age.	Reported Residence, Jan. 1, 1937. Street and Number.
	B	Palumbo Anthony	60	laborer	24	here
	C	*Palumbo Antonetta—†	60	housewife	43	“
	D	Palumbo Benedetta—†	60	stitcher	23	“
	F	*Palumbo Pasquale	60	laborer	51	
	E	Palumbo Raymond	60	“	21	
	G	*Pisano John	60	“	72	
	H	Sullivan John J	62	“	65	
	K	Sullivan Mary F—†	62	housewife	50	“
	L	Toomey John F	62	messenger	61	“
	M	Toomey Mary E—†	62	housewife	65	“
	N	Ford Alice G—†	62	operator	33	“
	O	Ford John J	62	laborer	47	
	P	Ford Theresa B—†	62	housewife	72	“
	R	*DelloRusso John	64	longshoreman	45	115 Everett
	S	Porcaro Agnes—†	64	at home	20	here
	T	Porcaro Emilio	64	barber	23	“
	U	Porcaro George	64	“	51	“
	V	*Porcaro Mary—†	64	housewife	46	“
	W	Porcaro Rose—†	64	packer	24	
	Y	*Grosso Mary—†	66	housewife	34	“
	Z	Grosso Saverio	66	laborer	40	
290						
	A	Gallagher Helen C—†	66	operator	29	
	B	Gallagher Mary A—†	66	finisher	59	
	C	Curran Catherine A—†	66	operator	45	“
	D	Daly Andrew A	66	manager	51	“
	E	Daly Francis W	66	shipper	44	
	F	McMullen George J	66	laborer	41	
	G	McMullen Marie J—†	66	housewife	40	“
	L	Montalto Joseph	82	mechanic	38	“
	M	*Montalto Josephine—†	82	housewife	31	“
	N	Rossi Concetta—†	82	“	38	
	O	Rossi Giuseppe	82	laborer	48	
	P	*Castanza Frank	82	retired	74	“
	R	D’Amico Angelina—†	84	housewife	28	43 Chelsea
	S	Conti Blanche—†	84	“	44	here
	T	Conti Carmello	84	laborer	44	“
	U	Balzano Adeline—†	84	housewife	32	“
	V	*Simione Jennie—†	86	“	57	
	W	Simione Nicholas	86	carpenter	66	“
	X	Ciampa James	86	laborer	27	

Page.	Letter.	FULL NAME.	Residence, Jan. 1, 1938.	Occupation.	Supposed Age.	Reported Residence, Jan. 1, 1937. Street and Number.

Bremen Street—Continued

	Y	Ciampa Rose O—†	86	housewife	24	here
	Z	Grieco Alice—†	86	clerk	25	146 Bremen
291						
	A	*Grieco Carmella—†	86	housewife	50	146 "
	C	DeAngelo Peter	88	engineer	32	here
	B	Ianniciello Pasquale	88	laborer	45	"
	D	DeFalco Anna—†	88	housewife	50	"
	E	*DeFalco Sabino	88	baker	54	
	F	Wilkins Warren	88	roofer	22	
	G	*Charone Stella—†	88	at home	65	
	H	*Iavola Josephine—†	88	"	72	
	K	Collins Mary J—†	90	housekeeper	65	"
	L	Jones Isabella—†	90	housewife	61	"
	M	Jones William F	90	foreman	62	
	N	Sammarco Carmelo	92	laborer	25	
	O	Sammarco Mary—†	92	housewife	25	"
	P	*DiPietro Elizabeth—†	92	"	58	414 Commerc'l
	R	DiPietro John	92	mechanic	24	414 "
	S	*Fabio Frank	92	retired	65	here
	T	*Sammarco Mary—†	92	housewife	70	"
	U	*Sammarco Vito	92	laborer	72	"

Chelsea Place

	V	Lamonica Clara—†	5	housewife	20	here
	W	Lamonica Filippo	5	laborer	24	"
	X	Maggio Josephine—†	5	housewife	32	"
	Y	Maggio Nicholas	5	laborer	34	
	Z	*Cuguliatta Rosario	5	"	56	
292						
	A	Dambrosio Ernest	6	"	21	276 Paris
	B	Dambrosio Mildred—†	6	housewife	20	276 "
	C	*DePremio Annie—†	6	"	48	Reading
	D	DePremio Anthony	6	retired	45	"
	E	DelGaudro Carmen	6	laborer	48	here
	F	Ferraro Joseph	6	"	34	"
	G	*Ferraro Margaret—†	6	housewife	30	"
	H	*Palcito Raffaelo	6	retired	62	"
	K	Gavin Frank J	7	clerk	43	13 Emmons
	L	Gavin Mary—†	7	housewife	29	6 "
	M	*Bonaccorso Anna—†	7	"	53	here

Chelsea Place—Continued

Page.	Letter.	Full Name.	Residence, Jan. 1, 1938.	Occupation.	Supposed Age.	Reported Residence, Jan. 1, 1937. Street and Number.
	N	Bonaccorso Anthony	7	retired	64	here
	O	Bonaccorso John	7	painter	23	"
	P	Bonaccorso Nancy—†	7	at home	29	"
	R	Bonaccorso Nunzio	7	attorney	27	"
	S	Barnes James	7	clerk	27	
	T	Barnes Parme—†	7	housewife	28	"
	U	Lezine Amelia—†	8	"	33	
	V	Lezine Edgar	8	chauffeur	35	"
	X	Severino Arthur	8	printer	28	121 Salem
	Y	Severino Concetta—†	8	housewife	25	121 "
	Z	*Genoves Camella—†	10	"	63	here
293						
	A	*Genoves Donata	10	laborer	62	
	B	Di Biasi Carl	10	operator	33	"
	C	Di Biasi Eleanor—†	10	housewife	32	"
	D	Piano Felix	10	operator	44	"
	E	Piano Mary—†	10	housewife	32	"

Chelsea Street

Page.	Letter.	Full Name.	Residence, Jan. 1, 1938.	Occupation.	Supposed Age.	Reported Residence, Jan. 1, 1937. Street and Number.
	N	Calsimitto Paul	5	shipper	23	64 Brooks
	O	Calsimitto Phyllis—†	5	housewife	23	148 Bayswater
	P	Presti Frank	5	operator	27	82 Brighton
	R	Presti Lena—†	5	housewife	24	82 "
	S	Lanzilli Albert	5	chauffeur	31	here
	T	Lanzilli Cornella—†	5	housewife	26	"
	U	*Grasso Anna—†	6	"	44	166 Putnam
	V	Grasso Michael	6	laborer	20	166 "
	W	Luongo Michael A	6	"	37	108 Chelsea
	X	*Opidee Joseph J	6	"	35	108 "
	Y	*Opidee Mary—†	6	housewife	33	108 "
294						
	B	*Bianchi Fidelia—†	7	"	44	here
	C	*Bianchi Michael	7	florist	56	"
	D	*Marino Charles	7	barber	46	"
	E	Marino Rose—†	7	housewife	39	"
	F	Capavella John	7	superintendent	30	"
	G	*Capavella Millie—†	7	housewife	29	"
	K	Spadoni Antonio	8	operator	52	
	L	*Spadoni Josephine—†	8	housewife	42	"
	M	*Apprignani Celeste—†	8	"	50	

Page.	Letter.	Full Name.	Residence, Jan. 1, 1938.	Occupation.	Supposed Age.	Reported Residence, Jan. 1, 1937. Street and Number.

Chelsea Street—Continued

	N	Apprignani Frank	8	laborer	60	here
	O	Indenarreli Jessie—†	8	operator	22	"
	P	Rapino Emanuela—†	9	houseworker	21	"
	R	Rapino Michelina—†	9	housewife	43	"
	S	Rapino Pasquale	9	undertaker	49	"
	T	Selvaggi Joseph	9	clerk	55	
	W	Altieri Adaline—†	10	housewife	33	"
	X	*Altieri Carlo	10	upholsterer	36	"
	Y	Cunningham Jeremiah J	10	laborer	45	
	Z	Cunningham Theresa—†	10	housewife	40	"
295						
	A	Gibbons Francis J	10	operator	42	"
	B	Gibbons George	10	clerk	40	"
	C	*Bonito Leah—†	11	housewife	47	"
	D	Bonito Ottone	11	operator	47	"
	E	*Cosentino Jennie—†	11	"	31	
	F	Draga Anthony	11	barber	48	
	G	Draga Mary—†	11	housewife	38	"
	H	Scionobra Pauline—†	11	operator	21	New York
	K	*Caliguire Angelo	11	tinsmith	51	here
	L	*Caliguire Elizabeth—†	11	housewife	39	"
	M	Caliguire Sadie—†	11	clerk	20	"
	N	D'Errico Anna—†	12	housewife	21	29 Princeton
	O	D'Errico Charles	12	laborer	22	29 "
	P	Chiano Domenic	12	"	59	203 Chelsea
	R	*Chaino Margaret—†	12	housewife	58	203 "
	S	Chiano Vittore	12	laborer	26	203 "
	T	*DeBonis Jennie—†	12	housewife	45	here
	U	*DeBonis Joseph	12	laborer	55	"
	V	DeBonis Rocco	12	clerk	21	"
	W	*DeBonis Vincent	12	painter	28	
	Y	Caggiano Louis	13	salesman	29	"
	Z	Guarini Evelyn—†	13	housewife	26	"
296						
	A	Guarini Peter	13	engineer	29	"
	B	*Principe Michael	13	operator	43	"
	C	*Principe Philomena—†	13	housewife	43	"
	D	Milano Peter	14	chauffeur	39	"
	E	Milano Phyllis—†	14	housewife	33	"
	F	Milano Antonetta—†	14	"	26	
	G	Milano Charles	14	laborer	49	

Page.	Letter.	Full Name.	Residence, Jan. 1, 1938.	Occupation.	Supposed Age.	Reported Residence, Jan. 1, 1937. Street and Number.

Chelsea Street—Continued

	H	Milano Daniel	14	chauffeur	29	here
	K	Milano Joseph	14	laborer	36	"
	L	Milano Patrick A	14	expressman	45	"
	M	DeFrancesco Anna—†	14	housewife	42	"
	N	DeFrancesco Anthony	14	painter	46	"
	O	*Fiore Filomena—†	15	housewife	60	257 Chelsea
	P	*Fiore Michael	15	retired	63	257 "
	R	*Hlabanis George	15	painter	37	here
	S	*Hlabanis Philomena—†	15	housewife	37	"
	T	*Gerollo Americo	15	laborer	22	"
	V	*Gerollo Celestina—†	15	housewife	48	"
	U	*Gerollo James	15	barber	58	
	W	*Caponigro Madeline—†	16	houseworker	45	"
	X	*Rossetti Florence—†	16	housewife	40	"
	Y	Rossetti Joseph	16	operator	47	"
	Z	Rossetti Maria—†	16	teacher	21	
297						
	A	Brignolo Josephine—†	16	housewife	37	"
	B	Brignolo Onnofrio	16	laborer	44	
	E	Nargi Rachael—†	18	housewife	34	"
	F	Aiello Helen—†	19	"	22	
	G	Aiello Leo	19	laborer	26	
	H	Trippi Josephine—†	19	housewife	45	"
	K	Trippi Salvatore	19	retired	47	
	L	DiMarzo Annetta—†	19	housewife	23	"
	M	DiMarzo Raymond	19	operator	27	"
	O	Speciale Ida—†	19	housewife	55	"
	N	Speciale James	19	laborer	20	
	R	Beninati Blanche—†	20	furrier	32	
	S	Beninati Frank	20	operator	32	
	T	Laurano Annie—†	20	housewife	48	"
	U	Laurano Anthony F	20	clerk	21	
	V	Laurano Catherine—†	20	housewife	74	"
	W	Laurano Frank	20	chauffeur	36	"
	X	Laurano Michael A	20	broker	54	
	Y	Laurano Michael A, jr	20	clerk	21	
	Z	Pisano Domenico	20	tailor	54	
298						
	A	*Pisano Pasqualina—†	20	housewife	44	"
	B	Laurano Emilio	20	chauffeur	30	"
	C	Laurano Florence—†	20	housewife	26	"

Page.	Letter.	Full Name.	Residence, Jan. 1, 1938.	Occupation.	Supposed Age.	Reported Residence, Jan. 1, 1937. Street and Number.

Chelsea Street—Continued

	D	Decoratio Frances—†	21	housewife	28	here
	E	Decoratio Rocco	21	barber	28	“
	F	Viglieroli Michael	21	cleaner	21	“
	G	*Viglieroli Thomas	21	retired	56	
	H	*Viglieroli Viola—†	21	housewife	60	“
	K	*Costa Louis	21	laborer	36	
	L	*Martello Lazzaro	21	“	70	
	M	*Martello Marie—†	21	housewife	65	“
	N	Martello Michael	21	laborer	23	
	P	Dotoli Ralph	22	“	38	
	R	*Cardillo Carmella—†	22	housewife	65	“
	S	Cardillo Domenic T	22	salesman	37	“
	T	Cardillo George	22	“	42	
	U	Cardillo Josephine—†	22	housewife	32	“
	V	Cardillo Michael	22	retired	75	
	W	Raphanella Joseph	22	chauffeur	34	“
	X	Raphanella Lillian—†	22	housewife	31	“
	Y	Picardi Carmino F	22	chauffeur	33	“
	Z	Picardi Emma M—†	22	housewife	29	“
299						
	A	Chiampa James	23	barber	30	
	B	Chiampa Margaret—†	23	housewife	25	“
	C	Pantano Camilla—†	23	stitcher	21	
	D	*Pantano Michelina—†	23	housewife	42	“
	E	Pantano Santo	23	laborer	49	
	F	*Cataldo Carmella—†	23	housewife	41	“
	G	*Cataldo Michael	23	expressman	44	“
	K	Calogaro Edith—†	24	operator	23	
	L	McDonald Rose—†	24	housewife	45	“
	M	McDonald Thomas	24	chauffeur	42	“
	N	Termini Charles	24	operator	20	
	O	Termini Louis	24	“	27	
	P	*Spampenato Carmella—†	24	housewife	41	“
	R	Spampenato Jennie—†	24	hairdresser	20	“
	S	Spampenato Joseph	24	salesman	21	“
	T	Spampenato Rosario	24	“	41	
	U	*Berardinelli Cesidio	25	pedler	66	
	V	Berardinelli Peter	25	clerk	36	
	W	*Berardinelli Rose—†	25	housewife	65	“
	X	Berardinelli Salvatore	25	laborer	23	
	Y	*Fiuma Josephine—†	25	housewife	46	“

Page.	Letter.	FULL NAME.	Residence, Jan. 1, 1938.	Occupation.	Supposed Age.	Reported Residence, Jan. 1, 1937. Street and Number.

Chelsea Street—Continued

	Z	*Fiuma Salvatore	25	storekeeper	58	here
300						
	A	DiMore Alphonso	25	carpenter	65	"
	B	*DiMore Lucy—†	25	housewife	55	"
	C	Ciampi Louis	25	gasman	30	
	D	Ciampi Susie—†	25	housewife	25	"
	F	*Tusa Dominic	26	carpenter	26	40 Chelsea
	G	Tusa Petrina—†	26	housewife	27	40 "
	H	DiBenedetto Inez—†	26	"	51	here
	K	DiBenedetto Sabina	26	barber	54	"
	L	*Cardosi Rose—†	26	at home	75	"
	M	DeVita Elvira—†	26	housewife	48	"
	N	DeVita Salvatore	26	laborer	46	"
	O	Falco Ralph	27	"	55	29 Chelsea
	P	*Perrotti Dominick	27	engineer	55	here
	R	Perrotti Giaconda—†	27	typist	20	"
	S	Perrotti Salvatore	27	laborer	22	"
	T	*Perrotti Vera—†	27	housewife	46	"
	W	Nicosia Grace—†	28	"	32	
	X	Nicosia Salvatore	28	salesman	39	"
	Y	*DeRosa Concetta—†	28	housewife	39	Italy
	Z	DeRosa Sebastian	28	laborer	38	142 Lexington
301						
	A	Campobasso Antonette—†	28	housewife	21	here
	B	Campobasso James	28	agent	29	"
	C	Ferrante Frank	28	operator	24	"
	D	Ferrante Giacomo	28	"	50	"
	E	O'Brien Patrick	29	retired	59	27 Chelsea
	F	White Fergus C	29	laborer	38	63 W Eagle
	G	McCormick Harold	29	painter	25	here
	H	McCormick Isabelle—†	29	housewife	55	"
	K	McCormick John	29	painter	35	"
	L	McCormick Lawrence	29	undertaker	28	"
	M	McCormick Lillian—†	29	housewife	21	"
	N	*Petrosino Josephine—†	29	operator	52	
	O	DiVita Anthony	29	"	43	
	P	DiVita Josephine—†	29	housewife	43	"
	R	Stefano Ethel—†	31	"	25	Maine
	S	Stefano Fred	31	supervisor	28	24 Bremen
	T	*Calafato Marion—†	31	housewife	51	here

Page.	Letter.	FULL NAME.	Residence, Jan. 1, 1938.	Occupation.	Supposed Age.	Reported Residence, Jan. 1, 1937. Street and Number.

Chelsea Street—Continued

	U	Calafato Michael	31	laborer	64	here
	V	Spinelli Frank G	31	operator	31	"
	W	Spinelli Pauline—†	31	housewife	30	"
	X	Cefalo Angeline—†	31	"	26	
	Y	Cefalo Saverio	31	operator	26	"
	Z	Marascia John	31	stitcher	20	24 Charter
302						
	A	Scoffi John	33	storekeeper	46	here
	B	Scoffi Louise—†	33	housewife	41	"
	C	Scoffi Salvatore	33	baker	23	"
	D	Calafato Eva—†	33	housewife	25	"
	E	Calafato Thomas	33	musician	29	"
	F	Garofalo Concetta—†	33	housewife	23	"
	G	Garofalo Dominic F	33	janitor	27	
	H	Scoffi Alphonse	33	laborer	25	
	K	*Scoffi Mary—†	33	housewife	24	"
	L	Royster Angeline—†	35	"	25	225 Lexington
	M	Royster Ernest E	35	clerk	25	225 "
	N	*Giampapa Charles	35	painter	41	here
	O	*Giampapa Constance—†	35	housewife	38	"
	P	*Tringale Antoinette—†	35	operator	28	"
	R	Romano Charles	35	laborer	23	"
	S	Bassilo Alexander	35	"	42	
	T	*Bassilo Rose—†	35	housewife	40	"
	U	DiGregio Alphonse	35	laborer	45	"
	V	Grosso Nicola	37	"	42	62 Gove
	W	Ruggiero Laura—†	37	housewife	28	here
	X	*Ruggiero Ralph	37	painter	38	"
	Y	Biancucci Mary—†	37	operator	27	1201 Bennington
	Z	*Lazzaro Antonio	37	baker	38	here
303						
	A	Lazzaro Theresa—†	37	housewife	29	"
	B	*Morano Catherine—†	37	"	52	
	C	Morano Joseph	37	clerk	30	
	D	Morano Michael	37	operator	24	"
	E	Morano Rocco	37	laborer	60	
	F	Morano Rose—†	37	saleswoman	21	"
	G	Morelli Giuseppe	39	laborer	48	
	H	Spataro Jennie—†	39	housewife	29	"
	K	Spataro Philip	39	broker	38	
	L	*Patti Catherine—†	39	housewife	23	"

Page.	Letter.	Full Name.	Residence, Jan. 1, 1938.	Occupation.	Supposed Age.	Reported Residence, Jan. 1, 1937. Street and Number.

Chelsea Street—Continued

Page.	Letter.	Full Name.	Residence, Jan. 1, 1938.	Occupation.	Supposed Age.	Reported Residence, Jan. 1, 1937. Street and Number.
	M	Patti Joseph	39	barber	25	here
	N	*Mergiotti Rose—†	39	housewife	62	"
	O	*Halforce Josephine—†	40	housekeeper	68	95 Princeton
	P	Ryan Anna—†	40	housewife	36	95 "
	R	Ryan Daniel	40	engineer	30	122 Hunt'n av
	S	*D'Amico Feruri	40	cook	54	here
	T	*D'Amico Peter	40	laborer	59	"
	U	Galante Silvio	40	bartender	48	"
	V	Femino Mary—†	40	stitcher	27	960 Saratoga
	W	*Femino Nancy—†	40	housewife	62	960 "
	X	*Femino Santo	40	laborer	65	960 "
	Y	Femino Stella—†	40	stitcher	24	960 '
	Z	Femino Theresa—†	40	"	31	960 '
304						
	A	Palladino Emily—†	41	housewife	25	130 Porter
	B	*Palladino John	41	retired	87	here
	C	Palladino Salvatore	41	exterminator	28	"
	D	*Prattola Antonio	41	operator	38	68 Webster
	E	Prattola Mary—†	41	housewife	34	68 "
	F	*Bonaffine Joseph	41	retired	80	here
	G	*Bonaffine Josephine—†	41	housewife	55	"
	H	*Morelli Anthony	41	laborer	62	"
	K	Ginensky Jacob H	42	salesman	50	"
	L	Ginensky Lena—†	42	housewife	50	"
	M	Kaplan Harold	42	salesman	24	"
	N	Femino Andrew	42	operator	39	
	O	Femino Margaret—†	42	housewife	36	"
	P	Tortolano Anna—†	42	dressmaker	29	"
	R	Tortolano Celia—†	42	"	20	"
	S	Tortolano Elivra—†	42	packer	25	"
	T	Tortolano Frederick	42	operator	22	"
	U	Tortolano Hilda—†	42	at home	22	
	V	Tortolano Mary—†	42	dressmaker	27	"
	W	*Cravotta Joseph	43	laborer	50	
	X	*Cravotta Sadie—†	43	housewife	40	"
	Y	Rigione Anna—†	43	"	33	
	Z	Rigione Dominic	43	dealer	45	
305						
	A	*Vitagliona Amelia—†	43	housewife	72	"
	B	*Vitagliona Paul	43	printer	65	"
	C	Paglieroni Josephine—†	43	housewife	42	57 Chelsea

Page.	Letter.	Full Name.	Residence, Jan. 1, 1938.	Occupation.	Supposed Age.	Reported Residence, Jan. 1, 1937. Street and Number.

Chelsea Street—Continued

	D	Paglieroni Julio	43	operator	41	57 Chelsea
	E	Fischer Florence—†	45	housewife	38	here
	F	Fischer William W	45	laborer	48	"
	G	Bruschette Anna—†	45	beautician	31	"
	H	*Bruschette Girolomo	45	retired	70	"
	K	Bruschette Josephine—†	45	stenographer	25	Springfield
	L	*Bruschette Mary—†	45	housewife	69	here
	M	Bruschette Andrew	45	machinist	28	"
	N	Bruschette Louise—†	45	housewife	28	"
	O	Amante Angelina—†	45	"	37	
	P	Amante Joseph	45	packer	38	"
	R	Maggio Antonio	46	cutter	28	
	S	Maggio Grace—†	46	housewife	23	"
	T	Modica Mario	46	operator	51	
	U	*Modica Mary—†	46	housewife	42	"
	V	D'Ambrosia Joaquin	46	barber	63	
	W	D'Ambrosia Maria—†	46	housewife	67	"
	X	*Porrovecchia John	47	retired	68	
	Y	*Porrovecchia Rose—†	47	housewife	63	"
	Z	*Simonelli Concetta—†	47	"	29	
306						
	A	Simonelli Joseph	47	tailor	34	179 Havre
	B	LaConte Nicholas	47	laborer	32	55 Maverick
	C	LaConte Rose—†	47	housewife	29	here
	D	Amoroso Angelo	47	retired	62	133 Everett
	E	Amoroso Angelo	47	baker	20	133 "
	F	*Amoroso Rose—†	47	housewife	45	133 "
	G	LaBella Dominic	48	laborer	30	88 Trenton
	H	LaBella Esther—†	48	housewife	29	400 Walk Hill
	K	Langone Florence M—†	48	"	38	here
	L	Langone James F	48	laborer	42	"
	M	Angelo Joseph	48	tailor	46	"
	N	Angelo Mary—†	48	housewife	42	"
	O	LaMonica Mildred—†	49	"	33	
	P	LaMonica Salvatore	49	painter	34	
	R	Mazzio Antonio	49	laborer	43	
	S	Mazzio Josephine—†	49	housewife	43	"
	T	*Carusella Antonette—†	49	"	40	
	U	*Carusella Pasquale	49	tailor	41	
	V	D'Ambrosio Ernest	49	shoemaker	58	"
	W	D'Ambrosio Filomena—†	49	operator	24	

Page.	Letter.	Full Name.	Residence, Jan. 1, 1938.	Occupation.	Supposed Age.	Reported Residence, Jan. 1, 1937. Street and Number.

Chelsea Street—Continued

Page.	Letter.	Full Name.	Residence, Jan. 1, 1938.	Occupation.	Supposed Age.	Reported Residence, Jan. 1, 1937. Street and Number.
	X	D'Ambrosio Maria—†	49	housewife	56	here
	Y	D'Ambrosio Rosaria—†	49	seamstress	23	"
	Z	*Sullivan James	50	longshoreman	47	"
307						
	A	*Sullivan Margaret—†	50	housewife	32	"
	C	Daboisio Emily—†	50	operator	20	"
	D	*Deboisio Mary—†	50	housewife	51	"
	E	Annunziata Frank	51	laborer	23	"
	F	Annunziata Santa—†	51	housewife	24	"
	G	*LaMonica Calogera—†	51	"	53	85 Paris
	H	LaMonica Rosario	51	laborer	20	85 "
	K	LaMonica Santo	51	"	58	85 "
	L	Cericola Joseph	51	waiter	25	here
	M	Cericola Stella—†	51	housewife	24	"
	N	*Maglio Carmella—†	51	"	74	"
	O	*LaVita Angelina—†	52	"	68	244 Havre
	P	*LaVita Pasquale	52	laborer	61	244 "
	R	*Gangi Carmella—†	52	housewife	37	here
	S	*Gangi Manuel	52	laborer	47	"
	T	Simione James	52	chauffeur	30	"
	U	Simone Minnie—†	52	housewife	32	"
	V	*Gentile Elvira—†	53	"	27	
	W	Gentile Francis	53	artist	33	
	X	*Gentile Domenic	53	retired	65	
	Y	Gentile Marshall	53	laborer	22	
	Z	Amoroso Archangelo	53	blacksmith	60	"
308						
	A	*Amoroso Jennie—†	53	housewife	47	"
	B	Festa Henry	53	operator	42	
	C	Festa Jennie—†	53	housewife	37	"
	D	Damiano Anthony	53	operator	32	
	E	Damiano Mary—†	53	housewife	27	"
	F	*Lampiani Josephine—†	53	housekeeper	60	"
	G	*Saia Maria—†	53	"	65	"
	H	Cutrone Marie—†	53	housewife	55	"
	K	Cutrone Orazio	53	storekeeper	60	"
	N	DiMargo Catherine—†	54	housewife	29	"
	O	DiMargo Romolo	54	operator	32	"
	P	Barrasso Americo	54	laborer	23	
	R	Barrasso Ida—†	54	tailoress	21	
	S	*Barrasso Julia—†	54	housewife	61	"

Page.	Letter.	Full Name.	Residence, Jan. 1, 1938.	Occupation.	Supposed Age.	Reported Residence, Jan. 1, 1937. Street and Number.

Chelsea Street—Continued

Page.	Letter.	Full Name.	Residence, Jan. 1, 1938.	Occupation.	Supposed Age.	Reported Residence, Jan. 1, 1937. Street and Number.
	T	*Pino Concetta—†	56	housewife	37	here
	U	Pino Stephen	56	salesman	44	"
	V	Tango Michael	58	painter	42	"
	W	Quattrocchi Rose—†	58	housewife	31	"
	X	*Macaluso Mary—†	58	"	63	
	Y	Tango Anna—†	58	"	28	
	Z	Tango James	58	chauffeur	29	"
309						
	A	Anzaldi Nancy—†	60	housewife	24	"
	B	*Anzaldi William	60	plumber	26	"
	C	Fiorino Emanuel	60	laborer	52	
	D	*Fiorino Mary—†	60	housewife	42	"
	E	Fiorino Salvatore	60	laborer	20	
	F	*Forgione Antonetta—†	60	housewife	32	"
	G	Forgione Salvatore	60	laborer	39	"
	H	LaCourt Peter	62	realtor	65	8 Edward
	K	LaMonica Joseph	64	janitor	27	here
	L	LaMonica Rose—†	64	housewife	23	"
	M	Paradiso Alexander	64	laborer	36	"
	N	*Paradiso Vincenza—†	64	housewife	30	"
	O	*Langini Michelina—†	64	"	61	"
	P	Langini Phillip	64	retired	61	"
	S	*Siciliano Carmella—†	66	housewife	39	"
	T	Siciliano Rocco	66	laborer	52	
	U	*Salvo Vita—†	66	housewife	35	"
	V	Salvo Vito	66	shoemaker	44	"
	W	*Colangelo Harry	68	janitor	41	
	X	*Colangelo Jennie—†	68	housewife	37	"
	Y	Leonardi Angelo	68	laborer	40	"
	Z	*Martello Mary—†	68	housewife	37	"
310						
	A	Martello Nicholas	68	operator	39	"
	B	*Paridiso Julia—†	68	housewife	64	"
	C	Paridiso Luigi	68	laborer	64	
	D	*Carbono Isabella—†	68	housewife	52	"
	E	*Carbono Michael	68	painter	48	
	F	Frasicca Frances—†	68	housewife	28	"
	G	Frasicca Mario	68	laborer	36	
	H	Romanelli Carmen	68	clerk	23	
	K	Romanelli Charles	68	musician	26	"
	L	Noviello Charles	68	tailor	49	

Page.	Letter.	FULL NAME.	Residence, Jan. 1, 1938.	Occupation.	Supposed Age.	Reported Residence, Jan. 1, 1937. Street and Number.

Chelsea Street—Continued

Page.	Letter.	FULL NAME.	Residence, Jan. 1, 1938.	Occupation.	Supposed Age.	Reported Residence, Jan. 1, 1937. Street and Number.
	M	Varallo Assunta—†	68	housewife	42	here
	N	Varallo Humbert	68	carver	45	"
	O	*Fuccillo Anthony	70	butcher	55	"
	P	Fuccillo Carmen	70	painter	22	
	R	Fuccillo Emma—†	70	stitcher	20	
	S	*Fuccillo Fannie—†	70	housewife	48	"
	T	DaVolio Mary—†	70	"	43	Chelsea
	U	DaVolio Michael	70	painter	45	"
	V	Gioia Carmela—†	70	operator	26	here
	W	Gioia Eugenia—†	70	at home	20	"
	X	*Gioia John	70	painter	56	"
	Y	Gioia John	70	operator	27	"
	Z	Gioia Joseph	70	painter	21	"
311						
	A	*Gioia Vincenza—†	70	housewife	49	"
	B	*Bellafatto Concetta—†	70	"	38	230 Maverick
	C	Bellafatto Louis	70	tailor	44	230 "
	D	Zambello Anna—†	72	housewife	22	here
	E	Zambello Frank	72	butcher	22	48 Porter
	F	Durante Theresa—†	72	dressmaker	42	here
	G	*Galendo Bennie	72	salesman	41	"
	H	Lauria Henry	72	laborer	26	218 Bremen
	K	Lauria Josephine—†	72	housewife	21	74 Chelsea
	L	Indorato Lena—†	74	"	43	here
	M	Indorato Mario	74	tailor	51	"
	N	Indorato Salvatore	74	"	26	"
	O	Wahlquist Eva—†	74	housewife	26	"
	P	*Wahlquist Nils	74	engineer	39	
	R	*Pittella Josephine—†	74	housewife	40	"
	S	*Pittella Stephen	74	laborer	50	"
	T	Volpe Peter	74	stenographer	22	303 Princeton
	U	Freada Dominic	76	painter	26	8 Chelsea pl
	V	Freada Helen—†	76	housewife	27	8 "
	W	Ciarcia Anthony	76	laborer	22	here
	X	*Ciarcia Antoinette—†	76	housewife	38	"
	Y	Ciarcia Paul	76	laborer	44	"
	Z	*Odice Vincenza—†	76	housekeeper	60	"
312						
	A	*Baldini Assunta—†	76	housewife	51	"
	B	*Baldini Attilio	76	laborer	54	
	C	Baldini Carl	76	machinist	23	"

Page.	Letter.	Full Name.	Residence, Jan. 1, 1938.	Occupation.	Supposed Age.	Reported Residence, Jan. 1, 1937. Street and Number.

Chelsea Street—Continued

Page.	Letter.	Full Name.	Residence, Jan. 1, 1938.	Occupation.	Supposed Age.	Reported Residence, Jan. 1, 1937. Street and Number.
	D	Baldini Girolamo	76	operator	24	here
	E	Donovan Charles A	78	policeman	29	"
	F	Donovan Louise V—†	78	housewife	29	"
	G	Glufling Frances C—†	78	operator	25	134 I
	H	Hurley Catherine V—†	78	stenographer	29	here
	K	Hurley James J	78	fireman	25	"
	L	Hurley Margaret M—†	78	at home	27	"
	M	Spada Bartholomew	78	student	20	"
	N	*Spada Catherine—†	78	housewife	45	"
	O	Spada Frank	78	laborer	50	
	P	Spada Sergio	78	woodturner	23	"
	R	*Scudiero Louisa—†	80	housewife	50	"
	S	*Scudiero Vincenzo	80	cutter	54	"
	T	*Mondovano Rose—†	80	housekeeper	49	158 Chelsea
	U	Faldetta Carmela—†	80	housewife	40	here
	V	Faldetta John	80	laborer	22	"
	W	Faldetta Salvatore	80	carpenter	45	"
	Y	Daddario Julia—†	82	housewife	43	"
	Z	Daddario Matthew	82	chauffeur	20	"
313						
	A	*Daddario Salvatore	82	"	48	
	B	Salerno Ernest	82	laborer	46	
	C	Salerno Mary—†	82	housewife	39	"
	E	Belusca Antoinetta—†	84	at home	65	here
	F	Gulino Angela	84	shoemaker	40	53 Bennington
	G	*Gulino Mary C—†	84	housewife	28	53 "
	K	*Grillo Joseph	86	retired	68	here
	L	Correale Anna—†	86	housewife	32	"
	M	Correale Samuel	86	laborer	35	"
	N	Schillaci Catherine—†	86	at home	22	
	O	Schillaci Stefana—†	86	housewife	49	"
	P	Schillaci Vincent	86	finisher	51	
	R	*LaGrasso Lena—†	86	housewife	36	"
	S	LaGrasso Vincenzo	86	baker	46	
	U	Aloi Catina—†	88	at home	24	
	V	Aloi Mary—†	88	housewife	50	"
	W	*Lamattina Josephine—†	88	"	31	
	X	Lamattina Louis	88	candymaker	38	"
	Y	*Lipizzi Grace—†	88	housewife	45	196 Paris
	Z	*Lipizzi Michael	88	laborer	44	196 "

Page.	Letter.	Full Name.	Residence, Jan. 1, 1938.	Occupation.	Supposed Age.	Reported Residence, Jan. 1, 1937. Street and Number.

314
Chelsea Street—Continued

314	A	Cinseruli Ella—†	90	housewife	34	here
	B	Cinseruli Vincent	90	bartender	41	"
	C	Basillio Anabilo	90	"	53	"
	D	Basillio Josephine—†	90	housewife	42	"
	E	*Nota Nancy—†	90	"	54	94 Chelsea
	F	*Nota Salvatore	90	salesman	54	94 "
	G	Nota Vincenza—†	90	operator	22	94 "
	H	Riccio Angela—†	92	housewife	29	here
	K	Riccio Carmen	92	laborer	42	"
	L	*Pistone Marie—†	92	housewife	48	"
	M	*Pistone Paul	92	laborer	58	"
	N	Pistone Tino	92	musician	21	Chelsea
	O	Brencola Angelina—†	92	packer	26	here
	P	Brencola Anna—†	92	"	22	"
	R	Brencola Anthony	92	laborer	25	"
	S	Brencola Leo	92	tailor	28	
	T	Brencola Lucy—†	92	housewife	54	"
	U	*Dampolo Fortunato	94	laborer	35	174 Bremen
	V	*Dampolo Mary—†	94	housewife	31	174 "
	W	Pace Dominick	94	laborer	44	82 London
	X	*Pace Mary—†	94	housewife	31	82 "
	Y	Fiorino Josephine—†	94	"	34	here
	Z	Fiorino Vincent	94	baker	39	"
315	A	*Luciano Harry	96	laborer	42	
	B	Luciano Margaret—†	96	housewife	32	"
	C	*Abbate Frances—†	96	"	36	
	D	*Abbate Louis	96	laborer	42	
	E	Smith Robert	96	salesman	26	"
	F	Smith Sarah—†	96	housewife	27	"
	G	*Curzi Biagio	98	laborer	43	47 Park
	H	*Curzi Santa—†	98	housewife	38	47 "
	K	Oliver Charles	98	salesman	45	156 Saratoga
	L	*Oliver Inez—†	98	housewife	29	156 "
	M	*Senna John	102	retired	74	here
	N	DeMarino Josephine—†	102	housewife	24	"
	O	DeMarino Phillip	102	clerk	25	"
	R	Capuzzo Inez—†	102	housewife	28	"
	S	*Capuzzo Ubaldo	102	painter	35	
	T	Ciccarello Angelina—†	102	housewife	38	"

Page.	Letter.	FULL NAME.	Residence, Jan. 1, 1938.	Occupation.	Supposed Age.	Reported Residence, Jan. 1, 1937. Street and Number.

Chelsea Street—Continued

	U	Ciccarello Frank	102	laborer	40	here
	V	*Malino Concetta—†	102	housewife	47	"
	W	*Malino Frank	102	laborer	53	"
	X	*Pisapia Grace—†	104	housewife	39	"
	Y	*Pisapia Louis	104	baker	43	
	Z	*Rodriguez Alida—†	104	housewife	30	"
316						
	A	*Rodriguez Joseph	104	engineer	34	"
	B	*Pompeo Angelo	104	laborer	42	76 Frankfort
	C	*Pompeo Anna—†	104	housewife	36	76 "
	D	*Bondanza Ciriaco	104	laborer	63	184 Cottage
	E	*Bondanza Phyllis—†	104	housewife	61	184 "
	F	*Bossi Orlando	104	clerk	25	154 Chelsea
	G	*Bossi Theresa—†	104	housewife	23	361 Princeton
	H	Sporza Antonio	104	laborer	32	here
	K	Sporza Elvira—†	104	housewife	26	"
	L	Minichiello Albert	106	seaman	24	"
	M	Minichiello Arthur	106	student	21	
	N	*Minichiello Emelia—†	106	housewife	52	"
	O	Minichiello Generoso	106	laborer	57	
	P	Celeste Joseph	106	"	27	
	R	Celeste Julia—†	106	housewife	24	"
	S	Giusti Anna—†	106	"	27	
	T	*Giusti Dominick	106	laborer	37	
	U	*Ciummei Lila—†	106	housewife	30	"
	V	*Ciummei Tito	106	laborer	41	
	W	*DiFrancesco Alfred	106	baker	38	
	X	*DiFrancesco Diana—†	106	housewife	35	"
	Y	Gambardella Theresa—†	106	"	24	
	Z	Gambardella Vincent	106	operator	25	
317						
	A	Gallo Marie—†	108	housewife	22	266 Bremen
	B	Gallo Salvatore	108	laborer	24	1 Unity
	C	Memolo John	108	"	24	here
	D	DiPietro Catherine—†	108	housewife	46	"
	E	DiPietro Ralph	108	longshoreman	38	"
	F	*Balba Agrippina—†	108	housewife	55	"
	G	*Balba Josephine—†	108	operator	29	"
	H	Barone Christopher	108	laborer	37	185 Gladstone
	K	Barone Mary—†	108	housewife	32	185 "
	L	Loduca Alphonse	108	laborer	27	2 Paris ct

Page.	Letter.	Full Name.	Residence, Jan. 1, 1938.	Occupation.	Supposed Age.	Reported Residence, Jan. 1, 1937. Street and Number.

Chelsea Street—Continued

	M	Loduca Lillian—†	108	housewife	32	Malden
	N	Russo Ciriaco	110	tailor	66	here
	O	*Russo Rachael—†	110	housewife	53	"
	P	Ciampa Anthony	110	machinist	39	"
	R	Ciampa Marion—†	110	housewife	40	"
	S	Latorraca Dominick	110	janitor	39	
	T	*Latorraca Henrietta—†	110	housewife	40	"
	W	*Mason Fannie—†	122	"	68	
	X	*Mason Matthew	122	retired	70	
	Y	Nicoletti Alice—†	122	housewife	31	"
	Z	Nicoletti Salvatore	122	laborer	33	
318						
	C	*Zagorsky Isaac	124	glazier	59	
	B	*Zagorsky Rebecca—†	124	housewife	59	"
	D	Puopolo Angelo	124	laborer	58	"
	E	*Puopolo Carmela—†	124	housewife	57	"
	F	*Puopolo Carmeno	124	operator	24	"
	G	*Vostro Dominick	126	retired	69	
	H	LaSala Carmello	126	barber	38	
	K	LaSala Louise—†	126	housewife	34	"
	L	Manganaro Anna—†	126	bookbinder	29	"
	M	Orlando Albert	126	operator	25	"
	N	*Orlando Carmelo	126	laborer	59	
	O	Orlando John	126	printer	28	
	P	*Orlando Josephine—†	126	housewife	52	"
	S	*Tramontana Mary—†	128	"	43	
	T	Tramontana Vincenzo	128	laborer	44	
	V	*Smith Isaac	130	glazier	80	
	W	*Smith Sarah—†	130	housewife	76	"
	X	Martinelli Henry	130	clerk	42	
	Y	*Martinelli Margaret—†	130	housewife	40	"
	Z	*Gioiosa Antonio	130	painter	53	
319						
	A	Gioiosa Daniel	130	clerk	25	
	B	*Gioiosa Mary—†	130	housewife	50	"
	C	Belmont Carmen	132	laborer	26	
	D	Belmont Patricia—†	132	housewife	25	"
	E	Mattivello Joseph	132	operator	30	"
	F	Mattivello Louis	132	dealer	20	
	G	Mattivello Martin	132	cabinetmaker	22	"
	H	*Mattivello Petrina—†	132	housewife	53	"

Page.	Letter.	Full Name.	Residence, Jan. 1, 1938.	Occupation.	Supposed Age.	Reported Residence, Jan. 1, 1937. Street and Number.

Chelsea Street—Continued

Page.	Letter.	Full Name.	Residence, Jan. 1, 1938.	Occupation.	Supposed Age.	Reported Residence, Jan. 1, 1937. Street and Number.
	K	Mattivello Russell	132	salesman	33	here
	L	*Mattivello Salvatore	132	laborer	55	"
	M	Mattivello Salvatore	132	cabinetmaker	25	"
	N	*Barresi Joseph	132	shoemaker	40	"
	O	*Barresi Sarah—†	132	housewife	38	"
	P	*Tarzia Mary—†	134	"	38	"
	R	Tarzia Pasquale	134	laborer	39	
	S	Carso Croce	134	"	34	
	T	Carso Gilorama—†	134	packer	24	
	U	Carco John	134	butcher	21	
	V	*Carco Joseph	134	laborer	65	
	W	*Carco Josephine—†	134	housewife	59	"
	X	Carco Paul	134	laborer	22	
	Y	*Genzale Carmella—†	134	housewife	48	"
	Z	Genzale Rose—†	134	stitcher	20	
320						
	B	*Martino Constantina—†	136	housewife	40	"
	C	*Martino Saverio	136	carpenter	48	"
	E	Matarazzo Agostino	138	chauffeur	28	"
	F	Matarazzo Antonetta—†	138	operator	26	"
	G	*Matarazzo Margaret—†	138	housewife	59	"
	H	Matarazzo Orlando	138	operator	22	
	K	*Matarazzo Ralph	138	retired	65	
	L	Matarazzo Ralph, jr	138	clerk	20	"
	M	Farina Joseph	138	tailor	35	
	N	*Farina Josephine—†	138	housewife	44	"
	O	DelloRusso Carmen	138	laborer	43	
	P	*DelloRusso Matilda—†	138	housewife	43	"
	S	Iacovino Frank	140	laborer	38	
	T	*Iacovino Josephine—†	140	housewife	32	"
	U	*Orlandino Amelia—†	140	"	49	216 Bremen
	V	Orlandino Concetta—†	140	operator	21	here
	W	*Orlandino Edmund	140	laborer	27	"
	X	*Orlandino Joseph	140	barber	49	216 Bremen
	Y	Orlandino Theodore	140	laborer	20	here
321						
	A	Matarazzo Angelo	142	operator	24	"
	B	Matarazzo James	142	inkmaker	52	"
	C	Matarazzo Joseph	142	operator	27	"
	D	*Matarazzo Mary—†	142	housewife	52	"
	E	Matarazzo Mary—†	142	stenographer	25	"

Page.	Letter.	Full Name.	Residence, Jan. 1, 1938.	Occupation.	Supposed Age.	Reported Residence, Jan. 1, 1937. Street and Number.

Chelsea Street—Continued

	F	*Matarazzo Theresa—†	142	housewife	83	here
	G	*Marino Mary—†	142	"	41	"
	H	*Marino Nicholas	142	laborer	46	"
	K	Marino Theresa—†	142	stitcher	21	
	L	*Cannella Charles	144	operator	25	"
	M	Cannella Domenica—†	144	housewife	23	"
	N	Martori Marie—†	144	"	40	
	O	Martori Vincenzo	144	pressman	51	"
	P	Pasciscia Antonio	144	machinist	20	"
	R	Pasciscia Joseph	144	laborer	50	
	S	Pasciscia Josephine—†	144	housewife	43	"
	T	Pasciscia Mary—†	144	tailoress	22	
	V	Gioiosa Margaret—†	152	housewife	21	"
	W	Gioiosa Michael	152	laborer	23	
	X	*Esposito Frances—†	152	housewife	53	"
	Y	*Esposito Frank	152	laborer	54	
	Z	*Esposito Mary—†	152	housewife	27	"
322						
	A	Esposito William	152	plumber	27	"
	C	Nappi John	154	laborer	52	
	D	*Nappi Pauline—†	154	housewife	52	"
	F	Bossi Anna—†	154	operator	20	"
	G	*Bossi Antonetta—†	154	housewife	52	"
	H	Bossi Frank	154	pedler	52	
	L	*Manganello Concetta—†	156	housewife	39	"
	M	Manganello George	156	laborer	48	
	N	Vozella John	156	"	45	
	O	Vozella Josephine—†	156	housewife	42	"
	P	Cresta Genereno	158	laborer	20	"
	R	*Cresta James	158	"	56	3 Wash'n av
	S	*Cresta Mary—†	158	housewife	43	3 "
	T	Carnevale Salvatore	158	plasterer	25	Rhode Island
	U	*DiDonato Alphonse	158	laborer	55	here
	V	DiDonato Eleanor—†	158	at home	21	"
	W	DiDonato Florence—†	158	cigarmaker	24	"
	X	LaConte Viola—†	158	at home	28	"
	Y	Pericolo Joseph	158	florist	43	200 Marion
	Z	*Pericolo Philomena—†	158	housewife	44	here
323						
	B	*Gagliardi Rose—†	162	"	40	"
	C	Gagliardi Sabino	162	laborer	40	499 Sumner

Page.	Letter.	Full Name.	Residence, Jan. 1, 1938.	Occupation.	Supposed Age.	Reported Residence, Jan. 1, 1937. Street and Number.

Chelsea Street—Continued

	D	Dineen Arthur	164	operator	23	Needham
	E	Dineen Delphine—†	164	housewife	25	"
	F	Scopa Carmen	164	laborer	40	here
	G	Scopa Laura—†	164	housewife	43	"
	H	Scopa John	164	foreman	38	"
	K	Scopa Lucy—†	164	housewife	33	"
	L	*Pagliarulo Marie—†	164	"	51	
	M	Pagliarulo Paul	164	laborer	50	"
	N	*Falzarano Angelo	164A	butcher	32	67 Burrell
	O	Falzarano Julia—†	164A	housewife	27	67 "
	P	Lucca Leo	164A	cabinetmaker	34	here
	R	Lucca Louise—†	164A	housewife	34	"
	S	Scopa Elizabeth—†	164A	"	36	"
	T	Scopa Frances—†	164A	"	70	
	U	Scopa Ralph	164A	mechanic	36	"
	Y	*Caggiano Amelia—†	166	housewife	45	"
	W	*Caggiano Angelo	166	chauffeur	46	"
	X	Caggiano Antonio	166	laborer	44	
	Z	Caggiano Samuel	166	"	23	
324						
	A	Dampolo Joseph	166	upholsterer	32	"
	B	Dampolo Mary—†	166	housewife	29	"
	C	*Comperchio Jennie—†	166A	"	35	
	D	Comperchio Vito	166A	machinist	36	"
	E	Russo Phillip	166A	laborer	54	
	F	*Russo Theresa—†	166A	housewife	38	"
	G	Buonopane Joseph	166A	laborer	43	
	H	Buonopane Margaret—†	166A	housewife	30	"
	K	DiStefano Angelo	168	storekeeper	47	160 Chelsea
	L	*DiStefano Mary—†	168	housewife	35	160 "
	M	Alberelli Arturo	168	tailor	58	here
	N	*Alberelli Jennie—†	168	housewife	52	"
	O	Celata Bernard	168	electrician	38	"
	P	Celata Josephine—†	168	housewife	32	"
	R	*Piana Antonio	168	cheesemaker	50	"
	S	*Piana Emma—†	168	housewife	50	"
	V	Spolsino Jennie—†	170	"	40	
	W	Spolsino Michael	170	laborer	44	
	X	*Mazza Angelina—†	170	housewife	34	"
	Y	Mazza Joseph	170	painter	42	
	Z	*Mazza Peter	170	retired	71	

Page.	Letter.	Full Name.	Residence, Jan. 1, 1938.	Occupation.	Supposed Age.	Reported Residence, Jan. 1, 1937. Street and Number.
325		**Chelsea Street**—Continued				
	A	*Mazza Rose—†	170	housewife	65	here
	B	Sponpinato Anna—†	174	"	25	154 Chelsea
	C	*Sponpinato Joseph	174	laborer	29	154 "
	D	Drago Charles	174	tailor	60	here
	E	Drago Charles J, jr	174	"	20	"
	F	Drago Josephine—†	174	housewife	51	"
	G	*Privitero Florence—†	174	"	61	
	H	*Privitero Joseph	174	baker	61	
	K	*Privitero Josephine—†	174	operator	20	
	L	*Cataldo Carlo	176	storekeeper	47	"
	M	Cataldo Louise—†	176	housewife	34	"
	N	Rapino Jerry	176	machinist	55	"
	O	Rapino Margaret—†	176	housewife	40	"
	P	Geraci Charles	176	carpenter	45	"
	R	*Geraci Columbia—†	176	housewife	47	"
	S	DeFronzo Joseph	180	tailor	60	
	T	DeFronzo Sarah—†	180	housewife	59	"
	U	*Bruno Alphonse	180	operator	26	
	V	*Bruno Gabriel	180	chauffeur	48	"
	W	*Bruno Jennie—†	180	operator	28	
	X	*Bruno Mary—†	180	housewife	48	"
	Y	Catarozolo Angelina—†	180	"	45	
	Z	Catarozolo Felix	180	laborer	49	
326						
	A	Catarozolo Florence—†	180	seamstress	21	"
	B	*DiStefano Charles	182	laborer	23	62 Brooks
	C	DiStefano Mary—†	182	housewife	21	Medford
	D	Petitto Rocco	182	laborer	42	292 Chelsea
	E	*Petitto Rose—†	182	housewife	38	292 "
	F	Lorina Anthony	182	barber	31	here
	G	Lorina Josephine—†	182	housewife	30	"
	H	*Celeste Anna—†	184	"	46	221 Marion
	K	Celeste Charles	184	clerk	25	221 "
	L	Paterano Angelo	184	laborer	37	255 "
	M	Paterano Anna—†	184	housewife	28	255 "
	N	Mari Dominick	184	carpenter	59	here
	O	Mari Eugenia—†	184	housewife	54	"
	P	Bodkins Morris H	186	electrician	28	"
	R	Bodkins Pauline—†	186	housewife	25	"
	S	Guerriero Christopher	186	operator	45	

Page.	Letter.	Full Name.	Residence, Jan. 1, 1938.	Occupation.	Supposed Age.	Reported Residence, Jan. 1, 1937. Street and Number.

Chelsea Street—Continued

Page.	Letter.	Full Name.	Residence, Jan. 1, 1938.	Occupation.	Supposed Age.	Reported Residence, Jan. 1, 1937. Street and Number.
	T	Guerriero Florence—†	186	housewife	38	here
	U	Burke Grace—†	186	"	37	"
	V	Burke John P	186	shipper	38	"
	W	Stasio Mary—†	186	at home	66	"
	Y	Santarpio Emily—†	188A	housewife	30	40 Gladstone
	Z	Santarpio Frank	188A	garageman	21	40 "
327						
	A	*Santarpio Incoronata—†	188A	housewife	59	40 "
	B	Santarpio Sandrina—†	188A	clerk	25	40 "
	C	Cuperagio James	188A	barber	50	here
	D	Guerra Frances—†	188A	tailoress	25	"
	E	*Virgino Filomena—†	188A	housewife	48	"
	F	Virgino Leo	188A	laborer	48	"

Drake Place

Page.	Letter.	Full Name.	Residence, Jan. 1, 1938.	Occupation.	Supposed Age.	Reported Residence, Jan. 1, 1937. Street and Number.
	G	*Addario Antonetta—†	1	housewife	57	here
	H	Addario Nicholas	1	laborer	60	"
	K	Drago Anna—†	1	housewife	20	199 Marion
	L	Drago William	1	cutter	20	199 "
	M	*Deraedt Edmund	1	operator	30	here
	N	Deraedt Rose—†	1	housewife	24	"
	O	*Jardin Julia—†	1	"	37	"
	P	*Jardin Julius	1	operator	38	
	R	*Galati Catherine—†	1	housewife	53	"
	S	Galati Joseph	1	laborer	47	
	T	*Lagroppra Rocco	1	"	49	
	V	*Lopelato Adeline—†	2	housewife	52	"
	U	*Lopelato Anthony	2	retired	78	
	W	*Lopelato Sebastian	2	laborer	56	
	X	Lopelato Anthony	2	salesman	25	"
	Y	Lopelato Manuel	2	laborer	21	
	Z	Mirabella Amelio	2	"	36	
328						
	A	Mirabella Joseph	2	seaman	33	
	B	Morelli Antonetta—†	3	stenographer	22	"
	C	Morelli Guy	3	laborer	28	"
	D	Morelli Michael	3	machinist	24	"
	E	Morelli Orozio	3	laborer	60	
	F	Morelli Palmina—†	3	operator	26	
	G	Avola Charles	4	laborer	58	

Page.	Letter.	Full Name.	Residence, Jan. 1, 1938.	Occupation.	Supposed Age.	Reported Residence, Jan. 1, 1937. Street and Number.
		Drake Place—Continued				
	H	*Avola Rose—†	4	housewife	41	here
	K	*Albanese Angelina—†	4	"	41	"
	L	Albanese Severino	4	laborer	43	"
	M	Ricci Anthony	5	retired	30	
	N	Ricci Mary—†	5	housewife	26	"
	O	*Ricci Antonetta—†	5	"	29	
	P	Ricci Ralph	5	engraver	39	"
	R	Barletta Ferdinands	5	laborer	37	
	S	Barletta Rose—†	6	housewife	31	"
	T	Cravotta Giuseppe	6	laborer	49	
	U	*Cravotta Mary—†	6	housewife	37	"
	V	*Ingala Filippa—†	7	housekeeper	69	"
	W	DiRuose Dominica—†	7	housewife	42	"
	X	DiRuose Sylvester	7	printer	42	"
	Y	Antonucci Angelo	8	laborer	42	171 Trenton
	Z	*Antonucci Gaetana—†	8	housewife	38	Italy
329						
	A	*Grasso Emilio	8	expressman	45	here
	B	*Grasso Febronia—†	8	housewife	48	"
		Elbow Street				
	C	*Salamone Lawrence	2	retired	74	here
	D	*Salamone Marie—†	2	housewife	70	"
	E	Apicco Angelina—†	2	operator	44	"
	F	Apicco James	2	"	42	
	G	Apicco Michael	2	"	22	
	H	*Giannusa Concetta—†	2	housewife	49	"
	K	*Giannusa Vincent	2	laborer	49	"
	L	Joyce Annie—†	4	housewife	67	18 London
	M	Joyce Jeffrey	4	carpenter	69	18 "
	N	Coppola Salvatore	4	cook	44	here
	O	*Poccio Enrico	4	laborer	42	"
	P	*Poccio Sebastiana—†	4	housewife	41	"
		Emmons Street				
	R	*D'Agostino Anthony	1	tailor	45	here
	S	D'Agostino Virginia—†	1	housewife	36	"
	T	Passananti Carmine	1	merchant	49	"
	U	Imparato Louis	3	operator	28	"

Page.	Letter.	Full Name.	Residence, Jan. 1, 1938.	Occupation.	Supposed Age.	Reported Residence, Jan. 1, 1937. Street and Number.

Emmons Street—Continued

	V	Imparato Marguerite—†	3	housewife	30	here
	W	Passannanti Ralph	3	retired	71	"
	X	*Deveau Beatrice—†	5	housewife	38	"
	Y	*Deveau Henry	5	carpenter	42	"
	Z	Lacona Florence—†	7	housewife	27	"
330						
	A	Lacona James	7	merchant	29	"
	B	Bucci Frank B	8	retired	71	
	C	*Bucci Rose—†	8	housewife	74	"
	D	*Bartolo Antonetta—†	8	"	30	
	E	Bartolo Charles	8	chauffeur	30	"
	F	Sgroi John	8	laborer	30	
	G	Sgroi Rose—†	8	operator	29	"
	H	Bucci Anna—†	8	housewife	51	"
	K	Bucci James	8	laborer	48	
	L	*Graziano Nicholas	9	"	60	
	M	*Callabrese Adeline—†	9	at home	76	
	N	*Vozzelle Mary—†	10	housewife	32	"
	O	Vozzelle Ralph	10	printer	32	
	P	Cafarelli Mary—†	10	housewife	26	"
	R	Cafarelli Romeo	10	printer	30	
	S	DeFranzo Michael	10	collector	36	"
	T	DeFranzo Isabel—†	10	housewife	34	"
	U	Messina Josephine—†	10	at home	25	"
	V	*Messina Lucy—†	10	housewife	45	"
	W	Messina Nicholas	10	laborer	48	"
	X	Marcella Domenic	11	seaman	27	"
	Y	*Marcella Joseph	11	laborer	64	
	Z	Famiglietti Joseph	11	"	45	
331						
	A	Famiglietti Joseph	11		22	
	B	Morelli Anthony	11	"	40	"
	C	*Parziale Carmino	12	clerk	34	
	D	Marullo Elvira—†	12	housewife	29	"
	E	Marullo Michael	12	baker	34	
	F	*Maggio Andrew	12	laborer	39	
	G	*Maggio Josephine—†	12	housewife	75	"
	H	Domenico Amelio	12	teacher	40	
	K	Domenico Rose—†	12	housewife	30	"
	L	*Luizza Frances—†	12	"	35	
	M	*Luizza Leonardo	12	laborer	43	

Page.	Letter.	Full Name.	Residence, Jan. 1, 1938.	Occupation.	Supposed Age.	Reported Residence, Jan. 1, 1937. Street and Number.
		Emmons Street—Continued				
	N	*Amari Peter	12	operator	44	here
	O	*Amari Rose—†	12	housewife	34	"
	P	*Vanalli Nina—†	12	at home	75	"
	R	*Rubino Joseph	12	laborer	44	
	S	Rubino Josephine—†	12	housewife	33	"
		Gove Street				
	V	*Carrillo Domenico	11	laborer	60	here
	W	*Carrillo Veneranda—†	11	housewife	45	"
	Y	Giardina Angelo	11	chauffeur	22	191 Porter
	Z	Giardina Frances—†	11	packer	23	191 "
332						
	A	Gaspie John, jr	21	seaman	20	Worcester
	B	Gaspie Ruth—†	21	housewife	24	"
	C	McCormack Archibald	21	laborer	29	44 Terrace
	D	McCormack Lillian—†	21	housewife	24	44 "
	E	Coppney Charles	25	laborer	25	here
	F	Coppney Jennie—†	25	housewife	25	"
	G	DeRocco Mary—†	25	"	34	"
	H	DeRocco Peter	25	carpenter	39	"
	K	Colombo Frederick	25	laborer	55	
	L	*Colombo Rose—†	25	housewife	55	"
	N	*DiDonato Carmella—†	36	"	51	
	O	DiDonato Felix	36	operator	23	
	P	*DiDonato Joseph	36	painter	51	
	R	DiDonato Louis	36	woodcarver	25	"
	S	DiDonato Ralph	36	painter	21	
	T	Caliendo Carlo	36	barber	49	
	U	Caliendo Felix	36	glassblower	22	"
	V	*Caliendo Maria—†	36	housewife	47	"
	W	*Uccello Salvatore	36	laborer	40	
	X	*Uccello Theresa—†	36	housewife	30	"
	Y	Cammarata Calogero	38	laborer	52	
	Z	*Cammarata Frances—†	38	housewife	52	"
333						
	A	*Bellino Antonetta—†	38	"	42	
	B	*Bellino Paul	38	laborer	63	
	C	Bellino Salvatore	38	clerk	23	
	D	*Alba Agnes—†	38	housewife	26	"
	E	Alba James	38	laborer	32	

Page.	Letter.	Full Name.	Residence, Jan. 1, 1938.	Occupation.	Supposed Age.	Reported Residence, Jan. 1, 1937. Street and Number.

Gove Street—Continued

Page.	Letter.	Full Name.	Residence, Jan. 1, 1938.	Occupation.	Supposed Age.	Reported Residence, Jan. 1, 1937. Street and Number.
	F	Capobianco Anthony	40	chauffeur	30	here
	G	Capobianco Josephine—†	40	housewife	25	"
	H	*Capobianco Jessie—†	40	"	54	"
	H[1]	Capobianco Pasquale	40	laborer	56	
	K	Simonelli Jessie—†	40	housewife	26	"
	L	Simonelli Salvatore	40	laborer	27	"
	M	Correalle Alphonse	42	"	44	"
	N	*Correalle Concetta—†	42	housewife	47	"
	O	*DeLuca John	42	retired	73	
	P	DeLuca Michael	42	laborer	33	
	R	Bevere Nicholas	42	"	24	
	S	Geralomo Josephine—†	42	housewife	27	"
	T	*Geralomo Mary—†	42	"	64	
	U	Geralomo Patrick	42	chauffeur	31	"
	V	Petrucci Florindo	43	carpenter	46	"
	W	*Fuccillo Annie—†	43	housewife	40	"
	X	Fuccillo Massimino	43	laborer	44	
	Y	D'Apice Carmine	43	mechanic	31	"
	Z	D'Apice Edith—†	43	housewife	29	"
334						
	A	*Frieni Mary—†	44	"	43	
	B	Frieni Stephen	44	laborer	47	
	C	Collura Grace—†	44	housewife	32	"
	D	*Collura Rosario	44	retired	62	
	E	Collura Vincent	44	printer	32	"
	F	Ventre Mary—†	44	housewife	29	"
	G	Ventre Rocco	44	laborer	34	
	H	*Maffeo Celia—†	59	housewife	76	"
	K	*Maffeo Pasquale	59	retired	78	"
	L	*Maffeo Alphonso	59	painter	36	"
	M	*Maffeo Mary—†	59	housewife	29	"
	N	Mascuzza Josephine—†	59	at home	25	"
	O	*Jacinto Andriana—†	61	housewife	59	59 Chelsea
	P	*Jacinto Manuel	61	seaman	45	59 "
	R	Spinazzola Mary—†	61	housewife	32	here
	S	Spinazzola Pasquale	61	barber	32	"
	T	Salamone Angelo	61	laborer	45	"
	U	Salamone Vincenza—†	61	housewife	45	"
	V	Rizza Angelina—†	63	"	60	Reading
	W	*Rizza Salvatore	63	laborer	61	"
	Y	Salamone Louis	63	operator	38	Revere

Page.	Letter.	Full Name.	Residence, Jan. 1, 1938.	Occupation.	Supposed Age.	Reported Residence, Jan. 1, 1937. Street and Number.
		Gove Street—Continued				
	z	*Salamone Mary—†	63	housewife	29	here
335						
	A	*Martino Anthony	65	laborer	45	
	B	*Gimilaro Alice—†	65	housewife	36	"
	C	*Gimilaro Peter	65	laborer	47	
	D	*Meoli Pasquale	65	retired	79	
	E	Morelli Annie—†	65	housewife	32	"
	F	Morelli Joseph	65	laborer	38	
		Henry Street				
	H	McGuire James	10	laborer	23	here
	K	McGuire Jennie—†	10	housewife	22	"
	L	*Carabello Agrippino	10	baker	57	"
	M	Carabello Concetta—†	10	stitcher	21	
	N	*Carabello Louise—†	10	housewife	50	"
	O	Carabello Nancy—†	10	operator	24	
	P	*Sennato Concetta—†	10	housewife	41	"
	R	Sennato Paul	10	painter	43	
	S	*Vella Fanny—†	10	housewife	24	"
	T	Vella Salvatore	10	laborer	31	
	U	Bergh Charles	11	seaman	41	"
	V	Brysen Richard	11	"	23	S America
	W	Carlson Hjalmar	11	"	45	here
	X	Clausen Axel	11	"	35	82 Everton
	Y	*Derane John	11	clerk	26	18 Milford
	Z	*Egel Victor	11	seaman	24	here
336						
	A	Franklin Edward D	11	"	26	Maryland
	B	*Frederickson Edwin	11	carpenter	39	Cuba
	C	*Hansen Chris	11	seaman	42	Georgia
	D	*Johansön Axel	11	"	43	here
	E	*Jorgensen Asmond	11	"	25	"
	F	*Karlson John	11		43	England
	G	*Larson Oscar	11	"	55	here
	H	Lindberg Anna—†	11	housewife	46	"
	K	Lindberg Walter	11	clergyman	60	"
	L	Nielsen Nels	11	seaman	30	"
	M	*Olamson Oswald H	11	"	40	Everett
	N	Ottowson Carl	11	"	40	here
	O	*Reilecke Hans	11	"	35	"

Page.	Letter.	Full Name.	Residence, Jan. 1, 1938.	Occupation.	Supposed Age.	Reported Residence, Jan. 1, 1937. Street and Number.

Henry Street—Continued

	P	*Rosenvinde Peter M	11	seaman	48	here
	R	Shawno Haakon	11	"	28	New York
	S	Johnson Nils	12	laborer	40	here
	T	Johnson Victoria—†	12	housewife	29	"
	U	*Viola Anthony	12	operator	38	"
	V	*Viola Constanza—†	12	housewife	63	"
	W	Viola Joseph	12	laborer	22	
	X	Zelandi Ralph J	12	printer	28	
	Y	*Zelandi Virginia—†	12	housewife	57	"
	Z	Martino Gerolimo	12	operator	25	"
337						
	A	Martino Susan—†	12	housewife	23	"
	B	Petitto Joseph	16	laborer	40	
	C	Petitto Mary—†	16	housewife	36	"
	D	DiGiorgio Christina—†	16	"	30	
	E	DiGiorgio Leonard	16	laborer	35	"
	F	*Capizzi Josephine—†	16	housewife	68	37 Decatur
	G	*Capizzi Isabel—†	16	operator	27	37 "

Lewis Street

	K	*Lynch Frederick	3	retired	72	here
	L	Lynch Frederick F	3	clerk	27	"
	M	Lynch Ida N—†	3	bookkeeper	32	"
	N	*Lynch Margaret—†	3	housewife	59	"
	O	Lynch Michael J	3	laborer	23	
	P	Wolfson Louis	3	druggist	52	

338 Marion Street

	A	*Greco Annie—†	213	storekeeper	48	here
	B	Greco Biagio	213	laborer	47	"
	C	Salerno Ferdinando	213	retired	72	"
	D	Salerno Pasqualina—†	213	housewife	69	"
	E	Vertuccio Domenico	213	laborer	54	"
	F	Vertuccio Ralph	213	"	20	
	H	Capanese Anthony	219	"	29	
	K	Capanese Lena—†	219	housewife	24	"
	L	Rossetti Alfred	219	shoemaker	24	"
	M	*Rossetti Theresa—†	219	housewife	50	"
	N	Rossetti Fannie—†	219	"	25	

Marion Street—Continued

Page.	Letter.	Full Name.	Residence, Jan. 1, 1938.	Occupation.	Supposed Age.	Reported Residence, Jan. 1, 1937. Street and Number.
	O	Rossetti George	219	shoemaker	29	here
	P	Schraffa Doenta—†	221	housekeeper	52	125 Trenton
	R	Schraffa Gaetano	221	laborer	54	125 “
	S	Schraffa Vito	221	“	25	125 “
	T	*Soldano Angelina—†	221	housewife	44	here
	U	*Soldano Gabriel	221	laborer	45	“
	V	Soldano Theresa—†	221	operator	20	“
	X	Paluso Joseph	rear 221	laborer	30	
	Y	Paluso Mary—†	“ 221	housewife	30	“
	Z	*Giardullo Liberato	“ 221	laborer	71	
339						
	A	Giardullo Mary—†	“ 221	operator	21	“
	B	*Giardullo Theresa—†	“ 221	housewife	56	“
	D	*Blanco Anna—†	223	“	37	
	E	*Blanco Stellario	223	laborer	50	
	F	Cahill Eugenie—†	223	housewife	30	“
	G	Cahill Thomas	223	guard	31	
	H	*Grieco Emanuel	223	operator	51	
	K	*Grieco Margaret—†	223	housewife	42	“
	L	*Goldenberg Morris	225	merchant	60	“
	M	Goldenberg Myers	225	clerk	30	
	N	*Goldenberg Rose—†	225	housewife	56	“
	O	Goldstein Maurice	225A	laborer	34	
	P	Goldstein Sarah—†	225A	housewife	61	“
	R	*Arnone Peter	225A	laborer	42	
	S	*Arnone Theresa—†	225A	housewife	37	“
	T	Rizzo Bertha—†	227	“	50	
	U	Rizzo Mary—†	227	stitcher	23	
	V	Avila Antonio	227	retired	68	
	W	Avila Rose—†	227	housewife	58	“
	X	*Figliolina Antonio	227	painter	40	
	Y	*Figliolina Carmella—†	227	housewife	27	“
	Z	Finamore Adeline—†	229	“	40	
340						
	A	Finamore Joseph	229	tailor	43	
	B	Barrasso Laura—†	229	housewife	45	“
	C	Barrasso Pasquale	229	barber	52	“
	D	Fiorillo Monica M—†	229	housewife	30	126 Trenton
	E	Fiorillo Salvatore	229	policeman	27	126 “
	F	*Midus Annie—†	237	housewife	59	here
	G	*Midus David	237	retired	68	“

Page.	Letter.	Full Name.	Residence, Jan. 1, 1938.	Occupation.	Supposed Age.	Reported Residence, Jan. 1, 1937. Street and Number.

Marion Street—Continued

Page.	Letter.	Full Name.	Residence, Jan. 1, 1938.	Occupation.	Supposed Age.	Reported Residence, Jan. 1, 1937. Street and Number.
	H	Feldman Eva—†	237	housewife	39	here
	K	Feldman Hyman	237	student	20	"
	L	Feldman Max	237	mattressmaker	39	"
	M	*Goodman Bessie—†	237	housekeeper	65	"
	N	Catanese Gaetano	237	laborer	22	"
	O	Catanese Joseph	237	"	20	
	P	Catanese Mary—†	237	at home	26	
	R	*Inzana Concetta—†	237	housewife	48	"
	S	Inzana Frank	237	laborer	52	

Maverick Square

Page.	Letter.	Full Name.	Residence, Jan. 1, 1938.	Occupation.	Supposed Age.	Reported Residence, Jan. 1, 1937. Street and Number.
	V	Belmonte Concetta—†	3	housewife	37	119 Benningt'n
	W	Belmonte Vincenzo	3	tavernkeeper	37	119 "
	X	Campbell Edward	3	longshoreman	58	254 Sumner
	Y	*Campbell Elizabeth—†	3	housewife	62	here
	Z	DiPietro Michael	3	laborer	41	"
341						
	A	Riley Christopher	3	longshoreman	44	"
	B	Spain Daniel	3	operator	48	"
	F	DeLacy Ida M—†	7	housekeeper	64	"
	G	O'Hanley Bernard	7	laborer	27	"
	H	O'Hanley Blanche—†	7	housewife	53	"
	K	O'Hanley Gladys—†	7	waitress	30	"
	O	Barrett Mary C—†	11	housewife	52	156 Falcon
	P	Barrett Mary E—†	11	stitcher	30	156 "
	R	Donovan Margaret—†	11	housekeeper	74	here
	S	Weiner Ernest	11	porter	24	"
	T	White Dorothy—†	11	bookkeeper	26	"
	U	White Emma—†	11	housewife	67	"
	Y	Lelos Margaret—†	15	"	40	
	Z	Lelos Michael	15	counterman	40	"
342						
	A	Bellevue Elizabeth F—†	15	housekeeper	68	"
	B	Bellevue Mary F—†	15	"	65	"
	G	Langone Anthony	21	operator	24	"
	H	*Langone Caroline—†	21	housewife	52	"
	K	Langone Frank	21	operator	22	"
	L	*Langone Joseph	21	laundryman	52	"
	M	McCleave Mary A—†	21	housekeeper	67	"
	N	*Torrone Angela—†	21	housewife	79	"

Page.	Letter.	FULL NAME.	Residence, Jan. 1, 1938.	Occupation.	Supposed Age.	Reported Residence, Jan. 1, 1937. Street and Number.

Maverick Square—Continued

	O	*Torrone Antonetta—†	21	housewife	43	here
	P	Torrone Nicholas	21	laundryman	49	"
	R	DellaRusso Joseph	21	florist	29	"
	S	DellaRusso Mary—†	21	housewife	27	"
	T	Poto Louis D	21	clerk	25	"
	W	Carrozza Amico	27	laborer	32	
	X	Carrozza David	27	"	58	
	Y	Carrozza Enrico	27	longshoreman	25	"
	Z	Carrozza Frances—†	27	housewife	52	"
343						
	A	Carrozza John	27	agent	30	
	B	Carrozza Lesandrina—†	27	housewife	27	"
	C	Lifave Angelo	27	barber	28	
	D	*Lifave Paulina—†	27	housewife	53	"
	E	*Screnci Agrippina—†	27	"	32	
	F	Screnci Domenic G	27	tailor	38	
	G	Giaquinto Angelo	27	operator	49	"
	H	Giaquinto Jennie—†	27	housewife	32	2A Baldwin pl
	K	*DiCiccio Anna—†	29	"	42	here
	L	DiCiccio Pasquale	29	plasterer	46	"
	M	Caprera Anthony	29	laborer	40	"
	N	Caprera Frances—†	29	housewife	30	"
	O	*Monoca Agrippina—†	29	housekeeper	83	"
	P	*DeVita Marie—†	29	housewife	48	"
	U	Clark John J	33	laborer	20	
	V	Clark William D	33	"	22	
	W	*Walsh John J	33	longshoreman	58	"
	X	Walsh John J, jr	33	clerk	21	
	Y	Walsh Marie—†	33	housewife	54	"
	Z	McNamara Mary—†	33	housekeeper	54	9 Winthrop
344						
	A	Kingston Julia A—†	33	housewife	54	54 London
	B	Kingston Thomas T	33	laborer	21	54 "
	K	*Gallo Carmella—†	41	housekeeper	42	here
	L	*Fiore Domenic	41	carpenter	54	"
	M	*Fiore Filomena—†	41	housewife	55	"
	U	Trevisonne Clementina-†	47	"	40	
	V	Trevisonne Louis	47	woodcarver	53	"
	W	Cimmino Emma—†	47	housewife	33	"
	X	*Cimmino Joseph	47	chef	43	
	Y	Palma Helen—†	48	housewife	28	"

Page.	Letter.	Full Name.	Residence, Jan. 1, 1938.	Occupation.	Supposed Age.	Reported Residence, Jan. 1, 1937. Street and Number.

Maverick Square—Continued

Page.	Letter.	Full Name.	Residence, Jan. 1, 1938.	Occupation.	Supposed Age.	Reported Residence, Jan. 1, 1937. Street and Number.
	Z	*Palma William	48	painter	30	here
345						
	A	Silva Frank	48	retired	76	107 Moore
	D	DellaRusso Louise—†	51	housewife	30	389 Sumner
	E	Walsh Catherine—†	51	houseworker	25	here
	F	Walsh Jane—†	51	saleswoman	21	"
	G	*Young Alexander	51	fisherman	43	"
	H	Young Cecelia—†	51	housewife	49	"
	L	*Lomio Louis	55	laborer	46	383 Sumner
	M	*Lomio May—†	55	housewife	36	383 "
	N	Laracy Cyril	55	longshoreman	26	here
	O	*Laracy Elizabeth—†	55	housewife	66	"
	P	Laracy Frank	55	painter	30	"
	R	Laracy William	55	operator	27	
	S	Stott Gertrude—†	55	housekeeper	33	"
	U	LaFratta Caroline—†	59	seamstress	24	"
	V	*LaFratta Frances—†	59	housewife	47	"
	W	LaFratta John	59	laborer	22	
	X	*LaFratta Joseph	59	retired	53	
	Y	LaFratta Winifred—†	59	operator	20	"
	Z	DeMasie Michael	59	painter	43	
346						
	A	*DeMasie Rose—†	59	housewife	37	"
	B	Celeste Gaetano	59	laborer	23	"
	C	Celeste Joseph	59	clerk	21	"
	D	*Celeste Josephine—†	59	housewife	43	"
	E	*Celeste Philip	59	operator	53	
	F	*Bourletos John	61	baker	46	
	G	*Bourletos Rose—†	61	housewife	45	"
	H	Dorazio John	61	laundryman	45	"
	K	Dorazio John, jr	61	operator	22	"
	L	*Dorazio Rose—†	61	housewife	45	"
	M	Rossetta Augustus	61	operator	26	"
	N	*Rossetta Fred	61	dealer	47	
	O	Rossetta Jean—†	61	examiner	21	"
	P	Rossetta Marie—†	61	stitcher	22	
	R	Rossetta Philip	61	operator	24	"
	S	*Rossetta Theresa—†	61	housewife	44	"
	V	*Carlson Frances—†	67	"	49	174 Webster
	W	Carlson Olaf	67	longshoreman	64	174 "
	X	Saunders Gertrude—†	67	nurse	29	174 "

Page.	Letter.	FULL NAME.	Residence, Jan. 1, 1938.	Occupation.	Supposed Age.	Reported Residence, Jan. 1, 1937. Street and Number.

Maverick Square—Continued

	Y	DeStefano Arthur	67	hatter	23	here
	Z	DeStefano Dora—†	67	clerk	25	"
347						
	A	DeStefano Louise—†	67	housewife	59	"
	B	DeStefano Peter	67	hatter	60	
	C	Vernaccio Mildred—†	67	housewife	33	"
	D	Vernaccio Philip	67	chauffeur	33	"
	E	Cardinalle Anna—†	67	operator	20	38 London
	F	Cardinalle Bernard	67	fisherman	22	38 "
	G	*Cardinalle Dominic	67	"	52	38 "
	H	*Cardinalle Josephine—†	67	housewife	43	38 "
	M	Salvatore Angelina—†	73	"	42	here
	N	Salvatore Louis	73	secretary	47	"
	O	*Lambrese Henry S	73	photographer	45	"

Maverick Street

	T	*Laurano Grace—†	117	housewife	44	4 Paris ct
	U	Laurano Rocco M	117	tailor	51	4 "
	V	Onessimo Erminia—†	117	housewife	49	here
	W	Onessimo Patrick	117	plumber	51	"
	X	DiLorenzo Beatrice—†	117	at home	23	"
	Y	DiLorenzo Dominick	117	retired	70	
	Z	DiLorenzo Jennie—†	117	clerk	29	"
348						
	A	DiLorenzo William	117	plumber	26	"
	B	Nicchinella Anthony	117	"	22	Saugus
	C	Nicchinella Mary—†	117	housewife	21	"
	D	Coppola Ninetta—†	119	"	24	here
	E	Coppola Vincent	119	baker	29	"
	F	*Delprato Nicola	119	shoemaker	45	"
	G	Moscone Leona—†	119	housewife	33	"
	H	Moscone Peter	119	operator	40	
	M	Gueli Rocco	125	laborer	48	
	N	Taschetta Joseph	125	operator	22	"
	O	Taschetta Salvatore	125	laborer	51	
	P	Taschetta Vita—†	125	housewife	41	"
	R	Corey Nellie—†	127	at home	57	
	S	St George John	127	retired	83	
	T	*Whelan Elizabeth—†	127	at home	70	
	U	Yellen Helen—†	127	housewife	21	"

Page.	Letter.	Full Name.	Residence, Jan. 1, 1938.	Occupation.	Supposed Age.	Reported Residence, Jan. 1, 1937. Street and Number.

Maverick Street—Continued

Page.	Letter.	Full Name.	Residence, Jan. 1, 1938.	Occupation.	Supposed Age.	Reported Residence, Jan. 1, 1937. Street and Number.
	x	Greene Margaret—†	144	at home	20	38 Paris
	y	McArdle William	144	printer	40	Cambridge
349						
	A	Buono Stanislao	146	laborer	49	here
	B	Freeze Harry	146	"	38	"
	D	Poto Joseph H	147	"	50	"
	E	Saracino Anna—†	147	housewife	32	"
	F	*Saracino Emilio	147	shoemaker	34	"
	G	Amato Peter	148	storekeeper	42	"
	H	Previte Grace—†	148	housewife	40	"
	K	Previte John J	148	storekeeper	51	"
	L	Previte John J, jr	148	salesman	24	"
	M	Previte Matthew	148	"	23	"
	N	DiMarzo Dominick	149	laborer	22	151 Maverick
	O	DiMarzo Lena—†	149	housewife	22	151 "
	P	DiMarzo Joseph	149	laborer	25	here
	R	DiMarzo Margaret—†	149	housewife	23	"
	S	DiMarzo Michael	149	laborer	31	"
	T	DiMarzo Rose—†	149	housewife	57	"
	V	Christina James	151	laborer	34	New York
	W	Christina Santa—†	151	housewife	56	"
	X	Muro Beatrice—†	151	housekeeper	45	125 Cottage
	Y	*DeMarco Carmen	153	laborer	61	here
	Z	*DeMarco Rose—†	153	housewife	62	"
350						
	A	Curtin Frances—†	153	"	63	
	B	Curtin Thomas W	153	checker	65	
	D	Giannoccaro Almina—†	157	housewife	53	"
	E	Giannoccaro Florence—†	157	saleswoman	21	"
	F	Giannoccaro Vito	157	laborer	58	
	G	Spano Leo	157	"	40	
	H	Spano Sadie—†	157	housewife	35	"

Meridian Street

Page.	Letter.	Full Name.	Residence, Jan. 1, 1938.	Occupation.	Supposed Age.	Reported Residence, Jan. 1, 1937. Street and Number.
	S	Chamberlain Agnes J—†	5	housewife	45	here
	T	Chamberlain Mabel A—†	5	stenographer	21	"
	U	Crowley Mary G—†	5	at home	51	"
351						
	A	McIntyre John J	11	longshoreman	23	236 Webster
	B	McIntyre Nora J—†	11	housewife	45	here

Page.	Letter.	FULL NAME.	Residence, Jan. 1, 1938.	Occupation.	Supposed Age.	Reported Residence, Jan. 1, 1937. Street and Number.

Meridian Street—Continued

	C	Mullen Elizabeth A—†	11	at home	62	here
	E	*Axelsson Bror	13A	seaman	23	Finland
	F	*Anue Nils	13A	"	28	"
	K	Samuels Philip	20	attorney	57	49 Meridian
	P	Forrest Jane—†	49	housewife	69	here
	R	Forrest John	49	retired	76	"
	S	Sullivan Christina—†	49	saleswoman	37	"
	T	Sullivan Fred	49	laborer	30	
	U	Morin Joseph F	49	salesman	40	"
	V	Morin Marie—†	49	housewife	40	"
352						
	E	Akerberg Chester	65	laborer	29	212 Chelsea
	F	Akerberg Mary—†	65	housewife	30	212 "
	G	Nocito Clara—†	65	"	35	here
	H	*Nocito Joseph	65	painter	42	"
	L	Lannagan Patrick	67	fireman	49	"
	M	Lannagan Sarah E—†	67	housewife	43	"
	O	*Maurice Rose—†	71	"	34	
	P	Hovesepian Ella M—†	71	"	30	
	R	Hovesepian Harry	71	mechanic	32	"
	S	Parks Elizabeth—†	71	housewife	45	"
	T	Parks James A	71	letter carrier	44	"
	W	O'Leary Hannah—†	77	at home	52	
	X	Maher Annie M—†	77	housewife	53	"
	Y	Maher Daniel J	77	seaman	54	
	Z	Maher Rita M—†	77	saleswoman	21	"
353						
	B	Brown George	77	laborer	35	
	A	Petronella Blanche—†	77	nurse	37	

Orleans Street

	K	Citron Joseph A	28	clerk	58	here
	L	Citron Rose I—†	28	housewife	50	"
	M	Barrett Alice—†	28	housekeeper	83	"
	N	Jones Ruth L—†	28	housewife	37	"
	O	Jones Thomas R	28	longshoreman	42	"
	P	Lomba Concetta—†	30	housewife	24	343 Sumner
	R	*Lomba Marcelino	30	carpenter	34	343 "
	S	Martolo Agnes—†	30	housewife	26	here
	T	Martolo Vincent	30	laborer	26	"

Page.	Letter.	FULL NAME.	Residence, Jan. 1, 1938.	Occupation.	Supposed Age.	Reported Residence, Jan. 1, 1937. Street and Number.

Orleans Street—Continued

	U	*Petrizzi Mary—†	30	housewife	68	here
	V	*Petrizzi Nicolo	30	laborer	71	"
	W	Briana Charles	32	"	26	"
	X	*Briana Frank	32	"	67	"
	Y	*Briana Mary—†	32	housewife	63	"
	Z	Petrilli Alfred	32	laborer	53	Pennsylvania
354						
	A	Petrilli Anna—†	32	housewife	40	"
	B	Briana James	32	laborer	34	here
	C	Briana Mary—†	32	housewife	31	"

Paris Court

	D	Dodge Marguerite—†	2	at home	44	4 Bremen
	E	*Iavolo Avis	2	housewife	31	12 Derne
	F	Iavolo Ferdinand	2	operator	40	here
	H	*Delisa Frank	4	laborer	48	227 Border
	K	*Gregorio Eva—†	4	housekeeper	42	227 "

Paris Place

	L	*Varichino Vincent	1	pedler	57	here
	M	*Berile Biagio	1	laborer	59	"
	N	*Agrela Frank	1	"	52	"
	O	*Freitas Manuel	1	"	55	"
	R	Cimino Joseph	3	clerk	36	355 Chelsea
	S	Crowley John J	3	laborer	42	5 Paris pl
	T	Gorman Mary—†	3	housewife	43	5 "
	U	Gorman Michael	3	machinist	43	5 "
	V	Kingsbury Harold	5	fisherman	43	89 Liverpool
	W	Kingsbury Mabel—†	5	housewife	44	89 "
	X	*Dyke Mary—†	5	at home	33	11 Maverick
	Y	Silva Emily—†	5	housewife	21	here
	Z	*Silva Manuel	5	operator	34	"
355						
	A	*Rendonio Francesca—†	6	housewife	74	100 Sumner
	B	*Rendonio Frank	6	retired	78	100 "
	C	*Fraragia Joseph	6	"	66	here
	D	*Gulino Salvatore	6	"	75	"
	E	Feolo Ellen—†	6	housewife	40	"
	F	*Feolo Frank	7	retired	65	

Page.	Letter.	Full Name.	Residence, Jan. 1, 1938.	Occupation.	Supposed Age.	Reported Residence, Jan. 1, 1937. Street and Number.

Paris Place—Continued

Page.	Letter.	Full Name.	Residence, Jan. 1, 1938.	Occupation.	Supposed Age.	Reported Residence, Jan. 1, 1937. Street and Number.
	K	Shepard Robert	7	carpenter	59	here
	G	Tubilleja Ellen—†	7	at home	39	294 Paris
	H	Williams Mary A—†	7	"	62	294 "

Paris Street

Page.	Letter.	Full Name.	Residence, Jan. 1, 1938.	Occupation.	Supposed Age.	Reported Residence, Jan. 1, 1937. Street and Number.
	L	*Whynot Abbie—†	11	housewife	65	here
	M	Whynot Beulah—†	11	forewoman	32	"
	N	Whynot Elsie—†	11	packer	23	"
	O	*Whynot Ira	11	longshoreman	57	"
	P	Whynot Mae—†	11	packer	26	
	R	Brogna Dorothy—†	11	housewife	26	"
	S	Brogna Henry	11	dealer	29	
	T	*McInnis Vincent	11	seaman	31	"
	U	Voto Alfred	11	operator	21	39 Haynes
	V	Voto Josephine—†	11	stitcher	22	126 Bremen
	Z	*Ferrara Angelina—†	78	housewife	37	170 Lexington
356						
	A	Ferrara Vincent	78	glazier	38	170 "
	B	*Allatte Angelina—†	78	housewife	46	here
	C	Allatte Joseph	78	storekeeper	56	"
	K	Maupas John	83	laborer	29	147 Webster
	L	Maupas Phyllis—†	83	housewife	23	147 "
	M	Sullivan John	83	oiler	46	36 Paris
	N	Sullivan Mary—†	83	housekeeper	36	Rhode Island
	R	Thibeau George	84	laborer	28	108 Bremen
	S	Thibeau Grace—†	84	housewife	21	108 "
	T	Visconte Michael	84	painter	36	87 Paris
	U	Visconte Mildred—†	84	housewife	33	87 "
	V	Myers Edward G	85	engineer	55	Randolph
	W	Myers Ethel E—†	85	clerk	20	"
	X	Myers Georgia A—†	85	housewife	55	"
	Z	McDonough Emily—†	87	"	23	30 Bremen
357						
	A	Merlino Mary C—†	87	housekeeper	37	62 London
	B	Riley Mary A—†	87	"	58	62 "
	C	*Amato Mary—†	127	housewife	26	here
	D	Amato Salvatore	127	letter carrier	40	"
	E	Marino Rose—†	127	housekeeper	34	"
	F	Rymill Mary—†	127	"	49	"
	G	Rotondo Concetta—†	127	saleswoman	24	"

Page	Letter.	Full Name.	Residence, Jan. 1, 1938.	Occupation.	Supposed Age.	Reported Residence, Jan. 1, 1937. Street and Number.

Paris Street—Continued

Page	Letter.	Full Name.	Residence, Jan. 1, 1938.	Occupation.	Supposed Age.	Reported Residence, Jan. 1, 1937. Street and Number.
	H	Rotondo Josephine—†	127	at home	22	here
	K	*Rotondo Mary—†	127	housewife	52	"
	L	Rotondo Phillip	127	pedler	55	"
	M	*Bruno Luigi	rear 127	laborer	55	
	N	Amato Albina—†	" 127	housewife	37	"
	O	Amato Andrew	" 127	bookbinder	43	"
	P	*LaDuca Charles	" 127	laborer	55	"
	R	LaDuca Joseph	" 127	"	26	"
	S	Berner Edward O	133	timekeeper	26	69 W Seventh
	T	Berner Emma E—†	133	housewife	47	here
	U	Berner Joseph E	133	laborer	49	"
	V	Giordano Charles	133	"	50	"
	W	Giordano Jennie—†	133	packer	22	
	X	*Giordano Maria—†	133	housewife	45	"
	Y	Giordano Salvatore	133	laborer	20	
	Z	DeVincentis Mafalda—†	133	housewife	25	"
358						
	A	DeVincentis Vincent	133	architect	26	"
	B	*Salamone John	133	retired	75	
	C	*Salamone Maria—†	133	housewife	65	"
	D	Martorana John	135	cutter	21	148 Bremen
	E	Megna John	135	laborer	32	here
	F	Megna Lena—†	135	housewife	29	"
	G	Megna Antonio	135	barber	49	"
	H	Megna Lena—†	135	operator	22	
	K	Megna Mildred—†	135	housewife	29	"
	N	Spitaleri Concetta—†	137	packer	22	
	O	Spitaleri Frank	137	manager	26	"
	P	Spitaleri Michael	137	laborer	56	
	R	Spitaleri Nancy—†	137	housewife	54	"
	M	*Barrasso Mary—†	137	housekeeper	38	"
	S	*DePalma Theresa—†	137A	"	57	"
	T	Vasapolli Joseph	137A	mattressmaker	45	"
	U	*Vasapolli Mary—†	137A	housewife	34	"
	V	*LaMonica Antonio	137A	laborer	36	
	W	*LaMonica Mary—†	137A	housewife	35	"
	X	*Capobianco Angelo	139	retired	71	41 Chelsea
	Y	*Capobianco Giuseppina—†	139	housewife	70	41 "
	Z	*Veneziano Catherine—†	139	"	32	here
359						
	A	*Veneziano Charles	139	manufacturer	42	"

Paris Street—Continued

Page.	Letter.	Full Name.	Residence, Jan. 1, 1938.	Occupation.	Supposed Age.	Reported Residence, Jan. 1, 1937. Street and Number
	B	*Grassa Beatrice—†	139	housewife	47	here
	C	Grassa Nicola	139	tilesetter	48	"
	D	DeGregorio Pasquale	141	painter	29	"
	E	DeGregorio Rose—†	141	housewife	27	"
	F	*Oppiddo John	141	painter	34	173 Havre
	G	*Defeo Costanza—†	141	housewife	47	here
	H	Defeo Frank	141	operator	43	"
	K	Peppe Lawrence	141	laborer	22	"
	L	Peppe Phyllis—†	141	housewife	21	"
	M	*DeVingo Filomena—†	143	housekeeper	48	"
	N	Zirpolo Angelina—†	143	housewife	28	21 Gove
	O	Zirpolo John	143	painter	34	21 "
	P	Russo James	143	"	26	here
	R	Russo Josephine—†	143	housewife	24	"
	U	Conte Joseph	149	laborer	49	"
	V	*Conte Rose—†	149	housewife	53	"
	T	Giso Domenic	149	retired	79	
	W	*Todisco Celeste—†	149	housekeeper	78	"
	X	Todisco Joseph	149	constable	50	"
	Y	*Todisco Mary—†	149	housewife	41	"
	Z	Todisco Michael	149	storekeeper	55	"
360						
	A	Todisco Catherine—†	149	housewife	20	here
	B	Todisco Joseph A	149	operator	24	"
	D	*Beggelman Abraham	153	sorter	59	"
	E	Beggelman Eva—†	153	bookkeeper	28	"
	F	Beggelman Reuben	153	laborer	22	"
	G	Beggelman Samuel	153	glazier	24	
	H	*Beggelman Sarah—†	153	housewife	54	"
	K	Beggelman William	153	machinist	31	"
	L	*Kaplan Rose—†	163	housekeeper	52	"
	M	Dievitch Bessie—†	163	housewife	38	"
	N	Dievitch Solomon B	163	clerk	40	
	O	*Hoffman Dora—†	163	housekeeper	68	"
	P	Hoffman Phillip	163	storekeeper	32	"
	R	Samuels Mamie—†	163	housewife	52	"
	S	Doble Henry	165	mechanic	45	"
	T	Pittella Joseph	165	laborer	39	"
	U	*Pittella Victoria—†	165	housewife	31	"
	V	*Libbero Arivardo	165	fisherman	55	"
	W	*Libbero Gracia—†	165	housewife	52	"

Page.	Letter.	FULL NAME.	Residence, Jan. 1, 1938.	Occupation.	Supposed Age.	Reported Residence, Jan. 1, 1937. Street and Number.

Paris Street—Continued

	X	*Rugnetta Giuseppe	165	retired	76	here
	Y	Alfieri Josephine—†	167	housewife	34	"
	Z	Alfieri Louis A	167	reporter	39	"
361						
	A	Pascarella Louise—†	167	packer	23	
	B	*Carfagna Amelia—†	167	housekeeper	67	"
	C	Carfagna Arturo	167	laborer	35	"
	D	*Amaroso Angelina—†	167	housewife	83	173 Paris
	E	Salerno Angela—†	167	housekeeper	22	here
	F	Ferreira Joaquin	169	dealer	69	"
	G	Taylor Mary—†	169	housewife	54	"
	H	Taylor William	169	baggagemaster	50	"
	K	Fratus Rose M—†	169	attendant	64	10 Harris
	L	Bush Esther—†	169	housewife	29	here
	M	Bush Henry	169	clerk	29	"
	N	Hasset Ida—†	171	bookkeeper	20	"
	O	*Hasset Jennie—†	171	housewife	54	"
	P	*Hasset William	171	polisher	55	
	R	Goldberg Esther—†	171	operator	20	"
	S	*Goldberg Etta—†	171	housewife	45	"
	T	*Goldberg Joseph	171	hostler	50	
	U	DiLeo Joseph	173	laborer	42	
	V	DiLeo Josephine—†	173	housewife	38	"
	W	Castelluccio Michael	173	laborer	38	
	X	*Castelluccio Rosa—†	173	housewife	42	"
	Y	Cigna Catherine—†	173	"	44	
	Z	Cigna Joseph	173	laborer	47	
362						
	A	Foster Carmella—†	175	housewife	29	"
	B	Foster Joseph R	175	chauffeur	31	"
	C	*Prisco Maria A—†	175	at home	72	
	D	Prisco Theresa—†	175	clerk	25	"
	E	Mario Benny	175	laborer	50	84 Chelsea
	F	*Mario Rosina—†	175	housewife	49	84 "
	G	*Privitera Charles	177	laborer	54	47 "
	H	*Privitera Josephine—†	177	housewife	46	47 "
	K	Ormond Catherine—†	177	housekeeper	30	here
	L	*Ormond Elizabeth—†	177	housewife	66	"
	M	Ormond Francis	177	machinist	27	"
	N	Ormond Mary—†	177	clerk	25	
	O	*Ormond Patrick	177	retired	76	

Page.	Letter.	Full Name.	Residence, Jan. 1, 1938.	Occupation.	Supposed Age.	Reported Residence, Jan. 1, 1937. Street and Number.

Paris Street—Continued

	P	Ormond Thomas	177	laborer	24	here
	R	Kenney Andrew J	177	retired	82	"
	S	Kenney Andrew J, jr	177	painter	45	"
	T	Mastone Angelo	179	clerk	36	
	U	Mastone Rose—†	179	housewife	29	"
	V	Vecchio Angelina—†	179	"	31	
	W	*Vecchio Florence—†	179	"	65	
	X	Vecchio Michael	179	operator	39	
	Y	*Covotta Angelina—†	179	housewife	65	"
	Z	*Covotta Michael	179	operator	58	
363						
	A	*Akell Anna—†	181	housewife	26	251 Marion
	B	Akell Harold	181	laborer	25	251 "
	C	*Macchione Concetta—†	181	housewife	56	251 "
	D	Macchine Ernest	181	laborer	22	251 '
	E	Macchione Mario	181	clerk	24	251 "
	F	Abramo Frank	181	dealer	24	here
	G	*Abramo Grace—†	181	housewife	42	"
	H	*Abramo Natale	181	dealer	47	"
	K	Abramo Salvatore	181	"	21	
	L	Ferullo John	181	salesman	.20	"
	M	Ferullo Joseph	181	expressman	52	"
	N	Ferullo Mary—†	181	stitcher	21	
	O	Ferullo Palma—†	181	seamstress	23	"
	P	Ferullo Susie—†	181	housewife	48	"
	S	Cunningham John	183	messenger	23	178 Paris
	T	Cunningham Mary—†	183	housewife	55	178 "
	U	Cunningham Thomas	183	laborer	24	178 "
	V	Ginsberg Albert	183	storekeeper	58	here
	W	Ginsberg Flora—†	183	housewife	55	"
	X	Ginsberg Ida—†	183	bookkeeper	33	"
	Y	*Buck Mary—†	183	housewife	53	"
	Z	Buck Michael	183	longshoreman	60	"
364						
	A	Cambria Frank	185	baker	32	
	B	*Cambria Lena—†	185	housewife	31	"
	C	Scarpa Antonio	185	machinist	25	"
	D	*Scarpa Carmella—†	185	housewife	46	"
	E	*Scarpa Carmine	185	laborer	51	
	F	Incatasciato Carmella—†	185	housewife	20	"
	G	Incatasciato Joseph	185	barber	27	

Page.	Letter.	FULL NAME.	Residence, Jan. 1, 1938.	Occupation.	Supposed Age.	Reported Residence, Jan. 1, 1937. Street and Number.

Paris Street—Continued

	K	Bosco Caroline—†	207	housewife	32	here
	L	Bosco John	207	machinist	35	"
	M	Luongo Anthony	207	operator	21	"
	N	Luongo Carmine	207	"	27	
	O	*Luongo Filomina—†	207	housewife	51	"
	P	Luongo Joseph	207	operator	27	"
	R	Luongo Pasquale	207	laborer	55	
	S	DeFalco Anna—†	207	housewife	39	"
	T	DeFalco Nunzio	207	bartender	48	"
	U	Zocco Nellie—†	209	housewife	36	"
	V	Zocco Thomas	209	cutter	40	
	W	Dalelio Fiore	209	laborer	53	
	X	*Dalelio Grace—†	209	housewife	53	"
	Y	Dalelio John	209	chauffeur	22	"
	Z	*Dellesandro Alfred	209	blacksmith	51	"
365						
	A	*Dellasandro Elvira—†	209	housewife	48	"
	B	Cahill Anna T—†	217	"	66	
	C	Cahill Edward J	217	inspector	66	"
	D	Cahill Frederick C	217	clerk	30	
	E	Cahill Mary T—†	217	saleswoman	23	"
	F	Cahill Regina—†	217	housewife	23	11A Armstrong
	G	Cahill Richard T	217	clerk	23	here
	H	Cahill Robert W	217	decorator	27	11A Armstrong
	L	*Indingaro Clorinda—†	221	housewife	43	here
	M	Indingaro Leo	221	messenger	20	"
	N	Indingaro Michael	221	bootblack	46	"
	O	*Lacascia Angelo	223	laborer	53	
	P	*Lacascia Croce—†	223	housewife	49	"
	R	*Scimone Angelina—†	223	"	37	
	S	Scimone Domenico	223	operator	44	
	T	*Abate Jennie—†	223	housewife	40	"
	U	*Abate Joseph	223	operator	54	
	V	Lannon Mary—†	225	housewife	43	"
	W	Lannon Walter	225	inspector	46	"
	X	*Ademo Annie—†	225	housewife	45	"
	Y	*Ademo Carmello	225	retired	52	
	Z	Ademo Peter	225	plumber	22	
366						
	A	Ademo Sebastian	225	barber	25	
	B	Mazzarella Anthony J	225	timekeeper	32	"
	C	Mazzarella Mary—†	225	housewife	32	"

Page.	Letter.	FULL NAME.	Residence, Jan. 1, 1938.	Occupation.	Supposed Age.	Reported Residence, Jan. 1, 1937. Street and Number.

Porter Street

Page.	Letter.	FULL NAME.	Residence, Jan. 1, 1938.	Occupation.	Supposed Age.	Reported Residence, Jan. 1, 1937. Street and Number.
	G	*Valanzola Josephine—†	94	housewife	62	here
	H	*Valanzola Salvatore	94	retired	75	"
	K	LoBue Josephine—†	94	housewife	37	"
	L	LoBue Luigi	94	proprietor	41	"
	N	*Cardarella Joseph	96	laborer	56	
	O	*Cardarella Lucy—†	96	housewife	50	"
	P	*Mosconi Anna—†	96	"	32	
	R	*Mosconi Frederick	96	laborer	37	
	S	Borisowsky Abraham	103	teacher	30	
	T	Borisowsky Israel	103	storekeeper	64	"
	U	Borisowsky Lena—†	103	housewife	64	"
	V	Amori Caroline—†	103	"	27	Chelsea
	W	*Amori Guy	103	barber	45	"
367						
	B	Iarrobino Florinda—†	110	domestic	20	172 Paris
	C	*Iarrobino Lorenza—†	110	housewife	44	172 "
	D	Iarrobino Vincenzo	110	operator	51	172 "
	E	Freitas Carl	110	laborer	55	here
	F	*Freitas Lena—†	110	housewife	48	"
	G	Badolato Domenic	111	laborer	21	"
	H	*Badolato Frank	111	expressman	50	"
	K	*Badolato Mary—†	111	housewife	43	"
	M	Odierno Elsie—†	112	operator	23	
	N	Odierno Grace—†	112	clerk	22	
	O	Odierno Louis	112	chauffeur	29	"
	P	Odierno Paolo	112	storekeeper	50	"
	R	Odierno Susie—†	112	housewife	50	"
	S	*Frustaglia Antonio	112	nickelplater	48	"
	T	Frustaglia Elizabeth—†	112	seamstress	34	"
	U	*Alongi Alphonso	113	laborer	35	
	V	*Alongi Anna—†	113	housewife	68	"
	X	*Lunata Elizabeth—†	115	"	68	37 Chelsea
	Y	*Lunata Salvatore	115	retired	79	37 "
	Z	*Nicoletti Barbara—†	115A	housewife	60	here
368						
	A	Nicoletti Philip	115A	laborer	67	
	B	Pepi Michael	117	"	29	
	C	Pepi Santa—†	117	housewife	23	"
	D	Tuberosa Catherine—†	117	"	54	
	E	Tuberosa Ernest	117	laborer	21	
	F	Tuberosa Salvatore	117	"	55	
	G	*Young Mary—†	117	housewife	29	"

Page.	Letter.	Full Name.	Residence, Jan. 1, 1938.	Occupation.	Supposed Age.	Reported Residence, Jan. 1, 1937. Street and Number.

Porter Street—Continued

Page.	Letter.	Full Name.	Residence, Jan. 1, 1938.	Occupation.	Supposed Age.	Reported Residence, Jan. 1, 1937. Street and Number.
	L	*Tuck Henry	122	storekeeper	45	here
	M	*Tuck Sadie—†	122	housewife	40	“

Savage Court

Page.	Letter.	Full Name.	Residence, Jan. 1, 1938.	Occupation.	Supposed Age.	Reported Residence, Jan. 1, 1937. Street and Number.
	N	Casalletto James	1	laborer	21	233 Cheslea
	O	Gargiulo Florence—†	1	housewife	31	here
	P	*Gargiulo Giro	1	cabinetworker	49	“
	R	*Gianpietro Amelia—†	2	housewife	44	87 Orleans
	S	*Gianpietro Giuseppe	2	laborer	56	87 “
	T	Iovanna John	2	barber	52	158 Bremen
	U	Iovanna Margaret—†	2	housewife	56	158 “
	V	*Gulli Michael	2	laborer	68	here
	W	Gulli Paul	2	mechanic	35	“
	X	Sgrow Anthony	3	baker	23	“
	Y	Sgrow Joseph	3	pedler	56	“
	Z	*Jannis James	3	laborer	40	294 Bremen
369						
	A	Jannis Mary—†	3	housewife	36	294 “
	B	Calindo Frances—†	3	housekeeper	34	174 Gove

Sumner Street

Page.	Letter.	Full Name.	Residence, Jan. 1, 1938.	Occupation.	Supposed Age.	Reported Residence, Jan. 1, 1937. Street and Number.
	M	Barry Bridget—†	190	housewife	48	here
	N	Barry John	190	laborer	51	“
	O	Barry John J	190	“	22	“
	P	Greene Thomas	190	fisherman	30	“
	R	Hayes Michael	190	“	35	
	S	Lee James	190	“	47	
	T	*Sampson Robert	190	“	49	“
	U	Carlson Elsie—†	190½	housewife	32	“
	V	Carlson Ingvald	190½	painter	38	“
	W	*Gilbert Theodore	190½	seaman	66	Sweden
	X	*Iverson Nils	190½	“	37	here
	Y	*Ulwick Tideman	190½	longshoreman	52	“
	Z	Alders Frank	191	laborer	42	“
370						
	A	Carrigan Peter	191		52	
	B	Cramp Peter	191	“	50	
	C	Defelice Frank	191	machinist	42	“
	D	Gablin Minnie—†	191	at home	52	

Page.	Letter.	Full Name.	Residence, Jan. 1, 1938.	Occupation.	Supposed Age.	Reported Residence, Jan. 1, 1937. Street and Number.
		Sumner Street—Continued				
	E	Marafino Pasquale	191	laborer	38	here
	F	Sheehan Timothy	191	"	55	"
	H	Aldus Mary A—†	193	at home	37	"
	K	*Borgeson William	193	seaman	38	Louisiana
	L	Burke Patrick	193	laborer	50	here
	M	Cyr Eva—†	193	housewife	44	"
	N	*Cyr Joseph	193	fisherman	49	"
	O	Doherty James	193	laborer	55	"
	P	*Gregorio Michael	193	"	54	10 Havre
	R	Kelley John	193	"	56	here
	S	Thompson John	193	retired	84	"
	T	Cooper John J	195	"	70	"
	U	Donavan William F	195	laborer	53	
371						
	B	Giudicianni John	221	"	26	
	C	*Giudicianni Justina—†	221	housewife	60	"
	D	*Giudicianni Michael	221	retired	63	
	E	Giudicianni Michael, jr	221	chauffeur	22	"
	F	Giudicianni Sidney	221	storekeeper	28	"
	G	Giudicianni Ulysses	221	laborer	24	"
	L	*Fontana Mary—†	228	housewife	48	"
	M	*Fontana Michael	228	laborer	48	
	N	*Chillemi Mary—†	228	housewife	34	"
	O	Chillemi Tindaro	228	laborer	41	
	P	*Panto Bernadina—†	230	housewife	46	"
	R	Panto Peter	230	laborer	55	
	S	Panto Rosalie—†	230	inspector	21	"
	T	Panto Santa—†	230	floorwoman	26	"
	U	LaMarco Alphonse	230	retired	67	
	V	LaMarco Anthony M	230	barber	21	
	W	LaMarco Armand	230	laborer	25	
	X	LaMarco Clorinda—†	230	housewife	58	"
		Washington Avenue				
	Z	*Barisano Bernardina—†	1	housewife	26	here
372						
	A	Barisano Salvatore	1	laborer	29	
	B	Colasanti Assunta—†	1	housewife	31	"
	C	Colasanti Bonaventuri	1	carpenter	42	"
	D	Brun Albert	1	storekeeper	32	"

Page.	Letter.	FULL NAME.	Residence, Jan. 1, 1938.	Occupation.	Supposed Age.	Reported Residence, Jan. 1, 1937. Street and Number.

Washington Avenue—Continued

	E	Brun Albina—†	1	housewife	27	here
	F	LoChiatto Angelo A	2	laborer	34	"
	G	*LoChiatto Rose—†	2	housewife	32	"
	H	*Russo Lucia—†	2	"	53	201 Chelsea
	K	*Russo Michael	2	laborer	50	201 "
	L	*Petrola Palmira—†	2	housewife	38	here
	M	Petrola Umberto	2	laborer	50	"
	N	*Nocilla Charles	3	retired	76	182 Chelsea
	O	*Nocilla Paulina—†	3	housewife	68	182 "
	P	*Pascarella Hilda—†	3	"	52	here
	R	Pascarella John	3	operator	29	118 Paris
	S	Pascarella Joseph	3	"	21	here
	T	*Pascarella Louis	3	"	59	"
	U	*Ferullo John	3	retired	66	"
	V	Ferullo Mary—†	3	operator	34	
	W	Ferullo Samuel	3	presser	23	

Webster Street

	Z	*DeAngelis Nellie—†	40	housewife	47	here
373						
	A	Riley Anne B—†	42	housekeeper	69	"
	B	O'Donnell Hugh E	42	photographer	41	"

Winthrop Street

	E	Beath William	4	clerk	55	72 Trenton
	F	Collins Dennis	4	laborer	67	here
	G	Keenan Frank	4	clerk	42	"
	H	Layhe Elizabeth—†	4	housekeeper	51	"
	K	Layhe George	4	watchman	26	"
	L	Locke George	4	machinist	50	"
	M	Olsen Hans	4	fisherman	57	"
	N	*Riley Richard	4	laborer	85	"
	O	Rodrigues Manuel	4	cook	33	New Bedford
	P	Safrin Manuel	4	clerk	50	N Hampshire
	R	Youngstrom Maurice	4	painter	38	here
	S	*Giangregorio Carmella—†	6	housewife	60	"
	T	Giangregorio Raphael	6	laborer	47	"
	U	Belmonte Angelo	6	foreman	49	
	V	Belmonte Carmella—†	6	housewife	70	"
	W	Belmonte Carmella—†	6	clerk	22	

Page.	Letter.	Full Name.	Residence, Jan. 1, 1938.	Occupation.	Supposed Age.	Reported Residence, Jan. 1, 1937. Street and Number.

Winthrop Street—Continued

	X	*Belmonte Jennie—†	6	housewife	48	here
	Y	Belmonte Natalie—†	6	at home	20	"
	Z	Pucillo Sabato	6	laborer	36	"
374						
	A	Giglio Josephine—†	6	housekeeper	34	"
	B	Allen Fred	8	chef	55	"
	C	Buckley John	8	longshoreman	52	39 Monmouth
	D	Buckley Lillian—†	8	housewife	48	39 "
	E	Bulger Patrick	8	retired	66	here
	F	Fraser George	8	seaman	30	"
	G	*Jacobson John	8	machinist	40	9 Winthrop
	H	Murphy William T	8	navigator	32	here
	K	*Nelson Charles	8	watchman	60	"
	L	*Quits John	8	contractor	52	8 Sumner
	M	*Rose John	8	seaman	25	20 Havre
	N	Smith William	8	roofer	56	here
	O	*DiMartini Almeda—†	9	stitcher	46	"
	P	Graf Richard V	9	printer	67	"
	R	*Millen Frank	9	machinist	67	6 London
	S	Murray William	9	longshoreman	38	30 Hawkins
	T	Silva Manuel	9	retired	84	here
	U	*Sinclair Alice—†	9	housekeeper	65	"
	V	Vallen Joseph	9	longshoreman	38	414 Sumner
	W	*Salerno Philip	10	retired	77	here
	X	*Salerno Phyllis—†	10	housewife	67	"
	Y	*Cuozzo Ivolli	10	laborer	20	350 Sumner
	Z	Pepe Pasquale	10	"	26	here
375						
	A	Pepe Pauline—†	10	housewife	26	"
	B	*Piguatone Antonette—†	10	"	25	
	C	Piguatone Louis	10	packer	29	"
	D	Cady John P	11	laborer	38	Cambridge
	E	Farnum Gleason	11	student	23	here
	F	Habberley Josephine E–†	11	artist	70	"
	G	Leighton E Louise—†	11	housekeeper	73	"
	H	Green Edward	13	longshoreman	40	131 Main
	K	McKenna John	13	sealer	26	here
	L	McNeil John	13	retired	64	193 Sumner
	M	Pope Roger	13	laborer	61	8 Paris
	N	Walsh David	13	machinist	48	here
	O	Webber Ella M—†	13	housewife	56	"
	P	Webber Franklin B	13	proprietor	67	"

1

1

14

15

51

7

8

9

2

2

1

Ward 1—Precinct 5

CITY OF BOSTON

LIST OF RESIDENTS
20 YEARS OF AGE AND OVER

(NON-CITIZENS INDICATED BY ASTERISK)
(FEMALES INDICATED BY DAGGER)

AS OF

JANUARY 1, 1938

JOSEPH F. TIMILTY, } *Listing*
FREDERIC E. DOWLING, } *Board.*

CITY OF BOSTON PRINTING DEPARTMENT

Page.	Letter.	Full Name.	Residence, Jan. 1, 1938.	Occupation.	Supposed Age.	Reported Residence, Jan. 1, 1937. Street and Number.
385		**Appian Place**				
	A	*Ingalo Camilla—†	1	housewife	42	here
	B	Ingalo Concetta—†	1	at home	21	"
	C	Ingalo Lillian—†	1	clerk	23	"
	D	*Ingalo Salvatore	1	salesman	48	"
	E	Carney George F	2	conductor	36	"
	F	Carney John	2	ironworker	74	"
	G	Thomas William T	2	laborer	46	
	H	Tassoni Joseph	2	"	43	
	K	*Tassoni Mary—†	2	housewife	38	"
	L	Marino Albert	3	baker	21	Revere
	M	Mondello Elizabeth—†	3	housewife	22	110 Marion
	N	Mondello John	3	laborer	29	110 "
	O	*Lacascia Anna—†	4	housewife	25	28 Seneca
	P	*Lacascia Matteo	4	barber	27	28 "
	R	Martello Joseph	4	laborer	56	here
	S	*Martello Maria—†	4	housewife	54	"
	T	Martello Mary—†	4	packer	23	"
386		**Bennington Street**				
	C	Kirby Richard C	15	director	35	here
	D	McDonnell Leo T	15	"	36	"
	H	Schraffa Joseph J	19	clerk	36	"
	K	Schraffa Thomassina—†	19	housewife	32	"
	L	Sunstrom Vivian H—†	19	nurse	27	
	M	Burns Jennie S—†	21	housewife	57	"
	N	Andrews William	21	guard	66	
	O	Doull Louise B—†	21	housewife	55	"
	P	*Bailey Elizabeth—†	21	dressmaker	50	"
	R	*Bailey Patrick	21	shoemaker	69	"
	S	Arno Constance M—†	23	housewife	26	94 Armandine
	T	Arno Samuel R	23	attorney	29	94 "
	U	Desmond Frederick	23	bartender	50	here
	V	Desmond Mary—†	23	housewife	75	"
	W	*Penprase Mary—†	23	"	52	"
	X	Conlin James F	25	retired	74	
	Y	Conlin Nellie E—†	25	housewife	71	"
	Z	Peddle Bridget M—†	25	"	68	
387						
	A	Peddle Francis J	25	mechanic	35	"

Page.	Letter.	Full Name.	Residence, Jan. 1, 1938.	Occupation.	Supposed Age.	Reported Residence, Jan. 1, 1937. Street and Number.

Bennington Street—Continued

	B	Becker Doris L—†	25	stenographer	28	here
	C	Becker Ludivine—†	25	housewife	48	“
	E	Freese Charles H	29A	shipper	21	“
	F	Freese Francis J	29A	painter	23	
	G	Freese Harry J	29A	laborer	45	
	H	Freese Mary E—†	29A	operator	42	
	M	Hopkins I Chester	35	engineer	57	
	N	Sweeney Alice M—†	35	housewife	36	“
	O	Sweeney Frederick L	35	teacher	39	
	P	Sweeney Margaret E—†	35	housewife	67	“
	R	Little Alice J—†	37	“	30	
	S	Little John J	37	mechanic	32	“
	T	McGrath Margaret J—†	37	housewife	66	“
	U	McGrath William	37	storekeeper	72	“
	V	*Driscoll Hannah A—†	37	housewife	67	“
	W	Driscoll Michael A	37	machinist	72	“
	Y	O'Connor Lawrence F	41	longshoreman	48	163 Byron
	Z	O'Connor Nora—†	41	housewife	49	163 “
388						
	A	Russell Edward	41	painter	22	163 “
	B	Russell Helen—†	41	packer	20	163 “
	C	Morgera Dominic	41	mechanic	23	47 Lexington
	D	Morgera Mary—†	41	housewife	23	47 “
	E	Bellusci Michael	43	agent	56	2 Thurston
	F	Bellusci Nicholas	43	realtor	26	2 “
	G	*LaMonica Concetta—†	43	housewife	37	57 Bennington
	H	LaMonica Joseph	43	chauffeur	42	57 “
	L	Block David R	45	bartender	23	here
	M	Block Ethel—†	45	housewife	21	“
	N	Simonelli Eleanor—†	45	“	30	“
	O	Simonelli Theodore	45	musician	33	“
	R	*Colontono Lawrence	47	laborer	50	
	S	*Colontono Mary—†	47	housewife	40	“
	T	Scaparatto Gabriel	47	laborer	53	
	U	Crumley Anna—†	47	housewife	46	“
	V	Zarrella Christine—†	49	“	55	
	W	*Caccialino Albina—†	49	“	60	
	X	*Caccialino Peter	49	laborer	49	
	Y	Block Ralph	49	“	21	
	Z	Diaz Esther—†	49	housewife	42	“
389						
	A	Diaz Frederick E	49	chauffeur	35	“

Page.	Letter.	FULL NAME.	Residence, Jan. 1, 1938.	Occupation.	Supposed Age.	Reported Residence, Jan. 1, 1937. Street and Number.
		Bennington Street—Continued				
	B	*Rose Adeline—†	51	housewife	58	here
	C	*Rose Alexander	51	laborer	64	"
	E	Rose George	51	shoemaker	29	"
	D	Rose Phoebe—†	51	operator	27	"
	F	Fratas James	51	"	48	"
	H	*Marotta Alfonso	53	storekeeper	51	73 London
	K	Marotta Joseph	53	musician	27	73 "
	L	Marotta Leo	53	"	22	73 "
	M	*Marotta Vincenzo—†	53	housewife	44	73 "
	N	McCarthy Frances—†	53	"	42	here
	O	Geer Mary—†	57	"	33	"
	P	Alba Andrew	57	laborer	59	"
	R	*Alba Maria—†	57	housewife	50	"
	S	*DeMonti Eleanor—†	57	"	45	33 Paris
	T	DeMonti Mario	57	shoemaker	21	33 "
	U	*DeMonti Ralph	57	laborer	50	33 "
	V	DeMonti Ralph	57	shoemaker	23	33 "
	W	Laurasi Carolina—†	57	housewife	25	here
	X	Laurasi Frank	57	laborer	27	"
	Y	Rondino Anthony	59	"	21	"
	Z	Rondino Vincent	59	tailor	50	
390						
	A	Barbaro Anthony	59	laborer	50	
	B	DeBenedetto Alfred	59	"	49	
	C	DeBenedetto Josephine—†	59	housewife	49	"
	D	Morgera Charles E	59	locksmith	51	"
	E	Morgera Ernestina—†	59	housewife	44	"
	F	Morgera Louise—†	59	saleswoman	21	"
	G	Fiandaca Frederick	59	carpenter	63	"
	H	Fiandaca Nunzio	59	salesman	22	"
	L	DeGregorio Antionetta—†	61	saleswoman	27	84 Porter
	M	*DeGregorio Camilla—†	61	housewife	54	84 "
	N	DeGregorio Margaret—†	61	operator	22	84 "
	O	*DiCenso Costanza—†	61	housewife	27	here
	P	DiCenso Ercolo	61	laborer	35	"
	R	*DiCenso Paul	61	retired	75	"
	S	*Turco Anthony	67	laundryman	43	"
	T	*Turco Mary—†	67	housewife	44	"
	U	Vaporakis Angela—†	67	"	41	225 London
	V	Vaporakis Kyriakos	67	waiter	45	225 "

Page.	Letter.	FULL NAME.	Residence, Jan. 1, 1938.	Occupation.	Supposed Age.	Reported Residence, Jan. 1, 1937. Street and Number.

Bennington Street—Continued

	X	Pistoni Rosario	69	storekeeper	43	here
	Y	Cosaccio Michael	69	laborer	28	114 Lexington
	Z	*Cosaccio Millie—†	69	housewife	25	New York
391						
	A	*Belliveau Louise—†	71	"	47	here
	B	*Belliveau Roger	71	fishcutter	36	"
	C	*Georgopulos Bertha—†	71	housewife	39	"
	D	Georgopulos Peter	71	storekeeper	39	"
	F	Murphy Alice D—†	89	teacher	37	"
	G	Murphy Margaret A—†	89	housewife	53	"
	H	Hegner Albert	91	laborer	23	
	K	Hegner Andrew	91	"	82	
	L	Hegner Francis	91	engineer	27	
	M	Hegner Mary N—†	91	housewife	61	"
	N	*Rizzo Florence—†	95	"	64	
	O	Rizzo Frederick	95	clerk	34	
	P	Rizzo George	95	pressman	28	"
	R	Pomponi Mary—†	95	housewife	33	"
	S	Pomponi Vincent	95	tailor	39	
	T	*Mirro Carmella—†	97	housewife	69	"
	U	Mirro Martin	97	operator	39	
	V	Malfy Anna—†	97	housewife	23	"
	W	Malfy Rocco	97	laborer	27	
	X	Ballarobe Joseph	99	seaman	40	
	Y	Perez Anthony	99	fireman	48	
	Z	*Perez Concetta—†	99	housewife	38	"
392						
	A	*Perez Frank	99	carpenter	28	"
	B	Perez Rose—†	99	clerk	20	"
	C	DeDominicas Nicholas	101	musician	32	215 Saratoga
	D	DeDominicas Violet—†	101	housewife	22	215 "
	E	Kelly Ethel M—†	101	"	48	here
	F	Kelly John C	101	janitor	48	"
	G	Mogan Catherine—†	101	teacher	23	291 Havre
	H	Mogan James W	101	broker	50	291 "
	K	Mogan Theresa—†	101	housewife	45	291 "
	L	Carrozza Anthony	103	millhand	22	here
	M	Carrozza James	103	letter carrier	24	"
	N	*Carrozza Santo	103	floorman	61	"
	O	Delsie Anthony	105	laborer	24	

Page.	Letter.	Full Name.	Residence, Jan. 1, 1938.	Occupation.	Supposed Age.	Reported Residence, Jan. 1, 1937. Street and Number.

Bennington Street—Continued

Page.	Letter.	Full Name.	Residence, Jan. 1, 1938.	Occupation.	Supposed Age.	Reported Residence, Jan. 1, 1937. Street and Number.
	P	Walsh Ellen—†	105	housewife	82	here
	R	Forziati Alfonso F	107	student	25	“
	S	Forziati Frank	107	tailor	53	“
	T	Forziati Ida—†	107	housewife	51	“
	U	Miccichi John	109	chauffeur	23	219 Saratoga
	V	Miccichi Josephine—†	109	housewife	21	179 Princeton
	W	*Foote Bella—†	109	“	26	“
	X	*Foote Leonard	109	fisherman	34	“
	Y	DiAngelis Eleanor—†	109	operator	22	“
	Z	*DiAngelis Joseph	109	shoemaker	55	“
393						
	A	DiAngelis Mary—†	109	housewife	43	“
	B	DiOrio Mary—†	111	“	40	
	C	DiOrio Thomas	111	printer	46	“
	D	DiOrio Adam	111	shipper	23	
	E	DiOrio John	111	student	21	
	F	Nappi Isadore	113	merchant	23	“
	H	Russo John	113	printer	31	305 Havre
	G	Russo Mary—†	113	housewife	29	305 “
	K	*Gravallese John	115	tailor	52	here
	L	*Gravallese Linda—†	115	housewife	47	“
	M	McNeil Andrew T	117	operator	65	“
	N	McNeil Elizabeth F—†	117	housewife	60	“
	P	Marmoud Emma—†	119	“	22	219 Lexington
	R	Marmoud Joseph	119	operator	28	219 “
	S	Beranger Florence G—†	119	housewife	27	6 Coleman
	T	Beranger Phillip Leon	119	fishcutter	29	6 “
	U	Martinello Filomena—†	121	housewife	26	306 Chelsea
	V	*Martinello Orazio	121	laborer	36	306 “
	W	*Cioffi Giatno	123	“	47	54 Brooks
	X	D'Amelio Dominic	123	“	20	54 “
	Y	*D'Amelio James	123	“	52	54 “
	Z	D'Amelio Rose—†	123	housewife	45	54 “
394						
	A	D'Amelio Theodore	123	painter	23	54 “
	B	Ristino Arthur	125	clerk	23	here
	C	*Ristino Concetta—†	125	housewife	52	“
	D	*Ristino Joseph	125	laborer	52	“
	E	Ristino Pasquale	125	“	29	
	F	Ristino Rose—†	125	clerk	21	

Page.	Letter.	FULL NAME.	Residence, Jan. 1, 1938.	Occupation.	Supposed Age.	Reported Residence, Jan. 1, 1937. Street and Number.
		Brooks Street				
	H	Sen Alice—†	52	housewife	56	here
	K	Sen James	52	laborer	24	"
	L	*Sen John	52	storekeeper	68	"
	M	Sen Mary—†	52	teacher	29	"
	N	MacKay Hilma—†	52	housewife	22	"
	O	MacKay James	52	laborer	21	"
	P	Goglia Agnes—†	54	housewife	21	293 Paris
	R	Goglia James	54	operator	21	112 Falcon
	S	Petrone Antonio	54	barber	43	302 Paris
	T	Petrone Nancy—†	54	housewife	40	302 "
	T1	Ebba John	54	laborer	40	here
	U	Ebba Philomina—†	54	housewife	39	"
	W	DiStasio Albert	62	chauffeur	22	"
	X	DiStasio Frank	62	bartender	47	"
	Y	DiStasio Mary—†	62	housewife	47	"
	Z	*DiStefano Jennie—†	62	"	41	251 Lexington
395						
	A	DiStefano Jennie—†	62	operator	21	251 "
	B	*DiStefano Salvatore	62	shoemaker	43	251 "
	C	*Lachiavo Mary—†	62	housewife	45	here
	D	Lachiavo Peter	62	laborer	45	"
	E	Wise James	64	"	29	"
	F	Wise Mary—†	64	housewife	24	"
	G	Lavita Anthony	64	laborer	32	
	H	Lavita Mary—†	64	housewife	30	"
	K	Forshner Alma—†	68	"	34	
	L	Forshner Harold	68	tinsmith	45	
	M	Riccardelli John	68	plumber	26	"
	N	Riccardelli Rose—†	68	housewife	26	"
	O	Meaney Alice—†	68	"	48	
	P	Meaney Thomas	68	fisherman	51	"
		Davis Court				
	P1	Sylvester Gertrude—†	1	housewife	25	199 London
	R	Sylvester Samuel	1	laborer	28	199 "
	S	Faretra Richard	1	"	25	here
	T	Faretra Thomas	1	clerk	21	"
	U	Faretra Virginia—†	1	at home	23	"
	V	Pinto Joseph	3	laborer	21	
	W	*Pinto Mary G—†	3	housewife	56	"

Davis Court—Continued

Page.	Letter.	Full Name.	Residence, Jan. 1, 1938.	Occupation.	Supposed Age.	Reported Residence, Jan. 1, 1937. Street and Number.
	X	Pinto Nicholas	3	laborer	22	here
	Y	Guerreri Josephine—†	3	operator	21	"
	Z	*Guerreri Philip	3	laborer	55	"
396						
	A	*Guerreri Susie—†	3	housewife	43	"

Havre Street

Page.	Letter.	Full Name.	Residence, Jan. 1, 1938.	Occupation.	Supposed Age.	Reported Residence, Jan. 1, 1937. Street and Number.
	C	*Messina Jennie—†	110	housewife	38	here
	D	Messina Mariano	110	storekeeper	48	"
	F	*Petronio Catherine—†	112	housewife	68	"
	G	*Petronio Gregorio	112	shoemaker	73	"
	E	*Antelmi Frances—†	112	housewife	26	"
	H	*Antelmi Frederick	112	salesman	26	"
	K	*Petronio Gregory, jr	112	shoeworker	36	"
	L	*Petronio Mary S—†	112	housewife	29	"
	M	Vigri Armino	113	laborer	46	
	N	Vigri Carmella—†	113	housewife	39	"
	O	Pecorella Angelina—†	113	"	29	
	P	Pecorella Salvatore	113	storekeeper	36	"
	R	*McDonough Marcella—†	113	housewife	65	"
	S	McDonough Thomas J	113	constable	65	"
	T	Caci Angelo	rear 113	upholsterer	22	205 Princeton
	U	Caci Petrina—†	" 113	housewife	20	here
	V	*DeLorenzo Frank	" 113	laborer	33	"
	W	DeLorenzo Sarah—†	" 113	housewife	30	"
	X	Wellings Francis J	114	bartender	68	"
	Y	Wellings Nora A—†	114	housewife	67	"
	Z	Rodriguez Juanita—†	115	at home	29	
397						
	A	Giordano Caroline—†	115	housewife	65	"
	B	Giordano Phillip	115	bricklayer	69	"
	C	*Giordano Raymond	115	laborer	29	
	D	*Lalicata Angelo	115	"	49	
	E	Lalicata Salvatore	115	busboy	21	
	F	*Palermo Mary—†	rear 115	housewife	37	"
	G	*Palermo Salvatore	" 115	laborer	45	
	H	Testa Mary—†	" 115	at home	42	
	K	Tesca Charles	" 115	laborer	62	
	L	*Tesca Lena—†	" 115	housewife	54	"
	M	Tesca Mary—†	" 115	stenographer	21	"

Page.	Letter.	Full Name.	Residence, Jan. 1, 1938.	Occupation.	Supposed Age.	Reported Residence, Jan. 1, 1937. Street and Number.

Havre Street—Continued

	N	Scola Mary—†	2d r 115	housewife	23	here
	O	Scola Samuel	2d " 115	laborer	25	"
	R	Melia Andrew	2d " 115	"	53	"
	S	*Melia Carmela—†	2d " 115	housewife	41	"
	T	Lynch William C	116	student	21	"
	U	Rezendes Joseph	116	longshoreman	64	109 Meridian
	V	Thorburn Nelson	116	retired	67	here
	W	*Bracale Vincent	117	"	87	"
	X	Caprera Mario	117	laborer	47	"
	Y	*Caprera Mary—†	117	housewife	37	"
	Z	*Pizzo Concetta—†	117	"	47	
398						
	A	Pizzo Paul	117	shoeworker	52	"
	B	Miles Frederick E	118	salesman	37	"
	C	Miles Henry	118	laborer	47	
	D	Miles Josephine—†	118	housewife	32	"
	E	Miles Stephen	118	retired	72	
	F	Bruno Daniel	119	gilder	33	
	G	Bruno Pauline—†	119	housewife	33	"
	H	Bruno Anna—†	119	tailoress	23	
	K	*Bruno Mary—†	119	housekeeper	46	"
	L	Bruno Nicholas	119	candymaker	52	"
	M	Bruno Vetta—†	119	stenographer	26	"
	N	*Poto Palma—†	119	at home	81	"
	O	Bruno Lucy—†	119	stenographer	32	"
	P	Bruno Michael	119	laborer	60	"
	R	Bruno Mildred—†	119	operator	22	"
	T	Camerlingo Alfonso	120	painter	29	
	U	Camerlingo Clementina-†	120	housewife	25	"
	V	*LoConte Antionetta—†	120	"	52	
	W	*LoConte Vincent	120	laborer	62	"
	X	Camerlingo Benjamin	121	painter	35	314 Meridian
	Y	Parenti Dominick	121	machinist	24	here
	Z	Parenti Mildred—†	121	housewife	24	"
399						
	A	Verro Louise—†	121	"	24	
	B	*Verro Pasquale	121	shoeworker	24	"
	C	*Camerlengo Angelina—†	121	housewife	55	"
	D	*Camerlengo Anthony	121	retired	74	
	E	Camerlengo Margaret—†	121	seamstress	20	"
	F	Fera Lucy—†	122	housewife	25	"

Page.	Letter.	Full Name.	Residence, Jan. 1, 1938.	Occupation.	Supposed Age.	Reported Residence, Jan. 1, 1937. Street and Number.

Havre Street—Continued

Page.	Letter.	Full Name.	Residence, Jan. 1, 1938.	Occupation.	Supposed Age.	Reported Residence, Jan. 1, 1937. Street and Number.
	G	Fera Martin	122	operator	26	here
	H	*Guarenti Andrea	122	laborer	53	"
	K	Guarenti Daniel	122	"	22	"
	L	*Guarenti Florence—†	122	housewife	48	"
	M	Guarenti John	122	cutter	21	"
	N	Bruno Aniello	122	laborer	42	23 Princeton
	O	Bruno Fidella—†	122	housewife	32	23 "
	P	Bellone Antonio	126	baker	24	here
	R	Bellone Virginia—†	126	housewife	23	"
	S	Pepe Joseph	126	laborer	40	1 Drake pl
	T	Pepe Lena—†	126	housewife	34	1 "
	U	*Pepe Patricia—†	126	housekeeper	66	1 "
	V	Uccello Concettina—†	126	at home	22	here
	W	Uccello Concetto	126	laborer	48	"
	X	*Uccello Filomena—†	126	housewife	40	"
	Z	*Messina Antonio	128	fisherman	59	100 Sumner
400						
	A	*Messina Gracia—†	128	housewife	56	100 "
	B	*Santos Aldegundes—†	128	"	45	220 Havre
	C	Santos John, jr	128	fisherman	20	220 "
	D	*Santos John W	128	"	48	220 "
	E	*DeMeo Alfonsina—†	128	housekeeper	56	here
	F	Fungilo Albino	128	barber	25	"
	G	Fungilo Mary—†	128	housewife	20	"
	H	*Modica Angela—†	131	at home	77	
	K	*Modica Joseph	131	laborer	79	
	L	Modica Carmela—†	131	housewife	31	"
	M	Modica Joseph	131	painter	35	"
	N	*Valletta Frank	131	storekeeper	49	126 Havre
	O	*Valletta Mary—†	131	housewife	49	here
	P	Seracuse Alice—†	132	"	22	"
	R	Seracuse Joseph	132	clerk	22	"
	S	Dantona Frances—†	132	housewife	41	"
	T	Dantona Leo R	132	salesman	21	"
	U	Dantona Liborio	132	tailor	47	
	V	Pascucci Joseph	132	laborer	42	
	W	Pascucci Olympia—†	132	housewife	42	"
	X	*Caruso Catherine—†	133	"	44	
	Y	*Caruso Natale	133	laborer	46	
	Z	Barber Frank	133	chauffeur	41	"

Page.	Letter.	FULL NAME.	Residence, Jan. 1, 1938.	Occupation.	Supposed Age.	Reported Residence, Jan. 1, 1937. Street and Number.

401
Havre Street—Continued

	A	Barber Marie—†	133	housewife	31	here
	B	Cunho Mary E—†	133	at home	66	"
	C	DeCarlo Elizabeth—†	134	housekeeper	41	"
	D	DeFilippi Anne—†	134	housewife	45	"
	E	DeFilippi Pasquale	134	laborer	50	
	F	*Spina Caroline—†	134	housewife	44	"
	G	Spina Gaetano	134	pedler	48	"
	H	LaMonica Salvatore	135	laborer	23	184 London
	K	Lewis Arthur	135	"	39	here
	L	Lewis Josephine—†	135	housewife	38	"
	M	*Pantano Nazarina—†	135	"	40	"
	N	*Pantano Santo	135	mason	43	
	O	Bellevue Anna J—†	136	housekeeper	70	"
	P	Callahan Laura—†	136	"	58	"
	R	Lanning Ellen—†	136	"	48	"
	S	Arcaro Nellie—†	137	housewife	34	Medford
	T	*Arcaro Pasquale	137	tailor	42	"
	U	Pasqualino Angelo	137	laborer	52	here
	V	*Pasqualino Frances—†	137	housewife	45	"
	W	Pasqualino Rose—†	137	tailoress	20	"
	X	Salvaggio Leonardo	137	laborer	39	6 Salutation
	Y	*Salvaggio Phillipa—†	137	at home	70	6 "
402						
	A	Silva Blanche—†	138	housewife	24	1008 Bennington
	B	Silva John	138	painter	24	1008 "
	C	*Ferraro John	138	shoemaker	43	102 Chelsea
	D	Ferraro Mary—†	138	housewife	31	102 "
	E	Romonelli Charles	138	musician	27	68 "
	F	Scozella Angelina—†	139	housewife	24	here
	G	Scozella Louis	139	plumber	29	"
	H	Purnell Mildred—†	139	housewife	24	"
	K	Purnell William	139	freighthandler	29	"
	L	Chiango Frank	139	shipper	27	
	M	Chiango Helen—†	139	housewife	25	"
	O	*Tomasella Josephine—†	141	"	45	
	P	*Tomasella Luigi	141	laborer	52	
	R	Tomasella Santa—†	141	at home	20	
	S	Pitari Agreppina—†	141	housewife	43	"
	T	Pitari Agreppino	141	laborer	45	

Page.	Letter.	Full Name.	Residence, Jan. 1, 1938.	Occupation.	Supposed Age.	Reported Residence, Jan. 1, 1937. Street and Number.

Havre Street—Continued

Page.	Letter.	Full Name.	Residence, Jan. 1, 1938.	Occupation.	Supposed Age.	Reported Residence, Jan. 1, 1937. Street and Number.
	U	Pitari Marie—†	141	at home	21	here
	V	Vella Frances—†	141	housewife	24	32 Orleans
	W	Vella Joseph	141	barber	30	32 “
	X	*DelVento Incoronata—†	142	housewife	37	here
	Y	DelVento Nicola	142	laborer	46	“
	Z	DeLucca Hilda—†	142	housewife	33	“
403						
	A	DeLucca John	142	bartender	35	“
	B	Valiante George	143	laborer	30	25 Eutaw
	C	Valiante Nina—†	143	housewife	23	25 “
	D	Augusto Anthony	143	secretary	32	148 London
	E	Augusto Celia—†	143	housewife	28	148 “
	F	Feulo Salvatore	143	laborer	43	103 Liverpool
	H	*Cataldo Antonio	144	pedler	52	here
	K	*Cataldo Mary—†	144	housewife	48	“
	L	Antonucci Corinna—†	144	“	36	93 Webster
	M	Antonucci Giacinto	144	bricklayer	45	93 “
	N	Cianciulli Louis	145	shoeworker	38	6 William J Kelly sq
	O	Giampitro Joseph	145	baker	20	here
	P	*Giampitro Lewis	145	laborer	45	“
	R	*Piaza Catrina—†	145	housewife	37	“
	S	*Piaza Joseph	145	laborer	43	
	T	Coco Anthony	145	shoeworker	21	“
	U	Coco Joseph	145	“	52	“
	V	Salini Antonia—†	147	housewife	20	Malden
	W	Salini Lewis	147	laborer	21	“
	X	*LaRosa Antonio	147	tailor	37	here
	Y	*LaRosa Grace—†	147	housewife	29	“
	Z	*Cali Rose—†	147	“	37	“
404						
	A	Cali Vincenzo	147	laborer	40	
	B	Mancuso Mary—†	148	housewife	38	“
	C	Mancuso Salvatore	148	operator	47	“
	D	Briana Caroline—†	148	housewife	42	“
	E	Briana William	148	operator	45	“
	F	*Recupero Frank	149	pedler	51	
	G	*Recupero Laura—†	149	housewife	53	“
	H	Ferrara Anna—†	149	“	24	
	K	Ferrara Joseph	149	laborer	25	
	L	*Mischio Antonetta—†	149	at home	43	
	M	*Mischio Michael	149	laborer	53	

Page.	Letter.	Full Name.	Residence, Jan. 1, 1938.	Occupation.	Supposed Age.	Reported Residence, Jan. 1, 1937. Street and Number.

Havre Street—Continued

	N	Mischio Philomena—†	149	candymaker	22	here
	O	Loconte Gertrude H—†	153	housewife	20	256 E Eagle
	P	Loconte Joseph O	153	pedler	24	here
	R	Loconte Arthur	153	laborer	56	"
	S	*Loconte Concetta—†	153	housewife	49	"
	T	Sawyer Marie—†	153	"	34	
	U	Sawyer Walter	153	laborer	35	
	V	Meloni Fred	155	leatherworker	25	"
	W	Meloni Phyllis—†	155	housewife	27	"
	X	Santora Arthur	155	shipper	24	
	Y	Santora Gilda—†	155	housewife	26	"
	Z	Capone Anthony	155	operator	32	
405						
	A	Capone Mary—†	155	housewife	33	"
	B	*Lopaz Epolito	157	retired	82	
	C	*Barrasso Emmanuela—†	157	housewife	44	"
	D	*Barrasso Frank	157	shoeworker	49	"
	E	Barrasso Rosario	157	clerk	20	
	F	*Zacchiara Josephine—†	157	housekeeper	47	"
	G	*Ripa Lucy—†	159	housewife	64	"
	H	Ripa Sebastian	159	retired	64	
	K	Diorio Joseph	159	laborer	41	"
	L	Diorio Minnie—†	159	housewife	40	"
	M	*DeStefano Giuseppe	159	laborer	50	
	N	*DeStefano Leboria—†	159	housewife	40	"
	O	*Mannuccia Cosmo	161	laborer	58	
	P	*Mannuccia Mary—†	161	housewife	61	"
	R	Barone Canio	161	pedler	44	
	S	Doherty Frank	161	operator	32	"
	T	Doherty Rita—†	161	housewife	21	"
	V	Nickerson Clara—†	175	at home	67	Lowell
	W	Tramonte Albert	175	shoecutter	45	here
	X	Tramonte Albert, jr	175	fishcutter	21	"
	Y	Tramonte Nellie—†	175	housewife	42	"
	Z	*DiCino Anthony	175	laborer	55	
406						
	A	DiCino Margaret—†	175	housewife	34	"
	B	Stokes John C	176	lather	32	
	C	Stokes Eva—†	176	housewife	34	"
	D	Salerno Madaline—†	176	"	28	
	E	Salerno Michael	176	chauffeur	34	"

Havre Street—Continued

Page.	Letter.	Full Name.	Residence, Jan. 1, 1938.	Occupation.	Supposed Age.	Reported Residence, Jan. 1, 1937. Street and Number.
	F	Puzzo Lena—†	178	housewife	27	here
	G	Puzzo Salvatore	178	laborer	37	"
	H	Diapolito Pasquale	178	"	27	"
	K	Diapolito Rocco	178	pedler	49	
	L	Diapolito Rosaria—†	178	housewife	47	"
	M	Cresenzi Adam	178	painter	46	
	N	Cresenzi Adam A, jr	178	"	22	"
	O	Cresenzi Angelina M—†	178	housewife	42	"
	P	DiMartino Marino	178	pressman	42	"
	R	Bertulli Alfred	179	clerk	28	"
	S	Bertulli Arthur	179	laborer	25	
	T	*Bertulli Elsie—†	179	housewife	53	"
	U	Bertulli Louise—†	179	packer	27	
	V	*Bertulli Nazarino	179	meatcutter	59	"
	W	Bertulli Angelina—†	179	packer	21	
	X	Bertulli Patrick	179	varnishmaker	23	"
	Y	*Crisafulli Epifaneo	179	printer	21	81 Chelsea
	Z	*Crisafulli Philomena—†	179	at home	54	81 "
407	A	*Donatelli Celia—†	181	housewife	60	here
	B	Donatelli Gaetano	181	laborer	62	"
	C	Donatelli Louis	181	"	21	"
	D	Donatelli Mary—†	181	at home	26	
	E	Jensen Eric A	183	rigger	68	
	F	Jensen Mary A—†	183	housewife	64	"
	G	Deluple Florence—†	183	"	32	
	H	Delupe John	183	fishcutter	40	"
	K	Gleason Catherine—†	183	housewife	32	"
	L	Gleason George	183	letter carrier	37	"
	M	*Falzone Elsie—†	184	housewife	28	"
	N	*Falzone Vincent	184	pedler	30	
	O	*Falzone Louis	184	laborer	65	
	P	Falzone Rego	184	"	20	
	R	*Rialli Anthony	184	storekeeper	34	"
	S	*Rialli Theresa—†	184	housewife	26	"
	T	Batchelder Frank J	185	laborer	61	
	U	Batchelder Margaret E–†	185	housewife	61	"
	V	*Pandolfo Angelina—†	185	"	40	
	W	*Pandolfo Matteo	185	laborer	49	"
	X	Pandolfo Victoria—†	185	clerk	22	
	Y	*Ciarcia Anna—†	185	housewife	39	"

Page.	Letter.	Full Name.	Residence, Jan. 1, 1938.	Occupation.	Supposed Age.	Reported Residence, Jan. 1, 1937. Street and Number.

Havre Street—Continued

Page.	Letter.	Full Name.	Residence, Jan. 1, 1938.	Occupation.	Supposed Age.	Reported Residence, Jan. 1, 1937. Street and Number.
	Z	Ciarcia Michael	185	laborer	47	here
408						
	A	*Minichiello Nancy—†	186	housewife	37	“
	B	Minichiello Salvatore	186	candymaker	39	“
	C	*Sciortino Angelina—†	187	housewife	45	“
	D	Sciortino Joseph	187	laborer	45	
	E	Vella Alphonse L	187	“	33	
	F	*Vella Rose—†	187	housewife	29	“
	G	*Leonardi John	187	retired	74	
	H	*Leonardi Rose—†	187	housewife	53	“
	K	*Ruggiero Antonetta—†	189	at home	43	
	L	Ruggiero Lewis	189	laborer	23	
	M	Palagreco Joseph	189	“	25	
	N	*Palagreco Lena—†	189	at home	31	
	O	*Palagreco Phillip	189	retired	76	
	P	*Palagreco Phillipa—†	189	housewife	66	“
	R	*Palagreco Charles	189	chauffeur	36	“
	S	Palagreco Josephine—†	189	housewife	31	“
	T	Annese Carmen	194	carpenter	45	“
	U	Caparelle Cesero	194	laborer	20	
	V	Covino James	194	chauffeur	44	“
	W	Covino Louis	194	“	21	
	X	*Covino Mary—†	194	housewife	54	“
	Y	Trifari Almerinda—†	195	“	70	
	Z	Trifari Joseph	195	rubberworker	60	“
409						
	A	Mazzarello Angelo	195	shoemaker	32	“
	B	*Mazzarella Francesco	195	shoeworker	58	“
	C	*Mazzarella Mary—†	195	housewife	48	“
	D	Albescia Grace—†	195	“	23	
	E	Albescia Louis A	195	manager	25	
	G	Nealon Catherine D—†	196	housekeeper	65	“
	H	Ryder Patrick H	196	retired	67	“
	K	*Pomodoro Frank	197	laborer	52	
	L	*Pomodoro Josephine—†	197	housewife	42	“
	M	*DeLario Carmela—†	197	at home	76	
	N	DeSalvo Michael	197	grocer	40	
	O	*DeSalvo Sarah—†	197	housewife	36	“
	P	Amato Frank	197	cabinetmaker	28	“
	R	Amato Marion—†	197	housewife	24	“
	S	Lacorazza Anthony	198	nickelplater	26	“

Page.	Letter.	Full Name.	Residence, Jan. 1, 1938.	Occupation.	Supposed Age.	Reported Residence, Jan. 1, 1937. Street and Number.

Havre Street—Continued

Page.	Letter.	Full Name.	Residence, Jan. 1, 1938.	Occupation.	Supposed Age.	Reported Residence, Jan. 1, 1937.
	T	Lacorazza Lena—†	198	housewife	22	here
	U	Romano Anna—†	198	"	31	Connecticut
	V	Romano Paul	198	storekeeper	35	"
	W	*Roberto Clara—†	198	housewife	49	here
	X	*Roberto Louis	198	pedler	44	"
	Y	Falzarano Angelo	199	laborer	24	"
	Z	*Falzarano Dominick	199	"	60	
410						
	B	*Falzarano Frances—†	199	housewife	58	"
	C	Falzarano Henry	199	laborer	20	
	D	*Giampapa Alphonse	201	"	41	
	E	*Giampapa Rose—†	201	housewife	37	"
	F	Walker Samuel	201	retired	56	
	G	Corsi Angelo	201	laborer	50	
	H	Cuozzo Mary—†	201	stenographer	23	"
	K	*Cuozzo Rose—†	201	housewife	47	"
	L	*Cuozzo Valentino	201	laborer	49	"
	N	*Coombs Anna—†	202	housewife	28	128 Princeton
	O	*Coombs John	202	fisherman	34	128 "
	P	*Quarantiello Celia—†	202	housewife	47	here
	R	Quarantiello Domenic	202	laborer	21	"
	S	*Quarantiello William	202	"	48	"
	T	*Falzarano Angelina—†	202	housewife	31	"
	U	*Falzarano Vincent	202	chauffeur	34	"
	V	Rialli Jennie—†	206	clerk	20	
	W	Rialli Joseph	206	mason	66	
	X	Rialli Mary—†	206	housewife	56	"
	Y	Arinella Anna—†	206	"	47	
	Z	Arinella Genaro	206	longshoreman	54	"
411						
	A	Arinella Mildred—†	206	candyworker	26	"
	B	DiChristiforo Carmella-†	206	housewife	46	"
	C	DiChristiforo Mildred—†	206	packer	24	
	D	DiChristiforo Peter	206	stonecutter	49	"
	E	DiChristiforo Peter	206	laborer	21	
	F	Giangrande John	207	"	45	
	G	*Giangrande Mary—†	207	housewife	38	"
	H	Mustone Alfred	208	pedler	23	
	K	Mustone Angelo	208	chauffeur	25	"
	L	Mustone Mary—†	208	housewife	43	"
	M	Mustone Saverio	208	laborer	52	"

Page.	Letter.	Full Name.	Residence, Jan. 1, 1938.	Occupation.	Supposed Age.	Reported Residence, Jan. 1, 1937. Street and Number.

Havre Street—Continued

Page.	Letter.	Full Name.	Residence, Jan. 1, 1938.	Occupation.	Supposed Age.	Reported Residence, Jan. 1, 1937. Street and Number.
	N	Mustone Susie—†	208	saleswoman	21	here
	O	Heres Rose—†	208	housewife	28	86 Bremen
	P	Heres William	208	laborer	28	86 "
	R	Sacco Rocco	209	"	35	here
	T	Greco Anthony	209	retired	68	"
	U	*Greco Catherine—†	209	housewife	54	"
	V	*Holden Blanche—†	rear 209	"	24	508 Sumner
	W	Holden Frederick	" 209	machinist	39	508 "
	X	Gallo James	" 209	tilesetter	29	168 Putnam
	Y	Gallo Margaret—†	" 209	housewife	24	168 "
	Z	Gioiso Phyllis—†	" 209	"	21	here
412						
	A	Gioiso Vincent	" 209	laborer	25	
	B	Russo Angelo	210	candymaker	45	"
	C	*Russo Frances—†	210	housewife	39	"
	D	Russo Salvatore	210	laborer	20	
	E	*Finocchio Anna—†	211	at home	45	
	F	Finocchio Anthony	211	laborer	22	"
	G	Juliano Joseph	213	bartender	37	163 Chelsea
	H	Juliano Lena—†	213	housewife	33	163 "
	K	Elesio Edward	213	retired	79	here
	K[1]	Elesio Edward, jr	213	marblesetter	27	"
	L	Elesio Euphemia—†	213	housewife	67	"
	M	Croswell William	214	operator	48	"
	N	Lippert Elizabeth—†	214	housewife	46	"
	O	Lippert Rudolph	214	mechanic	55	"
	P	Casiello Alvera—†	215	candymaker	23	"
	R	Casiello Anthony	215	pedler	56	
	S	*Casiello Filomena—†	215	housewife	58	"
	T	Casiello John	215	clerk	20	"
	U	Recca Angelo	215	laborer	22	476 Saratoga
	V	Recca Joseph	215	"	54	476 "
	W	Recca Marie—†	215	operator	21	476 "
	X	*Recca Mary—†	215	housewife	47	476 "
	Y	Rossetti Angelina—†	215	clerk	21	here
	Z	Rossetti Flora—†	215	saleswoman	24	"
413						
	A	*Rossetti Jennie—†	215	housewife	55	"
	B	Rossetti Leanora—†	215	operator	26	
	C	Rossetti Thomas	215	retired	63	
	D	O'Neil Ada M—†	216	housewife	56	"

Page.	Letter.	Full Name.	Residence, Jan. 1, 1938.	Occupation.	Supposed Age.	Reported Residence, Jan. 1, 1937. Street and Number.
		Havre Street—Continued				
	E	O'Niel John	216	boilermaker	60	here
	F	Trainor Dorothy A—†	216	housewife	27	“
	G	Trainor Owen J	216	longshoreman	28	“
	H	Irwin Francis W	216	clerk	32	
	K	Irwin Julia—†	216	housekeeper	65	“
	L	Monahan William B	216	clerk	35	“
	M	O'Farrell Mary J—†	216	housewife	28	“
	N	Taft Margaret—†	216	“	30	
	O	Tigges Herman	216	clerk	45	
	P	*Provinsano Margaret–†	r 216	housewife	45	“
	R	*Provinsano Salvatore	“ 216	laborer	46	“
	S	*Quartarone Frank	217	barber	50	
	T	*Quartarone Jennie—†	217	housewife	51	“
	U	DelloRusso Lucy—†	217	“	22	“
	V	*DelloRusso Orlando	217	printer	37	
	W	DelloRusso Amedeo	217	laborer	33	
	X	*DelloRusso Carlo	217	retired	64	
	Y	DelloRusso Emelia—†	217	packer	26	“
	Z	DelloRusso Matilda—†	217	“	31	“
414						
	A	*DelloRusso Raffaella—†	217	housewife	63	“
	B	DelloRusso Romeo	217	printer	23	
	C	O'Neill Albert	218	cook	28	
	D	O'Neill Harriet—†	218	housewife	27	“
	E	*Crescenzo Bragio	218	laborer	41	“
	F	*Crescenzo Rose—†	218	housewife	30	“
	G	*Maienza Rose—†	218	“	48	
	H	Maienza Salva	218	laborer	65	“
	K	Aronson Jacob	220	salesman	23	“
	L	Aronson Muriel—†	220	at home	26	“
	M	Aronson Robert	220	retired	68	
	N	*Aronson Rose—†	220	housewife	58	“
	O	Quigley Helen—†	220	“	31	“
	P	Quigley William	220	packer	35	“
	S	Pederson Herbert	rear 220	woodcarver	30	325 Bremen
	T	*Pederson Zita—†	“ 220	housewife	29	325 “
	U	*Nigro Nicholas	“ 220	laborer	48	here
	V	*Cerullo Antonio	“ 220	machinist	56	“
	W	*Cerullo Clara—†	“ 220	housewife	47	“
	X	*Devincentis Ann—†	“ 220	“	68	6 Lexington pl
	Y	French Anna—†	“ 220	“	22	19 Trenton

Page.	Letter.	Full Name.	Residence, Jan. 1, 1938.	Occupation.	Supposed Age.	Reported Residence, Jan. 1, 1937. Street and Number.

Havre Street—Continued

Page.	Letter.	Full Name.	Residence, Jan. 1, 1938.	Occupation.	Supposed Age.	Reported Residence, Jan. 1, 1937. Street and Number.
	z	French Roy	rear 220	electrician	27	19 Trenton
415						
	A	*Fenno Virginia—†	“ 220	housewife	59	here
	B	LaGrassa Peter	221	laborer	21	10 Battery
	C	LaGrassa Virginia—†	221	housewife	22	52 Porter
	D	*Durante Celia—†	221	“	54	here
	E	Durante Helen—†	221	clerk	21	“
	F	*Durante Pasquale	221	laborer	51	“
	G	Hay Catherine—†	221	housewife	20	“
	H	Hay Charles	221	laborer	21	
	K	Carroll Mary A—†	223	at home	70	
	L	Mahoney Mary E—†	223	“	73	
	N	Dioguardi Clara—†	226	operator	29	“
	O	Dioguardi Ida—†	226	“	26	
	P	Dioguardi Nicholas	226	carpenter	33	“
	R	*Dioguardi Otina—†	226	housekeeper	69	“
	S	McCarthy Florence J	227	retired	80	“
	T	Rutsky Abraham	228	ironworker	37	“
	U	*Rutsky Gertrude—†	228	housewife	69	“
	V	Rutsky Jacob	228	retired	66	“
	W	Rutsky Joseph	228	machinist	39	“
	X	*Ferlino Frank	228	laborer	55	
	Y	Ferlino Margaret—†	228	operator	21	“
	Z	*Ferlino Mary—†	228	housewife	53	“
416						
	A	*Grasso Angelina—†	228	“	43	
	B	Grasso Dominic	228	chauffeur	21	“
	C	*Grasso Philip	228	barber	53	
	D	*Bowen Mary—†	229	housewife	64	“
	E	*Bowen Patrick	229	fishcutter	59	“
	F	Cox Francis	229	freighthandler	22	“
	G	Hazlewood Annie—†	229	housewife	66	“
	H	Hazlewood Charles	229	laborer	66	
	K	*King Catherine—†	229	housewife	49	“
	L	*King Thomas	229	laborer	57	“
	M	Mainieri Nicholas	230	“	22	369 Chelsea
	N	*DePerri Palma—†	230	housewife	54	here
	O	*DePerri Salvatore	230	retired	57	“
	P	DePerri Salvatore, jr	230	clerk	21	“
	R	*Neves Anna—†	230	housewife	41	“
	S	*Neves Lawrence	230	seaman	51	“

Page.	Letter.	Full Name.	Residence, Jan. 1, 1938.	Occupation.	Supposed Age.	Reported Residence, Jan. 1, 1937. Street and Number.

Havre Street—Continued

Page.	Letter.	Full Name.	Residence, Jan. 1, 1938.	Occupation.	Supposed Age.	Reported Residence, Jan. 1, 1937. Street and Number.
	V	Lippert Charles R	236	caretaker	27	here
	W	Lippert Edna—†	236	housewife	26	"
	X	Doherty James	236	laborer	35	"
	Y	*Doherty Margaret—†	236	housekeeper	76	"
	Z	Donovan Catherine—†	236	housewife	65	"
417						
	A	*Hennessey Catherine T–†	236	clerk	34	
	B	*Amoroso Catherine—†	238	housewife	42	"
	C	Amoroso Salvatore	238	laborer	57	
	D	Amoroso Salvatore	238	toymaker	20	"
	E	*Mancuso Mary—†	238	housewife	38	"
	F	*Adragna John	238	laborer	43	
	G	*Adragna Filippa—†	238	housewife	36	"
	H	Doucette Charlotte—†	239	at home	73	
	K	*Kelly Delia—†	239	"	65	
	L	Critch Charles W	239	chauffeur	22	"
	M	Critch Josephine—†	239	housewife	21	"
	N	Frizzi Anthony	240	laborer	46	
	O	*Frizzi Elvira—†	240	housewife	46	"
	P	Kennedy Anna M—†	241	at home	71	
	R	*Melanson Anthony	241	laborer	21	"
	S	*Melanson Mary—†	241	at home	65	
	T	Boyne Patrick	241	freighthandler	55	"
	U	*Sears Mary—†	243	housekeeper	68	"
	V	*Reardon Lillian—†	243	"	52	"
	W	Lewis Eva—†	243	housewife	37	"
	X	Lewis Glenn	243	operator	47	"
	Y	*Gozzo Rosita—†	244	housewife	44	"
	Z	*Gozzo Sebastiano	244	salesman	59	"
418						
	A	Vaccaro Charles	244	weaver	27	
	B	*Vaccaro Mary—†	244	housewife	40	"
	C	*Vaccaro Salvatore	244	retired	60	
	D	*Bishop Bernard	244	laborer	47	
	E	*Bishop Maud—†	244	housewife	47	"
	F	DelloRusso Jean—†	rear 244	"	27	
	H	*Decarro Lena—†	245	housekeeper	52	"
	K	*Mingoia Salvatore	245	laborer	44	"
	L	*Mingoia Stella—†	245	housewife	32	"
	M	*Mancusa Francesca—†	245	housekeeper	79	"
	N	*Repoli Albina—†	246	housewife	34	"

Page.	Letter.	Full Name.	Residence, Jan. 1, 1938.	Occupation.	Supposed Age.	Reported Residence, Jan. 1, 1937. Street and Number.

Havre Street—Continued

Page.	Letter.	Full Name.	Residence, Jan. 1, 1938.	Occupation.	Supposed Age.	Reported Residence, Jan. 1, 1937. Street and Number.
	o	*Repoli Frank	246	finisher	44	here
	p	*Milillo Elvira—†	246	housewife	46	"
	r	Milillo Guy	246	clerk	21	"
	s	*Scimone Angelo	247	machinist	24	"
	t	*Scimone Calogero	247	retired	72	
	u	*Scimone Johanna—†	247	housewife	62	"
	v	*Pita Manuel C	247	weaver	45	169 Paris
	w	*Rosa Joseph	247	laborer	21	here
	x	*Rosa Mary—†	247	housekeeper	38	"
	y	Mini Andrew	259	chauffeur	26	"
	z	Mini Lena—†	259	housewife	22	"
419						
	c	DiLorenzo Fortunato	259	clerk	32	
	d	DiLorenzo Frances—†	259	housewife	26	"
	a	Fortunato Joseph	259	retired	74	
	b	*Fortunato Maria—†	259	housewife	67	"
	e	*Salimbene Anne—†	259	"	45	
	f	*Salimbene Benjamin	259	laborer	47	
	g	Salimbene Charles	259	mechanic	24	"
	h	Rossette Mary—†	261	housewife	31	587 Benningt'n
	k	Rossette Ralph	261	shoeworker	32	587 "
	l	Zona Alvira—†	261	stitcher	21	here
	n	Zona Frances—†	261	at home	20	"
	m	*Zona Grace—†	261	housewife	45	"
	o	Zona Jennie—†	261	laundress	24	"
	p	Zona Michael	261	polisher	51	
	r	Zona Rose—†	261	laundress	23	"
	s	*Barrese Mary—†	261	housewife	51	149 Cottage
	t	*Barrese Nicola	261	laborer	48	149 "
	u	Barrese Roy	261	"	22	149 "
	v	Quartarone Mario	262	"	31	here
	w	*Quartarone Minnie—†	262	housewife	37	"
	x	McPhee Joseph	262	laborer	32	186 Marion
	y	McPhee Rose—†	262	housewife	25	186 "
	z	Schepici Rose—†	262	"	21	here
420						
	a	Schepici Salvatore	262	toymaker	25	"
	b	Beck Harry	263	electrician	50	"
	c	Beck Ida—†	263	housewife	43	"
	d	Schlosberg Samuel	263	chauffeur	48	"
	e	Stone Rose—†	263	housewife	31	"

Page.	Letter.	Full Name.	Residence, Jan. 1, 1938.	Occupation.	Supposed Age.	Reported Residence, Jan. 1, 1937. Street and Number.

Havre Street—Continued

	F	Stone Samuel	263	druggist	37	here
	G	Wolf Ethel—†	263	housekeeper	48	"
	H	Wolf Leo	263	druggist	26	"
	K	Wolf Milton	263	chemist	22	
	L	*Giambusso Carmella—†	263	housewife	40	"
	M	*Giambusso Charles	263	laborer	50	"
	N	Fahey Edward	264	"	34	
	O	Fahey Martha—†	264	housewife	28	"
	P	DiSilvestro Joseph	264	laborer	27	
	R	DiSilvestro Theresa—†	264	housewife	22	"
	S	Sindoni Anthony	264	finisher	36	
	T	Sindoni Domenica—†	264	housewife	31	"
	U	Stellato Betty—†	265	"	25	
	V	Stellato Frank	265	painter	28	
	W	*Avola Anna—†	265	housewife	42	"
	X	Avola John	265	shoeworker	44	"
	Y	*Miraglila Carmella—†	265	housewife	33	"
	Z	*Miraglila Josephine—†	265	housekeeper	69	"
421						
	A	*Miraglila Rocco	265	cobbler	42	
	B	Panzini Dominic	266	laborer	30	
	C	Panzini Philomena—†	266	housewife	25	"
	D	Colotti Anthony	266	shoemaker	22	"
	E	Colotti Carmen	266	laborer	25	
	F	Colotti Josephine—†	266	packer	21	"
	G	Colotti Mary—†	266	candymaker	23	"
	H	Colotti Michael	266	laborer	53	"
	K	*Colotti Sarah—†	266	housewife	48	"
	L	*Costello Elizabeth—†	267	"	30	"
	M	Costello Valentine	267	laborer	42	"
	N	Avola Liborio	267	shoeworker	50	"
	O	Avola Rosalia—†	267	housewife	42	"
	P	Brignolo Cero	267	barber	32	Lawrence
	R	Brignolo Mary—†	267	housewife	26	91 Chelsea
	S	Simmons Abel	268	seaman	55	here
	T	Simmons Frances—†	268	clerk	22	"
	U	*Simmons Mary—†	268	housewife	59	"
	V	*Edmonds Sadie—†	270	"	44	
	W	*Edmonds William	270	laborer	57	
	X	Lawless Olive—†	270	housewife	46	"
	Y	Lawless Oliver	270	laborer	48	

Page.	Letter.	FULL NAME.	Residence, Jan. 1, 1938.	Occupation.	Supposed Age.	Reported Residence, Jan. 1, 1937. Street and Number.

Havre Street—Continued

	z	*Loscocco Manuel	271	laborer	49	here
422						
	A	*Loscocco Philomena—†	271	housewife	42	"
	B	Mondello Ethel—†	271	"	38	
	C	Mondello Frank	271	carpenter	46	"
	D	Mondello James F	271	musician	20	"
	E	*Lazzaro Anna—†	271	housewife	41	"
	F	Lazzaro Philip	271	laborer	47	
	G	Rotondo Salvatore	271	chauffeur	41	"
	H	Caulfield John	272	letter carrier	59	"
	K	Caulfield Mary E—†	272	housewife	56	"
	L	Caulfield Nellie—†	272	at home	39	
	M	Griffiths Catherine—†	273	housekeeper	86	"
	N	Griffiths Walter F	273	painter	57	"
	O	Griffiths William J	273	attendant	21	"
	P	Murphy Elizabeth—†	274	housewife	54	"
	R	Murphy Helen—†	274	at home	27	
	S	Murphy John H	274	shipper	22	
	T	Murphy Joseph W	274	clerk	25	
	U	Terriciano Angelina—†	275	housekeeper	62	"
	V	Terriciano Salvatore	275	laborer	20	"
	W	Sciome Helen—†	275	stitcher	26	
	X	Russo George	275	tailor	28	
	Y	Russo Margaret—†	275	housewife	23	"
	Z	Battista Emilio	rear 275	attendant	40	"
423						
	A	Battista Rose—†	" 275	housewife	35	"
	B	D'Angelo Vincenzo	276	laborer	52	
	C	Pace Antonio	276	"	52	
	D	*Pace Rachel—†	276	housewife	57	"
	E	Ianello Pasquale	277	laborer	35	
	F	*Ianello Santa—†	277	housewife	32	"
	G	*Avila Anna—†	277	"	45	
	H	Avila Josephine—†	277	dressmaker	21	"
	K	Avila Michael	277	laborer	54	
	L	Buccheri Joseph	277	carpenter	34	"
	M	*Buccheri Mary—†	277	housewife	29	"
	N	Merchant Agnes—†	278	"	34	
	O	Merchant Edward	278	laborer	40	
	P	*Norcott Peter	278	fisherman	27	"
	R	Seminatore Joseph	279	operator	42	

Page.	Letter.	Full Name.	Residence, Jan. 1, 1938.	Occupation.	Supposed Age.	Reported Residence, Jan. 1, 1937. Street and Number.

Havre Street—Continued

	s	*Seminatore Susie—†	279	housewife	35	here
	T	Stella Angie—†	279	"	36	"
	U	Stella Charles	279	barber	46	"
	V	Pesce Carmella—†	279	operator	21	"
	W	Pesce Ignazio	279	laborer	50	
	X	Pesce Joseph	279	painter	23	
	Y	*Pesce Josephine—†	279	housewife	49	"
	Z	Beatrice Salvatore	280	laborer	44	"
424						
	A	*Memmolo Pasquale	280	"	41	
	B	*Memmolo Peter	280	"	44	
	C	Collyer Mary—†	280	at home	71	
	D	Mulcahy Loretta—†	281	housekeeper	50	"
	E	Shea Mary—†	281	accountant	29	"
	F	Shea Maurice	281	laborer	74	
	G	Carlton Marion A—†	281	entertainer	24	"
	H	Carlton Sarah T—†	281	housewife	56	"
	K	Carlton William H	281	pedler	54	
	L	Gessner Bernard	283	policeman	36	"
	M	Gessner Mary T—†	283	housewife	37	"
	N	Ferguson William J	283	clerk	58	"
	O	Lyons Edward H	283	mechanic	50	176 Poplar
	P	Winterston Catherine F–†	283	housekeeper	44	here
	R	Harkens Anna L—†	283	at home	49	"
	S	Harkens Anne M—†	283	housekeeper	77	"
	T	Reed Anne E—†	289	housewife	72	647 Saratoga
	U	Reed Benjamin	289	retired	84	647 "
	V	White Edward	289	"	80	here
	W	White Ellen—†	289	housewife	47	"
	X	White Simon J	289	baker	46	"
	Y	MacKay Mary A—†	289	housewife	24	385 Ashmont
	Z	MacKay Samuel W	289	laborer	50	385 "
425						
	A	White Everett J	291	fisherman	33	here
	B	White Mary J—†	291	housewife	61	"
	C	White Uriel	291	carpenter	62	"
	D	Swan Catherine—†	291	housewife	21	"
	E	Swan Edwin A, jr	291	shipper	29	
	F	*Figliolini Antonetta—†	291	housewife	49	"
	G	*Figliolini Constantine	291	tailor	22	
	H	*Figliolini Pasquale	291	"	48	

Page.	Letter.	Full Name.	Residence, Jan. 1, 1938.	Occupation.	Supposed Age.	Reported Residence, Jan. 1, 1937. Street and Number.

Havre Street—Continued

	K	*Figliolini Salvatore	291	upholsterer	25	here
	L	*Garofalo Charles	293	engineer	54	"
	M	*Garofalo Donata—†	293	housewife	53	"
	N	*Garofalo Pasquale	293	retired	69	
	O	Garofalo Vincent G	293	shoeworker	41	"
	P	*Ruo Dora—†	293	housewife	34	"
	R	*Ruo Frank	293	shoeworker	37	"
	T	Navarro Celia—†	295	housewife	20	2 Barnes
	U	Navarro Michael	295	chauffeur	23	2 "
	V	DePalma Alice H—†	295	housewife	31	179 Putnam
	W	DePalma Philip	295	painter	38	179 "
	X	Bruno Felice	295	laborer	62	here
	Y	*Bruno Filomena—†	295	housewife	52	"
	Z	*Moscaritolo Emma—†.	297	"	43	"
426						
	A	Moscaritolo Pasquale B	297	bartender	46	"
	C	Deveau Florence—†	301	housewife	34	"
	D	*Deveau Peter B	301	diver	35	
	E	Hueke Mary—†	301	secretary	26	"
	F	Hueke Warren	301	draftsman	26	"
	H	Meloni Rose—†	305	housewife	27	"
	K	Meloni Victor	305	printer	27	"
	L	Anzalone Eleanor—†	305	housewife	21	223 Saratoga
	M	Anzalone Pasquale	305	chauffeur	21	223 "
	N	*Furtado Francis	307	laborer	55	here
	O	Furtado Francis, jr	307	"	20	"
	P	*Furtado Mary—†	307	housewife	55	"
	R	*Chevarie Domenic	307	blacksmith	49	77 Brooks
	S	*Chevarie Helen—†	307	housewife	46	77 "

London Court

	T	*Farina Bella—†	1	at home	69	here
	W	Caruso Enis—†	3	housewife	27	"
	V	Caruso Stephen	3	chauffeur	26	"
	X	Mucci Anthony	3	painter	24	253 Lexington
	Y	Mucci Lena—†	3	housewife	23	here
	Z	*Poli Octavio	3	cook	53	"
427						
	A	*Poli Theresa—†	3	housewife	51	"

Page	Letter	Full Name.	Residence, Jan. 1, 1938.	Occupation.	Supposed Age.	Reported Residence, Jan. 1, 1937. Street and Number.

London Street

Page	Letter	Full Name.	Residence, Jan. 1, 1938.	Occupation.	Supposed Age.	Reported Residence, Jan. 1, 1937. Street and Number.
	D	Burke Gladys F—†	119	clerk	35	here
	E	Burke Joseph I	119	manager	34	"
	F	Golden Edward	119	"	40	"
	G	Golden Estelle—†	119	housewife	38	"
	H	*Bordanzo Emma—†	119	"	43	
	K	*Bordanzo Manuel	119	cook	52	
	N	Montalto Camille	125	upholsterer	26	"
	O	Montalto Jennie—†	125	housewife	21	"
	P	Farmer Elizabeth—†	125	housekeeper	60	"
	R	Farmer John	125	toymaker	38	"
	S	Farmer Mary—†	125	boxmaker	40	"
	T	Monaco Americo	125	laborer	22	
	U	Monaco Frances—†	125	housewife	24	"
	V	*Frank Ada—†	127	"	62	
	W	Frank Doris—†	127	bookkeeper	25	"
	X	*Frank Harry	127	dealer	70	"
	Y	Frank Marion—†	127	bookkeeper	22	"
	Z	Frank Samuel	127	clerk	30	"
428						
	A	Frank David	127	manager	40	"
	B	Frank Lena—†	127	housewife	35	"
	C	Cautrell Jesse	127	laborer	35	
	D	Cautrell Mary—†	127	operator	28	
	F	DiRocco Concetta—†	131	housewife	31	"
	G	DiRocco Gaetano	131	bootblack	35	"
	H	Scolletta Angelina—†	131	housewife	29	"
	K	Scoletta Leo	131	laborer	34	
	L	Magaldi Florence—†	131	housewife	28	"
	M	Magaldi Samuel	131	shipper	29	
	N	Field Ellen A—†	133	housekeeper	71	"
	O	Scott Agnes G—†	133	housewife	33	"
	P	Scott Rufus W	133	chauffeur	46	"
	R	Shanahan Leo	133	longshoreman	34	"
	S	Shanahan Lillian—†	133	housewife	33	"
	T	Dooley David J	135	director	71	
	U	Dooley Katherine L—†	135	housewife	68	"
	V	McDonough Katherine—†	135	cook	65	
	W	Morris Anna—†	135	operator	63	"
	X	Sullivan John	135	retired	63	
	Y	Ramirez Lillian—†	137	housewife	45	"
	Z	Ramirez Mary—†	137	clerk	23	

London Street—Continued

Page.	Letter.	Full Name.	Residence, Jan. 1, 1938.	Occupation.	Supposed Age.	Reported Residence, Jan. 1, 1937. Street and Number.
429						
	A	Ramirez Pauline—†	137	bookkeeper	30	here
	B	Ramirez Rosario	137	laborer	56	"
	C	Ramirez Salvatore L	137	engineer	25	"
	D	Breen James J	137	seaman	63	"
	E	Breen Julia—†	137	housewife	62	"
	F	*Reitano Jennie—†	137	at home	72	
	G	*Reitano Monica—†	138	housewife	40	"
	H	*Reitano Sylvester	138	cablemaker	41	"
	K	*Toomey Gregory	138	fisherman	36	"
	L	Barbanti Maria—†	138	housekeeper	50	"
	M	Barbanti Rosaria—†	138	stitcher	20	"
	N	*Anastasio Anna—†	139	housekeeper	67	"
	O	Anastasio Joseph	139	barber	36	"
	P	Anastasio Margaret—†	139	housewife	32	"
	R	*DePaula Mary—†	139	finisher	30	
	S	Livolsi Henry	139	barber	42	
	T	*Livolsi Josephine—†	139	housewife	38	"
	U	Doyle Susan—†	140	housekeeper	60	"
	V	McGrane Thomas J, jr	140	machinist	44	"
	W	Mongiello Giacomo	140	carpenter	41	"
	X	*Mongiello Philomena—†	140	housewife	44	"
	Y	Ricciardello Antonio	140	laborer	29	
	Z	*Ricciardello Benedetto	140	"	72	
430						
	A	Ricciardello Elvira—†	140	housewife	25	"
	B	*Ricciardello Giuseppina—†	140	"	72	
	C	McCarthy Katherine—†	141	"	62	
	D	McCarthy Richard	141	porter	29	
	E	McCarthy Simon	141	retired	67	
	F	Troy Rose—†	141	attendant	45	"
	G	Maloney Ellen—†	141	housewife	53	"
	H	Maloney John	141	laborer	50	
	K	McCarthy Helen—†	142	operator	34	"
	L	McGrane Helen—†	142	clerk	25	
	M	McGrane Mary E—†	142	housewife	63	"
	N	McGrane Thomas J	142	machinist	62	"
	P	*Lasala Bridget—†	143	housewife	42	"
	R	Lasala Joseph	143	laborer	20	
	S	Lasala Josephine—†	143	laundress	21	"
	T	Lasala Louis	143	barber	47	

Page.	Letter.	Full Name.	Residence, Jan. 1, 1938.	Occupation.	Supposed Age.	Reported Residence, Jan. 1, 1937. Street and Number.

London Street—Continued

	U	Scennamo Fannie—†	143	packer	23	here
	V	Scennamo Mary—†	143	stitcher	21	"
	W	*Scennamo Salvatore	143	laborer	48	"
	X	Iannacone Mary—†	143	housewife	34	"
	Y	Iannacone Michael	143	candyworker	42	"
	Z	Morrison Catherine—†	144	housekeeper	28	"
431						
	A	Morrow Alma—†	144	seamstress	48	"
	B	Morrow Everett	144	woodworker	47	"
	C	*Comeau Annette—†	144	seamstress	25	"
	D	*Comeau Delia—†	144	housekeeper	62	"
	E	*Comeau Joseph A	144	fishcutter	26	"
	F	*Comeau Maurice	144	cutter	22	
	G	Miller Edward F	144	laborer	25	
	H	Miller Emma—†	144	housewife	67	"
	K	Miller Louis C	144	janitor	77	"
	L	*Surette Leslie J	146	seaman	45	"
	M	*Surette Pheobe—†	146	housewife	35	"
	N	Boisoneau Henry G	146	laborer	71	
	O	Boisoneau Mathilda—†	146	housewife	65	"
	P	Boisoneau Ralph C	146	engineer	43	
	R	Rose Agnes M—†	146	housewife	46	"
	S	Rose John A	146	machinist	22	"
	T	Rose Violet G—†	146	clerk	23	
	U	*Potenza Assunta—†	148	housekeeper	78	"
	V	Potenza Louis	148	laborer	53	"
	W	Augusta Biaglio	148	shipper	27	150 London
	X	Augusta Evelyn—†	148	packer	32	150 "
	Y	Augusta Helen—†	148	at home	22	here
	Z	*Augusta Madeline—†	148	housewife	52	"
432						
	A	*Augusta Pasquale	148	laborer	55	"
	B	Boisoneau Cecelia R—†	148	housewife	38	"
	C	Boisoneau William H	148	foreman	46	
	D	Nappa Augustino	150	shoeworker	32	"
	E	Nappa Michelena—†	150	housewife	23	"
	F	Nappa Carmen	150	shoeworker	48	"
	G	Nappa Michael	150	"	25	
	H	*Nappa Patronella—†	150	housewife	59	"
	K	Amico Josephine—†	150	"	30	"
	L	Amico Philip	150	beautician	30	"

Page.	Letter.	Full Name.	Residence, Jan. 1, 1938.	Occupation.	Supposed Age.	Reported Residence, Jan. 1, 1937. Street and Number.

London Street—Continued

Page.	Letter.	Full Name.	Residence, Jan. 1, 1938.	Occupation.	Supposed Age.	Reported Residence, Jan. 1, 1937. Street and Number.
	M	Penta Josephine—†	152	housewife	20	here
	N	Penta Salvatore	152	chauffeur	23	"
	O	*Penta Sabina—†	152	housewife	47	"
	P	Penta Samuel	152	shoeworker	21	"
	R	Penta Saverio	152	candymaker	48	"
	S	Capozzi Carmella—†	152	"	25	
	T	Capozzi Peter	152	"	27	
	U	*Festa Carmella—†	158	packer	42	
	V	*Festa Frank	158	shoeworker	44	"
	W	Marino Nicholas	158	laborer	49	
	X	Marino Raffaela—†	158	housewife	37	"
	Y	*DiDonato Nicoletta—†	158	"	50	
	Z	DiDonato Vincenzo	158	pedler	44	
433						
	A	Obino Carmen	158	laborer	27	1 Maverick sq
	B	Coggio Anna—†	160	housewife	31	here
	C	Coggio Jerome	160	painter	31	"
	D	Celata Frederick	160	tailor	42	"
	E	Celata Lena—†	160	housewife	38	"
	F	Scrima Frank A	160	laborer	24	
	G	*Scrima Frank P	160	foreman	63	
	H	*Scrima Mary—†	160	housewife	63	"
	L	*Scimone Camella—†	165	"	37	
	M	*Scimone Leo	165	laborer	47	
	N	Vitagliano Filomena—†	165	housewife	30	"
	O	Vitagliano Orlando	165	meatcutter	30	"
	S	DeRenzo Frank	171	candyworker	38	"
	T	*DeRenzo Rosario—†	171	housewife	38	"
	U	*Guarino Elizabeth—†	171	at home	82	
	V	Shea Mary A—†	172	housewife	66	"
	W	Shea Michael J	172	retired	70	
	X	Buckley Anna A—†	172	housewife	64	"
	Y	Buckley John H	172	surveyor	67	"
	Z	Harding Annie A—†	172	at home	65	
434						
	A	*Gaternicolo Filomena—†	173	housewife	34	"
	B	Gaternicolo Nicola	173	laborer	44	"
	C	Landolfi Frances—†	173	laundress	21	192 Paris
	D	*Landolfi Mary—†	173	housewife	38	192 "
	E	Landolfi Vincenzo	173	laborer	48	192 "
	F	Nugent Edward	174	sorter	21	here

London Street—Continued

Page.	Letter.	Full Name.	Residence, Jan. 1, 1938.	Occupation.	Supposed Age.	Reported Residence, Jan. 1, 1937. Street and Number.
	G	Nugent John	174	engineer	51	Cambridge
	H	Nugent Nellie M—†	174	housewife	51	here
	K	Nugent Richard J	174	laborer	57	"
	L	DeRosa Archie	174	tailor	43	"
	M	DeRosa Edward	174	stockman	20	"
	N	DeRosa Margaret—†	174	housewife	41	"
	O	Donahue Mary—†	174	housekeeper	56	"
	P	White Arthur F	177	operator	20	"
	R	White Cecelia—†	177	housewife	60	"
	S	White James W	177	machinist	22	"
	T	White Lawrence P	177	carpenter	61	"
	U	White Peter	177	clerk	27	
	V	*Micciche Jennie—†	177	housewife	38	"
	W	Micciche Pasquale	177	barber	45	
	X	Emma Philip	177	operator	34	
	Y	*Emma Sadie—†	177	housewife	29	"
	Z	Palladino Frank	179	candyworker	32	"
435						
	A	Palladino Mary—†	179	housewife	22	"
	B	Rosso Antonio	179	shoemaker	48	"
	C	*Rosso Carmela—†	179	housewife	37	"
	D	*D'Apice Elsie—†	179	"	39	
	E	D'Apice Rudolph	179	laborer	48	
	F	Dalessio Gaetano	180	"	56	
	G	*Dalessio Josephine—†	180	housewife	41	"
	H	Noel Davis	180	rigger	31	Chelsea
	K	Noel Evelyn—†	180	housewife	27	"
	L	Wessling Anna G—†	180	"	57	here
	M	Wessling Herman	180	painter	28	"
	N	Wessling John B	180	"	53	"
	O	Casaletto Michael	181	laborer	30	
	P	*Casaletto Vincenza—†	181	housewife	27	"
	R	Moscillo James	181	tailor	34	
	S	Moscillo Mary—†	181	housewife	31	"
	T	Panzina Josephine—†	181	tailoress	37	
	U	McKenna Rose M—†	182	clerk	50	
	V	Carrabes Agnes—†	183	housewife	32	"
	W	Carrabes Carmine	183	cook	38	
	X	*Gurliaccio Josephine—†	183	housewife	42	"
	Y	Gurliaccio Lazzaro	183	laborer	53	
	Z	*Palermo Joseph	183	butcher	48	"

Page.	Letter.	Full Name.	Residence, Jan. 1, 1938.	Occupation.	Supposed Age.	Reported Residence, Jan. 1, 1937. Street and Number.
436		**London Street—Continued**				
	A	*Palermo Josephine—†	183	housewife	42	here
	B	*LaMonica Esther—†	184	housekeeper	60	"
	C	LaMonica Lawrence	184	laborer	22	"
	D	Parisi Frances—†	184	housewife	41	"
	E	Parisi Joseph	184	laborer	46	
	G	Cannata Michael	185	"	27	
	H	Cannata Rose—†	185	housewife	24	"
	K	Campana Mary—†	185	"	22	
	L	Campana Patrick	185	marketman	20	"
	M	*Cannata Antonio	185	laborer	67	
	N	*Cannata Mary A—†	185	housewife	47	"
	O	*Tamagna Annie—†	186	"	34	
	P	*Tamagna Dominic	186	salesman	39	"
	S	Tamagna Andreane—†	186	clerk	23	
	T	Tamagna Angelina—†	186	"	25	
	U	*Tamagna Anthony	186	laborer	58	
	V	*Tamagna Josephine—†	186	at home	58	
	W	Tamagna Victor	186	candyworker	24	"
	X	Recupero Paul	187	painter	30	125 Chelsea
	Y	*Recupero Rose—†	187	housewife	27	125 "
	Z	LaCedra Ida—†	187	at home	20	185 London
437						
	A	Marrone Mariana—†	187	housewife	47	here
	B	Marrone Paul	187	baker	22	791 Saratoga
	C	Lima Elsie—†	187	housewife	29	134 Falcon
	D	Lima John	187	assembler	32	134 "
	E	Boudreau Felix	188	dealer	75	here
	F	Boudreau Margaret—†	188	housewife	81	"
	G	Graves John	188	clerk	48	"
	H	Graves Lester	188	laborer	33	
	K	Graves Mary—†	188	housewife	31	"
	L	Marrana Lena—†	189	"	21	
	M	Marrana Ugo	189	sorter	33	
	N	Stornaieolo Albert	189	laborer	64	
	O	Stornaieolo Dora—†	189	shoeworker	25	"
	P	Stornaieolo Jennie—†	189	housewife	61	"
	R	Stornaieolo Molly—†	189	at home	20	
	S	Stornaieolo Pasquale	189	laborer	22	
	T	Mendum Adelaide—†	189	housewife	45	"
	U	Mendum Benjamin	189	painter	49	

Page.	Letter.	FULL NAME.	Residence, Jan. 1, 1938.	Occupation.	Supposed Age.	Reported Residence, Jan. 1, 1937. Street and Number.
		London Street—Continued				
	V	Ramos Calisto	190	spinner	43	here
	W	Ramos Ondina—†	190	housewife	32	"
	X	Alu Catina—†	191	"	32	"
	Y	Alu Michael	191	pressman	41	"
	Z	Buttiglieri Carmela—†	191	housewife	59	"
438						
	A	Buttiglieri Carmelo	191	leatherworker	22	"
	B	Buttiglieri Louis	191	salesman	21	"
	C	*Buttiglieri Phyllis—†	191	dipper	29	
	D	Rizzuto Anthony	191	laborer	26	
	E	Rizzuto Mary—†	191	housekeeper	44	"
	F	Fariole Ella—†	192	housewife	56	"
	G	Fariole Lawrence	192	chauffeur	22	"
	H	Fariole Robert	192	repairman	57	"
	K	*Perretti Angelina—†	193	housewife	44	"
	L	*Briana Mary—†	193	"	38	"
	M	Briana Thomas	193	laborer	40	
	N	Bernhardt Leonard	193	clerk	23	
	O	*Bernhardt Rose—†	193	housewife	62	"
	P	*Lottero Joseph	194	shoeworker	58	"
	R	Lottero Michael	194	machinist	25	"
	S	*Lottero Rose—†	194	housewife	55	"
	T	Lottero Albert	194	operator	20	
	U	Lottero Louis	194	painter	23	
	V	Lottero Marie—†	194	secretary	27	"
	W	Dias John	196	toymaker	23	149 Marion
	X	*Dias Manuel	196	retired	60	149 "
	Y	*Dias Mary—†	196	housewife	57	149 "
	Z	Love James	196	chauffeur	28	149 "
439						
	A	Love Mary—†	196	housewife	30	149 "
	B	Costa Joseph	197	musician	48	here
	C	Costa Sebastiana—†	197	housewife	48	"
	D	Gilmore Margaret—†	197	housekeeper	34	"
	E	DiCicco Henry	197	carpenter	32	151 Marion
	F	*DiCicco Nellie—†	197	housewife	31	151 "
	G	Cali Charles	198	pressman	25	here
	H	Cali Fannie—†	198	housewife	23	"
	K	DeMattia Anna—†	198	at home	39	"
	L	DeLuca Helen—†	198	housewife	24	"
	M	DeLuca Michael	198	chauffeur	22	"

Page.	Letter.	Full Name.	Residence, Jan. 1, 1938.	Occupation.	Supposed Age.	Reported Residence, Jan. 1, 1937. Street and Number.

London Street—Continued

Page.	Letter.	Full Name.	Residence, Jan. 1, 1938.	Occupation.	Supposed Age.	Reported Residence, Jan. 1, 1937. Street and Number.
	N	Giampetro Anthony	198	toyworker	25	162 Chelsea
	O	Tstrious Ernest	198	baker	42	here
	P	Terminello Anthony	199	painter	24	191 Marion
	R	Terminello Dena—†	199	housewife	21	191 "
	S	Coroniti Rose—†	199	"	25	here
	T	*Coroniti Samuel	199	tinsmith	39	"
	U	Fasciano Alfonse	199	shoemaker	42	"
	V	*Fasciano Mary—†	199	housewife	34	"
	W	Santaniello Alice—†	200	"	21	
	X	Santaniello Michael	200	chauffeur	27	"
	Y	*Santaniello Nunzo	200	retired	61	
	Z	DiChristoforo Amelia—†	200	housewife	22	"
440						
	A	DeChristoforo Frederick	200	laborer	26	
	B	*Vasapolli Fannie—†	200	housewife	37	"
	C	*Vasapolli Josephine—†	200	at home	71	
	D	Vasapolli Vincent	200	rubberworker	48	"
	E	*Cali Anthony	202	pressman	21	"
	F	Cali Virginia—†	202	housewife	20	"
	G	Calabria Joseph	202	chauffeur	31	"
	H	*Calabria Mary—†	202	housewife	26	"
	K	Bevilacqua Joseph	202	pressman	47	"
	L	*Bevilacqua Josephine—†	202	housewife	35	"
	M	Mascis Marie—†	203	marker	21	
	N	Mascis Valerio	203	leatherworker	26	"
	O	Scozzaro Benedette	203	operator	31	202 Paris
	P	Scozzaro Mary—†	203	housewife	22	202 "
	R	Emma Lucy—†	203	"	29	here
	S	*Emma Paul	203	retired	71	"
	T	*Emma Phillp	203	rubberworker	34	"
	U	Capello Anthony	205	laborer	24	
	V	Capello Frances—†	205	housewife	22	"
	W	Scrima Mary—†	205	"	22	
	X	*Grimaldi Gloria—†	207	"	53	
	Y	Grimaldi James	207	laborer	52	
	Z	Mennella Margaret—†	207	housewife	36	"
441						
	A	Mennella Randolph	207	operator	45	"
	B	Marques John	207	seaman	45	
	C	Rossetti Angelo	209	laborer	23	
	D	Rossetti Josephine—†	209	shoeworker	21	"

Page.	Letter.	Full Name.	Residence, Jan. 1, 1938.	Occupation.	Supposed Age.	Reported Residence, Jan. 1, 1937. Street and Number.

London Street—Continued

Page.	Letter.	Full Name.	Residence, Jan. 1, 1938.	Occupation.	Supposed Age.	Reported Residence, Jan. 1, 1937. Street and Number.
	E	Rossetti Raffaela—†	209	housekeeper	65	here
	F	Errobino Mary—†	209	housewife	36	“
	G	Errobino Pasquale	209	shoeworker	40	“
	H	Puglio Albert	209	clerk	23	
	K	Puglio Barbarino	209	retired	53	“
	L	*Puglio Louisa—†	209	housewife	48	“
	M	Puglio Mario	209	musician	24	“
	N	*Blotti Domenico	211	blacksmith	45	119 Havre
	O	*Blotti Gracia—†	211	housewife	39	119 “
	P	*Bonelli Christine—†	211	“	78	here
	R	Bonelli Cosimo	211	laborer	68	“
	S	Ippolito Antonetta—†	211	operator	25	279 Chelsea
	T	Ippolito Rose—†	211	at home	21	279 “
	U	Morgera Frank	212	laborer	26	here
	V	Morgera Mary—†	212	housewife	24	“
	X	Prinnos John	221	fireman	55	19 Marion
	Y	*Prinnos Mary—†	221	operator	58	19 “
	Z	*Adreani Anita—†	221	housewife	52	here
442						
	A	Adreani Jennie—†	221	at home	27	
	B	Adreani Luigi	221	storekeeper	60	“
	C	Adreani Yolanda—†	221	clerk	20	“
	D	LeBlanc Willis	223	proprietor	59	“
	E	Shaughnessy William	223	retired	55	
	F	Surette Howard	223	bartender	41	“
	G	Surette Lena—†	223	housewife	40	“
	H	Mennella Annie—†	223	“	50	
	K	Mennella Anthony	223	conductor	48	“
	L	Matarazzo Joseph	223	meatcutter	21	“
	M	Matarazzo Mary—†	223	housewife	38	“
	N	Matarazzo Michael	223	decorator	40	“
	O	Pereira Joaquim B	225	weaver	34	“
	P	*Grimes Paul	225	laborer	70	27 Central sq
	R	Merchant Charles E	225	“	26	27 “
	S	Merchant Lucy A—†	225	housekeeper	64	27 “
	T	Merchant Simon A	225	shipper	23	27 “
	U	Lipson Fanny—†	225	housewife	70	here
	V	Lipson Michael	225	tailor	69	“
	W	Lipson William	225	finisher	37	“
	X	Silvae Emma—†	227	housewife	52	“
	Y	Silvae Louise—†	227	operator	30	“

Page.	Letter.	Full Name.	Residence, Jan. 1, 1938.	Occupation.	Supposed Age.	Reported Residence, Jan. 1, 1937. Street and Number.
		London Street—Continued				
	z	Rose Albert	227	chauffeur	37	here
443						
	A	Rose Naomi—†	227	housewife	36	"
	B	Panopoulos Julia—†	227	"	32	"
	C	Panopoulos Theodore	227	fireman	41	
	D	Steph Mary—†	229	housewife	23	"
	E	Steph William	229	laborer	23	
	F	Murphy Grace—†	229	at home	28	
	G	*Trapuzzano Antonio	229	laborer	51	"
	H	*Trapuzzano Catherine—†	229	housewife	53	"
	K	Salvaggio Phillip	231	laborer	22	
	L	Casaletto Joseph M	231	musician	45	"
	M	Casaletto Mary G—†	231	housewife	33	"
	N	*Salvaggio Josephine—†	231	"	40	
	O	Salvaggio Rocco	231	candymaker	49	"
	P	*Musto Joseph	233	laborer	39	81 Princeton
	R	Musto Pasqua—†	233	housewife	29	81 "
	S	Lemar Manuel K	233	laborer	63	here
		Marion Street				
	U	*Bunder Bessie—†	172	housewife	61	here
	V	Bunder Charles	172	mechanic	22	"
	W	*Bunder Harris	172	shoemaker	64	"
	X	Leone Rocco	172	laborer	36	
	Y	*Leone Rosaria—†	172	housewife	29	"
	Z	*Musiello Carmella—†	174	housekeeper	58	"
444						
	A	Goldberg Nathan	174	metalworker	47	"
	B	*Levenstein Ida—†	174	housewife	63	"
	C	*Levenstein Louis	174	dealer	57	
	D	Mangino Caroline—†	174	housewife	29	"
	E	*Mangino John	174	operator	40	"
	G	Venuti Florence—†	176	housewife	22	184 Havre
	H	Venuti Sabato	176	operator	23	here
	K	*Sano Angelina—†	176	housekeeper	44	"
	L	Sano Antonio	176	packer	25	"
	M	*Sano Frank	176	laborer	58	
	N	Sano Rosario	176	"	22	
	O	*Venuti Carmella—†	176	housewife	49	"
	P	*Venuti Joseph	176	foreman	53	

Page.	Letter.	Full Name.	Residence, Jan. 1, 1938.	Occupation.	Supposed Age.	Reported Residence, Jan. 1, 1937. Street and Number.

Marion Street—Continued

Page.	Letter.	Full Name.	Residence, Jan. 1, 1938.	Occupation.	Supposed Age.	Reported Residence, Jan. 1, 1937. Street and Number.
	R	Venuti Raffaela—†	176	at home	21	here
	S	Cestone Anthony	178	laborer	24	"
	T	Cestone Theresa—†	178	housewife	23	"
	U	Boncore Angelo	178	tailor	31	
	V	Boncore Frances—†	178	at home	24	"
	W	*Siracusa Antonio	178	laborer	69	"
	X	Siracusa Carmelo	178	"	36	
	Y	Siracusa Joseph	178	"	20	
	Z	Siracusa Mary T—†	178	operator	27	
445						
	A	*Siracusa Salvatore—†	178	housewife	62	"
	B	Mazzeo Angelo A	179	bartender	58	Worcester
	C	Mazzeo Angie—†	179	housewife	56	"
	D	Mayo Joseph	179	laborer	45	Pennsylvania
	E	*Mayo Mary—†	179	housekeeper	37	"
	F	Puleio Anthony	179	barber	54	here
	G	Puleio Joseph	179	mechanic	21	"
	H	*Puleio Mary—†	179	at home	70	"
	K	Puleio Mary—†	179	marker	26	
	L	Puleio Rose—†	179	housewife	42	"
	M	Conaxis Josephine—†	180	at home	22	35 Vaughan av
	N	*Pecci Frank	180	retired	74	here
	O	*Pecci Philomena—†	180	housewife	70	"
	P	*Pecci Concetta—†	180	"	39	"
	R	*Pecci Paul	180	shoemaker	44	"
	S	Marciano Michael	181	laborer	24	
	T	Marciano Sophie—†	181	housewife	22	"
	U	Panarese John	181	laborer	43	"
	V	Panarese Mary—†	181	housewife	31	"
	W	Davola Angelina—†	181	operator	20	"
	X	Davola Phillip	181	laborer	46	
	Y	Davola Stella—†	181	housewife	42	"
446						
	A	*Marconi Anna—†	182	"	45	
	B	*Marconi Jerry	182	laborer	55	
	C	Anzalone Anna—†	182	housewife	42	"
	D	Anzalone John	182	barber	45	"
	E	*Dellorfano Carmella—†	183	housewife	43	"
	F	Dellorfano Carmen	183	laborer	21	"
	G	Dellorfano Catherine—†	183	operator	23	"
	H	*Marottole Mary—†	183	housewife	38	"

Page.	Letter.	FULL NAME.	Residence, Jan. 1, 1938.	Occupation.	Supposed Age.	Reported Residence, Jan. 1, 1937. Street and Number.

Marion Street—Continued

	K	*Marottole Oresti	183	tinsmith	38	here
	L	LaMonica Joseph L	183	laborer	20	"
	M	*LaMonica Sabia—†	183	housewife	43	"
	N	LaMonica Salvatore	183	laborer	52	"
	O	Iona Frank	184	"	22	Arlington
	P	Vistola Luigi R	184	"	56	here
	R	*Vistola Pasqualina—†	184	housewife	54	"
	S	Ciriello Antonio	184	operator	50	"
	T	*Ciriello Mary—†	184	housewife	51	"
	U	Dionizio Josephine—†	185	"	25	331 Paris
	V	Dionizio Manuel	185	laborer	29	331 "
	W	LaRocca Gaetano	185	"	21	here
	X	*LaRocca John	185	retired	58	"
	Y	LaRocca Joseph	185	laborer	23	"
	Z	LcRocca Mar —†	185	operator	28	
447y						
	A	*LaRocca Nora—†	185	housewife	58	"
	B	LcRocca Nora—†	185	at home	20	"
	C	*Perretti Philomena—†	185	housewife	48	244 Paris
	D	Perretti Ralph	185	laborer	45	244 "
	E	Grillo Samuel	186	"	25	205 E Eagle
	F	*DeAngelo Domenic	186	"	55	here
	G	*DeAngelo Louise—†	186	housewife	55	"
	H	Terriciano Benjamin	186	operator	28	"
	K	Terriciano Theresa—†	186	housewife	27	"
	L	Mancusa John	187	baker	27	
	M	Mancusa Philip	187	rubberworker	25	"
	N	Fiore Angela—†	187	housewife	33	"
	O	Fiore Maurice	187	musician	35	"
	P	Mastrangelo Philomena–†	188	housewife	28	"
	R	Mastrangelo Rocco	188	mechanic	30	"
	S	*Cambria Lillian—†	188	housewife	46	"
	T	*Cambria Pasquale	188	pedler	57	
	U	*DeAngelo Nicholas	188	laborer	21	
	V	DeAngelo Pasquale	188	shoemaker	24	"
	W	*Cappucci Dominic	188	bootblack	52	"
	X	*Cappucci Rose—†	188	housewife	48	"
	Y	Cappucci Thomas	188	painter	21	
448						
	B	Silva Josephine—†	191	housewife	22	376 Chelsea
	C	Silva Paul	191	laborer	27	376 "

Page.	Letter.	Full Name.	Residence, Jan. 1, 1938.	Occupation.	Supposed Age.	Reported Residence, Jan. 1, 1937. Street and Number.

Marion Street—Continued

	D	*Silva Sarah—†	191	housekeeper	59	376 Chelsea
	E	Finamore Anna—†	191	at home	23	here
	F	Finamore Angelina—†	191	"	34	"
	G	Finamore Gaetano	191	barber	33	"
	H	Finamore Margaret—†	191	shoeworker	32	"
	K	Finamore Mary—†	191	housewife	52	"
	M	*Benincasa Carmella—†	192	"	55	"
	N	*Benincasa Paul	192	shoemaker	68	"
	O	Barbarisi Amelio	192	laborer	20	
	P	Porcaro Edward	192	"	39	
	R	*Porcaro Florence—†	192	housewife	35	"
	S	Porcaro Frances—†	192	at home	22	
	T	Porcaro Mary—†	192	"	23	
	U	Porcaro Minnie—†	192	"	20	
	V	*Farro Andrew	192	laborer	56	
	W	Farro Carmella—†	192	at home	20	
	X	Farro Frank	192	laborer	22	"
	Y	Farro Michael	192	"	32	
	Z	*Farro Rose—†	192	housewife	52	"
449						
	A	*Dangelico Anna—†	193	"	48	
	B	*Dangelico Carl	193	barber	51	
	C	Dangelico Dominic	193	laborer	24	
	D	Dangelico Guy	193	"	22	
	E	Thirens Edith—†	193	housewife	32	"
	F	Thirens George	193	operator	42	
	G	*Tutela Mary—†	193	at home	58	
	K	Giunta Louis	194	laborer	47	
	L	*Giunta Mary—†	194	housewife	46	"
	M	Giunta Phyllis—†	194	operator	24	"
	N	DiPesa Alexander	194	U S A	21	"
	O	DiPesa Patrick	194	roofer	44	
	P	DiPesa Phoebe—†	194	housewife	41	"
	R	DiPesa Ralph	194	toymaker	22	"
	T	Robbins Llewellyn—†	195	calendarman	23	Chelsea
	U	Lombardi Anthony	195	carpenter	48	here
	V	*Lombardi Emma—†	195	housewife	42	"
	W	Lombardi Vincent A	195	carpenter	21	"
	X	*Anoroso Angelina—†	195	housekeeper	55	Malden
	Y	Anoroso Josephine—†	195	operator	26	"
	Z	Anoroso Natalie—†	195	housewife	21	"

Page.	Letter.	Full Name.	Residence, Jan. 1, 1938.	Occupation.	Supposed Age.	Reported Residence, Jan. 1, 1937. Street and Number.

450
Marion Street—Continued

	A	Fiandaca Domenic	196	laborer	49	here
	B	*Fiandaca Lena—†	196	housewife	47	"
	C	Pignataro Anna—†	196	at home	22	"
	D	*Gangi Annette—†	196	housewife	56	"
	E	*Gangi Nicholas	196	laborer	59	
	F	Gangi Samuel	196	operator	25	"
	H	LaFrazia Francisco	197	laborer	43	
	K	LaFrazia Josephine—†	197	housewife	33	"
	L	Finamore Arthur	197	plumber	29	218 Saratoga
	M	Finamore Mary—†	197	housewife	26	218 "
	O	Rocco Eleanor—†	198	"	34	here
	P	Barker Oline—†	198	"	24	"
	R	Barker William T	198	chauffeur	31	"
	T	Pasqualetto Matto	199	laborer	50	5 Cross
	U	*Pasqualetto Nora—†	199	housewife	39	5 "
	V	*Ardito Crucifixa—†	199	"	47	195 Marion
	W	Ardito John	199	laborer	47	195 "
	X	*Arone Catherine—†	199	at home	67	here
	Y	Pungitore Giovanni	199	laborer	46	"
	Z	Pungitore Rose—†	199	housewife	33	"
451						
	A	*Cutrone Grace—†	200	"	36	151 Chelsea
	B	*Cutrone Paul	200	barber	41	151 "
	C	Villani Louise—†	200	housewife	27	here
	E	Grandolfi Cyrio	201	chauffeur	26	"
	F	Grandolfi Mary—†	201	housewife	25	"
	G	Conti Angelo	201	laborer	22	
	H	*Conti Josephine—†	201	housewife	50	"
	K	Conti Ralph	201	laborer	23	
	L	Hawes Edward J	201	"	31	
	M	Hawes Francis	201	"	37	
	N	Hawes Margaret—†	201	at home	65	
	O	Hawes Russell J	201	laborer	27	
	S	*DePari Pauline—†	205	housewife	25	"
	T	DePari Sebastian	205	barber	28	
	U	*Brazzo Fannie—†	205	housewife	31	"
	V	*Brazzo Salvatore	205	ironworker	40	"
	W	Rao Frank	205	"	27	
	X	Rao Mary—†	205	housewife	22	"
	Y	Rao Nunzio	205	storekeeper	60	"

Page.	Letter.	Full Name.	Residence, Jan. 1, 1938.	Occupation.	Supposed Age.	Reported Residence, Jan. 1, 1937. Street and Number.

Marion Street—Continued

	Z	Cioffi Angelo—†	206	clerk	20	here
452						
	A	Cioffi John	206	baker	51	
	B	Cioffi Joseph	206	"	25	
	C	Cioffi Sigismondo	206	"	23	
	D	*Cioffi Theresa—†	206	housewife	45	"
	E	Durante Emily—†	206	"	27	
	F	Durante Pasquale	206	laborer	25	
	H	*Caccamesi Giacomo	207	retired	62	
	K	Caccamesi Peter	207	shoemaker	26	"
	L	*Caccamesi Salvatrice—†	207	housewife	54	"
	M	*Caccamesi Charles	207	shoemaker	28	"
	N	*Caccamesi Josephine—†	207	housewife	29	"
	O	Weiner Annie—†	209	"	42	
	P	Weiner Louis	209	storekeeper	44	"

Meridian Place

	S	Ramsdell George F	3	chauffeur	43	here
	T	Ramsdell Winifred D—†	3	housewife	48	"
	U	Zellers Robert L	3	chauffeur	24	"

Meridian Street

	W	*Rogers John J	95	longshoreman	60	here
	X	Rogers Marie—†	95	waitress	20	"
	Y	Rogers Michael	95	longshoreman	24	"
	Z	Rogers William	95	"	29	
453						
	A	Calderone August	97	fishcutter	36	"
	B	*Hunter James	97	laborer	63	
	C	*Keith Bertha—†	97	housewife	55	"
	D	Keith Ford W	97	meatcutter	56	"
	E	Messina Mario	97	tailor	30	"
	F	O'Neil John J	97	painter	38	
	H	*Baccardax Peter	101	fisherman	42	"
	K	*Howard Frederick	101	steward	50	
	L	McDonald Edward	101	fisherman	60	"
	M	McLaughlin Mary A—†	101	housekeeper	70	"
	N	McLaughlin Philip H	101	machinist	40	"

Page.	Letter.	Full Name.	Residence, Jan. 1, 1938.	Occupation.	Supposed Age.	Reported Residence, Jan. 1, 1937. Street and Number.

Meridian Street—Continued

	S	Noonan James F	107	chauffeur	46	24 London
	T	Noonan Mary—†	107	housewife	57	24 "
	V	Amarosi Angelo	109	tailor	25	80 Havre
	W	Amarosi Mary—†	109	housewife	25	80 "
	X	*Doyle Mary—†	109	"	34	here
	Y	Lynch Jessie B—†	109	housekeeper	49	"
	Z	Macri John	109	carpenter	43	144 Maverick
454						
	A	Murphy Frederick J	109	clerk	49	here
	B	Nevell Frank	109	plumber	43	116 Havre
	C	*Rizzo Augustus	109	weaver	36	here
	D	Shannon Jeanette—†	109	clerk	30	143 Meridian
	E	Willis James A	109	bartender	50	here
	G	*Pedell Abraham	111	tailor	47	"
	H	*Pedell Ida—†	111	housekeeper	41	"
	K	Donahoe Mary H—†	111	"	32	33 Maverick sq
	N	Gallo Annie—†	141	housewife	46	here
	O	*Gallo Ralph	141	baker	46	"
	P	*Dwyer Angelo	141	ironworker	29	"
	R	Dwyer Lillian—†	141	housewife	26	"
	S	Joy Austin	143	laborer	21	
	T	Joy Catherine—†	143	housekeeper	60	"
	U	Joy James	143	laborer	63	"
	V	Parsons Frances—†	143	operator	25	
	W	*Parsons William	143	painter	59	
	Z	*Bishop Celia A—†	149	housekeeper	53	"
455						
	A	*Bishop Geraldine—†	149	at home	27	
	B	*Bishop Harold J	149	clerk	24	
	C	*Breen John	149	fisherman	45	"
	D	Dobbins Catherine—†	149	housewife	50	"
	E	Dobbins David J	149	carpenter	62	"
	F	*Fagan Peter	151	fisherman	40	"
	G	Riggs Frances—†	151	housekeeper	54	"
	H	Riggs William	151	painter	66	"
	K	Sweeney Warren	151	letter carrier	32	"
	L	Gambetta Anthony	151	tailor	43	
	M	Gambetta Josephine—†	151	housekeeper	35	"
	N	Burge Walter	157	fishcutter	20	"
	O	Perry Jennie—†	157	housekeeper	34	"

Page.	Letter.	Full Name.	Residence, Jan. 1, 1938.	Occupation.	Supposed Age.	Reported Residence, Jan. 1, 1937. Street and Number.
		Meridian Street—Continued				
	P	*Perry Joseph	157	fisherman	59	here
	R	Willis James A	157	bartender	50	"
	S	*Willis Stella—†	157	housewife	34	"
		Model Place				
	W	*Chiango Augustino	3	laborer	62	here
	X	Chiango Carmen	3	"	22	"
	Y	*Chiango Jennie—†	3	housewife	62	"
456						
	A	*Petti Joseph	4	laborer	50	
	B	Savoia Mary—†	4	operator	28	"
	C	*Savoia Vittorio	4	retired	69	
		Paris Street				
	E	Bernardinelli Nellie—†	98	housewife	54	Revere
	F	Bernardinelli Pasquale	98	machinist	39	"
	G	Nazzaro Emidio	98	barber	57	here
	H	Reppucci Herbert	98	porter	23	"
	K	Reppucci Joseph	98	candymaker	57	"
	L	Reppucci Lydia—†	98	teacher	25	
	M	Reppucci Michael	98	candymaker	54	"
	N	Forti Catherine—†	98	at home	45	
	O	Forti Frank	98	laborer	48	
	P	Forti Paul	98	machinist	20	"
	R	Forti Vincent	98	shipper	22	
	S	*Gazzara Paul	98	retired	68	
	T	Gazzara Rose—†	98	stitcher	30	
	U	*Catinazzo Annie—†	100	housewife	50	"
	V	Catinazzo James	100	shoeworker	21	"
	W	Catinazzo Josephine—†	100	"	23	
	X	*Catinazzo Nicholas	100	laborer	54	
	Y	Cassetina Annie—†	100	clerk	25	
	Z	*Cassetina Catherine—†	100	housewife	60	"
457						
	A	Cassetina Joseph	100	laborer	67	
	B	Cassetina Ruth—†	100	student	20	
	C	Fewer Arthur	100	fisherman	23	"
	D	Fewer James	100	machinist	54	"
	E	Fewer Mary—†	100	housewife	47	"

Page.	Letter.	FULL NAME.	Residence, Jan. 1, 1938.	Occupation.	Supposed Age.	Reported Residence, Jan. 1, 1937. Street and Number.

Paris Street—Continued

Page.	Letter.	FULL NAME.	Residence, Jan. 1, 1938.	Occupation.	Supposed Age.	Reported Residence, Jan. 1, 1937. Street and Number.
	F	Logan Addie—†	102	at home	65	here
	G	Mealey Mary J—†	102	housekeeper	72	"
	H	Ciaburri Carmella—†	102	housewife	46	"
	K	Ciaburri Ralph	102	glassworker	52	"
	L	Bellone Fannie—†	102	housewife	43	"
	M	Bellone Joseph	102	laborer	53	
	N	*Genco Josephine—†	102	at home	68	
	O	Savoia Frank	104	laborer	32	
	P	Savoia Miranda—†	104	housewife	28	"
	R	Dell'Orfano Evelyn—†	104	operator	25	
	S	Dell'Orfano Hilda—†	104	"	24	
	T	Dell'Orfano Luigi	104	blacksmith	54	"
	U	Dell'Orfano Maria—†	104	housewife	53	"
	V	Dell'Orfano Oresto	104	jeweler	27	
	W	Micciche Annie—†	104	housewife	26	"
	X	*Micciche Santi	104	shoeworker	38	"
	Y	Buttiglieri Nellie—†	106	housewife	30	"
	Z	Buttiglieri Rocco	106	machinist	34	"
458						
	A	Minichiello Antoinetta—†	106	housewife	41	"
	B	Minichiello Nunzio	106	laborer	48	
	C	Vozella Theodore	106	"	21	"
	D	Lopresti Adeline—†	106	housewife	23	Everett
	E	Lopresti Anthony	106	chiropodist	25	here
	F	Lopresti Frances—†	106	housewife	49	"
	G	Lopresti Frank	106	barber	63	"
	H	Lopresti Lillian—†	106	dressmaker	29	"
	K	Lopresti Virginia—†	106	operator	27	
	L	Sirianni Pasquale	108	chauffeur	31	"
	M	Sirianni Thomasena—†	108	housewife	27	"
	N	Abate Albert	108	shoeworker	23	"
	O	*Abate Esther—†	108	housewife	47	"
	P	Abate Ida—†	108	tailoress	21	
	R	*Abate Joseph	108	barber	54	"
	S	Vaccaro Giovanni	108	carpenter	48	70 Chelsea
	T	Vaccaro Mary—†	108	housewife	40	70 "
	U	*Amisto Angelina—†	110	"	42	109 "
	V	*Amisto Antonio	110	laborer	48	109 "
	W	Amisto Frank	110	"	22	109 "
	X	Morabito Domenic	110	cutter	48	here
	Y	Morabito Rose—†	110	housewife	43	"

Page.	Letter.	FULL NAME.	Residence, Jan. 1, 1938.	Occupation.	Supposed Age.	Reported Residence, Jan. 1, 1937. Street and Number.

Paris Street—Continued

Page.	Letter.	Full Name.	Residence, Jan. 1, 1938.	Occupation.	Supposed Age.	Reported Residence, Jan. 1, 1937.
	Z	Morabito Sadie—†	110	at home	22	here
459						
	A	Corino Anthony	110	painter	34	
	B	Corino Rose—†	110	housewife	27	"
	C	DiPasquale John	110	laborer	21	
	E	*Zappulla Rose—†	132	housewife	30	"
	F	*Zappullo Vincenzo	132	rubberworker	40	"
	G	Barrasso Edward	132	student	23	
	H	Barrasso Louise—†	132	operator	20	"
	K	Barrasso Lucy—†	132	housewife	48	"
	L	Barrasso Phyllis—†	132	secretary	25	"
	M	Barrasso Thomas	132	shoeworker	49	"
	N	Phillips Bessie—†	132	housewife	47	"
	O	Phillips Jacob	132	merchant	54	"
	P	Rotondo Caroline—†	134	housewife	27	"
	R	Rotondo Michael	134	barber	29	
	S	Guarino Dorothy—†	134	clerk	20	
	T	Guarino Maria L—†	134	housewife	53	"
	U	Guarino Nicholas	134	salesman	62	"
	V	Maraggia Albert	134	operator	25	
	W	*Maraggia Lucy—†	134	housewife	24	"
	X	Pungente Domenic	136	candymaker	32	"
	Y	Pungente Mary—†	136	housewife	29	"
	Z	*Pungente Theresa—†	136	at home	56	
460						
	A	Umbrello Domenic	136	candymaker	42	"
	B	*Umbrello Emma—†	136	housewife	36	"
	C	Antonacci Giacomo	136	tailor	43	
	D	*Antonacci Louisa—†	136	housewife	40	"
	E	*Dannolfo Carlo	138	tailor	33	
	F	Dannolfo Theresa—†	138	housewife	32	"
	G	Lavorgna Mary—†	138	at home	56	
	H	Montuori Aniello	138	laborer	45	
	K	Montuori Rose—†	138	housewife	32	"
	L	Weldon Elizabeth—†	138	at home	67	
	M	Wiseman Frederick	138	shipper	36	
	N	Wiseman Muriel—†	138	housewife	30	"
	O	*Petruzillo Mary—†	140	"	65	
	P	*Petruzillo Pasquale	140	retired	68	
	R	Pergola Mary—†	140	clerk	22	
	S	Pergola Petrina—†	140	housewife	40	"

Page.	Letter.	FULL NAME.	Residence, Jan. 1, 1938.	Occupation.	Supposed Age.	Reported Residence, Jan. 1, 1937. Street and Number.

Paris Street—Continued

	T	Pergola Philip	140	storekeeper	45	here
	U	Pergola Phyllis—†	140	clerk	20	"
	V	Petruzillo Annie—†	140	housewife	32	357 Chelsea
	W	Petruzillo Laurence	140	laborer	38	357 "
	X	Abitabile Concetta—†	142	at home	20	here
	Y	*Abitabile Jennie—†	142	housewife	41	"
	Z	*Abitabile John	142	laborer	43	"
461						
	A	Abitabile Marion—†	142	stitcher	22	"
	B	Petrucelli Angelo	142	shoeworker	28	Maine
	C	Petrucelli Daniel E	142	"	35	here
	D	Petrucelli Joseph	142	baker	60	"
	E	Petrucelli Mary—†	142	at home	22	"
	F	Sacco Joseph	142	laborer	40	
	G	*Sacco Mary—†	142	housewife	40	"
	H	Marcotullio Albert	144	tailor	28	
	K	*Marcotullio Beatrice—†	144	housewife	27	"
	L	Micciche Joseph	144	laborer	65	
	M	*Micciche Joseph S	144	shoeworker	27	"
	N	*Micciche Josephine—†	144	housewife	57	"
	O	Micciche Mary G—†	144	teacher	24	
	P	Vitale Mary F—†	144	housewife	36	"
	R	Vitale Rocco	144	shoeworker	40	"
	S	Carrabino Angelina—†	146	housewife	33	"
	T	Carrabino Angelo	146	dealer	33	
	U	Scozzello Angelina—†	146	housewife	62	"
	V	Scozzello Joseph	146	retired	70	
	W	Flood Bror H	146	engineer	31	
	X	Flood Carmella—†	146	housewife	31	"
	Y	Nicoletti Anthony	166	barber	37	
	Z	Nicoletti Rose—†	166	saleswoman	36	"
462						
	A	*Daddario Louis	166	laborer	55	
	B	*Daddario Marie—†	166	housewife	52	"
	C	Cioffi Joseph	166	candymaker	23	"
	D	Cioffi Mary—†	166	packer	26	
	E	Cioffi Nicholas	166	painter	47	
	F	Cioffi Rose—†	166	housewife	49	"
	G	Anderson Albert	168	bookkeeper	37	"
	H	Anderson Evelyn—†	168	"	26	"
	K	Anderson Matilda—†	168	at home	61	

Page.	Letter.	Full Name.	Residence, Jan. 1, 1938.	Occupation.	Supposed Age.	Reported Residence, Jan. 1, 1937. Street and Number.

Paris Street—Continued

	L	Imbrescia Michael	168	laundryman	38	here
	M	*Imbrescia Rigoletta—†	168	tailoress	37	"
	N	Diaz Manuel V	168	fireman	55	"
	O	*Diaz Maria—†	168	housewife	47	"
	P	Mercendante Celia—†	170	"	30	
	R	Mercendante John	170	plasterer	30	"
	S	*Cogliani Antonetta—†	170	housewife	49	"
	T	*Cogliani Michael	170	laborer	54	
	U	Umbro Antonio	170	pedler	46	
	V	Umbro Elizabeth—†	170	housewife	36	"
	W	Muse Mary—†	172	"	28	
	X	Muse Philip	172	plumber	29	
	Y	Altieri Ferdinand	172	salesman	21	"
	Z	Altieri Frank	172	pedler	40	
463						
	A	Altieri Philomena—†	172	housewife	45	"
	B	*Fumicello Anna—†	172	"	30	166 Chelsea
	C	*Fumicello Nunzio	172	candymaker	35	166 "
	D	Arinella Carmen	174	retired	87	here
	E	*Cocaco Barbara—†	174	at home	62	"
	F	*Cocaco Nicholas	174	laborer	52	"
	G	Cocaco Susan—†	174	housewife	45	"
	H	Cocaco William	174	laborer	50	
	K	Arinella Joseph	174	painter	52	
	L	Arinella Mary—†	174	operator	45	"
	M	Pascucci Henry	176	electrician	33	"
	N	Pascucci Josephine—†	176	housewife	28	"
	O	*Carfagna Josephine—†	176	"	42	
	P	*Carfagna Richard	176	porter	45	
	R	Pascucci Antoinette—†	176	nurse	25	
	S	Pascucci Ida—†	176	housewife	58	"
	T	Pascucci Philip	176	retired	63	
	U	Barry Ellen M—†	178	housewife	29	"
	V	Barry Lawrence	178	clerk	30	"
	W	Warner Ernest C	178	watchman	29	"
	X	Greco Frank	178	shoeworker	48	222 Paris
	Y	Greco Grace—†	178	housewife	37	222 "
	Z	Kaplan Pearl—†	178	"	36	163 "
464						
	A	Kaplan Samuel	178	storekeeper	40	163 "
	B	Venuti Anna M—†	180	operator	23	here

Page.	Letter.	Full Name.	Residence, Jan. 1, 1938.	Occupation.	Supposed Age.	Reported Residence, Jan. 1, 1937. Street and Number.

Paris Street—Continued

	C	Venuti Anthony D	180	leatherworker	30	here
	D	Venuti Celia M—†	180	housewife	29	"
	E	Lombardo Helen—†	180	"	21	"
	F	Lombardo Joseph	180	cabinetmaker	29	"
	G	Capobianco Angelo	180	candymaker	26	"
	H	*Capobianco John	180	shoeworker	47	"
	K	*Capobianco Lucy—†	180	housewife	44	"
	L	Capobianco Pasquale	180	laborer	20	
	M	Capobianco Philomena-†	180	at home	22	
	N	Terranova Carmella—†	182	housewife	28	"
	O	*Terranova Joseph	182	laborer	35	
	P	DeChristoforo Emilio	182	milkman	31	"
	R	DeChristoforo Emma—†	182	housewife	30	"
	S	*Calvagno Anthony	182	operator	32	
	T	Calvagno Theresa—†	182	housewife	25	"
	U	*DeStefano Joseph	184	baker	42	
	V	*DeStefano Mary Ann—†	184	housewife	38	"
	W	*Maroni Mary—†	184	at home	70	
	X	Adamo Frank	184	shoeworker	21	"
	Y	Adamo Gabriel	184	foreman	63	
	Z	Adamo Mary—†	184	housewife	50	"
465						
	A	*Cosco Andrew	184	retired	73	
	B	Iannone Sarah—†	184	packer	35	
	C	*Ledonne John	184	retired	81	
	D	*Montalto Mary—†	184	housewife	32	"
	E	*Montalto Nicholas	184	laborer	42	
	F	*Samrona Amelia—†	186	at home	75	
	G	Ottana Joseph	186	laborer	50	
	H	Ottana Mary—†	186	housewife	35	"
	K	Accardi Annette—†	186	at home	25	160 Putnam
	L	*Accardi Joseph	186	iceman	64	160 "
	M	*Accardi Marie—†	186	housewife	59	160 "
	N	Spadorcia Domenic	190	pressman	26	here
	O	Spadorcia Palmina—†	190	housewife	26	"
	P	Puzzo Ida—†	190	at home	27	Fitchburg
	R	*Puzzo Mary—†	190	housewife	56	"
	S	*Puzzo Salvatore	190	laborer	59	"
	T	*Puzzo Vito	190	operator	34	"
	U	D'Agostino Arthur	190	painter	40	here
	V	D'Agostino Olimpia—†	190	housewife	48	"

Page.	Letter.	FULL NAME.	Residence, Jan. 1, 1938.	Occupation.	Supposed Age.	Reported Residence, Jan. 1, 1937. Street and Number.

Paris Street—Continued

	W	DeLorenzo Concetta—†	190	housewife	22	here
	X	DeLorenzo Vincent	190	painter	25	"
	Y	*Riccio Anthony	rear 190	laborer	53	"
	Z	Riccio Joseph	" 190	student	20	
466						
	A	*Riccio Mary—†	" 190	housewife	43	"
	B	Riccio Michael	" 190	clerk	22	
	C	Diminico Jennie—†	192	operator	21	
	D	*Diminico Pasqualina—†	192	housewife	46	"
	E	*Diminico Sabato	192	laborer	56	"
	F	*Giunta Beatrice—†	192	housewife	36	196 Paris
	G	Giunta Salvatore	192	laborer	44	196 "
	H	Costa Josephine—†	192	packer	20	here
	K	*Costa Mary—†	192	housewife	53	"
	L	Costa Rose—†	192	packer	22	"
	M	*Costa Salvatore	192	laborer	57	
	O	Fabrizio Antonio	196	storekeeper	50	"
	P	Fabrizio Carmella—†	196	at home	23	"
	R	Fabrizio Thomasina—†	196	"	26	"
	S	Marotta Anna—†	196	housewife	28	197 Marion
	T	Marotta Louis	196	laborer	32	197 "
	U	Chingo Joseph	196	"	26	here
	V	Chingo Rose—†	196	housewife	27	"
	W	Michetti Gasper	196	mechanic	26	"
	X	Michetti Sylvia—†	196	housewife	24	"
	Y	*DeLeo Achille	196	musician	51	"
	Z	*DeLeo Julia—†	196	housewife	46	"
467						
	A	Dagnino Frank	196	chauffeur	33	"
	B	Dagnino Margaret—†	196	housewife	36	"
	D	Szymanski Anthony	196	laborer	25	
	C	Szymanski Elvera—†	196	housewife	26	"
	E	Piermatti Agnes—†	196	packer	23	
	F	Piermatti Domenic	196	laborer	25	
	G	*DeRosa Michael	196	painter	40	
	H	DeRosa Rose—†	196	housewife	29	"
	K	*Gangemi Antoinetta—†	196	at home	57	184 Paris
	L	Gangemi Joseph	196	shoemaker	37	184 "
	N	Ricupero Antonio	202	painter	30	here
	O	Ricupero Mary—†	202	housewife	27	"
	R	Cheverie Agnes—†	206	"	66	"

Page.	Letter.	Full Name.	Residence, Jan. 1, 1938.	Occupation.	Supposed Age.	Reported Residence, Jan. 1, 1937. Street and Number.

Paris Street—Continued

Page.	Letter.	Full Name.	Residence, Jan. 1, 1938.	Occupation.	Supposed Age.	Reported Residence, Jan. 1, 1937. Street and Number.
	S	Cheverie William	206	retired	65	here
	T	Longo Joseph	206	laborer	41	"
	U	Longo Mary—†	206	housewife	39	"
	V	Fucillo Marto	206	shipper	40	"
	W	Fucillo Rita—†	206	teacher	21	
	X	Fucillo Ruth—†	206	housewife	40	"
	Y	Murray Anna L—†	210	"	27	
	Z	Murray Henry	210	painter	27	
468						
	A	*Flanagan Mary A—†	210	nurse	31	
	B	Ryan Daniel J	210	ironworker	61	"
	C	Ryan Daniel J, jr	210	laborer	25	
	D	Ryan Marion—†	210	packer	31	
	E	Ryan Mary A—†	210	housewife	60	"
	F	Grace Andrew	210	clerk	49	
	G	*Grace Bridget—†	210	at home	78	
	H	Cahill Edward J	216	clerk	35	
	K	Cahill June—†	216	housewife	25	"
	L	Sugerman Bernard	216	dealer	22	
	M	Sugerman Israel	216	"	49	
	N	Sugerman Rose—†	216	housewife	47	"
	O	Sugerman Samuel	216	model	23	"
	P	Waddingham Arthur	216	laborer	36	147 Princeton
	R	Waddingham Sadie—†	216	housewife	43	147 "
	S	*Tasi Delia—†	218	"	54	here
	T	Tasi John	218	laborer	32	"
	U	Tasi Mary—†	218	packer	24	"
	V	*Tasi Peter	218	carpenter	54	"
	W	*Cecere Camella—†	218	housewife	50	"
	X	Cecere Louis	218	printer	23	
	Y	*Cecere Paul	218	laborer	56	
	Z	Pascarella Florence—†	218	operator	27	"
469						
	A	Capprini Josephine—†	220	housewife	20	142 Paris
	B	Capprini Leo	220	ironworker	24	142 "
	C	Cohen Abraham	220	retired	65	here
	D	Cohen Ida—†	220	housewife	56	"
	E	Cohen Rose I—†	220	bookkeeper	26	"
	F	Cowin Philip	220	attorney	34	"
	G	Gerace Angelina—†	220	housewife	21	Medford
	H	Gerace Anthony	220	laborer	25	"

Page.	Letter.	FULL NAME.	Residence, Jan. 1, 1938.	Occupation.	Supposed Age.	Reported Residence, Jan. 1, 1937. Street and Number.

Paris Street—Continued

	K	Gold Rae—†	222	at home	27	here
	M	*DiAngelo Carmine	222	laborer	36	288 Chelsea
	N	*Cordischi Angelina—†	222	housewife	26	288 "
	O	Cordischi Archie	222	cutter	36	288 "
	P	D'Angelico Flora—†	224	housewife	31	here
	R	D'Angelico Michael	224	cleaner	43	"
	S	*Fusco Camella—†	224	housewife	48	"
	T	Fusco Joseph	224	candymaker	51	"
	U	Fusco Vincent	224	laborer	24	
	V	Sciarappo Angelo	224	"	44	"
	W	*Sciarappo Camella—†	224	housewife	38	"
	X	Sacco Clara—†	226	packer	24	
	Y	Sacco Lucy—†	226	housewife	65	"
	Z	Sacco Mildred—†	226	teacher	35	
470						
	A	Sacco Ralph	226	laborer	65	
	B	Sacco Ralph	226	entertainer	27	"
	C	Criscolo Antonio	226	shoeworker	42	"
	D	Criscolo Jennie—†	226	housewife	37	"
	E	Camuso Margaret—†	226	"	37	
	F	Camuso Pasquale	226	secretary	37	"
	G	Cusolito Felix	226	chauffeur	45	"
	H	Sgro Maria—†	236	housewife	42	"
	K	Sgro Natale	236	laborer	49	
	L	Antonuccio John	236	"	30	
	N	Sgro Anthony	236	"	22	
	M	Sgro Antonina—†	236	operator	26	"
	O	*Antonuccio Peter	236	laborer	49	"
	P	*Antonuccio Sarah—†	236	housekeeper	37	"
	R	Marcoccio Antoinetta—†	240	housewife	31	19 Chaucer
	S	Marcoccio Domenic	240	dealer	34	19 "
	T	Weinstein Esther—†	242	at home	74	here
	U	Brass Bernice—†	242	saleswoman	22	"
	V	*Brass Myer	242	dealer	57	"
	W	*Brass Sarah—†	242	housewife	45	"
	X	Grasso Mary—†	242	"	22	Malden
	Y	Grasso Victor	242	shoeworker	26	"
	Z	Weinberg Abraham	244	salesman	40	here
471						
	A	*Weinberg Katie—†	244	housewife	36	"
	B	Bloom Charlotte—†	244	at home	35	

Page.	Letter.	FULL NAME.	Residence, Jan. 1, 1938.	Occupation.	Supposed Age.	Reported Residence, Jan. 1, 1937. Street and Number.

Paris Street—Continued

Page.	Letter.	FULL NAME.	Residence, Jan. 1, 1938.	Occupation.	Supposed Age.	Reported Residence, Jan. 1, 1937. Street and Number.
	C	Donovan Marcella—†	244	at home	37	161 Putnam
	D	Vernacchio Frank	252	mechanic	30	228 Saratoga
	E	Vernacchio Lucy—†	252	housewife	22	Somerville
	F	Russo Armando	252	shipper	24	154 Brooks
	G	Russo Lucy—†	252	housewife	24	Medford
	H	Pacci Mary A—†	252	"	24	37 Decatur
	K	Pacci Salvatore J	252	laborer	24	37 "
	L	Forgione Alfonso	254	shoeworker	50	here
	M	Forgione Delia—†	254	housewife	43	"
	N	Forgione Joseph J	254	laborer	22	"
	O	Parenteau Matilda—†	254	at home	83	"
	P	Pascarella Annetti—†	256	housewife	32	3 Murray ct
	R	Pascarella Louis	256	tailor	33	3 "
	S	Brunco Esther—†	256	housewife	30	here
	T	*Brunco Joseph	256	laborer	41	"
	U	Rivers Guy M	256	cook	34	416 Shawmut av
	V	Luciano Augustino	256	laborer	43	here
	W	Luciano Joseph	256	"	20	"
	X	Luciano Theresa—†	256	housewife	40	"
	Y	Kenney Harry	rear 256	laborer	38	
	Z	Kenney Theresa—†	" 256	housewife	37	"
472						
	A	Barnes Charles	258	laborer	25	
	B	Barnes Josephine—†	258	housewife	51	"
	C	Silvagni Alexander	258	electrician	36	"
	D	*Silvagni Ascenzio	258	retired	72	
	E	Silvagni Rose—†	258	housewife	35	"
	F	Caucci Angelina—†	258	bookkeeper	24	"
	G	Caucci Marion—†	258	housewife	43	"
	H	Caucci Thomas	258	laborer	46	
	K	Caucci William	258	"	20	
	L	Francis Ellen—†	260	housewife	23	"
	M	Francis George	260	usher	22	
	N	Carr Blanche—†	260	housewife	25	"
	O	Francis Anthony G	260	woodworker	48	"
	P	Francis Joseph L	260	chauffeur	20	"
	R	Francis Mary E—†	260	housewife	47	"
	S	Gill Dennis A	260	printer	42	
	T	Littlewood Mary—†	260	at home	73	
	U	*Gallo Mary—†	262	housewife	35	"
	V	Gallo Pasquale	262	shoeworker	40	"

Page.	Letter.	Full Name.	Residence, Jan. 1, 1938.	Occupation.	Supposed Age.	Reported Residence, Jan. 1, 1937. Street and Number.
		Paris Street—Continued				
	W	*Zollo Florence—†	262	housewife	34	here
	X	Zollo James	262	laborer	34	"
	Y	Mastromarino Donato	262	meatcutter	41	"
	Z	*Mastromarino Margaret—†	262	housewife	41	"
473						
	A	DeDominicis Alfred	264	printer	29	
	B	DeDominicis Helen—†	264	housewife	26	"
	C	*Chiarenza Mary—†	264	"	33	
	D	Chiarenza Vincenzo	264	cutter	41	
	E	*Nappi Alfonzo	264	chauffeur	34	"
	F	Nappi Dora—†	264	housewife	31	"
	G	Castagiana Concetta—†	266	"	36	
	H	Castagiana Frank	266	barber	40	"
	K	*Cuozzo Angelo	266	laborer	22	242 E Eagle
	L	Cuozzo Mary—†	266	housewife	22	242 "
	M	Tiano Florence—†	266	packer	27	here
	N	*Tiano Jennie—†	266	housewife	57	"
	O	Tiano Samuel	266	laborer	24	"
	P	Fenno Laurence	268	clerk	23	
	R	Coviello Angelo	268	laborer	34	
	S	Coviello Catherine—†	268	housewife	24	"
	T	Delaney Louise—†	268	"	38	"
	V	Barbaro Angelo	276	baker	29	209 Havre
	W	Barbaro Jennie—†	276	housewife	25	209 "
	X	Mazzone Antoinetta—†	276	at home	21	here
	Y	Mazzone Joseph	276	laborer	46	"
	Z	*Mazzone Margaret—†	276	housewife	46	"
474						
	A	Alfano Alfonzo	276	tailor	49	
	B	*Alfano Rose—†	276	housewife	35	"
		Porter Street				
	K	Farrell James	14	clerk	39	here
	N	*Minichiello Angelina—†	24	housewife	46	"
	O	Minichiello Antonio	24	machinist	44	"
	R	Caggiano Antonio	26	laborer	52	
	S	Caggiano Bernard	26	"	25	
	T	*Caggiano Rose—†	26	at home	85	"
	U	DeVingo Edward J	26	cutter	28	24 Porter
	V	DeVingo Josephine—†	26	housewife	20	24 "

Page.	Letter.	Full Name.	Residence, Jan. 1, 1938.	Occupation.	Supposed Age.	Reported Residence, Jan. 1, 1937. Street and Number.

Porter Street—Continued

Page.	Letter.	Full Name.	Residence, Jan. 1, 1938.	Occupation.	Supposed Age.	Reported Residence, Jan. 1, 1937. Street and Number.
	w	*Lozzi Joseph	28	tailor	38	here
	x	Lozzi Teresa—†	28	housewife	32	"
	y	Santiano Anthony	28	chauffeur	26	"
	z	*Santiano Leona—†	28	housewife	57	"
475						
	A	*Santiano Louis	28	carpenter	68	"
	B	Santiano Madeline—†	28	housewife	35	"
	C	Santiano Michael J	28	electrician	35	"
	D	Santiano Sadie—†	30	housewife	27	"
	E	Santiano Vito	30	chauffeur	28	"
	F	Caruso Angelo	30	laborer	40	
	G	Caruso Philomena—†	30	housewife	28	"
	L	Stellato Constance—†	40	packer	23	
	M	*Stellato Frank	40	storekeeper	61	"
	N	*Stellato Pasquale	40	shoeworker	37	"
	O	*Stellato Pasqualina—†	40	housewife	54	"
	R	*Amato Concettina—†	42	"	36	
	S	*Amato Frank	42	laborer	38	"
	T	Ciampa Arthur	42	pedler	21	33 Haynes
	U	Ciampa Rose—†	42	housewife	20	149 Havre
	W	*Ciriello Linda—†	46	"	42	here
	X	Ciriello Nicholas	46	operator	23	"
	Y	*Ciriello Peter	46	laborer	45	"
	Z	Ciriello Vito	46	shipper	21	
476						
	A	Giordano Mafalda—†	46	operator	23	"
	B	Giordano Mary—†	46	housewife	54	"
	C	Giordano Salvatore	46	painter	22	
	F	Zambello Francesca—†	48	sorter	20	
	G	Zambello Joseph	48	storekeeper	48	"
	H	*Zambello Lucia—†	48	housewife	38	"
	K	Colombo Mario	52	laborer	23	131 Havre
	L	Avellino Frank	52	"	50	here
	M	*Avellino Greta—†	52	housewife	41	"
	N	Cavalieri Dominic	54	laborer	24	"
	O	Cavalieri Frank	54	"	53	
	P	*Cavalieri Maria—†	54	housewife	50	"
	R	Gatti Almo	60	roofer	43	240 Bremen
	S	*Gatti Lena—†	60	housewife	38	240 "
	T	*Zangetti Renato	60	roofer	45	240 "
	U	*Frustaglia Electra—†	62	housewife	53	here

Page.	Letter.	Full Name.	Residence, Jan. 1, 1938.	Occupation.	Supposed Age.	Reported Residence, Jan. 1, 1937. Street and Number.

Porter Street—Continued

	V	Gallucci Josephine—†	62	operator	22	here
	W	*Umbro Isabella—†	62	housewife	35	Italy
	X	Umbro Joseph	62	laborer	45	13 Hanover
477						
	A	Annella Anna—†	72	housewife	28	here
	B	Annella Edward	72	shoeworker	31	"
	C	Guidara Concetta—†	72	housewife	22	"
	D	Guidara William	72	bricklyer	29	"
	E	Petrocchi Cleofe—†	72	housewife	40	"
	F	Petrocchi Samuel	72	janitor	32	"
	G	*Lombardi Filippa—†	72	housewife	31	5 Battery
	H	*Lombardi Lebalo	72	presser	39	5 "
	K	*Baudanza Gesualdo	72	baker	67	here
	L	*Baudanza Joseph	72	"	35	"
	M	*Baudenza Mary—†	72	housewife	57	"
	N	Baudenza Mary—†	72	attorney	25	
	O	Baudenza Rose—†	72	clerk	36	
	P	Incerto Genaro	72	shoeworker	28	"
	R	Incerto Nancy—†	72	housewife	25	"
	T	Maimone Domenic	76	cook	46	
	U	Maimone Margaret—†	76	housewife	44	"
	V	*Coco Carmella—†	76	"	41	
	W	*Coco Mario	76	laborer	47	
	X	*Montelione Manuel	80	storekeeper	44	"
	Y	*Montelione Mary—†	80	housewife	26	"
	Z	DeMarco Alfred	80	chauffeur	22	77 Brooks
478						
	A	DeMarco Theresa—†	80	housekeeper	49	77 "
	C	DePaolis Lena—†	82	housewife	45	here
	D	DePaolis Ugo	82	mechanic	45	"
	E	DePaolis Virginia—†	82	maid	22	"
	F	Pieri Concetta—†	82	housewife	41	"
	G	Pieri Noe	82	pedler	46	
	H	Sansone Andrew	84	laborer	64	"
	K	Sansone Sylvia—†	84	housewife	58	"
	O	*Gallo Joseph	86	tailor	67	326 Bremen
	P	Gallo Joseph	86	baker	47	326 "
	R	Gallo Thomasina—†	86	housewife	40	326 "
	S	*Amerino Anna A—†	86	at home	75	here
	T	Cardosi Henry	86	metalworker	36	391 Lexington
	U	Cardosi Jennie—†	86	housewife	38	291 "

Page.	Letter.	Full Name.	Residence, Jan. 1, 1938.	Occupation.	Supposed Age.	Reported Residence, Jan. 1, 1937. Street and Number.
		Porter Street—Continued				
	V	*Gallo Giuseppe	87	laborer	46	here
	W	*Gallo Thomasina—†	87	housewife	39	"
	X	*Giuffre Giuseppe	87	presser	67	"
479						
	A	Schwartz Morris	88	grocer	39	
	B	Schwartz Tillie—†	88	housewife	33	"
	C	*DeLuigi Joseph	88	storekeeper	53	"
	D	*DeLuigi Mary—†	88	housewife	46	"
	E	Zarrella Ciriaco	90	retired	70	
	F	Zarrella Consiglia—†	90	housewife	63	"
		Sharon Court				
	H	Hiscock John	1	laborer	44	here
	K	*Hiscock Eliza—†	2	housewife	66	"
	L	*Hiscock Richard	2	laborer	65	"
	M	Falzarano Domenica—†	3	housewife	49	"
	N	Falzarano Ralph	3	laborer	27	
	O	Falzarano Sabatino	3	"	60	
		William J Kelly Square				
	P	Orlandi Pasquale	6	laborer	45	here
	R	Polazzo James	6	operator	46	"
	S	Rizza Edith—†	6	housewife	20	Winthrop
	T	Rizza Salvatore	6	laborer	24	69 Frankfort
	U	*Wilcox Margaret—†	6	housekeeper	49	here
	W	Bonner Bernard F	7	painter	38	"
	X	Bonner Margaret F—†	7	housewife	38	"
	Y	Bonner William E	7	printer	38	"
	Z	Curcio Pasquale M	7	barber	38	208 Princeton
480						
	A	Dietrich Ernest R	7	foreman	52	here
	B	Kearns Frank J	7	bartender	35	"
	C	Noone Patrick F	7	engineer	69	"
	D	Pecora Thomas	7	welder	39	Chelsea
	E	Regan Dorothy M—†	7	laundress	23	here
	F	Stephen William T	7	machinist	50	37 W J Kelly sq
	M	Mess Charles	13	foreman	40	Chelsea
	N	Mess Helen—†	13	housewife	43	"
	O	Rizzo Angelina—†	13	"	42	here

Page.	Letter.	Full Name.	Residence, Jan. 1, 1938.	Occupation.	Supposed Age.	Reported Residence, Jan. 1, 1937. Street and Number.

William J Kelly Square—Continued

Page.	Letter.	Full Name.	Residence, Jan. 1, 1938.	Occupation.	Supposed Age.	Reported Residence, Jan. 1, 1937. Street and Number.
	P	Rizzo Michael	13	foreman	40	here
	R	Nevola Alfred	13	attendant	24	"
	S	*Ciccarelli Cesere	13	mechanic	40	"
	T	Cogliano Alfonso	13	laborer	41	62 Bennington
	U	*DiOna Ralph	13	"	57	here
	V	Pastori John	13	carpenter	28	"
	X	Stack Hannah T—†	14	housewife	54	279 Paris
	Y	Stack Michael J	14	fireman	51	279 "
	Z	Morelli Nieda—†	14	shoeworker	25	here
481						
	A	Morelli Theodore	14	chauffeur	24	"
	B	Valianti Alfred	14	laborer	23	
	C	Valianti Edith—†	14	dressmaker	25	"
	D	Valianti Louise—†	14	housewife	27	"
	E	Valianti Peter	14	chauffeur	32	"
	F	Valianti Robert	14	laborer	21	
	G	*Valianti Rose—†	14	housewife	53	"
	K	*Fazio Josephine—†	17	housekeeper	70	Revere
	L	Fazio Salvatore	17	barber	45	35 W J Kelly sq
	M	*Pilsos Stephen	17	cook	40	38 Paris
	N	Shiveree Mary C—†	17	housekeeper	34	35 W J Kelly sq
	O	Sprague Rodella—†	17	operator	51	6 "

15

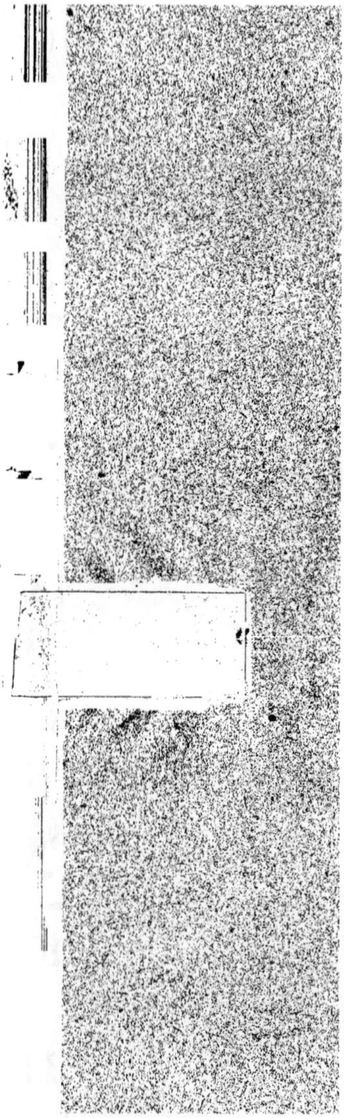

Ward 1—Precinct 6

CITY OF BOSTON

LIST OF RESIDENTS
20 YEARS OF AGE AND OVER

(NON-CITIZENS INDICATED BY ASTERISK)
(FEMALES INDICATED BY DAGGER)

AS OF

JANUARY 1, 1938

JOSEPH F. TIMILTY, } *Listing*
FREDERIC E. DOWLING, } *Board.*

CITY OF BOSTON PRINTING DEPARTMENT

Page.	Letter.	Full Name.	Residence, Jan. 1, 1938.	Occupation.	Supposed Age.	Reported Residence, Jan. 1, 1937. Street and Number.

490

Bennington Street

Page.	Letter.	Full Name.	Residence, Jan. 1, 1938.	Occupation.	Supposed Age.	Reported Residence, Jan. 1, 1937. Street and Number.
490	E	*Azzelino Filomena—†	18	housewife	52	here
	F	*Azzelino Joseph	18	laborer	52	"
	G	Mennella Charles M	22	jeweler	41	"
	H	Mennella Edith—†	22	housewife	36	"
	R	Berman Charles	34	druggist	30	
	S	Berman Eva—†	34	housewife	25	"
	T	*Cohen Esther—†	34	"	48	
	U	Cohen Ethel—†	34	saleswoman	27	"
	V	*Cohen Max	34	storekeeper	52	"
	W	Jason Margaret—†	34	housewife	60	"
	X	St George Alice M—†	34	"	40	"
	Y	St George Edward B	34	laborer	45	"
	Z	St George Maria I—†	34	clerk	22	"
491	H	Cleary Christopher	56	painter	36	
	K	Cleary Jeanette—†	56	housewife	32	"
	L	Whitten Louise—†	56	domestic	37	"
	M	Whitten Margaret—†	56	housewife	63	"
	U	Gardas Catherine—†	56	"	44	304 Maverick
	O	Gardas William H	56	fireman	45	304 "
	P	Pero Henry	56	factoryhand	28	304 "
	R	Hall Alma F—†	56	clerk	20	72 Bennington
	S	Hall Elmer	56	painter	54	72 "
	T	Hewitt Fannie M—†	56	housewife	65	72 "
	U	Green Harold	58	attendant	30	61 "
	V	Green Rose—†	58	housewife	25	here
	W	*Nicosia Josephine—†	58	"	52	"
	X	Nicosia Josephine—†	58	saleswoman	24	"
	Y	LaMotta Anna A—†	58	housewife	31	"
	Z	LaMotta Leonard E	58	clerk	37	
492	A	Zeringis Anthony	58	chauffeur	26	"
	B	Liddy Francis	60	mechanic	32	"
	C	Liddy Mary—†	60	housewife	62	"
	D	*Schiff Bessie—†	60	"	58	
	E	Schiff Jacob	60	retired	60	
	F	Laurasi James	62	plumber	27	
	G	Laurasi Mary—†	62	housewife	27	"
	H	Acunzo Salvatore	62	musician	52	"
	K	Laurasi Agnes—†	62	stitcher	25	

Page.	Letter.	FULL NAME.	Residence, Jan. 1, 1938.	Occupation.	Supposed Age.	Reported Residence, Jan. 1, 1937. Street and Number.

Bennington Street—Continued

Page.	Letter.	FULL NAME.	Residence, Jan. 1, 1938.	Occupation.	Supposed Age.	Reported Residence, Jan. 1, 1937. Street and Number.
	L	Laurasi Alveria—†	62	stitcher	23	here
	M	*Laurasi Assunta—†	62	housewife	59	"
	N	*Scala Angelina—†	64	"	54	"
	O	Scala John	64	retired	61	
	P	Scala John	64	student	23	
	R	Scala Anthony	64	"	20	
	S	Scala Mildred—†	64	stenographer	27	"
	T	Goshgarian Serop	64	storekeeper	48	"
	X	Marotta Charles	70	baker	29	"
	Y	Marotta Michael	70	stitcher	27	
	Z	Marotta Phyllis—†	70	clerk	25	
493						
	A	Marotta Salvatore	70	bookkeeper	23	"
	E	Keating Charlotta M—†	72	housewife	65	"
	F	Keating Florence F—†	72	saleswoman	40	"
	G	Keating Michael E	72	inspector	61	"
	H	*Bonia Mary—†	74	housewife	40	"
	K	*Bonia Michael	74	fisherman	43	"
	L	*Kalland Anna—†	74	housewife	65	"
	M	*Kalland John	74	mechanic	65	"
	N	Wright Christine—†	74	housewife	47	"
	O	Wright John F	74	clerk	50	
	P	Pitts Florence—†	76	housewife	26	"
	R	Pitts John E	76	watchman	38	"
	S	*Botta Carmen	76	fisherman	29	300 Chelsea
	T	Botta Mary—†	76	housewife	26	300 "
	V	Murigan Catherine—†	78	at home	50	here
	W	Lynch Alice—†	78	operator	29	56 Putnam
	X	Lynch Julia—†	78	housewife	60	56 "
	Y	Lynch William J	78	laborer	60	56 "
	Z	Festa Arthur	80	meatcutter	22	here
494						
	A	*Festa Michael	80	"	62	
	B	Enos Joseph	80	packer	69	
	C	Reyendes Mary L—†	80	housekeeper	43	"
	E	Altri Frank	82	laborer	31	54 Cottage
	F	Altri Rose—†	82	housewife	26	54 "
	G	Plant Lucy—†	82	"	34	N Hampshire
	H	Plant Wilfred	82	electrician	36	"
	M	Sullivan Ethel—†	84C	housewife	44	here
	N	Sullivan John	84C	laborer	47	"

Page.	Letter.	Full Name.	Residence, Jan. 1, 1938.	Occupation.	Supposed Age.	Reported Residence, Jan. 1, 1937. Street and Number.

Bennington Street—Continued

Page.	Letter.	Full Name.	Residence, Jan. 1, 1938.	Occupation.	Supposed Age.	Reported Residence, Jan. 1, 1937. Street and Number.
	S	Gorman Alice M—†	90	housewife	49	here
	T	Gorman Margaret—†	90	typist	25	"
	U	Gorman Richard	90	chauffeur	22	"
	V	Keough Patrick	90	laborer	50	
	W	Laffey John	90	"	28	
	X	Laffey Joseph W	90	finisher	29	
	Y	Mazzola Anna—†	90	clerk	21	
	Z	Mazzola Phyllis—†	90	"	25	
495						
	A	*Mazzola Vincenza—†	90	at home	58	
	B	Mazzola Vinzenza—†	90	dressmaker	26	"
	C	Charotas Mary—†	92	housewife	59	"
	D	Charotas Stephen	92	merchant	57	"
	E	Donis Arthur	92	counterman	45	"
	F	Kitas Nicolas	92	rigger	44	
	G	Alves Henrietta—†	92	housewife	45	"
	H	Alves Joseph	92	laborer	60	
	K	Burke Margaret M—†	92	operator	27	
	L	Burke Margaret T—†	92	at home	65	
	M	Campana Filippo	94	finisher	45	"
	N	Campana Louise—†	94	housewife	43	"
	O	Harris Fred J	94	deckhand	46	"
	P	Harris Winifred—†	94	housewife	32	"
	R	Porfido Concetta—†	94	"	30	
	S	Porfido Eugene	94	storekeeper	37	"
	T	Wise Catherine—†	96	at home	57	"
	U	Wise John	96	laborer	34	
	V	Farrell Michael	96	"	64	
	W	Moran Mary—†	96	at home	70	
	X	Smith Catherine—†	96	"	58	
	Y	Smith John	96	laborer	28	
	Z	Quinn Dorcas E—†	100	at home	78	
496						
	A	Rubin Hyman	100	laborer	23	"
	B	Rubin Max	100	glasscutter	58	"
	C	Rubin Rose—†	100	housewife	57	"
	D	Marino Marion—†	100	"	22	
	E	Marino Patrick	100	engraver	29	"
	F	DiMarino Mary—†	104	housewife	25	"
	G	DiMarino Vincent	104	laborer	24	"
	H	Codagnone Joseph	104	"	47	

Page.	Letter.	Full Name.	Residence, Jan. 1, 1938.	Occupation.	Supposed Age.	Reported Residence, Jan. 1, 1937. Street and Number.

Bennington Street—Continued

Page.	Letter.	Full Name.	Residence, Jan. 1, 1938.	Occupation.	Supposed Age.	Reported Residence, Jan. 1, 1937. Street and Number.
	K	Codagnone Robert	104	artist	23	here
	L	Codagnone Silvia—†	104	housewife	39	"
	M	Cardone Anna—†	104	candyworker	24	"
	N	Cardone Anthony	104	shoeworker	21	"
	O	*Cardone Bessie—†	104	housewife	48	"
	P	*Cardone Pasquale	104	laborer	48	
	R	Cipriano Joseph	108	broker	40	
	S	Cipriano Mary L—†	108	housewife	32	"
	T	Marino Americo	108	laborer	30	
	U	Marino Elvera—†	108	candymaker	22	"
	V	Marino Emma—†	108	shoeworker	29	"
	W	Marino Esta—†	108	saleswoman	21	"
	X	Marino Mary—†	108	at home	25	
	Y	Marino Millie—†	108	stitcher	28	
	Z	Marino Rose—†	108	at home	70	
497						
	A	Marino Virginia—†	108	saleswoman	24	"
	B	Faretra Arthur	108	barber	38	
	C	Faretra Sarah—†	108	housewife	38	"
	D	Grillo Joseph	110	shoemaker	27	229 Benningt'n
	E	Marino Emilo	110	tailor	38	here
	F	Marino Emma—†	110	housewife	33	"
	G	Dalosio Alfred	110	laborer	29	"
	H	Dalosio Eleanora—†	110	housekeeper	24	"
	K	Dalosio Ernest	110	laborer	20	"
	L	Dalosio Mafalda—†	110	shoeworker	21	"
	M	Dalosio Ralph	110	laborer	47	
	N	Constant Emma H—†	114	housewife	62	"
	O	Constant Thomas B	114	retired	73	"
	P	Creigh Mary—†	114	housemaid	48	Arlington
	R	Marliave Anna—†	114	housewife	40	here
	S	Marliave Daniel	114	fireman	42	"
	T	Lamb Elizabeth F—†	116	clerk	23	276 Prescott
	U	Lamb Nina M—†	116	housewife	54	276 "
	V	Lamb William	116	boilermaker	56	276 "
	W	Lamb William A	116	"	21	276 "
	Y	Russell Catherine B—†	116	housewife	51	here
	Z	Russell Joseph L	116	metalworker	49	"
498						
	A	Grillo Mary—†	118	housewife	29	24 Eutaw
	B	Grillo Stephen	118	laborer	33	24 "

Page.	Letter.	Full Name.	Residence, Jan. 1, 1938.	Occupation.	Supposed Age.	Reported Residence, Jan. 1, 1937. Street and Number.

Bennington Street—Continued

	C	Camerlingo Angelina—†	118	housewife	28	here
	D	Camerlingo Ralph	118	laborer	34	"
	E	Cleary Elizabeth—†	118	housewife	65	"
	F	Cleary Glynn	118	clerk	28	
	G	Cleary James R	118	mechanic	31	"
	H	Cleary William	118	carpenter	66	"
	K	Cleary William L	118	mechanic	36	"
	L	Mudge Sadie—†	118	at home	69	
	M	Bagnera Joseph	120	actor	42	
	N	Cogswell Anna—†	120	clerk	20	
	O	Cogswell Annie—†	120	at home	57	
	P	Cogswell Edward	120	counterman	23	"
	S	Nealon Leo	120	laborer	31	
	R	Nealon Mildred—†	120	housewife	30	"
	T	Broussard Anna—†	120	at home	48	
	U	Broussard Edward	120	painter	26	"
	V	Cahill John J	120	chauffeur	51	4 Jeffries
	W	McNeil Leo	120	bartender	33	here
	X	Preshong Albert	124	watchman	60	"
	Y	Preshong Joseph	124	seaman	25	"
	Z	Preshong Josephine—†	124	housewife	55	"
499						
	A	Prejean Theresa—†	124	"	23	
	B	Prejean Willard	124	shipper	30	
	C	Torre Angelo	128	jeweler	36	
	D	Torre Silvia—†	128	housewife	29	"
	E	Manfredonia Adelaide—†	132	"	48	
	F	Manfredonia Leopoldo	132	manager	55	"
	G	Zakarian Massup	136	storekeeper	61	"
	K	Chafity Dora—†	138	housewife	55	"
	L	Chafity Harry	138	manager	60	"
	M	Sheehan Mary E—†	138	at home	53	
	N	Sheehan William G	138	operator	24	"
	O	St George Alice M—†	140	at home	38	
	P	St George Joseph J	140	laborer	53	
	R	Powell Elizabeth—†	140	at home	45	

Border Street

	S	McDonald John	219	cook	45	here
	T	McDonald Murdock	219	blacksmith	75	"

Page.	Letter.	Full Name.	Residence, Jan. 1, 1938.	Occupation.	Supposed Age.	Reported Residence, Jan. 1, 1937. Street and Number.

Border Street—Continued

Page.	Letter.	Full Name.	Residence, Jan. 1, 1938.	Occupation.	Supposed Age.	Reported Residence, Jan. 1, 1937. Street and Number.
	V	Bruno Antonio	219	laborer	51	here
	W	*Bruno Esther—†	219	housewife	48	"
	X	Bruno Natalie—†	219	operator	21	"
	Y	Reale Manuel	221	laborer	25	
	Z	*Reale Sebastiano	221	"	57	
500						
	E	Buccheri Joseph	221	plumber	23	
	A	Buccheri Paul	221	pedler	55	
	B	*Buccheri Pauline—†	221	housewife	50	"
	C	Buccheri Samuel	221	laborer	22	379 Meridian
	D	Buccheri Victor	221	"	21	here
	F	Buswell Dorothy—†	223	waitress	21	47 Saratoga
	G	Oxley Edith—†	223	housewife	41	47 "
	H	Oxley Ralph	223	engineer	47	47 "
	K	Fortini Jennie—†	223	packer	23	here
	L	Fortini Joseph	223	laborer	50	"
	M	*Fortini Mary—†	223	housewife	48	"
	N	Stewart Leo L	223	mechanic	33	"
	O	Stewart Rose M—†	223	housewife	25	"
	P	Emma Cologero	225	laborer	44	
	R	*Emma Lucy—†	225	housewife	34	"
	S	Turco Charles	225	gardener	47	"
	T	*Turco Filippa—†	225	at home	82	
	U	*Turco Ida—†	225	housewife	39	"
	V	Viola Marianna—†	225	"	24	
	W	*Viola Mary—†	225	housekeeper	61	"
	X	Viola Vito	225	painter	24	"
	Y	*Cipriano Mickeln—†	227	housewife	43	217 Webster
	Z	Cipriano Nicholas	227	laborer	51	217 "
501						
	A	Cipriano Phillip	227	factoryhand	21	217 "
	C	McPhee Elizabeth—†	255	housekeeper	64	here
	D	*Whalen Mary—†	255	stitcher	58	"
	E	Wilkie Frederick S	255	boilermaker	46	"
	F	Gallo Battisto	257	laborer	33	
	G	*Gallo Joseph	257	retired	70	"
	H	Johnson Laura—†	257	laundryworker	39	28 Liverpool
	K	Russell Charles B	257	painter	66	275 Border
	L	Gallo Mary—†	257	housewife	28	here
	M	Gallo Michael	257	laborer	31	"
	N	*DiPeietro Filippa—†	259	housekeeper	63	"

Page.	Letter.	Full Name.	Residence, Jan. 1, 1938.	Occupation.	Supposed Age.	Reported Residence, Jan. 1, 1937. Street and Number.
		Border Street—Continued				
	O	*Fendo Angeline—†	259	housewife	37	here
	P	*Fendo James	259	laborer	44	"
	R	Rizzuto Joseph	259	"	27	"
	S	*Rizzuto Mafalda—†	259	housewife	29	"
	T	Aiello Ignazio	261	laborer	42	"
	U	Lauria Anthony	261	electrician	35	11 Gove
	V	Lauria Hazel—†	261	housewife	24	11 "
	W	Viola Joseph	261	laborer	30	here
	X	Viola Phyllis—†	261	housewife	24	"
	Y	*Buttigliole Mary—†	263	"	37	"
	Z	Buttiglioie Rocco	263	laborer	45	"
502						
	A	*Spada Catina—†	263	housewife	41	"
	B	Spada Leo	263	laborer	46	"
	C	*Lopes Cezar	263	operator	35	28 Decatur
	D	Marshall Marie—†	265	housekeeper	31	here
	E	Pries Albert	265	garageman	39	Greenbush
	F	Jones Anna G—†	265	housewife	34	28 Pleasant
	G	Jones Daniel N	265	clerk	40	28 "
	K	Cassara Peter	265	leatherworker	29	here
	H	Cassara Tina—†	265	housewife	22	"
		Brooks Street				
	L	Daddario Nicolas	76	mechanic	42	here
	M	*Femino Charles	76	baker	23	"
	N	Femino Jennie—†	76	saleswoman	24	"
	O	*Femino Mary—†	76	clerk	29	
	P	*Femino Minnie—†	76	housewife	51	"
	R	*Femino Paul	76	baker	51	
	S	Bennett Margaret—†	78	housewife	65	"
	T	Bennett Mark	78	retired	71	
	U	Rose Fannie—†	78	housewife	63	"
	V	Rose Silas	78	laborer	58	
	W	*Russo Priso	78	"	48	
	X	*Russo Venice—†	78	housewife	57	"
	Y	White Margaret—†	80	housekeeper	55	"
	Z	*Yappheria Esta—†	80	housewife	36	"
503						
	A	*Yappheria Salvatore	80	shoeworker	47	"
	B	Costa Margaret—†	80	student	21	284 Lexington

Page.	Letter.	FULL NAME.	Residence, Jan. 1, 1938.	Occupation.	Supposed Age.	Reported Residence, Jan. 1, 1937. Street and Number.

Brooks Street—Continued

	C	Laskey Charles	80	salesman	21	110 Trenton
	D	Laskey Helen—†	80	housewife	22	24 Lexington
	E	Laskey Herbert	80	electrician	23	110 Trenton
	F	Donners Elizabeth—†	82	at home	74	here
	G	Bombaci Lucy—†	82	nurse	24	"
	H	Bombaci Rose—†	82	at home	58	"
	K	Bombaci Virgilio	82	locksmith	21	"
	L	DeLucia Jennie—†	82	packer	24	164 Benningt'n
	M	DeLucia Rose—†	82	housewife	48	164 "
	N	DeLucia Thomaso	82	laborer	53	164 "
	O	Benvissuto Viola—†	84	housewife	25	here
	P	Benvissuto William	84	laborer	28	"
	R	Capezzuto Benjamin	84	"	43	"
	S	Capezzuto Louise—†	84	housewife	42	"
	T	Simonelli Dominic	84	sailor	42	
	U	Simonelli Jennie—†	84	housewife	40	"
	V	Mastrangelo Mary—†	86	"	42	
	W	Mastrangelo Michael	86	laborer	40	
	X	Scorzello Joseph	86	"	22	
	Y	Scorzello Michael	86	manager	23	"
	Z	Marruzzo Angelina—†	86	at home	24	
504						
	A	Marruzzo Angelo	86	laborer	23	
	B	*Marruzzo Joseph	86	"	53	
	C	*Goon Charlie	88	laundryman	66	"
	D	Carpenito Anthony	88	merchant	34	"
	E	Carpenito Mary—†	88	housewife	30	"
	F	Minichello Anthony	88	manager	29	"
	G	Minichello Emily—†	88	housewife	21	"
	L	Sears Amelia—†	100	"	23	50 Taylor
	M	Sears Frank	100	laborer	26	50 "
	O	Rose Emily—†	102	at home	68	here
	P	Rose Mary—†	102	candymaker	35	"
	R	*Pantano Carmela—†	104	housewife	49	"
	S	*Pantano Frank	104	laborer	62	
	T	McCormack Annie—†	104	housewife	47	"
	V	McCormack Harold	104	laborer	25	
	U	McCormack John	104	rigger	49	
	W	McCormack Leo	104	laborer	21	
	X	McCormack Leonard	104	"	27	
	Y	Kelly Helen—†	106	housewife	40	"

Page.	Letter.	Full Name.	Residence, Jan. 1, 1938.	Occupation.	Supposed Age.	Reported Residence, Jan. 1, 1937. Street and Number.

Brooks Street—Continued

Page.	Letter.	Full Name.	Residence, Jan. 1, 1938.	Occupation.	Supposed Age.	Reported Residence, Jan. 1, 1937. Street and Number.
	Z	Kelly John	106	fisherman	47	here
505						
	A	Muise Anthony	106	laborer	42	"
	B	Muise Margaret—†	106	at home	26	"
	C	Muise Mary—†	106	housewife	36	"
	D	Joyce Harriet E—†	106	"	52	"
	E	Joyce Joseph S	106	fireman	52	"
	F	St Croix Henry	108	packer	22	72 Prescott
	G	St Croix Ruth—†	108	housewife	21	here
	H	Duca Ida—†	108	"	30	"
	K	Duca Joseph	108	painter	32	"
	N	*Cerulo Nicolas	108	retired	81	"
	L	*DePhilips Marie J—†	108	housewife	55	"
	M	*DePhilips Michael	108	laborer	56	"

Lexington Avenue

Page.	Letter.	Full Name.	Residence, Jan. 1, 1938.	Occupation.	Supposed Age.	Reported Residence, Jan. 1, 1937. Street and Number.
	O	McCarthy John J	1	laborer	29	18 Brigham
	P	McCarthy Mabel—†	1	housewife	30	18 "
	R	DiPerri Charles	1	laborer	21	here
	S	DiPerri Lorenzo	1	"	55	"
	T	*DiPerri Mary—†	1	housewife	42	"
	U	Jenning Augusta—†	2	"	78	"
	V	McEachern Joseph A	2	painter	49	"
	W	McEachern Joseph A, jr	2	"	24	"
	X	McEachern Reta A—†	2	housewife	41	"
	Y	*Silva Gertrude—†	3	"	41	"
	Z	*Silva Manuel	3	seaman	57	"
506						
	B	Fothergel Mary J—†	4	housewife	51	"
	C	*McMillan Allen D	4	corker	59	"
	D	*Brennan Catherine—†	4	housewife	32	"
	E	Brennan Frederick	4	laborer	35	"
	F	*Keefe Margaret—†	5	housewife	52	164 Marion
	G	Vitale John	5	laborer	42	here
	H	*Vitale Mary—†	5	housewife	35	"
	K	Brennan Mary F—†	6	"	32	"
	L	Brennan William H	6	storekeeper	31	"
	M	Brennan Blanche—†	6	housewife	63	343 Border
	N	Brennan Emma—†	6	dressmaker	22	343 "
	O	Brown Margaret—†	7	housewife	68	here

Page.	Letter.	Full Name.	Residence, Jan. 1, 1938.	Occupation.	Supposed Age.	Reported Residence, Jan. 1, 1937. Street and Number

Lexington Avenue—Continued

	P	Brown William H	7	laborer	66	here
	R	*Cordowano Jennie—†	7	housewife	63	"
	S	*Cordowano Salvatore	7	retired	76	"
	T	*Vietro Esther—†	8	housewife	33	180 Princeton
	U	*Baglio Lillian—†	8	"	37	here
	V	*Baglio Louis	8	tailor	42	"
	W	Bronfield Annie T—†	9	housewife	68	"
	X	*Genualdo Arthur	9	painter	24	220 Lexington
	Y	Genualdo Rose—†	9	housewife	23	220 "
	Z	Crowell Ernest	10	fireman	52	here
507						
	A	Crowell Lottie—†	10	inspector	63	"
	B	*Callari Josephine—†	10	housewife	48	"
	C	Callari Philip	10	laborer	52	
	D	Callari Philip	10	"	21	
	E	*Carra Maria—†	10	houseworker	69	"

Lexington Place

	F	Lapoint Joseph	1	painter	41	Malden
	G	Moulton Ella—†	1	housewife	43	Medford
	H	Collins Arthur	1	laborer	21	here
	K	Collins John	1	fireman	32	"
	L	Collins Mary E—†	1	housewife	55	"
	M	Collins William	1	engineer	57	
	N	Minichello Angelo	2	laborer	30	
	O	Minichello Marie A—†	2	clerk	29	
	P	*Minichello Michael	2	mason	58	
	R	Minichello Philomena—†	2	housewife	51	"
	S	Vitale Lena—†	2	clerk	32	
	T	Vitale Mary—†	2	housewife	26	"
	U	Vitale Michael	2	boilermaker	36	"
	V	*Barrett Mildred—†	3	housewife	42	"
	W	*Barrett Peter	3	painter	55	"
	X	Smith Horace	3	mariner	63	98 Marion
	Y	Lightbody Charles A	3	engineer	51	here
	Z	Lightbody Charles T	3	molder	24	"
508						
	A	Lightbody Edith M—†	3	housewife	49	"
	B	*Murray Mary—†	4	"	31	
	C	*Murray Roderick	4	fisherman	30	"

Page.	Letter.	FULL NAME.	Residence, Jan. 1, 1938.	Occupation.	Supposed Age.	Reported Residence, Jan. 1, 1937. Street and Number.

Lexington Place—Continued

	D	McKillop Kenneth	4	carpenter	65	here
	E	*LaBlanc Rose—†	5	housewife	26	"
	G	Surette Esther—†	5	"	26	"
	H	*Surette Reginald	5	fisherman	43	"
	F	Usher Mary—†	5	housewife	39	"
	K	*Devincentes Frank	6	laborer	33	
	L	Devincentes Philomena—†	6	housewife	23	"
	M	Comeau Ambrose	6	fishcutter	41	"
	N	Comeau Mary—†	6	housewife	43	"
	O	Bosco Edith—†	6	"	33	"
	P	D'India Mildred—†	7	"	26	75 Border
	R	D'India Ralph	7	laborer	29	75 "
	S	Platt Mary M—†	7	housewife	59	here

Lexington Street

	U	Kelly Francis	21	seaman	32	here
	V	MacDonald Marie—†	21	housewife	69	103 Marion
	W	MacDonald Robert H	21	inspector	68	103 "
	X	Beacham Helen G—†	21	housewife	39	here
	Y	Amico Luciano	23	bartender	27	"
	Z	Amico Mary—†	23	saleswoman	24	"
509						
	A	Amico Philip	23	barber	60	
	B	Swett Charles W	23	machinist	67	"
	C	Swett Lizzie M—†	23	housewife	54	"
	E	Sulkey Evelyn—†	rear 23½	"	35	169 Princeton
	F	Sulkey William	" 23½	ironworker	39	169 "
	H	Bonin Amelia—†	27	housewife	71	Chelsea
	G	Snow Alfred	27	laborer	37	"
	K	Snow Evelyn—†	27	housewife	39	"
	L	Durgin Charles	27	salesman	52	here
	M	Durgin Helen L—†	27	housewife	43	"
	N	Johnson Esther—†	29	housekeeper	34	"
	O	Sandmo Beryl	29	housewife	32	"
	P	*Sandmo Karsten	29	fishhandler	32	"
	R	*Youngquist Elizabeth—†	29	housewife	66	"
	S	DeCosta Harry	31	dredger	37	
	T	*Hancock Deborah—†	31	housewife	50	"
	U	*Hancock Joseph	31	carpenter	56	"
	V	*Hancock Mary—†	31	operator	24	"

Page.	Letter.	Full Name.	Residence, Jan. 1, 1938.	Occupation.	Supposed Age.	Reported Residence, Jan. 1, 1937. Street and Number.

Lexington Street—Continued

	W	Soley Cecil	31	storekeeper	37	Everett
	X	Barker Frank A	31A	carpenter	58	here
	Y	*Bickford Herbert B	31A	laborer	43	"
	Z	Casino Matthew J	31A	clerk	25	431 Benningt'n
510						
	A	Hughes Addie M—†	31A	housewife	55	here
	B	Hughes John W	31A	retired	75	"
	C	Stacey Roland	31A	clerk	25	51 Eutaw
	D	*Surette Robert	31A	deckhand	33	here
	E	*Martell Julia—†	31A	at home	90	"
	F	*Martell Leo	31A	brushmaker	56	"
	G	Nolan Arthur	31A	helper	21	
	H	Nolan John F	31A	printer	51	"
	K	Nolan Margaret—†	31A	clerk	25	
	L	Nolan Victoria—†	31A	housewife	50	"
	M	Ferri Pasquale	33	retired	65	
	N	McVey James	33	laborer	31	
	O	McVey Mary—†	33	housewife	56	"
	P	Succolillo Dominic	33	retired	77	
	R	Mason James E	33	guard	60	
	S	Mason William	33	tree surgeon	22	"
	T	McDonnell John	33	foreman	24	62 Trenton
	U	McDonnell Mildred F—†	33	housewife	23	62 "
	V	Fitzgerald Mary E—†	45	housekeeper	47	here
	W	Nardo Anthony	45	shipper	22	"
	X	*Nardo Mary—†	45	housewife	47	"
	Y	Preshong Mabelle—†	45	houseworker	47	"
	Z	McLaughlin Angela—†	47	housewife	27	46 Cameron
511						
	A	McLaughlin John	47	boilermaker	38	46 "
	B	*Cardone Esther—†	47	housewife	30	294 Paris
	C	*Cardone Rocco	47	laborer	40	294 "
	D	Vito Marco S	47	"	57	here
	E	Vito Mary—†	47	housewife	66	"
	F	*Keefe John	49	carpenter	55	55 Call
	G	*Keefe Nathan	49	retired	72	111 Meridian
	H	*Marcis Catherine—†	49	housewife	40	here
	K	Marcis Dominic	49	laborer	42	"
	L	Iovanna Charles	49	"	45	"
	M	Iovanna Louise—†	49	housewife	42	"
	N	Murray Annie E—†	51	"	63	235 Benningt'n

Page.	Letter.	Full Name.	Residence, Jan. 1, 1938.	Occupation.	Supposed Age.	Reported Residence, Jan. 1, 1937. Street and Number.

Lexington Street—Continued

	O	Murray John J	51	fisherman	33	11 Havre
	P	Vilar Joseph J	51	timekeeper	24	11 "
	R	Vilar Julia—†	51	housewife	22	Chelsea
	S	*Sousa Anthony	51	longshoreman	58	67 Marion
	T	Sousa Mary—†	51	housewife	50	67 "
	U	Sousa Mary—†	51	factoryhand	23	67 "
	V	Pistone Fannie—†	51	housewife	25	204 Benningt'n
	W	Pistone Frank	51	laborer	29	204 "
	X	Bromfield Jennie M—†	53	housewife	55	here
	Y	Bromfield John F	53	laborer	47	"
	Z	*Tobin Martin	53	fisherman	36	"
512						
	A	*Tobin Mary—†	53	housewife	34	"
	B	Preilli Rosamando—†	53	housekeeper	60	"
	C	Leno Henry	61	mechanic	29	"
	D	Leno Mary —†	61	housewife	31	"
	E	Zaccaria Anthony	61	laborer	49	"
	F	Zaccaria Mary—†	61	housewife	43	"
	G	Zaccaria Rose—†	61	factoryhand	23	"
	H	*Amari Joseph	61	laborer	48	
	K	*Amari Peter	61	retired	80	
	L	*Amari Rose—†	61	housewife	44	"
	M	Pomet James	63	fishcutter	27	"
	N	Pomet Mildred—†	63	housewife	25	"
	O	Beale Abby—†	63	houseworker	58	"
	P	McPherson John	63	fireman	34	
	R	McPherson Madeline I—†	63	housewife	29	"
	S	Psihogois Mary—†	63	"	42	
	T	Psihogois Peter	63	laborer	45	
	U	Mannetta Eugene	65	chauffeur	25	"
	V	Mannetta Phyllis—†	65	housewife	23	"
	W	Smith Mary—†	65	"	31	
	X	Smith Raymond R	65	engineer	31	
	Y	Mannetta Anna—†	65	factoryhand	23	"
	Z	Mannetta George	65	meatcutter	22	"
513						
	A	Casiello Louise—†	67	housewife	34	"
	B	Casiello Samuel	67	laborer	34	
	C	Giannotti Angela—†	67	housewife	38	"
	D	Giannotti George A	67	laborer	46	
	E	Moscarito Philomena—†	67	houseworker	72	"

Page.	Letter.	Full Name.	Residence, Jan. 1, 1938.	Occupation.	Supposed Age.	Reported Residence, Jan. 1, 1937. Street and Number.
		Lexington Street—Continued				
	F	Puzzo Anna—†	67	housewife	32	10 Lexington av
	G	Puzzo Vincent	67	laborer	45	10 "
	H	McDonald Daniel J	69	operator	47	here
	K	McDonald Mary E—†	69	housewife	41	"
	L	McDonald Stephen A	69	carpenter	43	"
	M	Bloom John	71	retired	75	
	N	Currier Frederick	71	B F D	39	
	O	Currier Mary—†	71	housewife	39	"
	P	Mann Edward	71	laborer	50	Arlington
		Marion Street				
	S	Giordano Antoinette—†	103	housewife	24	here
	T	Giordano Wilfred	103	factoryhand	25	"
	U	*Leavitt David	103	chef	50	"
	V	*Leavitt Sonia—†	103	housewife	45	"
	W	Mingoia Joseph	103	laborer	48	
	X	Mingoia Phyllis—†	103	factoryhand	48	"
	Y	*Spampinato Johana—†	103	housewife	80	"
	Z	Graham Ethel—†	105	"	23	90 Marion
514						
	A	Graham Richard	105	shipper	28	90 "
	B	Chieppo Antonio	105	carpenter	57	here
	C	*Chieppo Theresa—†	105	housewife	52	"
	D	Savino Charles	105	painter	30	"
	E	Savino Rose—†	105	housewife	24	"
	F	Bozzi Helen—†	107	"	22	
	G	Bozzi John	107	factoryhand	26	"
	H	Kelley Agnes—†	107	housewife	49	"
	K	Murphy Thomas	107	fireman	59	
	L	Iantosca Consalata—†	107	housewife	38	"
	M	Iantosca Felice	107	laborer	38	
	N	Iantosca Philip	107	boxmaker	53	"
	P	Tabbi Charles	126	clerk	23	
	R	Tabbi Frank	126	reporter	21	
	S	Tabbi Mary—†	126	stitcher	29	
	T	*Tabbi Rosaria—†	126	housewife	54	"
	U	Tabbi Salvatore	126	merchant	61	"
	V	Tabbi Sarah—†	126	stitcher	24	"
	W	Giampapa Marie—†	126	housekeeper	49	165 Marion
	Y	*Deveau Daisy—†	130	housewife	35	here

Z	Deveau Frank	130	carpenter	42	here
	515				
A	Deveau Isaie	130	"	45	
B	Deveau Mary—†	130	housewife	40	"
C	Dame Emma—†	130	"	43	
D	Dame William	130	dyesetter	46	"
E	Nuskey John J	130	fisherman	61	"
F	*Silva Joseph	132	longshoreman	51	"
G	*Silva Mary—†	132	housewife	45	"
H	Mason John F	132	plumber	30	97 Trenton
K	Mason Margaret—†	132	housewife	26	97 "
L	Barros Zulmira—†	132	housekeeper	37	4 Paris ct
N	Driscoll Agnes C—†	134	"	25	here
O	Driscoll Julia M—†	134	clerk	33	"
P	Driscoll Lillian L—†	134	operator	28	"
R	Driscoll Margaret J—†	134	clerk	32	
S	*Tirone Georgiana—†	134	housewife	41	"
T	Tirone Mary—†	134	nurse	23	
U	*Tirone Michael	134	storekeeper	49	"
V	Paris Charles	149	shipper	24	508 Benningt'n
W	Paris Frances—†	149	housewife	20	Chelsea
X	Hurley Blanche—†	149	"	32	86 Trenton
Y	*Hurley Sylvester	149	longshoreman	29	86 "
	516				
A	*Pothier Michael	151	counterman	33	249 Meridian
B	*Surette John	151	fishhandler	60	212 Saratoga
C	*Surette Winifred—†	151	housewife	60	212 "
E	McCaffrey Joseph	151	electrician	29	116 Benningt'n
D	McCaffrey Joseph J	151	"	55	116 "
F	Cunha Joseph	151	laborer	25	2 London ct
G	Cunha Octavia—†	151	housewife	28	2 "
H	Silva Albert	153	fireman	50	here
K	Silva Annie—†	153	housewife	45	"
M	Glock John	153	baker	62	"
N	Glock Mary—†	153	housewife	48	"
O	*Armento Marie—†	155	housekeeper	66	"
P	Penta Louisa—†	155	factoryhand	23	"
R	Penta Michael	155	laborer	67	
S	*Penta Rose—†	155	housewife	60	"
T	Cunha Alfred	155	laborer	30	
U	Cunha Anthony	155	shipper	34	

Page.	Letter.	FULL NAME.	Residence, Jan. 1, 1938.	Occupation.	Supposed Age.	Reported Residence, Jan. 1, 1937. Street and Number.

Marion Street—Continued

	V	Cunha Mary—†	155	housekeeper	59	here
	W	McKay Marie R—†	156	secretary	35	116 Saratoga
	X	Kretenberg Ernest	156	laborer	38	here
	Y	Kretenberg Louise—†	156	housewife	27	"
	Z	*Mascis Antonio	157	laborer	66	"
517						
	A	*Mascis Marguerite—†	157	housewife	60	"
	B	Mascis Michael	157	laborer	22	
	C	Catalana Dominic	157	shoemaker	35	"
	D	*Catalana Geraldine—†	157	housekeeper	62	"
	E	Catalana Mary—†	157	housewife	23	"
	G	Proto Salvatore	157	laborer	49	
	F	Proto Theresa—†	157	housewife	48	"
	L	*Nolan Caroline—†	159	"	27	90 Eutaw
	M	*Nolan William J	159	fisherman	44	90 "
	N	Zerolla Anna—†	159	shoeworker	21	here
	O	Zerolla Antonio	159	laborer	49	"
	P	Zerolla Bruno	159	shoeworker	23	"
	R	*Zerolla Mary—†	159	housewife	47	"
	S	Baptista Alice—†	159	"	25	47 Lexington
	T	*Baptista Manuel	159	cook	40	47 "
	U	*Crouse Spurgeon	162	clerk	20	here
	V	*Ivory Eva—†	162	housewife	41	"
	W	Ivory John R	162	longshoreman	51	"
	X	Healy Agnes F—†	162	fitter	47	
	Y	Healy Mary E—†	162	housekeeper	49	"
518						
	B	Hankard Mary—†	166	housewife	39	109 Benningt'n
	A	Hankard Thomas F	166	longshoreman	43	109 "
	C	Deveau Zoe—†	166	housekeeper	40	here
	D	Anderson Stella—†	168	"	56	701 Mass av
	E	*LeBlanc Edward	168	fishcutter	41	here
	F	*LeBlanc Ely	168	longshoreman	43	"
	G	*LeBlanc Julia—†	168	housewife	42	"

Meridian Street

	K	McNeil Madeline—†	234	housekeeper	27	here
	L	Carnabuci Leo	234	painter	20	"
	M	*Cecchinelli Clara—†	234	housekeeper	38	"
	N	Cecchinelli Frank	234	painter	20	"

Page.	Letter.	Full Name.	Residence, Jan. 1, 1938.	Occupation.	Supposed Age.	Reported Residence, Jan. 1, 1937. Street and Number.

Meridian Street—Continued

	o	Bell Francis C	236	manager	39	here
	p	Bell Gertrude E—†	236	housewife	43	"
	r	Baldwin George F	236	electrician	57	"
	s	McGowan Josephine—†	236	waitress	30	
	w	Melanson Edmund	242	musician	22	"
	x	Melanson Gerald	242	laborer	20	
	y	Melanson John L	242	cook	56	
	z*	Melanson Mary—†	242	housewife	46	"
519						
	a	Cappuccio Vincenzo A	244	barber	54	
	b	Butts Vincent	244	physician	48	"
	c*	Lauria Carmelo	244	merchant	39	"
	d	Roccuzzo Alfio	244	"	42	
	e	Roccuzzo Gioacchino	244	shoemaker	44	"
	f*	Ehler Anna—†	244	housewife	53	"
	g*	Ehler James	244	fisherman	58	"
	h	Lee George	244A	laundryworker	60	"
	k*	Lee Wong—†	244A	housewife	40	"
	m*	Boudreau Edward	249	fishcutter	27	"
	n	Studley Evelyn—†	249	factoryhand	46	1 Morton pl
	p	Gurevich Gertrude—†	251	housewife	47	here
	r	Gurevich Harry	251	merchant	57	"
	s	Gurevich Ralph	251	salesman	22	"
	t	Shatz Charles	251	meatcutter	23	"
	u	Shatz Ida A—†	251	housewife	24	"
	v*	Valletta Louis	251	laborer	20	126 Havre
	x	Mariani Filomena—†	257	housewife	37	here
	y	Mariani Peter	257	boilermaker	48	"
	z	Ferraro Angelo	257	stonecutter	21	7 Lexington pl
520						
	a	Ferraro Antonette—†	257	candyworker	24	7 "
	b	Ferraro Nunzio	257	painter	23	7 '
	c*	Ferraro Virginia—†	257	housewife	60	7 "
	f	Keating Anna—†	259	at home	69	here
	g	McCluskey Harry	259	clerk	25	"
	d	Pinhkam Edward	259	painter	50	"
	e	Pinkham Hilda—†	259	housewife	45	"
	h	Cantare Lucy—†	259	operator	23	96 Homer
	k	Cantare Phoebe—†	259	"	48	96 "
	l	Clark Annie—†	259	at home	62	here

Meridian Street—Continued

Page.	Letter.	Full Name.	Residence, Jan. 1, 1938.	Occupation.	Supposed Age.	Reported Residence, Jan. 1, 1937. Street and Number.
	M	Clark Stella—†	259	at home	60	here
	N	Connelly Joseph	259	shipper	38	"
	O	Coyle Frances—†	259	housewife	29	"
	P	Coyle Hugh J, jr	259	shipper	29	
	R	Mahoney Daniel	259	clerk	58	
	S	Rumney Gideon	259	retired	86	"
	W	Shaw Daniel F	265	steelworker	42	24 Princeton
	X	*Shaw Mary—†	265	housewife	33	24 "
521						
	B	Donovan Helen L—†	269	"	33	59 W Eagle
	C	Stewart Frances—†	269	"	21	here
	D	Stewart Millet	269	clerk	24	"
	H	Greenwood Edna—†	274	housewife	65	"
	K	Greenwood Lester	274	seaman	30	
	L	Greenwood Reginald	274	engineer	36	
	M	Greenwood Valetta—†	274	at home	34	
	N	Swimm Margaret—†	274	decorator	34	"
	O	*Nickerson Alberta W—†	274	packer	26	
	P	*Nickerson Benjamin L	274	fisherman	57	"
	R	*Nickerson Elsie M—†	274	decorator	28	"
	S	Nickerson Rose A—†	274	housewfe	59	"
	T	Payne Frederick W	274	chauffeur	23	"
	U	Payne Rita M—†	274	housewife	22	"
	W	*Olsen Ella—†	277	"	50	
	X	*Olsen Olaf	277	seaman	50	
522						
	C	Brown Albert M	284	chauffeur	32	144 Maverick
	D	Murphy Florence—†	284	housewife	31	Indiana
	E	Murphy James A	284	electrician	34	"
	F	Nolan Louis A	285	salesman	42	715 Benningt'n
	G	Nolan Thomas H	285	clerk	37	715 "
	H	Synnott William H	285	mason	43	715 "
	K	Gallo Bernard C	285	engineer	41	here
	L	Dunn Charles P	285	laborer	24	68 Centre
	M	Dunn Margaret M—†	285	housewife	20	68 "
	P	Byer Frank	287A	tailor	67	here
	R	Dean Annie—†	288	housekeeper	72	"
	S	Dean Emily—†	288	housewife	43	"
	T	Dean Norman	288	painter	49	
	U	Young Benjamin A	288	"	45	

Page.	Letter.	Full Name.	Residence, Jan. 1, 1938.	Occupation.	Supposed Age.	Reported Residence, Jan. 1, 1937. Street and Number.

Meridian Street—Continued

	V	Young Mary E—†	288	housewife	49	here
	W	Batson Elizabeth J—†	288	"	75	"
	X	Dean Edith M—†	288	"	42	"
	Y	Dean George R	288	laborer	23	"
	Z	Dean Joseph R	288	inspector	45	"
523						
	A	Gibbs Edward L	289	retired	86	
	B	Gibbs Nellie A—†	289	housewife	74	"
	D	Marshall Ellen—†	290	at home	80	
	F	*Burke Lydia—†	291A	housewife	75	"
	G	Burke William H	291A	bookkeeper	45	71 Walnut av
	K	Green Arthur J	293	electrician	45	Winthrop
	L	Jansen Lena—†	293	at home	75	here
	M	Jansen Lillian M—†	293	hairdresser	37	"
	N	Stillings Pearl—†	293	laundryworker	38	"
	O	Stillings Ray	293	salesman	45	"
	R	Barnes Blanche V—†	294	housewife	66	284 Meridian
	P	Barnes George H	294	retired	67	284 "
	S	*Guiditta Angeline—†	294	shoeworker	22	here
	T	*Guiditta Frank	294	shoemaker	46	"
	U	Guiditta Jennie—†	294	student	20	"
	V	Guiditta Mary—†	294	housewife	44	"
	X	Gannon Catherine—†	296	operator	31	
	Y	Gannon Cecilia T—†	296	florist	28	
	Z	Gannon Mary M—†	296	housewife	62	"
524						
	A	Gannon Timothy H	296	florist	62	
	B	Quinn Isabella F—†	296	at home	74	
	D	King Charles	297	plumber	77	
	E	King Florence M—†	297	housewife	65	"
	G	Cohen Beatrice—†	298	baker	45	
	H	Cohen Julius	298	"	44	
	K	Parker Lincoln E	298	undertaker	33	"
	L	Parker Rose M—†	298	housewife	29	"
	M	MacNamara George	299	dentist	45	"
	N	Brown Elizabeth—†	299	housewife	40	286 Meridian
	O	Brown Frank E	299	undertaker	60	286 "
	R	Rollins Emma C—†	300	"	70	here
	S	Grant Alphonso C	300	cook	42	456 Meridian
	T	Grant Stella M—†	300	housewife	40	456 "

Page.	Letter.	Full Name.	Residence, Jan. 1, 1938.	Occupation.	Supposed Age.	Reported Residence, Jan. 1, 1937. Street and Number.

Morton Place

Page.	Letter.	Full Name.	Residence, Jan. 1, 1938.	Occupation.	Supposed Age.	Reported Residence, Jan. 1, 1937. Street and Number.
	U	Sinkeldan Mary—†	1	stitcher	43	104 Eutaw
	V	Davis Catherine—†	1	housekeeper	71	here
	W	Coyle Margaret—†	2	stitcher	44	"
	X	Carey Ellen—†	2	housekeeper	52	"
	Y	Carey Peter	2	machinist	48	"
	Z	*McGuinness Elizabeth—†	3	housekeeper	69	"
525						
	A	Francis Mary E—†	3		69	

Princeton Street

Page.	Letter.	Full Name.	Residence, Jan. 1, 1938.	Occupation.	Supposed Age.	Reported Residence, Jan. 1, 1937. Street and Number.
	B	Hardy James	4	cook	52	here
	C	Hardy Virginia—†	4	housewife	45	"
	D	Harloff Nellie—†	4	"	31	"
	E	Harloff William	4	fisherman	27	"
	G	Bonney Robert	7	physician	78	"
	H	Hayden Frederick	7	retired	78	
	K	Robichaud Marie C—†	7	housekeeper	29	"
	N	Doyle Robert	9	laborer	60	"
	L	Driscoll Frances C—†	9	housewife	30	"
	M	Driscoll John M	9	longshoreman	35	"
	O	Zuccola Eva—†	9	factoryhand	36	"
	P	Zuccola William	9	laborer	30	
	R	Boudreau Eleanor—†	10	at home	21	
	S	*Boudreau Elias	10	fisherman	63	"
	T	Boudreau John	10	packer	22	
	U	*Boudreau Virginia—†	10	housewife	63	"
	V	Courie Edward F	10	chauffeur	32	"
	W	Courie Elizabeth—†	10	at home	28	
	Y	O'Brien Albert	10	porter	26	
	X	O'Brien Ethel V—†	10	housewife	26	"
	Z	Tait William	11	machinist	75	"
526						
	A	Tait Winifred—†	11	housewife	63	"
	B	Gowdy Alonzo	11	retired	67	
	C	Gowdy George	11	manager	34	"
	D	Gowdy Sarah—†	11	housewife	60	"
	E	Gurney Alton L	12	clerk	29	
	F	Gurney Olive M—†	12	housewife	21	"
	G	Layhe Francis	12	metalworker	21	"
	H	Layhe Sarah—†	12	housewife	25	"

Page.	Letter.	Full Name.	Residence, Jan. 1, 1938.	Occupation.	Supposed Age.	Reported Residence, Jan. 1, 1937. Street and Number.

Princeton Street—Continued

Page.	Letter.	Full Name.	Residence, Jan. 1, 1938.	Occupation.	Supposed Age.	Reported Residence, Jan. 1, 1937. Street and Number.
	K	Clancy Edward A	12	longshoreman	30	here
	L	Clancy Helen R—†	12	housewife	25	"
	M	Barker Emily—†	13	housekeeper	65	"
	N	Rollins Annie—†	13	housewife	68	"
	O	Rollins Lendall	13	gateman	61	"
	P	Jones Frederick	14	laborer	31	
	R	Jones Ruth—†	14	housewife	25	"
	S	Hines Ernest	14	clerk	35	"
	T	*Hines Margaret—†	14	housewife	24	"
	U	Maguire Francis N	14	clerk	25	
	V	Maguire Jennie A—†	14	housewife	24	"
	W	Gambacorta Adalgisa—†	15	"	50	
	X	Gambacorta Leopold	15	physician	57	"
	Y	Gambacorta Otto	15	student	23	
	Z	Harper Catherine C—†	16	housewife	36	"
527						
	A	*Parsons William I	16	retired	69	
	B	Parsons Williams S	16	proprietor	44	"
	C	Goggin Adele M—†	16	housewife	29	"
	D	Goggin John J	16	cutter	38	
	E	Stone Mary E—†	17	housekeeper	76	"
	F	McLellan Bessie M—†	17	housewife	58	"
	G	McLellan William A	17	engineer	54	
	H	Waters Jennie R—†	17	housekeeper	59	"
	K	Schwartz Annie—†	19	"	69	"
	L	Schwartz George H	19	physician	45	"
	M	DeLeskey Ernest	19	watchman	45	"
	N	Donahue Thomas	19	machinist	35	"
	O	Fothergill John W	19	gateman	56	166 Marion
	P	Gurney Alice—†	19	housewife	53	here
	R	Gurney Harry	19	retired	63	"
	S	Marshall Albert	19	teamster	21	"
	T	Marshall Willard	19	laborer	28	
	U	*Fitzpatrick Peter	19	fisherman	45	"
	V	*Garron Austin	19	"	50	
	W	Hines Ashton	19	"	47	
	X	*Hines Evangeline—†	19	housewife	34	"
	Y	*Nickerson Florence—†	19	housekeeper	54	"
	Z	Fagan Bernard	19A	fisherman	55	"
528						
	A	*St Croix Andrew F	19A	"	51	

Page.	Letter.	Full Name.	Residence, Jan. 1, 1938.	Occupation.	Supposed Age.	Reported Residence, Jan. 1, 1937. Street and Number.

Princeton Street—Continued

Page.	Letter.	Full Name.	Residence, Jan. 1, 1938.	Occupation.	Supposed Age.	Reported Residence, Jan. 1, 1937. Street and Number.
	B	*St Croix Elizabeth A—†	19A	housewife	45	here
	C	Campbell Evelyn M—†	19A	"	41	"
	D	Campbell John W	19A	policeman	46	"
	E	Campbell John W, jr	19A	machinist	22	"
	F	Dodge Emma—†	19A	housewife	31	"
	G	Dodge Howard	19A	engineer	35	
	H	Tully Catherine—†	20	housekeeper	50	"
	K	Walker Arthur J	20	laborer	57	Somerville
	L	Walker Charles F	20	"	29	"
	M	Walker Eliwait A—†	20	housewife	59	"
	N	Olafson Gertrude—†	20	operator	26	here
	P	Bowden Charles	22	printer	46	61 W Eagle
	R	Bowden Mary E—†	22	housewife	38	61 "
	S	*Cleary Jeremiah	22	fisherman	33	here
	T	Doherty Joseph	22	retired	67	"
	U	Drake Albert J	22	mechanic	54	"
	V	Drake Anna M—†	22	housewife	46	"
	W	*Enos Joseph	22	laborer	45	38 Princeton
	X	*Enos Mary—†	22	housewife	43	38 "
	Y	Murphy William	22	entertainer	43	here
	Z	Gambino Joseph	23	shoeworker	39	"
529						
	A	Gambino Pauline—†	23	housewife	30	"
	B	Norbiet Adam	24	machinist	45	"
	C	Orlando Dominic	24	retired	46	Winthrop
	D	*Rowe Betty—†	24	at home	45	Canada
	E	*Rowe Jackson	24	fisherman	40	"
	F	Smart Thomas	24	engineer	50	here
	G	Unsworth Ethel E—†	24	housekeeper	55	"
	H	Unsworth William J	24	accountant	24	"
	K	*Cotreau Gilbert	25	retired	70	
	L	Taylor Ashford	25	engineer	38	
	M	*Taylor Rose—†	25	housewife	40	"
	N	Cann Jesse C	25	engineer	24	
	O	Cann Joseph S	25	retired	54	
	P	Cann Sarepta—†	25	housewife	57	"
	R	DellaGrotte Albert	26	laborer	20	
	S	DellaGrotte Anthony	26	druggist	27	
	T	*DellaGrotte Josephine—†	26	housewife	65	"
	U	Marganelli Marie—†	26	at home	32	
	V	Condakes Peter	26	proprietor	56	"

Page.	Letter.	Full Name.	Residence, Jan. 1, 1938.	Occupation.	Supposed Age.	Reported Residence, Jan. 1, 1937. Street and Number.

Princeton Street—Continued

	W	Condakes Stella—†	26	housewife	43	here
	X	Mazzarino Frances—†	26	"	48	"
	Y	Mazzarino Joseph J	26	teacher	24	"
	Z	Mazzarino Pasquale B	26	presser	51	
530						
	A	Manfra Joseph	27	laborer	22	93 Princeton
	B	Manfra Lucy—†	27	housewife	22	93 "
	C	*Visconte Mary—†	27	"	67	here
	D	Visconte Vincenzo	27	retired	76	"
	E	Cleary James	27	custodian	52	"
	F	Cleary Sadie—†	27	housewife	58	"
	G	Murray Homer	28	engineer	34	Wareham
	H	Murray Margaret M—†	28	housewife	26	"
	K	Finizio Blanche—†	28	operator	33	here
	L	*Finizio Frances—†	28	at home	75	"
	M	Finizio Mary—†	28	operator	39	"
	N	Hallrean Ambrose J	28	longshoreman	54	265 Meridian
	O	Hallrean Mary H—†	28	housewife	54	265 "
	P	Lavalle Anna J—†	28	at home	27	265 "
	R	*O'Boyle Michael	28	retired	61	265 "
	S	Williams Joseph	28	laborer	62	265 "
	T	Lawler George C	29	accountant	31	285 "
	U	Lawler Pearl M —†	29	housewife	25	285 "
	V	*Armstrong Ellen—†	29	"	32	here
	W	*Armstrong William P	29	fisherman	35	"
	X	*Ruo Carmello—†	29	housewife	62	"
	Y	*Ruo Michael	29	retired	62	"
531						
	A	Whitton Alfred J	31	watchman	43	92 Byron
	B	Whitton Minnie L—†	31	housewife	67	92 "
	C	Whitton William I	31	watchman	65	92 "
	D	Johnson Bernard F	31	investigator	41	here
	E	Ohlson James H	31	laundryworker	36	"
	F	Ohlson Margaret—†	31	housewife	30	"
	G	*Benenati Mary—†	32	"	29	
	H	Benenati Rocco	32	tailor	41	
	K	Vertullo Mary—†	32	housewife	32	"
	L	Vertullo Pasquale	32	laborer	42	"
	M	Cardone Phillip	33	chauffeur	33	153 Saratoga
	N	Caruso Adam E	33	steamfitter	45	here
	O	Caruso Margaret—†	33	housewife	39	"

Page.	Letter.	Full Name.	Residence, Jan. 1, 1938.	Occupation.	Supposed Age.	Reported Residence, Jan. 1, 1937. Street and Number.

Princeton Street—Continued

	P	Caruso Vincent	33	student	22	here
	R	Viola Albert	33	salesman	33	24 Princeton
	S	Donovan Frank	33	auditor	32	here
	T	Donovan Gretta—†	33	housewife	32	"
	U	Coy Edward L	34	retired	43	"
	V	Coy Grace M—†	34	housekeeper	70	"
	W	Murphy Christine—†	34	housewife	32	96 Trenton
	X	Murphy Thomas	34	fisherman	40	96 "
	Z	Jeddery Edward	35	carpenter	59	24 Princeton
532						
	A	Jeddery Laura—†	35	housekeeper	25	110 Minden
	B	Nesky Aleck	35	policeman	45	110 "
	C	Giovino Patrick	36	storekeeper	33	here
	D	Giovino Rose—†	36	housewife	29	"
	E	*Adinolfi Joseph A	36	milkman	31	"
	F	Adinolfi Lydia—†	36	housewife	30	"
	G	Adinolfi Prisco	36	retired	66	
	H	*Adinolfi Tomasina—†	36	housewife	73	"
	K	*Cardinal Anthony	36	factoryhand	30	"
	L	Cardinal Mary—†	36	housewife	26	"
	M	Braff Jacob	37	salesman	51	"
	N	Hewey Leon N	37	janitor	53	
	O	Hewey Mildred H—†	37	housewife	47	"
	P	Swimm Emma E—†	37	supervisor	34	"
	R	Swimm Herbert J	37	shipper	46	
	S	*Seward Bridget—†	38	housewife	34	"
	T	Seward Walter E	38	ironworker	35	"
	U	Bennett James	38	painter	35	
	V	Butts Mary J—†	38	housekeeper	60	"
	W	*Cardiner John	38	fisherman	30	Canada
	X	*Cardiner Richard	38	"	28	here
	Y	McNabb Mary—†	38	dressmaker	39	"
	Z	McPhee John	38	meatcutter	40	"
533						
	A	Goodwin Maud L—†	39	housewife	71	"
	B	Goodwin Wilfred W	39	physician	77	"
	C	McLenna Mildred—†	40	at home	31	
	D	McCarthy Florence A—†	40	housewife	34	"
	E	McCarthy John L	40	undertaker	46	"
	F	Spagnoulo Carmen	40	carpenter	24	"
	G	Spagnoulo Constantine	40	laborer	43	

Page.	Letter.	Full Name.	Residence, Jan. 1, 1938.	Occupation.	Supposed Age.	Reported Residence, Jan. 1, 1937. Street and Number.

Princeton Street—Continued

Page.	Letter.	Full Name.	Residence, Jan. 1, 1938.	Occupation.	Supposed Age.	Reported Residence, Jan. 1, 1937. Street and Number.
	H	*Spagnoulo Olympia—†	40	housewife	46	here
	K	Stevenson Helen B—†	41	at home	67	"
	L	Stevenson J Estelle—†	41	"	66	"
	M	Donaldson Albert L	44	clerk	31	
	N	Donaldson Ernest D	44	salesman	33	"
	O	Donaldson Ernest M	44	cook	60	"
	P	Donaldson Mary A—†	44	housewife	29	"
	R	Haskell Judson T	44	pilot	68	
	S	Allen Edward	46	fishcutter	56	"
	T	Karatlanes Nicholas	46	laborer	50	
	U	Whelan Alexander	46	ironworker	65	"
	V	Whelan Annie—†	46	housewife	57	"
	W	Whelan Elmer F	46	clerk	26	"
	X	Cariedo Genevieve—†	48	housewife	21	99 Trenton
	Y	Gallagher Emma—†	48	housekeeper	42	32 Princeton
	Z	Sanford Ruth—†	48	waitress	35	32 "
534						
	A	Montague Cecil	48	foreman	30	86 Lexington
	B	*Montague Laura—†	48	housewife	58	86 "
	C	*Montague Vera—†	48	at home	21	86 "
	D	*Albert Stanley	50	porter	21	Maine
	E	Bradley Emily M—†	50	housewife	38	here
	F	Bradley Frederick V	50	laborer	38	"
	G	Bradley James	50	"	48	"
	H	Elder Gladys—†	50	factoryhand	31	Everett
	K	*Geer Catherine—†	50	at home	64	"
	L	Strickland Dorothy A—†	50	housewife	21	52 Rockland
	M	*Strickland George W	50	laborer	23	52 "
	N	*Barrett Morris	54	retired	72	35 Princeton
	O	Crowell Arnold	54	fisherman	37	35 "
	P	Crowell Mary—†	54	housewife	44	35 "
	R	Gallagher Joseph	54	seaman	28	186 Lexington
	S	*Healey Thomas	54	fisherman	34	35 Princeton
	T	McQue Agnes—†	54	factoryhand	24	35 "
	U	Mistred William	54	rigger	35	35 "
	V	Sullivan Helen—†	54	waitress	45	Reading
	W	Bergstrom Annie—†	56	housewife	55	here
	X	Bergstrom Harold N	56	electrician	41	"
	Y	Bergstrom Regina V—†	56	clerk	35	"
	Z	Currier Edward	56	machinist	38	"

Page.	Letter.	Full Name.	Residence, Jan. 1, 1938.	Occupation.	Supposed Age.	Reported Residence, Jan. 1, 1937. Street and Number.

535
Princeton Street—Continued

	A	McLaughlin Alton W	56	electrician	42	here
	B	McLaughlin George	56	printer	35	"
	C	Nichols Earl	56	laborer	45	"
	D	Solstrand Nicholas	56	fisherman	40	"
	E	Ruddock Clarence P	58	foreman	34	220 Lexington
	F	Ruddock Ethel M—†	58	housewife	29	220 "
	G	*Marino Amato	58	laborer	62	here
	H	Marino Anthony	58	"	24	"
	K	*Marino Marie—†	58	housewife	62	"
	L	Marino Salvatore	58	laborer	21	
	M	*Cavanaugh Elizabeth—†	60	housewife	49	"
	N	*Cavanaugh Patrick	60	longshoreman	51	"
	O	*Connors Anna—†	60	factoryhand	36	"
	P	Pulao Robert	60	laborer	29	146 Paris
	S	*Faraci Angelina—†	62	housewife	49	here
	T	Faraci Charles	62	reporter	22	"
	U	Faraci Joseph	62	barber	50	"
	V	Chiaramont Carmel	62	laborer	25	160 Putnam
	W	*Chiaramont Mary—†	62	housewife	25	160 "
	X	*Caristo Asunta—†	77	"	62	here
	Y	*Caristo Vincent	77	printer	25	"
	Z	Schraffa Joseph H	77	shoefitter	30	"
536						
	A	Schraffa Rose M—†	77	housewife	30	"
	B	*Alvaris Antonio	79	mason	65	
	C	*Alvaris Rose—†	79	housewife	45	"
	D	DeMatteo Anthony	81	chauffeur	23	Medford
	E	DeMatteo Margaret E—†	81	housewife	23	"
	F	*Ferrera Josephine—†	81	"	34	here
	G	Ferrera Pasquale	81	bricklayer	42	"
	H	*Agostino Margaret C—†	81	housewife	34	"
	K	*Agostino Nicholas	81	tailor	42	"
	L	*Boudreau Evangeline—†	83	housewife	29	Canada
	M	Boudreau George	83	fisherman	35	146 Princeton
	N	Landry Arthur	83	rigger	37	Everett
	O	*Landry Freda—†	83	housewife	33	"
	P	Impemba John	83	shoemaker	41	222 Paris
	R	Impemba Mary—†	83	housewife	38	222 "
	S	Bernard Ralph	87	seaman	46	here

Page.	Letter.	Full Name.	Residence, Jan. 1, 1938.	Occupation.	Supposed Age.	Reported Residence, Jan. 1, 1937. Street and Number.

Princeton Street—Continued

Page.	Letter.	Full Name.	Residence, Jan. 1, 1938.	Occupation.	Supposed Age.	Reported Residence, Jan. 1, 1937. Street and Number.
	T	Hanagan Dennis	87	retired	71	92 Meridian
	U	Hosea Mary—†	87	housekeeper	62	here
	V	Lund James G	87	painter	31	544 Saratoga
	W	McInnis Daniel	87	manager	59	New York
	X	McInnis Ronald	87	operator	57	here
	Y	Sousa Manuel	87	factoryhand	28	"
	Z	Gravallese Charles M	89	plumber	29	"
537						
	A	Gravallese Rose—†	89	housewife	27	"
	B	Palmierr Lena—†	89	"	27	102 Marion
	C	*Palmierr Rico	89	shoemaker	28	102 "
	D	Scarfo Geraldine—†	89	housewife	39	here
	E	Scarfo Nicholas	89	tailor	49	"
	F	Scarfo Philip	89	painter	21	"
	G	Giansiracusa Joseph	91	shoemaker	42	"
	H	Giansiracusa Nicholas	91	ironworker	39	"
	K	*Giansiracusa Nicola—†	91	housekeeper	80	"
	L	Britten Henry M	93	engineer	49	"
	M	Poirier Edith—†	93	factoryhand	23	159 Princeton
	N	Poirier Mary—†	93	housewife	56	159 "
	O	Poirier Wallace	93	painter	57	159 "
	P	Pignato Dominic	93	laborer	56	here
	R	*Pignato Josephine—†	93	housewife	48	"
	S	*Granese Mary—†	93	housekeeper	48	"
	T	Cassidy Robert J	rear 93	retired	85	"
	U	Teed Frederick B	" 93	clerk	50	
	V	Teed Mabel E—†	" 93	housewife	49	"
	X	Tasha Anthony	95	laborer	46	149 Princeton
	Y	Tasha Grace—†	95	housewife	39	149 "
	Z	French Catherine—†	95	inspector	28	here
538						
	A	French Celia—†	95	operator	21	"
	B	*Fringuella Nicola	97	retired	53	
	C	Brazil Gertrude—†	97	housewife	34	"
	D	Brazil Thomas E	97	longshoreman	36	"
	E	*Bennissuto Theresa—†	101	housekeeper	67	"
	F	Pasquale John	101	fishcutter	28	"
	G	Pasquale Josephine—†	101	housewife	24	"
	H	*Pesaturo Angelina—†	103	"	43	
	K	Pesaturo Emma—†	103	factoryhand	23	"
	L	Pesaturo Giovanni	103	shoemaker	45	"

Page.	Letter.	Full Name.	Residence, Jan. 1, 1938.	Occupation.	Supposed Age.	Reported Residence, Jan. 1, 1937. Street and Number.

Princeton Street—Continued

Page.	Letter.	Full Name.	Residence, Jan. 1, 1938.	Occupation.	Supposed Age.	Reported Residence, Jan. 1, 1937. Street and Number.
	M	Pesaturo Salvatore	103	printer	21	here
	N	*Giusto Filippa—†	103	housewife	48	"
	O	Giusto Rose—†	103	stitcher	23	"
	P	Beath James	105	machinist	53	107 Princeton
	R	Fisher Daniel F	105	laborer	34	107 "
	S	Willis Andrew	105	clerk	31	107 "
	T	Willis Christine R—†	105	housewife	29	107 "
	U	Brown Ethel M—†	105	"	45	here
	V	Brown Harold R	105	seaman	50	"
	W	Brown Harold R, jr	105	shipper	21	"
	X	Tacelli Anastasia—†	107	supervisor	34	Cambridge
	Y	Tacelli Arthur	107	clerk	33	here
	Z	Tacelli Albert	107	agent	30	"
539						
	A	Tacelli Benjamin	107	barber	63	
	B	*Tacelli Carmella—†	107	housewife	70	"
	C	Tacelli Edith—†	107	at home	27	
	D	Tacelli Joseph	107	machinist	67	"
	E	Tacelli William	107	clerk	32	
	F	Butler Margaret—†	109	housewife	54	"
	G	Butler Thomas	109	laundryman	20	"
	H	*Jackman Gerald	109	fisherman	38	"
	K	*Larsen Axel	109	seaman	60	Sweden
	L	*Melanson John R	109	fisherman	46	4 Lexington pl
	M	Melanson Raymond	109	fishcutter	23	4 "
	N	Sweeney Arlene M—†	109	housewife	22	43 Monum'nt
	O	Serra Joseph P	111	carpenter	24	113 Brooks
	P	Serra Mary O—†	111	housewife	26	113 "
	R	Preziosi Alphonzo	111	butcher	22	here
	S	Preziosi Andrew	111	"	24	"
	T	Preziosi Angelo	111	"	51	"
	U	*Preziosi Columbia—†	111	housewife	45	"
	V	Preziosi John	111	butcher	20	
	W	Barranco Amando	113	factoryhand	23	"
	X	*Barranco Augustino	113	laborer	58	
	Y	Barranco Charles	113	boilermaker	21	"
	Z	Barranco John	113	carpenter	27	"
540						
	A	*Barranco Sadie—†	113	housewife	52	"
	B	Nason Elizabeth M—†	113	waitress	21	
	C	Nason Francis J	113	longshoreman	54	"

Page.	Letter.	FULL NAME.	Residence, Jan. 1, 1938.	Occupation.	Supposed Age.	Reported Residence, Jan. 1, 1937. Street and Number.

Princeton Street—Continued

	D	Nason Margaret M—†	113	housewife	53	here
	E	DeSantis Ida A—†	113	teacher	31	"
	F	DeSantis Vito	113	barber	61	"
	G	Carrozza Josephine—†	115	factoryhand	22	"
	H	*Carrozza Philimena—†	115	housewife	47	"
	K	Carrozza Philip	115	bricklayer	48	"
	L	Bongiovanni Amelia—†	115	housewife	39	"
	M	Bongiovanni Anthony	115	shoemaker	47	"
	N	O'Hanley Cyril J	117	laborer	25	11 Gove
	O	O'Hanley Margaret F—†	117	housewife	25	11 "
	P	Hunter James A	117	machinist	21	here
	R	Hunter Jean—†	117	stenographer	23	"
	S	Hunter Lettie M—†	117	housewife	51	"
	T	Bickley Alma M—†	117	"	42	
	U	Bickley Joseph W	117	engineer	38	
	V	Capasso Luigina—†	119	housewife	34	"
	W	Capasso Vincent	119	laborer	44	
	X	Foster Adeline—†	119	housewife	38	"
	Y	Foster Arthur J	119	laborer	36	
	Z	Chaffee Della—†	121	housewife	63	"
541						
	A	Chaffee Dora L—†	121	at home	35	
	B	Chaffee Frederick W	121	retired	64	
	C	Delehanty Annie G—†	121	housewife	70	"
	D	Delehanty Catherine A-†	121	at home	49	
	E	Delehanty John J	121	electrician	44	"
	F	Delehanty Joseph J	121	laborer	37	
	G	Delehanty Pierce B	121	checker	41	"
	H	Schwarz Clara—†	123	housewife	25	Cambridge
	K	Schwarz William	123	clerk	30	"
	L	Paglialonga Dominic	123	laborer	41	here
	M	*Maglio Emily—†	123	housewife	43	"
	N	Maglio Frank	123	shoemaker	41	"
	O	*Rotondo Anna C—†	125	shoeworker	36	"
	P	*Rotondo Anna G—†	125	housewife	63	"
	R	*Rotondo Nellie G—†	125	at home	32	
	S	Rotondo Rosario	125	laborer	68	
	T	Nastri Carlo A	125	foreman	34	
	U	Nastri Ralph P	125	clerk	27	
	V	Nastri Stella—†	125	at home	33	
	W	Lazzaro Frances—†	125	"	23	

Page.	Letter.	Full Name.	Residence, Jan. 1, 1938.	Occupation.	Supposed Age.	Reported Residence, Jan. 1, 1937. Street and Number.

Princeton Street—Continued

Page.	Letter.	Full Name.	Residence, Jan. 1, 1938.	Occupation.	Supposed Age.	Reported Residence, Jan. 1, 1937. Street and Number.
	X	Lazzaro Rose—†	125	housewife	46	here
	Y	Lazzaro Thomas	125	butcher	55	"
	Z	Driscoll Patrick J	127	laborer	72	"
542						
	A	McGrath Mary F—†	127	housekeeper	74	"
	B	*Pelligrini Leona—†	127	housewife	40	"
	C	*Pelligrini Ralph	127	tailor	50	
	D	Gunning Margaret R—†	127	housewife	37	"
	E	Gunning Robert J	127	deckhand	38	"
	F	Hillegass John J	131	retired	58	
	G	Moore Jennie E	131	housekeeper	61	"
	H	Delcore Alice—†	131	nurse	22	"
	K	Delcore Bettina—†	131	housewife	47	"
	L	Delcore Guido	131	machinist	21	"
	M	Delcore Louis	131	laborer	49	
	N	Delcore Paredo	131	"	24	
	O	Murray James F	133	engineer	74	
	P	Murray Mary A—†	133	housewife	71	"
	R	DeDeo Denis D	133	carpenter	27	"
	S	DeDeo Gemma—†	133	at home	30	
	T	DeDeo Leonardo	133	printer	63	
	U	DeDeo Visletta—†	133	secretary	35	"
	V	Giuseppe Rudolph C	133	chauffeur	32	"

Saratoga Place

Page.	Letter.	Full Name.	Residence, Jan. 1, 1938.	Occupation.	Supposed Age.	Reported Residence, Jan. 1, 1937. Street and Number.
	W	Indigaro Edward	1	seaman	35	here
	X	Indigaro Hazel—†	1	housewife	37	"
	Y	Montero Antonio	1	fisherman	27	"
	Z	Montero Eleanor—†	1	waitress	20	
543						
	A	Lattore Liberio	1	laborer	56	
	B	Lattore Marie—†	1	housewife	46	"
	C	Young Sarah L—†	2	housekeeper	66	11 Trenton
	D	Keith Lulu—†	2	housewife	32	here
	E	Keith Ralph	2	laborer	32	"
	F	Peterson George	2	steamfitter	39	"
	G	Peterson Mary—†	2	housekeeper	69	"
	H	Foley Catherine M—†	3	houseworker	57	"
	K	McDonald Harry L	3	dyemaker	33	"
	L	McDonald Simon J	3	carpenter	61	"

Page.	Letter.	FULL NAME.	Residence, Jan. 1, 1938.	Occupation.	Supposed Age.	Reported Residence, Jan. 1, 1937. Street and Number.
		Saratoga Place—Continued				
	M	Keith Donald	3	laborer	27	here
	N	Keith Kathleen—†	3	housewife	23	"
	P	Hamilton Christina—†	4	"	70	"
	R	Hamilton James	4	laborer	34	
	U	LaRosa Alphonso	5	mechanic	25	"
	V	LaRosa Lillian—†	5	housewife	24	"
	W	Berry George E	5	fisherman	21	"
	X	Berry Ida—†	5	housekeeper	45	102 Saratoga
		Saratoga Street				
	Y	Costello Thomas	9	carpenter	55	here
	Z	Malone Helen J—†	9	housewife	30	"
544						
	A	Malone Thomas J	9	contractor	39	"
	B	Ryan James	9	clerk	49	
	C	Carter Edith M—†	9	housewife	67	"
	D	Carter Samuel	9	janitor	56	
	E	Day Charles F	9	mason	60	
	F	Day Jennie—†	9	housewife	51	"
	G	Parks David F	9	painter	56	
	H	Lawler Harold	9	clerk	23	"
	K	Lawler Mary E—†	9	housewife	49	"
	L	Lawler Patrick G	9	fireman	51	
	P	Trainor Lawrence A	15	shipper	21	
	R	Trainor Mary O—†	15	matron	49	
	S	Goff Edward J	15	orderly	24	
	T	Goff Jane E—†	15	housewife	40	"
	U	Goff Leo F	15	operator	45	
	V	Goff Leo F, jr	15	clerk	21	
	W	Goff Marie C—†	15	factoryhand	20	"
	X	Moore Harold R	17	laborer	35	
	Y	Moore Madeline F—†	17	housekeeper	31	"
	Z	Ricci Anthony	17	laborer	50	"
545						
	A	*Ricci Josephine—†	17	housewife	44	"
	B	Ricci Leo	17	clerk	24	
	C	Ricci Michael	17	laborer	20	
	D	Ricci Phyllis—†	17	clerk	22	
	E	King Frank R	19	shipper	49	
	F	King Mildred A—†	19	housewife	42	"

Page.	Letter.	Full Name.	Residence, Jan. 1, 1938.	Occupation.	Supposed Age.	Reported Residence, Jan. 1, 1937. Street and Number.

Saratoga Street—Continued

	G	O'Neill John F	19	foreman	59	here
	H	O'Neill Mary E—†	19	housewife	57	"
	K	Siertson Ole A	19	fireman	64	France
	L	White Helen—†	20	saleswoman	40	here
	M	Burke Elizabeth I—†	20	housewife	32	"
	N	Burke George R	20	chauffeur	25	"
	O	Deering Emily—†	20	housewife	42	"
	P	Deering Richard	20	fisherman	43	"
	R*	Barrett Dennis	21	painter	50	
	S*	Barrett Mary—†	21	housewife	67	"
	T	Crowell James	21	seaman	55	
	U	Stevenson Charles	21	fisherman	43	"
	V	Malloy Harry	22	shoeworker	52	"
	W	Malloy Mary C—†	22	housewife	36	"
	X	Alexander Maud—†	22	housekeeper	64	"
	Y	MacDonald Bertha—†	22	"	40	54 Brooks
	Z	Boland Evelyn—†	25	housewife	30	here
546						
	A	Boland Thomas	25	laborer	32	
	B	Lowell Alice M—†	25	operator	31	
	C	Lowell Bridget A—†	25	housewife	57	"
	D	Lowell Henry L	25	technician	29	"
	E	Lowell James R	25	clerk	33	"
	F*	Douglas Harold E	26	counterman	23	101 Saratoga
	G*	Douglas Mary—†	26	housewife	50	101 "
	H	Doyle Arthur H	26	laborer	51	here
	K	Inman Caroline—†	26	at home	73	11 Tolman pl
	L	Webber Aaron	26	teacher	56	Indiana
	M	Corrado Carlo	27	manager	24	68 White
	N	Corrado Helen—†	27	housewife	24	68 "
	O	Fronduto Antonio	27	chauffeur	23	here
	P	Fronduto John	27	laborer	54	"
	R*	Fronduto Rose—†	27	housewife	54	"
	S*	Senior Charles	28	fisherman	30	"
	T*	Senior Loretta—†	28	housewife	29	"
	U	Kartenberg George	28	janitor	38	
	V	Keough Edward W	28	clerk	26	
	W	Keough Helen G—†	28	housewife	50	"
	X	Winston James F	28	inspector	45	"
	Y	Cardullo Dominic	30	factoryhand	32	"
	Z*	Cardullo Margaret—†	30	housewife	30	"

Page.	Letter.	FULL NAME.	Residence, Jan. 1, 1938.	Occupation.	Supposed Age.	Reported Residence, Jan. 1, 1937. Street and Number.
547		**Saratoga Street**—Continued				
	A	Marino Adagisa—†	30	secretary	21	here
	B	*Marino Amedo	30	painter	57	"
	C	Marino Americo	30	factoryhand	20	"
	D	*Marino Antonio	30	painter	25	
	E	*Marino Jennie—†	30	housewife	58	"
	F	*Marino Rose M—†	30	dressmaker	23	"
	G	Lasco Anna—†	31	housewife	28	"
	H	Lasco Joseph	31	barber	30	"
	K	Regan Catherine—†	32	housewife	33	159 Marion
	L	Regan Herbert	32	candyworker	24	159 "
	M	Murphy Edward J	32	boilermaker	34	here
	N	Murphy Gertrude M—†	32	stenographer	35	"
	O	Murphy Leo F	32	B F D	42	"
	P	Murphy Mary F—†	32	housewife	70	"
	R	Tekulsky Anna H—†	34	stenographer	33	"
	S	Tekulsky Jacob	34	messenger	32	"
	U	*Bolan Catherine—†	36	housewife	50	"
	V	Bolan Lawrence	36	fisherman	50	"
	W	Holm Marie—†	38	housekeeper	50	"
	X	Thompson Anna—†	41	"	32	"
	Y	Thompson Mary—†	41	housewife	70	"
	Z	Campbell Susie—†	41	"	50	
548						
	A	Campbell Walter	41	fisherman	43	"
	B	Driver John	41	chauffeur	27	"
	C	Pagington Jenny—†	42	social worker	36	152 Hyde Park av
	D	Wilson Isabel—†	42	"	23	New Jersey
	E	Bickford Edwin	43	watchman	62	here
	F	Bickford Lillian A—†	43	librarian	55	"
	G	Bickford Mabel—†	43	housekeeper	44	"
	H	Wurl Adelia—†	43	housewife	72	"
	K	Wurl Adelia A—†	43	"	42	"
	L	Wurl Frederick C	43	clergyman	74	"
	M	McCarthy Nellie G—†	rear 43	housekeeper	68	"
	N	Sullivan Mary T—†	" 43	governess	41	"
	O	Jedrey Elias H	" 43	engineer	43	
	P	Jedrey Lillian M—†	" 43	housewife	47	"
	R	Harding Gertrude—†	44	"	26	
	S	Harding Gustave	44	fisherman	26	"
	T	Langley Gustave	44	longshoreman	39	73 Horace

Page.	Letter.	Full Name.	Residence, Jan. 1, 1938.	Occupation.	Supposed Age.	Reported Residence, Jan. 1, 1937. Street and Number.

Saratoga Street—Continued

	U	Martell Florence J—†	44	housewife	44	here
	V	Martell Howard D	44	painter	47	"
	W	Bouchie Joseph	45	repairman	25	Medford
	X	Martell Daniel	45	retired	78	"
	Y	Martell Philomena—†	45	housewife	69	"
	Z	*Muise Margaret—†	45	"	33	
549						
	A	*Muise Raymond J	45	chef	36	here
	B	Storapoldi Joseph	45	laborer	43	"
	C	*Storapoldi Josephine—†	45	housewife	33	"
	D	*Micastro Mary D—†	46	"	49	
	E	Micastro Michael	46	machinist	51	"
	F	Micastro Vincenzio—†	46	bookkeeper	23	"
	G	*Huey Caleb M	46	laborer	39	"
	H	Jones Clara—†	46	cook	49	
	K	Jones Thomas	46	clerk	21	
	L	Bennett Donald	47	fishcutter	34	"
	M	Bennett Mae—†	47	housewife	40	"
	N	*Giordano Antonio	47	chauffeur	54	159 Marion
	O	*Giordano Carmella—†	47	housewife	53	159 "
	P	Principe Albert	47	laborer	47	here
	R	*Principe Celia—†	47	housewife	40	"
	S	Boland Celia—†	48	"	50	"
	T	Boland John	48	laborer	54	"
	U	Boland Mary—†	48	stitcher	23	
	V	Boland Stephen	48	clerk	20	
	W	Dolaher Albert J	49	attendant	26	"
	X	Hedrington Annie A—†	49	housekeeper	71	"
	Y	Hedrington Eleanor E—†	49	saleswoman	30	"
	Z	*D'Entremont Albine	49A	fisherman	35	"
550						
	A	Maillet Jerome	49A	carpenter	60	"
	B	Maillet Josephine—†	49A	housewife	56	"
	C	Maillett Robert	49A	carpenter	30	"
	D	*Pottie Malcolm	49A	fisherman	35	"
	E	Conran Andrew	49A	retired	54	
	F	Conran Catherine—†	49A	housewife	57	"
	G	McGrath John J	49A	laborer	40	
	H	*Cosco Christiforo	51	barber	50	
	K	*Cosco Lucy—†	51	housewife	49	"
	L	*Falzerano Antonio	51	shoeworker	63	"

Page.	Letter.	FULL NAME.	Residence, Jan. 1, 1938.	Occupation.	Supposed Age.	Reported Residence, Jan. 1, 1937. Street and Number.

Saratoga Street—Continued

	M	*Falzerano Sylvia—†	51	housewife	52	here
	N	Santora Sadie—†	52	housekeeper	50	"
	O	Shapiro Anna—†	52	housewife	37	"
	P	Shapiro Joseph	52	chauffeur	39	"
	R	Crawford William	56	secretary	41	"
	S	Miller Catherine—†	56	housewife	43	"
	T	Miller Dorothy—†	56	typist	21	
	U	Miller Harry	56	longshoreman	48	"
	V	Gewran Peter	56	attorney	29	"
	W	*Gonis Peter	56	merchant	39	"
	X	*Gonis Rose—†	56	housewife	31	"
	Y	Famiglietti Alfred R	56	metalworker	21	"
	Z	Famiglietti Antonetta—†	56	housewife	47	"
551						
	A	Famiglietti Joseph A	56	student	25	
	B	Famiglietti Mary H—†	56	secretary	24	"
	C	Famiglietti Raffaele	56	butcher	57	
	D	*Boucher Louis	57	retired	72	
	E	Ingersoll Charles G	57	machinist	25	"
	F	Ingersoll James W	57	porter	27	
	G	Ingersoll John W	57	operator	22	"
	H	Ingersoll Sarah J—†	57	housewife	45	"
	K	Ingersoll Walter F	57	sailmaker	55	"
	L	Abbatessa Anthony	57	operator	30	"
	M	Abbatessa Catherine M—†	57	housewife	27	"
	N	Luongo Alvira—†	57	candymaker	22	"
	O	Luongo Josephine—†	57	housewife	51	"
	P	Luongo Michael	57	laborer	48	
	R	Luongo Pasquale	57	"	26	
	S	*Powers Leo	59	fisherman	27	"
	T	Powers Mary—†	59	housewife	25	"
	U	Colantonio Christopher	59	laborer	29	
	V	Colantonio Phyllis—†	59	housewife	27	"
	W	Pearson Alfred E	59	policeman	48	"
	X	Pearson Alfred W	59	electrician	24	"
	Y	Pearson Edward J	59	clerk	20	
	Z	Pearson Josephine—†	59	housewife	43	"
552						
	A	Blake John F	61	operator	27	"
	B	Blake Nora—†	61	housewife	53	"
	C	Giangregorio Antonio	61	chauffeur	20	"

Page.	Letter.	Full Name.	Residence, Jan. 1, 1938.	Occupation.	Supposed Age.	Reported Residence, Jan. 1, 1937. Street and Number.

Saratoga Street—Continued

	D	Giangregorio Dante	61	agent	57	here
	E	Giangregorio Giulbert	61	student	23	"
	F	Giangregorio Lawrence	61	clerk	25	"
	G	Giangregorio Millie—†	61	housewife	48	"
	H	Manning Alice—†	63	clerk	21	
	K	Manning Blanche—†	63	housekeeper	40	"
	L	Hickey John	65	retired	75	"
	M	Hickey Mary J—†	65	waitress	52	
	N	Reddy Johanna M—†	65	housekeeper	67	"
	O	Martin Gertrude—†	67	bookkeeper	20	"
	P	Martin Josephine F—†	67	student	21	"
	R	*Martin Mary A—†	67	housewife	49	"
	S	Martin Mary A—†	67	stenographer	21	"
	T	*Martin Thomas	67	engineer	50	"
	U	Allison Ruth—†	69	teacher	35	
	V	Boudreau Anna—†	69	housekeeper	68	"
	W	Hewes Nettie—†	69	housewife	63	"
	X	*Jones John	69	retired	64	
	Y	Mulieri Andrew	69	machinist	28	"
	Z	Salerno Frank	69	laborer	21	
553						
	A	Salerno Joseph	69		23	"
	B	Devan Charles J	71	"	39	53 Neptune rd
	C	Saulnier Lawrence	71	fisherman	42	here
	D	Saulnier Mary E—†	71	housewife	33	"
	E	Carnevale Edna—†	71	operator	26	"
	F	*Carnevale Frank	71	barber	42	
	G	*Carnevale Salvatore	71	laborer	55	
	H	*Mazzie Antonio	71	"	43	
	K	*Mazzie Rose—†	71	housewife	42	"
	L	*LaRosa Lena—†	75	housekeeper	46	"
	M	LaRosa Rosario	75	laborer	63	"
	N	Poto Santa—†	75	housewife	23	"
	R	McGillicuddy Daniel	101	riveter	21	Winthrop
	S	McLaren Donald J	101	clerk	21	"
	T	McLaren James S	101	"	56	here
	U	McLaren Lillian C—†	101	housewife	54	Winthrop
	V	Cowan Christina C—†	101	bookkeeper	21	here
	W	Cowan Emma E—†	101	housewife	52	"
	X	Cowan Lyman W	101	engineer	52	"
	Y	Hughes Grace—†	102	housewife	37	"

Page.	Letter.	Full Name.	Residence, Jan. 1, 1938.	Occupation.	Supposed Age.	Reported Residence, Jan. 1, 1937. Street and Number.

Saratoga Street—Continued

Page.	Letter.	Full Name.	Residence, Jan. 1, 1938.	Occupation.	Supposed Age.	Reported Residence, Jan. 1, 1937. Street and Number.
	z	Hughes Thomas	102	seaman	42	here
554						
	A	Kelley George	102	electrician	42	"
	B	Burke Arthur P	102	laborer	20	122 Saratoga
	C	Burke Elmer	102	shipper	27	122 "
	D	*Burke Isabel S—†	102	housewife	60	122 "
	E	Burke Marion E—†	102	"	24	122 '
	F	Burke W Raymond	102	laborer	21	122 '
	G	Burke William R	102	carpenter	67	122 "
	H	Sullivan Beatrice—†	102	housewife	31	122 "
	K	Sullivan William	102	watchman	31	122 "
	L	*DeChristoforo Amadeo	103	laborer	58	here
	M	DeChristoforo Frank	103	metalworker	23	"
	N	DeChristoforo Joseph	103	steamfitter	25	"
	O	DeChristoforo Mary—†	103	housewife	48	"
	P	Smith Anna F—†	103	"	59	
	R	Smith Lewis B	103	salesman	59	"
	S	Vella Violet—†	103	housekeeper	24	Revere
	T	Derome Anna—†	104	housewife	44	187 Benningt'n
	U	Derome Arthur L	104	laborer	44	187 "
	V	Gardner Helen E—†	105	housekeeper	62	here
	W	Gardner William B	105	fisherman	29	"
	X	Hogan Eugene	105	butcher	63	"
	Y	Joy William	105	laborer	65	"
	Z	Bodkins Dora—†	106	housewife	45	130 Saratoga
555						
	A	Bodkins Harry	106	machinist	45	130 "
	B	Bodkins Irving	106	laborer	21	130 "
	C	Bremer Adele J— †	106	saleswoman	46	38 Lonsdale
	D	Mann Gertrude C—†	106	at home	62	here
	E	Shaneck Johanna M—†	106	"	77	"
	F	Knowles Nathaniel E	107	clerk	57	"
	G	Moore Lillian J—†	107	housekeeper	57	"
	H	Warnock Hugh	107	retired	77	"
	K	Hendrickson Charles	109	"	64	
	L	Paulson Hanna—†	109	at home	78	
	M	Burke Georgia—†	110	housewife	37	"
	N	Burke James D	110	shipper	38	
	O	Lavoie Annie—†	110	housewife	39	"
	P	Lavoie Edward F	110	machinist	49	"
	R	Currier Mary E—†	111	at home	77	

Page.	Letter.	FULL NAME.	Residence, Jan. 1, 1938.	Occupation.	Supposed Age.	Reported Residence, Jan. 1, 1937. Street and Number.

Saratoga Street—Continued

	S	Furtado Louise—†	111	waitress	27	here
	T	Horgan Daniel J	111	laborer	61	"
	U	McLaughlin Mary—†	111	at home	80	"
	V	Morse Edna G—†	111	"	58	
	W	White Henry	111	laborer	37	
	X	DePalma Anthony	113	painter	24	
	Y	DePalma Eleanor—†	113	housekeeper	22	"
	Z	Brennan Catherine A—†	114	"	64	"
556						
	A	Greenbaum Joseph	114	oiler	41	
	B	Kelley James J	114	clerk	59	
	C	McLaughlin Harold G	114	finisher	33	
	D	Miglionico Joseph	114	plumber	31	"
	E	Smith Louis	114	timekeeper	33	"
	F	Smith Mary C—†	114	housewife	30	"
	G	Cardinale Joseph	115	baker	50	
	H	Cardinale Josephine—†	115	housewife	45	"
	K	Cardinale Pasquale	115	baker	23	"
	L	McCarthy John B	116	chauffeur	42	46 Monmouth
	M	McCarthy Mary E—†	116	housewife	40	46 "
	N	Mann Elizabeth L—†	116	secretary	34	here
	O	Mann Henry C	116	grocer	69	"
	P	Mann Minna G—†	116	housewife	66	"
	R	*Daddieco Angelina—†	117	at home	83	
	S	*Daddieco Josephine—†	117	housewife	52	"
	T	Daddieco Louis	117	shoeworker	27	"
	U	Daddieco Mary—†	117	housekeeper	26	"
	V	*Daddieco Sabino	117	retired	63	"
	W	Bruse Isabella—†	119	waitress	24	
	X	MacDonald Catherine—†	119	at home	65	
	Y	MacDonald James G	119	candler	43	
	Z	MacDonald James J	119	carpenter	72	"
557						
	A	*MacDonald William	119	retired	70	
	B	Simmons Amelia—†	119	at home	99	
	C	Cardinale James	120	baker	25	
	D	Cardinale Mary—†	120	housewife	25	"
	E	Leventhal Jacob	120	storekeeper	49	"
	F	Leventhal Louis	120	clerk	22	"
	G	*Leventhal Sarah—†	120	housewife	48	"
	H	Trask Ada M—†	121	"	63	

Page.	Letter.	Full Name.	Residence, Jan. 1, 1938.	Occupation.	Supposed Age.	Reported Residence, Jan. 1, 1937. Street and Number.
		Saratoga Street—Continued				
	K	Trask Ada M—†	121	stitcher	30	here
	M	*Mortenson Neils P	123	cleaner	79	“
	N	Cucughata Charles	125	blacksmith	53	“
	O	Cucughata Charles, jr	125	upholsterer	25	“
	P	Cucughata Eleanor—†	125	clerk	20	
	R	Cucughata Grace—†	125	housekeeper	48	“
	S	Cucughata Lucy—†	125	finisher	28	“
	T	Cucughata Marie—†	125	stitcher	23	
	U	Peterson Eleanor—†	126	housewife	30	“
	V	Peterson Frederick W	126	installer	33	
	W	Matson Gustaf	126	ironworker	61	“
	X	Watson Mary—†	126	housewife	60	“
	Z	Crowley Annie—†	129	housekeeper	40	“
558						
	A	Crowley Michael	129	carpenter	53	“
	B	Magnuson Oscar	129	“	53	
	C	*Mason Edward	129	laborer	60	“
	D	Pascucci Albert J	129	factoryhand	30	83 Lexington
	E	Pothies Julius	129	stevedore	50	here
	F	Shakaran Thomas	129	clerk	50	“
	G	Lally James A	130	guard	46	“
	H	Lally Loretta E—†	130	stenographer	20	“
	K	Lally Margaret M—†	130	teacher	23	“
	L	Lally Mary A—†	130	housewife	44	“
	M	*Bodkins Gutel—†	130	housekeeper	67	“
	N	Stoddard Florence—†	130	housewife	21	131 Trenton
	O	Stoddard Reginald	130	scaler	27	131 “
	P	*Andolina Angelo	131	retired	69	here
	R	Andolina Charles	131	shipper	39	“
	S	Andolina Josephine—†	131	operator	41	“
	T	Andolina Mary—†	131	“	26	
	U	*Andolina Rosina—†	131	housewife	65	“
	V	*Terravecchia Marie—†	133	housekeeper	70	“
	W	Paolini Anthony	134	shoeworker	29	“
	X	Paolini Mildred—†	134	housewife	21	“
	Y	*Panzini Antonetta—†	134	“	65	
	Z	Panzini Henry	134	clerk	31	
559						
	A	Panzini Mafalda—†	134	at home	21	
	B	*Panzini Pasquale	134	laborer	65	
	C	Panzini Thomas	134	operator	25	

Page.	Letter.	Full Name.	Residence, Jan. 1, 1938.	Occupation.	Supposed Age.	Reported Residence, Jan. 1, 1937. Street and Number.
		Saratoga Street—Continued				
	D	*Taccardo Anna—†	134	housewife	53	here
	E	*Taccardo Joseph	134	laborer	51	"
	F	Pardo Angelo	135	guard	47	"
	G	Pardo Emma—†	135	housekeeper	37	"
	H	Stretton Grace E—†	135	leatherworker	47	"
	K	*Giusto Jennie—†	136	housewife	36	"
	L	Giusto Joseph	136	dealer	43	
	M	Harris Frances—†	136	housewife	37	"
	N	Harris Timothy	136	caterer	36	
	O	Guppy Laura—†	136	housewife	50	"
	P	*Salvaggio Salvatrice—†	137	housekeeper	74	"
	R	Salvaggio Eleanor—†	137	housewife	25	"
	S	*Salvaggio Paul	137	shoeworker	42	"
	T	*Bates Amy L—†	139	housewife	70	"
	U	Bates David S	139	machinist	69	"
	V	Corcoran Simon	139	fisherman	37	"
	W	Ferri Carl	139	laborer	27	
	X	Price John	139	"	60	
	Y	Ridini Leonard	140	milkman	30	"
	Z	Ridini Mary—†	140	housewife	30	"
560						
	B	Russo Gaetano	140	barber	54	
	A	Russo Jennie—†	140	factoryhand	24	"
	C	Russo Stefani	140	housewife	52	"
	D	Russo Tina—†	140	factoryhand	23	"
	E	Barbarisi Joseph	140	laborer	35	
	F	Barbarisi Margaret—†	140	housewife	32	"
	G	*Cavalieri Frank	141	dealer	63	
	H	*Cavalieri Mary—†	141	housekeeper	48	"
	K	Vozzella Antonetta—†	141	housewife	43	"
	L	Vozzella Charles	141	blacksmith	46	"
	M	Lazzaro Phillipa—†	143	housewife	56	"
	N	Lazzaro Salvatore	143	laborer	66	
	O	Gangi Grace—†	143	dressmaker	25	"
	P	Gangi Phyllis—†	143	stenographer	23	"
	R	Gangi Rose—†	143	housewife	53	"
	S	*Gangi Salvatore	143	cabinetmaker	62	"
	T	Gangi Salvatore, jr	143	"	33	
	U	DiCocco Joseph	144	laborer	49	
	V	DiCocco Loretta—†	144	operator	22	
	W	*DiCocco Rita—†	144	housewife	40	"

Page	Letter	Full Name.	Residence, Jan. 1, 1938.	Occupation.	Supposed Age.	Reported Residence, Jan. 1, 1937. Street and Number.

Saratoga Street—Continued

Page	Letter	Full Name.	Residence, Jan. 1, 1938.	Occupation.	Supposed Age.	Reported Residence, Jan. 1, 1937. Street and Number.
	X	Dantona Alphonsus	144	printer	31	here
	Y	*Dantona Maria—†	144	housekeeper	63	"
	Z	*Dantona Marie—†	144	housewife	29	"
561						
	A	*Spencer Gertrude—†	144	housekeeper	52	"
	B	Horne Marie—†	145	housewife	33	"
	C	Horne Walter	145	boilermaker	35	"
	D	*Vecchio Carmen	145	housewife	38	"
	E	Vecchio Michael	145	watchman	50	"
	F	D'Amato Albert	146	draftsman	34	"
	G	D'Amato Dravinia—†	146	housewife	34	"
	H	Abate Cesare	146	stockman	22	"
	K	*Abate Grace—†	146	housewife	46	"
	L	*Abate John	146	shoeworker	51	"
	M	*Dugas Concetta—†	146	housewife	35	"
	N	Dugas Walter	146	carpenter	37	"
	O	*Davis Patrick	147	fisherman	28	"
	P	Joy John	147	"	60	
	R	Murphy Mary—†	147	housekeeper	55	"
	S	*LaRosa Marie—†	148	housewife	53	"
	T	LaRosa Roasario	148	bricklayer	63	"
	U	*Cannata Jennie—†	149	housewife	42	"
	V	Cannata John	149	operator	48	
	W	* Sambooni Vita—†	149	housekeeper	60	"
	X	Vanelli Anna—†	149	"	37	"
	Y	*Vanelli Benjamin	149	pedler	42	
	Z	*Stoico Libera—†	149	housewife	45	"
562						
	A	*Stoico Louis	149	painter	23	
	B	*Stoico Nicholas	149	laborer	49	"
	D	DiLorenzo Alice—†	151	housekeeper	28	46 Everett
	E	DiLorenzo William	151	plumber	31	117 Maverick
	F	*Paolini Anselmo	151	laborer	54	here
	G	Paolini Emma—†	151	operator	28	"
	H	Paolini Esther—†	151	"	23	"
	K	*Paolini Lucy—†	151	housewife	54	"
	L	Paolini Marion—†	151	operator	21	"
	M	Terrazzano Francesco	151	factoryhand	42	166 Gove
	N	Vitale Giuseppi	151	laborer	45	153 Saratoga
	O	*Vitale Nicolina—†	151	housewife	38	153 "
	P	MacDonald Elinor—†	152	"	26	175 Benningt'n

Page.	Letter.	Full Name.	Residence, Jan. 1, 1938.	Occupation.	Supposed Age.	Reported Residence, Jan. 1, 1937. Street and Number

Saratoga Street—Continued

	R	MacDonald John	152	clerk	23	109 Eutaw
	S	Corbett Florence—†	153	housewife	46	here
	T	Corbett James H	153	boilermaker	46	"
	U	Corbett Margaret—†	153	saleswoman	25	"
	V	Consilvio Benjamin	153	laborer	64	
	W	*Consilvio Concetta—†	153	housewife	58	"
	X	Consilvio Emerico	153	goldbeater	28	"
	Y	Consilvio Felix	153	student	24	
	Z	Consilvio Francis	153	electrician	27	"
563						
	A	Consilvio Joseph	153	typist	21	
	B	Consilvio Vincenzo	153	stonecutter	39	"
	C	Mirabella Carl A	153	laborer	28	217 Webster
	D	Mirabella Marie—†	153	housewife	28	217 "
	E	McDonald Edward	154	calker	53	here
	F	McDonald John	154	retired	89	"
	G	McDonald Mary—†	154	housewife	91	"
	H	McDonald Thomas	154	painter	44	
	K	Leville Alice C—†	155	housewife	27	"
	L	Leville William T	155	helper	28	164 Lexington
	M	Coelho Antonio	155	rigger	51	here
	N	*Coelho Mary—†	155	housewife	47	"
	O	*Kehoe Eugene	155	machinist	58	Somerville
	P	*Kehoe Mary—†	155	housewife	61	"
	R	*Kehoe Richard	155	machinist	32	"
	S	Albanese Betty—†	156	housewife	28	163 Chelsea
	T	Albanese Francis	156	orderly	28	163 "
	U	Salerno Michael	156	counterman	21	96 Saratoga
	V	Hayes Alice—†	157	housekeeper	20	here
	W	Hayes John	157	fisherman	53	"
	X	Hayes Valentine	157	laborer	22	"
	Y	Fasciano Alfonse	157	painter	21	
	Z	Fasciano Beatrice—†	157	operator	28	"
564						
	A	*Fasciano Domina—†	157	housekeeper	53	"
	B	Fasciano John	157	laborer	58	"
	C	Tontodonato Albert	158	clerk	22	
	D	Tontodonato Anthony	158	"	24	
	E	Tontodonato Camilla—†	158	housewife	50	"
	F	Tontodonato Luigi	158	tilesetter	53	"
	G	Tontodonato Joseph	158	clerk	28	

Page.	Letter.	Full Name.	Residence, Jan. 1, 1938.	Occupation.	Supposed Age.	Reported Residence, Jan. 1, 1937. Street and Number.

Saratoga Street—Continued

	H	Tontodonato Louise—†	158	housewife	25	here
	K	Rizzari Giacamo	159	laborer	44	32 Liverpool
	L	*Rizzari Michaelena—†	159	housewife	33	32 "
	M	Cannon Cornelius S	160	chauffeur	45	here
	N	Cannon James W	160	shipfitter	40	"
	O	Cannon John J	160	manager	50	"
	P	Cannon Mary E—†	160	housekeeper	56	"
	R	DiGirolamo Eleanor—†	161	housewife	37	"
	S	DiGirolamo Joseph	161	tilesetter	38	"
	T	Messina Dora—†	161	housewife	33	167 Cottage
	U	Messina Joseph	161	laborer	31	163 Saratoga
	V	*Brobecker Helen—†	162	housekeeper	58	here
	W	Tracey Agnes—†	162	examiner	40	"
	X	*Tracey Catherine—†	162	housewife	60	"
	Y	*Messina Christine—†	163	"	54	"
	Z	Messina Sylvester	163	tilesetter	57	"
565						
	A	Messina Frank	163	laborer	23	"
	B	Messina Mary—†	163	laundress	20	"
	C	O'Connell Josephine—†	163	housewife	24	83 Brooks
	D	O'Connell Thomas E	163	laborer	27	83 "
	E	*LaCascia Catherine—†	165	housewife	32	203 Saratoga
	F	LaCascia Frank	165	proprietor	36	203 "
	G	Fingerman Irving	165	merchant	35	here
	H	*Fingerman Rose—†	165	housewife	34	"
	L	Sanders Alta—†	174	"	58	"
	M	Sanders Ernest	174	clerk	64	
	N	Glennon Joseph	174	"	50	
	O	Cobb Mabel—†	174	"	54	

William J. Kelly Square

	V	Consolo Anna—†	27	hairdresser	38	here
	W	Consolo Vincent	27	dealer	32	430 Hanover
	X	DePari Ralph	27	laborer	20	here
	Y	DePari Victor	27	hairdresser	22	"
	Z	Flynn Elizabeth—†	27	housewife	73	"
566						
	A	Flynn James	27	retired	68	
	B	*Deering Katherine—†	27	housewife	57	"
	C	Deering Michael	27	expressman	30	"

Page.	Letter.	Full Name.	Residence, Jan. 1, 1938.	Occupation.	Supposed Age.	Reported Residence, Jan. 1, 1937. Street and Number.

William J. Kelly Square—Continued

Page.	Letter.	Full Name.	Residence, Jan. 1, 1938.	Occupation.	Supposed Age.	Reported Residence, Jan. 1, 1937. Street and Number.
	D	Ahlberg Eric W	27	coppersmith	40	59 E Brookline
	E	Ahlberg Signe—†	27	housewife	47	59 "
	E1	Johnson Raymond	27	mechanic	29	8 Gayland
	F	*Carroll Joseph	27	fisherman	53	27 Lexington
	G	Grant Alice—†	27	housekeeper	33	27 "
	N	A'Hearn Lillian—†	35	at home	70	here
	O	*Bergh Charles	35	seaman	38	Ohio
	P	Brogatti Steven	35	meatcutter	30	here
	R	*Ceyons David	35	fisherman	35	New York
	S	Dalton Florence—†	35	housekeeper	27	here
	T	DelRusso Michael	35	undertaker	43	"
	U	Gardner Anna—†	35	housewife	43	"
	V	Gardner Edward	35	shipfitter	45	"
	W	Lacey Dorothy—†	35	waitress	28	Haverhill
	X	Licari Ignazio	35	contractor	48	124 Benningt'n
	Y	Rockett Edward J	35	salesman	40	here
	Z	Tedescia Oligante	35	cobbler	32	"
567						
	A	Zorzy Grace—†	35	housewife	21	"
	B	Zorzy Ralph	35	waiter	23	"
	F	Villani Michael	40	proprietor	29	76 Havre
	G	Bernazani Ethel M—†	40	housewife	40	here
	H	Fellows Nettie L—†	40	at home	83	"
	K	Stevens Ida M—†	40	housewife	64	"
	L	Stevens William H	40	retired	66	
	M	Vitale Anthony A	40	manager	45	"

1

14

15

1(

17

18

1

11

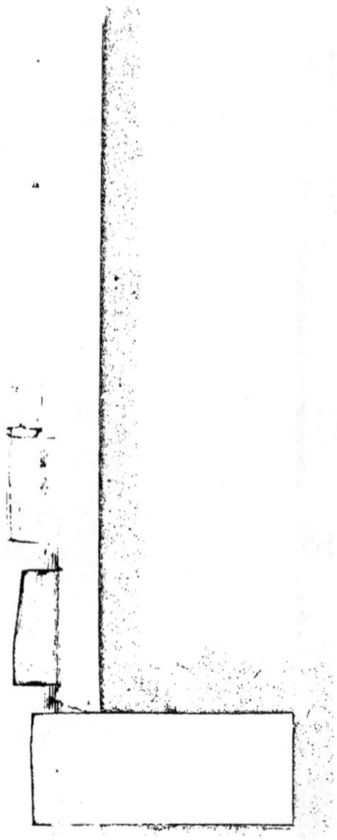

Ward 1—Precinct 7

CITY OF BOSTON

LIST OF RESIDENTS
20 YEARS OF AGE AND OVER

(NON-CITIZENS INDICATED BY ASTERISK)
(FEMALES INDICATED BY DAGGER)

AS OF

JANUARY 1, 1938

JOSEPH F. TIMILTY, } *Listing*
FREDERIC E. DOWLING, } *Board.*

CITY OF BOSTON PRINTING DEPARTMENT

Page.	Letter.	Full Name.	Residence, Jan. 1, 1938.	Occupation.	Supposed Age.	Reported Residence, Jan. 1, 1937. Street and Number.
579						
		Border Street				
	B	*Aia Mary	275	housewife	42	here
	C	Aia Michael	275	laborer	50	"
	E	*Silva Alice—†	319	housewife	32	"
	F	*Silva Manuel	319	longshoreman	42	"
	G	August Albina—†	319	housewife	42	"
	H	August Joseph F	319	accountant	47	"
	K	Cuscianotta Anthony	319	packer	24	
	L	Cuscianotta Theresa—†	319	housewife	23	"
	M	Firth Geraldine—†	321	"	23	147 Princeton
	N	Marley Frank J	321	carpenter	38	23 Monmouth
	O	Marley Margaret A—†	321	housewife	40	23 "
	P	McCoy Agnes J—†	321	"	49	here
	R	McCoy John E	321	instructor	25	"
	S	McCoy Lawrence J	321	"	22	"
	T	McCoy Thomas E	321	scaler	20	"
	U	*Wheaton Anna—†	323	at home	62	381 Meridian
	V	Wheaton Charles E	323	seaman	38	381 "
	W	Duffy Maud—†	323	housewife	43	here
	X	Duffy William P	323	steamfitter	43	"
	Y	Duffy William P, jr	323	helper	20	"
	Z	Burns Gerald F	323	chauffeur	40	"
580						
	A	Burns Lillian M—†	323	housewife	39	"
		Brooks Street				
	B	Carmen Israel	116	storekeeper	44	here
	C	Carmen Sarah—†	116	housewife	37	"
	D	Sheehan Anna L—†	116	"	54	"
	E	Sheehan Daniel J	116	blacksmith	54	"
	F	DeDonato Joseph	118	laborer	40	
	G	DeDonato Mary—†	118	housewife	40	"
	H	D'Apice Gerardo	120	laborer	54	
	K	D'Apice Jennie—†	120	operator	24	
	L	D'Apice Mary—†	120	housewife	47	"
	M	Hulke Benjamin, jr	122	policeman	41	"
	N	Hulke Florence—†	122	housewife	35	"
	O	Campbell Clinton D	126	captain	46	
	P	Campbell Jennie S—†	126	housewife	45	"
	R	Johannson Gudmund	126	fisherman	35	"

Page.	Letter.	Full Name.	Residence, Jan. 1, 1938.	Occupation.	Supposed Age.	Reported Residence, Jan. 1, 1937. Street and Number.

Brooks Street—Continued

Page.	Letter.	Full Name.	Residence, Jan. 1, 1938.	Occupation.	Supposed Age.	Reported Residence, Jan. 1, 1937. Street and Number.
	S	Sigborson Olaf	126	fisherman	38	here
	T	Keane Mary F—†	127	at home	50	"
	U	McDonnell Alphonso J	127	undertaker	34	"
	V	McDonnell Mary H-†	127	housewife	30	"
	W	Peterson Marion—†	127	saleswoman	38	150 Princeton
	X	Splaine John J	128	pedler	43	here
	Y	Splaine Mary E—†	128	at home	45	"
	Z	Doherty Mary A—†	128	housewife	66	118 Benningt'n
581						
	A	Doherty Philip	128	laborer	60	118 "
	B	Sirnes Bjarne	129	"	29	here
	C	*Sorenson Andrew	129	fisherman	48	"
	D	*Sorenson Bina—†	129	housewife	49	"
	E	Murphy Elizabeth—†	130	at home	58	
	F	Stone Fletcher L	130	retired	65	
	H	Rosalbo Lucy—†	131	housewife	44	"
	K	*Avolla Michael	131	shoemaker	48	90 Lexington
	L	*Avolla Ola—†	131	housewife	45	90 "
	M	DiGirolamo Dorothy—†	133	dressmaker	23	here
	N	DiGirolamo Erminio	133	tailor	50	"
	O	DiGirolamo Mary—†	133	housewife	59	"
	P	LaMotta Harold A	133	clerk	31	"
	R	LaMotta Michael	133	laborer	40	
	S	LaMotta Violet—†	133	stenographer	29	"
	T	Johnson Arthur D	135	chauffeur	39	"
	U	Johnson Marion T—†	135	housewife	40	"
	V	Fogg Lena—†	135	at home	84	
	W	Lacedra Barbara—†	137	housewife	23	"
	X	Lacedra Patrick	137	laborer	27	"
	Y	Rabasco Josephine—†	137	housewife	39	Winthrop
	Z	Rabasco Patrick	137	laborer	49	"
582						
	A	Faber John A	139	salesman	21	here
	B	Faber John T	139	dealer	48	"
	C	Faber Mary E—†	139	housewife	51	"
	D	Bonsey Charles M	140	baker	42	
	E	Bonsey Theresa—†	140	housewife	40	"
	F	Swamberg Dwight K	140	carpenter	52	"
	G	Huggan Mary R—†	144	at home	50	
	H	Ryder Grace M—†	144	"	51	
	K	Swett Lillian A—†	144	housewife	48	"

Page.	Letter.	Full Name.	Residence, Jan. 1, 1938.	Occupation.	Supposed Age.	Reported Residence, Jan. 1, 1937. Street and Number.

Brooks Street—Continued

	L	Swett Robert W	144	salesman	55	here
	M	Riley Michael F	146	mechanic	40	"
	N	Riley Rita—†	146	housewife	39	"
	O	*Melanson Daniel	146	carpenter	45	117 Princeton
	P	Melanson Rebecca—†	146	housewife	40	117 "
	R	Boudreau Adelaide—†	147	"	27	here
	S	Boudreau John	147	laborer	30	"
	T	*Hyslop Caroline A—†	147	housewife	43	"
	U	Hyslop Harold J	147	laborer	43	
	V	Hyslop James H	147	"	67	
	W	Hyslop Serenna—†	147	housekeeper	64	"
	X	Bergh Axel	148	clergyman	64	"
	Y	Bergh Herbert A	148	clerk	25	
	Z	Bergh Inga—†	148	housewife	60	"
583						
	A	Joyce Margaret A—†	149	at home	74	
	B	Joyce Melvin J	149	printer	42	
	C	Driscoll Catherine A—†	149	housewife	71	"
	D	Driscoll John P	149	laborer	66	
	E	Mortimer Anna—†	151	saleswoman	24	"
	F	Mortimer Catherine—†	151	clerk	29	
	G	Mortimer John	151	retired	67	
	H	Mortimer Mary—†	151	clerk	28	
	K	Mortimer Nora—†	151	operator	30	
	L	King Annie—†	153	housewife	54	"
	M	King Helen—†	153	at home	23	
	N	King James R	153	fisherman	63	"
	O	King John	153	"	27	

Eutaw Street

	R	*Newell Hazel—†	19	folder	32	24 Eutaw
	P	*Newell Sylvester	19	laborer	37	24 "
	S	*Luciano Elvira—†	19	housewife	25	here
	T	*Luciano John	19	shoeworker	31	"
	V	Fawcett Irene D—†	19	housewife	30	"
	U	Fawcett Peter W	19	shipworker	31	"
	W	Lyons Arnold	21	fishcutter	25	"
	X	*Lyons Evanell—†	21	housewife	28	"
	Z	Loricio Marion—†	21	"	24	"
	Y	Loricio Pasquale	21	chauffeur	26	"

Page.	Letter.	FULL NAME.	Residence, Jan. 1, 1938.	Occupation.	Supposed Age.	Reported Residence, Jan. 1, 1937. Street and Number.

584

Eutaw Street—Continued

584	A	Tarr Augusta—†	21	storekeeper	26	here
	B	Tarr Jennie—†	21	"	52	"
	C	Culleton Dorothy—†	23	housewife	38	"
	D	Culleton Wilfred	23	carpenter	36	"
	E	Fitzgerald Rose—†	23	housekeeper	28	191 Brooks
	F	Fitzgerald William	23	cooper	63	191 "
	G	Conte Frank	23	finisher	35	here
	H	Conte Mary—†	23	housewife	32	"
	K	Leary James	25	printer	25	349 Meridian
	L	Leary Margaret—†	25	housewife	23	349 "
	M	Siraco John	25	tilesetter	48	here
	N	*Siraco Lucy—†	25	housewife	44	"
	O	Siraco Mary—†	25	waitress	26	"
	P	Siraco Philomena—†	25	typist	20	
	R	Siraco Vincenza—†	25	"	21	
	S	Siraco Anthony	25	tilesetter	53	"
	T	Siraco Camillo	25	helper	20	
	U	*Siraco Vincenza—†	25	housewife	51	"
	V	Amerau Harold F	27	shipfitter	23	"
	W	Dobbins Helen K—†	27	housewife	30	"
	X	Dobbins William J	27	examiner	32	"
	Y	Carino Joseph	27	tailor	53	"
	Z	*Carino Margaret—†	27	housewife	38	606 Dor av
585	A	Frevold Eleanor—†	29	"	23	here
	B	Frevold Stanley	29	attendant	23	"
	C	*Mello Charles	29	cabinetmaker	44	227 Lexington
	D	*Mello Ethel—†	29	housewife	43	227 "
	E	Mello James	29	laborer	20	227 "
	F	*Pierro Carmen	29	meatcutter	45	here
	G	*Pierro Elena—†	29	housewife	41	"
	H	Kenneally Francis X	31	letter carrier	34	"
	K	Kenneally John F	31	B F D	43	
	L	Kenneally Mary E—†	31	housekeeper	30	"
	M	Kenneally Timothy	31	retired	70	"
	N	McKenna John J	31	laborer	45	"
	O	Tedesco Anna—†	33	housewife	22	35 Eutaw
	P	Tedesco Anthony	33	chauffeur	24	35 "
	R	Abramovitch Basil	33	laborer	50	here
	S	Abramovitch Francis	33	"	23	"

Page.	Letter.	FULL NAME.	Residence, Jan. 1, 1938.	Occupation.	Supposed Age.	Reported Residence, Jan. 1, 1937. Street and Number.

Eutaw Street—Continued

	T	Abramovitch Margaret—†	33	housewife	50	here
	U	*DeBay Rex	33	millhand	28	8 Lexington av
	W	*Burke Catherine—†	35	housewife	45	26 Trenton
	X	Burke Joseph P	35	pipefitter	43	26 "
	Y	Penney Mary—†	37	housewife	60	here
	Z	*Penney William	37	fisherman	55	"
586						
	A	Stasio Evelyn—†	37	bookkeeper	23	"
	B	Facchino Angelo	37	presser	49	"
	C	*Facchino Marie—†	37	housewife	45	"
	D	Siraco Joseph	37	shipper	24	109 Trenton
	E	Siraco Rose—†	37	housewife	25	109 "

Lexington Street

	G	Doucette Edith—†	4	housewife	26	here
	H	*Doucette Wilfred	4	laborer	28	"
	K	Barry Adelaide—†	4	housewife	35	"
	L	Barry Joseph	4	boilermaker	42	"
	M	Levins Herbert	4	photographer	38	Malden
	N	Dougherty James	4	laborer	44	Quincy
	O	Ritchie Arlene—†	4	housewife	37	here
	P	Ritchie Harry L	4	painter	49	"
	R	Davidson Ellen M—†	4	housewife	35	"
	S	Davidson Joseph J	4	messenger	31	"
	T	O'Malley Thomas	4	clerk	30	64 Putnam
	U	Dondero Gladys—†	8	housewife	20	24 Harwood
	V	Dondero Ralph	8	floorwalker	25	24 "
	W	Roach Carrier—†	20	housewife	55	here
	X	Roach Charles	20	retired	75	"
	Y	Walsh Frank	20	laborer	45	"
	Z	Angell Catherine—†	26	at home	65	Malden
587						
	A	Ennis Annie—†	26	housewife	65	here
	B	Pomeroy Alice—†	26	"	71	"
	C	Riley Emma—†	26	at home	65	"
	D	*Sullivan Catherine—†	26	cook	30	"
	E	DiNicola Elena—†	28	housewife	27	202 E Eagle
	F	DiNicola Rocco	28	tailor	37	202 "
	H	Bell Evelyn—†	30	housewife	29	here
	K	Bell William E	30	mechanic	40	238 Webster

Page.	Letter.	Full Name.	Residence, Jan. 1, 1938.	Occupation.	Supposed Age.	Reported Residence, Jan. 1, 1937. Street and Number.

Lexington Street—Continued

Page.	Letter.	Full Name.	Residence, Jan. 1, 1938.	Occupation.	Supposed Age.	Reported Residence, Jan. 1, 1937. Street and Number.
	L	Bell William R	30	retired	83	here
	M	Gorman Judith—†	30	nurse	24	"
	N	Safrin Diana—†	30	housewife	44	238 Webster
	P	Aylward Catherine E—†	34	"	30	34 Linwood
	R	Brothers Arthur	34	chauffeur	29	here
	S	Brothers Cecelia—†	34	housewife	24	"
	T	Dalton Isabel—†	34	"	54	68 Centre
	U	Dalton Thomas	34	sprayer	27	68 "
	V	Ciampa Joseph	36	shoeworker	42	here
	W	Ciampa Louise—†	36	housewife	33	"
	X	Vozzello Giuseppe	36	laborer	58	"
	Y	Bonapano Romano	36	"	61	
	Z	Shannon Francis A	36	salesman	39	"
588						
	A	Shannon James	36	laborer	63	
	B	*Troigero Columba—†	36	housewife	49	"
	C	Anderson Andrew C	38	clerk	22	
	D	Anderson Mary A—†	38	housewife	48	"
	E	Anderson William R	38	laborer	26	"
	F	Bartolino Jennie—†	38	nurse	22	Westfield
	G	McMahon Alice M—†	38	factoryhand	20	315 Saratoga
	H	McMahon Lillian E—†	38	housekeeper	26	315 "
	K	McMahon Richard L	38	watchman	52	315 "
	M	Frederick Dolores—†	40	housewife	24	here
	N	Frederick Howard	40	accountant	31	"
	O	Roche Dora—†	40	housewife	52	"
	P	Roche Frank	40	inspector	53	"
	R	*Chapman Fannie—†	42	housewife	41	"
	S	Freda Charles	42	laborer	24	
	T	Freda Ethel—†	42	housewife	24	"
	U	Doyle William	42	salesman	51	"
	V	Kiernan Henry A	42	electrician	56	"
	W	Kiernan James	42	laborer	51	
	X	Cuccinotta Arthur	42	musician	30	"
	Y	Cuccinotta Flora—†	42	housewife	60	"
	Z	*Brigioni Frank	44	cook	38	
589						
	A	*Capezzuto Beatrice—†	44	housewife	22	"
	B	Capezzuto Joseph	44	laborer	24	
	C	Chase Nellie—†	44	at home	75	
	D	*Lynch Michael	44	fisherman	33	"

Page.	Letter.	FULL NAME.	Residence, Jan. 1, 1938.	Occupation.	Supposed Age.	Reported Residence, Jan. 1, 1937. Street and Number.

Lexington Street—Continued

	E	Meuse Leo	44	painter	34	50 Princeton
	F	*Meuse Lillian—†	44	housewife	24	50 "
	G	Ryder William E	44	mariner	64	here
	H	Sanders Herman	44	retired	63	"
	K	Stewart Annie E—†	44	housekeeper	35	"
	L	Wilson Alfreida—†	44	hairdresser	35	"
	M	Curran Emma M—†	46	housewife	51	"
	N	Curran Henry P	46	serviceman	53	"
	O	Curran Julia E—†	46	housewife	77	"
	R	Boyer Francis	70	fishcutter	32	"
	S	Boyer Mary—†	70	housewife	28	"
	T	MacPhee Mary—†	70	"	37	"
	U	MacPhee William A	70	seaman	42	
	V	*Goarlabasso Mary—†	70	housewife	36	"
	W	Goarlabasso Stefano	70	laborer	42	
	X	Surrette Adolph	72	waiter	35	
	Y	Surrette Louise—†	72	housewife	40	"
	Z	Bellino John	72	laborer	35	
590						
	A	Bellino Mary—†	72	housewife	29	"
	B	*Bellino Agrippino	72	mason	63	"
	C	*Bellino Jennie—†	72	housewife	57	"
	E	Walsh Albina—†	74	"	43	
	F	Walsh Robert	74	coast guard	22	"
	G	Walsh William	74	welder	45	
	H	Beach Darwin	78	clerk	53	
	K	Dobbins Frank E	78	timekeeper	23	"
	L	Dobbins Thelma M—†	78	saleswoman	24	"
	M	Hagar Elson	78	fisherman	45	"
	N	McLeish Charlotte—†	78	housewife	51	"
	O	Snow Clarence	78	B F D	35	
	P	Frame Catherine—†	78	housewife	30	"
	R	Frame Paul	78	mechanic	32	"
	S	Carrigan Daisy—†	78	housewife	40	"
	T	Carrigan Richard	78	cook	35	"
	U	Rideout Sarah—†	78	housewife	55	2 Lexington av
	V	Rideout William	78	watchman	65	2 "
	W	Keely Joseph	78	laborer	35	here
	X	Keely Roseann—†	78	housewife	27	"
	Z	Comeau Albert	81	carpenter	49	"

Page.	Letter.	Full Name.	Residence, Jan. 1, 1938.	Occupation.	Supposed Age.	Reported Residence, Jan. 1, 1937. Street and Number.
591		**Lexington Street—Continued**				
	A	*Comeau Mary—†	81	housewife	53	here
	B	Comeau Wallace	81	fishcutter	40	383 Meridian
	C	*Crowell Ivan	81	fisherman	36	here
	D	Deveau Patrick	81	carpenter	35	62 Bennington
	E	Ford Elsie—†	81	housewife	20	178 Broadway
	F	Ford John F	81	carpenter	24	Long Island
	G	George Harry	81	waiter	38	62 Bennington
	H	*Meuse Sylvain	81	fishcutter	35	here
	K	Namislo John	81	baker	40	44 Lexington
	L	*Pastore Anthony	83	carpenter	38	here
	M	Pastore Rose—†	83	housewife	32	"
	N	Fronduto Nicholas	83	tailor	31	"
	O	Staff Anna—†	83	housewife	28	"
	P	Staff Leonard	83	driver	28	
	R	Roy Armandine—†	85	housewife	43	"
	S	*Roy Elias	85	cook	67	
	T	Roy Elizabeth—†	85	housewife	37	"
	U	Roy Mary—†	85	clerk	31	
	V	Roy Thelma—†	85	stitcher	30	
	W	Roy Thomas G	85	fireman	37	"
	X	Joyce Clancy	85	"	43	Watertown
	Y	Monson Albertine—†	85	housewife	35	here
	Z	Monson Henry	85	painter	43	"
592						
	A	*Pickler Mary E—†	86	housewife	45	"
	C	Saunier Anna—†	88	"	43	
	D	Saunier Melvin	88	machinist	44	"
	E	Whelan John	88	retired	75	
	F	Whelan Mary—†	88	housewife	70	"
	G	*Swindle Samuel	88	laborer	50	
	H	*Molloy Robert	89	fisherman	25	"
	K	*Molloy Sadie—†	89	housewife	42	"
	L	*Molloy Sylvester	89	fisherman	27	"
	M	Molloy Thomas	89	"	38	"
	N	Arcari Anthony	89	electrician	36	62 Eutaw
	O	Arcari Christine—†	89	housewife	27	here
	P	*Lanni Angelo	89	shoeworker	45	"
	R	*Lanni Nancy—†	89	housewife	45	"
	S	Fabiano Anna—†	90	"	34	

Page	Letter.	Full Name.	Residence, Jan. 1, 1938.	Occupation.	Supposed Age.	Reported Residence, Jan. 1, 1937. Street and Number.

Lexington Street—Continued

	T	Fabiano Joseph	90	bartender	34	here
	U	*Bartolino Concetta—†	90	housewife	70	"
	V	Modeo Louis	90	laborer	63	"
	W	Young Catherine—†	92	housewife	56	"
	X	Young John	92	blacksmith	45	"
	Y	Keyes Milton	92	helper	24	
	Z	Keyes Rita—†	92	housewife	22	"
593						
	A	Shea Edward	92	laborer	37	"
	B	*Pugliese Andrew	93	carpenter	55	268 Princeton
	C	Pugliese John	93	clerk	21	268 "
	D	*Pugliese Joseph	93	carpenter	50	268 "
	E	*Pugliese Julia—†	93	housewife	45	268 "
	F	Pugliese Olympai—†	93	operator	24	268 "
	G	McGrath John	93	fisherman	44	here
	H	McGrath Theresa—†	93	housewife	41	"
	K	DiBiccari Edith—†	94	"	22	"
	L	DiBiccari Frank	94	shoeworker	27	"
	M	Martucci Anthony	94	painter	40	
	N	Martucci Josephine—†	94	housewife	32	"
	P	Krueger James	94	painter	40	
	O	Krueger Lena—†	94	housewife	30	"
	R	Pierce Evangeline A—†	95	"	56	11 Saratoga
	S	Pierce Joseph F	95	janitor	68	11 "
	T	Foster Henry B	95	clerk	28	here
	U	Olson Bonoria—†	95	housewife	58	"
	V	*Johanson Aagot—†	95	"	32	"
	W	Johanson Helmer	95	pipefitter	38	"
	X	*Cold Annie—†	96	housewife	51	"
	Y	*Cold John	96	fisherman	50	"
	Z	Dobbins Leo	96	laborer	25	
594						
	A	Ettman Nellie—†	96	housewife	46	"
	B	Ettman Robert	96	fisherman	53	"
	D	Crowell Dorothea—†	96	operator	20	"
	F	Crowell Thelma—†	96	stenographer	23	"
	C	*King Anna B—†	96	housewife	89	20 Marion
	E	*King Sarah J—†	96	at home	53	20 "
	G	McKenna Ernest A	96	supervisor	31	here
	H	McKenna Harrietta—†	96	housewife	63	"
	K	McKenna James A	96	foreman	63	"

Page.	Letter.	FULL NAME.	Residence, Jan. 1, 1938.	Occupation.	Supposed Age.	Reported Residence, Jan. 1, 1937. Street and Number.

Lexington Street—Continued

Page.	Letter.	FULL NAME.	Residence, Jan. 1, 1938.	Occupation.	Supposed Age.	Reported Residence, Jan. 1, 1937. Street and Number.
	L	Vecchione Arthur	96	foreman	23	here
	M	Vecchione Elveria L—†	96	teacher	30	“
	N	Vecchione Jennie—†	96	housewife	52	“
	O	Vecchione Olympia G—†	96	student	21	
	P	Gross Calvin G	97	messenger	42	“
	R	McGloan Frederick	97	retired	67	
	S	McGloan Martha J—†	97	housewife	50	“
	T	Foster Avis L—†	97	housekeeper	27	“
	U	Foster Hattie L—†	97	housewife	51	“
	V	Foster William	97	B F D	51	
	W	Scott Anthony L	98	seaman	43	
	X	Scott Marie—†	98	housewife	35	“
	Y	Cooley Francis T	98	packer	22	“
	Z	Duffy Annie—†	98	housewife	55	“
595						
	A	Duffy Thomas F	98	retired	63	
	B	Hagen Elizabeth—†	98	houseworker	55	“
	D	Reed Emma M—†	99	clerk	61	
	C	Reed Gertrude E—†	99	housewife	63	“
	E	Sheridan Margaret J—†	100	“	39	
	F	Nickerson Marion—†	103	“	44	
	G	Nickerson Nicholas	103	chauffeur	44	“
	H	Nicastro Cosimo D	104	attorney	41	“
	K	Nicastro Esther F—†	104	housewife	37	“
	L	Pizzuto Frank L	105	clergyman	40	“
	M	Pizzuto Santina—†	105	housewife	28	“
	N	Wetherbee Emily—†	106	“	68	“
	O	*Dias Joseph	107	spinner	22	571 Benningt'n
	P	Hunt Herbert L	107	manager	64	here
	R	Hunt Rosamond—†	107	housewife	64	“
	S	Johnson Helen—†	107	at home	76	“
	T	Ottorson Sofus	107	seaman	68	
	U	Wallace Theresa—†	107	dealer	38	
	V	O'Brien Edward J	108	retired	75	
	W	O'Brien Francis J	108	salesman	44	“
	X	O'Brien Julia—†	108	housewife	78	“
	Y	Bowman Carl V	109	attorney	35	“
	Z	Gage Gertrude—†	109	housekeeper	64	“
596						
	A	Roberts Blanchard R	109	retired	72	
	B	Maguire Thomas B	110	B F D	49	

Page.	Letter.	Full Name.	Residence, Jan. 1, 1938.	Occupation.	Supposed Age.	Reported Residence, Jan. 1, 1937. Street and Number.

Lexington Street—Continued

	C	McCoy Mary—†	110	housewife	41	here
	D	McAlpine Effie—†	111	at home	70	"
	E	McCarthy Callahan	111	chauffeur	45	"
	F	White Walter	111	cook	36	
	G	Yeaton Clinton	111	painter	21	"
	H	Yeaton Josephine—†	111	houseworker	49	"
	K	Emery Emerald	114	B F D	47	
	L	Farwell Martha—†	114	housewife	71	"
	M	Crozier Charlotte M—†	116	teacher	30	
	N	Crozier Grace E—†	116	housekeeper	59	"
	O	Crozier Grace E—†	116	teacher	25	"
	P	*DeSimone Pasqualine—†	117	housekeeper	48	394 Benningt'n
	R	Monaco Anthony	117	laborer	28	41 Salem
	S	Monaco Mary—†	117	housewife	23	10 Lexington av
	T	Powers Cecil	117	laborer	39	here
	U	Powers Harold	117	pipeman	41	"
	V	*Warren Elsie—†	117	housekeeper	42	"
	W	Warren Harold	117	boilermaker	43	"
	X	McEwen Mary A—†	118	at home	62	
	Y	Nichols Emma J—†	118	housewife	65	"
	Z	Nichols John S	118	attorney	66	"
597						
	A	*Thibodeau Annie—†	119	housewife	60	"
	B	*Thibodeau Charles	119	carpenter	26	"
	C	*Thibodeau Elizabeth—†	119	stitcher	22	
	D	*Thibodeau Henry	119	carpenter	52	"
	E	*Thibodeau Hilda—†	119	student	21	
	F	*Comeau Eva—†	119	housewife	34	"
	G	Comeau Leo	119	carpenter	33	"
	H	Cote Dorthy—†	119	housewife	28	"
	K	Cote Paul	119	cook	38	
	L	Francis Fred	119	retired	64	
	M	Powell Laura—†	119	housewife	53	"
	N	Powell William E	119	seaman	56	
	O	Robichaud Charles	119	painter	35	
	P	*Robichaud Zita—†	119	housewife	38	"
	R	Anerau Arthur	119	shipfitter	36	"
	S	Anerau Frances—†	119	housewife	33	"
	T	Anerau Robert	119	painter	33	
	U	Hargrave John W	123	embalmer	51	"
	V	Staples George F	123	mason	75	

Page.	Letter.	Full Name.	Residence, Jan. 1, 1938.	Occupation.	Supposed Age.	Reported Residence, Jan. 1, 1937. Street and Number.

Lexington Street—Continued

Page.	Letter.	Full Name.	Residence, Jan. 1, 1938.	Occupation.	Supposed Age.	Reported Residence, Jan. 1, 1937. Street and Number.
	W	Walsh Joseph	123	retired	58	here
	X	Woods Fred E	123	engineer	72	"
	Y	Woods Isabel M—†	123	housewife	65	"
	Z	Hargrave Cora M—†	124	"	65	
598						
	A	Hargrave George W	124	retired	85	
	B	McCallum Malcolm L	124	clerk	32	
	C	McCallum Minnie B—†	124	at home	71	
	D	*D'Entremont Anna—†	125	housewife	38	"
	E	D'Entremont Edward J	125	clerk	44	
	F	*Amirault Annie A—†	125	maid	39	
	G	Glass Evalina F—†	125	at home	76	
	H	Nutter Caroline—†	125	"	76	
	K	Forster Barbara D—†	126	forewoman	45	"
	L	Forster Edward W	126	retired	67	
	M	Forster Gertrude—†	126	housewife	41	"
	N	Forster Mary A—†	126	"	71	
	O	Forster Rita G—†	126	clerk	21	
	P	Forster William J	126	B F D	43	
	R	Story Oliver E	127	musician	52	"
	S	Story T Parker	127	retired	77	
	T	Bourdeau Esther—†	128	maid	30	
	U	Boudreau Simon	128	retired	62	
	V	Edmunds Alvin	128	bartender	39	"
	W	Edmunds Lillian—†	128	housewife	35	"
	X	Lee Dolores L—†	128	"	35	
	Y	Lee Robert J	128	engineer	45	"
	Z	Hughes Mary—†	129	housewife	44	89 Trenton
599						
	A	Hughes Thomas	129	steamfitter	45	89 "
	B	Hughes Thomas	129	clerk	21	89 "
	C	Peterson Ella—†	129	millhand	57	34 Princeton
	D	*Johnson Joseph B	136	painter	43	here
	E	*Johnson Marion F—†	136	inspector	21	"
	F	Johnson Mary T—†	136	housewife	42	"
	G	*McDonald Anselm	136	carpenter	45	"
	H	McDonald Sadie—†	136	housewife	35	"
	K	Impeduglia Lillian—†	138	"	23	
	L	Impeduglia Lorenza	138	millhand	25	"
	N	DiCicco Lawrence	138	laborer	34	141 Saratoga
	M	DiCicco Marie A—†	138	housewife	30	141 "

Page.	Letter.	Full Name.	Residence, Jan. 1, 1938.	Occupation.	Supposed Age.	Reported Residence, Jan. 1, 1937. Street and Number.

Lexington Street—Continued

	o	Amico Annie—†	138	housewife	45	here
	p	Amico Anthony	138	laborer	24	"
	r	Amico Peter	138	"	55	"
	s	*Doucette Grace—†	140	housewife	41	"
	t	*Doucette Norman	140	calker	40	"
	u	*Surette Clifford	140	fishcutter	29	200 Lexington
	v	*Surette Margaret—†	140	housewife	25	200 "
	w	Lalli Joseph	140	painter	45	here
	x	Lalli Josephine—†	140	housewife	32	"
	y	*Benoit Anna—†	141	"	23	"
	z	Benoit Joseph	141	packer	24	
600						
	a	Gavaghan Edward	141	watchman	31	"
	b	Gavaghan Frank	141	"	33	
	c	Gavaghan Julia—†	141	housewife	31	"
	d	Minichiallo Antonio	142	salesman	58	"
	e	*Minichiallo Rose—†	142	housewife	57	"
	f	Belmonte Angelina—†	142	"	33	65 Frankfort
	g	Belmonte Genarosa	142	bartender	42	65 "
	h	Gallinaro Salvatore	142	shoeworker	24	here
	k	*Gallinaro Sylvia—†	142	housewife	25	"
	l	Bartollo Frank	143	laborer	20	"
	m	*Bartollo Tina—†	143	housewife	51	190 Chelsea
	n	Viglione Americo	143	laborer	30	here
	o	*Viglione Domenic	143	"	53	"
	p	*Viglione Rose—†	143	housewife	51	"
	r	Marks Frank	144	operator	42	N Easton
	s	*Marks Mary G—†	144	housewife	38	"
	t	*Rubicco Antonio	144	shoeworker	54	here
	u	Rubicco Sylvio	144	laborer	22	"
	v	*Rubicco Theresa—†	144	housewife	48	"
	w	*Tisi Joseph	144	laborer	69	
	x	Tisi Pasquale	144	"	29	
	y	*Tisi Philomina—†	144	housewife	63	"
	z	Mandi Josephine—†	145	"	40	
601						
	a	*Maurano Caroline—†	145	"	70	
	b	Maurano Peter	145	retired	70	
	c	Laura Domenic	145	mechanic	35	"
	d	*Laura Emma—†	145	housewife	33	"
	e	Parsons Chester	146	laborer	29	

Page.	Letter.	Full Name.	Residence, Jan. 1, 1938.	Occupation.	Supposed Age.	Reported Residence, Jan. 1, 1937. Street and Number.
		Lexington Street—Continued				
	F	*Parsons Evelyn—†	146	housewife	28	here
	G	DeVita Annette—†	146	"	33	123 Trenton
	H	DeVita Joseph	146	electrician	33	123 "
	K	Dunbar Mary—†	146	housewife	46	here
	L	Dunbar Mildred—†	146	clerk	22	"
	M	Garisto Theresa—†	147	housewife	35	"
	N	*Nadile Louis	147	laborer	68	
	O	*Nadile Mary—†	147	housewife	68	"
	P	Schieppa Joseph	147	bartender	46	"
	R	Jones Edmund	148	shipfitter	43	"
	S	Jones Elsie—†	148	housewife	35	"
	T	Mazzarino Adalina—†	148	clerk	22	128 Marion
	U	Mazzarino Joseph	148	"	20	128 "
	V	Mazzarino Pasquale	148	florist	54	128 "
	W	*Mazzarino Rosalie—†	148	housewife	46	128 "
	X	Jones Mary—†	148	"	56	here
	Y	Jones William	148	laborer	22	"
	Z	*Zeuli Adolph	149	barber	47	"
602						
	A	Zeuli Philomena—†	149	housewife	48	"
	B	DeFeo Arnold	149	candymaker	53	"
	C	DeFeo Arthur	149	shipper	21	
	D	DeFeo Grace—†	149	packer	23	
	E	DeFeo Jennie—†	149	housewife	52	"
	F	DeFeo Mary—†	149	candyworker	26	"
	G	DeFeo Ralph	149	shoeworker	25	"
	H	*Clark Burton	150	mechanic	32	92 Lexington
	K	Clark Elizabeth M—†	150	housewife	33	92 "
	L	*Clark Thomas W	150	clerk	35	92 "
	M	Goodwin Etta—†	150	housewife	61	4 Saratoga pl
	N	Murphy Violet—†	150	"	33	4 "
	O	Murphy William M	150	roofer	40	4 "
	P	McGuiness Francis	150	laborer	31	here
	R	McGuiness Mary A—†	150	housewife	52	"
	S	McGuiness William	150	leatherworker	28	"
	T	Fitzpatrick James F	152	engineer	63	"
	U	Marmaud Francis B	152	laborer	43	273 Lexington
	V	Marmaud Frederick F	152	retired	76	273 "
	W	Marmaud Rebecca A—†	152	housewife	66	273 "
	X	Ohlson Anna C—†	153	clerk	45	here
	Y	Vaglia Alfred	153	cashier	50	"

Page.	Letter.	Full Name.	Residence, Jan. 1, 1938.	Occupation.	Supposed Age.	Reported Residence, Jan. 1, 1937. Street and Number.

Lexington Street—Continued

Page.	Letter.	Full Name.	Residence, Jan. 1, 1938.	Occupation.	Supposed Age.	Reported Residence, Jan. 1, 1937. Street and Number.
	z	*Dillon Clifford	154	steward	33	here
603						
	A	*Dillon Georgia—†	154	housewife	33	"
	B	Nalen Anthony W	154	clerk	35	"
	C	Nalen Gertrude M—†	154	housewife	27	"
	D	Nichols George W	154	clerk	68	
	E	Nichols Mary E—†	154	housewife	63	"
	F	*Ahearn Abraham	156	fishcutter	28	"
	G	Ahearn Theresa—†	156	housewife	21	"
	H	*Chiffilo Frank	156	fishcutter	44	"
	K	O'Meara Hattie M—†	156	housewife	39	"
	L	O'Meara Michael H	156	pipefitter	40	"
	M	Rollins Charles A	156	retired	75	152 Lexington
	O	Bickley Elfrida—†	157	housewife	32	here
	P	Bickley William W	157	laborer	35	Connecticut
	R	*Doucette Edward	157	musician	42	here
	S	Gillette Louise—†	157	housewife	28	"
	T	Mulcahy Albert B	157	laborer	23	"
	U	*Mulcahy Mary—†	157	housewife	53	"
	V	*Ramirez Lena—†	158	"	60	"
	W	Ramirez Leo	158	floorlayer	60	"
	X	Ramirez Sally—†	158	bookkeeper	32	"
	Y	Ramirez Salvatore	158	draftsman	28	"
	Z	Ramirez Theresa—†	158	dressmaker	27	"
604						
	A	DeSimone Helen—†	159	clerk	21	
	B	DeSimone Joseph	159	butcher	45	"
	C	DeSimone Louise—†	159	clerk	24	
	D	DeSimone Mary—†	159	housewife	45	"
	E	Pagliuca Caroline—†	162	"	24	"
	F	Pagliuca Gerald	162	physician	32	Medford
	G	Pignotti John	162	tailor	47	here
	H	*Pignotti Olympia—†	162	housewife	39	"
	K	Fuccillo Carlo	162	candymaker	52	"
	L	*Fuccillo Carmella—†	162	housewife	74	"
	M	Fuccillo Carmella—†	162	"	44	
	N	Muto Michael	163	blacksmith	38	"
	O	Nota Angelo	163	finisher	48	"
	P	Nota Anna—†	163	stitcher	48	
	R	*Nota Josephine—†	163	housewife	44	"
	S	*D'Entremont Eli	163	fishcutter	39	"

Page.	Letter.	Full Name.	Residence, Jan. 1, 1938.	Occupation.	Supposed Age.	Reported Residence, Jan. 1, 1937. Street and Number.

Lexington Street—Continued

	T	*D'Entremont Exilda—†	163	housewife	33	here
	U	*LeBlanc Edward	163	fishcutter	45	"
	V	*Daley Clement	164	fisherman	31	254 Saratoga
	W	*Daley Gertrude—†	164	housewife	35	254 "
	X	*Clare Annie—†	164	"	52	249 Lexington
	Y	Clare John	164	fish handler	56	249 "
	Z	DeSisto Alice—†	164	operator	23	here
605						
	A	DeSisto Joseph	164	U S N	24	
	B	*Pavone Prisco	164	laborer	52	
	C	*Pavone Rose—†	164	housewife	49	"
	D	Brown Edna—†	165	stenographer	33	"
	E	Brown Sabine—†	165	housekeeper	65	"
	F	Oxley Emma L—†	165	waitress	59	
	H	White Mary—†	167	housewife	23	"
	K	White Thomas	167	carpenter	27	"
	L	*Servata Leo	167	shoemaker	55	"
	M	*Servata Rose—†	167	housewife	53	"
	N	Piro Joseph	170	chauffeur	33	21 Shrimpton
	O	Piro Mary—†	170	housewife	24	21 "
	P	*Ferrara Anthony	170	retired	70	here
	R	Ferrara Anthony B	170	electrician	35	"
	S	Ferrara Joseph	170	laundryman	35	"
	T	*Stoico Anthony	170	laborer	26	149 Saratoga
	U	Stoico Theresa—†	170	housewife	29	here
	V	Sullivan Edward	170	chauffeur	33	"
	W	Sullivan Rose—†	170	wrapper	26	"
	X	Theodore Michelina—†	170	housewife	25	38 Sumner
	Y	Theodore Nicolo	170	seaman	44	50 Border
	Z	Buckley Dennis	171	watchman	63	here
606						
	A	Buckley Dennis, jr	171	attendant	22	"
	A[1]	Buckley John L	171	watchman	25	"
	B	Buckley Joseph D	171	clerk	29	
	C	Ferullo Carrie—†	173	housewife	28	"
	D	Ferullo Michael	173	expressman	32	"
	E	Viglione Anthony	173	tailor	30	
	F	Viglione Josephine—†	173	housewife	24	"
	G	*Mirabelo Antonio	173	laborer	47	
	H	*Mirabelo Antonio, jr	173	barber	23	
	K	*Mirabelo Gasparina—†	173	housewife	41	"

Page.	Letter.	Full Name.	Residence, Jan. 1, 1938.	Occupation.	Supposed Age.	Reported Residence, Jan. 1, 1937. Street and Number.
		Lexington Street—Continued				
	L	Anthes Naomi—†	174	housewife	36	here
	M	Anthes Philip E	174	clergyman	37	"
	N	Spack David	174	storekeeper	50	"
	O	*Spack Ida—†	174	housewife	47	"
	P	Golden Catherine—†	174	"	47	
	R	Golden James D	174	chauffeur	47	"
	S	McGoldrick John	174	retired	70	
	T	Jackson Laura—†	176	housewife	63	"
	U	Jackson William H	176	meatcutter	56	"
	V	Smith Jane—†	177	housewife	57	"
	W	Smith William	177	banker	67	
	X	Hansen Edwin	178	chauffeur	23	"
	Y	Hansen Esther—†	178	bookkeeper	20	"
	Z	Hansen Niles	178	rigger	59	
607						
	A	*Hansen Olga—†	178	housewife	46	"
	B	Beamish Florence—†	179	seamstress	35	"
	C	Murphy Bertha R—†	179	housewife	54	"
	D	Murphy George	179	draftsman	66	"
	E	Laurano Anthony	179	chauffeur	46	"
	F	Laurano Catherine—†	179	student	20	
	G	Laurano Rita—†	179	housewife	42	"
	H	*Crowley Agnes—†	179	"	38	166 Putnam
	K	*Crowley William	179	carpenter	48	166 "
	L	*Fusco Mary—†	180	housewife	45	194 Maverick
	M	*Fusco Ralph	180	laborer	46	194 "
	N	Burke Felix	182	meatcutter	42	here
	O	Burke Helen—†	182	housewife	37	"
	P	DeEntremont Rita—†	184	clerk	29	"
	R	*Trahan Angelina—†	184	housewife	43	"
	S	Trahan John	184	carpenter	39	"
	T	*Trahan Mary—†	184	housewife	69	"
	U	*Melchionda Angelo	185	cutter	46	208 Lexington
	V	*Melchionda Louise—†	185	housewife	40	208 "
	W	Melchionda Michael	185	student	22	208 "
	X	*Casucci Caesar	185	carpenter	51	267 Havre
	Y	*Casucci Rose—†	185	housewife	49	267 "
	Z	Redman Mary—†	186	"	70	here
608						
	A	*Scimone Carmella—†	186	"	51	
	B	Scimone Frank	186	glazier	26	

Page.	Letter.	FULL NAME.	Residence, Jan. 1, 1938.	Occupation.	Supposed Age.	Reported Residence, Jan. 1, 1937. Street and Number.

Lexington Street—Continued

	C	Scimone Gasper	186	shipper	20	here
	D	*Scimone Joseph	186	laborer	54	"
	E	Hoffman John	187	engineer	55	"
	F	Swansburg Dora G—†	187	at home	55	
	G	Swansburg Edna J—†	187	"	44	
	H	Swansburg James	187	custodian	39	"
	K	Swansburg Margaret—†	187	housewife	83	"
	L	Vega Antonette—†	188	"	42	
	M	Vega Pasquale	188	laborer	47	
	N	*Peraino Margaret—†	188	housewife	50	"
	O	Sozio Josephine—†	188	"	30	
	P	Sozio Louis	188	printer	34	
	R	*Dexter Preston C	188	clerk	65	"
	S	Doane William B	188	fisherman	41	407 Saratoga
	T	Newhall James A	190	tailor	79	here
	U	Scott Annie L—†	190	housewife	74	"
	V	Masucci Amedo	191	laborer	23	"
	W	Masucci Anthony	191	retired	68	
	X	*Masucci Frances—†	191	housewife	60	"
	Y	Masucci Guido	191	stonecutter	31	"
	Z	Masucci Leonita—†	191	operator	28	"
609						
	A	Masucci Loretta—†	191	at home	26	
	B	Masucci Mary—†	191	nurse	30	"
	C	Masucci Mary—†	191	housewife	25	109 Liverpool
	D	Masucci Orlando	191	carpetlayer	29	here
	E	Licciardi Laura—†	191	housewife	25	226 Princeton
	F	Licciardi Oscar	191	machinist	27	226 "
	G	Powers Francis E	192	engineer	28	here
	H	Powers Mary F—†	192	housewife	26	"
	K	Shea Ambrose	192	carpenter	48	"
	L	*Shea Mary—†	192	housewife	38	"
	M	*Cohen Belle—†	193	"	23	Chelsea
	N	Cohen Joseph	193	storekeeper	32	"
	O	*Tusa Frank	193	carpenter	64	40 Chelsea
	P	*Tusa Rose—†	193	housewife	61	40 "
	R	Tusa Victor	193	woodcarver	28	40 "
	S	*Palidino Jennie—†	193	housewife	39	40 "
	T	Palidino Victor	193	barber	37	40 "
	U	DiFuria Anthony	194	mason	29	470 Sumner
	V	*DiFuria Marion—†	194	housewife	32	470 "

Page.	Letter.	Full Name.	Residence, Jan. 1, 1938.	Occupation.	Supposed Age.	Reported Residence, Jan. 1, 1937. Street and Number.

Lexington Street—Continued

Page.	Letter.	Full Name.	Residence, Jan. 1, 1938.	Occupation.	Supposed Age.	Reported Residence, Jan. 1, 1937. Street and Number.
	w	*Cardoza Gertrude—†	194	housewife	68	75 Morris
	x	Placet Adalina—†	194	"	29	75 "
	y	Placet Armando	194	laborer	28	75 "

610 Marion Street

Page.	Letter.	Full Name.	Residence, Jan. 1, 1938.	Occupation.	Supposed Age.	Reported Residence, Jan. 1, 1937. Street and Number.
610	c	*D'Amato Gaetano—†	53	stagehand	61	49 Eutaw
	d	D'Amato Josephin	53	housewife	59	49 "
	e	D'Amato Vincent	53	musician	23	49 "
	f	Holland Charles H	53	chef	59	here
	g	Holland Jennie G—†	53	housewife	48	"
	h	McCluskey Charles W	53	foundryworker	53	"
	k	*McCluskey Margaret—†	53	housewife	74	"
	l	George Manuel	55	laborer	64	
	m	Terry Anna—†	55	housewife	28	"
	n	*Terry Stephen	55	chauffeur	33	"
	o	Flanagan John	55	pressman	41	548 Benningt'n
	p	Coffin Ellen—†	57	housewife	67	here
	r	Coffin James	57	retired	72	"
	s	Coffin Margaret E—†	57	forewoman	26	"
	t	Kinnear Alice—†	57	saleswoman	57	"
	u	*Dahlroth Siama—†	59	housekeeper	45	233 Condor
	v	*Lindgram Emil	59	mechanic	50	233 "
	w	Canney Helen M—†	59	housekeeper	27	here
	x	Renberg Ann—†	59	clerk	25	"
	y	*Renberg John	59	longshoreman	57	"
	z	*Renberg Olga M—†	59	housewife	57	"
611						
	b	Walpole Margaret—†	61	houseworker	34	"
	c	Canney Helen M—†	61	housewife	27	"
	d	McWeeny Edward L	61	laborer	25	
	e	McWeeny Ella E—†	61	housewife	62	"
	f	McWeeny Harold J	61	glazier	30	
	g	Marden Clayton	63	operator	23	"
	h	Marden Mary—†	63	housewife	51	"
	k	Nickerson Ralph	63	fishcutter	26	"
	l	Nickerson Violet—†	63	housewife	26	"
	m	DeGiacomo Rose—†	63	houseworker	23	"
	n	Maffeo Antonio	63	laborer	62	
	o	*Maffeo Mary—†	63	housewife	48	"
	p	*Ceruldolo Marie—†	63	"	36	

Page.	Letter.	FULL NAME.	Residence, Jan. 1, 1938.	Occupation.	Supposed Age.	Reported Residence, Jan. 1, 1937. Street and Number.

Marion Street—Continued

	R	Ceruldolo Salvatore	63	laborer	42	here
	S	Atkins Annie T—†	65	housewife	51	"
	T	*Atkins Ervin L	65	fisherman	52	"
	U	*Calla Deana—†	65	housewife	54	"
	V	Calla Dominick	65	cashier	21	
	W	Calla Orlando	65	laborer	24	
	X	Calla Ernest	65	machinist	26	"
	Y	Calla Phyllis—†	65	housewife	25	33 Eutaw
	Z	McGinn Frances—†	67	"	38	49 Lexington
612						
	A	Porter Christian—†	67	mechanic	23	49 Eutaw
	B	Porter Grace—†	67	housewife	21	49 "
	C	Amaral Irene—†	67	houseworker	22	33 "
	D	Cox Joseph	67	laborer	50	33 '
	E	Cox Vincenza—†	67	housewife	49	33 "
	F	*Porcelli Elizabeth—†	69	"	35	here
	G	*Porcelli Joseph	69	laborer	41	"
	H	Salerno Annette—†	69	housewife	35	"
	K	Salerno Camillo	69	laborer	47	
	L	Celete Anna—†	69	housewife	42	"
	M	Celete Marion—†	69	student	20	
	N	*Celete Pasquale	69	laborer	60	
	O	Reppucci Claire—†	71	housewife	22	"
	P	Reppucci Joseph	71	foreman	25	
	R	*Salemme Lucy—†	71	housewife	37	"
	S	*Salemme Saverio	71	storekeeper	44	"
	T	Walsh Annie—†	75	houseworker	75	"
	U	Walsh Francis	75	finisher	32	
	V	Walsh Mary A—†	75	housekeeper	68	"
	W	Creamer Jeremiah	75	chauffeur	40	"
	X	Creamer Mary—†	75	housewife	34	"
	Y	Lawrence Emily—†	77	"	71	
	Z	Lawrence Louise V—†	77	dressmaker	43	"
613						
	A	Hunt James	77	painter	52	
	B	*Martin Mary—†	77	checker	58	
	C	Bourne Grace—†	79	teacher	62	
	D	Pote Leontine T—†	79	social worker	63	"
	E	Thompson Grace M—†	80	housewife	70	"
	F	Thompson Ruth H—†	80	bookkeeper	46	"
	G	Durbeck Nettie M—†	80	housewife	65	"

Page.	Letter.	Full Name.	Residence, Jan. 1, 1938.	Occupation.	Supposed Age.	Reported Residence, Jan. 1, 1937. Street and Number.

Marion Street—Continued

	H	Candeliere Lillian—†	82	housewife	36	here
	K	Candeliere Pasquale	82	laborer	34	"
	L	Candeliere Attilio F	82	boxmaker	29	"
	M	Candeliere Ettore	82	student	21	
	N	Candeliere Sarah—†	82	housewife	56	"
	P	Calla Albert	87	clerk	27	
	R	*Calla Angelina—†	87	housewife	50	"
	S	Calla Emma—†	87	houseworker	30	"
	T	*Calla John	87	candyworker	68	"
	U	Chapman Albert	90	watchman	44	82 Myrtle
	V	Noll Henry W	90	operator	56	27 Havre
	W	Osterle Bertha—†	98	housewife	60	here
	X	Osterle Frank	98	butcher	59	"
	Y	Halliday Ida E—†	98	housewife	76	"
	Z	*Cohen Abraham	100	retired	75	
614						
	A	*Cohen Rose—†	100	housewife	63	"
	B	Tarr Beatrice—†	100	"	29	
	C	Tarr Herman	100	chauffeur	31	"
	E	Cinelli James	102	fisherman	25	Cambridge
	F	Cinelli Rocco	102	wrapper	22	132 Marginal
	G	*Pasquariello Adelaide—†	102	housewife	45	here
	H	*Torrone Angelina—†	102	"	49	"
	K	*Torrone Anthony	102	candymaker	22	"
	L	Torrone John	102	clerk	24	
	M	Torrone Louis	102	candymaker	48	"
	N	Censullo Angelo	104	laborer	22	
	O	Censullo Frank	104	"	26	
	P	Censullo Rose—†	104	housewife	42	"
	R	Barry John	104	candymaker	27	"
	S	Barry Julia—†	104	housewife	47	"
	T	LeGrasse Antonio	104	laborer	43	41 Benningt'n
	U	LeGrasse Elizabeth—†	104	housewife	38	41 "
	V	Bolwell Verna F—†	106	"	43	here
	W	Reynolds Dana L	106	stockman	26	"
	X	Reynolds George L	106	retired	72	"
	Y	Reynolds Mary E—†	106	housewife	65	"
	Z	McArdle Elizabeth M—†	110	"	43	
615						
	A	McArdle James J	110	clerk	46	
	B	White James F	110	B F D	36	

Page.	Letter.	Full Name.	Residence, Jan. 1, 1938.	Occupation.	Supposed Age.	Reported Residence, Jan. 1, 1937. Street and Number.

Marion Street—Continued

	C	White Marguerite—†	110	housewife	33	here
	D	DeCristoforo Adeline—†	110	"	26	"
	E	DeCristoforo Americo	110	shipper	26	"
	F	Mannetta Anthony	110	beautician	38	36 Ashley
	G	Mannetta Eleanor—†	110	housewife	37	36 "
	H	Hart Patrick	112	laborer	58	here
	K	Murray Arthur	112	chauffeur	23	"
	L	Murray Hannah—†	112	housewife	59	"
	M	Murray John D	112	painter	64	
	N	Murray John L	112	laborer	34	
	O	Quinn James	112	"	45	
	P	Damelgo Frank L	112	bookkeeper	29	"
	R	Damelgo Josephine—†	112	housewife	46	"
	S	Shelley Harry D	112	baker	52	
	T	Bennett Henry	112	operator	45	
	U	Ford Daniel	112	carpenter	48	"
	V	*Ford Mary L—†	112	housewife	51	"

Meridian Street

	X	Amato Sebastian	306	tailor	47	here
	Y	Atkinson Fred B	306	seaman	55	"
	Z	Babbin Benjamin	306	laborer	70	"
616						
	A	Carlson Charles	306	"	68	78 Lexington
	B	Comeau William H	306	fishworker	52	153 Dorchester
	C	*Giffin S Etta—†	306	dressmaker	69	here
	D	*Giffin Livia—†	306	housekeeper	61	"
	E	Guthrie Edward S	306	retired	77	"
	F	Kenney Ray	306	laborer	58	
	G	McAllister Charles	306	seaman	45	
	H	Peacock William	306	bartender	47	"
	K	Smith Erland	306	seaman	45	
	L	Taylor Charles	306	"	51	
	M	Mitchell George	308	retired	85	
	N	Mullen Edward	308	laborer	44	
	O	Mullen Joseph	308	"	42	
	P	Walker Helen N—†	308	housewife	44	"
	R	Walker John J	308	carpenter	56	"
	T	Ferri Benjamin G	309A	seaman	28	
	U	Ferri Ernest	309A	plumber	38	

Page.	Letter.	FULL NAME.	Residence, Jan. 1, 1938.	Occupation.	Supposed Age.	Reported Residence, Jan. 1, 1937. Street and Number.

Meridian Street—Continued

Page.	Letter.	FULL NAME.	Residence, Jan. 1, 1938.	Occupation.	Supposed Age.	Reported Residence, Jan. 1, 1937. Street and Number.
	V	Ferri Jennie—†	309A	housewife	39	here
	W	*Repucci Concetta—†	309A	"	62	"
	X	Repucci George	309A	laborer	29	"
	Y	DeMarco Vincent	310	longshoreman	43	113 Havre
	Z	McMullen Margaret—†	310	at home	50	here
617						
	A	Lorizio Anna—†	310	packer	24	"
	B	Lorizio Anthony	310	bartender	26	"
	C	Lorizio Edith—†	310	operator	22	"
	D	Lorizio Emma—†	310	housewife	48	"
	E	Lorizio James	310	cook	47	
	F	Lorizio Joseph	310	clerk	20	
	G	Lorizio Vito	310	shoeworker	27	"
	H	Bransfield William	311	retired	68	46 Cameron
	K	Eldridge Frank	311	policeman	48	55 Chaucer
	L	Feeley Alfred F	311	fisherman	30	here
	M	Feeley Caroline C—†	311	housewife	68	"
	N	Feeley Elizabeth C—†	311	clerk	26	"
	O	Feeley James P	311	retired	71	
	P	Quinlan Sophie—†	311	at home	71	
	R	Bulger Augustine J	312	dentist	70	
	S	Bulger Esther A—†	312	at home	35	
	T	Jenkins Loyal L	312	dentist	60	
	U	Kiley Claire B—†	312	housewife	40	"
	V	Kiley Harry F	312	clerk	43	
	X	Kennedy Matthew H	313A	chauffeur	36	"
	Y	Lovett Eva F—†	313A	at home	41	
	Z	Lovett Sarah A—†	313A	"	76	
618						
	A	McLaughlin James	313A	meatcutter	42	"
	B	*O'Hanley Agnes—†	314	housewife	32	"
	C	*O'Hanley Roy	314	welder	29	"
	D	Fatkin Mary E—†	314	at home	80	19 Trenton
	E	*LeBlanc Delia—†	314	housewife	24	Canada
	F	LeBlanc Edward	314	fishcutter	23	"
	H	Ankenbauer Irma M—†	315	secretary	29	Ohio
	G	Ankenbauer Mary T—†	315	at home	64	"
	K	Backman Wesley	315	electrician	38	here
	L	Boyd Avery L	315	retired	72	"
	M	Boyd James A	315	clerk	43	"
	N	McDonald Elizabeth O—†	315	housewife	39	"

Page.	Letter.	Full Name.	Residence, Jan. 1, 1938.	Occupation.	Supposed Age.	Reported Residence, Jan. 1, 1937. Street and Number.

Meridian Street—Continued

	O	McDonald Henry F	315	B F D	39	here
	P	Murphy John W	315	repairman	39	"
	S	Fife Frances R—†	317	housewife	54	"
	T	Fife John E	317	painter	22	
	U	Fife John W	317	guard	55	
	V	Fife Mary F—†	317	operator	25	
	W	Higgins Joseph H	319	salesman	32	"
	X	McKillop Catherine—†	319	housewife	61	"
	Y	McKillop William G	319	laborer	39	
	Z	Whalen Margaret—†	319	at home	69	
619						
	B	Furlong Mary M—†	323	"	25	
	C	Furlong Michael P	323	laborer	52	
	D	Furlong Mildred—†	323	saleswoman	22	"
	G	Rose Mary—†	326	housewife	25	332 Meridian
	H	Campbell John F	326	shipper	49	here
	K	Tino Antonio	326	cook	29	"
	L	Tino Dominic	326	clerk	21	"
	M	Tino Frank	326	porter	54	
	N	*Tino Mary—†	326	housewife	56	"
	O	Tino Virginia—†	326	"	29	
	P	Repucci Joseph	326	roofer	36	
	R	Repucci Lillian—†	326	housewife	30	"
	S	Moore Charles V, jr	328	electrician	27	"
	T	Moore Ruth M—†	328	housewife	25	"
	U	*Burridge Emma—†	328	"	56	
	V	*Burridge Henry	328	carpenter	58	"
	W	*Maragioglio Gasparina–†	328	housewife	47	"
	X	Maragioglio Josephine–†	328	tailoress	23	"
	Y	Maragioglio Stefano	328	laborer	54	"
	Z	Blaquiere Francis P	330	chauffeur	28	35 Ashley
620						
	A	Blaquiere Lillian—†	330	stitcher	21	Chelsea
	B	*Cameron David E	330	laborer	30	31A Lexington
	C	Coulon Albert	330	operator	28	here
	D	Coulon Eugene	330	"	41	"
	E	Doyle Frank A	330	shipper	32	"
	F	*Doyle William O	330	surveyor	26	"
	G	Ford Frank F	330	electrician	37	"
	H	Ford Percy E	330	cook	41	
	K	*Sinclair Susie C—†	330	housewife	62	"

Page.	Letter.	Full Name.	Residence, Jan. 1, 1938.	Occupation.	Supposed Age.	Reported Residence, Jan. 1, 1937. Street and Number.

Meridian Street—Continued

Page.	Letter.	Full Name.	Residence, Jan. 1, 1938.	Occupation.	Supposed Age.	Reported Residence, Jan. 1, 1937. Street and Number.
	L	Sinclair Whit T	330	carpenter	74	here
	N	*Censullo Jennie—†	332	housewife	39	“
	O	Censullo Peter	332	laborer	50	“
	P	Tortorici Alice—†	332	housewife	24	138 Adams
	R	Tortorici William	332	packer	30	138 “
	S	Simonian Agnes—†	333	housewife	48	here
	T	Simonian Kane	333	accountant	25	“
	U	Simonian Whynott	333	storekeeper	27	“
	V	*McGray Dorcas—†	334	housewife	48	“
	W	McGray Avard T	334	seaman	22	
	X	McGray Charles A	334	fireman	55	
	Y	Melanson Raymond	334	seaman	22	
	Z	*Theriault Elsie—†	334	housewife	35	“
621						
	A	Theriault Joseph	334	carpenter	37	“
	B	Porras Margaret—†	334	housewife	38	101 Leverett
	C	Porras Perfecto	334	cook	49	101 “
	D	Rizzuto Margaret—†	334	at home	71	101 “
	E	Wyner Anna L—†	335	housewife	23	here
	F	Wyner James J	335	laborer	28	“
	K	Simpson Maria—†	335	“	73	“
	G	Simpson Matthew, jr	335	waiter	35	“
	H	Simpson Matthew K	335	machinist	55	“
	L	Krafve William	336	seaman	33	“
	M	Robicheau Zacharie	336	“	56	
	N	Moore Helen F—†	336	housewife	36	“
	O	Moore John R	336	painter	40	
	P	*Nunes Frank	336	barber	26	“
	R	*Nunes Hector	336	retired	56	
	S	*Nunes Mina—†	336	housewife	57	“
	T	Bogasian Armen	337	student	28	
	U	Bogasian Kazar	337	clerk	31	
	V	Bogosian Marian—†	337	“	27	
	W	Bogosian Mary—†	337	housewife	49	“
	X	Bogosian Paul	337	tailor	60	
	Y	Fawcett Dorothy—†	338	housewife	30	“
	Z	Fawcett John J	338	chauffeur	33	“
622						
	A	Domegan John	338	fishcutter	24	“
	B	Domegan Mary—†	338	housewife	32	“
	C	Domegan Patrick	338	laborer	54	

Page.	Letter.	Full Name.	Residence, Jan. 1, 1938.	Occupation.	Supposed Age.	Reported Residence, Jan. 1, 1937. Street and Number.

Meridian Street—Continued

Page.	Letter.	Full Name.	Residence, Jan. 1, 1938.	Occupation.	Supposed Age.	Reported Residence, Jan. 1, 1937. Street and Number.
	D	Domegan Thomas	338	laborer	30	here
	E	Domegan Winifred—†	338	housewife	50	"
	G	*Lasalla Isabelle—†	338	at home	23	26 Trenton
	F	*McDonald Andrew	338	clerk	25	26 "
	H	McDonald Luke	338	operator	26	26 "
	K	*McDonald Mary—†	338	housewife	48	26 "
	L	Ranahan Alice—†	339	"	42	here
	M	Ranahan William	339	longshoreman	41	"
	N	McCormick Anna—†	339	housewife	37	"
	O	McCormick Joseph	339	wool handler	48	"
	P	Poirier Charles	340	engineer	42	
	R	Poirier Isaura—†	340	housewife	39	"
	S	Forte James	340	laborer	26	75 Neptune rd
	T	*Forte Jennie—†	340	housewife	62	75 "
	U	Forte Michael	340	dyemaker	22	75 "
	V	Forte Paul	340	laborer	29	75 "
	W	Hanley John A	340	operator	43	here
	X	Hanley Mary C—†	340	housewife	40	"
623						
	A	*Amero Lena—†	342	"	32	34 Trenton
	B	Amero William	342	carpenter	41	34 "
	C	Bryant Gertrude R—†	342	housewife	26	here
	D	Bryant William C	342	laborer	29	"
	E	McCluskey Eleanor—†	342	operator	21	"
	G	Peterson Emery	345	coppersmith	37	"
	H	Peterson Phyllis—†	345	waitress	36	
	K	Bozza Josephine—†	345	housewife	31	"
	L	Bozza Michael	345	barber	35	
	M	Crescy Catherine—†	347	housewife	27	"
	N	Crescy Herbert	347	seaman	35	
	O	*Cavalieri Joseph	347	laborer	50	
	P	*Cavalieri Rose—†	347	housewife	38	"
	R	*Chiarello Annie—†	347	"	55	233 Chelsea
	S	Chiarello Frank	347	tailor	21	233 "
	T	*Chiarello Peter	347	laborer	57	233 "
	U	*Lavangie Charles	349	shipper	52	here
	V	Lavangie Mary—†	349	housewife	53	"
	W	Loomer Dorothy—†	349	clerk	35	"
	X	*Clericuzio Gloriano	349½	laborer	47	145 Princeton
	Y	*Clericuzio Mary—†	349½	housewife	44	145 "
	Z	Sciacca Anna M—†	349½	cutter	26	here

Page.	Letter.	Full Name.	Residence, Jan. 1, 1938.	Occupation.	Supposed Age.	Reported Residence, Jan. 1, 1937. Street and Number.
624		**Meridian Street**—Continued				
	A	*Sciacca John	349½	tailor	63	here
	B	*Sciacca Josephine—†	349½	housewife	54	"
	C	Sciacca Millie—†	349½	operator	24	"
	D	Dingley Ada Mae—†	351	housewife	52	"
	E	Dingley Albert F	351	seaman	50	"
	F	Campbell Helen A—†	351	housewife	34	"
	G	Campbell Robert L	351	locksmith	41	"
		Princeton Street				
	K	*Eld Marie—†	80	cook	60	here
	L	Morrison Almira E—†	80	at home	78	"
	M	Morrison Jean E—†	80	"	49	"
	O	Cashman Laura—†	94	milliner	51	
	P	Cashman Phoebe—†	94	at home	81	
	R	Cashman Thomas	94	retired	84	
	S	Sanderson Caroline—†	96	at home	88	
	T	Tedford Minnie—†	96	"	56	"
	U	Bradley Alice—†	98	housewife	38	"
	V	Bradley Frederick	98	chauffeur	40	"
	W	Crawford Myron	98	operator	41	"
	X	Crawford Ruth A—†	98	housewife	40	"
625						
	A	*Serrapica Celia—†	102	"	44	
	B	*Serrapica Sebastian	102	baker	52	
	C	Asci Filippo	104	longshoreman	40	"
	D	Asci Vincenza—†	104	housewife	40	"
	E	*Caravella Lorenza—†	104	at home	82	
	F	Cerullo Gabriel	104	laborer	21	
	G	*Cerullo Mary—†	104	housewife	59	"
	H	Cerullo Mary—†	104	operator	22	"
	K	*Cerullo Nicholas	104	laborer	60	
	L	*Grant Mary—†	104	housewife	35	"
	M	Grant Nathan S	104	shipper	33	
	N	Rolfe Alberta—†	106	nurse	66	
	O	Towlson Agnes—†	106	housewife	24	"
	P	Towlson Lester	106	chauffeur	25	"
	R	Chiappa Frederick	108	cutter	40	
	S	Chiappa Nellie—†	108	housewife	34	"
	T	D'Amico Louise—†	108	"	35	

Page.	Letter.	Full Name.	Residence, Jan. 1, 1938.	Occupation.	Supposed Age.	Reported Residence, Jan. 1, 1937. Street and Number.

Princeton Street—Continued

Page.	Letter.	Full Name.	Residence, Jan. 1, 1938.	Occupation.	Supposed Age.	Reported Residence, Jan. 1, 1937. Street and Number.
	U	*Asci Diomira—†	110	housewife	36	here
	V	Asci Gaetano	110	engineer	45	“
	W	Castruci Biagio	110	ironworker	47	“
	X	Taurono Angelo	110	shoeworker	39	“
	Y	*D'Andrew Andrew	110	laborer	44	
	Z	*D'Andrew Olympia—†	110	housewife	41	“
626						
	A	Sofia Ernest	110	laborer	22	
	B	Bochner Gordon W	112	cutter	48	
	C	Bochner Minnie C—†	112	housewife	47	“
	D	Wallace Gladys M—†	112	clerk	28	
	E	Wallace James E	112	painter	33	
	F	Cordiner Annie—†	112	beautician	59	“
	G	Malanson George L	112	bartender	55	“
	H	Malanson Madelon—†	112	housewife	47	“
	K	Bassett Florence—†	114	“	51	
	L	Bassett Herbert	114	clerk	53	
	M	Bassett Merrill	114	“	22	
	N	Raymond John	116	laborer	51	
	O	Raymond Mary—†	116	housewife	47	“
	P	Hannon Edmund F	116	longshoreman	20	“
	R	Hannon Edward F	116	stevedore	43	“
	S	Hannon Gertrude—†	116	housewife	40	“
	T	Muttart George M	118	physician	74	“
	U	Brown John	118	machinist	43	“
	V	Hanson Einar	118	painter	34	
	W	Robertson Ella W—†	118	housekeeper	65	“
	X	Snow Albert C	120	laborer	56	“
	Y	Tyrar Charles H	120	operator	39	
	Z	Tyrar Dorothy—†	120	presser	32	
627						
	A	Tyrar Joseph E	120	laborer	37	
	B	Tyrar Lettie J—†	120	at home	63	
	C	Russell Clara—†	124	“	70	
	D	Waltman Blanche—†	124	housewife	40	“
	E	Waltman Carl	124	machinist	38	“
	F	*Matsolo Salvatore	126	retired	63	
	K	Scarmella Girolamo	126	laborer	60	
	G	Tritto Frank	126	operator	48	“
	H	*Tritto Mary—†	126	housewife	37	“
	L	Ceresi Angelo	126	pressman	52	“

Page.	Letter.	Full Name.	Residence, Jan. 1, 1938.	Occupation.	Supposed Age.	Reported Residence, Jan. 1, 1937. Street and Number.

Princeton Street—Continued

	M	Ceresi Anthony	126	laborer	23	here
	N	Ceresi Joseph	126	"	24	"
	O	Ceresi Justine—†	126	housekeeper	43	"
	P	Ceresi Salvatore	126	seaman	21	"
	R	Salonen Gustave	128	electrician	33	41 White
	S	Salonen Martha—†	128	housewife	35	41 "
	T	McNamara John	128	laborer	21	here
	U	Powell Mary E—†	128	housewife	71	"
	V	Powell Robert H	128	retired	72	"
	W	Cotter Catherine L—†	128	housewife	28	56 Marion
	X	Cotter Frederick	128	laborer	34	56 "
	Y	*Ciampi Frederick	130	beautician	49	here
	Z	*Ciampi Mary—†	130	housewife	44	"
628						
	A	Mazzolla Mary—†	130	"	23	75 Cottage
	B	Mazzolla Michael	130	operator	30	90 Bennington
	E	Gushue Bridget—†	142	housewife	45	here
	F	Gushue Gerald	142	machinist	21	"
	G	Boudreau Bander	144	fisherman	38	"
	H	*Boudreau Violet—†	144	housewife	26	"
	K	Landry Irene—†	144	"	33	
	L	Landry Wilfred	144	engineer	34	
	M	Boudreau Joseph B	146	"	40	
	N	Boudreau Mary A—†	146	housewife	38	"
	O	Goyetche Emma—†	146	operator	30	"
	P	Sampson Edith B—†	146	housewife	38	"
	R	Sampson Leo W	146	machinist	47	"
	S	Driscoll Florence J—†	148	at home	63	
	T	Driscoll John	148	retired	60	"
	U	Driscoll Margaret E—†	148	at home	48	"
	V	Lenoce Domenic	150	foreman	48	153 Putnam
	W	Lenoce Nunzia—†	150	housewife	42	153 "
	X	Socci Anna—†	150	at home	20	here
	Y	*Socci Lucy—†	150	housewife	50	157 Putnam
	Z	Socci Paul	150	pressman	27	153 "
629						
	A	Socci Stephen	150	laborer	50	153 "
	B	DeMartini John	150	metalworker	37	here
	C	DeMartini Vincent	150	butcher	41	"
	D	*Giannattasio Angelina-†	150	housewife	40	"
	E	Giannattasio Antonio	150	upholsterer	44	"

Page.	Letter.	Full Name.	Residence, Jan. 1, 1938.	Occupation.	Supposed Age.	Reported Residence, Jan. 1, 1937. Street and Number.

Princeton Street—Continued

	F	Harrington Mary—†	150	at home	84	here
	G	Katz Harry C	150	salesman	52	"
	H	*DePietro Lucy—†	154	at home	52	"
	K	*DePietro Rocco	154	laborer	52	
	L	DePietro Rose—†	154	at home	22	
	M	*McGrath Jennie—†	154	housewife	27	"
	N	*McGrath William	154	fisherman	38	"
	O	*Martin Elizabeth—†	154	housewife	55	159 Benningt'n
	P	Martin Lawrence	154	fisherman	56	159 "
	R	Papeo Frank	158	teacher	44	here
	S	*Papeo Matilda—†	158	housewife	45	"
	T	Tonon Livia—†	158	social worker	32	"
	U	*Tonon Pasqua—†	158	at home	58	
	V	Bluhm Morris	160	finisher	62	
	W	Bluhm Philip	160	chauffeur	27	"
	X	Bluhm Rita—†	160	housewife	20	1447 Blue Hill av
	Y	Dobbins Ernest	166	cutter	22	here
	Z	Dobbins Margaret—†	166	housewife	21	"
630						
	A	Argot Frank	166	cook	64	
	B	Bennett Mary—†	166	housewife	45	"
	C	Bennett Peter	166	engineer	53	
	D	Timmons Edward	166	fisherman	39	"
	E	Gracie Julius	168	"	52	
	F	Gracie Mary—†	168	housewife	51	"
	G	Bluhm Julia—†	168	"	24	
	H	Bluhm Solomon	168	salesman	30	"
	K	Cordeau Henry	168	retired	79	
	L	Sampson Alfred N	168	engineer	63	
	M	Sampson Mary—†	168	housewife	50	"
	N	Crocker Walter	172	expressman	31	"
	O	Ekman Carl	172	fisherman	44	"
	P	Erskine Thelma—†	172	housewife	49	"
	R	Erskine Walter	172	engineer	49	
	S	Hemenway Annie—†	172	operator	49	"
	T	Hogan Doris—†	172	waitress	22	
	U	Magnesson John	172	fisherman	45	"
	V	O'Neil Harold	172	laborer	44	
	W	O'Neil William	172	"	30	
	X	Reddey Edward	172	seaman	52	
	Y	*Mackillop Neil	174	fisherman	36	"

Page.	Letter.	Full Name.	Residence, Jan. 1, 1938.	Occupation.	Supposed Age.	Reported Residence, Jan. 1, 1937. Street and Number.

Princeton Street—Continued

	z	Wild James	174	machinist	34	here
631						
	A*	Wild Jessie—†	174	housewife	32	"
	B	Rake Charles	174	operator	35	"
	C	Rake John, jr	174	chauffeur	37	"
	D	Rake John L	174	laborer	68	
	E	Zuccarino Rocco	176	"	40	
	F*	Zuccarino Thomasina—†	176	housewife	42	"
	G	Mazzarino Paulina—†	176	"	46	
	H	Mazzarino Sebastian	176	operator	48	"
	K	DiMunzio Amelia—†	178	housewife	23	"
	L	DiMunzio Clement	178	cutter	28	
	M	Blasi Angelina—†	178	housewife	69	"
	N	Blasi Michael	178	laborer	71	
	O	Nappi Armando	178	"	31	
	P	Nappi Mary—†	178	housewife	31	"
	R	Katz Abraham	180	manager	23	"
	S*	Katz Annie—†	180	housewife	58	"
	T	Katz Frances—†	180	at home	21	
	U	Katz Irving	180	attorney	29	"
	V	Katz Lillian—†	180	at home	27	
	W*	Katz Max	180	retired	60	
	X	Katz Sadie—†	180	saleswoman	24	"
	Y	Mitchell Cora—†	180	housekeeper	34	Medford
	Z*	DeFilippo Joseph	182	cutter	42	here
632						
	A*	DeFilippo Rita—†	182	housewife	38	"
	B	Cordeau Ada—†	182	"	32	
	C	Cordeau Arthur	182	ironworker	39	"
	D	Cipriano Carmella—†	184	housewife	26	"
	E*	Cipriano Pasquale	184	laborer	29	
	F	Salzo Arline—†	184	operator	24	"
	G*	Salzo Concordia—†	184	housewife	49	"
	H	Salzo Flora—†	184	operator	22	
	K	Salzo John	184	laborer	21	
	L*	Salzo Nicholas	184	"	57	
	M*	Babine Earl	186	chauffeur	27	"
	N	Babine Margaret—†	186	housewife	28	"
	O	Caplan Abraham N	186	physician	36	"
	P	Stone Daniel F	186	chauffeur	22	"

Page.	Letter.	Full Name.	Residence, Jan. 1, 1938.	Occupation.	Supposed Age.	Reported Residence, Jan. 1, 1937. Street and Number.

Princeton Street—Continued

Page.	Letter.	Full Name.	Residence, Jan. 1, 1938.	Occupation.	Supposed Age.	Reported Residence, Jan. 1, 1937. Street and Number.
	R	*Boudreau Alice—†	190	housewife	62	here
	S	Boudreau Arcade	190	carpenter	64	"
	T	Boudreau Marie—†	190	stenographer	30	"

Putnam Street

Page.	Letter.	Full Name.	Residence, Jan. 1, 1938.	Occupation.	Supposed Age.	Reported Residence, Jan. 1, 1937. Street and Number.
	U	Melanson Georgina—†	87	housewife	27	here
	V	Melanson Joseph E	87	diver	33	"
	W	*Melanson Mary A—†	87	housewife	66	"
	X	*Melanson Thomas	87	carpenter	72	"
	Y	*Fernandes John	87	longshoreman	57	"
	Z	Fernandes John, jr	87	clerk	25	
633						
	A	*Fernandes Lucy—†	87	housewife	23	"
	B	Fernandes Manuel	87	fishworker	20	"
	C	*Fernandes Marie R—†	87	housewife	57	"
	D	*Portella Anthony	87	ironworker	41	"
	E	Portella Mary—†	87	housewife	31	"
	F	O'Neill Abraham J	87	seaman	28	
	G	O'Neill Arthur J	87	laborer	22	
	H	O'Neill Mary A—†	87	housewife	51	"
	K	O'Neill William P	87	laborer	60	
	L	Ferande Frank	89	entertainer	40	"
	M	Finamore Antoinette—†	89	housewife	37	"
	N	Finamore Gaetano	89	electrician	46	"
	O	*Simonelli Rosilda—†	89	housewife	76	"
	P	*Panteleeff Natalia—†	91	"	70	
	R	*Panteleeff Nicola	91	operator	66	"
	S	Giardina Mickelina—†	91	housewife	34	"
	T	Giardina Vincenzo	91	laborer	46	
	U	Daddieco Anthony	107	foreman	33	
	V	Daddieco Laura—†	107	housewife	27	"
	W	Banks Ellen P—†	107	"	73	
	X	Banks Ellen V—†	107	secretary	48	"
	Y	Forlenza Clara—†	109	housewife	32	108 Putnam
	Z	Forlenza Mario	109	pedler	33	108 "
634						
	A	Denehy Alice—†	111	housewife	29	here
	B	Denehy Henry J	111	chauffeur	32	"

Page.	Letter.	FULL NAME.	Residence, Jan. 1, 1938.	Occupation.	Supposed Age.	Reported Residence, Jan. 1, 1937. Street and Number.

Trenton Street

	D	Coffin Mary E—†	4	at home	72	here
	E	Indingaro Thomas	4	waiter	38	"
	F	Lynch James E	4	retired	67	"
	G	Morgan Annie L—†	4	at home	70	
	H	O'Hara Arthur	4	chauffeur	21	"
	K	O'Hara Ronald	4	"	20	"
	L	Drew Ora—†	4	at home	45	
	M	Ricco Vincenzo	4	bricklayer	55	"
	N	Caruso Carmine	4	clerk	20	
	O	Caruso Frederick	4	shoemaker	45	"
	P	Caruso Marie—†	4	housewife	39	"
	R	*Scioscia Camille—†	4	dressmaker	26	"
	S	Santiano Grace—†	6	housewife	30	"
	T	Santiano Joseph	6	printer	33	
	U	Cuzzi Anthony N	6	cutter	29	
	V	Cuzzi Lucy—†	6	housewife	29	"
	W	Colbert Edward	6	laborer	22	
	X	Colbert Mary—†	6	housewife	49	"
	Y	Colbert Philip J	6	fisherman	38	"
	Z	Ryan Peter J	6	"	36	
635						
	A	*Curtis Michael	7	laborer	36	
	B	*Curtis Violet—†	7	housewife	35	"
	C	Delehanty James M—†	7	laborer	43	
	D	Delehanty Louise T—†	7	housewife	39	"
	E	Costigan Bernard	7	laborer	46	
	F	Costigan Mary—†	7	housewife	42	"
	G	Ciancuilli Liberto	9	mechanic	29	"
	H	Ciancuilli Margaret—†	9	housewife	28	"
	L	Materese Concetta—†	9	operator	20	
	M	*Materese Jennie—†	9	housewife	46	"
	N	Materese Mary—†	9	operator	22	"
	O	*Materese Michael	9	polisher	56	
	P	Powers John	11	fishcutter	34	"
	R	Powers Kathleen—†	11	housewife	32	"
	S	Powers Morris	11	scaler	36	"
	T	Dodge Charles G	11	operator	50	15 Trenton
	U	Dodge Lena M—†	11	housewife	49	15 "
	V	Dodge Lewis	11	laborer	20	15 "
	W	Burge George J	12	"	29	here
	X	Burge Margaret J—†	12	housewife	26	"

Page.	Letter.	Full Name.	Residence, Jan. 1, 1938.	Occupation.	Supposed Age.	Reported Residence, Jan. 1, 1937. Street and Number.

Trenton Street—Continued

	Y	Fawcett Elizabeth—†	12	housewife	60	here
	Z	Fawcett Patrick A	12	packer	23	"
636						
	A	Fawcett Richard N	12	retired	63	
	C	Simms Mary—†	15	at home	45	
	E	Gleason Michael	16	retired	78	
	H	Bailey Elizabeth—†	17	housewife	58	"
	F	Bailey Harry C	17	clerk	61	
	G	Bailey Harry C, jr	17	"	20	"
	K	Alves Caroline—†	18	housewife	23	334 Lexington
	L	Alves Napoleon	18	cook	25	334 "
	M	Ross May—†	18	at home	40	4 W Eagle
	N	Fougere Grace—†	18	housewife	27	67 Bennington
	O	Fougere Thomas A	18	scaler	33	67 "
	S	Winer Frances—†	20	housewife	26	here
	T	Winer George E	20	laborer	27	"
	U	DiCicco Evelyn—†	20	saleswoman	22	"
	V	DiCicco Helen—†	20	beautician	24	"
	W	*D'Errico Antoinette—†	20	housewife	46	"
	X	*D'Errico Tubio	20	laborer	55	
	Y	Lacoco Alfred	21	mechanic	27	"
	Z	Lacoco Josephine—†	21	housewife	23	"
637						
	A	Costantino Ann—†	21	at home	20	
	B	*Costantino Concetta—†	21	housewife	52	"
	C	Costantino Francesco	21	contractor	55	"
	D	Costantino Joseph	21	carpenter	24	"
	E	Costantino Matthew	21	laborer	22	
	F	Costantino Rose—†	21	operator	26	"
	G	*Pothier Jane—†	22	housewife	34	"
	H	Pothier Lawrence A	22	cutter	38	
	K	*Imbriano Lena—†	22	housewife	52	"
	L	Imbriano Margaret—†	22	packer	29	
	M	Imbriano Pasquale	22	candyworker	52	"
	N	Imbriano Ralph	22	dishwasher	21	"
	O	DiPaolo Margaret—†	22	housewife	23	339 North
	P	DiPaolo Pasquale	22	salesman	26	82 Havre
	R	Constantine Henry	24	longshoreman	26	here
	S	Constantine Louise—†	24	housewife	26	"
	T	Capodilupo Angelina—†	24	"	28	"
	U	Capodilupo Anthony	24	cook	33	

Page.	Letter.	Full Name.	Residence, Jan. 1, 1938.	Occupation.	Supposed Age.	Reported Residence, Jan. 1, 1937. Street and Number.

Trenton Street—Continued

	v	Capodilupo Peter	24	shoeworker	60	here
	w	Ciampolillo John R	24	machinist	47	"
	x	Ciampolillo Sarah—†	24	housewife	37	"
	y	Fitzgerald Anne A—†	26	stenographer	28	"
	z	Fitzgerald Bridget J—†	26	housewife	65	"
638						
	A	*German Hermeline—†	26	housewife	42	58 Eutaw
	B	*German Thomas	26	laborer	47	58 "
	D	Nichols Agnes—†	28	housewife	40	here
	E	Nichols John	28	welder	45	"
	F	O'Brien Marion—†	28	housewife	49	"
	G	O'Brien Mary—†	28	operator	22	
	H	O'Brien Patrick	28	laborer	46	
	K	Crosby Francis M	28	printer	45	
	L	Crosby Josephine—†	28	housewife	40	"
	M	Hamilton Phillip	28	retired	74	"
	N	Hamilton Phillip F, jr	28	mechanic	38	19 Dillingham
	O	Kincaide Richard	28	clerk	22	here
	P	Conners Mabel—†	30	housewife	42	40 Eutaw
	S	Conners Michael J	30	chauffeur	42	40 "
	R	Conners Mary H—†	30	housewife	35	here
	T	Conners Stephen E	30	chauffeur	38	"
	U	Napier John P	30	retired	64	"
	V	Foote Gertrude—†	32	operator	20	145 Falcon
	W	*Foote John	32	fisherman	48	145 "
	X	*Foote Mary D—†.	32	housekeeper	52	145 "
	Y	Gifford Mary E—†	32	housewife	69	here
	Z	Gifford Winfield W	32	engineer	64	"
639						
	A	*D'Eon Nathan	34	cutter	29	77 Trenton
	B	D'Eon Pauline—†	34	housewife	22	77 "
	C	Vega Emily—†	34	"	45	here
	D	Vega Pellegrino	34	laborer	49	"
	E	*Vega Carolina—†	34	housewife	35	"
	F	*Vega Domenic	34	laborer	32	
	G	Petre Alphonse	36	retired	60	
	H	Petre Mary—†	36	tailoress	24	
	K	Petre Rosa—†	36	housewife	50	"
	L	D'Eon Albert	36	painter	35	
	M	*D'Eon Ida—†	36	housewife	34	"
	O	*Della Grotta Emily—†	57	"	42	

Page.	Letter.	FULL NAME.	Residence, Jan. 1, 1938.	Occupation.	Supposed Age.	Reported Residence, Jan. 1, 1937. Street and Number.

Trenton Street—Continued

	P	Della Grotta Peter	57	painter	40	here
	R	*Santoro Carmella—†	57	housewife	59	"
	S	Santoro John	57	attorney	37	"
	T	Santoro Joseph	57	retired	65	
	U	Santoro Salvatore	57	laborer	23	
	V	Santoro Thomasina—†	57	teacher	34	
	W	Santoro Vincenza—†	57	operator	32	"
	X	Biancardi Virginia—†	61	"	26	
	Y	Picardi Amorino	61	shoeworker	35	"
	Z	Picardi Eva—†	61	housewife	33	"
640						
	A	Parziale Josephine—†	61	"	65	
	B	Parziale Lillian—†	61	at home	35	
	C	Parziale Louis	61	engineer	23	
	D	Parziale Luigi	61	bricklayer	68	"
	G	Richard Goldie—†	75	housewife	46	"
	H	Richard Maurice	75	grocer	48	
	K	Richard Stanley	75	clerk	21	"
	L	Sandquist Dorothy F—†	77	housewife	22	59 White
	M	Sandquist Eric J	77	pressman	24	59 "
	N	*Thibodeau Edward	77	cutter	67	here
	O	Thibodeau Joseph	77	"	26	"
	P	Thibodeau Lillian—†	77	at home	24	"
	R	*Thibodeau Nelsie—†	77	housewife	66	"
	S	Beattie Margaret I—†	77	at home	69	
	T	*Levenson Dora—†	81	housewife	62	"
	U	Levenson Ethel—†	81	clerk	24	
	V	Levenson George	81	student	22	
	W	Levenson Harry	81	shipper	27	
	X	Levenson Henry	81	salesman	29	"
	Y	*Levenson Joseph	81	retired	60	
	Z	Lomas Harry	85	policeman	40	"
641						
	A	Lomas Mildred—†	85	housewife	37	"
	B	Benson Helen—†	85	operator	24	"
	C	*Dafilo Manuel	85	engineer	57	"
	D	Dafilo Sarah J—†	85	housewife	57	"
	E	*Fraquela Manuel G	85	fireman	48	
	F	Bellino Agrippino	85	laborer	71	
	G	Bellino Josephine—†	85	dressmaker	36	"
	H	Bellino Lucia—†	85	housewife	65	"

Page.	Letter.	Full Name.	Residence, Jan. 1, 1938.	Occupation.	Supposed Age.	Reported Residence, Jan. 1, 1937. Street and Number.

Trenton Street—Continued

	K	DeLucia Amedio	87	tavernkeeper	50	here
	L	DeLucia Grace—†	87	housewife	49	"
	M	DeLucia Mary—†	87	at home	22	"
	N*	Hansen Fritz	87	laborer	51	
	O	Hansen Marie—†	87	housewife	54	"
	P*	Stoddard Evangeline—†	87	"	32	
	R*	Stoddard William	87	laborer	38	"
	S	McCully James	89	retired	81	33 W Eagle
	T	McCully Sarah—†	89	housewife	80	33 "
	U	Sullivan Anna G—†	89	at home	43	128 Brooks
	V	Sullivan Mary E—†	89	operator	53	128 "
	W	Gunn Medora C—†	89	at home	71	33 W Eagle
	X*	Thibodeau Augustine	91	painter	36	here
	Y*	Thibodeau Mary Ann—†	91	housewife	30	"
	Z	Delucia Benjamin	91	baker	23	"
642						
	A	Delucia John	91	baker	22	
	B*	Delucia Josephine—†	91	housewife	50	"
	C*	Delucia Leonard	91	shoemaker	54	"
	D	Migliore Anna—†	91	housewife	37	206 E Eagle
	E	Migliore Joseph	91	shoeworker	47	206 "
	F	Flynn Katherine T—†	93	clerk	52	here
	G	Greer Alice H—†	93	housewife	50	"
	H	Greer Frank B	93	guard	56	"
	L	Spencer Joseph E	95	laborer	24	
	M	Spencer Martha E—†	95	housewife	22	"
	N	Spencer Mary—†	95	waitress	20	
	O	Spencer Ruth—†	95	clerk	22	
	P	Langford Katherine—†	95	at home	38	
	R	McGlue Mary—†	95	housewife	48	"
	S	McGlue William	95	laborer	43	"
	T*	DeAmbrosio John	97	machinist	23	96 Sumner
	U	DeAmbrosio Mary—†	97	housewife	24	96 "
	V	Connolly Phyllis—†	97	"	29	here
	W	Connolly Thomas	97	machinist	30	"
	X	Welling Agnes—†	97	housekeeper	50	"
	Y	Airello Josephine—†	99	housewife	25	45 White
	Z	Airello Peter	99	musician	26	45 "
643						
	A	Letterie Nora—†	99	at home	21	here
	B	Letterie Philomena—†	99	housewife	41	"

Page.	Letter.	Full Name.	Residence, Jan. 1, 1938.	Occupation.	Supposed Age.	Reported Residence, Jan. 1, 1937. Street and Number.

Trenton Street—Continued

	c	Letterie Vincenzo	99	operator	49	here
	D	Giovino Anna—†	101	"	26	"
	E	Giovino Edward	101	shoeworker	29	"
	F	Corrado Esther—†	101	housewife	37	"
	G	Corrado John	101	chauffeur	42	"
	H	Giovino Armando	103	musician	26	"
	K	Giovino Concetta—†	103	clerk	24	
	L	*DeFeo Christne—†	103	housewife	50	"
	M	*DeFeo Eppolito	103	photographer	60	"
	N	DeFeo Ferdinand	103	laborer	24	"
	P	DeFeo Margaret—†	103	packer	24	
	O	DeFeo Michael	103	painter	29	
	S	Lewis Evelyn—†	107	clerk	22	
	T	Lewis George	107	salesman	55	"
	U	Lewis Gertrude—†	107	housewife	50	"
	V	Weinstein George	107	laborer	40	
	W	Weinstein Rachael—†	107	housewife	38	"
	X	Bona Daniel J	109	fisherman	36	89 Falcon
	Y	Bona Mildred—†	109	housewife	35	89 "
	Z	Viola Anthony	109	shoemaker	27	here
644						
	A	Viola Joseph	109	candymaker	56	"
	B	Viola Mary—†	109	housewife	45	"
	C	Logan Annie—†	111	at home	63	
	D	Logan Julia A—†	111	teacher	66	
	E	McCallum John E	111	painter	42	
	F	McCallum Josephine—†	111	housewife	39	"
	G	Gavagan Edward	113	lineman	38	
	H	Gavagan Mary—†	113	housewife	39	"
	K	Collins Dennis A	113	salesman	34	"
	L	Collins Jeremiah	113	retired	69	
	M	Collins John J	113	salesman	36	"
	N	Collins Charles J	113	clerk	32	
	O	Collins Thomas T	113	"	29	
	P	Lauricella Rose—†	115	housewife	25	"
	R	Lauricella Salvatore	115	salesman	25	"
	S	*Analoro Joseph	115	laborer	46	
	T	*Analoro Theresa—†	115	housewife	39	"
	U	Rossetti Albert F	115	foreman	35	64 Brooks
	V	Rossetti Rose—†	115	housewife	36	64 "
	X	Babin Edmund	117	cutter	67	here

Page.	Letter.	Full Name.	Residence, Jan. 1, 1938.	Occupation.	Supposed Age.	Reported Residence, Jan. 1, 1937. Street and Number.

Trenton Street—Continued

	Y	*Babin Elizabeth—†	117	housewife	58	here
	Z	*Babin Leamus	117	cutter	33	"
645						
	A	*Surette Augustine	117	"	27	"
	B	Gannon Leonard	117	surveyor	21	206 Saratoga
	C	Gannon Rose—†	117	at home	20	here
	D	Pius Peter	117	cutter	22	"
	E	*Capasso Eleanor—†	119	housewife	35	"
	F	Capasso Eugene	119	tailor	42	
	G	*Mallett Clara—†	119	housewife	40	"
	H	Mallett Ernest	119	fisherman	36	"
	K	*Avila Camillo	119	tailor	42	
	L	*Avila Rose—†	119	housewife	40	"
	M	*McLaughlin John	121	cutter	54	
	N	*McLaughlin Theresa—†	121	housewife	38	"
	O	*LaBlanc Eve	121	laborer	54	
	P	*LaBlanc Naomi—†	121	housewife	53	"
	R	*McCue Norman	121	fisherman	26	"
	S	*Murray Anna—†	121	housekeeper	66	"
	T	Ring Estella—†	121	housewife	38	"
	U	Ring James F	121	fisherman	46	"
	V	McDonald Archie	123	waiter	28	158 W Brookline
	W	McDonald Claire—†	123	housewife	28	158 "
	X	Nickerson Lester	123	seaman	27	63 Condor
	Y	Fioravanti Elizabeth—†	123	housewife	59	here
	Z	Fioravanti Fera	123	laborer	56	"
646						
	A	Casazza Deodato	125	shoeworker	37	"
	B	Casazza Victoria R—†	125	housewife	27	"
	C	Nevola Arthur	125	shoeworker	21	13 Central sq
	D	Nevola Carmella—†	125	housewife	20	385 Meridian
	E	Cuscinotta Mary—†	125	"	42	here
	F	Cuscinotta Peter	125	cutter	50	"
	G	Brazil Bernard J	129	laborer	35	"
	H	Brazil Mary—†	129	housewife	31	"
	K	Scanlon John J	129	carpenter	37	"
	L	Scanlon Mary E—†	129	housewife	36	"
	N	Geer Alden	131	mechanic	37	"
	O	*Geer Anna—†	131	housewife	29	"
	P	*Morrissey Catherine—†	131	at home	28	134 Trenton
	R	Caristo Mary—†	133	housewife	33	here

Page.	Letter.	Full Name.	Residence, Jan. 1, 1938.	Occupation.	Supposed Age.	Reported Residence, Jan. 1, 1937. Street and Number.

Trenton Street—Continued

	s	Caristo Salvatore	133	shoeworker	35	here
	u	Ventre Charles	139	leatherworker	32	"
	v	Ventre Lillian—†	139	housewife	29	"
	w	Chillemi John	139	tailor	31	
	x	Chillemi Josephine—†	139	housewife	31	"
	y	*Ventre Carmella—†	139	"	58	
	z	*Ventre Christopher	139	laborer	36	
647						
	A	*Ventre Massimino	139	retired	65	
	B	Ventre Peter	139	leatherworker	25	"
	C	Young Eleanor M—†	141	housewife	39	"
	D	Young Elmer H	141	painter	41	
	E	Taurasi Carmen	141	cableworker	45	"
	F	Taurasi Katherine—†	141	housewife	33	"
	G	Taurasi Peter	141	laborer	40	
	H	Russo Joseph J	141	chauffeur	38	"
	K	Russo Mary—†	141	housewife	31	"
	L	Myett Frank	143	clerk	34	
	M	Myett Margaret—†	143	housewife	33	"
	N	Sheffield Catherine—†	143	saleswoman	50	"
	O	Sheffield James	143	engineer	52	
	P	Sheffield Pauline—†	143	stenographer	30	"
	R	Dow Nettie F—†	143	housewife	74	"
	S	Dow Winthrop	143	laborer	36	"
	U	Williams Edward H	145	"	26	7 Prescott
	W	Williams James J	145	"	36	7 "
	V	Williams James T	145	retired	74	7 "
	X	Williams Margaret H—†	145	housewife	32	7 "
	Y	Baker Charles S	145	mechanic	22	here
	Z	Baker George R	145	chauffeur	25	"
648						
	A	Baker Herbert F	145	"	28	
	B	Baker Jennie E—†	145	at home	63	
	C	Waldron Michael	145	inspector	55	"
	D	*Coffin Lucy—†	147	housewife	48	"
	E	*Coffin Melbourne	147	welder	39	
	G	LaBlanc George H	147A	cutter	53	
	F	LaBlanc George T	147A	laborer	21	
	H	LaBlanc Joseph E	147A	"	23	
	K	LaBlanc Mary—†	147A	housewife	47	"
	L	Sheffield Emma J—†	147A	"	54	

Page.	Letter.	Full Name.	Residence, Jan. 1, 1938.	Occupation.	Supposed Age.	Reported Residence, Jan. 1, 1937. Street and Number.

Trenton Street—Continued

	M	Sheffield James A	147A	retired	83	here
	N	*DiBiccari Albert	149	shoeworker	53	"
	O	DiBiccari Eda—†	149	operator	20	"
	P	*DiBiccari Jean—†	149	"	29	
	R	*DiBiccari Leanora—†	149	housewife	50	"
	S	DiBiccari Louis	149	laborer	24	
	T	*DeEntremont Edgar	151	cutter	34	
	U	*D'Eon Clayton	151	"	28	
	V	Surette Damien	151	"	42	
	W	*Surette Rose—†	151	housewife	39	"
	X	Orlando Carmella—†	151	"	49	43 Sea View av
	Y	Orlando John	151	laborer	24	43 "
	Z	*Abreu Anna—†	151	housewife	69	here
649						
	A	*Abreu John	151	laborer	65	
	B	Abreu John, jr	151	operator	34	"
	C	Mealey Madeline—†	153	housewife	24	165 Hamilton
	D	Mealey Thomas	153	clerk	32	524 Sumner
	E	Piacenza Francis	153	laborer	22	here
	F	Piacenza Carlo	153	mechanic	49	"
	G	Piacenza Josephine—†	153	housewife	43	"
	H	*DeEntremont Edmond	155	ironworker	50	"
	K	*DeEntremont Rose—†	155	housewife	49	"
	L	Romano Pauline—†	155	saleswoman	24	"
	M	Romano Principio	155	barber	26	
	N	Spinazzola Caroline—†	155	dressmaker	27	"
	O	Spinazzola Josephine—†	155	housewife	55	"
	P	Spinazzola Pasquale	155	laborer	57	
	R	*Melanson Alexander	157	retired	71	
	S	*Melanson Edward	157	machinist	38	"
	T	*Melanson Emily—†	157	housewife	35	"
	U	*Melanson James	157	draftsman	27	"
	V	*Melanson Jennie—†	157	housewife	59	"
	W	Carano Frederick	157	waiter	31	144 Trenton
	X	Cataldo Annette—†	157	packer	26	here
	Y	Cataldo Carmella—†	157	housewife	49	"
	Z	Cataldo Eleanor—†	157	clerk	25	"
650						
	A	Cataldo Ernest	157	butcher	54	
	B	Cataldo John	157	"	27	
	C	Deveau Frank J	157A	carpenter	35	"
	D	*Deveau Marie C—†	157A	beautician	38	"

1

14

15

1(

17

18

19

20

1(

1

W

LIST

Ward 1—Precinct 8

CITY OF BOSTON

LIST OF RESIDENTS
20 YEARS OF AGE AND OVER

(NON-CITIZENS INDICATED BY ASTERISK)
(FEMALES INDICATED BY DAGGER)

AS OF

JANUARY 1, 1938

JOSEPH F. TIMILTY, } *Listing*
FREDERIC E. DOWLING, } *Board.*

CITY OF BOSTON PRINTING DEPARTMENT

Page.	Letter.	Full Name.	Residence, Jan. 1, 1938.	Occupation.	Supposed Age.	Reported Residence, Jan. 1, 1937. Street and Number.
660						
		Border Street				
	F	Lepore Angelo	325	laborer	23	77 Falcon
	G	Lepore Matthew	325	"	28	Cambridge
	H	Mosca Joseph	325	clerk	28	here
	K	*Mosca Maria—†	325	housewife	27	"
	L	Allen Josephine—†	325	"	49	"
	M	Allen Roderick	325	counterman	21	"
	N	*LeBlanc Alphie	327	laborer	39	308 Princeton
	O	*LeBlanc Elizabeth—†	327	housewife	30	308 "
	P	Caruso Joseph	329	salesman	25	here
	R	*Caruso Mary—†	329	housewife	64	"
	S	Cappannelli George	329	salesman	24	"
	T	Cappannelli Mary—†	329	housewife	22	"
	U	Gartland George	329	metalworker	26	"
	V	Gartland John	329	mechanic	24	"
	W	Gartland Thomas	329	metalworker	23	"
	X	Gartland William	329	laborer	20	
	Y	Grady Catherine—†	329	housewife	54	"
	Z	Grady Elizabeth—†	329	"	48	"
661						
	C	Barry Emma G—†	336	"	70	
	D	Barry Michael J	336	retired	70	
	E	Barry Catherine A—†	336	matron	66	
	F	Barry Hannah T—†	336	at home	68	"
	G	Hoy Bertha—†	339	housewife	22	48 Maverick sq
	H	Hoy Charles	339	laborer	21	347 Border
	K	Cushman Oscar M	339	chauffeur	63	343 "
	L	Noone Helen—†	339	housewife	32	305 Lexington
	M	Noone John T	339	chauffeur	34	305 "
	N	Thornell Blanche—†	339	housewife	34	here
	O	Thornell James	339	lineman	36	"
	P	Whippen Marian—†	341	housewife	20	373 Border
	R	Whippen William	341	mechanic	24	373 "
	S	Landers John	341	laborer	42	here
	T	Landers Mary—†	341	housewie	45	"
	U	Smith Stella—†	341	"	85	"
	V	Clancy Gladys—†	343	"	22	Randolph
	W	Clancy Peter	343	welder	25	"
	X	King Louis	343	laborer	36	here
	Y	Morani Eva—†	343	housewife	41	"
	Z	*Morani Thomas	343	plumber	53	"

Page.	Letter.	Full Name.	Residence, Jan. 1, 1938.	Occupation.	Supposed Age.	Reported Residence, Jan. 1, 1937. Street and Number.
662		**Border Street**—Continued				
	A	Morani Thomas	343	fishcutter	23	here
	B	Caristinos Amelia—†	343	housewife	23	67 Border
	C	Caristinos Michael	343	seaman	33	67 "
	D	*Marshall Mary—†	343	housewife	59	67 "
	E	Moran Martin	345	retired	58	here
	F	King Anna F—†	345	operator	40	"
	G	King Gertrude F—†	345	housewife	59	"
	H	Kenney Ada—†	345	waitress	31	"
	K	Thomas John	345	laborer	40	62 Princeton
	L	Morris Frank	347	clerk	32	107 Eutaw
	M	Morris Mary—†	347	housewife	35	107 "
	N	Rue Ethel L—†	347	waitress	20	112 Chelsea
	P	Rue Lena—†	347	housewife	40	112 "
	R	Hoy James D	347	janitor	51	here
	S	Hoy Margaret—†	347	housewife	48	"
	T	Hoy Walter J	347	manager	23	"
663						
	A	Coffin Beatrice A—†	364	housewife	42	"
	B	Coffin William M	364	shipfitter	43	"
	C	Coffin William T	364	clerk	20	
	D	Malley Anna—†	364	housewife	71	"
	E	Malley John J	364	retired	70	
	F	Malley Thomas F	364	inspector	65	"
	G	Grifone James	366	laundryworker	38	"
	H	Grifone Lulu—†	366	housewife	54	"
	K	Oliver Charlotte C—†	366	"	22	
	L	Oliver Stanley P	366	clerk	28	
	M	Minscalo Anthony	366	laborer	58	
	N	Minscalo Domenica—†	366	housewife	56	"
	O	Wilband Fred	367	laborer	77	"
	P	Richard Hannah E—†	367	housewife	73	148 Pleasant
	R	Davis Walter W	367	seaman	52	Chelsea
	S	Lindsey Elsie E—†	367	housewife	27	here
	T	Lindsey James W	367	seaman	27	"
	U	Lindgren Chester	368	porter	25	"
	V	Lindgren Robert	368	carpenter	58	"
	W	Fullerton David F	368	fisherman	39	"
	X	Fullerton Mary A—†	368	housewife	31	"
	Y	Cotreau Adeline—†	368	"	32	
	Z	Cotreau Charles	368	fisherman	39	"

Page.	Letter.	Full Name.	Residence, Jan. 1, 1938.	Occupation.	Supposed Age.	Reported Residence, Jan. 1, 1937. Street and Number.

664

Border Street—Continued

	B	*Muise Eli	369	fishcutter	43	here
	C	*Muise Matta—†	369	housewife	36	"
	D	Epps Catherine—†	369	"	53	"
	E	Epps Charles H	369	retired	68	
	F	Epps Charles H	369	salesman	33	"
	G	Epps Helen G—†	369	domestic	21	"
	H	Cresey Edna—†	370	operator	45	
	K	Cresey Lottie—†	370	housekeeper	75	"
	L	McAuley Bertha—†	370	housewife	38	"
	M	McAuley Lawrence	370	laborer	38	
	P	Whippen Frank A	373	painter	58	
	R	Whippen Franklin H	373	mechanic	24	"
	S	Whippen Rachael—†	373	packer	48	"

Brooks Street

	Z	Thomas Beatrice—†	166	housewife	24	1034 Saratoga
665						

Page.	Letter.	FULL NAME.	Residence, Jan. 1, 1938.	Occupation.	Supposed Age.	Reported Residence, Jan. 1, 1937. Street and Number.

Brooks Street—Continued

	Z	Staffiere Michael	171	laborer	25	here
666						
	A	Staffiere Ralph	171	"	21	
	B	Miller David	171	draftsman	32	"
	C	*Moggi Umberto	171	laborer	56	
	D	Costagliola Josephine—†	171	housewife	25	"
	E	Costagliola Peter	171	laborer	26	
	G	Macrina Frances—†	174	operator	20	
	H	Macrina Johanna—†	174	inspector	22	"
	K	Macrina Lena—†	174	housewife	40	"
	L	Murphy John	174	laborer	38	115 Porter
	M	*Murphy Laura—†	174	housewife	31	115 "
	N	*Sinkeldam John	174	carpenter	39	104 Eutaw
	O	Catalano Ernest	176	salesman	24	281 Lexington
	P	Catalano Lucy—†	176	housewife	22	281 "
	R	Giorgio Joseph	176	chauffeur	23	208 Havre
	S	Giorgio Ralph	176	laborer	54	208 "
	T	Marino Celia—†	176	housewife	26	121 Eutaw
	U	Marino Leonard	176	barber	33	121 "
	V	Lightbody Hazel E—†	178	housewife	24	here
	W	Lightbody J Edward	178	engineer	26	"
	X	*Belliveau Frances—†	178	housewife	32	"
	Y	Belliveau Frank	178	foreman	32	
	Z	Adams Dorothy—†	178	housewife	28	"
667						
	A	Adams John	178	machinist	37	"
	B	Dahringer Herman	178	fireman	71	
	C	Welch Edward R	188	teacher	29	
	D	Welch Loretta J—†	188	housewife	31	"
	E	Burgess Katherine S—†	190	at home	62	
	F	Cadigan Florence—†	190	maid	22	
	G	Pomeroy Bridget M—†	190	housewife	58	"
	H	Pomeroy Elmer J	190	painter	22	
	K	Pomeroy Esther K—†	190	attendant	20	"
	L	Pomeroy Frank C	190	reporter	27	
	M	Pomeroy Joseph A	190	mechanic	24	"
	N	*Muliera Nicholas	192	painter	53	
	O	*Meuse Antoinette—†	192	housewife	33	"
	P	Meuse John S	192	fishcutter	39	"
	R	Phelan George	192	chauffeur	31	"
	S	Phelan Josephine—†	192	housewife	22	"

Page.	Letter.	Full Name.	Residence, Jan. 1, 1938.	Occupation.	Supposed Age.	Reported Residence, Jan. 1, 1937. Street and Number.

Brooks Street—Continued

Page.	Letter.	Full Name.	Residence, Jan. 1, 1938.	Occupation.	Supposed Age.	Reported Residence, Jan. 1, 1937. Street and Number.
	T	*McLellan Leo G	194	molder	30	here
	U	*McLellan Margaret—†	194	housewife	33	"
	V	*Bonaiuto Antoinette—†	194	housekeeper	55	"
	W	Ricardo Anthony	194	clerk	25	"
	X	Lembo Mary—†	194	housewife	27	"
	Y	Lembo Michael	194	pressman	40	"
	Z	Garcia Jennie—†	196	housewife	25	"
668						
	A	Garcia John	196	laborer	33	
	B	Catoggio Antoinette—†	196	housewife	27	"
	C	Catoggio Nicholas	196	shoecutter	33	"
	D	Catoggio Frank	196	laborer	54	
	E	*Catoggio Mary—†	196	housewife	50	"
	F	Sciaraffa Filomena—†	198	at home	30	"
	G	Hopkins Frank K	198	seaman	66	
	H	Hopkins Katherine E—†	198	housewife	54	"
	K	Bennett Margaret—†	198	"	56	
	L	Bennett Simon E	198	shoeworker	47	"
	M	Bennett William	198	"	58	
	N	Diorio Dominic	200	painter	50	
	O	Diorio Susie—†	200	housewife	49	"
	P	Toby Bertha—†	200	"	34	342 Meridian
	R	Toby Harry	200	laborer	35	342 "
	S	Nardo Annette—†	200	housewife	27	here
	T	Nardo Frank	200	musician	31	"

Eutaw Place

Page.	Letter.	Full Name.	Residence, Jan. 1, 1938.	Occupation.	Supposed Age.	Reported Residence, Jan. 1, 1937. Street and Number.
	U	Williams Helen J—†	1	housewife	27	here
	V	Williams Joseph A	1	lineman	35	"
	W	Casey Margaret E—†	2	housewife	78	"
	X	Fortier Eliza—†	2	"	76	
	Y	Fortier Lester	2	laborer	25	
	Z	Fabrano Joseph	3	operator	31	"
669						
	A	Grasso Josephine—†	3	housewife	22	"
	B	Grasso Louis	3	operator	26	"
	C	*Violetto Concetta—†	3	housewife	48	"
	D	*Pisano Antonio	3	laborer	45	
	E	Pisano Leonard	3	pedler	24	
	F	Pisano Louis	3	laborer	20	

Eutaw Place—Continued

Page.	Letter.	Full Name.	Residence, Jan. 1, 1938.	Occupation.	Supposed Age.	Reported Residence, Jan. 1, 1937. Street and Number.
	G	*Pisano Maria—†	3	housewife	45	here
	H	Poirier Irene—†	4	"	35	"
	K	Gelormini Louie	5	carpenter	43	"
	L	Molino Armando	5	blacksmith	33	"
	M	Stella Charles	5	weaver	27	
	N	Stella John	5	laborer	55	
	O	*Stella Lucy—†	5	housewife	44	"
	R	Mattina Fannie—†	6	typist	20	
	S	*Mattina John	6	laborer	50	
	T	Mattina Peter	6	weaver	22	"
	U	Doherty Kathleen—†	7	housewife	28	11 Marion
	V	Newman Elizabeth—†	7	"	40	here
	W	Newman John F	7	calker	45	"
	X	Barry Augustine W	7	retired	72	"
	Y	Crosby Mary R—†	8	housewife	35	"

Eutaw Street

Page.	Letter.	Full Name.	Residence, Jan. 1, 1938.	Occupation.	Supposed Age.	Reported Residence, Jan. 1, 1937. Street and Number.
	Z	Baker Alice—†	6	housewife	60	here
670						
	A	Baker John	6	boilermaker	62	"
	B	*Amero Roger	6	engineer	40	
	C	*Baudro Benjamin	6	cook	54	
	D	Rose Joseph	6	pedler	60	
	E	Wilkie William	6	boilermaker	38	"
	F	Beck Dorothy—†	20	stenographer	31	"
	G	Beck Nathan	20	dealer	65	"
	H	Beck Rose—†	20	housewife	55	"
	K	*Kenney Geneva—†	20	"	49	
	L	Kenney Isabelle—†	20	clerk	21	
	M	*Kenney Minard	20	carpenter	53	"
	N	Brown Amy E—†	20	housewife	52	"
	O	Brown Edward C	20	clerk	26	
	P	Brown Helen H—†	20	at home	24	
	R	Brown Louise P—†	20	operator	21	"
	S	Allen Joseph F	24	retired	68	145 Trenton
	T	*Keefe Lillian—†	24	housekeeper	45	145 "
	V	Finn Mary—†	24	"	49	here
	W	Arena Josephine—†	26	"	56	"
	X	Grover Harold L	26	painter	37	"
	Y	Grover Josephine—†	26	housewife	37	"

Page.	Letter.	Full Name.	Residence, Jan. 1, 1938.	Occupation.	Supposed Age.	Reported Residence, Jan. 1, 1937. Street and Number.

Eutaw Street—Continued

Page.	Letter.	Full Name.	Residence, Jan. 1, 1938.	Occupation.	Supposed Age.	Reported Residence, Jan. 1, 1937. Street and Number.
	z	*Gentile Armando	26	operator	44	here
671						
	A	*Gentile Grace—†	26	housewife	36	"
	B	Madison Edward J	28	longshoreman	62	"
	C	Madison Evelyn—†	28	housekeeper	31	"
	D	Madison Herbert	28	mechanic	24	"
	E	Madison Hilda—†	28	housewife	58	"
	F	Mason Louis A	28	mechanic	39	"
	G	Gifford Orianna—†	30	at home	82	
	H	Gifford Ella—†	30	housekeeper	34	"
	K	LaVoie Alice M—†	32	housewife	43	148 Lexington
	L	LaVoie Norbert J	32	painter	40	148 "
	M	*Cerrato Elizabeth—†	34	housewife	44	here
	N	Cerrato Francis	34	packer	21	"
	O	Cerrato Joseph	34	clerk	20	"
	P	*Cerrato Pasquale	34	packer	49	
	R	Harrigan Harriet—†	34	at home	74	
	S	Marchesi Felix	36	chauffeur	45	"
	T	Marchesi Margaret M—†	36	housewife	40	"
	U	*Maggio Angeline—†	38	"	62	
	V	*Maggio Michael	38	laborer	53	
	W	Marchesi Dominic	38	"	39	"
	X	Coombs Alexander	40	pipefitter	25	132 Marion
	Y	Coombs Bridget—†	40	housewife	55	132 "
	Z	Coombs Edward	40	painter	22	132 "
672						
	A	Coombs Eli	40	retired	65	132 '
	B	Coombs William	40	painter	23	132 '
	C	Coombs Winifred—†	40	at home	21	132 "
	D	Noble Harry E	42	printer	29	55 Call
	E	Noble Mary J—†	42	housewife	50	55 "
	F	Noble Thomas S	42	painter	28	55 "
	G	Silinsky William W	44	laborer	40	here
	H	Accettullo Angela M—†	46	housewife	55	"
	K	Accettullo Anna—†	46	operator	23	"
	L	Accettullo Antoinette—†	46	at home	23	
	M	Accettullo Domenico	46	merchant	55	"
	N	Accettullo Dora—†	46	at home	23	
	O	Accettullo Mary—†	46	operator	22	"
	P	Winsor Allan	48	statistician	28	"
	R	Winsor Frank	48	mechanic	60	"

Page.	Letter.	Full Name.	Residence, Jan. 1, 1938.	Occupation.	Supposed Age.	Reported Residence, Jan. 1, 1937. Street and Number.

Eutaw Street--Continued

Page.	Letter.	Full Name.	Residence, Jan. 1, 1938.	Occupation.	Supposed Age.	Reported Residence, Jan. 1, 1937. Street and Number.
	S	Winsor Rebecca—†	48	housewife	50	here
	U	Crowley Anna M—†	49	"	21	186 Benningt'n
	V	Crowley Edward J	49	dairyworker	21	689 Saratoga
	W	Barsons Charles	50	retired	67	here
	W1	Kierstead George	50	machinist	30	"
	X	Kierstead Ida—†	50	housewife	73	"
	Y	Keenan Margaret—†	50	"	54	
	Z	Keenan Walter	50	electrician	53	"
673						
	A	O'Brien Agnes G—†	50	housekeeper	62	"
	B	Crotty Andrew J	51	installer	39	"
	C	Crotty Evelyn I—†	51	housewife	37	"
	D	*Salerno Florence—†	52	"	53	
	E	Salerno Nicholas	52	laborer	51	
	F	Salerno Andrew	52	barber	25	
	G	Salerno Carmella—†	52	housewife	25	"
	K	Guiggio Joseph	54	laborer	56	"
	L	*Guiggio Louise—†	54	housewife	45	"
	M	Guiggio Theresa—†	54	operator	23	"
	N	Magnell Hilma C—†	56	housewife	39	173 Princeton
	O	Magnell Joseph N	56	printer	39	173 "
	R	Bianco Catherine—†	58	housewife	48	here
	S	Bianco Katherine—†	58	clerk	22	"
	T	Bianco Nicholas	58	dealer	51	"
	U	Staretz Leah—†	60	housewife	31	"
	V	Staretz Samuel	60	plumber	33	"
	W	Adelman Bertha—†	60	clerk	20	
	X	Adelman David	60	carpenter	22	"
	Y	Adelman Max H	60	"	56	
	Z	Ademan Sarah D—†	60	housewife	51	"
674						
	A	Rogers Anna—†	60	operator	40	"
	B	Jacobs Jacob	62	tailor	60	
	C	Jacobs Miriam—†	62	at home	29	"
	D	*Duccini Arthur	62	sculptor	52	72 Frankfort
	E	*Landano Mary—†	62	housewife	26	72 "
	F	Landana Michael	62	operator	24	72 "
	G	Landano Gerald	62	"	29	143 Cottage
	H	Landano Sophia—†	62	housewife	25	143 "
	K	Pecora Nicholas	64	baker	20	404 Meridian
	L	Pecora Rosalie—†	64	housewife	20	411 Saratoga

Page	Letter.	Full Name.	Residence, Jan. 1, 1938.	Occupation.	Supposed Age.	Reported Residence, Jan. 1, 1937. Street and Number.

Eutaw Street—Continued

	M	Sullivan John	64	machinist	26	here
	N	Sullivan Rose—†	64	housewife	23	"
	O	Cimo Jane—†	64A	"	51	"
	P	Cimo Salvatore	64A	merchant	50	"
	S	*Re Avira—†	66	operator	30	
	T	Re Celso	66	bartender	57	"
	U	*Re Julia—†	66	operator	27	
	V	*Re Mary—†	66	housewife	55	"
	W	Alexander Marie J—†	68	teacher	45	
	X	Alexander Robert R	68	superintendent	43	"
	Y	Alexander Robert R, jr	68	clerk	20	"
	Z	*Boudreau Louise M—†	68	maid	46	
675						
	A	*Contini Jennie—†	70	housewife	50	"
	B	Contini Louis	70	clerk	20	
	C	Contini Michael	70	carpenter	60	"
	D	Contini Eleanor—†	70	housewife	32	"
	E	Contini Paul	70	printer	32	
	F	Sacco Carlo	71	shoemaker	39	"
	G	*Sacco Nellie—†	71	housewife	33	"
	H	*Pedro Anna F—†	71	"	55	
	K	*Pedro Antonio F	71	packer	63	
	L	Pedro Emily—†	71	operator	21	
	M	Pedro Joseph	71	painter	24	
	N	Pedro Mary—†	71	inspector	28	"
	O	Perry John	71	merchant	36	"
	P	Megna Ferdinand	72	printer	36	
	R	Megna Marie—†	72	housewife	34	"
	S	LoVetere Anthony	72	barber	61	"
	T	*LoVetere Rose—†	72	housewife	55	"
	U	LoVetere Anthony, jr	72	engineer	31	
	V	LoVetere John	72	student	21	
	W	LoVetere Marietta—†	72	bookkeeper	26	"
	X	Crotty Anna J—†	73	stenographer	29	"
	Y	Crotty Mary E—†	73	housewife	64	"
	Z	Crotty Mary H—†	73	teacher	34	"
676						
	A	Nihen Margaret—†	73	seamstress	65	"
	B	Sullivan Elinor M—†	73	housewife	32	92 Oakland
	C	Sullivan John J	73	clerk	42	92 "
	D	*Nazzaro Eugene	74	barber	48	here

Page.	Letter.	Full Name.	Residence, Jan. 1, 1938.	Occupation.	Supposed Age.	Reported Residence, Jan. 1, 1937. Street and Number

Eutaw Street—Continued

Page.	Letter.	Full Name.	Residence, Jan. 1, 1938.	Occupation.	Supposed Age.	Reported Residence, Jan. 1, 1937.
	E	*Nazzaro Mary—†	74	housewife	41	here
	F	Barranco Angela—†	74	operator	28	"
	F[1]	*Barranco Angelo	74	retired	75	"
	G	*Barranco Josephine—†	74	housewife	65	"
	H	Barranco Salvatore	74	painter	33	
	K	Tantosca Anna—†	74	operator	26	
	L	Tantosca Felix	74	"	27	
	M	Johnson Henry W	75	carpenter	44	"
	N	Johnson Viola B—†	75	housewife	48	"
	O	Doherty Nora F—†	75	"	49	
	P	Londrigan Annabelle M–†	75	"	63	
	R	Londrigan John	75	laborer	71	
	S	Murphy Mary M—†	75	housewife	58	"
	S[1]	Murphy Michael H	75	retired	60	
	T	Murphy Niel M	75	chauffeur	37	"
	U	Dame Abbie—†	76	housewife	67	"
	V	Dame Charles	76	retired	78	
	W	Dame Della F—†	76	at home	52	
	X	Field Ada—†	76	candymaker	65	"
	Y	McGuire Daniel	77	B F D	39	
	Z	McGuire Lillian—†	77	housewife	33	"
677						
	A	Rubino Alfred	77	clerk	21	
	B	Rubino Angelina—†	77	operator	23	"
	C	Rubino Antonette—†	77	stenographer	21	"
	D	*Rubino Jennie—†	77	housewife	52	"
	E	Rubino Louis P	77	laborer	55	
	F	Rubino Mary—†	77	clerk	25	
	G	*Norris Anna—†	79	housewife	36	"
	H	*Norris Michael	79	fisherman	36	"
	K	Ward Rose—†	79	housewife	34	"
	L	*Levy Bertha—†	79	"	39	
	M	Joyce Mary F—†	80	housekeeper	37	"
	N	O'Niel Henry F	80	woodworker	20	235 Saratoga
	O	Sprague Florence N—†	80	attendant	21	here
	P	Sprague Forest C	80	printer	45	"
	R	Sprague Madeline E—†	80	housewife	41	"
	S	Regan Annie—†	81	nurse	30	
	T	Regan Daniel	81	bellboy	29	
	U	Regan John	81	porter	31	
	V	Snowdon Emma M—†	81	housewife	52	"

Page.	Letter.	FULL NAME.	Residence, Jan. 1, 1938.	Occupation.	Supposed Age.	Reported Residence, Jan. 1, 1937. Street and Number.

Eutaw Street—Continued

Page.	Letter.	FULL NAME.	Residence, Jan. 1, 1938.	Occupation.	Supposed Age.	Reported Residence, Jan. 1, 1937. Street and Number.
	W	Snowdon Wallace E	81	retired	61	here
	X	Snowdon Wallace E, jr	81	dealer	24	"
	Y	Elkins Eva—†	82	waitress	48	"
	Z	Ryan Margaret—†	83	housewife	65	"
678						
	A	*Albino Edith—†	83	"	38	
	B	Albino George	83	cobbler	44	"
	C	Albino James	83	"	21	
	D	*Lewis Gordon	83	fisherman	26	"
	E	Lewis Mary—†	83	housewife	26	"
	F	Moore Catherine A—†	84	operator	49	"
	G	Durgin Carrie H—†	84	housekeeper	63	"
	H	Gatchell Hazel M—†	84	clerk	38	"
	K	Connors Mary—†	84	housewife	43	"
	L	Connors Timothy	84	porter	53	"
	M	*Cole Jennie—†	85	at home	70	59 Marion
	N	*Cacciatore Angelina—†	85	housewife	43	here
	O	Cacciatore Giacomo	85	clerk	22	"
	P	Cacciatore Raymond	85	laborer	55	"
	R	Cacciatore Stephen	85	"	24	
	S	Stasio A Ralph	86	foreman	48	
	T	Stasio Mary—†	86	housewife	44	"
	U	*Cheivers Margaret—†	86	"	68	
	V	Cheivers Nicholas	86	retired	68	
	W	*Markis Charles	86	shoemaker	41	"
	X	*Markis May—†	86	housewife	36	"
	Y	*Nadi Agozio	87	candymaker	52	"
	Z	*Nadi Mary—†	87	housewife	42	"
679						
	A	Bickford Edward S	87	cook	38	11 Monmouth
	B	Bickford Mildred A—†	87	housewife	33	11 "
	C	*Bailey Dorothy—†	87	"	39	here
	D	Bailey John	87	laborer	49	"
	E	Ciampa Joseph	88	attendant	21	210 Bremen
	F	Ciampa Mary—†	88	housewife	21	210 "
	G	Marotta Albert	88	barber	35	here
	H	Marotta Mary A—†	88	housewife	29	"
	K	Russo Domenico	88	laborer	55	"
	L	Russo Margaret—†	88	candymaker	23	"
	M	O'Leary Jessie A—†	90	housewife	28	13 Haynes
	N	O'Leary John J	90	longshoreman	29	13 "

Page.	Letter.	Full Name.	Residence, Jan. 1, 1938.	Occupation.	Supposed Age.	Reported Residence, Jan. 1, 1937. Street and Number.

Eutaw Street—Continued

Page.	Letter.	Full Name.	Residence, Jan. 1, 1938.	Occupation.	Supposed Age.	Reported Residence, Jan. 1, 1937. Street and Number.
	O	McIntyre Edgar F	90	chauffeur	31	75 W Eagle
	P	McIntyre Rhoda M—†	90	housewife	27	75 "
	R	Borgess Henry L	90	cabinetmaker	47	here
	S	Borgess Louise V—†	90	housewife	45	"
	T	Frevold Clarence	92	machinist	28	"
	U	Frevold Margaret—†	92	operator	29	"
	V	Frevold Olivia—†	92	housekeeper	59	"
	W	Cohan Florence—†	96	housewife	21	"
	X	Cohan John T	96	shipper	23	37 Glendon
	Y	MacDonald Catherine—†	96	housekeeper	52	here
680						
	A	Zavarelli Frances—†	105	housewife	26	"
	B	Zavarelli Philip	105	laborer	22	
	C	Mancuso Pasquale	105	"	32	
	D	*Napoli Rose—†	105	housewife	44	"
	E	Napoli Vincenzo	105	shoemaker	49	"
	F	Surette Jeremiah	107	shipper	24	109 Eutaw
	G	Surette Mary—†	107	housewife	24	109 "
	H	D'Agosta Joseph	107	butcher	21	853 Saratoga
	K	Antonoucci Andrew	107	presser	27	here
	L	Antonucci Clara—†	107	housewife	22	"
	M	*Welsh Gabriel	109	fisherman	41	"
	N	*Welsh Helen—†	109	housewife	31	"
	O	DePalma Luigi	109	laborer	45	
	P	DePalma Mario	109	clerk	20	
	R	*DePalma Mary—†	109	housewife	45	"
	S	Gentuso Leo	111	chauffeur	24	"
	T	Gentuso Lucy—†	111	housewife	24	"
	U	Gentuso Ignacio	111	laborer	56	
	V	*Gentuso Rose—†	111	housewife	52	"
	W	DeMarco Michael	111	laborer	38	
	X	DeMarco Theresa—†	111	housewife	35	"
	Y	Caristo Ottavina—†	113	"	34	
	Z	*Caristo Salvatore	113	tailor	29	
681						
	A	Camerlengo Anna—†	113	clerk	20	
	B	Camerlengo Louise C—†	113	housewife	43	"
	C	Camerlengo Philip J	113	assessor	44	
	D	Daley John B	113	bookbinder	43	"
	E	Daley Mary—†	113	housewife	45	"
	F	Campagna Alfred	115	clerk	23	173 Maverick

Page.	Letter.	Full Name.	Residence, Jan. 1, 1938.	Occupation.	Supposed Age.	Reported Residence, Jan. 1, 1937. Street and Number.

Eutaw Street—Continued

Page.	Letter.	Full Name.	Residence, Jan. 1, 1938.	Occupation.	Supposed Age.	Reported Residence, Jan. 1, 1937. Street and Number.
	G	Campagna Marie—†	115	housewife	20	119 Trenton
	H	Dilwin Margaret E—†	115	housekeeper	60	here
	K	Gallagher Sarah A—†	115	housewife	59	"
	L	O'Brien Frederick L	115	probat'n officer	50	"
	M	O'Brien William H	115	clerk	52	
	N	*Berrigan Leo	117	fisherman	29	"
	O	Berrigan Rita—†	117	housewife	21	"
	P	Slaney John	117	fisherman	33	"
	R	*Comunali Antoinetta—†	117	housewife	34	"
	S	Comunali Joseph	117	laborer	43	"
	T	Gillis Christina B—†	119	housewife	43	614 Beningt'n
	U	Gillis John	119	laborer	22	614 "
	V	Greenwood Samuel	119	fireman	27	123 Eutaw
	W	Whiteway Arthur E	119	retired	69	here
	X	Whiteway Martha—†	119	housewife	68	"
	Y	Cady Nora—†	119	packer	28	"
	Z	Cady William	119	dealer	30	
682						
	A	*Smith Herbert	121	machinist	32	207 Princeton
	B	Smith Nora—†	121	housewife	31	207 "
	C	Miraglia Joseph	121	bacteriologist	26	here
	D	Miraglia Lucy—†	121	housewife	49	"
	E	Miraglia Vincent	121	tailor	49	"
	F	Taveno Antonio	121	operator	47	
	G	Tavano Josephine—†	121	housewife	44	"
	H	Tavano Michelina—†	121	clerk	21	
	K	*Banks Esmeralda—†	123	housewife	34	"
	L	*Banks James A	123	fishcutter	35	"
	M	Giglio Grace—†	123	knitter	27	"
	N	*Giglio Ida—†	123	housewife	63	"
	O	Giglio Roger	123	repairman	30	"
	P	Iozzo Joseph	123	laborer	45	
	R	Iozzo Joseph, jr	123	chauffeur	22	"
	S	Montoni Francesco	125	tailor	46	
	T	Ruggiero Elvira—†	125	housewife	33	"
	U	Ruggiero Fiorentino	125	bartender	42	"
	V	*Caruccio Angelina—†	125	housewife	40	"
	W	Caruccio Frank	125	presser	45	
	X	*Comunale Rosina—†	127	housewife	64	"
	Y	*Comunale Vincenzo	127	laborer	64	"
	Z	McCormick John W	127	painter	43	

Page.	Letter.	Full Name.	Residence, Jan. 1, 1938.	Occupation.	Supposed Age.	Reported Residence, Jan. 1, 1937. Street and Number.
683						
		Eutaw Street—Continued				
	A	McCormick Mary V—†	127	housewife	41	here
	B	*Farulla Helen—†	127	"	35	Framingham
	C	Kennedy John J	129	waterproofer	23	666 Saratoga
	D	Kennedy Ruth M—†	129	housewife	23	437 Lubec
	E	Kehoe Annie E—†	129	"	68	here
	F	Kehoe James F	129	machinist	37	"
	G	Kehoe William S	129	boilermaker	73	"
	H	Barbere Angelo	129	clerk	25	
	K	Barbere Theresa—†	129	housewife	24	"
	L	Centracchio Celia—†	131	"	30	
	M	Centracchio Nicolas	131	supervisor	37	"
	N	*Iminza Mary—†	131	at home	34	"
	O	Banks Joseph	131	laborer	22	78 Trenton
	P	Taurasi Mary—†	133	at home	20	here
	R	Taurasi Salvatore	133	bootblack	55	"
	S	Taurasi Virginia—†	133	housewife	46	"
	T	*Russi Salvatore	133	cabinetmaker	54	198 Maverick
	U	*Russi Theresa—†	133	housewife	43	198 "
	V	*Caprarella Mary—†	133	"	37	here
	W	Caprarella Thomas	133	manufacturer	39	"
	X	*Perrisco Anna—†	135	housewife	45	"
	Y	*Perrisco Michael	135	laborer	46	
	Z	*Battaglia Frank	135	"	61	
684						
	A	Battaglia John	135	packer	23	
	B	Battaglia Samuel	135	chauffeur	25	"
	C	Waters Joseph	135	salesman	42	"
	D	Waters Mary—†	135	housewife	32	"
	E	*Vila John	137	fireman	41	
	F	Vila Vita—†	137	packer	28	
	G	Votta Antonio	137	laborer	53	
	H	*Votta Rose—†	137	housewife	43	"
	K	*Quinlan Catherine—†	137	"	46	
	L	*Quinlan John	137	fisherman	51	"
	M	Gillespie Florence—†	139	inspector	27	"
	N	Gillespie Paul	139	laborer	29	
	O	McDonald John W	139	B F D	45	
	P	McDonald Sarah—†	139	at home	40	
	R	McDonald Teresa—†	139	housewife	40	"
	S	McDonald William	139	clerk	21	

Page.	Letter.	FULL NAME.	Residence, Jan. 1, 1938.	Occupation.	Supposed Age.	Reported Residence, Jan. 1, 1937. Street and Number.

Eutaw Street—Continued

	T	Griffin Annie F—†	141	housewife	56	here
	U	Garbaley Bridget E—†	143	at home	74	"
	V	Garbaley Sarah A—†	143	storekeeper	70	"
	W	Gehm Gertrude—†	145	housewife	46	"
	X	Gehm John	145	custodian	40	"

Marion Street

	Y	*Chin Lee	1	laundryman	54	here
685						
	A	Brown Frederick E	3	laborer	37	"
	B	Brown Sophia—†	3	housewife	34	"
	C	*Abric Grace K—†	5	"	29	
	D	*Abric Louis P	5	fishcutter	35	"
	E	*Stark Olive L—†	5	housekeeper	38	8 W Eagle
	F	Cotreau Frederick	5	fireman	34	here
	G	Cotreau Joshua	5	fishcutter	37	"
	H	Cotreau Rita—†	5	housewife	28	"
	K	*Smith Edward G	5	fishcutter	34	1 White
	L	*Smith Ethel—†	5	housewife	34	1 "
	M	Flaherty Lavinia A—†	9	"	49	here
	N	Flaherty William H	9	laborer	55	"
	O	Shute Annie M—†	11	housewife	65	"
	P	Verdy Edward	11	guard	58	"
	R	Verdy George	11	chauffeur	30	"
	S	Verdy Lena—†	11	housewife	58	"
	T	Wyse Marguerite P—†	12	"	55	
	U	Wyse Michael	12	seaman	61	
	V	Leighton Arthur L	13	clerk	42	
	W	Leighton Grace A—†	13	at home	72	
	X	Driscoll John E	14	baker	65	
	Y	Fariolio Clara—†	14	clerk	50	
	Z	Fariolio William	14	repairman	42	"
686						
	A	Moriarty Elizabeth—†	14	housekeeper	62	"
	B	*Surette Eva J—†	15	housewife	32	"
	C	*Surette Sylvester J	15	fishcutter	31	"
	D	*Vitello Fannie—†	15	at home	86	
	E	Vitello Fannie—†	15	typist	24	
	F	Vitello Joseph	15	pressman	53	"
	G	*Vitello Mary—†	15	housewife	49	"

Page.	Letter.	Full Name.	Residence, Jan. 1, 1938.	Occupation.	Supposed Age.	Reported Residence, Jan. 1, 1937. Street and Number.

Marion Street—Continued

	H	Duann Violet—†	16	operator	35	217 Lexington
	K	Webb Irma M—†	16	clerk	21	217 "
	L	Webb James O	16	sprayer	23	217 "
	M	*Webb Marie—†	16	housewife	51	217 "
	N	Webb Patrick X	16	cook	57	217 "
	O	Doran John	17	fisherman	28	361 Meridian
	P	Doran Julia—†	17	housewife	28	361 "
	R	Doucette Melbourne J	17	cook	36	here
	S	Joyce George P	17	steamfitter	31	"
	T	Joyce Marie A—†	17	housewife	28	"
	U	LeBlanc Blanche—†	17	"	55	
	V	LeBlanc Gordon P	17	electrician	26	"
	W	LeBlanc Louis C	17	chef	61	
	X	*Surette Ernest P	17	machinist	29	"
	Y	Surette Marion—†	17	housewife	27	"
	Z	*Gray David	18	operator	64	
687						
	A	Gray Mildred—†	18	secretary	27	"
	B	Smith Edith—†	18	housewife	35	"
	C	Smith Paul	18	optometrist	42	"
	D	Melanson Gretchen—†	19	housewife	29	"
	E	*Melanson John	19	fishcutter	32	"
	F	Chindos Florence—†	19	housewife	34	"
	G	Chindos Nicholas	19	painter	45	"
	H	Pearson Walter	19	molder	22	261 Havre
	K	DeCristoforo Angelina—†	20	housewife	24	here
	L	DeCristoforo Raymond	20	salesman	28	"
	N	Tedesche Gaetano	20	painter	25	"
	O	Tedesche Gerardo	20	laborer	21	"
	P	Gillis Dorothy A—†	21	housewife	24	221 Webster
	R	Gillis John C	21	laborer	30	221 "
	S	Gillis Peter	21	retired	57	221 "
	T	Fischer Minnie—†	21	housewife	38	here
	U	Fischer Vincent	21	laborer	46	"
	V	Munn Edna—†	21	housewife	24	Revere
	W	Munn William	21	watchman	33	"
	X	Nicholason Edith—†	22	at home	20	here
	Y	Nicholson Frederick M	22	meatcutter	35	"
	Z	Nicholson Marion—†	22	housewife	45	"
688						
	A	Nicholson William	22	machinist	46	"

Page.	Letter.	Full Name.	Residence, Jan. 1, 1938.	Occupation.	Supposed Age.	Reported Residence, Jan. 1, 1937. Street and Number.

Marion Street—Continued

	B	Keyes Bertha—†	22	at home	71	here
	C	Keyes Chester	22	engineer	46	"
	D	Keyes Edith—†	22	housewife	43	"
	E	Bonzagni Leo A	24	broker	44	"
	F	Lane Anne M—†	24	housewife	68	"
	G	Lane Henry B	24	salesman	47	"
	H	Lane Ruth M—†	24	housewife	39	"
	K	Lane Walter M	24	foreman	45	
	L	Quinn Edna—†	24	housewife	35	"
	M	Quinn Lawrence P	24	letter carrier	39	"
	N	Swift Caroline—†	24	at home	70	
	O	Gannon Augustine S	26	policeman	41	"
	P	Gannon Helen E—†	26	housewife	38	"
	R	*Wallpurger Hilda—†	37	"	33	Germany
	S	*Wallpurger Rudolf	37	mechanic	31	"
	U	Amicangelo Helen—†	40	at home	22	here
	V	Mondello Anthony	40	laborer	43	"
	W	*Mondello Frances—†	40	housewife	47	"
	X	*Tramonte Leo	40	barber	38	
	Y	*Tramonte Mary—†	40	housewife	25	"
	Z	*Giardiello Fannie—†	40	"	45	
689						
	A	Giardiello Michael	40	tailor	46	
	B	Eaton George	41	pipefitter	54	"
	C	Eaton Mary—†	41	housewife	73	"
	D	Ebert Michael	43	retired	75	
	E	Horgan Ellen—†	43	at home	78	
	F	O'Brien Catherine—†	43	housewife	48	"
	G	Sullivan William J	43	shipper	49	
	H	Dichieara Nicola	44	laborer	46	
	K	*Dichiara Philomena—†	44	housewife	46	"
	L	Howe Emma—†	44	"	50	
	M	Howe Harry R	44	blacksmith	52	"
	N	Howe Thelma L—†	44	operator	21	
	O	DiPaola Michelina—†	44	housewife	35	"
	P	DiPaola Nicholas A	44	carpenter	40	"
	R	Hurley Margaret—†	48	housewife	45	165 Byron
	S	Rich August	48	laborer	44	here
	T	Rich Mary B—†	48	housewife	46	"
	U	*DiChiara Ralph	48	laborer	47	"
	V	*DiChiara Rose—†	48	housewife	38	"

Page.	Letter.	FULL NAME.	Residence, Jan. 1, 1938.	Occupation.	Supposed Age.	Reported Residence, Jan. 1, 1937. Street and Number.

Marion Street—Continued

	W	Tuttle Anna—†	52	housewife	35	here
	X	Tuttle Harold	52	painter	44	"
	Y	*Grifone Anthony	52	butcher	38	"
	Z	*Grifone Lucy—†	52	housewife	31	"
690						
	A	*Delio Filomena—†	52	"	36	
	B	Delio Michael	52	laborer	38	
	C	Dexter Evelena—†	54	clerk	70	
	D	Dexter Myrtle—†	54	at home	45	"
	E	Cerulli Nancy—†	56	housewife	30	50 Wadsworth
	F	Cerulli Thomas	56	engineer	30	53 "
	G	Williams Elizabeth—†	58	housewife	55	here
	H	Williams John	58	operator	56	"
	K	Maffei Alphonse	58	cook	21	"
	L	Maffei Camilla—†	58	housewife	45	"
	M	Maffei Peter	58	laborer	45	
	N	Repucci Carlo	60	bootblack	51	"
	O	*Repucci Mary—†	60	housewife	52	"
	P	Smallcomb Bernard	68	fisherman	47	"
	R	*Smallcomb Mary—†	68	housewife	48	"

Meridian Street

	V	Cook Claude F	358	machinist	54	here
	W	Cook Claude T	358	candymaker	25	"
	X	Cook George	358	laborer	27	"
	Y	Cook Julia—†	358	housewife	53	"
	Z	Oldanie Celia—†	358	"	31	
691						
	A	Ross Howard M	358	foreman	50	
	B	Ross Mertie C—†	358	housewife	43	"
	C	Donahue John H	358	plumber	33	
	D	Donahue Madeline C—†	358	housewife	33	"
	F	*Ohearn Malcolm	359A	fisherman	33	"
	G	*Ohearn Rose—†	359A	housewife	33	"
	H	Hackett Johanna—†	359A	"	73	
	K	McInnis John	359A	seaman	57	
	L	McInnis Madeline F—†	359A	housewife	47	"
	N	Richard Emily S—†	361	"	61	
	O	Richard Newall A	361	laborer	68	
	P	*Winer Celia—†	361	housewife	55	"

Page.	Letter.	Full Name.	Residence, Jan. 1, 1938.	Occupation.	Supposed Age.	Reported Residence, Jan. 1, 1937. Street and Number.
		Meridian Street—Continued				
	R	*Winer Myer	361	cobbler	65	here
	S	Oliver Mary—†	361	housewife	65	Winthrop
	T	Quinn John F	362	mechanic	53	here
	U	Quinn John F, jr	362	laundryman	25	"
	V	Quinn Mary D—†	362	clerk	24	"
	W	Quinn Mary E—†	362	housewife	50	"
	Y	Boyan Catherine J—†	362	"	46	
	Z	Boyan Dorothy J—†	362	waitress	23	
692						
	A	Boyan Edward	362	chef	22	
	B	Boyan John J	362	boilermaker	59	"
	C	Boyan Thomas A	362	fisherman	28	"
	D	Desmond Francis	362	laborer	65	
	E	Ross Alice B—†	363	housewife	57	"
	F	Zeigler Howard	363	mechanic	29	"
	G	Zeigler Mary M—†	363	housewife	23	"
	H	Warner Joseph	363	clerk	24	
	K	Warner Mary D—†	363	housewife	23	"
	L	*Cavanagh Christina—†	363	houseworker	25	Chelsea
	M	Pike Campbell	363	laborer	38	63 Condor
	N	*Pike Mary—†	363	housewife	34	63 "
	O	*Hyde Thomas	364	chef	36	Stoughton
	P	Leith John	364	janitor	41	Revere
	R	McDonald Mary—†	364	operator	48	here
	S	Preble Elizabeth—†	364	housewife	77	"
	T	Dexter Clytie L—†	364	"	41	"
	U	Dexter David A	364	cook	52	
	V	*Aiello Frances—†	364	housewife	52	"
	W	Aiello Joseph	364	accountant	21	"
	X	Aiello Lorenzo	364	pressman	52	"
	Y	Amerena Maud M—†	365	housewife	45	"
	Z	Amerena Vincent J	365	teacher	42	
693						
	A	Alfama Asa	365	messboy	22	332 Meridian
	B	Alfama Dorothy—†	365	saleswoman	21	332 "
	C	Alphonso Mary—†	365	housewife	46	332 "
	D	Maielino Florence—†	365	housekeeper	43	here
	E	Masoli Salvatore	365	barber	53	"
	F	Donahoe David A	366	merchant	52	"
	G	Donahoe David S	366	clerk	30	
	H	Surabian Alice—†	366A	student	21	

Page.	Letter.	Full Name.	Residence, Jan. 1, 1938.	Occupation.	Supposed Age.	Reported Residence, Jan. 1, 1937. Street and Number.

Meridian Street—Continued

	K	Surabian Elizabeth—†	366A	stenographer	27	here
	L	Surabian Lazarus K	366A	butcher	54	"
	M	Surabian Lillian—†	366A	secretary	26	"
	N	Surabian Rose—†	366A	housewife	46	"
	O	*Almond Jennie—†	366A	"	48	
	P	Almond Norma—†	366A	operator	22	
	R	Almond Peter	366A	blacksmith	60	"
	S	*Cussack Timothy	366A	"	39	
	T	Rose Fred	366A	chef	42	"
	U	Sheedy George	366A	mechanic	43	321 Border
	V	Sheedy John	366A	painter	39	321 "
	W	Byrne Joseph L	368	ironworker	38	here
	X	Flynn Michael J	368	retired	74	"
	Y	Gorman Frank A	368	clerk	55	"
	Z	Gorman James L	368	"	60	
694						
	A	*Johnson Annie—†	368A	housekeeper	76	"
	B	Laidlaw Frederick W	368A	painter	49	"
	C	Laidlaw Lillian—†	368A	clerk	22	
	D	Laidlaw Lillian J—†	368A	housewife	45	"
	E	Laidlaw Loretta G—†	368A	clerk	25	
	F	Demerjian Alice—†	368A	housewife	40	"
	G	Demerjian Max	368A	shipper	42	
	H	Cooke Clarence	369	boilermaker	47	"
	K	Cooke Olivetta—†	369	housewife	45	"
	L	Alves Anna—†	369	"	38	
	M	Alves Jesse J	369	laborer	41	
	N	Alves John J	369	student	21	
	O	Alves Mary—†	369	at home	69	
	P	Davidson John J	369	timekeeper	31	"
	R	DiVirgilio Mary—†	369	operator	23	"
	S	DiVirgilio Peter	369	baker	24	
	T	Dearing Ann—†	370	teacher	57	
	U	Andrews George	370	chef	24	
	V	*Andrews Thomas	370	"	60	
	W	*Attwood Angus	370	retired	75	
	X	*Attwood Nancy—†	370	housewife	71	"
	Y	Morrison Alice—†	370	clerk	32	
	Z	Smith Georgia M—†	370	operator	60	
695						
	A	Cameron Alice—†	370	housewife	54	"

Page.	Letter.	Full Name.	Residence, Jan. 1, 1938.	Occupation.	Supposed Age.	Reported Residence, Jan. 1, 1937. Street and Number.

Meridian Street—Continued

Page.	Letter.	Full Name.	Residence, Jan. 1, 1938.	Occupation.	Supposed Age.	Reported Residence, Jan. 1, 1937. Street and Number.
	B	Cameron Ruth—†	370	teacher	30	here
	C	Hunter Cora E—†	370	agent	56	"
	D	*Palmer Albert	371	painter	49	"
	E	Palmer Mary—†	371	housewife	51	"
	F	Palmer Mildred—†	371	laundryworker	24	"
	G	Ruggiero Anna—†	371	housewife	23	25 White
	H	Ruggiero Anthony	371	painter	25	189 Havre
	K	Cunningham Mary—†	372	housewife	76	here
	L	Cunningham Thomas H	372	retired	76	"
	M	Johnson Charles	372	laundryworker	39	Arlington
	N	McCormack Elizabeth A—†	372	housewife	51	here
	O	McCormack John J	372	mechanic	51	"
	P	Claus May—†	372	housewife	25	"
	R	Claus Paul	372	printer	27	
	S	Cunningham Claire—†	372	clerk	23	
	T	Cunningham Helen—†	372	"	21	
	U	Cunningham Eva—†	372	housewife	46	"
	V	Cunningham Thomas	372	clerk	49	
	W	Olsen Carl	373	laborer	55	"
	X	DiBenedetto Mary L—†	379	housewife	24	"
	Y	DiBenedetto Vencenzo	379	chef	44	"
	Z	Shaw Clarence	379	salesman	62	153 Trenton
696						
	A	Shaw Delia—†	379	housewife	62	153 "
	B	*DiBenedetto Mary—†	379	"	38	here
	C	*DiBenedetto Ralph	379	tailor	46	"
	D	Parma John	379	laborer	44	"
	E	*Parma Mary—†	379	housewife	44	"
	F	*Walker Catherine—†	381	"	50	
	G	*Walker John	381	laborer	49	
	H	Walker Mark	381	clerk	21	
	L	Beveilacqua Anna—†	381	housewife	34	"
	M	*Bevilacqua Salvatore	381	laborer	44	
	N	*Catinazzo Louis	383	lather	31	
	O	Catinazzo Margaret—†	383	housewife	35	"
	P	*Comeau Augustus	383	calker	53	Chelsea
	R	*Comeau Joseph	383	carpenter	57	here
	S	Comeau Simon	383	"	40	"
	T	Hayes Warren	383	machinist	46	191 Sumner
	U	Maggio Catherine—†	383	waitress	27	284 Meridian
	V	*Saulneir Agnes—†	383	housewife	40	here

Page.	Letter.	Full Name.	Residence, Jan. 1, 1938.	Occupation.	Supposed Age.	Reported Residence, Jan. 1, 1937. Street and Number.

Meridian Street—Continued

	w	Saulneir Alfred	383	carpenter	44	here
	x	*Sbriglio Conchetta—†	385	housewife	48	“
	y	*Sbriglio Paul	385	laborer	58	“
	z	O'Brien Dennis J	385	“	37	
697						
	A	*O'Brien Mary L—†	385	housewife	37	“
	B	*Lento Marie—†	385	“	50	
	C	*Lento Pasquale	385	laborer	56	
	E	Zazzaretti Joseph	387	“	25	
	F	Zazzaretti Pietrina—†	387	housewife	25	“
	G	Fazio Aurelio	387	shoemaker	52	“
	H	*Fazio Josephine—†	387	housewife	45	“
	K	*Perma Josephine—†	387	“	47	
	L	Perma Nicholas	387	plasterer	50	“
	M	Graves Janet H—†	388	secretary	40	“
	N	Graves Jennie H—†	388	housewife	60	“
	O	Bar Charles R	388	retired	81	
	P	Greenslaide Ralph S	388	student	22	
	R	Kieling John	388	janitor	61	
	S	Kieling Lillian E—†	388	housewife	54	“
	U	Whalen Margaret—†	389	“	47	362 Meridian
	V	Whalen Thomas J	389	fisherman	47	362 “
	W	Goldenberg Edward B	389	salesman	42	here
	X	Goldenberg Lillian—†	389	housewife	44	“
	Y	*Longo Theresa—†	389	“	67	“
	Z	Minichino Louis	389	receiver	26	
698						
	A	Minichino Margaret—†	389	housewife	26	“
	B	Wellington Alfred E	390	banker	65	
	C	*Palladino Jeremiah	391	barber	76	
	D	Palladino Joseph	391	pedler	38	
	E	Palladino Ann—†	391	operator	25	
	F	*Palladino Constance—†	391	housewife	65	“
	G	Palladino Victor	391	packer	32	
	H	Shannon John B	391	chauffeur	38	“
	K	Shannon Theresa—†	391	housewife	35	“
	N	Hartigan Imelda—†	393A	saleswoman	23	“
	O	Hartigan Veronica—†	393A	housewife	50	“
	P	Hartigan William	393A	seaman	50	
	R	Fronglio Louis	393A	electrician	33	“
	S	Safrin Annie M—†	393A	housewife	54	“

Page.	Letter.	Full Name.	Residence, Jan. 1, 1938.	Occupation.	Supposed Age.	Reported Residence, Jan. 1, 1937. Street and Number.

Meridian Street—Continued

	T	Safrin Francis E	393A	clerk	36	here
	U	Safrin Frank A	393A	laborer	57	"
	V	Benoit Alexander	394	painter	32	"
	W	Benoit Victoria—†	394	housewife	23	"
	X	DePlacido Frank	394	laborer	52	
	Y	*DePlacido Mary—†	394	houseworker	28	"
	Z	DePlacido Prudence—†	394	housewife	54	"
699						
	A	Flynn Ethel B—†	394	"	49	37 Falcon
	B	McMahon Helen—†	394	maid	38	50 "
	C	Yeo Jennie M—†	394	housewife	58	50 "
	D	Porter Clarence	395	laborer	25	here
	E	*Porter Elizabeth—†	395	housewife	58	"
	F	Hunt Daniel	395	watchman	45	"
	G	Hunt Ethel—†	395	housewife	40	"
	H	Harney Edward J	395	painter	40	
	K	Harney Elizabeth—†	395	housewife	39	"
	L	Roskilly Colin	396	shipper	60	
	M	Sloan Ann—†	396	housewife	66	"
	N	Sloan Margaret—†	396	bookkeeper	58	"
	P	Brown Bertha—†	398	housewife	68	"
	R	Brown Wallis	398	engineer	74	
	S	Ross Mabel E—†	398	housewife	50	"
	T	Ross Thomas	398	seaman	38	
	U	McElman Allen	398	welder	24	
	V	McElman Anna—†	398	housewife	24	"
	W	*Hughes Willa—†	401	"	36	101 Benningt'n
	X	*Hughes William	401	watertender	31	101 "
	Y	*Muise Dorothy—†	401	housewife	26	here
	Z	Muise Lester	401	seaman	33	"
700						
	A	Forrest Elizabeth—†	401	housewife	67	"
	B	Forrest Frederick	401	retired	73	
	C	Forrest Leroy	401	clerk	25	
	D	Forrest Lucille—†	401	sorter	23	
	E	Forrest Maud S—†	401	operator	38	
	F	Belmonte Frada E	402	machinist	28	"
	G	Belmonte Helen—†	402	bookkeeper	36	"
	H	Bordonaro Joseph	402	laborer	53	"
	K	Bordonaro Peter	402	clerk	23	
	L	Bordonaro Tina—†	402	housewife	24	"

Page.	Letter.	FULL NAME.	Residence, Jan. 1, 1938.	Occupation.	Supposed Age.	Reported Residence, Jan. 1, 1937. Street and Number.

Meridian Street—Continued

	M	*Harnich Leona—†	402	housewife	36	here
	N	*Harnich Robert	402	foreman	43	"
	O	Papasodoro Mary—†	402	housewife	29	"
	P	Papasodoro Onofrio	402	laborer	30	
	R	Siracusa Nicholas	402	shoeworker	27	"
	S	*Siracusa Palma—†	402	housewife	27	"
	T	Morley Eva—†	403	teacher	67	
	U	Dean Benjamin	404	welder	27	
	V	Dean Mildred—†	404	housewife	25	"
	W	Prato Dominick	404	laborer	27	
	X	Prato Mary—†	404	dressmaker	25	"
	Y	Santienello Conchetta—†	404	housewife	42	"
	Z	Santienello Michael	404	merchant	49	"
701						
	A	Manfredonia Grace—†	404	housewife	24	74 Eutaw
	B	Manfredonia Ralph	404	chauffeur	27	132 Benningt'n
	C	Vege Andrew	404	seaman	40	here
	D	Vege Evelyn—†	404	housewife	39	"
	E	Silver Anthony	404	clerk	33	"
	F	Silver Julia—†	404	housewife	28	"
	K	Rutherford Barbara—†	406	"	27	
	L	Rutherford Robert	406	social worker	28	"
	M	Bluhm Martha—†	407	housewife	24	"
	N	Bluhm Samuel	407	merchant	29	"
	O	Comeau Arthur	407	fishcutter	30	"
	P	Comeau Helen—†	407	housewife	36	"

Monmouth Street

	U	Bennett Mary—†	1	housekeeper	66	here
	V	Boudreau Henry	1	carpenter	42	"
	W	Morris Elisha	1	salesman	23	"
	X	Tahash Eugene	1	clerk	24	
	Y	Stewart Ethel F—†	1	stenographer	26	"
	Z	Stewart Mary—†	1	housewife	62	"
702						
	A	Stewart William R	1	checker	30	"
	B	Busquets Antonio	1	engineer	55	394 Meridian
	C	Busquets Catelena—†	1	housewife	38	394 "
	D	Iverson Frederick	3	engineer	68	321 Border
	E	Iverson Freida—†	3	housewife	60	321 "

Page.	Letter.	Full Name.	Residence, Jan. 1, 1938.	Occupation.	Supposed Age.	Reported Residence, Jan. 1, 1937. Street and Number.

Monmouth Street—Continued

	F	Leman Arthur A	3	manufacturer	66	here
	G	Leman Dorothy M—†	3	at home	21	"
	H	Leman Maude L—†	3	housewife	56	"
	K	Sawyer Joseph L	3	pilot	43	
	L	Sawyer Sarah A—†	3	housewife	58	"
	O	Swim Evelyn—†	7	waitress	23	"
	P	Swim Herbert	7	cook	37	
	R	*Swim Joseph	7	bartender	30	"
	S	Lawless Agnes G—†	7	housewife	55	"
	T	Lawless John J	7	mover	45	
	U	Vega Nicholas	8	barber	55	"
	V	Vega Rose—†	8	housewife	53	"
	W	Killeen Gertrude—†	8	hairdresser	22	"
	X	Killeen Lena—†	8	housekeeper	44	"
	Y	Parmenter Charles R	9	pilot	60	"
	Z	Parmenter Edith D—†	9	housewife	59	"
703						
	A	Crosby Effie G—†	9	housekeeper	59	"
	B	McDonald Margaret—†	9	seamstress	66	"
	C	Moseley Elsie—†	9	nurse	58	"
	D	Martell Harold A	10	gardener	23	37 Eutaw
	E	Martell Helen—†	10	housewife	61	37 "
	F	Martell William F	10	laborer	29	37 "
	G	*Lindstrom Dorothy—†	10	housewife	33	54 Putnam
	H	*Lindstrom Fred	10	fisherman	34	54 "
	K	*Lindstrom Walter	10	"	30	54 "
	L	Hodney Andrew	11	engineer	58	here
	M	McLaughlin Margaret—†	11	housekeeper	35	"
	N	Cotillo Evelyn—†	11	housewife	47	"
	O	Cotillo Jennie—†	11	clerk	21	"
	P	Cotillo Ralph	11	barber	47	"
	R	Finney Charles B	11	foreman	59	"
	S	Finney Clarinda—†	11	housewife	63	"
	T	Antonelli Edith—†	12	inspector	31	"
	U	Antonelli Esther—†	12	operator	26	
	V	*Antonelli Mary—†	12	housewife	64	"
	W	Antonelli William	12	operator	27	"
	X	Melisi Jennie—†	12	housewife	33	"
	Y	Melisi Thomas	12	mechanic	35	"
	Z	Flynn Annie—†	13	housewife	64	232 Lexington

Page.	Letter.	Full Name.	Residence, Jan. 1, 1938.	Occupation.	Supposed Age.	Reported Residence, Jan. 1, 1937. Street and Number.
704		**Monmouth Street**—Continued				
	A	Flynn James J	13	clerk	33	232 Lexington
	B	Flynn James S	13	watchman	63	232 "
	C	Flynn William H	13	laborer	28	232 "
	D	*Poirier Francis W	13	fisherman	32	76 Trenton
	E	*Poirier Georgina—†	13	housewife	65	76 "
	F	*Poirier Hubert S	13	fisherman	28	76 "
	G	*Poirier Margaret A—†	13	clerk	22	76 "
	H	*Burke Emily—†	13	presser	30	38 Lexington
	K	Poirier Albanie	13	painter	30	38 "
	L	*Poirier Marie—†	13	housewife	25	38 "
	M	*DiSimone Louis	14	painter	44	251 '
	N	Rogers Herbert W	14	cutter	34	251 '
	O	Rogers Mary—†	14	housewife	31	251 "
	P	Belkner Paul	14	baker	42	266 Princeton
	R	Belkner Violet—†	14	housewife	36	266 "
	S	Foley Elizabeth C—†	15	housekeeper	65	here
	T	Ingalls Bernard	15	laborer	65	"
	U	Ingalls Margaret—†	15	housewife	62	"
	V	Kenney Earl E	15	laborer	48	
	W	Kenney Marie—†	15	housewife	46	"
	X	Reed Annie C—†	17	"	63	
	Y	Reed Gilbert C	17	engineer	63	
	Z	Greenwood Leonard G	17	patternmaker	53	"
705						
	A	Greenwood Margaret P–†	17	housewife	53	"
	B	Vallen Concehtta—†	21	housekeeper	26	"
	C	Spalvero Albert	21	laborer	41	"
	D	Spalvero Grace—†	21	housewife	29	"
	E	Cogswell Francis	21	seaman	24	
	F	Cogswell Mary—†	21	housewife	21	"
	G	Zaino Angelena—†	21	"	55	
	H	Zaino Elizabeth—†	21	dressmaker	20	"
	K	Zaino Frank	21	laborer	58	
	L	Cucchiara Gaetano	22	"	55	
	M	Cucchiara Mary—†	22	operator	22	
	N	*Cucchiara Paul	22	hairdresser	25	"
	O	*Cucchiara Rose—†	22	housewife	48	"
	P	Anzaldi Guy	22	machinist	22	"
	R	*Anzaldi Josephine—†	22	housewife	40	"

Page.	Letter.	FULL NAME.	Residence, Jan. 1, 1938.	Occupation.	Supposed Age.	Reported Residence, Jan. 1, 1937. Street and Number.

Monmouth Street—Continued

	S	Anzaldi Louis	22	laborer	49	here
	T	Buontempo Anna—†	23	housewife	33	10 Winthrop
	U	Buontempo Patrick	23	painter	36	10 "
	V	Boudreau Anna—†	23	candyworker	30	here
	W	*Boudreau Emma—†	23	housewife	67	"
	X	Boudreau Joseph	23	laborer	23	"
	Y	Buontempo Albert	23	chauffeur	25	"
	Z	*Buontempo Filomena—†	23	housewife	65	"
706						
	A	*Buontempo Frank	23	laborer	65	
	B	Stone Margaret—†	25	housekeeper	71	"
	C	Hamilton Jeanette—†	26	housewife	52	"
	D	Hamilton Linwood S	26	seaman	53	
	E	Cline James H	26	broker	76	
	F	McClements John W	26	nurse	49	
	G	Porper Susie—†	26	housekeeper	67	"
	H	Sullivan Frank E	26	teacher	56	"
	K	O'Brien Elizabeth A—†	27	housewife	37	"
	L	O'Brien Thomas F	27	manager	39	"
	M	Sullivan Irvin J	27	seaman	38	"
	N	Anzalone Ernestina—†	28	housewife	24	35 Liverpool
	O	Anzalone Joseph	28	salesman	30	35 "
	P	Cabone Alfred	28	barber	55	here
	R	Cabone Antonetta—†	28	housewife	29	"
	S	Cabone Carmelia—†	28	"	52	"
	T	Cabone Vincent	28	painter	29	
	U	Miller Elizabeth—†	29	saleswoman	25	"
	V	Miller John	29	boilermaker	54	"
	W	Miller Priscilla—†	29	housewife	59	"
	X	Miller Sarah I—†	29	at home	23	
	Y	Coffin Seymour	29	janitor	72	
	Z	Coffin Susanna P—†	29	housewife	67	"
707						
	A	Comeau George	30	bellboy	28	
	B	Comeau Verna—†	30	housewife	25	"
	C	D'Entremont Bernard	30	carpenter	32	"
	D	*D'Entremont Irene—†	30	housewife	32	"
	E	*D'Entremont Louis	30	fisherman	31	"
	F	*Deon Emeline—†	30	housekeeper	65	"
	G	Dattler James	30	laborer	44	"
	H	Dattler Lillian—†	30	housewife	42	"

Page.	Letter.	Full Name.	Residence, Jan. 1, 1938.	Occupation.	Supposed Age.	Reported Residence, Jan. 1, 1937. Street and Number.

Monmouth Street—Continued

	K	Duffy Frank	30	shipper	43	here
	L	*Ryan Renie—†	31	housewife	34	"
	M	*Ryan Thomas	31	longshoreman	32	"
	N	*LePeron Henrietta—†	31	housekeeper	60	"
	O	*Dalton Hazel—†	32	housewife	27	"
	P	Dalton William	32	fishcutter	33	"
	R	Scopa Anthony	32	laborer	58	
	S	Scopa Antonetta—†	32	at home	21	
	T	*Scopa Filomena—†	32	housewife	58	"
	U	*Scopa Joseph	32	laborer	33	
	V	Scopa Lucy—†	32	milliner	26	
	W	Scopa Mary—†	32	"	24	
	X	Ballem Edna—†	33	clerk	23	
	Y	Ballem John	33	retired	72	
	Z	Ballem Mary G—†	33	housewife	65	"
708						
	A	Nuzzolo Charles	34	operator	37	
	B	Nuzzolo Jean—†	34	"	28	
	C	Nuzzolo Josephine—†	34	candyworker	22	"
	D	*Nuzzolo Mary—†	34	housewife	65	"
	E	*Pisco Clara—†	34	"	52	
	F	Pisco Elizabeth—†	34	dressmaker	21	"
	G	Pisco Francesco	34	expressman	58	"
	H	Guarnera Carmella—†	36	seamstress	21	"
	K	Guarnera Catherine—†	36	housewife	56	"
	L	Guarnera Charles	36	bricklayer	57	"
	M	Guarnera Conchetta—†	36	entertainer	25	"
	N	Guarnera Guy	36	salesman	28	"
	O	Parrelli Frank	36	"	31	"
	P	Parrelli Stephanie—†	36	housewife	30	"
	R	Guarnera Joseph	36	clerk	24	
	S	Guarnera Mary—†	36	housewife	25	"
	T	Wessling Frank	37	laborer	43	
	U	Wessling Margaret—†	37	housewife	47	"
	V	Kennedy Anne—†	37	"	66	
	W	Kennedy Bernard	37	retired	68	
	X	Kennedy William	37	bookkeeper	25	"
	Y	Bulens Harry	38	laborer	33	"
	Z	Bulens Nellie—†	38	housewife	30	"
709						
	A	Chase Mary L—†	38	at home	72	

Page.	Letter.	Full Name.	Residence, Jan. 1, 1938.	Occupation.	Supposed Age.	Reported Residence, Jan. 1, 1937. Street and Number.

Monmouth Street—Continued

	B	*Andrade Manuel	38	longshoreman	37	here
	C	*Andrade Mary—†	38	housewife	35	"
	D	*Francis Manuel V	rear 38	longshoreman	52	"
	E	Francis Mary—†	" 38	housewife	20	"
	F	*Amerault Elsie—†	39	"	36	
	G	*Amerault Leslie T	39	laborer	36	"
	H	Hanrahan Ruth—†	39	cutter	33	453 Meridian
	K	Maggin Edward	39	retired	72	here
	L	McCarthy Bessie—†	39	housewife	36	453 Meridian
	M	McCarthy James	39	B F D	40	453 "
	N	Memmolo Grace—†	40	housewife	31	here
	O	Memmolo Thomas	40	chauffeur	31	"
	P	Pascucci Edward	40	cleaner	22	"
	R	Pascucci Henry	40	machinist	24	"
	S	*Pascucci Nicoletta—†	40	housewife	49	"
	T	Pascucci Sabino	40	laborer	55	"
	U	*Boland Julia—†	41	housewife	39	"
	V	Boland Vincent	41	seaman	37	
	W	Bartley Allen	41	retired	84	
	X	Martin Katherine—†	41	housekeeper	60	"
	Y	Delaney Anne L—†	41	"	73	"
	Z	Maginn Charles H	42	patternmaker	59	"
710						
	A	Call Maria A—†	43	housekeeper	75	"
	B	Herzig Joseph M	43	electrician	71	"
	C	Burr Elizabeth K—†	43	hairdresser	66	"
	D	Schluter Doris—†	44	housewife	27	"
	E	Schluter Harry	44	seaman	36	
	F	Tracy May M—†	44	housewife	50	"
	G	Tracy Paul D	44	machinist	57	"
	H	Crocker Carlton W	45	pharmacist	63	"
	K	Crocker Carlton W, jr	45	seaman	26	
	L	Crocker Eliza M—†	45	housewife	61	"
	M	Crocker Harvey J	45	student	20	
	N	Crocker Jean E—†	45	at home	22	
	O	Murphy Edwin J	45	mechanic	40	"
	P	McCarthy Edward J	46	teacher	44	
	R	McCarthy Mary—†	46	housewife	71	"
	S	McCarthy William E	46	teacher	32	
	T	Grasse Lillian—†	47	housewife	25	"
	U	Grasse Maynard	47	laborer	34	

Page.	Letter.	FULL NAME.	Residence, Jan. 1, 1938.	Occupation.	Supposed Age.	Reported Residence, Jan. 1, 1937. Street and Number.

Monmouth Street—Continued

	V	Hagen Alvah	47	fishcutter	44	here
	W	Hagen Mary—†	47	housewife	46	"
	X	Furniss Catherine J—†	48	bookkeeper	65	"
	Y	Power Gertrude—†	48	stenographer	27	"
	Z	Power Mabel—†	48	operator	29	"
711						
	A	Power Stephen	48	retired	65	
	B	Power Susie—†	48	housewife	59	"
	C	Campbell Jospeh	49	B F D	39	
	D	Campbell Margaret A—†	49	housewife	39	"
	E	Norman William	49	painter	45	
	F	Thivierge Edward	49	retired	89	
	G	Thivierge Virginia—†	49	housewife	75	"
	H	Stokes Ellen T—†	50	"	31	
	K	Stokes Walter	50	printer	31	
	L	Ferris Antone L	50	guard	59	
	M	Lombard Anthony W	50	barber	25	
	N	Lombard Frances—†	50	housewife	41	"
	O	Lombard Robert A	50	clerk	21	
	P	*Costa Vivian—†	51	housekeeper	64	"
	R	Ingalls Mary—†	51	housewife	37	"
	S	Ingalls Reginald	51	chauffeur	33	"
	T	Nazzaro Bessie—†	51	housewife	31	"
	U	Nazzaro Robert	51	electrician	35	"
	V	Sullivan Francis J	51	seaman	37	
	W	Sullivan Violet J—†	51	housewife	27	"
	X	Narroway Rose—†	52	housekeeper	78	"
	Y	Strong James H	52	physician	65	"
	Z	Strong Mary L—†	52	housewife	62	"
712						
	A	O'Brien Alice—†	53	secretary	32	"
	B	O'Brien Anne M—†	53	housewife	73	"
	C	O'Brien David L	53	installer	39	
	D	O'Brien Michael J	53	retired	84	
	E	Sorensen George	55	engineer	23	
	F	Sorensen Olive—†	55	housewife	60	"
	G	Sorensen Theodore	55	machinist	48	"
	H	Sullivan Thomas C	57	retired	59	
	K	Wellings John S	57	policeman	44	"
	L	Wellings Lauretta M—†	57	teacher	24	
	M	Wellings Mary A—†	57	housewife	43	"

Page.	Letter.	FULL NAME.	Residence, Jan. 1, 1938.	Occupation.	Supposed Age.	Reported Residence, Jan. 1, 1937. Street and Number.

Monmouth Street—Continued

	N	Warren Fred L	59	salesman	42	here
	O	Warren George W	59	clergyman	77	"
	P	Warren Marjorie C—†	59	social worker	44	"
	R	*Robicheau Edith—†	61	housewife	25	90 Morris
	S	*Robicheau Joseph B	61	carpenter	32	90 "
	T	*Gomes Braz	61	longshoreman	42	here
	U	*Gomes Mary—†	61	housewife	40	"
	V	D'Entremont Elmer	61	foreman	27	"
	W	Hutchinson Margaret—†	61	housewife	24	"
	X	Hutchinson Richard	61	laborer	31	"
	Y	Pisello Carmine	63	carpenter	40	8 Liverpool
	Z	Pisello Mary—†	63	housewife	34	8 "
713						
	A	Repucci Edith—†	63	candyworker	23	here
	B	*Repucci Joseph	63	laborer	72	"
	C	Grainger Harry	63	custodian	63	"
	D	Repucci Alfred	63	"	39	
	E	Repucci Caroline—†	63	housewife	35	"
	F	Repucci John	63	chauffeur	41	"
	G	Repucci Rose—†	63	housewife	30	"

Putnam Street

	H	*Morella Marino	65	laborer	72	here
	K	Russo Agatino	65	chauffeur	32	"
	L	Russo Florence—†	65	housewife	26	"
	M	Lepore Antonio	67	operator	44	
	N	Lepore Conchetta—†	67	housewife	27	"
	O	*Fitzgerald Catherine—†	67	"	36	
	P	Fitzgerald Francis	67	chauffeur	49	"
	R	Sheehy Catherine—†	69	housewife	65	39 Marion
	S	Jones George	69	dentist	30	here
	T	Jones Rose—†	69	housewife	30	"
	U	Moreschi Lena—†	69	"	43	"
	V	Moreschi Raffaele	69	laborer	47	
	W	Perkins Harry F	71	engineer	62	
	X	Perkins Josephine L—†	71	housewife	63	"
	Y	Rutledge Almyra H—†	71	"	62	
	Z	Rutledge Harold B	71	clerk	40	
714						
	A	Maxwell Effie—†	73	houseworker	68	"

Page.	Letter.	Full Name.	Residence, Jan. 1, 1938.	Occupation.	Supposed Age.	Reported Residence, Jan. 1, 1937. Street and Number.

Putnam Street—Continued

Page.	Letter.	Full Name.	Residence, Jan. 1, 1938.	Occupation.	Supposed Age.	Reported Residence, Jan. 1, 1937. Street and Number.
	B	*Wyman Della—†	73	houseworker	58	here
	C	Bertino Andrew	75	salesman	23	193 Lexington
	D	*Bertino Antonetta—†	75	housewife	46	193 “

Trenton Street

Page.	Letter.	Full Name.	Residence, Jan. 1, 1938.	Occupation.	Supposed Age.	Reported Residence, Jan. 1, 1937. Street and Number.
	G	*Druken Patrick	56	fisherman	39	here
	H	*Powers Augustus	56	“	32	“
	K	Shanahan Rose—†	56	housekeeper	44	“
	L	*Barros Anna—†	56	housewife	35	“
	M	*Barros Antonio	56	operator	52	“
	N	*Barros Henry	56	cook	47	
	O	*Barros Theofido	56	“	45	
	P	Constien Margaret—†	58	operator	25	“
	R	Cronin Catherine—†	58	housewife	32	“
	S	Cronin James F	58	policeman	34	“
	T	Giovino Alfred	58	boxmaker	32	“
	U	*Giovino Carmeno	58	retired	67	
	V	*Giovino Jennie—†	58	housewife	60	“
	W	Giovino Lillian—†	58	operator	25	“
	X	Giovino Louis	58	“	27	
	Y	*Miller Henry P	60	shipfitter	39	“
	Z	*Miller Mildred—†	60	housewife	29	“
715						
	A	Nesbitt Clement B	60	laborer	24	
	B	*Nesbitt George A	60	fisherman	60	“
	C	*Nesbitt Georgina—†	60	housewife	52	“
	E	Stacey Bessie—†	62	“	43	94 Trenton
	F	Stacey Hubbard	62	machinist	51	94 “
	G	*Colatrella Carmine	62	operator	46	here
	H	*Colatrella Jennie—†	62	housewife	41	“
	K	*Robicheau Lucy—†	rear 62	“	31	94 Lexington
	L	Robicheau Wilbourn	“ 62	carpenter	34	94 “
	M	Bellino James	64	salesman	30	here
	N	Bellino Mary—†	64	housewife	27	“
	O	Campagna Adelaide—†	64	cashier	40	“
	P	*Campagna Marie—†	64	housewife	66	“
	R	Campagna Robert	64	printer	31	“
	S	Iocco Rocco	64	rubberworker	43	“
	T	*Iocco Theresa—†	64	housewife	44	“
	U	*Carvalho August	66	seaman	26	

Page.	Letter.	Full Name.	Residence, Jan. 1, 1938.	Occupation.	Supposed Age.	Reported Residence, Jan. 1, 1937. Street and Number.

Trenton Street—Continued

Page.	Letter.	Full Name.	Residence, Jan. 1, 1938.	Occupation.	Supposed Age.	Reported Residence, Jan. 1, 1937. Street and Number.
	v	*Carvalho Johanna—†	66	housewife	51	here
	w	*Carvalho Mario	66	repairman	42	"
	x	Gillespie Arthur	66	musician	36	81 Lexington
	y	Santos Manuel	66	seaman	56	here
	z	McNeely Madeline—†	68	housekeeper	34	9 Trenton
716						
	A	Insley Aphra	68	seaman	50	327 Paris
	B	Insley Lessie—†	68	housewife	45	327 "
	C	Insley Sarah—†	68	laundryworker	22	327 "
	D	Swimm Harriet—†	68	housekeeper	33	Everett
	E	Porrazzo Anna—†	70	housewife	22	75 Webster
	F	Porrazzo Joseph	70	printer	26	70 "
	G	DiNicola Albert	70	clerk	21	here
	H	Mariani Domenic	70	printer	24	"
	K	Mariani Sebatino	70	mechanic	56	"
	L	Elberfeld Isabel—†	72	housewife	62	"
	M	Elberfeld John	72	teacher	34	
	N	Elberfeld Richard B	72	student	20	
	O	Elberfeld Samuel L	72	clergyman	69	"
	P	Jollimore Alma—†	74	housekeeper	26	"
	R	Morrow Irving A	74	chauffeur	31	"
	S	*Morrow Nina—†	74	housewife	54	"
	T	Saggese Anthony	74	barber	28	
	U	*Saggese Sestina B—†	74	housewife	26	"
	V	Catania Joseph L	74	shipper	23	
	W	Catania Marie—†	74	housewife	25	"
	X	*Beranger Frances—†	76	"	26	8 W Eagle
	Y	Beranger Paul	76	fisherman	27	8 "
717						
	A	*Banks Elsie—†	78	housewife	45	48 Marion
	B	Banks Oran	78	chauffeur	55	2 Paris
	C	*DiFazio Carmella—†	78	housewife	40	68 Trenton
	D	DiFazio Carmello	78	tileworker	39	68 "
	F	Blake Frank	80	mechanic	36	here
	G	Harrison Annie F—†	80	housekeeper	40	"
	H	Riggs Anna—†	80	waitress	31	"
	L	*Frato Conchetta—†	82	housewife	46	"
	M	Frato John	82	laborer	54	
	N	Frato Joseph	82	operator	24	
	O	Frato Orlando	82	"	21	
	P	*Ferri Jennie—†	82	housewife	28	"

Page.	Letter.	Full Name.	Residence, Jan. 1, 1938.	Occupation.	Supposed Age.	Reported Residence, Jan. 1, 1937. Street and Number.

Trenton Street—Continued

	R	Ferri Umberto	82	tailor	41	here
	S	Porreca Sebastian	82	barber	50	"
	T	Harney Genevieve N—†	86	housewife	30	"
	U	Harney John F	86	painter	35	
	V	*Alberti Angelina—†	86	housewife	49	"
	W	Alberti Edith—†	86	operator	20	
	X	Alberti Jennie—†	86	at home	24	
	Y	*Alberti Rocco	86	laborer	54	"
	Z	DiBilio Gaetano	86	watchman	55	226 Chelsea
718						
	A	DiBilio Grace—†	86	teacher	21	226 "
	B	*DiBilio Maria—†	86	housewife	45	226 "
	C	*Fabrizio Margaret—†	88	retired	79	here
	D	Rasetti Luigi	88	engineer	41	"
	E	Rasetti Mary—†	88	housewife	40	"
	F	LaBella Anthony	88	barber	54	
	G	LaBella Charles	88	manager	29	"
	H	LaBella Erminia—†	88	housewife	54	"
	K	LaBella Gerardo	88	butcher	24	
	M	Marchand Marie A—†	90	housewife	37	"
	L	Marchand Narcisse	90	freighthandler	37	"
	N	Buono Antonio	90	laborer	43	
	O	Buono Mary—†	90	housewife	40	"
	P	Baccardax Juanita—†	92	housekeeper	38	"
	R	*Lamberti Mary—†	92	housewife	45	"
	S	*Lamberti Philip	92	operator	52	
	T	Puorro Antonio	94	retired	44	
	U	*Puorro Filomena—†	94	housewife	36	"
	V	Govoni John	94	B F D	42	
	W	*Govoni Mildred—†	94	housewife	37	"
	X	Rose Jessie—†	94	"	26	70 Trenton
	Y	Rose Manuel	94	steward	32	70 "
719						
	A	Carroll Agnes—†	96	housewife	28	21 Marion
	B	*Carroll Joseph	96	chauffeur	31	21 "
	C	Daye Ruth—†	96	housewife	22	here
	D	*Daye Wilfred	96	ironworker	35	"
	E	*McCormack Catherine—†	96	housewife	27	20 Morris
	F	McCormack Ronald	96	machinist	33	20 "
	G	Hardy Charles O	98	foreman	44	here
	H	Hardy Lillian B—†	98	housewife	41	"

Page.	Letter.	Full Name.	Residence, Jan. 1, 1938.	Occupation.	Supposed Age.	Reported Residence, Jan. 1, 1937. Street and Number.

Trenton Street—Continued

	K	Hardy William	98	operator	21	here
	L	Poor Charles	98	laborer	55	"
	M	Thompson Anne—†	100	housewife	64	"
	N	Thompson Helen I—†	100	teacher	30	
	O	Ford John	102	mechanic	44	"
	P	Winnerberg Emil F	102	engineer	70	
	R	Winnerberg Mattie—†	102	housewife	70	"
	U	Sannella Ralph	110	tailor	48	Revere
	V	Sannella Thomasina—†	110	housewife	35	"
	W	*Hurley Daniel J	110	longshoreman	43	here
	X	*Hurley Laura M—†	110	housewife	41	"
	Y	Perelli Philip	112	retired	65	"
	Z	*Whiffen Catherine—†	112	housewife	29	"
720						
	A	*Whiffen John	112	fisherman	32	"
	B	*Whiffen Thomas	112	"	29	
	C	Elvey John	112	fireman	42	
	D	Elvey Milton	112	fishcutter	40	"
	E	Elvey Stella—†	112	housewife	39	"
	F	Driscoll Evelyn—†	112	at home	23	36 Beachview rd
	G	Madison Catherine—†	112	housewife	28	36 "
	H	Madison Edwin	112	longshoreman	29	36 "
	K	Maylor Ernest G	114	chauffeur	34	here
	L	*Zuccola Josephine—†	114	housewife	54	"
	M	Zuccola Katie—†	114	tailoress	24	"
	N	Stymest Albert	114	mechanic	27	249 Lexington
	O	Stymest Nancy—†	114	housewife	22	249 "
	P	Maylor Clyde	116	attorney	32	here
	R	Maylor Elizabeth H—†	116	housewife	24	"
	S	*Dinn John	116	laborer	36	76 Havre
	T	*Dinn Mary—†	116	housewife	35	76 "
	U	Smith John	116	fisherman	33	76 "
	V	Micciche Diego	116	laborer	45	here
	W	Micciche Lena—†	116	housewife	39	"
	X	Boudreau Clifford	118	fisherman	32	"
	Y	Boudreau Rose—†	118	housewife	26	"
	Z	*Muise Mary C—†	118	"	32	
721						
	A	*Muise Peter B	118	fishcutter	38	"
	B	Garvey Anna—†	118	housewife	23	"
	C	Garvey Robert E	118	operator	28	"

Page.	Letter.	Full Name.	Residence, Jan. 1, 1938.	Occupation.	Supposed Age.	Reported Residence, Jan. 1, 1937. Street and Number.
		Trenton Street—Continued				
	D	LaBella Gino	120	barber	26	here
	E	LaBella Louise—†	120	housewife	24	"
	F	Morgan Daniel J	120	shipfitter	39	"
	G	Morgan Gertrude—†	120	candyworker	41	"
	H	*Ristano Antonio	120	longshoreman	45	"
	K	*Ristano Carmella—†	120	housewife	43	"
	L	McEwen Allen W	122	cooper	72	
	M	McEwen Mary E—†	122	housewife	57	"
	N	Reagan Frederick	122	waiter	31	329 Saratoga
	O	*Reagan Harriet—†	122	housewife	32	329 "
	P	Reagan James M	122	bellboy	27	329 "
	R	Losanno John	124	clerk	27	here
	S	Losanno Lena—†	124	housewife	27	"
	T	Santangelo Savino	124	shoemaker	65	"
	U	Santangelo Victoria—†	124	housewife	59	"
	V	Carroll Alice—†	124	"	42	
	W	Carroll John	124	mechanic	41	"
	X	Driver Arthur R	126	sorter	26	41 Saratoga
	Y	Driver Mildred—†	126	housewife	25	Mansfield
	Z	*Muise Bertha—†	126	"	28	here
722						
	A	Muise George	126	fishcutter	30	"
	B	*Gall Charles	126	spinner	40	
	C	*Gall Olga—†	126	housewife	44	"
	D	Marino Josephine—†	128	"	26	149 Paris
	E	Marino Vito	128	tilesetter	35	149 "
	F	*D'Antone Grace—†	128	housewife	38	here
	G	*D'Antone Joseph	128	candymaker	44	"
	H	Monkiewicz Edward	128	tailor	21	"
	K	*Monkiewicz Julia—†	128	housewife	48	"
	L	Monkiewicz Stanley	128	manufacturer	52	"
	M	Enos Mary C—†	130	clerk	45	"
	N	Enos Palmeda M—†	130	"	41	
	O	Enos Virginia C—†	130	housewife	69	"
	P	Enos William	130	retired	78	
	R	Enos William L	130	salesman	32	"
	S	McGillvray Alexander	130	laborer	53	
	T	McGillvray Estella—†	130	housewife	53	"
	U	Ward Bertha E—†	130	usher	57	
	V	*Ward John E	130	blacksmith	55	"
	W	Cooke Carlton	132	repairman	28	"

Page.	Letter.	Full Name.	Residence, Jan. 1, 1938.	Occupation.	Supposed Age.	Reported Residence, Jan. 1, 1937. Street and Number.

Trenton Street—Continued

	X	Cooke Irene—†	132	housewife	26	here
	Y	Joyce Anna—†	132	"	45	"
	Z	Joyce Harry	132	fireman	55	"
723						
	A	Serra Lillian Q—†	132	housewife	26	"
	B	Serra Thomas A	132	painter	26	
	C	Costello Howard	134	messenger	22	"
	D	Costello Rita—†	134	housewife	23	"
	E	Marmaud Edith—†	134	"	21	5 Lexington av
	F	Marmaud Edward	134	clerk	25	5 "
	G	Hawes Annie—†	134	operator	54	here
	H	McNamee Elizabeth—†	134	forewoman	52	"
	K	Bondi Joseph	136	janitor	42	"
	L*	Bondi Josephine—†	136	housewife	33	"
	M	Amenta Anthony	136	clerk	20	
	N	Amenta Lucy—†	136	operator	23	"
	O*	Amenta Michelina—†	136	housewife	61	"
	P	Caputo Antonio	136	counterman	21	"
	R	Caputo Josephine—†	136	housewife	25	"
	S	Caputo Paul	136	laborer	28	
	T	Silva Anthony	138	"	62	
	U	Silva Margaret—†	138	housewife	57	"
	V	Coletta Antonio	138	cabinetmaker	45	"
	W*	Coletta Theresa—†	138	housewife	46	"
	X	Moralis John	138	mason	50	
	Y	Moralis Joseph	138	engraver	25	"
	Z	Moralis Mary—†	138	operator	22	"
724						
	A*	Moralis Sebastiana—†	138	housewife	50	"
	B*	DiMauro Antonetta—†	140	"	58	
	C	DiMauro Joseph	140	carpenter	31	"
	D	DiMauro Sebastian	140	mason	62	"
	E*	Romano Jennie—†	140	housewife	41	305 Saratoga
	F	Romano Phillip	140	laborer	43	305 "
	G	Rizzo Charles	140	clerk	24	here
	H	Rizzo Conchetta—†	140	housewife	22	"
	K	DeLuca Anthony	142	painter	24	"
	L	DeLuca Dorothy—†	142	housewife	22	"
	M	Francis Esther—†	142	"	65	
	N	Francis Joseph	142	expressman	63	"
	O	Griffin Michael	142	B F D	61	

Page.	Letter.	Full Name.	Residence, Jan. 1, 1938.	Occupation.	Supposed Age.	Reported Residence, Jan. 1, 1937. Street and Number.

Trenton Street—Continued

	P	Williams Agnes—†	142	seamstress	22	here
	R	Hayden Nellie—†	144	housewife	34	"
	S	Hayden Richard	144	foreman	33	"
	T	*Lynch Eliza—†	144	at home	75	"
	U	Carino Bernice M—†	144	stenographer	27	13 W J Kelly sq
	V	Carino Marino R	144	butcher	25	13 "
	W	Florentino Angelo	144	chauffeur	42	here
	X	Florentino Mary—†	144	housewife	36	"
	Y	*Deveau Charles	146	carpenter	53	"
	Z	*Deveau Fannie—†	146	housewife	49	"
725						
	A	*Gillen Marietta—†	146	"	28	
	B	Gillen Martin	146	longshoreman	31	"
	C	O'Neil Arthur F	146	laborer	25	158 Webster
	D	Dempsey Raymond	148	B F D	36	here
	E	Ellsworth Edna V—†	148	housewife	43	"
	F	Ellsworth George A	148	court officer	51	"
	G	*McFarlane Mary—†	148	secretary	24	"
	H	Wilkie Edward J	148	retired	47	81 Morris
	K	Wilson Alexander W	148	B F D	40	here
	L	Godbold C Agnes—†	150	secretary	62	"
	M	Schuler Leonard J	150	retired	81	"
	N	Freethy Isabella C—†	152	housewife	44	"
	O	Freethy Roy H	152	engineer	53	"
	P	Robinson Lester N	152	B F D	53	57 Monmouth
	R	Robinson Mary E—†	152	hosuewife	52	57 "
	S	Rogers Maurice S	152	retired	79	here
	T	Testa Myrtle—†	154	housewife	43	"
	U	Testa Robert F	154	merchant	47	"
	V	Testa Robert F, jr	154	clerk	20	
	W	Bernardi Alfred	154	waiter	29	
	X	Bernardi Mary—†	154	housewife	26	"
	Y	Lake Marion P—†	156	"	40	Chelsea
	Z	Panzini Rocco	156	chauffeur	40	"
726						
	A	Perkins Alfreda—†	156	at home	22	

White Street

	C	Hipwell Gertrude—†	1	housewife	37	here
	D	Hipwell Joseph	1	laborer	36	"

Page.	Letter.	Full Name.	Residence, Jan. 1, 1938.	Occupation.	Supposed Age.	Reported Residence, Jan. 1, 1937. Street and Number.

White Street—Continued

	E	Trott Albert	1	retired	69	here
	F	*Salvage Arcene—†	1	housewife	50	"
	G	*Salvage Arthur	1	clerk	49	"
	H	*Costigan John	1	longshoreman	54	401 Meridian
	K	Fitzpatrick Thomas M	17	laborer	53	here
	L	McCarthy Michael	17	fireman	39	"
	M	McCarthy Ruth M—†	17	housewife	30	"
	O	*Ferraro Frances—†	21	"	41	
	P	Ferraro Frank	21	merchant	45	"
	R	Chalmers Catherine J—†	21	housewife	70	"
	S	Chalmers William A	21	seaman	71	
	T	Foster Emma—†	21	housewife	33	"
	U	Foster Ralph G	21	fireman	31	
	V	Carfagna Helen—†	23	housewife	28	"
	W	Carfagna Henry	23	laborer	28	
	X	*Cochrane Catherine—†	23	housewife	39	"
	Y	*Cochrane Frank	23	longshoreman	37	"
	Z	Viglione Catherine—†	23	housewife	28	162 Lexington
727						
	A	Viglione Louis	23	salesman	31	162 "
	B	McAllister Thomas	25	rigger	40	here
	C	Nunes Lucille—†	25	housekeeper	33	"
	D	Joyce Charles	25	fireman	24	"
	E	Joyce Frederick J	25	engineer	51	
	F	Joyce Matilda A—†	25	housewife	47	"
	G	Thibeault Ernest L	25	seaman	34	306 Meridian
	H	Ducharme Elric	27	laborer	44	here
	K	Ducharme Leo	27	clerk	21	"
	L	Grace Anna—†	27	waitress	25	"
	M	Grace Elizabeth—†	27	housewife	54	"
	N	Grace George	27	clerk	32	
	O	Grace Joseph	27	laborer	22	
	P	Grace William	27	operator	28	"
	R	Dalton Martin J	29	laborer	20	42 Eutaw
	S	Dalton Mary—†	29	at home	24	42 "
	T	Dalton Robert	29	clerk	34	42 "
	U	*Nugent Margaret—†	29	housewife	54	42 "
	V	*Nugent William	29	carpenter	58	42 "
	W	Shea Elizabeth—†	31	housewife	60	here
	X	Shea James F	31	engineer	69	"
	Y	Shea Jeremiah L	31	salesman	53	"

Page.	Letter.	FULL NAME.	Residence, Jan. 1, 1938.	Occupation.	Supposed Age.	Reported Residence, Jan. 1, 1937. Street and Number.

White Street—Continued

	Z	Shea Thomas J	31	electrician	57	here
728						
	A	Sinopole Mary—†	33	housewife	30	"
	B	Sinopole Michael	33	polisher	37	
	C	*Testa Catherine—†	33	housewife	62	"
	D	*Testa Domenic	33	retired	79	
	E	Stone Amanda—†	33	housewife	39	"
	F	Stone Harry	33	laborer	45	
	G	O'Connell Cornelius	35	bartender	30	"
	H	O'Connell Marjorie—†	35	housewife	26	"
	K	Coyle Claire J—†	35	at home	24	
	L	Coyle Joseph A	35	joiner	66	
	M	Coyle Joseph A, jr	35	chauffeur	28	"
	N	Coyle Lawrence F	35	clerk	24	
	O	Coyle Mary E—†	35	housewife	56	"
	P	Perry Louise—†	35	housekeeper	74	"
	R	Carter Lawrence	37	bartender	35	"
	S	Cayon Rosalie—†	37	housewife	46	"
	T	Cayon Roy	37	cook	53	
	U	Lemery Mary E—†	39	housekeeper	60	"
	V	McLaughlin Rose G—†	39	at home	42	"
	W	*Polm Susan—†	41	housekeeper	58	"
	X	Salnon Arthur A	41	laborer	28	"
	Y	Davis David	41	shoeworker	55	"
	Z	Davis Rose—†	41	housewife	54	"
729						
	A	Sullivan Samuel	41	clerk	62	
	B	Bichy Ella G—†	43	nurse	39	
	C	Garrity Katherine V—†	43	"	28	
	D	Sullivan Mary F—†	43	"	31	
	F	Held Jessica P—†	87	housekeeper	39	"

15

1(

17

18

19

2

1(

11

9

Ward 1—Precinct 9

CITY OF BOSTON

LIST OF RESIDENTS
20 YEARS OF AGE AND OVER

(NON-CITIZENS INDICATED BY ASTERISK)
(FEMALES INDICATED BY DAGGER)

AS OF

JANUARY 1, 1938

JOSEPH F. TIMILTY, } *Listing*
FREDERIC E. DOWLING, } *Board.*

CITY OF BOSTON PRINTING DEPARTMENT

Page.	Letter.	Full Name.	Residence, Jan. 1, 1938.	Occupation.	Supposed Age.	Reported Residence, Jan. 1, 1937. Street and Number.
740						
		Bennet Place				
	A	Caton Bertha M—†	1	housekeeper	57	here
	B	Caton Frances E—†	1	factoryhand	20	"
	C	Caton Harold L	1	clerk	22	"
	D	Caton Helen J—†	1	packer	35	
	E	Caton Manuel F	1	ironworker	67	"
	F	Hodgkins Carrie—†	2	housewife	27	69 Falcon
	G	Hodgkins Rupert	2	fireman	34	69 "
	H	Scott Mary—†	3	housekeeper	36	here
	M	Ford Clarence P	4	student	25	"
	N	Ford Daniel G	4	B F D	23	"
	O	Ford Jerome	4	clerk	21	
	K	*Kennedy Alphonsus M	4	rigger	52	
	L	Kennedy Catherine—†	4	housewife	54	"
		Border Street				
	U	Whynot Britton	445	carpenter	62	here
	V	Whynot Lettie—†	445	housewife	56	"
		Brooks Street				
	W	Murray Isabelle—†	185	housewife	40	here
	X	Murray William F	185	truckman	27	"
	Y	*Costigan Nora—†	185	housewife	38	"
	Z	*Costigan Patrick F	185	longshoreman	39	"
741						
	A	Ewing Harriet—†	187	housewife	24	Somerville
	B	Ewing Ronald	187	seaman	24	"
	C	Silvey Pauline—†	187	housewife	26	here
	D	Silvey William	187	painter	30	"
	E	Budreau William	189	retired	60	44 Liverpool
	F	*Theriault Joseph W	189	carpenter	33	here
	G	*Theriault Lena—†	189	housewife	30	"
	H	*O'Brien Catherine—†	189	"	49	"
	K	*O'Brien Michael J	189	laborer	49	
	L	McGuire Alice A—†	191	housewife	74	"
	M	McGuire William J	191	retired	80	
	N	Ciampa John G	191	clerk	22	
	O	Ciampa Mary—†	191	housewife	42	"
	P	Ciampa Nicholas	191	bricklayer	46	"

Page.	Letter.	Full Name.	Residence, Jan. 1, 1938.	Occupation.	Supposed Age.	Reported Residence, Jan. 1, 1937. Street and Number.

Brooks Street—Continued

	R	Costanza Annie C—†	193	stitcher	63	here
	S	Sousa Frederick M	193	clerk	21	"
	T	Sousa Manuel M	193	butcher	61	"
	U	*DiGiovanni Anthony	195	chauffeur	36	172 Cottage
	V	DiGiovanni Mary—†	195	housewife	36	172 "
	W	Erikson Irene G—†	195	"	36	here
	X	Erikson Roy W	195	longshoreman	38	"
	Y	Baker Josephine—†	195	housewife	45	"
	Z	Mooney Arthur F	195	retired	61	
742						
		Mooney Arthur J	195	porter	31	
		Mooney Claire—†	195	housewife	27	"
		Netto Florence A—†	214	"	31	
		Netto Thomas S	214	clerk	37	
		Lanieri Antonetta—†	214	housewife	50	"
		Lanieri Carl	214	physician	24	"
	G	Lanieri Jean—†	214	factoryhand	26	"
	H	Lanieri Renaldo	214	upholsterer	49	"
	K	Curelli Biago	214	waiter	42	
	L	Curelli Fausta—†	214	housewife	42	"
	M	*Guiffrida Frances—†	216	houseworker	66	190 Benningt'n
	N	Sinatra Mario	216	foreman	38	190 "
	O	Sinatra Sarah—†	216	housewife	34	190 "
	P	McEachern Duncan	216	repairman	22	here
	R	McEachern Elizabeth—†	216	housewife	46	"
	S	McEachern Ronald	216	B F D	46	"
	T	*Thibeau Celina—†	218	housewife	64	"
	U	Thibeau Clifford	218	mechanic	34	"
	V	Thibeau Mildred—†	218	clerk	35	
	W	Silva Edith—†	218	housewife	30	"
	X	Silva Joseph	218	chauffeur	35	"
	Y	King Florence—†	220	housewife	34	338 Meridian
	Z	King John	220	chauffeur	34	338 "
743						
	A	Connolly Mary A—†	220	housewife	62	here
	B	Connolly Patrick J	220	dealer	58	"
	C	Connolly Patrick J, jr	220	"	30	"
	D	Doucette Bertha—†	220	housewife	47	184½ Sumner
	E	Doucette Frederick	220	janitor	47	184½ "
	F	Muse Edward	224	seaman	37	here
	G	*Muse Elizabeth—†	224	housewife	25	"

Page.	Letter.	Full Name.	Residence, Jan. 1, 1938.	Occupation.	Supposed Age.	Reported Residence, Jan. 1, 1937. Street and Number.

Brooks Street—Continued

Page.	Letter.	Full Name.	Residence, Jan. 1, 1938.	Occupation.	Supposed Age.	Reported Residence, Jan. 1, 1937. Street and Number.
	H	Nadeau Alfred	224	seaman	33	here
	K	Nadeau Catherine—†	224	housewife	28	"
	L	Hill Manda—†	224	"	43	"
	M	Hill Toivo F	224	clerk	20	
	N	Selin Francis	rear 224	salesman	21	"
	O	*Selin Hulda—†	" 224	housewife	49	"
	P	*Selin Richard	" 224	ironworker	48	"

Condor Street

Page.	Letter.	Full Name.	Residence, Jan. 1, 1938.	Occupation.	Supposed Age.	Reported Residence, Jan. 1, 1937. Street and Number.
	R	Leville Annie T—†	5	housewife	57	here
	S	Leville Charles J	5	retired	58	"
	T	*DeCoste Rachel—†	5	houseworker	62	"
	U	Hawes Alice M—†	5	housewife	37	"
	V	Hawes Richard J	5	clerk	36	
	W	Barrett Eleanor—†	5	housewife	29	"
	X	Barrett James J	5	chauffeur	28	"
	Y	Magee Florence G—†	7	housekeeper	65	"
744						
	A	Riley William	7	shipper	58	
	B	Emmons Frederick	7	accountant	55	"
	C	Emmons Muriel—†	7	housewife	40	"
	D	Garcia Abrozine D—†	9	"	70	
	E	Garcia John A	9	watchman	70	"
	F	*Crosby Edith—†	9	housewife	36	"
	G	Losco Mary—†	13	"	37	
	H	Losco William	13	laborer	39	
	K	Nuner Albert J	13	mechanic	34	"
	L	Hanhy Harold A	13	pipecutter	28	118 Falcon
	M	Hanhy Pauline—†	13	housewife	22	118 "
	N	Tallman Ethel—†	13	"	45	156 "
	O	Tallman Harry	13	accountant	50	156 "
	P	Lawson Herbert	15	stevedore	28	here
	R	Lawson Lucille—†	15	housewife	23	"
	S	Craven Louis C	15	fireman	30	"
	T	Heeck Cornelius	15	printer	66	
	U	Heeck Florence L—†	15	housewife	54	"
	V	Kelleher Catherine A—†	15	typist	28	
	W	Kelleher Cornelius J	15	plumber	50	
	X	Kelleher Joseph E	15	policeman	27	"
	Y	Kelleher Lawrence F	15	laborer	22	

Condor Street—Continued

Page.	Letter.	Full Name.	Residence, Jan. 1, 1938.	Occupation.	Supposed Age.	Reported Residence, Jan. 1, 1937. Street and Number.
	z	Kelleher Margaret M—†	15	housewife	50	here
745						
	A	White James E	21	operator	37	“
	B	White Rose—†	21	housewife	33	“
	D	Mahoney Julia M—†	30	“	34	
	E	Mahoney Timothy	30	laborer	40	
	F	Murphy Daniel F	30	retired	73	
	G	Murphy Mary—†	30	at home	65	
	H	Murphy Tina—†	32	housewife	40	“
	K	Murphy William F	32	chauffeur	39	“
	L	Coogan Lawrence J	33	machinist	57	“
	M	Coogan Mary—†	33	housewife	55	“
	N	Coogan Mary C—†	33	nurse	21	
	O	Kane Emma E—†	33	housewife	40	“
	P	Kane Joseph A	33	engineer	39	
	R	MacLean Rita—†	33	clerk	20	
	S	Leary Arlene P—†	33	“	22	
	T	Leary Florence E—†	33	housewife	48	“
	U	Leary Lewis B	33	painter	54	
	W	Johnson Karl	34	social worker	27	“
	V	Johnson Marie—†	34	cutter	25	
	X	Johnson Andrew	36	retired	60	
	Y	Johnson Harold	36	clerk	22	
	Z	Melville Hazel A—†	37	housewife	49	“
746						
	A	Melville James A	37	machinist	49	“
	B	Smith Sarah M—†	37	dressmaker	55	“
	C	Ellis Frank A	37	clerk	49	
	D	Ellis Marion M—†	37	“	41	
	E	Smith Ella—†	37	housewife	69	“
	F	Smith Nema—†	37	housekeeper	43	“
	G	Forrey Lillian—†	38	housewife	36	“
	H	Forrey Patrick	38	proprietor	37	“
	K	Bengston Alice—†	40	housewife	21	“
	L	Bengston Irving	40	seaman	22	
	M	Mathisen Olaf	40	longshoreman	59	“
	N	Foster Annie—†	41	housewife	52	“
	O	Foster Ralph	41	oiler	62	
	P	Foster William	41	dyeworker	27	“
	R	Smith Evelyn—†	41	decorator	23	“
	S	Smith Lillian—†	41	housewife	46	“

Page.	Letter.	Full Name.	Residence, Jan. 1, 1938.	Occupation.	Supposed Age.	Reported Residence, Jan. 1, 1937. Street and Number.

Condor Street—Continued

Page.	Letter.	Full Name.	Residence, Jan. 1, 1938.	Occupation.	Supposed Age.	Reported Residence, Jan. 1, 1937. Street and Number.
	T	Stoodley Doris—†	41	inspector	29	here
	U	Stoodley Madeline—†	41	housewife	45	"
	V	Stoodley Thomas J	41	operator	45	"
	W	Thornton Elizabeth M—†	42	housewife	44	"
	X	Thornton James	42	engineer	60	
	Y	McKinnon Daniel F	44	laborer	51	
	Z	McKinnon Mary—†	44	housewife	26	"
747						
	A	Groom Helena—†	46	"	34	
	B	Groom Robert J	46	agent	45	
	C	Hulke William A	46	chauffeur	45	"
	D	Kearns Thomas J	46	shipper	25	
	E	Daggett Thomas H	47	retired	67	
	F	Murphy Catherine R—†	47	housewife	53	"
	G	Murphy John J	47	machinist	29	"
	K	LaMoure Abigail F—†	47B	housewife	47	"
	L	LaMoure Catherine—†	47B	clerk	21	
	M	LaMoure Francis	47B	timekeeper	23	"
	N	LaMoure Joseph	47B	clerk	25	63 Condor
	O	LaMoure Thomas E	47B	bartender	51	here
	P	LaMoure Thomas J	47B	laborer	21	"
	S	Zimmer Albert	49	"	31	379 Meridian
	T	Zimmer George	49	"	27	379 "
	U	Zimmer George W	49	"	54	379 "
	V	Zimmer Sarah L—†	49	housewife	53	379 "
	W	Sanford Grace—†	51	"	46	here
	X	Sanford William E	51	salesman	55	"
	Y	Hall Edna—†	57	clerk	20	"
	Z	Hall Edward	57	ironworker	59	"
748						
	A	Hall Olivia—†	57	housewife	51	"
	B	Cash Frank E	61	repairman	32	"
	C	Cash Mildred R—†	61	housewife	26	"
	D	Grady Catherine—†	61	clerk	21	
	E	Grady Daniel	61	laborer	61	
	F	Grady Jessie—†	61	housewife	47	"
	G	Boudreau Edith—†	61	"	24	163A Falcon
	H	Boudreau Wilfred	61	fishcutter	29	163A "
	L	Tanner Ernest	63	laborer	31	32 White
	M	Tanner Rita—†	63	housewife	29	32 "
	N	Botchie Carmen—†	63	housekeeper	28	477 Meridian

Page.	Letter.	Full Name.	Residence, Jan. 1, 1938.	Occupation.	Supposed Age.	Reported Residence, Jan. 1, 1937. Street and Number.

Condor Street—Continued

	O	Whitten Louise—†	63	housewife	60	here
	P	Whitten Robert	63	engineer	69	477 Meridian
	R	*Johnson William	63	fisherman	40	here
	T	Matthews Martha—†	65	housewife	21	"
	U	Matthews Walter	65	mechanic	20	"
	V	Cullen Elizabeth M—†	65	saleswoman	44	"
	W	Cullen Leo	65	longshoreman	48	"
	X	Pendlebury Burt	65	packer	39	
	Y	Pendlebury Dorothy—†	65	housewife	25	"
	Z	Crouse James E	67	carpenter	57	"
749						
	A	Crouse Lillian—†	67	housewife	58	"
	B	Connolly Anna—†	67	"	34	
	C	Connolly George	67	pipefitter	38	"
	D	Dow Hazel A—†	67	maid	50	
	E	Peterson Emma L—†	75	housewife	62	"
	F	Peterson John T	75	foreman	65	
	G	*Fitzgerald Anastasia—†	77	housewife	60	"
	H	Fitzgerald Joseph	77	machinist	30	"
	K	Peterson Alice—†	77	housewife	25	"
	L	Peterson John F	77	teacher	28	
	M	Hagerty Edith—†	79	housewife	50	"
	N	Hagerty Edward	79	expressman	57	"
	O	Hagerty Edward T	79	"	20	"
	P	Paradis John	79A	laborer	28	197 London
	R	Paradis Mildred—†	79A	housewife	27	197 "
	S	Clark Florence M—†	79A	operator	26	here
	T	Curtin Michael	79A	fireman	48	"
	V	Bagaroza Frederick	81	cutter	27	"
	W	Bagaroza Thora—†	81	housewife	22	"
	X	Clark Francis L	81	clerk	58	"
	Y	Napier Rita—†	81	"	23	1093 Saratoga
	Z	West Catherine—†	81	housewife	48	here
750						
	A	West James H	81	engineer	47	"
	B	Scott William T	85	retired	80	
	C	Dooley John	85	shipper	31	
	D	Whalen John J	85	engineer	53	
	E	Whalen Mary J—†	85	housewife	47	"
	F	McDermott John F	87	laborer	65	
	G	McDermott Mary A—†	87	housewife	58	"

Page.	Letter.	FULL NAME.	Residence, Jan. 1, 1938.	Occupation.	Supposed Age.	Reported Residence, Jan. 1, 1937. Street and Number.

Condor Street—Continued

	H	Corbett George	89	foreman	60	here
	K	Corbett George T	89	fishcutter	30	"
	L	Corbett Mary E—†	89	housewife	51	"
	M	Corbett William G	89	carpenter	22	"
	N	*DePaolo Carmello	91	retired	85	
	O	Lucido Angelina—†	91	housewife	43	"
	P	Lucido Angelina—†	91	clerk	24	
	R	Flammia Michael	91	operator	40	"
	S	Flammia Virginia—†	91	housewife	38	"
	T	DeFeo Carolina—†	93	"	36	
	U	DeFeo Pasquale	93	laborer	41	
	W	Thompson Mabel—†	97	housekeeper	52	"
	X	Thompson Viola—†	97	clerk	33	"
	Y	Fielding Catherine—†	97	proofreader	21	"
	Z	Fielding Gertrude—†	97	housekeeper	43	"

751 Eutaw Street

	B	Somers Amy—†	104	housewife	35	204 Bremen
	C	Somers Roy	104	laborer	40	204 "
	D	Froio John	106	"	52	174 Benningt'n
	E	Froio John A	106	"	27	174 "
	F	*Froio Rose—†	106	housewife	53	174 "
	G	Froio Teresa—†	106	at home	23	174 "
	H	LaBrie Georgina—†	108	houseworker	55	here
	K	McLean Catherine—†	108	seamstress	57	"
	L	McNeil Emily—†	108	at home	47	"
	M	Burke Albert	110	laborer	21	
	N	Burke Augustus	110	watchman	63	"
	O	Burke Barbara—†	110	housewife	58	"
	P	McLaughlin Aloysius	112	letter carrier	44	"
	R	McLaughlin Margaret—†	112	housewife	44	"
	S	Shea Ellen C—†	112	"	44	
	T	Shea Helen T—†	112	boxmaker	40	"
	U	Shea John J	112	custodian	50	"
	V	Shea Mary L—†	112	forewoman	48	"
	W	Shea Timothy J	112	watchman	39	"
	X	Donahue Bridget—†	116	housewife	70	"
	Y	Donahue Richard	116	retired	73	
	Z	Donahue William J	116	"	75	

Page.	Letter.	Full Name.	Residence, Jan. 1, 1938.	Occupation.	Supposed Age.	Reported Residence, Jan. 1, 1937. Street and Number.
752		**Eutaw Street**—Continued				
	A	Miller Joseph	116	laborer	40	here
	B	Miller Mary E—†	116	housewife	36	"
	C	Partland Joseph H	116	laborer	68	"
	D	DeCamillo Camillo	118	"	54	
	E	DeCamillo Lena—†	118	factoryhand	22	"
	F*	DeCamillo Mary—†	118	housewife	49	"
	G	DeCamillo Vincenzo	118	factoryhand	24	"
	H	Fallavollita Lucy—†	120	housewife	24	"
	K	Fallavollita Paulino	120	mechanic	24	"
	L	Palmizio Vincenzo	120	laborer	36	
	M	Fallavollita Angelina—†	120	housewife	45	"
	N	Fallavollita Antonio	120	electrician	25	"
	O	Fallavollita Catherine—†	120	packer	22	
	P	Buonagurio Julia—†	122	housewife	59	"
	R	Buonagurio Julia—†	122	clerk	24	
	S	Buonagurio Sabino	122	painter	63	
	T	Hamilton George U	124	storekeeper	67	"
		Falcon Street				
	U	Bragdon Clifford	5	retired	62	here
	V	Bragdon Sarah—†	5	housewife	62	"
	W	Pushaw James H	5	operator	54	"
	X	Pushaw Martha A—†	5	housewife	48	"
	Y	Pushaw Olive M—†	5	typist	20	
	Z*	D'Entremont Catherine—†	7	housewife	26	"
753						
	A	D'Entremont Charles	7	laborer	35	
	B*	D'Entremont Dometille—†	7	housewife	33	"
	C	D'Entremont Elmer	7	fishcutter	28	"
	D	McIntyre Clarence T	9	steamfitter	36	"
	E	McIntyre Eva M—†	9	housewife	36	"
	F*	Campbell Catherine—†	12	"	55	
	G*	Campbell Margaret—†	12	operator	56	
	H	Crosby Sarah E—†	12	housewife	56	"
	K	King Anna—†	14	"	60	220 Brooks
	L	Lang Beatrice B—†	14	"	38	220 "
	M	Lang Edward P	14	inspector	42	220 "
	N	Moran Florence D—†	14	waitress	38	220 "
	O	Moran James F	14	manager	43	220 "

Page.	Letter.	Full Name.	Residence, Jan. 1, 1938.	Occupation.	Supposed Age.	Reported Residence, Jan. 1, 1937. Street and Number.

Falcon Street—Continued

	P	Lannelli Charles M	22	shipper	29	here
	R	Lannelli Evelyn—†	22	houseworker	26	"
	S	Lannelli James	22	salesman	30	"
	T	Lannelli Louise—†	22	housewife	50	"
	U	Lannelli Silvio	22	barber	52	
	V	Lannelli Ugo	22	student	21	
	W	*Healey James	22	laborer	24	
	X	McCarthy Callahan	22	"	42	
	Y	Riley Elizabeth—†	22	clerk	22	
	Z	Riley Joseph P	22	porter	63	
754						
	A	Riley Julia—†	22	housewife	59	"
	B	Danner Edward D	22	B F D	50	
	C	Danner Nina M—†	22	housewife	38	"
	D	*Grifone Anibal	24	tailor	72	
	E	Grifone Carlo	24	"	30	
	F	Grifone Emma—†	24	stitcher	33	"
	G	Grifone Jennie—†	24	housewife	36	"
	H	McPhee Charles	25	steelworker	47	"
	K	*McPhee Mary—†	25	housewife	46	"
	L	McPhee Melvin	25	clerk	24	
	M	Beekman Alice—†	25	radio tester	21	"
	N	Beekman Genevieve—†	25	at home	26	
	O	Beekman George A	25	shipper	50	
	P	Beekman Mary—†	25	housewife	48	"
	R	Johnson Paul	26	fishcutter	24	"
	S	Tribuna Bartholomew	26	packer	36	
	T	Tribuna Marion—†	26	housewife	33	"
	U	LaBohn Catherine M—†	27	at home	81	
	V	LaBohn Willard J	27	inspector	49	"
	W	Hoyt Eva C—†	27	housewife	56	"
	X	Hoyt George M	27	checker	59	
	Y	Nelson August E	27	clerk	53	
	Z	Nelson Helen E—†	27	operator	28	"
755						
	A	Nelson Helen M—†	27	housewife	54	"
	B	Nelson Warren F	27	baker	22	
	C	Cutcliffe Charles R	28	laborer	37	
	D	Cutcliffe Mary E—†	28	housewife	32	"
	E	*Hansen Barbara—†	28	"	56	
	F	Hansen Heeakon	28	operator	23	

Page.	Letter.	Full Name.	Residence, Jan. 1, 1938.	Occupation.	Supposed Age.	Reported Residence, Jan. 1, 1937. Street and Number.
		Falcon Street—Continued				
	G	Hansen John	28	painter	57	here
	H	Hansen Ruth B—†	28	houseworker	22	"
	K	Dore Joseph	29	shoemaker	60	"
	L*	Dore Margaret—†	29	housewife	54	"
	M	Dore Peter	29	cabinetmaker	39	"
	N	Grace Gerald A	29	electrician	39	54 Jewett
	O	Grace Mildred P—†	29	housewife	35	54 "
	P	Johnson Theresa—†	30	clerk	32	here
	R	Linstead Alma—†	30	at home	71	"
	S	Linstead Beatrice—†	30	cashier	36	"
	T	Snodgrass Inez—†	30	housewife	33	"
	U	Snodgrass Robert W	30	tinsmith	41	
	V	Parker Charles M	30	manager	65	"
	W	Parker Grace I—†	30	housewife	63	"
	X	Bruce Ellen K—†	31	"	39	
	Y	Bruce William	31	seaman	40	
	Z*	O'Brien Bridget—†	31	housekeeper	70	"
756						
	A*	McBournie John W	31	watchman	70	"
	B*	McBournie Margaret—†	31	housewife	70	"
	C	McBournie Walter S	31	clerk	35	
	D	McRae Ira	31	operator	45	"
	E	McRae Jessie—†	31	housewife	37	"
	F	Olsson Charles	32	hygienist	41	"
	G	Olsson Ruth—†	32	housewife	20	"
	H	Denehy Daniel A	33	woodworker	42	"
	K	Denehy Josephine M—†	33	housewife	37	"
	L	McCormack Ella W—†	33	"	52	
	M	McCormack Helen M—†	33	teacher	25	
	N	McCormack John	33	grocer	63	
	O	McCormack Norma E—†	33	student	21	
	P	Elliott Jennie—†	33	housewife	45	"
	R	Elliott Robert A	33	motorman	48	"
	S	Wall Alfred M	34	mechanic	27	"
	T	Wall Amy J—†	34	stenographer	24	"
	U	Wall Constance W—†	34	housekeeper	56	"
	V	Wall Mary E—†	34	packer	32	"
	W	Abbott Clarence F	34	chauffeur	20	"
	X	Abbott Susan J—†	34	housewife	58	"
	Y	Bonner Edward L	35	tollman	51	
	Z	Bonner Ella A—†	35	housewife	47	"

Page.	Letter.	Full Name.	Residence, Jan. 1, 1938.	Occupation.	Supposed Age.	Reported Residence, Jan. 1, 1937. Street and Number.

757

Falcon Street—Continued

	A	Cancellieri Eleanor M—†	35	housewife	23	here
	B	Cancellieri Romeo G	35	chauffeur	22	"
	C	Flynn Margaret L—†	35	waitress	45	"
	D	Kelley Patrick J	35	seaman	63	
	E	Landrigan Michael J	35	painter	57	
	F	Sullivan Ella V—†	35	housewife	54	"
	G	Sullivan Helen R—†	35	clerk	23	
	H	Sullivan John J	35	oiler	57	
	K	Bonner Anna T—†	35	housewife	44	"
	L	Bonner George J	35	janitor	43	
	M	Johnson Clara—†	36	housewife	66	"
	N	Johnson Florence—†	36	waitress	31	
	O	Johnson Harry	36	laborer	42	
	P	Johnson Helen—†	36	saleswoman	28	"
	R	Sullivan Joseph H	36	seaman	43	
	S	Sullivan Robert L	36	"	20	
	T	Sullivan Stella M—†	36	housewife	45	"
	U	Griffin Harold	37	electrician	23	59 W Eagle
	V	Powers Harold	37	longshoreman	47	59 "
	W	Powers Mary—†	37	housewife	45	59 "
	X	McGurnin Harriet F—†	37	at home	85	here
	Y	Noyes Vera L—†	37	housekeeper	40	"
	Z	McElman Allan B	37	mechanic	54	"
758						
	A	McElman Katherine A—†	37	operator	25	"
	B	McElman Nellie J—†	37	housewife	52	"
	C	McElman Thomas H	37	electrician	20	"
	D	Gage Laura L—†	38	bookkeeper	47	"
	E	Gage Winthrop H	38	mechanic	45	"
	F	Logan Blanche E—†	38	clerk	45	"
	G	Logan Jane E—†	38	at home	76	
	H	Logan Julia M—†	38	housewife	39	"
	K	Logan Leslie D	38	grocer	46	
	L	Logan Virginia M—†	38	clerk	20	
	M	Denehy Alice E—†	39	operator	26	"
	N	Denehy Edward J	39	fisherman	24	"
	O	Denehy Louise M—†	39	housewife	32	"
	P	Denehy Mary M—†	39	operator	36	"
	R	*D'Entremont Albert	40	fishcutter	31	17 Marion
	S	*D'Entremont Margaret—†	40	housewife	28	17 "

Page.	Letter.	FULL NAME.	Residence, Jan. 1, 1938.	Occupation.	Supposed Age.	Reported Residence, Jan. 1, 1937. Street and Number.

Falcon Street—Continued

Page.	Letter.	FULL NAME.	Residence, Jan. 1, 1938.	Occupation.	Supposed Age.	Reported Residence, Jan. 1, 1937.
	T	Kane Addie L—†	40	housewife	51	here
	U	Kane Thomas V	40	chauffeur	54	"
	V	Scopa Albert	40	"	25	154 Cottage
	W	*Scopa Jennie—†	40	housewife	53	here
	X	Scopa Mary—†	40	at home	24	154 Cottage
	Y	Parker Agnes C—†	41	housewife	32	here
	Z	Parker Delia W—†	41	at home	87	Maine
759						
	A	Parker Donald W	41	mechanic	35	here
	B	Clemens Edward J	41	ironworker	39	"
	C	Clemens Helen F—†	41	housewife	32	"
	D	Kehoe Julia D—†	42	"	21	
	E	Kehoe William H	42	manager	22	"
	F	McRae Mary L—†	42	housewife	47	"
	G	McRae William D	42	machinist	49	"
	H	Hoffman Barbara—†	42	operator	40	
	K	Hoffman Christie—†	42	at home	70	
	L	Hoffman Donald	42	laborer	34	
	M	Hoffman Lucy—†	42	housewife	28	"
	N	Hoffman Sarah—†	42	boxmaker	32	"
	O	*Alves Antonio	42	retired	76	
	P	*Alves Leo	42	toolmaker	36	"
	R	*Alves Marie—†	42	housewife	73	"
	S	Gillogly Mildred B—†	44	"	38	
	T	Gillogly William	44	electrician	45	"
	U	McDonnell Annie E—†	44	housewife	68	"
	V	McDonnell Edward A	44	policeman	42	"
	W	McDonnell Richard	44	mechanic	68	"
	X	Ellis Edith V—†	44	housewife	38	647 Saratoga
	Y	Ellis John J	44	seaman	42	647 "
	Z	Ellis Margaret—†	44	housewife	62	647 "
760						
	A	Gillogly Helen—†	44	cashier	30	here
	B	Gillogly James	44	woodworker	72	"
	C	Gillogly Mary—†	44	housewife	68	"
	D	Gustafson Marion—†	44	at home	40	
	E	Nagle Ann—†	44	cashier	34	
	F	Marini Alice A—†	47	housewife	37	"
	G	Marini John	47	marbleworker	50	"
	H	*Nickerson Ivan	48	laborer	38	
	K	*Nickerson Matilda—†	48	housewife	34	"

Page.	Letter.	FULL NAME.	Residence, Jan. 1, 1938.	Occupation.	Supposed Age.	Reported Residence, Jan. 1, 1937. Street and Number.

Falcon Street—Continued

	L	Nickerson Nellie—†	48	housekeeper	28	90 Eutaw
	M	Crosby Dedrick C	48	painter	67	here
	N	Crosby Lillian M—†	48	housewife	70	"
	O	Brannen Clissie—†	48	housekeeper	65	"
	P	Brannen Estella—†	48	housewife	25	"
	R	Brannen Shirley—†	48	painter	35	"
	S	Fobert Jennie M—†	49	housewife	45	60 Falcon
	T	Fobert Josephine—†	49	operator	21	60 "
	U	Fobert Leo	49	plater	25	60 "
	V	Fobert Roy	49	machinist	23	60 "
	W	Chase Fred J	50	dispatcher	57	here
	X	Chase Josephine I—†	50	housewife	56	"
	Y	Baptista Adeline—†	50	"	43	51 Falcon
	Z	Baptista Adeline E—†	50	designer	22	51 "
761						
	A	Baptista John	50	superintendent	47	51 "
	B	O'Connell Alfred C	51	metalworker	31	Lowell
	C	O'Connell Nellie—†	51	housewife	32	"
	D	Trainor Florence E—†	51	"	37	53 Falcon
	E	Trainor William J	51	bartender	41	53 "
	F	Ledwell Francis	52	fisherman	45	131 "
	G	*Ledwell Gertrude—†	52	housewife	42	131 "
	H	Malfy Fred	53	operator	52	here
	K	Malfy Fred, jr	53	laborer	20	"
	L	Malfy Helen—†	53	saleswoman	22	"
	M	Malfy Mabel—†	53	housewife	45	"
	N	Leonard Alice—†	53	"	25	
	O	Leonard Frank	53	chauffeur	27	"
	P	Stapleton Edna—†	54	housewife	32	Chelsea
	R	Stapleton Leo J	54	serviceman	37	"
	T	Halstead Charles A	55	guard	40	here
	U	Halstead Edith J—†	55	housewife	39	"
	S	Halstead Bertha M—†	55	"	63	"
	V	Halstead William F	55	seaman	70	"
	W	Quindley Andrew L	56	engineer	38	98 Princeton
	X	Quindley Marion—†	56	housewife	37	98 "
	Y	MacAuley Franklin A	57	engineer	34	118 Falcon
	Z	MacAuley Verna E—†	57	housewife	34	118 "
762						
	A	Hamel Angie V—†	57	"	37	here
	B	Hamel Donald T	57	ironworker	37	"

Falcon Street—Continued

Page.	Letter.	Full Name.	Residence, Jan. 1, 1938.	Occupation.	Supposed Age.	Reported Residence, Jan. 1, 1937. Street and Number.
	C	Perrier Kenneth	57	mechanic	27	here
	D	Gilbrook John	58	B F D	41	40 Ashley
	E	Gilbrook Mary J—†	58	housewife	40	40 "
	H	Dunbar Florence C—†	60	housekeeper	22	here
	F	Dunbar Ralph	60	chauffeur	23	"
	G	Dunbar Stella—†	60	housewife	67	"
	K	Powell Clarence E	60	salesman	29	"
	L	Powell Mary—†	60	housewife	27	"
	M	*Barretta Catherine—†	60	at home	80	477 Meridian
	N	Page Frank	60	clerk	43	477 "
	O	Page Louise—†	60	housewife	40	477 "
	P	Irvine Gertrude—†	62	"	41	here
	R	Irvine Margaret—†	62	at home	70	"
	S	Irvine William H	62	electrician	46	"
	T	Heffron Cecelia—†	62	at home	89	
	U	Heffron Frederick L	62	tollman	52	
	V	Heffron Margaret—†	62	housewife	47	"
	W	Heffron William	62	laborer	62	
	X	Flynn Ellen—†	63	housewife	50	"
	Y	Flynn Joseph P	63	brassworker	55	"
	Z	Preston Blanche L—†	63	housewife	24	"
763						
	A	Preston Michael J	63	serviceman	28	"
	B	Ryan Charles J	63	chauffeur	37	850 Saratoga
	C	Ryan Rose—†	63	housewife	36	here
	D	Preston John F	63	clerk	22	"
	E	Preston Mary E—†	63	housewife	46	"
	F	*Condon Richard	64	laborer	35	
	G	Tobin Nora—†	64	housewife	52	"
	H	Tobin Patrick	64	laborer	54	
	K	Delaney Elizabeth—†	64	forewoman	37	"
	L	Gardiner Edward	64	chauffeur	32	"
	M	Gardiner Jane—†	64	housewife	73	"
	N	Gardiner Jefferson	64	laborer	44	
	O	Gardiner John	64	steamfitter	42	"
	P	Heffron Catherine—†	64	housewife	65	"
	R	Heffron James	64	custodian	37	"
	S	Melvin Edward M	64	chauffeur	48	"
	T	Melvin Lena—†	64	housewife	40	"
	U	*Hanson Anna—†	66	"	35	
	V	Hanson Arndt	66	laborer	40	

Page.	Letter.	FULL NAME.	Residence, Jan. 1, 1938.	Occupation.	Supposed Age.	Reported Residence, Jan. 1, 1937. Street and Number.

Falcon Street—Continued

	W	Marshall Cornelius B	66	baggageman	62	here
	X	Marshall Ena M—†	66	clerk	20	"
	Y	Marshall Gertrude E—†	66	laundress	34	"
	Z	Hanson Christian	68	laborer	38	36 Haynes
764						
	A	Darling Dora—†	68	housewife	63	48 White
	B	Darling Frank M	68	retired	65	48 "
	C	Donahue Ruth—†	68	housekeeper	37	48 "
	D	Joy Mary—†	69	housewife	23	516 Sumner
	E	*Joy William	69	fisherman	30	516 "
	F	*Penney Joseph	69	retired	52	516 "
	G	Patz Clara—†	69	housewife	40	here
	H	Patz John	69	mason	46	"
	K	Hodgkins Louise—†	69	housewife	41	"
	L	Hodgkins William	69	engineer	47	"
	N	Healey Monica—†	71	housewife	32	"
	O	Healey Phillip J	71	longshoreman	37	"
	P	LeBlanc Roy	71	fisherman	42	"
	R	Surette Ely	71	fishcutter	40	"
	S	*Surette Lennie—†	71	housewife	35	"
	T	Boyle Margaret—†	71	housekeeper	54	"
	U	Powers John S	71	ironworker	50	"
	V	Powers Margaret—†	71	housewife	37	"
	W	Powers Robert J	71	retired	37	
	X	Krestofferson Agnes—†	74	housewife	50	"
	Y	Krestofferson Kaare	74	manager	26	"
	Z	Krestofferson Mathias	74	watchman	55	"
765						
	A	Osborne George	74	fireman	35	
	B	Flaherty Anita—†	77	housewife	28	"
	C	Flaherty William L	77	machinist	32	"
	D	Tarquinio Amedeo	77	blacksmith	58	"
	E	Tarquinio Frank	77	messenger	27	"
	F	Tarquinio Jean—†	77	housewife	23	"
	G	Colotti Geraldine—†	77	"	36	"
	H	Colotti Pasquale	77	pressman	41	"
	K	Sadoff Abraham	78	foreman	30	"
	L	Sadoff Gertrude—†	78	housewife	29	"
	M	Butler Leslie I	78	clerk	39	
	N	Butler Viola J—†	78	housewife	43	"
	O	Keyes Henry L	78	retired	69	

Page.	Letter.	Full Name.	Residence, Jan. 1, 1938.	Occupation.	Supposed Age.	Reported Residence, Jan. 1, 1937. Street and Number.

Falcon Street—Continued

Page.	Letter.	Full Name.	Residence, Jan. 1, 1938.	Occupation.	Supposed Age.	Reported Residence, Jan. 1, 1937. Street and Number.
	P	D'Addieco Assunta—†	79	housewife	45	here
	R	D'Addieco Louis	79	operator	24	"
	S	D'Addieco Michael	79	pressman	52	"
	T	Millar Nellie—†	79	housewife	50	"
	U	Millar Thomas	79	repairman	56	"
	V	Millar Thomas P	79	laborer	23	
	W	Foley Ellen—†	81	housewife	47	"
	X	Foley John F	81	B F D	50	
	Y	Haley Gertrude—†	81	bookkeeper	42	"
	Z	Lyons Jeremiah T	81	messenger	63	"
766						
	A	*McHugh Catherine—†	87	housewife	25	"
	B	*McHugh Patrick	87	fisherman	28	"
	C	Duke James	87	"	50	
	D	Duke Mary—†	87	housewife	47	"
	E	*LaTorre Filippa—†	87	at home	73	82 Bennington
	F	*LaTorre Josephine—†	87	housewife	33	82 "
	G	LaTorre Salvatore	87	baker	40	82 "
	H	Cianciarullo Gerardo	89	piano tuner	37	77 W Eagle
	K	Cianciarullo Mary—†	89	housewife	36	77 "
	L	Cianciarullo Raffaele—†	89	housekeeper	58	77 "
	M	Lane Anthony	89	laborer	31	here
	N	*Lane Elizabeth—†	89	housekeeper	58	"
	O	Lane Joseph	89	retired	71	"
	P	*Lane Rose—†	89	housewife	31	"
	R	Repetto Batista	89	pressman	52	"
	S	Repetto Maria—†	89	housewife	47	"
	T	Maher Elsie—†	93	"	28	"
	U	Maher Michael	93	seaman	32	
	V	Doherty Bernard L	93	clerk	20	
	W	Doherty Grace E—†	93	"	26	
	X	Doherty Helen M—†	93	"	28	
	Y	Doherty Joseph L	93	messenger	29	"
	Z	Doherty Margaret C—†	93	operator	23	"
767						
	A	Doherty Margaret J—†	93	housewife	60	"
	B	Lewis Miriam C—†	95	packer	24	
	C	Lewis Miriam E—†	95	housewife	46	"
	D	Lewis William A	95	inspector	49	"
	E	Lewis William T	95	salesman	28	"
	F	Irving Herbert E	95A	foreman	63	

Page.	Letter.	Full Name.	Residence, Jan. 1, 1938.	Occupation.	Supposed Age.	Reported Residence, Jan. 1, 1937. Street and Number.

Falcon Street—Continued

	G	Irving Viola P—†	95A	housewife	62	here
	H	Roome Ethel G—†	95A	saleswoman	23	"
	K	Bailey Benjamin	97	machinist	50	"
	L	Bailey Benjamin A	97	clerk	26	
	M	Bailey Elizabeth C—†	97	housewife	45	"
	N	Bailey Lawrence C	97	clerk	22	
	O	Curry George L	97	"	37	
	P	Curry Mary M—†	97	operator	39	"
	R	Alexander John	99	inspector	70	"
	S	McBournie Ina—†	99	housewife	42	"
	T	McBournie William	99	clerk	42	
	U	McBournie William, jr	99	"	20	
	V	Pitts Florence A—†	101	housewife	34	"
	W	Pitts George D	101	engineer	38	"
	X	Long Alice F—†	101	housewife	55	"
	Y	Long Thomas G	101	cutter	22	
768						
	A	Long William C	101	operator	49	
	Z	Long William F	101	cutter	23	
	B	Hulke Almeda—†	103	housewife	44	"
	C	Hulke Eleanor—†	103	clerk	22	
	D	Hulke Thelma—†	103	plater	20	
	E	Pease Warren	103	retired	76	
	F	Turpin Ella J—†	103	housewife	47	"
	G	Turpin John E	103	engineer	50	
	H	Grady Alice—†	103	housewife	41	"
	K	Grady William F	103	metalworker	45	"
	L	Broussard James	105	salesman	39	"
	M	Broussard Mary—†	105	housewife	38	"
	N	Doherty Jennie—†	105	housekeeper	53	"
	O	Clarke Christine—†	105	housewife	30	117 Lexington
	P	Clarke George	105	welder	31	117 "
	R	Keough Annie F—†	105	housewife	55	here
	S	Keough Mary E—†	105	clerk	25	"
	T	Keough William	105	laborer	57	"
	U	Martinez Domingo	107	machinist	52	"
	V	Martinez Eugene	107	clerk	20	
	W	*Martinez Manuela—†	107	housewife	41	"
	X	Fernandez Joseph	107	engineer	52	
	Y	*Fernandez Virginia—†	107	housewife	46	"
	A	Renzi Constantino	109	laborer	26	

Page.	Letter.	Full Name.	Residence, Jan. 1, 1938.	Occupation.	Supposed Age.	Reported Residence, Jan. 1, 1937. Street and Number.

Falcon Street—Continued

Page.	Letter.	Full Name.	Residence, Jan. 1, 1938.	Occupation.	Supposed Age.	Reported Residence, Jan. 1, 1937. Street and Number.
	z	Renzi Diamanta—†	109	housewife	26	here
769						
	B	Vellotti Paul	109	shipper	21	"
	C	Erickson Arthur	109	steamfitter	26	65 W Eagle
	D	Erickson Emma—†	109	housewife	22	65 "
	E	Sullivan John J	111	B F D	40	25 Falcon
	F	Sullivan Ruth—†	111	housewife	38	25 "
	G	Benson Charles	111	retired	74	here
	H	Benson Herbert B	111	carpenter	40	"
	K	Benson Mabel L—†	111	housewife	43	"
	L	Fagan Anna—†	117	"	34	859 Saratoga
	M	Fagan Gerald	117	fisherman	34	859 "
	N	Enos Deolda—†	117	housewife	37	here
	O	Enos John	117	fireman	42	"
	P	Keating Louise—†	117	housekeeper	41	299 Lexington
	R	Keating Thomas	117	social worker	20	299 "
	S	Cleary Ethel I—†	119	housewife	33	55 Putnam
	T	Cleary George A	119	janitor	41	55 "
	U	Trevor Edward	119	fishcutter	30	here
	V	Trevor Margaret—†	119	housewife	30	"
	W*	Doucette Francis	119	fisherman	50	236 Saratoga
	X*	Doucette Mary H—†	119	housewife	46	236 "
	Y	Doucette Peter R	119	repairman	24	236 "
	Z	Piva Joseph S	119	mechanic	36	666 Summer
770						
	B	Fulliginiti Christine—†	121	housewife	37	here
	C*	Fulliginiti James	121	plasterer	44	"
	D	Garofano Frank	121	chauffeur	39	"
	E	Garofano Mary—†	121	housewife	32	"
	F	Pagliarulo Evelyn—†	121	"	33	
	G	Pagliarulo George	121	broker	26	
	H	Pagliarulo Lillian—†	121	stenographer	23	"
	K	Pagliarulo Michael	121	mechanic	22	"
	L	Pagliarulo Adelaide—†	121	housewife	55	"
	M	Pagliarulo Anthony	121	retired	63	
	N	Pagliarulo Joseph F	121	engineer	35	
	O	Pagliarulo Rose—†	121	teacher	31	
	P	Sweeney Helen—†	129	housewife	64	"
	R	Sweeney Michael	129	retired	74	
	S*	Molloy Clara—†	129A	housewife	38	"
	T	Molloy George J	129A	build'g wrecker	37	"

Page.	Letter.	Full Name.	Residence, Jan. 1, 1938.	Occupation.	Supposed Age.	Reported Residence, Jan. 1, 1937. Street and Number.

Falcon Street—Continued

	U	Carroll Anna—†	131	housewife	33	416 Saratoga
	V	Carroll John	131	fisherman	44	416 "
	W	Gray Joseph	131	"	66	here
	X	Powers Austin	131	"	42	86 Trenton
	Y	*Furlong Mary—†	131A	housewife	33	133 Falcon
	Z	*Furlong Thomas	131A	fishcutter	32	133 "
771						
	A	McLaughlin Alice—†	133	housewife	37	here
	B	McLaughlin Charles	133	iceman	45	"
	C	McLaughlin William	133	chauffeur	21	"
	D	Copithorne Charlotte—†	133A	housewife	28	5 Haverhill
	E	Copithorne Richard J	133A	chauffeur	31	5 "
	F	Brennan Amy—†	135	housewife	32	here
	G	Brennan Winston	135	laborer	37	"
	H	Rolfe Delma L—†	135A	housewife	26	Winthrop
	K	Rolfe Leon C	135A	U S A	29	"

Meridian Street

	L	Carey Margaret E—†	414	domestic	69	here
	M	Foley Elizabeth A—†	414	housewife	65	"
	N	Foley Henry E	414	storekeeper	62	"
	P	Eagan Anastasia—†	417	housewife	72	"
	R	Eagan James	417	retired	78	
	S	Eagan James J	417	janitor	44	
	T	Eagan Rita—†	417	stenographer	34	"
	U	Chillemi Anthony	418	jeweler	33	36 Liverpool
	V	Chillemi Mary—†	418	housewife	20	Brookline
	W	Orr Donald	418	mechanic	35	here
	X	Orr Irene—†	418	housewife	32	"
	Y	Campbell John	418	laborer	35	"
	Z	*McCullen Eliza—†	418	factoryhand	25	Somerville
772						
	A	*Muse Helen—†	418	domestic	31	here
	B	Persson Edith—†	418	housewife	57	"
	C	Persson Nelson	418	cook	60	"
	D	Reid Frank	418	clerk	32	
	E	Marcucilli Anthony	419	carpenter	24	"
	F	Marcucilli Henry	419	bartender	29	"
	G	Marcucilli James	419	"	25	"
	H	*Marcucilli Joseph	419	realtor	61	

Page.	Letter.	Full Name.	Residence, Jan. 1, 1938.	Occupation.	Supposed Age.	Reported Residence, Jan. 1, 1937. Street and Number.

Meridian Street—Continued

Page.	Letter.	Full Name.	Residence, Jan. 1, 1938.	Occupation.	Supposed Age.	Reported Residence, Jan. 1, 1937. Street and Number.
	K	*Marcucilli Margaret—†	419	housewife	60	here
	L	Ciarfella Anna—†	419	"	31	"
	M	Ciarfella Henry	419	salesman	35	"
	N	O'Rourke Catherine—†	421	housewife	44	"
	N	O'Rourke Joseph P	421	foreman	42	
	P	O'Rourke Mary—†	421	at home	74	
	R	O'Rourke Mary E—†	421	seamstress	48	"
	S	Greenwood Anna E—†	421	housewife	35	82 W Eagle
	T	Greenwood John W	421	engineer	37	82 "
	U	Marcucella Guy	421	bartender	27	here
	V	Marcucella Mary—†	421	housewife	26	"
	W	*Kovacen Angelina—†	422	"	48	"
	X	*Kovacen Joseph	422	storekeeper	56	"
	Y	Kovacen Nathaniel	422	laborer	22	"
	Z	Kovacen Tony	422	storekeeper	24	"
773						
	A	*Askin Frances—†	422	housewife	50	"
	B	Askin John	422	bartender	52	"
	C	Elms Florence H—†	422	housewife	37	"
	D	Elms Winslow	422	salesman	36	"
	E	Jenkins George	423	retired	65	
	F	Lurvey Albert	423	student	21	
	G	Lurvey Ellen—†	423	housewife	51	"
	H	Lurvey Mary—†	423	seamstress	23	"
	K	Lurvey Reginald	423	engineer	47	
	L	Cocorochio Antoinette—†	423	domestic	25	"
	M	Cocorochio Louis	423	laborer	33	
	N	*Cocorochio Thomas	423	butcher	65	
	P	Harris Elizabeth—†	425	housewife	64	"
	P1	Harris George C	425	cook	64	
	R	Harris George L	425	bookkeeper	33	"
	S	McNear Georgia—†	425	housewife	62	"
	T	Ladd Louis A	426	laborer	48	
	U	Quirk James W	426	motorman	65	"
	V	Quirk Mary E—†	426	housewife	67	"
	W	Murphy Eunice—†	426	operator	28	
	X	Murphy Martha—†	426	"	27	
	Y	Guillon Bertha—†	426	housewife	38	"
	Z	Guillon Francis	426	laborer	40	
774						
	A	Pulsifer Fred	426	"	48	

Page.	Letter.	Full Name.	Residence, Jan. 1, 1938.	Occupation.	Supposed Age.	Reported Residence, Jan. 1, 1937. Street and Number.

Meridian Street—Continued

	B	Nolan Florence—†	427	housewife	22	31 Lexington
	C	Nolan Frank	427	mechanic	22	31 "
	D	Wilson James P	427	welder	26	396 Meridian
	E	Wilson John R	427	boilermaker	66	396 "
	F	Wilson Susie M—†	427	housewife	60	396 "
	H	McInnis Beatrice—†	427	clerk	23	here
	K	McInnis Edward	427	electrician	24	"
	L	McInnis Francis	427	laborer	21	"
	M	McInnis Helen—†	427	housewife	50	"
	N	McInnis John	427	electrician	25	"
	O	McInnis Lillian—†	427	clerk	26	"
	P	Connell Dennis	427	laborer	45	119 Falcon
	G	Hoy John	427	"	25	195 Condor
	R	Smith Lillian M—†	428	teacher	50	here
	S	Libby Adelbert L	428	technician	26	"
	T	Libby Caroline M—†	428	operator	35	"
	U	Libby Mary J—†	428	cleaner	45	
	V	Strong Grace M—†	428	teacher	58	
	W	Fitzgibbons Richard B	430	operator	67	"
	X	Grant Margaret B—†	430	designer	50	
	Y	Hall Charles H	430	printer	50	
	Z	Kerr Catherine L—†	430	at home	79	
775						
	A	Kerr Mary L—†	430	clerk	47	"
	B	McCarthy Edward J	430	printer	34	45 Saratoga
	C	Riley Elizabeth —†	432	housewife	48	here
	D	Riley Frederick	432	policeman	49	"
	E	McKeogh Cecelia—†	432	at home	77	"
	F	McKeogh Josephine—†	432	operator	37	
	G	McKeogh Margaret—†	432	domestic	39	"
	H	Croak Mary A—†	432	housewife	34	"
	K	Croak Rose—†	432	at home	75	
	L	Croak Thomas J	432	accountant	34	"
	M	Donahoe Thomas H	434	retired	69	366 Meridian
	N	Douglass James A	434	inspector	60	here
	O	Kincaid Frank	434	clerk	52	"
	P	Kincaid Sarah C—†	434	housewife	47	"
	R	Angelosanto Emily—†	436	"	29	"
	S	Angelosanto Joseph	436	serviceman	39	"
	T	Barrett John	436	mechanic	37	"
	U	*Barrett Margaret—†	437	housewife	58	"

Page.	Letter.	FULL NAME.	Residence, Jan. 1, 1938.	Occupation.	Supposed Age.	Reported Residence, Jan. 1, 1937. Street and Number.

Meridian Street—Continued

	V	Barrett Margaret—†	436	bookkeeper	25	here
	W	*Barrett Robert	436	carpenter	58	"
	X	Barrett Thomas	436	chemist	33	"
	Y	Phillips Daniel	437	policeman	37	"
	Z	Phillips Ethel—†	437	housewife	34	"
776						
	A	Nolan Esther—†	437	clerk	40	
	B	Nolan John	437	mechanic	47	"
	C	Norris John	437	mason	58	
	D	Sullivan Mary—†	437	housekeeper	63	"
	E	*Bozzi Matilda—†	437	housewife	43	"
	F	Bozzi Vincent	437	tailor	22	"
	G	Tedeschi Joseph	437	carpenter	48	20 Marion
	H	DeAngelis Amelia—†	438	housewife	40	here
	K	DeAngelis Henry	438	shoemaker	42	"
	L	Hanson Anna—†	438	housewife	70	"
	M	Hanson Rangwell	438	laborer	32	
	N	Mullen Arthur	438	chauffeur	36	"
	O	Mullen Sadie—†	438	housewife	30	"
	P	Colantuono Catherine—†	438	"	73	
	R	Colantuono Charles A	438	storekeeper	39	"
	S	Colantuono Edith G—†	438	seamstress	32	"
	T	O'Connor Cyril J	439	student	20	
	U	O'Connor Ellen M—†	439	housewife	64	"
	V	O'Connor Louise E—†	439	clerk	47	
	W	Mullane David	439	laborer	20	
	X	Mullane John R	439	"	21	
	Y	Mullane Michael J	439	chauffeur	26	"
	Z	*Mullane Thomas	439	hostler	61	
777						
	A	Mullane Thomas P	439	laborer	24	
	C	Sullivan Patrick J	440	chauffeur	22	"
	D	Sullivan Susan A—†	440	housewife	49	"
	E	Sullivan William F	440	chauffeur	49	"
	F	Vichy Theodore L	440	mechanic	46	"
	G	Pearson Alfred	440	agent	27	
	H	Pearson Veronica—†	440	housewife	25	"
	K	Wasgatt Thomas	440	janitor	70	
	L	*Birss Gladys—†	440	secretary	33	"
	M	May Mary—†	440	housewife	57	"
	N	May William	440	mechanic	62	"

Page.	Letter.	Full Name.	Residence, Jan. 1, 1938.	Occupation.	Supposed Age.	Reported Residence, Jan. 1, 1937. Street and Number.

Meridian Street—Continued

	O	McCarthy Charles	440	clerk	54	here
	P	McCarthy Mabel—†	440	housewife	57	"
	R	Alfama August	441	cook	49	"
	S	*Alfama Maria—†	441	housewife	49	"
	T	Camilo Frank	441	cook	35	
	U	Camilo Louise—†	441	housewife	21	"
	V	*Smith Augusta—†	441	waitress	26	
	W	*Smith Charles	441	laborer	24	
	X	*Smith Gladys—†	441	housewife	45	"
	Y	*Smith Harold	441	laborer	23	
	Z	*Smith Lewis	441	"	21	
778						
	A	Smith Randall	441	"	32	
	B	*Smith Ross A	441	foreman	50	
	C	Swan Arthur	441	laborer	21	
	D	Price Doris M—†	441	student	24	
	E	Price Edith M—†	441	factoryhand	27	"
	F	Price Frank E	441	laborer	33	
	G	Price Jennie L—†	441	housewife	55	"
	H	Price Phyllis—†	441	"	23	61 Marion
	K	Rigg Harry A	441	motorman	48	here
	L	Lafferty William	443	foreman	60	"
	M	McClellan George B	443	storekeeper	31	"
	N	McClellan Mildred—†	443	housewife	31	"
	O	Moore Arthur E	443	cook	29	
	P	Moore Charles P	443	laborer	67	
	R	Moore Lillian—†	443	housewife	66	"
	S	*Babon Leo	443	fisherman	30	"
	T	*Comeau Leo	443	carpenter	58	"
	U	*Comeau Leona—†	443	housewife	65	"
	V	*Richard Pius	443	fisherman	30	"
	W	Keating James	445	proprietor	55	"
	X	Tierney Irene—†	445	housewife	36	"
	Y	Tierney William	445	B F D	44	
	Z	Woods Esther—†	445	housewife	55	"
779						
	A	Mann Bertha L—†	445	"	60	
	B	Mann Diedrich H	445	grocer	64	
	C	Wiegand Frieda V—†	445	housewife	58	"
	D	Wiegand Louise A—†	445	clerk	48	
	E	Cooney William L	445	"	44	

Page.	Letter.	Full Name.	Residence, Jan. 1, 1938.	Occupation.	Supposed Age.	Reported Residence, Jan. 1, 1937. Street and Number.
		Meridian Street—Continued				
	F	Dolaher Frederick	445	B F D	53	here
	G	Dolaher Jennie F—†	445	housewife	54	"
	H	DeRota Clăra—†	447	factoryhand	20	"
	K*	DeRota Ettore	447	laborer	54	
	L	DeRota Maria—†	447	factoryhand	22	"
	M*	DeRota Rachel	447	housewife	48	"
	N	Morella Anthony	447	chauffeur	39	87 White
	O	Morella Anthony C	447	secretary	34	87 "
	P	Morella Laura—†	447	housewife	31	87 "
	R	Morella Ralph	447	clerk	32	87 "
	S	Miller Anna E—†	451	housewife	67	here
	T	Miller Peter	451	retired	78	"
	U	Troy Anna—†	451	housewife	40	"
	V	DeSimone Eleanor—†	451	clerk	23	
	W	DeSimone Rita—†	451	"	23	
	X	DeSimone Sarah—†	451	housewife	60	"
	Y	Grasso Edward	451	chauffeur	22	"
	Z	Ohlson Alexander F	451	seaman	43	
780						
	A	Ohlson Alexander F	451	laborer	21	
	B	Ohlson Elizabeth M—†	451	housewife	43	"
	C	Parmenter Charles	452	retired	67	
	D	Parmenter Fannie—†	452	housewife	66	"
	E	Keyes Clement R	453	motorman	43	"
	F	Keyes Ethel D—†	453	waitress	23	
	G	Keyes Thelma M—†	453	clerk	20	
	H	Keyes Winifred M—†	453	housewife	41	"
	K	Pitts Ethel V—†	453	"	35	
	L	Pitts Herbert A	453	seaman	37	
	N	Lang Joseph E	454	clerk	36	
	O	Lang Mary E—†	454	housewife	71	"
	P	Lang Patrick A	454	plumber	70	"
	R	Sanchez Frank	455	engineer	53	68 Montmorenci av
	S	Sanchez Mary—†	455	housewife	52	68 "
	T	Portello Josephine—†	455	"	41	here
	U	Portello Mary D—†	455	clerk	21	"
	V	Portello Michael	455	painter	48	"
	W	Bartolo Julia—†	456	housewife	21	502 Sumner
	X	Bartolo Michael	456	laborer	24	504 "
	Y	Butler Frank	456	clerk	24	here
	Z	Butler Margaret—†	456	housewife	65	"

Page.	Letter.	Full Name.	Residence, Jan. 1, 1938.	Occupation.	Supposed Age.	Reported Residence, Jan. 1, 1937. Street and Number.
781		**Meridian Street**—Continued				
	A	Butler Mary—†	456	teacher	28	here
	B	Butler Robert	456	retired	67	"
	C	Butler Thomas	456	clerk	40	"
	E	Beatrice James	458	laborer	28	
	F	Palmieri Anthony	458	painter	46	
	G	Palmieri Louise—†	458	housewife	40	"
	H	McGregor Matilda—†	459	clerk	41	
	K	Oldford Elizabeth—†	459	waitress	52	
	L	Oldford Reba H—†	459	housewife	51	"
	M	Tolman Clifford A	459	engineer	55	
	N	Dawe Christopher	459	carpenter	53	"
	O	Worthy Alice—†	460	housewife	22	"
	P	Worthy Edward	460	seaman	25	
	R	Bradley Manassah E	460	clerk	37	"
	S	Bradley Mary T—†	460	housewife	35	"
	T	Perry Hattie B—†	460	"	45	
	U	Perry Ivan M	460	B F D	38	"
	V	Brown Alice M—†	462	housewife	59	Hingham
	W	Smith Doris—†	462	"	36	here
	X	Smith Garfield	462	mechanic	39	"
	Y	Newhook Charles	462	engineer	44	"
	Z	Newhook Charles T	462	mechanic	22	"
782						
	A	Newhook Emma—†	462	housewife	44	"
	B	Cadigan Mary G—†	463	domestic	41	"
	C	Collins John J	463	cable splicer	38	"
	D	Collins Lillian A—†	463	housewife	33	"
	E	Randall Anna—†	463	"	46	
	F	McCabe Bernard G	463	chauffeur	26	"
	G	McCabe Rose D—†	463	housewife	24	"
	H	Mills William J	463	pressman	20	"
	K	Norcott John	464	laborer	45	214 Chelsea
	L	Norcott Mary—†	464	housewife	42	214 "
	M	Rafuse Earle	464	riveter	28	36 Amory
	N	Rafuse Elizabeth—†	464	housewife	24	36 "
	O	Fox Calvin C	464	operator	27	14 Monmouth
	P	Fox Edna M—†	464	housewife	30	14 "
	R	Foote Charles	465	seaman	44	here
	S	*Fraser Maude—†	465	housewife	54	"
	T	Buontempo Edward	465	chauffeur	22	"

Page.	Letter.	Full Name.	Residence, Jan. 1, 1938.	Occupation.	Supposed Age.	Reported Residence, Jan. 1, 1937. Street and Number.

Meridian Street—Continued

	U	Buontempo Grace—†	465	housewife	20	here
	W	Day Emma F—†	469	at home	67	"
	X	Gambino Angelina—†	469	housewife	40	"
	Y	Gambino Anthony	469	laborer	48	
	Z	Moon Mary E—†	469	at home	67	
783						
	A	Ryan Edward L	469	machinist	52	"
	B	Ryan Ruth M—†	469	stenographer	25	"
	C	Coffey James S	469	inspector	39	"
	D	Coffey Mary G—†	469	housewife	37	"
	E	Ferry Beatrice—†	469	clerk	24	
	F	Denaro Bertha—†	471	housewife	30	"
	G	Denaro Manuel	471	laborer	32	
	H	*Fulginiti Frances—†	471	housewife	35	"
	K	*Fulginiti Joseph	471	plasterer	38	"
	L	Creamer Anna—†	471	candymaker	39	"
	M	Creamer Edward	471	laborer	35	
	N	Creamer Mary—†	471	candymaker	35	"
	O	Norcott Catherine—†	473	housewife	51	Chelsea
	P	Norcott Lawrence	473	laborer	22	"
	R	Norcott Michael J	473	fisherman	29	"
	S	Norcott William	473	"	66	"
	T	Hayden Alice—†	473	housewife	50	here
	U	Hayden Patrick J	473	rigger	52	"
	V	Cadigan Anna—†	475	housewife	32	114 Bayswater
	W	Cadigan John	475	chauffeur	31	114 "
	X	Cadigan Mary A—†	475	operator	35	114 "
	Y	Flaherty Bertha M—†	475	housewife	34	here
	Z	Flaherty Thomas F	475	foreman	38	"

784 West Eagle Street

	L	Nelson Edith—†	2	housekeeper	59	here
	M	Newbury Etta—†	2	at home	62	"
	N	Day Agnes—†	2	housewife	40	"
	O	Day Bert	2	engineer	42	"
	P	Day James	2	fishcutter	23	"
	R	Snow William H	2	retired	83	"
	S	*Fougere Gustave	4	seaman	29	Medford
	T	*Fougere Joseph	4	counterman	32	111 Princeton
	U	Fougere Madeline—†	4	housewife	26	111 "

Page.	Letter.	Full Name.	Residence, Jan. 1, 1938.	Occupation.	Supposed Age.	Reported Residence, Jan. 1, 1937. Street and Number.

West Eagle Street—Continued

Page.	Letter.	Full Name.	Residence, Jan. 1, 1938.	Occupation.	Supposed Age.	Reported Residence, Jan. 1, 1937. Street and Number.
	V	Fidler Ethel M—†	4	secretary	27	here
	W	MacDonald Alfred A	4	engineer	52	"
	X	MacDonald Laura A—†	4	housewife	49	"
	Y	Pedersen Elizabeth—†	6	"	43	
	Z	Pedersen Thomas	6	machinist	49	"
785						
	A	Scali Joseph	6	tailor	45	
	B	*Scali Theresa—†	6	housewife	38	"
	C	Doherty Francis C	8	shipper	32	39 W Eagle
	D	Doherty Kathleen G—†	8	housewife	30	39 "
	E	Jewkes Anna—†	8	"	25	here
	F	Jewkes Benjamin	8	clerk	24	"
	G	Kelly Dorothy—†	8	secretary	21	"
	H	Kelly Earl B	8	engineer	51	
	K	Kelly Hilda—†	8	housewife	50	"
	M	Graves Mabel F—†	23	housekeeper	45	"
	N	Pendleton Ella—†	23	at home	83	"
	O	Morrisroe Bertha—†	26	teacher	56	
	P	Stewart James H	26	laborer	43	
	R	Stewart Katheleen—†	26	housewife	39	"
	S	Begley Edward J	27	longshoreman	40	"
	T	Begley Elizabeth F—†	27	housewife	69	"
	U	Begley Michael F	27	engineer	38	
	V	Begley Thomas	27	machinist	42	"
	W	O'Hare George	28	chauffeur	31	"
	X	O'Hare Helen—†	28	housewife	32	"
	Y	McQuillian Catherine—†	28	seamstress	60	28 Maverick
	Z	McQuillian John	28	retired	64	28 "
786						
	A	Quigley Catherine L—†	28	secretary	34	here
	B	Quigley Mary G—†	28	housewife	67	"
	C	Quigley Mary G—†	28	bookkeeper	31	"
	D	Quigley Thomas J	28	retired	70	"
	E	Quigley William H	28	chauffeur	28	"
	F	Conway John T	29	foreman	50	
	G	Greene Anna J—†	29	housewife	37	"
	H	Greene Francis D	29	laborer	41	
	K	Greene John P	29	electrician	40	"
	L	McClellan Mary A—†	29	housekeeper	36	"
	M	Regan Ellen E—†	29	housewife	58	"
	N	Regan James J	29	electrician	31	"

Page.	Letter.	Full Name.	Residence, Jan. 1, 1938.	Occupation.	Supposed Age.	Reported Residence, Jan. 1, 1937. Street and Number.

West Eagle Street—Continued

	o	Regan Margaret L—†	29	seamstress	39	here
	P	Capobianco Jennie—†	30	housewife	35	"
	R	Capobianco Thomas	30	shoemaker	40	"
	S	Hoffman Frances—†	30	bookkeeper	37	"
	T	Yeaton Charles L	30	superintendent	59	"
	U	Yeaton Marie A—†	30	housewife	58	"
	V	Dolan Mary E—†	31	operator	25	"
	W	Lang Anna G—†	31	bookkeeper	38	"
	X	McEachern Duncan R	31	retired	81	"
	Y	Dingwell Chester N	31	expressman	40	"
	Z	Dingwell Elsie M—†	31	housekeeper	42	"
787						
	A	Dingwell Harold C	31	expressman	39	"
	B	Dingwell Mary E—†	31	housewife	33	"
	C	Mullen Helen—†	32	"	28	
	D	Mullen John	32	laborer	30	
	E	Bonanno Louise—†	32	operator	30	"
	F	Canariato Anna—†	32	housewife	38	"
	G	Canariato George	32	shoeworker	40	"
	H	Canariato James	32	laborer	46	
	K	*Canariato Josephine—†	32	housewife	47	"
	L	Canariato Lawrence	32	clerk	20	
	M	Barnet Vernie—†	33	housewife	50	"
	N	Barnet William	33	operator	75	"
	P	Juckett Harvey	33	gardener	70	Vermont
	O	McFarran Aimee—†	33	housekeeper	76	here
	R	*Ryan Albert	33	fisherman	60	"
	S	Thomas William	33	longshoreman	75	"
	T	Tovey John F	33	retired	78	22 Paris
	U	Massaro Henry	34	mason	30	here
	V	Massaro Louise—†	34	housewife	26	"
	W	Mannetta Angelo	34	candyworker	57	"
	X	Mannetta Rose—†	34	housewife	54	"
	Y	Clifford Sarah—†	34	housekeeper	67	"
	Z	Weeks Frederick	35	engineer	76	98 Falcon
788						
	A	Weeks Margaret M—†	35	housewife	50	98 "
	B	Weeks Robert	35	lineman	23	98 "
	C	Hines Albert L	35	seaman	56	here
	D	Hines Albert L	35	laborer	26	"
	E	Hines Annie B—†	35	housewife	53	"

Page.	Letter.	Full Name.	Residence, Jan. 1, 1938.	Occupation.	Supposed Age.	Reported Residence, Jan. 1, 1937. Street and Number.

West Eagle Street—Continued

	F	Hines Arnold L	35	bookkeeper	32	here
	G	Hines Wilfred H	35	seaman	30	"
	H	Gibbons Catherine—†	35	housewife	71	"
	K	Gibbons Hazel M—†	35	clerk	44	
	L	Gibbons John J	35	laborer	46	
	M	Gibbons Morgan	35	watchman	71	"
	N	Stewart George	35	engineer	30	
	O	Woodside William R	35	printer	70	"
	P	Massaro Camella—†	36	housewife	25	146 Everett
	R	Massaro Herman J	36	mason	30	146 "
	S	DeStefano Josephine—†	36	housewife	33	here
	T	DeStefano Ralph	36	barber	37	"
	U	Faretra Ann—†	36	housewife	23	159 Trenton
	V	Faretra Armando	36	clerk	27	159 "
	W	Flaherty Catherine—†	37	housewife	33	here
	X	Flaherty James	37	ironworker	37	"
	Y	Cranitch Daniel M	37	retired	78	"
	Z	Cranitch George L	37	letter carrier	49	"
789						
	A	Cranitch Helen L—†	37	housewife	47	"
	B	Hegner Andrew G	37	laborer	51	
	C	Hegner Lawrence G	37	chauffeur	22	"
	D	Hegner Sarah J—†	37	housewife	48	"
	E	Hegner Thomas A	37	laborer	23	
	F	*Cotreau Andrew L	38	carpenter	49	"
	G	Cotreau Andrew L, jr	38	fishcutter	21	"
	H	*Cotreau Lucy—†	38	housewife	52	"
	K	*LeBlanc Agnes—†	38	"	28	321 Paris
	L	*LeBlanc Louis	38	fishcutter	28	321 "
	M	Munroe Fred U	39	clerk	38	93 Lexington
	N	*Munroe Margaret F—†	39	housewife	37	93 "
	O	Pitts Dorothy E—†	39	"	27	here
	P	Pitts Joseph L	39	fishcutter	32	"
	R	Souza Joseph	39	laborer	30	32 Eutaw
	S	Souza Mary—†	39	housewife	52	32 "
	T	Souza Matilda—†	39	clerk	27	32 "
	U	*Souza Salvadore	39	laborer	55	32 "
	V	Souza William	39	clerk	22	32 "
	W	Barbarossa Della—†	40	bookkeeper	26	here
	X	Barbarossa Evelyn—†	40	factoryhand	29	"
	Y	Barbarossa Louis D	40	carpenter	27	"

Page.	Letter.	FULL NAME.	Residence, Jan. 1, 1938.	Occupation.	Supposed Age.	Reported Residence, Jan. 1, 1937. Street and Number.

West Eagle Street—Continued

	Z	Barbarossa Luigi	40	laborer	68	here
790						
	A	Barbarossa Mary—†	40	housewife	55	"
	B	Nadeau Austin	40	seaman	21	
	C	Nadeau Bernard	40	"	24	
	D	Nadeau Edgar	40	"	26	
	E	Nadeau John	40	laborer	57	
	F	*Nadeau Mary—†	40	housewife	58	"
	G	DeChristoforo Celia—†	40	"	33	
	H	DeChristoforo Paul	40	carpenter	32	"
	K	McNeil Mabel—†	41	housewife	30	"
	L	McNeil Milton	41	laundryman	33	"
	M	Wyse David	41	seaman	47	
	N	Wyse Elizabeth—†	41	housewife	42	"
	O	*Tedesco Frances—†	41	"	57	
	P	Tedesco Joseph	41	carpenter	59	"
	R	Tedesco Santo	41	tailor	57	"
	S	Moulton Addie F—†	42	housekeeper	75	Northampton
	T	Trafton Lillian M—†	42	at home	60	here
	U	*D'Entremont Donald	42	chauffeur	37	"
	V	*D'Entremont Margaret—†	42	housewife	32	"
	W	Brainard Ellen—†	42	instructor	55	"
	X	Harrington Timothy	43	retired	76	
	Y	Mitchell Joseph E	43	fisherman	44	"
	Z	Mitchell Mary C—†	43	housewife	40	"
791						
	A	Orensteen Francis	43	retired	64	
	B	Orensteen Mary A—†	43	housewife	64	"
	C	*Huey Annie E—†	44	housekeeper	82	"
	D	Huey Forrest W	44	seaman	56	"
	E	Aitken Florence E—†	44	housewife	60	14 Sutherland rd
	F	Aitken Joseph	44	chauffeur	29	14 "
	G	*Dunkerton James E	44	dealer	50	14 "
	H	Dow George	44	chauffeur	34	here
	K	Dow Jean—†	44	housewife	37	"
	L	Snow Leonard	49	engineer	44	"
	M	*Snow Mildred—†	49	housewife	39	"
	N	Roche Anna—†	49	housekeeper	67	"
	O	Roche Helen T—†	49	stitcher	42	"
	P	Roche James E	49	calker	44	
	R	Danielian George	49	grocer	65	

Page.	Letter.	Full Name.	Residence, Jan. 1, 1938.	Occupation.	Supposed Age.	Reported Residence, Jan. 1, 1937. Street and Number.

West Eagle Street—Continued

	s	*Nalbandian Bagdasar	49	grocer	74	here
	T	*Nalbandian Mary B—†	49	housewife	56	"
	U	Russo Alice—†	51	clerk	27	"
	V	Russo Lucy—†	51	"	24	
	W	Viggiano Carmela—†	51	housewife	60	"
	X	Viggiano Joseph	51	painter	66	
	Y	Stevens Ernest	51	instructor	30	"
	Z	Stevens Rose M—†	51	housewife	30	"
792						
	A	Buccafusca Frank	51	laborer	41	
	B	Buccafusca Jennie—†	51	housewife	36	"
	C	George Aubrey	52	rigger	56	37 Prescott
	D	George Aubrey A	52	shipper	26	37 "
	E	George Hope—†	52	housewife	51	37 "
	F	McDonald Charles R	52A	student	21	here
	G	McDonald Edward R	52A	engineer	59	"
	H	McDonald Harold	52A	clerk	22	"
	K	McDonald Marie—†	52A	at home	20	
	L	McDonald Mary B—†	52A	housewife	58	"
	N	*Crupi Angelina—†.	53	housekeeper	57	"
	O	Scarcella Antonio	53	laborer	60	"
	P	Blowers Eliza—†	53	housewife	69	"
	R	Blowers James	53	laborer	76	
	S	Blowers James E	53	"	28	
	T	Blowers Anna—†	53	housewife	26	"
	U	Blowers Reginald	53	machinist	34	"
	V	Bartolomeo Helen—†	54	housewife	22	258 E Eagle
	W	Bartolomeo Lawrence	54	laborer	24	258 "
	X	Keenan Arthur F	54A	accountant	27	365 Meridian
	Y	Keenan Edward J	54A	merchant	20	365 "
	Z	Keenan Ida M—†	54A	housewife	55	365 "
793						
	A	Keenan Robert G	54A	seaman	35	365 "
	B	Botto Mary—†	54A	housewife	41	119 Falcon
	C	Botto Michael	54A	laborer	51	119 "
	D	Portrait George A	54A	"	24	119 "
	E	Roche Catherine T—†	55	housewife	53	here
	F	Roche Thomas A	55	laborer	69	"
	G	*Mombourquette Charles	55	fisherman	37	"
	H	*Mombourquette Hannah—†	55	housewife	34	"
	K	Doucette Ella—†	55	"	39	Wakefield

Page.	Letter.	FULL NAME.	Residence, Jan. 1, 1938.	Occupation.	Supposed Age.	Reported Residence, Jan. 1, 1937. Street and Number.

West Eagle Street—Continued

	L	Doucette Stanley	55	cutter	43	Wakefield
	M	Boudreau Corinne—†	55	housewife	29	Wilmington
	N	Boudreau Martin	55	plumber	30	"
	O	Brow Helen—†	56	housekeeper	34	here
	P	Petitti Charles	56	laborer	35	"
	R	Petitti Gertrude—†	56	housewife	31	"
	S	*Costa Mary—†	56	"	38	
	T	Costa Paulino	56	proprietor	45	"
	U	*Irving Margaret—†	57	housekeeper	36	"
	V	Giambusso Frank	57	shoeworker	47	"
	W	*Giambusso Sarah—†	57	housewife	38	"
	X	Rooney Edward	57	timekeeper	26	"
	Y	Rooney Jessie—†	57	housewife	21	"
	Z	Chamness Ambrosine—†	58	housekeeper	40	"
794						
	A	*Menezes Laurenza J—†	58	housewife	40	"
	B	*Menezes Louis A	58	longshoreman	54	"
	C	*Cabral James	58	millhand	37	106 Putnam
	G	Luzinski Frank P	60	policeman	39	here
	H	Luzinski Henrietta—†	60	housewife	33	"
	K	Kelley Jean—†	61	"	28	Vermont
	L	Kelley Harold	61	laborer	31	"
	M	Lagammo Joseph	61	shoeworker	29	here
	N	Lagammo Theresa—†	61	housewife	27	"
	O	Delcore Elvira—†	61	"	27	67 E Eagle
	P	Delcore John	61	butcher	31	67 "
	R	Clifford Sadie—†	62	housekeeper	72	here
	S	Simington Charles	62	janitor	32	"
	T	*Stoddard David	63	fisherman	63	"
	U	*Stoddard Jennie—†	63	housewife	59	"
	V	*Haddock Agnes—†	63	"	30	
	W	*Haddock Walter	63	boilermaker	32	"
	X	Andrade Gabriel	63	porter	40	
	Y	*Andrade Helen—†	63	housewife	35	"
	Z	Visco Domenica—†	64	"	37	
795						
	A	Visco Frank	64	laborer	44	
	B	Penney George K	64	"	25	
	C	Penney Thomas	64	mechanic	26	"
	D	Perham Lloyd	64	rigger	57	
	E	Perham Theresa—†	64	housewife	53	"

Page.	Letter.	Full Name.	Residence, Jan. 1, 1938.	Occupation.	Supposed Age.	Reported Residence, Jan. 1, 1937. Street and Number.

West Eagle Street—Continued

	F	Visco Anna—†	64	seamstress	35	here
	G	*Visco Camella—†	64	housewife	69	"
	H	Visco Mary—†	64	stenographer	30	"
	K	Visco Rose—†	64	seamstress	33	"
	L	Kearney Althea—†	65	housewife	23	188 Falcon
	M	Kearney John J	65	storekeeper	23	188 "
	N	Wilson Gordon	65	laborer	24	Vermont
	O	Zagarella Anna—†	65	housewife	23	989 Benningt'n
	P	Zagarella James	65	laborer	25	989 "
	R	Zagarella Louise—†	65	housewife	30	here
	S	*Zagarella Peter	65	presser	32	"
	T	Tanner Elmer	66	laborer	49	"
	U	Tanner Virginia—†	66	cashier	21	
	V	*Costantino Alice—†	66	housewife	48	"
	W	Costantino Antonio	66	clerk	20	
	X	Costantino Pasquale	66	laborer	48	
	Y	Costantino Vincent	66	counterman	22	"
	Z	*Keough Andrew	66	cook	23	
796						
	A	*Keough Ellen—†	66	housewife	47	"
	B	*Keough James	66	ironworker	49	"
	D	Ross Charles	67	fireman	29	"
	C	Ross Emma—†	67	housewife	29	"
	E	Penney Edward M	67	timekeeper	38	307 Lexington
	F	*Penney Mary J—†	67	housewife	28	307 "
	G	*Burrone Charles	67	painter	53	here
	H	*Burrone Josephine—†	67	housewife	48	"
	K	Burrone Mary—†	67	seamstress	23	"
	L	Bostrom Ambia—†	69	housewife	54	"
	M	Bostrom Fred	69	laborer	26	"
	N	Larson George	69	longshoreman	40	"
	O	Carusone John	69	laborer	62	
	P	Carusone Josephine—†	69	housewife	49	"
	S	Aitken Catherine E—†	70	"	34	
	T	Aitken Frank D	70	mechanic	36	"
	U	*Poirier Ina—†	70	housekeeper	42	"
	V	*DesJardins Nellie—†	70	housewife	31	"
	W	*DesJardins Oscar	70	fireman	39	
	X	Clements Cerita—†	71	housewife	46	"
	Y	Clements Richard	71	laborer	22	
	Z	*Clements William	71	millhand	58	"

Page.	Letter.	Full Name.	Residence, Jan. 1, 1938.	Occupation.	Supposed Age.	Reported Residence, Jan. 1, 1937. Street and Number.
797						

West Eagle Street—Continued

Page.	Letter.	Full Name.	Residence, Jan. 1, 1938.	Occupation.	Supposed Age.	Reported Residence, Jan. 1, 1937. Street and Number.
	A	*Doucette Levi	71	fisherman	51	here
	B	Vitello Frank	72	painter	34	"
	C	Vitello Theresa—†	72	housewife	29	"
	D	Laville Henry W	72	shipper	49	
	E	Laville Mary A—†	72	housewife	49	"
	F	*Jaakola Edwin	72	laborer	43	
	G	Jaakola Edwin	72	"	21	
	H	*Jaakola Elsie—†	72	housewife	40	"
	K	*Iaderosa Mary—†	73	housekeeper	40	"
	L	Morante Anna—†	73	seamstress	24	"
	N	McIntire Daniel P	75	carpenter	38	"
	O	McIntire Herbert J	75	"	35	
	P	McIntire Mary E—†	75	clerk	22	
	R	Rose Frances M—†	75	operator	31	..
	S	Cooper Daniel A	76	mariner	55	
	T	Cooper Jessie H—†	76	housewife	53	"
	U	Morse Mabel M—†	76	librarian	45	"
	V	*Frost Leander	77	laborer	28	61 W Eagle
	W	*Frost Margaret—†	77	housewife	26	61 "
	X	*Amirault Edgar	77	fishcutter	35	here
	Y	*Amirault Mary—†	77	housewife	34	"
	Z	*LaRaia Anna—†	77	housekeeper	48	"
798						
	A	Nolan Louis F	81	realtor	60	
	B	Nolan Mary E—†	81	housekeeper	55	"
	D	Hardy Elizabeth T—†	81	housewife	82	"
	C	Hardy Howard	81	retired	80	
	E	Hemeon Edith H—†	81	housewife	51	"
	F	Hemeon Edward B	81	fisherman	55	"
	G	Greenwood Helen G—†	82	secretary	42	"
	H	Greenwood Jennie M—†	82	housekeeper	75	"
	K	Forbes Arthur H	82	chauffeur	43	74 W Eagle
	L	Forbes Mary J—†	82	housewife	45	74 "
	M	Whittendale Ruth L—†	84	"	79	here
	N	Whittendale Walter B	84	carpenter	46	"
	O	Tanner Hattie E—†	84	housewife	48	"
	P	Tanner Louis A	84	engineer	53	
	R	Tanner Louis A, jr	84	foreman	23	"
	S	Dennis Millie—†	84	housewife	57	117 Falcon
	T	Nickerson J Ashton	86	teller	31	here

Page.	Letter.	Full Name.	Residence, Jan. 1, 1938.	Occupation.	Supposed Age.	Reported Residence, Jan. 1, 1937. Street and Number.

West Eagle Street—Continued

Page.	Letter.	Full Name.	Residence, Jan. 1, 1938.	Occupation.	Supposed Age.	Reported Residence, Jan. 1, 1937. Street and Number.
	U	Nickerson Mildred—†	86	housewife	30	here
	V	Crowell Elizabeth E—†	86	"	81	"
	W	Crowell Ritty W	86	shoeworker	46	"

White Street

Page.	Letter.	Full Name.	Residence, Jan. 1, 1938.	Occupation.	Supposed Age.	Reported Residence, Jan. 1, 1937. Street and Number.
	Y	Baretta Esther—†	24	housewife	42	here
	Z	Baretta Leonard	24	metalworker	45	"
799						
	A	Baretta Louise—†	24	clerk	20	"
	B	Scaperotti Edith—†	26	housewife	26	190 Paris
	C	Scaperotti Sidney	26	bricklayer	31	190 "
	D	Ventola Arthur	26	entertainer	22	13 Hanover av
	E	Dunbar Lawrence	26	fireman	36	Deer Island
	F	Kaeneman Mary—†	26	housewife	34	170 Brooks
	G	Kaeneman Robert	26	engineer	37	170 "
	H	Tallman Daniel	26	laborer	64	170 "
	K	LeBlanc Frank L	28	fishcutter	30	here
	L*	LeBlanc Regina—†	28	housewife	25	"
	M	O'Driscoll Catherine—†	28	clerk	29	"
	N	O'Driscoll Edward T	28	"	27	
	O	O'Driscoll James M	28	"	33	
	P	O'Driscoll Mary—†	28	housewife	59	"
	R	O'Driscoll Mary E—†	28	at home	37	
	S	O'Driscoll Thomas W	28	clerk	23	"
	T	Stubbs Anna M—†	28	at home	31	New York
	U	D'Entremont Leonce	32	fishcutter	29	here
	V*	D'Entremont Virginia—†	32	housewife	24	"
	W*	Comeau Joseph E	32	storekeeper	30	"
	X*	Comeau Laura—†	32	housewife	31	"
	Y*	Comeau Leander	32	carpenter	62	"
	Z*	Comeau Philomene—†	32	housewife	64	"
800						
	A	Hopkins Freeman	32	engineer	44	
	B*	Hopkins Hazel—†	32	housewife	31	"
	C	D'Entremont Joseph	34	fishcutter	33	Chelsea
	D*	D'Entremont Theresa—†	34	housewife	34	"
	E	Ceruola Angelina—†	34	"	30	200 Brooks
	F	Ceruolo Nicholas	34	foreman	32	200 "
	G	Vaccaro Angelina—†	34	housewife	40	here
	H	Vaccaro Francesco	34	bricklayer	49	"

Page.	Letter.	Full Name.	Residence, Jan. 1, 1938.	Occupation.	Supposed Age.	Reported Residence, Jan. 1, 1937. Street and Number.

White Street—Continued

	K	Vaccaro Isabelle—†	34	packer	22	here
	M	Cahalane Catherine—†	36	housewife	67	"
	N	Cahalane Cornelius F	36	chauffeur	34	"
	O	Cahalane Helen—†	36	nurse	23	Chelsea
	P	Cahalane Robert J	36	chauffeur	31	here
	R	McLaughlin Charles B	36	salesman	35	"
	S	Murray Edward H	38	laborer	48	"
	T	Murray Helen E—†	38	housewife	42	"
	V	Panzini Barbara—†	42	"	31	
	W	*Panzini John	42	candymaker	36	"
	X	Grasso Frank	42	electrician	25	"
	Y	Grasso Joseph	42	helper	22	
	Z	*Grasso Martin	42	laborer	62	
801						
	A	Grasso Mildred—†	42	seamstress	21	"
	B	*Grasso Sophie—†	42	housewife	52	"
	C	Norcott Mary—†	44	"	20	33 Lexington
	D	*Norcott Ronald	44	fisherman	27	33 "
	E	Norcott Timothy	44	"	31	278 Havre
	F	Sawyer Cora M—†	44	housewife	77	here
	G	Sawyer Edward T	44	retired	76	"
	H	*MacLean Jeanette—†	44	housewife	31	"
	K	*MacLean John	44	chauffeur	36	"
	L	Kelley Thomas F	46	laborer	29	6 Prescott
	M	Raleigh Rosamond—†	46	supervisor	34	6 "
	N	Ward Florence R—†	46	housewife	54	6 "
	O	Ward Richard N	46	machinist	22	6 "
	P	Burke Margaret E—†	46	matron	54	here
	R	Burke Thomas F	46	investigator	57	533 Benningt'n
	S	McCaul Edward J	46	clerk	30	here
	T	*McCaul Josephine A—†	46	housewife	59	"
	U	McCaul Thomas M	46	clerk	23	"
	V	McCaul William J	46	laborer	32	"
	W	Kearns Annie—†	46	at home	30	48 Condor
	X	Loomis Isabella—†	46	housewife	27	48 "
	Y	*Pipi Antoinetta—†	48	"	47	here
	Z	Pipi Joseph	48	barber	26	"
802						
	A	Pipi Michael	48	operator	49	"
	C	Basil Anthony	48	laborer	26	
	D	Basil Carmella—†	48	housewife	53	"

Page.	Letter.	FULL NAME.	Residence, Jan. 1, 1938.	Occupation.	Supposed Age.	Reported Residence, Jan. 1, 1937. Street and Number.

White Street—Continued

	E	Basil Mary—†	48	clerk	21	here
	F	Basil Peter	48	"	22	"
	G	Basil Salvatore	48	operator	23	"
	H	Basil Vincenzo	48	laborer	57	"
	K	Driscoll John	52	investigator	58	21 Lexington
	L	Jackson Harry	52	checker	55	here
	M	Joyce Marcella F—†	52	housewife	40	"
	N	Joyce Wilfred P	52	proprietor	43	"
	O	Kehoe Louise—†	52	operator	39	129 Eutaw
	P	Kelly Frank	52	collector	42	here
	R	McAuliffe Dennis	52	counterman	37	Somerville
	S	Ottiano James	52	machinist	40	here
	T	Sheridan Frank	52	collector	43	"
	U	Hegner Agnes—†	53	packer	56	212 Saratoga
	V	*Hegner Annie—†	53	housewife	48	212 "
	W	Hegner Walter J	53	laborer	48	212 "
	X	DeMatteo Anna—†	53	clerk	20	here
	Y	*DeMatteo Carmella—†	53	housewife	45	"
	Z	Nicosia Beatrice—†	53	seamstress	24	"
803						
	A	Nicosia Edmund	53	laborer	22	
	B	Nicosia Sarah—†	53	housewife	45	"
	C	Picardi Violet—†	53	clerk	28	"
	D	DeFronzo Clara—†	55	housewife	27	168 Putnam
	E	DeFronzo James	55	painter	27	168 "
	F	Tompkins Anna—†	55	at home	28	here
	G	*Tompkins John	55	retired	71	"
	H	Tompkins Joseph	55	laborer	32	"
	K	*Tompkins Margaret—†	55	housewife	60	"
	L	Tompkins Mary—†	55	laundryworker	34	"
	M	Cady Agnes—†	55	housewife	26	"
	N	Cady Joseph	55	chauffeur	30	"
	O	*Escorcio John	57	longshoreman	44	"
	P	*Escorcio Margaret—†	57	housewife	26	"
	R	Barros John	57	cook	50	
	S	*Barros Mary—†	57	operator	36	"
	T	*Souza Mary—†	57	at home	60	
	U	Pigeon Abram S	58	superintendent	30	"
	V	Pigeon Elizabeth W—†	58	housewife	61	"
	W	Pigeon Fred L	58	merchant	63	"
	X	West Newton P	58	retired	88	

Page.	Letter.	Full Name.	Residence, Jan. 1, 1938.	Occupation.	Supposed Age.	Reported Residence, Jan. 1, 1937. Street and Number.

White Street—Continued

	Y	McGunigle Mary J—†	59	housewife	24	here
	Z	McGunigle William G	59	machinist	27	"
804						
	A	Sandquist Catherine L—†	59	housewife	43	"
	B	Sandquist Eric T	59	mailer	47	
	C	Sandquist William O	59	salesman	21	"
	D	Fagone Joseph	60	asphalt worker	25	"
	E	Fagone Phyllis—†	60	housewife	23	12 Chelsea
	G*	Blanciforte Annie—†	60	"	43	here
	F	Fagone John S	60	instructor	23	"
	H	Fagone Angelina—†	60	packer	22	"
	K	Fagone Charles	60	operator	27	"
	L	McInnis Donald R	61	painter	37	
	M	McInnis Violet M—†	61	housewife	38	"
	N	Preshong Ephraim	61	painter	40	
	O	Preshong Louise—†	61	housekeeper	62	"
	P	Flammia Caroline—†	63	housewife	29	"
	R	Flammia William A	63	laborer	29	
	S	Hawes Margaret A—†	63	housewife	37	"
	T	Hawes Stephen P	63	laborer	41	
	U	Dalton Grace M—†	68	clerk	54	
	V	Dalton Joseph H	68	"	31	
	W	Ham Gordon R	68	artist	33	
	X	Corrado Alphonse	68	fishcutter	20	"
	Y	Corrado John	68	physician	29	"
	Z*	Corrado Pasqualina—†	68	housewife	58	"
805						
	A	Corrado Anna—†	68	"	34	
	B	Corrado Louis	68	mason	34	
	C*	Fenton Ellen—†	68	at home	72	
	E*	Giancristiano Ida—†	75	housewife	41	"
	F	Giancristiano Louise—†	75	clerk	21	
	G	Giancristiano Michael	75	steamfitter	47	"
	H	Worthy Doris V—†	75	stenographer	26	"
	K	Worthy Elsa A—†	75	housewife	49	"
	L*	Monkewitz Antonina—†	76	"	48	
	M*	Monkewitz Constanti	76	operator	56	"
	N	Grosso Vincent	76	shoemaker	65	"
	O	Zollo Fidele	76	laborer	41	
	P	Zollo Malvina—†	76	forewoman	37	"
	R*	Kazis Evelyn—†	76	housewife	32	"

Page.	Letter.	Full Name.	Residence, Jan. 1, 1938.	Occupation.	Supposed Age.	Reported Residence, Jan. 1, 1937. Street and Number.

White Street—Continued

	s	*Kazis George	76	packer	45	here
	T	*Kazis John	76	chef	47	"
	U	Limone Joseph	77	machinist	38	"
	V	*Limone Susie—†	77	housewife	38	"
	W	*Pagliccia Emidio	77	pedler	42	
	X	Shea Dorothy—†	77	housewife	32	"
	Y	Shea John P	77	engineer	33	
	Z	*Hirtle Clayton	78	shipper	20	
806						
	A	*Hirtle Florence—†	78	housewife	44	"
	B	*Hirtle Louis	78	carpenter	49	"
	C	*Hirtle Robert	78	at home	21	
	D	Flaherty Hannah—†	79	"	69	
	E	Kelleher Mary—†	79	"	68	
	F	*Parker Burton	79	carpenter	66	"
	G	Saklad Mary—†	80	housewife	56	"
	H	Saklad Sarah L—†	80	bookkeeper	33	Maine
	K	Burnis Benjamin	80	foreman	45	here
	L	Burnis Sophie—†	80	housewife	39	"
	M	Feins Daniel S	80	student	21	"
	N	Feins Lillian—†	80	saleswoman	45	"
	O	*Polonsky Anna—†	80	housewife	59	"
	P	Polonsky Emma—†	80	saleswoman	37	"
	R	Polonsky Frank	80	druggist	42	"
	S	Polonsky Jacob	80	"	30	Cambridge
	T	Polonsky Louis	80	physician	27	here
	U	Polonsky Mildred E—†	80	nurse	26	"
	V	O'Brien Elizabeth—†	81	housewife	83	"
	W	O'Brien Patrick D	81	laborer	60	"
	X	McGowan Catherine—†	81	operator	65	29 Maverick
	Y	Lipinsky Fannie—†	82	housewife	46	here
	Z	Lipinsky Samuel	82	operator	53	"
807						
	A	*Severino Alessandra—†	82	at home	70	"
	B	Severino Erminia—†	82	seamstress	30	"
	C	*Severino Eugene P	82	shoeworker	44	"
	D	Severino Sarah—†	82	"	40	"
	F	Coite Beatrice—†	85	domestic	50	407 Saratoga
	G	*Udelson Jennie—†	85	housewife	65	here
	H	Udelson Nathan	85	operator	66	"

Page.	Letter.	FULL NAME.	Residence, Jan. 1, 1938.	Occupation.	Supposed Age.	Reported Residence, Jan. 1, 1937. Street and Number.

White Street Place

	K	Doucette Arthur R	1	seaman	29	here
	L	Doucette Mary—†	1	housewife	38	"
	M	Deveau Enos J	2	fishcutter	62	"
	N	*Deveau Joseph S	2	cutter	25	
	O	*Doucette Annie—†	4	housewife	57	"
	P	*Doucette Arthur	4	carpenter	53	"

1

14

15

1(

17

18

19

2(

1(2

11

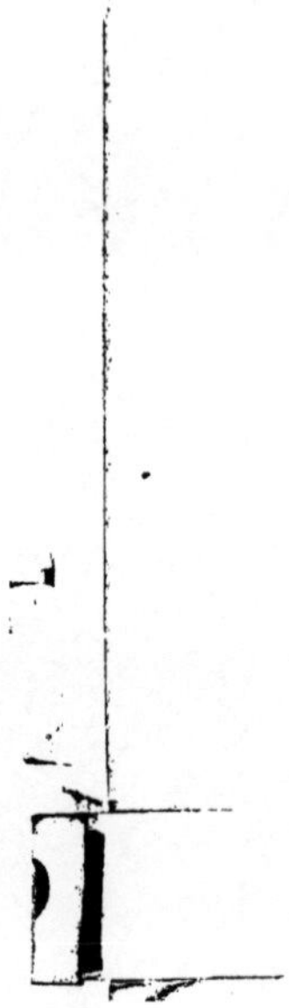

Ward 1—Precinct 10

CITY OF BOSTON

LIST OF RESIDENTS

20 YEARS OF AGE AND OVER

(NON-CITIZENS INDICATED BY ASTERISK)
(FEMALES INDICATED BY DAGGER)

AS OF

JANUARY 1, 1938

JOSEPH F. TIMILTY, } *Listing*
FREDERIC E. DOWLING, } *Board.*

CITY OF BOSTON PRINTING DEPARTMENT

Page.	Letter.	Full Name.	Residence, Jan. 1, 1938.	Occupation.	Supposed Age.	Reported Residence, Jan. 1, 1937. Street and Number.
815						
		Brooks Street				
	A	Nickerson Bradford	223	fishcutter	32	here
	B	Repetto Nicolas	223	laborer	24	"
	C	Repetto Florence—†	223	housewife	20	"
	D	*Salmi Emil	223	longshoreman	42	"
	E	Nickerson Alston	225	laborer	25	
	F	Nickerson Mary—†	225	housewife	26	"
	G	Towlson Charles	225	laborer	40	
	H	Towlson Estelle—†	225	housewife	40	"
	K	Eccleston Laura—†	227	at home	44	"
	L	Eccleston Ada—†	227	housewife	27	159 Falcon
	M	Eccleston Charles	227	fishcutter	27	159 "
		Condor Street				
	R	King Margaret F—†	121	housewife	33	here
	S	King Mary F—†	121	"	58	"
	T	King William C	121	machinist	36	"
	U	King William T	121	foreman	58	
	W	Gillis John	133	mechanic	31	"
	X	Gillis Lillian—†	133	housewife	25	"
	Y	Cowan Annie—†	133A	"	50	
	Z	Driscoll Mary—†	133A	housekeeper	73	"
816						
	B	Gillis Margaret A—†	133A	housewife	68	"
	A	McCarthy Jeremiah A	133A	B F D	41	
	C	McCarthy Patrick J	133A	"	43	
	D	Engley Frank W	135	retired	82	
	E	Engley Mary F—†	135	housewife	58	"
	F	Wainwright Charles E	135A	laborer	24	
	G	Wainwright Lottie—†	135A	housewife	58	"
	H	Werner Margaret—†	135A	"	32	
	K	Werner William	135A	milkman	35	"
	L	Duffy Annie—†	137	housewife	36	"
	M	*Duffy Patrick	137	laborer	49	
	P	Aitken Alice—†	139	housewife	35	"
	R	Aitken William	139	laborer	40	
	S	Merrigan Mary—†	139A	housewife	20	"
	T	Merrigan Thomas F	139A	reporter	26	
	U	Merrigan William	139A	printer	25	
	V	Ryan John J	139A	engineer	60	

Page.	Letter.	FULL NAME.	Residence, Jan. 1, 1938.	Occupation.	Supposed Age.	Reported Residence, Jan. 1, 1937. Street and Number.

Condor Street—Continued

Page.	Letter.	FULL NAME.	Residence, Jan. 1, 1938.	Occupation.	Supposed Age.	Reported Residence, Jan. 1, 1937. Street and Number.
	W	Ryan Margaret A—†	139A	housewife	46	here
	Z	Bonzagni Anthony J	155	clerk	56	"
817						
	A	Bonzagni Catherine—†	155	housewife	55	"
	B	Bonzagni Frank	155	bookkeeper	22	"
	C	Bonzagni John	155	surveyor	26	"
	D	Moore Albertina—†	157	housekeeper	60	"
	E	Simons Alexander D	157	retired	74	"
	F	Simons Robert	157	janitor	37	
	G	Simons Rosella—†	157	housewife	73	"
	H	*Bateman Laura—†	163	"	27	Nova Scotia
	K	Bateman Smith	163	seaman	29	40 Falcon
	L	*Williams Gladys A—†	165	housewife	36	here
	M	*Williams Frank A	165	mechanic	37	"
	N	*Boudreau Clayton	167	fishcutter	33	"
	O	*Boudreau Gladys—†	167	housewife	27	"
	P	Nolfo Joseph	169	laborer	55	
	R	Nolfo Josephine—†	169	housewife	51	"
	S	Calabria Gene	171	clerk	28	Medford
	T	Calabria Mafalda—†	171	housewife	28	"
	U	Albargo Angelina—†	173	"	50	here
	V	*Albargo Philip	173	fisherman	58	"
	W	Calabria Peter	173	clerk	20	"
	X	Ambrosio John	175	musician	29	"
	Y	Ambrosio Josephine—†	175	housewife	26	"
	Z	Leone Anthony	177	houseman	43	"
818						
	A	Leone Lena—†	177	housewife	33	"
	B	Veeder Mary—†	179	"	35	153 Falcon
	C	Veeder Perry L	179	watchman	37	153 "
	D	Cunningham Rose—†	181	housekeeper	63	here
	E	MacNeill Francis X	181	engineer	29	109 Falcon
	F	MacNeill Margaret R—†	181	housewife	24	109 Condor
	G	Phillips Mary F—†	181	operator	31	220 Brooks
	L	Benoit Annetta—†	195	housewife	32	458 Meridian
	M	Benoit Charles	195	carpenter	33	458 "
	N	*LaBlanc Lorenzo	195	fisherman	34	458 "
	O	*Currier Joseph	195	barber	65	here
	P	Currier Matilda—†	195	housewife	58	"
	R	Adams Albert A	197	binder	36	"
	S	Adams Alice M—†	197	housewife	29	"

Page.	Letter.	Full Name.	Residence, Jan. 1, 1938.	Occupation.	Supposed Age.	Reported Residence, Jan. 1, 1937. Street and Number.

Condor Street—Continued

Page.	Letter.	Full Name.	Residence, Jan. 1, 1938.	Occupation.	Supposed Age.	Reported Residence, Jan. 1, 1937. Street and Number.
	U	Goodwin Burns J	203	gardener	54	here
	V	Goodwin George G	203	clerk	20	"
	W	Goodwin Kenneth B	203	"	29	"
	X	Goodwin Lillian L—†	203	housewife	50	"
	Y	Anderson Andrew	203	mechanic	62	"
	Z	Anderson Jennie C—†	203	housewife	62	"
819						
	B	*Marjottie Carmella—†	213	"	48	
	C	*Marjottie Frank	213	laborer	48	"
	D	Sciacca Hugh	213	"	35	190 Cottage
	E	Sciacca Mary—†	213	housewife	24	190 "
	G	Flammia Antonio	225	clerk	32	here
	H	Flammia Frances—†	225	housewife	29	"
	K	Flammia Mary—†	225	at home	65	"
	L	Flammia Michael A	225	laborer	66	
	M	Flammia Theresa—†	225	housewife	25	"
	T	*Brutus Adolph E	237	engineer	56	"
	U	Brutus Annie M—†	237	housewife	55	"
	V	Fraser Mary P—†	237	housekeeper	53	"
	W	Pitts Charlotte B—†	237	operator	50	"
	X	Sullivan James M	237	musician	30	"
	Z	*Candido Ignazia—†	243	housewife	58	"
820						
	A	Candido Salvatore	243	laborer	54	
	C	DeLucca Amadio	243	"	29	
	D	DeLucca Pauline—†	243	housewife	22	"

East Eagle Street

Page.	Letter.	Full Name.	Residence, Jan. 1, 1938.	Occupation.	Supposed Age.	Reported Residence, Jan. 1, 1937. Street and Number.
	H	Gooby James	202	cook	48	206 White
	K	Hawco Louis	202	laborer	39	65 W Eagle
	L	Hawco Winfred—†	202	housewife	33	65 "
	M	Cattanese Dominick	204	chauffeur	23	336 Mass av
	N	Cattanese Mary—†	204	housewife	24	336 "
	O	Mondi Antonio	204	laborer	43	here
	P	Mondi Josephine—†	204	housewife	41	"
	R	Meo Alberto	204	laborer	42	"
	S	Meo Mary—†	204	housewife	27	"
	T	Cucinotta Mary—†	205	"	74	26 Barton
	U	Healy Laura—†	205	"	42	here
	V	Healy Matthew	205	rigger	48	"

Page.	Letter.	FULL NAME.	Residence, Jan. 1, 1938.	Occupation.	Supposed Age.	Reported Residence, Jan. 1, 1937. Street and Number.

East Eagle Street—Continued

	W	Grande Joseph	205	shoeworker	39	here
	X	*Grande Pauline—†	205	housewife	36	"
	Y	*Boland Jeremiah	206	fisherman	40	151 Saratoga
	Z	*Boland Violet—†	206	housewife	29	151 "
821						
	A	*DiLorenzo Fred	206	carpenter	61	154 Cottage
	B	DiLorenzo Jennie—†	206	stitcher	22	154 "
	C	DiLorenzo Josephine—†	206	"	25	154 "
	D	DiLorenzo Rachel—†	206	packer	24	154 '
	E	*DiLorenzo Yola—†	206	housewife	50	154 "
	F	*Cucinotta Celia—†	206	"	40	48 Billerica
	G	*Cucinotta Joseph	206	laundryman	47	48 "
	H	Cucinotta Sadie—†	206	clerk	21	48 "
	K	*Morrocco Mary—†	207	housewife	52	here
	L	Morrocco Vincent	207	laborer	43	"
	M	Gomez Helen—†	207	housewife	32	"
	N	Gomez Manuel	207	machinist	45	"
	O	Berardi Angela—†	207	housewife	26	"
	P	Berardi Frank	207	rubberworker	33	"
	R	*Berardi Mary—†	207	housewife	54	"
	S	*McCormick Helen B—†	208	"	46	206 E Eagle
	T	*McCormick Patrick	208	laborer	42	206 "
	U	*Catone Clara—†	208	housewife	40	here
	V	Catone Guy	208	laborer	52	"
	W	Catone Lena—†	208	clerk	21	"
	X	Catone Michael	208	laborer	21	
	Y	Catone Minnie—†	208	dressmaker	23	"
822						
	B	Shephard Edmund L	210	painter	29	
	C	Shephard Lillian M—†	210	housewife	26	"
	D	Dlott Dorothy—†	210	"	32	
	E	Dlott Samuel	210	storekeeper	37	"
	F	McDonald John	210	retired	60	"
	G	McDonald Margaret—†	210	housewife	57	"
	H	McDonald William	210	laborer	25	
	K	Sacco Rose—†	211	housewife	29	"
	L	Sacco Salvatore J	211	helper	38	
	M	Zeuli Henry	211	barber	43	
	N	*Zeuli Rose—†	211	housewife	38	"
	O	Milroy Bertram	212	chauffeur	44	"
	P	Milroy Margaret—†	212	housewife	42	"

East Eagle Street—Continued

Page.	Letter.	Full Name.	Residence, Jan. 1, 1938.	Occupation.	Supposed Age.	Reported Residence, Jan. 1, 1937. Street and Number.
	R	Milroy Mildred—†	212	at home	24	here
	S	*Surette Alice—†	212	housewife	27	221 Princeton
	T	*Surette Roger	212	painter	28	221 "
	U	*Surette Charles	212	carpenter	59	221 "
	V	*Surette Rose—†	212	housewife	50	221 "
	W	King Elmer A	212	chauffeur	43	here
	X	King Grace M—†	212	housewife	43	"
	Y	King Horace W	212	laborer	23	"
	Z	DeLuca Eleanor—†	213	shoeworker	22	"
823						
	A	DeLuca Ettore	213	tailor	51	
	B	*DeLuca Ignatius	213	pharmacist	26	"
	C	DeLuca Lucia—†	213	housewife	44	"
	D	Franklin Emanuel	213	agent	29	Somerville
	E	Franklin Patricia—†	213	housewife	24	here
	F	Cameron Roderick	214	carpenter	58	"
	K	Benoit August	214	seaman	55	"
	G	Pitts James	214	chauffeur	31	"
	H	Pitts Margaret—†	214	at home	67	
	L	Goodwin Dexter	214	laborer	31	
	M	Goodwin Gladys—†	214	housewife	24	"
	N	Stasio Henry	216	steamfitter	25	168 Falcon
	O	Stasio Lillian—†	216	housewife	25	168 "
	P	Callari Joseph	216	laborer	25	225 Condor
	R	Callari Louise—†	216	housewife	25	225 "
	T	Lugrin Bertrand	217	shipper	65	here
	U	Lugrin Elizabeth—†	217	housewife	60	"
	V	Lugrin Fred	217	laborer	40	"
	W	Santirocco George	217	engineer	44	
	X	Santirocco Theresa—†	217	housewife	22	"
	Y	*Breda Joseph	217	photographer	54	"
	Z	Breda Mary—†	217	housewife	57	"
824						
	A	Grancristiano Lillian—†	218	"	42	"
	B	Grancristiano Nicholas	218	laborer	42	"
	C	Primavera Frances—†	218	housewife	35	Lynn
	D	Primavera Pasquale	218	tailor	52	"
	E	Catalano Emilio	218	laborer	24	here
	F	Catalano Ernesto	218	"	56	"
	G	Catalano Mary—†	218	housewife	53	"
	H	Catalano Vera—†	218	at home	21	

Page.	Letter.	Full Name.	Residence, Jan. 1, 1938.	Occupation.	Supposed Age.	Reported Residence, Jan. 1, 1937. Street and Number.

East Eagle Street—Continued

Page.	Letter.	Full Name.	Residence, Jan. 1, 1938.	Occupation.	Supposed Age.	Reported Residence, Jan. 1, 1937. Street and Number.
	K	Finney Arthur	220	blacksmith	57	here
	L	Finney Ethel M—†	220	housewife	55	"
	M	Finney Warren	220	chauffeur	29	"
	N	Finney William A	220	painter	36	
	P	DeSantis Assunta—†	220	housewife	48	"
	R	DeSantis Frank	220	contractor	49	"
	S	DeSantis Trieste—†	220	student	21	
	T	DeSantis Vera—†	220	stenographer	25	"
	U	Bevere Marian—†	221	operator	27	"
	V	Melchiano Alphonse	221	pedler	34	
	W	Melchiano Fannie—†	221	housewife	32	"
	X	*Fuccillo Louis	221	retired	68	
	Y	Renzi Palmira—†	221	housewife	35	"
	Z	Renzi Philip	221	accountant	34	"
825						
	A	*Lacorazza Anna—†	221	housewife	55	"
	B	Lacorazza Daniel	221	clerk	21	
	D	Lacorazza Fannie—†	221	stitcher	23	
	C	*Lacorazza Frank	221	repairman	55	"
	E	Lacorazza Joseph	221	mechanic	25	"
	F	Lacorazza Josephine—†	221	candyworker	28	"
	G	DeCesare Emily—†	222	housewife	24	"
	H	DeCesare Henry	222	laborer	31	
	K	Pirello Carmen	222	"	26	
	L	Pirello Joseph	222	"	24	
	M	Pirello Mary—†	222	at home	49	
	N	DeLellis Ida—†	222	housewife	22	"
	O	DeLellis Michael	222	pressman	49	"
	P	Marasca Albert	223	helper	22	
	R	Marasca Antonio	223	laborer	24	
	S	*Marasca Christina—†	223	housewife	62	"
	T	Marasca Ferdinand	223	machinist	41	"
	U	Mercurio Adelaide—†	223	housewife	36	"
	V	Mercurio Michael	223	boilermaker	39	"
	W	Marasca Louis	223	machinist	39	"
	X	Marasca Margaret—†	223	housewife	28	"
	Y	Bovaro Jessie—†	224	houseworker	22	"
	Z	*Bovaro John	224	laborer	49	
826						
	A	*Bovaro Josephine—†	224	housewife	45	"
	B	Saccardo Adeline—†	224	at home	58	63 Monmouth

Page.	Letter.	Full Name.	Residence, Jan. 1, 1938.	Occupation.	Supposed Age.	Reported Residence, Jan. 1, 1937. Street and Number.

East Eagle Street—Continued

	C	Saccardo Anthony	224	laborer	27	63 Monmouth
	D	Saccardo Arcata—†	224	candymaker	22	63 "
	E	Saccardo Felix	224	laborer	25	63 "
	F	Saccardo Joseph	224	"	21	63 "
	G	Saccardo Teresa—†	224	operator	28	63 "
	L	Giordano Jennie—†	224	at home	60	here
	H	Ready Daniel M	224	machinist	28	174 Hamilton
	K	Ready Mary—†	224	housewife	23	here
	M	*DiBilio Carmello	225	longshoreman	32	"
	N	DiBilio Mary—†	225	housewife	32	"
	O	*DiBilio Mary—†	225	"	31	
	P	DiBilio Philip	225	laborer	35	
	R	Zuccala Anna—†	225	housewife	32	"
	S	Zuccala Giacomo	225	manufacturer	35	"
	T	DeSantis Frank	230	tailor	42	
	U	DeSantis Santina—†	230	housewife	41	"
	V	Bellina James	230	laborer	24	
	W	Bellina Mary—†	230	housewife	21	"
	X	*Freitas Manuel	235	longshoreman	37	"
	Y	*Freitas Mary—†	235	housewife	34	"
	Z	Vena Constance—†	235	"	27	
827						
	A	Vena Louis	235	laborer	29	
	B	Bordieri Jennie—†	235	housewife	22	"
	C	Bordieri Salvatore	235	welder	23	
	D	Busheme Anne—†	242	housewife	24	"
	E	Busheme Paul	242	bricklayer	26	"
	F	Vecchio Frank	242	tailor	48	
	G	Vecchio Geraldine R—†	242	housewife	35	"
	H	DeSimone Charles	242	salesman	32	Medford
	K	DeSimone Mary—†	242	housewife	27	"
	L	Milligan Annie—†	250	at home	68	here
	M	Milligan Frederick R	250	laborer	42	"
	N	Healy Henry G	250	"	39	"
	O	Healy Sarah—†	250	housewife	40	"
	P	Joyce Andrew	252	laborer	25	179 Trenton
	R	Joyce Elizabeth—†	252	at home	62	179 "
	S	Joyce Frank	252	laborer	21	179 "
	T	Joyce Lawrence	252	"	32	179 "
	U	Joyce Mary—†	252	clerk	29	179 "
	V	Joyce Peter	252	pipefitter	37	179 "

Page.	Letter.	Full Name.	Residence, Jan. 1, 1938.	Occupation.	Supposed Age.	Reported Residence, Jan. 1, 1937. Street and Number.

East Eagle Street—Continued

	W	Cunha Manuel	252	laborer	52	here
	X	Cunha Mary—†	252	housewife	50	"
	Y	Murphy Anna G—†	252	"	27	"
	Z	Murphy Paul	252	laborer	30	
828						
	A	Magaletti Albert	254	policeman	41	7 Morris
	B	Magaletti Rose—†	254	housewife	40	7 "
	C	Mazzone Eugene	254	laborer	49	here
	D	Mazzone Mary—†	254	housewife	46	"
	E	Mazzone Nicholas	254	baker	21	"
	F	Fontes Alfred	258	painter	36	
	G	Fontes Josephine—†	258	housewife	35	"
	H	Iandoli Guy	258	jeweler	32	
	K*	Iandoli Josephine—†	258	housewife	33	"
	L*	Vasquez Alponso	258	fishcutter	24	Beachmont
	M	Vasquez Augusta M—†	258	housewife	22	110 White
	N	Mozzetta Albert	262	laborer	35	here
	O	Mozzetta Dina—†	262	housewife	31	"
	P	Consolo Mary—†	262	"	21	216 Saratoga
	R	Consolo Philip	262	baker	24	430 Hanover
	S	Cianfrocca Assunta—†	262	housewife	43	here
	T	Cianfrocca Emilio	262	tailor	48	"
	U	Cianfrocca Linda—†	262	dressmaker	22	"
	V	Jones Lillian G—†	264	housewife	53	"
	W	Jones Thomas A	264	chauffeur	55	"
	X	Cashman Catherine—†	266	operator	26	"
	Y	Cashman Joseph M	266	timekeeper	28	"
	Z	Cashman Michael J	266	clerk	23	"
829						
	A	Cashman Richard M	266	"	23	
	B	Downing Rita L—†	266	at home	23	
	C	Lauber William	268	laborer	43	
	D	Butler Ernest J	270	"	45	
	E	Butler Mary F—†	270	housewife	53	"
	F	Favale Joseph	272	laborer	50	
	G	Favale Rose—†	272	housewife	48	"
	H	LaConte John	272	chauffeur	29	"
	K	LaConte Lina—†	272	housewife	29	"
	L	Curcio Annie—†	272	"	34	
	M	Curcio John	272	tailor	39	
	N	Sciortino Joseph	274	waiter	24	

Page.	Letter.	Full Name.	Residence, Jan. 1, 1938.	Occupation.	Supposed Age.	Reported Residence, Jan. 1, 1937. Street and Number.

East Eagle Street—Continued

	O	Sciortino Mary—†	274	housewife	21	here
	P	Sullo Caroline—†	274	"	22	"
	R	Sullo Marco	274	laborer	24	"
	S	Sciortino Gaetano	274	"	45	
	T	Sciortino Giuseppe	274	retired	69	
	U	Sciortino Rosalina—†	274	at home	40	
	V	Correia Antonio	278	laborer	48	
	W	Correia Delfina—†	278	housewife	34	"
	X	Chaison Augustus J	278	policeman	39	"
	Y	Chaison Helen F—†	278	housewife	35	"
	Z	Luciano Alexander	278	laborer	30	
830						
	A	Luciano Evelyn—†	278	housewife	21	"
	B	Gibson John	280	manager	27	"
	C	Gibson Josephine—†	280	housewife	22	"
	D	Sampson Dorothy—†	280	clerk	27	
	E	Sampson William	280	fisherman	27	"
	F	Canha Frank F	280	laborer	50	
	G	Canha Mary—†	280	housewife	40	"
	H	Sulprizio Caroline—†	280	"	30	
	K	Sulprizio George	280	plumber	38	
	L	Magner Emily F—†	291	housewife	47	"
	M	Magner John H	291	mechanic	47	"
	N	Elo John	291	ironworker	48	"
	O	Elo Rose—†	291	housewife	42	"
	P	McCormack Allen J	291	retired	71	
	R	McCormack Flora—†	291	housewife	62	"
	S	McCormack Hugh J	291	laborer	32	
	T	McCormack Loretta—†	291	operator	21	"
	U	McCormack Sarah—†	291	packer	33	
	V	DeAngelis Anthony	297	laborer	40	
	W	DeAngelis Margaret—†	297	housewife	30	"
	X	Quilty Evelyn—†	297	"	23	
	Y	Quilty George	297	machinist	27	"
	Z	Beach Clayton	297	carpenter	54	"
831						
	A	Beach Jabez	297	"	55	"
	B	Boyle John J	301	clerk	42	
	C	Boyle John J, jr	301	seaman	20	
	D	Boyle Mary A—†	301	housewife	68	"
	E	Boyle Patrick J	301	laborer	30	

Page.	Letter.	Full Name.	Residence, Jan. 1, 1938.	Occupation.	Supposed Age.	Reported Residence, Jan. 1, 1937. Street and Number.

East Eagle Street—Continued

	F	Sodergren Anna—†	303	housewife	56	here
	G	Sodergren George	303	electrician	30	"
	H	Sodergren Henry	303	"	31	"
	K	Sodergren John	303	retired	60	
	L	Thomas Beatrice—†	305	housewife	21	"
	M	Thomas Joseph	305	painter	24	"
	N	Sweeney Margaret—†	305	operator	42	77 Condor
	O	Sullivan Robert L	307	seaman	20	36 Falcon
	P	*Grandi Ernestina—†	307	housewife	36	here
	R	Grandi Ralph	307	laborer	42	"
	S	*Doucette Christina—†	309	housewife	24	"
	T	Doucette Clifford	309	metalworker	35	"
	W	Lally Frank	313	chauffeur	41	177 Paris
	X	Lally Mary—†	313	housewife	38	177 "
	Y	*Palzerazo Sarah—†	313	"	29	here
	Z	Day Winfield	315	machinist	55	"
832						
	A	Simonson Celia—†	315	housewife	63	"
	B	Dorin Ruth E—†	317	"	36	
	C	Dorin William J	317	laborer	46	
	D	McGlinchey Catherine–†	317	housewife	67	"
	E	McGlinchey William F	317	machinist	32	"

Falcon Street

	G	Hayden Charles F	84	machinist	50	here
	H	Hayden Clifford W	84	clerk	20	"
	K	Hayden John F	84	shipper	24	"
	L	Hayden Lillian—†	84	housewife	52	"
	M	Ewing Edna—†	84	"	44	
	N	Ewing Muriel—†	84	clerk	20	
	O	Ewing Robert	84	fireman	44	
	P	Ewing Ruby—†	84	clerk	22	
	R	Meuse Ruben	84	fireman	64	
	S	Larsen Ruth—†	86	saleswoman	20	"
	T	Larsen Signe—†	86	at home	47	
	U	Midgett Cecil A	86A	machinist	49	"
	V	Midgett Gladys—†	86A	housewife	43	"
	W	Knox Albert C	88	painter	42	614 Benningt'n
	X	Knox Margaret—†	88	housewife	39	614 "
	Y	*Atkins Annie—†	88A	"	70	here

Page.	Letter.	Full Name.	Residence, Jan. 1, 1938.	Occupation.	Supposed Age.	Reported Residence, Jan. 1, 1937. Street and Number.

Falcon Street—Continued

Page.	Letter.	Full Name.	Residence, Jan. 1, 1938.	Occupation.	Supposed Age.	Reported Residence, Jan. 1, 1937. Street and Number.
	z	*Atkins James	88A	retired	71	here
833						
	A	*Garcia Evelyn—†	90	housewife	42	"
	B	Garcia John W	90	electrician	38	"
	C	Nelson Francis	90½	tinsmith	22	
	D	Nelson Isabelle—†	90½	clerk	24	
	E	Nelson Joseph E	90½	B F D	54	
	F	Nelson Mary A—†	90½	housewife	53	"
	G	Moraitopoulos George	92	counterman	43	"
	H	*Moraitopoulos Lavonia—†	92	housewife	35	"
	K	Whitman Margaret—†	92	at home	57	
	L	Gallagher Frances R—†	92A	bookkeeper	25	"
	M	Gallagher Mary L—†	92A	at home	54	"
	N	Gallagher Richard	92A	salesman	30	"
	O	*Smith Enos C	94	machinist	37	"
	P	*Smith Lela M—†	94	housewife	35	"
	R	*Hollohan Michael	94	machinist	44	"
	S	*Hollohan Monica—†	94	housewife	37	"
	T	Sciarappa Elizabeth—†	96	tailor	23	
	U	Sciarappa Rinaldo	96	"	47	
	V	*Muratore Frank	96	laborer	21	
	W	*Muratore Lucy—†	96	housewife	46	"
	X	Muratore Michael	96	operator	49	"
	Y	Riley Thomas J	98	clerk	50	"
	Z	Crowley Gertrude—†	98	housewife	38	153 Falcon
834						
	A	Crowley John	98	laborer	39	153 "
	B	Crowley John, jr	98	clerk	20	here
	C	Allen Dorothy—†	102	bookkeeper	29	"
	D	Allen Frances L—†	102	at home	68	"
	E	Fariole Alfred	104	laborer	30	
	F	Fariole Louise—†	104	housewife	34	"
	G	*Sozia Annie—†	104	"	53	
	H	Sozia Carlo	104	clerk	26	
	K	Sozia George	104	"	22	
	L	Sozia Jeremiah	104	candymaker	56	"
	M	Sozia Santa—†	104	housewife	22	"
	N	Bonner Joseph	106	laborer	35	
	O	Bonner Lillian—†	106	housewife	34	"
	P	Possehl Fred W	108	machinist	48	"
	R	Possehl Vivian—†	108	housewife	37	"

Page.	Letter.	Full Name.	Residence, Jan. 1, 1938.	Occupation.	Supposed Age.	Reported Residence, Jan. 1, 1937. Street and Number.

Falcon Street—Continued

	S	Rogers William E	108	cook	55	here
	T	Mattson Mary M—†	112	at home	57	"
	U	*Goglia Julian	112	candymaker	44	"
	V	*Goglia Louise—†	112	housewife	43	"
	W	Marino Josephine—†	112	stitcher	22	"
	X	*Marino Marie—†	112	housewife	58	447 Meridian
	Y	Marino Rose—†	112	stitcher	26	here
	Z	Marino Theresa—†	112	"	24	"
835						
	A	*Marino Vincent	112	laborer	60	447 Meridian
	B	Gioiosa Domenico	114	"	45	here
	C	Gioiosa Rose—†	114	housewife	40	"
	D	Long Margaret—†	114	"	49	"
	E	Long Mary—†	114	clerk	21	
	F	Long William J	114	carpenter	53	"
	G	*Consolo Fannie—†	114	housewife	43	"
	H	Consolo Filice	114	barber	23	
	K	*Consolo Giuseppe	114	"	48	
	L	Consolo Phyllis—†	114	operator	20	"
	M	Amodeo Amelia—†	116	housewife	50	"
	O	Amodeo Marinda—†	116	clerk	25	
	P	Amodeo Nicholas	116	barber	51	
	N	Amodeo Teresa—†	116	at home	22	
	R	Colarossi Nicholas	116	clerk	40	
	S	*Colarossi Vanda—†	116	housewife	36	"
	T	Pastore Carmen	116	operator	34	"
	U	Pastore Eleanor—†	116	at home	34	
	V	Pastore Frank	116	retired	63	
	W	Pastore Julia—†	116	housewife	66	"
	X	Pastore Yolanda—†	116	seamstress	28	"
	Y	Singer Angelina—†	116	housewife	24	"
	Z	Ferriani Lillian—†	118	"	26	24 Shrimpton
836						
	A	Ferriani William	118	foreman	23	24 "
	B	Galia Anna—†	118	housewife	34	here
	C	Galia Frank	118	laborer	47	"
	D	Tiano Dominick	118	draftsman	30	5 Marion
	E	Tiano Helen—†	118	housewife	26	here
	F	Hudson John M	120	electrician	38	"
	G	Hudson Lillian E—†	120	housewife	43	"
	H	Melling Margaret L—†	120	operator	26	"

Page.	Letter.	FULL NAME.	Residence, Jan. 1, 1938.	Occupation.	Supposed Age.	Reported Residence, Jan. 1, 1937. Street and Number.

Falcon Street—Continued

	K	Melling Mildred M—†	120	cashier	20	here
	L	Cruise William A	120	operator	68	"
	N	Miller Gladys K—†	120	clerk	34	"
	M	Miller Helen J—†	120	housewife	66	"
	O	Miller Michael J	120	retired	69	"
	P	Nugent Anna—†	120	proprietor	40	"
	R	Facteau Pamela—†	122	hairdresser	38	"
	S	Meyer Ernest	122	cutter	27	
	T	Ferris Hugh	122	ironworker	58	"
	U	Ferris Hugh, jr	122	welder	25	
	V	Ferris Nellie—†	122	housewife	56	"
	W	Ferris Thomas	122	chauffeur	26	"
	X	*Donato Antonetta—†	124	housewife	38	"
	Y	Donato Frisco	124	boilermaker	47	"
	Z	Donato Mario	124	tailor	21	
837						
	B	Gilchrist Robert G	124	chef	59	
	C	Powers Christine E—†	124	housewife	41	"
	D	Powers Francis J	124	fishcutter	53	"
	E	Powers Lillian F—†	124	clerk	21	
	F	Powers William E	124	laborer	23	
	G	*Nickerson Eva—†	126	housewife	40	"
	H	*Nickerson Wallace	126	cooper	49	
	K	*Crowell Alfred	126	clerk	20	
	L	*Crowell Celia—†	126	saleswoman	21	"
	M	*Crowell Merle	126	gardener	52	"
	N	Crowell Myrta—†	126	housewife	49	"
	O	*Goodwin Olive—†	126	at home	22	"
	R	Collyer Frederick	128	instructor	28	27 Falcon
	P	Collyer Helen A—†	128	housewife	26	27 "
	S	*Boudreau Augustus	128	fisherman	52	here
	T	Boudreau Dennis	128	"	55	"
	U	*Todd John W	128	"	57	"
	V	Todd Leonard	128	laborer	22	
	W	*Todd Mary—†	128	housewife	58	"
	X	Todd Stanley W	128	baker	24	
	Y	Costa Joseph	128	operator	50	"
	Z	Costa Martha—†	128	housewife	40	"
838						
	A	Costa Nicholas	128	mechanic	21	"
	B	Pye Dexter	130	"	20	"

Page.	Letter.	Full Name.	Residence, Jan. 1, 1938.	Occupation.	Supposed Age.	Reported Residence, Jan. 1, 1937. Street and Number.
		Falcon Street—Continued				
	C	Reekast August	130	fisherman	42	here
	D	Reekast Grace L—†	130	housewife	42	"
	G	Pye Clayton	134	clerk	22	"
	F	Pye Grace—†	134	operator	31	"
	H	Pye Jesse	134	retired	72	188 Falcon
	K	Johnson Catherine—†	134	saleswoman	22	here
	L	Madaj Mary—†	134	housewife	42	"
	M*	Chetwynd Samuel	136	seaman	45	"
	N*	Goodwin Mildred—†	136	at home	36	
	O	Folger Eben A	136	proprietor	61	"
	P	Folger Ethel—†	136	housewife	54	"
	R	Folger Gladys C—†	136	student	46	
	S	Fortier Esther M—†	136	houseworker	47	"
	T	Frongillo Dorothy—†	137	housewife	21	21 Marion
	U	Frongillo Ralph T	137	mechanic	28	21 "
	V	Baxter Mary—†	137	at home	73	here
	W	Sciortino Elizabeth—†	137	housewife	37	"
	X	Sciortino Guy	137	operator	39	"
	Y	Dasey Clara—†	138	laundress	49	"
	Z	Dasey Rita—†	138	"	24	
839						
	A	Melanson Agnes—†	138	housewife	24	240 Lexington
	B	Melanson Joseph	138	chef	28	240 "
	C	Anderson Annie—†	139	housewife	27	here
	D	Anderson Arthur	139	letter carrier	36	"
	E	Anderson Alfred	139	retired	72	"
	F	Anderson Alfred H	139	janitor	27	"
	G	Ryan Joseph	140	pressman	25	16 Paul Gore
	H	Ryan Marian—†	140	waitress	22	16 "
	K	McKurdy Alice—†	140	housewife	25	here
	L	McKurdy William	140	salesman	27	"
	M	O'Dell Annie L—†	140	housewife	67	"
	N	O'Dell William A	140	clerk	43	
	O	O'Dell William H	140	brassfinisher	71	"
	P*	Benttila Hilma—†	140	housewife	47	"
	R	Benttila Isaac	140	retired	52	
	S	Anderson Esther V—†	141	housewife	26	"
	T	Anderson Gustav H	141	asbestos worker	31	"
	U	Anderson Ellen V—†	141	housewife	48	"
	V	Anderson John E	141	machinist	23	"
	W	Anderson John W	141	asbestos worker	49	"

Page.	Letter.	Full Name.	Residence, Jan. 1, 1938.	Occupation.	Supposed Age.	Reported Residence, Jan. 1, 1937. Street and Number.

Falcon Street—Continued

	X	Driver George	142	lithographer	27	here
	Y	Driver Sylvia—†	142	housewife	22	"
	Z	Houlihan Edna—†	142	"	30	"
840						
	A	Houlihan Thomas	142	seaman	33	
	B	Heino Henry	142	ironworker	49	"
	C	*Heino Impi—†	142	housewife	47	"
	D	Marks Frances—†	143	proprietor	56	"
	E	Marks Margaret—†	143	at home	24	
	F	Teevens Eugene	144	salesman	40	"
	G	Teevens Margaret—†	144	housewife	37	"
	H	Mangin Ernest	144	proprietor	47	"
	K	Mangin Mary—†	144	housewife	45	"
	L	Kelly Charles J	145	chauffeur	37	439 Benningt'n
	M	Kelly Ethel M—†	145	housewife	34	439 "
	N	McCormack Thomas	145	contractor	26	Medford
	O	Bellvich Anthony	145	packer	22	47A Condor
	P	*Bellvich John	145	plumber	25	47A "
	R	*Bellvich Mary—†	145	housewife	47	47A "
	S	Bellvich Stanley	145	painter	53	47A "
	T	*Elixson Gustave	145	carpenter	55	here
	U	*Elixson Mandy—†	145	housewife	49	"
	V	Elixson Toivo	145	boilermaker	24	"
	W	Hope Evelyn—†	146	laundryworker	21	"
	X	Hope Margaret—†	146	housewife	58	"
	Y	Hope Walter J	146	painter	59	
	Z	*Ivany Althea—†	146	housewife	52	"
841						
	A	Ivany Florence—†	146	waitress	21	
	B	Ivany Harry	146	builder	52	
	C	Murphy Mildred—†	148	laundryworker	34	"
	D	Murphy Morris	148	clerk	36	
	E	Stanton William	148	laborer	51	
	F	McGuire John J	148	ironworker	61	"
	G	McGuire Susan I—†	148	housewife	54	"
	H	McGuire William J	148	clerk	20	"
	K	Mastrogiovanni Carlo	149	operator	22	
	L	Mastrogiovanni Carmine	149	laborer	60	
	M	Mastrogiovanni Elvira—†	149	seamstress	27	"
	O	Mastrogiovanni Margherita—†	149	housewife	53	"
	N	Mastrogiovanni Silvio	149	clerk	20	

Page.	Letter.	FULL NAME.	Residence, Jan. 1, 1938.	Occupation.	Supposed Age.	Reported Residence, Jan. 1, 1937. Street and Number.

Falcon Street—Continued

Page.	Letter.	FULL NAME.	Residence, Jan. 1, 1938.	Occupation.	Supposed Age.	Reported Residence, Jan. 1, 1937. Street and Number.
	P	McAdams Charles	150	laborer	32	here
	R	McAdams Elizabeth—†	150	housewife	25	"
	S	McAdams Emma E—†	150	at home	70	"
	T	McAdams Thomas	150	clerk	27	
	U	Flot Lewis A	151	fireman	38	
	V	Flot Lillian M—†	151	housewife	42	"
	W	Robicheau David	151	laundryworker	33	"
	X	Loconte Luigi	152	finisher	48	
	Y	Loconte Mary—†	152	saleswoman	20	"
	Z	Loconte Philomena—†	152	housewife	37	"
842						
	A	Ventola Anthony	152	steamfitter	34	"
	B	Ventola Josephine—†	152	housewife	32	"
	C*	Rapp Carlton	153	fishcutter	33	163 Falcon
	D	Rapp Laura—†	153	housewife	24	163 "
	E	Doucette Joseph	153	laborer	29	60 White
	F	Doucette Mildred—†	153	housewife	26	60 "
	H	Brennan Lawrence	154	foreman	37	here
	K	Brennan Ragnhild—†	154	housewife	39	"
	L	Sindoni Frank	154	carpenter	38	"
	M	Sindoni Mary—†	154	housewife	31	"
	O	Carson Clara—†	156	at home	47	51 Lexington
	P	Carson Robert	156	clerk	24	here
	N	Clark Harriet—†	156	saleswoman	22	330 Meridian
	R	McConnell Catherine—†	156	at home	21	here
	S*	McConnell Nora—†	156	housewife	48	"
	T	Eide John	156	laborer	44	216 Brooks
	U	Eide Margaret—†	156	housewife	41	216 "
	V	Giles George	158	mechanic	38	here
	W	Giles Margaret—†	158	housewife	37	"
	X	DeNietolis Camilla—†	158	"	35	"
	Y	DeNietolis Nicholas	158	plumber	35	
	Z	Bithell William G	159	laborer	27	
843						
	A	Bithell Evelyn—†	159	housewife	30	"
	B	Bithell William P	159	plasterer	54	"
	C	Eldridge Annabelle—†	160	housewife	20	Winthrop
	D	Eldridge Francis	160	seaman	22	"
	L	Netto John S	160	retired	75	here
	E	O'Brien Anna E—†	160	housewife	43	"
	F	O'Brien Edward J	160	watchman	44	"

Page.	Letter.	Full Name.	Residence, Jan. 1, 1938.	Occupation.	Supposed Age.	Reported Residence. Jan. 1, 1937. Street and Number.

Falcon Street —Continued

Page.	Letter.	Full Name.	Residence, Jan. 1, 1938.	Occupation.	Supposed Age.	Reported Residence. Jan. 1, 1937. Street and Number.
	G	O'Brien Frederick	160	laborer	40	here
	H	O'Brien James F	160	machinist	62	“
	K	O'Brien Mary L—†	160	clerk	22	“
	M	Trahan Anna—†	162	housewife	25	“
	N	*Trahan Clarence	162	seaman	28	“
	O	Critch Mary—†	163	housewife	40	58 W Eagle
	P	*Critch Richard	163	clerk	20	58 “
	S	Rodrigues Anthony	163A	longshoreman	36	274 E Eagle
	R	*Rodrigues Antonette—†	163A	housewife	28	274 “
	T	*Ferriera Cleo—†	163A	“	35	154 Falcon
	U	Ferriera John	163A	fireman	39	154 “
	V	Dunbar Margaret—†	164	housewife	31	here
	W	Lunden Jalmar	164	seaman	56	“
	X	*Vranken Impi—†	164	housewife	47	“
	Y	*Vranken John F	164	cook	45	
	Z	*Perry Oliver	166	laborer	62	
844						
	A	*McKenzie Colin	167	seaman	53	“
	B	*McKenzie Susan—†	167	housewife	40	“
	C	Squires Arthur	167A	salesman	35	“
	D	Squires Jean—†	167A	housewife	33	“
	E	O'Brien Annie—†	167A	at home	60	
	F	O'Brien Isabelle—†	167A	operator	32	
	G	O'Brien John E	167A	clerk	30	
	H	O'Brien Margaret—†	167A	saleswoman	40	“
	K	O'Brien William	167A	salesman	27	“
	M	*Perry Bessie—†	168	housewife	31	“
	L	Perry Roy	168	laborer	38	
	N	*Hudson Elizabeth—†	170	housewife	62	“
	O	*Hudson William P	170	rigger	62	
	P	*Deon Adelbert	171	fishcutter	31	“
	R	*Deon Laura—†	171	housewife	31	“
	S	Cole John	171A	clerk	25	
	T	Page Helen—†	171A	housekeeper	42	“
	U	Joyce Joanna—†	171A	housewife	62	“
	V	Joyce Stewart	171A	foreman	64	
	W	Gallagher James	172	laborer	25	
	X	Gallagher Margaret—†	172	housewife	65	“
	Y	Lewis Herbert H	174	watchman	43	“
	Z	Lewis John	174	retired	77	

Page.	Letter.	Full Name.	Residence, Jan. 1, 1938.	Occupation.	Supposed Age.	Reported Residence, Jan. 1, 1937. Street and Number.
845						

Falcon Street—Continued

Page.	Letter.	Full Name.	Residence, Jan. 1, 1938.	Occupation.	Supposed Age.	Reported Residence, Jan. 1, 1937. Street and Number.
	A	Lewis Margaret—†	174	housewife	74	here
	C	Walker Harry B	174	mason	47	"
	B	Walker Ida A—†	174	housewife	47	"
	D	D'Entremont Arthur	175	seaman	40	
	E	*D'Entremont Mildred—†	175	housewife	40	"
	F	McCusker Catherine—†	175A	"	65	
	G	McCusker James M	175A	retired	76	
	H	DiGregorio Anthony	175A	B F D	44	"
	K	DiGregorio Mary—†	175A	housewife	34	1493 River
	L	Murphy Wilhelmina—†	175A	at home	35	here
	M	Bruttini Gertrude—†	176	housewife	47	149 Chelsea
	N	Bruttini Joseph	176	molder	49	149 "
	O	Goodwin Albert	176	seaman	54	12 Dorr
	P	*Goodwin Elizabeth—†	176	housewife	38	12 "
	R	Williams Anna T—†	178	"	39	here
	S	Williams Charles A	178	fireman	44	"
	T	*Leary Cecelia—†	180	housewife	47	"
	U	*Leary Richard J	180	longshoreman	48	"
	V	Gushue George	180	"	52	
	W	*Gushue Lorna—†	180	at home	20	
	X	*Gushue Mary—†	180	housewife	42	"
	Y	Stapleton Mildred—†	180	houseworker	54	"
	Z	*Santos Carmelita—†	182	tailoress	45	
846						
	A	*Santos Joseph T	182	longshoreman	46	"
	B	Rose Frank	182	boilermaker	35	307 E Eagle
	C	Rose Minnie—†	182	housewife	36	307 "
	D	Hayes Helen—†	188	"	24	15 Havre
	E	Hayes John	188	watchman	28	15 "
	F	Collins Edna—†	188	housewife	28	12 Marion
	G	Collins William L	188	laborer	29	12 "
	K	Clee Gertrude—†	188	housewife	21	Medford
	L	Clee Walter	188	repairman	20	392 Chelsea
	M	Tamick Alice—†	191	packer	23	here
	N	Tammick Martin	191	seaman	54	"
	O	Tammick William	191	mechanic	21	"
	P	*Dove Lempi—†	191	housewife	34	"
	R	Dove Mattie	191	ironworker	46	"
	S	Wilson Dorothea T—†	192	housewife	31	"

Page.	Letter.	Full Name.	Residence, Jan. 1, 1938.	Occupation.	Supposed Age.	Reported Residence, Jan. 1, 1937. Street and Number.

Falcon Street—Continued

Page.	Letter.	Full Name.	Residence, Jan. 1, 1938.	Occupation.	Supposed Age.	Reported Residence, Jan. 1, 1937. Street and Number.
	T	Wilson John H	192	shipper	33	here
	U	Amerina Alma—†	192	housewife	31	"
	V	Amerina John	192	foreman	35	"
	W	Merritt Grace—†	192	housewife	31	263 Princeton
	X	*Page Gladys—†	192	"	20	here
	Y	Page Lawrence	192	laborer	25	"
	Z	*Ferriani Dena—†	194	housewife	28	118 Marine rd
847						
	A	Ferriani Peter	194	chauffeur	28	118 "
	B	Enos Mario	194	laborer	47	here
	C	*Enos Virginia—†	194	housewife	37	"
	D	DiFrancisco Mary—†	194	"	24	"
	E	DiFrancisco Stephen	194	salesman	25	"
	F	Boyle Elizabeth—†	195	housewife	38	"
	G	Boyle John M	195	attorney	39	"
	H	Boyle Mary A—†	195	housewife	64	"
	K	Rogers Albert T	196	longshoreman	42	"
	L	Rogers Mary J—†	196	housewife	42	"
	M	Mello Olivia—†	196	"	50	
	N	Curtin John	197	longshoreman	52	"
	O	Driscoll Florence	197	laborer	57	
	P	Driscoll Mary—†	197	housewife	53	"
	R	Thibodeau Edith—†	198	"	39	"
	S	Thibodeau Joseph W	198	carpenter	40	"
	T	*Meuse John E	198	"	65	
	U	*Meuse Mary—†	198	housewife	67	"
	V	Nelson Howard	198	steward	28	
	W	Leonard Catherine—†	199	housewife	36	"
	X	Leonard John	199	inspector	45	"
	Y	McCarthy Margaret—†	199	candymaker	25	"
	Z	McCarthy Mary—†	199	"	32	
848						
	A	Meyer Frances—†	200	housewife	28	"
	B	Meyer Paul	200	painter	28	
	C	Stapleton Peter J	200	retired	78	"
	D	Manganelli Alfredo	200	painter	27	68 Chelsea
	E	Manganelli Maria C—†	200	operator	22	68 "
	F	*Manganelli Peter	200	cook	72	68 "
	G	MacDonald Duncan A	201	operator	47	here
	H	MacDonald Margaret—†	201	nurse	22	"
	K	MacDonald Margaret A—†	201	housewife	34	"

Page.	Letter.	Full Name.	Residence, Jan. 1, 1938.	Occupation.	Supposed Age.	Reported Residence, Jan. 1, 1937. Street and Number.

Falcon Street—Continued

Page.	Letter.	Full Name.	Residence, Jan. 1, 1938.	Occupation.	Supposed Age.	Reported Residence, Jan. 1, 1937. Street and Number.
	L	McCabe Francis P	202	barber	30	here
	M	McCabe Loretta C—†	202	housewife	30	"
	N	Keleher Albert F	202	laborer	22	"
	O	Keleher Edwin M	202	"	28	
	P	Keleher Francis J	202	machinist	25	"
	R	Keleher Lawrence M	202	seaman	34	
	S	Keleher Susan—†	202	housewife	63	"
	T	Guazzerotti Fred	203	laborer	40	249 River
	U	*Guazzerotti Mary—†	203	housewife	33	here
	V	Muldoon Edward	204	silversmith	22	"
	W	Muldoon Joseph	204	painter	24	"
	X	Muldoon Lawrence	204	laborer	27	
	Y	Muldoon Mary—†	204	housewife	47	"
	Z	Murray Charles	204	retired	57	
849						
	A	Sullivan Katherine—†	204	waitress	36	
	B	Thornton George	204	fishcutter	38	"
	C	Thornton Margaret—†	204	waitress	35	
	D	O'Brien Catherine L—†	205	housewife	34	"
	E	O'Brien John J	205	policeman	37	"
	F	Welch Elizabeth—†	206	housewife	47	34 Mead
	G	Welch Leo J	206	machinist	55	34 "
	H	Tobe Esther—†	206	housewife	53	here
	K	Tobe Phineas	206	teacher	27	"
	L	Tobe Samuel	206	watchman	54	"
	M	*Bloom Lena—†	206	at home	75	
	N	Olsen Margaret—†	206	housewife	56	"
	O	Olsen Ole	206	watchman	55	"
	P	Ahern Marie B—†	207	housewife	42	"
	R	Ahern William H	207	letter carrier	52	"
	S	Healy Mary E—	207	at home	75	

Glendon Street

Page.	Letter.	Full Name.	Residence, Jan. 1, 1938.	Occupation.	Supposed Age.	Reported Residence, Jan. 1, 1937. Street and Number.
	T	Foster Clarence W	6	engineer	53	here
	U	Smith Bertha—†	6	housewife	46	"
	V	Smith Mary L—†	6	at home	77	"
	W	Lopardi Angelina—†	6	housewife	34	"
	X	Lopardi Anthony	6	painter	39	
	Z	Deveau Irene	24	carpenter	45	"

Page.	Letter.	Full Name.	Residence, Jan. 1, 1938.	Occupation.	Supposed Age.	Reported Residence, Jan. 1, 1937. Street and Number.

850

Glendon Street—Continued

	A	*Deveau Lucy—†	24	housewife	39	here
	B	Cohan Margaret—†	24	"	47	"
	C	Cohan Maurice	24	retired	86	"
	D	Cohan Maurice	24	machinist	49	"
	E	Boczkowski Mary—†	28	housewife	48	"
	F	Boczkowski Stanley	28	machinist	52	"
	G	Nigrelli John	28	painter	53	"
	H	Nigrelli Joseph	28	shoeworker	24	"
	K	Nigrelli Maria—†	28	housewife	44	"
	L	Nigrelli Phyllis—†	28	stitcher	21	

Lexington Square

	M	O'Niel Catherine A—†	1	housewife	50	here
	N	O'Niel Daniel J	1	clerk	56	"
	O	Peterson Annie—†	2	housewife	42	"
	P	Downing Lillian—†	2	"	26	
	R	Downing Sanford	2	agent	28	"
	S	McEachern John	2	laborer	24	235 Benningt'n

Lexington Street

	T	DeMattia Anna—†	198	housewife	34	here
	U	*DeMattia Joseph	198	laborer	35	"
	V	O'Brien Joseph J	198	"	28	"
	W	O'Brien Mabel—†	198	housewife	26	"
	X	DeFelice Guy	200	operator	27	
	Y	DeFelice Margaret—†	200	housewife	25	"
	Z	*Belmonti Christine—†	200	"	45	
851						
	A	Belmonti Frank	200	shoemaker	44	"
	B	*Belmonti Grace—†	200	operator	21	"
	C	Coviello Louis	200	"	29	375 Hanover
	D	Coviello Louise—†	200	housewife	29	52 Neptune rd
	E	McManus Alice—†	202	"	53	here
	F	McManus John S	202	longshoreman	61	"
	G	Hamilton Edith—†	202	housewife	49	"
	H	Hamilton Margaret—†	202	at home	22	
	K	Hamilton Robert	202	longshoreman	49	"
	L	Melanson Mary—†	202	housewife	26	"

Page.	Letter.	Full Name.	Residence, Jan. 1, 1938.	Occupation.	Supposed Age.	Reported Residence, Jan. 1, 1937. Street and Number.

Lexington Street—Continued

Page.	Letter.	Full Name.	Residence, Jan. 1, 1938.	Occupation.	Supposed Age.	Reported Residence, Jan. 1, 1937. Street and Number.
	M	Melanson William	202	machinist	36	here
	N	Doyle Amanda M—†	204	housewife	47	"
	O	Doyle James M	204	seaman	51	"
	P	*Landry Edna—†	204	stitcher	38	
	R	*Landry Peter	204	laborer	47	
	S	Ayers Edward	204	chauffeur	25	"
	T	Ayers Evelyn—†	204	housewife	25	"
	U	Helmsdorf Lorenzo—†	206	at home	64	
	V	Ruud Matilda—†	206	"	66	"
	W	Bowen Martha—†	206	forewoman	60	210 Lexington
	X	Wilson Mary—†	206	housewife	69	210 "
	Y	Clinco Peter	206	chef	41	32 Falcon
	Z	Clinco Selma—†	206	housewife	31	32 "
852						
	A	*Olsson Julia—†	206	at home	61	32 Falcon
	B	Giusti Americo	208	painter	23	291 Sumner
	C	*Giusti Augusta—†	208	housewife	58	291 "
	D	*Giusti Joseph	208	retired	63	291 "
	E	Giusti Susie—†	208	saleswoman	26	291 "
	F	Hickey Edward B	208	machinist	22	here
	G	Hickey Joseph F	208	chauffeur	26	"
	H	Hickey Mary F—†	208	housewife	52	"
	K	Scarpetta Anthony	208	clerk	20	
	L	*Scarpetta Michael	208	laborer	58	
	M	*Scarpetta Sarah—†	208	housewife	51	"
	N	Lewis Frederick	210	laborer	60	
	O	Lewis Mary C—†	210	housewife	45	"
	P	O'Hara Mary—†	210	operator	20	
	S	Alves George H	210	foreman	69	
	R	Alves Sarah R—†	210	housewife	69	"
	V	MacDougal Elizabeth—†	210	"	47	68 Trenton
	T	Surette Elizabeth—†	210	at home	22	123 Princeton
	U	Surette William	210	operator	25	123 "
	W	Parziale Adalfo	212	laborer	29	here
	X	*Parziale Anne—†	212	housewife	21	"
	Y	Corvi Adruino	212	carpenter	59	"
	Z	Corvi Anna—†	212	dressmaker	23	"
853						
	A	Corvi Iris—†	212	dressmaker	24	"
	B	Corvi Iveno	212	mechanic	21	"
	C	Corvi Libero	212	clerk	25	

Page.	Letter.	Full Name.	Residence, Jan. 1, 1938.	Occupation.	Supposed Age.	Reported Residence, Jan. 1, 1937. Street and Number.

Lexington Street—Continued

	D	*Corvi Madaline—†	212	housewife	49	here
	E	Caplan Anna—†	218	"	40	"
	F	Caplan Harry	218	manager	41	"
	G	McCarthy Jeremiah F	218	gateman	60	
	H	McCarthy Paul J	218	clerk	21	
	K	McCarthy Sarah—†	218	housewife	55	"
	M	Haberlin John P	218	machinist	30	"
	L	Haberlin John T	218	sexton	54	
	O	Haberlin Mary—†	218	housewife	54	"
	N	Haberlin Rita—†	218	student	20	
	P	*Rafuse Alice—†	220	housewife	44	"
	R	Rafuse Frank	220	cook	44	
	S	Rafuse Robert	220	clerk	20	
	U	Siracusa Anthony	220	shoeworker	21	"
	T	*Siracusa Antoinetta—†	220	housewife	45	"
	V	*Siracusa Salvatore	220	shoeworker	25	"
	W	Tosta Celia—†	220	housewife	35	"
	X	Tosta Martin	220	stonemason	39	"
	Y	O'Brien Helen—†	222	housewife	44	"
	Z	O'Brien Jeremiah	222	fisherman	42	"
854						
	A	La Rocca Camello	222	laborer	44	99 London
	B	*La Rocca Sarah—†	222	housewife	42	99 "
	D	Giuliano Carl	222	operator	26	here
	C	*Giuliano Concetta—†	222	housewife	49	"
	E	*Giuliano Joseph	222	laborer	58	"
	F	Pulio Frances—†	224	housewife	26	"
	G	Pulio James	224	fishcutter	26	"
	H	Alonzo Nicolo	224	laborer	37	
	K	Ciardo Jennie—†	224	housewife	36	"
	L	Ciardo Peter	224	marketman	41	"
	M	Silver Hyman	224	cabinetmaker	35	"
	N	Silver Israel	224	brassworker	23	"
	O	Silver Molly—†	224	housekeeper	44	"
	P	Silver Sadie—†	224	bookkeeper	20	"
	S	Bartolo Joseph	226	repairman	32	"
	T	Bartolo Lucy—†	226	housewife	25	"
	U	Spano Adamo A	226	laborer	40	62 Brooks
	V	*Spano Frances—†	226	housewife	30	62 "
	W	Hancock Anna—†	226	"	29	156 Lexington
	X	Hancock Reuben	226	boilermaker	31	156 "

Page.	Letter.	FULL NAME.	Residence, Jan. 1, 1938.	Occupation.	Supposed Age.	Reported Residence, Jan. 1, 1937. Street and Number.

Lexington Street—Continued

	Z	Bruce Harold	rear 228	painter	28	87 Falcon
855						
	A	Bruce Mary O—†	" 228	housewife	37	87 "
	B	Ricciardelli Joseph	230	laborer	24	145 Lexington
	C	Ricciardelli Louise—†	230	housewife	21	145 "
	D	Pray Delia—†	230	"	63	here
	E	Pray Frank	230	retired	72	"
	F	Mattera Madaline—†	230	housekeeper	47	"
	G	Llewellyn Elsie—†	232	housewife	30	71 Savin
	H	Llewellyn John	232	laborer	37	71 "
	K	Carroll John H	232	ironworker	53	here
	L	Carroll Walter R	232	laborer	39	"
	M	DiGirolamo Antoinette—†	234	housewife	20	93 Waldemar av
	N	DiGirolamo Joseph	234	laborer	22	249 Prescott
	O	Donnarummo Benjamin	234	"	43	here
	P	Donnarummo Mary—†	234	housewife	39	"
	R*	Covino Catherine—†	234	"	24	188 Marion
	S	Covino Pasquale	234	laborer	32	188 "
	T*	Covino Thomasina—†	234	retired	70	188 "
	U	Kearney James	236	laborer	46	here
	V	Kearney Josephine—†	236	housewife	43	"
	W	Carbone Marion—†	236	at home	22	"
	X*	Carbone Rose—†	236	housewife	41	"
	Y	Carbone Sabato	236	mason	48	"
	Z	Romano Louis	236	chauffeur	26	240 Princeton
856						
	A	Romano Mary—†	236	housewife	22	240 "
	B*	Palange Matteo	238	laborer	41	174 Brooks
	C*	Palange Theresa—†	238	housewife	31	174 "
	D*	Mercuri Joseph	238	musician	25	163 Benningt'n
	E*	Mercuri Lucy—†	238	housewife	50	163 "
	F*	Curcio Anna—†	240	"	34	317 Saratoga
	G	Curcio Ettore	240	printer	34	317 "
	H	Curcio Linda—†	240	at home	32	317 "
	K	Neal Charles	240	fishcutter	34	here
	L	Neal Mary—†	240	housewife	29	"
	M	Gannon Ellen G—†	240	"	53	"
	N	Gannon Margaret P—†	240	salesman	21	"
	O	Gannon Michael J	240	woolworker	53	"
	P	Keller Agnes G—†	242	housewife	43	"
	R	Keller James B	242	carpenter	49	"

Page.	Letter.	FULL NAME.	Residence, Jan. 1, 1938.	Occupation.	Supposed Age.	Reported Residence, Jan. 1, 1937. Street and Number.

Lexington Street—Continued

	S	Loring Benjamin	242	entertainer	59	here
	T	Loring Ethel—†	242	housewife	36	"
	U	Willington Arland	242	mechanic	55	"
	V	Pulio Angelina—†	244	housewife	25	"
	W	Pulio Charles	244	laborer	31	
	X	DeMeo Dominic	244	"	21	"
	Y	DeMeo Frances—†	244	housewife	26	245 Lexington
	Z	DeMeo Frank	244	chauffeur	24	here
857						
	A	DeMeo Ralph	244	"	27	245 Lexington
	B	Taylor Gertrude—†	246	housewife	29	here
	C	Taylor William	246	laborer	30	"
	D	Ventresca Anthony	246	salesman	26	"
	E	Ventresca Frank	246	laborer	22	
	F	*Ventresca Mary—†	246	housewife	64	"
	G	Ventresca Nellie—†	246	at home	23	
	H	*Ventresca Philip	246	retired	66	"
	K	*Miniscalco Anna—†	250	housewife	41	104 Marion
	L	*Miniscalco Vincent	250	laborer	56	104 "
	M	*DiGirolano Gaetano	250	manager	25	146 Trenton
	N	*DiGirolano Irene—†	250	housewife	59	146 "
	O	DiGirolano Nicholas	250	tailor	36	146 "
	P	*DiGirolano Restituto	250	cobbler	63	146 "
	R	*Venuti Angelina—†	250	housewife	23	17 Frankfort
	S	Venuti Stallario	250	printer	22	17 "
	T	*Verbanas Caroline—†	250	housewife	35	35 Eutaw
	U	Verbanas Desideria—†	250	clerk	20	35 "
	V	Verbanas John	250	waiter	43	35 "
	X	*Ducey Catherine—†	256	housewife	32	here
	Y	Ducey Thomas	256	laborer	43	"
	Z	D'Alessandro Biagio	256	tailor	38	"
858						
	A	*D'Alessandro Helena—†	256	housewife	37	"
	B	Walsh William E	256	carpenter	36	"
	C	Pasciscia Salvatore	258	electrician	26	275 Chelsea
	D	*Pasciscia Tina—†	258	housewife	25	275 "
	E	Costa Venero A	258	mechanic	57	314 Harvard
	F	Tarentino Ambrose	258	cabinetmaker	24	170 Lexington
	G	Tarentino Ida—†	258	housewife	23	170 "
	H	Powers Edward W	260	operator	22	here
	K	Powers Nicholas L	260	boilermaker	41	"

Page.	Letter.	Full Name.	Residence, Jan. 1, 1938.	Occupation.	Supposed Age.	Reported Residence, Jan. 1, 1937. Street and Number.

Lexington Street—Continued

	L	Powers Robert J	260	chauffeur	20	here
	M	Powers Rose A—†	260	housewife	43	"
	N	Sharis Daniel	260	baker	23	"
	O	*Sharis George	260	laborer	55	
	P	*Sharis Helen—†	260	housewife	45	"
	R	Sharis Nicholas	260	mechanic	24	"
	S	Lawrence Arthur	262	chauffeur	25	6 Neptune rd
	T	Lawrence Edith—†	262	stenographer	23	6 "
	U	Lawrence Ernest	262	engineer	45	6 "
	V	Lawrence Margaret—†	262	housewife	43	6 "
	Y	Baker Ruth—†	264	"	29	here
	Z	Baker William R	264	salesman	34	"
	W	Welsh Alice L—†	264	housewife	51	"
	X	Welsh John W	264	printer	51	
859						
	A	Vieti Michael	266	laborer	47	80 Princeton
	C	Bickford John	266	salesman	46	here
	B	Walters Amy—†	266	housewife	53	"
	D	Walters James	266	calker	65	"
	F	McInnis Sarah—†	270	cook	46	
	G	McPherson Frederick L	270	realtor	54	
	H	McPherson Mary E—†	270	housewife	41	"
	K	Melcher Florence A—†	270	clerk	40	
	L	Deveau Alfred	274	carpenter	60	"
	M	Deveau Alfred A	274	plumber	30	
	N	Deveau Josephine—†	274	housewife	59	"
	O	McPherson Clara E—†	274	"	50	
	P	McPherson Ralph C	274	engineer	58	
	R	MacDougall George A	276	U S A	28	
	S	MacDougall Mary—†	276	housewife	60	"
	T	MacDougall Murdock	276	chauffeur	61	"
	U	Earl Everett	276	laborer	72	218 E Eagle
	V	Roome Annie E—†	276	housewife	43	218 "
	W	Roome Frank	276	weigher	56	218 "
	X	Ryan Joseph P	278	buffer	38	here
	Y	Ryan Marion B—†	278	housewife	39	"
	Z	Baker Clarence T	278	watchman	51	"
860						
	A	Baker Clarence T, jr	278	longshoreman	25	"
	B	Baker Flora E—†	278	at home	22	
	C	Baker Margaret M—†	278	housewife	48	"

Page.	Letter.	Full Name.	Residence, Jan. 1, 1938.	Occupation.	Supposed Age.	Reported Residence, Jan. 1, 1937. Street and Number.

Lexington Street—Continued

	D	MacDonald Mary A—†	278	secretary	35	here
	E	Barranco Joseph J	280	chauffeur	24	“
	F	Barranco Josephine—†	280	housewife	25	“
	G	Elwell James H	280	laborer	34	
	H	Elwell Josephine—†	280	housewife	35	“
	K	Taimi Eino	280	ironworker	46	“
	L	*Taimi Hilda—†	280	housewife	51	“
	M	Walsh James	282	retired	60	
	N	Walsh James, jr	282	shipper	26	“
	O	Walsh Nellie—†	282	housewife	59	“
	P	Pace Mildred—†	282	“	32	“
	R	Pace William	282	steamfitter	38	“
	S	Tiano Antoinetta—†	282	packer	24	
	T	Tiano John	282	clerk	27	
	U	Tiano Joseph	282	retired	63	
	V	*Tiano Mary—†	282	housewife	60	“
	W	Bellino James	282A	baker	25	
	X	Bellino Laura—†	282A	housewife	24	“
	Y	*LaRosa Jennie—†	282A	“	40	
	Z	LaRosa Joseph	282A	tailor	43	
861						
	A	Burke John J	282A	operator	42	“
	B	Burke Mary O—†	282A	housewife	41	“
	C	McCormack Anna—†	282A	packer	34	
	D	DeFeo Frederick	284	mechanic	41	“
	E	Thornton Catherine—†	284	housewife	69	“
	F	Thornton Ellen—†	284	“	45	
	G	Thornton Frederick	284	clerk	40	
	H	Gleason Alice—†	284	“	29	
	K	Gleason Edmund	284	laborer	38	
	L	Gleason Ina—†	284	housewife	33	“
	M	Trott Andrew	284	fishcutter	29	“
	N	*Fiore Angelina—†	286	housewife	44	“
	O	Fiore Camilla—†	286	at home	20	
	P	*Fiore James	286	laborer	53	
	R	Paiva Frank T	286	clerk	34	
	S	Paiva Mary—†	286	housewife	72	“
	T	Flamingo Amelia—†	286	“	38	198 Marion
	U	Flamingo Leonard	286	molder	41	198 “
	V	Hanlon Albert A	288	operator	45	here

Page.	Letter.	Full Name.	Residence, Jan. 1, 1938.	Occupation.	Supposed Age.	Reported Residence, Jan. 1, 1937. Street and Number.

Lexington Street—Continued

Page.	Letter.	Full Name.	Residence, Jan. 1, 1938.	Occupation.	Supposed Age.	Reported Residence, Jan. 1, 1937. Street and Number.
	W	Hanlon Albert A, jr	288	clerk	20	here
	X	Hanlon Mary C—†	288	housewife	45	"
	Y	Hanlon William F	288	shipper	22	"
	Z	Dalton Helen—†	290	nurse	27	
862						
	A	Dalton John H	290	mechanic	42	"
	B	Dalton Margaret—†	290	nurse	30	
	C	Gleason Francis	292	janitor	29	
	D	Gleason Josephine—†	292	housewife	22	"
	E	Kane Daniel J	292	fireman	29	
	F	Kane John W	292	chauffeur	24	"
	G	Kane Walter	292	coppersmith	32	"
	H	Smith Mary—†	294	operator	27	
	K	Smith Mildred—†	294	dressmaker	22	"
	L	Ravencroft Helena—†	294	at home	72	
	M	O'Connor Hannah—†	296	proprietor	64	"
	N	Howes Maud—†	296	housekeeper	27	"
	O	*Moscatelli Felicia—†	298	"	43	"
	P	Moscatelli Michael	298	marbleworker	48	"
	R	Moscatelli Thomas	298	manager	22	"
	S	Cuzziere Alice—†	300	housewife	23	280 Chelsea
	T	Cuzziere John	300	laborer	27	280 "
	U	LaRusso Joseph	300	candymaker	58	8 Sackville
	V	Ridge Colman	302	laborer	26	here
	W	Ridge Mary—†	302	housewife	54	"
	X	Ridge Patrick	302	chauffeur	34	"
	Y	Ridge Thomas	302	laborer	68	
	Z	Ridge Thomas	302	"	22	
863						
	A	Werner Elizabeth—†	306	housewife	50	"
	B	Werner John	306	inspector	61	"
	C	Almeida Anthony	306	operator	47	"
	D	Almeida Mary M—†	306	"	20	
	E	Almeida Rhoda M—†	306	housewife	42	"
	F	Almeida Roderick	306	merchant	22	"
	G	*McLeod John	306	retired	74	
	H	McLeod John B	306	steamfitter	24	"
	K	Morrison Margaret A—†	306	housewife	30	"
	L	Morrison Robert A	306	chauffeur	32	"

Page.	Letter.	Full Name.	Residence, Jan. 1, 1938.	Occupation.	Supposed Age.	Reported Residence, Jan. 1, 1937. Street and Number.

Prescott Street

	O	Walsh William P	3	painter	42	here
	N	Kennedy Catherine—†	3	housekeeper	46	"
	P	Neal William A	3	laborer	20	"
	R	Regan Patrick	3	operator	32	
	S	Sheehan Catherine A—†	3	clerk	40	"
	T	Cusenza Anna—†	5	housewife	21	225 Mass av
	U	Cusenza Joseph	5	laborer	33	225 "
	V	Capucci Mary—†	5	operator	37	here
	W	Velona Anna—†	5	"	24	"
	X	Velona Grace—†	5	hairdresser	22	"
	Y	Washl Hilja—†	5	housewife	22	"
	Z	Walsh Patrick J	5	fishcutter	24	"
864						
	A	*Dell'Aria Charles	6	shoemaker	38	"
	B	*Dell'Aria Sadie—†	6	housewife	40	"
	F	Wilcox Guy	6	blacksmith	56	"
	D	Zimmer Albert W	6	laborer	23	
	E	Zimmer Lillian—†	6	housewife	59	"
	G	Ricciardi Clorinda—†	7	candyworker	22	114 Trenton
	H	Ricciardi Domenic	7	shoeworker	26	285 Chelsea
	K	Valenti Antonio	7	foreman	46	here
	L	Valenti Helen—†	7	clerk	21	"
	M	*Valenti Margaret—†	7	housewife	40	"
	N	Valenti Theresa—†	7	clerk	24	
	O	Battaglia Joseph	8	laborer	30	
	P	Battaglia Julia—†	8	housewife	27	"
	R	Capolupo John	8	barber	43	
	S	*Capolupo Mary—†	8	housewife	30	"
	T	Capolupo Antonio	8	operator	45	"
	U	*Capolupo Filomena—†	8	housewife	37	"
	W	Carroll Florence—†	10	"	29	
	X	Carroll John H	10	repairman	29	"
	Y	Silva Joseph	10	weaver	38	151 Trenton
	Z	Silva Philomena—†	10	housewife	27	151 "
865						
	A	Spadaro Joseph	10	printer	32	here

Putnam Street

	B	Frasier Frank H	2	fireman	64	here
	C	Frasier Mary E—†	2	housewife	67	"

Page.	Letter.	Full Name.	Residence, Jan. 1, 1938.	Occupation.	Supposed Age.	Reported Residence, Jan. 1, 1937. Street and Number.

Putnam Street—Continued

	D	*Murphy Mary C—†	2	housewife	45	here
	E	*Murphy Robert J	2	laborer	48	"
	F	*Medeiros Anthony	7	chauffeur	38	Saugus
	G	*Medeiros Mary—†	7	housewife	36	"
	H	Beard Curtis A	7	repairman	36	here
	K	*Beard Verna F—†	7	housewife	30	"
	L	*Crowell Lottie E—†	7	"	48	"
	M	*Crowell Murray A	7	mechanic	50	"
	N	Nuuttila Anna I—†	8	librarian	23	
	O	*Nuuttila Lydia—†		nurse	51	
	P	Lilja Amanda—†	8	housewife	63	"
	R	Lilja Taimi—†	8	librarian	32	
	S	Penney Clinton E	10	fisherman	34	"
	T	*Penney Verna—†	10	housewife	31	"
	U	McAdams Lawrence E	10	chauffeur	28	"
	V	McAdams Virginia P—†	10	housewife	26	"
	W	Alberghini Alfred	47	machinist	22	"
	X	Alberghini Arthur	47	mechanic	47	"
	Y	Alberghini Eva—†	47	at home	26	
	Z	Alberghini Harold	47	machinist	24	"
866						
	A	Alberghini Mary—†	47	housewife	47	"
	B	Zuccaro Frank	48	painter	29	52 Chelsea
	C	Zuccaro Rose—†	48	housewife	26	52 "
	D	Patterson Florence G—†	48	"	23	here
	E	Paterson Robert A	48	laborer	25	"
	F	Scala Edward H	48	shoeworker	34	"
	G	Scala Inez M—†	48	housewife	29	"
	H	Alberghini Joseph	49	machinist	41	"
	K	Alberghini Mary—†	49	housewife	35	"
	L	Lopilato George	49	chauffeur	45	"
	M	Lopilato Lillian—†	49	housewife	32	"
	N	Laine Margaret—†	50	"	22	
	O	Laine Olga—†	50	"	49	
	P	Laine Onni A	50	machinist	24	"
	R	*DiPaola Carmella—†	50	housewife	47	"
	S	DiPaola Jennie—†	50	operator	21	"
	T	*DiPaola Pasquale	50	laborer	53	
	V	*Asci Catherine—†	50	housewife	27	"
	U	Asci Ernest	50	laborer	31	
	W	Olga Gabriel T	50	chauffeur	25	"

Page.	Letter.	FULL NAME.	Residence, Jan. 1, 1938.	Occupation.	Supposed Age.	Reported Residence, Jan. 1, 1937. Street and Number.

Putnam Street—Continued

	X	Brown Mary S—†	51	housewife	43	here
	Y	*Cianciulli Mary—†	52	"	29	"
	Z	Cianciulli Salvatore	52	chauffeur	37	"
		867				
	B	DiBacco Filomena—†	52	housewife	33	"
	A	DiBacco Mario	52	laborer	45	"
	C	Blase Anthony	52	machinist	21	"
	D	Blase James	52	laborer	56	
	E	Blase Jennie—†	52	housewife	52	"
	F	Romano Albert	52	chauffeur	21	"
	G	Romano Elizabeth—†	52	stitcher	23	
	K	Emery Effie M—†	53	housewife	50	"
	L	Emery Laura B—†	53	at home	30	
	H	Emery Rufus B	53	engineer	55	
	M	McInnes Angus	53	electrician	65	"
	N	Patterson Catherine M—†	53	housewife	50	"
	O	Patterson Jean E—†	53	operator	23	"
	P	McCormack Dorothy M-†	54	housewife	29	213 E Eagle
	R	McCormack Edward J	54	carpenter	35	213 "
	S	Law Elizabeth L—†	54	housewife	27	here
	T	Law John	54	repairman	34	"
	U	Nelson Howard J	54	watchman	40	"
	V	Anzalone John	54	bricklayer	30	220 Paris
	W	Anzalone Josephine C—†	54	housewife	28	220 "
	X	Hutchins Kenneth	55	fireman	25	337 E Eagle
	Y	Hutchins Stella M—†	55	housewife	26	337 "
	Z	Clifford Theodore C	56	checker	23	285 Lexington
		868				
	A	O'Brien Angela—†	56	housewife	33	here
	B	O'Brien Maurice J	56	laborer	35	"
	C	Roy Edward A	56	chauffeur	32	223 Border
	D	Roy Victoria A—†	56	housewife	27	223 "
	E	Barry Catherine M—†	58	"	58	here
	F	Barry Josephine—†	58	at home	20	"
	G	Barry Mary F—†	58	"	26	"
	H	Lidback George S	60	janitor	37	57 Neptune rd
	K	Lidback Isabel W—†	60	housewife	26	57 "
	L	Stamm Henry J	61	fireman	76	here
	M	Stamm Mary E—†	61	housewife	52	"
	N	Noble Florence V—†	61	"	29	"
	O	Noble John H	61	operator	27	"

Page.	Letter.	Full Name.	Residence, Jan. 1, 1938.	Occupation.	Supposed Age.	Reported Residence, Jan. 1, 1937. Street and Number.

Putnam Street—Continued

Page.	Letter.	Full Name.	Residence, Jan. 1, 1938.	Occupation.	Supposed Age.	Reported Residence, Jan. 1, 1937. Street and Number.
	P	*Clouter George	62	blacksmith	62	230 Lexington
	R	Thomas Edgar W	62	mechanic	35	34 White
	S	*Thomas Effie M—†	62	housewife	30	34 "
	T	Garrity Lillian B—†	63	"	63	here
	U	Garrity Thomas M	63	pressman	39	"
	V	Ryan James	63	laborer	53	"
	W	Doran Ellen N—†	63	housewife	57	"
	X	Doran Mary E—†	63	at home	29	
	Y	Doran William	63	laborer	59	"
	Z	LaVee Minnie—†	63	housekeeper	58	312 Bremen
869						
	A	Scarfo Mary—†	86	housewife	28	here
	B	*Scarfo Philip	86	operator	30	"
	C	Lombardi Albert	86	"	21	"
	D	Lombardi Henry	86	"	48	
	E	Lombardi Henry	86	"	20	
	F	Lombardi Mary—†	86	housewife	44	"
	G	Lombardi Sarah—†	86	clerk	24	
	H	Lombardi Tony	86	musician	23	"
	K	Yanelli Albert	88	operator	27	"
	L	Yanelli Anna—†	88	housewife	24	"
	M	*DeGruttola Carmella—†	88	"	65	
	N	DeGruttola Frank	88	bartender	29	"
	O	DeGruttola Joseph	88	repairman	32	"
	P	*DeGruttola Nicholas	88	baker	64	
	S	Colluccini Josephine—†	88	housewife	34	"
	R	*Colluccini Pasquale	88	candyworker	46	"
	T	Moore Christine L—†	90	teacher	27	
	U	Moore Harold F	90	plumber	35	
	V	Moore William J	90	retired	71	
	W	*Capolupo Emanuela—†	92	housewife	37	"
	X	Capolupo Vincent	92	shoemaker	39	"

Trenton Street

Page.	Letter.	Full Name.	Residence, Jan. 1, 1938.	Occupation.	Supposed Age.	Reported Residence, Jan. 1, 1937. Street and Number.
	Z	Cipriano Alice M—†	159	housewife	21	1065 Bennington
870						
	A	Cipriano Joseph A	159	machinist	23	here
	B	*Cipriano Maria—†	159	housekeeper	63	"
	C	Joyce James P	159	longshoreman	50	"
	D	Joyce Josephine—†	159	housewife	39	"

Page.	Letter.	Full Name.	Residence, Jan. 1, 1938.	Occupation.	Supposed Age.	Reported Residence, Jan. 1, 1937. Street and Number.

Trenton Street—Continued

Page.	Letter.	Full Name.	Residence, Jan. 1, 1938.	Occupation.	Supposed Age.	Reported Residence, Jan. 1, 1937. Street and Number.
	E	Joyce William P	159	laborer	20	here
	G	Tyman James	159	"	30	77 Falcon
	F	Tyman Mary—†	159	housewife	29	77 "
	H	Genovese Adolph	161	cabinetmaker	41	here
	K	Genovese Olympia—†	161	housewife	37	"
	L	*Fioritto Concetta—†	161	"	67	"
	M	Fioritto Oreste	161	painter	67	"
	N	*Altobelli Caroline—†	161	housewife	42	220 E Eagle
	O	*Altobelli Natale	161	watchmaker	46	220 "
	P	Ferraro Carmine	163	laborer	42	here
	R	*Ferraro Lucy—†	163	housewife	37	"
	S	Magee Elizabeth R—†	163	"	37	"
	T	Magee James J	163	foreman	36	
	U	Cipriani Louise—†	163	housewife	30	"
	V	Cipriani Victor	163	shoeworker	33	"
	W	Edmunds Hattie—†	165	housekeeper	58	"
	X	Benner Abbie E—†	165	housewife	82	"
	Y	Benner George F	165	custodian	78	"
	Z	Churchvig Hans	167	engineer	50	New York
871	A	Farsta Frederick	167	carpenter	62	here
	B	Farsta Louise—†	167	housewife	63	"
	C	Connelly Henry	169	expressman	37	"
	D	Connelly Theresa—†	169	housewife	33	"
	E	Viglione Adelaide—†	169	tailoress	34	
	F	*Viglione Angelo	169	tailor	67	
	G	Viglione Edmond	169	timekeeper	27	"
	H	*Viglione Julia—†	169	housewife	56	"
	K	Viglione Lillian—†	169	at home	29	
	L	Potito Alfio	169	butcher	22	
	M	Potito Domenic	169	physician	30	"
	N	*Potito Epifanio	169	tailor	53	"
	O	Potito Leonora—†	169	housewife	21	2 Thurston
	P	*Potito Margaret—†	169	"	53	here
	R	Potito Stella—†	169	dressmaker	24	"
	S	Clark Charles	171	U S A	32	Fort Andrews
	T	Clark Helen—†	171	housewife	27	"
	U	Fossett John F	171	mechanic	21	90 White
	V	Costello Anne C—†	171	housewife	48	here
	W	Costello Michael	171	repairman	49	"
	X	*Cronin Patrick F	171	carpenter	27	Canada

Page.	Letter.	Full Name.	Residence, Jan. 1, 1938.	Occupation.	Supposed Age.	Reported Residence, Jan. 1, 1937. Street and Number.

Trenton Street—Continued

Page.	Letter.	Full Name.	Residence, Jan. 1, 1938.	Occupation.	Supposed Age.	Reported Residence, Jan. 1, 1937. Street and Number.
	Y	*Grinkevich Michael	171	mechanic	49	here
	Z	*Grinkevich Victoria—†	171	housewife	38	"
872						
	A	Capolo Anna—†	173	housekeeper	25	"
	B	*Rondilone Lucia—†	173	housewife	43	"
	C	Rondilone Savino	173	laborer	43	
	D	DiMaggio Antonio	173	clerk	49	
	E	DiMaggio Sadie—†	173	housewife	33	"
	F	Polimeno Lena—†	173	"	29	
	G	*Polimeno Matteo	173	tailor	38	
	H	Trainito Cologero	175	barber	38	
	K	*Trainito Gaetana—†	175	housewife	68	"
	L	*Trainito Gaspero	175	retired	78	
	M	*Trainito Maria—†	175	housewife	25	"
	N	*Trainito Rosa—†	175	"	35	
	O	*Trainito Stefano	175	storekeeper	47	"
	P	Ford Daniel	175	laborer	32	
	R	Ford Edward	175	"	20	
	S	Ford Mary—†	175	housewife	58	"
	T	Ford Michael	175	rigger	59	
	U	*Mele Carmella—†	179	housewife	41	"
	V	Mele Carmella—†	179	waitress	20	
	W	Mele Morris	179	engineer	44	"
	X	Luongo Angelina—†	179	housewife	48	24 Morris
	Y	Luongo Filipo	179	laborer	48	24 "
	Z	Luongo Louis	179	"	21	24 "
873						
	A	Luongo Louise—†	179	dressmaker	23	24 "
	B	*DiMattia Maria—†	179	housekeeper	70	127 Paris
	C	*DeLeo Lena—†	189	housewife	45	here
	D	*DeLeo Pasquale	189	carpenter	49	"
	E	Frongillo Amando	189	cook	26	"
	F	Frongillo Andrew	189	chauffeur	30	"
	G	*Angelini Angelina—†	189	housewife	31	262 E Eagle
	H	*Angelini Stefano	189	mechanic	39	262 "
	K	*Avila Joseph	189	retired	64	here
	L	*Avila Josephine—†	189	housewife	53	"
	M	Contino Mary—†	189	housekeeper	38	"
	N	Siciliano Louis	189	proprietor	45	"
	O	Daddario Guerino	191	dealer	54	
	P	Daddario Louis	191	salesman	24	"

Page.	Letter.	Full Name.	Residence, Jan. 1, 1938.	Occupation.	Supposed Age.	Reported Residence, Jan. 1, 1937. Street and Number.

Trenton Street—Continued

Page.	Letter.	Full Name.	Residence, Jan. 1, 1938.	Occupation.	Supposed Age.	Reported Residence, Jan. 1, 1937. Street and Number.
	R	*Daddario Maria—†	191	housewife	55	here
	S	Rubbico Joseph	191	salesman	27	"
	T	D'Agostino Angelo	193	chauffeur	24	"
	U	D'Agostino Mary—†	193	housewife	22	"
	V	*Mancini Alice—†	193	housekeeper	22	"
	W	*Mancini Palma—†	193	housewife	50	"
	X	*Mancini Santino	193	tailor	52	"
	Y	Donahue George	195	janitor	27	"
	Z	Donahue Louise—†	195	housewife	25	"
874						
	A	Condon Alice—†	195	"	21	"
	B	Condon John	195	inspector	26	131 Addison
	C	*Lawson George	195	carpenter	48	here
	D	*Lawson Pearl—†	195	housewife	41	"
	E	Kanall Agnes—†	196	"	47	"
	F	Kanall Paul T	196	dealer	47	"
	G	Kelley Mary I—†	196	saleswoman	40	Somerville
	H	Chiofito Samuel	196	barber	24	216 Lexington
	K	Surette Frances—†	196	clerk	21	66 Trenton
	L	Surette John W	196	laborer	22	66 "
	M	*Surette Laura—†	196	housewife	53	66 "
	N	Golden Helen—†	197	"	31	here
	O	Golden Michael L	197	agent	34	"
	P	Golden Isaac	197	"	77	"
	R	Golden Rebecca—†	197	housewife	71	"
	S	Young Catherine B—†	197	"	59	
	T	Young Erving W	197	brakeman	59	"
	U	Dell'Orfano Antonio	198	musician	50	
	V	Dell'Orfano Helen—†	198	at home	20	
	W	Dell'Orfano Louisa—†	198	housewife	46	"
	X	Thiffault Charles L	198	chauffeur	33	"
	Y	Thiffault Emily—†	198	housewife	27	"
	Z	*Tomeo Alfred L	198	meatcutter	40	"
875						
	A	*Tomeo Mary—†	198	housewife	38	"
	B	Coolin Albert T	199	longshoreman	47	"
	C	Coolin Edward J	199	laborer	54	
	D	Coolin Harold L	199	"	35	
	E	Coolin Sophia—†	199	housewife	76	"
	F	McPhee Helen T—†	199	candyworker	43	"
	G	Piretti Elizabeth G—†	199	housewife	31	"

Page.	Letter.	Full Name.	Residence, Jan. 1, 1938.	Occupation.	Supposed Age.	Reported Residence, Jan. 1, 1937. Street and Number.

Trenton Street—Continued

Page.	Letter.	Full Name.	Residence, Jan. 1, 1938.	Occupation.	Supposed Age.	Reported Residence, Jan. 1, 1937. Street and Number.
	H	Piretti Raymond E	199	agent	33	here
	K	Scanzillo Louis	199	operator	21	“
	L	McDonald Eugenie L—†	207	“	39	“
	M	McDonald William L	207	mechanic	39	“
	N	McDonald Francis L	207	salesman	35	“
	O	McDonald George W	207	clerk	28	
	P	McDonald Hannah E—†	207	housewife	63	“
	R	McDonald Joseph A	207	engineer	70	
	S	McDonald Joseph A, jr	207	clerk	30	“
	U	Monkewicz Charles	209	pressman	21	38 Staniford
	V	Monkewicz Ruth—†	209	housewife	23	38 “
	W	Fenton Loretta L—†	209	“	37	here
	X	Fenton Michael E	209	clerk	38	“
	Y	Grant Edith F—†	211	waitress	46	131 Falcon
	Z	Coelho Mary E—†	211	housekeeper	61	here
876						
	A	Coelho William L	211	chauffeur	36	“
	B	Souza Manuel	211	longshoreman	37	“
	C	Souza Marie—†	211	housewife	37	“
	D	*Visione Anthony	213	proprietor	42	“
	E	*Visione Jennie—†	213	housewife	40	“
	F	Visione Mary—†	213	at home	20	“
	G	Rubico Amelia—†	213	housewife	28	“
	H	Rubico Jerome	213	repairman	25	“
	M	Park Catherine A—†	217	housewife	45	“
	N	Park George C	217	baker	46	
	O	McNeil Edmond L	217	watchman	41	“
	P	McNeil Frederick P	217	retired	77	
	R	McNeil Viola M—†	217	housewife	37	“
	S	Galvin Paul	219	engineer	40	“
	T	*Galvin Winifred—†	219	housewife	30	“
	U	Minichello Elvira—†	219	“	41	“
	V	Minichello Frank	219	marblesetter	45	“
	W	Minichello Nicholas	219	electrician	20	“
	X	*Pinfold James L	219	painter	54	
	Y	*Pinfold Mary—†	219	housewife	56	“
	Z	Balboni Gladys—†	221	“	38	“
877						
	A	Balboni Joseph	221	laborer	33	
	B	Reed Charles	221	rigger	60	
	C	Reed Clarabel—†	221	housewife	52	“

Page.	Letter.	Full Name.	Residence, Jan. 1, 1938.	Occupation.	Supposed Age.	Reported Residence, Jan. 1, 1937. Street and Number.

Trenton Street—Continued

Page.	Letter.	Full Name.	Residence, Jan. 1, 1938.	Occupation.	Supposed Age.	Reported Residence, Jan. 1, 1937. Street and Number.
	D	Velona Anna—†	221	shoeworker	27	here
	E	*Velona Antonetta—†	221	at home	20	“
	F	Velona Celeste—†	221	operator	25	“
	G	*Velona Cesira—†	221	housewife	62	“
	H	*Velona Rocco	221	laborer	58	
	K	DiPalma Mary—†	223	housewife	28	“
	L	DiPalma Nicholas	223	laborer	33	“
	M	Keough Thomas	223	collector	55	“
	N	O'Brien Marion—†	223	housekeeper	40	“
	O	*Favale Angela—†	227	housewife	48	“
	P	*Favale Maria—†	227	stitcher	23	“
	R	Favale Michael	227	carver	52	“
	S	Tartarini Gino	227	laborer	26	21 Unity
	T	Tartarini Mary—†	227	housewife	25	60 Gove
	X	Santelmo Anna—†	233	“	38	here
	Y	Santelmo Frank	233	electric welder	42	“
	V	Reed Earle	233	rigger	26	“
	W	Reed Olga—†	233	housewife	23	“
	Z	Digan Bernard	235	mechanic	25	137 Webster
878						
	A	Digan Catherine—†	235	housewife	25	409 Chelsea
	B	Fancher Dorothy—†	235	“	20	172 Border
	C	Olsen Henry	235	longshoreman	40	172 “
	D	Evans Mary A—†	237	housekeeper	76	here
	E	Downing Catherine E—†	237	housewife	45	112 Trenton
	F	Downing Eugene	237	laborer	51	112 “
	G	Murphy Lena—†	237	housekeeper	45	212 Saratoga
	H	Palmer Annie—†	239	housewife	69	here
	K	Palmer Joseph L	239	retired	78	“
	L	Pye Chester	239	operator	26	146 Putnam
	M	Dalton Michael L	239	fishcutter	30	29 White
	N	Dalton Philomina—†	239	housewife	21	249 Lexington
	O	*D'Amico Nunziata—†	241	“	54	313 “
	P	*D'Amico Sebastiano	241	laborer	59	313 “
	R	Pedoto Josephine—†	241	housekeeper	32	114 Trenton
	S	Clifford Mazie—†	241	“	43	285 Lexington
	U	*Murphy Arthur	243	laborer	35	319 Benningt'n
	T	*Murphy Bridget—†	243	housewife	33	319 “
	V	Nazzaro Ellen—†	243	“	32	209 Havre
	W	Nazzaro James	243	laborer	34	209 “
	X	Corkum Frances—†	243	housewife	39	68 Falcon
	Y	Corkum Lester	243	seaman	44	68 “

Page.	Letter.	Full Name.	Residence, Jan. 1, 1938.	Occupation.	Supposed Age.	Reported Residence, Jan. 1, 1937. Street and Number.

Trenton Street—Continued

Page.	Letter.	Full Name.	Residence, Jan. 1, 1938.	Occupation.	Supposed Age.	Reported Residence, Jan. 1, 1937. Street and Number.
	z	*Daley Mary—†	247	housewife	38	here
879						
	A	Daley Timothy	247	porter	41	“
	B	Seppa Oscar	247	engineer	50	
	c	*Seppa Rikka—†	247	housewife	53	“
	D	Cullinane Helen G—†	247	teacher	23	
	E	Cullinane Jennie M—†	247	housewife	48	“
	F	Cullinane William J	247	clerk	50	

White Street

Page.	Letter.	Full Name.	Residence, Jan. 1, 1938.	Occupation.	Supposed Age.	Reported Residence, Jan. 1, 1937. Street and Number.
	G	Wilson David	88	manager	55	here
	H	Wilson Margaret—†	88	operator	25	“
	K	Wilson Rosemond—†	88	teacher	21	“
	L	Cooper Mary E—†	rear 88	at home	77	
	M	Langley Capitola—†	“ 88	“	75	
	N	Fossett Frieda—†	90	housewife	46	“
	O	Fossett John	90	chauffeur	46	“
	P	Mastrolio Libby	90	laborer	20	
	R	*Mastrolio Nicholas	90	“	46	
	S	Mastrolio Phyllis—†	90	housewife	34	“
	T	Saggese Alfred	92	tailor	28	
	U	Saggese Dorothy—†	92	housewife	27	“
	V	Amiro Harold	92	engineer	35	
	W	Amiro Julia—†	92	housewife	31	“
	X	Saggese Margaret—†	92	teacher	32	
	Y	Saggese Mary—†	92	housewife	65	“
	Z	Saggese Michael	92	salesman	40	“
880						
	A	Saggese Nicholas	92	operator	42	“
	B	Saggese Victoria—†	92	at home	30	
	C	Carr Della—†	102	housewife	44	“
	D	Carr Ralph	102	salesman	23	“
	E	Kearney Phyllis—†	102	housewife	25	“
	F	Martin Hector	102	laborer	41	“
	G	Marani Antonette—†	104	housewife	21	“
	L	Marani Joseph	104	shipper	23	
	H	Nazzaro Antonio	104	janitor	41	
	K	Nazzaro Carmella—†	104	housewife	35	“
	M	Buontempo Americo	106	machinist	22	“
	N	Buontempo John	106	carpenter	60	“
	O	Buontempo Julia—†	106	housewife	62	“

Page.	Letter.	Full Name.	Residence, Jan. 1, 1938.	Occupation.	Supposed Age.	Reported Residence, Jan. 1, 1937. Street and Number.

White Street—Continued

Page.	Letter.	Full Name.	Residence, Jan. 1, 1938.	Occupation.	Supposed Age.	Reported Residence, Jan. 1, 1937. Street and Number.
	P	Buontempo Lucy—†	106	saleswoman	23	here
	R	Buontempo Romeo	106	machinist	20	"
	S	*Salierno Louise—†	106	housewife	41	"
	T	Salierno Savino	106	chemist	46	
	U	Coffin Elizabeth—†	108	social worker	23	"
	V	Deraney Ruth—†	108	"	24	"
	W	Powers Dorothea—†	108	"	28	"
	X	White Isabel—†	108	"	25	New York
	Y	Wright Lucy—†	108		61	here
881						
	A	Nelson Irene—†	110		44	
	C	Nelson S Max	110		48	"
	Z	Woodbury Alice—†	110	"	28	Connecticut
	B	Woodbury Lawrence	110	"	28	"
	D	Blasi Anna—†	112	housewife	39	271 Lexington
	E	Blasi Orlindo C	112	investigator	40	271 "
	F	Campbell Alice—†	112	clerk	27	1183 Bennington
	G	Kavin Catherine—†	112	housewife	57	1183 "
	H	Kavin Mary—†	112	librarian	31	1183 "
	K	Kavin William J	112	instructor	29	1183 "
	L	Bradley Dennis	112	chauffeur	36	1183 "
	M	Bradley Louise—†	112	housewife	31	1183 "
	N	Ippolito John	114	mechanic	28	279 Chelsea
	O	Ippolito Rose—†	114	housewife	21	118 White
	P	Clemente Angelo	114	mechanic	43	here
	R	*Clemente Nicoletta—†	114	housewife	40	"
	S	Surette Dora L—†	114	"	24	478 Saratoga
	T	Surette John B	114	carpenter	32	478 "
	U	Twombly George W	116	machinist	68	here
	V	Twombly Ida M—†	116	housewife	73	"
	W	Roselli Etta—†	116	"	24	254 E Eagle
	X	Roselli Louis	116	molder	27	10 Margaret
	X[1]	DiLeonardo Rosina—†	116	housewife	47	here
	Y	DiLeonardo Salvatore	116	collector	51	"
	Z	Ferranti Augustine	116	shoeworker	36	"
882						
	B	Sacco Charles	118	painter	27	
	C	*Sacco Mary—†	118	housewife	58	"
	D	*Sacco William	118	laborer	61	
	E	Colosi Frank	118	machinist	40	"
	F	Colosi Josephine—†	118	housewife	31	"
	G	Colosi Nancy—†	118	housekeeper	70	"

1

14

15

1(

17

18

19

2(

2

11

Ward 1—Precinct 11

CITY OF BOSTON

LIST OF RESIDENTS
20 YEARS OF AGE AND OVER

(NON-CITIZENS INDICATED BY ASTERISK)
(FEMALES INDICATED BY DAGGER)

AS OF

JANUARY 1, 1938

JOSEPH F. TIMILTY, } *Listing*
FREDERIC E. DOWLING, } *Board.*

CITY OF BOSTON PRINTING DEPARTMENT

Page.	Letter.	Full Name.	Residence, Jan. 1, 1938.	Occupation.	Supposed Age.	Reported Residence, Jan. 1, 1937. Street and Number.
889		**Bennington Street**				
	B	Doyle Annie—†	194	housekeeper	63	Wm J Kelly sq
	C	*Lamonica Josephine—†	194	housewife	44	16 Henchman
	D	Lamonica Santo	194	barber	45	16 "
	E	Cardoza Manuel T	194	constable	35	here
	F	Giordano Angelo	194	polisher	23	"
	G	Giordano Christine—†	194	housewife	21	"
	H	*Bossone Frances—†	196	"	48	"
	K	*Bossone Saverio	196	laborer	56	"
	L	Amodeo Sadie—†	196	housewife	30	208 E Eagle
	M	Amodeo Zaccario	196	laborer	31	208 "
	O	Cassidy Julia A—†	198	housewife	61	here
	P	Cassidy Thomas A	198	storekeeper	70	"
	R	Driscoll Paul T	198	laborer	21	"
	S	Cardosa Theresa—†	198	housewife	64	"
	T	Cardosa Thomas	198	laborer	35	
	U	Fiorentino Anna M—†	198	housewife	34	"
	V	Fiorentino Charles	198	laborer	41	
	X	*Scire Carmello	202	storekeeper	53	"
	Y	Scire Frank	202	clerk	20	"
	Z	*Scire Mary—†	202	housewife	49	"
890						
	A	*Zappulla Salvatore	202	printer	25	108A Orleans
	B	Zappulla Viola—†	202	housewife	20	148 London
	C	Scott Charlotte M—†	204	laundress	54	5 Col sq
	D	Scott Walter F	204	laborer	21	5 "
	E	Wooley Catherine A—†	204	laundress	36	5 "
	F	Surette Joseph	204	cutter	36	194 Benningt'n
	G	Surette Margaret—†	204	housewife	32	194 "
	H	Vargus Edmund	204	cutter	26	51 Princeton
	K	McGarrity Margaret—†	204	housewife	43	206 Benningt'n
	M	Mastascusa Frank	206	laborer	60	here
	N	*Silva Manuel	206	longshoreman	42	"
	O	*Silva Mary—†	206	housewife	39	"
	P	Scanzillo Luigi	206	shoemaker	50	"
	R	*Scanzillo Mary G—†	206	housewife	38	"
	T	*Diogo Carlos	208	longshoreman	52	"
	U	*Diogo Justina—†	208	housewife	57	"
	V	DiBernardini Antonio	208	laborer	46	310 Saratoga
	W	*DiBernardini Victoria—†	208	housewife	41	310 "
	X	*Rezendes Helen—†	210	"	38	here

Page.	Letter.	Full Name.	Residence, Jan. 1, 1938.	Occupation.	Supposed Age.	Reported Residence, Jan. 1, 1937. Street and Number.

Bennington Street—Continued

Page.	Letter.	Full Name.	Residence, Jan. 1, 1938.	Occupation.	Supposed Age.	Reported Residence, Jan. 1, 1937. Street and Number.
	Y	*Rezendes William	210	finisher	39	here
891						
	A	*Oliver Joseph	210	operator	59	
	B	*Oliver Mary—†	210	“	27	
	C	*Oliver Rose—†	210	housewife	61	“
	D	Smith Dennis J	212	plumber	48	“
	E	Smith Mary J—†	212	housewife	45	“
	F	Murnane Mary J—†	212	“	47	
	G	Murnane Maurice	212	storekeeper	73	“
	H	Gildea Mary—†	212	housewife	72	“
	K	Ambrosino Anthony	214	laborer	44	
	L	Ambrosino Mary—†	214	housewife	44	“
	M	Bowden Edward L	214	laborer	50	477 Meridian
	N	Bowden Hannah—†	214	housewife	43	477 “
	O	Riley Daniel F	214	guard	45	here
	P	Riley Mary E—†	214	housewife	49	“
	R	Moran Frank	215	laborer	33	“
	S	Moran Irene—†	215	housewife	30	“
	T	*Puopolo Alesio	215	operator	41	“
	U	Puopolo Anna—†	215	housewife	36	“
	V	Pignato Minnie—†	215	houseworker	22	“
	W	*Pignato Sebastian	215	laborer	49	
	X	Coady Harold	216	mechanic	31	“
	Y	*Coady Mary—†	216	housewife	28	“
	Z	Podeia Frank	216	laborer	43	
892						
	A	*Podeia Mary—†	216	housewife	38	“
	B	Fratto Anthony	216	operator	28	211 Princeton
	C	Fratto Marie—†	216	housewife	23	211 “
	D	Maloney Catherine—†	217	housekeeper	59	here
	E	Maloney Theresa—†	217	operator	29	“
	F	*Mulcahy Ann—†	217	housekeeper	79	“
	G	*Vertullo Florence—†	217	housewife	31	“
	H	*Vertullo Nicholas	217	shoemaker	33	“
	K	Zevlo Constantina—†	217	operator	20	“
	L	Zevlo Pasquale	217	laborer	45	
	M	Zevlo Rose—†	217	operator	21	
	N	*Zevlo Thomasina—†	217	housewife	41	“
	O	*Hollohan Catherine—†	219	“	42	
	P	Hollohan Edmund	219	laborer	21	
	R	Hollohan Thomas	219	carpenter	46	“

Page.	Letter.	Full Name.	Residence, Jan. 1, 1938.	Occupation.	Supposed Age.	Reported Residence, Jan. 1, 1937. Street and Number.

Bennington Street—Continued

Page.	Letter.	Full Name.	Residence, Jan. 1, 1938.	Occupation.	Supposed Age.	Reported Residence, Jan. 1, 1937. Street and Number.
	s	*Mahoney Sadie—†	219	laundress	37	here
	T	McCarthy Frances G—†	219	housewife	56	"
	U	McCarthy Frederick T	219	fireman	62	"
	V	Regan Catherine—†	219	housekeeper	74	"
	W	Regan Helen—†	221	housewife	38	"
	X	Regan William J	221	laborer	40	
	Z	Regan Margaret—†	221	operator	34	
893						
	A	Regan Michael	221	manager	46	
	B	Souza George L	223	longshoreman	42	"
	C	Souza Mary A—†	223	housewife	41	"
	D	McCormick Annie—†	223	"	49	115 Princeton
	E	McCormick James	223	painter	24	115 "
	F	McCormick John	223	carpenter	63	115 "
	G	Smith Arthur J	223	student	22	here
	H	Smith Arthur L	223	salesman	40	"
	K	Smith Bernard F	223	laborer	20	"
	L	Smith Ernest F	223	clerk	37	
	M	Smith George	223	agent	76	
	N	Smith Mary A—†	223	stitcher	45	
	O	*Smith Robert J	223	clerk	42	
	P	Smith Ruth J—†	223	housewife	74	"
	R	Smith William G	223	laborer	25	
	S	*Guiffrida Mary—†	225	housewife	36	"
	T	Guiffrida Sebastian	225	laborer	37	
	U	*D'Amico Concetta—†	225	housewife	64	"
	V	*D'Amico Felix	225	carpenter	68	"
	W	*D'Amico Josephine—†	225	housewife	39	"
	X	D'Amico Peter	225	carpenter	43	"
	Y	D'Amico Rose—†	225	seamstress	24	"
	Z	Zona Joseph	225	laborer	42	
894						
	A	Zona Theresa—†	225	housewife	38	"
	D	Burditt Mary J—†	226	bookbinder	41	"
	B	Flot Rose—†	226	housekeeper	74	"
	C	Munn George M	226	laborer	35	"
	E	Carroll Albert	226	"	35	
	F	Carroll Edward	226	clerk	40	
	G	Carroll Sarah J—†	226	housewife	67	"
	H	Saulnier Hannah C—†	226	"	37	
	K	Saulnier Joseph N	226	fisherman	40	"

Page.	Letter.	Full Name.	Residence, Jan. 1, 1938.	Occupation.	Supposed Age.	Reported Residence, Jan. 1, 1937. Street and Number.

Bennington Street—Continued

Page.	Letter.	Full Name.	Residence, Jan. 1, 1938.	Occupation.	Supposed Age.	Reported Residence, Jan. 1, 1937. Street and Number.
	M	Barrett Emma—†	228	housewife	48	here
	N	Barrett Florence V—†	228	clerk	27	“
	O	Barrett Joseph	228	chauffeur	60	“
	P	Barrett Mary V—†	228	clerk	30	
	R	Grillo Domenic	229	laborer	23	
	S	Grillo Francesca—†	229	housewife	62	“
	T*	Grillo John	229	laborer	64	“
	U*	Balduzzi Julia—†	229	housekeeper	49	106 Benningt'n
	V	Addario Carmen	229	chauffeur	23	169 Chelsea
	W	Addario Mary—†	229	housewife	23	169 “
	Y	Shlager Anna—†	230	“	40	here
	Z	Shlager Charles	230	clerk	40	“
895						
	A	DiPompo Peter	231	laborer	23	
	B	Mastrocola Domenic	231	“	43	
	C*	Mastrocola Marie—†	231	housewife	33	“
	D*	Mastrocola Frank	231	operator	52	“
	E*	Mastrocola Rose—†	231	housewife	43	“
	F	Mangino Frank	231	operator	22	“
	G	Mangino John	231	laborer	20	
	H	Russell Harry F	232	foreman	48	
	K	Russell Mary A—†	232	housewife	47	“
	L	Silva Anastasia A—†	232	“	37	
	M	Silva Anthony A	232	cutter	45	
	N	McInnis Catherine—†	232	clerk	33	
	O	Delehanty Mary A—†	233	housekeeper	35	“
	P	Maguire John	233	cooper	71	“
	R	Driscoll Hannah—†	233	matron	59	
	S	Willis Frances—†	233	“	58	
	T	Rochford Johanna—†	233	housekeeper	49	“
	U*	Ford Bridget—†	234	housewife	30	“
	V	Ford Clarence E	234	operator	29	“
	W	Ford Patrick F	234	laborer	62	
	X	Walsh Doris W—†	234	teacher	32	
	Y	Walsh Stephen E	234	manager	30	“
	Z	Walsh Stephen P	234	retired	64	
896						
	A	Walsh Veronica M—†	234	nurse	26	
	B	Mulholland Peter J	235	laborer	56	
	C	Mulholland Sarah C—†	235	housewife	43	“
	D*	Shaw John C	235	carpenter	54	“

Page.	Letter.	Full Name.	Residence, Jan. 1, 1938.	Occupation.	Supposed Age.	Reported Residence, Jan. 1, 1937. Street and Number.

Bennington Street—Continued

Page.	Letter.	Full Name.	Residence, Jan. 1, 1938.	Occupation.	Supposed Age.	Reported Residence, Jan. 1, 1937. Street and Number.
	E	*Shaw Mary—†	235	housewife	55	here
	F	Shaw Mary C—†	235	operator	20	"
	G	Skane Gertrude—†	235	housewife	44	249 Benningt'n
	H	Skane John	235	clerk	22	249 "
	K	Skane Richard	235	welder	45	249 "
	L	Skane Richard T	235	clerk	23	249 "
	M	Goglia Alfred A	236	physician	29	here
	N	Gallagher Elizabeth—†	236	housekeeper	50	138 Lexington
	O	Gallagher Elizabeth—†	236	stenographer	22	138 "
	P	Goglia Ernest	236	student	24	here
	R	Goglia Lucy—†	236	housewife	52	"
	S	Goglia Nicholas	236	laborer	54	"
	T	*Lauricella Anthony	237	barber	59	
	U	*Lauricella Frances—†	237	housewife	48	"
	V	Lauricella Frances—†	237	operator	21	"
	W	*Lauricella Theresa—†	237	"	28	
	X	DeFelice Anthony	237	printer	26	"
	Y	DeFelice Domenic	237	barber	20	
	Z	*DeFelice Leo	237	"	67	
897						
	A	*DeFelice Lucy—†	237	housewife	53	"
	B	DeFelice Michael	237	barber	24	
	C	Riccoli Domenic	237	hairdresser	33	"
	D	*Riccoli Mary—†	237	housewife	30	"
	E	Rich Agnes M—†	239	collector	42	"
	F	Rich Charles J	239	machinist	29	"
	G	Rich Annie—†	239	housewife	67	"
	H	Rich Margaret—†	239	"	38	
	K	Rich Webster A	239	carpenter	35	"
	L	Rich William W	239	buyer	38	
	N	Gordon Lawrence	247	laborer	28	
	O	*Gordon Michael	247	"	64	
	M	Portrait Catherine—†	247	housewife	25	"
	P	Diaz Mary—†	247	"	24	272 Princeton
	R	Diaz Morin	247	operator	27	272 "
	S	*Passariello Concetta—†	247	housewife	43	here
	T	*Passariello Emilio	247	laborer	45	"
	U	*Organ Catherine—†	249	housekeeper	80	"
	V	Riley Fred	249	laborer	37	313 E Eagle
	W	Riley Marion—†	249	housewife	32	313 "
	X	Riley Celia—†	249	"	34	146 Lexington

Page.	Letter.	Full Name.	Residence, Jan. 1, 1938.	Occupation.	Supposed Age.	Reported Residence, Jan. 1, 1937. Street and Number.

Bennington Street—Continued

Page.	Letter.	Full Name.	Residence, Jan. 1, 1938.	Occupation.	Supposed Age.	Reported Residence, Jan. 1, 1937. Street and Number.
	Y	Riley Edward	249	chauffeur	39	146 Lexington
	Z	Marshall Anna V—†	251	housekeeper	48	35 Central sq
898						
	A	*Barletta Alice—†	251	housewife	52	here
	B	*Barletta John	251	laborer	62	"
	C	Barletta Lawrence	251	"	24	"
	D	Ford George E	251	longshoreman	29	"
	E	Ford Thetla C—†	251	housewife	26	"
	F	*Patterson John	253	laborer	78	
	G	*Scarpa Rosario	253	"	44	
	H	*Scarpa Rose—†	253	housewife	44	"
	K	Gravalese Josephine—†	253	stitcher	20	
	L	*Gravalese Rose—†	253	housewife	58	"
	M	Colangelo August	255	laborer	22	
	N	Colangelo Mary—†	255	housewife	23	"
	O	*Antignano Josephine—†	255	"	40	
	P	*Antignano Luigi	255	laborer	45	
	R	*DelVecchio Flora—†	255	housewife	29	"
	S	DelVecchio Joseph	255	laborer	40	
	T	*Viola Theresa—†	257	housekeeper	37	"
	U	*Silva Filomena—†	257	"	40	247 Benningt'n
	V	*Repucci Filomena—†	257	housewife	32	here
	W	*Repucci Pasquale	257	laborer	34	"
	Y	*Cohen Israel	259	collector	47	"
	Z	*Cohen Mollie—†	259	housewife	38	"

899 Bremen Street

Page.	Letter.	Full Name.	Residence, Jan. 1, 1938.	Occupation.	Supposed Age.	Reported Residence, Jan. 1, 1937. Street and Number.
	A	DeRosa Alphonsina—†	326	housewife	44	here
	B	DeRosa Antonio	326	chauffeur	24	"
	C	DeRosa Eleanor—†	326	operator	20	"
	D	DeRosa Pasquale	326	counterman	22	"
	E	DeRosa Raymond	326	laborer	54	"
	G	Gomes Anthony	326	shoemaker	21	61 W Eagle
	H	*Gomes Manuel	326	longshoreman	48	61 "
	K	*Gomes Mary—†	326	housewife	44	61 "
	L	Kelley John J	344	chauffeur	46	here
	M	Ranahan John J	344	longshoreman	29	"
	N	Ranahan Mary—†	344	housewife	48	"
	O	Wilson George F	344	engineer	47	"
	P	Wilson Mona E—†	344	at home	20	

Page.	Letter.	Full Name.	Residence, Jan. 1, 1938.	Occupation.	Supposed Age.	Reported Residence, Jan. 1, 1937. Street and Number.

Bremen Street—Continued

	R	Grace Arthur F	350	pharmacist	45	here
	S	Grace Edward L	350	jeweler	47	"
	T	Grace Elizabeth—†	350	housewife	71	"
	U	Grace Julia F—†	350	decorator	33	"
	V	Grace Walter G	350	surgeon	38	"
	W	Garisto Helen I—†	352	housewife	22	134 Marion
	X	Garisto Joseph F	352	clerk	27	134 "
	Y	Papa Mary R—†	352	housewife	22	307 Saratoga
	Z	Papa Patrick A	352	printer	25	307 "

900 Chelsea Street

900	E	Latorella Anthony	305	laborer	58	here
	F	Latorella Henry	305	"	23	"
	G	Latorella John	305	physician	25	"
	H	Latorella Marie—†	305	housewife	55	"
	K	Scenna Agata—†	305	"	37	
	L	Scenna Rocco	305	laborer	43	
	M	Cardullo Antonetta—†	307	at home	56	
	N	Genavitch John	307	laborer	21	
	O	Genavitch Mary—†	307	housewife	53	"
	P	Genavitch Stephen	307	laborer	53	
	R	*Speranza Josephine—†	307	housewife	40	"
	S	Speranza Santo	307	laborer	49	
	T	Brown Joseph F	309	clerk	32	
	U	Brown Louise F—†	309	housewife	32	"
	V	McGunigle Agnes J—†	309	at home	42	
	W	McGunigle Mary J—†	309	"	69	
	X	Redmond Francis	309	clerk	38	
	Y	Redmond Mary—†	309	housewife	38	"
	Z	*Drago Guy	311	laborer	24	
901	A	Drago Pauline—†	311	housewife	24	"
	B	*Bonafino Frank	311	laborer	67	
	C	*Bonafino Rose—†	311	housewife	65	"
	D	Simili Lorenzo	311	laborer	51	
	E	Simili Marie—†	311	packer	21	
	F	*Simili Mary—†	311	housewife	45	"
	G	Maffeo Christe	313	shoemaker	35	"
	H	Maffeo Helen—†	313	housewife	30	"
	K	Consolo Concetta—†	313	"	30	

Page.	Letter.	FULL NAME.	Residence, Jan. 1, 1938.	Occupation.	Supposed Age.	Reported Residence, Jan. 1, 1937. Street and Number.

Chelsea Street—Continued

Page.	Letter.	FULL NAME.	Residence, Jan. 1, 1938.	Occupation.	Supposed Age.	Reported Residence, Jan. 1, 1937. Street and Number.
	L	Consolo Felice	313	cutter	34	here
	M	Consolo Josephine—†	313	at home	64	"
	N	Simole Angelina—†	313	stitcher	22	"
	O	*Simole Anna—†	313	housewife	50	"
	P	*Simole Mario	313	laborer	53	
	S	Francis Joseph	317	painter	39	
	T	Francis Margaret—†	317	housewife	38	"
	V	Casaletto John	320	laborer	27	
	W	Casaletto Rose—†	320	housewife	25	"
	X	Nuttoli Harry	320	laborer	52	
	Y	Nuttoli Helen—†	320	at home	21	
	Z	Nuttoli Lucy—†	320	housewife	47	"
902						
	A	McGonagle Ethel—†	320	"	28	
	B	McGonagle Hilary J	320	policeman	30	"
	C	Currie Harriet—†	322	housewife	22	"
	D	Currie Lawrence	322	laborer	22	
	E	Mosca Barbara—†	322	housewife	22	"
	F	Mosca Thomas	322	laborer	28	
	G	Broomstein Abraham	322	"	21	
	H	*Broomstein Esther—†	322	housewife	55	"
	K	*Capelo Angelo	324	laborer	69	
	L	*Capelo Anna R—†	324	housewife	69	"
	M	Velona Anna—†	324	"	24	
	N	Velona Bruno	324	operator	25	"
	O	Velona Dominic	324	"	51	
	P	*Velona Mary—†	324	housewife	48	"
	R	Velona Nicholas	324	laborer	22	
	S	Caruso Alphonso	324	tailor	50	
	T	Caruso Dominick	324	cutter	24	
	U	Caruso Mary—†	324	housewife	46	"
	V	Caruso Rose—†	324	clerk	26	
	W	Vincent Bertha—†	326	housewife	43	"
	X	Vincent William	326	laborer	60	
	Y	Fagone Charles	326	barber	40	
	Z	Fagone Edith—†	326	housewife	40	"
903						
	A	Loduca Cosmo	326	printer	26	
	B	*Loduca Mary—†	326	housewife	70	"
	C	Loduca Mary—†	326	operator	28	"
	D	DiMarino Anthony	328	laborer	29	

Page	Letter	Full Name.	Residence, Jan. 1, 1938.	Occupation.	Supposed Age.	Reported Residence, Jan. 1, 1937. Street and Number.
		Chelsea Street—Continued				
	E	DiMarino Teresa—†	328	housewife	25	here
	F	Coriani Catherine—†	328	“	24	“
	G	Coriani Dimerio	328	operator	29	“
	H	*DiMarino Antonetta—†	328	housewife	61	“
	K	*DiMarino Constance—†	328	at home	65	“
	L	Fagone Joseph	328	laborer	24	“
	M	Fagone Mary—†	328	housewife	28	“
	N	Jones Lillian—†	330	operator	40	“
	O	Jones Mary M—†	330	housewife	72	“
	P	Fagone Georgia—†	330	“	27	“
	R	Fagone Louis	330	meter reader	30	“
	S	Fagone Agrapino—†	330	student	21	“
	T	Fagone Frank	330	laborer	61	“
	U	Fagone Marie—†	330	housewife	55	“
	W	Cioffi Joseph	331	storekeeper	49	“
	X	Cioffi Rose—†	331	housewife	47	“
	Y	Fox Emma—†	332	at home	71	“
	Z	Rose Manuel J	332	retired	63	“
904						
	A	Fielding Annie J—†	332	operator	49	“
	B	Fielding Esther T—†	332	“	41	“
	C	Sullivan Frances J—†	332	housewife	58	“
	D	Sullivan Mary J—†	332	clerk	20	“
	E	Sullivan William L	332	salesman	58	“
	F	Sacco Daniel	333	baker	38	“
	G	Sacco Viola—†	333	housewife	29	“
	H	Mascoile Mary—†	333	at home	60	“
	K	Marmand Marie—†	334	“	37	“
	L	Barron Bessie—†	334	saleswoman	28	“
	M	Barron Fannie—†	334	housewife	55	“
	N	Barron Jacob	334	manager	35	“
	O	Kandler Harriett—†	334	stenographer	24	“
	P	Kandler Lottie—†	334	at home	48	“
	R	Maggi Helen—†	334	“	26	“
	S	*Balino Anna—†	335	“	65	“
	T	Riley Gertrude M—†	337	finisher	43	“
	V	White James T	339	retired	81	“
	W	Collins Arthur H	339	chauffeur	28	“
	X	Collins Margaret H—†	339	housewife	60	“
	Y	Collins William C	339	policeman	37	“
	Z	Coughlan Catherine F—†	339	housewife	68	345 Chelsea

Page.	Letter.	Full Name.	Residence, Jan. 1, 1938.	Occupation.	Supposed Age.	Reported Residence, Jan. 1, 1937. Street and Number
905		**Chelsea Street**—Continued				
	A	Coughlan Matthew J	339	laborer	42	345 Chelsea
	B	LaBlanc Albert S	341	cook	52	here
	C	LcBlanc Maude—†	341	housewife	48	"
	D	Duann Arthur	341	painter	29	"
	E	Duann Marie—†	341	housewife	24	"
	F	Cioffi Orlando	342	manager	22	"
	G	Cioffi Teresa—†	342	housewife	22	"
	H	Torelli Concetta—†	342	"	44	
	K	Torelli Jeanne—†	342	operator	25	
	L	Torelli Linda—†	342	"	21	
	M	Torelli Phyllis—†	342	packer	24	
	N	Torelli Vincent	342	laborer	50	
	O	Addario Josephine—†	342	housewife	25	"
	P	Addario Santino	342	printer	28	
	R	Dalton Elmer D	344	cutter	25	
	S	Dalton Florence—†	344	housewife	21	"
	T	Davella Albert	344	clerk	21	
	U	Davella Joseph	344	mechanic	22	"
	V	*Davella Margaret—†	344	housewife	52	"
	W	Davella Pasquale	344	laborer	53	
	X	Sacco Marie—†	344	housewife	25	"
	Y	Sacco Peter	344	laborer	30	
	Z	Reidy Nora M—†	346	at home	64	
906						
	A	Moran Mary E—†	346	maid	29	
	B	Reidy Margaret—†	346	housewife	33	"
	C	Reidy Patrick J	346	porter	35	
	D	Doyle Mary L—†	346	housewife	30	"
	E	Doyle Paul F	346	operator	34	
	G	*Parsons Robert	352	laborer	48	
	H	*Parsons Violet—†	352	housewife	46	"
	K	*DiNatale Catherine—†	352	at home	28	204 Benningt'n
	L	*Vacca Nicolina—†	352	housewife	31	here
	M	Vacca Pasquale	352	laborer	40	"
	N	Sanson Jeremiah	354	salesman	29	"
	O	Sanson Josephine—†	354	housewife	27	"
	P	Ruggiero Antonio	354	finisher	49	
	R	*Ruggiero Rose—†	354	housewife	47	"
	S	Salerno Americo	354	laborer	24	15 Neptune rd
	T	Salerno Mary—†	354	housewife	22	15 "

Page.	Letter.	FULL NAME.	Residence, Jan. 1, 1938.	Occupation.	Supposed Age.	Reported Residence, Jan. 1, 1937. Street and Number.

Chelsea Street—Continued

	U	*Grasso James	356	laborer	63	here
	V	*Grasso Marion A—†	356	housewife	62	"
	W	*Terranova Michelina—†	356	at home	43	"
	X	Barletta Alphonso	356	clerk	25	"
	Y	*Barletta Gerardo	356	laborer	56	"
	Z	Agreste Gaetano	358	machinist	22	246 Princeton
907						
	A	*Agreste Louis	358	retired	64	246 "
	B	Agreste Mary—†	358	operator	27	246 "
	C	*Theotakake Pauline—†	358	teacher	42	here

Lexington Street

	F	*Hearn Helen—†	195	housewife	30	279 Princeton
	G	*Hearn John J	195	fisherman	33	279 "
	H	*Barbera Catherine—†	195	housewife	45	here
	K	*Barbera John	195	butcher	51	"
	L	*Chin Oland	197	laundryman	46	"
	M	Frongillo Andrew G	197	operator	30	
	N	Frongillo Jennie—†	197	housewife	28	"
	O	Merola Guido	197	operator	47	"
	P	*Merola Michelina—†	197	housewife	44	"
	R	*Raimondi Joseph	199	retired	81	
	S	*Raimondi Mary—†	199	housewife	35	"
	T	Raimondi Tancredi	199	laborer	38	
	U	Ricciardelli Angelo	199	cutter	23	
	V	Ricciardelli Antonio	199	laborer	47	
	W	Ricciardelli Mary—†	199	housewife	43	"
	X	Giorgio Domnick	199	cutter	25	"
	Y	Giorgio Marie—†	199	housewife	23	"
	Z	Powers Mary E—†	201	"	60	
908						
	A	Murphy Annie—†	203	"	83	
	B	Murphy Elizabeth J—†	203	teacher	53	
	C	Pinder Leon	203	operator	48	"
	D	Pinder Madalena—†	203	housewife	54	"
	E	*Tobin Catherine—†	205	"	27	
	F	Tobin Thomas	205	clerk	30	
	G	*Fonte Joseph	207	operator	37	
	H	*Fonte Vincenza—†	207	housewife	29	"
	K	*Giangreco Diega—†	207	"	49	

Page.	Letter.	Full Name.	Residence, Jan. 1, 1938.	Occupation.	Supposed Age.	Reported Residence, Jan. 1, 1937. Street and Number.

Lexington Street—Continued

	L	*Giangreco Josephine—†	207	stitcher	24	here
	M	*Giangreco Santina—†	207	"	22	"
	N	Capezuto Charles	207	tailor	38	"
	O	Capezuto Helen—†	207	housewife	33	"
	P	Capezuto Maria—†	207	"	64	
	R	Capezuto Nicholas	207	cleaner	65	
	U	*Surette Celina—†	209	housewife	42	"
	V	Surette William F	209	fisherman	43	"
	S	Giacchetto Ignazio	209	baker	36	
	T	Giacchetto Thomasina—†	209	housewife	27	"
	W	Pagliarulo Antonetta—†	211	"	24	335 Paris
	X	Pagliarulo Euplio	211	laborer	62	here
	Y	Pagliarulo Saverio	211	chauffeur	24	335 Paris
	Z	French Annie—†	213	housewife	76	here
909						
	A	French John J	213	retired	71	
	B	French William J	213	nurse	23	
	C	Vino Edward	213	cook	21	
	E	Camuso Nina—†	213	bookkeeper	20	"
	D	Camuso Olga—†	213	housewife	53	"
	F	Camuso Pasquale	213	tailor	53	
	G	Camuso Romeo	213	machinist	23	"
	H	Barravecchio Angelo	213A	operator	31	"
	K	Barravecchio Jennie—†	213A	housewife	71	"
	L	Barravecchio Joseph	213A	retired	78	
	M	Barravecchio Vito	213A	operator	34	
	N	Mercandande, Michael	215	foreman	37	
	O	Mercandande Theresa—†	215	housewife	38	"
	P	Mercandande Anthony	215	operator	56	
	R	Mercandande Antonetta–†	215	housewife	55	"
	S	Courtoglous Annie—†	215	"	41	
	T	Courtoglous Theodore	215	cook	46	
	U	*D'Agostino Grace—†	217	housewife	58	"
	V	D'Agostino Pasquale	217	operator	29	"
	W	D'Agostino Philomena–†	217	"	27	"
	X	D'Agostino Rosario	217	laborer	25	
	Y	D'Agostino Salvatore	217	retired	69	"
	Z	D'Agostino Josephine—†	217	housewife	31	75 Neptune rd
910						
	A	D'Agostino Salvatore, jr	217	plumber	31	75 "
	B	Bonasera Joseph	217	tailor	43	here

Page.	Letter.	Full Name.	Residence, Jan. 1, 1938.	Occupation.	Supposed Age.	Reported Residence, Jan. 1, 1937. Street and Number.

Lexington Street—Continued

	C	Bonasera Theresa—†	217	housewife	33	here
	D	Trainor Anna G—†	219	"	34	"
	E	Trainor James	219	longshoreman	38	"
	F	Cotter Frederick E	219	salesman	60	"
	G	Cotter Frederick J	219	pedler	23	
	H	Cotter James F	219	student	21	
	K	Cotter Mary J—†	219	housewife	60	"
	L	Cotter Thomas B	219	pedler	27	
	M	Malone Mary C—†	221	housewife	65	"
	N	Malone William	221	oiler	60	
	O	Malone William	221	chauffeur	24	"
	P	Brown Lawrence	221	laundryman	30	"
	R	*Doucette Simon	221	retired	84	
	S	Geddry Frank	221	carpenter	65	"
	T	*Geddry Sarah—†	221	housewife	55	"
	U	Preshong Elizabeth A—†	221	folder	22	314 Meridian
	V	Preshong Zetha—†	221	housewife	49	314 "
	W	Thorne Pauline—†	223	"	25	here
	X	Thorne Richard	223	butcher	30	"
	Y	Callahan Catherine F—†	223	houseworker	46	"
	Z	Callahan Isabel M—†	223	stenographer	44	"
911						
	A	Sullivan Olive—†	223	"	31	
	B	Letteriello Joseph	225	actor	52	
	C	Letteriello Louis	225	mechanic	28	"
	D	Letteriello Nora—†	225	knitter	26	
	E	Duchi Anita—†	225	houseworker	22	"
	F	*Duchi Julia—†	225	housewife	48	"
	G	Duchi Santina—†	225	bookkeeper	23	"
	H	Duchi Ugo	225	operator	56	"
	K	*Ferrari Fidalina—†	225	housewife	70	"
	L	Milder Bertha—†	225	"	42	
	M	Milder Edward	225	mechanic	21	"
	N	Milder Leo	225	hostler	43	"
	O	DeGregorio Mario	227	carpenter	30	186 Benningt'n
	P	DeGregorio Olga—†	227	housewife	30	186 "
	R	*Romano Angelina—†	235	"	54	here
	S	Romano John	235	laborer	60	"
	T	Lane John	235	carpenter	50	Chelsea
	U	*Saulnier Alfonze	235	"	48	here
	V	*Saulnier Leonie—†	235	housewife	43	"

Page.	Letter.	Full Name.	Residence, Jan. 1, 1938.	Occupation.	Supposed Age.	Reported Residence, Jan. 1, 1937. Street and Number.

Lexington Street—Continued

	W	MacFee Thomas	237	retired	70	156 Benningt'n
	X	Roache Henry	237	salesman	48	234 Lexington
	Y	Roache Sarah—†	237	housewife	45	234 "
	Z	Dalton Helen—†	237	"	22	68 Center
912						
	A	Dalton John W	237	clerk	23	68 "
	B	*Powers Nicolas	237	fisherman	44	here
	C	*Powers Stella—†	237	housewife	40	"
	D	Perry Frank	239	painter	37	"
	E	Perry Helen A—†	239	housewife	29	"
	F	Butare Angelo	239	operator	27	
	G	*Butare John	239	finisher	57	
	H	Butare Joseph	239	operator	22	"
	K	Butare Louis	239	chauffeur	25	"
	L	*Butare Mary—†	239	housewife	48	"
	M	Butare Mary—†	239	"	22	
	N	Fallon Julia M—†	241	"	45	
	O	Fallon Mildred M—†	241	houseworker	22	"
	P	Beresford Ellen—†	241	housewife	52	"
	R	Beresford Joseph B	241	carpenter	59	"
	S	Beresford Joseph B, jr	241	student	22	Oregon
	T	Beresford Vincent	241	laborer	24	here
	U	Henebury John	241	fishcutter	25	"
	V	Roland Charles	241	watchman	41	"
	W	Roland Grace—†	241	housewife	38	"
	X	Ricciardelli Anthony	243	tailor	38	9 Breed
	Y	*Ricciardelli Jennie—†	243	housewife	31	9 "
913						
	B	Tennerini Celia—†	243½	stitcher	22	344 Saratoga
	C	*Tennerini Joseph	243½	laborer	51	344 "
	D	*Tennerini Maria—†	243½	housewife	47	344 "
	E	Tennerini Sabina—†	243½	operator	24	344 "
	F	Tennerini Theresa—†	243½	assembler	21	344 "
	G	Tennerini Viola—†	243½	houseworker	22	344 "
	H	*Cestone Pasquale	245	operator	47	here
	K	*Cestone Pauline—†	245	housewife	46	"
	M	Falzarano Jennie—†	245	"	21	Lynn
	N	Falzarano Lawrence	245	laborer	23	"
	O	Daddio Gennaro	247	barber	46	here
	P	Daddio Rose—†	247	housewife	31	"
	R	DeNicola Anna—†	247	"	36	"

Page.	Letter.	Full Name.	Residence, Jan. 1, 1938.	Occupation.	Supposed Age.	Reported Residence, Jan. 1, 1937. Street and Number.
		Lexington Street—Continued				
	s	*DeNicola Louis	247	barber	45	here
	T	*Daddio Josephine—†	247	housewife	31	Italy
	U	Daddio Louis	247	laborer	43	"
	V	Pomelli Emily—†	249	saleswoman	26	451 Saratoga
	W	*Pomelli John	249	laborer	57	451 "
	X	*Sano Josephine—†	249	housewife	43	here
	Y	Sano Rocco	249	shoemaker	45	"
	Z	Toland Mary D—†	249	housewife	59	164 Lexington
914						
	A	*Gifun Charles	251	tailor	44	Revere
	B	*Gifun Grace—†	251	housewife	40	"
	C	Toppi Andriana—†	251	"	25	236 Lexington
	D	Toppi Joseph	251	merchant	36	236 "
	E	*Mucci Celia—†	253	operator	27	here
	F	*Mucci Frank	253	retired	61	"
	G	*Mucci Lena—†	253	clerk	30	"
	H	Centracchio Celia—†	253	housewife	33	"
	K	Centracchio John	253	laborer	34	
	L	*Centracchio Angelina—†	253	housewife	48	"
	M	Centracchio Dominick	253	retired	73	
	N	Christian Charles	263	operator	36	
	O	Christian Mary—†	263	housewife	31	"
	P	Newman Benjamin L	263	stitcher	46	
	R	Newman Ida—†	263	housewife	42	"
	S	*Zaff Bessie—†	263	"	56	
	T	*Zaff Harry	263	storekeeper	58	"
	U	Shannon Jeanette—†	265	housewife	30	"
	V	Shannon Joseph J	265	operator	36	44 W Newton
	W	Pengue Anthony	265	salesman	26	here
	X	*Pengue John	265	carpenter	62	"
	Y	*Pengue Mary—†	265	housewife	58	"
	Z	*Varitimo Angela—†	265	"	45	
915						
	A	*Varitimo Anna—†	265	stitcher	27	
	B	*Varitimo George	265	counterman	22	"
	D	Gates Gertrude—†	267	saleswoman	26	"
	E	Mercandante Lucy—†	267	housewife	30	"
	F	Galluccio Amelia—†	269	"	36	
	G	Galluccio Egidio	269	laborer	42	
	H	Colantuoni Ida—†	269	housewife	29	"
	K	Colantuoni Samuel	269	operator	34	"

Page.	Letter.	FULL NAME.	Residence, Jan. 1, 1938.	Occupation.	Supposed Age.	Reported Residence, Jan. 1, 1937. Street and Number.

Lexington Street—Continued

Page.	Letter.	FULL NAME.	Residence, Jan. 1, 1938.	Occupation.	Supposed Age.	Reported Residence, Jan. 1, 1937. Street and Number.
	L	*Galligan Victoria—†	269	housewife	42	here
	M	Galligan William	269	counterman	50	"
	N	*Willis John	269	salesman	27	"
	P	DeMarco Philip	271	butcher	47	
	R	DeMarco Rose—†	271	housewife	37	"
	S	Peretti Louis	271	laborer	30	283 Lexington
	T	Peretti Mary—†	271	housewife	29	here
	U	Amico Pasquale	273	laborer	45	"
	V	Nunes Anna—†	273	housewife	44	"
	W	Nunes Joseph	273	laborer	44	
	X	Nunes Margaret—†	273	stitcher	22	"
	Y	McDonald Catherine M–†	273	housewife	26	68 Trenton
	Z	McDonald Walter F	273	fisherman	28	68 "
916						
	A	*Payne Frances—†	273	housewife	28	here
	B	*Payne Thomas L	273	fisherman	26	"
	C	Wood Charles J	275	laborer	46	"
	D	Wood Ethel M—†	275	housewife	35	"
	E	Nickerson Elmer	275	chauffeur	37	"
	F	*Nickerson John	275	retired	67	
	G	Nickerson Mary A—†	275	housewife	34	"
	H	Silva Americo	275	shipper	30	
	K	Silva Mary—†	275	housewife	26	"
	L	DeNeo Anthony	279	laborer	38	
	M	DeNeo Margaret—†	279	housewife	29	"
	N	*Bordieri Angelina—†	279	"	43	
	O	Bordieri Josephine—†	279	seamstress	21	"
	P	Bordieri Paul	279	laborer	47	
	R	Busheme Frank	279	"	21	
	S	Busheme Paul	279	"	48	
	T	*Mazzarella Frank	281	"	54	
	U	*Mazzarella Josephine—†	281	housewife	50	"
	V	Pellegrino Frances—†	281	"	32	
	W	Pellegrino Joseph	281	laborer	33	
	X	Bardiani Conchetta—†	281	housewife	48	"
	Y	Bardiani Sebastiano	281	laborer	49	"
	Z	DeStefano Margaret—†	283	housewife	23	Medford
917						
	A	DeStefano Peter	283	laborer	25	"
	B	Iengo Anna—†	283	housewife	39	here
	C	*Iengo Joseph	283	barber	39	"

Page.	Letter.	Full Name.	Residence, Jan. 1, 1938.	Occupation.	Supposed Age.	Reported Residence, Jan. 1, 1937. Street and Number.

Lexington Street—Continued

	D	Danilchuk Ignatz	283	laborer	48	here
	E	*Danilchuk Laura—†	283	housewife	37	"
	F	Rossi Andrew	285	chauffeur	24	Winthrop
	G	Rossi Doris—†	285	housewife	20	"
	H	Kayander Hilda M—†	285	"	45	here
	K	Kayander John D	285	machinist	45	"
	L	Kayander Thomas	285	"	23	"
	M	Bonner Loretta—†	285	housewife	33	"
	N	Bonner William	285	printer	38	
	O	Machado John F	287	laborer	29	
	P	Machado Marie S—†	287	housewife	56	"
	R	Machado Zeferino	287	retired	76	
	S	Nuccitelli Anthony	289	laborer	50	
	T	*Nuccitelli Mary—†	289	housewife	41	"
	U	Hoey Albert	291	laborer	26	256 Paris
	V	Hoey Evelyn—†	291	housewife	28	256 "
	X	O'Keefe Anna E—†	293	"	42	here
	Y	O'Keefe David	293	laborer	44	"
	Z	McLaren Ellen—†	293	housewife	70	"
918						
	A	McLaren John G	293	machinist	70	"
	B	Downey Catherine E—†	293	housewife	68	"
	C	Downey John F	293	retired	72	"
	D	Fiore Anthony	295	laborer	24	
	E	Fiore Irene—†	295	housewife	23	"
	F	Matt Lucy—†	295	"	29	
	G	Matt Sullivan	295	mechanic	34	"
	H	Gallo Eugene	295	cutter	42	
	K	*Gallo Rose—†	295	housewife	44	"
	L	Inacio Flora—†	297	"	26	
	M	*Inacio John	297	operator	36	"
	N	*Freitas Augustine	297	longshoreman	41	"
	O	*Freitas Mary—†	297	housewife	36	"
	P	Polito Genaro	297	laborer	24	"
	R	Polito Joseph	297	"	49	
	S	*Polito Philomena—†	297	housewife	48	"
	T	Mills Irving J	299	decorator	36	"
	U	Mills Mary L—†	299	housewife	31	"
	W	*Fahey Margaret—†	299	"	57	"
	X	Fahey Philip	299	longshoreman	68	"
	Y	Mietzner Olga—†	301	housewife	31	Everett

Page.	Letter.	Full Name.	Residence, Jan. 1, 1938.	Occupation.	Supposed Age.	Reported Residence, Jan. 1, 1937. Street and Number.

Lexington Street—Continued

Page.	Letter.	Full Name.	Residence, Jan. 1, 1938.	Occupation.	Supposed Age.	Reported Residence, Jan. 1, 1937. Street and Number.
	Z	Mietzner William	301	electrician	35	Everett
919						
	A	Palmunen Marie—†	301	housewife	66	here
	B	Palmunen Otto L	301	laborer	57	"
	C	Coady James T	301	"	53	"
	D	Coady Mary L—†	301	housewife	59	"
	E	Keough Charles F	303	serviceman	42	"
	F	Keough Marie C—†	303	housewife	39	"
	H	*Romano Edmund	307	chauffeur	23	163 Condor
	K	Romano Etta—†	307	housewife	23	163 "
	L	*Melvin David	307	fisherman	36	here
	M	*Melvin Mary—†	307	housewife	33	"
	N	*Walsh John	307	fisherman	32	"
	O	*Wall Elizabeth A—†	307	housewife	41	25 Brooks
	P	*Maher Agnes—†	309	"	28	here
	R	Maher Daniel	309	fisherman	32	"
	S	*Sampson William	309	laborer	30	"
	T	Kelsen Annie—†	309	housewife	53	"
	U	Kelsen Margaret—†	309	houseworker	23	"
	V	Kelsen Virginia—†	309	nurse	21	
	W	Cunha Manuel E	309	operator	22	"
	X	Cunha Wanda—†	309	housewife	25	"
	Y	Britt Mary E—†	311	"	42	
	Z	Britt Michael	311	teamster	44	"
920						
	A	Sleeper Alice—†	311	housewife	48	"
	B	Sleeper Fred W	311	salesman	52	"
	C	Capprine Pasquale J	311	welder	28	
	D	Capprine Rose—†	311	housewife	23	"
	E	Capo Anthony	313	mechanic	27	284 Princeton
	F	Capo Louise—†	313	housewife	24	103 Orleans
	G	Matt Caroline—†	313	"	24	93 Neptune rd
	H	Matt Michael	313	assembler	26	93 "
	K	*Scarpa Incenza—†	313	housewife	33	here
	L	Scarpa Ralph	313	laborer	46	"

Prescott Street

Page.	Letter.	Full Name.	Residence, Jan. 1, 1938.	Occupation.	Supposed Age.	Reported Residence, Jan. 1, 1937. Street and Number.
	M	*Caruso Carmen	31	laborer	49	here
	N	Caruso Ignatius	31	cutter	24	"
	O	*Caruso Lillian—†	31	housewife	42	"

Page.	Letter.	Full Name.	Residence, Jan. 1, 1938.	Occupation.	Supposed Age.	Reported Residence Jan. 1, 1937. Street and Number.

Prescott Street—Continued

	P	Venezia Albert	31	cutter	23	43 Orleans
	R	Venezia Rose—†	31	housewife	23	here
	S	Diaz Frank R	33	chauffeur	45	"
	T	Diaz Irene—†	33	housewife	45	"
	U	*Diaz Mary J—†	33	"	74	
	V	Meads Julia—†	33	"	35	
	W	Meads Manuel	33	fireman	45	"
	X	Silva Alfred F	35	operator	24	403 Saratoga
	Y	Silva Alice A—†	35	clerk	27	403 "
	Z	Silva Mary C—†	35	housewife	55	403 "
921						
	A	Kerrigan Louis A	35	laborer	47	295 Havre
	B	Kerrigan Mary A—†	35	housewife	43	295 "
	C	Boudreau Agnes—†	37	"	34	146 Brooks
	D	Boudreau William	37	laborer	38	146 "
	E	McArdle Andrew P	37	inspector	40	here
	F	McArdle Charles J	37	laborer	24	"
	G	McArdle Irene G—†	37	housewife	38	"
	H	McArdle Mary E—†	37	operator	20	"
	K	Farley Richard	47	laborer	53	
	L	Fielding Joseph F	47	printer	48	
	M	Gannon James	47	laborer	65	"
	N	Hamilton John	47	"	58	"
	O	Morse Joseph S	47	"	62	
	P	Oliver George	47		69	
	R	Wilson Archibald J	47	"	48	
	S	Wilson Elizabeth—†	47	housewife	56	"
	T	Murray Anna C—†	49	"	45	
	U	Murray Arthur C	49	laborer	49	"
	V	*Manzelli Mary—†	51	housewife	47	137 Brooks
	W	Manzelli Vincenzo	51	laborer	52	137 "
	X	Stoumbelis Helen—†	77	housewife	42	here
	Y	Stoumbelis Nicholas E	77	storekeeper	34	"
	Z	Stoumbelis Peter	77	"	53	"
922						
	B	*Mustos Angelo	79	photographer	40	"
	C	Carroll Agnes M—†	79	housekeeper	62	"
	D	Mitchell Anna E—†	79	"	69	"
	G	DeFoe Irene—†	93	operator	27	
	H	DeFoe Joseph	93	baker	26	
	K	Garuti Agnes—†	93	saleswoman	29	"

Page.	Letter.	Full Name.	Residence, Jan. 1, 1938.	Occupation.	Supposed Age.	Reported Residence, Jan. 1, 1937. Street and Number.

Prescott Street—Continued

Page.	Letter.	Full Name.	Residence, Jan. 1, 1938.	Occupation.	Supposed Age.	Reported Residence, Jan. 1, 1937. Street and Number.
	L	Lamborghini Mary—†	93	housekeeper	49	here
	M	*Buono Elvira—†	95	housewife	52	"
	N	*Buono Gabriel	95	operator	26	"
	O	Buono Mildred—†	95	housewife	25	"
	P	Buono Pasquale	95	operator	29	"
	R	*Lanney Josephine—†	97	housewife	42	"
	S	Lanney Nicholas	97	dealer	52	
	T	Parcella Antonio	97	barber	44	
	U	Parcella Frank	97	operator	22	"
	V	*Fucci Josephine—†	97	housewife	46	"
	W	Fucci Michael	97	laborer	48	

Princeton Place

Page.	Letter.	Full Name.	Residence, Jan. 1, 1938.	Occupation.	Supposed Age.	Reported Residence, Jan. 1, 1937. Street and Number.
	X	Gugliucciello Anna—†	1	clerk	23	here
	Y	Gugliucciello Jessie—†	1	"	27	"
	Z	Gugliucciello Josephine—†	1	at home	25	"
923						
	A	*Gugliucciello Sabato	1	bootblack	69	"

Princeton Street

Page.	Letter.	Full Name.	Residence, Jan. 1, 1938.	Occupation.	Supposed Age.	Reported Residence, Jan. 1, 1937. Street and Number.
	B	Stacks Anne—†	200	housewife	58	here
	C	Stacks Kova	200	storkeeper	72	"
	D	Balzatti Charles	200	clerk	25	"
	E	Balzatti Nancy—†	200	housewife	23	"
	F	Cody Anne—†	200	"	62	
	G	Cody Frank	200	clerk	23	
	H	*Cotreau Adrian S	201	fisherman	45	"
	K	*Cotreau Bernard J	201	cutter	38	
	L	Cotreau George S	201	fisherman	42	"
	M	*Cotreau Herman R	201	cutter	33	
	N	*Cotreau Mark A	201	fisherman	47	"
	O	*Cotreau Mary—†	201	housewife	69	"
	P	*Wastafero Angelo	201	laborer	60	"
	R	Wastafero Angelo	201	barber	24	
	S	Wastafero Giacomo	201	shoemaker	26	"
	T	*Wastafero Josephine—†	201	housewife	55	"
	U	Wastafero Rose—†	201	stitcher	21	
	V	Wastafero Sadie—†	201	at home	20	
	W	Polcari Anthony	201	operator	38	

Page.	Letter.	Full Name.	Residence, Jan. 1, 1938.	Occupation.	Supposed Age.	Reported Residence, Jan. 1, 1937. Street and Number.

Princeton Street—Continued

	X	Polcari Carmen	201	cook	24	here
	Y	*Polcari Gerard	201	retired	74	"
	Z	Polcari Louis	201	clerk	32	"
924						
	A	*Polcari Marie—†	201	housewife	62	"
	B	Polcari Theresa—†	201	operator	25	"
	C	*Vella Josephine—†	202	housewife	24	3 Appian pl
	D	Vella Rosario	202	operator	28	3 "
	E	*Ruggiero Carlo	202	laborer	36	here
	F	*Ruggiero Raphaella—†	202	housewife	30	"
	G	Principato Henrietta—†	203	"	43	"
	H	Principato Joseph	203	plumber	40	"
	K	Duffy Elizabeth A—†	203	housewife	35	"
	L	Duffy John J	203	operator	37	"
	M	Hayes Eugene	203	clerk	46	
	N	Sullivan Mary E—†	203	corsetiere	39	"
	O	Duffy Catherine—†	203	housewife	66	"
	P	Duffy Thomas J	203	laborer	66	
	R	Cleary Dorothy K—†	204	operator	26	"
	S	Cleary Sarah—†	204	housewife	56	"
	T	*DeCologero Jennie—†	204	"	51	
	U	DeCologero Salvatore	204	musician	20	"
	V	Curran Beatrice A—†	204	housewife	34	"
	W	Curran James J	204	coppersmith	38	"
	X	*D'Entremont Caroline–†	205	housewife	43	"
	Y	D'Entremont Joseph	205	cutter	46	
	Z	DiBartolomea Antoinette—†	205	typist	20	
925						
	A	*DiBartolomea Grace—†	205	housewife	40	"
	B	DiBartolomea Nicholas	205	laborer	43	
	C	Caci Benjamin	205	"	54	
	D	Caci Joseph	205	upholsterer	24	"
	E	*Caci Louise—†	205	housewife	53	"
	F	Caci Salvatore	205	upholsterer	30	"
	G	Marliave Mary A—†	206	housekeeper	79	"
	H	Johnson Elizabeth A—†	206	housewife	37	"
	K	Johnson Herbert W	206	laborer	42	
	L	*Borick Frances—†	206	domestic	45	"
	M	Lang Edward	206	laborer	55	
	N	*Inserra Angelina—†	207	housewife	50	"
	O	Inserra Jennie—†	207	at home	20	"

Page.	Letter.	Full Name.	Residence, Jan. 1, 1938.	Occupation.	Supposed Age.	Reported Residence, Jan. 1, 1937. Street and Number.

Princeton Street—Continued

Page.	Letter.	Full Name.	Residence, Jan. 1, 1938.	Occupation.	Supposed Age.	Reported Residence, Jan. 1, 1937. Street and Number.
	P	Inserra Luigi	207	laborer	55	here
	R	Porreca Anna—†	207	housewife	43	270 Princeton
	S	Porreca Guido	207	carpenter	21	270 "
	T	Porreca John	207	barber	46	270 "
	U	Porreca Louis	207	draftsman	23	270 "
	V	Luongo Anthony	207	constable	41	here
	W	*Luongo Nellie—†	207	housewife	36	"
	Z	*Caulfield Elizabeth—†	208	housekeeper	75	"
	X	Curcio Catherine—†	208	operator	36	"
	Y	Curcio Pasquale	208	barber	38	
926						
	A	Connelly Emilie—†	208	housewife	36	"
	B	Connelly Martin	208	laborer	40	
	C	Connelly Mary A—†	208	housewife	50	"
	D	*Simons Louis	208	tailor	59	
	E	*Simons Pearl—†	208	housewife	50	"
	F	*Ribaudo Maria—†	211	housekeeper	38	"
	G	Trunfio Etta—†	211	stenographer	21	"
	H	Trunfio Filomena—†	211	housewife	40	"
	K	Trunfio Paul	211	laborer	46	
	L	*Scopa Carmella—†	211	housewife	61	"
	M	Scopa Elvira—†	211	operator	21	"
	N	*Scopa Paul	211	laborer	57	
	O	Matthews Catherine—†	212	housewife	39	"
	P	Matthews Wallace J	212	mechanic	38	"
	R	Carter George	212	laborer	31	
	S	Carter Loretta—†	212	saleswoman	24	"
	T	Reagan Daniel	213	laborer	22	
	U	Reagan Ellen—†	213	housewife	25	"
	V	Reagan James J	213	longshoreman	81	"
	W	Reagan Margaret—†	213	housewife	50	"
	X	*Marraffino Filomena—†	213	"	79	
	Y	*Marraffino Vincent	213	retired	76	
	Z	*Racca Rose—†	213	housewife	39	"
927						
	A	*Racca Salvatore	213	operator	41	
	B	Bartholomew Anthony W	213	assembler	31	"
	C	Bartholomew Carmella-†	213	housewife	27	"
	E	Graziano Anne—†	214	clerk	26	
	F	Graziano Gerardo	214	laborer	25	
	G	*Graziano Josephina—†	214	housewife	50	"

Page.	Letter.	Full Name.	Residence, Jan. 1, 1938.	Occupation.	Supposed Age.	Reported Residence, Jan. 1, 1937. Street and Number.

Princeton Street—Continued

	H	*Graziano Otino	214	painter	50	here
	K	DiAngelis Mary—†	214	housewife	43	"
	L	DiAngelis Nicholas	214	laborer	45	"
	M	Paldo Caroline—†	215	shipper	20	
	N	Paldo Domenic	215	laborer	50	
	O	Paldo Florence—†	215	housewife	50	"
	P	Paldo Liberato	215	shipper	22	
	R	*Radino Carlo	215	laborer	52	
	S	*Radino Mary—†	215	housewife	49	"
	T	*Saporito Concetta—†	215	"	46	
	U	Saporito Joseph	215	operator	21	"
	V	Saporito Rocco	215	laborer	51	
	W	Lemo Mary—†	216	housekeeper	48	"
	X	Cipriani Isabel—†	216	operator	20	"
	Y	Cipriani Mary—†	216	housewife	21	"
	Z	*Cipriani Tullio	216	storekeeper	36	"
928						
	A	Vincentino Adelino	216	laborer	50	
	B	Napier Gladys—†	217	housewife	28	"
	C	Napier John	217	B F D	35	
	D	Cassetta Palma—†	217	housewife	38	"
	E	Cassetta Salvatore	217	barber	40	229 Marion
	F	Ellis Abraham	217	salesman	24	here
	G	Ellis Alexander	217	tailor	56	"
	H	Ellis Sarah—†	217	housewife	49	"
	K	Ellis Sydney	217	physician	29	"
	L	*Lynch David	218	painter	38	
	M	*Lynch Marjorie—†	218	housewife	29	"
	N	Hatch Jeanette—†	218	"	23	
	O	Hatch Linwood	218	operator	26	"
	P	Biancucci Antonio	218	carpenter	25	"
	R	Biancucci Pauline—†	218	housewife	20	"
	S	Hancock George E	221	chauffeur	31	176 Brooks
	T	Hancock Helen—†	221	housewife	30	176 "
	U	Zeringis Alice—†	221	operator	27	176 "
	V	*DeBattista Joseph	222	laborer	42	here
	W	*DeBattista Margaret—†	222	housewife	40	"
	X	*Mosca Carmella—†	222	"	40	"
	Y	*Mosca Peter	222	foreman	42	
	Z	*Viscione Mary—†	222	housekeeper	83	"

Page.	Letter.	Full Name.	Residence, Jan. 1, 1938.	Occupation.	Supposed Age.	Reported Residence, Jan. 1, 1937. Street and Number.
929		**Princeton Street**—Continued				
	A	Babin Nellie—†	223	housewife	36	here
	B	Babin Simon M	223	laborer	38	"
	C	Larizza Lillian—†	rear 223	housewife	31	"
	D	Larizza Rudolph	" 223	barber	44	
	E	*Bellabona Clementina—†	2d " 223	housewife	50	"
	F	*Bellabona Genoraso	2d " 223	carpenter	48	"
	G	Bellabona Joseph	2d " 223	"	26	
	H	Bellabona Leo	2d " 223	operator	23	"
	K	Intoppa Antonetta—†	224	stitcher	23	
	L	*Intoppa Ernest	224	laborer	51	
	M	*Intoppa Leonora—†	224	housewife	43	"
	N	Intoppa Louis	224	cutter	21	
	O	Smith Josephine—†	226	housewife	24	"
	P	Smith Wilfred	226	assembler	29	"
	R	Scarfo Adolfo	226	pedler	21	62 Princeton
	S	Scarfo Angelina—†	226	housewife	53	62 "
	T	Scarfo Joseph	226	laborer	23	62 "
	U	Cobb Charles	226	"	30	119 Benningt'n
	V	Cobb Mary—†	226	housewife	24	119 "
	W	Lessa Adeline—†	227	"	56	here
	X	Lessa Carlo	227	operator	56	"
	Y	Lessa Clara—†	227	typist	23	"
	Z	Lessa Josephine—†	227	operator	21	"
930						
	A	Lessa Mary—†	227	"	25	
	B	Lessa Michael	227	laborer	20	
	C	Lessa Vera—†	227	stenographer	24	"
	D	Giodarno Angelo	227	operator	27	"
	E	Giodarno Josephine—†	227	housewife	27	"
	F	Merchant Edward	227	laborer	72	
	G	Merchant Mary—†	227	housewife	64	"
	H	Schraffa Florence—†	228	"	30	
	K	Schraffa Thomas	228	laborer	30	
	L	*Bonanno Carmella—†	228	housewife	43	"
	M	Bonanno Salvatore	228	operator	54	
	N	*Geraci Santa—†	228	housekeeper	78	"
	O	Smeldone Emelio	228	carpenter	32	"
	P	Smeldone Florence—†	228	housewife	30	"
	R	Marinelli Frank	229	laborer	42	

Page.	Letter.	Full Name.	Residence, Jan. 1, 1938.	Occupation.	Supposed Age.	Reported Residence, Jan. 1, 1937. Street and Number.

Princeton Street—Continued

Page.	Letter.	Full Name.	Residence, Jan. 1, 1938.	Occupation.	Supposed Age.	Reported Residence, Jan. 1, 1937. Street and Number.
	S	Marinelli Mary—†	229	housewife	38	here
	T	Faretra Carmen	229	laborer	21	"
	U	Faretra Joseph	229	"	54	"
	V	*Faretra Mary—†	229	housewife	46	"
	W	Faretra Thomas	229	laborer	24	
	X	DeGregorio George	229	butcher	25	
	Y	DeGregorio Jennie—†	229	housewife	24	"
	Z	Kinnear Esther M—†	231	"	63	
931						
	A	Kinnear George E	231	laborer	62	
	B	Kinnear Ralph E	231	welder	30	
	C	Rogers John T	233	barber	66	
	D	Rogers Joseph	233	laborer	22	
	E	Rogers Mary—†	233	housewife	62	"
	F	Miles Louise—†	234	dressmaker	27	"
	G	Miles Michael J	234	attorney	38	"
	H	Miles William	234	painter	40	
	K	Doherty James	234	laborer	60	
	L	*Natola Antonetta—†	236	housewife	26	"
	M	*Natola Frank	236	operator	30	
	N	*Barranco Frank	236	laborer	32	
	O	*Barranco Mary—†	236	housewife	28	"
	P	Coluccino John	236	salesman	20	"
	R	*Coluccino Michael	236	machinist	46	"
	S	*Coluccino Rose—†	236	housewife	46	"
	T	*DiTomasso Joseph	237	operator	30	"
	U	DiTomasso Rose—†	237	housewife	30	"
	V	Sarno Angelina—†	237	"	46	
	W	Sarno Carmen	237	laborer	24	"
	X	Sarno Mary—†	237	seamstress	21	"
	Y	Sarno Onofrio	237	laborer	52	
	Z	Maccette Edward	238	printer	28	
932						
	A	Maccette Sadie—†	238	housewife	24	"
	B	Gianino Lena—†	238	"	23	
	C	Gianino Ralph	238	cutter	26	
	E	Geraci Augustino	rear 238	painter	47	
	F	Geraci Jennie—†	" 238	housewife	44	"
	G	Geraci Santa M—†	" 238	operator	21	
	H	DeCrescenzo Augusta-†	" 238	housewife	28	"
	K	*DeCrescenzo Sirio	" 238	laborer	33	

Page.	Letter.	Full Name.	Residence, Jan. 1, 1938.	Occupation.	Supposed Age.	Reported Residence, Jan. 1, 1937. Street and Number.
		Princeton Street—Continued				
	L	Anderson Alice C—†	239	housewife	45	207 Saratoga
	M	Anderson Oscar C	239	carpenter	45	207 "
	N	Mackell Catherine—†	239	housewife	24	207 "
	O	Mackell Edward	239	laborer	23	207 '
	P	O'Leary Michael	239	longshoreman	68	207 "
	R	Bossi Domenic	240	laborer	23	here
	S	Bossi Guido	240	salesman	21	"
	T	*Bossi Joseph	240	laborer	60	"
	U	*Bossi Pauline—†	240	housewife	56	"
	V	Mercadante Ethel C—†	240	"	23	220 E Eagle
	W	Mercadante Pasquale J	240	operator	25	215 Lexington
	Y	Casillo Albert	241	painter	32	here
	Z	Casillo Esther—†	241	housewife	30	"
933						
	A	Fiore Filomena—†	241	"	49	571 Benningt'n
	B	Fiore Luigi	241	laundryman	20	571 "
	C	Fiore Ralph	241	"	49	571 "
	D	*Sargeant Catherine—†	242	housewife	25	335 Paris
	E	*Sargeant Joseph	242	fisherman	34	335 "
	F	*Jesus Alfred S	242	operator	39	247 Havre
	G	*Jesus Maria—†	242	housewife	36	247 "
	H	*Muse John J	243	cutter	30	here
	K	*Muse Loretta—†	243	housewife	27	"
	L	Roach Herbert	243	laborer	22	"
	M	Roach Lawrence	243	pressman	30	"
	N	Roach Mary—†	243	operator	28	
	O	Roach Sarah—†	243	housewife	50	"
	P	Shannon Edward P	244	electrician	39	"
	R	Shannon Frances M—†	244	operator	29	"
	S	Shannon Frederick L	244	mechanic	32	"
	T	Shannon Mary—†	244	housewife	70	"
	U	Stevenson Anne—†	244	housekeeper	67	"
	W	*Fidalgo John	246	baker	32	132 Sumner
	X	*Fidalgo Regina—†	246	housewife	23	132 "
	Y	*DiSimone Domenica—†	246	"	59	here
	Z	*DiSimone Frank	246	storekeeper	64	"
934						
	A	O'Donnell James H	247	cook	49	
	B	O'Donnell Mary E—†	247	housewife	37	"
	C	*Doucette Margaret—†	247	"	42	161 Saratoga
	D	*Doucette Philip	247	cutter	45	161 "

Page.	Letter.	Full Name.	Residence, Jan. 1, 1938.	Occupation.	Supposed Age.	Reported Residence, Jan. 1, 1937. Street and Number.

Princeton Street—Continued

	E	Burnham George	247	letter carrier	48	here
	F	Burnham Grace—†	247	housewife	45	"
	G	Hatch Henry	247	laborer	27	"
	H	Despony Paul	248	clergyman	62	"
	K	Kelley Henry L	249	B F D	40	
	L	Kelley Marie M—†	249	housewife	31	"
	M	Pumfret Alice L—†	249	teacher	30	
	N	Pumfret Michael J	249	retired	74	
	O	McInnis George F	250	laborer	36	
	P	McInnis Gertrude—†	250	housewife	34	"
	R	Greene Catherine M—†	250	"	32	"
	S	Greene Walter J	250	salesman	30	306 Meridian
	T	Penny Elizabeth J—†	250	housewife	60	here
	U	Penny John C	250	laborer	29	"
	V	Penny William L	250	carpenter	60	"
	W	Peterson Mary—†	250	housewife	43	"
	X	Peterson Sigurd	250	engineer	49	
	Y	Owen Aloyse—†	251	teacher	50	
	Z	Owen Cecelia—†	251	housewife	80	"
935						
	A	Owen John F	251	retired	80	"
	B	Anderson Mary F—†	252	at home	41	"
	C	Stevenson Anne J—†	252	housewife	65	"
	D	Stevenson Henry	252	clerk	22	
	E	Neal Charles W	252	engineer	66	
	F	Neal Claire—†	252	bookkeeper	22	"
	H	Neal John	252	cutter	25	"
	G	Neal Mary—†	252	housewife	55	"
	K	Beaudro Daniel	252	carpenter	45	"
	L	Beaudro Emma—†	252	clerk	22	
	M	Beaudro Mabel—†	252	housewife	42	"
	N	Villani Constantino	253	laborer	50	
	O	*Corcoran Thomas	253	"	65	
	P	*Griffin Richard	253	"	75	
	R	Quinn Bridget—†	253	housewife	59	"
	S	Quinn Hugh	253	watchman	38	"
	T	Malgioglio Joseph	255	laborer	33	
	U	Malgioglio Theresa—†	255	housewife	27	"
	V	DeFranza Joseph	255	operator	21	"
	W	DeFranza Leonardo A	255	laborer	57	
	X	DeFranza Saveria—†	255	housewife	54	"

Page.	Letter.	Full Name.	Residence, Jan. 1, 1938.	Occupation.	Supposed Age.	Reported Residence, Jan. 1, 1937. Street and Number.

Princeton Street—Continued

	Y	Barnes John	255	clerk	24	here
	Z	Barnes Margaret—†	255	housewife	24	"
936						
	B	Dunphy Cecelia E—†	262	stenographer	30	"
	C	Dunphy James A	262	accountant	33	"
	D	Dunphy John L	262	clerk	25	
	E	Dunphy Sarah F—†	262	housewife	56	"
	F	Gordon Helen—†	262	waitress	23	
	G	Palange Antonio	262	cook	53	
	H	Palange Josephina—†	262	housewife	51	"
	K	Mazzone Carmen	262	salesman	37	"
	L	Mazzone Mary—†	262	housewife	33	"
	M	Ledoux Angela—†	266	"	24	"
	N	Ledoux Rosario	266	operator	31	"
	O	*Vena Antonia—†	266	housewife	55	"
	P	*Vena Pellegrino	266	laborer	60	
	R	Kelly John	266	"	43	
	S	Kelly John L	266	attendant	20	"
	T	Kelly Margaret—†	266	housewife	43	"
	U	O'Brien John J	268	laborer	23	33 Neptune rd
	V	O'Brien Margaret—†	268	housekeeper	48	33 "
	W	*Petralia Frances—†	268	housewife	44	here
	X	*Petralia Sebastanio	268	laborer	64	"
	Y	Livingstone Duncan	268	watchman	52	"
	Z	Livingstone Mary—†	268	housewife	51	"
937						
	A	Livingstone Mary A—†	268	clerk	25	
	B	Tuscano Angelo	270	operator	58	
	C	Tuscano Dominic	270	laborer	21	
	D	Ferrera Angelina—†	270	stitcher	22	
	E	Ferrara Angelo	270	laborer	43	
	F	*Ferrera Mary—†	270	housewife	46	"
	G	Palazzolo Connie—†	270	operator	21	101 Leverett
	H	Palazzolo Jacquelina—†	270	decorator	25	101 "
	K	*Palazzolo Jennie—†	270	housewife	47	101 "
	L	Palazzolo Joseph	270	laborer	27	101 '
	M	Palazzolo Paul	270	"	52	101 "
	N	Searle Bertha M—†	272	housewife	43	218 Princeton
	O	Searle Edwin R	272	clerk	43	218 "
	P	Colicchio Agnes—†	272	housewife	47	here
	R	Colicchio Joseph	272	barber	22	"

Page.	Letter.	Full Name.	Residence, Jan. 1, 1938.	Occupation.	Supposed Age.	Reported Residence, Jan. 1, 1937. Street and Number.

Princeton Street—Continued

	S	Colicchio Nicholas	272	barber	59	here
	T	*DiFuria Angelina—†	272	housewife	50	"
	U	DiFuria Carmelo	272	laborer	53	"
	X	*DeRibas Fred	274	"	71	"
	V	Ganno Concetta—†	274	housewife	38	"
	W	Ganno Salvatore	274	chauffeur	40	"
	Y	D'Avolio Frank	274	musician	34	"
	Z	D'Alvolio Lucy—†	274	housewife	33	"
938						
	A	Marcella Arthur	274	laborer	27	
	B	Marcella Helen—†	274	operator	37	
	C	*Marcella Nicolina—†	274	housewife	58	"
	D	Saggese Adelina—†	276	"	56	"
	E	Saggese Giuseppe	276	laborer	60	74 Trenton
	F	Saggese Pasquale	276	"	20	here
	G	Chalmers Fred W	276	fireman	39	"
	H	Chalmers Mary A—†	276	housewife	38	"
	K	*Coscia Alphonso	276	operator	40	241 Princeton
	L	*Coscia Carmella—†	276	housewife	34	241 "
	M	Stenberg Anna—†	278	housekeeper	70	here
	N	Anderson Edwin L	rear 278	machinist	24	180 Leyden
	O	Anderson Ruth M—†	" 278	housewife	24	180 "
	P	Travaglini Albert	284	laborer	33	here
	R	Travaglini Margaret—†	284	housewife	28	"
	S	*Capo Angelina—†	284	"	57	"
	T	Capo John	284	operator	55	
	U	Messenger Mary—†	286	housekeeper	75	"
	X	Barry William B	288	retired	78	"
	V	*Silva Caroline—†	286	housewife	54	"
	W	*Silva Hypolite	286	operator	51	"
	Y	Cooper Arthur	288	seaman	33	
	Z	Cooper Cecelia—†	288	housewife	25	"
939						
	A	Cooper Mary J—†	288		73	
	B	Genzale Ann—†	288	"	25	
	C	Genzale Anthony	288	laborer	24	
	D	Alexander Ellen—†	292	housewife	38	"
	E	Alexander Ernest L	292	B F D	37	
	F	Donnelly Frances—†	292	at home	74	
	G	Carrigan Marie—†	294	stitcher	40	
	H	Dean Gertrude M—†	294	housewife	36	"

Page.	Letter.	FULL NAME.	Residence, Jan. 1, 1938.	Occupation.	Supposed Age.	Reported Residence, Jan. 1, 1937. Street and Number.

Princeton Street—Continued

	K	Dean Ralph M	294	B F D	42	here
	L	Keenan William E	294	"	45	"
	M	Alexander Victor	296	laborer	34	"
	N	Alexander Winifred—†	296	housewife	32	"
	O	Smith Irene—†	298	"	22	
	P	Smith Marie—†	298	at home	59	
	R	*Rossi Louis B	300	laborer	53	
	S	Rossi Louis B, jr	300	timekeeper	25	"
	T	*Rossi Rose—†	300	housewife	52	"
	U	Sullivan Clara R—†	310	"	23	
	V	Sullivan Lawrence J	310	serviceman	21	"
	W	Lavender Doris—†	310	stenographer	23	"
	X	Lavender Marie—†	310	storekeeper	65	"
	Y	Orlando Frank	310	contractor	48	43 Sea View av
	Z	O'Neil Delia—†	310	housewife	54	here
940						
	A	O'Neil John J	310	retired	63	
	C	Moynihan Francis F	312	salesman	30	"
	D	Moynihan Mary L—†	312	housewife	29	"
	E	Fabeno Carmella—†	312	operator	26	
	F	Fabeno Joseph	312	"	23	
	G	Fabeno Rose—†	312	housewife	45	"
	H	*Vitale Dorothy—†	312	"	70	
	K	Vitale Mary—†	312	"	35	
	L	Vitale Michael	312	laborer	34	"
	M	Dillon Ruth—†	312	housekeeper	27	216 E Eagle
	N	Albanese Grace—†	314	housewife	24	here
	O	Albanese Philip	314	shipper	25	"
	P	Bolino Nicholas	314	cook	44	"
	R	Bolino Rose—†	314	housewife	36	"
	S	*Albanese Domenic	314	retired	60	
	T	*Albanese Madeline—†	314	housewife	50	"
	U	Albanese Raymond	314	operator	21	
	V	Clark Edward P	316	painter	35	
	W	Clark Lena—†	316	housewife	35	"
	X	Gannon Charles J	316	laborer	57	407 Saratoga
	Y	Gannon Sadie—†	316	housewife	47	407 "
	Z	*Perry Guillermina—†	316	"	51	here
941						
	A	*Perry Joseph	316	longshoreman	58	"
	B	Fahey Gladys—†	318	housewife	30	"

Page.	Letter.	Full Name.	Residence, Jan. 1, 1938.	Occupation.	Supposed Age.	Reported Residence, Jan. 1, 1937. Street and Number.

Princeton Street—Continued

	C	Fahey James	318	bartender	30	here
	D	*Siraco Domenic	318	laborer	64	"
	E	Siraco Frank	318	operator	36	"
	F	*Siraco Mary—†	318	housewife	63	"
	G	Tasso Mary—†	318	"	32	
	H	Tasso Samuel	318	operator	41	"
	K	Baldinale Angelina—†	320	housekeeper	48	"
	L	Siraco Joseph	320	tinsmith	34	"
	M	Siraco Mary—†	320	housewife	29	"
	N	DeMayo Carmella—†	320	"	39	
	O	DeMayo Chester	320	barber	39	
	P	Campbell Florence—†	322	housewife	58	"
	R	Campbell Jerome	322	clerk	52	California
	S	Casucci Augusto	322	laborer	28	here
	T	Casucci Louise—†	322	housewife	22	"
	V	Wainwright Elizabeth—†	324	housekeeper	65	306 Princeton
	W	*Thompson Cora—†	324	"	25	106 Saratoga

Putnam Street

	Y	*Amirault Mary—†	106	housewife	28	here
	Z	*Amirault Roy	106	cutter	34	"
942						
	A	*LeBlanc Josephine—†	106	operator	22	317 Saratoga
	B	Coluntino Arthur	106	decorator	23	here
	C	*Coluntino Leo	106	operator	58	"
	D	*Coluntino Mary—†	106	housewife	50	"
	E	Cerrato Carmella—†	108	"	29	
	F	Cerrato Louis	108	painter	34	
	G	Cerrata Maria—†	108	at home	26	
	H	Frisoli Domenico	108	salesman	51	"
	K	Frisoli Gilda—†	108	housewife	40	"
	L	Benvissuto John	108	barber	44	131 Eutaw
	M	Benvissuto Mary—†	108	housewife	37	131 "
	N	*Hollander Emil	110	laborer	59	here
	O	*Hollander Hilma—†	110	housewife	58	"
	P	Hollander John E	110	machinist	32	"
	R	Amundsen Andrew	112	foreman	52	"
	S	Eggertsen Grimur	112	seaman	33	
	T	Jensen Annie M—†	112	housewife	51	"
	U	Jensen Anton	112	carpenter	58	"

Page.	Letter.	Full Name.	Residence, Jan. 1, 1938.	Occupation.	Supposed Age.	Reported Residence, Jan. 1, 1937. Street and Number.

Putnam Street—Continued

	V	Jensen Helen A—†	112	operator	22	here
	W	Adagnia Rosario	126	"	40	"
	X	Amoroso Anna—†	126	clerk	21	"
	Y	Amoroso Joseph	126	laborer	46	
	Z	*Amoroso Rose—†	126	operator	42	"
943						
	A	*Blunda Frances P—†	126	housewife	63	"
	B	Blunda Francesco	126	laborer	64	
	C	Blunda Josephine—†	126	clerk	24	
	D	Blunda Mary—†	126	"	26	
	E	Matthews Joseph J	126	laborer	32	
	F	Matthews Mary G—†	126	housewife	30	"
	G	Ruotolo Louis	128	plumber	28	
	H	Ruotolo Rose—†	128	housewife	25	"
	K	Ruotolo Frank	128	laborer	55	
	L	Ruotolo Mary—†	128	housewife	57	"
	M	Ruotolo Nancy—†	128	stenographer	20	"
	N	Ruotolo Gerardo	128	electrician	31	"
	O	Ruotolo Helen—†	128	housewife	30	"
	P	Cotreau Caleb L	130	coppersmith	42	"
	R	*Cotreau Lennie—†	130	housewife	40	"
	S	DiPesa Josephine—†	130	"	39	"
	T	DiPesa Michael	130	painter	40	
	U	Nolan Catherine M—†	130	clerk	24	
	V	Nolan James R	130	"	48	
	W	Nolan Mary M—†	130	housewife	43	"
	Y	Benvissuto Alfred	140	chauffeur	31	"
	Z	Benvissuto Serafina—†	140	housewife	27	"
944						
	A	Silano Grace—†	140	packer	27	
	B	Silano Ralph	140	laborer	56	
	C	*Silano Rose—†	140	housewife	54	"
	D	Tranquillino Luca	140	blacksmith	38	"
	E	*Staffier Christina—†	141	at home	80	
	F	Staffier Edith—†	141	housewife	46	"
	G	Staffier Frank	141	manager	45	"
	H	Staffier Anthony	141	barber	43	
	K	Staffier Christina—†	141	at home	20	
	L	Staffier Mary—†	141	housewife	43	"
	M	Staffier Thomasina—†	141	at home	21	
	N	Antonelli Joseph	142	pedler	40	

Page.	Letter.	FULL NAME.	Residence, Jan. 1, 1938.	Occupation.	Supposed Age.	Reported Residence, Jan. 1, 1937. Street and Number.

Putnam Street—Continued

	o	*Ardita Antonio	142	laborer	64	here
	p	*Ardita Mary—†	142	housewife	58	"
	r	Ardita Michael	142	clerk	20	"
	s	*Ciampa Nicholas	142	laborer	68	
	t	Santoro Alesio	143	painter	22	
	u	*Santoro Frances M—†	143	housewife	46	"
	v	Nazzaro Caroline—†	143	"	26	
	w	Nazzaro Joseph	143	laborer	27	
	x	*Calvano Antonetta—†	143	housewife	45	"
	y	Calvano John	143	laborer	49	"
	z	Lamb Hannah—†	144	housekeeper	67	678 Benningt'n
945						
	a	Moseley Lotta—†	144	housewife	33	174 Brooks
	d	Flammia Angelina—†	145	"	32	here
	e	Flammia Joseph	145	laborer	35	"
	f	Lotisi Christina—†	145	housewife	34	"
	g	Lotisi Joseph	145	laborer	39	
	k	Vena Ella—†	146	housewife	32	"
	l	Vena John	146	mechanic	33	"
	m	Silva Arthur	146	operator	24	
	n	Silva Madeline—†	146	packer	22	
	o	Silva Manuel	146	longshoreman	52	"
	p	Silva Sarah—†	146	housewife	50	"
	r	Puopolo John	147	laborer	28	
	s	Puopolo Nicholas	147	retired	72	
	t	Puopolo Rocco	147	manager	40	"
	u	Puopolo Jennie—†	147	housewife	26	"
	v	Puopolo Ralph A	147	laborer	29	
	w	McCarthy Jane—†	147	housewife	43	"
	x	Tapper Frieda—†	148	clerk	30	
	y	Tapper William H	148	storekeeper	38	"
	z	Antonucci Rose—†	148	housewife	49	"
946						
	a	Antonucci Salvatore	148	laborer	49	
	b	Johannessen Christian	148	machinist	45	"
	c	Johannessen Elsie—†	148	at home	20	
	d	Johannessen Henrietta–†	148	housewife	41	"
	e	Schraffa Angelo	149	butcher	23	
	f	Schraffa Antonio	149	tailor	62	
	g	Schraffa David F	149	laborer	27	
	h	Schraffa Francis P	149	physician	25	"

Page.	Letter.	Full Name.	Residence, Jan. 1, 1938.	Occupation.	Supposed Age.	Reported Residence, Jan. 1, 1937. Street and Number.

Putnam Street—Continued

	K	Schraffa Louis E	149	physician	34	here
	L	Schraffa Louise M—†	149	clerk	21	"
	M	Schraffa Rocco J	149	tailor	29	"
	N	Grasso Angelo	149	machinist	37	"
	O	Grasso Josephina—†	149	housewife	36	"
	P	*Lucca Anthony	150	barber	44	
	R	*Lucca Frances—†	150	housewife	46	"
	S	Nosworthy Donald	150	laborer	32	319 Benningt'n
	T	Nosworthy Isabelle—†	150	housewife	25	319 "
	V	*Goveia Mary—†	151	housekeeper	32	here
	W	D'Laria Giacomo	151	laborer	58	"
	X	D'Laria James V	151	clerk	20	"
	Y	*D'Laria Jennie—†	151	housewife	52	"
	Z	*Carvotta Cosimo	151	laborer	44	10 Havre ct
947						
	A	*Carvotta Rose—†	151	housewife	37	10 "
	B	Cimmino Mary A—†	152	"	25	here
	E	Lasalle Elvira—†	152	seamstress	29	140 Paris
	C	Smaldoni John C	152	cutter	30	here
	D	Smaldoni Mildred—†	152	housewife	29	"
	F	Pezzella Ann—†	152	at home	22	"
	G	Pezzella Carmen	152	foreman	52	
	H	Pezzella Violet—†	152	operator	20	
	K	*Abate John	153	storekeeper	54	"
	L	Abate Josephine—†	153	stenographer	25	"
	M	Abate Rose—†	153	secretary	26	"
	N	*Abate Rosina—†	153	housewife	52	"
	O	*Ferrari Barbara—†	153	"	44	216 Princeton
	P	*Ferrari Mario	153	cutter	53	216 "
	R	Mascatelli Michael	153	operator	47	216 "
	S	DeDeo Anthony A	154	lithographer	39	here
	T	DeDeo Jeannette—†	154	housewife	36	"
	U	Montecalvo Marciano	154	laborer	29	52 London
	V	Montecalvo Selma—†	154	housewife	26	52 "
	W	*Cerose Carmillo	154	laborer	53	here
	X	*Cerose Josephine—†	154	housewife	44	"
	Y	DeRosa Joseph	156	laborer	22	"
	Z	DeRosa Mary—†	156	housewife	21	"
948						
	A	Flaherty Agnes—†	156	saleswoman	23	"
	B	Flaherty Nellie—†	156	housewife	53	"

Page.	Letter.	Full Name.	Residence, Jan. 1, 1938.	Occupation.	Supposed Age.	Reported Residence, Jan. 1, 1937. Street and Number.

Putnam Street—Continued

	c	Salvo Domenic	156	laborer	43	here
	d	*Salvo Rose—†	156	housewife	40	"
	e	Hancock James	158	carpenter	40	"
	f	Hancock Victoria—†	158	operator	37	"
	g	Iodice Nicholas	158	"	31	
	h	Iodice Rose—†	158	"	27	
	k	*Vitello Concetta—†	158	housewife	53	"
	l	Vitello Pasquale	158	laborer	54	"
	n	Viola Frank	160	"	42	84 Havre
	o	*Viola Mary—†	160	housewife	44	84 "
	p	*Grimaldi Filomena—†	160	at home	75	216 Paris
	r	*Masci Angelina—†	160	housewife	38	216 "
	s	*Masci Antonio	160	operator	42	216 "
	t	*Grande Christopher	162	cutter	24	here
	u	Grande Emily—†	162	housewife	22	"
	v	Corvino Giacomo	162	laborer	25	"
	w	Corvino Josephine—†	162	housewife	21	"
	x	Pontrandolfo Frank	162	barber	50	
	y	*Pontrandolfo Rose—†	162	housewife	50	"
	z	*Maniaci Salvatore	164	baker	24	
949						
	a	Maniaci Tina—†	164	housewife	22	"
	b	*Clemente Egidio	164	salesman	28	"
	c	Clemente Ida—†	164	housewife	25	"
	d	*Doucette Elizabeth—†	164	"	59	
	e	*Doucette Joseph	164	fisherman	60	"
	g	Cappannelli Lucy—†	166	housewife	27	"
	h	Cappannelli Nicholas	166	laborer	26	
	k	*Cornetta Angelo	166	retired	67	
	l	Cornetta John	166	welder	36	
	m	*Cornetta Rose—†	166	housewife	71	"
	n	*Cornetta Rose—†	166	"	31	"
	o	Whitehead Bella—†	168	laundress	66	1829 Wash'n
	p	Flammia Anthony	168	laborer	27	here
	r	Flammia Helen—†	168	housewife	34	"
	s	*Doble Angelo	168	cook	37	229 Benningt'n
	t	Doble Antonette—†	168	housewife	28	229 "
	u	*Carallo Angelina—†	170	operator	50	here
	v	Carallo Luciano	170	retired	61	"
	w	*Pulso Gaetano	170	operator	40	"
	x	*Pulso Mary—†	170	"	32	

Page.	Letter.	Full Name.	Residence, Jan. 1, 1938.	Occupation.	Supposed Age.	Reported Residence, Jan. 1, 1937. Street and Number.

Putnam Street—Continued

	Y	Cappola Filomena—†	170	housewife	29	here
	Z	Cappola Peter	170	operator	31	"
950						
	B	Brass Bette—†	172	saleswoman	30	"
	C	Brass Minnie—†	172	"	31	
	D	Miller David	172	grocer	57	
	E	Miller Sarah—†	172	housewife	57	"
	F	Brass Barnett	172	clerk	45	
	G	*Brass Rose—†	172	housewife	80	"
	H	Eddels Jeannette—†	172	"	40	
	M	Tango Maria F—†	198	housekeeper	47	"
	N	*Balliro Joseph	198	finisher	53	"
	O	*Balliro Mary—†	198	housewife	46	"

Saratoga Street

	P	McLaughlin Mary A—†	251	housekeeper	62	25 Chelsea
	R	D'India Ida—†	251	housewife	25	here
	S	D'India Louis	251	operator	27	"
	T	*Mammucci Samuel	251	retired	64	"
	U	*Rizzo Elizabeth M—†	251	housewife	37	"
	V	*Rizzo Martin	251	laborer	40	
	W	*Aquino Annie—†	253	housewife	37	"
	X	*Aquino Arcorino	253	laborer	37	
	Y	Ciampi Charles	253	"	21	
	Z	Ciampi Mildred—†	253	housewife	22	"
951						
	A	*Manganella Louise—†	253	housekeeper	60	"
	B	*Ciampi Filomena—†	253	housewife	40	"
	C	*Ciampi Louis	253	operator	50	"
	D	Longo John R	255	mechanic	23	278 Chelsea
	E	Longo Mary M—†	255	housewife	20	278 "
	F	Nobile G Rudolph	255	attorney	33	526 Newbury
	G	Nobile Raffaela—†	255	housewife	29	526 "
	H	Guardabasso Antonio	255	artist	27	here
	K	Guardabasso Frank	255	laborer	25	"
	L	Guardabasso Giovanni	255	"	53	"
	M	*Guardabasso Pasqualina—†	255	housewife	55	"
	N	DeCrescenzo Mary—†	257	"	23	
	O	DeCrescenzo Michael A	257	janitor	26	
	P	Bossi Genevieve—†	257	at home	21	

Page.	Letter.	Full Name.	Residence, Jan. 1, 1938.	Occupation.	Supposed Age.	Reported Residence, Jan. 1, 1937. Street and Number.

Saratoga Street—Continued

	R	Robinson Helen G—†	257	housewife	45	here
	S	Robinson Ralph M	257	laborer	25	"
	T	Robinson William H	257	foreman	49	"
	U	Indingaro Arthur D	259	laborer	27	169 Benningt'n
	V	Indingaro Caroline—†	259	housewife	25	169 "
	W	DiNatale Emma—†	259	"	28	305 Saratoga
	X	DiNatale Michael	259	laborer	27	305 "
952						
	A	Sambrone Mary—†	301A	housewife	31	here
	B	Sambrone Roy	301A	shoemaker	43	"
	C	Gambino John	301A	barber	44	"
	D	Gambino Nellie—†	301A	housewife	43	"
	E	Crescenzo Albino—†	302	"	33	
	F	Crescenzo James	302	dealer	37	
	G	DiBenedetto Josephine—†	302	housewife	31	"
	H	DiBenedetto Rombolo	302	laborer	33	
	L	Clark Julia A—†	303	housekeeper	38	"
	K	Crumley Grace E—†	303	"	64	"
	M	*Zarrella Angie—†	303	housewife	68	240 Princeton
	N	Zarrella Marie—†	303	clerk	31	240 "
	O	*Asgrizzi Josephine—†	303	housewife	51	here
	P	Asgrizzi Salvatore	303	contractor	57	"
	R	Pastore Anthony	304	laborer	24	"
	S	Pastore Norma E—†	304	housewife	23	"
	T	Zambuto Antonio	304	operator	21	"
	U	*Zambuto Carmella—†	304	housewife	40	"
	V	Zambuto Joseph	304	operator	46	
	W	Gullifa Grace—†	304	housewife	34	"
	X	Gullifa Ludo	304	chauffeur	35	"
	Y	*DiNatale Marie—†	305	housewife	60	"
	Z	*DiNatale Salvatore	305	retired	62	"
953						
	A	*Puzzo Rocca—†	305	housewife	35	"
	B	Puzzo Vito	305	laborer	44	
	C	*Bareletto Agnes—†	305	housewife	41	"
	D	Brouillard Gertrude A—†	306	"	23	
	E	*Brouillard Paul	306	mechanic	27	"
	F	*Lombardo Florence—†	306	housewife	39	"
	G	Lombardo Florence—†	306	tailoress	20	
	H	Lombardo Philip	306	laborer	53	
	K	Pastone Guy	306	painter	24	

Page.	Letter.	Full Name.	Residence, Jan. 1, 1938.	Occupation.	Supposed Age.	Reported Residence, Jan. 1, 1937. Street and Number.

Saratoga Street—Continued

Page.	Letter.	Full Name.	Residence, Jan. 1, 1938.	Occupation.	Supposed Age.	Reported Residence, Jan. 1, 1937. Street and Number.
	L	Pastone Stephanie—†	306	housewife	23	here
	M	Costa Carlos P	307	retired	67	194 Falcon
	N	Costa Gaeda G—†	307	waitress	33	194 "
	O	Coelho John P	307	operator	25	155 Saratoga
	P	Coelho Lucille—†	307	housewife	22	268 Princeton
	R	*DeAngelis Carmella—†	307	"	58	here
	S	DeAngelis Carmen	307	laborer	20	"
	T	DeAngelis Crescenzo	307	bootblack	24	"
	U	DeAngelis Mary—†	307	at home	23	
	V	*DeAngelis Masimino	307	retired	57	..
	W	DeAngelis Michael	307	laborer	27	
	X	*Tucci Maria—†	307	at home	104	'
	Y	*Staffieri Francisco	308	retired	76	
	Z	*Staffieri Phyllis—†	308	housewife	72	"
954						
	A	Nazzaro Clarence W	308	student	22	
	B	Nazzaro Joseph	308	shoemaker	43	"
	C	Nazzaro Mary E—†	308	housewife	43	"
	D	Gregory Samuel	308	salesman	38	"
	E	*Staffieri Agnes E—†	308	housewife	48	"
	F	Staffieri Angelo	308	shoemaker	50	"
	G	Trehan Elizabeth—†	309	at home	90	
	H	Telesforo Joseph	309	laborer	60	
	K	*Telesforo Mary—†	309	housewife	70	"
	L	Telesforo Pasquale	309	clerk	37	"
	M	LaVoie John A	309	laborer	53	110 Saratoga
	N	Reardon Joseph J	309	chauffeur	67	here
	O	Reardon Lawrence K	309	laborer	28	"
	P	*Riggillo Alice—†	310	housewife	33	131 Trenton
	R	Riggillo Joseph	310	painter	36	131 "
	S	Alfano Antonio	310	laborer	50	here
	T	Alfano Dominic	310	student	22	"
	U	Alfano Jennie—†	310	housewife	47	"
	V	*Riggillo Anthony	310	laborer	59	"
	W	Riggillo Rocco	310	foreman	32	286 Chelsea
	X	Riggillo Yolanda—†	310	housewife	21	286 "
	Y	Manfredonia Florence M—†	311	"	24	here
	Z	Manfredonia Joseph	311	clerk	24	"
955						
	A	Grande Anastasia—†	311	housewife	47	"
	B	Grande Frances—†	311	bookkeeper	23	"

Page.	Letter.	Full Name.	Residence, Jan. 1, 1938.	Occupation.	Supposed Age.	Reported Residence, Jan. 1, 1937. Street and Number.

Saratoga Street—Continued

Page.	Letter.	Full Name.	Residence, Jan. 1, 1938.	Occupation.	Supposed Age.	Reported Residence, Jan. 1, 1937. Street and Number.
	C	Grande Gaetano G	311	student	21	here
	D	Grande Sebastiano	311	chauffeur	52	"
	E	Pierro Annette—†	311	housewife	24	"
	F	Pierro Joseph	311	printer	26	
	G	Mackey Elizabeth—†	312	housewife	40	"
	H	Mackey Richard F	312	fisherman	41	"
	K	Collins Ellen—†	312	housewife	74	"
	L	Collins Peter F	312	retired	84	
	M	Collins Thomas	312	plumber	34	
	N	Riley Helen V—†	312	operator	38	"
	O	Colucci Carl J	312	clerk	22	
	P	Colucci Genevieve—†	312	housewife	53	"
	R	Colucci George A	312	barber	27	
	S	Colucci Gerado	312	"	55	
	T	Coleman David B	313	policeman	54	"
	U	Coleman Ida E—†	313	housewife	54	"
	V	Peraino Gemma—†	313	"	26	
	W	Peraino John	313	operator	29	
	X	*Babine Helen—†	314	housewife	34	"
	Y	*Babine James	314	fisherman	48	"
	Z	Jacobs Helen I—†	314	at home	34	
956						
	A	Jacobs Ida E—†	314	housewife	60	"
	B	Jacobs Samuel S	314	teamster	59	
	C	Jacobs William R	314	clerk	32	
	D	Banks Margaret L—†	314	stitcher	32	
	E	Sousa John A	314	chauffeur	24	"
	F	Sousa Mary T—†	314	housewife	20	"
	G	Shea Anna G—†	315	"	47	72 Robinwood av
	H	Shea Richard F	315	inspector	59	72 "
	K	McMahon Sarah J—†	315	housekeeper	84	here
	L	Davenport Emory M	315	laborer	60	"
	M	Twomey George	315	retired	57	"
	N	Hender Mary E—†	316	housewife	45	"
	O	Hender Walter J	316	salesman	46	"
	P	*McDonnell Daniel	316	retired	80	
	R	Pasquariello Alfred G	316	laborer	22	
	S	Pasquariello Charles	316	cook	53	
	T	Gallo Jennie—†	316	housewife	34	"
	U	*Gallo John	316	plasterer	43	"
	V	Rottollo Angelina—†	317	operator	24	"

Page.	Letter.	Full Name.	Residence, Jan. 1, 1938.	Occupation.	Supposed Age.	Reported Residence, Jan. 1, 1937. Street and Number.

Saratoga Street—Continued

	W	Rottollo Julia—†	317	housewife	50	here
	X	Rottollo Charles	317	laborer	27	"
	Y	Rottollo Joseph	317	"	57	"
	Z	Rottollo Rocco	317	operator	22	"
957						
	A	Delvecchio Marie—†	317	housewife	51	"
	B	Delvecchio Ottavio	317	operator	53	"
	C	Laquaglia Antonio	319	tailor	56	
	D	Laquaglia Margaret—†	319	at home	26	
	E	*Laquaglia Rose—†	319	housewife	54	"
	F	Laquaglia Theresa—†	319	tailoress	29	
	G	Richard Ethel F—†	319	housewife	25	"
	H	Richard Harold F	319	packer	26	
	K	Laquaglia Carmen	319	"	23	
	L	Laquaglia Joseph	319	messenger	24	"
	M	Laquaglia Rocco	319	packer	22	
	N	*St Croix Charlotte—†	320	housewife	51	"
	O	St Croix James W	320	operator	20	"
	P	*St Croix William	320	longshoreman	57	"
	R	Bruno Lucy—†	320	housewife	53	"
	S	Bruno Nicholas N	320	librarian	21	"
	T	Bruno Paul F	320	"	23	
	U	Bruno Ricardo	320	cabinetmaker	51	"
	V	Bruno Rose—†	320	at home	24	
	W	Abruzese Jennie—†	320	"	22	
	X	Abruzese Marion R—†	320	operator	23	"
	Y	*Abruzese Mary—†	320	housewife	45	"
	Z	Abruzese Pasquale V	320	butcher	21	
958						
	A	*Abruzese Peter	320	shoemaker	59	"
	B	Pattipas Louis	321	carpenter	63	"
	C	Pattipas Marie S—†	321	housewife	62	"
	D	Banks Gertrude V—†	322	"	26	
	E	Banks John R	322	decorator	31	"
	F	Pucciarello Emmaline—†	322	housewife	28	"
	G	*Pucciarello Laurence	322	retired	75	
	H	Pucciarello Louis	322	bartender	40	"
	K	Pucciarello Elizabeth R—†	322	clerk	20	
	L	Pucciarello Mary J—†	322	housewife	44	"
	M	Pucciarello Pasquale	322	operator	44	"
	N	Jeffrey Florence R—†	323	housewife	39	"

Page.	Letter.	Full Name.	Residence, Jan. 1, 1938.	Occupation.	Supposed Age.	Reported Residence, Jan. 1, 1937. Street and Number.

Saratoga Street—Continued

	O	Jeffrey William J	323	engineer	41	here
	P	Caggiano Annie—†	324	typist	22	"
	R	Caggiano Antonio	324	retired	59	"
	S	Caggiano Concetta—†	324	at home	25	"
	T	*Caggiano Frances—†	324	housewife	55	326 Saratoga
	U	Caggiano Saverio	324	laborer	26	here
	V	Caggiano Theresa—†	324	clerk	28	"
	W	*Camarda Gasper	324	pedler	55	"
	X	Camarda James	324	decorator	21	"
	Y	*Camarda Louise—†	324	housewife	37	"
	Z	*Venza Anna—†	324	"	36	
959						
	A	Venza Peter	324	salesman	43	"
	B	*Pizzano Antonio	rear 325	retired	65	
	C	Pizzano Elvira—†	" 325	housewife	58	"
	D	Pizzano Susan—†	" 325	operator	29	"
	E	DeMarco Anna—†	326	at home	33	171 Condor
	F	*Privetero Lucy—†	326	housewife	30	165 Saratoga
	G	Privetero Samuel	326	chauffeur	39	165 "
	H	Fitzgerald Herbert	329	laborer	20	5 Saratoga pl
	K	Fitzgerald Mary E—†	329	housewife	46	5 "
	L	Jeffrey John E	329	laborer	38	here
	M	Jeffrey Joseph H	329	retired	72	"
	N	Jeffrey Walter J	329	laborer	35	"
	O	Wagner Mary A—†	329	housekeeper	45	"
	R	Haggett Alice—†	330	housewife	31	"
	S	Haggett Reginald	330	salesman	30	"
	T	Ahern James J	330	longshoreman	40	"
	U	Ahern William F	330	policeman	44	"
	V	Bly Catherine A—†	330	housewife	61	"
	W	Donovan George A	330	clerk	31	
	X	Grant Josephine M—†	330	housewife	46	"
	Y	Grant Patrick J	330	policeman	49	"
	Z	Keenan Frances L—†	331	operator	25	
960						
	A	Keenan Henry P	331	student	21	
	B	Keenan Jane F—†	331	operator	36	
	C	Keenan John T	331	retired	65	
	D	Keenan Katherine M—†	331	clerk	27	
	E	Keenan Katherine W—†	331	housewife	64	"
	F	Keenan Leo B	331	messenger	24	"

Page.	Letter.	FULL NAME.	Residence, Jan. 1, 1938.	Occupation.	Supposed Age.	Reported Residence, Jan. 1, 1937. Street and Number.

Saratoga Street—Continued

	G	Dwyer Margaret L—†	333	bookkeeper	42	here
	H	Dwyer Timothy D	333	guard	76	"
	L	Marino Anthony J	340	painter	27	"
	M	Marino Marie—†	340	housewife	24	"
	N	Caliri Joseph	340	barber	48	
	O	Caliri Lucy—†	340	housewife	45	"
	P	Lovetere John	340	machinist	44	"
	R	Lovetere Josephine—†	340	housewife	31	"
	S	Rossi Frances—†	342	at home	22	
	T	Rossi Josephine M—†	342	clerk	28	
	U	Rossi Mary—†	342	at home	22	
	V	Rossi Michael A	342	laborer	26	
	W	Rossi Stella—†	342	housewife	50	"
	X	Rossi Vito	342	barber	53	
	Y	Puopolo Angelina—†	342	at home	21	
	Z	Puopolo Anna—†	342	housewife	40	"
961						
	A	Puopolo Anthony	342	barber	23	
	B	Puopolo Rocco	342	"	48	
	C	Marino Angelina—†	344	housewife	27	"
	D	Marino James	344	painter	29	
	E	Alphas Georgia—†	344	at home	20	
	F	*Alphas Harriet—†	344	housewife	41	"
	G	*Alphas Louis	344	salesman	47	"
	H	*Amoroso Michael	344	laborer	46	
	K	*Paras George	344	cook	56	"
	L	Velardo Anthony	344	machinist	23	215 Havre
	M	Velardo Frank	344	laborer	60	215 "
	N	Velardo Joseph G	344	clerk	29	215 "
	O	*Velardo Rose—†	344	housewife	52	215 "
	P	Hogan Lillian N—†	346	clerk	25	here
	R	*Hogan Michael J	346	longshoreman	57	"
	S	McCaffery Arthur S	346	electrician	22	116 Benningt'n
	T	Miller Florence C—†	346	housewife	40	here
	U	Miller James E	346	laborer	44	"
	V	McGrath Anna F—†	346	housewife	40	"
	W	McGrath John F	346	longshoreman	40	"
	Y	Prudente Anna M—†	348	supervisor	30	"
	Z	Prudente Antonio	348	retired	68	
962						
	A	Prudente Florence—†	348	housewife	65	"

Page.	Letter.	Full Name.	Residence, Jan. 1, 1938.	Occupation.	Supposed Age.	Reported Residence, Jan. 1, 1937. Street and Number.

Saratoga Street—Continued

	B	Prudente Julia G—†	348	at home	29	here
	C	Prudente William S	348	engineer	24	"
	D	Frusciante Joseph J	348	laborer	26	"
	E	Marotta Pasquale	348	bartender	22	"
	F	*Romano Angelina—†	348	housewife	29	"
	G	Romano Salvatore	348	laborer	46	
	K	Cataldo Frances—†	400	housewife	37	"
	L	Cataldo Joseph E	400	attorney	43	"
	N	Cornetta Angelo	400	barber	63	
	O	Cornetta Anna—†	400	operator	31	
	P	Cornetta Christine—†	400	housewife	60	"
	R	Cornetta Henry C	400	operator	37	

Shelby Street

	S	Cheverie Catherine A—†	5	housewife	29	here
	T	Cheverie Percy J	5	foreman	29	"
	U	Hawes Edward J	5	laborer	21	"
	V	Hawes Thomas F	5	"	60	
	W	Hawes Thomas M	5	fireman	23	"
	X	Starrett Frances J—†	5	waitress	25	238 Hemenw'y

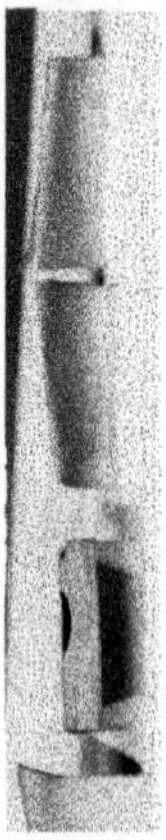

Ward 1—Precinct 12

CITY OF BOSTON

LIST OF RESIDENTS
20 YEARS OF AGE AND OVER

(NON-CITIZENS INDICATED BY ASTERISK)
(FEMALES INDICATED BY DAGGER)

AS OF

JANUARY 1, 1938

JOSEPH F. TIMILTY, } *Listing*
FREDERIC E. DOWLING, } *Board.*

CITY OF BOSTON PRINTING DEPARTMENT

Page.	Letter.	Full Name.	Residence, Jan. 1, 1938.	Occupation.	Supposed Age.	Reported Residence, Jan. 1, 1937. Street and Number.
		976				
		Bennington Street				
	A	Stopplone Joseph	149	salesman	49	here
	B	*Stopplone Mary—†	149	housewife	43	"
	C	Totoria Antoinetta—†	149	operator	27	"
	D	*Totoria Antonio	149	finisher	59	
	E	Totoria Jennie—†	149	operator	24	
	F	*Totoria Josephine—†	149	housewife	54	"
	H	Laquidara John	151	shoemaker	34	"
	K	*Laquidara Sylvia—†	151	housewife	32	"
	L	*Cagna Albino	151	laborer	48	
	M	*Cagna Maria—†	151	housewife	56	"
	P	Maze George L	153	timekeeper	31	371 Meridian
	R	Maze Thelma E—†	153	housewife	29	371 "
	S	Pepe Antoinetta—†	153	"	48	here
	T	Pepe Carmella—†	153	at home	21	"
	U	Pepe John	153	laborer	26	"
	V	Pepe Pellegrino	153	"	28	
	W	Pepe Philomena—†	153	at home	23	
	X	Pepe Vincenzo	153	fireman	60	"
	Z	Albano Angelina—†	154	housewife	52	"
		977				
	A	Albano Anna—†	154	operator	25	
	B	Albano Anthony	154	clerk	21	
	C	Albano Philomena—†	154	packer	26	
	D	DeFalco Raffaela—†	154	housewife	23	"
	E	Hogan Elizabeth A—†	154	packer	27	
	F	Hogan Sarah—†	154	housewife	59	"
	G	Hogan Thomas	154	carpenter	59	"
	H	*Ferrera Grace—†	154	housewife	47	"
	K	*Ferrera Ignazio	154	cutter	51	
	L	Rinella Joseph	155	plumber	34	
	M	Rinella Mary—†	155	housewife	30	"
	N	Rinella Samuel	155	plumber	24	
	O	Cashman Eleanor—†	155	housewife	48	"
	P	Cashman Frank A	155	laborer	49	
	S	Jerrier Catherine—†	156	housekeeper	34	"
	T	Petruzeilo Gerardo	156	laborer	35	"
	U	Petruzeilo Gertrude—†	156	housewife	28	"
	V	Rizzo Carmine	156	laborer	56	
	W	*Rizzo Rosa—†	156	housewife	48	"
	X	Sava John	156	proprietor	40	151 Benningt'n

Page.	Letter.	Full Name.	Residence, Jan. 1, 1938.	Occupation.	Supposed Age.	Reported Residence, Jan. 1, 1937. Street and Number.

Bennington Street—Continued

Page.	Letter.	Full Name.	Residence, Jan. 1, 1938.	Occupation.	Supposed Age.	Reported Residence, Jan. 1, 1937. Street and Number.
	Y	*Staffieri Luigia—†	157	housewife	47	here
	Z	Staffieri Mary—†	157	operator	21	"
978						
	A	*Perry Manuel	157	laborer	64	
	B	*Perry Maria—†	157	operator	37	
	C	Perry Natalie—†	157	laundress	21	"
	E	Barrett Catherine—†	158	domestic	49	"
	F	Perez Alice—†	158	housewife	49	"
	G	Perez Rose—†	158	clerk	21	
	H	Pellegrino Bernardino	158	operator	43	"
	K	*Pellegrino Frances—†	158	housewife	41	"
	N	Lane Dorothy—†	159	"	21	4 Lexington
	O	Lane Wilfred J	159	laborer	26	4 "
	M	Smith Leon S	159	"	39	Lynnfield
	P	Foster Malvern H	159	cook	49	New York
	R	Nickerson Alice M—†	159	waitress	36	here
	S	*Nickerson Arthur D	159	fisherman	52	"
	U	Picariello Jennie—†	160	housewife	27	"
	V	Picariello Joseph	160	painter	27	
	W	Pepe Amelia—†	160	housewife	52	"
	X	Pepe Enrico	160	student	20	
	Y	Marino Anthony	rear 160	cleanser	33	
	Z	Marino Kathleen—†	" 160	housewife	25	"
979						
	A	*Mouleson Moses	161	laborer	68	
	B	*Mouleson Rose—†	161	at home	28	
	C	*Impemba Antonio	161	shoemaker	49	"
	D	*Impemba Assunta—†	161	housewife	42	"
	E	*Impemba Martin	161	laborer	21	
	F	Bozzi John	161	"	29	
	G	Bozzi Rose—†	161	housewife	26	"
	H	Moynihan Bridget G—†	162	"	52	
	K	Moynihan Lillian G—†	162	operator	24	"
	L	Moynihan Maurice E	162	laborer	32	
	M	Moynihan Ruth E—†	162	collector	23	"
	N	Doucette Doris—†	163	housewife	27	257 Benningt'n
	O	Doucette William E	163	cutter	27	257 "
	P	DiBacco Giustino	163	laborer	44	here
	R	DiBacco Lucy—†	163	housewife	36	"
	S	Lombardi Mary—†	163	"	35	111 Boardman
	T	Massano Georgiana—†	164	"	64	here

Page.	Letter.	Full Name.	Residence, Jan. 1, 1938.	Occupation.	Supposed Age.	Reported Residence, Jan. 1, 1937. Street and Number.

Bennington Street—Continued

Page.	Letter.	Full Name.	Residence, Jan. 1, 1938.	Occupation.	Supposed Age.	Reported Residence, Jan. 1, 1937. Street and Number.
	U	*Massano Samuel	164	retired	84	here
	V	DiGregorio Mary—†	164	housewife	30	125 Chelsea
	W	DiGregorio Salvatore	164	laborer	42	125 "
	X	Kehoe Henry	164	"	29	here
	Y	Kehoe Mary F—†	164	housewife	30	"
	Z	*Morro Antoinetta—†	165	sorter	52	"
980						
	A	*DiGregio Anthony	165	janitor	45	
	B	*DiGregio Crucifica—†	165	housewife	35	"
	C	*Maglio Dominic	165	laborer	43	
	D	*Maglio Raffaela—†	165	housewife	41	"
	E	Stapleton Helen A—†	166	waitress	34	
	F	Stapleton James	166	cook	36	
	G	*Pagliarulo John	166	laborer	53	
	H	*Pagliarulo Josephine—†	166	housewife	55	"
	K	Pagliarulo William	166	salesman	23	"
	L	*Erikson Elena—†	166	housewife	55	169 W Eagle
	M	Erikson Ernest	166	fireman	56	169 "
	N	Erikson Francis E	166	clerk	24	169 "
	O	*Giusto Giuseppe	167	retired	75	here
	P	Imperioso Joseph	167	clerk	21	"
	R	*Imperioso Mary—†	167	housewife	40	"
	S	Minolla Ciriaco	167	laborer	62	
	T	Minolla Palmina—†	167	housewife	42	"
	U	*Reilly Catherine—†	168	"	45	
	V	Reilly James J	168	retired	70	
	W	Pimentel Mary—†	168	housewife	58	"
	X	Silva Isabella—†	168	"	37	
	Y	Silva Manuel	168	laborer	38	
	Z	McMullen Hugh A	168	salesman	56	"
981						
	A	McMullen Margaret A–†	168	housewife	54	"
	B	*McMullen Philomena—†	168	"	86	
	C	Emmert Anna—†	169	at home	20	
	D	Emmert Anna M—†	169	housewife	44	"
	E	Emmert Thomas E	169	painter	44	
	F	Crawford Mary T—†	170	secretary	55	"
	G	Leddy Joseph M	170	welder	36	
	H	Leddy Julia—†	170	housewife	68	"
	K	Leddy Mary—†	170	operator	32	
	L	Leddy Mildred E—†	170	housewife	35	"

Page.	Letter.	Full Name.	Residence, Jan. 1, 1938.	Occupation.	Supposed Age.	Reported Residence, Jan. 1, 1937. Street and Number.

Bennington Street—Continued

	M	Kennedy John	170	laborer	69	here
	N	West Albert H	173	clerk	28	“
	O	West Ann F—†	173	housewife	61	“
	P	Coriani Louis	173	laborer	35	
	R	Coriani Raffaela—†	173	housewife	32	“
	S	Gunning Catherine—†	174	“	56	102 Meridian
	T	Gunning Robert W	174	engineer	59	102 “
	U	Drohan Joseph P	174	laborer	20	here
	V*	Drohan Mary—†	174	housewife	57	“
	W	Drohan William T	174	policeman	34	“
	X	Corkery Louise A—†	174	at home	30	Somerville
	Y	Donovan Timothy F	174	teamster	66	here
	Z	McPhee Margaret—†	175	clerk	39	184 Marion
982						
	A	Kinder Cecil F	175	timekeeper	36	82 Brooks
	B	Kinder Ethel F—†	175	housewife	31	82 “
	C	McDonald Alice—†	177	seamstress	24	here
	D*	McDonald Bridget—†	177	housewife	51	“
	E	McDonald David	177	laborer	23	“
	F	McDonald Martin	177	fisherman	48	“
	G	Kirby Maurice	178	undertaker	32	Winthrop
	H	Curran Bridget—†	178	housewife	67	here
	K	Curran Catherine T—†	178	at home	31	“
	L	Curran Charles J	178	painter	32	“
	M	Curran Edward	178	clerk	26	
	N	Curran Ethel—†	178	saleswoman	29	“
	O	Curran Josephine—†	178	operator	30	
	P	Curran Leo M	178	laborer	33	
	R	Curran William H	178	salesman	34	“
	S	O'Keefe Margaret C—†	178	housewife	44	“
	T	O'Keefe William E	178	longshoreman	45	“
	U*	Zambello Antonio	180	laborer	55	
	V*	Zambello Concetta—†	180	housewife	52	“
	W*	Ferrara Nellie—†	180	dressmaker	37	“
	X	Ferrara Nicholas	180	barber	50	
	Y*	Gretsky Bessie—†	180	housewife	48	“
	Z	Gretsky Harold	180	laborer	30	
983						
	A	Gretsky Henry	180	clerk	28	
	B	Gretsky Joseph	180	salesman	26	“
	C*	Gretsky Morris	180	manager	58	“

Page.	Letter.	Full Name.	Residence, Jan. 1, 1938.	Occupation.	Supposed Age.	Reported Residence, Jan. 1, 1937. Street and Number.

Bennington Street—Continued

Page.	Letter.	Full Name.	Residence, Jan. 1, 1938.	Occupation.	Supposed Age.	Reported Residence, Jan. 1, 1937. Street and Number.
	D	Silva Marion F—†	181	at home	38	here
	E	Silva Mary E—†	181	housewife	68	“
	F	Levin Celia—†	182	“	54	“
	G	Levin Lena—†	182	beautician	26	“
	H	Levin Mary—†	182	clerk	27	
	K	Levin Nellie—†	182	saleswoman	25	“
	L	*Nickerson Clara—†	182	housewife	57	“
	M	*Nickerson Frieda—†	182	“	24	3 Monmouth
	N	*Nickerson George	182	watchman	58	here
	O	*Nickerson John A	182	laborer	27	3 Monmouth
	P	Jacques Florence C—†	184	housewife	34	here
	R	Jacques Manuel M	184	laborer	36	“
	S	Cunha Joseph	184	“	47	“
	T	*Cunha Lordes—†	184	housewife	36	“
	U	*Ferrara Joseph	184	fireman	47	
	V	*Ferrara Mary—†	184	housewife	32	“
	W	Sentner Henry	rear 184	laborer	25	116 Moore
	X	Sentner Margaret—†	“ 184	housewife	25	116 “
	Y	Gillespie Eileen—†	185	“	37	here
	Z	Gillespie Joseph	185	laborer	35	“
984						
	A	*Lane Leo	185	operator	40	“
	B	*Lane Sarah—†	185	housewife	42	“
	C	Guiffrida Grace—†	185	operator	28	“
	D	Guiffrida Joseph	185	“	32	
	E	Curran John J	186	laborer	42	“
	F	McKenna Elizabeth—†	186	housewife	37	“
	G	*Raimondi Mary—†	186	“	43	
	H	Raimondi Peter	186	laborer	55	“
	K	Sarro Angelina—†	186	seamstress	22	123 Benningt'n
	L	Sarro Carmella—†	186	packer	23	123 “
	M	Sarro Carmen	186	laborer	20	123 “
	N	Sarro Charles	186	“	42	123 “
	O	Sarro Teresa—†	186	housewife	44	123 “
	R	McPhee George H	187	longshoreman	40	193 Lexington
	S	McPhee Helen E—†	187	housewife	41	181 “
	T	*Martin Gloria—†	187	housekeeper	59	here
	U	Martin Julia—†	187	“	20	“
	W	*Gannon Mary—†	188	housewife	30	“
	X	*Gannon Robert	188	seaman	36	
	Y	Purcell Mary—†	188	housewife	42	“

Page.	Letter.	Full Name.	Residence, Jan. 1, 1938.	Occupation.	Supposed Age.	Reported Residence, Jan. 1, 1937. Street and Number.

Bennington Street—Continued

Page.	Letter.	Full Name.	Residence, Jan. 1, 1938.	Occupation.	Supposed Age.	Reported Residence, Jan. 1, 1937. Street and Number.
	Z	Purcell Thomas J	188	laborer	48	here
985						
	A	Mascetta Elizabeth—†	188	at home	20	"
	B	*Mascetta Ferdinando	188	tailor	55	
	C	Mascetta Philomena—†	188	packer	26	
	D	Mascetta Remigio	188	cutter	22	
	E	*Mascetta Romilda—†	188	housewife	50	"
	F	Mascetta Thomasina—†	188	tailoress	24	
	G	Avellar John F	190	packer	33	
	H	*Avellar Marie—†	190	housewife	34	"
	K	Lewis Caroline—†	190	designer	24	Cambridge
	L	LeBlanc Ralph	190	waiter	23	Canada
	M	*Muise Frank P	190	watchman	67	161 Saratoga
	N	*Muise Jane—†	190	housewife	66	161 "
	O	*Muise John F	190	waiter	21	161 "
	P	Forgione Frank	190	laborer	31	here
	R	Forgione Mary—†	190	housewife	37	"
	S	French Frank	192	painter	34	19 Trenton
	T	French Jennie—†	192	housewife	57	19 "
	U	DeFillippo Grace—†	192	"	23	11 Emmons
	V	DeFillippo Joseph	192	operator	25	11 "
	W	Masello Mary—†	192	"	25	11 "

Bremen Street

Page.	Letter.	Full Name.	Residence, Jan. 1, 1938.	Occupation.	Supposed Age.	Reported Residence, Jan. 1, 1937. Street and Number.
	X	Cardarelli Grace—†	236	housewife	30	here
	Y	Cardarelli Ralph	236	laborer	29	"
	Z	Forgione Joseph	236	chauffeur	37	"
986						
	A	Forgione Rose—†	236	housewife	33	"
	B	Fracia Charles	236	chauffeur	37	"
	C	Fracia Marcella—†	236	housewife	37	"
	D	Pepi Anna—†	238	"	55	17 Morris
	E	Pepi Augustina	238	laborer	60	17 "
	F	*Albanese Antonio	238	retired	83	here
	G	*Sellazzo Antonio	238	"	66	"
	H	*Sellazzo Emma—†	238	housewife	57	"
	K	LoConte Clara—†	238	packer	23	
	L	LoConte Dora—†	238	"	22	
	M	LoConte John	238	laborer	50	
	N	LoConte Lena—†	238	housewife	41	"

Page.	Letter.	Full Name.	Residence, Jan. 1, 1938.	Occupation.	Supposed Age.	Reported Residence, Jan. 1, 1937. Street and Number.

Bremen Street—Continued

	o	Silva Emanuel	240	engineer	44	here
	p	Silva Mary C—†	240	housewife	40	"
	r	Silva Theophilus	240	clerk	22	"
	s	DiDonato Phyllis—†	240	housewife	39	71 Chelsea
	t	*DiDonato Stephen	240	laborer	41	71 "
	u	*Polizzi Josephine—†	240	housewife	38	here
	v	Polizzi Philip	240	laborer	42	"
	w	DiMonde Angelo	242	"	48	"
	x	DiMonde Rose—†	242	housewife	36	"
	y	*Terramagra Louis	242	laborer	52	
	z	*Terramagra Stella—†	242	housewife	49	"
987						
	a	Izzo Mary—†	242	"	34	22 Brooks
	b	Izzo Paul	242	laborer	42	22 "
	c	Graziano Alice—†	244	housewife	36	here
	d	Graziano James	244	laborer	36	"
	e	Barresi Angelo	244	"	52	"
	f	Barresi Frank	244	clerk	22	
	g	Barresi Josephine—†	244	housewife	48	"
	h	Barresi Rose—†	244	packer	26	
	k	Vitale Felix	244	pedler	51	
	l	Vitale Josephine—†	244	housewife	45	"
	m	Vitale Philip	244	laborer	24	"
	n	*Catrone Giuseppe	246	retired	71	4 Appian pl
	o	*Catrone Marion—†	246	housewife	66	4 "
	p	Silva Edmund	246	laborer	28	here
	r	Silva Marie—†	246	housewife	24	"
	s	*Bellitti Frances—†	246	"	46	"
	t	Bellitti Josephine—†	246	stenographer	23	"
	u	Bellitti Vito	246	painter	53	"
	w	*DeVita Emmanuela—†	252	housewife	71	"
	x	*DeVita Vincenzo	252	retired	77	
	y	Scaramella Fioravante	252	"	65	
	z	DeVita James	252	clerk	29	
988						
	a	DeVita Rose—†	252	housewife	30	"
	b	DeVita Mary—†	252	"	41	
	c	DeVita Michael	252	printer	43	
	d	Raffaele James	254	laborer	32	"
	e	Raffaele Jean—†	254	housewife	27	"
	f	Napolitano Clement	254	laborer	33	"

Page.	Letter.	FULL NAME.	Residence, Jan. 1, 1938.	Occupation.	Supposed Age.	Reported Residence, Jan. 1, 1937. Street and Number.

Bremen Street—Continued

Page.	Letter.	FULL NAME.	Residence, Jan. 1, 1938.	Occupation.	Supposed Age.	Reported Residence, Jan. 1, 1937. Street and Number.
	G	Napolitano Ida—†	254	housewife	29	here
	H	Massara Carlo	254	laborer	49	"
	K	Massara Maria—†	254	housewife	50	"
	L	Massara Peter	254	laborer	21	
	O	O'Neil Caroline F—†	264	housewife	39	"
	P	O'Neil William G	264	chauffeur	41	"
	R	*Carli Frank	266	laborer	32	4 Cottage pl
	S	*Carli Theresa—†	266	housewife	32	4 "
	T	Joy Clement	268	laborer	34	here
	U	Joy Hannah—†	268	housewife	75	"
	V	Joy Joseph	268	retired	78	"
	W	Sullivan Alice—†	268	housewife	48	"
	X	Sullivan Daniel	268	laborer	52	
	Y	Sullivan Francis	268	"	26	
	Z	Sullivan Joseph	268	"	29	
989						
	A	Sullivan Leo	268	"	24	"
	D	Familiare Augusta—†	284	at home	54	163 Byron
	E	Familiare Inez—†	284	clerk	33	163 "
	F	Rogers Anthony J	284	"	50	217 E Eagle
	G	Rogers Mary—†	284	housewife	54	217 "
	H	Donnarumma John	286	storekeeper	45	here
	K	Donnarumma Rose—†	286	housewife	38	"
	L	Donnarumma Amelia—†	286	laundress	20	"
	M	*Donnarumma John	286	laborer	45	
	N	*Donnarumma Rose—†	286	housewife	39	"
	O	Corbett Elizabeth—†	288	"	48	
	P	Corbett Henry	288	painter	48	
	R	Corbett Robert	288	laborer	22	
	S	Vecchione Felix	290	student	34	
	T	Vecchione Salvatore	290	barber	25	
	U	Jackson Florence—†	290	housewife	23	"
	V	Jackson William	290	laborer	24	
	W	Kiernan Beatrice M—†	292	housewife	46	"
	X	Kiernan John E	292	foreman	51	
	Y	Carco Dorothy—†	294	housewife	21	"
	Z	Carco Louis	294	finisher	29	
990						
	A	Brigante Joseph	294	carpenter	58	"
	B	Brigante Theresa—†	294	housewife	49	"
	C	Carco Constance—†	294	operator	23	

Page.	Letter.	Full Name.	Residence, Jan. 1, 1938.	Occupation.	Supposed Age.	Reported Residence, Jan. 1, 1937. Street and Number.

Bremen Street—Continued

	D	Carco Emanuel	294	laborer	55	here
	E	Carco Josephine—†	294	housewife	48	"
	F	Costa Mary—†	294	operator	22	"
	G	Costa Peter	294	printer	24	
	H	*Costa Stephen	294	laborer	56	
	O	Simington Arthur	310	"	44	
	P	Simington Edith—†	310	housewife	43	"
	R	Clark Edna—†	310	"	45	279 Chelsea
	S	Clark Edward	310	retired	70	279 "
	T	DeViller Ada—†	310	at home	54	here
	U	Muise John	310	clerk	21	"
	V	Powers Anna—†	312	operator	29	"
	W	Powers Eva—†	312	housewife	65	"
	X	Powers John	312	laborer	25	"
	Y	Lombardo Edward	312	"	22	180 Paris
	Z	Powers Anna—†	312	housewife	31	181 "
991						
	A	Powers Michael	312	operator	33	181 "
	B	Powers Joseph	312	"	31	here
	C	Powers Josephine—†	312	housewife	27	"

Brooks Street

	D	DeNapoli Joseph	2	laborer	32	here
	E	DeNapoli Mary—†	2	housewife	30	"
	F	O'Keefe Cornelius H	2	longshoreman	43	"
	G	Shephard James F	2	operator	22	"
	H	Shephard Mary E—†	2	housewife	46	"
	K	Shephard Mary E—†	2	houseworker	26	"
	L	*Festa Carmella—†	2	housewife	52	"
	M	*Festa Gaetano	2	laborer	45	"
	N	Pothier George I	4	operator	26	Rhode Island
	O	Pothier Isadore	4	seaman	54	"
	P	Pothier Madeline—†	4	housewife	30	"
	R	Salvatore Catherine—†	4	"	30	305 Chelsea
	S	*Salvatore John	4	cutter	36	305 "
	T	*DeGloria Immacolata—†	4	housewife	42	here
	U	DeGloria Rosario	4	laborer	46	"
	V	Boncore Charles	6	tailor	48	"
	W	Boncore Louisa—†	6	student	20	"
	X	*Boncore Louise—†	6	housewife	42	"

Page.	Letter.	FULL NAME.	Residence, Jan. 1, 1938.	Occupation.	Supposed Age.	Reported Residence, Jan. 1, 1937. Street and Number.

Brooks Street—Continued

	Y	Boncore Tina—†	6	saleswoman	24	here
992						
	A	*Lariviere Eugene	6	laborer	53	
	B	Lariviere Lydia—†	6	housewife	44	"
	E	Tracia Angelina—†	19	"	25	"
	F	Tracia Louis	19	laborer	25	
	G	Girla Louis	19	"	22	
	H	Girla Margaret—†	19	housewife	46	"
	K	Girla Pasquale	19	storekeeper	46	"
	L	*Cirillo Mary—†	19	housewife	40	"
	M	Cirillo Raymond	19	chauffeur	44	"
	N	Cirillo Rosalie—†	19	stenographer	22	"
	O	Cirillo Virginia—†	19	saleswoman	21	"
	P	Cappuccio Mathilda—†	20	housewife	38	"
	R	Cappuccio Nicholas	20	laborer	45	
	S	Minichiello Angelo	20	"	28	
	T	Minichiello Carolina—†	20	student	21	
	U	*Minichiello Ralph	20	laborer	56	
	V	*Minichiello Rose—†	20	housewife	50	"
	W	Barrett John J	21	laborer	52	
	X	Barrett Margaret A—†	21	housewife	51	"
	Y	Barrett Mary A—†	21	operator	23	"
993						
	A	*Anzalone Rose—†	21	housekeeper	62	"
	Z	D'Avolio Esther—†	21	"	27	"
	B	*Manzo Alphonso	21	retired	58	183 Chelsea
	C	*Manzo Jennie—†	21	housewife	48	183 "
	D	Manzo Marie—†	21	operator	21	183 "
	E	Manzo Salvatore	21	"	24	183 "
	F	Markovitz Celia—†	22	clerk	20	here
	G	*Markovitz Charles	22	laborer	44	"
	H	*Markovitz Eva—†	22	housewife	43	"
	K	Murphy Fred	22	timekeeper	32	"
	L	Perry George T	22	custodian	65	"
	M	Perry Margaret T—†	22	housewife	53	"
	N	Falzone Anna—†	22	"	29	152 Chelsea
	O	Falzone Rosario	22	laundryman	45	152 "
	P	Boncora Guy	23	printer	27	here
	R	Boncora Josephine—†	23	housewife	26	"
	S	Kushner Albert	23	salesman	27	"
	T	*Kushner Anna—†	23	housewife	65	"

Page.	Letter.	Full Name.	Residence, Jan. 1, 1938.	Occupation.	Supposed Age.	Reported Residence, Jan. 1, 1937. Street and Number.

Brooks Street—Continued

Page.	Letter.	Full Name.	Residence, Jan. 1, 1938.	Occupation.	Supposed Age.	Reported Residence, Jan. 1, 1937. Street and Number.
	U	Kushner Max	23	salesman	25	here
	V	Kushner Sally—†	23	saleswoman	22	“
	W	Driver Harold	23	engineer	28	“
	X	Driver Stella—†	23	housewife	23	“
	Y	Crowley Albert M	25	retired	63	319 Paris
	Z	Crowley Albert M, jr	25	chauffeur	29	319 “
994						
	A	Crowley Henry R	25	clerk	25	319 ·
	B	Crowley Margaret J—†	25	housewife	54	319 “
	C	Dollin Celia—†	25	bookkeeper	26	30 Garden
	D	Dollin William	25	upholsterer	28	30 “
	E	*Sandler Eva—†	25	housewife	53	here
	F	*Sandler Morris	25	dealer	53	“
	G	Sandler Tilda—†	25	clerk	23	“
	H	Grazino Agnes—†	25	operator	20	
	K	*Grazino Albert	25	laborer	42	
	L	*Grazino Mary—†	25	housewife	45	“
	M	Donohue James E	26	clerk	36	
	N	McDonald Margaret M–†	26	housewife	65	“
	O	McDonald Thomas	26	laborer	44	
	P	Mogan Helen F—†	26	stenographer	35	“
	S	Mogan J Winston	26	clerk	20	”
	R	Mogan Joseph F	26	guard	44	
	U	Alpert Alexander	27	attorney	32	“
	V	*Alpert Annie—†	27	housewife	63	“
	W	Perullo Frank	27	operator	22	430 Chelsea
	X	*Perullo Louis	27	laborer	60	430 “
	Y	Perullo Louise—†	27	housewife	21	430 “
	Z	*Perullo Mary—†	27	“	48	430 ‘
995						
	A	Klee Ernest	28	pinboy	20	here
	B	Klee Gretchen—†	28	houseworker	21	“
	C	Klee Henry J	28	baker	56	“
	D	Klee Madeline—†	28	houseworker	23	“
	E	Klee Nellie—†	28	housewife	57	“
	H	Gallagher M Genevieve–†	35	maid	36	
	K	Garrahan Thomas C	35	clergyman	64	“
	L	McCabe M Ultan	35	“	29	
	M	Moran Francis P	35	“	32	
	O	O'Brien James	35	bookkeeper	31	“
	N	O'Donnell Walter J	35	clergyman	32	“

Page.	Letter.	Full Name.	Residence, Jan. 1, 1938.	Occupation.	Supposed Age.	Reported Residence, Jan. 1, 1937. Street and Number.

Brooks Street—Continued

	P	Smith Sarah G—†	35	housekeeper	68	here
	R	Ferrino Enrico	44	laborer	53	"
	S	*Ferrino Josephine—†	44	housewife	51	"
	T	Ferrino Peter J	44	student	23	
	U	*Lopicato Nellie—†	44	housewife	34	"
	V	Lopicato Salvatore	44	laborer	40	
	X	*Gugluciello Paul	46	retired	75	
	Y	*Gugluciello Rose—†	46	housewife	72	"
	Z	*Porcelline Carmella—†	46	"	42	
996						
	A	*Porcelline Joseph	46	buyer	46	
	B	*Villari Nunzio	46	laborer	56	
	C	*Santosuosso Louis	48	"	48	
	D	*Santosuosso Theresa—†	48	housewife	55	"
	E	Cerasso Josephine—†	48	"	36	
	F	*Cerasso Julio	48	pedler	44	"
	G	Lepore John	48	operator	28	85 Putnam
	H	Lepore Phyllis—†	48	"	25	85 "
	K	Costantino Angelina—†	57	housewife	57	here
	L	Costantino James	57	laborer	57	"
	M	Cooper James B	57	longshoreman	24	Medford
	N	Cooper Regina M—†	57	housewife	22	"
	O	DiGiovanni Mary—†	57	housekeeper	25	here
	P	Nagle Anna—†	59	saleswoman	37	"
	R	Kurgan Anthony J	59	operator	27	"
	S	*Kurgan Mary J—†	59	housekeeper	67	"
	T	Karish Alfred	59	machinist	39	"
	U	*Karish Mary—†	59	housewife	37	"
	V	Sullivan Catherine O—†	61	"	67	
	W	Sullivan Martin J	61	longshoreman	48	"
	X	Sullivan Patrick J	61	seaman	28	
	Y	Cappucci Joseph	61	inspector	39	"
	Z	Cappucci Lucy—†	61	housewife	38	"
997						
	A	DiGiorgio Domenic	61	laborer	49	
	B	DiGiorgio Maria—†	61	housewife	46	"
	C	Trocano Flora—†	63	"	28	
	D	Trocano Pasquale	63	laborer	32	
	E	DiNapoli Alfred	63	operator	28	
	F	DiNapoli Esther—†	63	housewife	26	"
	G	*Pepe Angelina—†	63	"	67	

Page.	Letter.	FULL NAME.	Residence, Jan. 1, 1938.	Occupation.	Supposed Age.	Reported Residence, Jan. 1, 1937. Street and Number.

Brooks Street—Continued

Page.	Letter.	FULL NAME.	Residence, Jan. 1, 1938.	Occupation.	Supposed Age.	Reported Residence, Jan. 1, 1937. Street and Number.
	H	Pepe Antonio	63	cutter	57	here
	K	Baldassare Angela—†	63	housewife	42	"
	L	Baldassare Marcello	63	laborer	48	"
	M	Baldassare Pasquale	63	student	20	
	N	Barrasso Andrew	65	janitor	33	
	O	Barrasso Nellie—†	65	operator	26	"
	P	Barrasso Jeremiah	65	laborer	28	
	R	*Barrasso Raffaella—†	65	housekeeper	59	"
	S	Schepici Carmella—†	65	housewife	21	"
	T	Schepici Mario	65	laborer	23	"
	V	Fariole Catherine—†	77	housekeeper	45	61 Bennington
	W	Greene Francis	77	clerk	21	61 "
	X	Regan Mary—†	77	housewife	30	402 Saratoga
	Y	Regan Thomas D	77	laborer	31	402 "
	Z	Dempsey Agnes M—†	79	at home	79	here
998						
	A	Dempsey Helen M—†	79	"	45	
	B	*Rosa Concetta—†	79	housewife	53	"
	C	*Rosa Joseph	79	laborer	60	"
	D	*D'Agostino Jennie—†	79	housekeeper	51	71 Morris
	E	D'Agostino Nancy—†	79	typist	24	71 "
	F	*Orlando Edward	81	upholsterer	27	216 Bremen
	G	Viglione Louise—†	81	housewife	36	here
	H	Carney John J	81	clerk	49	"
	K	Carney John J, jr	81	laborer	23	"
	L	Carney Margaret A—†	81	housewife	48	"
	M	Brady John	81	engineer	27	
	N	Brady Mary—†	81	housewife	46	"
	O	O'Neil Joseph	81	porter	33	Medford
	P	Ferrara Margaret—†	83	housewife	27	221 Havre
	R	Ferrara Rocco	83	chauffeur	30	221 "
	S	Gannon Lillian—†	83	housewife	30	here
	T	Gannon Matthew	83	longshoreman	33	"
	U	*Waldron Beatrice—†	83	housewife	32	"
	V	Waldron Clark	83	cook	33	
	W	*Marciano Grace—†	85	housewife	47	"
	X	*Marciano John	85	laborer	55	
	Y	Marciano Josephine—†	85	cutter	22	
	Z	Festa Edith—†	85	housewife	27	"
999						
	A	Festa Gabriel	85	chauffeur	30	"

Page.	Letter.	Full Name.	Residence, Jan. 1, 1938.	Occupation.	Supposed Age.	Reported Residence, Jan. 1, 1937. Street and Number.

Brooks Street—Continued

	B	Margherita Anthony	85	laborer	31	here
	C	*Margherita Margaret—†	85	housewife	30	"
	G	Pupke August H	101	grocer	45	"
	H	Pupke Helene—†	101	housewife	72	"
	K	Caggiano James	103	butcher	23	221 London
	L	Caggiano Rose—†	103	housewife	23	221 "
	M	Keohane Dennis J	103	blacksmith	58	here
	M[1]	Keohane John J	103	clerk	27	"
	N	Keohane Mildred F—†	103	operator	21	"
	R	Limole Helen—†	107	housewife	27	"
	T	Bennett Frances—†	111	"	26	
	U	Bennett Nola—†	111	"	62	
	V	Closson Warren	111	seaman	63	
	W	*Paolucci Louis	111	retired	61	"
	X	King Elizabeth M—†	113	bookbinder	36	Malden

Chelsea Street

	Y	Ferrarecchia Anna—†	194	dressmaker	28	133 Saratoga
	Z	Ferrarecchia John	194	operator	32	133 "
1000						
	A	Berman Edith—†	194	at home	21	191 Chelsea
	B	Berman Joseph	194	butcher	36	191 "
	C	*Berman Lena—†	194	housewife	70	191 "
	D	Amico Bernice—†	194	"	21	here
	E	Amico Joseph	194	clerk	25	"
	F	Fumicello Jennie—†	196	housewife	31	"
	G	Fumicello Joseph	196	operator	38	
	H	Salamone Joseph	196	laborer	52	
	K	*Salamone Josephine—†	196	housewife	47	"
	L	Campochiaro Joseph	196	laborer	26	
	M	*Rizzo Frank	196	retired	84	
	N	Rizzo John	196	storekeeper	53	"
	O	*Rizzo Stella—†	196	housewife	50	"
	P	Rizzo Viola—†	196	dressmaker	23	"
	R	Gagliolo Alphonse	197	shoemaker	56	"
	S	Gagliolo Mary—†	197	housewife	54	"
	T	Alviti Albina—†	197	"	30	
	U	Alviti Americo	197	photographer	31	"
	V	DeCristoforo John	197	plumber	20	103 Saratoga
	W	*DeCristoforo Mary—†	197	housewife	21	78 Trenton

Page.	Letter.	Full Name.	Residence, Jan. 1, 1938.	Occupation.	Supposed Age.	Reported Residence, Jan. 1, 1937. Street and Number.

Chelsea Street—Continued

Page.	Letter.	Full Name.	Residence, Jan. 1, 1938.	Occupation.	Supposed Age.	Reported Residence, Jan. 1, 1937. Street and Number.
	X	Vetrano Salvatore	198	operator	42	here
	Y	Vetrano Theresa—†	198	housewife	32	“
	Z	Guerra Americo	198	printer	24	Chelsea
1001						
	A	Guerra Angela—†	198	housewife	24	“
	C*	Guerra Clementina—†	198	“	57	here
	B	Guerra Louis	198	laborer	62	“
	D	Hibbard Harry E	199	“	20	“
	E	Hibbard Mary—†	199	housewife	20	“
	F*	Laferla Carmella—†	199	“	43	
	G	Laferla John	199	laborer	44	
	H*	Pagliaro Anthony	199	“	31	
	K*	Pagliaro Carmello	199	“	66	
	L*	Pagliaro Rose—†	199	housewife	58	“
	M	Pagliaro Santo	199	laborer	20	“
	N	Jackson Prudence—†	200	housewife	23	290 Bremen
	O	Jackson Thomas	200	clerk	23	290 “
	P	Walsh Patrick	200	laborer	47	here
	R	Walsh Theresa—†	200	housewife	48	“
	S	Walsh Theresa R—†	200	packer	22	“
	T	Pasquantonio Angelo	200	butcher	37	“
	U	Pasquantonio Margaret—†	200	housewife	35	“
	V	Perella Carmella—†	201	“	20	Revere
	W	Perella John	201	painter	23	here
	X	Perella Pellegrino	201	laborer	58	“
	Y*	Perella Robina—†	201	housewife	54	“
	Z	Saffiro Margaret—†	201	“	31	
1002						
	A	Saffiro Salvatore	201	chauffeur	34	“
	B	DeWart Antone	202	cutter	37	
	C	DeWart Mary—†	202	housewife	37	“
	D*	Cohen Max	202	laborer	53	
	E	Cohen Myer	202	bookkeeper	23	“
	F*	Muscarelli Frances—†	202	housewife	40	“
	G*	Muscarelli Salvatore	202	operator	43	“
	H*	Pinieri Antonetta—†	203	housewife	40	4 Brooks
	K	Pinieri George	203	laborer	22	here
	L	Pinieri Rosario	203	“	49	4 Brooks
	M*	Salemi Angelina—†	203	housewife	52	here
	N	Salemi Santo	203	laborer	61	“
	O	LaCascia Joseph	203	baker	34	“

Page.	Letter.	Full Name.	Residence, Jan. 1, 1938.	Occupation.	Supposed Age.	Reported Residence, Jan. 1, 1937. Street and Number.

Chelsea Street—Continued

Page.	Letter.	Full Name.	Residence, Jan. 1, 1938.	Occupation.	Supposed Age.	Reported Residence, Jan. 1, 1937.
	P	*LaCascia Sadie—†	203	housewife	30	here
	R	DelliPriscoli Girolomo	204	laborer	48	"
	S	*DelliPriscoli Virginia—†	204	housewife	42	"
	T	Levi Jennie—†	204	at home	75	
	U	Yellin Abraham	204	merchant	46	"
	V	Yellin Rose—†	204	housewife	42	"
	W	*Marchetti Jennie—†	205	"	34	
	X	*Marchetti John	205	tailor	38	
	Y	*Chianca Antonio	205	baker	54	
	Z	Chianca Arthur	205	"	20	
1003						
	A	*Chianca Carmella—†	205	housewife	50	"
	B	DeSalvo Diego	205	clerk	20	
	C	DeSalvo John	205	laborer	56	
	D	*DeSalvo Mary—†	205	at home	24	
	E	*DeSalvo Rose—†	205	housewife	44	"
	F	Carrigan Daniel W	206	carpenter	61	"
	G	Carrigan Mary A—†	206	housewife	59	"
	H	*Caprio Angela—†	206	"	74	
	K	Caprio Louise—†	206	at home	30	
	L	Caprio Nicholas	206	clerk	42	
	M	Caprio Fannie—†	206	housewife	45	"
	N	Caprio Joseph	206	clerk	50	
	O	Veator Clara—†	207	housewife	34	"
	P	Veator Joseph F	207	cutter	38	
	R	Rosata Carmen	207	barber	50	
	S	Rosata Louise—†	207	clerk	22	
	T	*Rosata Mary—†	207	housewife	48	"
	U	Rosata Nancy—†	207	stenographer	24	"
	V	Rosata Viola—†	207	"	20	"
	W	DeSena Mary—†	207	housewife	27	347 Meridian
	X	DeSena Thomas	207	cutter	34	347 "
	Y	*Lunetta Anna—†	207	at home	52	347 "
	Z	Magnano Gertrude—†	208	housewife	43	43 Orleans
1004						
	A	Magnano John	208	foreman	53	43 "
	B	*Renda Agrippina—†	208	housewife	64	here
	C	*Renda Augostino	208	retired	69	"
	D	Thomas John	208	laborer	21	"
	E	Thomas Josephine—†	208	housewife	20	"
	F	Torra Catherine—†	209	"	27	

Page.	Letter.	Full Name.	Residence, Jan. 1, 1938.	Occupation.	Supposed Age.	Reported Residence, Jan. 1, 1937. Street and Number.

Chelsea Street—Continued

Page.	Letter.	Full Name.	Residence, Jan. 1, 1938.	Occupation.	Supposed Age.	Reported Residence, Jan. 1, 1937. Street and Number.
	G	Torra Frank	209	upholsterer	26	here
	H	*Cali Catherine—†	209	housewife	51	"
	K	Cali James	209	chauffeur	26	"
	L	Cali Joseph	209	laborer	23	
	M	Cali Salvatore	209	"	21	
	N	Mugnano Annette—†	209	housewife	26	"
	O	Mugnano Charles	209	laborer	29	
	P	*Mugnano Joseph	209	"	59	
	R	*Mugnano Josephine—†	209	housewife	55	"
	S	*Sutherland Minnie—†	210	at home	75	
	T	*Losco Mary—†	210	"	66	
	U	*Lettieri Joseph	210	packer	49	
	V	*Lettieri Josephine—†	210	housewife	47	"
	W	DeRosa Celia—†	211	"	27	
	X	DeRosa Joseph	211	laborer	29	
	Y	Cangiano Lucy—†	211	operator	30	"
	Z	*Cangiano Michelene—†	211	housewife	59	"
1005						
	A	Cangiano Rose—†	211	operator	23	"
	B	Cangiano Stella—†	211	stenographer	27	"
	C	Morocco Carmella—†	211	at home	33	"
	D	*Ferrara Giuseppe	211	laborer	67	
	E	*Ferrara Josephine—†	211	housewife	54	"
	F	Ferrara Mary—†	211	nurse	21	
	G	Ferrara Rose—†	211	clerk	27	
	H	Thomas Frances—†	212	housewife	30	"
	K	Thomas Harold	212	laborer	32	
	L	*Fusaloro Rose—†	212	housewife	32	"
	M	*Fusaloro Victor	212	laborer	42	
	N	*Mancuso Marion—†	212	housewife	45	"
	O	Mancuso Peter	212	laborer	57	
	P	Bellavia Mary—†	213	housewife	47	"
	R	Bellavia Salvatore	213	laborer	53	
	S	Catonese Mary—†	213	housewife	22	"
	T	Catonese Peter	213	tailor	24	
	V	*DaIona Rosaria—†	214	at home	77	
	W	Averill Lewis	214	retired	70	
	X	Garron Agnes—†	214	at home	22	"
	Y	Garron Frances—†	214	"	20	"
	Z	Garron John C	214	glazier	45	

Page.	Letter.	FULL NAME.	Residence, Jan. 1, 1938.	Occupation.	Supposed Age.	Reported Residence, Jan. 1, 1937. Street and Number.

1006
Chelsea Street—Continued

	A	Gagliolo Alphonse	214	laborer	50	here
	B	Gagliolo Leo	214	operator	23	"
	C	*Gagliolo Theresa—†	214	housewife	44	"
	E	Ferrante Joseph	215	hatter	38	
	F	Ferrante Phyllis—†	215	housewife	27	"
	G	Ferrante Concetta—†	215	operator	30	"
	H	*Ferrante Florence—†	215	housewife	61	"
	K	Ferrante John	215	busboy	24	
	L	Ferrante Minnie—†	215	at home	22	
	M	Ferrante Rose—†	215	operator	33	"
	N	Brunaccini Dominic	215	barber	35	
	O	Brunaccini Josephine—†	215	housewife	36	"
	P	*Santosuosso Angelo	216	baker	37	
	R	*Santosuosso Frances—†	216	housewife	34	"
	S	Delsordo Anna—†	216	at home	20	
	T	*Delsordo Anthony	216	laborer	60	
	U	Delsordo Catherina—†	216	operator	23	"
	V	*Delsordo Josephina—†	216	housewife	52	"
	X	Zarrella Joseph	217	laborer	38	
	Y	Zarrella Natalie—†	217	housewife	30	"
	Z	*Phillips Abraham	217	chauffeur	37	"
1007						
	A	Phillips Sophia—†	217	housewife	36	"
	B	Martucci Augustino	217	laborer	28	89 Chelsea
	C	Martucci Lena—†	217	housewife	28	here
	D	Cuono Louis	218	laborer	48	"
	E	*Cimmino Antonetta—†	218	housewife	60	"
	F	Cimmino Helen—†	218	operator	21	"
	G	Cimmino Joseph J	218	florist	27	
	H	*Belmonte Louis	218	tailor	52	
	K	Belmonte Louise—†	218	at home	23	
	L	*Belmonte Mary—†	218	housewife	52	"
	N	*Belgiorne Alberico	219	shoemaker	56	"
	O	Belgiorne Albert	219	clerk	24	
	P	Belgiorne Anna—†	219	milliner	26	
	R	*Belgiorne Lucy—†	219	housewife	52	"
	S	Belgiorne Margaret—†	219	milliner	22	
	T	Belgiorne Vincent	219	clerk	20	
	U	Ferrullo Antonette—†	219	bookkeeper	22	"

Page.	Letter.	FULL NAME.	Residence, Jan. 1, 1938.	Occupation.	Supposed Age.	Reported Residence, Jan. 1, 1937. Street and Number.

Chelsea Street—Continued

	V	Ferrullo Concetta—†	219	operator	28	here
	W	*Ferrullo Emilio	219	laborer	59	"
	X	Ferrullo Lena—†	219	seamstress	23	"
	Y	*Ferrullo Marion—†	219	housewife	60	"
	Z	Ferrullo Phyllis—†	219	operator	29	
1008						
	A	Ferrullo Ralph	219	cutter	31	
	B	Ferrullo Elvira—†	219	housewife	28	"
	C	Ferrullo Louis	219	chauffeur	30	"
	D	*Cotreau Albertine—†	220	housewife	49	"
	E	*Cotreau Roy	220	cutter	50	
	G	Carmosino Angelina—†	221	housewife	23	"
	H	*Carmosino Anthony	221	salesman	24	"
	K	Carmosino Pasquale	221	"	22	
	L	Piscitelli Angela—†	221	housewife	29	"
	M	*Piscitelli Lucia—†	221	"	67	
	N	Piscitelli Pasquale	221	barber	29	
	O	Freda Angelina—†	221	clerk	28	
	P	Freda Leopold	221	laborer	31	"
	R	*Longo Nicoletta—†	221	housewife	62	"
	S	Longo Potito	221	laborer	60	
	T	Tuberosa Joseph	223	mechanic	30	"
	U	*Tuberosa Margaret—†	223	housewife	26	"
	V	Crusco Antonio	223	laborer	42	
	W	*Crusco Mary—†	223	housewife	38	"
	X	Grella Frank	223	shipfitter	38	"
	Y	Grella Susan J—†	223	housewife	35	"
	Z	DeAngelis Achille	224	laborer	28	196 Paris
1009						
	A	DeAngelis Salvatrica—†	224	housewife	24	196 "
	B	*DeBeneditis Blanche—†	224	"	45	here
	C	DeBeneditis Louis	224	operator	22	"
	D	*DeBeneditis Vincenzo	224	tailor	52	"
	E	*Cicatelli Marie—†	224	housewife	40	"
	F	Cicatelli Vincenzo	224	shoemaker	45	"
	G	*Maienza Frank	225	salesman	25	Everett
	H	Maienza Mary—†	225	housewife	21	here
	K	Trabucco Anthony	225	laborer	47	"
	L	*Trabucco Theresa—†	225	housewife	47	"
	M	DiCalogero Charles	225	shoemaker	48	"
	N	DiCalogero James	225	reporter	20	

Page.	Letter.	Full Name.	Residence, Jan. 1, 1938.	Occupation.	Supposed Age.	Reported Residence, Jan. 1, 1937. Street and Number.

Chelsea Street—Continued

Page.	Letter.	Full Name.	Residence, Jan. 1, 1938.	Occupation.	Supposed Age.	Reported Residence, Jan. 1, 1937. Street and Number.
	O	DiCalogero Josephine—†	225	bookkeeper	22	here
	P	*DiCalogero Rose—†	225	housewife	42	"
	R	*DeStefano Mary—†	226	"	30	"
	S	DeStefano Ralph	226	operator	29	"
	T	*DiMauro Grace—†	226	housewife	24	"
	U	*DiMauro John	226	laborer	35	"
	V	*Giambaresi Catherine—†	226	housewife	53	187 London
	W	*Giambaresi Joseph	226	laborer	60	187 "
	X	Tavella Joseph	227	shoemaker	50	here
	Y	Tavella Philip J	227	artist	25	"
	Z	*Tavella Rose—†	227	housewife	44	"
1010						
	A	Tavella Rose—†	227	dressmaker	20	"
	B	Pagliarulo Jennie—†	227	housewife	21	295 Havre
	C	Pagliarulo Michael	227	laborer	25	295 "
	D	*Damigello Florence—†	227	housewife	48	60 Porter
	E	*Damigello Joseph	227	baker	48	60 "
	F	Damigello Thomas	227	student	22	60 "
	H	Pilato Angelo	229	machinist	35	here
	K	Pilato Josephine—†	229	housewife	30	"
	L	Micciche Andrina—†	229	"	31	"
	M	Micciche Rocco	229	laborer	35	
	N	Micciche Esther—†	229	housewife	37	"
	O	*Micciche Mary G—†	229	"	66	
	P	Micciche Pasquale	229	clerk	74	
	R	Micciche Santo	229	operator	41	..
	S	Vertuccio Joseph V	231	salesman	32	"
	T	Vertuccio Margaret—†	231	housewife	31	"
	U	Desio Benjamin	231	laborer	43	
	V	*Desio Mary—†	231	housewife	36	"
	W	*DeVisi Filomena—†	231	"	45	
	X	DeVisi Nicholas	231	laborer	26	
	Y	DeVisi Sabino	231	"	22	
	Z	DeVisi Vincent	231	tailor	51	
1011						
	A	Minichino Domenic	232	laborer	64	
	B	Minichino Philomena—†	232	housewife	55	"
	C	DePlacido Elizabeth—†	232	"	30	
	D	DePlacido Peter	232	laborer	33	
	E	*DeVingo Flora—†	232	housewife	66	"
	F	DeVingo Vincenza—†	232	packer	27	

Page.	Letter.	Full Name.	Residence, Jan. 1, 1938.	Occupation.	Supposed Age.	Reported Residence, Jan. 1, 1937. Street and Number.

Chelsea Street—Continued

	H	Casaletto Eva—†	233	housewife	26	here
	K	Casaletto Joseph	233	storekeeper	30	"
	L	Casaletto Helen—†	233	housewife	21	245 Chelsea
	M	Casaletto Jerry	233	laborer	26	245 "
	N	Casaletto Amelia—†	233	housewife	49	here
	O	Casaletto John	233	storekeeper	53	"
	R	Calistro Ralph	235	barber	22	213 Havre
	S	Palermo Josephine—†	235	housewife	21	194 Chelsea
	T	Palermo Victor	235	barber	22	194 "
	U	*Calistro Angelina—†	235	housewife	44	138 Porter
	V	Calistro Anna—†	235	operator	24	138 "
	W	*Calistro Bruno	235	barber	55	138 "
	Y	Palazzolo Anthony	237	printer	23	101 Leverett
	Z	Palazzola Mary—†	237	housewife	21	214 Chelsea
1012						
	A	*Cannata Mary—†	237	"	45	here
	B	*Cannata Rosario	237	laborer	52	"
	C	*Anzaldi Frank	237	"	29	"
	D	*Anzaldi Gaetano	237	"	64	"
	E	Anzaldi Guy	237	operator	24	"
	F	*Anzaldi Joseph	237	salesman	31	"
	G	*Anzaldi Mamie—†	237	housewife	56	"
	H	Anzaldi Rose—†	237	operator	21	"
	K	Terilli Joseph	239	chauffeur	24	"
	L	Privite Carmello	239	laborer	43	
	M	Privite Jennie—†	239	housewife	36	"
	N	*Reifel Israel	239	salesman	47	"
	O	*Reifel Lena—†	239	housewife	45	"
	P	Reifel Nora—†	239	student	21	
	R	Shuel Christine—†	241	housewife	33	"
	S	Shuel James H	241	storekeeper	33	"
	V	LaPusata Alexander	243	laborer	57	"
	W	*LaPusata Angelina—†	243	housewife	41	"
	X	*LaPusata Salvatore	243	laborer	21	
	Y	*Ippolito Charles	243	barber	29	
	Z	Ippolito Jennie—†	243	housewife	50	"
1013						
	A	Ippolito Joseph	243	laborer	54	"
	B	Puzzullo John	245	"	34	77 Morris
	C	Puzzullo Virginia—†	245	housewife	29	77 "
	D	*Cutreau Delphine—†	245	"	31	here

Page.	Letter.	Full Name.	Residence, Jan. 1, 1938.	Occupation.	Supposed Age.	Reported Residence, Jan. 1, 1937. Street and Number.

Chelsea Street—Continued

Page.	Letter.	Full Name.	Residence, Jan. 1, 1938.	Occupation.	Supposed Age.	Reported Residence, Jan. 1, 1937. Street and Number.
	E	Cutreau John L	245	cutter	32	here
	F	Scatto Anna—†	245	housewife	33	"
	G	Scatto Charles	245	electrician	33	"
	H	*Nappa Mary—†	247	housewife	50	"
	K	Nappa Ralph	247	tinsmith	57	
	L	*Leone Antonio	247	laundryman	25	"
	M	Leone Lillian—†	247	housewife	24	"
	N	Silvano Arthur	247	manager	25	"
	O	Silvano Mary—†	247	housewife	22	"
	P	Farina Irene—†	249	"	25	
	R	Farina Joseph	249	laborer	26	
	S	*Graziana Edna—†	249	housewife	47	"
	T	Graziana Joseph	249	laborer	37	
	U	Grasso John	249	clerk	24	
	V	Grasso Palmina—†	249	housewife	22	"
	W	*Cuozzo Anthony	251	laborer	25	
	X	Cuozzo Florence—†	251	housewife	24	"
	Y	*Ciancuilli Mary—†	251	"	32	
	Z	Ciancuilli Nicholas	251	baker	35	
1014						
	A	*Capobianco Angelina—†	251	housewife	47	"
	B	*Capobianco Antonio	251	laborer	52	
	C	Capobianco Fred	251	pressman	22	"
	D	Capobianco Ralph	251	clerk	21	
	E	*Andrew Mary—†	253	at home	24	
	F	Montiero Anthony P	253	laborer	64	
	G	*Bettencourt Manuel C	253	clockmaker	62	"
	H	*Bettencourt Olympia—†	253	housewife	50	"
	K	Dunbar Anna—†	253	"	37	
	L	Dunbar George A	253	painter	42	
	M	Young Thomas	253	laborer	75	
	N	*Pimental John	255	painter	47	
	O	Pimental John	255	timekeeper	26	"
	P	*Pimental Mary—†	255	housewife	45	"
	R	Falzone Ida—†	255	operator	23	"
	S	Falzone Philip	255	clerk	21	
	T	*Falzone Theresa—†	255	housewife	50	"
	U	Brennan Emily T—†	255	"	59	
	V	Brennan James N	255	retired	71	
	W	Brennan Lillian A—†	255	at home	34	"
	X	Finelli Dominic	257	operator	45	309 Sumner

Page.	Letter.	FULL NAME.	Residence, Jan. 1, 1938.	Occupation.	Supposed Age.	Reported Residence, Jan. 1, 1937. Street and Number.

Chelsea Street—Continued

	Y	*Finelli Marie—†	257	housewife	39	309 Sumner
	Z	*Ciandella Giuseppe	257	laborer	37	255 Webster
1015						
	A	Ciandella Perina—†	257	housewife	31	here
	B	*Nicosia Charles	257	mechanic	26	58 Bennington
	C	Nicosia Susan—†	257	housewife	25	Revere
	D	Albanese Alfred	259	machinist	28	here
	E	Albanese Anthony	259	clerk	55	"
	F	Albanese Mary—†	259	housewife	46	"
	G	Albanese Michael	259	clerk	24	
	H	Albanese Raymond	259	machinist	27	"
	L	Cionti Frank	259	laborer	23	
	M	Cionti Giuseppe	259	"	50	
	N	*Cionti Josephine—†	259	housewife	47	"
	O	Veara Joseph	261	laborer	36	
	P	*Veara Mary—†	261	housewife	65	"
	R	*Safrin Cassie—†	261	at home	79	
	S	Veara Florence—†	261	housewife	33	"
	T	Veara John R	261	mechanic	38	"
	U	*Messina Catherine—†	263	housewife	42	"
	V	Messina Charles	263	storekeeper	48	"
	W	Messina Diega—†	263	at home	20	"
	Y	*Provenzano Joseph	263	laborer	31	
	Z	*Provenzano Virginia—†	263	housewife	26	"
1016						
	A	DeAngelis Amelia—†	263	"	24	
	B	DeAngelis Nicholas	263	baker	29	
	D	*Tarazano Michael	271	retired	65	
	E	*Tarazano Rose—†	271	housewife	77	"
	F	Rossetti Antonetta—†	271	"	37	
	G	Rossetti Pasquale	271	chauffeur	45	"
	H	*Kotkovitch Leo	273	laborer	64	145 Chelsea
	K	Nikus Michael	273	"	51	here
	L	Stone Bella—†	273	housewife	65	"
	M	Stone Jacob	273	attorney	27	"
	N	Kagan Ellis	273	clerk	35	
	O	Kagan Ethel—†	273	housewife	31	"
	P	Tracia Angelina—†	274	"	25	"
	R	Tracia Louis	274	laborer	25	"
	U	Hickey Helen—†	275	housewife	22	257 Chelsea
	V	Hickey Thomas F	275	chauffeur	23	257 "

Page.	Letter.	Full Name.	Residence, Jan. 1, 1938.	Occupation.	Supposed Age.	Reported Residence, Jan. 1, 1937. Street and Number.

Chelsea Street—Continued

Page.	Letter.	Full Name.	Residence, Jan. 1, 1938.	Occupation.	Supposed Age.	Reported Residence, Jan. 1, 1937. Street and Number.
	w	*Balbanti Frank	275	storekeeper	52	here
	x	*Balbanti Mary—†	275	housewife	65	"
	y	Stokes Frank	276	laborer	35	"
	z	Stokes Jennie—†	276	housewife	65	"
1017						
	A	Kergald Amelia—†	276	"	49	
	B	Kergald George	276	electrician	50	"
	C	Mastrangelo Angelo	276	laborer	23	
	D	Mastrangelo Anthony	276	"	20	
	E	Mastrangelo John	276	"	61	
	F	Mastrangelo Mary—†	276	housewife	54	"
	G	Mastrangelo Ralph	276	laborer	29	
	H	Mastrangelo Rose—†	276	at home	25	"
	K	Lineo Frances—†	277	housewife	22	251 Lexington
	L	*Lineo Louis	277	laborer	24	251 "
	M	*Cavalo Manuel	277	operator	48	here
	N	Brilliant Betty—†	277	housewife	29	"
	O	*Brilliant Maxwell	277	salesman	38	"
	P	*Fine Dora—†	278	housewife	78	"
	R	*Fine Max	278	retired	78	"
	S	Oliver Alfred	278	laborer	24	Malden
	T	*Oliver Mary—†	278	housewife	46	"
	U	Oliver Rose—†	278	at home	20	"
	V	*Kootkivitz Frederick	278	laborer	56	here
	W	Kootkivitz Margaret—†	278	operator	22	"
	X	Kootkivitz Olga—†	278	bookbinder	24	"
	Y	*Kootkivitz Pauline—†	278	housewife	47	"
	Z	Tango John	279	operator	22	215 Webster
1018						
	A	Tango Margaret—†	279	housewife	20	215 "
	B	*Pereira Emma—†	279	at home	40	21 Gove
	C	Castagna Enrico	279	barber	45	here
	D	Quartarone John	279	"	28	"
	E	Quartarone Theresa—†	279	housewife	27	"
	F	Walters Eleanor—†	280	at home	22	Everett
	G	*Pothier Charles	280	cutter	66	here
	H	*Pothier Rose—†	280	housewife	47	"
	K	Pastore Assilio	280	laborer	49	"
	L	*Pastore Concetta—†	280	housewife	49	"
	M	*Dell'Aria Jessie—†	281	"	36	
	N	*Rogowicz Amelia—†	281	"	38	

Page.	Letter.	Full Name.	Residence, Jan. 1, 1938.	Occupation.	Supposed Age.	Reported Residence, Jan. 1, 1937. Street and Number.

Chelsea Street—Continued

	o	*Rogowicz John	281	baker	48	here
	p	Spano Carmella—†	281	housewife	21	"
	r	Spano John	281	operator	24	"
	s	Oliver James R	282	salesman	26	156 Saratoga
	t	Oliver Vera—†	282	housewife	23	156 "
	u	Vasconcellos Annie L—†	282	"	62	here
	v	Vasconcellos Anthony J	282	engineer	32	"
	w	Vasconcellos Mary A—†	282	housewife	29	"
	x	Vasconcellos Catherine–†	282	"	23	
	y	Vasconcellos Charles F	282	salesman	36	"
	z	Sonn Joseph	283	cutter	24	
1019						
	a	*Sonn Katherine—†	283	housewife	67	"
	b	Bruno Joseph	283	laborer	32	
	c	Bruno Louisa—†	283	housewife	28	"
	d	Santosuosso Albert	283	chauffeur	26	8 Drake pl
	e	Santosuosso Theresa—†	283	housewife	23	8 "
	f	Poirier Anthony	284	painter	23	216 Princeton
	g	Poirier Lena—†	284	housewife	20	202 "
	h	Falzarano Columbia—†	284	"	20	137 Havre
	k	Falzarano Louis	284	operator	22	137 "
	l	Campannaro Frank	284	laborer	42	here
	m	Campannaro Mary—†	284	housewife	41	"
	n	Ricciardi Concetta—†	285	"	43	"
	o	Ricciardi Frank	285	barber	48	
	p	Ricciardi Joseph	285	"	52	
	r	Ricciardi Mary—†	285	housewife	37	"
	s	Ricciardi Virginia—†	285	clerk	24	
	t	Gill Joseph P	285	laborer	27	
	u	Gill Phyllis—†	285	housewife	28	"
	v	Cimmino Pasquale	286	chauffeur	23	Revere
	w	Gisetto Lena—†	286	housewife	26	here
	x	Gisetto William	286	foreman	26	"
	y	*Mennella Angelina—†	286	at home	55	"
	z	Spinazzola Henry	286	tailor	27	Framingham
1020						
	a	Spinazzola Theresa—†	286	tailoress	24	95 Prescott
	b	Traiger Frances—†	287	housewife	25	here
	c	Traiger Louis	287	packer	34	"
	d	Traiger Louis	287	salesman	32	"
	e	Anzalone Ernest	287	operator	29	21 Brooks

Page.	Letter.	Full Name.	Residence, Jan. 1, 1938.	Occupation.	Supposed Age.	Reported Residence, Jan. 1, 1937. Street and Number.
		Chelsea Street—Continued				
	F	Anzalone Jennie—†	287	housewife	28	21 Brooks
	G	Angelo Catherine—†	288	"	40	here
	H	Angelo Pasquale	288	laborer	49	"
	K	Barletta Carmen	288	"	41	"
	L	Barletta Susanna—†	288	housewife	50	"
	M	Cusatano Gaetano	288	laborer	46	"
	N	Colluccini Florence—†	288	operator	26	160 Putnam
	O	Ferranova Joseph	288	laborer	44	160 "
	P	Ferranova Josephine—†	288	housewife	35	160 "
	R	VanDael Jacob	289	laborer	34	here
	S	VanDael Mary G—†	289	housewife	38	"
	T	Adelman Jacob	289	laborer	54	"
	U	Adelman Sadie—†	289	housewife	39	"
	V	*Fiorito Filomena—†	289	"	32	
	W	Fiorito Leonardo	289	laborer	37	
	X	Salamone Ignatius	290	"	25	
	Y	*Salamone Luigi	290	"	55	
	Z	*Salamone Stella—†	290	housewife	50	"
1021	A	*Occhipinti Joseph	290	carpenter	53	"
	B	*Occhipinti Millie—†	290	housewife	50	"
	C	Avola Adeline—†	290	"	23	115½ Havre
	D	Avola Frank	290	operator	23	115½ "
	E	Romano Guy	290	laborer	28	140 Lexington
	F	Romano Josephine—†	290	housewife	25	140 "
	G	Clark Nellie—†	291	at home	49	here
	H	DeFreitas John	291	laborer	20	"
	K	DeFreitas Thomas	291	clerk	25	"
	L	*Muise Mary—†	291	housewife	43	"
	M	*Muise Wilfred	291	carpenter	61	"
	N	Raphanella Anthony	292	laborer	23	
	O	*Raphanella Carmen	292	retired	63	
	P	Raphanella Dominick	292	chauffeur	25	"
	R	Raphanella Lucy—†	292	at home	29	
	S	*Napolitano Frances—†	292	housewife	38	"
	T	Napolitano Pasquale	292	laborer	40	
	U	Ruggiero Augustine	292	"	44	
	V	Ruggiero Margaret—†	292	housewife	43	"
	W	Ruggiero Theresa—†	292	clerk	23	
	Y	DelVisco Anthony	294	mechanic	27	"
	Z	LaCortiglia Catherine—†	294	housewife	34	"

Page.	Letter.	Full Name.	Residence, Jan. 1, 1938.	Occupation.	Supposed Age.	Reported Residence, Jan. 1, 1937. Street and Number.
1022		**Chelsea Street**—Continued				
	A	LaCortiglia Dominic	294	laborer	36	here
	B	*Freda Carmella—†	294	housewife	52	"
	C	Freda Pasquale	294	laborer	22	"
	D	*Freda Pellegrino	294	operator	49	"
	F	Guarnaccia Carlo	294	laborer	41	"
	E	*Guarnaccia Ida—†	294	housewife	37	"
	G	*Pellizzotti Benjamin	296	retired	75	
	H	*Pellizzotti Jennie—†	296	housewife	74	"
	K	*Ranaldi Florence—†	296	"	42	98 Moore
	L	*Ranaldi Frank	296	baker	42	98 "
	M	Chiampi Frank	296	painter	29	144 Putnam
	N	Chiampi Helen—†	296	housewife	26	144 "
	O	Silva Frances P—†	298	"	84	here
	P	Silva William P	298	laborer	74	"
	T	Reagan James J	300	bartender	27	213 Princeton
	U	Reagan Josephine—†	300	housewife	22	Lynn
	V	D'Amico Jennie—†	300	"	85	here
	W	D'Amico John	300	laborer	47	"
	X	Bertolino Anna—†	300	nurse	21	"
	Y	Bertolino Benedetto	300	tailor	56	
	Z	Bertolino Donald B	300	"	23	
1023						
	A	Bertolino Helen—†	300	housewife	43	"
	B	Bertolino Nicholas D	300	accountant	24	"
	C	Lawton John	302	timekeeper	22	111 Eutaw
	D	*Lawton Marie—†	302	housewife	22	111 "
	E	Griecco Carmella—†	302	packer	22	here
	F	Griecco Felix	302	salesman	54	"
	G	Griecco Margaret—†	302	packer	21	"
	H	*Griecco Philomena—†	302	housewife	54	"
	K	*Adinolfi Josephine—†	302	"	24	
	L	*Adinolfi Nicholas	302	laborer	36	"
	N	DeRosa Arthur	304	engineer	54	Malden
	O	*Fasano Josephine—†	304	housewife	29	here
	P	*Fasano Michael	304	laborer	39	"
	R	Sarminto Fernando	306	retired	70	"
	S	Rose Evelyn A—†	306	operator	26	
	T	Rose Lillian B—†	306	saleswoman	22	"
	U	Rose Mary A—†	306	housewife	58	"
	V	Rose Otto J	306	laborer	58	

Page.	Letter.	Full Name.	Residence, Jan. 1, 1938.	Occupation.	Supposed Age.	Reported Residence, Jan. 1, 1937. Street and Number.

Chelsea Street—Continued

	W	Russo Leborio	306	operator	52	Wakefield
	X	Russo Mary—†	306	housewife	50	"
	Y	Ardita Frank	308	custodian	30	here
	Z	Ardita Theresa—†	308	housewife	25	"
1024						
	A	Incerto Dominic	308	chauffeur	27	"
	B	Incerto Josephine—†	308	housewife	50	"
	C	Incerto Mary—†	308	packer	22	
	D	*Incerto Vincent	308	mechanic	58	"
	E	Cammarota Anna—†	308	housewife	42	"
	F	Cammarota Gaetano	308	laborer	52	
	G	Mirasola James	310	"	29	
	H	*Mirasola Josephine—†	310	housewife	66	"
	K	Mirasola Mary—†	310	"	25	
	L	Mirasola Angelina—†	310	"	36	
	M	Mirasola Peter	310	blacksmith	40	"
	N	Mirasola Carmella—†	310	housewife	33	"
	O	Mirasola Joseph	310	blacksmith	42	"
	P	Flaschner Caroline—†	312	housewife	34	"
	R	Flaschner Leo	312	chauffeur	38	"
	S	Flynn Helena—†	312	at home	43	
	T	Nolan Herbert	312	laborer	23	
	U	Dunn Ruth—†	312	housewife	26	"
	V	Dunn Walter	312	laborer	29	
	W	Leary Thomas	312	"	37	
	X	Saulnier Edmund	314	painter	48	
	Y	Saulnier Levina—†	314	housewife	43	"

1025 Marion Street

	C	Micele John	230	operator	40	here
	D	Micele Minnie—†	230	housewife	35	"
	E	*Albanese Cecelia—†	230	"	38	"
	F	*Albanese Salvatore	230	laborer	42	
	H	*Matarazza Gabriel	232	retired	61	
	K	Matarazza Inez—†	232	at home	21	
	L	Matarazza Joseph	232	salesman	28	"
	M	Matarazza Michael	232	"	23	
	N	*Matarazza Rosina—†	232	housewife	59	"
	O	DeAngelis Alfred R	232	salesman	38	"
	P	DeAngelis Mollie—†	232	housewife	31	"

Page.	Letter.	Full Name.	Residence, Jan. 1, 1938.	Occupation.	Supposed Age.	Reported Residence, Jan. 1, 1937. Street and Number.

Marion Street—Continued

Page.	Letter.	Full Name.	Residence, Jan. 1, 1938.	Occupation.	Supposed Age.	Reported Residence, Jan. 1, 1937. Street and Number.
	R	Vigliotta Anna—†	234	housewife	27	202 Princeton
	S	Vigliotta Biagio	234	laborer	37	202 "
	T	Aloise Domenic	234	operator	26	here
	U	Aloise Rose—†	234	housewife	22	"
	V	*DiStolfo Antonette—†	234	"	64	"
	W	DiStolfo Leonardo	234	laborer	44	
	X	*DiStolfo Santo	234	"	56	
	Z	*Rotondo Ella—†	236	housewife	46	"
	Y	Rotondo Orazio	236	garageman	55	"
1026						
	A	Albanese Angelina—†	236	saleswoman	32	"
	B	*Albanese Carmella—†	236	housewife	65	"
	C	*Albanese Jeremiah	236	laborer	63	
	D	Albanese Joseph	236	"	57	
	E	Albanese Joseph	236	bartender	33	"
	F	Graseano Frank	236	laborer	39	
	G	Padowitz Harry	236	merchant	58	"
	H	Padowitz Maurice	236	clerk	30	
	K	Padowitz Rose—†	236	housewife	60	"
	L	Padowitz Rose—†	236	"	31	
	M	Fallica John	238	storekeeper	49	"
	N	*Miccicche Domiana—†	238	housewife	39	"
	O	Miccicche Giuseppe	238	laborer	41	
	R	Bartolo Charles	252	chauffeur	30	"
	S	Bartolo Helen—†	252	housewife	25	"
	T	Forgione Battista	252	laborer	53	
	U	Forgione John	252	operator	22	
	V	Forgione Joseph	252	machinist	28	"
	W	Forgione Margaret—†	252	housewife	47	"
	X	Forgione Mary—†	252	operator	25	
	Y	Forgione Angelo	252	laborer	33	
	Z	Forgione Christina—†	252	housewife	30	"
1027						
	A	Gambino Angelo	254	operator	39	
	B	*Gambino Eva—†	254	housewife	33	"
	C	*Pisano Frank J	254	laborer	47	
	D	*Pisano Parmenia—†	254	housewife	40	"
	E	Burke John G	254	janitor	39	
	F	Burke Mary—†	254	housewife	33	"
	G	*Chiero Angelo	256	laborer	72	
	H	*Chiero Maria—†	256	housewife	73	"

Page.	Letter.	Full Name.	Residence, Jan. 1, 1938.	Occupation.	Supposed Age.	Reported Residence, Jan. 1, 1937. Street and Number.
		Marion Street—Continued				
	K	Chiello Joseph	256	shoemaker	48	here
	L	*Cobino Amelia—†	256	housewife	34	"
	M	*Cobino Angelo	256	laborer	43	"
	N	*Simili Angelina—†	258	housewife	37	"
	O	Simili Frank	258	storekeeper	46	"
	P	Balba Andrew	258	laborer	31	"
	R	Balba Philomena—†	258	housewife	30	"
	S	Sachs David	258	clerk	28	
	T	Sachs Edward R	258	attorney	25	"
	U	Sachs Maurice	258	clerk	27	
	V	Sachs Rachel—†	258	housewife	48	"
		Morris Street				
	W	Blizzi John	3	laborer	64	225 Paris
	X	Pazzo Anita—†	5	housewife	28	here
	Y	*Pazzo Peter	5	clerk	31	"
	Z	Emma Columbus	5	repairman	23	"
1028						
	A	Emma Gaetano	5	"	61	
	B	*Emma Vincenza—†	5	housewife	61	"
	C	*Chiuve Julia—†	5	"	40	
	D	Chiuve Mario	5	laborer	47	
	E	*Singerella Josephine—†	5	housewife	64	"
	F	*Singerella Mario	5	laborer	66	
	G	*Cassaro Frances—†	7	housewife	40	"
	H	*Cassaro Joseph	7	laborer	50	
	K	Casato John J	7	tailor	33	
	L	Casato Madeline—†	7	housewife	33	"
	N	Bavaro Anna—†	13	"	32	
	O	Bavaro Peter	13	laborer	36	
	P	Scirro Frances—†	13	housewife	34	"
	R	Scirro Ralph	13	laborer	38	
	S	Barrasso Antonio	13	"	57	
	T	Barrasso Antonio	13	"	24	
	U	*Barrasso Maria—†	13	housewife	54	"
	V	Oliveri Anthony	15	laborer	31	Everett
	W	Oliveri Arduina—†	15	housewife	23	213 Havre
	X	Yancovitz Charlotte—†	15	saleswoman	24	here
	Y	*Yancovitz Dominic	15	laborer	49	"
	Z	Yancovitz John	15	"	27	"

Page.	Letter.	Full Name.	Residence, Jan. 1, 1938.	Occupation.	Supposed Age.	Reported Residence, Jan. 1, 1937. Street and Number.

1029
Morris Street—Continued

Page.	Letter.	Full Name.	Residence, Jan. 1, 1938.	Occupation.	Supposed Age.	Reported Residence, Jan. 1, 1937. Street and Number.
	A	Yancovitz Joseph	15	laborer	28	here
	B	*Yancovitz Minnie—†	15	housewife	43	"
	C	*Cacaio Angelo	15	storekeeper	44	"
	D	*Cacaio Josephine—†	15	housewife	40	"
	E	*Nesti Lena—†	17	"	48	
	F	*Nesti Louis	17	laborer	48	"
	G	Salvati Dominic	17	"	21	95 Chelsea
	H	Salvati Frank	17	"	52	95 "
	K	Salvati Louise—†	17	operator	22	95 "
	L	*Salvati Mary—†	17	housewife	45	95 "
	M	Schena Samuel	17	laborer	42	here
	N	Schena Theresa—†	17	housewife	40	"
	O	Jones Emma—†	19	"	36	"
	P	Jones James D	19	tailor	35	
	R	Milano Biagio	19	laborer	22	
	S	*Milano Lena—†	19	housewife	43	"
	T	*Milano Vincent	19	laborer	54	
	U	Indoratto Filedelfio	19	"	20	
	V	Indoratto Julia—†	19	housewife	42	"
	W	Indoratto Salvatore	19	laborer	24	
	X	Indoratto Sebastiano	19	"	50	
	Y	*Fumicello Concetta—†	20	housewife	30	"
	Z	Fumicello Michael	20	timekeeper	32	"
1030						
	A	Magaletta Mary—†	21	housewife	21	"
	B	Magaletta Vovito	21	laborer	28	
	C	*Fumicello Philippa—†	21	housewife	60	"
	D	Fumicello Salvatore	21	laborer	20	
	E	*Milano Mary—†	21	housewife	42	"
	F	Milano Philip	21	laborer	41	
	G	*White George	22	painter	39	
	H	*White Philomena—†	22	housewife	33	"
	K	*Piccorella Eliza—†	22	"	50	"
	L	Piccorella Salvatore	22	laborer	56	
	M	*Castelluccio Sadie—†	23	housewife	32	"
	N	Castelluccio Samuel	23	operator	38	
	O	*Amico Josephine—†	23	housewife	25	"
	P	Amico Michael	23	operator	33	
	R	Mancuso Joseph	23	laborer	45	
	S	*Mancuso Philippa—†	23	housewife	30	"

Page.	Letter.	Full Name.	Residence, Jan. 1, 1938.	Occupation.	Supposed Age.	Reported Residence, Jan. 1, 1937. Street and Number.

Morris Street—Continued

	T	*Benedetti Alfred	24	cutter	31	128 Chelsea
	U	Benedetti Phyllis—†	24	housewife	29	128 "
	V	Accomando Ida—†	24	seamstress	22	128 "
	W	*DiPerri Angelina—†	24	housewife	27	here
	X	*DiPerri John	24	cutter	32	"
	Y	LaPlaca Russell F	24	operator	23	787 E Sixth
	Z	Morris Elizabeth—†	25	housewife	32	here
1031						
	A	*Morris James	25	laborer	29	"
	B	*Torname Joseph	25	"	62	Medford
	C	*Torname Maria—†	25	housewife	52	"
	D	Torname Salvatore	25	laborer	20	"
	E	*LaPlaca Clara—†	25	housewife	34	here
	F	LaPlaca John	25	laborer	43	"
	G	*Aste Louis	26	"	48	"
	H	*Meloni Enrico	27	"	75	
	K	*Meloni Mary—†	27	housewife	70	"
	L	Meloni Amelia—†	27	domestic	38	"
	M	Meloni John	27	laborer	30	
	N	Miranto Dionizio	27	"	38	
	O	Miranto Mary—†	27	housewife	34	"
	P	LaMarca Alfred	28	laborer	26	71 Liverpool
	R	LaMarca Mary—†	28	housewife	24	71 "
	S	Parisso Alesio	28	laborer	30	86 Porter
	T	Parisso Marion—†	28	housewife	32	86 "
	U	Mazza Antoinette—†	28	"	28	here
	V	Mazza John	28	laborer	33	"
	W	*Pizzello Filomena—†	30	housewife	41	"
	X	Pizzello Francesco	30	laborer	43	"
	Y	*Tedesco Anthony	30	"	60	Italy
	Z	Tedesco Anthony	30	"	37	here
1032						
	A	*Tedesco Molly—†	30	housewife	29	"
	B	*DeMarco Angelina—†	30	"	55	
	C	*DeMarco Benjamin	30	laborer	75	
	D	DeRosa Armando	30	"	26	
	E	DeRosa James	30	chauffeur	24	"
	F	Gioioso Frances—†	32	housewife	26	28 Morris
	G	Gioioso Patrick	32	pressman	28	28 "
	H	Dushane Anna—†	32	housewife	63	here
	K	Dushane Louis	32	laborer	65	"

Page.	Letter.	Full Name.	Residence, Jan. 1, 1938.	Occupation.	Supposed Age.	Reported Residence, Jan. 1, 1937. Street and Number.

Morris Street—Continued

Page.	Letter.	Full Name.	Residence, Jan. 1, 1938.	Occupation.	Supposed Age.	Reported Residence, Jan. 1, 1937. Street and Number.
	L	Dushane Sallie—†	32	saleswoman	29	here
	M	Gioioso Joseph	32	operator	26	"
	N	Gioioso Josephine—†	32	housewife	22	"
	O	Susi Frances—†	33	"	40	
	P	Susi Frank	33	laborer	44	
	R	*Agave Minnie—†	33	housewife	38	"
	S	Agave Umberto	33	waiter	43	
	T	*Gomes Bonvinda—†	34	housewife	37	"
	U	*Gomes Manuel	34	laborer	44	
	V	Collura Anthony	34	printer	27	
	W	Collura Esther—†	34	housewife	23	"
	X	Aguiar Augustino	34	longshoreman	37	"
	Y	Mello James	36	painter	37	1048 Saratoga
	Z	Mello Josephine—†	36	housewife	36	1048 "
1033						
	A	Collins Marion E—†	36	"	53	here
	B	Muldoon Thomas	36	operator	42	"
	C	Muldoon Victorio—†	36	housewife	41	"
	D	Springer Louis	37	laborer	54	
	E	Springer Rose—†	37	housewife	43	"
	F	*Scarpetuella Carmen	37	laborer	33	
	G	Scarpetuella Josephine—†	37	housewife	29	"
	H	*Chenine Anna—†	37	"	48	
	K	Chenine Joseph	37	laborer	47	
	L	Chenine Josephine—†	37	operator	20	"
	M	*Bandini Antoinetta—†	38	housewife	61	"
	N	*Bandini Paul	38	laborer	60	
	O	*Pimentel John	38	"	34	
	P	Pimentel Mary—†	38	housewife	34	"
	R	DeSimone Jennie—†	38	"	28	
	S	DeSimone John	38	laborer	29	
	T	Venute Anthony	40	"	25	
	U	Venute Margaret—†	40	housewife	23	"
	V	*Fumicello Josephine—†	40	"	32	
	W	*Fumicello Paul	40	laborer	40	
	X	*DePari Mary—†	40	housewife	53	"
	Y	*DePari Vito	40	laborer	58	
	Z	*Barrone Carmella—†	41	housewife	49	"
1034						
	A	Barrone Philomena—†	41	clerk	20	
	B	*Barrone Vito	41	laborer	59	

Page.	Letter.	Full Name.	Residence, Jan. 1, 1938.	Occupation.	Supposed Age.	Reported Residence, Jan. 1, 1937. Street and Number.

Morris Street—Continued

	C	Pasquantonio Phyllis—†	42	housewife	22	here
	D	Pasquantonio William	42	chauffeur	25	“
	E	Bonura Joseph	42	operator	41	“
	F	*Bonura Madeline—†	42	housewife	27	“
	G	*Pasquantonio Antonio	42	laborer	69	
	H	*Pasquantonio Jennie—†	42	housewife	61	“
	K	Dumas Alice—†	43	“	23	
	L	Dumas Godfrey	43	laborer	36	
	M	Russo Angelo	43	“	28	
	N	Russo Gabriella—†	43	operator	22	“
	O	*Russo Laura—†	43	housewife	50	“
	P	Russo Louise—†	43	operator	26	
	R	Russo Mary—†	43	“	30	
	S	Russo Thomas	43	laborer	24	
	T	*Incerto Antonio	44	“	60	
	U	Incerto Rose—†	44	clerk	20	
	V	*Cerbone Mary—†	44	housewife	44	“
	W	*Çerbone Michael	44	laborer	54	
	X	Fratto Josephine—†	44	clerk	21	
	Y	Fratto Peter	44	laborer	27	
	Z	Fratto Thomas	44	“	67	
1035						
	A	*Aliano Concetta—†	45	housewife	58	“
	B	*Aliano Santo	45	laborer	33	“
	C	*Marino Frank	45	“	43	
	D	*Marino Phyllis—†	45	housewife	39	“
	E	*Cappozi James	45	laborer	68	60 Lubec
	F	*Cappozi Rose—†	45	housewife	69	60 “
	G	Selvitella Ralph	46	laborer	43	here
	H	Selvitella Virginia—†	46	housewife	41	“
	K	*Corrao Frank	46	operator	38	“
	L	Corrao Jennie—†	46	housewife	31	“
	M	O'Connor Rose—†	46	“	34	
	N	O'Connor William T	46	clerk	38	
	O	*Golizano Angelo	51	laborer	42	
	P	Perrone Dominic	51	“	48	
	R	*Perrone Josephine—†	51	housewife	42	“
	S	*Perrone Susan—†	51	“	70	“
	T	Mancuso Charles	51	laborer	41	
	U	*Mancuso Jennie—†	51	housewife	33	“
	W	Harkins Anna—†	65	“	27	

Page.	Letter.	Full Name.	Residence, Jan. 1, 1938.	Occupation.	Supposed Age.	Reported Residence, Jan. 1, 1937. Street and Number.

Morris Street—Continued

Page.	Letter.	Full Name.	Residence, Jan. 1, 1938.	Occupation.	Supposed Age.	Reported Residence, Jan. 1, 1937. Street and Number.
	x	Harkins William H	65	cutter	27	here
	z	Cella Anthony	65	laborer	28	"
	y	Cella Elizabeth—†	65	housewife	26	"
1036						
	A	*Quarino Lena—†	65	"	34	
	B	*Quarino Prisco	65	laborer	48	
	C	Saggese Amando	67	chauffeur	25	"
	D	Saggese Helen—†	67	housewife	24	"
	E	Ruggiero Fortunato	67	fireman	43	
	F	Ruggiero Jennie—†	67	housewife	43	"
	1F	*Polito Theresa—†	67	"	60	
	G	DeChristoforo Anthony	69	operator	26	"
	H	DeChristoforo Fannie—†	69	housewife	24	"
	K	*Levine Louis	69	tailor	42	
	L	*Levine Sarah—†	69	housewife	43	"
	M	Columba Angela—†	69	"	27	
	N	Columba Frank	69	laborer	27	
	O	Graziano Helen—†	69	operator	25	
	P	*Graziano Louise—†	69	"	46	
	S	*Rappi Concetta—†	71	housewife	64	"
	T	Rappi Joseph	71	laborer	26	
	U	*Rappi Michael	71	"	61	"
	V	*Aleo Alice—†	71	clerk	30	3 Appian pl
	W	*Aleo Stella—†	71	housewife	56	3 "
	X	Tracia Anthony	71	laborer	27	197 Chelsea
	Y	Tracia Carmella—†	71	housewife	21	197 "
	Z	*Costigan Margaret—†	73	"	33	here
1037						
	A	*Costigan Thomas J	73	fisherman	39	"
	B	Cardoza Ferdinand	73	foreman	38	
	C	Cardoza Helen—†	73	housewife	33	"
	D	Gallagher Catherine—†	73	"	33	
	E	Gallagher William	73	laborer	37	
	F	Sousa Meda—†	75	operator	37	"
	G	Molino Charles	75	laborer	51	33 Morris
	H	*Molino Rose—†	75	housewife	42	33 "
	K	Lynch Ellen J—†	75	domestic	80	here
	L	Lynch Jane F—†	75	housewife	72	"
	M	*Delsie Antonetta—†	77	"	53	"
	N	*Delsie Philip	77	laborer	51	
	O	Doucette Charles	77	"	27	

Page.	Letter.	Full Name.	Residence, Jan. 1, 1938.	Occupation.	Supposed Age.	Reported Residence, Jan. 1, 1937. Street and Number.
		Morris Street—Continued				
	P	Doucette Josephine—†	77	housewife	24	here
	R	White Catherine B—†	77	"	63	"
	S	White Catherine R—†	77	operator	27	"
	T	White George F	77	teacher	33	
	U	White James J	77	laborer	62	
	V	White James J, jr	77	machinist	32	"
	W	White Mary V—†	77	clerk	29	
	X	White William J	77	"	35	"
	Y	Morrison Doris—†	79	housewife	38	196 Trenton
	Z	Morrison Warren	79	laborer	38	here
1038						
	A	Cocozza Charles	79	messenger	24	"
	B	Cocozza Dominic	79	laborer	57	
	C	*Cocozza Frances—†	79	housewife	56	"
	D	Cocozza William	79	messenger	21	"
	E	*Mitchell Lillian—†	79	housewife	39	"
	F	*Mitchell Percy	79	laborer	40	
	G	Mitchell Thomas	79	"	21	
	H	*Agri Antonio	81	"	60	
	K	*Agri Frances—†	81	housewife	60	"
	L	Harrington Robert E	81	chauffeur	41	"
	M	McGuire Catherine—†	81	housewife	49	"
	N	McGuire James W	81	laborer	51	
	O	Hennessey Emma—†	81	housewife	31	"
	P	Hennessey John	81	laborer	32	
	R	Romaine Joseph H	83	cook	44	
	S	Romaine Mary E—†	83	housewife	44	"
	T	Shapiro Anna—†	83	saleswoman	30	"
	U	Shapiro Minnie—†	83	"	28	
	V	Shapiro Samuel	83	merchant	62	"
	W	Pappallardo Josephine—†	83	clerk	21	
	X	*Pappallardo Mary—†	83	housewife	40	"
	Y	Pappallardo Vincent	83	laborer	50	
	Z	Indingaro Isabelle—†	87	housewife	57	"
1039						
	A	Indingaro Lawrence	87	restaurateur	29	"
	B	Keough John	87	storekeeper	61	"
	C	Russo Alma—†	87	housewife	32	"
	D	Russo Anthony	87	operator	32	"
	E	Russo Frank	87	musician	25	66 Eutaw
	F	Barone John	89	laborer	27	here

Morris Street—Continued

Page.	Letter.	Full Name.	Residence, Jan. 1, 1938.	Occupation.	Supposed Age.	Reported Residence, Jan. 1, 1937. Street and Number.
	G	Barone Rose—†	89	housewife	25	here
	H	Phillips Blanche—†	89	"	35	"
	K	Serra Alba—†	89	"	27	180 Paris
	L	Serra Pasquale	89	laborer	30	180 "
	M	Belton Helen M—†	90	housewife	29	91 Morris
	N	Belton Thomas P	90	printer	33	91 "
	O	Bratt Gustaf L	90	laborer	67	here
	P	Bratt Lena—†	90	housewife	67	"
	R	Amese Anthony	90	laborer	30	"
	S	Amese Celia—†	90	housewife	33	"
	T	McCarthy Charles	91	laborer	55	Chelsea
	U	McCarthy Jennie—†	91	housewife	34	325 Paris
	V	McCarthy Timothy J	91	laborer	39	325 "
	W	Ferranti Graziano	91	"	66	here
	X*	Ferranti Jennie—†	91	housewife	64	41 McLean
	Y*	Ruggiero Nicholas	91	laborer	55	here
	Z	LaCourtiglia Harry	91	chauffeur	30	"
1040	A	LaCourtiglia Louise—†	91	housewife	27	"
	B	Genova Anthony	99	chauffeur	22	"
	C	Genova Josephine—†	99	dressmaker	20	"
	D	Genova Pasquale	99	baker	58	
	E*	Genova Pasqualina—†	99	housewife	57	"
	F	Bernardinelli Anna—†	99	"	31	
	G	Bernardinelli William	99	machinist	43	"
	H	Lanagan Elizabeth C—†	101	housewife	37	327 Paris
	K	Lanagan Henry J	101	laborer	43	327 "
	L*	Walsh Mary—†	101	housewife	39	107 Eutaw
	M*	Walsh Michael	101	shoemaker	38	107 "
	N	Francis Elizabeth—†	101	housewife	46	here
	O	Francis John L	101	laborer	67	"
	R*	Barbanti Alfreda—†	103	housewife	23	"
	S	Barbanti John	103	cabinetmaker	29	"
	T	Mandella Helen—†	103	housewife	39	"
	U*	Mandella Patrick	103	laborer	57	
	V	Barbanti Antonio	103	retired	71	
	W	Barbanti Josephine—†	103	housewife	67	"
	X	Moynihan Elizabeth F–†	106	"	45	
	Y	Fine Anna—†	106	attorney	28	"
	Z	Fine Elizabeth—†	106	housewife	27	"

Page.	Letter.	Full Name.	Residence, Jan. 1, 1938.	Occupation.	Supposed Age.	Reported Residence, Jan. 1, 1937. Street and Number.
1041						
		Morris Street—Continued				
	A	Fine Harry M	106	merchant	40	here
	B	Fine Maurice	106	laborer	22	"
	C	Filippone Frances—†	106	housewife	50	"
	D	Filippone Henry	106	laborer	50	
		Paris Street				
	E	Martino Angela—†	253	housewife	33	here
	F	*Martino Peter	253	barber	40	"
	G	Ricciardi Fannie—†	253	housewife	20	5 Prescott
	H	Ricciardi James	253	engineer	21	here
	K	Ricciardi Joseph	253	chauffeur	26	5 Prescott
	L	Ricciardelli Antonio	253	mechanic	25	here
	M	Ricciardelli Luigi	253	laborer	52	"
	N	*Ricciardelli Michelina—†	253	housewife	47	"
	O	*Boncore Ida—†	255	"	33	91 Trenton
	P	Boncore Philip	255	tailor	39	91 "
	R	Pastore Angela—†	255	hairdresser	21	here
	S	*Pastore Rose—†	255	housewife	43	"
	T	Pastore Vito	255	hairdresser	48	"
	U	Puzzaghera Charles	255	laborer	53	
	V	Puzzaghera Gaetano	255	operator	23	
	W	*Puzzaghera Mary—†	255	housewife	47	"
	X	Puzzaghera Salvatore	255	operator	27	"
	Y	Puzzaghera Sarah—†	255	seamstress	21	"
	Z	Carrozza Carmella—†	257	housewife	33	"
1042						
	A	*Carrozza Gerardo	257	laborer	32	
	B	Casamassima Amelia—†	257	at home	26	
	C	Casamassima Dominick	257	shoemaker	34	"
	D	*Casamassima Gaetana—†	257	housewife	63	"
	E	Casamassima Michael	257	shoemaker	64	"
	F	*Lauletta Catherine—†	257	at home	57	
	G	*Miraglia Vincenza—†	257	"	78	
	H	*Albanese Carmella—†	259	housewife	59	"
	K	Albanese Frances—†	259	student	20	
	L	Albanese Fred	259	laborer	27	
	M	Albanese John	259	carpenter	22	"
	N	Albanese Lewis	259	engraver	24	"

Page.	Letter.	Full Name.	Residence, Jan. 1, 1938.	Occupation.	Supposed Age.	Reported Residence, Jan. 1, 1937. Street and Number.

Paris Street—Continued

Page.	Letter.	Full Name.	Residence, Jan. 1, 1938.	Occupation.	Supposed Age.	Reported Residence, Jan. 1, 1937. Street and Number.
	O	Pardi Frank	259	laborer	44	here
	P	*Pardi Mary—†	259	housewife	43	"
	R	Cedrone Dominick	259	laborer	52	"
	S	*Cedrone Mary—†	259	housewife	47	"
	T	Cedrone Severio	259	druggist	24	
	U	Picariello Felix	261	laborer	26	
	V	Picariello Irene—†	261	housewife	23	"
	W	Pastore Angelina—†	261	"	31	
	X	Pastore Lorenzo	261	laborer	46	
	Y	Mongiello Angelo	261	musician	28	"
	Z	Mongiello Concetta—†	261	housewife	49	"
1043						
	A	Mongiello John	261	operator	50	..
	B	Festa Alfred	263	cutter	26	
	C	Festa Julia—†	263	housewife	27	"
	D	Capezutto Carmen	263	printer	27	
	E	Capezutto James	263	laborer	20	
	F	Capezutto John	263	"	48	"
	G	Capezutto Nicholas	263	tailor	23	
	H	*Capezutto Theresa—†	263	housewife	80	"
	K	Pazzanese Anthony	263	operator	23	
	L	*Pazzanese Carmen	263	laborer	51	
	M	*Pazzanese Florence—†	263	housewife	44	"
	N	Pazzanese Francis	263	mechanic	21	"
	O	Ventullo Anthony	265	laborer	33	
	P	Ventullo Margaret—†	265	housewife	30	"
	R	*Palermo Paul	265	laborer	48	143 Paris
	S	*Palermo Rose—†	265	housewife	47	143 "
	T	*O'Brien Mary A—†	265	"	67	here
	U	O'Brien Peter J	265	clerk	44	"
	V	Prudente Anthony	267	longshoreman	33	"
	W	Prudente Rose—†	267	housewife	34	"
	X	*Guarino Ciriaco	267	laborer	60	
	Y	*Guarino Mary—†	267	housewife	46	"
	Z	Guarino Phyllis—†	267	bookkeeper	23	"
1044						
	A	Guarino Salvatore	267	laborer	22	
	B	*Gobbe Carmella—†	267	housewife	33	"
	C	*Gobbe Frank	267	laborer	47	
	D	Scaduto Agrippina—†	269	housewife	24	"
	E	Scaduto Salvatore	269	laborer	28	

Page.	Letter.	FULL NAME.	Residence, Jan. 1, 1938.	Occupation.	Supposed Age.	Reported Residence, Jan. 1, 1937. Street and Number.

Paris Street—Continued

	F	O'Brien Nancy—†	269	housewife	23	274 Saratoga
	G	O'Brien William	269	clerk	23	274 "
	H	*Bove Christina—†	269	housewife	56	here
	K	*Bove Joseph	269	laborer	60	"
	L	Kelly Mary—†	271	cook	43	"
	M	*Dwyer James	271	longshoreman	34	"
	N	*Dwyer Madeline—†	271	housewife	32	"
	O	Bird Honora—†	271	"	51	
	P	Bird William	271	laborer	22	
	R	Brown Catherine—†	273	at home	40	
	S	DeMarco Annie—†	273	housewife	43	"
	T	DeMarco Pasquale	273	operator	45	"
	U	*Silva Filomena—†	273	at home	74	
	V	Cannon Alice—†	275	clerk	21	
	W	Cannon Annie—†	275	housewife	53	"
	X	Cannon Herbert	275	clerk	25	
	Y	Cannon Joseph	275	laborer	23	
	Z	Cannon Phoebe—†	275	social worker	29	"
1045						
	A	Cannon Thomas	275	chauffeur	53	"
	B	*Bruno Eleanor—†	275	housewife	35	"
	C	Bruno Ignazio	275	shoeworker	44	"
	D	Ricupero Irene—†	277	housewife	22	"
	E	Ricupero Salvatore	277	merchant	24	"
	F	Caturano Dorinda—†	277	housewife	25	"
	G	Caturano James	277	chauffeur	24	"
	H	*DiPlacido Bernardo	277	laborer	47	
	K	DiPlacido Mary—†	277	housewife	38	"
	L	Dillon Catherine—†	279	"	65	
	M	Dillon Francis	279	chauffeur	24	"
	N	DeRosa Anna—†	279	housewife	24	Chelsea
	O	DeRosa Michael	279	chauffeur	27	"
	R	Scopa Filomena—†	292	housewife	27	here
	S	*Scopa Henry	292	laborer	30	"
	T	DeRosa Lena—†	292	operator	23	"
	U	*DeRosa Mary F—†	292	housewife	48	"
	V	DeRosa Mary G—†	292	operator	25	"
	W	DeRosa Pasquale	292	storekeeper	53	"
	X	DeRosa Rose—†	292	operator	21	"
	Y	*Lerro Annie—†	292	housewife	46	"
	Z	Lerro Vito	292	coffee roaster	45	"

Page.	Letter.	Full Name.	Residence, Jan. 1, 1938.	Occupation.	Supposed Age.	Reported Residence, Jan. 1, 1937. Street and Number.
1046		**Paris Street**—Continued				
	A	Collins Anna C—†	294	housewife	50	312 Princeton
	B	Collins William F	294	laborer	51	312 "
	C	*Ferreira Elizabeth M—†	294	housewife	58	here
	D	Ferreira Henry A	294	laborer	59	"
	E	Meaney David M	294	policeman	35	88 Bartlett
	F	Meaney Theresa A—†	294	housewife	35	here
	G	Hegner Edward	296	machinist	26	"
	H	Hegner Mary—†	296	housewife	20	"
	K	Flaherty Martin	296	B F D	49	
	L	Flaherty Mary—†	296	housewife	69	"
	M	Shepard Robert M	296	laborer	30	
	N	Shepard Sarah—†	296	housewife	36	"
	O	McArthur Edgar T	298	laborer	33	
	P	McArthur Mary—†	298	housewife	69	"
	R	Cogswell Alfred J	298	printer	27	
	S	Cogswell Frances—†	298	housewife	22	"
	T	Olsen Frances—†	298	at home	56	
	U	Porter Mildred—†	298	housewife	24	"
	V	Porter Roy	298	laborer	28	"
	W	Sullivan John	298	"	28	339 Border
	X	Schultz William	300	"	24	here
	Y	Forgione Angelina—†	300	housewife	34	"
	Z	*Forgione James	300	laborer	42	"
1047						
	A	Gallant Cyrus	300	"	47	
	B	Capozzoli Marie—†	302	housewife	28	"
	C	Capozzoli Robert J	302	laborer	33	
	D	*Young Jennie—†	302	housewife	59	"
	E	Young Robert	302	seaman	55	
	F	Dicks Elizabeth—†	302	operator	35	
	G	Dicks Francis	302	laborer	33	
	H	Cadigan Mary—†	303	teacher	44	
	K	Costigan Mary J—†	303	"	34	
	L	Crowley Julia—†	303	"	40	
	M	Ford Marion—†	303		33	
	N	Horvath Martha—†	303	"	29	
	O	Johnson Anna—†	303	"	37	
	P	Keefe Ellen—†	303		41	
	R	Kerens Loretta—†	303		45	
	S	Lafayette Mary J—†	303	"	37	

Page.	Letter.	FULL NAME.	Residence, Jan. 1, 1938.	Occupation.	Supposed Age.	Reported Residence, Jan. 1, 1937. Street and Number.

Paris Street—Continued

	T	Lyons Olive—†	303	teacher	41	here
	U	Meehan Helen G—†	303	"	47	"
	V	Murnane Catherine T—†	303	"	63	"
	W	Murray Catherine—†	303	"	33	
	X	Riley Margaret—†	303	"	62	
	Y	Salmon Mary—†	303		39	
	Z	Scott Mary F—†	303		60	
1048						
	A	Sheehan Julia—†	303	"	43	"
	B	Spalding Mary—†	303	principal	67	Illinois
	C	Sullivan Julia—†	303	teacher	42	here
	D	Tuttle Mary—†	303	"	31	"
	E	Weeks Anna—†	303	houseworker	39	Lynn
	F	*Hagan Mamie—†	306	housewife	37	here
	G	Hagan William	306	guard	42	"
	H	*Pedrazzi Henrietta—†	306	housewife	58	"
	K	Pedrazzi Henry	306	laborer	27	
	L	Pedrazzi Louis	306	"	30	
	M	Cullen Margaret M—†	308	at home	56	
	N	Timmins Richard	308	seaman	24	
	O	Nappa Carmen	308	operator	37	"
	P	Nappa Lucy—†	308	housewife	28	"
	R	Hodson Harry R	310	painter	38	"
	T	*Pitts Josephine—†	310	housewife	78	300 Paris
	S	Pitts Paul	310	laborer	23	here
	U	Hodson Clara—†	312	housewife	71	"
	V	Hodson Henry N	312	painter	75	"
	W	Hodson Margaret—†	312	housewife	38	"
	X	Hodson William E	312	engraver	42	"
	Y	*Nolan Aaron J	315	laborer	38	
	Z	*Nolan Anna—†	315	housewife	38	"
1049						
	A	Becker Albert	315	laborer	40	
	B	Becker Jacob	315	clerk	36	
	C	*Becker Mary—†	315	housewife	31	"
	D	*Becker Rebecca—†	315	"	60	
	E	*Fiore Delia—†	317	"	27	
	F	Fiore Dominick	317	chauffeur	25	"
	G	Connors Francis N	317	fisherman	38	"
	H	*Connors Mary—†	317	housewife	37	"
	K	Ryan Elizabeth—†	317	"	41	

Page.	Letter.	FULL NAME.	Residence, Jan. 1, 1938.	Occupation.	Supposed Age.	Reported Residence, Jan. 1, 1937. Street and Number.

Paris Street—Continued

	L	Ryan Michael	317	longshoreman	49	here
	M	Corumbo Catherine—†	319	at home	38	"
	N	DeAngelis Pasquale	319	chauffeur	45	"
	O	*DeAngelis Rose—†	319	housewife	38	"
	P	*Belardino Concetta—†	319	"	52	180 London
	R	Belardino James	319	laborer	25	here
	S	*Belardino John	319	"	62	180 London
	T	Belardino Mary—†	319	at home	20	180 "
	U	Belardino Thomas	319	laborer	23	here
	V	Filippone Henry F	321	welder	22	229 Benningt'n
	W	Filippone Margaret—†	321	housewife	24	229 "
	X	Sfarzo Angelina—†	321	"	47	here
	Y	Sfarzo Carmen	321	laborer	55	"
	Z	Sfarzo Frank	321	student	20	"
1050						
	A	Sfarzo Helen—†	321	operator	27	
	B	Sfarzo Margaret—†	321	"	23	
	C	Sfarzo Mary—†	321	tailoress	22	"
	D	Muise Ernest	325	cook	39	352 Bremen
	E	*Muise Loretta—†	325	housewife	39	here
	F	Vargus James	325	painter	20	"
	G	Vargus Joseph	325	"	66	"
	H	Vargus William	325	cutter	23	
	K	*Garron Florence—†	325	packer	32	
	L	*Garron Ida—†	325	housewife	55	"
	M	*Garron Kenneth	325	operator	28	"
	N	Garron Walter	325	laborer	24	"
	O	*Adamo Anthony	325	storekeeper	45	"
	P	George Elizabeth—†	325	stitcher	49	"
	R	Grant George	325	salesman	36	"
	S	Griffin Helen—†	325	housewife	38	"
	T	Griffin Michael	325	longshoreman	40	"
	W	LeBlanc James D	327	laborer	48	100 Brooks
	X	*LeBlanc Mary—†	327	housewife	43	here
	Y	Lawrence Julia—†	327	at home	48	"
	Z	*Costa James	327	laborer	48	110 Trenton
1051						
	A	*Costa Rose—†	327	housewife	47	110 "
	C	*Gubitosi Charles	329	tailor	52	here
	D	Gubitosi Enrico	329	shipper	22	"
	E	*Gubitosi Marie—†	329	housewife	52	"

Page.	Letter.	Full Name.	Residence, Jan. 1, 1938.	Occupation.	Supposed Age.	Reported Residence, Jan. 1, 1937. Street and Number.

Paris Street—Continued

Page.	Letter.	Full Name.	Residence, Jan. 1, 1938.	Occupation.	Supposed Age.	Reported Residence, Jan. 1, 1937. Street and Number.
	F	Gubitosi Samuel	329	bookbinder	26	here
	G	Gubitosi Guy	329	"	29	"
	H	Gubitosi Theresa—†	329	housewife	27	"
	K	*Caruso Irene—†	329	"	65	
	L	Caruso Mary—†	329	"	29	
	M	Caruso Nicholas	329	shoemaker	33	"
	N	McGilvery Isadore	331	chauffeur	25	579 Saratoga
	O	Ligotti Angelo	331	pedler	50	here
	P	*Ligotti Ida—†	331	housewife	47	"
	R	Ligotti John	331	clerk	21	"
	S	*Ligotti Joseph	331	barber	29	
	T	*Stroscia Michael	333	laborer	46	
	U	*White Ellen—†	333	housewife	50	"
	V	*White James	333	carpenter	54	"
	W	*Cheronis Olympia—†	333	housewife	47	"
	X	Cheronis Photis	333	retired	65	"
	Y	Coltraro Anthony	335	clerk	27	Beverly
	Z	Coltraro Josephine—†	335	housewife	25	329 Paris
1052						
	A	Grasso Frank	335	storekeeper	30	61 Chelsea
	B	*Grasso Rose—†	335	housewife	30	here

Princeton Street

Page.	Letter.	Full Name.	Residence, Jan. 1, 1938.	Occupation.	Supposed Age.	Reported Residence, Jan. 1, 1937. Street and Number.
	D	Carbone Ralph	137	laborer	57	here
	E	Carbone Rose—†	137	housewife	43	"
	F	Maio Anna—†	137	"	21	"
	G	Maio Frank	137	tailor	27	
	H	D'Entremont Joseph	139	carpenter	52	"
	K	D'Entremont Mary—†	139	housewife	53	"
	L	D'Entremont William E	139	seaman	25	
	M	Barrett Benjamin	139	laborer	27	"
	N	Barrett Helen—†	139	housewife	22	154 Wordsworth
	O	*Edison Dorothy—†	141	"	30	here
	P	*Edison Thomas	141	engineer	35	"
	R	Nazzaro Rose—†	141	housekeeper	68	"
	S	Fiorillo Christina—†	141	housewife	39	"
	T	Fiorillo James	141	laborer	40	
	U	DeProspo Jennie—†	143	housewife	26	"
	V	DeProspo Michael	143	chauffeur	28	"
	W	Perillo John	143	laundryman	29	"

Page.	Letter.	Full Name.	Residence, Jan. 1, 1938.	Occupation.	Supposed Age.	Reported Residence, Jan. 1, 1937. Street and Number.

Princeton Street—Continued

Page.	Letter.	Full Name.	Residence, Jan. 1, 1938.	Occupation.	Supposed Age.	Reported Residence, Jan. 1, 1937. Street and Number.
	x	Perillo Petrina—†	143	housewife	27	here
	y	Delcore Arthur	143	laborer	28	“
	z	Delcore Gertrude—†	143	housewife	27	“
1053						
	a	Ceccarossi Carmello	145	laborer	40	
	b	Ceccarossi Madeline—†	145	housewife	37	“
	f	Dispensiero Charles	149	musician	25	“
	g	Dispensiero Emily—†	149	housewife	24	“
	h	Siraco Filomeno	149	storekeeper	55	“
	k	Siraco Michelina—†	149	housewife	48	“
	l	Tontodonato Anna—†	149	“	28	“
	m	Tontodonato Nicholas	149	laborer	30	144 Lexington
	n	Martelo Frank	151	painter	23	here
	o	Martelo Mary—†	151	housewife	20	“
	p	*Parsons George	151	fisherman	34	32 Princeton
	r	*Parsons Madeline—†	151	housewife	26	32 “
	s	George Edward	151	laborer	29	here
	t	George Lillian—†	151	housewife	25	“
	u	Munn Edith—†	151	laundress	28	“
	v	*McCue John P	153	laborer	38	
	w	*McCue Mary—†	153	housewife	35	“
	x	DeMita Louis	153	laborer	46	
	y	DeMita Rose—†	153	“	36	
	z	Sullivan Eliza G—†	153	housekeeper	33	“
1054						
	a	Giardini Amelia—†	157	housewife	44	“
	b	Giardini Dante	157	mechanic	45	“
	c	Gaeta Arthur	157	laborer	24	
	d	Gaeta Edward	157	clerk	21	
	e	Gaeta Fiore	157	laborer	48	
	f	Gaeta Lucy—†	157	housewife	48	“
	g	*Francis Augusta—†	157	“	47	
	h	*Francis John	157	laborer	52	
	k	Pignato James	159	chauffeur	27	“
	l	Pignato Theresa—†	159	housewife	26	“
	m	Guide Joseph	159	barber	24	93 Princeton
	n	Guide Margaret—†	159	housewife	26	93 “
	o	*Picceo Anna—†	159	housekeeper	44	here
	p	*Sarravia Anthony	159	watchman	40	“
	r	*McKee John	165	manager	30	“
	s	Moore Ellen—†	165	housewife	31	“

Page.	Letter.	FULL NAME.	Residence, Jan. 1, 1938.	Occupation.	Supposed Age.	Reported Residence, Jan. 1, 1937. Street and Number.

Princeton Street—Continued

Page.	Letter.	Full Name.	Residence, Jan. 1, 1938.	Occupation.	Supposed Age.	Reported Residence, Jan. 1, 1937.
	T	Moore Henry	165	laborer	35	here
	U	Barcelles Edward	165	retired	62	"
	V	Barron Mary—†	165	operator	32	"
	W	Barron Thomas	165	fisherman	35	"
	X	Waldron Lucy—†	165	at home	70	
	Y	*Cuoco Elvira—†	167	housewife	33	"
	Z	Cuoco John	167	laborer	41	
1055						
	A	*Capponigro Geralamo	167	retired	91	
	B	Capponigro Rose—†	167	housewife	91	"
	C	LaRosa Margaret—†	167	"	45	
	D	LaRosa Vincent	167	foreman	47	
	E	Emma Rose—†	167	operator	33	"
	F	Emma Salvatore	167	shoemaker	36	"
	G	*DiLuigi Domenic	169	laborer	57	
	H	DiLuigi Rose—†	169	housewife	46	"
	K	Caraganio Anna—†	169	"	34	128 Princeton
	L	Caraganio James	169	fireman	44	128 "
	M	*Garofolini Lena—†	169	housewife	36	here
	N	*Garofolini Louis	169	painter	43	114 White
	O	Neagle Edmund H	171	chauffeur	65	here
	P	Neagle Gertrude—†	171	housewife	62	"
	R	Neagle Doris L—†	171	"	28	"
	S	Neagle Edmund H, jr	171	chauffeur	30	"
	T	*Zafarana Frances—†	173	housewife	45	"
	U	*Zafarana Giacomo	173	baker	55	
	V	Zafarana James	173	barber	24	
	W	Paterno Joseph	173	tailor	20	
	X	*Paterno Rose—†	173	housewife	40	"
	Y	Queenan Francis L	173	operator	50	236 Benningt'n
	Z	Queenan Sarah E—†	173	housewife	43	236 "
1056						
	A	Boyan John	175	teacher	45	here
	B	Boyan Mary—†	175	housewife	70	"
	C	Boyan Timothy	175	retired	78	"
	D	Morrissey Elizabeth—†	175	at home	80	
	E	Malone Harry	175	laborer	30	
	F	Malone Hibbard	175	"	58	
	G	Malone Lydia—†	175	housewife	50	"
	H	Malone Marshall N	175	foreman	28	"
	K	*Iudica Carmello	179	operator	43	169 Princeton

Page.	Letter.	Full Name.	Residence, Jan. 1, 1938.	Occupation.	Supposed Age.	Reported Residence, Jan. 1, 1937. Street and Number.

Princeton Street—Continued

Page.	Letter.	Full Name.	Residence, Jan. 1, 1938.	Occupation.	Supposed Age.	Reported Residence, Jan. 1, 1937. Street and Number.
	L	*Iudica Theresa—†	179	housewife	33	169 Princeton
	M	Tosto John	179	laborer	35	here
	N	Tosto Lena—†	179	housewife	31	"
	O	*Vaccaro Anthony	179	laborer	36	"
	P	Vaccaro Carmella—†	179	dressmaker	22	"
	R	*Vaccaro Giuseppe	179	laborer	65	
	S	*Vaccaro Mary—†	179	clerk	27	
	T	*Cucchiello Frank	181	laborer	29	
	U	*Cucchiello Michelina—†	181	housewife	27	"
	V	*LaPorta Agostino	181	laborer	49	
	W	*LaPorta Philomena—†	181	housewife	46	"
	X	Donovan Anna—†	181	"	22	161 Saratoga
	Y	Donovan James	181	baker	25	161 "
	Z	Lazzaro Joseph	183	laborer	26	here
1057						
	A	Lazzaro Mary—†	183	housewife	25	"
	B	Iannuzzi Grace—†	183	"	27	
	C	Iannuzzi John	183	operator	27	
	D	Datow Hannah—†	185	housewife	69	"
	E	Datow Otto A	185	retired	79	
	F	Smither Louise H—†	185	secretary	37	"
	G	Gomes Aurelia—†	187	housewife	43	215 Princeton
	H	Gomes Eugene	187	cook	52	215 "
	K	Colangelo Michael	187	laborer	24	here
	L	*Nigro Mary—†	187	housekeeper	45	"
	M	Gorgoni Anna—†	189	housewife	55	"
	N	Gorgoni Anna—†	189	clerk	39	
	O	Gorgoni Lorenzo	189	storekeeper	63	"
	P	Gorgoni Lucy—†	189	clerk	26	"
	R	LaCasia Peter	189	storekeeper	39	"
	S	LaCasia Philomena—†	189	housewife	29	"

Putnam Street

Page.	Letter.	Full Name.	Residence, Jan. 1, 1938.	Occupation.	Supposed Age.	Reported Residence, Jan. 1, 1937. Street and Number.
	V	Cotreau Frances—†	125	waitress	33	252 Marion
	W	Pannesi Anna—†	125	packer	23	here
	X	Pannesi Donald	125	chauffeur	29	"
	Y	Pannesi Mary—†	125	housewife	51	"
	Z	Pannesi Pasquale	125	watchman	55	"
1058						
	A	Brangiforte John	127	laborer	27	

Putnam Street—Continued

Page.	Letter.	Full Name.	Residence, Jan. 1, 1938.	Occupation.	Supposed Age.	Reported Residence, Jan. 1, 1937. Street and Number.
	B	Brangiforte Ruth—†	127	housewife	23	here
	C	Limole Agrippino	127	laborer	53	32 Shelby
	D	*Limole Ambrosina—†	127	housewife	50	32 "
	E	*Zagami Mary—†	127	"	36	here
	F	Zagami Rosario	127	laborer	45	"
	G	Ferrarra Joseph	129	clerk	25	"
	H	Ferrarra Sarah—†	129	housewife	22	"
	K	DeMattia Angelo	129	chauffeur	42	"
	L	*DeMattia Grace—†	129	housewife	40	"
	M	Anzalone Philomena—†	129	at home	35	
	N	Volo James	131	laborer	24	
	O	Volo Mary—†	131	housewife	23	"
	P	Radosta John	131	operator	22	
	R	Radosta Mary—†	131	"	23	
	S	Radosta Charles	131	tailor	25	
	T	Radosta John	131	operator	59	
	U	Radosta Josephine—†	131	housewife	49	"
	W	Michalis Dennis	133	fireman	51	
	X	*Michalis Sophia—†	133	housewife	43	"
	Y	Pagano John	133	butcher	42	
	Z	Pagano Lena—†	133	housewife	34	"
1059						
	B	DeRosa Louise—†	163	"	29	
	C	DeRosa Pasquale	163	laborer	32	
	D	*Columbo Rose—†	163	housewife	46	"
	E	*Columbo Salvatore	163	laborer	45	
	F	Columbo Theresa—†	163	dressmaker	21	"
	G	*Freni Minnie—†	163	housewife	46	"
	H	*Freni William	163	laborer	57	
	K	Piccarello Joseph	165	chauffeur	32	"
	L	Piccarello Josephine—†	165	housewife	32	"
	O	Green Beatrice—†	165	at home	22	219 Princeton
	P	Politano Joseph	165	laborer	42	here
	R	*Politano Josephine—†	165	housewife	44	"
	S	*Cassaro Theresa—†	167	"	34	"
	T	*Cassaro Vincent	167	chauffeur	34	"
	U	Caggiano Anthony	167	packer	27	
	V	Caggiano Mary—†	167	housewife	26	"
	W	*Schena Michael	167	shoemaker	40	"
	X	*Schena Vincenza—†	167	housewife	40	"
	Y	Murphy Timothy	177	laborer	65	

Page.	Letter.	Full Name.	Residence, Jan. 1, 1938.	Occupation.	Supposed Age.	Reported Residence, Jan. 1, 1937. Street and Number.

Putnam Street—Continued

	z	*Dettore Concetta—†	177	housewife	44	here
1060						
	A	Dettore John	177	laborer	49	
	B	Cunningham Clara—†	177	housewife	30	"
	C	Cunningham Clifford	177	laborer	33	
	E	Winn Doris—†	179	housewife	23	"
	F	Winn Harold	179	laborer	29	
	G	Connolly Anthony	179	cutter	25	
	H	Connolly John	179	fireman	44	
	K	Connolly Katherine—†	179	housewife	44	"
	L	Dorgan Florence—†	195	"	24	
	M	Dorgan James	195	cutter	25	
	N	Ferrara Concordia—†	195	mender	23	
	O	*Ferrara Henry	195	operator	55	"
	P	Ferrara Josephine—†	195	"	25	
	R	*Ferrara Rose—†	195	housewife	49	"
	S	Colangelo Antonio	195	laborer	46	
	T	Colangelo Palmina—†	195	housewife	37	"
	U	Bertucceli Angela—†	197	"	69	
	V	Bertucceli Joseph	197	retired	65	
	W	Lane Albert	197	machinist	21	"
	X	*Lane Helen—†	197	housewife	46	"
	Y	Ruggiero Carmella—†	197	"	52	
	Z	Ruggiero John	197	barber	50	
1061						
	A	Muise Dorothy—†	199	housewife	24	"
	B	Muise Vincent	199	laborer	26	
	C	Veiria Louise—†	199	operator	38	"
	D	Veiria Manuel	199	pedler	40	
	E	Silva Delphine V—†	199	housewife	56	"
	F	Silva John F	199	laborer	37	
	G	*Silva John G	199	painter	58	

Saratoga Street

	H	Brooks Edward E	201	laborer	45	here
	K	Kehoe Edward A	201	teamster	50	"
	L	Kehoe Mary A—†	201	housewife	30	"
	M	Shafer Bertha—†	201	"	63	
	N	Shafer David	201	retired	68	
	O	Kehoe Lawrence	201	operator	34	"

Page.	Letter.	Full Name.	Residence, Jan. 1, 1938.	Occupation.	Supposed Age.	Reported Residence, Jan. 1, 1937. Street and Number.

Saratoga Street—Continued

	P	Kehoe Margaret—†	201	housewife	33	here
	R	Brown Marshall	202	retired	86	"
	S	Partridge Frank	202	painter	57	"
	T	Partridge Lena—†	202	housewife	48	"
	U	Raymond Marion C—†	202	"	69	
	V	Lavoie Charles A	203	custodian	55	"
	W	Lavoie Della—†	203	housewife	55	"
	X	Moran Augustus	203	B F D	55	"
	Y	Cerullo Margaret—†	203	housewife	24	191 London
	Z	Cerullo Marino	203	laborer	24	181 Salem
1062						
	A	Tedesco Mildred—†	203	housewife	32	here
	B	Tedesco Pasquale	203	painter	31	"
	C	DeBernardis Fiore	204	laborer	57	"
	D	*DeBernardis Lucy—†	204	housewife	58	"
	E	Costigan Albert	204	cutter	21	
	F	*Costigan James	204	longshoreman	45	"
	G	*Costigan Margaret—†	204	housewife	42	"
	H	DeFilippis Mary—†	204	"	28	
	K	DeFilippis Nicholas	204	operator	33	
	L	Rinoni Joseph	205	printer	26	
	M	Rinoni Philip	205	clerk	28	
	N	*Rinoni Vincenza—†	205	housewife	50	"
	O	*Rinoni Vincenzo	205	laborer	58	
	P	Pazol Benjamin	205	pedler	43	
	R	Pazol Mary—†	205	housewife	34	"
	S	Cordaro Margaret—†	205	"	39	
	T	Cordaro Sebastian	205	cabinetmaker	40	"
	U	*Corbosiero Louis	206	operator	35	"
	V	*Corbosiero Rose—†	206	housewife	30	"
	W	DelVisco Antonio	206	laborer	52	
	X	DelVisco Emily—†	206	operator	25	"
	Y	*DelVisco Maria—†	206	housewife	55	"
	Z	Kelley Alice—†	206	operator	30	
1063						
	A	Kelley Joseph	206	longshoreman	40	"
	B	Rando Domenic E	207	draftsman	32	Rhode Island
	C	Rando Emily M—†	207	housewife	31	"
	D	Laffey Doris M—†	207	"	23	4 Frothingham av
	E	Laffey Raymond R	207	chauffeur	25	4 "
	F	Panzini Margaret—†	207	housewife	24	Revere

Page.	Letter.	Full Name.	Residence, Jan. 1, 1938.	Occupation.	Supposed Age.	Reported Residence, Jan. 1, 1937. Street and Number.

Saratoga Street—Continued

Page.	Letter.	Full Name.	Residence, Jan. 1, 1938.	Occupation.	Supposed Age.	Reported Residence, Jan. 1, 1937. Street and Number.
	G	Panzini Vito	207	laborer	27	Revere
	H	Sacco Marcus	208	"	35	here
	K	Sacco Margaret—†	208	housewife	28	"
	L	*Babine Adolph	208	cutter	32	"
	M	*Babine Gertrude—†	208	housewife	28	"
	N	*Silva Rose—†	208	housekeeper	50	195 Brooks
	O	Tutela Jennie—†	209	housewife	30	here
	P	Tutela Richard	209	laborer	31	"
	R	Lambunos Anna—†	209	housewife	38	"
	S	Lambunos William	209	fireman	58	"
	T	Kurland Morris S	209	chauffeur	39	"
	U	Kurland Sadie—†	209	housewife	39	"
	V	*DeVeau Harvey J	210	cook	29	
	W	*DeVeau Leah—†	210	housewife	28	"
	X	Church Ernestine—†	210	"	44	
	Y	Church James V	210	fireman	42	
	Z	McNeill James B	210	usher	23	
1064						
	A	*McNeill James J	210	carpenter	70	"
	B	*McNeill Lillian—†	210	housewife	50	"
	C	Limoli Florence—†	211	"	26	
	D	Limoli Louis	211	operator	26	
	E	Mirra Alice—†	211	housewife	34	"
	F	Mirra Anthony	211	tailor	37	
	G	*Mirra Antonette—†	211	tailoress	28	
	H	Mirra Florence—†	211	at home	21	
	K	*Mirra Paul	211	laborer	27	
	L	*Mirra Vito	211	retired	66	"
	M	McCarthy Nicholas	212	cook	30	100 Princeton
	O	*Biscay Antonia—†	212	housewife	57	here
	P	Biscay Joseph	212	oiler	28	"
	R	Biscay Richard	212	operator	22	"
	U	Venedam Charles	214	painter	25	
	V	Venedam Rose—†	214	housewife	20	"
	W	*Dove Antonetta—†	214	"	40	"
	X	Dove John	214	merchant	49	"
	Y	Dove Vincent	214	student	21	
	Z	*Solinos Salvatore	214	laborer	55	
1065						
	A	DeDomenicis Appolania—†	215	housewife	61	"
	B	DeDomenicis Edith—†	215	proofreader	26	"

Page.	Letter.	Full Name.	Residence, Jan. 1, 1938.	Occupation.	Supposed Age.	Reported Residence, Jan. 1, 1937. Street and Number.

Saratoga Street—Continued

Page.	Letter.	Full Name.	Residence, Jan. 1, 1938.	Occupation.	Supposed Age.	Reported Residence, Jan. 1, 1937. Street and Number.
	C	DeDomenicis Elvira—†	215	at home	30	here
	D	DeDomenicis Rose—†	215	student	20	"
	E	DeDomenicis Secondino	215	laborer	63	"
	F	Eriksen Helen—†	215	housekeeper	36	41 Wordsworth
	G	*Glatis Anna—†	215	housewife	36	here
	H	Glatis William	215	clerk	40	"
	K	Nicholson Evelyn—†	216	housewife	30	"
	L	Nicholson John	216	seaman	35	
	M	Robinson Mary—†	216	housewife	24	"
	N	Robinson Raymond	216	chauffeur	27	"
	O	Vaccari Dante	216A	salesman	29	"
	P	Vaccari Edna—†	216A	housewife	27	"
	R	Coluntino Helen—†	216A	"	24	
	S	Coluntino Ralph	216A	painter	30	
	T	*Siracuse Joseph	217	mattressmaker	31	"
	U	Siracuse Rose—†	217	housewife	30	"
	V	*Davolio Charles	217	laborer	41	
	W	Davolio Margaret—†	217	housewife	40	"
	X	Beranger Charles	217	cook	62	
	Y	*Beranger Lillian—†	217	housewife	58	"
	Z	Beranger Pearl—†	217	waitress	20	
1066						
	A	Beranger Peter	217	cutter	25	"
	B	Vitello Albert	218	operator	23	249 Lexington
	C	Vitello Stella—†	218	housewife	21	249 "
	D	*Lush Mary—†	218	"	35	here
	E	*Lush William	218	laborer	35	"
	F	*Smith Alton	218	fisherman	34	182 Benningt'n
	G	*Smith Margaret—†	218	housewife	27	here
	H	Haskell Herbert S	219	clerk	49	"
	K	Haskell Mary F—†	219	housewife	55	"
	N	*Peddle Patrick J	220	fisherman	38	"
	O	Rice Moses	220	"	57	
	P	Sullivan Joseph V	220	laborer	27	
	R	Sullivan Mary—†	220	housewife	45	"
	S	Pebrucco Angelo	220	laborer	49	332 Saratoga
	T	*Pebrucco Rose—†	220	housewife	39	here
	U	Elms Edward	220	seaman	29	"
	V	Elms Madeline—†	220	housewife	32	"
	X	Miller Lelia—†	221	attorney	52	"
	Y	Carlson Natalie—†	223	housewife	22	516 Saratoga

Page.	Letter.	Full Name.	Residence, Jan. 1, 1938.	Occupation.	Supposed Age.	Reported Residence, Jan. 1, 1937. Street and Number.

Saratoga Street—Continued

	z	Carlson Walter	223	cutter	23	516 Saratoga
1067						
	A	Petrillo Jennie—†	223	housewife	32	here
	B	*Petrillo Pasquale	223	painter	43	"
	C	Hondins Marie—†	223	at home	52	"
	D	Cannizzaro Rose—†	225	housewife	22	"
	E	Cannizzaro Santo	225	barber	22	
	F	Dellago Henry M	225	clerk	29	
	G	Dellago Velia—†	225	housewife	26	"
	H	Cannizzaro Adele—†	225	"	46	
	K	Cannizzaro Domenic	225	clerk	21	
	L	Cannizzaro Ralph	225	barber	56	
	M	Cannizzaro Sarah—†	225	forewoman	26	"
	N	*Halstead Mary—†	226	housekeeper	65	"
	O	*Hyder Emily—†	226	operator	44	"
	P	*Boudreau Albert	226	fisherman	35	31 Lovett
	R	Coilty Alice—†	226	domestic	24	here
	S	*Coilty Matilda—†	226	housewife	57	"
	T	*Coilty William	226	longshoreman	72	"
	U	Coilty William	226	laborer	22	
	V	O'Keefe Gertrude—†	226	at home	30	
	W	Thomas Fred	226	fisherman	30	"
	X	*Cannizzaro Jennie—†	227	housewife	38	"
	Y	*Cannizzaro Santo	227	operator	37	"
	Z	LoConte Anthony	227	pedler	50	
1068						
	A	LoConte John	227	student	20	"
	B	*LoConte Maria—†	227	housewife	50	"
	C	Cambria Lena—†	227	"	23	
	D	Cambria Pasquale	227	baker	23	
	E	Cino Gaetano	228	operator	31	"
	F	Cino Ursula—†	228	housewife	28	"
	G	Vernacchio Gerald	228	printer	21	
	H	*Vernacchio Jennie—†	228	housewife	58	"
	K	Vernacchio Mary—†	228	clerk	23	
	L	Vernacchio Pasquale	228	laborer	59	
	M	Santoro Filomena—†	229	clerk	21	
	N	*Santoro Mary—†	229	housewife	58	"
	O	*Santoro Raffaelo	229	laborer	57	
	P	Marino Frank	229	"	72	
	R	*Marino Sabato	229	"	60	

Page.	Letter.	Full Name.	Residence, Jan. 1, 1938.	Occupation.	Supposed Age.	Reported Residence, Jan. 1, 1937. Street and Number.

Saratoga Street—Continued

Page.	Letter.	Full Name.	Residence, Jan. 1, 1938.	Occupation.	Supposed Age.	Reported Residence, Jan. 1, 1937. Street and Number.
	S	*Rossi Theresa—†	229	housekeeper	41	here
	T	DeMelio Emma—†	230	operator	24	"
	U	*DeMelio James	230	"	27	"
	V	Lombardozzi Angelina—†	230	"	27	
	W	Lombardozzi Angelo	230	painter	38	
	X	Lombardozzi Marco	230	waiter	36	
	Y	*Lombardozzi Mary—†	230	housewife	64	"
	Z	Lombardozzi Mary—†	230	operator	35	"
1069						
	A	Lombardozzi Michael	230	"	28	
	B	*Olitsky Abraham	230	merchant	60	"
	C	Olitsky Harry	230	pedler	25	
	D	Olitsky Henry	230	"	27	
	E	*Olitsky Minnie—†	230	housewife	58	"
	F	Antonucci Mildred—†	231	at home	24	90 Chelsea
	G	Frizzi Gaetano	231	painter	48	90 "
	H	*Frizzi Jennie—†	231	housewife	48	90 "
	K	*Patti Rose—†	231A	housekeeper	39	59 W Eagle
	L	Viscio Domenic	231A	painter	56	here
	M	Viscio Ernest	231A	laborer	21	"
	N	*Viscio Louisa—†	231A	housewife	53	"
	O	Viscio Michael	231A	laborer	23	"
	P	Disario Emma—†	232	housewife	41	220 Saratoga
	R	Disario Gabriel A	232	laborer	46	220 "
	S	Garbati Edward P	232	"	54	here
	T	Aronson Abraham I	232	salesman	22	"
	U	*Aronson Dora—†	232	housewife	60	"
	V	Oster Sidney	232	salesman	35	"
	W	Vaccari Christopher	232	"	32	49 Cottage
	X	Vaccari Jennie—†	232	housewife	33	49 "
	Y	Fumicello Beatrice—†	233	"	24	25 Morris
	Z	Fumicello John	233	attorney	24	21 "
1070						
	A	*Coppola Mary—†	233	housewife	38	here
	B	Coppola Mary R—†	233	saleswoman	20	"
	C	Coppola Pasquale	233	laborer	39	"
	D	*Purgano Anthony	233	upholsterer	42	231 Saratoga
	E	*Purgano Rose—†	233	housewife	42	here
	F	Varone Grace—†	234	packer	26	"
	G	Varone Salvatore	234	mechanic	26	"
	H	Fisher Harold	234	painter	35	

Page.	Letter.	Full Name.	Residence, Jan. 1, 1938.	Occupation.	Supposed Age.	Reported Residence, Jan. 1, 1937. Street and Number.

Saratoga Street—Continued

Page.	Letter.	Full Name.	Residence, Jan. 1, 1938.	Occupation.	Supposed Age.	Reported Residence, Jan. 1, 1937. Street and Number.
	K	Fisher Herbert	234	accountant	20	here
	L	Fisher Lewis J	234	attorney	23	"
	M	*Fisher Molly—†	234	housewife	49	"
	N	*Fisher Samuel	234	painter	50	"
	O	Bosco Joseph	234	salesman	29	"
	P	*Bosco Mary—†	234	housewife	72	"
	R	Dwyer Florence—†	235	at home	20	"
	S	Dwyer Mary—†	235	housekeeper	50	"
	T	*Alfano Anna—†	235	housewife	45	"
	U	Alfano Joseph	235	laborer	48	
	V	*Favorito Angelina—†	235	housewife	51	"
	W	Favorito Emilio	235	laborer	40	
	X	Favorito Philip	235	clerk	20	"
	Y	DeStefano Joseph	236	baker	25	Winthrop
	Z	Hess Abner	236	electrician	43	"
1071						
	A	Hess Isabella—†	236	housewife	38	"
	B	Benson John E	236	chauffeur	40	here
	C	Benson Marion—†	236	housewife	38	"
	D	DiGregorio Margaret—†	236	operator	20	"
	E	DiGregorio Vincent	236	clerk	22	
	F	Frye Abbie—†	236	housekeeper	75	"
	G	Hemenway Nahum D	236	janitor	72	"
	H	Interbartolo Gaetina—†	238	housewife	23	420 Chelsea
	K	Interbartolo Marie—†	238	operator	47	here
	L	Interbartolo Michael	238	electrician	29	"
	M	Rose Mae—†	238	operator	33	"
	N	*Amico Angelina—†	238	housewife	48	"
	O	Amico Charles	238	shoemaker	52	"
	P	Amico Michael	238	"	27	
	R	*Marotta Charles	238	laborer	35	
	S	*Marotta Mary—†	238	housewife	26	"
	T	Breen Andrew	242	machinist	28	"
	U	Breen Hilda—†	242	housewife	28	"
	V	Alabiso James	242	operator	46	"
	W	*Alabiso Nora—†	242	housewife	36	"
	X	Damico Alexandro	242	laborer	47	
	Y	*Damico Jennie—†	242	housewife	47	"
	Z	Damico Lena—†	242	operator	24	
1072						
	A	Ricci Anna—†	243	"	23	"

Page.	Letter.	Full Name.	Residence, Jan. 1, 1938.	Occupation.	Supposed Age.	Reported Residence, Jan. 1, 1937. Street and Number.

Saratoga Street—Continued

Page.	Letter.	Full Name.	Residence, Jan. 1, 1938.	Occupation.	Supposed Age.	Reported Residence, Jan. 1, 1937. Street and Number.
	B	Ricci Assunta—†	243	at home	21	here
	C	Ricci Carmella—†	243	housewife	41	"
	D	Ricci Frank	243	laborer	43	"
	E	Natkil Alberta—†	244	housewife	36	"
	F	Natkil Benjamin	244	operator	38	"
	G	Sauchella Assunta—†	244	at home	27	
	H	Sauchella Gavino	244	shoemaker	66	"
	K	Sauchella Paolo	244	bootblack	29	"
	L	Sauchella Pasqualina—†	244	housewife	64	"
	M	*Puzzanghera Mary—†	244	"	46	
	N	Puzzanghera Salvatore	244	tailor	49	
	O	Puzzanghera Salvatore, jr	244	clerk	20	
	P	*Coggio Charles	245	laborer	63	
	R	*Coggio Marion—†	245	housewife	63	"
	S	Coggio Rose—†	245	at home	30	
	T	*Ciriardo Carmello	246	laborer	62	
	U	Ciriardo Concetta—†	246	operator	27	"
	V	Ciriardo Elizabeth—†	246	"	25	
	W	*Ciriardo Frances—†	246	housewife	53	"
	X	Ciriardo Pasquale	246	cutter	24	
	Z	Martin John	246	laborer	42	
1073						
	A	Martin Michael	246	operator	42	Lowell
	B	Leibman Julius	247	storekeeper	43	here
	C	Leibman Mary—†	247	housewife	38	"
	D	*Brown Gorley W	248	laborer	54	"
	E	*Brown Sadie—†	248	housewife	52	"
	F	Tracia Mazie—†	248	at home	26	
	G	*Interbartolo Rosario	248	clerk	51	
	H	*Panopoulas Anna—†	248	housewife	23	"
	K	*Panopoulas George	248	cook	40	131 Putnam
	L	Serra Francesco	249	laborer	57	here
	M	Serra John	249	operator	27	"
	N	Serra Marion—†	249	housewife	54	"
	O	Serra Mary—†	249	seamstress	22	"
	P	Serra Natale	249	printer	21	"
	R	Cuozzo Gaetano	250	operator	24	201 Havre
	S	*Cuozzo Phyllis—†	250	housewife	28	201 "
	T	*Costa John	250	carpenter	53	here
	U	*Costa Josephine—†	250	housewife	44	"
	V	Costa Mary—†	250	at home	20	"

Page.	Letter.	FULL NAME.	Residence, Jan. 1, 1938.	Occupation.	Supposed Age.	Reported Residence, Jan. 1, 1937. Street and Number.

Saratoga Street—Continued

	W	*Mello Mary—†	250	operator	53	here
	X	Lynch Frances—†	250	"	26	"
	Y	Lynch Maria—†	250	housewife	62	"
	Z	*Mercurio Agnes—†	252	"	74	
1074						
	A	*Mercurio Anna—†	252	"	39	
	B	Mercurio James	252	constable	43	"
	C	*DiNapoli Catherine—†	252	housewife	39	"
	D	*DiNapoli Pasquale	252	operator	44	"
	E	*Ferenda Antonio	254	"	52	242 Princeton
	F	*Ferenda Clementina—†	254	housewife	40	242 "
	G	*Poriera Manuel	254	operator	40	242 "
	H	Silverman Gertrude—†	254	housewife	45	259 Saratoga
	K	Silverman Philip	254	clerk	25	259 "
	L	Silverman Robert	254	storekeeper	57	259 "
	N	*Fernandez James	254	operator	32	here
	M	*Freitas Frank	254	"	45	"

2

3

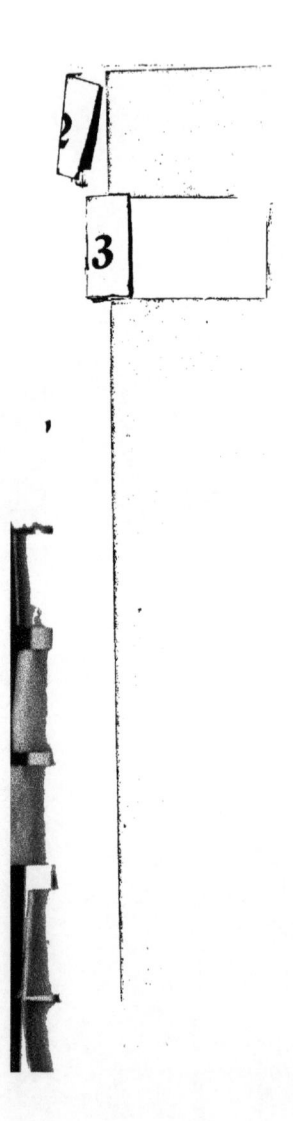

Ward 1—Precinct 13

CITY OF BOSTON

LIST OF RESIDENTS
20 YEARS OF AGE AND OVER

(NON-CITIZENS INDICATED BY ASTERISK)
(FEMALES INDICATED BY DAGGER)

AS OF

JANUARY 1, 1938

JOSEPH F. TIMILTY, } *Listing*
FREDERIC E. DOWLING, } *Board.*

CITY OF BOSTON PRINTING DEPARTMENT

Page.	Letter.	FULL NAME.	Residence, Jan. 1, 1938.	Occupation.	Supposed Age.	Reported Residence. Jan. 1, 1937. Street and Number.
1082						
		Bennington Street				
	B	Nagle Catherine J—†	256	housewife	77	here
	C	Ruggiero Antonio	256	barber	34	"
	D	Ruggiero Louisa—†	256	housewife	31	"
	F	Zampatella Mamie—†	260	cook	32	
	G	Zampatella Ralph	260	plumber	33	
	H	Keough Michael	260	laborer	52	
	K	Keough Nellie M—†	260	housewife	57	"
	L	Keough Rita—†	260	typist	23	"
	M	Deeran Gasper	262	storekeeper	56	"
	N	Deeran Martin	262	clerk	22	"
	O	Deeran Tarviz—†	262	housewife	48	"
	R	Saulnier John	266	laborer	41	
	S	Saulnier Mary—†	266	housewife	43	"
	Z	Quigley Augustine J	290	clerk	48	
1083						
	A	Quigley Ellen J—†	290	storekeeper	49	"
	B	Quigley Margaret M—†	290	housewife	51	"
	D	Machado Elizabeth A—†	292	"	50	
	E	Machado Frank J	292	painter	51	
	F	Machado Frank W	292	"	30	
	G	Machado Joseph H	292	tailor	22	
	H	Thornton Abigail—†	293	waitress	25	
	K	Thornton Helen—†	293	housewife	57	"
	L	Thornton John R	293	seaman	60	
	M	Thornton Thomas	293	porter	24	
	N	Thornton Virginia—†	293	operator	21	
	O	Cosgrove Alice E—†	293	housewife	57	"
	P	Cosgrove Daniel A	293	salesman	58	"
	R	Cosgrove Daniel F	293	clerk	22	"
	V	Tonelli Alice—†	297	operator	30	
	W	Tonelli Angelo	297	laborer	22	
	X	*Tonelli Annie—†	297	housewife	61	"
	Y	Tonelli Fred	297	laborer	29	"
	Z	Tonelli Joseph	297	retired	37	Bedford
1084						
	A	*Tonelli Lawrence	297	"	62	here
	B	Tonelli Lawrence	297	laborer	27	"
	C	O'Connell George H	297	electrician	30	66 Armandine
	D	O'Connell Rita—†	297	housewife	35	66 "
	E	Dolan Margaret A—†	301	"	38	here
	F	Dolan Thomas A	301	laborer	37	"

Page.	Letter.	Full Name.	Residence, Jan. 1, 1938.	Occupation.	Supposed Age.	Reported Residence, Jan. 1, 1937. Street and Number.

Bennington Street—Continued

	G	Hagerty Dorothea E—†	301	secretary	30	here
	H	Hagerty Johanna E—†	301	housewife	62	"
	K	DeWitt Ernestine W—†	301	"	54	"
	L	DeWitt Herman W	301	laborer	62	
	M	DeWitt Margaret—†	301	at home	89	
	O	*Doucette Ernest H	305	laborer	35	
	P	*Doucette Marie—†	305	housewife	32	"
	R	Mandell Anthony	305	chef	34	"
	S	*Mandell Margaret—†	305	housewife	31	158 Walnut av
	V	Austin Catherine M—†	315	"	58	here
	W	Austin Michael J, jr	315	chauffeur	51	"
	Y	*DeAngelo Mary—†	319	housewife	63	"
	Z	*DeAngelo Michael	319	retired	62	
1085						
	A	Lanzetta Jeremiah	319	laborer	33	"
	B	Lucisano Angelina—†	319	housewife	25	168 Cottage
	C	Lucisano Nicholas	319	laborer	26	168 "
	D	Florentino Elmer	321	"	37	here
	E	Florentino Ernestine—†	321	housewife	35	"
	F	Messer Arthur E	323	retired	72	"
	G	Messer Arthur E, jr	323	laborer	32	
	H	Messer Johanna—†	323	housewife	65	"
	K	Messer Sarah M—†	323	stenographer	34	"
	L	Connors Irene—†	325	housewife	30	"
	M	Connors Joseph	325	cook	37	
	N	Foley Daniel A	325	operator	60	"
	O	Hartnett Mary—†	325	seamstress	60	"
	P	Jarvis Charles	325	painter	54	
	R	Toomey John A	327	laborer	57	"
	S	Benson Harry A	329	contractor	36	32 Neptune rd
	T	Benson Ruth—†	329	housewife	35	32 "
	U	Dinsmore William A	329	clerk	38	1042 Saratoga
	W	Alessandroni Angelina—†	360	housewife	36	here
	X	Alessandroni Joseph	360	retired	67	"
	Y	Alessandroni Nino	360	instructor	44	"

Bremen Street

	Z	*Greenberg Celia—†	364	houseworker	50	here
1086						
	A	*Jacobs Sarah—†	364	at home	80	
	B	Weker Lottie—†	364	housewife	60	"

Page.	Letter.	Full Name.	Residence, Jan. 1, 1938.	Occupation.	Supposed Age.	Reported Residence, Jan. 1, 1937. Street and Number.

Bremen Street—Continued

	C	Weker Max	364	pedler	64	here
	D	Weker Morris	364	clerk	22	"
	E	Weker Myer	364	attorney	31	"
	F	Weker Simon	364	student	24	
	G	Benson Frank A	364A	auditor	32	
	H	Benson Selma D—†	364A	housewife	39	"
	K	Benson Sven H	364A	retired	72	
	L	Lynch Bernice—†	364A	clerk	20	
	M	Lynch Bridget—†	364A	housewife	57	"
	N	Lynch Helen—†	364A	saleswoman	22	"
	O	Green Theresa—†	364A	housewife	56	"
	P	Green William J	364A	tailor	58	
	R	DeLuca Anna—†	366	housewife	41	"
	S	DeLuca Dominick	366	clerk	21	
	T	Alley Anna M—†	368	housewife	39	"
	U	*Alley Robert	368	fireman	49	
	V	Gennaco Joseph	374	operator	25	
	W	Gennaco Pauline—†	374	housewife	22	"
	X	Rizzo Fannie—†	374	"	35	
	Y	Rizzo Joseph	374	operator	39	
	Z	*Rizzo Palma—†	374	housewife	74	"
1087						
	A	Flood Mary—†	376	at home	67	334 Chelsea
	B	Caggiano Frank	376	fireman	28	284 "
	C	Caggiano Rose—†	376	housewife	26	284 "
	D	Bailey John T	398	retired	68	376 Bremen
	E	Russell James	398	longshoreman	56	here
	F	Russell Rose—†	398	housewife	48	"
	G	Longini Julio	400	laborer	27	"
	H	Longini Marco	400	entertainer	23	"
	K	*Longini Nina—†	400	housewife	47	"
	L	Longini Umberto	400	operator	47	
	M	Ford Rose A—†	400	clerk	43	
	N	Gaffney James	400	electrician	33	"
	O	Gaffney Mabel—†	400	housewife	59	"
	P	*Amodeo Anna—†	408	"	33	..
	R	Amodeo Edward	408	barber	48	"
	S	Kelly Cornelius J	412	laborer	47	289 Havre
	T	Kelly Mary C—†	412	housewife	44	289 "
	U	Smith John	412	longshoreman	46	376 Bremen
	V	Higgins George	416	laborer	33	here

Bremen Street—Continued

Page.	Letter.	Name.	Residence, Jan. 1, 1938.	Occupation.	Supposed Age.	Reported Residence, Jan. 1, 1937. Street and Number.
	w	Higgins Mary—†	416	operator	38	here
	x	*Fairchild Bessie—†	416	at home	74	"
	y	DeBoli Mary—†	452	housewife	56	"
	z	McCassion Daniel	452	laborer	65	38 Paris

Chelsea Street

Page.	Letter.	Name.	Residence, Jan. 1, 1938.	Occupation.	Supposed Age.	Reported Residence, Jan. 1, 1937. Street and Number.
1088						
	c	Dellorfano Joseph	345	laborer	40	here
	d	Dellorfano Mary—†	345	housewife	34	"
	e	Dung Hin	347	laundryman	37	26 Oxford
	f	Yee Mon	347	"	30	Cambridge
	k	Gould Charles B	351	foreman	62	here
	l	Gould Margaret—†	351	housewife	59	"
	m	*Bagenski William J	351	laborer	50	"
	n	*Buttigliere Mary—†	353	tailoress	54	
	o	*Loconzolo Celia—†	353	housewife	55	"
	p	*Loconzolo Joseph	353	salesman	66	"
	r	Wilcox John	353	splicer	26	
	s	Badolato Anna—†	353	housewife	29	"
	t	Dorato Gennaro	355	pedler	42	358 Chelsea
	u	*Dorato Vincenza—†	355	housewife	32	358 "
	v	Siraco Michael	355	laborer	35	here
	w	Siraco Philomena—†	355	housewife	30	"
	x	*Puopolo Carmella—†	355	"	40	283 Chelsea
	y	*Puopolo Pasquale	355	laborer	50	283 "
	z	LaSala Amelia—†	357	housewife	23	here
1089						
	a	LaSala Marie—†	357		65	
	b	Timbone Anna—†	357	"	46	
	c	Timbone Vincent	357	cutter	48	"
	d	*Zarba James	357	laborer	41	253 Marion
	e	*Zarba Josephine—†	357	housewife	31	253 "
	g	*Geon Hong	365	laundryman	72	here
	h	McIntyre Wilfred	367	laborer	40	291 Lexington
	k	*Young Margaret—†	367	housewife	38	291 "
	l	Young Ruth—†	367	student	21	291 "
	m	Young Stanley	367	cleaner	43	291 "
	n	Morgan Helen—†	367	housewife	36	here
	o	Morgan Malcolm	367	fisherman	34	"
	p	Censale Domenick	369	upholsterer	30	"
	r	*Censale Yolanda—†	369	housewife	23	"

Page.	Letter.	Full Name.	Residence, Jan. 1, 1938.	Occupation.	Supposed Age.	Reported Residence, Jan. 1, 1937. Street and Number.

Chelsea Street—Continued

	s	*Moiniere Filomena—†	369	housewife	60	here
	T	Moiniere Leonardo	369	shoemaker	65	"
	V	Ryan Eugene F	373	laborer	35	235 Chelsea
	W	Ryan Rose—†	373	housewife	31	235 "
	X	Smith James J	373	teamster	39	here
	Y	Smith Julia M—†	373	housewife	37	"
1090						
	A	Burgess Alice A—†	376	waitress	27	464 Meridian
	B	Walsh John F	376	laborer	20	464 "
	C	Sullivan John J	376	merchant	56	here
	D	Sullivan Mary E—†	376	housewife	39	"
	F	Bloom Abraham	378	custodian	45	"
	G	Bloom Elizabeth—†	378	housewife	80	"
	H	Shore Esther—†	378	"	33	
	K	Shore Samuel	378	storekeeper	40	"
	M	Doherty Catherine T—†	380	housewife	44	"
	N	Doherty William F	380	florist	45	
	O	Doherty William G	380	chauffeur	22	"
	P	Riccioli Grace—†	380	housewife	23	235 Condor
	R	Riccioli Joseph	380	laborer	23	235 "
	S	Richards Loretta—†	382	housewife	42	here
	T	Richards William	382	laborer	42	"
	U	McGregor John F	382	clerk	66	"
	V	McGregor Mary—†	382	housewife	65	"
	Z	Olsen Frances—†	390A	stitcher	23	
1091						
	A	Olsen Helen—†	390A	housewife	54	"
	B	Wright Arthur	390A	fisherman	30	"
	C	Shea Agnes A—†	390A	housewife	38	"
	D	Shea James J	390A	laborer	39	"
	F	*Morse Annie—†	391	housewife	70	654 Saratoga
	G	*Morse John	391	laborer	30	654 "
	H	Morse William	391	"	42	654 "
	K	Henderson Edith—†	392	housewife	35	here
	L	Henderson Roderick	392	laundryman	39	"
	M	Musco Charles	392	barber	52	"
	N	Musco Mary—†	392	housewife	49	"
	O	Musco Mary—†	392	secretary	23	"
	P	Musco William	392	clerk	20	"
	R	Clee Hazel—†	392	saleswoman	25	"
	S	Clee Jennie E—†	392	housewife	45	"

Page.	Letter.	Full Name.	Residence, Jan. 1, 1938.	Occupation.	Supposed Age.	Reported Residence, Jan. 1, 1937. Street and Number.

Chelsea Street—Continued

Page.	Letter.	Full Name.	Residence, Jan. 1, 1938.	Occupation.	Supposed Age.	Reported Residence, Jan. 1, 1937. Street and Number.
	T	Gordinier Emerson	397	fireman	42	here
	U	Gordinier Hazel—†	397	housewife	35	"
	V	Murphy Agnes—†	397	operator	50	"
	W	O'Rourke Florence—†	397	housewife	45	"
	Y	Riccioli Constance—†	399	entertainer	23	"
	Z	*Riccioli Fannie—†	399	housewife	53	"
1092						
	A	*Riccioli Frederick	399	barber	64	
	B	Riccioli Salvatore	399	"	27	
	C	*Staffieri Carmine	399	tailor	39	
	D	*Staffieri Mary—†	399	housewife	34	"
	E	Manoli Charles P	399	laborer	44	
	F	Manoli Martin	399	mechanic	22	"
	G	*Cunningham Elizabeth–†	401	housewife	69	"
	H	Cunningham Frederick	401	clerk	29	"
	K	Cashman Bridget—†	401	housewife	69	85 Westglow
	L	*Texeira Edmund	403	laborer	26	187 Princeton
	M	*Texeira Mary—†	403	housewife	46	187 "
	N	Texeira Mary—†	403	"	25	187 "
	O	Coia Pietro	403	operator	50	here
	P	*Cordishi Maria—†	403	housewife	45	"
	R	Cordishi Nicholas	403	laborer	56	"
	S	Scarfo Domenick	403	"	27	
	T	Scarfo Ida—†	403	housewife	26	"
	V	Rotondi Antonio	405	storekeeper	55	"
	W	*Rotondi Maria—†	405	housewife	55	"
	X	Rotondi Victoria—†	405	saleswoman	23	"
	Z	McGregor Catherine—†	407	housewife	34	"
1093						
	A	McGregor John F	407	machinist	36	"
	B	Govoni Caroline—†	407	housewife	25	"
	C	*Govoni John	407	retired	72	
	D	Govoni Rose—†	407	inspector	33	"
	E	Lightbody Annie E—†	407	"	36	
	F	Lightbody Catherine A–†	407	housewife	75	"
	G	Lightbody Frederick H	407	compositor	34	"
	K	Norcross Catherine—†	409	housewife	53	251 Lexington
	L	Gillespie Dennis	409	retired	67	here
	M	Gillispie Frank	409	laborer	30	"
	N	Gillispie James	409	clerk	23	"
	O	Gillispie Margaret—†	409	housewife	67	"

Page.	Letter.	Full Name.	Residence, Jan. 1, 1938.	Occupation.	Supposed Age.	Reported Residence, Jan. 1, 1937. Street and Number.

Chelsea Street—Continued

	T	O'Regan Johanna—†	413	housewife	65	here
	U	O'Regan Mary A—†	413	"	73	"
	W	*Nastari Annie—†	415	"	37	"
	X	Nastari Gennaro	415	laborer	45	
	Z	Moran Edward E	417	merchant	42	"
1094						
	A	Moran Helen M—†	417	housewife	33	"
	B	Palumbo Anthony	420	mechanic	23	"
	C	Palumbo Jennie—†	420	housewife	22	"
	D	Arbia Anthony	420	tailor	48	
	E	Arbia Louise—†	420	operator	25	
	F	Arbia Pasquale	420	student	20	"
	G	Cirrone Santo	420	assembler	24	Everett
	H	Siraco Angelo	420	laborer	23	here
	K	Siraco Antonio	420	retired	60	"
	L	Siraco Delores—†	420	housewife	56	"
	M	Gordon Ellen—†	422	"	20	
	N	Gordon Henry P	422	chauffeur	29	"
	O	Lucius Manuel P	422	laborer	36	
	P	*Lucius Margaret R—†	422	housewife	33	"
	R	DeModena Frances—†	422	"	31	
	S	DeModena Leonard	422	engineer	38	
	T	Pascucci Alphonso	422	laborer	49	"
	U	Pascucci John	422	chauffeur	22	"
	V	Pascucci Louis	422	"	24	
	W	Pascucci Theresa—†	422	housewife	47	"
	Y	DiGiovanni Amedeo	424	storekeeper	46	"
	Z	DiGiovanni Mary—†	424	housewife	44	"
1095						
	A	*Budreau Lena—†	426	"	39	
	B	Budreau Raymond	426	laborer	21	"
	C	*Impeduglia Joseph	426	"	41	5 Shelby
	D	*Impeduglia Josephine—†	426	housewife	33	here
	E	Russo Anna—†	426A	"	23	"
	F	Russo James	426A	attendant	53	"
	G	Russo Pasquale	426A	chauffeur	21	"
	H	Russo Thomas L	426A	laborer	25	
	K	*Consolante Anna—†	428	housewife	38	"
	L	Consolante Pietro	428	machinist	41	"
	M	DiCesare Concetta—†	428	housewife	30	"
	N	DiCesare Fortunato	428	operator	35	"

Page.	Letter.	Full Name.	Residence, Jan. 1, 1938.	Occupation.	Supposed Age.	Reported Residence, Jan. 1, 1937. Street and Number.

Chelsea Street—Continued

Page.	Letter.	Full Name.	Residence, Jan. 1, 1938.	Occupation.	Supposed Age.	Reported Residence, Jan. 1, 1937. Street and Number.
	o	DiCesare Nunziata—†	428	housewife	63	here
	P	DiCesare Pasquale	428	retired	67	"
	R	DiCesare Rose—†	428	packer	27	"
	U	Giubileo Michael	430	laborer	37	
	V	Olive Vincenza—†	430	housewife	33	"
	W	Olive Vincenzo	430	machinist	46	"
	X	*Fucillo Constanzo	432	storekeeper	73	"
	Y	*Fucillo Filomena—†	432	housewife	64	"
	Z	Lamb Kenneth H	432	laborer	25	265 Border
1096						
	A	*Lamb Maude—†	432	housewife	24	265 "
	B	*Ippolito Frank	rear 432	laborer	55	here
	C	*Ippolito Grace—†	" 432	housewife	44	"
	D	Ippolito Vincenza—†	" 432	houseworker	20	"
	E	Porter Mildred—†	434	housewife	37	"
	F	*Porter Raeine	434	laborer	52	"
	G	*Bossi Antonette—†	434	housewife	30	100 E Newton
	H	*Bossi Joseph	434	chauffeur	30	100 "
	K	*Kilmartin Bridget—†	434	housewife	60	here
	L	*Kilmartin Michael	434	guard	76	"

Cleveland Street

Page.	Letter.	Full Name.	Residence, Jan. 1, 1938.	Occupation.	Supposed Age.	Reported Residence, Jan. 1, 1937. Street and Number.
	N	Feriani Daniel	3	chauffeur	27	here
	O	Feriani Henry	3	laborer	20	"
	P	*Feriani Louis	3	"	59	"
	R	*Feriani Mary—†	3	housewife	51	"

Eagle Square

Page.	Letter.	Full Name.	Residence, Jan. 1, 1938.	Occupation.	Supposed Age.	Reported Residence, Jan. 1, 1937. Street and Number.
	T	Cimmino Frances—†	4	houseworker	26	here
	U	*Sabbatine Carmella—†	4	housewife	52	"
	V	Sabbatine Ettore	4	merchant	54	"

East Eagle Street

Page.	Letter.	Full Name.	Residence, Jan. 1, 1938.	Occupation.	Supposed Age.	Reported Residence, Jan. 1, 1937. Street and Number.
	W	LaCortiglia Anthony	325	operator	29	here
	X	LaCortiglia Theresa—†	325	housewife	23	"
	Y	Bompane Armand	325	student	20	"
	Z	Bompane Bruno	325	machinist	24	"

Page.	Letter.	Full Name.	Residence, Jan. 1, 1938.	Occupation.	Supposed Age.	Reported Residence, Jan. 1, 1937. Street and Number.
1097		**East Eagle Street**—Continued				
	A	Bompane Charles	325	laborer	22	here
	B	*Bompane Giocchino	325	retired	63	“
	C	*Bompane Viola—†	325	operator	27	“
	D	Damico Angie—†	325	housewife	28	“
	E	Damico Charles	325	operator	29	
	F	Venuti Jennie—†	327	housewife	24	“
	G	Venuti Joseph	327	laborer	24	
	H	Polito Charles	327	“	21	
	K	Polito Marie—†	327	operator	22	
	L	*Polito Peter	327	“	53	
	M	*Polito Theresa—†	327	housewife	54	“
	N	Matt Elizabeth—†	327	“	22	
	O	Matt Nicholas	327	laborer	28	
	P	Arena Josephine—†	329	housewife	45	“
	R	*Romano Anthony	329	laborer	53	
	S	Romano Gaetano	329	operator	28	“
	T	Romano Sophie—†	329	“	24	
	U	*Romano Susan—†	329	housewife	50	“
	V	*Ciulla Lucy—†	329	“	71	
	W	Miraldi Anna—†	329	“	31	
	X	Miraldi Anthony	329	merchant	40	“
	Y	Areana Edith—†	331	housewife	27	“
	Z	Areana Joseph	331	clerk	27	
1098						
	A	*Lenzi Lillian—†	331	housewife	31	“
	B	Lenzi Thomas	331	packer	33	
	C	*Mainiero Carmella—†	331	housewife	32	“
	D	Mainiero Michael	331	barber	35	
	E	*Cormo Hilda—†	333	housewife	63	“
	F	Cormo Robert E	333	laborer	30	“
	G	Gould Mary—†	333	housewife	27	188 Falcon
	H	Gould Stephen	333	fireman	29	188 “
	K	Frati Augustine	333	chauffeur	40	360 Princeton
	L	Frati Margaret—†	333	housewife	29	here
	M	Maglitta Fred	335	packer	35	“
	N	Maglitta Mary—†	335	housewife	28	“
	O	*Gello Leona—†	335	“	35	
	P	DeStefano Edith—†	335	operator	23	
	R	DeStefano John	335	barber	55	
	S	DeStefano John J, jr	335	laborer	27	

Page.	Letter.	Full Name.	Residence, Jan. 1, 1938.	Occupation.	Supposed Age.	Reported Residence, Jan. 1, 1937. Street and Number.

East Eagle Street—Continued

Page.	Letter.	Full Name.	Residence, Jan. 1, 1938.	Occupation.	Supposed Age.	Reported Residence, Jan. 1, 1937. Street and Number.
	T	DeStefano Josephine—†	335	housewife	53	here
	U	McMillan Helen—†	337	"	25	"
	V	McMillan James	337	clerk	38	"
	W	Malzone Jennie—†	337	housewife	37	"
	X	*Malzone John	337	laborer	47	"
	Y	Tobin Annette—†	337	housewife	21	Arlington
	Z	Tobin James J	337	painter	31	342 Benningt'n
1099						
	A	Bertucelli Florindo	341	retired	71	here
	B	Sarro Frank C	341	foreman	38	"
	C	Sarro Josephine—†	341	housewife	38	"
	D	Dolan Marion E—†	341	"	39	
	E	Dolan Walter M	341	watchman	47	"
	F	Scotti Angelina—†	341	housewife	38	"
	G	Scotti John	341	painter	39	
	H	Balboni Barbara C—†	345	housewife	41	"
	K	Balboni John J	345	laborer	47	
	L	Balboni John J, jr	345	mechanic	21	"
	M	*Cerruti Angelina—†	345	housewife	24	"
	N	Cerruti Charles	345	laborer	40	"
	O	Doucette Edna—†	347	housewife	30	67 Porter
	P	Doucette George	347	fishcutter	29	67 "

Frankfort Street

Page.	Letter.	Full Name.	Residence, Jan. 1, 1938.	Occupation.	Supposed Age.	Reported Residence, Jan. 1, 1937. Street and Number.
	R	Vaccardio Marie—†	373	housewife	68	here
	S	Vaccardio Samuel	373	retired	67	"
	T	Mascetta Mabel—†	373	stitcher	21	"
	U	Mascetta Nicholas	373	tailor	49	
	V	Mascetta Renata—†	373	housewife	48	"
	W	Caprio Nicholas	373	chauffeur	32	262 Havre
	X	Caprio Philomena—†	373	housewife	33	262 "
	Y	Ianniciello Louis	375	laborer	27	here
	Z	Ianniciello Sadie—†	375	housewife	23	"
1100						
	A	Silva Joseph	375	laborer	38	260 Benningt'n
	B	Silva Philomena—†	375	housewife	37	260 "
	C	Soares Giacinto	375	laborer	44	260 "
	D	Marino Armond	375	operator	39	here
	E	Marino Louise—†	375	housewife	38	"
	F	Aragona Fred	377	plumber	38	"

Page.	Letter.	Full Name.	Residence, Jan. 1, 1938.	Occupation.	Supposed Age.	Reported Residence, Jan. 1, 1937. Street and Number.

Frankfort Street—Continued

Page.	Letter.	Full Name.	Residence, Jan. 1, 1938.	Occupation.	Supposed Age.	Reported Residence, Jan. 1, 1937. Street and Number.
	G	Aragona Marion—†	377	housewife	35	here
	H	Dolimount Edmund	377	clerk	22	"
	K	Dolimount Frances H—†	377	teacher	26	"
	L	Dolimount George I	377	clerk	24	
	M	Dolimount Isaac	377	engineer	59	
	N	Rose Dorothy—†	377	housewife	43	"
	O	Rose James	377	laborer	43	
	P	Natale Linda—†	379	housewife	32	"
	R	Natale Vincent	379	chauffeur	34	"
	S	Scanzillo Mary—†	379	housewife	47	"
	T	Scanzillo Michael	379	tailor	52	
	U	Russo Angelina—†	379	housewife	29	"
	V	Russo Angelo	379	chauffeur	32	221 Marion
	W	Pasquale Edward	381	laborer	24	here
	X	Pasquale Manuel	381	retired	65	"
	Y	Pasquale Marie—†	381	housewife	48	"
	Z	Graziano Anthony F	381	tailor	51	
1101						
	A	Graziano Mary A—†	381	housewife	49	"
	B	Moe Magna—†	381	"	33	
	C	Moe Ralph	381	tinsmith	36	
	D	DiPietro James	383	tailor	40	
	E	DiPietro Josephine—†	383	housewife	40	"
	F	DeStefano Clementina—†	383	"	70	
	G	DeStefano Rose—†	383	"	42	
	H	DeStefano Vincenzo	383	retired	76	
	K	Porzio Constantino	383	serviceman	29	"
	L	Porzio Margaret—†	383	housewife	28	"
	M	Doucette Alice—†	385	"	48	
	N	Doucette Henry	385	cutter	43	
	O	Surette Charles H	385	"	56	
	P	Calello Angelina—†	385	housewife	37	"
	R	Calello Gerald	385	guard	40	"
	S	Olivero Domenic	385	salesman	40	28 Hull
	T	Olivero Margaret—†	385	housewife	31	28 "

Lawson Place

Page.	Letter.	Full Name.	Residence, Jan. 1, 1938.	Occupation.	Supposed Age.	Reported Residence, Jan. 1, 1937. Street and Number.
	U	*Allie Nellie—†	1	housewife	31	here
	V	Allie William D	1	operator	30	"
	W	Alexander David	2	retired	67	"

Page.	Letter.	Full Name.	Residence, Jan. 1, 1938.	Occupation.	Supposed Age.	Reported Residence, Jan. 1, 1937. Street and Number.

Lawson Place—Continued

	X	Alexander Dorothy—†	2	operator	33	here
	Y	Alexander Rose L—†	2	housewife	63	"
	Z	Gatchell Merritt E	2	chauffeur	34	235 Webster
1102						
	A	Gatchell Rose—†	2	housewife	29	here
	B	Eldridge Celia—†	3	"	25	"
	C	Eldridge Daniel F	3	laborer	26	"
	D	Eldridge Joseph K	3	seaman	24	55 Chaucer
	E	Eldridge Sophie—†	3	housewife	48	55 "
	F	*Lopes Joseph	4	operator	52	here
	G	*Lopes Lucy—†	4	housewife	39	"
	H	Noble Annie—†	5	"	62	"
	K	Noble Florence A—†	5	packer	38	
	L	Goodrow Margaret F—†	5	housewife	53	"
	M	Goodrow Thomas F.	5	retired	64	
	N	Leary Catherine—†	5	packer	51	
	O	*Frazier Elizabeth—†	6	housewife	59	"
	P	*Frazier Frederick	6	retired	65	
	R	Johnson Ellen—†	6	housewife	42	"
	S	Frazier Annie J—†	7	"	71	
	T	Frazier Mary E—†	7	"	40	
	U	Frazier Peter	7	operator	45	

Lexington Street

	W	Garchinsky Charles	317	seaman	25	here
	X	Garchinsky Loretta—†	317	housewife	22	"
	Y	*Garchinsky Anna—†	317	"	30	"
	Z	Garchinsky John P	317	carpenter	32	"
1103						
	A	Garchinsky Joseph	317	laborer	20	
	B	Garchinsky Walter F	317	mechanic	34	"
	C	Holt Dorothy—†	317	operator	20	"
	D	Holt Elizabeth—†	317	housewife	46	"
	E	Holt Richard	317	laborer	23	
	F	Holt Robert	317	engineer	54	

Lovell Street

	G	Cammarano Angelina—†	371	housewife	40	here
	H	Cammarano Vito	371	laborer	44	"

Lovell Street—Continued

Page.	Letter.	Full Name.	Residence, Jan. 1, 1938.	Occupation.	Supposed Age.	Reported Residence, Jan. 1, 1937. Street and Number.
	K	Collaci Mario	371	student	23	Cambridge
	L	Jameson Robert J, jr	371	laborer	23	here
	M	Panetta Caroline—†	371	housewife	29	"
	N	Panetta Nicadimo	371	furrier	39	"
	O	Burke Frederick J	372	laborer	34	
	P	Burke Helen C—†	372	housewife	34	"
	R	Giella Marie A—†	372	milliner	36	274 Lovell
	S	Giella Marie S—†	372	housewife	67	274 "
	T	Flamia Alberico	372	blacksmith	41	here
	U	Flamia Mary—†	372	housewife	42	"
	V	Falsini Amelia—†	372	"	48	"
	W	Falsini Ateo	372	operator	25	"
	X	Falsini Egidia—†	372	"	22	
	Y	Falsini Libera—†	372	"	23	
	Z	Falsini Louis	372	laborer	50	"
1104						
	A	Falsini Maria—†	372	operator	22	
	B	DeCristoforo Anthony	373	clerk	30	
	C	DeCristoforo Mary C—†	373	housewife	29	"
	D	DeFronzo Louis	373	chauffeur	42	"
	E	DeFronzo Mary—†	373	housewife	33	"
	F	Pasquale Angelo A	373	welder	30	
	G	Saggese Elizabeth—†	373	operator	26	
	H	Saggese Lawrence	373	laborer	21	
	K	Saggese Louise—†	373	operator	28	
	L	Saggese Minnie—†	373	housewife	52	"
	M	Saggese Nicholas	373	retired	60	"
	N	Alessi Arthur	374	laborer	40	371 Frankfort
	O	Alessi Helen—†	374	housewife	40	371 "
	P	Trunfio Helen—†	374	"	28	115 Eutaw
	R	Trunfio Michael	374	laborer	45	115 "
	S	O'Brien Alice M—†	374	housewife	39	5 Blackinton
	T	O'Brien Richard T	374	laborer	42	5 "
	U	Fiandaca Frank	375	"	29	here
	V	Fiandaca Josephine—†	375	housewife	53	200 Chelsea
	W	Fiandaca Loretta—†	375	stitcher	25	200 "
	X	Amato Frank	375	laborer	43	here
	Y	Amato Vincenza	375	housewife	36	"
	Z	Luongo Antoinette—†	375	"	47	"
1105						
	A	Luongo Dominick	375	laborer	48	

Page.	Letter.	Full Name.	Residence, Jan. 1, 1938.	Occupation.	Supposed Age.	Reported Residence, Jan. 1, 1937. Street and Number.

Lovell Street—Continued

Page.	Letter.	Full Name.	Residence, Jan. 1, 1938.	Occupation.	Supposed Age.	Reported Residence, Jan. 1, 1937. Street and Number.
	B	Luongo Felix	375	laborer	22	here
	C	Gallerani Albert	376	printer	38	"
	D	Gallerani Cesira—†	376	housewife	62	"
	E	Gallerani James	376	operator	27	"
	F	Gallerani Louis	376	retired	73	
	G	Gallerani Alfred	376	policeman	41	"
	H	Gallerani Nellie J—†	376	housewife	39	"
	K	D'Eramo Andrew	376	manager	30	"
	L	D'Eramo Rose—†	376	housewife	30	"
	M	Miraglia Albert F	377	machinist	28	"
	N	Miraglia Lena—†	377	housewife	26	"
	O	Tutela Giramondo F	377	electrician	37	"
	P	Tutela Sarah—†	377	housewife	39	"
	R	Bettini Laura—†	377	"	29	
	S	Bettini Nicholas	377	operator	31	"
	T	DeStefano Margaret—†	378	housewife	21	347 Princeton
	U	DeStefano Vincent	378	chauffeur	24	347 "
	V	Salerno Anthony	378	salesman	28	here
	W	Salerno Constance—†	378	operator	21	"
	X	Salerno Joseph	378	mechanic	26	"
	Y	Salerno Marion—†	378	housewife	29	"
	Z	Salerno Mary—†	378	"	55	
1106						
	A	Salerno Peter	378	salesman	57	"
	B	Cianciulli Charles	378	laborer	50	
	C	Mastrogiovanni Anthony	379	foreman	25	
	D	Mastrogiovanni Lena—†	379	housewife	23	"
	E	Rusci Anna—†	379	"	42	
	F	Rusci Antonio	379	laborer	51	
	G	Rusci Ralph	379	student	22	
	H	Jeffrey Bertha—†	379	housewife	40	"
	K	Jeffrey Joseph F, jr	379	chauffeur	45	"
	L	Cocorocchio Albert	380	clerk	29	
	M	Cocorocchio Catherine-†	380	housewife	21	"
	N	Cocorocchio Clemente	380	clerk	58	
	O	Amato Angelina—†	380	at home	44	"
	P	Cornetta Benedetto	380	salesman	50	297 Cambridge
	R	Martocchio Angelo	380	toymaker	26	651 Benningt'n
	S	Martocchio Raffaela—†	380	housewife	23	651 "
	T	Dulong Joseph	381	electrician	32	here
	U	Dulong Pauline—†	381	housewife	28	"

Page.	Letter.	Full Name.	Residence, Jan. 1, 1938.	Occupation.	Supposed Age.	Reported Residence, Jan. 1, 1937. Street and Number.

Lovell Street—Continued

	V	DeSimone Anthony	381	operator	52	here
	W	DeSimone Mary—†	381	housewife	49	"
	X	DeSimone William	381	operator	25	"
	Y	Silva Alice—†	381	housewife	37	"
	Z	Silva Frank	381	photographer	37	"
1107						
	A	Kennedy Edward A	382	drawtender	51	"
	B	Kennedy Edward J	382	laborer	24	
	C	Kennedy Mary E—†	382	housewife	47	"
	D	Kennedy Miriam F—†	382	student	21	
	E	DeStefano Carmen	382	operator	48	"
	F	DeStefano Frances—†	382	housewife	47	"
	G	Mottola Jennie—†	382	"	52	
	H	Mottola Nelson	382	cutter	52	
	K	David John	382	stamper	29	
	L	David Mary—†	382	housewife	29	"
	M	Hedstrom Andrew J	383	retired	86	
	N	Hedstrom Ernest J	383	machinist	38	"
	O	Hedstrom Ida M—†	383	housewife	75	"
	P	Fuccillo Carmen	383	tailor	43	
	R	Fuccillo Isabella—†	383	housewife	42	"
	S	Fuccillo Albert	383	laborer	39	
	T	Fuccillo Edith—†	383	housewife	35	"
	U	Ghelfi Louis	384	chauffeur	26	Medford
	V	Ghelfi Madeline—†	384	housewife	23	"
	W	Marino Nelson	384	laborer	34	here
	X	Marino Rita—†	384	housewife	33	"
	Y	Morse Annie M—†	384	"	45	"
	Z	Morse Bernard B	384	laborer	23	
1108						
	A	Morse James	384	carpenter	46	"
	B	Morse John P	384	mechanic	26	"
	C	Morse William	384	laborer	21	

Neptune Road

	D	Rowe Herbert	15	waiter	28	409 Chelsea
	E	*Guidara Adalina—†	15	housewife	47	here
	F	Guidara Anna—†	15	at home	22	"
	G	Guidara John	15	plasterer	24	"
	H	Guidara Mary—†	15	at home	25	

Page.	Letter.	Full Name.	Residence, Jan. 1, 1938.	Occupation.	Supposed Age.	Reported Residence, Jan. 1, 1937. Street and Number.

Neptune Road—Continued

		Guidara Paul	15	laborer	58	here
	K	Ippolito Rose—†	15	at home	79	6 Neptune rd
	M	Luciano Anthony	15	tailor	40	6 "
	N	Luciano Helen—†	15	housewife	35	6 "
	O	Costello Bridget—†	17	"	64	here
	P	Costello Fred	17	operator	24	"
	R	Costello Martin J	17	longshoreman	62	"
	S	Costello Nicholas	17	"	27	
	T	Johnson Frederick	17	laborer	51	
	U	Johnson James H	17	retired	79	
	V	Johnson Winthrop	17	laborer	43	
	W	Sasso Joseph	17	cutter	48	
	X	Sasso Louise—†	17	at home	20	
	Y	Sasso Mary—†	17	packer	25	
	Z	Sasso Philomena—†	17	"	23	
1109						
	A	Toohig Catherine E—†	19	housewife	65	"
	B	Toohig Timothy A	19	retired	71	
	C	Toohig Warren A	19	B F D	40	
	D	O'Neil Catherine—†	19	at home	25	
	E	O'Neil Ethel—†	19	"	22	
	F	O'Neil Patrick J	19	laborer	62	
	G	Schrage James	19	machinist	35	"
	H	McPhail James D	19	checker	21	
	K	McPhail James J	19	superintendent	46	"
	L	McPhail Marion—†	19	assembler	20	"
	M	McPhail Mary—†	19	housewife	46	"
	N	Gleason John T	21	guard	45	
	O	Gleason Mary E—†	21	housewife	44	"
	P	Layne Ethel P—†	21	"	49	
	R	Granara Helena G—†	21	"	39	
	S	Granara William J	21	polisher	44	
	T	Leveroni Blanche D—†	21	operator	37	
	U	Leveroni Evelyn T—†	21	"	23	
	V	Leveroni Frederick J	21	welder	28	
	W	Leveroni Helena G—†	21	housewife	64	"
	X	Leveroni Rose B—†	21	at home	30	
	Y	*Vieira Anthony	23	fisherman	64	"
	Z	*Vieira Georgiana—†	23	housewife	63	"
1110						
	A	Giromini Garibaldi	23	laborer	53	

Page.	Letter.	Full Name.	Residence, Jan. 1, 1938.	Occupation.	Supposed Age.	Reported Residence, Jan. 1, 1937. Street and Number.

Neptune Road—Continued

	B	*Giromini Mary—†	23	housewife	52	here
	C	Postizzi Charles	23	chef	27	18 Frankfort
	D	Postizzi Mary—†	23	housewife	23	85 Westland av
	E	Austin Lillian M—†	25	matron	50	Billerica
	F	Murphy Johanna C—†	25	housewife	77	here
	G	Murphy Thomas	25	retired	79	“
	H	Cardinal Caroline—†	25	housewife	40	“
	K	Cardinal William	25	restaurateur	43	“
	L	Knudsen Anna C—†	27	at home	73	
	M	Currie John E	27	longshoreman	54	“
	N	Currie Mary E—†	27	housewife	56	“
	O	Lofgren Frederick	27	bookkeeper	42	“
	P	Lofgren Gladys—†	27	housewife	30	“
	R	Townsend James	27	engineer	54	167 Trenton
	S	*Babin Alexis J	33	fisherman	54	here
	T	Fougere Evelyn—†	33	housewife	31	“
	U	Fougere Napoleon A	33	bartender	31	“
	V	Irwin Edward F	33	clerk	34	
	W	Irwin Kathleen A—†	33	housewife	31	“
	X	Sweeney Frederick W	33	salesman	39	“
	Y	Sweeney Lawrence J	33	B F D	43	“
	Z	*Perdigan Manuel	33	longshoreman	33	6 Glendon
1111						
	A	*Perdigan Mary C—†	33	housewife	26	6 “
	B	Diaz Dorothy—†	35	“	25	here
	C	Diaz Manuel	35	chauffeur	31	“
	D	Vieira Manuel	35	longshoreman	37	“
	E	Vieira Mary—†	35	housewife	36	“
	F	Henry Emil	35	lithographer	53	“
	G	Popp John H	35	laborer	55	“
	H	Popp Virginia—†	35	housewife	51	“
	K	Vieira Mary—†	35	“	35	
	L	Vieira Matthew	35	longshoreman	36	“
	M	Crowley Catherine F—†	37	housewife	58	“
	N	Crowley Claire M—†	37	typist	27	
	O	Crowley Eileen G—†	37	“	25	
	P	Stasio Carlo	37	salesman	35	“
	R	Stasio Phyllis—†	37	housewife	33	“
	S	Gaeta Alphonso	37	laborer	28	
	T	Gaeta Emily—†	37	dressmaker	22	“
	V	Gaeta Michael	37	clerk	24	

Page.	Letter.	FULL NAME.	Residence, Jan. 1, 1938.	Occupation.	Supposed Age.	Reported Residence, Jan. 1, 1937. Street and Number.

Neptune Road—Continued

	W	Gaeta Theresa—†	37	housewife	53	here
	U	*Maglio Irene—†	37	"	73	"
	X	Marangiello Carmella—†	39	"	29	"
	Y	Marangiello Daniel	39	musician	30	"
	Z	Surette Alma—†	39	operator	22	
1112						
	A	Surette James	39	retired	63	
	B	*Surette Philomena—†	39	housewife	65	"
	C	Thibo Elizabeth—†	39	"	28	
	D	*Thibo James	39	operator	34	
	E	Vitale Frances F—†	39	housewife	42	"
	F	Vitale Joseph A	39	operator	43	"
	G	*Cardarelli Beatrice—†	41	housewife	63	"
	H	Cardarelli Frank	41	welder	26	
	K	Cardarelli Inez—†	41	at home	24	
	L	*Cardarelli Joseph	41	laborer	69	
	M	Cardarelli Michael	41	"	21	
	N	Johnson Anna—†	41	housewife	43	"
	O	Johnson James J	41	serviceman	42	"
	P	Kennedy Edward T	41	mechanic	35	"
	R	Cardarelli Lawrence	41	operator	43	"
	S	Cardarelli Vincenza—†	41	housewife	46	"
	U	Miraglia Antonio	45	storekeeper	61	"
	V	Miraglia Arthur	45	mechanic	32	"
	W	Miraglia Charles	45	laborer	30	
	X	Miraglia Eleanor—†	45	at home	20	
	Y	Miraglia Josephine—†	45	clerk	25	
	Z	Miraglia Leonora M—†	45	housewife	54	"
1113						
	A	Miraglia Richard	45	laborer	24	
	B	Miraglia Grace—†	45	housewife	28	"
	C	Miraglia James A	45	attorney	34	"
	D	Belt Helen—†	47	housewife	27	29 Decatur
	E	Belt James A	47	chauffeur	29	29 "
	F	Belt Laura J—†	47	housewife	61	218 Saratoga
	G	Hynes Beatrice M—†	47	operator	30	here
	H	Hynes Edward P	47	U S A	36	"
	K	Hynes Mary E—†	47	housewife	71	"
	L	*Shea Bridget—†	47	"	53	
	M	Shea Irene—†	47	waitress	30	
	N	*Shea Patrick	47	longshoreman	25	"

Page.	Letter.	Full Name.	Residence, Jan. 1, 1938.	Occupation.	Supposed Age.	Reported Residence, Jan. 1, 1937. Street and Number.

Neptune Road—Continued

Page.	Letter.	Full Name.	Residence, Jan. 1, 1938.	Occupation.	Supposed Age.	Reported Residence, Jan. 1, 1937. Street and Number.
	o	*Shea Raymond	47	laborer	20	here
	p	Carter Mary E—†	49	housewife	36	"
	r	Carter Robert J	49	clerk	37	"
	s	Oliver Francis G	49	"	22	"
	t	Oliver Frank R	49	serviceman	54	"
	u	Oliver Mary C—†	49	housewife	55	"
	v	Teixeira Phyllis L—†	49	packer	49	
	w	Churchill Thomas	49	laborer	60	
	x	Curran Sarah J—†	49	housewife	63	"
	y	D'Alessandro Ann—†	51	clerk	20	235 Chelsea
	z	*D'Alessandro Cecelia—†	51	housewife	55	235 "
1114						
	a	*D'Alessandro Ercolo	51	tailor	65	235 "
	b	D'Alessandro Yolanda—†	51	teacher	24	235 "
	c	Fickett Pilsbury C	51	retired	64	here
	d	McWhinnie James R	51	blacksmith	29	"
	e	McWhinnie Mary P—†	51	housewife	27	"
	f	Acres Charles J	51	chauffeur	29	"
	g	Acres Julia A—†	51	housewife	23	"
	h	Gomes Charlotte J—†	53	"	34	37 Faywood av
	k	Gomes George L	53	chauffeur	41	37 "
	l	Belyea Jessie M—†	53	seamstress	54	371 Lovell
	m	Landrigan Arthur W	53	bookkeeper	20	371 "
	n	Landrigan Mary E—†	53	housewife	50	371 "
	o	Landrigan Russell F	53	clerk	22	371 "
	p	Landrigan William R	53	laborer	56	371 "
	r	Howard Arthur W	53	B F D	38	here
	s	Howard Helen F—†	53	housewife	32	"
	t	*Cantalupo Annie—†	55	"	47	"
	u	*Cantalupo Carmen	55	operator	51	
	v	Cantalupo Lucy—†	55	clerk	20	
	w	Knox Marie—†	55	"	21	
	x	Knox Mary A—†	55	housewife	48	"
	y	Knox Sylvester J	55	printer	48	
	z	Knox Sylvester J, jr	55	foreman	23	
1115						
	a	Johnson Madeline—†	55	housewife	56	"
	b	Ryan Ellen S—†	55	"	26	
	c	Ryan J Gerard	55	clerk	27	
	d	Ryan Catherine—†	57	at home	56	

Page.	Letter.	Full Name.	Residence, Jan. 1, 1938.	Occupation.	Supposed Age.	Reported Residence, Jan. 1, 1937. Street and Number.

Neptune Road—Continued

	E	Ryan Nellie M—†	57	at home	60	here
	G	Olson Frank C	57	machinist	43	"
	H	Olson Josephine—†	57	housewife	78	"
	F	Olson Octavius	57	retired	82	
	K	Olson Vera C—†	57	bookkeeper	40	"
	L	Olson Victoria E—†	57	secretary	35	"
	M	Simmons Beatrice—†	57	housewife	20	Connecticut
	N	Simmons Lester M	57	engineer	42	101 Saratoga
	O	Grasso Serane—†	63	housewife	24	Everett
	P	Grasso Vincent	63	hairdresser	23	201 Havre
	R	*Gonsalves Alfred	63	operator	42	here
	S	*Gonsalves Lucy—†	63	"	44	"
	T	*Silva Caroline—†	63	at home	77	"
	U	Rizzo Amorino J	63	draftsman	34	"
	V	Rizzo Carmella—†	63	housewife	32	"
	W	*Pedro Alfred A	65	laborer	39	
	X	*Pedro Geronima B—†	65	housewife	35	"
	Y	Murphy Dorothy C—†	65	typist	22	
	Z	Murphy Mary E—†	65	housewife	50	"
1116						
	A	Murphy Michael	65	laborer	53	
	B	Quinlan Harvey	65	engineer	30	
	C	Quinlan Nora—†	65	housewife	28	"
	D	Butler Helen T—†	67	"	27	428 Frankfort
	E	Butler William E	67	chauffeur	32	428 "
	F	Sousa Mary J—†	67	at home	65	875 Saratoga
	G	*Vieira Andrew M	67	retired	79	here
	H	Vieira Andrew M, jr	67	barber	46	"
	K	Vieira Edward A	67	clerk	20	"
	L	*Bettini Peter	67	retired	62	
	M	*Bettini Rosina—†	67	housewife	63	"
	N	Moynihan Annie E—†	69	at home	75	
	O	Conway Helen M—†	69	housewife	40	"
	P	Conway John J	69	letter carrier	43	"
	R	Lynch Anna A—†	69	housewife	31	"
	S	Lynch Edward T	69	B F D	35	"
	T	*Johnson Carrie—†	75	clerk	25	412 Bremen
	U	*Johnson Charles	75	carpenter	49	412 "
	V	*Johnson Jean—†	75	packer	22	412 "
	W	*Johnson Maude—†	75	housewife	45	412 "

Page.	Letter.	Full Name.	Residence, Jan. 1, 1938.	Occupation.	Supposed Age.	Reported Residence, Jan. 1, 1937. Street and Number.

Neptune Road—Continued

	X	Bellizzia Vincent	75	chauffeur	42	here
	Y	*Marciano Concetta—†	75	housewife	30	"
	Z	Marciano Salvatore	75	chauffeur	32	"
1117						
	A	Rossano Frank	75	"	21	30 Horace
	B	Rossano Hazel—†	75	housewife	22	30 "
	C	Ruggiero Clara—†	93	"	33	here
	D	Ruggiero Matthew	93	bookbinder	36	"
	E	Pascucci Mary—†	93	housewife	46	"
	F	Pascucci Rocco M	93	operator	47	"
	G	Ruggiero Bella—†	93	housewife	22	214 Princeton
	H	Ruggiero Daniel	93	laborer	26	214 "
	K	Cianci Anthony	111	salesman	48	here
	L	Cianci Margaret—†	111	housewife	43	"
	M	Loschi Augustus	111	attorney	54	"
	N	Loschi Charles	111	storekeeper	40	"
	O	Loschi John	111	clerk	62	"
	P	Loschi Mary—†	111	teacher	44	"
	R	Loschi Victor	111	musician	49	"
	S	Tassinari Anna—†	115	operator	24	
	T	Tassinari Augustus	115	laborer	31	
	U	Tassinari Beatrice—†	115	at home	20	
	V	Tassinari Bernard	115	printer	31	
	W	*Tassinari Joseph	115	operator	61	
	X	*Tassinari Josephine—†	115	housewife	56	"
	Y	Tassinari William	115	busboy	22	
	Z	Sexton Richard J	115	policeman	38	"
1118						
	A	Sexton Ruth C—†	115	housewife	37	"
	B	Giggi Henry	115	laborer	34	
	C	Giggi Louise—†	115	housewife	26	"
	D	Casterina Sarah—†	131	operator	27	"
	E	*Mariotti Carmella—†	131	housewife	44	"
	F	*Mariotti Vasco	131	laborer	45	"
	G	Humphrey Annie—†	131	housewife	65	"
	H	Humphrey Harry H	131	laborer	69	
	K	Miller Sarah—†	131	at home	89	
	L	Humphrey Ethel—†	131	housewife	46	"
	M	Humphrey William L	131	laborer	47	
	N	Mahoney John H	131	"	26	"

Page.	Letter.	Full Name.	Residence, Jan. 1, 1938.	Occupation.	Supposed Age.	Reported Residence, Jan. 1, 1937. Street and Number.

Prescott Street

	R	*Amirault Augustin	50	cutter	32	here
	S	*Amirault Leon V	50	"	35	"
	T	*Amirault Rose—†	50	housewife	64	"
	U	*Amirault William J	50	fisherman	38	"
	V	Cavanagh Edward	50	operator	32	"
	W	*Cavanagh Margaret—†	50	housewife	30	"
	X	*Monahan Annie—†	50	cook	51	
	Y	*Monahan Patrick	50	laborer	28	
	Z	*Cain Eileen—†	50	housewife	31	"
1119						
	A	Cain John G	50	chauffeur	35	"
	B	Hartnett Edward D	62	physician	59	"
	C	Hartnett William J	62	retired	69	"
	E	*Jackson Agnes—†	68	housewife	47	290 Bremen
	F	Jackson Albert E	68	laborer	48	290 "
	G	Jackson Albert P	68	clerk	20	290 "
	H	Buonopane Eleanor—†	70	housewife	27	here
	K	Buonopane Vincent	70	salesman	28	"
	L	Rowe Frederick J	72	fisherman	29	"
	M	Rowe Mary—†	72	housewife	27	"
	N	West Florence—†	72	"	37	
	O	West Maurice E	72	B F D	40	
	P	Schatz Ada—†	72	housewife	60	"
	R	Schatz John	72	baker	65	
	S	Schatz John	72	clerk	24	
	T	Schatz Louise—†	72	operator	32	"
	U	Brooks Lillian—†	74	housewife	53	"
	V	Brooks Robert W	74	seaman	58	
	W	Curtis Ethel—†	74	housewife	24	"
	X	Lupu Cecilia—†	74	"	56	
	Y	Lupu Molly—†	74	operator	30	
	Z	Lupu Ruth—†	74	clerk	22	
1120						
	A	Lupu William	74	storekeeper	35	"
	B	Longmuir Jean	74	retired	73	
	C	Swadel Hannah—†	74	housewife	54	"
	D	Swadel Isabelle—†	74	maid	59	
	E	Swadel Isabelle—†	74	clerk	26	
	F	Swadel Robert	74	machinist	55	"
	G	Riley Edith A—†	90	housewife	54	"
	H	Riley James E	90	painter	57	

Page.	Letter.	FULL NAME.	Residence, Jan. 1, 1938.	Occupation.	Supposed Age.	Reported Residence, Jan. 1, 1937. Street and Number.

Prescott Street—Continued

	K	Riley Janet—†	90	bookkeeper	27	here
	L	Cone Carl	94	painter	34	"
	M	Cone Louise—†	94	housewife	30	"
	R	Higgins Helen—†	181	waitress	23	
	S	Higgins Joseph	181	laborer	20	
	T	Higgins Margaret Z—†	181	housewife	43	"
	U	Higgins Thomas H	181	inspector	48	"
	V	Hackett Peter J	181	engineer	42	
	W	Hackett Thomas	181	retired	71	
	X	Yocas Mary T—†	181	housewife	36	"
	Y	Yocas Paul	181	laborer	49	
	Z	Tucci Angelo M	209	retired	80	
1121						
	A	Tucci Angelo M, jr	209	laborer	32	
	B	Tucci Antonette—†	209	housewife	31	"
	C	*Tucci Palma—†	209	"	80	
	D	Ciampa Angelo R	249	retired	61	
	E	Ciampa Carmella—†	249	clerk	34	
	F	Ciampa Celia—†	249	housewife	54	"
	G	Ciampa Francis X	249	mechanic	30	"
	H	Ciampa Ignatius	249	clerk	33	
	K	*Nalli Adolfo	249	baker	49	
	L	Nalli Anthony	249	operator	21	
	M	Verra Patrick A	249	actor	23	
	N	DiGirolamo Anthony	249	chauffeur	25	"
	O	DiGirolamo Joseph	249	foreman	47	
	P	DiGirolamo Margaret—†	249	housewife	47	"
	R	DiGirolamo Mary—†	249	houseworker	21	"
	S	Tecci Antoinette—†	259	housewife	23	"
	T	Tecci Salvatore	259	laborer	24	
	U	DiFlumeri Joseph	259	"	29	
	V	DiFlumeri Luigi	259	"	55	
	W	*DiFlumeri Mary—†	259	housewife	52	"
	X	DiFlumeri Patrick	259	operator	28	"
	Y	Logue John A	259	mechanic	33	90 Neponset av
	Z	Logue Marie—†	259	housewife	35	Cambridge
1122						
	A	Crowley Annie—†	260	"	29	here
	B	Crowley George W	260	painter	32	"
	C	Bruno Domenica—†	260	stitcher	23	"
	D	Bruno Pasquelina—†	260	housekeeper	21	"

Page.	Letter.	Full Name.	Residence, Jan. 1, 1938.	Occupation.	Supposed Age.	Reported Residence, Jan. 1, 1937. Street and Number.

Prescott Street—Continued

	E	*Mackay Daniel	260	painter	46	here
	F	Mackay Rebecca—†	260	housewife	46	"
	G	Harrington Frederick J	261	carpenter	26	"
	H	Harrington John L	261	clerk	31	
	K	Harrington Rita A—†	261	stenographer	22	"
	L	Higgins Ellen N—†	261	housewife	56	"
	M	Higgins Joseph	261	laborer	52	
	N	Cowan James J	261	retired	72	
	O	Cowan Mary J—†	261	housewife	59	"
	P	Ventry Amelia—†	276	"	45	
	R	Ventry George	276	laborer	53	
	S	Honekamp Herman	276	"	63	
	T	Packard Frederick M	276	printer	47	
	U	Packard Mary F—†	276	housewife	68	"
	V	Packard Morton D	276	retired	82	

Princeton Street

	Y	Lawton Catherine—†	257	housewife	55	here
	Z	Lawton John J	257	operator	22	"
1123						
	A	Lawton Patrick	257	retired	63	
	B	Pascone Charlotte—†	257	housewife	27	"
	C	Pascone George	257	laborer	30	"
	E	Doluk Carroll	259	counterman	36	Chelsea
	F	Doluk Catherine—†	259	operator	33	"
	G	*Zebnik Anna—†	259	at home	69	"
	H	Ahern Bertha—†	259	operator	32	here
	K	Ahern Catherine—†	259	housewife	69	"
	L	Ahern Catherine—†	259	operator	36	"
	M	Ahern William J	259	clerk	30	
	N	Sartori Brunetta L—†	259	housewife	26	"
	O	Sartori James	259	teacher	28	
	P	Joyce Edith L—†	261	housewife	69	"
	R	Joyce George W	261	laborer	69	
	S	Joyce Jeannette—†	261	stenographer	30	"
	T	Joyce William L	261	mechanic	32	"
	U	DiMico Catherine—†	263	housekeeper	34	"
	V	Follo Anna—†	263	housewife	26	415 Frankfort
	W	Follo Salvatore	263	operator	27	447 "
	X	Sozio Joseph	263	"	53	here

Page.	Letter.	Full Name.	Residence, Jan. 1, 1938.	Occupation.	Supposed Age.	Reported Residence, Jan. 1, 1937. Street and Number.

Princeton Street—Continued

Page.	Letter.	Full Name.	Residence, Jan. 1, 1938.	Occupation.	Supposed Age.	Reported Residence, Jan. 1, 1937. Street and Number.
	Y	*Sozio Susie—†	263	housewife	47	here
	Z	Corby Alberta L—†	263	housekeeper	40	"
1124						
	A	Corby Frederick	263	laborer	45	
	B	MacLaren Jessie M—†	265	housewife	59	"
	C	MacLaren Rita L—†	265	clerk	25	
	D	Morrison Edward	265	chauffeur	31	"
	E	Morrison Helen—†	265	housewife	24	"
	F	Newman Mary A—†	265	housekeeper	44	58 Bennington
	G	Poirier Joseph C	265	chauffeur	28	Woburn
	H	Mazzone Claire—†	267	housewife	38	here
	K	Mazzone Onofrio	267	molder	38	"
	L	Steph Edward	267	laborer	24	"
	M	Steph Esmeralda—†	267	housewife	23	"
	N	Lacedra Celia M—†	269	"	24	
	O	Lacedra Daniel A	269	shoemaker	54	"
	P	Lacedra Dominic	269	painter	32	
	R	Lacedra Louis	269	"	34	
	S	Carroll Genevieve E—†	269	housewife	43	"
	T	Carroll James P	269	engineer	48	"
	U	Carroll James W	269	clerk	22	
	V	Hilton Mary C—†	271	housewife	41	"
	W	Shanahan Anastasia—†	271	"	72	
	X	Shanahan Edward	271	retired	84	"
	Z	Buchanan George W, jr	273	custodian	33	192 Benningt'n
1125						
	A	Buchanan Margaret A—†	273	housewife	33	192 Benningt'n
	B	O'Toole Ellen C—†	273	operator	27	1062 "
	C	*Bahrs Annie M—†	273	housewife	45	here
	D	Bahrs John H	273	painter	65	"
	E	Kruse Carl W	273	plumber	43	"
	G	Dobbins Henry M	277	fireman	56	
	H	Dobbins Ida L—†	277	housewife	75	"
	K	Wall Bertha M—†	277	"	27	
	L	Wall William E	277	longshoreman	32	"
	M	Burnette Mary—†	279	housekeeper	59	182 Falcon
	N	Caffrey Patrick	279	laborer	33	here
	O	McDonald Domenic	279	carpenter	52	412 Saratoga
	P	McDonald Jennie—†	279	housewife	55	412 "
	R	McDonald Ralph	279	laborer	27	412 "
	S	*Marino Mary A—†	279	housekeeper	67	Somerville

Page.	Letter.	Full Name.	Residence, Jan. 1, 1938.	Occupation.	Supposed Age.	Reported Residence, Jan. 1, 1937. Street and Number.

Princeton Street—Continued

Page.	Letter.	Full Name.	Residence, Jan. 1, 1938.	Occupation.	Supposed Age.	Reported Residence, Jan. 1, 1937.
	T	Schifano Anna—†	279	housewife	26	here
	U	Schifano Joseph	279	pressman	28	"
	V	Wheaton Lorenzo B	281	laborer	35	"
	W	Wheaton Viola A—†	281	housewife	34	"
	X	Huskins Joseph A	281	fisherman	51	"
	Y	Huskins Margaret E—†	281	housewife	48	"
	Z	Henrickson Thomas W	281	mechanic	45	"
1126						
	A	*Lanciotti Cecelia—†	283	dressmaker	54	"
	B	*Saveriana Agnes—†	283	housewife	46	"
	C	Saveriano Aniello	283	operator	51	"
	D	Saveriano Carmello	283	printer	20	
	E	Saveriano Eva—†	283	hairdresser	21	"
	F	*Gellese Guerino	283	blacksmith	25	"
	G	Gellese Josephine—†	283	at home	22	
	H	Gellese Nicholas	283	laborer	54	
	K	*Gellese Rosetta—†	283	housewife	53	"
	L	*Gellese Thomas	283	mechanic	31	"
	M	Gray Cecil	285	bookbinder	47	"
	N	Gray Mary—†	285	housewife	38	"
	O	Harris Ellen—†	285	"	40	
	P	Harris John	285	chauffeur	42	"
	R	Moriarty Clarence J	285	laborer	23	
	S	Moriarty Edward J	285	longshoreman	56	"
	T	Moriarty Julia A—†	285	clerk	22	
	U	Moriarty Mary E—†	285	housewife	46	"
	V	Moriarty William F	285	laborer	20	
	W	Faretra Joseph	301	"	31	
	X	Faretra Matilda—†	301	housewife	29	"
	Y	Bonito Annie—†	301	"	48	
	Z	Bonito Joseph A	301	clerk	20	
1127						
	A	Bonito Louis	301	"	27	
	B	Bonito Mary J—†	301	at home	30	"
	C	Farrand John E	303	laborer	26	680 Saratoga
	D	*Farrand Margaret—†	303	housewife	24	128 Lexington
	E	Ippolito Fred	303	laborer	57	680 Saratoga
	F	Volpe Michelina—†	303	operator	22	here
	G	Volpe Speranza—†	303	housewife	51	"
	K	*Johnson Alma—†	305	housekeeper	59	"
	L	*Gallagher Jeannette A—†	305	housewife	28	"

Page.	Letter.	Full Name.	Residence, Jan. 1, 1938.	Occupation.	Supposed Age.	Reported Residence, Jan. 1, 1937. Street and Number.

Princeton Street—Continued

Page.	Letter.	Full Name.	Residence, Jan. 1, 1938.	Occupation.	Supposed Age.	Reported Residence, Jan. 1, 1937. Street and Number.
	M	Gallagher Joseph L	305	mechanic	32	here
	N	King Max L	305	storekeeper	40	303 Princeton
	O	King Sirna L—†	305	housewife	40	303 "
	P	Bazzell Walter	336	pedler	58	here
	R	Labelle Ada—†	336	housewife	60	"
	S	Labelle Joseph R	336	longshoreman	29	"
	U	King Donald	342	laborer	20	
	V	Vargus John E	342	cutter	39	
	W	*Vargus Rose M—†	342	housewife	43	"
	X	Perricotti Charles	342	laborer	27	
	Y	Perricotti Edith—†	342	housewife	27	"
	Z	Ciasullo Eugene	rear 342	painter	36	
1128						
	A	Ciasullo Ida—†	" 342	housewife	25	"
	B	Pacifico Samuel	" 342	janitor	50	
	C	Pacifico Theresa—†	" 342	housewife	45	"
	D	*Caprini Adeline—†	345	"	47	
	E	*Caprini Joseph	345	laborer	55	
	F	Caprini Stanley	345	operator	22	"
	G	Larkin Helen—†	345	housewife	38	13 Condor
	H	Larkin James B	345	seaman	60	13 "
	K	Biancordi Elizabeth–†	rear 345	housekeeper	39	here
	L	Burdett Edward	347	operator	22	278 Benningt'n
	M	Ciampa Michael	347	laborer	47	here
	N	*Ciampa Pasqualina—†	347	housewife	40	"
	O	Iaconiello Marie—†	347	"	28	"
	P	Iaconiello Nicholas	347	laborer	33	
	R	Marzocchi Josephine—†	349	clerk	20	
	S	*Marzocchi Mary—†	349	housewife	37	"
	T	Marzocchi Samuel	349	painter	41	
	U	Hurley Helena M—†	352	housewife	26	"
	V	Hurley John F	352	operator	26	
	W	Steph Helena—†	352	housewife	42	"
	X	Steph Irene C—†	352	inspector	20	"
	Y	Arena Cosmo	356	salesman	35	"
	Z	*Arena Rose—†	356	housewife	33	"
1129						
	A	Gill Edward	356	clerk	30	
	B	Gill Lillian—†	356	housewife	25	"
	C	Caruso Ignazio	356	chauffeur	29	"
	D	Caruso Maria—†	356	housewife	21	"

Page.	Letter.	Full Name.	Residence, Jan. 1, 1938.	Occupation.	Supposed Age.	Reported Residence, Jan. 1, 1937. Street and Number.

Princeton Street—Continued

	E	Lyons Helen—†	357	candler	23	here
	F	Lyons James F	357	cutter	26	"
	G	Rothwell Annie—†	357	housewife	55	"
	H	Rothwell James S	357	packer	21	
	K	McGovern Helen—†	357	housewife	39	"
	L	McGovern Thomas L	357	electrician	39	"
	M	Monahan William	357	laborer	60	
	N	Visco Jennie—†	358	housewife	35	"
	O	Visco Joseph	358	plumber	39	
	P	Puopolo Mary—†	358	housewife	33	"
	R	Visto Hugh	358	tailor	46	
	S	Visto Rose—†	358	housewife	41	"
	T	Oricchio Angie—†	359	domestic	20	"
	U	Oricchio Harry	359	operator	46	"
	V*	Oricchio Lena—†	359	housewife	40	"
	W	Oricchio Michael	359	operator	26	"
	X	Ilmonen Helmar—†	360	housewife	41	"
	Y	Heino Fred	360	laborer	45	
	Z	Heino Ina—†	360	housewife	43	"
1130						
	A	Heino Reino	360	seaman	20	
	C	Filosa Albert	361	laborer	30	
	D*	Filosa Antonio	361	"	59	
	E	Filosa Elsie—†	361	housewife	29	"
	F*	Blundo Carmella—†	361	"	43	
	G	Blundo Joseph	361	laborer	52	
	H	Smith Selma—†	362	housewife	21	"
	K	Smith Welton	362	electrician	27	"
	L*	Maraldi Bridget—†	362	housewife	79	"
	M	Maraldi John	362	laborer	35	
	N	Carlson Mary—†	362	housewife	57	"
	O	Carlson Oscar	362	engineer	67	
	P	Love Alice M—†	362	housewife	49	"
	R	Love Lawrence H	366	clerk	25	
	S	Love Margaret A—†	366	operator	23	
	T	Havey Helen E—†	366	housewife	24	"
	U	Havey Helen M—†	366	nurse	45	
	V	Havey Walter A	366	clerk	29	"
	X	Rich Elizabeth M—†	368	housewife	50	53 Horace
	Y	Rich Herbert A	368	clerk	21	53 "
	Z	Rich Julius	368	laborer	53	53 "

Princeton Street—Continued

Page.	Letter.	Full Name.	Residence, Jan. 1, 1938.	Occupation.	Supposed Age.	Reported Residence, Jan. 1, 1937. Street and Number.
1131	A	Rich Robert J	368	operator	22	53 Horace
	B	Rich William G	368	clerk	25	53 "
	C	Rich Mary—†	368	housewife	26	here
	D	Rich Peter	368	laborer	27	"
	E	Gillis Mary—†	370	housewife	52	"
	F	Gillis William	370	blacksmith	49	"
	G	Thornton Margaret—†	370	housewife	32	"
	H	Thornton Patrick	370	engineer	32	
	K	O'Gorman Cora G—†	370	housewife	37	"
	L	O'Gorman James J	370	mechanic	38	"

Saratoga Street

Page.	Letter.	Full Name.	Residence, Jan. 1, 1938.	Occupation.	Supposed Age.	Reported Residence, Jan. 1, 1937. Street and Number.
	M	Wolfe Israel	401	storekeeper	49	here
	N	Wolfe Lillian—†	401	housewife	39	"
	O	Cohen Morris	401A	storekeeper	28	"
	P	Cohen Rose—†	401A	housewife	51	"
	R	Cohen Samuel	401A	bookkeeper	25	"
	S	LaCortiglia Peter	401A	watchman	60	"
	T	LaCortiglia Rose—†	401A	housewife	58	"
	U	Mastercuso John	401A	laborer	32	"
	V	Norris John L	402	operator	23	219 Trenton
	W	Norris Marion—†	402	housewife	23	219 "
	X	Nappa Joseph	402	shoemaker	59	here
	Y	Nappa Marie—†	402	housewife	59	"
	Z	Marshall Alfred	402	laborer	25	"
1132	A	Marshall Gertrude F—†	402	housewife	28	"
	B	Marshall William H	402	clerk	28	"
	C	Petrozzelle Angelo	403	oiler	34	133 Eutaw
	D	Petrozzelle Anna—†	403	housewife	33	here
	E	Quinn Lillian—†	404	housekeeper	48	"
	F	Curry Isabella—†	404	housewife	40	"
	G	Curry James L	404	inspector	40	"
	H	Rose Mary—†	404	housekeeper	57	"
	K	Mullins Elizabeth—†	404	housewife	37	"
	L	Mullins James	404	laborer	39	"
	M	*Petrozzelle Antonio	405	carpenter	23	133 Eutaw
	N	Petrozelle Ida—†	405	housewife	23	Fitchburg
	O	*Travers Manuel	406	laborer	52	here

Page.	Letter.	FULL NAME.	Residence, Jan. 1, 1938.	Occupation.	Supposed Age.	Reported Residence, Jan. 1, 1937. Street and Number.

Saratoga Street—Continued

	P	*Travers Mary—†	406	housewife	39	here
	R	Natale Carmella—†	406	"	39	"
	S	Natale Joseph	406	operator	44	"
	T	Brunaccini Angelina—†	406	housewife	38	"
	U	Brunaccini Anthony	406	operator	44	"
	V	DellaPiana Fred	407	assembler	22	775 E Sixth
	W	DellaPiana Mabel—†	407	housewife	20	775 "
	X	Crockett Charles L	407	constructor	47	238 Princeton
	Y	Crockett Emily L—†	407	housewife	34	here
	Z	*Souza Mary—†	407	"	43	"
1133						
	A	Souza Victor	407	carpenter	48	"
	B	*Lopez Manuel	408	seaman	34	
	C	Louvaris Charles	408	waiter	25	
	D	Louvaris Rose M—†	408	housewife	23	"
	E	Roberts Lawrence	408	seaman	42	
	F	Roberts Minnie—†	408	housewife	45	"
	G	Rose Thomas J	409	machinist	46	"
	H	Rose Valentina—†	409	housewife	41	"
	K	Ferrera Louis	409	laborer	40	"
	L	Ferrera Margaret—†	409	housewife	37	"
	M	*Trainor Bessie—†	409	"	43	
	N	Trainor Dorothy M—†	409	clerk	23	
	O	Trainor James H	409	"	24	
	P	Trainor James P	409	"	46	
	R	Trainor Raymond V	409	"	22	"
	S	McCarthy Edward	410	laborer	28	
	T	McCarthy Johanna—†	410	housewife	63	"
	U	McCarthy Lawrence	410	laborer	26	
	V	McCarthy Margaret—†	410	clerk	25	
	W	McCarthy Mortimer	410	laborer	32	"
	X	Collins Mary—†	410	housekeeper	68	178 Paris
	Y	Denehy John	410	longshoreman	34	178 "
	Z	Denehy Mary E—†	410	housewife	34	178 "
1134						
	A	*Padrenicola Mary—†	410	"	45	303 Saratoga
	B	*Padrenicola Philip	410	laborer	47	303 "
	C	DeCosta Mary—†	411	housewife	28	here
	D	DeCosta Richard	411	operator	33	"
	E	*Pecora Albert	411	laborer	54	"
	F	*Pecora Barbara—†	411	housewife	47	"

Page.	Letter.	Full Name.	Residence, Jan. 1, 1938.	Occupation.	Supposed Age.	Reported Residence, Jan. 1, 1937. Street and Number.

Saratoga Street—Continued

Page.	Letter.	Full Name.	Residence, Jan. 1, 1938.	Occupation.	Supposed Age.	Reported Residence, Jan. 1, 1937. Street and Number.
	G	Pecora Frank	411	clerk	21	here
	H	Pecora Samuel	411	machinist	28	"
	K	DeChristoforo Angelina–†	411	housewife	54	"
	L	DeChristoforo Angelina–†	411	stitcher	23	
	M	DeChristoforo Emanuel	411	clerk	22	
	N	DeChristoforo Joseph	411	"	20	"
	O	*Tammaro Angelo	412	laborer	48	68 Prescott
	P	*Tammaro Mary—†	412	housewife	35	68 "
	R	*Monteiro Frank	412	painter	48	here
	S	*Monteiro Frank, jr	412	"	23	"
	T	*Monteiro Mary—†	412	housewife	47	"
	U	LaBella Lena—†	412	clerk	20	
	V	LaBella Louis	412	laborer	25	
	W	*LaBella Luigi	412	"	48	
	X	*LaBella Theresa—†	412	housewife	46	"
	Y	Kibler Clarence	413	inspector	53	"
	Z	Kibler Irene E—†	413	operator	23	
1135						
	A	Kibler Joseph M	413	clerk	21	
	B	Kibler Nora E—†	413	housewife	49	"
	C	Wallace Elizabeth A—†	413	"	55	
	D	Wallace William J	413	chef	54	
	E	Green Catherine M—†	413	at home	78	
	F	Lunetta Mary—†	414	housewife	26	"
	G	Lunetta Michael	414	counterman	28	"
	H	Richard Charles	414	fisherman	47	"
	K	*Sampson Walter	414	longshoreman	42	"
	L	*Stone Beatrice—†	414	housewife	43	"
	M	Veiga Charles	414	laborer	24	
	N	*Veiga Limengos	414	operator	53	
	O	*Veiga Mary—†	414	housewife	47	"
	P	Veiga Paul	414	salesman	22	"
	R	Veiga William	414	laborer	21	"
	S	Vlogiare Aphrodite—†	416	waitress	21	
	T	*Vlogiare Fanny—†	416	housewife	45	"
	U	*Vlogiare George	416	operator	48	"
	V	Vlogiare Joan—†	416	housewife	22	"
	W	Coady Gladys—†	416	"	25	394 Meridian
	X	Coady William J	416	mechanic	30	394 "
	Y	DeFrancesco Joseph	416	salesman	27	here
	Z	DeFrancesco Lena—†	416	housewife	26	"

Page.	Letter.	FULL NAME.	Residence, Jan. 1, 1938.	Occupation.	Supposed Age.	Reported Residence, Jan. 1, 1937. Street and Number.

1136
Saratoga Street—Continued

	A	Piretti Ottino	416	laborer	58	here
	B	Nolan Coletta—†	420	clerk	29	"
	C	Nolan Elizabeth—†	420	housewife	73	"
	D	*Nolan John T	420	fisherman	30	"
	E	Cascieri Arcangelo	420	artist	35	
	F	*Cascieri Corrado	420	retired	75	
	G	*Cascieri Maria—†	420	housewife	71	"
	H	Cascieri Mary—†	420	dressmaker	28	"
	K	Reardon Anna—†	420	clerk	20	
	L	Reardon Frances—†	420	housewife	44	"
	M	Reardon Peter J	420	fisherman	49	"
	N	*Martins Anna—†	421	housewife	37	"
	O	*Martins Mario F	421	cutter	39	
	P	Amerena Joseph	421	salesman	53	"
	R	*Souza Mary—†	421	at home	68	
	S	Rosa Samuel	422	chauffeur	33	"
	T	Rosa Theresa—†	422	housewife	28	"
	U	DeLucia Frank	422	laborer	63	
	V	DeLucia Joseph	422	bartender	30	"
	W	DeLucia Mary—†	422	housewife	62	"
	X	DeLucia Mary—†	422	operator	25	"
	Y	Turco Alexander	422	machinist	41	"
	Z	Turco Angelina—†	422	housewife	35	"
1137						
	A	*Hamilton Anna E—†	423	"	31	132 Trenton
	B	Hamilton Peter C	423	chauffeur	34	132 "
	C	McKay John L	423	"	33	here
	D	Nealon Alice R—†	423	housewife	44	"
	E	Nealon Joseph B	423	seaman	45	"
	F	Trainor Georgianna—†	423	housewife	42	367 Chelsea
	G	Trainor John J	423	janitor	52	367 "
	H	Trainor Mary A—†	423	housewife	86	367 "
	K	Trainor Paul	423	chauffeur	21	367 "
	M	Sullivan Margaret—†	424	housewife	72	here
	N	Sullivan Michael B	424	laborer	38	"
	O	Belgiorno Adolphus	424	operator	28	"
	P	Belgiorno Concetta—†	424	housewife	51	"
	R	Belgiorno Edmundo	424	clerk	23	
	S	Belgiorno Pasquale	424	tailor	52	
	T	Coyle Barbara—†	425	operator	22	

Page.	Letter.	Full Name.	Residence, Jan. 1, 1938.	Occupation.	Supposed Age.	Reported Residence, Jan. 1, 1937. Street and Number.

Saratoga Street—Continued

Page.	Letter.	Full Name.	Residence, Jan. 1, 1938.	Occupation.	Supposed Age.	Reported Residence, Jan. 1, 1937. Street and Number.
	U	Coyle John	425	laborer	54	here
	V	Coyle John F	425	counterman	20	"
	W	Gaik Anna—†	425	housewife	41	"
	X	Gaik Stella—†	425	operator	25	"
	Y	Gaik Theodore J	425	repairman	46	"
	Z	*Giardella Divana—†	425	housewife	31	"
1138						
	A	Giardella Joseph	425	carpenter	34	"
	B	Giavalese Angelina—†	426	housewife	28	"
	C	Giavalese John	426	laborer	30	
	D	*Moschella Frank	426	mason	53	
	E	*Moschella Maria—†	426	housewife	48	"
	F	Moschella Ralph	426	laborer	23	
	G	Cronin Nora—†	rear 426	housewife	29	"
	H	Cronin William E	" 426	laborer	58	
	K	Cronin William F	" 426	"	35	
	L	Mosher Mary—†	" 426	housekeeper	56	"
	M	McGloan Catherine M—†	427	secretary	35	"
	N	McGloan James H	427	retired	73	
	O	McGloan Jeffrey J	427	salesman	27	"
	P	McGloan Mary E—†	427	housewife	63	"
	R	O'Connell Annie T—†	427	nurse	58	
	S	O'Connell Daniel J	427	retired	65	
	T	Reardon Alice J—†	427	at home	54	"
	U	*Cashin Elizabeth M—†	427A	housewife	28	455 Frankfort
	V	*Cashin Leo F	427A	molder	29	455 "
	W	Ferraro Antonio	428	"	41	here
	X	Ferraro Faustina—†	428	housewife	37	"
	Y	Stapleton Bridget—†	428	"	70	"
	Z	Stapleton Emma J—†	428	operator	34	
1139						
	A	Stapleton Lillian W—†	428	at home	38	
	B	Stapleton Mary C—†	428	operator	39	"
	C	Stapleton Patrick	428	retired	72	
	D	Provenzano Grace—†	428	stenographer	21	"
	E	Provenzano John	428	laborer	54	"
	F	Provenzano Mary—†	428	housewife	49	"
	G	Provenzano Tufano	428	clerk	24	
	H	Hulke Benjamin	429	retired	72	
	K	Nickerson Lillian—†	429	at home	43	
	L	Ducey Agnes—†	429A	clerk	30	

Page.	Letter.	FULL NAME.	Residence, Jan. 1, 1938.	Occupation.	Supposed Age.	Reported Residence, Jan. 1, 1937. Street and Number.

Saratoga Street—Continued

	M	Ducey Bridget—†	429A	housewife	68	here
	N	Ducey Nicholas	429A	operator	27	"
	O	Ducey Samuel A	429A	"	24	"
	P	Sexton Annie H—†	431	housewife	74	"
	R	Sexton Mary T—†	431	clerk	38	
	S	Sexton Robert E	431	inspector	56	"
	T	O'Neil James	431A	laborer	29	
	U	O'Neil Marion—†	431A	housewife	27	"
	V	Sexton Sarah E—†	431A	"	60	
	W	Sexton William H	431A	engineer	59	
	X	Tarquinio Clement	432	laborer	36	
	Y	Tarquinio Pasqualina—†	432	housewife	28	"
	Z	Tarquinio Antonio	432	laborer	64	
1140						
	A	*Tarquinio Beatrice—†	432	housewife	64	"
	B	*Tarquinio Mary—†	432	clerk	34	
	C	Tarquinio Sabatino	432	laborer	38	
	D	Costa Joseph	433	operator	24	"
	E	Costa Lucy—†	433	seamstress	52	"
	F	Vieira Adelaide—†	433	housewife	38	"
	G	Vieira Anthony J	433	laborer	40	
	H	*Bettencourt Joseph C	433	retired	64	
	K	*Bettencourt Mary—†	433	housewife	56	"
	L	Souza Margaret—†	433	housekeeper	44	"
	M	Thomas Beatrice—†	433	housewife	35	"
	N	Thomas Theodore	433	operator	35	"
	O	Anthony Claire G—†	433A	stenographer	23	"
	P	Anthony Edward J	433A	longshoreman	53	"
	R	Anthony Edward J, jr	433A	clerk	20	
	S	Anthony Mary E—†	433A	housewife	48	"
	T	Ottone Angelo	440	laborer	53	
	U	*Ottone Annie—†	440	housewife	63	"
	V	Ottone Mary—†	440	operator	22	"
	W	Ottone Michael	440	laborer	28	
	X	Almeida Frederick J	440	policeman	40	"
	Y	Almeida Isabella—†	440	housewife	37	"
	Z	Trabucco Alfred	440	student	23	
1141						
	A	Trabucco Carina—†	440	housewife	50	"
	B	Trabucco Gennaro	440	laborer	54	
	C	Trabucco Mary—†	440	dressmaker	22	"

Page.	Letter.	Full Name.	Residence, Jan. 1, 1938.	Occupation.	Supposed Age.	Reported Residence, Jan. 1, 1937. Street and Number.

Saratoga Street—Continued

	D	Petitpas Eva M—†	442	housewife	33	here
	E	Petitpas James H	442	packer	40	"
	F	Petitpas James S	442	clerk	24	"
	G	Caponigro George	442	dealer	31	"
	H	Caponigro Mary—†	442	housewife	25	"
	K	*Cultrera Lucy—†	442	"	19	
	L	*Cultrera Paul	442	laborer	62	
	M	Caponigro Andrew	442	dealer	62	
	N	Caponigro Mary—†	442	housewife	51	"
	O	DePaolo Albert	442	operator	28	120 Trenton
	P	DePaolo Mary—†	442	housewife	21	120 "
	R	*Fougere Eva—†	443	"	43	here
	S	Fougere Leo	443	clerk	38	"
	T	Ventre Anthony	443	"	20	"
	U	Ventre Christopher	443	mason	44	"
	V	Ventre Rose—†	443	housewife	43	"
	W	Flynn John J	445	laborer	32	Maine
	X	O'Brien Mary E—†	445	housewife	42	here
	Y	O'Brien William F	445	painter	49	"
	Z	Saari Paul	445	laborer	46	"
1142						
	A	Saari Saima—†	445	housewife	50	"
	B	Richards Alfred	445½	machinist	60	"
	C	Richards Annie—†	445½	housewife	63	"
	D	Silva Elvira—†	447	"	24	
	E	*Silva Peter	447	operator	33	"
	F	VanDyke Clarence M	447½	retired	75	
	G	VanDyke Mary A—†	447½	housewife	70	"
	H	Wolff Annie F—†	447½	housekeeper	48	287 Chelsea
	K	*Roccibene Ada—†	449	housewife	30	here
	L	*Roccibene Emelio	449	chauffeur	43	"
	M	DiMauro Mildred C—†	449	housewife	26	104 Brooks
	N	DiMauro Salvatore	449	machinist	28	140 Trenton
	O	Ettridge James	449	laborer	35	here
	P	*Ettridge Mary—†	449	housewife	31	"
	R	Cornetta Mary—†	451	"	40	"
	S	Cornetta Pasquale	451	laborer	42	
	T	Montalto Antonetta—†	451	housewife	28	"
	U	Montalto William	451	mechanic	49	"
	V	DiLorenzo Ida—†	451	housewife	24	449 Saratoga
	W	DiLorenzo Louis	451	operator	31	449 "

Page.	Letter.	Full Name.	Residence, Jan. 1, 1938.	Occupation.	Supposed Age.	Reported Residence, Jan. 1, 1937. Street and Number.
		Saratoga Street—Continued				
	X	Damato Albert	454	operator	36	here
	Y	*Damato Alphonso	454	retired	81	"
	Z	Damato Josephine—†	454	housewife	30	"
1143						
	A	Chafetz Frances—†	454	stenographer	21	"
	B	Chafetz Jacob	454	tailor	47	"
	C	Chafetz Mary—†	454	housewife	47	"
	D	*Polito Antonio	454	operator	56	"
	E	Polito Joseph	454	"	28	
	F	Polito Louise—†	454	housewife	24	"
	G	Polito Mary—†	454	clerk	26	
	H	Polito Minnie—†	454	housewife	48	"
	K	Polito Rose—†	454	dressmaker	23	"
	L	Caton Edward J	456	laborer	43	
	M	Connelly Andrew	456	"	40	
	N	Connelly Edward	456	machinist	38	"
	O	Connelly Sarah—†	456	housewife	70	"
	P	Connelly Sarah J—†	456	operator	39	"
	R	Melendy Catherine—†	456	housewife	44	"
	S	Melendy Charles H	456	teamster	43	"
	T	O'Hearn Catherine—†	458	housewife	43	"
	U	O'Hearn Michael	458	fisherman	45	"
	V	Scarpa Catherine—†	458	housewife	31	"
	W	*Scarpa Louis	458	retired	71	
	X	Scarpa Rosario	458	carpenter	43	"
	Y	Calliends Marie A—†	458	inspector	25	"
	Z	Connolly John J	458	laborer	46	
1144						
	A	Gayne Barbara M—†	458	housewife	51	"
	B	Gayne Harry D	458	guard	58	
	C	Scanlon John	458	chauffeur	25	"
	D	*Lento Angeline—†	460	housewife	42	"
	E	*Lento Antonio	460	laborer	55	
	F	Lento Frank	460	"	63	
	G	Lento Mary—†	460	stitcher	21	
	H	Faretra Joseph	460	chauffeur	44	"
	K	Faretra Rose—†	460	housewife	45	"
	L	Cuozzo Peter	460	operator	34	"
	M	Cuozzo Rose—†	460	housewife	26	"
	N	DeGruttola Anthony	462	operator	34	
	O	DeGruttola Ida—†	462	housewife	32	"

Page.	Letter.	Full Name.	Residence, Jan. 1, 1938.	Occupation.	Supposed Age.	Reported Residence, Jan. 1, 1937. Street and Number.

Saratoga Street—Continued

Page.	Letter.	Full Name.	Residence, Jan. 1, 1938.	Occupation.	Supposed Age.	Reported Residence, Jan. 1, 1937. Street and Number.
	P	*Francalagia Josephine—†	462	at home	87	here
	R	Vanodia Calogero	462	finisher	53	"
	S	*Vanodia Mary—†	462	housewife	42	"
	T	Pisatura Amedeo	462	bartender	27	"
	U	Pisatura Antoinette—†	462	stitcher	29	
	V	*Pisatura Pasqualina—†	462	housewife	56	"
	W	Banks Anna L—†	464	"	34	
	X	Banks Martin	464	mechanic	36	"
	Y	Pizzolante Domenic	464	laborer	43	
	Z	Pizzolante Mary E—†	464	housewife	33	"
1145						
	A	*Pizzolante Mary—†	464	"	38	
	B	Pizzolante Vincenzo	464	laborer	48	
	C	Fowler Alice F—†	466	housewife	31	"
	D	Fowler James S	466	mechanic	32	"
	E	Kirk Elizabeth J—†	466	housewife	41	"
	F	Hancock Edward H	466	salesman	22	"
	G	Hancock John W	466	laborer	27	
	H	Hancock Julia E—†	466	housewife	51	"
	K	Hancock Reuben J	466	laborer	56	
	L	*DeAngelis Pasquale	466	retired	71	
	M	*DelloPiana Eliza—†	466	housewife	46	"
	N	DelloPiana Leandro	466	laborer	52	
	O	DelloPiana Pasquale	466	clerk	21	
	P	Siltanen Amos	468	engineer	49	
	R	Siltanen Fannie—†	468	housewife	44	"
	S	Donahue Bridget F—†	468	"	47	
	T	Donahue John S	468	timekeeper	48	"
	U	Sacco Joseph	468	painter	37	
	V	Treavor Joseph H	468	laborer	38	
	W	Brennan Catherine—†	468	housewife	58	"
	X	Brennan Dorothy—†	468	clerk	29	
	Y	Brennan Ethel—†	468	waitress	25	
	Z	Brennan Joseph F	468	laborer	60	
1146						
	A	McGee Catherine—†	468	houseworker	39	"
	B	*Allegra Anthony	472	operator	35	
	C	Allegra Josephine A—†	472	housewife	31	"
	D	DiAngello Fiorindo	472	cobbler	49	
	E	*DiAngello Theresa—†	472	housewife	39	"
	G	Gallo Elizabeth A—†	474	bookkeeper	27	"

Page.	Letter.	Full Name.	Residence, Jan. 1, 1938.	Occupation.	Supposed Age.	Reported Residence, Jan. 1, 1937. Street and Number.

Saratoga Street—Continued

Page.	Letter.	Full Name.	Residence, Jan. 1, 1938.	Occupation.	Supposed Age.	Reported Residence, Jan. 1, 1937. Street and Number.
	H	Gallo George C	474	engineer	22	here
	K	Gallo Joseph A	474	designer	21	"
	L	Gallo Madeline—†	474	housewife	58	"
	M	Gallo Madeline R—†	474	bookkeeper	31	"
	N	Gallo Mary A—†	474	solicitor	37	"
	O	Gallo Pasquale	474	laborer	70	
	P	Gallo Rosa—†	474	operator	29	"
	R	Messer Charles	474	bookkeeper	30	323 Benningt'n
	S	Messer Regina—†	474	housewife	25	323 "
	T	Turco Jennie—†	474	"	29	here
	U	Turco Morris	474	pressman	42	"
	W	Gallo Agnes—†	476	housewife	34	"
	X	Gallo Michael	476	laborer	39	
	Y	*Riggi Julio	476	"	24	
	Z	*Riggi Liborio	476	"	50	
1147						
	A	*Riggi Theresa—†	476	housewife	43	"
	B	*Marcucci Adeline—†	476	"	46	299 Maverick
	C	*Marcucci Cesare	476	laborer	47	299 "
	D	Carroll Mary—†	478	housewife	31	here
	E	Carroll Wendell	478	laborer	31	259 Princeton
	F	Casey Daniel	478	fisherman	32	106 Saratoga
	G	Casey Mabel—†	478	housewife	29	106 "
	H	Caponigro Ada—†	478	teacher	30	here
	K	Caponigro Americo	478	pharmacist	28	"
	L	Caponigro Guido	478	manufacturer	21	"
	M	Caponigro Joseph	478	bartender	31	"
	N	Caponigro Liborato	478	manufacturer	27	"
	O	Caponigro Salvatore	478	student	24	
	P	Dumas Eugene	480	machinist	31	"
	R	*Dumas Somonne—†	480	housewife	26	"
	S	Siraco Frank	480	laborer	24	
	T	Siraco Silvatricia—†	480	housewife	63	"
	U	Siraco Stephen	480	laborer	28	
	V	Payne Frank	480	tester	50	
	W	Payne George	480	laborer	48	

Shelby Street

Page.	Letter.	Full Name.	Residence, Jan. 1, 1938.	Occupation.	Supposed Age.	Reported Residence, Jan. 1, 1937. Street and Number.
	Y	Abruzese Florence—†	4	clerk	24	here
	Z	Abruzese Gabriel	4	merchant	59	"

Page.	Letter.	Full Name.	Residence, Jan. 1, 1938.	Occupation.	Supposed Age.	Reported Residence, Jan. 1, 1937. Street and Number.
1148		**Shelby Street**—Continued				
	A	Abruzese James	4	clerk	29	here
	B	Abruzese Pasquale	4	butcher	34	"
	C	*Fusco Ralph	4	storekeeper	48	"
	D	*Fusco Sandrina—†	4	housewife	45	"
	E	*Vertullo Carmine	6	retired	61	"
	F	*Vertullo Gilorma—†	6	housewife	53	"
	G	Vertullo Carmella—†	6	operator	22	"
	H	Vertullo Mary M—†	6	"	27	
	K	Vertullo Rose—†	6	"	25	
	L	Purciello Augustine	6	"	38	
	M	Purciello Florence—†	6	housewife	36	"
	N	Sacco Salvatore	8	laborer	35	407 Chelsea
	O	Lee Carl	8	painter	26	here
	P	Lee Edith—†	8	housewife	25	"
	R	Bright Albert	8	seaman	21	"
	S	Bright Sarah—†	8	housewife	42	"
	T	Pimental Anthony	10	fireman	28	
	U	Pimental Lena—†	10	housewife	27	"
	V	Pettersen Ethel—†	10	"	24	
	W	*Pettersen Harold	10	laborer	40	
	X	*Blasi Margaret—†	10	housewife	52	"
	Y	*Blasi Rocco	10	tailor	55	
	Z	McGee Sarah—†	12	housekeeper	70	"
1149						
	A	Gallagher Annie—†	12	housewife	66	"
	B	Gallagher John	12	laborer	32	
	C	*Rodophele Jennie—†	12	housewife	54	"
	D	*Rodophele John	12	retired	67	
	E	Rodophele Luigi	12	operator	25	"
	F	Rodophele Sarah—†	12	"	23	
	G	*Johnston Charles	14	plumber	26	
	H	Johnston Lucy—†	14	housewife	25	"
	K	*Coombs Cecilia—†	14	"	37	
	L	Coombs Henry F	14	janitor	39	
	M	Coombs Ely	14	painter	28	
	N	Coombs Irene—†	14	housewife	24	"
	O	Coviello Nicholas	16	laborer	28	
	P	Coviello Phyllis—†	16	housewife	28	"
	R	Giardullo Frances—†	16	"	34	
	S	*Giardullo Mary—†	16	"	65	

Page.	Letter.	FULL NAME.	Residence, Jan. 1, 1938.	Occupation.	Supposed Age.	Reported Residence, Jan. 1, 1937. Street and Number.

Shelby Street—Continued

	T	Giardullo Nazzaro	16	laborer	38	here
	U	Intonti Americo	16	chauffeur	24	"
	V	Intonti Jennie—†	16	housewife	23	"
	W*	Saviano Aniello	18	operator	59	
	X	Saviano Frank	18	"	28	
	Y	Saviano Joseph	18	"	21	
	Z*	Saviano Sophie—†	18	housewife	50	"
1150						
	A	Saviano Angeline—†	18	"	23	
	B	Saviano Stephen	18	operator	29	"
	E	Manfra Anna—†	24	"	21	368 Princeton
	F	Manfra Jeremiah	24	barber	47	368 "
	G*	Manfra Rose—†	24	housewife	43	368 "
	H	Scarafone Gennaro	24	operator	42	here
	K	Scarafone Margaret—†	24	housewife	33	"
	L	Harlow Anna—†	26	"	35	"
	M	Harlow Joseph	26	chauffeur	31	"
	N	Festa Mario	26	tailor	33	
	O	Festa Mary—†	26	housewife	32	"
	P*	Cosco Anna—†	26	"	30	
	R	Cosco Salvatore	26	laborer	32	
	T	Bianco Margaret—†	32	housewife	35	"
	U	Bianco Michael	32	operator	37	532 Saratoga
	V*	Umana Annie—†	32	housewife	45	here
	W	Umana Samuel	32	barber	50	"
	X	Fanale Angeline—†	32	housewife	30	"
	Y	Fanale Anthony	32	chauffeur	33	"
	Z	Costa Joseph	34	laborer	23	110 Trenton
1151						
	A	Costa Margaret—†	34	housewife	22	here
	B	Fiorillo Madeline—†	34	stitcher	21	5 Shelby
	C	Petracco Alexander	34	retired	68	5 "
	D	Petracco Josephine—†	34	housewife	52	5 "
	E*	Velardo Anna—†	34	"	38	here
	F	Velardo Pasquale	34	chauffeur	49	"

Shrimpton Street

	G	Harrington John H	21	retired	65	65 Border
	H	Harrington Mary E—†	21	housewife	58	65 "
	K*	Murphy Annie—†	21	at home	79	here

Page.	Letter.	Full Name.	Residence, Jan. 1, 1938.	Occupation.	Supposed Age.	Reported Residence, Jan. 1, 1937. Street and Number.

Shrimpton Street—Continued

Page.	Letter.	Full Name.	Residence, Jan. 1, 1938.	Occupation.	Supposed Age.	Reported Residence, Jan. 1, 1937. Street and Number.
	L	Pope Annie—†	21	housekeeper	45	here
	M	Govoni Evelyn—†	22	clerk	22	"
	N	*Govoni John	22	laborer	57	"
	O	*Govoni Norma—†	22	housewife	53	"
	P	Usseglio John	24	painter	39	
	R	Usseglio Theresa—†	24	housewife	32	"
	S	Cavagnaro Francis P	24	laborer	42	
	T	Cavagnaro Mary E—†	24	housewife	62	"
	U	Cavagnaro Mary U—†	24	saleswoman	25	"
	V	Cavagnaro Nathaniel J	24	cutter	68	
	W	Marden Edwin	24	laborer	54	
	X	Marden Lillian—†	24	housewife	54	"

14

15

1

17

18

19

20

2

Ward 1—Precinct 14

CITY OF BOSTON

LIST OF RESIDENTS
20 YEARS OF AGE AND OVER

(NON-CITIZENS INDICATED BY ASTERISK)
(FEMALES INDICATED BY DAGGER)

AS OF

JANUARY 1, 1938

JOSEPH F. TIMILTY, } *Listing*
FREDERIC E. DOWLING, } *Board.*

CITY OF BOSTON PRINTING DEPARTMENT

Page.	Letter.	Full Name.	Residence, Jan. 1, 1938.	Occupation.	Supposed Age.	Reported Residence, Jan. 1, 1937. Street and Number.
1161		**Bennington Street**				
	C	*Cashin Ellen—†	387	housewife	64	here
	D	*Cashin Martina—†	387	laundress	26	"
	E	*Cashin Richard	387	watchman	39	"
	F	LaTorre Joseph	387	laborer	30	
	G	LaTorre Mary—†	387	housewife	21	"
	H	Holden George	387	chemist	23	
	K	Holden Gertrude—†	387	laundress	25	"
	L	Holden Mary—†	387	housewife	47	"
	N	*Scarafane Antonetta—†	394	"	49	
	O	Scarafane Dominic	394	operator	61	"
	P	Scarafane Dominic	394	laborer	23	10 Shelby
	R	Scarafane Joseph	394	"	29	10 "
	S	DiForte Carmella—†	396	housewife	25	here
	T	DiForte Salvatore	396	laborer	29	"
	V	Devizia Edmund C	398	welder	28	101 Benningt'n
	W	Devizia Helen—†	398	housewife	29	101 "
	X	Crump Anna—†	398	"	25	here
	Y	Crump Raymond	398	chauffeur	25	"
	Z	Crump Willard	398	welder	29	"
1162						
	A	Dunn Lena—†	398	housewife	31	"
	B	Dunn Patten	398	welder	30	
	C	Hoey Gertrude—†	400	housewife	24	"
	D	Hoey Paul	400	salesman	28	"
	E	Finneran Bridget F—†	400	housewife	70	"
	F	McDonald Nellie—†	400	"	94	
	G	Coughlin Susan T—†	402	"	65	
	H	Burke William	402	printer	30	
	L	*Powers Ellen—†	407	housewife	29	"
	M	*Powers Patrick	407	laborer	27	
	N	DePanfilis James	407	"	49	
	O	*DePanfilis Mary—†	407	housewife	39	"
	P	*Ilinitch Carolina—†	408	"	53	
	R	Ilinitch Joseph	408	laborer	55	
	S	*Bednarska Mary—†	408	housewife	45	"
	T	*Stoney Lena—†	408	"	27	
	U	*Stoney Walter	408	laborer	32	
	V	Malloy Anna M—†	408	cook	26	
	W	Malloy John J	408	butcher	58	
	X	Malloy Margaret—†	408	housewife	52	"

Page.	Letter.	FULL NAME.	Residence, Jan. 1, 1938.	Occupation.	Supposed Age.	Reported Residence, Jan. 1, 1937. Street and Number.

Bennington Street—Continued

	Y	Flanagan Helen—†	412	housewife	39	here
	Z	Flanagan Luke	412	reporter	39	"
1163						
	B	DeMartinio Anna—†	420	housewife	25	"
	C	DeMartinio Salvatore	420	butcher	34	
	D	Mazzone Alice—†	420	housewife	44	"
	E	Mazzone James	420	laborer	54	
	F	Mazzone James	420	butcher	22	
	G	Brothers Daniel F	423	chauffeur	33	"
	H	Brothers Mary—†	423	housewife	65	"
	K	Brothers Michael J	423	laborer	44	"
	L	Granara Louis A	423	chauffeur	39	Wilmington
	M	Stevenson Francis J	423	"	39	here
	N	Stevenson Marguerite H–†	423	housewife	38	"
	O	Carino Ernest	423	merchant	27	88 Trenton
	P	Carino Phyllis—†	423	housewife	24	88 "
	R	Cameron Agnes T—†	425	"	59	here
	S	Cameron Frederick J	425	tailor	43	"
	T	Cameron Marion G—†	425	clerk	39	"
	U	Cameron Pauline E—†	425	"	26	
	V	Cameron Ruth L—†	425	"	22	
	W	Cameron William T	425	tailor	71	
	X	O'Shea Evelyn—†	425	housewife	36	"
	Y	O'Shea Patrick J	425	printer	46	
	Z	McClellan Anna J—†	430	housewife	43	"
1164						
	A	McClellan Joseph A	430	laborer	45	"
	B	*Sturrock Jessie—†	430	housewife	45	171 Trenton
	C	*Sturrock Martin	430	engineer	47	171 "
	D	Granara John R	430	houseman	21	here
	E	Stewart Gertrude L—†	430	housewife	53	"
	F	Collins Margaret J—†	431	"	42	"
	G	Healey John H	431	carpenter	63	"
	H	Healey Mabel M—†	431	housewife	51	"
	K	Healey Thomas J	431	laborer	25	"
	L	Dellazoppa Anthony	431	seaman	33	380 Sumner
	M	*Dellazoppa Louis	431	laborer	65	here
	N	Dellazoppa Margaret—†	431	operator	24	"
	O	Dellazoppa Mary—†	431	"	30	"
	P	*Dellazoppa Nora—†	431	housewife	63	"
	R	McBride Abbie—†	432	typist	35	

Page.	Letter.	Full Name.	Residence, Jan. 1, 1938.	Occupation.	Supposed Age.	Reported Residence, Jan. 1, 1937. Street and Number.

Bennington Street—Continued

Page.	Letter.	Full Name.	Residence, Jan. 1, 1938.	Occupation.	Supposed Age.	Reported Residence, Jan. 1, 1937. Street and Number.
	S	McBride Daniel	432	clerk	37	here
	T	McBride Nora—†	432	housewife	67	“
	U	O'Shea Andrew J	432	laborer	43	“
	V	O'Shea Bridget—†	432	housewife	73	“
	W	O'Shea Nora G—†	432	operator	40	“
	X	Shaw Franklin J	433	laborer	48	
	Y	Shaw Mary G—†	433	housewife	48	“
	Z	Cabral Lena—†	433	designer	30	
1165						
	A	*Cabral Mary—†	433	housewife	52	“
	B	Cabral Rose—†	433	stenographer	25	“
	C	O'Brien Catherine I—†	433	clerk	39	“
	D	O'Brien Charles F	433	leatherworker	47	“
	E	O'Brien Edward F	433	printer	24	
	F	O'Brien Laura A—†	433	housewife	43	“
	G	*Viera Manuel	437	longshoreman	59	“
	H	Brown Vera—†	437	clerk	22	734 Benningt'n
	K	Graham Frank O	437	“	38	734 “
	L	Graham Muriel A—†	437	housewife	35	734 “
	M	Graham Walter H	437	clerk	25	734 “
	N	Winn Helen L—†	437	operator	21	734 “
	O	Balboni James	437	laborer	32	here
	P	Balboni Mary—†	437	housewife	24	“
	R	Kelly Nora A—†	439	operator	44	“
	S	Kidney Ellen—†	439	housewife	66	“
	T	*Kidney Mary—†	439	“	68	
	U	McCarthy Anna—†	439	domestic	55	“
	V	Twomey Mary F—†	441	housewife	50	“
	W	Twomey Joseph L	441	inspector	38	“
	X	Twomey Monica—†	441	housewife	33	“
	Y	Flaherty Hannah L—†	445	“	63	
	Z	Flaherty Mary G—†	445	clerk	26	“
1166						
	A	Marcella Charles	445	laborer	33	
	B	*Marcella Charoletta—†	445	housewife	30	“
	C	McNulty Bridget—†	447	druggist	51	
	D	Twomey Catherine H—†	447	housewife	48	“
	E	Shea Daniel F	447	laborer	37	
	F	Shea Dennis F	447	printer	47	
	G	Shea John F	447	clerk	42	
	H	Shea Patrick	447	retired	78	

Page.	Letter.	Full Name.	Residence, Jan. 1, 1938.	Occupation.	Supposed Age.	Reported Residence, Jan. 1, 1937. Street and Number.

Bennington Street—Continued

	K	Shea Patrick F	447	chauffeur	45	here
	L	Shea Thomas J	447	laborer	49	"
	M	Hickey Anna—†	449	housewife	40	"
	N	Hickey James	449	baker	41	
	O	Condon Esther—†	449	clerk	37	
	P	Coughlin Elizabeth—†	449	housewife	68	"
	R	Coughlin Patrick	449	laborer	68	
	S	Coughlin Thomas	449	timekeeper	28	"
	T	LeBlanc Alma—†	451	housewife	40	"
	U	LeBlanc Charles	451	engineer	40	
	V	Barretto William A	451	engraver	47	"
	W	Kepple Maude E—†	451	housewife	48	"
	X	Kepple Ruth E—†	451	clerk	25	
	Y	Kepple William F	451	laborer	51	
1167						
	A	Day Julia F—†	456	saleswoman	43	"
	B	Flanagan Agnes E—†	456	"	38	
	C	Flanagan Grace J—†	456	clerk	33	
	D	Flanagan Mary A—†	456	housewife	70	"
	E	Flanagan William A	456	clerk	45	
	G	Williams Isabella M—†	460	housewife	36	"
	H	Williams Joseph H	460	retired	72	
	K	Williams William J	460	laborer	40	
	L	Rochini Anunziata—†	490	clerk	25	
	M*	Rochini Diomira—†	490	housewife	52	"
	N	Rochini Nancy—†	490	hairdresser	23	"
	O	Rochini Santino	490	laborer	27	
	P	Maloney Mary J—†	496	housewife	30	"
	R	Maloney Theodore W	496	manager	31	"
	S	Hitchins George E	496	salesman	50	"
	T	Hitchins Laura I—†	496	housewife	38	"
	U	LaDuke Donald	498	mechanic	33	"
	V	LaDuke Edna—†	498	housewife	30	"
	W	Colbert Arthur	498	storekeeper	50	"
	X	Colbert Margaret—†	498	housewife	42	"
	Y	Hallahan James J	504	engineer	59	"
	Z	Hallahan John G	504	packer	22	
1168						
	A	Hallahan Margaret A—†	504	housewife	53	"
	B	Ezekiel Helena—†	506	clerk	29	
	C	Ezekiel James F	506	painter	27	

Bennington Street—Continued

Page.	Letter.	Full Name.	Residence, Jan. 1, 1938.	Occupation.	Supposed Age.	Reported Residence, Jan. 1, 1937. Street and Number.
	D	Ezekiel Michael	506	longshoreman	65	here
	E	Ezekiel Theresa—†	506	housewife	54	"
	G	Doyle Mary A—†	506	operator	43	"
	F	Doyle Mary M—†	506	housewife	72	"
	H	Paris Christie C—†	508	operator	46	
	K	Paris Margaret E—†	508	housewife	45	"
	L	Callahan John T	508	guard	54	
	M	Callahan Joseph T	508	clerk	21	
	N	Callahan Mary J—†	508	housewife	48	"
	O	Maher Stella—†	510	"	33	
	P	Powers Helen—†	510	"	40	
	R	Henderson Cornelius	512	laborer	33	
	S	Henderson Daniel	512	operator	23	"
	T	Henderson John	512	laborer	65	
	U	Henderson Josephine—†	512	housewife	63	"
	V	Henderson Mary—†	512	typist	24	
	W	Henderson Neil	512	clerk	37	
	X	Murphy Joseph H	516	laborer	38	
	Y	Murphy Madeline M—†	516	housewife	39	"
	Z	Memmolo Angelo	524	laborer	33	
1169						
	A	*Memmolo Delphine—†	524	housewife	29	"
	B	Memmolo Antonio	524	chauffeur	25	"
	C	Memmolo Camilla—†	524	packer	27	
	D	*Memmolo Mary—†	524	housewife	45	"
	E	Memmolo Stephen	524	laborer	62	
	F	Dixon Andrew	524	agent	52	
	G	Dixon Julia—†	524	housewife	49	"
	H	O'Connell John M	524	clerk	39	"
	K	Burke Catherine—†	528	housewife	56	45 Homes av
	L	Volpini Agosto	528	laborer	35	here
	M	*Volpini Emma—†	528	housewife	29	"
	N	Mullaley Agnes L—†	530	"	31	"
	O	Mullaley Daniel J	530	clerk	34	
	P	Mullaley Julia A—†	530	housewife	59	"
	R	Labello Grace—†	532	"	29	
	S	Labello Joseph	532	chauffeur	24	"
	T	Carideo Grace—†	532	housewife	26	"
	U	Carideo Joseph	532	foreman	28	
	V	Kondratsky Andrew	534	laborer	42	
	W	*Kondratsky Anna—†	534	housewife	38	"

Page.	Letter.	FULL NAME.	Residence, Jan. 1, 1938.	Occupation.	Supposed Age.	Reported Residence, Jan. 1, 1937. Street and Number.

Bennington Street—Continued

Page.	Letter.	FULL NAME.	Residence, Jan. 1, 1938.	Occupation.	Supposed Age.	Reported Residence, Jan. 1, 1937.
	X	Hildreth Maria—†	534	housewife	37	here
	Y	*Sergi Carmella—†	534	"	58	"
	Z	*Sergi Josephine—†	534	"	82	"
1170						
	A	Parziale Helen—†	536	"	24	Wash'n D C
	B	Parziale James	536	seaman	28	"
	C	Rizzo Anthony	536	tailor	26	here
	D	Rizzo Helen—†	536	housewife	23	"
	E	Puopolo Angelo	536	laborer	31	"
	F	Puopolo Mabel—†	536	housewife	35	"
	G	Carbone Gabriel	536	agent	33	28 Monmouth
	H	Carbone Mary—†	536	housewife	24	28 "
	K	Cook Elizabeth—†	540	"	59	here
	L	Cook James J	540	laborer	31	"
	M	Cook Margaret—†	540	packer	34	"
	N	*Abramo Clementina—†	540	housewife	26	"
	O	*Abramo Salvatore	540	laborer	30	
	P	Cataldo Charles	540	butcher	36	
	R	Cataldo Concetta—†	540	housewife	36	"
	S	Cantalupo Flora—†	544	"	33	
	T	*Cantalupo Maria—†	544	"	64	
	U	Cantalupo Ottavio	544	retired	43	
	V	Holden Jennie—†	546	housewife	78	"
	W	Donovan John	546	laborer	56	
	X	Donovan Sarah—†	546	housewife	57	"
	Y	McDonald John	546	laborer	51	
	Z	Carroll Anthony	546	tailor	57	
1171						
	A	Carroll Anthony	546	seaman	36	
	B	Carroll Mary—†	546	housewife	52	"
	C	Carroll Paul	546	seaman	22	
	D	McBridge Julia E—†	548	housewife	72	"
	E	McBride William H	548	laborer	77	
	G	Sweeney Edward	548	painter	39	
	H	Sweeney Esther—†	548	housewife	37	"

Chaucer Street

Page.	Letter.	FULL NAME.	Residence, Jan. 1, 1938.	Occupation.	Supposed Age.	Reported Residence, Jan. 1, 1937.
	M	Olsen Mary A—†	3	housewife	34	here
	N	Olsen William A	3	clerk	35	"
	O	Conway James J	3	laborer	29	"

Chaucer Street—Continued

Page.	Letter.	Full Name.	Residence, Jan. 1, 1938.	Occupation.	Supposed Age.	Reported Residence, Jan. 1, 1937. Street and Number.
	P	Conway John A	3	accountant	28	here
	R	Conway Mary J—†	3	housewife	65	"
	S	Conway Patrick J	3	oiler	65	"
	T	Conway Thomas J	3	electrician	30	"
	U	Ahearn Catherine—†	3	clerk	27	
	V	Ahearn Mary E—†	3	domestic	65	"
	W	Ahearn Mary E—†	3	clerk	36	
	X	Weagle C Maurice	5	laborer	53	
	Y	*Weagle Elizabeth—†	5	housewife	43	"
	Z	Llewellyn Anna—†	5	"	63	
1172						
	A	Llewellyn George	5	printer	29	
	B	Mierzykowski Joseph	5	laborer	44	
	C	*Mierzykowski Mary—†	5	housewife	40	"
	D	Mierzykowski Wladyslaw	5	operator	20	"
	E	Bissett Margaret A—†	9	clerk	42	"
	F	Gowdy Blanche L—†	9	housewife	45	"
	G	Gowdy Frank B	9	laborer	55	
	H	Keyes Annie J—†	9	matron	67	
	K	Curran Cecelia E—†	9	operator	46	
	L	Curran John	9	laborer	69	
	M	Curran John J, jr	9	"	43	
	N	*Curran Mary A—†	9	housewife	68	"
	O	*Duffy Mary—†	17	"	80	
	P	Duffy Thomas J	17	painter	50	
	S	Dwelley Eliza—†	17	housewife	88	"
	R	Dwelley Oscar W	17	laborer	65	
	T	Spear Louisa—†	17	housekeeper	52	"
	V	Flanagan Alice—†	25	clerk	21	"
	W	Flanagan Delia—†	25	housewife	49	"
	X	Flanagan Nicholas	25	laborer	56	
	Y	Phinney Catherine G—†	25	clerk	45	
	Z	Sullivan John H	25	engineer	55	
1173						
	A	Sullivan Paul	25	laborer	34	
	B	Tiffany Ann—†	25	housekeeper	37	"
	C	Mazza Theresa—†	25	storekeeper	43	405 Saratoga
	D	McCarthy Gertrude—†	25	saleswoman	20	405 "
	E	McCarthy Warren	25	laborer	24	405 "
	F	Murphy Emma—†	25	housekeeper	65	405 "

Page.	Letter.	FULL NAME.	Residence, Jan. 1, 1938.	Occupation.	Supposed Age.	Reported Residence, Jan. 1, 1937. Street and Number.

Chaucer Street—Continued

	G	Gill Helen T—†	27	clerk	29	here
	H	Gill Joseph F	27	policeman	35	"
	K	Gill Richard	27	laborer	65	"
	L	Lavelle Annie—†	27	cook	53	
	M	Pomeroy Andrew	27	packer	29	
	N	Pomeroy Estelle—†	27	clerk	25	
	O	Joy Margaret—†	31	seamstress	47	"
	P	Joy Mary	31	clerk	23	
	R	D'Alfonso Louise—†	31	bookbinder	20	"
	S	*D'Alfonso Theresa—†	31	operator	41	"
	T	Jannoni Joseph	31	"	24	6 Oswego
	U	Jannoni Mildred—†	31	milliner	27	117 Orleans
	V	Clingen Mildred—†	rear 35	stenographer	26	here
	W	Clingen Robert	" 35	watchman	57	"
	X	Clingen Sadie—†	" 35	housewife	46	"
	Y	Gay Frederick	" 35	chauffeur	42	"
	Z	Donovan Dennis F	" 35	clerk	60	
1174						
	A	Donovan Sarah—†	" 35	housewife	53	"
	B	Almeida Francis	37	teacher	25	
	C	Almeida Frank	37	carpenter	51	"
	D	Almeida Josephine—†	37	housewife	49	"
	E	*Furlong Mary—†	39	housekeeper	82	"
	F	Jensen Susan I—†	39	operator	39	"
	G	Thibault Gertrude E—†	39	housewife	40	"
	H	Thibault Horace J	39	policeman	46	"
	K	Gannon Catherine—†	39	bookkeeper	24	"
	L	Gannon John	39	engineer	51	"
	M	Gannon Martin J	39	mechanic	28	"
	N	Gannon Mary—†	39	housewife	49	"
	O	Gannon Mary—†	39	stenographer	22	"
	P	Lavalle Michael	39	fireman	49	"
	R	Velardo Frances—†	43	housekeeper	55	"
	S	Velardo Gaetano	43	chauffeur	25	"
	T	Velardo Joseph	43	baker	22	
	U	Werner Harold	47	policeman	39	"
	V	Werner Margaret F—†	47	housewife	41	"
	W	Werner Walter B	47	retired	41	
	X	Whitmarsh Fred C	49	machinist	54	"
	Y	Whitmarsh Mabel—†	49	housewife	51	"

Page.	Letter.	Full Name.	Residence, Jan. 1, 1938.	Occupation.	Supposed Age.	Reported Residence, Jan. 1, 1937. Street and Number.

Chelsea Street—Continued

	Z	Scannell Daniel P	49	seaman	37	here
1175						
	A	Scannell Elise—†	49	housewife	39	"
	B	Bowes James	49	machinist	41	"
	C	Bowes Margaret—†	49	housewife	36	"
	D	Martin Ella G—†	53	"	52	
	E	Martin Mary A—†	53	at home	78	"
	F	Howard James	55	laborer	34	Winthrop
	G	Howard Mildred—†	55	housewife	32	710 Saratoga
	H	Howard Richard	55	draftsman	36	710 "

Chelsea Street

	L	Busby Ella F—†	429	clerk	35	here
	M	Busby Ella M—†	429	housewife	62	"
	N	Busby John R	429	laborer	33	"
	O	Busby John W	429	"	73	"
	P	Boutchia Marjorie—†	429	operator	22	6 Lexington pl
	R	Smith Effie—†	429	housewife	50	here
	S	Smith Warren	429	assembler	23	"
	T	Simington Odina—†	429	housewife	40	"
	U	Simington Robert B	429	laborer	52	
	V	Dryden Cora B—†	431	housewife	63	"
	W	Dryden John W	431	retired	74	
	X	Cardinelli John	435	laborer	31	
	Y	Cardinelli Margaret—†	435	housewife	29	"
	Z	Morrelli Frank	435	laborer	28	
1176						
	A	*Morrelli Mary—†	435	housewife	51	"
	B	Morrelli Vincent	435	laborer	60	
	C	Scarpa Anna—†	437	housewife	31	"
	D	Scarpa Nazzaro	437	laborer	36	"
	E	Scarpa Carmen	437	"	23	
	F	*Scarpa Frances—†	437	housewife	65	"
	G	*Carpo Rosario	439	laborer	63	
	H	*Carpo Rose—†	439	housewife	59	"
	K	Sullo John C	439	laborer	30	
	L	Sullo Nicholas	439	"	58	

Page.	Letter.	Full Name.	Residence, Jan. 1, 1938.	Occupation.	Supposed Age.	Reported Residence, Jan. 1, 1937. Street and Number.

Curtis Street

Page.	Letter.	Full Name.	Residence, Jan. 1, 1938.	Occupation.	Supposed Age.	Reported Residence, Jan. 1, 1937.
	Z	Maguire Florence E—†	8	housewife	39	here
1177						
	A	Maguire William J	8	laborer	36	
	B	*Fagan Margaret—†	8	at home	76	
	C	Fagan Mary J—†	8	housewife	44	"
	D	Fagan Thomas F	8	laborer	49	
	E	Fowler Mary C—†	8	housewife	44	"
	F	Fowler William L	8	chauffeur	51	"
	G	Fowler William L, jr	8	laborer	21	
	H	McIntyre Alfred	11	"	65	
	K	McIntyre Alfred R	11	operator	33	"
	L	McIntyre Annie—†	11	housewife	66	"

Frankfort Street

Page.	Letter.	Full Name.	Residence, Jan. 1, 1938.	Occupation.	Supposed Age.	Reported Residence, Jan. 1, 1937.
	M	Norris Mary E—†	404	housewife	38	here
	N	Norris Thomas	404	laborer	42	"
	O	Finn Bernard J	404	clerk	29	"
	P	McGovern Anna—†	404	housewife	52	"
	R	McGovern Joseph	404	electrician	24	"
	S	McGovern Patrick	404	caretaker	55	"
	T	Sheremeta Henry	404	operator	52	"
	U	Sheremeta Johanna—†	404	housewife	43	"
	V	Sheremeta Vladimir	404	operator	24	"
	X	Magas Mary—†	406	housewife	25	384 Lovell
	Y	Magas Peter	406	laborer	28	384 "
	W	*Terzis Bertha—†	406	operator	45	384 "
	Z	*Pastore Angelo	406	bootblack	55	here
1178						
	A	Pastore Carmen A	406	jeweler	26	
	B	Pastore Eugene	406	foreman	23	
	C	Pastore James J	406	butcher	28	
	D	*Pastore Maria—†	406	housewife	53	"
	E	Ronayne Eileen J—†	406	"	40	
	F	Ronayne Robert F	406	laborer	51	
	G	Passaggio Alphonse	409	operator	24	
	H	Passaggio Nancy—†	409	housewife	24	"
	K	D'Addio Alexander	409	operator	55	
	L	*Cappannelli Elvira—†	409	housewife	49	"
	M	Cappannelli George	409	finisher	21	
	N	Cappannelli Sestilo	409	laborer	53	

Page.	Letter.	Full Name.	Residence, Jan. 1, 1938.	Occupation.	Supposed Age.	Reported Residence, Jan. 1, 1937. Street and Number.

Frankfort Street—Continued

	O	Mazzarella Ralph	411	porter	28	here
	P	*Mazzarella Rose—†	411	housewife	28	“
	R	*Cashin Mary A—†	411	“	66	“
	S	*Cashin Michael J	411	laborer	27	
	T	*Murphy Helen—†	411	operator	22	“
	U	Boissonneault Edward	411	clerk	51	603 Benningt'n
	V	Boissonneault Grace A–†	411	housewife	47	603 “
	W	Robertson John	411	counterman	29	603 “
	X	Butler Francis M	415	chauffeur	30	here
	Y	Butler Mary—†	415	housewife	28	“
	Z	Butler Edward L	415	chauffeur	28	“
1179						
	A	Butler Elizabeth M—†	415	housewife	50	“
	B	Butler William F	415	inspector	53	“
	C	Mazzarella Antonetta—†	415	packer	25	
	D	*Mazzarella Columbia—†	415	housewife	52	“
	E	Mazzarella Gerardo	415	operator	24	“
	F	*Mazzarella Vincenzo	415	laborer	54	
	G	Rubico Mary—†	415	at home	27	
	H	Dorgan Albert	417	operator	34	“
	K	Dorgan Edith—†	417	housewife	33	“
	L	Greene Elmer J	417	welder	36	
	M	Greene Mary T—†	417	housewife	34	“
	N	McDonough Elizabeth–†	417	at home	72	
	O	Connelly James T	417	timekeeper	24	“
	P	Connelly Mary F—†	417	housewife	54	“
	R	Turner Catherine—†	420	“	65	
	S	Turner Elizabeth—†	420	operator	25	“
	T	Turner Frederick	420	retired	82	
	U	McGrath Mary E—†	420	housewife	41	“
	V	McGrath Paul D	420	B F D	46	
	W	King John F	420	laborer	39	
	X	King Margaret—†	420	housewife	36	“
	Y	Campiglia Anthony	424	laborer	45	
	Z	Campiglia Giovina—†	424	housewife	35	“
1180						
	A	Ricci Anna—†	424	“	60	
	B	Ricci Louis	424	carpenter	62	“
	C	Dattoli Mary—†	424	housewife	31	“
	D	Dattoli Michael	424	operator	38	“
	E	*Lawrence Antone	425	painter	61	

Frankfort Street—Continued

Page.	Letter.	Full Name.	Residence, Jan. 1, 1938.	Occupation.	Supposed Age.	Reported Residence, Jan. 1, 1937. Street and Number.
	F	*Mosca Achilles, jr	426	chauffeur	29	here
	G	Mosca Romilda—†	426	housewife	24	"
	H	*Mosca Achilles	426	cobbler	59	"
	K	Mosca Constance—†	426	operator	24	"
	L	*Mosca Louise—†	426	housewife	63	"
	M	*Marranzini Carmella—†	426	"	40	
	N	Marranzini Carmine	426	operator	42	"
	P	Frati Anthony	428	"	30	
	R	Frati Giacomo	428	blacksmith	65	"
	S	Frati Giacomo, jr	428	electrician	22	"
	T	Dwelley Arthur F	428	printer	32	Winthrop
	U	Dwelley Josephine M—†	428	housewife	26	"
	V	Walsh John	428	retired	66	"
	W	Lumia Beatrice—†	428	clerk	21	Malden
	X	Lumia James	428	welder	25	"
	Y	Mambuca Catherine—†	429	housewife	26	"
	Z	Mambuca Francis	429	salesman	23	"
1181						
	A	*Mambuca James	429	laborer	47	
	B	Mambuca Nicholas	429	"	24	
	C	Bolivar Helen—†	430	housewife	38	"
	D	Bolivar Herbert	430	carpenter	36	"
	F	McLellan Henry P	431	chauffeur	41	"
	H	O'Keefe Edward F	433	retired	82	
	K	O'Keefe Thomas	433	watchman	64	"
	L	Fariole Angelina—†	435	housewife	38	"
	M	Fariole Robert	435	laborer	37	
	N	Petrillo Lena—†	435	housewife	57	"
	O	*Petrillo Vito	435	laborer	62	
	P	Keating Anna B—†	441	housewife	50	"
	S	Keating John T	441	seaman	53	
	R	Murray Grace A—†	441	housewife	22	"
	T	Bianchino Angelo	443	chauffeur	22	"
	U	Bianchino Ernest	443	laborer	25	
	V	*Bianchino Florindo	443	"	55	
	W	*Bianchino Jennie—†	443	housewife	56	"
	X	Capuana Agnes—†	447	at home	22	
	Y	Capuana Angelina—†	447	saleswoman	25	"
	Z	Capuana Ella—†	447	"	23	
1182						
	A	Capuana Serafina—†	447	housewife	45	"

Page.	Letter.	Full Name.	Residence, Jan. 1, 1938.	Occupation.	Supposed Age.	Reported Residence, Jan. 1, 1937. Street and Number.

Frankfort Street—Continued

Page.	Letter.	Full Name.	Residence, Jan. 1, 1938.	Occupation.	Supposed Age.	Reported Residence, Jan. 1, 1937. Street and Number.
	B	McGrath Dennis	447	longshoreman	64	246 Lexington
	C	McGrath Dennis F	447	laborer	31	246 “
	D	McGrath Elizabeth B—†	447	operator	23	246 “
	E	McGrath Irene B—†	447	“	28	246 “
	F	McGrath James B	447	clerk	25	246 “
	G	McGrath Joseph	447	longshoreman	33	246 “
	H	McGrath Louise M—†	447	at home	20	246 “
	K	McGrath Margaret A—†	447	housewife	61	246 “
	L	Liss George	447	laborer	45	here
	M	Liss Minnie—†	447	housewife	41	“
	N	Donnelly Elizabeth—†	449	“	55	“
	O	Donnelly William J	449	engineer	54	
	P	Scapa James A	453	laborer	37	
	R	Scapa Josephine J—†	453	housewife	31	“
	S	Pepicelli Pasquale L	453	laborer	27	
	T	Pepicelli Virginia—†	453	housewife	24	“
	U	Pepicelli Antonio	453	laborer	55	
	V	Pepicelli Lucy—†	453	housewife	54	“
	W	Pepicelli William	453	laborer	21	“
	X	*Leccese Lazzaro	455	operator	57	80 Chelsea
	Y	Leccese Michael	455	butcher	22	80 “
	Z	*Leccese Raffaela—†	455	housewife	50	80 “
1183	A	*Ricobene Agatha—†	455	seamstress	37	here
	B	Harris Dorothy—†	455	housewife	28	“
	D	Sharp Hugh	455	laborer	30	“
	C	Sharp Hugh A	455	machinist	62	“

Lubec Street

Page.	Letter.	Full Name.	Residence, Jan. 1, 1938.	Occupation.	Supposed Age.	Reported Residence, Jan. 1, 1937. Street and Number.
	E	LePage Elizabeth—†	428	housewife	48	here
	F	LePage William G	428	operator	52	“
	H	Coleman Charles J	437	carpenter	69	“
	K	Francis Mary E—†	438	housekeeper	52	“
	L	Gibbons Fannie—†	439	housewife	44	“
	M	Gibbons Joseph P	439	clerk	20	
	N	Gibbons Patrick	439	sexton	50	
	O	Cross Daisy—†	440	housewife	37	“
	P	Cross Richard	440	laborer	21	
	R	Clarke Ennis H	441	retired	77	
	S	Clarke Ennis W	441	photographer	41	“

Page.	Letter.	Full Name.	Residence, Jan. 1, 1938.	Occupation.	Supposed Age.	Reported Residence, Jan. 1, 1937. Street and Number.

Lubec Street—Continued

Page.	Letter.	Full Name.	Residence, Jan. 1, 1938.	Occupation.	Supposed Age.	Reported Residence, Jan. 1, 1937. Street and Number.
	T	*Clarke Gertrude—†	441	housewife	64	here
	U	Clarke Robert W	441	mechanic	40	"
	V	Beatrice Annie—†	442	housewife	38	"
	W	Beatrice Salvatore	442	carpenter	39	"
	X	Carter Delia L—†	443	housewife	57	"
	Y	Carter John M	443	chauffeur	26	"
	Z	*Hazel Agnes E—†	443	domestic	38	"
1184						
	A	Hazel Edward J	443	teamster	48	"
	B	Powers Mary A—†	443	housekeeper	47	"
	C	Jones Dorothy C—†	446	stenographer	26	"
	D	Jones Earl F	446	laborer	30	"
	E	Jones Mary A—†	446	housewife	69	"
	F	Jones Mildred—†	446	saleswoman	23	"

Moore Street

Page.	Letter.	Full Name.	Residence, Jan. 1, 1938.	Occupation.	Supposed Age.	Reported Residence, Jan. 1, 1937. Street and Number.
	G	Layman Margaret—†	30	housewife	35	here
	H	Layman Robert	30	laborer	35	"
	K	*Cammarano Mary—†	30	housewife	49	"
	L	*Cammarano Matthew	30	laborer	49	
	M	Cammarano Vincenzo	30	"	20	
	N	Donoghue Anna L—†	36	operator	36	
	O	Donoghue John F	36	broker	32	
	P	Donoghue Mary E—†	36	housewife	38	"
	R	Gaudet Clarence	36	machinist	33	"
	S	Gaudet Emile	36	welder	45	
	T	*Gaudet Mary E—†	36	operator	36	
	U	*Gaudet Monique—†	36	housewife	73	"
	V	Carney Catherine F—†	36	"	48	
	W	Carney Ellen F—†	36	teacher	29	
	X	Carney Frank W	36	decorator	50	"
	Y	Carney William F	36	chauffeur	28	"
	Z	Bullock Mary—†	38	at home	65	
1185						
	A	St Croix Mary E—†	38	housewife	29	"
	B	St Croix William J	38	salesman	29	"
	C	Murphy Joseph H	38	chauffeur	34	"
	D	Murphy Margaret A—†	38	housewife	34	"
	E	Gleeson Dennis F	42	rubberworker	50	"
	F	Gleeson Margaret J—†	42	housewife	48	"

Page.	Letter.	Full Name.	Residence, Jan. 1, 1938.	Occupation.	Supposed Age.	Reported Residence, Jan. 1, 1937. Street and Number.
		Moore Street—Continued				
	G	Clifford Elizabeth—†	58	teacher	33	N Hampshire
	H	Dee Joanna—†	58	"	49	here
	K	Dolan Margaret—†	58	"	41	"
	L	Heaphy Mary—†	58		35	N Hampshire
	M	Lindsey Martha—†	58		24	here
	N	Linen Margaret—†	58		38	"
	O	Loughlin Helen—†	58		47	"
	P	Mahoney Helen—†	58		41	
	R	McDonald Bridget—†	58	"	47	
	S	Mullane Esther—†	58	"	34	"
	T	O'Brien Mary—†	58		66	
	U	O'Leary Bridget—†	58		64	
	V	Pheur Mary—†	58	"	24	
	W	Stanton Mary—†	58	housekeeper	34	"
	X	Welsh Ellen—†	58	cook	60	"
		Neptune Road				
	Y	Burns Edward J	4	shipfitter	41	587 Saratoga
	Z	Burns Julia M—†	4	housewife	36	587 "
1186						
	B	Collins Dorothy—†	6	"	22	722 "
	C	Collins John H	6	clerk	26	516 Orleans
	D	Greeley Anna—†	6	housewife	47	here
	E	Greeley Eileen—†	6	manager	23	"
	F	Greeley Lloyd	6	chauffeur	21	"
	G	McCue Helen—†	6	housewife	22	Worcester
	H	McCue Henry J	6	fisherman	26	"
	K	*Mitchell Jabez	6	"	28	12 Border
	L	Cerrone Alfred	12	clerk	21	here
	M	Cerrone Elizabeth—†	12	corsetiere	25	"
	N	*Cerrone Elvira—†	12	housewife	50	"
	O	Cerrone Frederick	12	laborer	23	
	P	*Cerrone John	12	operator	50	
	R	Corriani Catherine—†	12	housewife	61	"
	S	Corriani Florence—†	12	operator	21	
	T	Corriani Leo	12	retired	67	
	U	Chaloner Mary—†	14	clerk	50	
	V	McIntosh Agnes—†	14	housewife	42	"
	W	McIntosh William	14	operator	43	
	X	Buono Joseph	14	laborer	38	

Page.	Letter.	FULL NAME.	Residence, Jan. 1, 1938.	Occupation.	Supposed Age.	Reported Residence, Jan. 1, 1937. Street and Number.

Neptune Road—Continued

	Y	Buono Lavinia—†	14	housewife	38	here
	Z	Schwamb Joseph	16	B F D	42	"
1187						
	A	Schwamb Margaret—†	16	housewife	41	"
	B	Grace Annie—†	16	"	69	
	C	Grace Clarence	16	laborer	35	
	D	Grace Gertrude—†	16	clerk	43	
	E	Grace Michael	16	fireman	67	
	F	Cotreau Albany	18	bartender	42	"
	G	Cotreau Delphis	18	fisherman	37	"
	H	*Cotreau Julia—†	18	housewife	35	"
	K	Mattina Angeline—†	18	"	24	"
	L	Mattina Joseph	18	inspector	23	"
	M	Picardi Florinda—†	18	housekeeper	66	"
	N	Fuccillo John	18	clerk	41	"
	O	Fuccillo Julia—†	18	housewife	40	"
	P	DiNatale Concetta—†	20	"	40	34 Liverpool
	R	DiNatale Frank	20	hairdresser	44	34 "
	S	DiNatale Phyllis—†	20	operator	20	34 "
	T	Benincasa Alphonse	20	tailor	45	here
	U	Benincasa Filomena—†	20	housewife	41	"
	V	Benincasa Matthew	20	tailor	37	"
	W	Hochbaum Esther—†	20	housewife	48	"
	X	Hochbaum Morris	20	storekeeper	50	"
	Y	Hochbaum Ray—†	20	bookkeeper	21	"
	Z	Morrison Annie W—†	22	housewife	65	"
1188						
	A	Morrison James E	22	watchman	65	"
	B	Morrison John R	22	chauffeur	35	"
	C	Puzzo Agnes—†	22	saleswoman	24	"
	D	Puzzo Albert	22	draftsman	29	"
	E	Puzzo Andrew R	22	guard	34	
	F	*Puzzo Angeline—†	22	housewife	62	"
	G	Puzzo James	22	retired	70	
	H	DiNucci Carl	22	engineer	38	
	K	DiNucci Delia—†	22	housewife	37	"
	L	Pugliese Joseph	24	laborer	60	
	M	Pugliese Rose—†	24	housekeeper	21	"
	N	Dykstra Harry M	24	laborer	53	"
	O	Dykstra Margaret L—†	24	housewife	47	"
	P	Struzziero Erminio	24	laborer	49	

Page.	Letter.	Full Name.	Residence, Jan. 1, 1938.	Occupation.	Supposed Age.	Reported Residence, Jan. 1, 1937. Street and Number.

Neptune Road—Continued

	R	Struzziero Ernest	24	clerk	21	here
	S	Struzziero Esther—†	24	housewife	49	"
	U	Vecchio Carmella—†	30	"	35	"
	V	Vecchio Jerome	30	guard	43	"
	W	Vecchio Marie—†	30	housewife	69	"
	X	Vecchio Rudolph	30	stitcher	39	
	Y	Ahearn Edgar	30	salesman	42	"
	Z	Ahearn Edgar, jr	30	operator	21	
1189						
	A	Ahearn Mary—†	30	housewife	41	"
	B	Massaro Anthony	32	laborer	34	
	C	Massaro Fannie—†	32	housewife	33	"
	D	Picardi Celia—†	32	"	58	
	E	Picardi Emma—†	32	operator	27	"
	F	Picardi Fred	32	laborer	24	
	G	Picardi Julia—†	32	operator	32	"
	H	Picardi Michael	32	retired	68	
	K	Picardi Olivia—†	32	operator	30	
	L	Picardi Onorina—†	32	"	21	
	M	Picardi Sabino	32	welder	29	"
	N	Walsh Edward F	32	painter	53	186 London
	O	Walsh Gertrude M—†	32	at home	20	186 "
	P	*August Rose—†	34	housewife	33	here
	R	*August William	34	laborer	52	"
	S	Picardi Amelia—†	34	at home	24	"
	T	Picardi George	34	foreman	26	
	U	*Picardi John	34	carpenter	73	"
	V	*Picardi Lucy—†	34	housewife	63	"
	W	Picardi Margaret—†	34	operator	28	"
	X	Silva John	34	laborer	20	
	Y	*Silva Joseph	34	longshoreman	47	"
	Z	Silva Joseph, jr	34	operator	24	"
1190						
	A	*Silva Mary—†	34	housewife	43	"
	B	*Silva Sefrina—†	34	at home	70	
	C	Caselden Daniel	36	B F D	40	
	D	Caselden Margaret—†	36	housewife	40	"
	E	Austin Esther M—†	36	"	45	
	F	Austin William H	36	operator	24	
	G	Austin William J	36	laborer	47	
	H	Bulgaris Arthur	36	accountant	25	"

Neptune Road—Continued

Page.	Letter.	Full Name.	Residence, Jan. 1, 1938.	Occupation.	Supposed Age.	Reported Residence, Jan. 1, 1937. Street and Number.
	K	Bulgaris Christopher	36	bartender	45	here
	L	Bulgaris Evangeline—†	36	housewife	44	"
	M	Howard Charles C	38	clerk	50	"
	N	Howard Margaret L—†	38	housewife	44	"
	O	Lynch Margaret—†	38	"	61	25 Neptune rd
	P	Lynch William J	38	retired	68	25 "
	R	Sullivan Catherine—†	38	saleswoman	51	25 "
	S	Chiampa Helen—†	38	typist	26	here
	T	Chiampa Henry	38	barber	22	"
	U	Chiampa Jennie—†	38	housewife	56	"
	V	Chiampa Rocco	38	barber	65	
	W	Chiampa Theresa—†	38	tailoress	24	
	X	Sampson Raymond	44	laborer	36	
	Y	Sampson Violet—†	44	housewife	27	"
	Z	*DiNublia Angelina—†	44	"	54	
1191						
	A	DiNublia Anthony	44	operator	23	"
	B	*DiNublia Frank	44	"	56	
	C	DiNublia Josephine—†	44	"	27	
	D	DiNublia Mary—†	44	"	28	
	E	*DiNublia Minnie—†	44	at home	32	
	F	DiNublia Rose—†	44	operator	25	"
	G	Tartiano Flora—†	44	housewife	24	"
	H	*Tartiano Joseph	44	baker	48	
	K	Redmond Florence N—†	46	housewife	44	"
	L	Redmond John	46	laborer	41	
	M	Redmond Susan—†	46	housewife	67	"
	N	Collins Charles H	46	clerk	23	
	O	Collins Dennis J	46	laborer	60	
	P	Collins Helen F—†	46	clerk	25	
	R	Collins Mary J—†	46	secretary	20	"
	S	Collins May—†	46	housewife	49	"
	T	Marshall Isabel—†	48	bookkeeper	27	"
	U	*Marshall Joaquin	48	retired	67	"
	V	Ferry Frank J	48	policeman	40	"
	W	Ferry Mary—†	48	housewife	38	"
	X	Fleming Alice—†	48	nurse	25	
	Y	Fleming Julia—†	48	housewife	59	"
	Z	Fleming Michael J	48	engineer	63	
1192						
	A	Elacqua Frank	50	clerk	53	

Neptune Road—Continued

Page.	Letter.	Full Name.	Residence, Jan. 1, 1938.	Occupation.	Supposed Age.	Reported Residence, Jan. 1, 1937. Street and Number.
	B	*Elacqua Victoria—†	50	housewife	43	here
	C	Venti Rose—†	50	“	27	“
	D	Venti Vincent	50	machinist	29	“
	E	Venti Americo	50	“	25	“
	F	Venti Biagio	50	laborer	50	
	G	Venti Emily—†	50	secretary	23	“
	H	Venti Frank	50	engineer	27	“
	K	Venti Micheline—†	50	housewife	52	“
	L	*Wilson Joseph	52	engineer	29	
	M	Wilson Mary—†	52	housewife	29	“
	N	Antico Amelia—†	52	“	54	
	O	Antico Guy	52	operator	25	
	P	Antico Joseph	52	laborer	56	
	R	Antico Lucy—†	52	packer	22	
	S	Musco Frances—†	52	housewife	41	“
	T	Musco Michael	52	salesman	24	“
	U	Musco Salvatore	52	baker	49	
	V	Musco Salvatore	52	salesman	23	“
	W	Collins Lawrence F	54	decorator	29	“
	X	Collins Vera—†	54	housewife	23	“
	Y	Cardarelli Caroline—†	54	“	37	
	Z	Cardarelli Gino	54	operator	36	“
1193						
	A	*Cardarelli Jennie—†	54	housewife	54	“
	B	Giardiello Emma—†	54	at home	24	
	C	Thistle Charles	54	seaman	30	
	D	Thistle Mary—†	54	housewife	31	“
	E	Pelham Helen L—†	56	“	32	
	F	Pelham Ivan	56	cook	39	
	G	Doherty Margaret—†	56	clerk	45	
	H	Hunter Betty—†	56	“	20	
	K	Hunter John H	56	manager	43	“
	L	Hunter Mary A—†	56	housewife	43	“
	M	Moran Charles H	56	checker	23	
	N	Rizzo Mary A—†	56	housewife	58	“
	O	Miranda Cora—†	60	housekeeper	41	“
	P	Racca Ralph	62	operator	45	“
	R	Racca Susan—†	62	seamstress	20	“
	S	Racca Viriginia—†	62	housewife	43	“
	T	*Miranda Celia—†	62	“	60	

Page.	Letter.	Full Name.	Residence, Jan. 1, 1938.	Occupation.	Supposed Age.	Reported Residence, Jan. 1, 1937. Street and Number.

Neptune Road—Continued

Page.	Letter.	Full Name.	Residence, Jan. 1, 1938.	Occupation.	Supposed Age.	Reported Residence, Jan. 1, 1937. Street and Number.
	U	Miranda Margaret—†	62	packer	24	here
	V	Miranda Michael	62	operator	55	"

Orleans Street

Page.	Letter.	Full Name.	Residence, Jan. 1, 1938.	Occupation.	Supposed Age.	Reported Residence, Jan. 1, 1937. Street and Number.
	X	Sanderson Alice—†	505	housewife	48	here
	Y	Sanderson Charles	505	clerk	21	"
	Z	Sanderson Frederick	505	chauffeur	49	"
1194	A	Fiatarone Anna—†	505	operator	22	"
	B	Fiatarone Lillian—†	505	clerk	20	
	C	Fiatarone Margaret—†	505	housewife	41	"
	D	Fiatarone Vincent	505	mechanic	48	"
	E	Vaccaro Anna—†	505	housewife	41	374 Lovell
	F	Vaccaro Nicholas	505	manager	43	374 "
	G	Smith Edward E	507	nurse	29	here
	H	Smith Margaret—†	507	housewife	24	"
	K	Cullen Gertrude B—†	507	matron	45	"
	L	Cullen Mary E—†	507	housewife	60	"
	M	Cullen Thomas H	507	laborer	61	
	N	*Borgosana Carmella—†	507	housewife	50	"
	O	Borgosano Guy	507	laborer	24	
	P	Borgosano Lillian—†	507	clerk	25	
	R	*Borgosano Stellario	507	laborer	62	"
	T	Dacey Anthony L	511	carpenter	37	238 Princeton
	U	Dacey Rita E—†	511	housewife	21	238 "
	V	Bevilacqua Jennie—†	511	"	44	here
	W	Bevilacqua Lena—†	511	stitcher	23	"
	X	Bevilacqua Libero	511	laborer	28	"
	Y	Bevilacqua Rose—†	511	stitcher	27	
	Z	Mazzone Fred	511	manager	23	"
1195	A	Mazzone Michelina—†	511	housewife	22	"
	B	McIsaac Francis C	513	assembler	41	"
	C	McIsaac Loretta—†	513	housewife	38	"
	E	Collins George E	517	clerk	24	
	F	Collins Helen M—†	517	"	29	
	G	Collins James J	517	laborer	73	
	H	Collins James J	517	"	28	
	K	Collins Mary A—†	517	housewife	65	"

Page.	Letter.	FULL NAME.	Residence, Jan. 1, 1938.	Occupation.	Supposed Age.	Reported Residence, Jan. 1, 1937. Street and Number.
		Orleans Street—Continued				
	L	Collins Walter E	517	chauffeur	24	here
	M	Coyle Charles F	517	operator	51	"
	N	Coyle Helen T—†	517	housewife	46	"
	O	Murphy Thomas A	517	guard	44	
		Saratoga Street				
	P	Tassinari Antenori	511	operator	21	here
	R	*Tassinari Mary—†	511	housewife	50	"
	S	Tassinari Max	511	welder	26	"
	U	Marsh Margaret J—†	514	druggist	52	
	V	Maguire Alice L—†	515	housekeeper	39	"
	W	Stock George	515	baker	67	"
	X	Paul Charles	515	assembler	53	"
	Y	Paul George	515	laborer	20	
	Z	Paul Margaret—†	515	housewife	40	"
1196						
	A	Silek Edwin	516	operator	24	368 Princeton
	B	Silek Elizabeth—†	516	housewife	25	368 "
	C	Scanzillo Florance	516	mechanic	25	here
	D	Scanzillo Madeline—†	516	housewife	22	"
	E	Abbott Helen—†	516	"	23	520 Saratoga
	F	Abbott William	516	laborer	27	520 "
	G	Crisci Catherine—†	518	housewife	32	here
	H	*Crisci Marie—†	518	"	74	"
	K	Crisci Ralph	518	laborer	37	"
	L	Graziano Elizabeth—†	518	operator	20	"
	M	*Graziano Felice—†	518	housewife	50	"
	N	Graziano Nicholas A	518	laborer	49	
	O	Botticelli Ralph	518	"	20	"
	P	Perricotti Anna—†	520	housewife	28	19 Eutaw
	R	Perricotti Peter J	520	painter	33	19 "
	S	Hazlett Sarah E—†	520	housewife	46	here
	T	Hazlett William	520	accountant	55	"
	U	Herrick Charlotte M—†	522	housewife	58	"
	V	Herrick Joseph C	522	laborer	65	
	W	O'Donnell Mary A—†	522	saleswoman	21	"
	X	O'Donnell Mary M—†	522	housewife	47	"
	Y	O'Donnell William F	522	baker	52	
	Z	Wignot John	522	"	46	

Page.	Letter.	Full Name.	Residence, Jan. 1, 1938.	Occupation.	Supposed Age.	Reported Residence, Jan. 1, 1937. Street and Number.

1197
Saratoga Street—Continued

	A	Apruzzese Domenic	524	carpenter	24	Everett
	B	Apruzzese Grace—†	524	housewife	20	here
	C	*Trifero Domenic	524	reedworker	51	"
	D	*Trifero Margaret—†	524	housewife	51	"
	E	Trifero Mary—†	524	forewoman	22	"
	F	Trifero Rose—†	524	stitcher	27	
	G	*Trifero Catherine—†	524	housekeeper	43	"
	H	Dame Bertha—†	526	"	47	"
	K	Dare John P	526	laborer	30	
	L	Quigley Margaret M—†	526	housekeeper	60	"
	M	Keane Mary—†	526	housewife	21	"
	N	Keane Matthew	526	counterman	23	"
	O	Henderson James E	534	asbestos worker	36	"
	P	Henderson Laura—†	534	housewife	33	"
	R	Cyr Albert	534	operator	49	"
	S	Cyr Bessie—†	534	housewife	45	"
	T	Gillis John J	534	packer	44	
	U	August Francis T	534	clerk	27	"
	V	August Irving J	534	U S A	20	California
	W	August Manuel	534	painter	54	here
	X	August Sarah F—†	534	housewife	53	"
	Z	DeFronzo Helen—†	538	housekeeper	23	"
1198						
	A	*Maiorano Louis	538	barber	34	
	B	*Maiorano Rose—†	538	housewife	34	"
	C	*Mancino Carmen	540	operator	50	"
	D	Mancino Frank	540	clerk	21	
	E	Mancino Joseph	540	stenographer	20	"
	F	Mancino Margaret—†	540	maid	24	"
	G	*Mancino Mary—†	540	housewife	45	"
	H	Marcella Benjamin	540	mechanic	26	Woburn
	K	Marcella Frances—†	540	housewife	23	"
	L	Lawson Mary E—†	540	housekeeper	38	here
	M	Lawson Michael J	540	retired	41	"
	N	Lawson William F	540	laborer	37	"
	O	Canty Oliver F	542	"	38	
	P	Canty Augustus T	542	auditor	34	
	R	Canty Chester D	542	inspector	45	"
	S	Canty Florence L—†	542	bookkeeper	30	"
	T	Canty Margaret E—†	542	housewife	67	"

Page.	Letter.	Full Name.	Residence, Jan. 1, 1938.	Occupation.	Supposed Age.	Reported Residence, Jan. 1, 1937. Street and Number.

Saratoga Street—Continued

Page.	Letter.	Full Name.	Residence, Jan. 1, 1938.	Occupation.	Supposed Age.	Reported Residence, Jan. 1, 1937. Street and Number.
	U	Gay John W	542	chauffeur	44	here
	V	Gay Theresa—†	542	housewife	45	"
	W	Tierney Annie—†	542	operator	43	"
	X	McHugh Andrew	544	fisherman	43	"
	Y*	McHugh Margaret—†	544	housewife	42	"
	Z	Capprini Florence—†	544	"	24	20 Shelby
1199						
	A	Capprini Galeano J	544	welder	26	345 Princeton
	B	Visco Alphonse	544	operator	20	here
	C*	Visco Assunta—†	544	housewife	40	"
	D	Visco Filomeno	544	operator	43	"
	E	McMillen Charles L	546	laborer	21	
	F	Schofield Charles R	546	policeman	48	"
	G	Schofield Margaret M—†	546	housewife	46	"
	H	Gill Albert T	551	carpenter	33	"
	K	Gill Anna E—†	551	operator	25	
	L	Gill Edmund F	551	salesman	27	"
	M	Gill James R	551	"	34	
	N	Gill Lillian D—†	551	operator	31	
	O	Gill Martin M	551	seaman	30	
	P	Flynn Mary A—†	553	housekeeper	84	"
	R	Goulland Carroll	553	laborer	21	"
	S	Goulland James	553	clerk	25	
	U	Trainor George	559	chauffeur	43	"
	V	Trainor Louis	559	laborer	31	
	W	Trainor Thomas	559	"	45	
	X	Hall Elizabeth—†	559	housewife	72	"
	Y	Hall Frederick O	559	painter	43	
	Z	Baracchini Charles	561	coppersmith	34	"
1200						
	A	Barracchini Charlotte—†	561	housewife	68	"
	B	Cohan Laura—†	561	"	29	
	D	Cohan William	561	foreman	29	
	C	Travers Mary—†	561	operator	31	"
	E	Delbon Alphonse	563	watchman	68	69 Maverick
	F	Delbon Mary—†	563	housewife	64	here
	G	Kenney Anna—†	563	housekeeper	36	"
	H	Sewara Mary—†	563	"	26	398 Benningt'n
	K	Comunale Frank	567	clerk	35	here
	L*	Comunale Theresa—†	567	housewife	32	"
	M*	Ricci Ippolita—†	567	"	74	"

Page.	Letter.	Full Name.	Residence, Jan. 1, 1938.	Occupation.	Supposed Age.	Reported Residence, Jan. 1, 1937. Street and Number.

Saratoga Street—Continued

	N	Ricci John	557	salesman	35	here
	O	Ricci Louis	567	"	37	"
	P	*Ricci Mariano	567	retired	82	"
	R	*Ricci Mary—†	567	housewife	32	"
	S	Bonanno Carmella—†	567	"	23	
	T	Bonanno Joseph	567	laborer	30	
	U	Burns Daniel	579	operator	34	"
	V	Sheehan John L	579	garageman	34	"
	W	Sheehan Mary M—†	579	housewife	32	"
	X	McGilvery Earl	579	laborer	21	
	Y	McGilvery Lawrence	579	"	31	
	Z	McGilvery Minnie—†	579	housewife	52	"
1201						
	A	Brems Catherine—†	579	operator	23	"
	B	Brems James	579	laborer	22	
	C	Brems Lillian—†	579	housewife	51	"
	D	Brems Philip E	579	printer	52	
	E	Brems Philip E, jr	579	laborer	20	"
	F	Fitzgerald Agnes M—†	585	housewife	31	153 Marion
	G	Fitzgerald John R	585	longshoreman	35	153 "
	K	Meads Helen—†	585	housewife	35	here
	L	Meads John	585	laborer	45	"
	H	Southard George	585	retired	82	"
	M	Daley John	585	laborer	27	
	N	Granara Eleanor—†	585	operator	20	"
	O	Granara Joseph E	585	chauffeur	42	"
	P	Granara Nora—†	585	housewife	37	"
	R	Quagliati Nicola	587	laborer	49	
	S	Quagliati Sophia—†	587	housewife	38	"
	T	*Hughes Catherine—†	587	"	59	
	U	Hughes Charles E	587	chauffeur	25	"
	V	*Hughes James E	587	glazier	62	
	W	Hughes Marion—†	587	decorator	21	"
	X	Meahan Mary—†	587	inspector	35	"
	Y	Termine Josephine—†	589	waitress	33	
	Z	Trevor Anna—†	589	housewife	40	"
1202						
	A	Trevor Evelyn—†	589	floorwoman	21	"
	B	McInnis James J	591	chauffeur	32	"
	C	McInnis Mary C—†	591	housewife	31	"
	D	Hogan Bridget—†	591	"	53	

Page.	Letter.	Full Name.	Residence, Jan. 1, 1938.	Occupation.	Supposed Age.	Reported Residence, Jan. 1, 1937. Street and Number.

Saratoga Street—Continued

Page.	Letter.	Full Name.	Residence, Jan. 1, 1938.	Occupation.	Supposed Age.	Reported Residence, Jan. 1, 1937. Street and Number.
	E	Hogan Patrick	591	longshoreman	59	here
	F	Hogan Henry	591	clerk	24	"
	G	Hogan Hugh	591	laborer	21	"
	H	Landry Sarah—†	593	housekeeper	48	"
	K	Sinclair Margaret—†	593	housewife	28	"
	L	Sinclair William	593	laborer	34	
	M	*Palma Frank	594	storekeeper	51	"
	N	*Palma Rose—†	594	housewife	52	"
	O	Gillispie Frank E	595	chauffeur	40	"
	P	Gillispie Mary A—†	595	housewife	45	"
	R	Swinerton Amos	595	retired	89	
	S	Melillo Charles	596	operator	25	"
	T	*Melillo Frances—†	596	housewife	57	"
	U	Melillo Frances—†	596	operator	30	
	V	Melillo Josephine—†	596	"	28	"
	W	Boissoneault Albert	596	laborer	28	32 Shelby
	X	Sousa Albert	596	janitor	24	32 "
	Y	Sousa Gabrielle—†	596	housewife	24	32 "
	Z	Dorgan John F	597	laborer	45	here
1203						
	A	Kane Edward J	597	operator	47	
	B	Kane John J	597	chauffeur	45	"
	C	Kane Margaret M—†	597	at home	22	
	E	*Abramson Rebecca—†	600	housekeeper	80	"
	F	*Shulman David	600	tailor	50	"
	G	Shulman Frieda—†	600	teacher	22	
	H	*Shulman Sarah—†	600	housewife	48	"
	K	Flynn Daniel	602	retired	75	
	L	Mahoney John P	602	checker	54	
	M	Keohane Arthur	604	longshoreman	58	"
	N	Keohane Ellen—†	604	housewife	47	"
	P	*Impemba Alfonzo	608	shoemaker	59	"
	R	Impemba Eleanor—†	608	at home	20	
	S	*Impemba Victoria—†	608	housewife	49	"
	T	Leno Jacqueline—†	608	"	23	
	U	Leno John	608	furrier	24	
	V	Ross Carl	610	printer	29	
	W	Ross Jennie—†	610	housewife	27	"
	X	Morante Ralph	612	operator	32	
	Y	Morante Rose—†	612	housewife	33	"
	Z	*Malgeri Carmella—†	614	"	38	

Page.	Letter.	Full Name.	Residence, Jan. 1, 1938.	Occupation.	Supposed Age.	Reported Residence, Jan. 1, 1937. Street and Number.
1204						

Saratoga Street—Continued

Page.	Letter.	Full Name.	Residence, Jan. 1, 1938.	Occupation.	Supposed Age.	Reported Residence, Jan. 1, 1937. Street and Number.
	A	Malgeri Vincenzo	614	laborer	43	here
	C	*Marry Catherine—†	616	housekeeper	37	"
	D	O'Hearn John J	616	fisherman	42	"
	E	*Turner Elizabeth—†	618	housewife	38	"
	F	Turner Michael	618	fisherman	49	"
	G	Lepore Henry J	619	laborer	23	
	H	Lepore Julia A—†	619	housewife	48	"
	K	Lepore Julia A—†	619	bookkeeper	21	"
	L	Lepore Peter A	619	machinist	53	"
	M	Grady Lena—†	619	housekeeper	51	"
	N	Wessling Elizabeth A—†	619	packer	31	"
	O	Wessling Henry B	619	operator	43	"
	P	Wessling Herman	619	machinist	50	"
	R	*Gentile Galliano	620	laborer	40	
	S	*Gentile Nancy—†	620	housewife	33	"
	U	Velardo Alice—†	624	"	27	2 Florence
	V	Velardo Domenic P	624	baker	29	2 "
	W	Reilly Dorothy—†	625	housewife	28	here
	X	Reilly Maurice	625	salesman	35	"
	Y	Titman Albert	625	printer	58	"
	Z	Titman Catherine—†	625	housewife	53	"
1205	A	*Cavaliere Camilla—†	625	housekeeper	75	"
	B	Laporta John	625	operator	22	"
	C	Dawson Catherine E—†	626–628	clerk	37	
	D	King Edward	626–628	guard	46	
	E	King Helen V—†	626–628	housewife	42	"
	F	Micarelli Elvira—†	629	teacher	24	
	G	Micarelli Maria—†	629	housewife	46	"
	H	Micarelli Nicola	629	storekeeper	52	"
	K	Joyce Mary E—†	630	housekeeper	35	182 Wordsworth
	L	Micarelli Catherine—†	631	housewife	32	here
	M	Micarelli James	631	butcher	25	"
	N	DeWolfe Frank	631	laborer	44	"
	O	DeWolfe May—†	631	housewife	41	"
	P	Ryan Sarah—†	632	"	37	
	R	Ryan Thomas J	632	operator	36	"
	S	Green Charles P	634	laborer	28	
	T	Green Elizabeth—†	634	housewife	30	"
	U	Green Florence E—†	634	operator	35	

Page.	Letter.	Full Name.	Residence, Jan. 1, 1938.	Occupation.	Supposed Age.	Reported Residence, Jan. 1, 1937. Street and Number.
		Saratoga Street—Continued				
	V	Fitzgerald Annie—†	634	housewife	56	here
	W	Fitzgerald Lawrence	634	watchman	65	“
	X	O'Brien George M	634	machinist	37	“
	Y	O'Reagan Anna—†	635	housewife	42	“
	Z	O'Reagan John	635	painter	45	
1206						
	A	Dundon Mary—†	635	secretary	50	“
	B	O'Donnell Agnes—†	636	operator	37	“
	C	O'Donnell Annie—†	636	housewife	67	“
	D	O'Donnell Charles	636	laborer	32	
	E	O'Donnell Johanna—†	636	operator	38	“
	F	DiGenio Anita—†	636	“	23	
	G	DiGenio Annibale	636	laborer	52	
	H	DiGenio Antonetta—†	636	housewife	40	“
	K	Marinelli Anna—†	637	stenographer	23	“
	L	Marinelli Ida—†	637	clerk	20	“
	M	*Marinelli Joseph	637	laborer	58	
	N	*Marinelli Josephine—†	637	housewife	47	“
	O	Marinelli Rose—†	637	clerk	22	“
	P	Murray Catherine—†	638	housewife	25	400 Saratoga
	R	Murray Harold	638	laborer	30	400 “
	S	Murray Jennie—†	638	candler	56	400 “
	T	Rothwell Harry	638	repairman	46	400 “
	U	Ambrogne Edward	638	chauffeur	47	here
	V	Ambrogne Rose A—†	638	housewife	43	“
	W	*Diorio Vincenzia—†	638	housekeeper	77	“
	X	Gioioso Edward J	638	clerk	23	“
	Y	Green Ella L—†	639	bookkeeper	54	“
	Z	Green Mary L—†	639	teacher	57	“
1207						
	A	Conte Grace—†	641	housewife	44	“
	B	Conte Julio	641	foreman	35	
	C	Daley Grace—†	643	housewife	25	“
	D	Daley Roy F	643	chauffeur	30	“
	E	*Daley Lillian—†	643	housewife	26	“
	F	*Daley Michael	643	painter	33	“
	G	Green Gertrude—†	643	housewife	21	44 Jeffries
	H	Green William	643	laborer	24	44 “
	L	*Balbone Emma—†	645	housewife	68	here
	M	*Balbone Romano	645	retired	80	“
	N	Balbone William	645	chauffeur	36	“

Page.	Letter.	FULL NAME.	Residence, Jan. 1, 1938.	Occupation.	Supposed Age.	Reported Residence, Jan. 1, 1937. Street and Number.

Saratoga Street—Continued

	O	LaCorte Domenic	647	plumber	36	Everett
	P	LaCorte Tina—†	647	housewife	29	"
	R	*Lombardo Carmella—†	647	"	33	679 Saratoga
	S	Lombardo Nunzio	647	operator	46	679 "
	T	Pagliarulo Louis	647	foreman	32	248 "
	U	Pagliarulo Pauline—†	647	housewife	27	248 "
	V	Neal Gertrude F—†	648	"	28	here
	W	Neal Joseph J	648	laborer	27	"
	X	Jones Herman W	648	"	46	"
	Y	Jones Rose M—†	648	housewife	49	"
	Z	Dutra Eugene P	648	laborer	22	
1208						
	A	Dutra Jerome	648	cigarmaker	51	"
	B	Dutra Mary A—†	648	housewife	54	"
	C	Leonard John F	650	timekeeper	38	"
	D	Leonard Theresa—†	650	housewife	38	"
	E	Kirby John T	650	laborer	31	
	F	Kirby Mary —†	650	housewife	31	"
	G	Cronin Annie—†	650	matron	48	
	H	Cronin Josephine—†	650	clerk	39	
	K	Diorio Emily—†	652	housewife	30	"
	L	Diorio Nicholas	652	operator	31	
	M	Dwelley Arthur G	652	laborer	57	
	N	Dwelley Elizabeth F—†	652	housewife	53	"
	O	Dwelley George	652	cook	24	
	P	Kane Jennie—†	652	housekeeper	43	"
	R	Bossi Eleanor—†	653	housewife	27	"
	S	Bossi Giacomo	653	laborer	35	"
	T	*DeFeo Angelina—†	653	housewife	48	375 Frankfort
	U	*DeFeo Antonio	653	laborer	55	375 "
	V	DeFeo Jennie—†	653	at home	21	375 "
	W	DeFeo William	653	laborer	26	375 "
	X	*O'Riordan Helen—†	653	housewife	63	here
	Y	O'Riordan John	653	operator	65	"
	Z	O'Riordan John	653	"	23	"
1209						
	A	*Joyce Anna—†	rear 653	housewife	67	"
	B	Joyce John J	" 653	laborer	42	
	C	Joyce Patrick J	" 653	retired	76	
	D	Joyce William F	" 653	engraver	37	"
	E	*Ventola Romana—†	" 653	housewife	84	"

Page.	Letter.	Full Name.	Residence, Jan. 1, 1938.	Occupation.	Supposed Age.	Reported Residence, Jan. 1, 1937. Street and Number.

Saratoga Street—Continued

Page.	Letter.	Full Name.	Residence, Jan. 1, 1938.	Occupation.	Supposed Age.	Reported Residence, Jan. 1, 1937. Street and Number.
	F	McCarthy Amy—†	654	housewife	56	here
	G	McCarthy Henry I	654	retired	68	"
	H	McCarthy Henry I, jr	654	laborer	21	"
	K	*Bossi Annie—†	654	housewife	24	661 Saratoga
	L	Bossi Carmen	654	chauffeur	28	661 "
	M	Hurley Daniel F	654	clerk	54	here
	N	Hurley John H	654	retired	88	"
	O	Hurley Mary A—†	654	housewife	52	"
	P	Hurley William J	654	operator	22	"
	S	Shea Brendan	656	fisherman	29	60 Bennington
	T	Shea Hilda—†	656	housewife	26	60 "
	U	McCarthy Catherine—†	656	"	41	here
	V	McCarthy Patrick	656	longshoreman	41	"
	W	Tierney Alice—†	656	nurse	57	"
	X	Tierney Bridget A—†	656	housewife	47	"
	Y	Tierney Francis J	656	fireman	51	
	Z	Fitzgerald Dennis A	658	laborer	46	
1210						
	A	*Fitzgerald Hannah—†	658	housewife	80	"
	B	Fitzgerald Lawrence A	658	laborer	52	
	C	Saviano Philip	658	chauffeur	26	"
	D	Saviano Phyllis—†	658	housewife	23	"
	E	Finn Evelyn—†	658	"	33	
	F	Finn John	658	bartender	32	"
	G	Ruggiero Carmine	660	laborer	44	
	H	Ruggiero Louise—†	660	housewife	46	"
	K	Ruggiero Barbara—†	660	"	30	
	L	*Ruggiero Gennaro	660	chauffeur	31	"
	N	French Alfred	661	mechanic	36	Chelsea
	O	French Dorothy—†	661	housewife	24	"
	R	*DiMauro Lucy—†	663	"	34	here
	S	DiMauro Vincent	663	cook	35	"
	T	Della Sala Attilio	663	cutter	37	Rockland
	U	*Della Sala Clara—†	663	housewife	37	"
	V	DeMarsks Mary—†	664	seamstress	50	154 Lexington
	W	Gustowski Harriet—†	664	housewife	44	here
	X	Hayes Wilfred A	664	draftsman	42	"
	Y	Hogan Alexander	664	bookbinder	38	192 Benningt'n
	Z	Hogan Madeline—†	664	housewife	38	here
1211						
	A	McMullen Joseph	664	storekeeper	47	"

Page.	Letter.	FULL NAME.	Residence, Jan. 1, 1938.	Occupation.	Supposed Age.	Reported Residence, Jan. 1, 1937. Street and Number.

Saratoga Street—Continued

Page.	Letter.	FULL NAME.	Residence, Jan. 1, 1938.	Occupation.	Supposed Age.	Reported Residence, Jan. 1, 1937. Street and Number.
	B	McMullen Margaret M–†	664	housewife	47	here
	C	McMullen William	664	guard	52	"
	E	Brennan Grace—†	666	housewife	24	"
	F	Brennan John	666	chauffeur	29	"
	G	Benson John A	666	clerk	65	
	H	Benson Mary N—†	666	housewife	62	"
	K	Kennedy Anna M—†	666	"	44	
	L	Kennedy Evelyn—†	666	at home	21	
	M	Kennedy John J	666	inspector	45	"
	N	*White Ellen—†	667	housewife	44	"
	O	*White William	667	longshoreman	53	"
	S	Porter Irene—†	669	at home	21	
	P	Porter Joseph R	669	fireman	39	
	R	Porter Margaret I—†	669	housewife	45	"
	T	O'Reagan Frederick	670	physician	42	"
	U	O'Reagan William L	670	dentist	46	
	V	Cronin Anna—†	671	housewife	27	"
	W	Cronin John	671	operator	29	"
	X	Blaquiere Annie—†	671	housewife	42	"
	Y	Blaquiere Maurice	671	carpenter	42	"
	Z	Boudreau Delphine—†	673	housewife	64	"
1212						
	A	Boudreau George H	673	retired	69	
	B	Dawber Joseph M	673	chauffeur	38	"
	C	Dawber Stephen W	673	"	35	
	D	Snow Arthur C	673	cook	56	
	E	Snow Sabina C—†	673	housewife	56	"
	F	Cabaliere Nicholas	674	retired	61	
	G	Cabaliere Rose—†	674	housewife	63	"
	H	Cabaliere Samuel	674	inspector	31	"
	K	Cabaliere Frank	674	operator	35	
	L	Cabaliere Josephine—†	674	housewife	28	"
	M	Nuzzo Elizabeth—†	675	"	27	
	N	Nuzzo Frank	675	operator	32	"
	O	Nuzzo Rose—†	675	housewife	67	"
	P	Sturniolo Charles	675	laborer	40	
	R	Sturniolo Mary—†	675	housewife	39	"
	S	DeMeo Josephine—†	675	"	36	
	T	DeMeo Michael	675	cutter	43	
	U	*DeNapoli Francesco	676	laborer	58	
	V	DeNapoli Ralph	676	"	21	

Page.	Letter.	FULL NAME.	Residence, Jan. 1, 1938.	Occupation.	Supposed Age.	Reported Residence, Jan. 1, 1937. Street and Number.

Saratoga Street—Continued

Page.	Letter.	FULL NAME.	Residence, Jan. 1, 1938.	Occupation.	Supposed Age.	Reported Residence, Jan. 1, 1937. Street and Number.
	W	*DeNapoli Rose—†	676	housewife	59	here
	X	Powers Anna—†	676	"	25	"
	Y	*Powers David	676	printer	24	"
	Z	Petrillo Anthony	676	baker	29	
1213						
	A	*Petrillo Concetta—†	676	housewife	24	"
	B	Ruggiero Jennie—†	677	"	47	
	C	Ruggiero Mary—†	677	seamstress	20	"
	D	Steffano Angelina—†	677	housewife	25	43 St Edward rd
	E	Steffano Joseph	677	chef	26	43 "
	F	Dooley Daniel	678	clerk	72	here
	G	Dooley Elizabeth—†	678	housewife	70	"
	H	*Salamone Joseph	678	barber	49	"
	K	*Salamone Lillian—†	678	housewife	45	"
	L	Salamone Mary—†	678	at home	22	
	M	Balboni Frederick	678	policeman	29	"
	N	Balboni Margaret—†	678	housewife	24	"
	O	Vansieleghem Josephine–†	679	"	29	
	P	Vansieleghem Julian	679	laborer	38	
	R	Catalanotto Joseph	679	barber	36	
	S	*Catalanotto Victoria—†	679	housewife	29	"
	T	Bruno Madeline—†	679	"	23	126 Saratoga
	U	Bruno Philip	679	tailor	24	119 Havre
	V	Pantos Mary—†	680	housewife	27	53 Byron
	W	Pantos Stephen	680	cook	37	53 "
	X	*Bondi Elvira—†	680	housewife	37	here
	Y	*Bondi Gino	680	painter	43	"
1214						
	A	*Santoro Patrick	681	laborer	48	
	B	Santoro Rose—†	681	at home	24	
	C	*Raymond Barbara—†	681	housewife	33	"
	D	Raymond John	681	laborer	37	
	E	Meninno Ambrozio	682	printer	23	
	F	Meninno Anthony	682	"	21	
	G	Meninno Carmella—†	682	housewife	41	"
	H	Meninno Domenic	682	retired	45	
	L	Ambrogne Annie B—†	687	housewife	40	"
	M	Ambrogne Jerome	687	retired	43	
	N	Peters Anna—†	687	housewife	21	"
	O	Peters Daniel H	687	U S A	31	666 Summer

Page.	Letter.	Full Name.	Residence, Jan. 1, 1938.	Occupation.	Supposed Age.	Reported Residence, Jan. 1, 1937. Street and Number.

Saratoga Street—Continued

Page.	Letter.	Full Name.	Residence, Jan. 1, 1938.	Occupation.	Supposed Age.	Reported Residence, Jan. 1, 1937. Street and Number.
	P	Newhook Esther—†	689	housewife	71	here
	R	Newhook Joseph	689	fireman	27	"
	S	Newhook Mary—†	689	housewife	28	"
	T	Newhook Robert J	689	laborer	30	
	U	Riley Edwin J	690	policeman	35	"
	V	Riley Florence J—†	690	housewife	35	"
	W	Riley Thomas A	690	inspector	68	"
	X	Turner Dorothy M—†	691	clerk	28	
	Y	Turner Jean—†	691	packer	46	
	Z	Turner Margaret—†	691	housewife	51	"
1215						
	A	Turner Robert T	691	mechanic	52	"
	B	Boudreau Harold A	691	manager	42	"
	C	Watson Agnes L—†	691	clerk	42	
	D	Turner Mary D—†	692	housewife	46	"
	E	Turner Rose C—†	692	"	82	
	F	Turner William L	692	engineer	52	"
	G	Butt Mae V—†	694	at home	50	
	H	Turner Charles E	694	clerk	32	
	K	Turner Edwin J	694	accountant	29	"
	L	Turner Flora A—†	694	housewife	59	"
	M	Turner Florence W—†	694	stenographer	27	"
	N	Turner Mae V—†	694	clerk	30	"
	O	Fife Mary—†	696	floorwoman	50	"
	P	*DeAngelis Clementine—†	696	housewife	75	"
	R	DeAngelis Grace—†	696	at home	22	
	S	DeAngelis Joseph	696	optician	35	
	T	*DeAngelis Ralph	696	retired	79	
	U	Kelley Anna A—†	702	merchant	46	"
	V	Kelley Dorothy—†	702	operator	21	"
	W	Zinna Concetta—†	704	packer	23	282 Maverick
	X	Zinna Frances—†	704	at home	25	282 "
	Y	Zinna James	704	clerk	20	282 "
	Z	Zinna Joseph	704	laborer	27	282 "
1216						
	A	*Zinna Mary—†	704	housewife	52	282 "
	B	*Zinna Nunzio	704	laborer	55	282 "
	E	Thompson Amelia M—†	710	housewife	35	39 Ashley
	F	Thompson Newell L	710	chauffeur	37	39 "

Page.	Letter.	Full Name.	Residence, Jan. 1, 1938.	Occupation.	Supposed Age.	Reported Residence, Jan. 1, 1937. Street and Number.

William F McClellan Highway

	K	Connelly Josephine M—†	47	housewife	25	here
	L	Connelly Lawrence P	47	clerk	27	"
	M	Dunn Harry	47	operator	25	"
	N	Dunn Ruth—†	47	"	23	
	O	Carmo Adeline—†	47	housewife	29	"
	P	Carmo Edward J	47	laborer	32	
	R	McMillan Johanna—†	47	housekeeper	65	"
	S	Driscoll Bridget—†	49	"	70	"
	T	Keenan Edward, jr	49	foreman	45	
	U	Keenan Mary J—†	49	housewife	36	"
	V	Jasus Etta—†	49	at home	26	
	W	*Rose Mary—†	49	housekeeper	46	"
	X	Puopolo Domenic	51	tailor	28	"
	Y	*Puopolo Mary—†	51	housewife	24	"
	Z	Kelly Esther—†	51	"	30	
1217						
	A	Kelly James	51	clerk	32	
	B	*Santos John T	51	fisherman	57	"
	C	*Santos Mary—†	51	housewife	53	"
	D	Granara Anna E—†	53	"	35	
	E	Granara Richard L	53	chauffeur	36	"
	F	DelBianco Catherine—†	53	housewife	25	"
	G	DelBianco Ernest	53	foreman	26	
	H	Reilly Catherine—†	53	housewife	26	"
	K	Reilly James	53	operator	30	
	L	Donovan Josephine—†	55	housewife	24	"
	M	Donovan Sylvester	55	packer	24	
	N	Doyle Gladys—†	55	housewife	31	"
	O	Doyle Walter	55	laborer	29	
	P	O'Connell Anna M—†	55	housewife	43	"
	R	O'Connell Florance E	55	calker	42	
	S	Henneberry Florence M-†	57	housekeeper	42	"
	T	Conroy Barbara—†	57	housewife	58	"
	U	Conroy Helen—†	57	assembler	24	"
	V	Conroy Joseph	57	clerk	27	
	W	Conroy Mary M—†	57	"	29	
	X	Fenton Bridget—†	57	housewife	50	"
	Y	Fenton Philip	57	laborer	30	
	Z	*Campbell Margaret—†	59	housewife	68	"
1218						
	A	*Campbell William C	59	retired	78	

Page.	Letter.	Full Name.	Residence, Jan. 1, 1938.	Occupation.	Supposed Age.	Reported Residence, Jan. 1, 1937. Street and Number.

William F McClellan Highway—Continued

	B	*Hodgson Ann—†	59	operator	49	here
	C	Laverson Anna—†	59	housewife	37	"
	D	Laverson John J	59	testman	35	"
	E	Laverson Mary—†	59	housewife	70	"
	F	Gallagher William F	59	retired	73	
	G	Gallagher William F, jr	59	laborer	36	
	H	Smith Catherine—†	59	housewife	38	"
	K	Smith Ethel—†	59	at home	21	

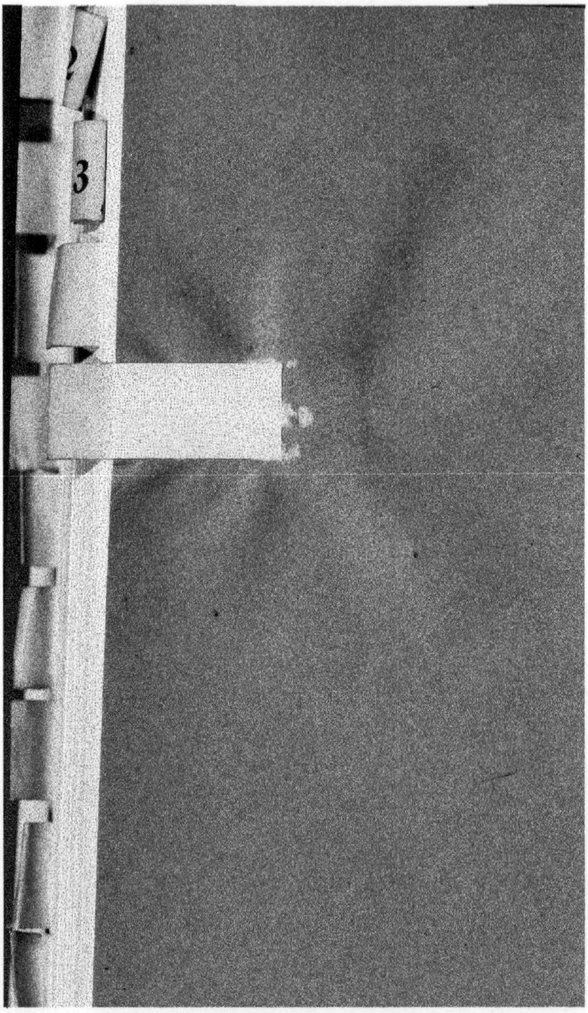
2
3

Ward 1—Precinct 15

CITY OF BOSTON

LIST OF RESIDENTS
20 YEARS OF AGE AND OVER

(NON-CITIZENS INDICATED BY ASTERISK)
(FEMALES INDICATED BY DAGGER)

AS OF

JANUARY 1, 1938

JOSEPH F. TIMILTY, } Listing
FREDERIC E. DOWLING, } Board.

CITY OF BOSTON PRINTING DEPARTMENT

Page.	Letter.	Full Name.	Residence, Jan. 1, 1938.	Occupation.	Supposed Age.	Reported Residence, Jan. 1, 1937. Street and Number.
1228						
		Ardee Street				
	A	Miles Catherine A—†	4	housewife	65	here
	B	Miles Lillian M—†	4	clerk	31	"
	C	Miles Ruth E—†	4	nurse	25	"
	D	Miles Sylvester C	4	clerk	27	
		Bennington Street				
	F	Carty Mary—†	519	housewife	43	here
	G	Carty Stephen	519	laborer	45	"
	H	Donnelly Ann—†	521	housewife	38	"
	K	Donnelly Daniel J	521	laborer	43	
	L	Murphy Elizabeth—†	521	at home	78	
	M	Barker Ellen—†	521	"	68	
	N	Burke John	521	foreman	61	
	O	Morris Ann—†	521	at home	73	
	P	Scaramella Christine—†	523	typist	28	
	R	Scaramella Domenica—†	523	housewife	61	"
	T	Marmo Ernestine—†	527	tailoress	21	"
	U	Marmo Jane—†	527	housewife	42	"
	V	Marmo Nicholas	527	laborer	44	
	W	*Cornetta Mary—†	527	at home	75	
	X	Esposito Peter	527	storekeeper	42	"
	Y	Vecchio Nicholas	527	"	34	"
	Z	Long Bridget—†	527	housewife	43	"
1229						
	A	Long Patrick J	527	engineer	55	
	B	Maher Bridget—†	529	housewife	65	"
	C	Maher Edward J	529	laborer	68	
	E	Alterisio Alexander	529	"	33	
	D	Alterisio Angelina—†	529	housewife	62	"
	F	Alterisio Anthony	529	laborer	62	
	G	Alterisio George	529	student	22	
	H	Alterisio John	529	chauffeur	27	"
	K	Alterisio Mary—†	529	operator	40	"
	L	*Mercurio Gerardo	529	shoemaker	48	"
	M	*Mercurio Josephine—†	529	housewife	37	"
	N	Beranger Adeline—†	531	"	25	
	O	Beranger Joseph	531	cutter	32	
	P	Carino Albert	531	porter	20	
	R	Carino Gaetano—†	531	housewife	53	"

Page.	Letter.	Full Name.	Residence, Jan. 1, 1938.	Occupation.	Supposed Age.	Reported Residence, Jan. 1, 1937. Street and Number.

Bennington Street—Continued

	S	Walsh Blanche M—†	531	clerk	30	here
	T	Walsh Harold	531	laborer	35	"
	U	Walsh Jane—†	531	housewife	65	"
	V	Winston James	533	laborer	56	
	W	*Dunn James L	533	retired	73	
	X	Dunn John P	533	operator	30	"
	Y	*Dunn Josephine—†	533	housewife	60	"
	Z	*Dunn Lillian M—†	533	at home	25	
1230						
	A	Winston Edward F	533	laborer	50	70 Montebello rd
	B	Winston Helen B—†	533	clerk	21	70 "
	C	Winston Sadie A—†	533	housewife	45	70 "
	D	Murray Bertha B—†	537	"	49	here
	E	Murray Henry B	537	cutter	54	"
	F	Fairchild Charles	537	laborer	45	Revere
	G	Fairchild Maude—†	537	at home	20	"
	H	Gundersen Dorothy S—†	537	housewife	33	here
	K	Gundersen Tallman H	537	waterproofer	39	"
	L	Visconti Anna—†	549	housewife	30	681 Saratoga
	M	Visconti Anthony	549	plumber	31	681 "
	N	Guerra Frank	549	laborer	41	here
	O	Guerra Mary—†	549	housewife	37	"
	P	Lazzaro Lillian—†	549	operator	27	"
	R	*Lazzaro Mary—†	549	housewife	54	"
	S	Lazzaro Nicholas	549	clerk	21	
	T	Previte Frank	551	chauffeur	46	"
	U	Previte Irene—†	551	housewife	38	"
	V	White Evelyn—†	553	"	33	
	W	White Robert	553	policeman	34	"
	X	Hankard Dorothy M—†	553	clerk	30	
	Y	Hankard Mary A—†	553	housewife	69	"
	Z	Hankard Walter M	553	policeman	32	"
1231						
	A	Hankard William M	553	laborer	43	
	B	Hearns Leo	553	policeman	34	"
	C	Hyland Emma I—†	555	housewife	50	"
	D	Hyland Frederick D	555	draftsman	47	"
	E	Hyland Mary A—†	555	housewife	70	"
	F	Hyland William J	555	retired	71	
	M	Eastwood Harry	557	B F D	53	
	H	Newby Thomas H	557	retired	88	

Page.	Letter.	Full Name.	Residence, Jan. 1, 1938.	Occupation.	Supposed Age.	Reported Residence, Jan. 1, 1937. Street and Number.

Bennington Street—Continued

	K	Gilgan Harriett A—†	557	housewife	55	here
	L	Gilgan James E	557	foreman	58	“
	N	Cook Georgiana—†	559	teacher	27	“
	O	Scott George	559	janitor	51	“
	P	Scott Herbert	559	operator	22	“
	R	Budd Emily—†	559	housewife	77	“
	S	Budd Emily E—†	559	operator	53	
	T	Budd Ruby V—†	559	clerk	37	
	U	McLaughlin Elizabeth–†	561	housewife	36	“
	V	McLaughlin Joseph F	561	laborer	36	
	W	Laundry George	561	printer	46	
	X	Laundry Gladys—†	561	operator	21	“
	Y	Laundry Helen—†	561	housewife	45	“
	Z	Donovan Margaret G—†	563	“	42	
1232						
	A	Donovan Richard J	563	machinist	44	“
	B	Donovan Rita M—†	563	secretary	20	“
	C	Farmer Hannah E—†	563	housewife	46	“
	D	Farmer John	563	machinist	51	“
	G	Clark Martha—†	569	housekeeper	50	“
	H	McCulpha John H	569	storekeeper	67	“
	K	Bohling Mary E—†	569	at home	72	“
	L	Murray Joseph W	569	operator	52	
	M	Murray Julia E—†	569	housewife	47	“
	N	Sullivan Catherine A—†	569	student	20	
	R	Mortimer Michael J	573	laborer	59	
	S	Mortimer Nellie A—†	573	housewife	49	“
	T	Mortimer Catherine G–†	573	bookkeeper	33	“
	U	Mortimer John A	573	laborer	31	“
	V	Mortimer Mary E—†	573	housewife	67	“
	W	Mortimer Peter J	573	laborer	68	
	X	Mortimer Peter J, jr	573	trustee	27	“
	Y	Nelson Alice G—†	573	housekeeper	30	“
	Z	McGee Catherine A—†	575	clerk	32	“
1233						
	A	McGee Mary A—†	575	housewife	36	“
	B	McGee Patrick	575	retired	74	“
	C	Tucci Mary—†	577	housewife	31	102 Orleans
	D	Tucci Nicholas	577	operator	34	102 “
	E	Burns John	579	painter	29	here
	F	Burns Marie—†	579	housewife	24	“

Page.	Letter.	FULL NAME.	Residence, Jan. 1, 1938.	Occupation.	Supposed Age.	Reported Residence, Jan. 1, 1937. Street and Number.

Bennington Street—Continued

Page.	Letter.	FULL NAME.	Residence, Jan. 1, 1938.	Occupation.	Supposed Age.	Reported Residence, Jan. 1, 1937. Street and Number.
	G	Rossano Frank P	579	laborer	52	here
	H	Rossano Louis R	579	"	20	"
	K	Rossano Madeline—†	579	housewife	49	"
	L	Ambrose Josephine—†	583	at home	35	
	M	Sullivan Helen C—†	585	clerk	36	
	N	Sullivan John J	585	retired	64	
	O	Sullivan Mary E—†	585	housewife	63	"
	P	Tierney Mary E—†	585	"	29	70 Horace
	R	Tierney Raymond J	585	adjuster	27	70 "
	S	McCauley John	587	laborer	37	73 Moore
	U	*McCauley Mary—†	587	housewife	62	73 "
	T	McCauley Mary J—†	587	operator	32	73 "
	V	Naples Elva—†	589	housewife	30	here
	W	Naples Joseph	589	operator	36	"
	X	Donovan Timothy X	591	laborer	37	"
	Y	Hamilton Elizabeth D–†	591	housewife	36	"
	Z	Hamilton John A	591	salesman	34	"
1234						
	A	Smith Mary—†	593	housewife	60	"
	B	Smith Michael	593	engineer	62	
	C	Curtis John	595	salesman	30	"
	D	Curtis Mary—†	595	housewife	30	"
	E	Gardner Lucy—†	595	at home	37	
	F	Gannon Frances—†	595	housewife	28	"
	G	Gannon Francis J	595	teacher	36	40 Holton
	H	Gannon Mark L	595	manager	40	here
	K	Butler Florence—†	597	housewife	24	"
	L	Butler John	597	operator	25	"
	M	Corliss Margaret—†	597	at home	59	"
	N	Phillips Franklin J	597	tester	26	220 Brooks
	O	Phillips Margaret—†	597	housewife	26	here
	P	Connelly Mary A—†	599	at home	73	"
	R	McLean Charles E	599	guard	50	"
	S	Sanderson Mary—†	599	housekeeper	50	"
	T	McLean Grace E—†	601	housewife	29	"
	U	McLean Harold P	601	B F D	31	107 Homer
	V	McLean William A	601	policeman	32	here
	W	Gormley Catherine—†	601	saleswoman	48	"
	X	Gormley James F	601	fireman	38	"
	Y	Gormley Mary—†	601	housewife	78	"
	Z	Howard John C, jr	603	mechanic	26	"

Page.	Letter.	Full Name.	Residence, Jan. 1, 1938.	Occupation.	Supposed Age.	Reported Residence, Jan. 1, 1937. Street and Number.
1235		**Bennington Street**—Continued				
	A	Howard Katherine J—†	603	housewife	22	here
	C	Cook Mary E—†	603	at home	40	"
	D	Durante Irene—†	605	housewife	32	"
	E	Durante Vincent	605	machinist	36	"
	F	Schieb Margaret—†	605	housewife	41	"
	G	Schieb William	605	electrician	41	"
	H	Hansford Leonard F	605	laborer	21	
	K	Hansford Mary C—†	605	housewife	46	"
	L	Hansford William H	605	electrician	51	"
	M	Hansford William R	605	laborer	25	
	N	Dunn Bridie—†	607	housewife	43	"
	O	Dunn James B	607	laborer	28	
	P	Dunn Mary—†	607	at home	27	
	R	Dunn William	607	laborer	42	
	S	*Bennambede Annie—†	607	housewife	38	"
	T	Bennambede Fabio	607	operator	42	
	U	Ripandelli Geralamo	607	"	41	"
	V	Alfieri Frank	609	laborer	29	16 Margaret
	W	Alfieri Nancy—†	609	housewife	24	291 Causeway
	X	Carresi Katherine—†	611	"	33	549 Benningt'n
	Y	Carresi Pasquale	611	painter	33	549 "
	Z	Silek Julia—†	613	housewife	27	677 "
1236						
	A	Silek Walter	613	counterman	31	677 "
	B	Hill Mary—†	613	at home	45	here
	C	Smith John	613	retired	76	"
	D	Smith William	613	mechanic	27	"
	E	Richardson Charles W	615	foreman	45	
	F	Richardson Hazel—†	615	housewife	31	"
	G	Bois Henry	615	operator	37	"
	H	Bois Madeline M—†	615	housewife	37	"
	K	Doyle Dorothy M—†	615	"	32	"
	L	Doyle Leo F	615	electrotyper	34	"
	M	Howard Joseph J	617	clerk	58	"
	N	Howard William F	617	laborer	51	
	O	Melanson Adeline—†	617	housewife	37	"
	P	Melanson Melvin J	617	chauffeur	38	"
	R	Murray Kathleen—†	617	clerk	34	
	S	Silva Mary A—†	617	at home	66	
	T	Murphy Edward J	617A	clerk	62	

Page.	Letter.	Full Name.	Residence, Jan. 1, 1938.	Occupation.	Supposed Age.	Reported Residence, Jan. 1, 1937. Street and Number.

Bennington Street—Continued

Page.	Letter.	Full Name.	Residence, Jan. 1, 1938.	Occupation.	Supposed Age.	Reported Residence, Jan. 1, 1937. Street and Number.
	U	Galzerano Adeline—†	619	student	20	here
	V	Galzerano Giuseppe	619	laborer	57	"
	W	Galzerano Viola—†	619	at home	24	"
	Y	Treanor Charles H	619	mortician	37	"
	Z	Treanor Louise G—†	619	housewife	37	"
1237						
	B	Potter Alice M—†	633	"	25	
	C	Potter Joseph E, jr	633	laborer	24	
	E	Smith Jean E—†	635	clerk	23	
	F	Smith Peter S	635	printer	65	
	G	Smith Sarah—†	635	housewife	63	"
	H	Smith William G	635	laborer	64	
	K	D'Ambrosio Antonio	641	mechanic	29	"
	L	D'Ambrosio Jennie—†	641	housewife	29	"
	M	D'Ambrosio Alice—†	641A	inspector	26	"
	N	*D'Ambrosio Amelia—†	641A	housewife	60	"
	O	D'Ambrosio Carmine	641A	laborer	59	
	P	D'Ambrosio Helen—†	641A	clerk	23	
	R	D'Ambrosio Leo	641A	foreman	48	
	S	D'Ambrosio Nancy—†	641A	inspector	20	"
	T	D'Ambrosio Sue—†	641A	bookkeeper	25	"
	U	Molino Ettore	641A	tailor	43	67 Byron
	V	Molino Rose—†	641A	housewife	40	67 "
	W	Geehan Agnes—†	643	"	37	here
	X	Geehan Richard J	643	mechanic	36	"
	Y	DeGregorio Albert	643	cook	27	"
	Z	DeGregorio Carmella—†	643	housewife	61	"
1238						
	A	DeGregorio Natalie—†	643	"	22	
	B	DeGregorio Vincenzo	643	retired	65	
	C	*Santosuosso Elizabeth—†	643	at home	83	
	D	Santosuosso Evelyn—†	643	housewife	42	"
	E	Santosuosso Principio	643	editor	45	
	F	McLaughlin Alfred P	645	conductor	33	"
	G	McLaughlin Alice R—†	645	housewife	34	"
	H	Skane Margaret M—†	645	"	46	
	K	Skane William I	645	operator	46	"
	L	DeGregorio Evelyn—†	645	stenographer	22	"
	M	DeGregorio Jerome	645	operator	49	"
	N	DeGregorio Rose—†	645	housewife	45	"
	O	Cody Catherine—†	647	"	29	864 Saratoga

Page.	Letter.	Full Name.	Residence, Jan. 1, 1938.	Occupation.	Supposed Age.	Reported Residence, Jan. 1, 1937. Street and Number.

Bennington Street—Continued

	P	Cody Joseph E	647	laborer	38	864 Saratoga
	R	Cody Thomas	647	cooper	65	864 "
	S	Peterson Mary L—†	647	at home	55	here
	T	Donnelly Anna—†	651	"	26	"
	U	Donnelly Lillian—†	651	saleswoman	25	"
	V	Donnelly Lillian L—†	651	housewife	53	"
	W	Donnelly Mary—†	651	saleswoman	28	"
	X	Terry Albert P	651	laborer	25	252 E Eagle
	Y	Terry Evelyn G—†	651	housewife	23	252 "
	Z*	Pisano Philip	651	shoemaker	25	20 Chelsea
1239						
	A*	Pisano Phyllis—†	651	housewife	22	809 Saratoga
	C	Drew Johanna M—†	653	seamstress	50	here
	D	Edwards James	653	U S A	22	"
	E	Edwards Lawrence	653	manager	24	"
	F	Edwards Margaret—†	653	bookkeeper	20	"
	G	O'Hare Arthur F	653	clerk	48	"
	H	O'Hare Christine A—†	653	housewife	47	"
	K	Flynn James	653	guard	43	
	P	Bagley Hugh J	673	retired	71	
	R	Briscoe Alfred	673	laborer	61	
	S	Briscoe Catherine L—†	673	housewife	63	"
	T*	Donadilli Antonetta—†	675	"	72	
	U	Donadilli Camello	675	laborer	32	
	V	Hudson Isabelle A—†	675	housewife	32	"
	W	Hudson Roy A	675	chauffeur	32	"
	X	Donadilli Frederick	675	shoemaker	22	"
	Y*	Donadilli Lydia—†	675	housewife	45	"
	Z*	Donadilli William	675	tailor	45	
1240						
	A	Pascucci Amelio	677	plumber	35	
	B	Pascucci Grace—†	677	housewife	36	"
	C	McDonald Kathryne—†	677	"	41	
	D	McDonald Raymond F	677	bartender	38	"
	E	Winer Louis I	677	seaman	36	
	F	Winer Richard L	677	"	32	"
	G	Nuzzo Bernard	677	salesman	26	528 Benningt'n
	H*	Nuzzo Mary—†	677	housewife	25	528 "
	K	Castagnola Alphonse	681	storekeeper	38	here
	L*	Castagnola Aurelia—†	681	housewife	38	"
	M	Moe Rosa C—†	683	dressmaker	46	"

Page.	Letter.	Full Name.	Residence, Jan. 1, 1938.	Occupation.	Supposed Age.	Reported Residence, Jan. 1, 1937. Street and Number.

Bennington Street—Continued

Page.	Letter.	Full Name.	Residence, Jan. 1, 1938.	Occupation.	Supposed Age.	Reported Residence, Jan. 1, 1937. Street and Number.
	N	Sorenson Frieda—†	683	housewife	52	here
	O	Sorenson Herman	683	clerk	28	“
	P	Sorenson John N	683	manager	54	“
	R	Sorenson Norman	683	clerk	23	
	S	Nebhen David	687	laborer	53	
	T	*Vliano Joseph	687	operator	54	“
	U	*Vliano Maria—†	687	housewife	49	“
	V	Leccese George	691	chauffeur	25	233 Saratoga
	W	Leccese Josephine—†	691	bookkeeper	23	233 “
	X	*Gallo Philomena—†	691	at home	75	here
	Y	Sena John	691	laborer	50	“
	Z	Sena John, jr	691	operator	21	New York
1241						
	A	Sena Mary—†	691	stenographer	26	here
	B	Sena Pompelia—†	691	housewife	49	“
	C	Sena Rose—†	691	at home	24	“
	D	Cancellieri Blanche—†	691	housewife	26	789 Saratoga
	E	Cancellieri Joseph G	691	bookkeeper	27	789 “
	F	Sanford Mary A—†	693	housewife	66	here
	G	Sanford Patrick F	693	engineer	62	“
	H	Sullivan James A	693	seaman	39	Somerville
	K	Trask Charles A	693	oiler	42	here
	L	Murphy Jean F—†	693	stenographer	35	“
	M	Murphy Raymond F	693	salesman	31	“
	N	Murphy Walter J	693	fisherman	58	“
	O	Gillespie Leila—†	693	housewife	28	“
	P	Gillespie Martin	693	clerk	30	
	R	Williams Florence—†	695	housewife	37	“
	S	Williams Harry E	695	mechanic	39	“
	T	Boudreau Daniel	695	student	23	
	U	Boudreau Mary M—†	695	housewife	50	“
	V	Boudreau Mary M—†	695	clerk	25	
	W	Boudreau William P	695	B F D	55	
	X	Boudreau Catherine G—†	695	at home	20	
	Y	Boudreau Elizabeth B—†	695	librarian	35	“
	Z	Boudreau Mary F—†	695	organist	47	
1242						
	A	Cotty William T	695	salesman	36	“
	B	Rogers Helen C—†	697	housewife	38	“
	C	Rogers William J	697	operator	52	“
	D	*Altirelli Guistina—†	697	at home	75	

Page.	Letter.	Full Name.	Residence, Jan. 1, 1938.	Occupation.	Supposed Age.	Reported Residence, Jan. 1, 1937. Street and Number.

Bennington Street—Continued

	E	Iapicca Bernadina—†	697	stenographer	22	here
	F	Iapicca Rocco	697	chauffeur	24	“
	G	*Iapicca Rose—†	697	housewife	45	“
	H	Iapicca Vincenzo	697	barber	46	“
	K	Powers Louise B—†	697	housewife	50	“
	L	Powers Patrick J	697	clerk	53	
	M	Curtin Eileen F—†	699	housewife	55	“
	N	Curtin John J	699	coppersmith	56	“
	O	Boyle Rose M—†	699	at home	45	
	P	McCarthy Gerald J	699	attorney	43	“
	R	Green Charles	699	salesman	58	“
	S	Green Elizabeth—†	699	housewife	46	“
	T	Green Rita—†	699	stenographer	23	“
	U	Currie Mary—†	701	housewife	62	“
	V	Currie William	701	retired	71	
	W	Currie William M	701	chauffeur	30	“
	X	Rogers Henry D	701	“	61	
	Y	Rogers Thomas	701	stereotyper	63	“
	Z	McLaughlin Charlotte A–†	701	housewife	60	“
1243						
	A	McLaughlin James E L	701	inspector	67	“
	B	McLaughlin Mary N—†	701	teacher	28	
	C	*LaCasscia Anna—†	703	housewife	67	“
	D	*LaCasscia Lena—†	703	operator	27	
	E	LaCasscia Salvatore	703	baker	24	
	F	Mirotta Rose—†	703	operator	46	“
	G	Fitzpatrick Dorothy M–†	703	“	27	
	H	Fitzpatrick Francis J	703	clerk	21	
	K	Fitzpatrick Gertrude R–†	703	operator	23	
	L	Fitzpatrick Julia E—†	703	housewife	52	“
	M	Ciampa Aminio	703	laborer	29	
	N	*Ciampa Jennie—†	703	housewife	29	“
	O	McKay Elizabeth A—†	705	“	59	
	P	McKay Henry F	705	inspector	35	“
	R	McKay Matthew W	705	laborer	30	“
	S	Velardo Catherine—†	705	housewife	59	“
	T	Velardo Frank	705	operator	32	“
	U	Velardo Jennie—†	705	bookkeeper	26	“
	V	Velardo Stefano	705	retired	71	“
	W	Murray Dora A—†	705	housewife	54	“
	X	Murray Franklin C	705	laborer	46	

Page.	Letter.	FULL NAME.	Residence, Jan. 1, 1938.	Occupation.	Supposed Age.	Reported Residence, Jan. 1, 1937. Street and Number.

Bennington Street—Continued

	Y	Murray Walter T	705	hostler	53	here
	Z	McGrath Mabel F—†	707	housewife	46	"
1244						
	A	McGrath Wilfred E	707	salesman	38	"
	B	Duffy Charles B	707	laborer	54	
	C	McCormack Francis T	707	clerk	36	
	D	McCormack Mary—†	707	housewife	70	"
	E	McDonald Alma M—†	707	"	35	
	F	McDonald John F	707	laborer	37	
	G	McDonald Mary C—†	707	housewife	46	"
	H	Goss Bridget—†	709	at home	72	
	K	Wickstrom Josephine—†	709	investigator	40	"
	L	Boudreau Helen M—†	709	housewife	39	"
	M	Boudreau William	709	policeman	39	"
	N	Colorusso Eleanor—†	709	housewife	41	"
	O	Colorusso Joseph	709	contractor	46	"

Byron Street

	P	Picciuolo Amelia—†	146	housewife	56	here
	R	Picciuolo Carmine	146	manager	30	"
	S	Picciuolo Stefano	146	retired	66	"
	T	Sexton Albert J	150	clerk	46	
	U	Sexton Frederick B	150	salesman	37	"
	V	Sexton Mary J—†	150	housewife	55	"
	W	Butler James L	163	gauger	27	677 Saratoga
	X	Butler Theresa M—†	163	housewife	26	677 "
	Y	McPhee John J	163	laborer	40	25 Morris
	Z	McPhee Marcella B—†	163	housewife	41	25 "
1245						
	A	Hines Corinne C—†	163	"	25	Newton
	B	Hines Frank H	163	manager	26	"
	C	Sacco Angelo	165	printer	33	29 Breed
	D	Sacco Mary—†	165	housewife	24	29 "
	E	*Davis Isabel—†	165	"	36	682 Benningt'n
	F	Davis Stephen	165	fisherman	44	682 "
	G	Matera Fred	165	bartender	37	549 "
	H	Matera Louise—†	165	housewife	37	549 "
	K	McNevin Isabel—†	167	"	44	here
	L	Regan Daniel	167A	operator	21	"
	M	Regan John J	167A	laborer	45	"

Page.	Letter.	FULL NAME.	Residence, Jan. 1, 1938.	Occupation.	Supposed Age.	Reported Residence, Jan. 1, 1937. Street and Number.

Byron Street—Continued

Page.	Letter.	FULL NAME.	Residence, Jan. 1, 1938.	Occupation.	Supposed Age.	Reported Residence, Jan. 1, 1937.
	N	Guthrie Bertha—†	169	housewife	36	837 Saratoga
	O	Guthrie Furn T	169	engineer	53	837 "
	P	Simonson Elizabeth—†	169A	housewife	27	here
	R	Simonson Joseph	169A	laborer	29	"
	S	Gallagher Catherine F—†	198	housewife	62	"
	T	Gallagher Catherine F—†	198	bookkeeper	34	"
	U	Gallagher Fred	198	salesman	21	"
	V	Gallagher Thomas F	198	retired	69	
	W	Gallagher Thomas F	198	laborer	29	
	X	Norton Elizabeth A—†	200	housewife	63	"
	Y	Norton James T	200	laborer	61	
	Z	Norton William F	200	merchant	47	"
1246						
	A	Norton Mary E—†	201	housewife	59	"
	B	Norton Mary E—†	201	teacher	24	
	C	Norton Thomas M	201	machinist	70	"
	D	Niland Anna M—†	202	principal	69	"
	E	Crowley Ellen T—†	206	waitress	21	754 Saratoga
	F	Crowley James F	206	janitor	25	754 "
	G	Crowley Margaret M—†	206	student	21	754 "
	H	Crowley Mary E—†	206	stenographer	27	754 "
	K	Crowley Patrick	206	engineer	63	754 "
	L	Cotter John H	206	fireman	46	here
	M	Manning Mary—†	206	housekeeper	78	"
	N	*Mendoza Bartholomew F	206	longshoreman	68	"
	O	Mendoza John J	206	clerk	26	
	P	*Mendoza Mary—†	206	housewife	59	"
	S	Cross James E	210	painter	20	440 Lubec
	R	Mullen Charles B	210	chauffeur	30	here
	T	Mullen Mabel T—†	210	housewife	24	"
	U	DiNuzzio Caroline—†	210	"	38	"
	V	DiNuzzio Francis	210	laborer	20	
	W	DiNuzzio Harry	210	operator	48	

Coleridge Street

Page.	Letter.	FULL NAME.	Residence, Jan. 1, 1938.	Occupation.	Supposed Age.	Reported Residence, Jan. 1, 1937.
	Y	Laskey Ellen—†	120	housewife	69	here
	Z	Laskey Raymond	120	machinist	24	"
1247						
	A	O'Leary Grace—†	124	housewife	42	"
	B	O'Leary Timothy	124	guard	51	

Page.	Letter.	FULL NAME.	Residence, Jan. 1, 1938.	Occupation.	Supposed Age.	Reported Residence, Jan. 1, 1937. Street and Number.

Coleridge Street—Continued

	C	Page Arthur J	126	retired	78	here
	D	Page Dorothy J—†	126	teacher	32	"
	E	Page Muriel M—†	126	"	29	"
	F	Page Sarah H—†	126	housewife	74	"
	G	McNabb Hugh J	130	policeman	40	"
	H	McNabb Madeline—†	130	housewife	37	"
	K	*Peterson Agnes—†	134	"	59	136 Coleridge
	L	Peterson Gilbert	134	machinist	25	136 "
	M	Lyons Gerald	134	fireman	31	here
	N	Lyons Ruth—†	134	housewife	29	"
	P	Roche Elizabeth—†	136	"	44	"
	R	Roche Michael T	136	clerk	51	
	S	Sloan Charles H	138	storekeeper	45	"
	T	Sloan Rose L—†	138	"	43	"
	U	McWilliams John H	138	carpenter	31	"
	V	McWilliams Marguerite—†	138	housewife	26	"
	W	Sullivan Christopher	148	painter	45	185 Wordsworth
	X	Sullivan Elizabeth—†	148	housewife	44	185 "
	Y	Czarnetski Florence—†	148	"	44	here
	Z	Czarnetski Fred	148	clerk	39	"
1248						
	A	Kline George H	148	painter	50	
	B	Kline Mary A—†	148	housewife	76	"
	C	Fowler Marcella—†	149	typist	36	
	D	Peterson Fred	149	clerk	27	
	E	Scigliano Frances—†	149	housewife	33	"
	F	Scigliano Frank	149	painter	32	
	G	McGunigle Phillip	149	laborer	59	
	H	Scigliano Alfred	149	attorney	37	"
	K	Scigliano Edward	149	operator	34	"
	L	Scigliano Eugene	149	student	21	
	M	Scigliano Joseph	149	painter	27	
	N	Scigliano Louise—†	149	student	23	
	O	Anderson John E	156	machinist	50	"
	P	Anderson Lilly—†	156	housewife	43	"
	R	Anderson Virginia—†	156	waitress	21	
	S	Barnard Charles H	156	seaman	22	
	T	Barnard Chester	156	millwright	47	"
	U	Barnard Chester S	156	machinist	22	"
	V	Barnard Marion—†	156	housewife	41	"
	W	Barnard Ruth W—†	156	saleswoman	20	"

Page.	Letter.	Full Name.	Residence, Jan. 1, 1938.	Occupation.	Supposed Age.	Reported Residence, Jan. 1, 1937. Street and Number.
		Coleridge Street—Continued				
	X	Musil Andrew H	157	retired	56	here
	Y	Musil Letitia—†	157	housewife	51	"
	Z	Musil Thomas H	157	ballplayer	23	"
1249						
	A	Harrington Dorothy M–†	157	housewife	29	196 Leyden
	B	Harrington Thaddeus L	157	clerk	31	196 "
	C	Ballam Evelyn R—†	163	housekeeper	35	here
	D	Leahy James H	163	electrician	40	"
	K	Lampman Mary—†	165	housekeeper	27	"
	E	Nagle Edward	165	clerk	20	"
	F	Nagle Harriett—†	165	housewife	51	"
	G	Nagle Horace	165	foreman	52	
	H	Nagle John	165	painter	21	
	L	Breault Arthur	167	chauffeur	26	"
	M	Breault John	167	longshoreman	58	"
	N	Breault Margaret—†	167	saleswoman	24	"
	O	Breault Mary—†	167	housewife	53	"
	P	Guptill Lewis H	167	operator	60	
	R	Reynolds Michael	167	laborer	50	"
	S	Brown Carrie—†	169	housewife	49	"
	T	Brown Ernest	169	clerk	50	
	U	Brown Lillian—†	169	"	20	
	V	Thompson Mary—†	171	housewife	48	"
	W	Thompson Mary—†	171	clerk	22	
	X	Thompson Robert	171	laborer	26	
	Y	Thompson S Carroll—†	171	teacher	24	
	Z	Shelton Constance I—†	173	saleswoman	26	"
1250						
	A	Shelton Elizabeth—†	173	housewife	70	"
	B	Bumpus Sarah—†	175	housekeeper	75	"
	C	McGunigle John E	176	mechanic	36	"
	D	McGunigle Robena—†	176	housewife	30	"
	E	Hicks Sebina—†	177	housekeeper	45	"
	F	Owens Charles W	177	laborer	65	"
		Cowper Street				
	M	Donohue Catherine—†	93	saleswoman	30	here
	N	Donohue Charles P	93	painter	32	"
	O	Donohue Jessie—†	93	housewife	61	"
	P	Donohue Rita—†	93	saleswoman	21	"

Page.	Letter.	Full Name.	Residence, Jan. 1, 1938.	Occupation.	Supposed Age.	Reported Residence, Jan. 1, 1937. Street and Number.

Cowper Street—Continued

Page.	Letter.	Full Name.	Residence, Jan. 1, 1938.	Occupation.	Supposed Age.	Reported Residence, Jan. 1, 1937. Street and Number.
	R	Donohue Thomas T	93	watchman	64	here
	S	Hildreth Mildred—†	93	packer	27	1 Monmouth
	U	Barron Ellen E—†	93	clerk	20	here
	T	Barron Ellen P—†	93	operator	47	"
	V	*Dieso Margaret—†	94	housewife	33	"
	W	Dieso Nicola	94	laborer	43	
	X	Roach George A	94	stevedore	46	"
	Y	Roach William A	94	"	48	
	Z	*Treunfio Concetta—†	94	housewife	28	"
1251						
	A	Treunfio Paul	94	laborer	41	
	B	Cataldo Albert F	95	"	34	
	C	Cataldo Dorothy—†	95	housewife	28	"
	D	Gagin Henry A	95	clerk	36	
	E	Gagin Josephine—†	95	housewife	26	"
	F	Gagin William	95	laborer	46	
	G	Cooper Albert	97	brakeman	51	"
	H	Cooper Eva—†	97	housewife	43	"
	K	Fenton John	97	painter	65	
	L	Trautz John G	97	"	34	
	M	Trautz Margaret—†	97	housewife	55	"
	N	Trautz Mary—†	97	"	33	"
	O	Jones Marion A—†	98	at home	32	209 Trenton
	P	Torredinare Adelaide—†	98	housewife	38	here
	R	Torredinare Frank	98	barber	42	"
	S	*Torredinare Michael	98	shoemaker	53	"
	T	Torredinare Rose A—†	98	teacher	20	
	U	McWilliams Daniel	99	retired	72	
	V	McWilliams Mary A—†	99	housewife	71	"
	W	McWilliams Mary A—†	99	operator	33	"
	X	Doherty Anna M—†	99	housewife	45	"
	Y	Doherty John N	99	student	20	
	Z	Doherty John P	99	mechanic	54	"
1252						
	A	Pascucci Antonio	100	seaman	25	
	B	Pascucci Mary—†	100	housewife	26	"
	C	Gilday Alice—†	100	at home	28	
	D	Gilday John	100	laborer	59	
	F	Lowell Ella F—†	101	at home	77	
	H	Williams Agnes M—†	104	housewife	48	"
	K	Williams John A	104	custodian	49	"

Page.	Letter.	Full Name.	Residence, Jan. 1, 1938.	Occupation.	Supposed Age.	Reported Residence, Jan. 1, 1937. Street and Number.

Cowper Street—Continued

	L	Love Merton W	106	retired	74	here
	M	Ray Tavia D—†	106	at home	67	"
	N	Holdsworth Helena R—†	110	housewife	43	"
	O	Holdsworth John R	110	clerk	44	
	P	Forshner Mabel B—†	114	at home	53	
	R	Osborne Dorothy E—†	114	housewife	29	"
	S	Osborne Merrill E	114	clerk	37	
	T	DeCosta Leander—†	118	housewife	75	"
	U	DeCosta Mary—†	118	at home	54	
	V	Hubbard Josephine—†	118	"	50	
	W	Bennett Clifford S	118	carpenter	40	"
	X	Bennett Jessie I—†	118	housewife	42	"
	Y	Wilson Douglas B	151	fireman	36	
	Z	Wilson Gertrude D—†	151	housewife	35	"
1253						
	A	Morgan Edmund J	151	laborer	39	
	B	Morgan Frances M—†	151	housewife	35	"
	C	McLean Mary M—†	155	"	45	
	D	McLean Thomas W	155	custodian	51	"
	E	Butt Dorothy—†	172	stenographer	27	"
	F	Butt James	172	laborer	28	"
	G	Butt Robert	172	"	38	Saugus
	H	Butt William	172	"	44	here
	K	Bagley Henry S	174	"	58	Michigan
	L	Bagley Sarah A—†	174	housewife	68	"
	M	DuWors Ellen E—†	174	"	72	here
	N	DuWors Robert J	174	retired	72	"
	O	Bagley Catherine G—†	176	housewife	59	"
	P	Bagley Catherine G—†	176	at home	23	
	R	Bagley James E	176	laborer	60	
	S	Bagley Robert J	176	plumber	32	
	T	Bagley William M	176	attorney	30	"
	U	Bagley Richard W	176	foreman	35	
	V	Bagley Ruth F—†	176	housewife	33	"
	W	Banks James E	177	laborer	66	
	X	Banks Mary A—†	177	housewife	62	"
	Y	Hagemeister Fred C	177	laborer	49	
	Z	Hagemeister James E	177	mechanic	22	"
1254						
	A	Hagemeister Josephine A—†	177	housewife	44	"
	B	Chase Annie R—†	179	"	50	

Page.	Letter.	FULL NAME.	Residence, Jan. 1, 1938.	Occupation.	Supposed Age.	Reported Residence, Jan. 1, 1937. Street and Number.

Cowper Street—Continued

	C	Chase Edward D	179	chauffeur	24	here
	D	Chase Florence A—†	179	lampmaker	20	"
	E	Chase George N	179	mechanic	51	"
	F	Chase George N, jr	179	"	22	
	G	Chase Warren	179	"	28	
	H	Harrison James J	179	laundryman	37	"
	K	Shea Eva M—†	181	housewife	31	"
	L	Shea William M	181	draftsman	34	"
	M	O'Donnell Elizabeth—†	181	housewife	25	165 Byron
	N	O'Donnell Thomas G	181	chauffeur	28	165 "
	O	Moran Lawrence J	184	inspector	49	here
	P	Moran Mary E—†	184	housewife	47	"
	R	Ryan Michael J	184	accountant	45	"

Homer Street

	S	Shea John J	58	operator	46	here
	T	Shea Marguerite—†	58	housewife	42	"
	U	Rogan Abbie J—†	58	housekeeper	69	"
	V	Rogan Abbie J—†	58	clerk	36	"
	W	Rogan Mary A—†	58	operator	31	
	X	Welch John F	63	publisher	47	"
	Y	Welch Lillian—†	63	housewife	42	"
	Z	Johnson James P	63	laborer	44	
1255						
	A	Johnson Margaret—†	63	housewife	38	"
	B	Johnson Mary T—†	63	housekeeper	79	Winthrop
	C	McLaughlin Edward J	64	electrician	54	here
	D	*Thompson Mary J—†	66	housewife	40	"
	E	Thompson Richard F	66	fireman	44	"
	F	Martin Edith L—†	67	housewife	43	"
	G	Martin Ellsworth J	67	clerk	49	"
	H	Stack John E	67	repairman	26	740 Saratoga
	K	Mealey Francis	69	clerk	37	here
	L	Mealey Mary—†	69	housewife	38	"
	M	Curran Andrew	69	corker	42	"
	N	*Curran Karin	69	laborer	50	
	O	Foley Joseph	69	"	27	
	P	Foley Mary—†	69	housewife	50	"
	R	Foley Patrick	69	chauffeur	25	"

Page.	Letter.	Full Name.	Residence, Jan. 1, 1938.	Occupation.	Supposed Age.	Reported Residence. Jan. 1, 1937. Street and Number.

Homer Street—Continued

Page.	Letter.	Full Name.	Residence, Jan. 1, 1938.	Occupation.	Supposed Age.	Reported Residence. Jan. 1, 1937. Street and Number.
	S	Mullaney Alice—†	69	operator	38	here
	T	Mullaney Bernard	69	laborer	32	"
	U	Mullaney James	69	printer	46	"
	V	Mullaney Louise—†	69	operator	47	"
	W	Mullaney Mary—†	69	housewife	70	"
	X	MacDonald Irene—†	70	"	26	2 Saratoga pl
	Y	MacDonald John	70	laborer	29	2 "
	Z	Supple Ellen T—†	71	housekeeper	59	here
1256						
	A	Doherty Henry J	71	wireman	32	"
	B	Doherty James G	71	painter	30	Lynn
	C	Doherty Marion F—†	71	housewife	28	here
	D	Czarnetzki Louis M	71	policeman	43	744 Benningt'n
	E	Czarnetzki Mary A—†	71	housewife	41	744 "
	G	Kiley Delores—†	72	at home	79	here
	H	Hartery Andrew T	72	plumber	47	"
	K	Hartery Eleanor T—†	72	housewife	44	"
	L	O'Hanley Elizabeth—†	73	"	38	
	M	O'Hanley John W	73	machinist	38	"
	N	Phalan John	73	engineer	37	Winthrop
	O	Brown Sarah—†	73	domestic	48	here
	P	Boyce Bridget—†	73	housewife	42	"
	R	Boyce Joseph	73	operator	42	"
	T	Miller Charles W	74	laborer	43	
	U	Miller Mary J—†	74	housewife	39	"
	V	Hughes Eleanor M—†	75	operator	22	
	W	Hughes Ellen M—†	75	housewife	44	"
	X	Hughes John W	75	clerk	44	
	Y	Hughes Mary S—†	75	saleswoman	20	"
	Z	Wren Thomas	75	B F D	57	
1257						
	C	Bouchie Jean—†	76	housekeeper	24	Connecticut
	A	Elias Marie—†	76	housewife	27	14 Laconia
	B	Elias Michael	76	repairman	28	14 "
	D	Laskey Helen—†	78	housewife	36	here
	E	Laskey Lloyd	78	policeman	36	"
	F	Hartery Eleanor—†	78	housewife	31	668 Benningt'n
	G	Hartery William J	78	plumber	35	668 "
	H	Ricciardi Annie—†	82	housewife	41	here
	K	Ricciardi Antonio	82	laborer	40	"
	L	Ricciardi Soccorso	82	"	56	"

Page.	Letter.	Full Name.	Residence, Jan. 1, 1938.	Occupation.	Supposed Age.	Reported Residence, Jan. 1, 1937. Street and Number.

Homer Street—Continued

Page.	Letter.	Full Name.	Residence, Jan. 1, 1938.	Occupation.	Supposed Age.	Reported Residence, Jan. 1, 1937. Street and Number.
	M	Kinsela Emma F—†	82	housewife	60	here
	N	Kinsela Emma H—†	82	teacher	25	"
	O	Kinsela James R	82	pressman	20	"
	P	Rothwell John J	82	retired	71	
	R	Duffy Elizabeth—†	83	housewife	31	"
	S	Duffy John P	83	foreman	30	
	T	*Meuse Estelle—†	83	housewife	43	"
	U	Meuse Raymond	83	engineer	49	"
	V	Meuse Raymond	83	laborer	21	
	W	Burns Edward	83	operator	24	"
	X	Burns John	83	guard	56	
	Y	Burns Martha—†	83	housewife	49	"
	Z	Burns Thomas	83	laborer	21	
1258						
	A	Miles Auranus F	87	operator	40	
	B	Morrison Adelia—†	87	housewife	72	"
	C	Morrison Charles W	87	timekeeper	47	"
	D	Mullen Bernard M	90	realtor	57	"
	E	Mullen Cecelia B—†	90	operator	25	
	F	Mullen Helena A—†	90	housewife	53	"
	G	Mullen Herbert F	90	chauffeur	26	"
	H	Cambria Luigi	91	cabinetmaker	54	"
	K	Cambria Mary—†	91	housewife	44	"
	L	Cambria Peter	91	clerk	29	
	M	Storin Bertha A—†	91	stenographer	26	"
	N	Storin Ellen C—†	91	housekeeper	50	"
	O	Storin George W	91	laborer	20	"
	P	McGurin Charles A	92	clerk	21	Everett
	R	McGurin John J	92	retired	62	here
	S	Murphy James P	92	policeman	37	"
	T	Murphy Sadie H—†	92	housewife	36	"
	U	*Scandurra Joseph	93	cabinetmaker	56	"
	V	*Scandurra Josephine—†	93	housewife	55	"
	W	Scandurra Peter	93	laborer	23	"
	X	Belli Nicholas	93	"	25	205 Orient av
	Y	Belli Rose—†	93	housewife	26	205 "
	Z	Gibbs Anna—†	94	"	37	here
1259						
	A	Gibbs Ivy	94	fireman	36	"
	B	Ferry Manuel	94A	salesman	50	"
	C	Newman Esther H—†	95	clerk	23	

Page.	Letter.	Full Name.	Residence, Jan. 1, 1938.	Occupation.	Supposed Age.	Reported Residence, Jan. 1, 1937. Street and Number.

Homer Street—Continued

Page.	Letter.	Full Name.	Residence, Jan. 1, 1938.	Occupation.	Supposed Age.	Reported Residence, Jan. 1, 1937. Street and Number.
	D	*Newman Gustaf	95	oiler	68	here
	E	Newman John H	95	machinist	25	"
	F	Sheehan Daniel H	96	clerk	36	125 Wordsworth
	G	Sheehan Mary A—†	96	housewife	34	125 "
	H	Hoff Karl	96A	laborer	32	here
	K	Hoff Marguerite—†	96A	housewife	25	"
	L	Harrington Sadie—†	97	"	51	"
	M	Harrington William H	97	laborer	65	
	N	Campbell Ann—†	99	clerk	21	
	O	McCormack Mary—†	99	housewife	55	"
	P	McCormack Raymond J	99	salesman	31	"
	R	Rowe Frederick A	101	mechanic	46	"
	S	Rowe George H	101	retired	79	
	T	Keating Daniel—†	103	laborer	55	
	U	Leonard Esther J—†	103	housewife	56	"
	V	Leonard Esther J—†	103	librarian	27	
	W	Leonard Mary M—†	103	clerk	21	
	X	Leonard Nicholas F	103	manager	57	"
	Y	Clayton Charles W	105	retired	65	
	Z	Clayton Constance M—†	105	at home	26	
1260						
	A	Clayton Dora M—†	105	housewife	63	"
	B	Marshall William J	107	B F D	56	
	C	Moran Mary L—†	107	at home	72	
	D	Riley Annie T—†	107	housewife	69	"
	E	Riley William J	107	retired	70	

Horace Street

Page.	Letter.	Full Name.	Residence, Jan. 1, 1938.	Occupation.	Supposed Age.	Reported Residence, Jan. 1, 1937. Street and Number.
	G	O'Connell Edmund F	53	laborer	22	here
	H	O'Connell William J	53	storekeeper	50	"
	K	Quinn George E	57	laborer	65	"
	L	Quinn Marjorie—†	57	nurse	30	"
	M	Rogers George	59	mechanic	41	"
	N	Rogers Mary—†	59	housewife	35	"
	O	O'Connell Lloyd	60	machinist	45	"
	P	O'Connell Matilda—†	60	housewife	43	"
	R	Smith Albert E	63	cook	57	
	S	Smith Alice M—†	63	housewife	55	"
	T	Hourigan Michael J	63	druggist	65	
	U	Coughlin Joseph	64	laborer	27	

Horace Street—Continued

Page.	Letter.	Full Name.	Residence, Jan. 1, 1938.	Occupation.	Supposed Age.	Reported Residence, Jan. 1, 1937. Street and Number.
	v	Coughlin Rena—†	64	housewife	24	here
	w	Gillespie Michael F	64	oiler	60	"
	x	McHugh Irene M—†	64	at home	40	"
	y	Coughlin Catherine G—†	65	housewife	56	"
	z	Coughlin Frank J	65	accountant	36	"
1261						
	A	Coughlin Helen—†	65	at home	31	
	B	Coughlin Mary—†	65	"	21	
	C	Coughlin Michael F	65	engineer	57	
	D	Gillespie Gertrude—†	65	accountant	33	"
	E	Fitzpatrick Anna—†	67	housewife	44	"
	F	Fitzpatrick Joseph	67	dealer	50	
	H	Norton Mary V—†	70	at home	22	
	K	Norton Nellie C—†	70	housewife	57	"
	L	Norton William F	70	operator	58	"
	M	Decker George M	70	proprietor	39	6 St Andrew rd
	N	Decker Joseph	70	policeman	43	6 "
	O	Sullivan Francis C	70	attendant	28	585 Benningt'n
	P	Sullivan Mary A—†	70	housewife	29	585 "
	S	Joyce Annie M—†	73	"	68	here
	T	Joyce Ellen M—†	73	"	28	"
	U	Joyce Joseph C	73	operator	33	"
	V	Joyce John F	73	painter	41	
	W	Joyce John F	73	clerk	20	
	X	McWilliams Mary M—†	74	housewife	28	"
	Y	McWilliams Richard D	74	laborer	35	
	Z	Austin Mary M—†	74	housewife	50	"
1262						
	A	Austin Richard J	74	laborer	50	
	B	Middleton Arthur F	75	clerk	23	
	C	Middleton Arthur L	75	laborer	54	
	D	Middleton Mary B—†	75	housewife	56	"
	E	Clark Doris E—†	75	nurse	23	
	F	Clark Janet D—†	75	housewife	54	"
	G	Clark Ruth F—†	75	secretary	29	"
	H	Clark Willard D	75	student	20	"
	L	Sweeney Emily M—†	77	housewife	26	"
	K	Sweeney Wilfred	77	packer	27	
	M	Farmer Ann M—†	77	typist	22	
	N	Farmer Mary E—†	77	housewife	50	"
	O	Farmer Thomas J	77	laborer	53	

Page.	Letter.	FULL NAME.	Residence, Jan. 1, 1938.	Occupation.	Supposed Age.	Reported Residence, Jan. 1, 1937. Street and Number.

Horace Street—Continued

	P	Corello Angelina—†	78	housewife	30	here
	R	Corello Erminio	78	laborer	38	"
	S	Sacco Jeremiah	78	retired	69	"
	T	Testa Albert	78	student	21	"
	U	Testa Florence—†	78	housewife	38	"
	V	Testa Joseph	78	laborer	48	
	W	McMillan Collin J	79	salesman	36	"
	X	McMillan Edith E—†	79	housewife	31	"
	Y	*McMillan Elizabeth A—†	79	"	62	
	Z	O'Donnell Mary C—†	79	at home	40	
1263						
	A	O'Donnell Rose E—†	79	"	69	
	B	Graf Catherine—†	80	housewife	69	"
	C	Graf Valentino	80	retired	69	
	D	Moran John J	80	laborer	59	
	E	Moran Joseph F	80	"	61	
	F	Moran Mary—†	80	housewife	56	"
	G	Flanagan Anna—†	81	"	39	
	H	Flanagan John	81	decorator	45	"
	K	Gilleo Anna—†	81	housewife	43	"
	L	Gilleo Edith A—†	81	clerk	30	
	M	Gilleo Martin	81	retired	82	
	N	Cunningham Eleanor—†	82	housewife	43	"
	O	Cunningham Timothy T	82	laborer	44	
	P	Doherty Margaret D—†	82	at home	77	
	R	Christopher Bridget F—†	84	housewife	50	"
	S	Christopher Dorothy M—†	84	packer	22	
	T	Christopher John	84	laborer	52	
	U	Christopher Joseph F	84	"	23	
	V	Christopher William H	84	policeman	30	"
	W	Kelly Beatrice—†	87	housewife	42	"
	X	Kelly Richard F	87	custodian	42	"
	Y	Reilly Agnes—†	87	housewife	68	"
	Z	Reilly Margaret L—†	87	stenographer	33	"
1264						
	A	Reilly William J	87	chauffeur	44	"
	B	Barnes Mary J—†	87	clerk	39	
	C	Kelly Frances L—†	87	"	32	
	D	Kelly Frances M—†	87	housewife	75	"
	E	Kelly Richard	87	retired	80	
	F	Aitken Harold	91	operator	29	"

Page.	Letter.	FULL NAME.	Residence, Jan. 1, 1938.	Occupation.	Supposed Age.	Reported Residence, Jan. 1, 1937. Street and Number.

Horace Street—Continued

	G	Aitken Loretta—†	91	housewife	28	here
	H	Hines Anna R—†	91	teacher	33	"
	K	Hines Catherine A—†	91	housewife	73	"
	L	Hines Edward J	91	teacher	49	
	M	Ahearn Margaret—†	95	housewife	40	"
	N	Ahearn Owen F	95	laborer	42	"
	O	Grimshaw Celia—†	97	housewife	37	76 Homer
	P	Grimshaw James	97	chauffeur	38	76 "
	R	Rothwell Louis	97	operator	34	here
	S	Rothwell Mary—†	97	housewife	33	"

Milton Street

	T	Colosi Antonetta—†	30	housewife	35	here
	U	Colosi Salvatore	30	laborer	42	"
	V	LaFay Frederick	30	"	26	45 Milton
	W	Murphy Florence—†	30	housewife	46	45 "
	X	Gallagher Eileen F—†	34	"	32	here
	Y	Gallagher Joseph N	34	laborer	33	"
	Z	Riley Joseph L	34	"	39	"
1265						
	A	Robicheau Dorothy—†	38	housewife	38	"
	B	Robicheau Peter	38	laborer	36	
	D	Nowosielski Alfred	45	student	20	
	E	*Nowosielski Boleslawa—†	45	housewife	42	"
	F	Nowosielski Walter	45	mechanic	46	"
	G	Warrino Amerise—†	45	housewife	30	"
	H	Warrino Dominic	45	laborer	42	
	L	Callahan Catherine—†	134	housewife	65	"
	M	Flynn Mary A—†	134	operator	34	"
	N	Sammon Christopher	137	seaman	35	
	O	Sammon James	137	"	45	
	P	Sammon Joseph	137	salesman	42	"
	R	Sammon Mary—†	137	housewife	73	"

Moore Street

	S	Greenwood Mary B—†	73	housewife	34	here
	T	Shannon Arthur	73	engineer	29	"
	U	Shannon Catherine—†	73	housewife	66	"
	V	Shannon Francis	73	laborer	25	

Page.	Letter.	Full Name.	Residence, Jan. 1, 1938.	Occupation.	Supposed Age.	Reported Residence, Jan. 1, 1937. Street and Number.

Moore Street—Continued

	W	Shannon Margaret—†	73	secretary	32	here
	X	McCaffrey Anna G—†	75	housewife	71	"
	Y	Rich Evelyn C—†	75	"	30	"
	Z	Rich Frank J	75	superintendent	35	"
1266						
	A	Sheehan Christopher A	75	manager	43	"
	B	Sheehan James H	75	clerk	37	
	D	Carlton Ellen H—†	76	operator	37	"
	E	Sullivan Florence W	76	seaman	57	
	F	Sullivan Mary A—†	76	domestic	36	"
	G	Stott Jessie G—†	78	housewife	26	"
	H	Stott John W	78	electrician	27	"
	L	Berry James	84	laborer	30	
	M	Berry Mary—†	84	housewife	28	"
	N	Stott Charlotte E—†	84	"	37	
	O	Stott Harry	84	mechanic	58	"
	P	Porter Elda—†	88	housewife	27	"
	R	Porter William	88	chemist	27	
	T	Rich John J	91	laborer	28	
	U	Rich Peter	91	"	51	
	V	Campbell Alice—†	91	housewife	38	"
	W	Campbell William	91	laborer	39	"
	X	Cohan Elizabeth E—†	92	housewife	83	"
	Y	Curran Edgar L	92	laborer	51	
	Z	Curran Mary M—†	92	housewife	53	"
1267						
	A	MacDonald Adelaide—†	92	bookkeeper	25	"
	B	MacDonald Clarence B	92	mechanic	20	"
	C	MacDonald Emma—†	92	housewife	45	"
	D	Fraga George	93	bookbinder	38	"
	E	Fraga Mary A—†	93	housewife	36	"
	F	Vieara George	96	longshoreman	37	"
	G	Vicara Mary—†	96	housewife	32	"
	H	Fougere Ethel L—†	98	"	36	28 Monmouth
	K	Fougere Philip A	98	cook	37	28 "
	L	O'Connell Arthur	106	welder	24	60 Horace
	O	O'Connell Catherine—†	106	housewife	22	60 "
	P	O'Connell William E	106	salesman	25	Winthrop
	M	Riley Helen T—†	106	housewife	29	here
	N	Riley Thomas A	106	mechanic	31	"
	R	Donahue Elizabeth M—†	107	housewife	35	"

Page.	Letter.	Full Name.	Residence, Jan. 1, 1938.	Occupation.	Supposed Age.	Reported Residence, Jan. 1, 1937. Street and Number.

Moore Street—Continued

	S	Donahue George F	107	oiler	37	here
	T	Vaugh John J	107	salesman	45	"
	U	Vaugh Pauline—†	107	housewife	40	"
	V	Costa Agnes—†	107	"	41	
	W	Costa John	107	painter	49	
	X	Costa John J	107	laborer	21	
	Y	Costa Manuel	107	"	53	
	Z	Ryan Peter	107	chauffeur	40	"
1268						
	A	Tassinari Horace V	108	"	27	
	B	Tassinari Maria—†	108	housewife	26	"
	C	Cotte Joseph	108	manufacturer	32	"
	D	Cotte Julia—†	108	housewife	32	"
	E	Dutra Eleanor M—†	109	"	35	
	F	Dutra John L	109	mechanic	46	"
	G	*Lovell Iva—†	109	housewife	36	"
	H	Lovell Raymond	109	cutter	36	
	K	*Rose Julia—†	109	housewife	59	"
	L	Gillis Anna E—†	110	operator	38	"
	M	Gillis Anthony A	110	chauffeur	37	"
	N	Gillis Jennie—†	110	housewife	71	"
	O	Lockwood Patricia—†	110	operator	21	"
	P	Sluckas John	111	mechanic	48	"
	R	DeLory Alice—†	111	housewife	33	247 Princeton
	S	DeLory Joseph	111	painter	42	247 "
	T	Currie Henry	112	fireman	39	here
	U	Currie Mildred E—†	112	housewife	37	"
	W	Driscoll Benjamin	113	storekeeper	60	"
	X	Driscoll Nellie—†	113	housewife	54	"
	V	Boyd Elizabeth—†	113	"	45	
	Y	Edwards George	114	retired	76	
	Z	Edwards George, jr	114	laborer	29	
1269						
	A	Edwards Jessie—†	114	housewife	69	"
	B	Edwards Walter	114	guard	35	
	C	Swift Margaret A—†	114	housewife	51	"
	D	Swift Margaret A—†	114	stenographer	25	"
	E	Swift Robert	114	laborer	51	"
	F	Walsh Alice M—†	115	housewife	33	"
	G	Walsh Patrick J	115	letter carrier	43	"
	H	Hawco Angela R—†	115	stenographer	29	"

Page.	Letter.	FULL NAME.	Residence, Jan. 1, 1938.	Occupation.	Supposed Age.	Reported Residence, Jan. 1, 1937. Street and Number.

Moore Street—Continued

	K	Hawco Mary B—†	115	housewife	67	here
	L	Hawco Mary L—†	115	domestic	26	"
	M	Hawco Thomas	115	fireman	64	"
	N	Green Mary—†	116	housewife	45	"
	O	Green William	116	laborer	49	
	P	Ritenour John	116	seaman	26	
	R	Ritenour Lena—†	116	housewife	23	"
	S	Clark George F	116	janitor	57	
	T	Clark Mabel—†	116	housewife	36	"
	U	Anderson John	116	fisherman	70	296 Paris
	V	Anderson Susan—†	116	housewife	66	296 "
	W	D'Avella Helen—†	118	"	23	here
	X	D'Avella Vincent	118	operator	24	"
	Y	Vieria Emilio	118	retired	66	"
	Z	Vieria Emily—†	118	housewife	64	"
1270						
	A	Heck Margaret E—†	118	"	64	
	B	Schroider Mary—†	118	housewife	60	"
	D	Bunn Edward	120	dealer	30	
	E	Bunn Florence—†	120	housewife	28	"
	F	Whitehead Vernice—†	120	waitress	32	
	G	*Deptula Joseph	120	laborer	56	
	H	*Deptula Mary A—†	120	housewife	50	"
	K	Deptula Walter	120	operator	28	

Wordsworth Street

	L	Benoit Augustus	125	laborer	23	67 Wordsworth
	M	Benoit Mary—†	125	housewife	23	114 Lexington
	N	Mottola Albert	125	laborer	21	391 Chelsea
	O	Mottola Archangel—†	125	housewife	47	391 "
	P	Mottola Ciriaco	125	operator	47	391 "
	R	Russo Frank	125	plasterer	47	here
	S	Russo Mary—†	125	housewife	36	"
	T	Doyle Alfred	127	carpenter	55	"
	U	Doyle Ella—†	127	housewife	50	"
	V	Doyle Greta—†	127	stenographer	23	"
	W	Doyle Joseph	127	laborer	24	"
	X	Doyle Thomas	127	"	20	
	Y	Gormley John J	128	longshoreman	34	"
	Z	Gormley Mary—†	128	housewife	33	"

Page.	Letter.	Full Name.	Residence, Jan. 1, 1938.	Occupation.	Supposed Age.	Reported Residence, Jan. 1, 1937. Street and Number.

1271

Wordsworth Street—Continued

	A	Rawson Mildred—†	130	housewife	38	here
	B	Rawson William	130	laborer	42	"
	C	Higer Lottie—†	130	housewife	53	"
	D	Higer Rita—†	130	bookkeeper	21	"
	E	Higer Ruth—†	130	"	25	"
	F	Higer Samuel	130	pedler	54	
	G	Callahan John F	140	carpenter	30	"
	H	Callahan Margaret T—†	140	housewife	27	"
	K	Gannon Mary—†	142	"	35	
	L	Andrews Blanche E—†	148	operator	30	
	M	Andrews Charles E	148	laborer	28	
	N	Andrews Ernest	148	carpenter	54	"
	O	Andrews Helen—†	148	housewife	40	"
	P	Andrews John	148	chemist	20	
	R	McCarthy Dennis F	148	laborer	65	
	S	McCarthy Josephine—†	148	housewife	67	"
	T	Miller Peter F	154	laborer	54	602 Benningt'n
	U	Pearson Alice C—†	154	housewife	39	602 "
	V	Pearson Arthur A	154	guard	39	602 "
	W	Beaulieu Hannah S—†	158	housewife	32	N Hampshire
	X	Beaulieu Joseph A	158	laborer	36	"
	Y	O'Kane James	158	custodian	65	here
	Z	O'Kane Mary—†	158	housewife	63	"
1272						
	A	Hagemeister Eleanor—†	178	"	24	"
	B	Hagemeister Frederick	178	manager	24	177 Cowper
	C	Nutile John R	178	laborer	26	799 Saratoga
	D	Nutile Mary F—†	178	housewife	26	799 "
	E	Conry Henry	182	laborer	42	178 Wordsworth
	F	King Delia—†	182	seamstress	41	178 "
	G	Murphy Michael	182	retired	80	178 "
	H	Murphy Susan M—†	182	housewife	53	178 "
	K	Murphy Warren M	182	attendant	29	178 "
	L	Murphy William	182	laborer	53	178 "
	M	Breault John R	185	assembler	29	here
	N	Breault Phyllis—†	185	housewife	24	"
	O	Maglio Ida—†	185	"	49	"
	P	Maglio Louis	185	laborer	23	
	R	Maglio Michael	185	"	49	
	S	Potter Edith E—†	186	housewife	56	"

Page.	Letter.	FULL NAME.	Residence, Jan. 1, 1938.	Occupation.	Supposed Age.	Reported Residence, Jan. 1, 1937. Street and Number.

Wordsworth Street—Continued

	T	Potter Hannah M—†	186	at home	31	here
	U	Potter Joseph E	186	guard	54	"
	V	DiVito Thomas	189	laborer	51	"
	W	Kacos Carl	189	proprietor	34	"
	X	Kacos Louise—†	189	housewife	32	"
	Y	Gilleo Leo	189	chauffeur	34	157 Coleridge
	Z	Gilleo Leona—†	189	housewife	32	157 "

1(

17

18

19

2

2

6

Ward 1—Precinct 16

CITY OF BOSTON

LIST OF RESIDENTS
20 YEARS OF AGE AND OVER

(NON-CITIZENS INDICATED BY ASTERISK)
(FEMALES INDICATED BY DAGGER)

AS OF

JANUARY 1, 1938

JOSEPH F. TIMILTY, } *Listing*
FREDERIC E. DOWLING, } *Board.*

CITY OF BOSTON PRINTING DEPARTMENT

Page.	Letter.	Full Name.	Residence, Jan. 1, 1938.	Occupation.	Supposed Age.	Reported Residence, Jan. 1, 1937. Street and Number.
1284						
		Addison Street				
	B	Mingotti Delia—†	81	operator	29	here
	C	Mingotti Eugene	81	welder	31	"
	D	Mingotti Frances—†	81	operator	23	"
	E	*Mingotti Gilda—†	81	housewife	55	"
	F	Mingotti Mary—†	81	operator	28	
	G	Mingotti Nellie—†	81	"	26	
	H	*Mingotti Vincent	81	cooper	58	
	K	*Mikus Amelia—†	95–97	cutter	51	
	L	*Pontolilo Teofila—†	95–97	operator	58	"
	M	King Charles R	95–97	"	24	Winthrop
	N	King Dorothy M—†	95–97	housewife	20	"
	O	Fenton Franklin	95–97	expressman	42	here
	P	Fenton Irene—†	95–97	housewife	38	"
	R	*Biskupek Virginia—†	95–97	"	43	"
	S	Biskupek Walter	95–97	operator	46	"
	T	Emerald Amelia—†	95–97	housewife	60	257 Border
	U	Reed Almond A	95–97	retired	77	257 "
	V	Myers Edward	95–97	laborer	24	256 E Eagle
	W	Myers Lillian—†	95–97	operator	20	357 Chelsea
	X	Myers Melvin H	95–97	manager	23	256 E Eagle
	Y	*Halle Mary—†	95–97	operator	46	here
	Z	Halle Michael	95–97	"	49	"
1285						
	D	Lada Mieczystaw	95–97	laborer	42	
	E	*Lada Stella—†	95–97	housewife	42	"
	F	*Zebniak Tillie—†	95–97	operator	31	"
	G	Zebniak Wasil	95–97	laborer	38	
	H	O'Connell Mary—†	99	housewife	26	"
	K	O'Connell Peter	99	bartender	26	"
	L	Moran Frank A	101	laborer	32	
	M	Moran Mary E—†	101	housewife	62	"
	N	Moran Stephen A	101	laborer	67	
	O	Mills Albert L	103	garageman	31	"
	P	Mills Mabel—†	103	housewife	30	"
	R	Salemme Agnes M—†	105	"	20	
	S	Salemme Mario	105	tree surgeon	22	"
	T	Michilopoulos Andrew	113	restaurateur	42	"
	U	*Michilopoulos Sophie—†	113	housewife	48	"
	V	*Repetto John	117	retired	81	
	W	*Repetto Louise—†	117	housewife	65	"

Page.	Letter.	FULL NAME.	Residence, Jan. 1, 1938.	Occupation.	Supposed Age.	Reported Residence, Jan. 1, 1937. Street and Number.

Addison Street—Continued

	X	Repetto Peter	117	chauffeur	29	here
	Y	Lafferty Florence—†	117	student	20	"
	Z	Piscatelli Mabel—†	117	housewife	39	"
1286						
	A	Cooper Edwin L	117	galvanizer	21	837 Saratoga
	B	Fleming Eleanor—†	117	housewife	21	here
	C	Fleming Russell	117	laborer	27	"
	D	*Silva Harriet—†	121	operator	25	"
	E	Silva William	121	laborer	30	
	F	Turpin Louise—†	121	housewife	53	"
	G	Barker Annie—†	125	at home	79	
	H	Gilleo Joseph	125	policeman	45	"
	K	Gilleo Joseph F	125	chauffeur	20	"
	L	Gilleo Mary I—†	125	housewife	43	"
	M	Condon Catherine J—†	131	clerk	48	
	N	Condon Elizabeth M—†	131	saleswoman	52	"
	O	Condon Joanna I—†	131	clerk	50	
	P	Condon Mary—†	131	housewife	60	"
	R	Swaine Thomas	131	operator	58	
	S	Cox Estella R—†	135	housewife	41	"
	T	Cox George L	135	policeman	42	"

Bennington Street

	X	Calhoun George W	602	retired	65	here
	Y	Calhoun George W, jr	602	clerk	31	"
	Z	*Cestroni Achilles	604	carpenter	42	619 Benningt'n
1287						
	A	*Cestroni Concetta—†	604	housewife	32	619 "
	B	Ferrari Anthony	604	laborer	59	619 "
	C	Costello Benjamin	606	longshoreman	32	here
	D	Costello Mary E—†	606	housewife	27	"
	E	Dalton Agnes—†	606	"	25	"
	F	Dalton Edmund E	606	laborer	29	
	G	Sullivan Mary A—†	606	housekeeper	52	"
	H	Sullivan Alice M—†	610	housewife	37	"
	K	Sullivan Patrick H	610	laborer	51	
	L	Donnell Agnes—†	610	housewife	56	"
	M	Donnell Thomas J	610	waiter	54	
	O	Madden John	614	laborer	22	
	P	Madden Theresa—†	614	housewife	21	"

Page.	Letter.	Full Name.	Residence, Jan. 1, 1938.	Occupation.	Supposed Age.	Reported Residence, Jan. 1, 1937. Street and Number.

Bennington Street—Continued

	R	Follo Carlo	614	laborer	33	447 Frankfort
	S	Follo Carmella—†	614	housewife	26	447 "
	T	*Follo Maria—†	614	"	62	447 "
	U	Canino Susan—†	614	"	46	here
	V	Canino Thomas	614	shoemaker	46	"
	Z	Gately George L	624	physician	43	"
1288						
	A	Martin Marie E—†	624	clerk	28	"
	B	Moran Rita—†	624	singer	22	New York
	C	Tierney Margaret—†	624	seamstress	43	here
	D	Tierney Marie T—†	624	housekeeper	54	"
	E	D'Amico Delia—†	624	housewife	40	"
	F	D'Amico Pasquale	624	laborer	45	
	G	O'Neil Minnie—†	626	housekeeper	60	"
	H	Furningham William	626	blacksmith	52	126 Meridian
	K	Nickerson Anna—†	626	housewife	38	here
	L	*Nickerson Harold	626	laborer	38	"
	M	Garden Manuel	626	operator	31	333 E Eagle
	N	Garden Mary—†	626	housewife	21	333 "
	O	Levangie Joseph D	628	laborer	48	here
	P	Levangie Margaret—†	628	housewife	49	"
	R	Phillips Catherine A—†	628	"	67	"
	S	Phillips Ernest F	628	mechanic	27	"
	T	Phillips Katherine I—†	628	designer	46	"
	U	Crouse Edward C	628	seaman	40	90 Byron
	V	Crouse Melvin F	628	chauffeur	27	here
	W	Crouse Mildred M—†	628	housewife	27	"
	X	Winn Lester	630	laborer	52	"
	Y	Winn Mary—†	630	housewife	50	"
	Z	McInnis Alice—†	630	"	30	
1289						
	A	McInnis Herman	630	laborer	34	"
	B	McInnis Lawrence	630	electrician	33	435 Meridian
	C	Puopolo Anthony	630	operator	38	here
	D	Puopolo Rose—†	630	housewife	34	"
	E	McHatton Alexander J	632	laborer	53	"
	F	McHatton Mary—†	632	housewife	57	"
	G	*Korsak Anna—†	632	"	61	
	H	*Korsak Roman	632	operator	61	
	K	*Statkum Josephine—†	632	housewife	31	"
	L	Burns Agnes—†	632	"	50	

Page.	Letter.	Full Name.	Residence, Jan. 1, 1938.	Occupation.	Supposed Age.	Reported Residence, Jan. 1, 1937. Street and Number.

Bennington Street—Continued

	M	Burns Daniel P	632	operator	48	here
	N	Byrne Angela—†	632	saleswoman	22	"
	O	Byrne Nelson	632	clerk	35	Cambridge
	P	Keane Anna—†	634	housewife	34	here
	R	Keane James	634	laborer	34	"
	S	Briggs Charles A	634	salesman	57	66 Ferrin
	T	Briggs Mary M—†	634	housewife	44	66 "
	U	O'Leary Rita—†	634	hairdresser	21	66 "
	V	Livesey Hannah—†	634	housewife	51	here
	W	Livesey Robert	634	teacher	51	"
	Y*	Cooney Anna—†	656	housekeeper	65	144 Maverick
	Z	Cooney Lawrence	656	laborer	29	144 "
1290						
	A	Cooney Mary—†	656	housewife	28	144 "
	B	Wahlberg Axel	656	operator	36	here
	C	Wahlberg Madeline—†	656	housewife	35	"
	D	Flynn Grace M—†	656	"	58	"
	E	Flynn John P	656	chauffeur	34	"
	F	Flynn Joseph J	656	blacksmith	24	"
	G	Flynn Margaret T—†	656	operator	28	"
	H	Flynn Warren F	656	chauffeur	33	"
	K	Schleicker Carl H	660	baker	69	
	L	Schleicker Charlotte R—†	660	at home	35	
	M	Schleicker Theresa M—†	660	housewife	71	"
	N	Ivers Carroll A	660	laborer	22	103 Faywood
	O	Schleicker Henry W	660	chauffeur	37	here
	P	Schleicker Margaret—†	660	housewife	26	"
	R	Moran Edmund F	664	physician	57	"
	S	Moran Grace S—†	664	housewife	45	"
	T	Stapleton James	664	retired	79	
	U	Stapleton Mary B—†	664	housewife	46	"
	V	Callahan Daniel	666	operator	39	
	W	Callahan Lillian—†	666	housewife	37	"
	X	Santamaria Adeline—†	668	operator	26	
	Z	Santamaria Amelia—†	668	housewife	52	"
	Y	Santamaria Arthur	668	clerk	23	
1291						
	A	Santamaria Michael	668	barber	60	
	B	Bagley James, jr	670	attorney	36	"
	C	O'Connor James J	670	druggist	38	
	D	Donoghue Daniel J	670	operator	50	

Page.	Letter.	Full Name.	Residence, Jan. 1, 1938.	Occupation.	Supposed Age.	Reported Residence, Jan. 1, 1937. Street and Number.
		Bennington Street—Continued				
	E	Donoghue Daniel J, jr	670	investigator	20	here
	F	Donoghue Mary A—†	670	housewife	50	"
	H	DeBenedetto John	678	chauffeur	34	"
	K	DeBenedetto Louis	678	laborer	27	
	L	DeBenedetto Pasquale	678	"	65	
	M	Souza John	680	operator	23	
	N	Souza Julia—†	680	housewife	49	"
	O	Desautelle Cecil	680	clerk	23	
	P	Desautelle Elizabeth—†	680	housewife	64	"
	R	Desautelle Ruby—†	680	"	22	
	S	Roche George	680	laborer	50	
	T	Ferrandi Domenic	680	student	20	
	U	Ferrandi Marino	680	engineer	46	"
	V	*Ferrandi Rose—†	680	housewife	44	"
	W	Stone Chester	682	painter	29	653 Benningt'n
	X	Stone Dorothy—†	682	housewife	28	653 "
	Y	Edwards Katherine T—†	682	housekeeper	51	166 Leyden
	Z	O'Connell Mary—†	682	"	68	166 "
1292						
	A	Cain Bernard J	684	machinist	45	here
	B	Cain Eileen—†	684	housewife	35	"
	C	Jenkinson John	684	operator	28	California
	D	Roach Mary—†	684	"	31	243 Princeton
	E	Squires Josephine—†	684	"	25	Maine
	F	Western Edmund	686	laborer	60	here
	G	Western Kathleen—†	686	secretary	28	"
	H	Western Lena—†	686	housewife	62	"
	K	*Scotti Arthur	688	machinist	47	"
	L	Scotti Elvira—†	688	housewife	38	"
	M	Scotti John	688	machinist	22	"
	N	Scotti Walter W	688	salesman	23	"
	O	Vermynck Florent	690	operator	62	789 Saratoga
	P	Vermynck Hazel—†	690	housewife	35	Brockton
	R	Vermynck Joseph	690	upholsterer	36	"
	S	Vermynck Louisa—†	690	housewife	66	789 Saratoga
	T	Duff James	692	printer	45	here
	U	Yeates Sarah J—†	692	housekeeper	46	"
		Byron Street				
	V	LaCroix Amedee	45	machinist	48	here
	W	LaCroix Eleanor—†	45	stitcher	21	"

Page.	Letter.	FULL NAME.	Residence, Jan. 1, 1938.	Occupation.	Supposed Age.	Reported Residence, Jan. 1, 1937. Street and Number.

Byron Street—Continued

	X	LaCroix Stella—†	45	housewife	42	here
	Y	Taylor Frederick A	45	retired	69	810 Saratoga
	Z	Cataldo Charles J	48	physician	32	here
1293						
	A	Cataldo Helene—†	48	housewife	32	"
	B	Pasqua Carmella—†	49	"	26	
	C	Pasqua John J	49	operator	30	
	D	*Merullo Angelina—†	49	housewife	52	"
	E	Merullo Carmen	49	laborer	53	
	F	Merullo Leonard	49	student	20	
	G	Merullo Roland	49	operator	23	
	H	Brosnan Alice C—†	52	housewife	28	"
	K	Brosnan Eugene T	52	laborer	31	"
	L	Crowley William	52	machinist	68	"
	M	*Cataldo Antonio	52	retired	71	
	N	*Cataldo Louis	52	"	73	
	O	Bobrek Edward	52	chauffeur	25	"
	P	*Bobrek John	52	laborer	56	
	R	LaVigneur Albert	52	longshoreman	25	"
	S	LaVigneur Rose—†	52	housewife	23	"
	T	Giardullo Emma—†	53	"	24	54 Neptune rd
	U	Giardullo Leo	53	salesman	25	54 "
	V	Wilcox Agnes—†	55	housewife	56	here
	W	Wilcox Gifford D	55	foreman	55	"
	X	Drohan Genevieve—†	56	housewife	35	"
	Y	Drohan John F	56	agent	36	
	Z	Mazza Francis	56	clerk	23	
1294						
	A	Mazza Marion—†	56	operator	22	
	B	Mazza Mary—†	56	housewife	44	"
	C	Alleas John	57	mechanic	60	"
	D	Alleas Rose—†	57	housewife	58	"
	E	Cahill Catherine—†	59	at home	23	
	F	Cahill Francis J	59	chauffeur	34	"
	G	Cahill Herbert C	59	laborer	61	
	H	Cahill Sophie M—†	59	housewife	59	"
	K	Cahill Thomas	59	operator	22	"
	L	Geggis Mary—†	60	housewife	44	"
	M	Geggis William	60	laborer	47	
	N	Czarnetzki Anna—†	60	housewife	40	"
	O	Czarnetzki Augustine	60	attendant	37	"
	P	Czarnetzki Mary—†	60	housewife	65	"

Page.	Letter.	FULL NAME.	Residence, Jan. 1, 1938.	Occupation.	Supposed Age.	Reported Residence, Jan. 1, 1937. Street and Number.

Byron Street—Continued

	R	Fennelly Dennis J	61	longshoreman	46	here
	S	*Fennelly Sarah—†	61	housewife	41	"
	T	Flynn Minnie—†	64	"	24	"
	U	Flynn Roland	64	laborer	26	
	V	Stoia Veronica—†	64	housewife	60	"
	W	Stoia Vincenzo	64	laborer	58	
	X	Stoia William	64	clerk	21	
	Y	Molino Frank	64	operator	44	
	Z	Molino Ida—†	64	housewife	36	"
1295						
	A	Wingard Alice—†	66	"	26	
	B	Wingard William	66	longshoreman	31	"
	C	Wilkes William	66	manager	55	"
	D	Wright Basil	66	painter	32	
	E	Wright Ruth—†	66	housewife	25	"
	F	Buldini Antoinette—†	66	"	20	
	G	Buldini Guido	66	laborer	24	
	H	*Marcantonio Dora—†	67	housewife	50	"
	K	Marcantonio Louis	67	barber	54	"
	L	Pagliccia Domenic	67	operator	46	Waltham
	M	*DiRitto Rose—†	67	housekeeper	41	here
	N	*Isasi Antonio	67	engineer	47	479 Sumner
	O	*Isasi Paula—†	67	housewife	36	479 "
	P	Joyce Thomas A	68	operator	20	here
	R	Morse Daniel	68	longshoreman	37	"
	S	Morse Mary F—†	68	housewife	41	"
	T	Barker George A	68	assembler	31	"
	U	Barker Harry	68	baker	59	
	V	Barker Henry R	68	laborer	29	"
	W	Barker Isabel R—†	68	clerk	22	
	X	Barker Susan—†	68	housewife	51	"
	Y	Barker William J	68	laundryman	25	"
	Z	Johnson Esther—†	70	stenographer	24	"
1296						
	A	*Johnson Sandra—†	70	housewife	53	"
	B	D'Agnelli Domenic	70	laborer	35	
	C	*D'Agnelli Maria—†	70	housewife	38	"
	D	*D'Orio Maria—†	70	housekeeper	70	"
	E	Iannone Domenic	70	laborer	41	"
	F	Rutledge Arthur E	71	"	42	
	G	Rutledge Nora C—†	71	housewife	40	"

Page.	Letter.	Full Name.	Residence, Jan. 1, 1938.	Occupation.	Supposed Age.	Reported Residence, Jan. 1, 1937. Street and Number.

Byron Street—Continued

Page.	Letter.	Full Name.	Residence, Jan. 1, 1938.	Occupation.	Supposed Age.	Reported Residence, Jan. 1, 1937. Street and Number.
	H	Vecchio Gioacchino	72	operator	45	here
	K	Berube Emile	72	laborer	39	"
	L	McCormick Alexander	72	"	40	"
	M	McCormick Florence—†	72	housewife	30	"
	N	McCormick William	72	retired	72	Connecticut
	O	McIntyre Anna—†	74	housewife	27	here
	P	McIntyre John	74	bookkeeper	27	"
	R	Jackson Eileen—†	74	stenographer	24	"
	S	*Jackson John H	74	laborer	59	"
	T	Jackson John J	74	"	23	
	U	*Jackson Mary—†	74	housewife	56	"
	V	Dorgan Annie L—†	76	"	50	
	W	Dorgan Michael	76	clerk	50	
	X	Flanigan Anna—†	76	housewife	40	"
	Y	Flanigan Charles H	76	laborer	48	
	Z	Flanigan Laura—†	76	housewife	46	"
1297						
	A	Cardillo Joseph	77	operator	35	"
	B	Cardillo Lucy—†	77	housewife	35	"
	C	Belange John	77	operator	38	"
	D	Belange Pauline—†	77	housewife	36	96 Byron
	E	Belange Peter	77	custodian	40	96 "
	F	Belange Anthony	77	plumber	45	here
	G	Belange Lucy—†	77	housewife	45	"
	H	Necco Annette F—†	79	"	49	"
	K	Necco John	79	retired	54	
	L	Necco John, jr	79	laborer	24	
	N	McDuffie Catherine—†	79	housewife	26	"
	O	McDuffie Daniel B	79	engineer	32	
	P	Lyng Michael	81	salesman	57	"
	R	McCormick Catherine F–†	81	saleswoman	47	"
	S	McCormick Mary—†	81	stitcher	45	
	T	Mulkerin Jane F—†	81	housekeeper	57	"
	U	Metcalfe Hannah—†	83	housewife	77	"
	V	Metcalfe Joseph A	83	designer	52	
	W	Maillet Emelie—†	84	housewife	37	"
	X	Maillet Joseph A	84	carpenter	38	"
	Y	Goodfellow Anna—†	84	housewife	37	"
	Z	Lane Dorothy—†	84	clerk	35	
1298						
	A	Lane Helen—†	84	"	29	

Page.	Letter.	Full Name.	Residence, Jan. 1, 1938.	Occupation.	Supposed Age.	Reported Residence, Jan. 1, 1937. Street and Number.
		Byron Street—Continued				
	B	Lane Mary E—†	84	housewife	71	here
	C	Lane Mary E—†	84	clerk	29	"
	D	Lane Robert	84	machinist	22	"
	E	Lane Thomas	84	retired	73	
	F	McIntire Alice E—†	85	housewife	33	"
	G	McIntire Frank C	85	chauffeur	33	"
	H	Lahti Charles A	85	calker	36	"
	K	Lahti Taimi—†	85	housewife	35	"
	L	Demontreux Edgar	87	messenger	22	"
	M	Demontreux Henry	87	calker	62	
	N	Demontreux Henry	87	manager	32	"
	O	Demontreux Louis	87	"	31	
	P	Demontreux Louise—†	87	housewife	60	"
	R	Bois Ernest	89	dealer	38	
	S	*Bois Sarah—†	89	housewife	38	"
	T	Bois Louis	89	operator	48	
	U	Bois Malvina—†	89	housewife	47	"
	V	Anderson Lillian—†	90	"	33	54 Putnam
	W	Anderson Martin F	90	longshoreman	35	54 "
	X	Clayton John J	93	printer	34	here
	Y	*Clayton Mabel A—†	93	housewife	31	"
	Z	Donovan John P	93	laborer	50	"
1299						
	A	Wilcox James	94	guard	21	55 Byron
	B	*Abrahams Joseph W	94	longshoreman	38	here
	C	Abrahams Lillian—†	94	housewife	37	"
	D	Brady Mary—†	94	at home	48	751 Benningt'n
	E	Irons Emily—†	95	housekeeper	37	here
	F	Aiken Irene G—†	96	housewife	31	239 Webster
	G	Aiken Leo C	96	salesman	32	239 "
	H	Amirault Clifford	96	messenger	21	here
	K	*Amirault Cyrus	96	welder	42	"
	L	*Amirault Gertrude—†	96	housewife	41	"
	M	McNeil Annie—†	96	laundress	42	"
	N	Kelley Walter B	96	gasman	45	
	O	McKenney Frances—†	96	housekeeper	25	"
	P	McKenney Mary J—†	96	housewife	64	"
	R	Lear George	97	laborer	29	
	S	Lear Sarah A—†	97	housewife	68	"
	T	Lear William H	97	finisher	67	
	U	O'Donnell Catherine C–†	104	housewife	75	"

Page.	Letter.	Full Name.	Residence, Jan. 1, 1938.	Occupation.	Supposed Age.	Reported Residence, Jan. 1, 1937. Street and Number.
		Byron Street—Continued				
	v	O'Donnell James F	104	inspector	41	here
	w	O'Donnell Joseph C	104	cutter	37	"
	x	Prendergast Frances—†	104	clerk	42	"
	y	Ciarlone Audrey—†	106	stenographer	21	"
	z	Ciarlone Emma—†	106	waitress	22	"
1300						
	A	Ciarlone Helen B—†	106	saleswoman	24	"
	B	Ciarlone Linda—†	106	housewife	49	"
	C	Ciarlone William A	106	draftsman	27	"
	D	Ciarlone William F	106	laborer	62	
	E	*DeMarco Celia—†	106	housewife	79	"
	F	DeMarco Guido	106	musician	43	"
	G	DeMarco Joseph	106	salesman	34	"
	H	Howard Catherine A—†	108	at home	67	"
	K	Stack Ellen—†	112	housewife	63	740 Saratoga
	L	Stack Raymond M	112	clerk	36	740 "
	M	Callahan Mary F—†	112	housewife	73	here
	N	Connerty Anna L—†	112	"	33	"
	O	Connerty John A	112	B F D	43	"
	P	Thornton Edwin J	114	clerk	42	
	R	Thornton Margaret R—†	114	housewife	38	"
	S	Wholley Mary E—†	114	housekeeper	69	"
	T	Morse Mary J—†	114	housewife	64	"
	U	Morse William P	114	clerk	39	"
	V	Rossiter Elizabeth—†	114	at home	84	300 Meridian
	W	*Impeduglia John	127	laborer	68	here
	X	Impeduglia Michael	127	"	22	"
	Y	*Impeduglia Sabastina—†	127	housewife	60	"
	Z	Impeduglia Salvatore	127	operator	24	
1301						
	A	Hagstrom Martha—†	129	housewife	37	"
	B	Hagstrom Oliver	129	laborer	42	"
	C	Goulet Albert	129	operator	22	Connecticut
	D	Goulet Eveda—†	129	housewife	55	"
	E	Goulet Odlon	129	operator	56	"
		Moore Street				
	F	*McDonald Alexander	1	laborer	58	here
	G	*McDonald Emma—†	1	housewife	58	"
	H	McDonald Emma T—†	1	clerk	29	"

Page.	Letter.	Full Name.	Residence, Jan. 1, 1938.	Occupation.	Supposed Age.	Reported Residence, Jan. 1, 1937. Street and Number.

Moore Street—Continued

	K	McDonald John C	1	steamfitter	26	here
	L	McDonald Joseph R	1	"	32	"
	M	McDonald Margaret I—†	1	clerk	24	"
	N	McDonald Robert E	1	"	21	
	O	Chase Helen—†	3	housewife	64	"
	P	Chase Mary M—†	3	hairdresser	31	"
	R	Chase William E	3	mechanic	35	"
	S	Chase William J	3	cook	68	"
	T	*White Isabel—†	5	housewife	28	206 Byron
	U	*White Terrence	5	longshoreman	29	206 "
	V	*Firth Esma—†	5	housewife	49	here
	W	*Firth George E	5	mechanic	24	"
	X	Firth Walter D	5	laborer	22	"
	Y	O'Rourke Doris G—†	15	operator	25	
	Z	Zarveson George	15	druggist	45	
1302						
	A	Zarveson Loretta B—†	15	housewife	45	"
	C	Lockwood Marie G—†	19	"	42	
	D	Lockwood Ralph F	19	laborer	42	
	E	MacMaster Charles H	19	painter	50	
	F	MacMaster Jane—†	19	milliner	54	
	G	*MacMaster Margaret—†	19	housewife	82	"
	H	Sheridan Mary—†	21	"	48	
	K	Sullivan Louise—†	21	operator	35	"
	L	Baldwin Harry	21	mechanic	25	"
	M	Baldwin Muriel—†	21	housewife	24	"
	N	*Cavanaugh Elizabeth—†	25	"	25	
	O	Cavanaugh Patrick	25	fisherman	30	"
	P	Cervizzi Pasquale	25	attorney	30	"
	R	Cervizzi Thelma—†	25	housewife	24	"
	S	Crowley Mary M—†	25	"	49	736 Saratoga
	T	Crowley Michael A	25	guard	50	736 "
	U	Crowley Nathaniel T	25	clerk	20	here
	V	Flynn Alice C—†	27	housewife	31	"
	W	Flynn Alice E—†	27	"	67	"
	X	Flynn David B	27	chauffeur	34	"
	Y	McGeney Anna E—†	27	seamstress	33	"
	Z	Crowley Anna—†	27	housewife	55	"
1303						
	A	Crowley Joseph R	27	clerk	24	"
	B	Barry Mary—†	27	housewife	53	"

Page.	Letter.	Full Name.	Residence, Jan. 1, 1938.	Occupation.	Supposed Age.	Reported Residence, Jan. 1, 1937. Street and Number.

Moore Street—Continued

Page.	Letter.	Full Name.	Residence, Jan. 1, 1938.	Occupation.	Supposed Age.	Reported Residence, Jan. 1, 1937. Street and Number.
	c	Crowley Catherine—†	27	housewife	45	here
	D	Crowley Timothy	27	mechanic	57	"
	E	Doyle Anna M—†	31	teacher	49	"
	F	Doyle Gertrude F—†	31	secretary	46	"
	G	Doyle Joseph F	31	carpenter	42	"
	H	Doyle Nora—†	31	housewife	76	"
	K	Barron Elizabeth—†	31	"	75	
	L	Beale Edward	35	packer	30	
	M	Beale Mildred—†	35	housewife	27	"
	N	DeLuca Florence—†	35	clerk	23	
	O	DeLuca John	35	barber	40	
	P	DeLuca Sophie—†	35	housewife	40	"
	R	McCarthy Charles J	39	mechanic	20	"
	S	McCarthy John E	39	seaman	58	
	T	Milward Anna P—†	39	clerk	21	
	U	Milward Edward M	39	"	46	
	V	Milward Marcella L—†	39	housewife	53	"
	W	Milward Paul E	39	clerk	22	"
	X	Willis John	39	retired	74	126 Lexington
	Y	Coakley Mark J	63	clergyman	35	here
	Z	*Doyle Malvinia—†	63	domestic	55	Greenwood
1304						
	A	Flynn Leo B	63	clergyman	35	here
	B	Kelley Mary—†	63	domestic	24	"
	C	McCarthy Patrick J	63	clergyman	50	"

Saratoga Street

Page.	Letter.	Full Name.	Residence, Jan. 1, 1938.	Occupation.	Supposed Age.	Reported Residence, Jan. 1, 1937. Street and Number.
	E	Newhook Arthur F	716	engineer	36	here
	F	Newhook Winifred—†	716	housewife	29	"
	G	Keating Hattie—†	716	"	53	"
	H	Keating James P	716	bartender	62	"
	K	Carrafiello Mary—†	718	housewife	43	"
	L	Carrafiello Rose—†	718	stitcher	22	
	M	Bibber Caroline—†	718	housewife	52	"
	N	Bibber Frank	718	laborer	21	"
	O	Wing Joseph	720	laundryman	32	China
	P	Stasio Domenic	722	laborer	46	here
	R	Stasio Robert	722	"	21	"
	S	Stasio Stella—†	722	housewife	44	"
	T	Stasio Annette—†	722	"	37	

Page.	Letter.	Full Name.	Residence, Jan. 1, 1938.	Occupation.	Supposed Age.	Reported Residence, Jan. 1, 1937. Street and Number.

Saratoga Street—Continued

Page.	Letter.	Full Name.	Residence, Jan. 1, 1938.	Occupation.	Supposed Age.	Reported Residence, Jan. 1, 1937. Street and Number.
	U	Stasio Arthur	722	glazier	38	here
	V	Nowe Eleanor T—†	722	housewife	46	"
	W	Nowe Lewis A	722	laborer	40	"
	X	Doherty Henry	724	"	26	
	Y	Merchant Ann—†	724	housewife	30	"
	Z	Merchant Thomas	724	laborer	37	
1305						
	A	*Pedersen Louis	724	fireman	43	"
	B	*Pedersen Margaret—†	724	housewife	28	"
	C	Gallagher Robert E	724	laborer	28	
	D	Kane Kathleen E—†	724	housewife	34	"
	E	Kane William J	724	machinist	42	"
	F	Plummer Henry L	726	physician	70	"
	G	Treanor Alice E—†	728	housewife	42	"
	H	Treanor William A	728	mortician	48	"
	K	Hollahan Mary—†	736	saleswoman	32	854 Saratoga
	L	Roche Peter	736	fisherman	39	854 "
	M	*Roche Violet—†	736	housewife	33	854 "
	N	Brady Joseph P	736	laborer	21	here
	O	Sands James	736	mechanic	47	"
	P	Sands Mary B—†	736	housewife	51	"
	R	Rego Anna—†	736	operator	23	5 Moore
	S	Rego Louise—†	736	"	20	5 "
	T	Rego Patrick	736	clerk	21	5 "
	U	Rego Rose—†	736	housewife	45	5 "
	W	Kelly Mary E—†	740	"	46	here
	X	Kelly Paul J	740	student	20	"
	Y	Hogan Mary T—†	740	housewife	43	"
	Z	Hogan William T	740	B F D	44	
1306						
	A	O'Brien William L	740	laborer	36	
	B	Sousa Manuel J	740	B F D	40	"
	C	Morgan Margaret G—†	740	housewife	33	46 Wordsworth
	D	Morgan William F	740	policeman	37	46 "
	E	Rauth Florence D—†	741	housewife	47	here
	F	Rauth William H	741	operator	50	"
	G	Milward Louis A	742	accountant	45	"
	H	Milward Louis A, jr	742	clerk	22	
	K	Milward Margaret—†	742	housewife	38	"
	L	Maher Bridget T—†	745	"	62	
	M	Maher Daniel J	745	clerk	71	

Page.	Letter.	Full Name.	Residence, Jan. 1, 1938.	Occupation.	Supposed Age.	Reported Residence, Jan. 1, 1937. Street and Number.

Saratoga Street—Continued

Page.	Letter.	Full Name.	Residence, Jan. 1, 1938.	Occupation.	Supposed Age.	Reported Residence, Jan. 1, 1937. Street and Number.
	N	Burns Arthur I	745	sheriff	39	here
	O	Keenan Hannah—†	745	housewife	64	"
	P	Keenan James H	745	bartender	67	"
	R	O'Connell Michael	745	"	42	
	S	*Coscia Aurora—†	746	housewife	52	"
	T	Coscia Ferdinand	746	plumber	23	
	U	*Coscia Generoso	746	laborer	66	
	V	Cohen Theresa—†	746	matron	40	
	W	Cohen William A	746	policeman	42	"
	X	Trinchitella Nicholas	746	clerk	42	
	Y	Trinchitella Rose—†	746	housewife	31	"
	Z	McGee Margaret M—†	749	"	35	
1307						
	A	McGee Michael J	749	timekeeper	38	"
	B	Crosby Marie A—†	749	housewife	38	"
	C	Crosby Robert E	749	manager	43	"
	D	Danihy Sarah J—†	749	at home	56	
	E	Crosby Catherine E—†	749	teacher	39	
	F	Crosby Edward H	749	retired	68	
	G	Coulombe Edward	750	checker	26	
	H	Coulombe Mary A—†	750	housewife	29	"
	K	Hamilton Amy—†	750	matron	55	
	L	Hoey Amy—†	750	housewife	27	"
	M	Hoey Matthew	750	porter	29	
	N	Park Mary J—†	753	housewife	59	"
	O	Murray John J	753	longshoreman	30	Lynn
	P	*Murray Marion—†	753	housewife	28	Swampscott
	R	Howard Sarah J—†	754	packer	52	here
	S	Splaine Lena—†	754	housekeeper	63	"
	T	DeLauretis Elizabeth—†	754	housewife	36	77 Byron
	U	DeLauretis John	754	machinist	42	77 "
	W	Duffy Arthur	754	clerk	23	here
	V	Duffy Arthur J	754	foreman	57	"
	X	Duffy Ellen—†	754	housewife	49	"
	Y	Duffy Ruth M—†	754	packer	20	
	Z	Hartman Eliza W—†	755	housewife	49	"
1308						
	A	Hartman James F	755	foreman	66	"
	B	Powell Ardella N—†	755	at home	83	
	C	Porter Agnes S—†	755	teacher	28	
	D	Porter Helen—†	755	operator	20	

Page.	Letter.	Full Name.	Residence, Jan. 1, 1938.	Occupation.	Supposed Age.	Reported Residence, Jan. 1, 1937. Street and Number.

Saratoga Street—Continued

	E	Porter James	755	clerk	24	here
	F	Porter Joseph	755	laborer	31	“
	G	Porter Margaret—†	755	operator	33	“
	H	Berry Anna J—†	755	“	24	
	K	Berry Bridget—†	755	housewife	62	“
	L	Berry Felix X	755	sorter	25	
	M	Berry George F	755	“	27	
	N	Berry John J	755	clerk	23	
	O	Berry Patrick J	755	laborer	59	
	P	Keough Mary C—†	756	housekeeper	70	“
	R	MacIsaac Anna I—†	756	clerk	38	“
	S	MacIsaac Frank A	756	repairman	39	“
	T	MacIsaac Nellie—†	756	housewife	72	“
	U	Murphy Evelyn—†	756	operator	57	
	V	Murphy Mary A—†	756	housewife	60	“
	W	Murphy Mary A—†	756	operator	37	
	Y	Guay Annie—†	759	housewife	59	“
	Z	Guay Catherine E—†	759	bookkeeper	24	“
1309						
	A	Guay Henry J	759	conductor	58	“
	B	Guay Joseph P	759	accountant	20	“
	C	Willis Alice—†	759	at home	80	
	D	McRea George	784	clerk	30	
	E	McRea Margaret—†	784	housewife	29	“
	F	Cavaliere Elizabeth—†	784	“	42	
	G	Cavaliere Joseph	784	operator	42	
	H	Duffy Edward	784	“	21	
	K	Duffy Mary—†	784	housekeeper	47	“
	L	Duffy May—†	784	operator	23	
	M	Dini Angelo	786	counterman	42	“
	N	Dini Julia—†	786	operator	38	
	O	McQueeney John V	786	letter carrier	63	“
	P	McQueeney John V	786	clerk	25	
	S	McQueeney Margaret A–†	786	librarian	26	
	R	McQueeney Margaret A–†	786	housewife	55	“
	T	McQueeney Rita M—†	786	operator	20	
	U	Goggin John J	786	printer	32	
	V	Goggin Margaret M—†	786	housewife	24	“
	W	O'Brien Mary A—†	786	dietitian	51	“
	X	Donahue Catherine M–†	788	stenographer	39	“
	Y	Donahue Cornelius V	788	foreman	57	“

Page.	Letter.	Full Name.	Residence, Jan. 1, 1938.	Occupation.	Supposed Age.	Reported Residence, Jan. 1, 1937. Street and Number.

Saratoga Street—Continued

	Z	Donahue Joseph G	788	clerk	46	here
1310						
	A	Donahue Julia—†	788	housewife	80	"
	B	Donahue Mary T—†	788	"	55	
	C	McCarthy Ellen F—†	788	bookbinder	64	"
	D	Thompson Delia A—†	788	housewife	46	"
	E	Thompson George F	788	custodian	46	"
	G	Silano Angelo	789	watchman	63	877 Saratoga
	H	*Silano Assunta—†	789	housewife	58	877 "
	K	Silano John	789	chauffeur	46	877 "
	M	Frazier Arthur S	790	B F D	39	34 Granfield av
	N	Frazier Hattie—†	790	housewife	65	here
	O	Gillespie John	790	decorator	34	"
	P	Gillespie Mary—†	790	housewife	28	"
	R	Gorman James A	790	repairman	52	"
	S	Gorman Louise H—†	790	housewife	52	"
	T	Gorman Margaret J—†	790	saleswoman	26	"
	U	Gorman William P	790	laborer	23	
	V	O'Connell Alfreda—†	790	inspector	20	"
	W	O'Connell Helen E—†	790	operator	25	"
	X	O'Connell Mary—†	790	housewife	58	"
	Y	O'Connell Mary—†	790	inspector	28	"
	Z	O'Connell Richard	790	mechanic	31	"
1311						
	A	O'Connell Rita—†	790	operator	22	"
	B	Bullock Rose—†	791	housewife	35	"
	C	Bullock William J	791	laborer	38	
	D	Grasso Rosalie—†	791	housewife	33	"
	E	Grasso Salvatore	791	constable	44	"
	G	*Hourihan Anna—†	792	housewife	22	533 Benningt'n
	H	Hourihan Joseph	792	counterman	33	106 Bennett
	K	Coveney Ellen F—†	792	housekeeper	55	here
	L	McLaughlin Dorothy—†	792	housewife	30	"
	M	McLaughlin Samuel	792	garageman	36	"
	N	MacDonald Anna L—†	793	housewife	25	361 Meridian
	O	MacDonald John R	793	laborer	29	361 "
	P	Jensen Agnes E—†	793	housewife	38	647 Benningt'n
	R	Jensen William	793	clerk	39	647 "
	S	Finn Katherine G—†	794	"	44	here
	T	Finn Margaret—†	794	bookkeeper	49	"
	U	Lee Dennis J	794	retired	64	"

Page.	Letter.	FULL NAME.	Residence, Jan. 1, 1938.	Occupation.	Supposed Age.	Reported Residence, Jan. 1, 1937. Street and Number.

Saratoga Street—Continued

	V	Cuneo Alfred	795	soapmaker	39	here
	W	Cuneo Catherine—†	795	at home	20	"
	X	Cuneo Helen—†	795	housewife	38	"
	Y	Cuneo Eva—†	795	operator	45	"
	Z	Cuneo Frederick	795	laborer	58	
1312						
	A	*Cuneo Joseph	795	retired	78	
	B	Cuneo Nellie—†	795	operator	48	
	C	Canavan Anna—†	796	housekeeper	37	"
	D	Welsh Mary L—†	796	housewife	47	"
	E	Welsh Walter J	796	inspector	55	"
	F	Canavan Catherine D—†	796	housewife	42	"
	G	Canavan Joseph I	796	B F D	46	
	H	Canavan Joseph I, jr	796	clerk	20	
	K	Moran Lawrence F	797	B F D	54	
	L	Moran Margaret H—†	797	decorator	48	"
	M	Moran Mary L—†	797	housewife	50	"
	N	Burke Eleanor—†	797	houseworker	39	"
	O	*Rockliff Charles	797	retired	71	"
	R	Walsh Mary R—†	799	housewife	30	95 Addison
	S	Walsh Timothy J	799	carpenter	33	95 "
	T	Cook Flora M—†	799	operator	60	here
	V	Rooney Marie L—†	801	housewife	24	"
	W	Rooney William F	801	operator	24	"
	X	Baum Harry	801	waiter	65	
	Y	Morey Emma—†	801	saleswoman	45	"
	Z	Barker Edwin J	801	chauffeur	52	"
1313						
	A	Barker Lillian G—†	801	housewife	47	"
	B	Hughes Brainerd F	801	editor	31	Belmont
	D	Barry Mary J—†	803	clerk	44	here
	E	Welling Augustine D	803	painter	57	"
	F	Welling Emily A—†	803	housewife	47	"
	L	*Capogrica Anna—†	809	"	40	65 Marion
	M	Capogrica Nicholas	809	carpenter	40	65 "
	N	*Ciccia Angela—†	809	housewife	44	21 Monmouth
	O	Ciccia Emilio	809	tailor	20	21 "
	P	Ciccia Nicholas	809	"	49	21 "
	R	Bruzzese Filiberto	809	operator	46	105 Marion
	S	*Bruzzese Nunciata—†	809	housewife	38	105 "
	T	Sabbagh Charles	810	laborer	21	here

Page.	Letter.	Full Name.	Residence, Jan. 1, 1938.	Occupation.	Supposed Age.	Reported Residence, Jan. 1, 1937. Street and Number.

Saratoga Street—Continued

Page.	Letter.	Full Name.	Residence, Jan. 1, 1938.	Occupation.	Supposed Age.	Reported Residence, Jan. 1, 1937. Street and Number.
	U	Sabbagh Fred	810	clerk	28	here
	V	Sabbagh George	810	entertainer	29	“
	W	*Sabbagh Richard	810	cook	57	“
	X	McLean Allen G	814	seaman	27	
	Y	McLean Mildred F—†	814	housewife	24	“
	Z	Canty Catherine T—†	814	“	38	
1314						
	A	Canty John A	814	laborer	43	
	B	Haynes Frank E	815	operator	47	“
	C	Haynes Margaret M—†	815	housewife	44	“
	D	*Iapicca Augustino	815	operator	63	“
	E	*Iapicca Nicoletta—†	815	housewife	60	“
	F	Iapicca Salvatore	815	barber	38	
	G	Iapicca Tancredi	815	engineer	27	
	H	Iapicca Rocco	815	laborer	37	
	K	Iapicca Theresa—†	815	housewife	34	“
	L	O'Brien Catherine—†	816	“	31	
	M	O'Brien James H	816	foreman	41	
	N	Rogers Florence—†	816	at home	21	
	O	Rogers Manuel	816	electrician	42	“
	P	Spadaro Ann—†	816	matron	35	Cambridge
	R	Dando Charles J	818	cigarmaker	78	here
	S	Dando Margaret—†	818	housewife	74	“
	T	Smith Margaret V—†	818	“	47	“
	U	Smith Robert C	818	chauffeur	44	“
	V	Ferragamo Pasquale	819	laborer	40	
	W	*Ferragamo Rose—†	819	housewife	35	“
	X	Maggiore Antonio	819	tailor	46	
	Y	Maggiore Imprimo	819	barber	21	
	Z	Maggiore Marie—†	819	teacher	22	
1315						
	A	*Maggiore Nellie—†	819	housewife	44	“
	B	Crawford Çatherine—†	819	“	36	
	C	Crawford John L	819	repairman	39	“
	D	Belton Arthur	820	student	21	
	E	Belton Francis J	820	electrician	35	“
	F	Belton William	820	seaman	58	
	G	Gustowski Lillian F—†	820	operator	24	“
	H	Gustowski Mary E—†	820	housekeeper	52	“
	K	Doyle Helen—†	820	housewife	46	“
	L	Doyle James J	820	repairman	46	“

Page.	Letter.	FULL NAME.	Residence, Jan. 1, 1938.	Occupation.	Supposed Age.	Reported Residence, Jan. 1, 1937. Street and Number.

Saratoga Street—Continued

	M	Jacobsen Elvina—†	820	housewife	63	here
	N	Jacobsen Marie—†	820	bookkeeper	27	"
	O	Jacobsen Walter	820	salesman	25	"
	P*	DiMinico James	821	laborer	39	
	R*	DiMinico Mary—†	821	housewife	31	"
	S	Pepi Antonio	821	barber	51	
	T	Pepi Frank	821	podiatrist	25	"
	U	Pepi John F	821	physician	27	"
	V	Pepi Sophie—†	821	housewife	46	"
	W	Cerella Anna—†	821	operator	24	162 Chelsea
	X*	Rubino Antonio	821	laborer	49	162 "
	Y	Rubino Mary—†	821	operator	21	162 "
	Z*	Rubino Philomena—†	821	housewife	56	162 "
1316						
	A	Grenier Catherine—†	822	"	39	here
	B	Grenier Joseph	822	operator	40	"
	C	Brown Charles R	822	retired	74	"
	D	Jacobson Frank E	822	chauffeur	36	"
	E	Jacobson Rose M—†	822	housewife	37	"
	F	Stewart Bertha I—†	822	clerk	27	
	G	Stewart Bessie B—†	822	housewife	69	"
	H	Stewart David H	822	laborer	24	
	K	Stewart Ralph S	822	upholsterer	37	"
	L	Fronk Bernice C—†	823	housewife	38	"
	M	Fronk Floyd T	823	mechanic	38	"
	N	Hunter David W	823	messenger	33	70 Bay State rd
	O	Hunter Mary M—†	823	bookkeeper	33	755 Saratoga
	P	Bonito Della—†	823	at home	24	989 Benningt'n
	R	Bonito Eugene	823	laborer	30	536 "
	S	Bonito Joseph	823	"	21	536 "
	T*	Bonito Rose—†	823	housewife	58	536 "
	U	Bonito Samuel	823	painter	28	536 "
	V	Heveran John	825	laborer	34	here
	W	Moloney Cornelius	825	"	31	"
	X*	Moloney Mary—†	825	housewife	33	"
	Y	Vieira Francis	825	laborer	23	
	Z	Vieira Francisco	825	barber	54	
1317						
	A	Vieira Ursula—†	825	housewife	50	"
	B	Jasus Justin S	825	operator	36	49 McClellan H'way
	C*	Jasus Ursula—†	825	housewife	67	here

Page.	Letter.	Full Name.	Residence, Jan. 1, 1938.	Occupation.	Supposed Age.	Reported Residence, Jan. 1, 1937. Street and Number.

Saratoga Street—Continued

	D	Stokes Madeline F—†	827	housewife	35	681 Benningt'n
	E	Stokes William W	827	electrotyper	38	681 "
	F	Dodd Patrick F	827	laborer	64	here
	G	Stack Agnes J—†	827	milliner	64	"
	H	Spindler John	827	barber	58	"
	K	Spindler M Barbara—†	827	teacher	27	
	L	Spindler Mary—†	827	housewife	56	"
	M	Kelley Helen J—†	829	secretary	34	"
	N	Kelley Patrick J	829	laborer	67	"
	O	Kelley Sarah A—†	829	housewife	64	"
	P	O'Hare Alice G—†	829	at home	47	
	R	O'Brien Catherine M—†	831	housewife	68	"
	S	O'Brien Edmund J	831	clerk	23	
	T	O'Brien George R	831	manufacturer	37	"
	U	McLaughlin John J	831	guard	60	
	V	McLaughlin Mary M—†	831	housewife	57	"
	W	McLaughlin Regina E—†	831	clerk	20	
	X	Palladino Josephine—†	833	housewife	21	"
	Y	Palladino Rocco	833	laborer	27	
	Z	Cipoletta Mar —†	833	housewife	37	"
1318y						
	A	Cipoletta Nicholas	833	chauffeur	44	"
	B	Newhall Cecelia—†	833	housewife	42	"
	C	Newhall Charles H	833	operator	47	"
	D	Newhall Helen E—†	833	"	20	
	E	*Ferretti Pierina—†	835	housewife	35	"
	F	*Ferretti Thomas	835	painter	41	
	G	Sabbag Philip	835	machinist	24	"
	H	*Sabbag Salemme—†	835	housewife	46	"
	K	Sabbag Samuel	835	laborer	26	
	L	Norton George J	835	"	28	"
	M	Norton Sarah—†	835	housewife	65	"
	N	Norton Thomas P	835	waiter	68	
	O	Gallagher Benjamin F	837	laborer	49	
	P	Gallagher James A	837	welder	20	
	R	Gallagher Susan A—†	837	housewife	42	"
	S	Payne James W	837	laborer	53	217 Saratoga
	T	Coe Janet—†	837	housewife	68	here
	U	Hanlon Eva M—†	837	saleswoman	39	"
	V	Hanlon Leonard	837	clerk	20	"
	W	Hanlon Virginia—†	837	stenographer	22	"

Page.	Letter.	Full Name.	Residence, Jan. 1, 1938.	Occupation.	Supposed Age.	Reported Residence, Jan. 1, 1937. Street and Number.

Saratoga Street—Continued

Page.	Letter.	Full Name.	Residence, Jan. 1, 1938.	Occupation.	Supposed Age.	Reported Residence, Jan. 1, 1937. Street and Number.
	X	Hanlon William	837	mechanic	45	here
	Y	Ramsay Albert E	837	printer	27	91 St Andrew
	Z	Ramsay David A	837	“	56	91 “
1319						
	A	Ramsay David A, jr	837	clerk	28	91 “
	B	Ramsay Lucy E—†	837	housewife	55	91 “
	C	Petitpas Albert B	839	operator	43	here
	D	*Petitpas Melina—†	839	housewife	38	“
	E	Cooper Mary A—†	839	“	51	“
	F	Cooper William E	839	operator	63	
	G	Cooper William F	839	clerk	28	
	H	Veiga Florence G—†	839	“	25	
	K	Cullen Catherine A—†	849	housewife	48	“
	L	Cullen George F	849	clerk	22	
	N	Cullen John J	849	accountant	24	“
	M	Cullen Joseph H	849	merchant	57	“
	O	Steiner Francis V	849	agent	23	
	P	Steiner Thomas N	849	salesman	49	“
	R	Murphy Elizabeth M—†	849	housewife	55	“
	S	Schuch Matthew C	849	teamster	66	“
	T	Culbert Frank J	850	bartender	61	789 Saratoga
	U	Culbert Frank J, jr	850	operator	21	789 “
	V	Culbert Sarah—†	850	housewife	57	789 “
	W	Mirakian Mary—†	850	“	70	here
	X	Mirakian Stephen	850	retired	79	“
	Y	Bonafini Sebastiano	851	laborer	37	“
	Z	*Bonafini Theresa—†	851	housewife	33	“
1320						
	A	Leone Annette—†	851	“	33	
	B	Leone Basil	851	operator	33	“
	C	*Vozzella Florindo	851	cobbler	70	
	D	Vozzella Joseph	851	operator	39	“
	E	Vozzella Mary—†	851	housewife	32	“
	F	Mascis Elsie—†	852	“	34	
	G	Mascis James	852	laborer	30	
	H	*Terry Marion—†	852	housewife	39	“
	K	Terry Rene	852	guard	37	
	L	Casa Anthony J	853	mechanic	34	“
	M	Casa Antoinetta—†	853	housewife	28	“
	N	Cutlip Susie—†	853	at home	70	
	O	Webber Carl	853	operator	26	“

Page.	Letter.	FULL NAME.	Residence, Jan. 1, 1938.	Occupation.	Supposed Age.	Reported Residence, Jan. 1, 1937. Street and Number.

Saratoga Street—Continued

	P	*D'Agosta Adeline—†	853	housewife	36	here
	R	D'Agosta Frank	853	cutter	35	"
	S	Burke Thomas J	854	laborer	37	857 Saratoga
	T	Nichols Joseph L	854	salesman	42	857 "
	U	*Nichols Kathleen—†	854	housewife	39	857 "
	V	Thomas Anna—†	854	clerk	23	here
	W	Thomas Mary—†	854	housewife	61	"
	X	Coon Catherine—†	855	"	36	"
	Y	Coon James B	855	operator	45	
	Z	Frattarole Elvira—†	855	housewife	38	"
1321						
	A	DiPietro Hilda—†	855	bookkeeper	21	"
	B	DiPietro Marion—†	855	operator	23	"
	C	DiPietro Michelina—†	855	housewife	45	"
	D	*Sullivan Agnes—†	856	"	26	
	E	*Sullivan Francis	856	laborer	31	
	F	Venezia John	856	"	47	
	G	Venezia Theresa—†	856	housewife	38	"
	L	Petrillo Anthony	857	painter	34	
	M	Petrillo Vienna—†	857	housewife	34	"
	N	McCarthy Daniel D	858	laborer	57	
	O	McCarthy Daniel J	858	clerk	22	
	P	McCarthy Nora—†	858	housewife	52	"
	R	Rice Harold E	858	assembler	34	"
	S	Rice John	858	finisher	65	
	T	Rice Louise—†	858	housewife	59	"
	U	Rice William A	858	clerk	24	
	V	Pasqua Margaret—†	859	operator	29	"
	W	Pasqua Philip	859	"	34	
	X	*Santoro Domenic	859	watchman	68	"
	Y	*Santoro Theresa—†	859	housewife	66	"
	Z	*Recupero Mary—†	859	"	43	Italy
1322						
	A	Recupero Michael	859	laborer	43	here
	B	*Recupero Prisco	859	"	23	"
	C	Piano Donato	860	"	50	"
	D	Piano Josephine—†	860	housewife	48	"
	E	McClements Eva—†	860	housekeeper	56	"
	F	Porter Madeline—†	860	waitress	29	"
	G	Shute Anna E—†	860	housewife	59	"
	H	Shute Francis	860	operator	22	"

Page.	Letter.	Full Name.	Residence, Jan. 1, 1938.	Occupation.	Supposed Age.	Reported Residence, Jan. 1, 1937. Street and Number.

Saratoga Street—Continued

	K	Shute Manuel J	860	chauffeur	60	here
	L	Panora Anna—†	861	housewife	39	“
	M	Panora Donato J	861	machinist	46	“
	N	Simione Alfred	861	chauffeur	24	“
	O	Anselone Frank	861	laborer	42	“
	P	Anselone Kathleen—†	861	housewife	38	“
	R	McNeil Alfred J	861	chauffeur	22	“
	S	McNeil Francis J	861	“	48	
	T	McNeil George F	861	attendant	24	“
	U	McNeil Nellie—†	861	housewife	47	“
	V	Wilcox Gifford	862	laborer	29	
	W	Wilcox Mildred—†	862	housewife	23	“
	X	Olivieri Angelo	862	laborer	44	
	Y	*Olivieri Rose—†	862	housewife	42	“
	Z	*Sepe Salvatore	863	laborer	67	
1323						
	A	*Sepe Sophia—†	863	housewife	68	“
	B	*Sepe Theresa—†	863	operator	29	“
	C	Sepe Marie—†	863	secretary	34	“
	D	Sepe Peter	863	foreman	34	
	E	Sabbagh Adele—†	863	housewife	44	“
	F	Sabbagh Elias	863	salesman	51	“
	G	Sabbagh Julia—†	863	stenographer	22	“
	H	McDonald Mary—†	864	housekeeper	55	“
	K	Perella Alphonse	864	painter	26	“
	L	Perella Angelina—†	864	housewife	26	“

William F. McClellan Highway

	M	English Alice—†	119	housewife	28	here
	N	English William	119	clerk	30	“
	O	Massuca Ernest F	121	laborer	27	“
	P	Massuca Helen—†	121	housewife	25	“
	R	Wilkes Frederick C	121	laborer	21	66 Byron

Wordsworth Street

	S	Gorman Barbara—†	7	clerk	26	12 Wordsworth
	T	Gorman Della—†	7	“	26	12 “
	U	Gorman Peter	7	oiler	65	12 “
	V	Mannix Dennis	7	carpenter	45	here

Page.	Letter.	Full Name.	Residence, Jan. 1, 1938.	Occupation.	Supposed Age.	Reported Residence, Jan. 1, 1937. Street and Number.

Wordsworth Street—Continued

	W	Mannix James	7	salesman	21	here
	X	Mannix Mary—†	7	housewife	43	"
	Y	DiGiso Florence—†	9	"	32	"
	Z	DiGiso Frank	9	laborer	33	
1324						
	A	*Wolochka Mary—†	9	housekeeper	39	"
	B	Wolochka Pauline—†	9	operator	22	"
	C	Mauro Anthony	9	chauffeur	33	"
	D	Mauro Mildred—†	9	housewife	26	"
	E	Wilson Alexander	9A	laborer	41	
	F	*Wilson Elizabeth—†	9A	housewife	38	"
	G	*Russell Ellen—†	9A	"	58	
	H	*Russell Thomas	9A	laborer	53	
	K	Foster Agnes—†	9A	housewife	43	"
	L	Foster Charles	9A	clerk	20	
	M	Foster Joseph	9A	chauffeur	44	"
	N	Jewkes Blanche—†	10	housewife	33	"
	O	Jewkes Joseph F	10	salesman	37	"
	P	Rogers Theresa—†	10	at home	60	
	R	Campbell Julia—†	10	"	63	"
	S	Cochran Theresa—†	10	housewife	31	"
	T	Cochran William	10	laborer	32	
	U	Gorman Mary—†	10	at home	28	"
	V	Tonello Evelyn—†	11	housewife	23	"
	W	Tonello Guido	11	operator	28	"
	X	Carter George H	11	chauffeur	35	"
	Y	Carter Rose—†	11	housewife	32	"
	Z	Julian Charles	11	salesman	36	"
1325						
	A	Anderson Emma—†	12	at home	63	793 Saratoga
	B	Layne Jennie—†	12	"	44	793 "
	C	Dawson Helen—†	12	housewife	39	here
	D	Dawson William L	12	dealer	39	"
	E	*Rebak Evdakim	13	laborer	49	"
	F	*Rebak Klavidia—†	13	housewife	37	"
	G	Farmer Beatrice—†	13	"	37	
	H	Farmer Edward	13	printer	36	
	K	Mezzocchi Alfred	13	salesman	27	"
	L	Mezzocchi Anna—†	13	housewife	25	"
	N	Tierney Edward	15	laborer	45	
	O	Tierney Nora—†	15	housewife	45	"

Page.	Letter.	Full Name.	Residence, Jan. 1, 1938.	Occupation.	Supposed Age.	Reported Residence, Jan. 1, 1937. Street and Number.

Wordsworth Street—Continued

Page.	Letter.	Full Name.	Residence, Jan. 1, 1938.	Occupation.	Supposed Age.	Reported Residence, Jan. 1, 1937. Street and Number.
	P	*Tedeschi Clara—†	15	at home	30	Italy
	R	Tedeschi Emilio	15	tailor	42	here
	S	*Tedeschi Fortuna—†	15	housewife	38	"
	T	*Riley Catherine—†	15	"	27	"
	U	Riley Henry	15	chauffeur	33	"
	V	Gatti Bruno	16	laborer	42	
	W	*Gatti Gina—†	16	housewife	35	"
	X	*Travaglini Attilio	16	storekeeper	63	"
	Y	Travaglini John	16	upholsterer	28	"
	Z	*Travaglini Lucia—†	16	housewife	63	"
1326						
	A	*Travaglini Tina—†	16	operator	23	
	B	*Camerano Filomena—†	17	housewife	51	"
	C	*Camerano Frank	17	operator	59	
	D	Camerano Rose—†	17	at home	21	
	E	*Mustone Angelina—†	17	housewife	45	"
	F	Mustone Nicholas	17	laborer	46	
	G	*Facardio Alvera—†	17	housewife	36	"
	H	Keenan James	18	retired	80	
	K	Keenan Mary E—†	18	housewife	71	"
	L	Rourke William J	18	fireman	42	
	M	Fleming Joseph	19	clerk	21	
	N	Fleming Margaret—†	19	housewife	23	"
	O	*DeSimone Flora—†	19	"	38	"
	P	DeSimone Gabriel	19	laborer	20	
	R	Barnes Charlotte E—†	19	at home	52	
	S	McGee George E	19	clerk	37	
	T	McGee Mary A—†	19	housewife	73	"
	U	*O'Hara Henry	20	watchman	65	"
	V	O'Hara John	20	storekeeper	55	"
	W	Seaberg Elfreda—†	20	housewife	54	"
	X	Seaberg Gustav	20	designer	50	"
	Y	Turner Frank	20	engineer	29	691 Saratoga
	Z	Turner Olga—†	20	housewife	27	here
1327						
	A	Chioccola Guy	21	barber	28	
	B	Chioccola Mary—†	21	housewife	26	"
	C	Manguso Frank	21	operator	44	
	D	*Manguso Mary—†	21	housewife	37	"
	E	Dalton Anna—†	21	"	21	
	F	Dalton Gordon	21	clerk	22	

Page.	Letter.	FULL NAME.	Residence, Jan. 1, 1938.	Occupation.	Supposed Age.	Reported Residence, Jan. 1, 1937. Street and Number.

Wordsworth Street—Continued

	G	*Turco Philip	21	mechanic	49	here
	H	*Turco Vincenza—†	21	housewife	44	"
	K	D'Avella Lewis	22	clerk	21	"
	L	*D'Avella Nicholas	22	laborer	44	
	M	Gardullo Anthony	22	"	25	
	N	Gardullo Gertrude—†	22	housewife	24	"
	O	McDonough Alfred	23	longshoreman	27	"
	P	McDonough Virginia—†	23	housewife	25	"
	R	*Moniz Emma S—†	23	"	39	
	S	*Moniz John B	23	grinder	36	
	T	*Fontana Anna—†	23	housewife	42	"
	U	Fontana Antonio	23	fireman	48	
	V	Kirby Helen—†	25	housewife	26	"
	W	Kirby James J	25	laborer	29	
	X	Picinisco Frances—†	25	housewife	62	"
	Y	*Picinisco John	25	laborer	59	
	Z	*Picinisco Thomas	25	clerk	25	
1328						
	A	*Bruno Libera—†	25	housewife	31	"
	B	Bruno Pasquale	25	operator	32	
	C	Keefe Esther—†	27	housewife	41	"
	D	Keefe Thomas	27	student	20	
	E	Story Cora—†	27	at home	27	
	F	Hawkins Ruth—†	27	housewife	43	"
	G	Hawkins William, jr	27	operator	43	"
	H	*Love Henry S	27	laborer	53	
	K	Incerto Lena—†	29	housewife	24	"
	L	Incerto Virgilio	29	clerk	28	
	M	*Degenaro Antonetta—†	29	housewife	40	"
	N	*Degenaro Peter	29	mechanic	53	"
	O	Petitpas Clara—†	30	housewife	45	"
	P	Petitpas Marie—†	30	clerk	20	
	R	Petitpas Wilfred	30	cutter	45	
	S	*Krystyan Catherine—†	30	housewife	50	"
	T	Krystyan Karol	30	student	20	
	U	Krystyan Mary—†	30	operator	28	
	V	Krystyan Sophie—†	30	tester	25	
	W	Nagle George F	31	installer	36	
	X	Nagle Marie—†	31	housewife	30	"
	Y	McCormick Cyril	33	oiler	21	
	Z	McCormick Edgar P	33	waiter	27	

Page.	Letter.	Full Name.	Residence, Jan. 1, 1938.	Occupation.	Supposed Age.	Reported Residence, Jan. 1, 1937. Street and Number.

1329
Wordsworth Street—Continued

A	McCormick James V	33	teacher	25	here
B	McCormick Margaret—†	33	housewife	48	"
C	McCormick Thomas J	33	student	23	"
D	Vickley Agnes J—†	35	operator	29	
E	Vickley Alice N—†	35	"	40	
F	Vickley Francis A	35	seaman	28	
G	Vickley Joseph F	35	painter	33	
H	Vickley Mary N—†	35	at home	34	
K	Vickley Rose V—†	35	"	32	
L	Paquet Edmund	37	mechanic	36	"
M	Paquet Emelda—†	37	housewife	33	"
N	Wildes Hazel—†	37	"	27	
O	Wildes Winslow	37	operator	28	"
P	Morante Anthony	39	custodian	30	367 Princeton
R*	Morante Frances—†	39	housewife	24	Medford
S	Mahoney Christina—†	39	clerk	40	here
T	Mitchell Mary—†	39	housewife	66	"
U	Smith Dorothy—†	41	"	27	"
V	Smith Edward A	41	operator	26	"
W	Buldini Daniel	41	engineer	25	951 Saratoga
X	Buldini Florence—†	41	housewife	24	951 "
Y	Allie Adelard	41	operator	69	here
Z	Allie James	41	laborer	23	"

1330

A	Allie Mary—†	41	clerk	27	
B	Allie Regina—†	41	housewife	59	"
C	Gormley Mary L—†	42	"	42	
D	Gormley Nathaniel F	42	letter carrier	51	"
E	Gould Michael J	42	fireman	47	
F	Harrington Annie—†	42	at home	48	
G	MacKay Eleonora F—†	43	housewife	46	"
H	MacKay Martin L	43	machinist	44	"
K	Aiello Leo	43	clerk	40	
L*	Aiello Margaret—†	43	housewife	65	"
M	LeClair Delia—†	45	"	54	
N	LeClair Ferdinand	45	operator	58	
O	LeClair Roger	45	electrician	24	"
P	Gonsalves Henry	45	operator	36	"
R	Gonsalves Mildred	45	housewife	30	"
S	Curry Jane E—†	46	"	38	"

Page.	Letter.	FULL NAME.	Residence, Jan. 1, 1938.	Occupation.	Supposed Age.	Reported Residence, Jan. 1, 1937. Street and Number.

Wordsworth Street—Continued

	T	Curry Joseph P	46	guard	41	here
	U	Donahue Bridget—†	46	housewife	63	"
	V	Donahue Catherine T—†	46	secretary	24	"
	W	Donahue Cecelia—†	46	operator	32	"
	X	Donahue Cornelius	46	policeman	40	"
	Y	Donahue Gerard	46	clerk	30	
	Z	Donahue Mary A—†	46	operator	36	
1331						
	A	Donahue William	46	fireman	68	
	B	Donahue William E	46	seaman	34	
	C	Swadel Annie—†	48	housewife	33	"
	D	Swadel Robert	48	letter carrier	33	"
	E	McKenna Catherine—†	48	housewife	29	9 Walker
	F	McKenna John F	48	laborer	30	17 Cottage
	G	Hansen Charles G	50	clerk	37	here
	H	Hansen Frances H—†	50	housewife	34	"
	K	Hansen Annie—†	50	"	65	"
	L	Hansen William	50	policeman	42	"
	M	Bennett Rachel—†	51	at home	55	
	N	Hurley Dorothy—†	51	housewife	26	"
	O	Hurley Patrick L	51	clerk	29	Winthrop
	P	Cody Jennie I—†	51	housewife	40	here
	R	Cody Thomas H	51	laborer	42	"
	S	Cody Walter L	51	clerk	21	"
	T	Houghton Edna F—†	52	operator	40	"
	U	Sullivan Arthur J	52	chauffeur	34	"
	V	Sullivan Dennis B	52	retired	73	
	W	Sullivan Mary A—†	52	housewife	72	"
	X	Sullivan Mildred C—†	52	operator	37	"
	Y	Scannell Daniel	53	retired	74	
	Z	*Scannell Elsie—†	53	housewife	25	"
1332						
	A	Scannell William J	53	laborer	32	"
	B	Amato Anthony	53	engineer	28	609 Benningt'n
	C	Amato Gertrude—†	53	housewife	23	609 "
	D	Andrade Antonio J	53	storekeeper	46	here
	E	*Andrade Rose—†	53	housewife	38	"
	F	Heaphy Bridget—†	54	"	74	"
	G	Heaphy Edward	54	laborer	39	
	H	Bambrick Henry J	54	mechanic	37	"
	K	Bambrick Marcella—†	54	housewife	32	"

Page.	Letter.	Full Name.	Residence, Jan. 1, 1938.	Occupation.	Supposed Age.	Reported Residence, Jan. 1, 1937. Street and Number.
		Wordsworth Street—Continued				
	L	Pinkham Arthur	55	manager	33	here
	M	Pinkham Hilda—†	55	housewife	29	"
	N	Mullen Catherine G—†	55	"	41	"
	O	Mullen James A	55	machinist	42	"
	P	Brennan Francis	56	laborer	50	
	R	Brennan Nellie—†	56	housewife	49	"
	S	Callaghan Catherine—†	56	"	48	
	T	Callaghan William J	56	laborer	56	
	U	Munroe Helen N—†	57	housewife	33	"
	V	Munroe Joseph	57	longshoreman	35	"
	W	Huyge Gustave	57	machinist	63	852 Saratoga
	X	Huyge Jennie—†	57	housewife	58	here
	Y	Coleman John	58	chauffeur	40	"
	Z	Coleman Julia—†	58	housewife	36	"
1333						
	A	Bradley Peter	58	retired	75	"
	B	Bottelsen Hilma—†	59	housewife	62	1075 Saratoga
	C	Bottelsen Olaf	59	machinist	62	1075 "
	D	Bottelsen Olaf, jr	59	operator	32	1075 "
	E	Barry Helen A—†	59	housewife	52	here
	F	Barry John F	59	laborer	22	"
	G	Barry Thomas F	59	druggist	53	"
	H	Fernald Catherine—†	59	at home	74	
	K	Bellavia Charles	60	upholsterer	25	"
	L	Bellavia Mildred—†	60	housewife	22	"
	M	Amato Ella—†	60	stitcher	26	
	N	Amato Frances—†	60	housewife	45	"
	O	Amato John	60	clerk	22	
	P	Amato Patrick	60	"	20	
	R	Doran Edward	61	fisherman	39	"
	S	Doran Mary—†	61	housewife	39	"
	T	*Benoit Evangeline—†	61	"	47	
	U	Benoit Joseph	61	operator	53	"
	V	Langley Wilfred	61	seaman	33	Canada
	W	Shelton Catherine—†	62	housewife	35	here
	X	Shelton George A	62	mechanic	42	"
	Y	Thompson Anthony L	63	fireman	51	"
	Z	Thompson Margaret L—†	63	housewife	51	"
1334						
	A	*Ducrow Charlotte—†	63	"	65	Winthrop
	B	*Ducrow James	63	operator	70	"

Page.	Letter.	Full Name.	Residence, Jan. 1, 1938.	Occupation.	Supposed Age.	Reported Residence, Jan. 1, 1937. Street and Number.

Wordsworth Street—Continued

	c	Joyce Florence—†	65	housewife	26	here
	D	Joyce John	65	manager	23	"
	E	Pennell Addie E—†	65	housewife	44	"
	F	Pennell Clayton V	65	mechanic	23	"
	G	Pennell John C	65	foreman	50	
	H	Yeo Margaret—†	67	housewife	27	"
	K	Yeo Warren	67	chauffeur	24	"
	L	Flynn Mary B—†	67	teacher	45	
	M	McGovern Annie N—†	67	housewife	53	"
	N	McGovern Joseph F	67	clerk	20	
	O	McGovern Michael F	67	operator	55	"
	P	Malloy Edward J	69	mechanic	45	160 Bayswater
	R	Malloy Mary—†	69	housewife	31	160 "
	S	Dunbar Frank B	69	B F D	50	here
	T	Olsen Charles E	69	"	48	"
	U	Olsen Florence D—†	69	housewife	40	"
	V	Palazzalo Leo	70	operator	30	"
	W	Palazzalo Rose—†	70	housewife	26	"
	X	*Piano Josephine—†	70	"	57	
	Y	*Piano Pasquale	70	operator	50	"
	Z	Fennell Catherine—†	70	housewife	35	"
1335						
	A	Fennell Michael	70	letter carrier	37	"
	B	DeFiore Anthony	70	laborer	23	
	C	DeFiore Edward	70	"	40	
	D	DeFiore Fannie—†	70	housewife	47	"
	E	DeFiore Frank	70	barber	52	
	F	Hastings Catherine M—†	71	housewife	56	"
	G	Hastings James F	71	laborer	32	
	H	Hastings James H	71	retired	67	
	K	Hastings John A	71	welder	33	
	L	Ryan Bridget A—†	71	housewife	60	"
	M	Ryan John J	71	laborer	27	
	N	Ryan Margaret A—†	71	stenographer	20	"
	O	*Gardullo Ida—†	72	housewife	53	"
	P	*Gardullo Joseph	72	operator	55	
	R	Molino Enrico	72	shoemaker	48	"
	S	Molino Josephine—†	72	housewife	28	"
	T	Sablone Alice—†	72	stitcher	21	
	U	*Sablone Angelina—†	72	housewife	47	"
	V	Sablone Antonio	72	dairyman	45	"

Page.	Letter.	FULL NAME.	Residence, Jan. 1, 1938.	Occupation.	Supposed Age.	Reported Residence, Jan. 1, 1937. Street and Number.

Wordsworth Street—Continued

Page.	Letter.	FULL NAME.	Residence, Jan. 1, 1938.	Occupation.	Supposed Age.	Reported Residence, Jan. 1, 1937. Street and Number.
	W	Driscoll Alice V—†	73	operator	31	here
	X	Driscoll Thomas H	73	laborer	27	"
	Y	McNabb Mary—†	73	housewife	67	"
	Z	McNabb William E	73	laborer	65	
1336						
	A	Smith Charles	74	mechanic	26	"
	B	Smith Mildred—†	74	housewife	25	"
	C	Cohan Alice—†	74	"	26	
	D	Cohan Henry J	74	cutter	27	
	E	Hardy Albert	75	electrician	34	"
	F	Hardy Ina—†	75	housewife	30	"
	G	Sweeney Gerald C	75	guard	38	
	H	Sweeney Susan L—†	75	housewife	38	"
	L	Chase Evelyn—†	78	forewoman	37	"
	M	Dunn Pauline—†	78	inspector	36	"
	N	O'Keefe Edward	78	retired	75	"
	O	O'Keefe Henry	78	laborer	26	
	P	O'Keefe Jennie—†	78	housewife	67	"
	R	O'Keefe Joseph	78	painter	38	"
	S	DeSisto Ciraco	80	engineer	54	704 Saratoga
	T	DeSisto Helen—†	80	housewife	34	704 "
	U	Gylling Selma P—†	86	"	61	here
	V	LaChance Edward	86	foreman	53	"
	W	Williams Albert L	86	operator	37	"
	X	Callahan James D	88	bookkeeper	33	"
	Y	Callahan James J	88	fireman	63	"
	Z	Callahan Joseph F	88	salesman	25	"
1337						
	A	Callahan Leo B	88	clerk	20	
	B	Callahan Margaret L—†	88	housewife	59	"
	C	Callahan Margaret L—†	88	clerk	27	
	D	Callahan Mary L—†	88	"	29	
	E	Callahan Rita T—†	88	operator	23	"
	F	Douglas John H	88	salesman	64	"
	G	Fennelly Anna—†	90	housewife	50	"
	H	Fennelly Canice J	90	policeman	46	"
	K	Harvender Grace M—†	92	housewife	36	"
	L	Harvender William H	92	clerk	21	
	M	Sullivan Agnes E—†	92	housewife	34	"
	N	Sullivan Alexander F	92	contractor	46	"
	O	Eaton Effie—†	96	housewife	56	"

Page.	Letter.	FULL NAME.	Residence, Jan. 1, 1938.	Occupation.	Supposed Age.	Reported Residence, Jan. 1, 1937. Street and Number.

Wordsworth Street—Continued

	P	Eaton Violet—†	96	housewife	24	78 White
	R	Eaton Walter	96	laborer	24	here
	S	Eaton William	96	clerk	29	"
	T	Murphy James J	96	operator	41	"
	U	McMahon Anna—†	96	housewife	68	"
	V	McMahon Catherine—†	96	"	66	
	W	Lammers Marion E—†	107	"	40	
	X	Lammers Walter F	107	bookbinder	37	"
	Y	Lammers William A	107	operator	74	
1338						
	A	Cecchino Angelina—†	109	housewife	24	51 Wordsworth
	B	Cecchino Hector J	109	manufacturer	26	51 "
	C	Pallozzi Dora—†	109	saleswoman	20	here
	D	Pallozzi Josephine—†	109	housewife	42	"
	E	Pallozzi Ralph	109	laborer	47	"

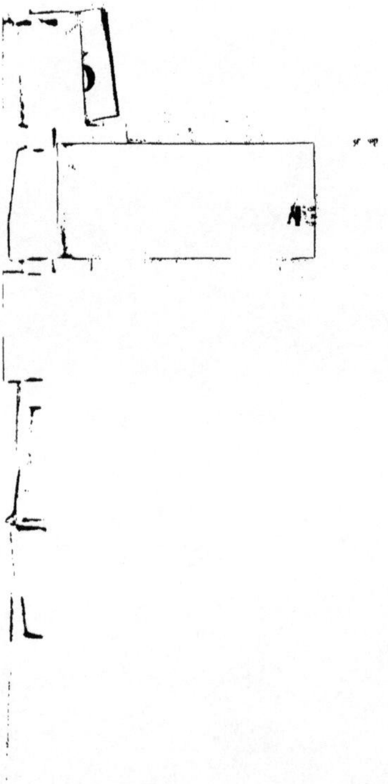

Ward 1–Precinct 17

CITY OF BOSTON

LIST OF RESIDENTS
20 YEARS OF AGE AND OVER

(NON-CITIZENS INDICATED BY ASTERISK)
(FEMALES INDICATED BY DAGGER)

AS OF

JANUARY 1, 1938

JOSEPH F. TIMILTY, } *Listing*
FREDERIC E. DOWLING, } *Board.*

CITY OF BOSTON PRINTING DEPARTMENT

Ashley Street

Page.	Letter.	Full Name.	Residence, Jan. 1, 1938.	Occupation.	Supposed Age.	Reported Residence, Jan. 1, 1937. Street and Number.
1348						
	A	*Carideo Angelina—†	19	housewife	50	here
	B	*Carideo Nicholas	19	operator	60	“
	C	Carideo Patrick	19	“	23	“
	D	Carideo Rose—†	19	“	30	“
	E	Gianino Frank	19	laborer	42	“
	F	*Gianino Mary—†	19	housewife	39	“
	G	Conley Florence—†	19	“	28	“
	H	Conley Harry	19	salesman	27	“
	K	Donovan Ambrose	19	laborer	23	
	L	*Puzzo Angelina—†	19A	housewife	67	“
	M	Puzzo Lillian—†	19A	operator	30	“
	N	*Capone Gaetano	19A	longshoreman	39	“
	O	*Capone Mary—†	19A	housewife	34	“
	P	McDonald Ellen—†	21	“	64	“
	R	McDonald Florence—†	21	“	35	
	S	*McDonald James A	21	carpenter	66	“
	T	McDonald James M	21	butcher	35	“
	U	*Cassaro Michael	21	laborer	51	231 Saratoga
	V	*Cassaro Santina—†	21	housewife	41	231 “
	W	*Censabella Carmella—†	21A	“	67	here
	X	*Censabella Domenic	21A	carpenter	67	“
	Y	*Covalucci Rose—†	21A	housewife	27	246½ Leyden
	Z	Covalucci Vito	21A	laborer	27	246½ “
1349						
	A	Iovanna Frank	23	finisher	47	here
	B	Iovanna Mary E—†	23	housewife	48	“
	C	Melvin Alfred	23A	watchman	85	“
	D	Venezia Patrick	23A	laborer	30	
	E	Venezia Rose—†	23A	housewife	35	“
	F	Sacco Grace—†	23A	“	29	142 Leyden
	G	Sacco Michael	23A	laborer	28	142 “
	H	Casale Elizabeth—†	25	housewife	32	23A Ashley
	K	Casale Richard	25	laborer	35	23A “
	L	*Minichiello Antoinette—†	27	housewife	35	here
	M	*Minichiello Ralph	27	longshoreman	50	“
	N	Gemelli Michael	29	laborer	49	1106½ Bennington
	O	Gemelli Raffaela—†	29	housewife	44	1106½ “
	P	Gemelli Rose—†	29	dressmaker	24	1106½ “
	R	Grande Joseph	31	laborer	22	here
	S	Grande Pauline—†	31	housewife	23	“

Page.	Letter.	Full Name.	Residence, Jan. 1, 1938.	Occupation.	Supposed Age.	Reported Residence, Jan. 1, 1937. Street and Number.

Ashley Street—Continued

	T	Velardo Giovanni	31	barber	50	here
	U	Velardo Jeunic—†	31	housewife	43	"
	W	Bradley Edward	35	operator	20	"
	X	Bradley Henry	35	longshoreman	39	"
	Y	Bradley Marie—†	35	housewife	40	"
	Z	*Giglio Caroline—†	39	"	41	15 North sq
1350						
	A	Giglio Domenic	39	operator	39	15 "
	B	Craviotto Margaret—†	39	housewife	29	167 Leyden
	C	Craviotto Silvio	39	laborer	30	167 "
	D	Pepe Martha—†	41	dressmaker	22	here
	E	*Pepe Nellie—†	41	housewife	44	"
	F	Pepe Pasqualina—†	41	operator	24	"
	G	Masone Pasqualina—†	41	housewife	46	"
	H	Masone Raffaele	41	laborer	49	
	K	Bellio Angela—†	rear 41	housewife	42	"
	L	Bellio Moses	" 41	operator	44	

Beachview Road

	M	Kraner Gladys—†	9	housewife	28	here
	N	*Brignati Ellen—†	11	"	68	"
	O	Brignati Lawrence	11	superintendent	69	"
	P	Brignati Lawrence C	11	decorator	30	"
	R	*Cook Alice H—†	15	clerk	44	
	S	*Cook Catherine W—†	15	housewife	69	"
	T	Smith Charles H	15	printer	56	
	U	Antonicci Ancella—†	23	housewife	25	"
	V	Antonicci Frank	23	painter	26	"
	W	Indrisano Margaret—†	23	housewife	33	"
	X	Indrisano Victor	23	laborer	37	
	Y	Biagiotti Alice—†	23	housewife	34	"
	Z	Biagiotti Victor	23	storekeeper	35	"
1351						
	A	Mainardi Omero	23	laborer	45	
	B	Groppi Ancleto	23	"	32	
	C	Groppi Erina—†	23	housewife	58	"
	D	Groppi John	23	laborer	21	
	E	Groppi Joseph	23	"	23	
	F	Groppi Oreste	23	cigarmaker	67	"
	G	*Biagiotti Mary—†	27	housewife	42	"

Page.	Letter.	FULL NAME.	Residence, Jan. 1, 1938.	Occupation.	Supposed Age.	Reported Residence, Jan. 1, 1937. Street and Number.

Beachview Road—Continued

	H	Biagiotti Ralph	27	mechanic	43	here
	K	Sardina Ida—†	27	housewife	30	"
	L	Sardina John	27	laborer	28	"
	M	Paterson Bessie—†	30–32	housewife	55	"
	N	Paterson Elizabeth—†	30–32	teacher	25	"
	O	Paterson Grace W—†	30–32	cook	23	
	P	Paterson John N	30–32	printer	56	
	R	Ford Arthur F	30–32	superintendent	54	"
	S	Ford Charles	30–32	laborer	24	
	T	Ford Jennie—†	30–32	housewife	55	"
	U	Ford Pearl—†	30–32	"	26	
	V	Ford Raymond	30–32	clerk	26	
	W	Ford Ruth—†	30–32	student	21	
	X	*Perricotti Fortunato	31	retired	80	
	Y	Perricotti John W	31	laborer	42	
	Z	*Perricotti Sarah—†	31	housewife	72	"
1352						
	A	Rando Anthony	36	laborer	50	
	B	Rando Margaret—†	36	clerk	21	
	C	Rando Mary—†	36	housewife	48	"
	D	*Rando Paul	36	laborer	74	
	E	Velardo Anthony	36	barber	60	
	F	Velardo John	36	dentist	24	
	G	*Velardo Josephine—†	36	housewife	52	"
	H	Velardo Natale—†	36	clerk	20	"
	K	Terry David	36	operator	34	145 Falcon
	L	Terry Nora—†	36	housewife	33	145 "
	M	Perce Angelo	47	painter	54	here
	N	Perce Charles	47	chauffeur	26	"
	O	Perce Mildred—†	47	clerk	20	"
	P	Perce Susan M—†	47	housewife	45	"
	R	Palladino Joseph	47	laborer	26	
	S	Palladino Pauline—†	47	housewife	28	"
	T	Hoyt Irving	53	policeman	46	"
	U	Hoyt Violetta—†	53	housewife	39	"

Bennington Street

	V	Abate Arthur	1144	salesman	44	here
	W	Abate Marietta—†	1144	housewife	40	"
	X	Casaletto Alfred	1144	laborer	32	129 Chiswick rd

Page.	Letter.	Full Name.	Residence, Jan. 1, 1938.	Occupation.	Supposed Age.	Reported Residence, Jan. 1, 1937. Street and Number.

Bennington Street—Continued

	Y	Casaletto Joseph	1144	clerk	28	129 Chiswick rd
	Z	Casaletto Josephine—†	1144	housewife	59	129 "
1353						
	A	Venditti Celia—†	1144	"	49	here
	B	Venditti Edward	1144	tailor	50	"
	C	Venditti Loretta—†	1144	saleswoman	21	"
	D	Queenan Agnes—†	1148	housewife	33	"
	E	Queenan John	1148	laborer	31	
	F	Tammans Charles	1148	"	35	
	G	Tammans Margaret—†	1148	housewife	33	"
	L	Ardolino Maria—†	1148	at home	48	
	H	*LaValle Anthony	1148	coppersmith	43	"
	K	LaValle Emma—†	1148	housewife	24	"
	M	*Savasta Antonetta—†	1150	"	50	
	N	*Savasta John	1150	laborer	59	
	O	Savasta Joseph	1150	"	22	
	P	Savasta Mary—†	1150	clerk	25	
	R	*Lanfranchi Antonetta–†	1150	housewife	37	"
	S	Lanfranchi John	1150	laborer	37	
	T	Bonanno Leo	1150	"	43	
	U	*Bonanno Mary—†	1150	housewife	37	"
	V	*DeBella Francesco	1150	retired	71	

Breed Street

	W	Allegra Joseph	29	laborer	20	here
	X	Ferrara Anthony	29	"	29	"
	Y	Ferrara Antonio	29	"	22	"
	Z	*Ferrara Frank	29		57	
1354						
	A	*Ferrara Mary—†	29	housewife	54	"
	B	Ferrara Salvatore	29	laborer	20	
	C	Rando Agnes—† .	31	housewife	49	"
	D	Rando Pasquale	31	barber	53	
	E	Kalman Louis	31	salesman	37	"
	F	Kalman Sonia—†	31	housewife	36	"
	G	Cushing Bertha F—†	33	"	52	
	H	Cushing Charles A	33	painter	64	
	K	Smith Alfred H	33	operator	59	"
	L	Smith Alfred H, jr	33	clerk	25	
	M	Smith Anne C—†	33	housewife	57	"

Page.	Letter.	Full Name.	Residence, Jan. 1, 1938.	Occupation.	Supposed Age.	Reported Residence, Jan. 1, 1937. Street and Number.

Breed Street—Continued

	N	Keating Christopher	35	retired	60	here
	O	Lial Josephine—†	35	seamstress	55	“
	P	Cerullo Louis	35	laborer	32	“
	R	Cerullo Mary—†	35	housewife	22	“

Faywood Avenue

	T	Labadini Alda—†	31	housewife	30	here
	U	Labadini Ernest	31	bartender	32	“
	V	Viveiros Paul A	31	laborer	23	“
	W	Azzatto Emma—†	31	housewife	31	“
	X	Azzatto Thomas	31	laborer	35	
	Y	Pearson Charles W	31	oiler	31	
	Z	Pearson Etta—†	31	housewife	60	“
1355						
	A	Pearson Frank W	31	clerk	23	
	B	Pearson Walter H	31	laundryman	26	“
	C	Leigh Amy—†	33	housewife	70	“
	D	Leigh Dorothy M—†	33	stenographer	38	“
	E	Leigh John	33	wharfinger	69	“
	F	Moran Henry F	33	foreman	36	“
	G	Moran Mary J—†	33	housewife	32	“
	H	Buresh Charles	33	foreman	30	
	K	Buresh Gladys—†	33	housewife	27	“
	L	Rogers Alfred	33	operator	55	
	M	Rogers Blanche—†	33	housewife	60	“
	N	Muse Mary E—†	35	“	38	
	O	Muse Wilfred F	35	seaman	44	
	P	Homeyer Henry N	35	proprietor	59	“
	R	Homeyer Henry N, jr	35	student	22	
	S	Homeyer Sarah E—†	35	housewife	50	“
	T	Stoliker Mary L—†	35	at home	72	“
	U	Breau Alice M—†	35	housewife	58	29 Orient av
	V	Breau Mary E—†	35	nurse	24	here
	W	Breau Robert J	35	machinist	22	29 Orient av
	X	Breau Thaddeus	35	engineer	65	29 “
	Y	Dennehy James F	37	clerk	56	here
	Z	Dennehy Sarah E—†	37	housewife	58	“
1356						
	A	*Butera Jennie—†	37	“	35	“
	B	*Butera Rocco	37	barber	39	

Page.	Letter.	Full Name.	Residence, Jan. 1, 1938.	Occupation.	Supposed Age.	Reported Residence, Jan. 1, 1937. Street and Number.
		Faywood Avenue—Continued				
	C	Capobianco Jennie—†	37	housewife	45	195 Webster
	D	Capobianco Joseph	37	manager	43	195 "
	E	Pesce Edith—†	43	housewife	35	here
	F	Pesce Geronima—†	43	"	64	"
	G	Pesce Louis	43	laborer	36	"
	H	Pesce Silvio	43	"	23	
	K	Sacco Theresa—†	43	housekeeper	31	"
	L	Williams Ralph	43	clerk	27	"
	M	Williams Rose—†	43	housewife	28	"
	N	Bianco Emma—†	45	"	24	727 Benningt'n
	O	Bianco James	45	laborer	29	727 "
	P	Campatelli Augusto	45	retired	72	here
	R	Campatelli Marjorie—†	45	houseworker	30	Chelsea
	S	Dundon Cornelius L	48	constable	56	here
	T	Dundon Joseph M	48	clerk	30	"
	U	Dundon Mary L—†	48	"	58	"
	V	Lemos Clarence	51	engraver	44	"
	W	Lemos Margaret—†	51	housewife	37	"
	X	Velardi Antonio	52	policeman	44	"
	Y	Velardi Mildred C—†	52	housewife	34	"
	Z	Campagnone Anthony	52	barber	56	
1357						
	A	Campagnone Carmella—†	52	housewife	60	"
	B	Campagnone Gennaro	52	machinist	28	"
	C	Campagnone John	52	"	24	
	D	Campagnone Mario	52	laborer	26	
	E	Campagnone Pasquale	52	draftsman	30	"
	F	Boudreau Sabina M—†	55	at home	65	
	G	Doherty Grace A—†	55	clerk	26	"
	H	Doherty Hugh	55	laborer	67	
	K	Kenney Alice K—†	56	housewife	35	"
	L	Kenney Nicholas E	56	policeman	42	"
	M	McCallum Helen—†	56	operator	55	
	N	Kenney Walter J	60	policeman	40	"
	O	McNealy Edward C	60	chauffeur	45	"
	P	McNealy Gertrude—†	60	housewife	43	"
	R	Lavery Agnes C—†	64	teacher	39	
	S	Tyrell John A	64	custodian	39	"
	T	Tyrell Marguerite—†	64	housewife	38	"
	U	Cosgrove Joseph F	67	inspector	41	"
	V	Cosgrove Margaret A—†	67	housewife	24	"

Page.	Letter.	Full Name.	Residence, Jan. 1, 1938.	Occupation.	Supposed Age.	Reported Residence, Jan. 1, 1937. Street and Number.

Faywood Avenue—Continued

Page.	Letter.	Full Name.	Residence, Jan. 1, 1938.	Occupation.	Supposed Age.	Reported Residence, Jan. 1, 1937.
	W	DeLeo Gaetano	67	musician	45	here
	X	Serignano Michael	67	storekeeper	47	"
	Y	Serignano Nancy—†	67	housewife	35	"
	Z	Chase George	68	engraver	48	"
1358						
	A	Chase Sarah—†	68	housewife	40	"
	B	Trevor Joseph A	68	retired	64	
	C	McDermott Francis H	69	compositor	37	"
	D	McDermott Harriet M—†	69	bookkeeper	43	"
	E	McDermott M Catherine—†	69	housewife	46	"
	F	McDermott Sylvia E—†	69	supervisor	40	"
	G	O'Malley Delia A—†	69	housewife	70	"
	H	O'Malley James	69	retired	72	
	K	O'Malley Lillian—†	69	bookkeeper	37	"
	L	Freeman Agnes L—†	73	housewife	66	"
	M	Freeman James H	73	retired	72	
	N	Warren Samuel A	73	inspector	44	"
	O	Warren Winifred F—†	73	housewife	43	"
	P	Wright Charles D	74	inspector	44	"
	R	Wright Margaret J—†	74	housewife	40	"
	S	Kelly Angela J—†	76	operator	33	"
	T	Kelly Richard T	76	retired	80	
	U	Kelly James J	76	seaman	65	
	V	Magee Mary F—†	76	clerk	45	
	W	Magee Rose F—†	76	at home	70	
	X	McGinley John	76	retired	84	
	Y	Newbury Warren C	79	superintendent	42	"
	Z	Williams Catherine M—†	79	clerk	35	"
1359						
	A	Cuttillo Alice—†	84	housewife	34	62 Webster
	B	Cuttillo Philomena—†	84	"	75	62 "
	C	Cuttillo William	84	proprietor	39	62 "
	D	Venezia Edna—†	85	at home	32	here
	E	Venezia Mary—†	85	operator	33	"
	F	Venezia Michael	85	"	24	"
	G	Venezia Nellie—†	85	stitcher	41	
	H	*Venezia Victoria—†	85	housewife	66	"
	K	DeLese Eugene	85	laborer	38	
	L	*DeLese Susan—†	85	housewife	33	"
	M	Ferrore Henrietta—†	87	"	35	
	N	Ferrore Joseph	87	clerk	36	

Page.	Letter.	Full Name.	Residence, Jan. 1, 1938.	Occupation.	Supposed Age.	Reported Residence, Jan. 1, 1937. Street and Number.

Faywood Avenue—Continued

Page.	Letter.	Full Name.	Residence, Jan. 1, 1938.	Occupation.	Supposed Age.	Reported Residence, Jan. 1, 1937. Street and Number.
	O	Ferry George	87	printer	21	here
	P	Schwarz Albert	87	laborer	26	"
	R	Schwarz Beatrice—†	87	operator	28	"
	S	Schwarz Catherine—†	87	housewife	55	"
	T	Schwarz George	87	optician	35	
	U	Faiella Anna—†	88	housewife	48	"
	V	Faiella Felix	88	barber	52	"
	W	Merullo Arthur	88	tailor	30	Quincy
	X	Merullo Mercedes—†	88	housewife	25	"
	Y	Fiella Ralph	88	barber	27	here
	Z	Fiella Theresa—†	88	housewife	24	"
1360						
	A	DeFelice Leo	92	printer	32	"
	B	DeFelice Mildred—†	92	housewife	32	161 Trenton
	C	*DiFazio Antonetta—†	92	"	36	215 Havre
	D	*DiFazio Michael	92	laborer	39	215 "
	E	Brems Florence—†	93	housewife	42	here
	F	Brems Louis	93	director	48	Winthrop
	G	Driscoll George	93	manager	38	here
	H	Driscoll Louise—†	93	housewife	38	"
	K	Sozio Fred	95	printer	33	"
	L	Sozio Lucy—†	95	housewife	30	"
	M	Lanno Clara—†	95	clerk	21	
	N	Lanno Gennaro	95	barber	54	
	O	*Lanno Madeline—†	95	housewife	54	"
	P	Lanno Michael	95	electrician	27	"
	R	Osganian George	100	butcher	43	
	S	Osganian Rose—†	100	housewife	33	"
	T	Thibeault Bertina	103	clerk	23	99 Orient av
	U	Thibeault Edward G	103	seaman	50	Maine
	V	Thibeault Edward P	103	laborer	21	99 Orient av
	W	Thibeault Elizabeth A–†	103	housewife	50	Maine
	X	Perrone Frances—†	108	houseworker	20	29 Ashley
	Y	Perrone Frank	108	salesman	55	29 "
	Z	Perrone Julia—†	108	housewife	50	29 "
1361						
	A	Puzzanghera Crucifessa–†	110	"	52	here
	B	Puzzanghera Giuseppe	110	laborer	57	"
	C	Puzzanghera James	110	musician	28	"
	D	Puzzanghera Joseph	110	clerk	20	
	E	Puzzanghera Salvatore	110	tailor	26	

Page.	Letter.	Full Name.	Residence, Jan. 1, 1938.	Occupation.	Supposed Age.	Reported Residence, Jan. 1, 1937. Street and Number.
		Faywood Avenue—Continued				
	F	Capillo Joseph	116	chauffeur	40	here
	G	Capillo Margaret—†	116	housewife	45	“
	H	Doto Horace J	116	messenger	24	“
	K	Doto Margaret—†	116	housewife	22	“
	L	Martin Edith—†	124	“	49	“
	M	Martin Wilfred	124	engineer	49	
	N	Shields William J	124	investigator	31	“
	O	Gradone Arthur B	150	laborer	49	
	P	Gradone Elvira—†	150	bookkeeper	22	“
	R	Gradone Mary—†	150	clerk	26	“
	S	Gradone Olympia—†	150	stenographer	23	“
	T	Maffei Rufina—†	153	housewife	55	“
	U	Maffei Salvatore	153	constable	53	“
	V	Gillis Dorothy—†	154	housewife	40	“
	W	Gillis Frank	154	clerk	42	
		Gladstone Street				
	X	Cutillo Mary—†	1	housewife	36	37 Gladstone
	Y	Cutillo Pasquale	1	shoemaker	37	37 “
	Z	Ciampa Anthony	1	barber	23	here
1362						
	A	Ciampa Eleanor—†	1	housewife	20	“
	B	Ciampa Frank	1	machinist	35	“
	C	*Ciampa Gennaro	1	retired	67	
	D	*Ciampa Lucia—†	1	housewife	60	“
	E	Ciampa Theresa—†	1	dressmaker	28	“
	H	DeWitt Margaret—†	5	operator	36	1071 Bennington
	K	Grady Alexander	5	clerk	42	1071 “
	L	Grady Mary—†	5	housewife	34	1071 “
	M	Kitson Jennie—†	7	at home	78	here
	N	Stavredis Christopher	7	dealer	50	“
	O	Stavredis Viola—†	7	housewife	47	“
	P	Monahan Daniel	8	laborer	65	
	R	Norton Agnes V—†	8	housewife	57	“
	S	Norton William L	8	operator	57	
	T	Anderson Abbie—†	9	clerk	35	
	U	Anderson Ethel—†	9	at home	27	
	V	Anderson Frank E	9	retired	66	
	W	Anderson Lillian J—†	9	housewife	65	“
	X	Perry Thomas J	9	fisherman	63	“

Page.	Letter.	FULL NAME.	Residence, Jan. 1, 1938.	Occupation.	Supposed Age.	Reported Residence, Jan. 1, 1937. Street and Number.

Gladstone Street—Continued

Page.	Letter.	FULL NAME.	Residence, Jan. 1, 1938.	Occupation.	Supposed Age.	Reported Residence, Jan. 1, 1937. Street and Number.
	Y	Goldberg Beatrice—†	9	housewife	23	here
	Z	Goldberg John	9	manager	28	“
1363						
	A	Goldstein Annie—†	9	housewife	48	“
	B	Goldstein Ruth—†	9	stenographer	21	“
	C	Goldstein Samuel	9	storekeeper	50	“
	D	Lentini Guy	10	teacher	29	17 Moseley
	E	Lentini Rose—†	10	housewife	25	here
	F	Maffeo Consiglia—†	10	“	52	“
	G	Maffeo Henry	10	student	21	“
	H	Maffeo Paul	10	florist	52	
	K	Maffeo Peter A	10	student	20	
	L	Maffeo Sylvia—†	10	teacher	23	
	M	Krebs John F	12	laborer	36	
	N	Kerbs Victoria E—†	12	housewife	35	“
	O	Lovett Estella—†	12	operator	44	“
	P	Lovett John	12	barber	70	
	R	Lovett Mary—†	12	housewife	48	“
	S	Breault Edna—†	16	“	25	Winthrop
	U	Breault Joseph	16	chauffeur	27	“
	T	Ciampa John	16	“	34	here
	V	Ciampa Mary—†	16	housewife	34	“
	W	Barboza Emma—†	17	timekeeper	28	“
	X	Barboza Helen—†	17	clerk	20	“
	Y	Barboza Joseph	17	manager	55	“
	Z	Barboza Marie—†	17	housewife	48	“
1364						
	A	Barboza Marie G—†	17	packer	27	
	B	Barboza Robert	17	cook	24	
	C	Piscopo Concettina—†	17	housewife	46	“
	D	Piscopo Nina—†	17	student	20	
	F	Berg Mabel E—†	18	housewife	45	“
	G	Berg Olaf D	18	painter	50	
	H	Harrington Arthur G	18	laborer	55	
	K	Ghelfi Alfred	20	hairdresser	24	“
	L	Ghelfi Anna—†	20	housewife	53	“
	M	Ghelfi Aristide	20	cook	62	
	N	Bonugli Anna—†	21	housewife	42	“
	O	Bonugli John	21	operator	47	
	P	Carbone Charles	21	“	40	
	R	Carbone Elizabeth—†	21	clerk	44	

Page.	Letter.	FULL NAME.	Residence, Jan. 1, 1938.	Occupation.	Supposed Age.	Reported Residence, Jan. 1, 1937. Street and Number.

Gladstone Street—Continued

	S	Crowley James J	21	letter carrier	29	50 Bayswater
	T	Crowley Sarah H—†	21	housewife	26	here
	U	Leary Dennis J	21	guard	57	"
	V	Leary Harriet A—†	21	clerk	28	"
	W	Leary Sarah A—†	21	housewife	57	"
	X	Lynch Edward M	21	B F D	40	520 La Grange
	Y	Shelley Stella A—†	22	housewife	39	here
	Z	Shelley Thomas M	22	clerk	39	"
1365						
	A	Sullivan John J	24	reporter	41	"
	B	Sullivan Margaret E—†	24	housewife	37	"
	C	Green Elizabeth M—†	24	at home	50	"
	D	Sullivan Alice M—†	24	teacher	46	"
	E	Sullivan Michael N	24	retired	79	"
	F	Guarino Frances—†	25	housewife	31	"
	G	Guarino John	25	engineer	32	"
	H	Caputo Angelina—†	25	artist	28	"
	K	Caputo Louis	25	laborer	65	"
	L	Caputo Philomena—†	25	clerk	34	"
	M	*Caputo Theresa—†	25	housewife	55	"
	N	Giarrusso Caroline C—†	26	"	38	"
	O	Giarrusso James	26	salesman	41	"
	P	Cataldo Agatha F—†	26	housewife	31	"
	R	Cataldo Angelina—†	26	"	59	"
	S	Cataldo John P	26	agent	35	"
	T	Cataldo Lawrence	26	jeweler	29	"
	U	Butt Cecelia—†	26	housewife	45	"
	V	Butt Joseph	26	laborer	45	"
	W	*Calamoneri Dominica—†	33	at home	74	"
	X	*Femino Bruno	33	barber	45	"
	Y	Femino Jennie—†	33	seamstress	22	"
	Z	Femino John	33	laborer	20	"
1366						
	A	*Femino Rose—†	33	housewife	42	"
	B	Paci Angelo	33	operator	23	"
	C	Paci Charles	33	"	27	"
	D	Paci Dominic	33	laborer	62	"
	E	Paci Dominica—†	33	housewife	21	"
	F	Paci Elizabeth—†	33	"	53	"
	G	Paci Joseph	33	operator	25	"
	H	Paci Salvatore	33	"	39	"

Page.	Letter.	Full Name.	Residence, Jan. 1, 1938.	Occupation.	Supposed Age.	Reported Residence, Jan. 1, 1937. Street and Number.

Gladstone Street—Continued

Page.	Letter.	Full Name.	Residence, Jan. 1, 1938.	Occupation.	Supposed Age.	Reported Residence, Jan. 1, 1937. Street and Number.
	K	Occhipinti Angelina—†	33	housewife	29	here
	L	Occhipinti Santo	33	glassworker	32	"
	M	DiGregorio Angelina—†	34	housewife	36	"
	N	DiGregorio Richard	34	laborer	42	
	O	*Marino Charles	37	barber	49	
	P	*Marino Flora—†	37	housewife	44	"
	R	Marino Michael	37	printer	21	
	S	Marino Mildred—†	37	operator	24	
	T	Venuti Carmella—†	37	at home	63	"
	U	Venuti Salvatore	37	operator	27	89 Orleans
	V	Caputo Andrew	37	"	23	here
	W	Caputo Elizabeth—†	37	housewife	48	"
	X	Caputo John	37	laborer	51	"
	Y	DeFonzo Angelina—†	37	housewife	24	"
	Z	DeFonzo Pasquale	37	operator	25	Revere
1367						
	A	*Cutillo Annette—†	37	housewife	28	here
	B	*Cutillo Celia—†	37	"	64	"
	C	Cutillo John	37	shoemaker	41	"
	D	*Cutillo Joseph	37	guard	64	
	E	*Cutillo Raymond	37	operator	22	"
	F	Bianco Joseph A	40	physician	55	"
	G	Bianco Mary D—†	40	housewife	41	"
	K	D'Allesandro Louis	40	laborer	29	146 Gove
	L	D'Allesandro Marion—†	40	housewife	25	146 "
	M	Giardinalli Mary—†	44	operator	21	here
	N	Giardinalli Nicholas	44	laborer	23	"
	O	Giardinalli Rosa—†	44	housewife	46	"
	P	Piscopo Alice—†	45	"	27	
	R	Piscopo Guy T	45	attorney	33	"
	S	Piscopo John	45	dealer	63	
	T	Piscopo Lillian C—†	45	clerk	38	
	U	Piscopo Louise G—†	45	"	31	
	V	Piscopo Mary L—†	45	at home	34	
	W	Piscopo Rachel—†	45	housewife	56	"
	X	Piscopo Thomas G	45	salesman	29	Lynn
	Y	*Guerrini Purifica—†	46	housewife	48	here
	Z	Guerrini Valentine	46	laborer	57	"
1368						
	A	Lowney Helen—†	46	housewife	39	"
	B	Lowney Herbert	46	laborer	38	

Page.	Letter.	Full Name.	Residence, Jan. 1, 1938.	Occupation.	Supposed Age.	Reported Residence, Jan. 1, 1937. Street and Number.

Gladstone Street—Continued

	C	Palladino Aldo F	51	clerk	22	here
	D	Palladino Amy L—†	51	teacher	26	"
	E	Palladino Irma J—†	51	bookkeeper	30	"
	F	Palladino Maria—†	51	housewife	61	"
	G	Ekholm Charles F	52	laborer	63	
	H	Ekholm Helen—†	52	at home	32	
	K	Ekholm Helena—†	52	housewife	57	"
	L	Ekholm Joseph G	52	salesman	33	"
	M	Gattuso Anna—†	56	housewife	28	"
	N	Gattuso Domenic	56	packer	28	
	O	Cummings Edward L	56	clerk	34	
	P	Cummings Ethel A—†	56	attorney	31	"
	R	Cummings John	56	retired	79	
	S	Cummings John A	56	broker	33	
	T	Cummings Joseph J	56	clerk	30	
	U	Cummings Katherine A-†	56	secretary	38	"
	V	Cummings Thomas B	56	clerk	36	
	W	Cummings William F	56	inspector	32	"
	X	Larkin Mary—†	57	housekeeper	48	"
	Y	McDonald Elias	57	engineer	62	"
	Z	McDonald Josephine—†	57	housewife	61	"
1369						
	A	McDonald Raymond	57	laborer	35	"
	C	Sacco Charles	60	mechanic	38	128 Gladstone
	D	Sacco Louise—†	60	housewife	33	here
	E	Bruno James	60	clerk	20	"
	F	*Bruno Joseph	60	storekeeper	57	"
	G	*Bruno Julia—†	60	housewife	45	"
	H	Leary Edward T	61	chauffeur	31	Quincy
	K	Leary Mary A—†	61	housewife	30	"
	L	Andrisano Anthony	61	musician	20	here
	M	Andrisano Carpina—†	61	housewife	52	"
	N	Andrisano Eleanor—†	61	at home	22	"
	O	Andrisano Joseph	61	laborer	52	
	P	Leary Elizabeth M—†	65	housekeeper	53	"
	R	Boushell Catherine—†	66	housewife	79	"
	S	Boushell Margaret I—†	66	clerk	35	
	T	Boushell William F	66	cleanser	46	
	U	Riley Charles H	66	dealer	52	
	V	Riley Frederick E	66	contractor	22	"
	W	Riley Mary A—†	66	housewife	52	"

Page.	Letter.	Full Name.	Residence, Jan. 1, 1938.	Occupation.	Supposed Age.	Reported Residence, Jan. 1, 1937. Street and Number.

Gladstone Street—Continued

Page.	Letter.	Full Name.	Residence, Jan. 1, 1938.	Occupation.	Supposed Age.	Reported Residence, Jan. 1, 1937. Street and Number.
	x	*Crosby Henry B	69	cutter	33	here
	y	Crosby Isabella V—†	69	housewife	27	“
	z	Murray Arthur	69	longshoreman	36	“
1370						
	A	Murray Lydia—†	69	housewife	34	“
	B	Marino Irene—†	69	“	34	
	C	Marino Joseph	69	mechanic	35	“
	D	Oakes Charles G	71	operator	40	“
	E	Oakes Henry J	71	retired	76	
	F	Oakes John L	71	clerk	33	
	G	Oakes Mary A—†	71	housewife	64	“
	H	Oakes Mary E—†	71	bookkeeper	35	“
	K	Farley Marie—†	72	housewife	27	“
	L	Farley Vincent H	72	optician	32	
	M	Cashman Gertrude M—†	72	stenographer	28	“
	N	Cashman Mae K—†	72	housewife	30	“
	O	Cashman Mary F—†	72	“	58	
	P	Cashman Maurice J	72	realtor	60	
	R	Cashman William J	72	attorney	30	“
	S	Luongo John	73	clerk	24	
	T	Luongo Margaret—†	73	housewife	50	“
	U	Luongo Ralph	73	manager	50	“
	V	Luongo Silvio	73	clerk	26	“
	W	Palladino Antonio	81	laborer	30	
	X	Palladino Frances—†	81	housewife	26	“
	Y	Pallacino Jennie—†	81	clerk	21	
	Z	*Palladino Joseph	81	laborer	65	
1371						
	A	Palladino Nunzio	81	“	29	
	B	*Cortese Frances—†	81	at home	87	
	C	Palladino Domenic	81	longshoreman	27	“
	D	Palladino Frank	81	“	21	
	E	*Palladino Josephine—†	81	housewife	46	“
	F	*Palladino Rocco	81	salesman	52	“
	G	Marino Delma—†	82	housewife	29	“
	H	Marino Frank	82	laborer	29	
	K	*Marino Grace—†	82	housewife	69	“
	L	Marino John	82	janitor	39	
	M	*Marino Leo	82	retired	79	
	N	*Marino Rose—†	82	housewife	34	“
	O	Marino Louise—†	82	“	42	

Page.	Letter.	Full Name.	Residence, Jan. 1, 1938.	Occupation.	Supposed Age.	Reported Residence, Jan. 1, 1937. Street and Number.

Gladstone Street—Continued

	P	Marino Samuel	82	barber	44	here
	R	Marino Anthony	85	fireman	46	"
	S	Marino Flavia—†	85	housewife	43	"
	T	Marino Angelina—†	85	nurse	22	
	U	Marino Esther—†	85	operator	20	"
	V	Marino Grace—†	85	stenographer	27	"
	W	Pratt Arthur W	86	engineer	61	"
	X	Pratt Mary—†	86	housewife	63	"
	Y	*Fredella Jennie—†	87	"	29	
	Z	*Fredella Lorenzo	87	tailor	35	
1372						
	A	Bird Mary E—†	88	teacher	66	
	B	Bird Sarah L—†	88	at home	70	
	C	Ottiano Pasquale	89	musician	47	"
	D	Sampson Blanche E—†	89	housekeeper	53	"
	E	*Ducio Joseph	90	operator	64	"
	F	*Ducio Mary—†	90	housewife	56	"
	G	*Marotta Anna—†	92	"	53	
	H	Marotta Louis	92	operator	21	
	K	*Marótta Vincent	92	shoemaker	60	"
	L	Breed Helen—†	93	housewife	24	"
	M	Breed James	93	printer	26	
	N	Eramo Fred	93	chauffeur	29	"
	O	Eramo George	93	"	30	
	P	Eramo Guido	93	proprietor	28	"
	R	Eramo John	93	operator	20	
	S	Eramo Mary—†	93	housewife	53	"
	T	Eramo Vincent	93	laborer	63	
	U	Eramo Viola—†	93	checker	22	
	V	Granato Carmello	94	operator	23	"
	W	*Granato Fanny—†	94	housewife	46	128 Trenton
	X	*Granato Joseph	94	operator	53	128 "
	Y	Granato Josephine—†	94	"	20	here
	Z	Granato Theresa—†	94	"	25	128 Trenton
1373						
	A	Granato Tina—†	94	"	22	here
	B	Indingaro Domenic	98	barber	53	"
	C	Indingaro Evelyn—†	98	operator	31	"
	D	Indingaro Margaret—†	98	housewife	52	"
	E	Indingaro Romeo	98	barber	23	
	F	Cragin Annie K—†	99	housewife	70	"

Page.	Letter.	Full Name.	Residence, Jan. 1, 1938.	Occupation.	Supposed Age.	Reported Residence, Jan. 1, 1937. Street and Number.

Gladstone Street—Continued

Page.	Letter.	Full Name.	Residence, Jan. 1, 1938.	Occupation.	Supposed Age.	Reported Residence, Jan. 1, 1937. Street and Number.
	G	Cragin Edward T	99	engineer	28	here
	H	Whalen Annie F—†	101	housewife	62	"
	K	Whalen Edmund L	101	student	24	"
	L	Whalen John I	101	foreman	69	
	M	Whalen Marion L—†	101	stenographer	32	"
	N	Bertagna Euba—†	111	nurse	24	"
	O	Bertagna Speranza—†	111	housewife	47	"
	P	Pastore Eva—†	111	housekeeper	28	"
	R	Mandra John	112	dealer	24	"
	S	Mandra Rita—†	112	housewife	23	"
	T	DeStefano Augustine	112	chauffeur	30	"
	U	DeStefano Sarah—†	112	housewife	28	"
	V	Skehan Alice V—†	112	"	47	
	W	Skehan James N	112	clerk	25	
	X	Skehan John J	112	B F D	48	
	Y	Skehan John J, jr	112	clerk	27	
	Z	Skehan Lawrence W	112	"	22	
1374						
	A	Riley Edna—†	114	housewife	30	"
	B	Riley Edward J	114	machinist	32	"
	C	Sacco Frank	114	engineer	41	
	D	Sacco Mary—†	114	housewife	41	"
	E	Allavesen Frederick L	114	laborer	47	
	F	Allavesen George A	114	assembler	42	"
	G	Allavesen John F	114	laborer	50	
	H	Allavesen Louise—†	114	housewife	40	"
	K	Joyce William J	114	laborer	48	
	L	Moretto John	116	clerk	36	
	M	*Moretto Mary—†	116	housewife	27	"
	N	McNamee Anna—†	116	"	32	
	O	McNamee James	116	mechanic	35	"
	P	*Viscione Antonetta—†	116	housewife	57	"
	R	*Viscione Domenic	116	laborer	59	
	S	Silvia Manuel	118	"	37	
	T	Silvia Shandra—†	118	housewife	38	"
	U	Perlupo Joseph	118	laborer	37	
	V	Perlupo Mary—†	118	housewife	30	"
	W	Faccini Charles	118	manager	40	"
	X	*Faccini Victoria—†	118	housewife	40	"
	Y	Mazzarella Grace—†	118	operator	22	
	Z	Mazzarella John	118	laborer	61	

Page.	Letter.	FULL NAME.	Residence, Jan. 1, 1938.	Occupation.	Supposed Age.	Reported Residence, Jan. 1, 1937. Street and Number.
		1375				
		Gladstone Street—Continued				
	A	Mazzarella Mary—†	118	housewife	31	here
	B	Mazzarella Stella—†	118	at home	24	"
	C	Silvia August	120	laborer	36	"
	D	Silvia Mary—†	120	housewife	37	"
	E	Moccia Anthony	120	decorator	32	"
	F	Moccia Maria—†	120	housewife	39	"
	G	Lemos Antonetta—†	120	"	28	
	H	Lemos George	120	timekeeper	33	"
	K	*Iannelli Domenic	120	tailor	44	
	L	*Iannelli Helen—†	120	housewife	37	"
	M	Casey Charles	122	laborer	31	
	N	Casey Marie L—†	122	housewife	28	"
	O	DiCillio Mary—†	122	"	36	
	P	DiCillio Raymond	122	blacksmith	39	"
	R	Golivieri Joseph	122	laborer	54	
	S	*Golivieri Josephine—†	122	housewife	45	"
	T	DiPerri Louis	122	laborer	23	7 Lexington
	V	Colucci Margaret—†	124	housewife	25	here
	U	Colucci Raymond	124	barber	31	"
	W	DeSimone Adelaide A—†	124	stenographer	29	"
	X	DeSimone Alexander H	124	agent	28	"
	Y	Nunes Joseph	124	barber	29	New Jersey
	Z	Nunes Phyllis—†	124	housewife	28	"
		1376				
	A	Ricciardi Fred	126–128	machinist	24	974 Benningt'n
	B	Ricciardi Grace—†	126–128	housewife	23	here
	C	Vitagliano Frank	126–128	laborer	21	"
	D	*Vitagliano Leo	126–128	machinist	48	"
	E	Vitagliano Mary V–†	126–128	housewife	41	"
	F	Savoia Frances—†	129	"	45	
	G	Savoia Vincent	129	counterman	22	"
	H	Sacco Frances—†	137	housewife	35	"
	K	Sacco Henry	137	engineer	33	
	L	Sacco Assunta—†	137	housewife	73	"
	M	Sacco Michael	137	retired	65	
	N	Sacco Patrick	137	clerk	31	
		Leyden Street				
	R	Goldstein Harry	150	storekeeper	50	here
	S	Goldstein Isaac	150	"	44	"

Page.	Letter.	Full Name.	Residence, Jan. 1, 1938.	Occupation.	Supposed Age.	Reported Residence, Jan. 1, 1937. Street and Number.

Leyden Street—Continued

	T	Goldstein Minnie—†	150	housewife	46	here
	U	Goldstein Sadie—†	150	"	48	"
	V	DeRose Concetta—†	150	"	41	"
	W	DeRose Domenic	150	laborer	47	
	X	Testa Gilda—†	150	stenographer	23	"
	Y	*Testa Joseph	150	electrician	58	"
	Z	Testa Joseph, jr	150	laborer	21	
1377						
	A	*Testa Mary—†	150	housewife	52	"
	B	*Testa Salvatore	150	electrician	25	"
	C	Kirk Otto	151	mechanic	33	"
	D	Kirk Rubina—†	151	housewife	30	"
	E	*Bosia Anita—†	151	"	38	
	F	*Bosia Joseph	151	clerk	41	
	G	*Bonoldi Attilio	151	retired	60	
	H	*Bonoldi Regina—†	151	housewife	58	"
	M	Montanari Elvira—†	151	operator	36	"
	K	Palasi Arthur	151	laborer	46	
	L	*Palasi Luiga—†	151	housewife	74	"
	N	Vadaro Henry	151	mechanic	31	"
	O	Vadaro Theresa—†	151	housewife	29	"
	P	Pignat Elizabeth—†	152	"	35	Winthrop
	R	Pignat John	152	laborer	35	"
	S	*Todesca Artenia—†	152	housewife	37	here
	T	Todesca Joseph	152	laborer	39	"
	U	Perschi Charles	152	storekeeper	51	"
	V	Perschi John	152	clerk	21	"
	W	Perschi Romilda—†	152	housewife	45	"
	X	Langone Edna M—†	153	"	28	
	Y	Langone Victor J	153	salesman	35	"
	Z	Alioto Joseph	153	barber	48	
1378						
	A	Alioto Mary—†	153	housewife	43	"
	B	Alioto Anthony	153	chauffeur	39	"
	C	Alioto Antonetta—†	153	housewife	38	"
	D	LaSpina Lillian—†	155	"	34	"
	E	LaSpina Paul J	155	operator	41	"
	F	Alioto Ernest	155	bartender	45	"
	G	Alioto Mary—†	155	housewife	39	"
	H	Sindoni Mary—†	155	"	51	
	K	Sindoni Thomas	155	salesman	54	"
	L	Booth Edward F	160	laborer	57	

Page.	Letter.	Full Name.	Residence, Jan. 1, 1938.	Occupation.	Supposed Age.	Reported Residence, Jan. 1, 1937. Street and Number.

Leyden Street—Continued

Page.	Letter.	Full Name.	Residence, Jan. 1, 1938.	Occupation.	Supposed Age.	Reported Residence, Jan. 1, 1937. Street and Number.
	M	Booth Helen B—†	160	housewife	34	here
	N	Fitzpatrick Katherine L–†	161	teacher	49	"
	O	Fitzpatrick Theresa A—†	161	"	50	"
	P	Fitzpatrick Thomas E	161	"	42	
	R	Donovan Elizabeth M—†	166	housewife	52	"
	S	Donovan John F	166	clerk	21	
	T	Cuneo Catherine—†	166	housekeeper	45	"
	U	Healy John	166	clerk	35	"
	V	Healy Sylvia—†	166	housewife	31	"
	W	Messina Joseph	166	baker	24	
	X	Messina Mary—†	166	housewife	24	"
	Y	Rossi Anthony	167	operator	23	
	Z	Rossi Augostino	167	retired	55	
1379						
	A	Rossi Jennie—†	167	clerk	26	
	B	Rossi Julia—†	167	operator	24	
	C	Rossi Mary—†	167	housewife	50	"
	D	DeSisto Joseph	167	laborer	21	
	E	*DeSisto Lena—†	167	housewife	45	"
	F	*DeSisto Thomas	167	laborer	41	"
	G	*Celoni Grace—†	168	housewife	30	Beverly
	H	*Celoni Stephen	168	laborer	35	"
	K	Carideo Augustino	168	mechanic	20	here
	L	Carideo Carmella—†	168	housewife	38	"
	M	Carideo Samuel	168	operator	46	"
	N	*Scarramuzzino Filippo	168	tailor	53	
	O	Scarramuzzino Joseph	168	operator	23	"
	P	*Scarramuzzino Mary—†	168	housewife	46	"
	R	Veneziano Emma—†	169	"	38	
	S	Veneziano Salvatore	169	machinist	40	"
	T	Felzani Anna—†	172	clerk	26	
	U	*Felzani Antonetta—†	172	housewife	49	"
	V	Felzani Dora—†	172	saleswoman	21	"
	W	Felzani Ernest	172	machinist	24	"
	X	*Felzani Louis	172	tailor	56	
	Y	DeCristoforo Carl	174	salesman	32	"
	Z	DeCristoforo Carmen	174	retired	65	
1380						
	A	DeCristoforo Dorothy—†	174	housewife	31	"
	B	DeCristoforo Rosa—†	174	"	60	
	C	Scotti Esther—†	174	saleswoman	40	"

Page.	Letter.	Full Name.	Residence, Jan. 1, 1938.	Occupation.	Supposed Age.	Reported Residence, Jan. 1, 1937. Street and Number.

Leyden Street—Continued

	D	Scotti Marion—†	174	at home	20	here
	E	Frassica Fillipa—†	175	stenographer	42	"
	F	Frassica Madeline—†	175	at home	29	"
	G	Frassica Marie—†	175	housewife	65	"
	H	Perricotti Louis	175	chauffeur	39	348 N Harvard
	K	Perricotti Mildred—†	175	housewife	37	348 "
	L	Emerson Catherine E—†	176	"	66	here
	M	Emerson Charles N	176	towerman	69	"
	N	Basso Eva—†	177	housewife	35	"
	O	Basso William	177	laborer	36	
	P	*Celona Dominica—†	177	housekeeper	42	"
	R	Memmolo Nellie—†	177	housewife	38	"
	S	Memmolo Ralph	177	laborer	42	
	T	Mantica Domenic	178	chauffeur	44	"
	U	Mantica Leo	178	"	24	
	V	Mantica Mary—†	178	housewife	25	"
	W	Mantica Sarah—†	178	"	45	"
	X	Paine Charles	180	clerk	25	"
	Y	Paine Dagma—†	180	housewife	22	Winthrop
	Z	DeGregorio Eileen—†	180	"	24	here
1381						
	A	DeGregorio Robert	180	aviator	27	
	B	Flaherty Adele—†	182	operator	21	"
	C	Flaherty Catherine M-†	182	housewife	50	"
	D	Flaherty Helen M—†	182	supervisor	27	"
	E	Flaherty Lawrence J	182	laborer	22	
	F	Flaherty Michael J	182	retired	62	
	G	Grieco Angelo	183	attorney	24	"
	H	*Grieco Domenic	183	salesman	49	"
	K	Grieco Michael	183	laborer	22	
	L	Grieco Vito	183	"	20	
	M	Sgroi Frances—†	183	housewife	35	"
	N	Sgroi Samuel	183	painter	42	
	O	*Grieco Josephine—†	183	housewife	38	"
	P	Grieco Mary—†	183	librarian	20	"
	R	*Grieco Michael	183	clerk	46	"
	S	Terriciano Angelina—†	186	housewife	34	"
	T	Terriciano Joseph	186	chauffeur	38	"
	U	DeAngelis Florence—†	186	housewife	36	"
	V	DeAngelis Henry C	186	draftsman	37	"
	W	Christopher John	186	clerk	27	72 Leyden

Page.	Letter.	Full Name.	Residence, Jan. 1, 1938.	Occupation.	Supposed Age.	Reported Residence, Jan. 1, 1937. Street and Number.

Leyden Street—Continued

Page.	Letter.	Full Name.	Residence, Jan. 1, 1938.	Occupation.	Supposed Age.	Reported Residence, Jan. 1, 1937. Street and Number.
	X	Christopher Mary—†	186	housewife	25	72 Leyden
	Y	Salerno Eleanor—†	188	typist	20	here
	Z	Salerno John P	188	clerk	28	"
1382						
	A	Salerno Linda—†	188	typist	23	
	B	Salerno Peter	188	waiter	48	
	C	Salerno Rose—†	188	housewife	47	"
	D	Fennell Anne—†	192	"	54	
	E	Fennell Edward	192	laborer	26	
	F	Fennell James	192	longshoreman	63	"
	G	Fennell William	192	"	31	"
	H	Frazier Marie—†	192	at home	24	34 Granfield av
	K	Smiddy Margaret H—†	194	housewife	41	here
	L	Smiddy Margaret H—†	194	operator	20	"
	M	Smiddy William P	194	longshoreman	44	827 Saratoga
	N	Maltedo Henry P	196	attorney	61	here
	O	Maltedo Katherine S—†	196	housewife	55	"
	P	Biggi Louis	198	laborer	48	"
	R	Riggi Peter	198	custodian	50	"
	S	Biggi Theresa—†	198	housewife	84	"
	T	Christoforo Nellie—†	198	housekeeper	42	"
	U	Maglitta Albert	200	musician	29	"
	V	*Maglitta Frank	200	retired	72	
	W	*Maglitta Salvatrice—†	200	housewife	67	"
	X	*Maglitta Viola—†	200	at home	33	"
	Y	McIntyre Beatrice—†	210	clerk	38	
	Z	McIntyre Ellen—†	210	housewife	65	"
1383						
	A	McIntyre Francis E	210	clerk	27	
	B	McIntyre Helen—†	210	"	31	
	C	McIntyre Irene—†	210	waitress	33	
	D	McIntyre Richard	210	salesman	41	"
	E	Cipoletta Anthony	214	laborer	22	
	F	Cipoletta Josephine—†	214	housewife	44	"
	G	Griffin Edward	226	laborer	24	146 St Andrew rd
	H	Griffin Elizabeth C—†	226	housewife	46	146 "
	K	Griffin John F	226	clerk	50	146 "
	L	Griffin Joseph J	226	chauffeur	26	146 "
	M	Fraga John J	226	clerk	33	here
	N	Fraga Josephine—†	226	housewife	48	"
	O	Fraga Manuel J	226	policeman	46	"

Page.	Letter.	Full Name.	Residence, Jan. 1, 1938.	Occupation.	Supposed Age.	Reported Residence, Jan. 1, 1937. Street and Number.

Leyden Street—Continued

	P	Fraga Mary—†	226	housewife	70	here
	R	McRae Anna K—†	226	bookbinder	32	"
	S	McRae Charles	226	clerk	25	"
	T	McRae Ella—†	226	saleswoman	27	"
	U	McRae Lillian—†	226	bookbinder	26	"
	V	McRae Mary L—†	226	housewife	54	"
	W	McRae Mildred M—†	226	bookbinder	33	"
	X	McRae Walter	226	laborer	21	
	Y	McRae William	226	clerk	23	
	Z	Ballerina Ernano	240	operator	28	
1384						
	A	Ballerina Rose—†	240	housewife	28	"
	B	*Cardinalle Mary C—†	240	stitcher	20	
	C	*Cardinalle Michael	240	retired	63	
	D	*Cardinalle Raffaela—†	240	housewife	59	"
	E	Mauceri Achille	240	laborer	64	
	F	Mauceri Constance—†	240	clerk	23	
	G	*Mauceri Corradina—†	240	housewife	63	"
	H	Mauceri Helen—†	240	clerk	26	
	K	Mauceri Joseph	240	laborer	30	"
	L	Palladino Domenic	240½	"	31	1229 Bennington
	M	Palladino Josephine—†	240½	housewife	25	1229 "
	N	Rapino Phyllis—†	242	"	22	here
	O	Rapino Vincent	242	mortician	25	"
	P	Mulone Antonio F	242	salesman	20	"
	R	Mulone Calogero	242	"	36	
	S	*Mulone Diega—†	242	housewife	36	"
	T	Dinarello Mary—†	242	"	46	
	U	Dinarello Victor	242	clerk	20	
	V	Ponti Gaetano	244	cook	58	
	W	Zunino Alfred J	244	salesman	48	"
	X	Zunino Gertrude—†	244	housewife	39	"
	Y	Zunino Joseph	244	laborer	43	
	Z	*Bruxelles Mary—†	244	housewife	43	"
1385						
	A	Bruxelles Pasquale	244	carver	45	"
	B	Giella Edward	246	laborer	33	374 Lovell
	C	Giella Ida—†	246	housewife	29	374 "
	D	*Zagarri Jennie—†	246	"	40	here
	E	Zagarri Salvatore	246	painter	21	"
	F	*Messina Jennie—†	246	housewife	46	6 Ford

Page.	Letter.	Full Name.	Residence, Jan. 1, 1938.	Occupation.	Supposed Age.	Reported Residence, Jan. 1, 1937. Street and Number.
		Leyden Street—Continued				
	G	Messina Santo	246	operator	48	6 Ford
	H	Stasio Anthony	250	draftsman	23	here
	K	Stasio Fannie—†	250	housewife	49	"
	L	Stasio Joseph	250	coppersmith	50	"
	M	Bianco Angelina—†	250	housewife	59	"
	N	Bianco Bartholomew	250	cutter	36	
	O	Bianco Carmen	250	attendant	24	"
	P	Bianco Eleanor—†	250	dressmaker	23	"
	R	Bianco Geraldine—†	250	bookkeeper	27	"
	S	Bianco Lawrence	250	clerk	38	"
	T	Grasso Angelina—†	250	"	30	
	U	Grasso Clara—†	250	"	24	
	V	Grasso Mary—†	250	operator	28	"
	W	*Grasso Rosa—†	250	housewife	66	"
	X	Messina James	256	salesman	37	"
	Y	*Messina Josephine—†	256	housewife	55	"
	Z	Messina Margaret—†	256	saleswoman	28	"
1386						
	A	Messina Mary—†	256	stitcher	27	
	B	Cincotti Joseph	256	laborer	28	"
	C	Cincotti Philip	256	musician	20	"
	D	*Cincotti Rose—†	256	seamstress	31	"
	E	*Cincotti Vincenza—†	256	housewife	62	"
	F	Lavezzo Mary F—†	258	"	40	
	G	Lavezzo Sylvester	258	bartender	50	"
	H	O'Brien Catherine—†	258	housewife	20	"
	K	O'Brien Edward	258	longshoreman	24	"
	L	Roper Martin A	258	seaman	38	
	M	Warren Catherine—†	258	housewife	42	"
	N	Warren John	258	fireman	44	"
	O	Warren William F	258	oiler	23	
		Montmorenci Avenue				
	R	Orio Frank	75	operator	49	here
	S	Orio Mary—†	75	housewife	54	"
	T	Orio Peter	75	mechanic	22	"
	U	Carco Constantino	91	machinist	36	"
	V	*Carco Josephine—†	91	housewife	38	"
	W	Phillips Anthony L	111	operator	48	
	X	Phillips Edna—†	111	housewife	44	"

Montmorenci Avenue—Continued

Page.	Letter.	Full Name.	Residence, Jan. 1, 1938.	Occupation.	Supposed Age.	Reported Residence, Jan. 1, 1937. Street and Number.
	Y	Cannellos Peter G	119	proprietor	41	here
	Z	Cannellos Pota—†	119	housewife	26	"

1387 Orient Avenue

Page.	Letter.	Full Name.	Residence, Jan. 1, 1938.	Occupation.	Supposed Age.	Reported Residence, Jan. 1, 1937. Street and Number.
1387	A	Hoey Catherine E—†	1	saleswoman	52	here
	B	Hoey Edward A	1	clerk	49	"
	C	Hoey Lawrence F	1	"	29	"
	D	Quirk Frances M—†	1	housewife	63	"
	E	Quirk Francis T	1	laborer	36	
	F	Quirk John	1	"	21	
	G	Quirk Margaret E—†	1	teacher	26	
	H	Quirk Paul	1	chauffeur	30	"
	K	Quirk William	1	laborer	33	
	L	Greenfield Anna V—†	1	clerk	27	
	M	Greenfield Charles H	1	checker	61	
	N	Greenfield Florence—†	1	housewife	25	"
	O	Greenfield Francis C	1	watchman	27	"
	P	Greenfield Mary B—†	1	housewife	51	"
	R	Greenfield Thomas R	1	bookkeeper	25	"
	S	Greenfield William G	1	laborer	24	"
	T	Johnson Amelia A—†	3	housewife	66	"
	U	Johnson Lawrence L	3	printer	32	
	V	Johnson Mary R—†	3	housewife	31	"
	W	McLaughlin Eleanor—†	3	operator	22	"
	X	McLaughlin John J	3	letter carrier	62	"
	Y	McLaughlin Mary—†	3	housewife	53	"
	Z	McLaughlin Walter J	3	clerk	25	
1388	A	Grant Henry	3	"	35	
	B	Grant Marie—†	3	operator	29	"
	E	Hooton Pearl M—†	5	housewife	22	"
	F	Hooton Walter R	5	oculist	25	
	C	Titcomb Charles A	5	musician	42	"
	D	Titcomb Mary C—†	5	housewife	38	"
	G	O'Brien Elizabeth M—†	5	"	58	
	H	O'Brien James E	5	investigator	34	"
	K	O'Brien Joseph R	5	mechanic	31	"
	L	Sears Margaret M—†	5	housewife	35	"
	M	Sears William W	5	chauffeur	37	"
	N	Murray George F	5	clerk	49	

Page.	Letter.	Full Name.	Residence, Jan. 1, 1938.	Occupation.	Supposed Age.	Reported Residence, Jan. 1, 1937. Street and Number.

Orient Avenue—Continued

	O	Verry John H	5	chauffeur	30	here
	P	Verry Pauline K—†	5	clerk	28	"
	R	Verry Sarah B—†	5	housewife	54	"
	S	O'Donnell Grace M—†	7	"	30	"
	T	O'Donnell James J	7	policeman	36	"
	U	O'Donnell William J	7	clerk	28	
	V	Cozzi Annette—†	7	housewife	32	"
	W	Cozzi James J	7	salesman	23	"
	X	Cozzi Louis	7	clerk	30	
	Y	*Cozzi Margaret—†	7	housewife	58	"
	Z	Cozzi Mary—†	7	hairdresser	25	"
1389						
	A	Cozzi Patrick	7	clerk	21	
	B	Hurley Edward J	7	laborer	62	
	C	Sampson John T	7	seaman	22	
	D	Sampson John W	7	contractor	50	"
	E	Sampson Margaret M—†	7	housewife	29	"
	F	Cespa Ida—†	8	"	47	
	G	Cespa Orlando	8	tailor	56	
	H	*Panosette Carmello	rear 8	"	62	
	K	*Panosette Philomena–†	" 8	housewife	54	"
	L	Mortimer Catherine J—†	11	clerk	22	
	M	Mortimer Catherine R—†	11	housewife	53	"
	N	Mortimer Percy H	11	mechanic	57	"
	O	Cray Eliza—†	11	housewife	74	"
	P	Cray Evelyn—†	11	"	24	
	R	Cray Richard S	11	carpenter	71	"
	S	Cray William R	11	guard	27	
	T	*Crowell Irene—†	11	domestic	28	"
	U	Fontes Manuel S	11	chauffeur	40	"
	V	Fontes Natalie—†	11	housewife	40	"
	W	Lanza Concetta—†	12	clerk	26	
	X	Lanza Frank	12	laborer	22	
	Y	Lanza Louis	12	contractor	48	"
	Z	Venezia Alfred	12	chauffeur	27	"
1390						
	A	Venezia Philomena—†	12	housewife	24	"
	B	Smallcomb Peter	12	clerk	27	
	C	Thompson Agnes—†	12	operator	32	
	D	Thompson James	12	clerk	23	
	E	*Thompson Margaret—†	12	housewife	81	"

Page.	Letter.	Full Name.	Residence, Jan. 1, 1938.	Occupation.	Supposed Age.	Reported Residence, Jan. 1, 1937. Street and Number.

Orient Avenue—Continued

Page.	Letter.	Full Name.	Residence, Jan. 1, 1938.	Occupation.	Supposed Age.	Reported Residence, Jan. 1, 1937. Street and Number.
	F	*Walsh Bridget—†	12	housewife	67	here
	G	Rasmussen Charlotte N-†	15	"	46	"
	H	Rasmussen Edna A—†	15	typist	21	"
	K	Rasmussen Robert	15	mechanic	50	"
	L	Callan Madeline L—†	19	clerk	34	
	M	Callan Mary—†	19	housewife	74	"
	N	Rowe George A	19	electrician	53	"
	O	Rowe George A	19	clerk	22	
	P	Rowe Margaret A—†	19	housewife	47	"
	R	Rowe Margaret A—†	19	clerk	20	
	S	O'Donnell Anastasia—†	21	housewife	44	"
	T	O'Donnell Edwin	21	clerk	20	
	U	O'Donnell George W	21	decorator	22	"
	V	O'Donnell John J	21	chauffeur	46	"
	W	Adreani Andrew	24	clerk	30	
	X	Adreani Eleanor—†	24	housewife	26	"
	Y	*Trongone Maria—†	24	"	51	
	Z	*Sampson Mary—†	27	"	80	
1391						
	A	*Sampson Paul	27	retired	78	"
	B	*Buchey Mary A—†	27	housewife	84	"
	C	Martell Mary F—†	27	seamstress	50	"
	D	Martell Mary P—†	27	housewife	78	"
	E	Martell Thomas P	27	retired	80	
	F	*Merchant Maria—†	27	housewife	82	"
	G	Smith Wilfred L	27	laborer	52	"
	H	Morrison Isabel—†	28	housewife	30	1100 Bennington
	K	Morrison John	28	operator	31	1100 "
	L	Giuffre Anna—†	28	housewife	25	here
	M	Giuffre John	28	painter	32	"
	N	Landry Mary M—†	29	housewife	44	"
	O	Landry Walter C	29	fireman	54	"
	P	Bernard Charles F	29	laborer	56	1102 Bennington
	R	Bernard Maria P—†	29	housewife	54	1102 "
	S	*Landry Edmund	29	retired	99	here
	T	Landry Mary B—†	29	saleswoman	49	"
	U	Landry Peter	29	laborer	52	"
	V	Polodec Mary S—†	29	housewife	65	"
	W	DiMari Mary—†	32	"	36	
	X	DiMari Sebastian	32	salesman	40	"
	Y	Staffier Angelo	32	tailor	52	

Page.	Letter.	Full Name.	Residence, Jan. 1, 1938.	Occupation.	Supposed Age.	Reported Residence, Jan. 1, 1937. Street and Number.

Orient Avenue—Continued

Page.	Letter.	Full Name.	Residence, Jan. 1, 1938.	Occupation.	Supposed Age.	Reported Residence, Jan. 1, 1937. Street and Number.
	Z	Staffier Ida—†	32	housewife	51	here
1392						
	A	Staffier Louis	32	agent	30	
	B	Staffier Philomena—†	32	domestic	22	"
	C	Staffier Thomasina—†	32	assembler	25	"
	D	McLellan Ronald	37	operator	67	"
	E	McLellan Sarah—†	37	housewife	67	"
	F	McDonald Elizabeth M–†	39	"	60	
	G	McDonald Thomas E	39	retired	72	"
	H	Moran Alice—†	39	secretary	30	112 Byron
	K	Moran Elizabeth R—†	39	"	35	112 "
	L	Boudreau Anna L—†	39	housewife	59	here
	M	Boudreau Elmer S	39	mechanic	22	"
	N	Boudreau Paul	39	chauffeur	27	"
	O	Boudreau Walter S	39	barber	59	
	P	*Boncorddo Dominica—†	40	housewife	50	"
	R	*Boncorddo Joseph	40	laborer	63	
	S	Vadala Ignazio	40	chauffeur	46	"
	T	Vadala Rose—†	40	housewife	28	"
	U	Boncorddo Joseph	40	salesman	23	"
	V	Boncorddo Maria—†	40	housewife	23	1219 Bennington
	W	Ciriello Aida—†	41	"	31	here
	X	Ciriello Harold	41	barber	25	"
	Y	*Nazzaro Jennie—†	41	housewife	51	"
	Z	Campatelli Gino	41	policeman	48	"
1393						
	A	Campatelli Stella—†	41	housewife	42	"
	B	*Grovallese Angelina—†	42	"	60	
	C	Luongo Elizabeth—†	42	"	38	
	D	Luongo John	42	restaurateur	46	"
	E	Mastrangelo Charles	44	physician	42	"
	F	Mastrangelo Mary—†	44	housewife	41	"
	G	Barker Regina V—†	48	"	48	
	H	Barker William H	48	clerk	45	
	K	Merlino Andrew	49	barber	46	
	L	Merlino Christine—†	49	housewife	41	"
	M	Testa Eugene F	49	grocer	66	
	N	Fiorentino Caroline—†	54	housewife	42	"
	O	Fiorentino Dominic	54	student	20	
	P	Fiorentino Frank S	54	baker	60	
	R	Fiorentino Raffaela—†	54	teacher	22	

Page.	Letter.	Full Name.	Residence, Jan. 1, 1938.	Occupation.	Supposed Age.	Reported Residence, Jan. 1, 1937. Street and Number.

Orient Avenue—Continued

	S	Peterson Albert	54	policeman	37	5 Gladstone
	T	Merluzzi Carlo	56	manager	58	here
	U	Merluzzi Gilda—†	56	teacher	30	"
	V	Merluzzi Gino	56	"	33	"
	W	*Merluzzi Ida—†	56	housewife	55	"
	X	Granata Flora—†	57	"	21	Beachmont
	Y	Granata James	57	salesman	30	"
	Z	Pilato Anthony	57	operator	39	here
1394						
	A	*Pilato Grace—†	57	clerk	28	
	B	Pilato Joseph	57	musician	23	"
	C	*Pilato Maria—†	57	housewife	70	"
	D	*Pilato Marion—†	57	domestic	38	"
	E	*Pilato Rosario	57	retired	74	
	F	Spinale Emma G—†	60	housewife	34	"
	G	Spinale Matthew D	60	manager	35	"
	H	Spinale Anna K—†	60	teacher	28	
	K	Spinale Carmello P	60	restaurateur	60	"
	L	Spinale Catherine—†	60	housewife	58	"
	M	Pilato Charles	63	operator	33	57 Orient av
	N	*Pilato Rose—†	63	housewife	31	New York
	O	*Pilato Louise—†	63	"	34	here
	P	Pilato Michael	63	operator	34	"
	R	Giannattasio Phyllis—†	68	secretary	21	"
	S	Lazzari Adeline—†	68	housewife	38	"
	T	Lazzari Stephen	68	salesman	40	"
	U	Leone Amelia—†	68	housewife	37	"
	V	Leone Patrick	68	storekeeper	48	"
	W	Giannattasio Jane—†	68	clerk	23	"
	X	Giannattasio Michael	68	mechanic	48	"
	Y	Giannattasio Michael	68	"	25	
1395						
	A	Giannattasio Philomena–†	68	housewife	42	"
	Z	Giannattasio Phyllis—†	68	bookkeeper	20	"
	B	Santarpio Edward H	72	investigator	34	"
	C	Santarpio Theresa—†	72	housewife	32	"
	E	Graziano Anthony	75	storekeeper	32	19 Thurston
	F	Graziano Camille—†	75	housewife	25	19 "
	G	Lanza Leo F	75	plumber	29	Winthrop
	H	Graziano Ruth—†	75	housewife	28	here
	K	Graziano William P	75	clerk	25	"

Page.	Letter.	Full Name.	Residence, Jan. 1, 1938.	Occupation.	Supposed Age.	Reported Residence, Jan. 1, 1937. Street and Number.

Orient Avenue—Continued

Page.	Letter.	Full Name.	Residence, Jan. 1, 1938.	Occupation.	Supposed Age.	Reported Residence, Jan. 1, 1937. Street and Number.
	L	DePaulo Gertrude R—†	76	housewife	31	here
	M	DePaulo John C	76	laborer	39	"
	N	*Marafino Mary A—†	76	housewife	78	"
	O	Marafino Nicholas	76	barber	45	
	P	Marafino Rose—†	76	housewife	34	"
	R	Selvitella Henry J	80	attorney	40	"
	S	Selvitella Lena—†	80	housewife	37	"
	T	Selvitella George	80	waiter	23	
	U	Selvitella Helen—†	80	clerk	29	
	V	*Selvitella Mary—†	80	housewife	64	"
	W	Selvitella Susan—†	80	clerk	24	
	X	Selvitella Vera—†	80	"	30	
	Y	Masullo Anthony	81	baker	29	
	Z	Masullo Benjamin	81	barber	58	
1396						
	A	Masullo Catherine—†	81	housewife	56	"
	B	Masullo Dominic	81	baker	28	
	C	Masullo Francis	81	hairdresser	23	"
	D	Bannon Ethel J—†	83	housewife	38	"
	E	Bannon Robert J	83	proprietor	45	"
	F	Evanson Dina J—†	83	housewife	57	"
	G	Lanza Alphonsus G	84	engineer	41	392 Chelsea
	H	Lanza Anna G—†	84	stenographer	34	here
	K	Lanza Concetta—†	84	housewife	67	"
	L	Lanza Elvira G—†	84	"	32	392 Chelsea
	M	Lanza Frank	84	contractor	65	here
	N	Lanza Theresa—†	84	clerk	36	"
	O	Pinardi Charles S	84	engineer	22	"
	P	Merlino Louis	86	restaurateur	53	"
	R	Merlino Mary—†	86	housewife	52	"
	S	Merlino Nunzia—†	86	student	20	
	T	*Viola Josephine—†	87	housewife	43	"
	U	Viola Salvatore	87	operator	52	
	V	Puleo Frances—†	89	housewife	42	"
	W	Puleo Samuel R	89	laborer	45	
	X	Staffieri Grace—†	90	housewife	41	"
	Y	Staffieri Rocco	90	proprietor	45	"
	Z	Forster Charles	90	clerk	45	
1397						
	A	McDonald Beatrice—†	90	teacher	30	
	B	McDonald Irene F—†	90	"	25	

Page.	Letter.	FULL NAME.	Residence, Jan. 1, 1938.	Occupation.	Supposed Age.	Reported Residence, Jan. 1, 1937. Street and Number.

Orient Avenue—Continued

	C	Reagan Anna—†	90	housewife	43	here
	D	Reagan Charles	90	salesman	50	"
	E	Marinelli Agostino T	94	policeman	52	"
	F	Marinelli Marguerita—†	94	housewife	43	"
	G	Pessella Concetta—†	98	"	35	
	H	Pessella Jeremiah	98	florist	30	
	K	Langlois Arthur	98	seaman	26	
	L	Langlois Edna—†	98	investigator	28	"
	M	Langlois Edward	98	seaman	35	
	N	Arsenault Adam	99	engineer	37	
	O	Arsenault Marcella—†	99	housewife	39	"
	P	Thibeault Chester L	99	salesman	26	"
	R	Thibeault Edward E	99	laborer	24	
	S	Thibeault Leo W	99	"	22	
	T	Thibeault Mary—†	99	housewife	52	"
	U	Dolan Edward	99	lineman	34	
	V	Dolan Evelyn—†	99	clerk	24	
	W	Dolan Florence—†	99	"	30	
	X	Dolan Francis	99	"	23	
	Y	Dolan Joseph	99	"	25	
	Z	Dolan Thomas	99	lineman	32	
1398						
	A	Ferrera Arthur	100	student	21	
	B	Ferrera James	100	dealer	46	
	C	Ferrera James	100	student	20	
	D	Ferrera Mary—†	100	housewife	44	"
	E	Perrier Ruth—†	112	"	37	
	F	Perrier Wilfred	112	mechanic	35	"
	G	Landry Estelle—†	112	waitress	21	
	H	Landry Helen—†	112	"	22	
	K	Perrier Delvenia—†	112	housewife	60	"
	L	Perrier Emily—†	112	cook	30	
	M	Perrier Evangeline—†	112	clerk	24	
	N	Perrier Ralph	112	mechanic	22	"
	P	Ayotte Delphine—†	150	teacher	29	
	R	*Campestrini Marie—†	150	cook	72	"
	S	*Cloutier Bernadette—†	150	teacher	40	
	T	DiMilla Pasquale	150	clergyman	68	"
	U	*Dorion Belzemine—†	150	houseworker	69	"
	V	*Gagne Claire—†	150	"	50	"
	W	Joy Lillian—†	150	teacher	39	Fall River

Page.	Letter.	Full Name.	Residence, Jan. 1, 1938.	Occupation.	Supposed Age.	Reported Residence, Jan. 1, 1937. Street and Number.
		Orient Avenue—Continued				
	X	*Killeen Margaret—†	150	houseworker	49	Rhode Island
	Y	*LaCroix Eva—†	150	dressmaker	58	here
	Z	Lattimer Catherine—†	150	houseworker	25	Rhode Island
1399						
	A	*Lavigne Nadia—†	150	nursemaid	37	“
	B	Montcalvo Elena—†	150	cook	23	“
	C	*Parayre Lucie—†	150	seamstress	52	here
	D	*Parzkiewiez Franciszka–†	150	laundryworker	46	“
	E	Pouliot Marie-Ange—†	150	nurse	38	“
	F	*Presseau Marie—†	150	houseworker	65	“
	G	*Sandyes Bridget—†	150	laundress	58	“
	H	Strunk Mary—†	150	teacher	22	Rhode Island
	K	*Talbot Alma—†	150	“	39	here
	L	*Thiriard Lucy—†	150	housekeeper	54	“
		Overlook Street				
	M	Larsen Alfred C	14	laborer	21	here
	N	Larsen Anna E—†	14	housewife	64	“
	O	Larsen Edith M—†	14	bookkeeper	32	“
	P	Larsen Hans C	14	carpenter	60	“
	R	Larsen Harry P	14	chauffeur	34	“
	S	Larsen Lewis H	14	student	23	
	T	Nielsen Frederica—†	18	stenographer	29	“
	U	Nielsen Heinrich V	18	laborer	61	“
	V	Nielsen Louise—†	18	housewife	63	“
	W	Nielsen Robert N	18	clerk	21	
	X	Cameron Archie	26	pharmacist	30	“
	Y	Cameron Christina—†	26	housewife	62	“
	Z	Cameron Winifred—†	26	“	29	
1400		**Sea View Avenue**				
	B	Maida Mary—†	1–3	housewife	46	here
	C	Maida Pasquale D	1–3	clergyman	56	“
	D	Maggio Maria—†	1–3	housewife	43	36 W Eagle
	E	*Maggio Michael	1–3	laborer	48	36 “
	F	Staffier Dominic T	5–7	physician	32	here
	G	Staffier Helen G—†	5–7	housewife	32	“
	H	Dinarello Joseph	5–7	realtor	40	“
	K	Dinarello Mary—†	5–7	housewife	38	“

Page.	Letter.	FULL NAME.	Residence, Jan. 1, 1938.	Occupation.	Supposed Age.	Reported Residence, Jan. 1, 1937. Street and Number.

Sea View Avenue—Continued

	L	Maggio Angelina—†	5–7	housewife	68	here
	M	Maggio Mario	5–7	tailor	40	"
	N	Barone Mary—†	11	housewife	33	"
	O	Barone Pasquale	11	foreman	37	"
	P	Giunta Samuel M	11	clerk	30	27 Everett
	R	Giunta Sylvia—†	11	housewife	25	here
	S	Taddonio Joseph	11	watchmaker	47	"
	T	Taddonio Rose—†	11	housewife	41	"
	U	Cavalieri Dorothy—†	15	at home	20	
	V	Cavalieri Frank	15	chauffeur	29	"
	W	Cavalieri Jennie—†	15	housewife	62	"
	X	Cavalieri Helen—†	15	"	27	
	Y	Cavalieri Henry	15	laborer	27	
	Z	Catrone Emma—†	19	housewife	33	"
1401						
	A	Catrone Joseph	19	salesman	35	"
	B	Rejo Ernest	19	manager	33	3 Sea View av
	C	Rejo Helen—†	19	housewife	33	3 "
	D	Berardi Joseph A	27	retired	67	here
	E	Conti Anthony	27	laborer	38	"
	F	Conti Liberta—†	27	housewife	33	"
	G	Cianciulli Antonio	31	shoemaker	32	367 Lovell
	H	*Cianciulli Louisa—†	31	housewife	68	367 "
	K	*Cianciulli Luigi	31	retired	72	367 "
	L	Calla Argia J—†	39	housewife	40	here
	M	Calla Francis J	39	tailor	42	"
	N	DePaolo Jennie—†	43	housewife	30	99 Orient av
	O	DePaolo Ottone	43	mechanic	32	99 "
	P	Murray Lawrence W	43	"	34	Malden
	R	Murray Marguerite—†	43	housewife	29	"

Selma Street

	S	Cragin Anna G—†	10	housewife	71	here
	T	Cragin Charles H	10	retired	70	"

Waldemar Avenue

	V	Boudreau Harold	17	clerk	24	here
	W	Martell Annie H—†	17	housewife	65	"
	X	Martell Louis D	17	retired	67	"

Page.	Letter.	Full Name.	Residence, Jan. 1, 1938.	Occupation.	Supposed Age.	Reported Residence, Jan. 1, 1937. Street and Number.

Waldemar Avenue—Continued

Page.	Letter.	Full Name.	Residence, Jan. 1, 1938.	Occupation.	Supposed Age.	Reported Residence, Jan. 1, 1937. Street and Number.
	Y	Muise Francis J	17	mechanic	42	here
	Z	Muise Maude—†	17	housewife	41	“
1402						
	A	Favello Louis	20	laborer	30	
	B	Favello Pauline—†	20	housewife	28	“
	C	Driscoll Arthur G	21	laborer	21	
	D	Driscoll Edna M—†	21	clerk	24	
	E	Driscoll Leonard G	21	“	23	
	F	Driscoll Margaret T—†	21	housewife	57	“
	G	Driscoll William M	21	clerk	26	“
	H	Fleming Ellen G—†	23	housewife	65	“
	K	Fleming George J	23	clerk	24	“
	L	Fleming William C	23	laborer	63	“
	M	Fleming William W	23	clerk	33	“
	N	Boyan Catherine—†	32	bookkeeper	40	“
	O	Magee David	32	laborer	46	“
	P	Magee Margaret M—†	32	housewife	37	“
	R	Magrath Frederick J	36	mortician	38	“
	S	Magrath Mary E—†	36	housewife	35	“
	T	Johnson Frank J	37	foreman	63	
	U	Johnson Mary A—†	37	housewife	61	“
	V	Murphy Mary M—†	40	“	62	
	W	Murphy Rita E—†	40	clerk	25	
	X	Olsen Carolyn H—†	40	housewife	40	“
	Y	Olsen Harry J	40	oiler	40	“
	Z	Foley James L	44	clerk	24	“
1403						
	A	Foley James P	44	“	65	
	B	Foley John T	44	cutter	29	
	C	Foley Patrick F	44	longshoreman	35	“
	D	Glassett Catherine M—†	44	housewife	33	“
	E	Glassett Walter T	44	checker	45	“
	F	Balboni Albert	52	operator	26	49 Ashley
	G	Balboni Alfred	52	janitor	27	here
	H	Balboni Anna—†	52	housewife	57	“
	K	Balboni Ivo	52	laborer	29	“
	L	Balboni Louis	52	counterman	31	“
	M	Balboni Sylvia—†	52	housewife	25	49 Ashley
	N	*Rondelli Adolfus	52	retired	74	here
	P	Caruso Pasquale	93	laborer	41	“
	R	Caruso Rose—†	93	housewife	37	“

Page.	Letter.	FULL NAME.	Residence, Jan. 1, 1938.	Occupation.	Supposed Age.	Reported Residence, Jan. 1, 1937. Street and Number.
		Waldemar Avenue—Continued				
	S	Vignoli Helen—†	116	housewife	42	here
	T	Vignoli John	116	laborer	41	"
	U	Harris James A	166	chemist	44	"
	V	Harris Winifred V—†	166	housewife	38	"
	W	King Elizabeth—†	230	"	43	
	X	King George T	230	chauffeur	45	"
	Y	Shea James J	254	"	31	
	Z	Shea Julia—†	254	housewife	29	"
1404						
	A	Watkins Arthur	254	laborer	52	
	B	Watkins Helen C—†	254	housewife	42	"
		Walley Street				
	D	Brady Edward	7	dentist	42	here
	E	LeBlanc Margaret—†	7	nurse	25	"
	F	O'Neil Valentine	7	fisherman	60	"
	G	O'Neil Mary—†	7	housewife	55	"
	H	O'Neil Virginia—†	7	stenographer	20	"
	K	Powers Austin	7	laborer	52	"
	L	Powers Peter	7	retired	62	
	M	McEnaney Lucy—†	7	secretary	44	"
	N	McEnaney Rose—†	7	teacher	54	
	O	McEnaney Thomas	7	attorney	50	
	P	Ciampa James	10	barber	26	
	R	Ciampa Mildred—†	10	housewife	24	"
	V	DeSimone Annette—†	18	"	37	
	W	DeSimone James	18	bartender	37	"

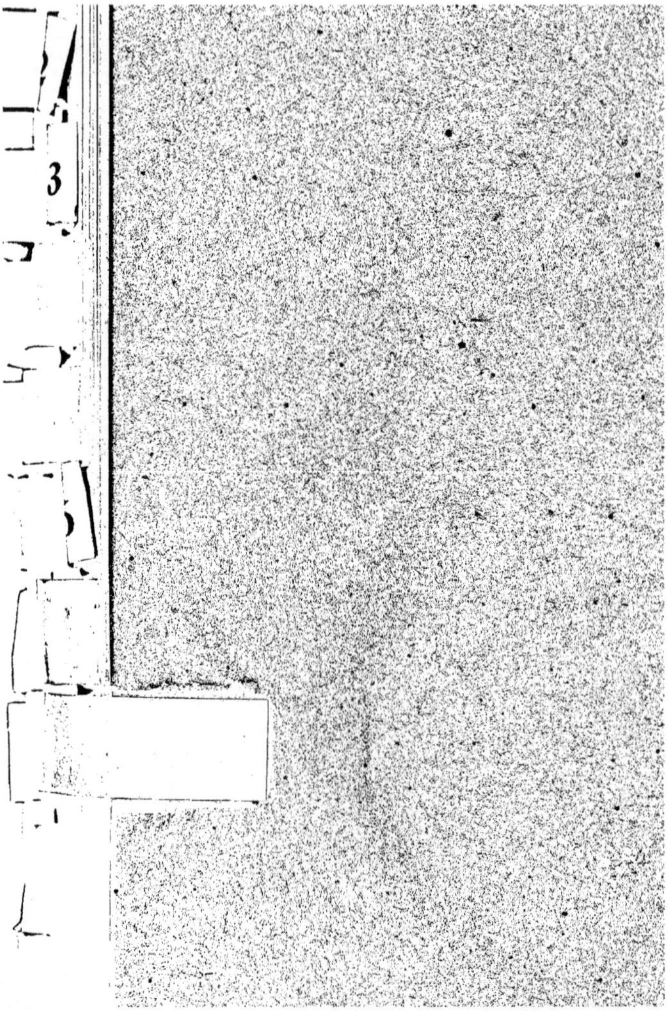
3
5

Ward 1—Precinct 18

CITY OF BOSTON

LIST OF RESIDENTS
20 YEARS OF AGE AND OVER

(NON-CITIZENS INDICATED BY ASTERISK)
(FEMALES INDICATED BY DAGGER)

AS OF

JANUARY 1, 1938

JOSEPH F. TIMILTY, } *Listing*
FREDERIC E. DOWLING, } *Board.*

CITY OF BOSTON PRINTING DEPARTMENT

Page.	Letter.	Full Name.	Residence, Jan. 1, 1938.	Occupation.	Supposed Age.	Reported Residence, Jan. 1, 1937. Street and Number.
1413						
		Barnes Avenue				
	B	Cochrane Edward	6	electrotyper	40	here
	C	Cochrane Josephine—†	6	housewife	40	“
	D	*Pizzano Theresa—†	6	candymaker	64	“
	E	Mason Margaret—†	6	housewife	36	“
	F	Mason Matthew V	6	surveyor	37	“
	G	Morrison Ann—†	10	housewife	30	“
	H	Morrison Paul	10	salesman	39	“
	K	Collins Mary—†	10	housewife	50	“
	L	Collins Robert	10	bookkeeper	50	“
	M	Crowley Anna A—†	14	housewife	49	“
	N	Crowley David J	14	clerk	52	
	O	Crowley Marie E—†	14	“	23	
	P	McCarthy James J	14	accountant	47	“
	R	Stewart Grace F—†	17	housewife	55	“
	S	Stewart John A	17	retired	70	
	T	Hines Agnes A—†	18	housewife	43	“
	U	Hines Claire W—†	18	at home	20	
	V	Hines Leo F	18	serviceman	23	“
	W	Hines Robert F	18	seaman	47	
	X	Giella Florence L—†	18	housewife	38	“
	Y	Giella Vincent J	18	surveyor	35	“
	Z	Hedrington Arthur J	18	laborer	35	
1414						
	A	Hedrington Nellie M—†	18	clerk	40	
	B	Corbett Dennis	18	laborer	41	
	C	Corbett Dennis P	18	rodman	23	
	D	Corbett George	18	clerk	25	
	E	Howland Nora—†	18	housekeeper	60	“
	F	*Cavicchi Adele C—†	21	housewife	68	“
	G	Cavicchi Edward	21	shipper	27	
	H	Cavicchi Evelyn—†	21	bookkeeper	30	“
	K	Cavicchi John	21	laborer	32	“
	L	Cavicchi Joseph	21	toolmaker	32	“
	N	Lambert Charles H	22	upholsterer	44	“
	O	Lambert Helen G—†	22	housewife	42	“
	P	O'Keefe Elizabeth M—†	22	cook	38	
	R	O'Keefe James	22	clerk	20	
	S	O'Shea James	22	“	37	
	T	O'Shea Julia—†	22	housekeeper	43	“
	U	Turvanen John W	22	contractor	40	“

Page.	Letter.	Full Name.	Residence, Jan. 1, 1938.	Occupation.	Supposed Age.	Reported Residence, Jan. 1, 1937. Street and Number.

Barnes Avenue—Continued

Page.	Letter.	Full Name.	Residence, Jan. 1, 1938.	Occupation.	Supposed Age.	Reported Residence, Jan. 1, 1937. Street and Number.
	V	Turvanen Mary E—†	22	housewife	39	here
	W	Perry Alton R	22	salesman	49	“
	X	Perry May—†	22	housewife	43	“
	Y	Malatesta Joseph	25	manager	55	“
	Z	Mangini Frederick	25	“	34	“
1415						
	A	Mangini Madeline—†	25	housewife	33	“
	B	Viverios Joseph	25	salesman	30	“
	C	Celata Joseph	25	policeman	41	“
	D	Celata Lucy—†	25	operator	22	
	E	Celata Paulina—†	25	housewife	41	“
	F	Carlson Carl A	26	patternmaker	26	“
	G	Carlson Carl S	26	carpenter	58	“
	H	Carlson Oscar V	26	rubberworker	24	“
	K	Rush Esther C—†	26	housewife	42	“
	L	Rush Thomas F	26	chauffeur	48	“
	M	Hagan Agnes F—†	26	housewife	28	“
	N	Hagan John L	26	B F D	35	
	O	Chisholm Andrew	30	mechanic	53	“
	P	Chisholm Annie—†	30	housewife	42	“
	R	Chisholm Virginia—†	30	operator	20	
	S	White Ellen—†	30	housewife	28	“
	T	White John	30	clerk	30	
	U	Pagliarulo Caroline—†	30	housewife	32	“
	V	Pagliarulo Joseph	30	salesman	35	“
	W	Foley Edward D	34	machinist	59	“
	X	Foley Mary T—†	34	housewife	80	“
	Y	Bowen Annie E—†	40	“	49	
	Z	Bowen John P	40	foreman	49	
1416						
	A	White Josephine—†	40	housewife	36	“
	B	White Nathaniel J	40	storekeeper	51	“
	C	Moschella Anna—†	42	housewife	36	“
	D	Moschella Michael	42	grocer	41	
	E	Indrisano Mary D—†	44	housewife	29	“
	F	Indrisano Mary P—†	44	“	57	
	G	Indrisano Pasquale	44	foreman	39	
	H	Indrisano Pietro	44	laborer	65	
	K	Indrisano Ruggiero	44	shipper	27	
	L	Whittington Chandler	50	letter carrier	56	“
	M	Whittington Edith E—†	50	housewife	59	“

Page.	Letter.	Full Name.	Residence, Jan. 1, 1938.	Occupation.	Supposed Age.	Reported Residence, Jan. 1, 1937. Street and Number.

Barnes Avenue—Continued

	N	Whittington John R	50	conductor	66	here
	O	McCormack Jessie—†	50	housewife	56	"
	P	McCormack Joseph	50	motorman	57	"
	R	Williamson Alice B—†	50	housewife	61	"
	S	Williamson Harry O	50	tinsmith	49	"
	T	Blackwell Louise—†	54	clerk	29	66 Barnes av
	U	Blackwell Mary—†	54	housewife	60	66 "
	V	O'Mara Agnes—†	54	boxworker	58	66 "
	W	MacCrossan Minnie—†	54	housewife	51	here
	X	MacCrossan Thomas F	54	machinist	52	"
	Y	Burns Howard W	54	B F D	38	"
	Z	Cahill Herbert J	54	"	37	
1417						
	A	Cahill Mary L—†	54	housewife	37	"
	B	*Mucci John	58	chauffeur	28	"
	C	Mucci Mary—†	58	housewife	25	"
	D	Capone Benjamin	58	clerk	20	
	E	Capone Dominic	58	engineer	26	
	F	Capone Guido	58	clerk	22	
	G	Capone Ralph	58	carpenter	53	"
	H	Capone Romilda—†	58	housewife	46	"
	K	*Mucci Angelina—†	58	"	44	
	L	Mucci Antonio	58	meatcutter	59	"
	M	Saggese Salvatore	58	chauffeur	24	"
	N	Nilson Elise—†	62	at home	73	
	O	Nordby Edith—†	62	housewife	41	"
	P	Nordby Sigwald	62	laborer	45	
	R	Crocker Ina—†	62	investigator	29	"
	S	McInnis Florence—†	62	operator	30	"
	T	Johnson Clifford	62	messenger	20	194 Leyden
	U	Johnson Dorothy—†	62	stenographer	23	194 "
	V	Johnson Helen—†	62	clerk	27	194 "
	W	*Johnson Jennie—†	62	housewife	56	194 "
	X	Johnson Lillian—†	62	nurse	30	194 "
	Z	McLaughlin Veronica M–†	66	housewife	30	here
1418						
	A	McLaughlin Walter L	66	pressman	31	"
	B	Sweeney Alice—†	66	housewife	34	96 Homes av
	C	Sweeney Jeremiah J	66	salesman	37	96 "
	D	West Catherine—†	66	clerk	37	96 "
	E	Rezendes Alfred	66	"	26	here

Page.	Letter.	FULL NAME.	Residence, Jan. 1, 1938.	Occupation.	Supposed Age.	Reported Residence, Jan. 1, 1937. Street and Number.

Barnes Avenue—Continued

	F	Rezendes Bento	66	serviceman	52	here
	G	Rezendes Ernest	66	clerk	28	"
	H	Rezendes Evelyn—†	66	at home	21	"
	K	Rezendes Rita—†	66	housewife	48	"
	L	Accetta Alice—†	69	"	55	
	M	Accetta Manfrede	69	salesman	54	"
	N	Muldoon Loretta E—†	70	housewife	46	"
	O	Muldoon William E	70	cutter	46	
	P	Perotti Charles	70	salesman	32	"
	R	Stone Edward J	70	chauffeur	36	"
	S	Stone James H	70	foreman	69	
	T	Stone James H, jr	70	salesman	34	"
	U	Stone Margaret M—†	70	housewife	69	"
	V	Fenockotti Alfred	73	electrotyper	55	"
	W	Fenockotti Alma A—†	73	teacher	26	"
	X	Fenockotti Leonard J A	73	engineer	24	
	Y	Fenockotti Mary—†	73	housewife	53	"
	Z	Lovezzola Frank	73	retired	81	
1419						
	A	Lovezzola Michael	73	engraver	44	"
	B	Lovezzola Teresa G—†	73	housewife	44	"
	C	Lamplough Katherine—†	74	"	29	
	D	Lamplough Lawrence G	74	salesman	32	"
	E	Lamplough Philip J	74	supervisor	29	"
	F	Callanan James J	74	painter	64	
	G	Callanan James J, jr	74	manager	26	
	H	Callanan John J	74	clerk	35	
	K	Callanan Mary A—†	74	housewife	59	"
	L	Abbott Everett M	74	chauffeur	27	"
	M	Abbott Mary E—†	74	housewife	27	"
	N	O'Connell James J	74	operator	58	
	O	O'Connell Margaret A—†	74	housewife	57	"
	P	Kelly Arthur M	78	student	21	
	R	Kelly Florence C—†	78	housewife	46	"
	S	Kelly Michael T	78	plumber	46	"
	T	Fitzpatrick Alice—†	78	housewife	37	"
	U	Fitzpatrick Edward J	78	policeman	38	"
	V	Mahoney William	78	"	41	
	W	Daly Anna P—†	78	housewife	50	"
	X	Daly Maurice A	78	engineer	50	
	Y	Daly Maurice H	78	student	21	

Page.	Letter.	Full Name.	Residence, Jan. 1, 1938.	Occupation.	Supposed Age.	Reported Residence, Jan. 1, 1937. Street and Number.
		Barnes Avenue—Continued				
	Z	Daly Rose A—†	78	teacher	23	here
1420						
	A	Pierce Ellen E—†	82	housewife	24	103 Brown av
	B	Pierce Francis R	82	guard	31	103 “
	C	Sanders William W	82	laborer	51	here
	D	Williams Catherine L—†	82	housewife	71	“
	E	Williams William J	82	custodian	71	“
	F	Coleman Frank K	82	bookkeeper	42	“
	G	Coleman Margaret—†	82	operator	52	“
	H	Coleman Mary—†	82	housewife	66	“
	K	Corrigan Grace M—†	86	teacher	25	
	L	Corrigan John J	86	carpenter	48	“
	M	Corrigan Nora F—†	86	housewife	48	“
	N	Corrigan Ruth F—†	86	bookkeeper	22	“
	O	Murray Margaret A—†	86	“	57	“
	P	Murray Mary A—†	86	housekeeper	60	“
	R	Murray William A	86	clerk	53	“
	S	Brown Sophie—†	86	housewife	55	“
	T	Brown William M	86	engineer	63	
	U	O'Connor Gertrude—†	90	housewife	37	“
	V	O'Connor Thomas	90	plasterer	38	“
	W	Kelley Annie M—†	90	at home	53	
	X	Lane David E	90	B F D	36	
	Y	Lane Katherine A—†	90	housewife	36	“
	Z	Murphy Edward G	90	lineman	20	
1421						
	A	Murphy Egbert R	90	B F D	45	
	B	Murphy Frances—†	90	stenographer	22	“
	C	Murphy Margaret B—†	90	housewife	45	“
		Bayswater Street				
	D	Landry Arthur J	15	B F D	43	here
	E	Landry Clarence	15	attendant	37	“
	F	Landry Genevieve—†	15	housewife	41	“
	G	Landry Mary A—†	15	“	70	
	H	Basile Michael A	16	retired	76	
	K	McMorrow Arthur D	16	laborer	38	
	L	McMorrow Mary E—†	16	housewife	43	“
	M	McMorrow William P	16	B F D	39	
	N	Reynolds Eleanor—†	16	clerk	38	

Page.	Letter.	FULL NAME.	Residence, Jan. 1, 1938.	Occupation.	Supposed Age.	Reported Residence, Jan. 1, 1937. Street and Number.

Bayswater Street—Continued

	O	August Mary T—†	16	houseworker	65	here
	P	Boardman Americus A	16	custodian	66	"
	R	Boardman Charles A	16	retired	68	"
	S	Boardman Marion A—†	16	housewife	55	"
	T	Croce Achille	21	operator	65	
	U	Croce Frederick	21	engineer	28	
	V	Croce Helen—†	21	teacher	29	
	W	Croce Matilda—†	21	housewife	52	"
	X	Bianco Alexander F	22	retired	67	
	Y	Bianco Carol A—†	22	houseworker	24	"
	Z	Bianco Jennie M—†	22	housewife	69	"
1422						
	A	*Avallone Mary—†	23	"	40	
	B	Avallone Matthew	23	tailor	43	
	C	Keller Andrew J	25	attendant	28	"
	D	Keller John J	25	shoecutter	42	"
	E	Keller Mary E—†	25	housewife	35	"
	F	Keller Robert J	25	photographer	37	"
	G	Keller Susan T—†	25	housewife	73	"
	H	Bowen Enos E	29	physician	55	"
	K	Bowen Margaret J—†	29	housewife	49	"
	L	Collins James P	31	teacher	43	
	M	Sullivan Benjamin	33	guard	33	
	N	Sullivan Charles	33	cashier	30	
	O	Sullivan John	33	clerk	23	
	P	Sullivan Joseph	33	carpenter	25	"
	R	Sullivan Mary—†	33	housewife	58	"
	S	Driscoll Catherine M—†	35	saleswoman	21	"
	T	Driscoll Irene—†	35	housewife	38	"
	U	Driscoll Timothy J	35	roofer	43	
	V	Pomfrey Timothy W	35	operator	34	"
	W	Braff Eva H—†	37	housewife	40	"
	X	Braff Max M	37	physician	45	"
	Y	Bertelsen Anna W—†	41	housewife	71	"
	Z	Bertelsen Christian W	41	estimator	37	"
1423						
	A	Bertelsen Marius D	41	retired	68	
	C	Meloni Charles	45	physician	38	"
	D	Meloni Mary—†	45	housewife	36	"
	E	*Castagniola Ruby—†	49	at home	78	6 Ford
	F	Gainor Joseph	49	laborer	27	Lynn

Page.	Letter.	Full Name.	Residence, Jan. 1, 1938.	Occupation.	Supposed Age.	Reported Residence, Jan. 1, 1937. Street and Number.
		Bayswater Street—Continued				
	G	Gainor Rose—†	49	housewife	29	Lynn
	H	Lombardi Humbert	49	clerk	34	6 Ford
	K	Lombardi Joanna—†	49	housewife	33	6 “
	L	*Lombardi Madalena—†	49	“	55	6 “
	M	Lombardi Peter	49	laborer	59	6 “
	N	Lombardi Peter, jr	49	clerk	22	here
	O	Lombardi William	49	student	20	“
	P	Dwyer Elizabeth G—†	50	housewife	66	“
	R	Dwyer John J	50	foreman	62	
	S	McGillicuddy Ruth—†	50	student	23	
	T	McGillicuddy William	50	salesman	60	“
	U	Pryor Matilda E—†	50	housewife	46	“
	V	Pryor Percy J	50	secretary	66	“
	W	Pryor Stanley F	50	clerk	23	“
	X	Lewis James W	53	policeman	63	“
	Y	O'Connell Daniel J	53	merchant	46	“
	Z	O'Connell Lillian S—†	53	housewife	46	“
1424						
	A	Herman Alta—†	54	“	50	
	B	Herman Henry	54	policeman	60	“
	C	Leahy Pauline—†	54	cashier	33	
	D	McGunigle Anna—†	54	housewife	56	“
	E	McGunigle Charles J	54	clerk	28	
	F	McGunigle Daniel H	54	supervisor	34	“
	G	McGunigle George E	54	attorney	36	“
	H	McGunigle John J	54	clerk	26	
	K	McGunigle Mary A—†	54	“	37	
	L	MacEachern Lottie—†	55	housewife	43	“
	M	MacEachern Peter A	55	custodian	48	“
	N	Evans George E	57	mason	47	
	O	Evans Mary F—†	57	clerk	57	
	P	Booth Elizabeth E—†	58	secretary	24	“
	R	Booth Ernest L	58	physician	53	“
	S	Booth Mary A—†	58	housewife	55	“
	T	Booth Mary P—†	58	secretary	24	“
	V	Keating Alice D—†	66	probat'n officer	37	“
	W	Keating Gertrude C—†	66	teacher	32	
	X	Keating Kathryn I—†	66	stenographer	34	“
	Z	Weafer Leonard E	70	attorney	37	“
1425						
	A	Weafer Margaret P—†	70	housewife	34	“

Page.	Letter.	Full Name.	Residence, Jan. 1, 1938.	Occupation.	Supposed Age.	Reported Residence, Jan. 1, 1937. Street and Number.

Bayswater Street—Continued

Page.	Letter.	Full Name.	Residence, Jan. 1, 1938.	Occupation.	Supposed Age.	Reported Residence, Jan. 1, 1937. Street and Number.
	B	Queenan Harold R	74	clerk	29	here
	C	Queenan John P	74	photographer	57	“
	E	Queenan Paul A	74	“	24	“
	D	Queenan Rosanna E—†	74	housewife	56	“
	F	Halbich Margaret—†	74	“	44	
	G	Grisdale Ada B—†	74	“	70	

Bennington Street

Page.	Letter.	Full Name.	Residence, Jan. 1, 1938.	Occupation.	Supposed Age.	Reported Residence, Jan. 1, 1937. Street and Number.
	H	Dinsmore Agnes G—†	715	housewife	35	here
	K	Dinsmore Robert	715	agent	40	“
	L	Healy Edward C	715	clerk	22	“
	M	Healy Francis P	715	“	27	
	N	Healy Margaret T—†	715	housewife	45	“
	O	Healy Peter H	715	supervisor	52	“
	P	Healy Peter H, jr	715	mechanic	24	“
	R	Healy Ruth M—†	715	stenographer	23	“
	S	Terry William J	719	longshoreman	21	“
	T	Lewis Frank W	719	draftsman	30	“
	U	Lewis Margaret H—†	719	housewife	32	“
	V	LoConte Lillian—†	723	“	64	
	W	LoConte Raymond	723	tailor	34	
	X	Nigro Costa	723	clerk	30	
	Y	Nigro Frank	723	blacksmith	64	“
	Z	Nigro Mary—†	723	housewife	64	“
1426	A	Daniels Charles H	727	machinist	37	411 Frankfort
	B	Daniels Evelyn J—†	727	housewife	39	411 “
	C	Trevor Francis J	727	packer	27	411 “
	D	Trevor Lawrence J	727	salesman	42	Revere
	E	Trevor William A	727	serviceman	68	411 Frankfort
	F	Daniels Charles H	727	mchinist	59	380 Chelsea
	G	Daniels Della—†	727	housewife	56	380 “
	H	Riley Grace—†	727	“	27	380 “
	K	Riley Lawrence	727	clerk	28	1593 Dor av
	L	Gazzara Joseph	731	bracemaker	35	1 Gladstone
	M	Gazzara Rita G—†	731	housewife	32	1 “
	N	O'Brien Edward	731	seaman	21	here
	O	O'Brien Edward A	731	clerk	55	“
	P	Driscoll John J	735	chauffeur	30	Winthrop
	R	Driscoll Margaret M—†	735	housewife	29	“

Page.	Letter.	Full Name.	Residence, Jan. 1, 1938.	Occupation.	Supposed Age.	Reported Residence, Jan. 1, 1937. Street and Number.

Bennington Street—Continued

	S	Rich Anthony	735	salesman	22	here
	T	*Rich Frank	735	tailor	52	"
	U	Rich Lillian—†	735	candymaker	25	"
	V	*Rich Mary—†	735	housewife	48	"
	W	Rich Rachel—†	735	tailoress	32	
	X	Winston Catherine A—†	739	hairdresser	40	"
	Y	Winston John J	739	fireman	56	
	Z	Winston Thomas A	739	letter carrier	50	"
1427						
	A	McCarthy Annie T—†	739	housewife	47	"
	B	McCarthy Charles J	739	engraver	48	"
	C	McCarthy Paul J	739	clerk	20	"
	D	Adams Annie G—†	743	housewife	37	Winthrop
	E	Adams George J	743	seaman	40	"
	F	Brogan James E	743	policeman	29	187 Webster
	G	Curran Barbara—†	743	housewife	49	here
	H	Curran Patrick M	743	guard	50	"
	K	DeFranco Anthony	747	policeman	45	"
	L	DeFranco Matilda—†	747	housewife	42	"
	M	*Calla Adeline—†	747	"	52	
	N	Calla Amelia—†	747	clerk	27	
	O	Calla Nicodemo	747	tailor	54	
	P	Calla Silvio	747	laborer	23	
	R	Calla William	747	sign painter	25	"
	S	Otis Ellen M—†	751	teacher	26	
	T	Otis Frank M	751	blacksmith	61	"
	U	Otis Mary C—†	751	housewife	51	"
	V	McLaughlin Albert J	751	conductor	43	"
	W	McLaughlin George W	751	clerk	41	
	X	McLaughlin Katherine A—†	751	housewife	70	"
	Y	McLaughlin Paul F	751	printer	27	
	Z	Bradley Elizabeth J—†	755	clerk	35	
1428						
	A	Bradley Susan A—†	755	housewife	72	"
	B	Donovan Florence T—†	755	clerk	41	
	C	Donovan Susan K—†	755	at home	42	
	D	McLaughlin Catherine A—†	755	housewife	57	"
	E	Ryan Mary A—†	755	clerk	57	
	G	Wall Agnes F—†	755	nurse	22	
	F	Wall Agnes T—†	755	housewife	46	"
	H	Wall James R	755	B F D	50	

Page.	Letter.	FULL NAME.	Residence, Jan. 1, 1938.	Occupation.	Supposed Age.	Reported Residence, Jan. 1, 1937. Street and Number.

Bennington Street—Continued

	K	Corson Anna L—†	759	housewife	49	here
	L	Corson Louis	759	machinist	44	"
	M	Brown Annie G—†	759	operator	59	"
	N	Stevens Louise—†	759	housewife	71	"
	O	Sweeney Lena—†	759	at home	69	
	P	Walker Annie—†	759	"	75	
1429						
	D	Forti Anthony	989	laborer	31	333 E Eagle
	E	Forti Theresa—†	989	housewife	27	333 "
	F	*Lamoly Catherine—†	989	saleswoman	23	here
	G	Hewitt James H	989	carpenter	70	"
	H	Hewitt Margaret—†	989	housewife	73	"
	K	Jensen Edward	989	chauffeur	32	"
	L	Jensen Sarah—†	989	housewife	73	"
	O	Mora John F	989	operator	36	
	P	Mora Walter J	989	"	27	
	R	Silvia Emma—†	989	housekeeper	40	"
	Y	Spadafora Anthony	1025	druggist	32	"
	Z	Spadafora Marion—†	1025	housewife	60	"
1430						
	A	Spadafora Mary—†	1025	clerk	28	
	B	Spadafora Michael	1025	retired	67	
	C	LaCerda Alice L—†	1025	housewife	54	"
	D	LaCerda Frederick F	1025	operator	54	
	E	LaCerda Frederick F, jr	1025	shipper	25	
	F	Morgner Edwin A	1027	laborer	53	
	G	Morgner Mary I—†	1027	housewife	53	"
	H	Morgner Richard R	1027	cabinetmaker	29	"
	K	Ronca Minnie V—†	1027	housekeeper	75	"
	L	Sasso John A	1027	painter	60	"
	M	Sasso Josephine A—†	1027	housewife	50	"
	N	Gallagher Catherine M–†	1027	"	52	
	O	Gallagher George A	1027	laborer	52	
	S	Collins Frances—†	1065	at home	47	
	T	McAuliffe Dennis	1065	retired	74	
	U	O'Rourke Daniel L	1065	bookkeeper	45	"
	V	O'Rourke Helen G—†	1065	operator	23	"
	W	O'Rourke Thomas C	1065	clerk	22	
	X	Powers Martin J	1067	B F D	40	
	Y	Powers Mary B—†	1067	housewife	38	"
	Z	Russo Albina—†	1069	"	40	

Page.	Letter.	Full Name.	Residence, Jan. 1, 1938.	Occupation.	Supposed Age.	Reported Residence, Jan. 1, 1937. Street and Number.
1431						
		Bennington Street—Continued				
	A	Russo Mary—†	1069	operator	23	here
	B	Russo Pauline—†	1069	clerk	21	"
	C	Russo Rocco	1069	barber	43	"
	D	Geary Edmond F	1071	starter	40	1056 Bennington
	E	Geary Marie E—†	1071	housewife	37	1056 "
	F	*Smarrella Josephine—†	1073	"	52	here
	G	*Smarrella Peter	1073	tailor	57	"
	H	Smarrella Phyllis N—†	1073	stitcher	26	"
	K	Smarrella Jennie—†	1075	housewife	29	"
	L	Smarrella Vincent	1075	optician	29	
	O	Hendricks Albert E	1088	chemist	47	
	P	Hendricks Florence—†	1088	housewife	50	"
	R	List Florence M—†	1088	teacher	25	"
	S	Marotta Aurelia—†	1088	housewife	47	"
	T	Marotta Michael A	1088	bartender	47	"
	U	Barnicle Edward A	1088	technician	41	"
	V	Barnicle Henry A	1088	musician	30	"
	W	Barnicle Leonard W	1088	clerk	35	
	X	Barnicle Mary E—†	1088	cashier	38	
	Y	Barnicle Thomas J	1088	painter	45	
	Z	Barnicle Thomas W	1088	retired	72	
1432						
	B	McNaughton May B—†	1092	at home	58	
	C	Pumphret Frances O—†	1092	housewife	58	"
	D	Pumphret Robert J	1092	foreman	67	
	E	Mullen Priscilla—†	1092	teacher	28	
	F	Mullen Virginia R—†	1092	at home	21	"
	G	Mullen Virginia V—†	1092	housewife	53	"
	H	Mullen William F	1092	clerk	60	"
	K	Mullen William F	1092	engineer	24	
	L	Cosgrove James	1092	motorman	67	"
	M	Cosgrove Mary—†	1092	housewife	67	"
	N	Cosgrove Mary L—†	1092	operator	37	
	O	Kiley Henry A	1092	stenographer	32	"
	P	Celona Cosimo	1096	finisher	54	"
	R	Celona Joseph	1096	teacher	29	
	S	Celona Josephine—†	1096	housewife	49	"
	T	MacDonald Johanna J—†	1096	"	87	
	U	MacDonald Mabel—†	1096	bookkeeper	49	"
	V	MacDonald Roderick J	1096	agent	54	"

Page.	Letter.	FULL NAME.	Residence, Jan. 1, 1938.	Occupation.	Supposed Age.	Reported Residence, Jan. 1, 1937. Street and Number.

Bennington Street—Continued

Page.	Letter.	FULL NAME.	Residence, Jan. 1, 1938.	Occupation.	Supposed Age.	Reported Residence, Jan. 1, 1937. Street and Number.
	W	Celona Florence—†	1096	housewife	33	here
	X	Celona Frank	1096	teacher	30	"
	Y	Giacoppo Anna—†	1098	housewife	43	"
	Z	Giacoppo Joseph	1098	operator	50	
1433						
	A	Del Bianco Eugene	1098	salesman	35	here
	B	Del Bianco Margaret—†	1098	housewife	32	"
	C	*Mazzeo Catherine—†	1098	"	51	"
	D	Mazzeo Dominic	1098	polisher	54	
	E	Mazzeo Dominic	1098	finisher	22	
	F	Mazzeo Mary—†	1098	at home	20	
	G	Mazzeo Nicholas	1098	shipper	27	
	H	Mazzeo Phillip	1098	hairdresser	29	"
	K	*Fasano Carmella—†	1100	housewife	33	"
	L	Fasano Nicholas	1100	shoecutter	41	"
	M	Bozza Anna—†	1100	housewife	30	38 Frankfort
	N	Bozza Samuel	1100	salesman	30	38 "
	O	D'Este Pauline—†	1100	operator	62	955 Saratoga
	P	Adelizzi Dante	1100	clerk	26	55 Chelsea
	R	Adelizzi Eugene	1100	printer	20	55 "
	S	*Adelizzi Giaconina—†	1100	housewife	78	55 "
	T	Adelizzi Josephine—†	1100	"	44	55 '
	U	Adelizzi Pasquale	1100	shoecutter	52	55 "
	V	Gozzi Giuseppe	1102	entertainer	40	here
	W	Gozzi Rose—†	1102	housewife	57	"
	X	Ferrara Anthony	1102	bartender	35	"
	Y	Ferrara Olga—†	1102	housewife	33	"
	Z	*Cassaro Diego	1102	carpenter	57	36 W Eagle
1434						
	A	Cassaro Josephine—†	1102	secretary	21	36 "
	B	Cassaro Liberia—†	1102	housekeeper	22	36 "
	C	Cassaro Michael	1102	attendant	25	36 "
	D	*Cassaro Rose—†	1102	housewife	45	36 "
	E	DiCosimo Biagio	1106	storekeeper	50	here
	F	*DiCosimo Jennie—†	1106	housewife	40	"
	G	Mini Alice M—†	1106½	"	24	406 Frankfort
	H	Mina William S	1106½	chauffeur	29	406 "
	K	Cook George L	1112	retired	81	here
	L	Cunningham Katherine W—†	1112	housewife	72	"
	M	Cunningham Kathryn W—†	1112	secretary	30	"
	N	Tyrell Lillian T—†	1114	housewife	55	"

Page.	Letter.	Full Name.	Residence, Jan. 1, 1938.	Occupation.	Supposed Age.	Reported Residence, Jan. 1, 1937. Street and Number.

Bennington Street—Continued

	O	Tyrell Thomas C	1114	guard	60	here
	P	Cowhig Charles C	1114	policeman	40	"
	R	Cowhig Margaret M—†	1114	housewife	37	"
	S	Gahen Francis J	1114	draftsman	30	"
	T	Gahen John B	1114	machinist	37	"
	U	Gahen Mary A—†	1114	housewife	75	"
	V	Graham Bertha—†	1118	"	30	
	W	Graham Raymond D	1118	foreman	32	
	X	Miller Annie C—†	1118	housewife	60	"
	Y	Miller Charles W	1118	policeman	62	"
	Z	Callahan Kathryn L—†	1124	at home	55	
1435						
	A	Callahan Mary A—†	1124	clerk	62	
	B	Murphy John D	1124	attendant	58	"
	C	Murphy Margaret L—†	1124	housewife	49	"
	D	Wallace Caroline V—†	1130	"	36	
	E	Wallace John	1130	engraver	42	"
	G	Caputo Gaetania—†	1183	housewife	42	"
	H	Caputo Michael	1183	machinist	21	"
	K	Caputo Paul	1183	blacksmith	49	"
	L	Caputo Vincent	1183	chauffeur	22	"
	M	Visconti Emma—†	1183	stitcher	22	271 Sumner
	N	Visconti James A	1183	longshoreman	43	271 "
	O	Visconti Mary—†	1183	housewife	40	271 "
	P	Visconti Vincent E	1183	mechanic	22	271 "
	R	Campatelli Joseph	1183	metalworker	34	45 Faywood av
	S	Campatelli Margaret—†	1183	housewife	31	45 "
	T	Coffee Edwin N	1185	retired	69	here
	U	Coffee Edwin N, jr	1185	clerk	31	"
	V	Coffee Margaret L—†	1185	housewife	64	"
	W	Coffee Mary H—†	1185	clerk	29	
	X	Shackelton Catherine M—†	1185	housewife	32	"
	Y	Leese Myrene E—†	1185	"	52	
	Z	Leese William A	1185	chauffeur	25	"
1436						
	A	Leese William H	1185	superintendent	54	"
	B	Love Margaret S—†	1185	operator	43	"
	C	Marshall Anna M—†	1185	housewife	41	"
	D	Marshall Joseph J	1185	B F D	51	
	E	Clapp Charles M	1189	salesman	21	"
	F	Clapp Elmer A	1189	steamfitter	40	"

Page.	Letter.	Full Name.	Residence, Jan. 1, 1938.	Occupation.	Supposed Age.	Reported Residence, Jan. 1, 1937. Street and Number.

Bennington Street—Continued

Page.	Letter.	Full Name.	Residence, Jan. 1, 1938.	Occupation.	Supposed Age.	Reported Residence, Jan. 1, 1937. Street and Number.
	G	Clapp Katherine M—†	1189	housewife	41	here
	H	Dolan Katherine A—†	1189	“	60	“
	K	Dolan Michael A	1189	starter	61	“
	M	Noyes Marie C—†	1193	at home	25	
	N	Noyes Marjorie T—†	1193	stenographer	23	“
	O	Brown James	1193	steamfitter	69	“
	P	Brown Lida P—†	1193	housewife	54	“
	R	Dibble Shirley W—†	1193	at home	37	
	S	Ragin Mary—†	1193	“	63	
	U*	Cambria Frank	1201	cabinetmaker	65	“
	V	San Lorenzo John	1201	retired	70	
	W	San Lorenzo Rose—†	1201	housewife	70	“
	X	Potenza Jennie—†	1201	stitcher	21	137 Gladstone
	Y	Potenza Mary M—†	1201	housewife	45	137 “
	Z	Potenza Vincent A	1201	roofer	51	137 “
1437						
	A*	Daddario Alice—†	1203	housewife	49	45 St Edward rd
	B	Daddario Gilda—†	1203	at home	20	here
	C	Daddario Motto	1203	laborer	24	“
	D	Daddario Pasquale	1203	clerk	22	“
	E	Lanzilli Carl	1205	student	22	
	F	Lanzilli Frank	1205	machinist	27	“
	G	Lanzilli Joseph	1205	tailor	56	
	H*	Lanzilli Theresa—†	1205	housewife	52	“
	K	Lawrence John L	1209	salesman	53	“
	L	Lawrence May C—†	1209	housewife	46	“
	M*	Trischitta Bernardina—†	1209	“	49	
	N	Trischitta Concetta—†	1209	hairdresser	24	“
	O	Trischitta Rosario	1209	carpenter	55	“
	P	Trischitta Violet—†	1209	at home	29	
	R	Spaziani Patricia—†	1211	housewife	24	“
	S	Spaziani Peter	1211	barber	34	
	T*	Lazzari Bettina—†	1211	housewife	44	“
	U*	Lazzari Salvatore	1211	tailor	52	
	V	Lazzari Victoria—†	1211	clerk	21	
	X	Contarino Anthony	1215	chauffeur	32	“
	Y	Contarino Mary—†	1215	operator	29	
	Z	Rosa Charles H	1215	baker	43	
1438						
	A	Rosa Lena M—†	1215	housewife	40	“
	B*	Girone Catherine—†	1219	“	37	

Page.	Letter.	Full Name.	Residence, Jan. 1, 1938.	Occupation.	Supposed Age.	Reported Residence, Jan. 1, 1937. Street and Number.

Bennington Street—Continued

Page.	Letter.	Full Name.	Residence, Jan. 1, 1938.	Occupation.	Supposed Age.	Reported Residence, Jan. 1, 1937. Street and Number.
	C	*Girone Nicholas	1219	carpenter	52	here
	D	Lauricella Anthony	1219	storekeeper	50	"
	E	Lauricella Sarah—†	1219	housewife	45	"
	F	Marley Edward F	1223	checker	50	18 Gladstone
	G	Marley Edward F, jr	1223	clerk	21	18 "
	H	Marley Mary G—†	1223	"	20	18 "
	K	Marley Mary J—†	1223	housewife	42	18 "
	M	Ciriello Carman	1229	barber	52	43 Sea View av
	N	Ciriello Esther—†	1229	housewife	47	43 "
	O	Buldini Armando	1229	meatcutter	23	here
	P	Buldini Nerina—†	1229	stenographer	26	"
	R	*Buldini Raffaele	1229	meatcutter	56	"
	S	*Buldini Venusta—†	1229	housewife	48	"

Blackinton Street

Page.	Letter.	Full Name.	Residence, Jan. 1, 1938.	Occupation.	Supposed Age.	Reported Residence, Jan. 1, 1937. Street and Number.
	V	Ratto Ernest	1	painter	41	here
	W	Ratto Sarah—†	1	housewife	34	"
	X	Wyke Elizabeth H—†	3	housekeeper	56	"
	Y	Wkye Ernest L	3	counterman	40	"
	Z	Wyke Herbert E	3	machinist	81	"
1439						
	A	Wyke Jesse	3	laborer	51	
	B	O'Brien Eileen M—†	5	at home	26	
	C	O'Brien John F	5	printer	40	
	D	O'Brien Kathleen A—†	5	operator	34	
	E	O'Brien Margaret—†	5	housewife	64	"
	F	O'Brien Mary A—†	5	bookkeeper	36	"
	G	O'Brien Maurice T	5	machinist	29	"
	H	Lagamasino John	7	manager	47	"
	K	Lagamasino Lillian E—†	7	librarian	21	
	L	Lagamasino Mildred B—†	7	housewife	48	"
	M	Roddo Frank L	7	manager	44	"
	N	Powell Clarence A	9	shipfitter	22	12½ Orient av
	O	Powell Marie B—†	9	housewife	24	3 "
	P	*Cerisola Gerolama—†	11	at home	73	here
	R	Lavezzo Rose—†	11	clerk	50	"
	S	MacPherson Donald W	11	cashier	39	"
	T	MacPherson Eugenia—†	11	housewife	38	"

Page.	Letter.	Full Name.	Residence, Jan. 1, 1938.	Occupation.	Supposed Age.	Reported Residence, Jan. 1, 1937. Street and Number.

Leyden Street

Page.	Letter.	Full Name.	Residence, Jan. 1, 1938.	Occupation.	Supposed Age.	Reported Residence, Jan. 1, 1937. Street and Number.
	z	Dondero Albert	215	machinist	36	here
1440						
	A	Dondero Frank	215	"	48	
	B	Dondero Theresa—†	215	housewife	47	"
	C	Favello Anthony	215	inspector	54	"
	D	Favello Grace—†	215	operator	35	
	E	Favello Nellie—†	215	housewife	52	"
	F	Disario Beatrice A—†	215	secretary	25	"
	G	Disario Caroline E—†	215	housewife	51	"
	H	Disario Marguerite A—†	215	decorator	23	"
	K	Disario Paul C	215	inspector	54	"
	L	Dondero Evelyn T—†	215	leatherworker	36	"
	M	Dondero William H	215	chauffeur	37	"
	N	Gillis Grace M—†	215	clerk	34	
	O	Solari Mary F—†	215	housekeeper	59	"
	P	*Vincenti Ambrose	219	chef	43	"
	R	Petito Catherine—†	219	housewife	28	"
	S	Petito Eugene	219	laborer	33	"
	T	Schwamb Clinton	221	builder	26	731 Benningt'n
	U	Schwamb Mildred—†	221	housewife	26	731 "
	V	Maguire George F	223	carpenter	58	370 Main
	W	McMillen Mary F—†	223	housewife	54	here
	X	McMillen Mary T—†	223	saleswoman	23	"
	Y	McMillen Thomas G	223	clerk	21	"
	Z	Courtois Lucille—†	225	housewife	26	71 Lubec
1441						
	A	Courtois Oscar	225	butcher	28	71 "
	B	Console Annie—†	225	housewife	42	here
	C	Console Antonio	225	barber	45	"
	D	Sergi Benjamin	225	laborer	23	"
	E	Kane Annie—†	231	operator	20	"
	F	McAteer Annie—†	231	housewife	74	"
	G	McAteer Elizabeth—†	231	clerk	30	
	H	McAteer John	231	longshoreman	43	"
	K	McDonald Alice—†	231	operator	38	"
	L	Brown Charles	235	engineer	44	76 Paris
	M	Ness Jennie N—†	235	housewife	52	76 "
	N	Ness John H	235	machinist	23	76 "
	O	Ness Peter H	235	builder	48	76 "
	P	Olson Nels	235	laborer	66	76 "
	R	Parker Anton D	235	engineer	45	76 "

Leyden Street—Continued

Page.	Letter.	Full Name.	Residence, Jan. 1, 1938.	Occupation.	Supposed Age.	Reported Residence, Jan. 1, 1937. Street and Number.
	S	Rovatti Fiore	239	carpenter	42	here
	T	Rovatti Louise—†	239	housewife	41	"
	U	Carlow Doris—†	239	"	26	"
	V	Carlow Lyman E	239	plumber	25	
	W	Beaton Alice M—†	241	operator	20	"
	X	Beaton Helen—†	241	housewife	48	"
	Y	Beaton Hugh F	241	clerk	57	
	Z	Beaton Marion—†	241	waitress	21	
1442						
	A	Ivers Angelina—†	249	housewife	37	"
	B	*Cazzaniga Angelo	249	retired	62	
	C	*Cazzaniga Petronilla—†	249	housewife	63	"
	D	*Lamborghini Alexander	249	laborer	58	
	E	*Lamborghini Elvira—†	249	housewife	50	"

Saint Andrew Road

Page.	Letter.	Full Name.	Residence, Jan. 1, 1938.	Occupation.	Supposed Age.	Reported Residence, Jan. 1, 1937. Street and Number.
	H	Sullivan Mary C—†	2	housewife	71	626 Benningt'n
	K	Sullivan Mary E—†	2	clerk	37	626 "
	L	Sullivan William J	2	"	34	626 "
	M	Mahoney Marie—†	2	housewife	42	Medford
	N	Mahoney Walter	2	salesman	45	"
	O	Schindhelm Henry J	6	clerk	31	here
	P	Schindhelm Louise E—†	6	telegrapher	37	"
	R	Schindhelm Mary E—†	6	housewife	69	"
	S	Farley Alice J—†	8	housekeeper	46	"
	T	Nugent Gertrude V—†	8	teacher	33	"
	U	Nugent William B	8	investigator	45	"
	V	DeDeyn Jules	10	longshoreman	39	"
	W	DeDeyn Julia—†	10	housewife	45	"
	X	Sofrine Edward	10	operator	31	"
	Y	Sofrine Eleanor—†	10	housewife	23	"
	Z	Sofrine Manuel E	10	retired	74	
1443						
	A	Sofrine Mary—†	10	housewife	69	"
	B	Hart Mary A—†	14	"	43	
	C	Hart William	14	policeman	47	"
	D	Ryan Catherine—†	16	clerk	26	
	E	Ryan Josephine R—†	16	supervisor	34	"
	F	Ryan Lawrence	16	clerk	26	
	G	Ryan Mary A—†	16	housewife	67	"

Page.	Letter.	Full Name.	Residence, Jan. 1, 1938.	Occupation.	Supposed Age.	Reported Residence, Jan. 1, 1937. Street and Number.

Saint Andrew Road—Continued

	H	Adams John Q	18	retired	74	here
	K	Adams Rose G—†	18	housewife	66	"
	L	Garbrino Anthony	18	motorman	68	"
	M	Wellings Bridget A—†	21	housewife	62	"
	N	Wellings Eileen F—†	21	student	21	
	O	Wellings Gladys D—†	21	teacher	26	
	P	Wellings John A	21	clerk	67	
	R	Brodbine Sarah J—†	24	housewife	64	"
	S	Whelan Catherine—†	24	"	35	
	T	Whelan Leo A	24	architect	37	"
	U	Frazer Annie—†	25	housewife	75	"
	V	Fraser Gertrude S—†	25	housekeeper	48	"
	W	Powe Thomas J	25	carpenter	73	"
	Y	Blue Dorothea A—†	26	librarian	29	"
	Z	Blue Irene A—†	26	housewife	59	"
1444						
	A	Blue James McD	26	clergyman	63	"
	B	Rego August	29	chauffeur	35	"
	C	Rego Madeline—†	29	housewife	35	"
	D	Scoppettuolo Albert	29	meatcutter	26	"
	E	Scoppettuolo Annette—†	29	saleswoman	29	"
	F	Scoppettuolo Anthony	29	clerk	64	
	G	Scoppettuolo Anthony	29	waiter	23	
	H	Scoppettuolo Carmella—†	29	housewife	64	"
	K	Scoppettuolo Charles	29	waiter	24	
	L	Scoppettuolo Lena—†	29	packer	31	
	M	Scoppettuolo Vera—†	29	"	27	
	N	Burmester Gladys—†	30	at home	47	
	O	Burns Fannie—†	30	"	73	
	P	Tellor Alice—†	30	"	69	
	R	Kelley Anna R—†	31	housewife	40	"
	S	Kelley Edward I	31	inspector	52	"
	T	Kelley Edward I	31	student	25	
	U	Kelley Mary M—†	31	secretary	22	"
	V	Sullivan Arthur W	32	registrar	52	
	W	Sullivan Helen J—†	32	housewife	53	"
	X	Mangini Edmund	33	bartender	27	"
	Y	Mangini Madeline—†	33	housewife	28	"
	Z	Brown Frank P	34	retired	69	
1445						
	A	Brown Henry H	34	"	72	

Page.	Letter.	Full Name.	Residence, Jan. 1, 1938.	Occupation.	Supposed Age.	Reported Residence, Jan. 1, 1937. Street and Number.
		Saint Andrew Road—Continued				
	B	Lawrence Helen—†	37	secretary	29	here
	C	Lawrence Herbert S	37	laborer	58	"
	D	Lawrence John H	37	electrician	31	"
	E	Lawrence Sarah S—†	37	secretary	33	"
	F	Carey Edward	38	broker	51	New York
	G	Carey Margaret—†	38	clerk	53	here
	H	Matroni Josephine—†	38	housewife	44	62 Barnes av
	K	*Jonasson Sophie—†	39	housekeeper	68	here
	L	Maguire Catherine A—†	41	housewife	63	"
	M	Maguire James E	41	attorney	65	"
	N	Maguire Richard	41	student	23	88 Bayswater
	O	Butler Bridie—†	44	housewife	47	here
	P	Butler Edward F	44	student	24	"
	R	Butler William J	44	engineer	53	"
	S	Lally Edward	44	printer	28	
	T	McCarthy Helen G—†	44	housewife	26	"
	U	McCarthy Joseph L	44	operator	29	
	V	McInnis Archibald	44	salesman	60	"
	W	McInnis Ellen E—†	44	housewife	52	"
	X	McInnis Evelyn E—†	44	stenographer	30	"
	Y	McInnis Kathryn—†	44	clerk	23	"
		Saint Edward Road				
	Z	McCarthy Charles P	32	bookkeeper	20	here
1446						
	A	McCarthy John F	32	student	23	
	B	McCarthy Margaret M—†	32	housewife	52	"
	C	McCarthy Mary A—†	32	secretary	22	"
	D	McCarthy Patrick J	32	laborer	57	
	E	Wilson Ellen—†	40	housewife	69	"
	F	Wilson George L	40	laborer	21	
	G	Wilson George N	40	printer	48	
	H	Wilson Mary A—†	40	housewife	48	"
	K	Nagle John E	40	laborer	58	
	L	Nagle Katherine L—†	40	operator	22	
	M	Nagle Rebecca—†	40	housewife	49	"
	N	Corbett Thomas	40	checker	39	
	O	Petzke August	40	salesman	63	"
	P	Petzke Hattie—†	40	housewife	55	"
	R	Petzke Henry	40	attendant	25	"

Page.	Letter.	Full Name.	Residence, Jan. 1, 1938.	Occupation.	Supposed Age.	Reported Residence, Jan. 1, 1937. Street and Number.

Saint Edward Road—Continued

Page.	Letter.	Full Name.	Residence, Jan. 1, 1938.	Occupation.	Supposed Age.	Reported Residence, Jan. 1, 1937. Street and Number.
	S	Petzke Julia—†	40	operator	27	here
	T	DeRosa Lena—†	44	housewife	24	"
	U	DeRosa Vito	44	agent	36	"
	V	*Zagarella Joseph	44	retired	77	
	W	*Zagarella Josephine—†	44	housewife	68	"
	X	Zagarella Mary—†	44	"	41	
	Y	Zagarella Peter	44	machinist	46	"
	Z	Quartarone John	44	candymaker	25	"
1447						
	A	Quartarone Joseph	44	operator	22	
	B	Quartarone Margaret—†	44	housewife	47	"
	C	Quartarone Samuel	44	barber	49	

Saratoga Street

Page.	Letter.	Full Name.	Residence, Jan. 1, 1938.	Occupation.	Supposed Age.	Reported Residence, Jan. 1, 1937. Street and Number.
	U	Lyons Isabelle—†	1042	housewife	42	here
	V	Lyons John J	1042	agent	42	"
	W	McGee John	1042	manager	48	142 St Andrew rd
	X	McGee Julia—†	1042	housewife	45	142 "
	Y	O'Shea Daniel	1042	laborer	45	here
	Z	Fenlon Herbert C	1042	clerk	38	"
1448						
	A	Fenlon Marion J—†	1042	housewife	33	"
	B	Lafayette Elizabeth—†	1042	at home	74	
	C	Shannon Catherine—†	1042	bookbinder	45	"
	D	Shannon Joseph	1042	clerk	23	
	F	Capone Richard	1044	laborer	25	
	G	Rocciolo Elvira—†	1044	housewife	41	"
	H	Rocciolo Pasquale	1044	musician	45	"
	L	Watchmaker Abraham	1045A	storekeeper	55	"
	M	McLaughlin Evangeline A—†	1046	operator	34	"
	N	O'Keefe Mary C—†	1046	housewife	30	"
	O	O'Keefe Maurice J	1046	policeman	39	"
	P	Cacchiotti Louise—†	1046	housewife	38	"
	R	Cacchiotti Orizio	1046	tailor	47	
	S	Eldridge Daniel K	1046	policeman	45	"
	T	Buswell Charles C	1047	seaman	31	
	U	Buswell John F	1047	clerk	27	
	V	Butterworth Clara J—†	1047	housewife	42	"
	W	Butterworth Harry	1047	B F D	43	
	X	Muldoon Anna L—†	1047	housekeeper	52	"

Page.	Letter.	Full Name.	Residence, Jan. 1, 1938.	Occupation.	Supposed Age.	Reported Residence, Jan. 1, 1937. Street and Number.

Saratoga Street—Continued

	Y	Muldoon Katherine I–†	1047	nurse	42	here
	Z	Muldoon James A	1047	lineman	45	"
1449						
	A	Wood Fred S	1047	pilot	49	
	B	Wood Mary M—†	1047	housewife	48	"
	C	Carpinella Adeline—†	1048	"	55	
	D	Carpinella Agnes—†	1048	at home	24	
	E	Carpinella Michael	1048	clerk	27	
	F	Maniglia Anthony	1048	barber	62	
	G	Maniglia Caroline—†	1048	housewife	54	"
	K	*D'Amelio Carmella–†	r 1050	"	67	41 Ashley
	L	D'Amelio Mary—†	" 1050	clerk	24	41 "
	M	Casella Frances—†	1051	tailoress	31	here
	N	Casella Josephine—†	1051	saleswoman	21	"
	O	Casella Natale J	1051	baker	26	"
	P	Casella Natalie—†	1051	saleswoman	23	"
	R	Casella Nicholas	1051	laborer	52	
	S	Casella Pauline—†	1051	housewife	52	"
	T	Casella Vincent	1051	baker	27	
	U	Mulkerron Elizabeth G–†	1051	stenographer	26	"
	V	Mulkerron Frank H	1051	clerk	23	"
	W	Mulkerron John J	1051	foreman	53	
	X	Mulkerron John J	1051	clerk	25	
	Y	Mulkerron Mary A—†	1051	housewife	52	"
	Z	O'Neil Margaret R—†	1051	clerk	26	
1450						
	A	O'Neil Michael J	1051	social worker	27	"
	B	Famolare Alexander	1051	hairdresser	27	"
	C	Famolare Mary—†	1051	housewife	23	"
	D	Vivenzio Nicholas	1051	tailor	51	
	E	Vivenzio Theresa—†	1051	housewife	50	"
	F	Keefe Anne E—†	1052	at home	49	
	G	Keefe Elizabeth G—†	1052	housewife	54	"
	H	Keefe Thomas P	1052	clerk	51	
	K	Dahnke Caroline—†	1052	housewife	69	"
	L	Dahnke Christian F	1052	foreman	46	
	M	Dahnke Christian H	1052	machinist	80	"
	N	Dahnke Frederick	1052	"	42	
	O	Haritos Bertha—†	1052	housewife	31	"
	P	Haritos Peter J	1052	policeman	43	"
	R	Fitzpatrick Catherine—†	1053	at home	30	

Page.	Letter.	Full Name.	Residence, Jan. 1, 1938.	Occupation.	Supposed Age.	Reported Residence, Jan. 1, 1937. Street and Number.

Saratoga Street—Continued

	s	Fitzpatrick Mary—†	1053	housekeeper	35	here
	t	Dowling Francis X	1053	engineer	28	"
	u	Dowling John J	1053	agent	29	"
	v	Dowling Margaret T—†	1053	clerk	24	
	w	Dowling Mary A—†	1053	buyer	29	
	x	Dowling Nora A—†	1053	housewife	62	"
	y	Dowling Rose J—†	1053	"	30	
	z	Dowling William L	1053	clerk	34	
1451						
	a	Hannerty Ida F—†	1053	"	30	
	b	Boucha Bridget—†	1053	at home	75	
	c	Burke John F	1053	retired	70	
	d	McKenna Elizabeth J–†	1055	housewife	60	"
	e	McKenna Patrick J	1055	carpenter	61	"
	f	McCarthy Elizabeth E–†	1055	housewife	42	613 Benningt'n
	g	McCarthy John J	1055	clerk	50	613 "
	h	Brendlemore Dorothy–†	1055	saleswoman	24	here
	k	Brendlemore Frank	1055	operator	29	"
	l	Dorgan Charlotte G—†	1055	housewife	56	"
	m	Dorgan Margaret—†	1055	saleswoman	29	"
	n	Dorgan Michael	1055	laborer	65	
	o	McGee Edward	1055	fishcutter	25	"
	p	McGee John	1055	laborer	23	
	r	Buckingham Florence–†	1057	clerk	36	
	s	Buckingham Lillian L–†	1057	"	27	
	t	Buckingham Louise J–†	1057	housewife	55	"
	u	Buckingham William R	1057	laborer	64	
	v	Buckingham William R	1057	clerk	23	
	w	McDonald Anthony T	1057	laborer	36	
	x	McDonald James E	1057	clerk	56	
	y	McDonald Winifred E–†	1057	operator	44	"
1452						
	a	Boudreau Flora G—†	1057	housewife	41	"
	b	Boudreau Francis R	1057	seaman	46	
	z	Clark Nita M—†	1057	clerk	27	"
	c	Venedam Alice—†	1059	housewife	48	4 Neptune rd
	d	Venedam Charles W	1059	carpenter	48	here
	e	Venedam Joseph A	1059	salesman	23	4 Neptune rd
	f	Venedam Warren A	1059	clerk	21	4 "
	g	Larson Clara M—†	1059	housewife	53	61 Gladstone
	h	Larson Frank O	1059	seaman	50	61 "

Saratoga Street—Continued

Page.	Letter.	Full Name.	Residence, Jan. 1, 1938.	Occupation.	Supposed Age.	Reported Residence, Jan. 1, 1937. Street and Number.
	K	Larson Frank O	1059	student	23	61 Gladstone
	L	Donoghue Bessie—†	1059	housewife	59	here
	M	Donoghue Charles W	1059	clerk	33	"
	N	Donoghue Margaret F–†	1059	"	31	"
	O	Donoghue Myron	1059	student	25	
	P	Cianci Edward	1060	electrician	32	"
	R	Cianci Rachel—†	1060	housewife	66	"
	S	DiMuro Antonio	1060	storekeeper	49	"
	T	DiMuro Bernard	1060	clerk	23	"
	U	DiMuro Jennie—†	1060	housewife	47	"
	V	Indrisano Anthony	1060	laborer	43	
	W	Indrisano Lena—†	1060	housewife	40	"
	X	Cianci Josephine—†	1060	"	38	
	Y	Cianco Louis	1060	operator	43	
	Z	Varalla Catherine—†	1060	at home	39	
1453						
	A	Varalla Domenico	1060	retired	72	
	B	Varalla Vincenza—†	1060	housewife	73	"
	C	Kirwan Arthur P	1061	policeman	39	"
	D	Kirwan Rose M—†	1061	housewife	29	"
	E	Miller Walter M	1061	engineer	48	
	F	Miller Winifred C—†	1061	housewife	48	"
	G	McDonald Mary F—†	1061	"	48	
	H	McDonald Thomas F	1061	foreman	48	
	K	McDonald Walter T	1061	laborer	26	
	L	Pierce Arthur	1061	painter	48	
	M	Winston Catherine A—†	1061	at home	50	
	N	Graceffa Argentine—†	1062	housewife	35	"
	O	Graceffa John	1062	painter	28	"
	P	Santo Doris—†	1062	housewife	30	"
	R	Santo Julio	1062	operator	32	"
	S	Cardillo Angelo	1062	laborer	37	
	T	Cardillo Irene—†	1062	housewife	33	"
	U	Abramo Angelo	1065	retired	72	
	V	Abramo Antonia—†	1065	housewife	62	"
	W	Abramo Josephine—†	1065	"	21	
	X	Abramo Santo	1065	cabinetmaker	32	"
	Y	Grady Anna M—†	1066	housewife	53	"
	Z	Grady Joseph J	1066	salesman	58	"
1454						
	A	Larkin Ruth E—†	1066	at home	22	

Page.	Letter.	Full Name.	Residence, Jan. 1, 1938.	Occupation.	Supposed Age.	Reported Residence, Jan. 1, 1937. Street and Number.

Saratoga Street—Continued

Page.	Letter.	Full Name.	Residence, Jan. 1, 1938.	Occupation.	Supposed Age.	Reported Residence, Jan. 1, 1937. Street and Number.
	B	Cohan Alice M—†	1068	housewife	59	here
	C	Cohan Alice M—†	1068	clerk	25	"
	D	Cohan Morris M	1068	shipper	59	"
	E	Fiamingo James F	1069	retired	60	
	F	Fiamingo Lila M—†	1069	housewife	55	"
	G	Mullane Mary T—†	1071	"	38	
	H	Mullane Patrick J	1071	attorney	54	"
	K	Murray Ann J—†	1071	operator	37	
	L	Murray Martin A	1071	teacher	35	
	M	Murray Patrick J	1071	electrician	42	"
	N	Craviotto Prospero	1072	retired	75	
	O	Craviotto Theresa—†	1072	housewife	74	"
	P	DiMarchi Mary A—†	1072	housekeeper	39	"
	R	Ardini Emma M—†	1072	housewife	49	"
	S	Ardini Joseph	1072	steamfitter	59	"
	T	Ardini Robert J	1072	teacher	24	
	U	Romolo Alma—†	1072	saleswoman	24	"
	V	Romolo Florence—†	1072	at home	21	
	W	Romolo Johanna—†	1072	housekeeper	23	"
	X	Romolo John	1072	clergyman	53	"
	Y	Crovo John M	1073	laborer	38	
	Z	Kerrigan John	1073	"	51	
1455						
	A	Kerrigan Margaret—†	1073	housewife	45	"
	B	McRury John	1073	counterman	28	"
	C	Wilson William	1073	retired	65	"
	D	Matthews Florence J—†	1075	teacher	32	214 Benningt'n
	E	Matthews Michael E	1075	retired	70	214 "
	F	Riley Arthur F	1075	laborer	33	214 "
	G	Bimber Angelina—†	1075	inspector	22	here
	H	Bimber Arthur	1075	salesman	27	"
	K	Bimber Madeline—†	1075	housewife	45	"
	L	Bimber Mary—†	1075	at home	24	
	M	Bimber Octavio	1075	merchant	59	"
	O	Ruggieri Anthony	1078	barber	50	
	P	Ruggieri Susan—†	1078	housewife	50	"
	R	Sacco Alfred	1078	laborer	29	
	S	Sacco Antonetta—†	1078	housewife	29	"
	T	Gallo Anthony	1078	meatcutter	42	108 Porter
	U	Gallo Josephine—†	1078	housewife	28	108 "
	W	Adams Edward	1084	laborer	30	here

Page.	Letter.	Full Name.	Residence, Jan. 1, 1938.	Occupation.	Supposed Age.	Reported Residence, Jan. 1, 1937. Street and Number.

Saratoga Street—Continued

Page.	Letter.	Full Name.	Residence, Jan. 1, 1938.	Occupation.	Supposed Age.	Reported Residence, Jan. 1, 1937. Street and Number.
	X	Bradley Edna—†	1084	housekeeper	34	here
	Y	Babine Benjamin	1084	fisherman	44	"
	Z	Babine Helen—†	1084	housewife	38	"
1456						
	A	Woods Catherine J—†	1084	at home	71	
	B	Guazzerotti Ambrosina—†	rear 1084	housewife	45	"
	C	*Guazzerotti Caesar	" 1084	laborer	52	
	D	Guazzerotti Edith—†	" 1084	clerk	23	
	E	Guazzerotti Irene—†	" 1084	saleswoman	21	"
	F	Guazzerotti Jean—†	" 1084	clerk	22	
	G	Bishop Edward L	1085	dentist	37	
	H	Riley Mary F—†	1085	housekeeper	45	"
	K	Riley Rose E—†	1085	teacher	45	"
	L	Riley William J	1085	dentist	60	
	M	Conlon John F	1085	retired	79	
	N	Bucolo Anna—†	1088	at home	27	
	O	Bucolo Joseph	1088	chauffeur	60	"
	P	Bucolo Joseph F	1088	laborer	22	
	R	Bucolo Josephine—†	1088	stitcher	29	
	S	Bucolo Mary—†	1088	housewife	60	"
	T	*Palandro Caesar	1088	shoemaker	50	"
	W	Palandro Dominic	1088	clerk	21	
	V	Palandro Esther—†	1088	waitress	23	
	U	*Palandro Martha—†	1088	housewife	47	"

Thurston Street

Page.	Letter.	Full Name.	Residence, Jan. 1, 1938.	Occupation.	Supposed Age.	Reported Residence, Jan. 1, 1937. Street and Number.
	Y	Roddy Gertrude—†	2	stenographer	27	736 Saratoga
	Z	Roddy Helen M—†	2	operator	30	736 "
1457						
	A	Roddy Mary E—†	2	clerk	25	736 "
	B	Roddy Mildred R—†	2	stenographer	21	736 "
	C	Roddy Nora M—†	2	housewife	65	736 "
	D	Olpin Bessie—†	3	clerk	49	here
	E	Scott Elizabeth—†	3	housewife	49	"
	F	Scott James N	3	carpenter	54	"
	G	Donnelly Anna T—†	3	stenographer	33	"
	H	Donnelly Charles J	3	retired	75	"
	K	Donnelly John F	3	inspector	42	"
	L	Donnelly Mary T—†	3	housewife	72	"
	M	Donnelly William L	3	fireman	40	

Page.	Letter.	Full Name.	Residence, Jan. 1, 1938.	Occupation.	Supposed Age.	Reported Residence, Jan. 1, 1937. Street and Number.

Thurston Street—Continued

	N	Streeter Mary G—†	3	clerk	38	here
	O	Anderson Louis A	4	laborer	46	"
	P	Anderson Rose—†	4	housewife	44	"
	R	Silva Gertrude—†	4	at home	72	
	S	Condon Ellen M—†	5	housewife	47	"
	T	Condon William J	5	drawtender	54	"
	U	Hollingsworth Daniel J	5	retired	61	
	V	Hollingsworth Mary C—†	5	envelopemaker	59	"
	W	Hollingsworth Sarah M—†	5	candyworker	57	"
	X	Sweeney Julia F—†	5	housekeeper	56	"
	Y	Enos Catherine G—†	6	housewife	32	"
	Z	Enos Edmund F	6	policeman	41	"
1458						
	A	Benker Alma M—†	7	cashier	30	
	B	Benker Charles G	7	retired	77	
	C	Benker Charles W	7	clerk	40	
	D	Benker Frederick W	7	"	39	
	E	Benker Jacob J	7	retired	67	
	F	Benker Mary E—†	7	housewife	65	"
	G	Benker William A	7	lineman	37	
	H	McNamara John J	7	B F D	27	
	K	Kelly Emmett J	7	clerk	36	
	L	Kelly Theresa C—†	7	housewife	33	"
	M	Lagamosino Margaret—†	7	operator	39	
	N	Leary John F	7	clerk	47	
	O	O'Connor Anna M—†	8	"	28	
	P	O'Connor Bridget A—†	8	housewife	70	"
	R	O'Connor Charles J	8	clerk	36	
	S	O'Connor Daniel P	8	plasterer	45	"
	T	Sullivan Robert	8	clerk	31	
	U	Mahoney George T	8A	salesman	44	"
	V	Mahoney Katherine A—†	8A	housewife	41	"
	W	Sullivan Mary W—†	8A	at home	23	
	X	Nolan Mary L—†	10	housewife	62	"
	Y	Nolan William S	10	broker	62	
	Z	Flood Edward J	10A	merchant	58	"
1459						
	A	Flood Margaret—†	10A	housewife	58	"
	B	Cullinane James F	11	chauffeur	28	91 St Andrew rd
	C	Cullinane Rita—†	11	housewife	22	91 "
	D	Dunn Helen M—†	11	"	54	91 "

Page.	Letter.	FULL NAME.	Residence, Jan. 1, 1938.	Occupation.	Supposed Age.	Reported Residence, Jan. 1, 1937. Street and Number.

Thurston Street—Continued

	E	Dunn John J	11	mechanic	62	91 St Andrew rd
	G	Barker Charles A	11A	clerk	57	182 Wordsworth
	F	*Sacco Annie—†	11A	housewife	58	here
	H	Sacco Henry	11A	manager	21	"
	K	Sacco Louisa—†	11A	bookkeeper	20	"
	L	Fennelly John	12	retired	75	"
	M	Mahoney Ellen G—†	12	at home	49	"
	N	Russell Annie M—†	12	housewife	53	"
	O	Russell George A	12	conductor	53	"
	P	Crowley Agnes T—†	12	housewife	64	"
	R	Crowley James T	12	seaman	64	
	S	Cantillo Maurice	14	grocer	27	
	T	Cantillo Rosaria—†	14	housewife	27	"
	U	Cantillo Alfonso	14	grocer	51	
	V	Cantillo Henrietta—†	14	housewife	47	"
	W	Cantillo James A	14	grocer	23	
	X	Cantillo Thomas R	14	"	21	
	Y	Rocco Florence—†	15	housewife	65	"
	Z	Rocco Leopold	15	retired	72	
1460						
	A	Rocco Florence C—†	15	at home	21	
	B	Rocco Josephine—†	15	housewife	38	"
	C	Rocco Michael	15	salesman	41	"
	D	Kincaid Elsie M—†	16	stenographer	32	"
	E	Kincaid George E	16	clerk	63	"
	F	Kincaid Mary S—†	16	housewife	61	"
	G	Kincaid Sterling J	16	upholsterer	34	"
	H	Murray John E	18	carpenter	40	"
	K	Sullivan Charles A	18	shipfitter	28	"
	L	Sullivan John F	18	supervisor	62	"
	M	Sullivan Katherine—†	18	stenographer	30	"
	N	Sullivan Mary E—†	18	housewife	52	"
	O	Calhoun Elizabeth J—†	18	at home	76	
	P	Calhoun George F	18	engineer	73	
	R	Calhoun Mary—†	18	housewife	70	"
	S	Roby George H	18	retired	81	
	T	Graziano Carmella—†	19	bookkeeper	32	"
	U	Graziano Emelia—†	19	housewife	60	"
	V	Graziano Ida—†	19	clerk	27	
	W	Graziano Mary—†	19	"	30	
	X	Downing Byron O	20	"	55	

Page.	Letter.	Full Name.	Residence, Jan. 1, 1938.	Occupation.	Supposed Age.	Reported Residence, Jan. 1, 1937. Street and Number.

Thurston Street—Continued

	Y	Downing Hiram	20	watchman	56	here
	Z	Downing Melissa—†	20	housewife	52	"
1461						
	A	Smith Justina S—†	20	"	73	
	B	Smith Willard M	20	retired	77	"
	C	Aronson Harry	21	superintendent	37	1118 Saratoga
	D	Devlin Louise—†	21	nurse	32	1118 "
	E	O'Rourke Helen F—†	21	operator	41	1118 "
	F	O'Rourke Irene M—†	21	clerk	36	here
	G	O'Rourke Mary A—†	21	housewife	64	1118 Saratoga
	H	O'Rourke Thomas L	21	inspector	33	1118 "
	K	Donovan Arthur J	22	laborer	38	here
	L	Donovan Ellen C—†	22	housewife	38	"
	M	Morrison Dorothy P—†	22	stenographer	29	"
	N	Morrison John P	22	engineer	71	"
	O	Morrison Julia F—†	22	teacher	33	
	P	Morrison Mary E—†	22	operator	43	
	R	Tigges Catherine A—†	25	housewife	39	"
	S	Tiggs Walter J	25	machinist	41	"
	T	*Alossi Ardena—†	26	housewife	32	"
	U	Alossi Umberto	26	agent	37	
	V	Giordano Mario	26	"	30	
	W	*Giordano Raffaela—†	26	housewife	70	"
	X	Rossi Angelo	26	tailor	47	
	Y	*Rossi Hilda—†	26	housewife	45	"

Ward 1—Precinct 19

CITY OF BOSTON

LIST OF RESIDENTS
20 YEARS OF AGE AND OVER

(NON-CITIZENS INDICATED BY ASTERISK)
(FEMALES INDICATED BY DAGGER)

AS OF

JANUARY 1, 1938

JOSEPH F. TIMILTY, } *Listing*
FREDERIC E. DOWLING, } *Board.*

CITY OF BOSTON PRINTING DEPARTMENT

Page.	Letter.	FULL NAME.	Residence, Jan. 1, 1938.	Occupation.	Supposed Age.	Reported Residence, Jan. 1, 1937. Street and Number.
1474						
		Annavoy Street				
	C	Cerullo Christie	10	laborer	28	75 St Andrew rd
	B	Cerullo Lilia—†	10	housewife	25	here
	C	Ruggieri Amelia—†	10	"	50	"
	D	Ruggieri Luigi	10	finisher	52	"
	E	Montgomery Edward N	26	B F D	51	
	F	Montgomery Helen B—†	26	housewife	47	"
		Barnes Avenue				
	G	McDonald Catherine—†	95	operator	35	here
	H	McDonald Clementine—†	95	secretary	40	"
	K	McDonald Mary—†	95	clerk	45	"
	L	Perrier Alice—†	95	housewife	56	"
	M	Perrier Eugene	95	operator	56	
	N	Riley Irene—†	95	housewife	23	"
	O	Riley William	95	mechanic	25	"
	P	Jannini Alice—†	99	housewife	32	"
	R	Jannini Christopher	99	cutter	33	
	S	Abate Angelo	99	operator	52	..
	T	Abate Frank	99	laborer	27	
	U	Abate Jeannette—†	99	clerk	26	
	V	Abate Laura—†	99	housewife	44	"
	W	Fenlon John J	102	fireman	36	
	X	Fenlon Mary E—†	102	housewife	70	"
	Y	Fenlon Warren F	102	attorney	39	"
	Z	Golden Katherine—†	102	at home	60	
1475						
	A	McCabe Walter	102	painter	29	Arlington
	B	Pendergast Catherine—†	102	housewife	60	here
	C	Pendergast Lillian—†	102	operator	37	"
	D	*Smiddy Catherine—†	103	housewife	49	"
	E	Smiddy Helen—†	103	librarian	29	
	F	*Smiddy John	103	clerk	51	
	G	Campbell Armina—†	103	housewife	70	"
	H	Campbell John L	103	retired	76	
	K	McDermott Armina—†	103	housewife	36	"
	L	McDermott John J	103	policeman	37	"
	M	Accettullo Louis	107	salesman	28	"
	N	Accettullo Sarah—†	107	waitress	25	
	O	Brady Edward	107	chauffeur	29	"

Page.	Letter.	FULL NAME.	Residence, Jan. 1, 1938.	Occupation.	Supposed Age.	Reported Residence, Jan. 1, 1937. Street and Number.

Barnes Avenue—Continued

	P	Collins Mary E—†	107	matron	49	here
	R	Hickey Catherine F—†	107	housewife	55	"
	S	Hickey Edward J	107	investigator	27	"
	T	Hickey Frances—†	107	housewife	27	"
	U	Hickey John T	107	laborer	63	
	V	Hickey Mary E—†	107	operator	28	
	W	Norman Herbert S	110	B F D	41	
	X	Norman Louise A—†	110	housewife	31	"
	Y	Merlino Angelina—†	110	at home	37	
	Z	Merlino Anthony	110	barber	52	
1476						
	A	Testa Anna—†	110	housewife	33	"
	B	Testa Frank	110	salesman	34	"
	C	Ahern Helen—†	111	saleswoman	42	"
	D	Ahern Margaret—†	111	at home	35	
	E	Ahern Michael	111	retired	80	
	F	Ahern Nora—†	111	saleswoman	45	"
	G	Dillon Joseph P	111	clerk	30	
	H	Dillon Mildred A—†	111	housewife	29	"
	K	Callanan Pauline A—†	115	"	32	
	L	Callanan William A	115	policeman	33	"
	M	Kerivan Elizabeth—†	115	domestic	60	"
	N	White John J	115	carpenter	63	"
	O	White Isabelle F—†	115	bookkeeper	29	"
	P	White Mary E—†	115	housewife	55	"
	R	White Mary R—†	115	clerk	27	
	S	Lehmann Arthur B	118	printer	47	
	T	Lehmann Dorothy M—†	118	stenographer	24	"
	U	Lehmann Grace—†	118	at home	23	"
	V	Lehmann Lillian A—†	118	housewife	46	"
	W	Lane Alice—†	118	dressmaker	53	"
	X	Lane Catherine—†	118	housewife	31	"
	Y	Lane Helen—†	118	operator	42	"
	Z	Lane James	118	laborer	32	
1477						
	A	Lane John	118	clerk	37	
	B	Lane Katheryn—†	118	operator	36	"
	C	Crawford Mary—†	126	at home	70	
	D	Ryan Helen G—†	126	housewife	34	"
	E	Ryan James	126	chauffeur	38	"
	F	Higgins Lillian—†	126	operator	41	"

Page.	Letter.	Full Name.	Residence, Jan. 1, 1938.	Occupation.	Supposed Age.	Reported Residence, Jan. 1, 1937. Street and Number.

Barnes Avenue—Continued

	G	Nolan Margaret R—†	126	at home	46	here
	H	Shannon Edward	126	salesman	37	"
	K	Shannon Edward P	126	retired	73	"
	L	Shannon Elizabeth—†	126	housewife	43	"
	M	Shannon George	126	chauffeur	34	"
	N	Shannon William	126	watchman	35	"

Bayswater Street

	O	Dondero Arthur J	80	clerk	28	here
	P	Dondero Elizabeth C—†	80	housewife	59	"
	R	Dondero Florence A—†	80	stenographer	34	"
	S	Dondero Joseph M	80	laborer	59	"
	T	Ahearn Bridget T—†	82	clerk	67	
	U	Conley Michael F	82	operator	63	
	V	Recomendes Annie E—†	82	housewife	65	"
	W	Recomendes Francis X	82	waiter	46	
	X	Recomendes Joseph A	82	salesman	38	"
	Y	O'Neill Nellie—†	84	housewife	64	"
	Z	O'Connor Anna M—†	86	operator	33	"
1478						
	A	Engren Theresa E—†	88	housewife	44	154 St Andrew rd
	B	Engren Walter F	88	engineer	43	154 "
	C	Mullen James	88	retired	76	154 "
	D	Mullen John J	88	storekeeper	46	154 "
	E	Mullen Marion K—†	88	stenographer	36	154 "
	F	Hamilton Charles J	94	carpenter	43	here
	G	Hamilton Evelyn M—†	94	housewife	40	"
	H	McMullen Annie—†	94	clerk	29	"
	K	McMullen Peter A	94	"	35	
	L	O'Brien Elizabeth—†	94	"	21	
	M	O'Brien Frank P	94	fireman	24	
	N	O'Brien John C	94	clerk	26	"
	N[1]	Campbell Agnes—†	98	housewife	24	326 Meridian
	O	Campbell Frank	98	electrician	28	326 "
	P	DiNucci Amirico	98	laborer	33	here
	R	DiNucci Antonetta—†	98	housewife	63	"
	S	DiNucci Antonio	98	mechanic	31	"
	T	DiNucci Ferdinand	98	salesman	24	"
	U	DiNucci Rose—†	98	clerk	35	
	V	DiNucci Victoria—†	98	"	29	"

Page.	Letter.	Full Name.	Residence, Jan. 1, 1938.	Occupation.	Supposed Age.	Reported Residence, Jan. 1, 1937. Street and Number.

Bayswater Street—Continued

	W	DiNucci Vincent	98	laborer	68	here
	X	McCarthy Leona E—†	100	housewife	57	"
	Y	McCarthy Timothy A	100	U S customs	58	"
	Z	Kincade Gerald F	102	student	20	
1479						
	A	Kincade William E	102	foreman	45	
	B	Kincade William E	102	"	22	"
	C	Nutile Edna V—†	104	housewife	41	22 Bayswater
	D	Nutile Thomas	104	salesman	54	22 "
	E	Chiccarelli Jennie—†	106	housewife	37	here
	F	Chiccarelli Joseph B	106	merchant	46	"
	G	Donahue Cornelius J	108	plumber	30	"
	H	Donahue Frances—†	108	nurse	30	"
	K	Kelly Brendon	110	operator	33	87 Horace
	L	Kelly Eileen—†	110	housewife	30	Winthrop
	M	Rossetta Angela—†	112	"	26	284 Maverick
	N	Rossetta Anthony	112	laborer	26	284 "
	O	Mogan Ethel D—†	112	housewife	46	here
	P	Mogan William H	112	realtor	49	"
	R	Stearns Henry	114	pressman	26	Winthrop
	S	Stearns Katherine—†	114	housewife	37	14 Embankment rd
	T	Stearns Morris	114	engraver	34	Winthrop
	U	Whalen Irene—†	114	secretary	26	here
	V	Whalen John J	114	"	30	"
	W	Brown Amy F—†	116	teacher	28	"
	X	Brown Francis T	116	retired	67	
	Y	Brown Margaret E—†	116	housewife	55	"
	Z	DiSimone Adeline—†	120	"	38	
1480						
	A	DiSimone Michael	120	merchant	39	"
	B	Lane Ellen—†	120	housewife	82	"
	C	Lane Mabel—†	120	secretary	40	"
	D	Pellegrini Helen—†	122	housewife	39	100 Belvidere
	E	Pellegrini Joseph	122	manager	41	100 "
	F	Herbert Agnes W—†	124	technician	23	here
	G	Herbert John	124	chauffeur	21	"
	H	Herbert Mary A—†	124	hostess	50	"
	K	Morton Evelyn G—†	126	housewife	33	"
	L	Morton Walter E	126	clerk	37	
	M	Digon Agnes—†	140	housewife	61	"
	N	Digon Freeman	140	storekeeper	60	"

Page.	Letter.	FULL NAME.	Residence, Jan. 1, 1938.	Occupation.	Supposed Age.	Reported Residence, Jan. 1, 1937. Street and Number.

Bayswater Street—Continued

	O	Digon Mary—†	140	teacher	26	here
	P	Phelan Helen A—†	140	housewife	39	"
	R	Phelan William M	140	B F D	51	"
	S	Whynot George A	144	machinist	56	"
	T	Whynot Lucinda—†	144	housewife	55	"
	U	Silva Anthony F	144	laborer	51	
	V	Silva Emily C—†	144	housewife	50	"
	W	Brown Hazel R—†	146	stenographer	21	"
	X	Brown James S	146	electrician	57	"
	Y	Burns Claire M—†	146	secretary	24	"
	Z	Burns Edward P	146	laborer	64	
1481						
	A	Burns Margaret A—†	146	housewife	59	"
	B	Clarke Estelle L—†	146	social worker	40	"
	C	Ciampa Elizabeth—†	148	houseworker	20	"
	D	Ciampa Emma—†	148	hairdresser	23	"
	E	Ciampa Evelyn—†	148	"	28	
	F	Ciampa Florence—†	148	clerk	27	
	G	Ciampa Joseph	148	salesman	25	"
	H	Montgomery Annie T—†	150	housewife	73	"
	K	Montgomery Hugh D	150	artist	48	
	L	Montgomery Rose E—†	150	housewife	47	"
	M	Montgomery Claire—†	152	"	40	
	N	Montgomery Eugene R	152	jeweler	45	
	O	Hines Mary F—†	154	housewife	68	"
	P	Hines Thomas J	154	laborer	31	
	R	Riley Catherine—†	156	housewife	31	"
	S	Riley Leonard P	156	plumber	30	"
	T	Broussard Clementine—†	160	housewife	67	105 Falcon
	U	Dolan Frank X	160	chemist	38	here
	V	Dolan Margaret—†	160	housewife	35	"
	W	Supple Henry L	160	editor	35	Winthrop
	X	Supple Mildred E—†	160	housewife	34	"
	Y	Sennett Arthur J	166	foreman	43	here
	Z	Sennett Margaret M—†	166	housewife	41	"
1482						
	A	Brosnahan Ann—†	166	"	27	
	B	Brosnahan Catherine—†	166	teacher	26	
	C	Brosnahan Frank	166	accountant	30	"
	D	Brosnahan Mary—†	166	housewife	50	"

Page.	Letter.	Full Name.	Residence, Jan. 1, 1938.	Occupation.	Supposed Age.	Reported Residence, Jan. 1, 1937. Street and Number.
		Bayswater Street—Continued				
	E	Brosnahan William	166	laborer	26	here
	F	Goodwin Carl D	170	engineer	37	"
	G	Goodwin Lorraine M—†	170	housewife	35	"
	H	Chalmers Hazen A	170	policeman	42	"
	K	Chalmers Julia C—†	170	housewife	42	"
	L	Cerulli Domenick	174	foreman	66	
	M	Cerulli Frederick	174	engineer	32	
	N	*Cerulli Marie—†	174	housewife	56	"
	O	Cerulli Rose M—†	174	"	33	
	P	Chiarini Henry	174	student	24	
	R	Chiarini Joseph	174	musician	49	"
	S	Chiarini Josephine—†	174	housewife	47	"
	T	Lowther Anne—†	174A	operator	29	
	U	Lowther Celia—†	174A	housewife	59	"
	V	Lowther Frances—†	174A	supervisor	32	"
	W	Lowther Grace—†	174A	operator	26	
	X	Lowther Margaret—†	174A	houseworker	34	"
	Y	Lafferty Matthew L	186	clerk	47	
	Z	Landry Jeffrey	186	manager	49	"
1483						
	A	Landry May E—†	186	housewife	46	"
	B	MacDonald Mary—†	186	"	67	
	C	McLaughlin Frances—†	186	"	47	
	D	McLaughlin James F	186	salesman	48	"
	E	Alla Helen—†	188	housewife	31	"
	F	Alla Vincent J	188	mechanic	41	"
	G	Antelmi Joseph	188	laborer	26	
	H	Antelmi Matthew	188	"	36	
	K	Antelmi Pasquale	188	"	25	
	L	Fantasia Benjamin	188	"	22	
	M	*Fantasia Clement	188	"	62	
	N	Hall Fritz S	190	painter	42	
	O	Hall Marion F—†	190	housewife	30	"
	P	Harrigan Julia—†	190	"	65	
		Benner Street				
	R	Hoffman Jack	8	fisherman	54	here
	S	Hoffman Sadie—†	8	housewife	52	"

Page.	Letter.	Full Name.	Residence, Jan. 1, 1938.	Occupation.	Supposed Age.	Reported Residence, Jan. 1, 1937. Street and Number.

Lillian Street

Page.	Letter.	Full Name.	Residence, Jan. 1, 1938.	Occupation.	Supposed Age.	Reported Residence, Jan. 1, 1937. Street and Number.
	V	Kelleher Catherine W—†	1	housewife	60	here
	W	Kelleher Dennis J	1	probat'n officer	61	"
	X	Kelleher Joseph	1	student	21	"
	Y	Kelleher Mary M—†	1	houseworker	22	"
	Z	Linehan Aurelia—†	14	housewife	45	"
1484						
	A	Linehan Daniel J	14	guard	55	
	B	Linehan Daniel L	14	operator	26	
	C	Linehan Walter W	14	busboy	21	
	D	Zagarella Gemma—†	14	housewife	40	"
	E	Zagarella Salvatore	14	barber	42	

Nancia Street

Page.	Letter.	Full Name.	Residence, Jan. 1, 1938.	Occupation.	Supposed Age.	Reported Residence, Jan. 1, 1937. Street and Number.
	F	Heggem Dagmar—†	2	housewife	39	here
	G	Heggem Lars	2	clergyman	50	"
	H	Nordly Alma—†	2	houseworker	70	"
	K	Greco Joseph	9	chauffeur	38	1055 Saratoga
	L	Greco Louis	9	laborer	40	1055 "
	M	Greco William	9	chauffeur	42	1055 "
	N	Romano Anna—†	9	housewife	35	1055 "
	O	Romano Philip	9	tailor	39	1055 "
	P	Bradley Joseph H	10	B F D	41	here
	R	Bradley Madeline—†	10	housewife	36	"

Saint Andrew Road

Page.	Letter.	Full Name.	Residence, Jan. 1, 1938.	Occupation.	Supposed Age.	Reported Residence, Jan. 1, 1937. Street and Number.
	T	Goodwin Frank	50	registrar	63	here
	U	Ciampa Domenico	50	realtor	56	"
	V	Ciampa Lillian—†	50	housewife	44	"
	W	Gietz Carl F	51	carpenter	28	Winthrop
	X	MacDonald Dorothy—†	51	attendant	26	here
	Y	MacDonald Margaret—†	51	social worker	50	"
	Z	MacDonald Miriam—†	51	operator	24	"
1485						
	A	MacDonald Thomas	51	constable	66	"
	B	Penta Ida—†	51	dressmaker	23	"
	C	Penta John	51	tailor	35	
	D	Penta Laura—†	51	tailoress	24	
	E	*Penta Mary—†	51	housewife	59	"
	F	*Penta Michael	51	laborer	58	

Page.	Letter.	Full Name.	Residence, Jan. 1, 1938.	Occupation.	Supposed Age.	Reported Residence, Jan. 1, 1937. Street and Number.
		Saint Andrew Road—Continued				
	G	Penta Pasquale	51	clerk	27	here
	H	Penta Theresa—†	51	tailoress	30	"
	K	Wey George	51	engineer	31	"
	L	Entwistle Agnes—†	53	housewife	56	"
	M	Entwistle James H	53	clerk	57	
	N	Entwistle Margaret—†	53	"	24	
	O	Winston James J	53	supervisor	52	"
	P	Winston John E	53	statistician	46	"
	R	Winston Katherine B—†	53	housewife	39	"
	S	Winston Mary F—†	53	bookkeeper	41	"
	T	Watts Gertrude H—†	55	housekeeper	45	"
	U	Leary Arthur F	55	teacher	47	"
	V	Reardon Walter F	55	investigator	41	"
	W	Regan Cornelius F	55	manager	49	"
	X	Regan Donald A	55	laborer	22	
	Y	Regan Herbert G	55	agent	23	
	Z	Regan Louise B—†	55	housewife	49	"
1486						
	A	Ryan Agnes M—†	56	"	36	
	B	Ryan Catherine—†	56	"	62	
	C	Ryan Thomas B	56	electrician	37	"
	D	Winston James B	56	clerk	62	
	E	Winston James B	56	inspector	23	"
	F	Segal Leah—†	57	housewife	38	"
	G	Segal Samuel L	57	attorney	42	"
	H	Corrigan Anna K—†	57	secretary	31	"
	K	Corrigan Catherine F—†	57	housewife	62	"
	L	Crowley Claire T—†	59	clerk	22	"
	M	Crowley Eva T—†	59	at home	48	Winthrop
	N	Crowley Margaret R—†	59	housewife	47	here
	O	Crowley Patrick L	59	guard	54	"
	P	Hart Helen S—†	59	housewife	31	"
	R	Hart Peter J	59	manager	32	"
	S	Sullivan James L	59	chauffeur	39	"
	T	Sullivan Jane A—†	59	nurse	41	
	U	Sullivan Lawrence T	59	seaman	38	
	V	Sullivan Susie A—†	59	housewife	70	"
	W	McLeavey Annie E—†	60	"	56	
	X	McLeavey Patrick F	60	fireman	69	
	Y	Love Roselena—†	60	clerk	37	
	Z	Plunkett Bernard	60	retired	72	"

Saint Andrew Road—Continued

Page.	Letter.	Full Name.	Residence, Jan. 1, 1938.	Occupation.	Supposed Age.	Reported Residence, Jan. 1, 1937. Street and Number.
1487						
	A	Reardon Catherine M—†	60	housewife	61	here
	B	Reardon John J	60	superintendent	62	"
	C	Reardon John J	60	clerk	27	"
	D	McCarthy Claire H—†	61	typist	26	1056 Bennington
	E	McCarthy John H	61	glazier	66	1056 "
	F	McCarthy Mary F—†	61	housewife	65	1056 "
	G	Gill Mary E—†	61	"	63	here
	H	Gill Richard F	61	watchman	64	"
	K	Gill Richard M	61	student	22	"
	L	Grifone Alice T—†	63	housewife	41	Swampscott
	M	Grifone Louis P	63	tailor	42	24 Falcon
	N	Musto Albert S	63	manager	30	here
	O	Musto Mary A—†	63	housewife	29	"
	P	*Nigrelli Elizabeth—†	63	"	24	251 Meridian
	R	Nigrelli Frank C	63	operator	28	251 "
	S	Francis Adelaide A—†	64	at home	62	here
	T	Lamb Ethel B—†	64	housewife	41	"
	U	Lamb Frank T	64	policeman	45	"
	V	Roome Mortimer	64	retired	73	
	W	Byrne Mary A—†	65	matron	59	
	X	Haley Arthur E	65	student	23	"
	Y	Haley Susan G—†	65	housewife	60	"
	Z	Haley Thomas F	65	engineer	60	
1488						
	A	McGovern Margaret A—†	65	clerk	40	
	B	Cummings Florence G—†	66	stenographer	44	"
	C	Cummings Nellie E—†	66	housewife	57	"
	D	Harris Catherine—†	68	saleswoman	23	"
	E	Harris Charles	68	salesman	21	"
	F	*Harris James	68	operator	47	
	G	*Harris Margaret—†	68	housewife	45	"
	H	McDonough Marguerite–†	68	nurse	22	
	K	Strong Annie—†	68	housewife	58	"
	L	Strong Ellen—†	68	"	62	
	M	Strong William H	68	dentist	48	
	N	Hoey Fred J	69	mechanic	25	"
	O	Hoey John W	69	B F D	50	
	P	Hoey Mary L—†	69	housewife	50	"
	R	Leary Helen L—†	69	clerk	39	
	S	Leary Matthew M	69	probat'n officer	59	"

Page.	Letter.	Full Name.	Residence, Jan. 1, 1938.	Occupation.	Supposed Age.	Reported Residence, Jan. 1, 1937. Street and Number.

Saint Andrew Road—Continued

	T	Caggiano Arthur	70	laborer	29	here
	U	Caggiano Florence—†	70	candymaker	27	"
	V	*Caggiano Grace—†	70	housewife	63	"
	W	Caggiano Joseph	70	barber	68	
	X	Schoenfeld Lena—†	70	stenographer	36	"
	Y	Caggiano Armando	70	fireman	34	"
	Z	Caggiano Catherine V—†	70	housewife	33	"
1489						
	A	Caggiano Evelyn—†	70	"	40	
	A[1]	Caggiano Generoso	70	salesman	43	"
	B	Cataldo Chiarina—†	72	housewife	65	"
	C	Cataldo Pasquale	72	retired	76	
	D	Zizza Ermalinda—†	72	housekeeper	32	"
	E	DiFronzo Albert	72	printer	26	"
	F	DiFronzo John	72	chauffeur	24	"
	G	DiFronzo Laura—†	72	clerk	20	
	H	DiFronzo Louise—†	72	hairdresser	22	"
	K	Callahan John J	73	manager	44	
	L	Callahan Rose M—†	73	housewife	43	"
	M	Abely Eleanor V—†	73	teacher	30	
	N	Dolan Anna L—†	73	bookkeeper	50	"
	O	Dolan Charles	73	clerk	68	"
	P	Dolan Patrick J	73	retired	62	
	R	McCarthy Mary F—†	73	housekeeper	65	"
	S	Carangelo Louise—†	74	teacher	31	"
	T	Miraldi Gerald	74	attorney	34	"
	U	Miraldi Olive—†	74	housewife	33	"
	V	Blackwell Herbert	75	clerk	34	
	W	Blackwell Theresa—†	75	housewife	33	"
	X	*Cerrullo Annie—†	75	"	61	
	Y	Cerrullo Antonio	75	operator	25	"
	Z	Cerrullo Sabata	75	retired	60	
1490						
	A	Clegg Anna—†	75	housewife	30	22 Breed
	B	Clegg Daniel	75	laborer	30	22 "
	C	DeStefano Albert	75	bartender	33	225 Leyden
	D	DeStefano Mary—†	75	housewife	33	here
	E	Giuliotti Adolph	76	policeman	39	"
	F	Giuliotti Mary V—†	76	housewife	34	"
	G	Kelleher Bridget—†	77	"	85	
	H	Kelleher Jeremiah J	77	laborer	53	

Page.	Letter.	Full Name.	Residence, Jan. 1, 1938.	Occupation.	Supposed Age.	Reported Residence, Jan. 1, 1937. Street and Number.

Saint Andrew Road—Continued

	K	Kelleher John V	77	waterman	56	here
	L	Kelleher Mary M—†	77	housewife	45	"
	M	Kelleher William P	77	guard	48	"
	N	Hanagan Elizabeth—†	77	housewife	41	"
	O	Hanagan John P	77	B F D	44	
	P	Hanagan Matthew	77	laborer	35	
	R	Kelley Joseph E	77	student	20	
	S	Tellier William	77	clerk	25	
	T	Elmore Joseph F	78	"	48	
	U	Elmore Margaret—†	78	housewife	77	"
	V	Elmore Mary G—†	78	clerk	40	
	W	McAdams Alfred J	78	"	45	
	X	McAdams Eleanor—†	78	housewife	45	"
	Y	Dawley Anastasia—†	80	"	74	
	Z	Dawley Anna F—†	80	operator	39	
1491						
	A	Dawley William J	80	inspector	41	"
	B	Kelley Christopher	80	retired	76	
	C	Kinnaly George W	81	manager	34	"
	D	Kinnaly Theresa M—†	81	housewife	29	"
	E	Cunningham Mary E—†	81	housekeeper	67	"
	F	Drowney Agnes C—†	81	dietitian	54	"
	G	Shaw Harry F	81	agent	48	
	H	Shaw Marie A—†	81	housewife	43	"
	K	Shaw Marie A—†	81	secretary	23	"
	L	Fowler Edward	82	foreman	50	
	M	Fowler Frances—†	82	housewife	32	"
	N	Compaino Charles	82	salesman	60	"
	O	Cucio Henry	82	tailor	35	
	P	McNeil Catherine—†	82	at home	65	"
	R	Musto Ralph R	82	attorney	32	109 Lexington
	S	Musto Renata A—†	82	housewife	26	Revere
	T	Stout Isabella—†	82	"	80	here
	U	Stout Lena G—†	82	"	48	"
	V	Stout Walter A	82	clerk	50	"
	W	Sullivan Beatrice F—†	83	housewife	36	"
	X	Sullivan William J	83	attorney	48	"
	Y	Labadesia Joseph	85	laborer	57	"
	Z	*Labadesia Lucia—†	85	housewife	56	"
1492						
	A	Labadesia Stella—†	85	clerk	26	

Page.	Letter.	Full Name.	Residence, Jan. 1, 1938.	Occupation.	Supposed Age.	Reported Residence, Jan. 1, 1937. Street and Number.

Saint Andrew Road—Continued

Page.	Letter.	Full Name.	Residence, Jan. 1, 1938.	Occupation.	Supposed Age.	Reported Residence, Jan. 1, 1937. Street and Number.
	B	Arnone Adele—†	86	housewife	25	here
	C	Arnone Angela—†	86	“	49	“
	D	Arnone Felice	86	clerk	29	“
	E	Arnone Nicholas J	86	foreman	52	
	F	Gomes John	86	retired	81	
	G	Gomes Mary G—†	86	teacher	45	
	H	Martins Anna M—†	86	housewife	44	“
	K	Martins John H	86	salesman	44	“
	L	Dunn Ann—†	87	housewife	27	“
	M	Dunn Joseph A	87	contractor	34	“
	N	Bellusci Josephine—†	89	housewife	45	“
	O	Bellusci Michael C	89	realtor	55	
	P	Bellusci Nicholas	89	agent	26	
	R	DeSimone Joseph	89	manager	45	“
	S	DeSimone Lucas	89	clerk	23	
	T	DeSimone Margaret—†	89	housewife	43	“
	U	Collyer Albert I	90	laborer	38	
	V	Stoner Elizabeth A—†	90	housewife	40	“
	W	Stoner George A	90	engineer	51	
	X	Stoner George H	90	student	20	
	Y	DiGrenier Abbie—†	90	housewife	57	“
1493						
	A	DiGrenier John E	90	chauffeur	27	“
	Z	DiGrenier Joseph	90	operator	57	
	B	DiGrenier Leo A	90	clerk	22	
	C	DiGrenier Mary—†	90	“	20	“
	D	Lavezzo Corinne—†	91–93	housewife	33	727 Benningt'n
	E	Lavezzo Frank	91–93	printer	42	727 “
	F	Smith Francis X	91–93	letter carrier	44	727 “
	G	Smith John E	91–93	salesman	42	727 “
	H	Smith Margaret V—†	91–93	clerk	38	727 “
	K	Smith Mary A—†	91–93	operator	39	727 “
	L	Smith Sarah A—†	91–93	housewife	38	727 “
	M	Whaland Helen E—†	92	“	37	here
	N	Whaland Philip	92	policeman	47	“
	O	Schlosberg Jessie—†	94	at home	25	“
	P	Schlosberg Leon	94	pharmacist	23	“
	R	Schlosberg Louis	94	salesman	52	“
	S	Schlosberg Sadie—†	94	housewife	48	“
	U	Zielinger Charles J	96	manager	34	“
	T	Zielinger Christine M—†	96	operator	32	

Page.	Letter.	Full Name.	Residence, Jan. 1, 1938.	Occupation.	Supposed Age.	Reported Residence, Jan. 1, 1937. Street and Number.
		Saint Andrew Road—Continued				
	v	Zielinger Isabella M—†	96	housewife	54	here
	w	Greer Andrew A	98	retired	68	"
	x	Greer Herbert A	98	clerk	21	"
	y	Greer Margaret—†	98	housewife	48	"
	z	Ryan Dorothy A—†	98	nurse	22	
1494						
	A	Ryan Nicholas J	98	letter carrier	58	"
	B	Lund Anna—†	100	housewife	89	"
	C	Lund Gustave E	100	retired	82	
	D	Lund Hilma E—†	100	operator	54	
	E	Lund Winnifred R—†	100	hairdresser	21	"
	F	Palladina Alfonsina—†	101	housewife	24	"
	G	Palladina Anthony	101	salesman	28	"
	H	Selvitella Joseph	103	manager	39	"
	K	Selvitella Matilda R—†	103	housewife	32	"
	L	Selvitella Adeline—†	103	"	30	
	M	Selvitella James	103	manager	37	"
	o	*Stasio Anna—†	105	housewife	65	"
	P	Stasio Helen—†	105	saleswoman	32	"
	R	Ianatuoni Florence—†	105	housewife	37	"
	S	Ianatuoni Joseph	105	operator	44	"
	T	Olson Margaret—†	106	housewife	43	144 St Andrew rd
	U	Olson Olof N	106	operator	49	144 "
	V	Rahn Joseph C	107	manufacturer	53	here
	W	Rahn Vera N—†	107	housewife	41	"
	X	*Valli Adella—†	108	"	65	"
	Y	Valli George	108	teamster	35	"
1495						
	A	Crane Joseph	109	manager	39	"
	B	Crane Mary—†	109	housewife	36	"
	C	Capuano Elizabeth—†	110	"	30	
	D	Capuano John	110	bartender	32	"
	E	Bianco Adeline—†	111	housewife	34	"
	F	Bianco Edward	111	constructor	48	"
	G	Taurasi Anthony	111	collector	29	Everett
	H	Frazier Dorothy—†	111	housewife	29	here
	K	Frazier Stephen	111	clerk	34	"
	L	Stone Betty L—†	112	housewife	31	"
	M	Stone Julius	112	attorney	36	"
	N	Catenacci John	114	laborer	41	
	O	*Catenacci Susie—†	114	housewife	43	"

Page.	Letter.	Full Name.	Residence, Jan. 1, 1938.	Occupation.	Supposed Age.	Reported Residence, Jan. 1, 1937. Street and Number.

Saint Andrew Road—Continued

Page.	Letter.	Full Name.	Residence, Jan. 1, 1938.	Occupation.	Supposed Age.	Reported Residence, Jan. 1, 1937. Street and Number.
	P	Abruzzese Luigi	117	dealer	50	here
	R	Abruzzese Marion—†	117	at home	24	"
	S	Abruzzese Susie—†	117	"	21	"
	T	*Abruzzese Theresa—†	117	housewife	41	"
	U	Abruzzese Assunta—†	119	"	36	
	V	Abruzzese Carlo	119	dealer	45	
	W	Carresi Gemma—†	121	housewife	35	"
	X	Carresi Leo	121	salesman	35	"
	Y	Carresi Michael	121	"	31	
	Z	Ciccarelli Michael	121	meatcutter	45	"
1496						
	A	Ciccarelli Rachel—†	121	housewife	35	"
	B	Blinn Ellen L—†	123	nurse	21	
	C	Blinn Katherine L—†	123	housewife	46	"
	D	Blinn William C	123	machinist	50	"
	E	Overlan Francis P	123	cutter	41	"
	F	Overlan Leo H	123	operator	43	92 Falcon
	G	Sinatra Carmen C	123	clerk	24	here
	H	Sinatra Constance—†	123	at home	29	"
	K	*Sinatra Gertrude—†	123	housewife	31	"
	L	*Sinatra James	123	cutter	31	
	M	Sinatra Josephine—†	123	operator	28	
	N	DiChristoforo Carmelina—†	125	housewife	30	"
	O	DiChristoforo Emilio	125	printer	37	
	P	Christopher Eleanor—†	127	housewife	22	"
	R	Christopher John	127	engineer	39	
	S	Brennan Mary F—†	127	housekeeper	57	"
	T	Shanahan James A	127	teacher	49	"
	U	Shanahan May E—†	127	buyer	42	
	V	Sawyer Edison F	140	attorney	45	"
	W	Sawyer Winifred—†	140	housewife	41	"
	Y	Kenefick Matthew J	140	clerk	45	
	Z	Kenefick Mildred M—†	140	"	25	
1497						
	A	Kenefick Violet M—†	140	housewife	45	"
	A[1]	Oteri Pauline—†	140	hairdresser	34	New York
	B	Bartlett Catherine—†	142	housewife	44	here
	C	Bartlett Grace—†	142	at home	23	"
	D	Bartlett John F	142	superintendent	48	"
	E	Bartlett John F	142	laborer	21	"
	F	Sacco Elizabeth—†	142	housewife	37	19 Ashley

Page.	Letter.	FULL NAME.	Residence, Jan. 1, 1938.	Occupation.	Supposed Age.	Reported Residence, Jan. 1, 1937. Street and Number.

Saint Andrew Road—Continued

	G	Sacco Frank	142	policeman	47	19 Ashley
	H	Caggiano Carmen A—†	144	housewife	36	11 Thurston
	K	Caggiano Michael S	144	towerman	37	11 "
	L	Blangio Albert	144	manager	52	here
	M	Blangio Alfred J	144	chauffeur	27	"
	N	Blangio Annie M—†	144	housewife	45	"
	O	Blangio Charles	144	clerk	24	
	P	Blangio John	144	U S A	25	
	R	Blangio Michael	144	clerk	22	
	S	Mosher Robert R	146	electrician	37	"
	T	Smith Alice—†	146	housewife	42	"
	U	Smith William	146	manager	42	"
	W	DeStefano Eleanor—†	146	housewife	37	383 Frankfort
	V	DeStefano George	146	foreman	39	383 "
	X	Bacciola Eliza—†	147	buyer	43	here
	Y	Bacciola Emma—†	147	clerk	39	"
	Z	Bacciola Giacoma	147	retired	73	"
1498						
	A	Bacciola Nellie—†	147	teacher	36	
	B	Bacciola Theodore	147	"	30	
	C	Costantino Bonifacio	148	foreman	63	
	D	Rapa Anita—†	148	housewife	32	"
	E	Rapa Fiore	148	manager	38	"
	F	Cancian Anna—†	148	housewife	37	"
	G	Cancian Frances—†	148	nurse	20	
	H	Cancian Frank	148	architect	43	"
	K	Winters Elmer F	150	watchman	29	"
	L	Winters Henry A	150	waiter	31	
	M	Winters Margaret—†	150	housewife	56	"
	N	Winters Sylvester J	150	undertaker	58	"
	O	Cancian Emma—†	150	housewife	40	"
	P	Cancian Ottavo	150	contractor	39	"
	R	Dahlgren Eric	150	salesman	28	"
	S	Montgomery Cyril	152	policeman	41	
	T	Montgomery Florence—†	152	housewife	33	"
	U	Carey Angelina—†	152	"	28	Winthrop
	V	Carey Thomas A	152	supervisor	43	38 St Andrew rd
	W	Kincaid Grace R—†	154	housewife	42	here
	X	Kincaid Paul	154	operator	21	"
	Y	Kincaid Paul E	154	foreman	43	"
	Z	Alexander William J	154	salesman	49	463 Meridian

Page.	Letter.	Full Name.	Residence, Jan. 1, 1938.	Occupation.	Supposed Age.	Reported Residence, Jan. 1, 1937. Street and Number.

Saint Andrew Road—Continued

	A	Donohue Cornelius J	154	plumber	65	109 Bayswater
	B	Donohue Harriet N—†	154	housewife	60	109 "
	C	Donohue Thomas F	154	agent	24	109 "
	D	Walters Rose M—†	154	clerk	47	289 Bremen

Saint Edward Road

	F	*Guarino Louisa—†	35	housewife	57	here
	G	Guarino Raffael	35	laborer	61	"
	H	Lagana Concetta—†	35	housewife	45	"
	K	Lagana Frances—†	35	examiner	20	"
	L	Lagana John	35	bookkeeper	22	"
	M	Lagana Placido	35	barber	50	"
	N	DePeppo Arietta—†	35	clerk	23	
	O	*DePeppo Concetta—†	35	housewife	50	"
	P	DePeppo John	35	tailor	54	
	R	DePeppo Victor	35	draftsman	26	"
	S	Albano Antonetta—†	37	housewife	54	"
	T	Albano Philip	37	chauffeur	28	"
	U	Genoesa Charles	37	barber	46	1088 Saratoga
	V	Genoesa Mary—†	37	housewife	34	1088 "
	W	*Bruno Mary—†	37	"	46	here
	X	Bruno Mary—†	37	clerk	20	"
	Y	*Bruno Peter	37	laborer	47	"
	Z	Mucci Adeline—†	39	housewife	27	"
1500						
	A	*Mucci Louis	39	butcher	37	
	B	DeLorenzo Carmine	39	laborer	23	
	C	DeLorenzo Stella—†	39	at home	24	
	D	DeLorenzo Theresa—†	39	housewife	47	"
	E	Caizza Thomas	39	chauffeur	22	"
	F	Nazzaro Raymond	39	clerk	23	
	G	Perrelli Catherine—†	39	housewife	36	"
	H	Perrelli Ernest	39	installer	34	
	K	Anderson Ellen M—†	41	at home	33	
	L	Anderson Sarah L—†	41	"	54	
	M	Downey Annie E—†	41	housewife	31	"
	N	Downey Frederick P	41	plumber	31	293 Lexington
	O	McCluskey Henry	41	bookkeeper	27	here
	P	Clark Arthur	41	salesman	46	"
	R	Clark Myrtle—†	41	housewife	44	"

Page.	Letter.	Full Name.	Residence, Jan. 1, 1938.	Occupation.	Supposed Age.	Reported Residence, Jan. 1, 1937. Street and Number.

Saint Edward Road—Continued

Page.	Letter.	Full Name.	Residence, Jan. 1, 1938.	Occupation.	Supposed Age.	Reported Residence, Jan. 1, 1937. Street and Number.
	s	Gallagher William	43	laborer	38	26 Overlook
	T	Gallagher Winifred M—†	43	housewife	36	26 "
	U	McGinnis Hazel—†	43	"	29	80 Trenton
	V	McGinnis John	43	packer	43	80 "
	W	Dalton Florence N—†	43	housewife	29	21 London
	X	Dalton James J	43	laborer	31	21 "
	Y	Savio Clara—†	43	decorator	23	here
	Z	Savio Domenica—†	43	housewife	47	"
1501						
	A	Savio Domenica—†	43	at home	20	
	B	Savio Joseph	43	waiter	54	
	C	*Bombaci Alvira—†	45	housewife	41	"
	D	Bombaci Carmella—†	45	at home	21	
	E	Bombaci Leo	45	cabinetmaker	48	"
	F	Bombaci Stella—†	45	nurse	22	"
	G	DeMaio Anthony	45	laborer	41	36 Cottage
	H	DeMaio James	45	clerk	31	36 "
	K	DeMaio Mary—†	45	housewife	69	36 "
	L	DiBiasi Ida—†	45	"	28	47 '
	M	DiBiasi Michael	45	salesman	30	47 "
	N	Costante Joseph	45	tailor	28	26 Ashley
	O	Costante Sarah—†	45	housewife	25	26 "

Saratoga Street

Page.	Letter.	Full Name.	Residence, Jan. 1, 1938.	Occupation.	Supposed Age.	Reported Residence, Jan. 1, 1937. Street and Number.
	P	Gillison Oscar	1093	fisherman	36	here
	R	Youngberg George	1093	"	34	"
	S	Donovan Daniel J	1093	manager	44	"
	T	Donovan John J	1093	longshoreman	22	"
	U	Donovan Julia A—†	1093	housewife	43	"
	W	Seix Marion F—†	1095	bookkeeper	48	"
	X	Coakley Harold J	1095	clerk	35	"
	Y	McHugh Edward J	1095	contractor	43	"
	Z	McHugh Joseph A	1095	teacher	41	
1502						
	A	McHugh Margurite M—†	1095	housewife	41	"
	B	*Frechette Annie M—†	1096	"	43	
	C	Frechette Emile A	1096	storekeeper	41	"
	D	Chisholm Annie—†	1096	at home	65	"
	E	Walker Dorothy—†	1097	operator	24	"
	F	Walker John	1097	clerk	25	

Saratoga Street—Continued

Page.	Letter.	Full Name.	Residence, Jan. 1, 1938.	Occupation.	Supposed Age.	Reported Residence, Jan. 1, 1937. Street and Number.
	G	Walker Lillian—†	1097	clerk	22	here
	H	Geggis Catherine C—†	1097	housewife	34	“
	K	Geggis Ellen—†	1097	“	78	“
	L	Geggis James S	1097	salesman	41	“
	M	Geggis John A	1097	laborer	55	
	N	Rego Charles E	1098	“	55	
	O	Rego Frances—†	1098	housewife	55	“
	P	Rego Mary F—†	1098	packer	21	
	R	Karasik Bessie L—†	1098	clerk	30	
	S	Karasik Hyman	1098	machinist	27	“
	T	*Karasik Nathan	1098	laborer	60	
	U	Baldassaro Elizabeth—†	1101	housewife	25	“
	V	Baldassaro Louis	1101	plumber	30	
	W	Lattore Frank	1101	storekeeper	43	“
	X	Lattore Mary—†	1101	housewife	37	“
	Y	Bednarsky Stanley	1102	cook	27	401 Benningt'n
	Z	Doyle Mary—†	1102	at home	70	here
1503						
	A	Gomes Arthur J	1102	operator	44	
	B	Gomes Madeline—†	1102	housewife	38	“
	C	Busalacchi Anthony	1105	dealer	55	
	D	Busalocchi Frank	1105	“	23	“
	E	Busalocchi Helen—†	1105	at home	21	
	F	Busalocchi Josephine—†	1105	housewife	59	“
	G	Mortimer Abraham	1105	salesman	28	“
	H	Mortimer Bridget—†	1105	housewife	59	“
	K	Mortimer John W	1105	salesman	25	“
	L	Mortimer Marie—†	1105	waitress	24	
	M	Mortimer Thomas J	1105	laborer	60	
	N	Cappuccio Luigi	1106	mechanic	24	“
	O	Morrelli Angelina—†	1106	housewife	55	“
	P	Morrelli John	1106	storekeeper	43	“
	R	Graff Edward	1109	B F D	40	823 Saratoga
	S	Graff Mary—†	1109	housewife	32	823 “
	T	Baldassaro Frank	1109	laborer	21	here
	U	*Baldassaro Pasquale	1109	“	50	“
	V	Fernald Agnes M—†	1110	housewife	50	“
	W	Fernald Marion E—†	1110	stenographer	23	“
	X	Fernald Robert A	1110	clerk	50	“
	Y	Leonard Christopher T	1110	gateman	61	
	Z	Parker John J	1110	foreman	23	

Page.	Letter.	Full Name.	Residence, Jan. 1, 1938.	Occupation.	Supposed Age.	Reported Residence, Jan. 1, 1937. Street and Number.

1504

Saratoga Street—Continued

	A	Parrell Catherine—†	1111	housewife	47	here
	B	Parrell Richard T	1111	retired	52	"
	C	Billings Anna—†	1111	housewife	37	"
	D	Billings Kenneth U	1111	chauffeur	37	"
	E	Leahy Catherine—†	1111	operator	33	
	F	Leahy Hugh T	1111	guard	45	
	G	Leahy Mary C—†	1111	clerk	30	
	H	Leahy Sarah A—†	1111	housewife	41	"
	K	Cushing John H	1114	designer	32	
	L	Hazelton James E	1114	engineer	47	
	M	Hazelton Mary M—†	1114	housewife	44	"
	N	Monahan Dennis J	1114	clerk	60	
	O	Monahan Francis L	1114	packer	23	
	P	Monahan John B	1114	clerk	26	
	R	Monahan Nellie F—†	1114	housewife	59	"
	S	Cairns James C	1115	printer	50	
	T	Cairns Theresa—†	1115	housewife	45	"
	U	Nelson Gardner N	1115	clerk	50	
	V	Nelson Norma A—†	1115	housewife	44	"
	W	Duffy Mary M—†	1116	"	34	
	X	Duffy Michael H	1116	clerk	39	
	Y	Arthur Joseph	1116	salesman	42	"
1505						
	A	Arthur Josephine—†	1116	student	20	
	B	Arthur Lawrence	1116	clerk	38	"
	C	Arthur Thomas	1116	foreman	40	
	D	Arthur Veronica—†	1116	housewife	38	"
	E	Flynn Annie B—†	1117	"	59	
	F	Flynn Anna M—†	1117	saleswoman	28	"
	G	Flynn Edna M—†	1117	"	27	
	H	Flynn Robert J	1117	clerk	21	
	K	Flynn Thomas J	1117	operator	26	"
	L	Flynn Walter F	1117	clerk	24	
	M	Aylward Alice R—†	1117	housewife	40	"
	N	Aylward Richard F	1117	B F D	46	
	O	Hamilton George J	1117	"	51	"
	P	Hanrahan Bernard F	1117	contractor	62	26A Bennington
	R	Hill Frederick J	1117	laborer	37	here
	S	Gavagan Ethel M—†	1118	operator	28	1126 Saratoga
	T	Gavagan Helen G—†	1118	housewife	38	1126 "

Page.	Letter.	FULL NAME.	Residence, Jan. 1, 1938.	Occupation.	Supposed Age.	Reported Residence, Jan. 1, 1937. Street and Number.

Saratoga Street—Continued

	U	Gavagan Katherine E–†	1118	operator	26	1126 Saratoga
	V	Gavagan Walter M	1118	clerk	37	1126 "
	W	Colbert Alice—†	1118	housewife	80	here
	X	Colbert John J	1118	laborer	45	1140 Saratoga
	Y	Colbert Nellie J—†	1118	housewife	50	here
	Z	Walsh John K	1119	retired	76	"
1506						
	A	Cleary Edward	1119	fisherman	39	155 Saratoga
	B	Sampson Alphonso	1119	"	34	155 "
	C	Sampson Margaret—†	1119	housewife	40	155 "
	D	Sampson Nicolas	1119	fisherman	40	155 "
	E	Jackson Edward H	1120	agent	31	here
	F	Jackson Mary L—†	1120	housewife	28	"
	G	Bartlett Francis	1120	blacksmith	64	"
	H	Bartlett Mary R—†	1120	housewife	56	"
	K	Walsh Edna—†	1121	at home	24	
	L	Walsh John P	1121	B F D	60	
	M	Walsh John P, jr	1121	laborer	29	
	N	McCauley Frank T	1121	salesman	43	"
	O	McCauley Gerald A	1121	"	37	
	P	McCauley Mary B—†	1121	nurse	50	
	R	McCauley Ruth A—†	1121	housewife	47	"
	S	Donnelly Catherine A–†	1122	"	68	1118 Saratoga
	T	Donnelly John J	1122	chauffeur	31	1118 "
	U	Donnelly Margaret M–†	1122	housewife	65	1118 "
	V	Sherry Francis J	1122	guard	53	1118 "
	X	Crowley George S	1123	letter carrier	46	here
	Y	Crowley Helen E—†	1123	housewife	40	"
	Z	Burns Clara J—†	1123	operator	32	"
1507						
	A	Burns John C	1123	clerk	33	
	B	Burns Julia A—†	1123	housewife	75	"
	C	McWilliams Anna L—†	1123	at home	38	
	D	Hutchinson Stacia—†	1124	housewife	33	"
	E	Hutchinson William	1124	laborer	34	
	F	Moran Mary A—†	1124	housewife	48	"
	G	Moran Thomas J	1124	fireman	56	
	H	Butler Lillian C—†	1125	clerk	43	
	K	Cashman Richard J	1125	foreman	60	
	L	Cashman Susan A—†	1125	housewife	47	"
	M	McCarthy Edward L	1125	laborer	56	

Page.	Letter.	Full Name.	Residence, Jan. 1, 1938.	Occupation.	Supposed Age.	Reported Residence, Jan. 1, 1937. Street and Number.

Saratoga Street—Continued

	N	McCarthy George F	1125	clerk	22	here
	O	McCarthy John F	1125	stenographer	25	"
	P	McCarthy Josephine B–†	1125	housewife	52	"
	R	Glennon John F	1126	laborer	26	72 Orient av
	S	Glennon Rita—†	1126	housewife	24	72 "
	T	McDonald William K	1126	tailor	61	here
	U	Grecco Anthony F	1127	operator	38	"
	V	Grecco Lucy—†	1127	housewife	32	"
	W	Abate Alfred	1127	salesman	46	"
	X	Abate Mary—†	1127	housewife	42	"
	Y	Sacchetti James V	1128	physician	36	"
1508						
	A	Sacchetti Melinda—†	1128	saleswoman	38	"
	B	*Sacchetti Raffaella—†	1128	housewife	65	"
	C	Collyer Annetta—†	1128	at home	63	
	D	Monk Esther M—†	1128	housewife	36	"
	E	Monk John	1128	laborer	38	
	F	Masucci Eliseo	1129	"	52	
	G	Masucci Ella—†	1129	housewife	46	"
	H	Masucci Richard	1129	laborer	21	
	K	Masucci Robert	1129	"	23	
	L	Vesci Frank	1129	salesman	21	"
	M	Vesci Joseph	1129	manufacturer	50	"
	N	Silipigni Grace—†	1130	housewife	58	"
	O	Silipigni Lawrence	1130	barber	61	
	P	Silipigni Leo	1130	laborer	21	
	R	Silipigni Mary—†	1130	clerk	29	
	S	Silipigni Nancy—†	1130	at home	27	
	T	Cogliani Anthony	1130	clerk	29	
	U	Cogliani Mary—†	1130	bookkeeper	27	"
	V	Cogliani Nicholas	1130	laborer	53	..
	W	Cogliani Vincenza—†	1130	housewife	51	"
	X	Hazelton Anna—†	1132	"	27	
	Y	Hazelton Charles K	1132	laborer	26	
	Z	*Cogliano Antonetta—†	1132	housewife	38	"
1509						
	A	Cogliano Joseph	1132	chauffeur	50	"
	B	*Morrella Petro	1132	laborer	46	Connecticut
	D	Horner Eileen—†	1141	secretary	28	here
	E	Horner Frederick	1141	superintendent	29	"
	F	Horner Josephine—†	1141	clerk	23	"

Page.	Letter.	Full Name.	Residence, Jan. 1, 1938.	Occupation.	Supposed Age.	Reported Residence, Jan. 1, 1937. Street and Number.

Saratoga Street—Continued

	G	Reardon William J	1141	operator	29	here
	H	Fenlon Ruth C—†	1143	housewife	34	"
	K	Fenlon William F	1143	electrician	40	"
	L	Sullivan Stephen C	1143	clerk	45	"
	M	Wagner Freeman	1143	B F D	61	136 St Andrew rd
	N	Rossetti Frank	1145	operator	40	here
	O	Lane Frederick J	1147	broker	43	"
	P	Rosa Albert V	1149	attorney	30	"
	R*	Rosa Armando	1149	chauffeur	32	"
	S	Rosa Catherine—†	1149	secretary	26	"
	T	Rosa Ercolino	1149	chauffeur	24	"
	U	Lyons Alice M—†	1151	housewife	42	97 Horace
	V	Lyons Charles E	1151	electrician	40	97 "
	W*	Riccobene Concetta—†	1179	housewife	30	here
	X	Riccobene Peter	1179	operator	39	"
	Y	Finn William	1179	clerk	23	"
	Z	Meaney Catherine—†	1179	housewife	31	"
1510						
	A	Meaney Joseph	1179	mechanic	32	"
	B	Wallace Edward	1179	laborer	68	
	C	Perrault Francis	1181	installer	37	
	D	Perrault Mary—†	1181	housewife	50	"
	E	Famolare Anthony	1181	hairdresser	32	"
	F	Famolare Mary—†	1181	housewife	29	"
	G	Pasillo Anna—†	1187	"	44	
	H	Pasillo Joseph	1187	waiter	51	
	K	Vmana Guy	1187	baker	28	
	L	Vmana Yolanda—†	1187	housewife	28	"
	M	Ciamma Ada—†	1189	clerk	21	
	N	Ciamma Arthur	1189	operator	57	
	O*	Ciamma Ida—†	1189	housewife	44	"
	P	Corsetti Angelio	1191	shoemaker	30	"
	R	Corsetti Laura—†	1191	housewife	50	"
	S	Corsetti Leo	1191	laborer	58	
	T	Corsetti Leo	1191	shoemaker	23	"
	U	DeMild Leonard	1193	machinist	34	"
	V	DeMild Thelma—†	1193	housewife	32	"
	W	Facelli Mary—†	1193	at home	61	
	X	Meoli Antonette—†	1195	housewife	32	"
	Y	Meoli Gaetano	1195	laundryman	42	"
	Z	Green Charles F	1197	laborer	23	

Page.	Letter.	Full Name.	Residence, Jan. 1, 1938.	Occupation.	Supposed Age.	Reported Residence, Jan. 1, 1937. Street and Number.
1511		**Saratoga Street**—Continued				
	A	Green John P	1197	clerk	27	here
	B	Green Maria—†	1197	housewife	59	"
	C	Green Mary E—†	1197	stenographer	25	"
	D	Green Rose E—†	1197	"	30	"
	E	Green Thomas J	1197	clerk	35	
	F	Palladino Eva—†	1199	housewife	36	"
	G	Palladino John	1199	dealer	41	
	H	Sacco Edward M	1201	operator	21	
	K	Sacco Frank J	1201	laborer	23	
	L	Sacco Joseph	1201	"	47	
	M	Sacco Mary A—†	1201	housewife	42	"
		Shawsheen Road				
	O	Driscoll Florence D	30	B F D	53	here
	P	Driscoll Katherine L—†	30	bookkeeper	49	"
	R	Shaw Christina M—†	30	housewife	40	"
	S	Shaw Frank P	30	dealer	41	
	T	Shaw Louis T	30	clerk	32	
		Teragram Street				
	U	Hedrington James	25	operator	38	21 Gardner
	V	Kirby John F	25	compositor	30	here
	W	Kirby Louise—†	25	housewife	36	"
	X	Berninger Catherine—†	25	"	51	"
	Y	Berninger Jacob G	25	B F D	57	
	Z	Berninger Mary—†	25	operator	21	"
1512						
	A	Ryan Joseph	25	dealer	55	"
	B	Halloran Bridget—†	26	housewife	35	Lynn
	C	Halloran Patrick	26	clerk	36	"
	D	Smith George	26	policeman	42	1151 Saratoga
	E	Smith Irene—†	26	housewife	37	1151 "
	F	*Mastrangella Agnes—†	30	"	37	here
	G	*Mastrangella Henry	30	druggist	39	"
	H	Hicks Alice—†	30	student	21	2 St Andrew rd
	K	Hicks Charles	30	clerk	34	2 "
	L	Hicks Helen—†	30	operator	22	2 "
	M	Solari Louis	30	"	62	2 "
	N	Solari Rose—†	30	housewife	46	2 "

20

2

22

Ward 1–Precinct 20

CITY OF BOSTON

LIST OF RESIDENTS
20 YEARS OF AGE AND OVER

(NON-CITIZENS INDICATED BY ASTERISK)
(FEMALES INDICATED BY DAGGER)

AS OF

JANUARY 1, 1938

JOSEPH F. TIMILTY, } *Listing*
FREDERIC E. DOWLING, } *Board.*

CITY OF BOSTON PRINTING DEPARTMENT

Page.	Letter.	Full Name.	Residence, Jan. 1, 1938.	Occupation.	Supposed Age.	Reported Residence, Jan. 1, 1937. Street and Number.
1523		**Castle Court**				
	B	DiSimone Joseph	3	laborer	43	here
	C	*DiSimone Lena—†	3	housewife	40	“
	D	Federico James	3	cook	30	70 Webster
	E	Federico Mildred—†	3	housewife	29	here
	F	*Ladue Mary—†	3	“	53	70 Webster
	G	Ladue Norman	3	orderly	27	70 “
	H	Severo Carlo	5	shoemaker	24	here
	K	Severo Flora—†	5	dressmaker	22	“
	L	*Severo Rose—†	5	housewife	53	“
	M	Severo Severio	5	laborer	58	
		Cottage Street				
	N	Ciarlone Carmine	57	retired	73	here
	O	Ciarlone Mary—†	57	housewife	72	“
	P	Cecere Ernest	57	laborer	42	“
	R	*Cecere Lucy—†	57	housewife	37	“
	T	Ferrara Fred	59	painter	48	
	U	Ferrara John	59	laborer	21	
	V	Ferrara Theresa—†	59	housewife	42	“
	W	Simonelli Carmine	59	barber	25	
	X	Simonelli Evelyn—†	59	bookkeeper	26	“
	Y	Simonelli Ferdinand	59	clerk	20	“
	Z	Simonelli Mary—†	59	housewife	28	“
1524						
	A	Simonelli Mary A—†	59	“	60	
	B	Simonelli Rubina—†	59	student	21	
	C	Simonelli Samuel	59	barber	56	
	E	DeMarcelles Louis	61	tailor	37	
	F	DeMarcelles Rose—†	61	housewife	36	“
	G	Selvitelli Carmen	61	storekeeper	36	“
	H	*Selvitelli Grace—†	61	housewife	46	“
	L	*Guido Gennaro	67	laborer	27	
	M	*Guido Vincenza—†	67	housewife	20	“
	N	DeNisco John	67	storekeeper	44	“
	O	DeNisco Natalina—†	67	housewife	32	“
	R	Morrelli Alfred	69	retired	56	
	S	Morrelli Anne—†	69	operator	25	“
	T	*Morrelli Beatrice—†	69	housewife	50	“
	U	Gambardella Dominic	69	seaman	21	

Page.	Letter.	Full Name.	Residence, Jan. 1, 1938.	Occupation.	Supposed Age.	Reported Residence, Jan. 1, 1937. Street and Number.

Cottage Street—Continued

	V	Gambardella Gaetano	69	cobbler	53	here
	W	Gambardella Josephine–†	69	operator	23	"
	X	*Gambardella Lucy—†	69	housewife	54	"
	Y	Simonelli Carmen	69	laborer	26	
	Z	Simonelli Filomena—†	69	housewife	24	"
1525						
	A	Triesi Joseph	73	cooper	72	
	B	*Triesi Mary—†	73	housewife	59	"
	C	Panzini Benedetto	73	laborer	30	135 Havre
	D	Panzini Grace—†	73	housewife	31	135 "
	E	*Capone Josephine—†	73	"	83	here
	H	*Costra John	75	laborer	48	"
	K	*Angelo Anna—†	75	housewife	38	"
	L	Angelo Leonardo	75	laborer	48	
	M	*Melito Domenic	75	"	57	
	N	*Melito Filomena—†	75	housewife	53	"
	P	*Serpentino Antonio	77	laborer	67	
	R	*Serpentino Grace—†	77	housewife	67	"
	S	*Scorziello Anna—†	77	"	31	
	T	Scorziello Nicholas M	77	merchant	33	"
	U	Mercurio Charles	77	laborer	36	
	X	*Adonizzo Gaetano	79	butcher	56	"
	Y	*Adonizzo Josephine—†	79	housewife	48	"
	Z	Abramo Anita—†	79	"	33	
1526						
	A	*Abramo Domenic	79	laborer	40	
	C	*Carnevale Carmella—†	81	housewife	40	"
	D	*Carnevale Jaquino	81	laborer	42	
	E	*Lamia Joseph	81	"	62	
	F	*Lamia Mary—†	81	housewife	62	"
	H	Mercurio John	87	laborer	28	
	K	Mercurio Rose—†	87	housewife	25	"
	L	Inzirillo Constance—†	87	at home	27	"
	M	*Inzirillo Mary—†	87	housewife	58	"
	N	*Inzirillo Sebastian	87	baker	66	"
	P	*Ciampa Angelo	89	laborer	58	59 Charter
	R	*Ciampa Antonnetta—†	89	housewife	50	59 "
	S	*Inzirillo Antonio	89	laborer	50	here
	T	*Inzirillo Josephine—†	89	housewife	38	"
	U	Russo Michael	89	laborer	31	"
	W	*Vellini Eliza—†	91	housewife	50	"

Page.	Letter.	Full Name.	Residence, Jan. 1, 1938.	Occupation.	Supposed Age.	Reported Residence, Jan. 1, 1937. Street and Number.

Cottage Street—Continued

Page.	Letter.	Full Name.	Residence, Jan. 1, 1938.	Occupation.	Supposed Age.	Reported Residence, Jan. 1, 1937. Street and Number.
	X	*Vellini Joseph	91	storekeeper	52	here
	Y	*Piazza Charles	91	laborer	61	"
	Z	*Piazza Margaret—†	91	housewife	54	"
1527						
	B	*Quarantello Angelo	93	operator	33	"
	C	Quarantello Sarah—†	93	housewife	27	"
	D	Annese Antonio	93	laborer	32	
	E	Annese Elsie—†	93	housewife	29	"
	G	*Zeuli Concetta—†	95	housekeeper	34	"
	H	*Zeuli Frank	95	laborer	80	"
	K	Capobianco Joseph	95	"	37	
	L	*Capobianco Mary—†	95	housewife	34	"
	N	Manzione Christine—†	97	operator	21	"
	O	*Manzione Frank	97	laborer	61	
	P	*Manzione Jennie—†	97	housewife	51	"
	R	Manzione Lawrence	97	laborer	23	
	S	Zeuli Antonio	97	storekeeper	50	"
	T	*Zeuli Michael	97	operator	21	"
	U	*Zeuli Vincenza—†	97	housewife	44	"
	W	Chioccola Anna M—†	99	"	42	
	X	Chioccola Domenic	99	barber	40	
	Z	Malzeri Theresa—†	101	housekeeper	75	"
1528						
	A	Guercio Angela—†	101	at home	34	
	B	*Guercio Calogera—†	101	housewife	73	"
	C	Guercio Ida—†	101	operator	32	
	D	Guercio Marie—†	101	designer	30	
	E	Vennacci Eleanor—†	103	clerk	28	
	F	Vennacci Ferdinando	103	retired	64	
	G	Parillo Domenic	103	operator	34	
	H	Parillo Jennie—†	103	housewife	34	"
	K	*Bibbo Caroline—†	103	"	28	
	L	*Bibbo Domenic	103	laborer	42	
	N	Altavilla Carmen	114	clerk	20	
	O	Altavilla John	114	operator	25	
	P	*Altavilla Olympia—†	114	housewife	48	"
	R	*Altavilla Ralph	114	musician	54	"
	S	*Scannelli Joseph	114	laborer	53	
	T	*Scannelli Josephine—†	114	housewife	52	"
	U	Sarro Edward	114	chauffeur	32	"
	V	Sarro Jennie—†	114	housewife	33	"

Page.	Letter.	Full Name.	Residence, Jan. 1, 1938.	Occupation.	Supposed Age.	Reported Residence, Jan. 1, 1937. Street and Number.

Cottage Street—Continued

	W	*Modugno Carmella—†	114	housewife	29	here
	X	Modugno Carmen	114	laborer	37	"
	Y	Cianfrocca Gustavo	114	tailor	42	"
	Z	*Cianfrocca Josephine—†	114	housewife	40	"
1529						
	A	Carco Carmella—†	114	"	22	121 Salem
	B	Carco Joseph	114	laborer	25	121 "
	D	*DePasquale Concetta—†	115	housewife	40	here
	E	DePasquale Frank	115	baker	46	"
	F	Freda Rocco	115	butcher	44	"
	G	Freda Susan—†	115	housewife	35	"
	H	Nazzaro Carl	117	barber	28	
	K	Nazzaro Grace—†	117	housewife	28	"
	L	Grasso Margaret—†	117	"	39	
	M	Grasso Michael	117	operator	41	"
	N	Bernabei Anna—†	117	housewife	29	"
	O	Bernabei Anthony	117	laborer	29	
	P	*DeDonati Angelina—†	117	housewife	67	"
	R	*DeDonati John	117	retired	70	
	S	DeDonati Rocco	117	laborer	25	"
	U	Balzotti Cecero	119	"	42	
	V	Balzotti Elizabeth—†	119	housewife	32	"
	W	Pascone Ferrara	119	chauffeur	27	42 Frankfort
	X	Pascone Rose—†	119	housewife	25	42 "
	Y	*Ciccone Carmella—†	119	"	39	here
	Z	Ciccone Nicholas	119	laborer	46	"
1530						
	A	Zompanti Arderino	119	blacksmith	51	"
	B	*Zompanti Madelena—†	119	housewife	49	"
	C	*DiTroia Bernice—†	119	"	41	
	D	DiTroia Peter	119	blacksmith	42	"
	E	*D'Amico Arline—†	119	housewife	30	"
	F	D'Amico Renato	119	storekeeper	35	"
	G	*Troiani Mary—†	119	housewife	43	"
	H	*Troiani Pasquale	119	laborer	48	
	K	*Pellegriti Angelo	121	merchant	66	"
	L	*Pellegriti Josephine—†	121	housewife	60	"
	M	DePaolo Antonetta—†	121	"	23	
	N	*DePaolo Pasquale	121	laborer	32	
	O	*Prisco Mary—†	121	housekeeper	69	"
	P	*Vinciguerra Adele—†	121	housewife	50	"

Page.	Letter.	Full Name.	Residence, Jan. 1, 1938.	Occupation.	Supposed Age.	Reported Residence, Jan. 1, 1937. Street and Number.
		Cottage Street—Continued				
	R	*Vinciguerra Ralph	121	cobbler	52	here
	S	*Pericelli Anna—†	121	housewife	64	123 Cottage
	T	Pericelli Antonio	121	carpenter	64	123 "
	U	Galasso Lawrence	121	laborer	56	here
	V	Galasso Victoria—†	121	housewife	54	"
	W	Liberatore Olive—†	123	"	25	"
	X	Liberatore Pompeo	123	laborer	25	
	Y	Milano Antonio	123	"	21	
	Z	Milano Calogero	123	"	59	
1531						
	A	*Milano Mary—†	123	housewife	59	"
	B	Boschitti Amelia—†	123	"	35	167 Cottage
	C	Boschitti Anthony	123	laborer	35	167 "
	D	Milano Biagio	123	timekeeper	32	here
	E	Milano Louise—†	123	housewife	27	"
	F	*Giangregorio Antonio	123	laborer	42	"
	G	*Giangregorio Jennie—†	123	housewife	31	"
	H	Morgante Albert	125	laborer	46	
	K	Morgante Anthony	125	"	21	
	L	*Morgante Felice—†	125	housewife	43	"
	M	*Martino Domenic	125	tailor	60	158 London
	N	*Martino Raffaela—†	125	housewife	56	158 "
	O	*LoConte Carmella—†	125	"	41	here
	P	*LoConte Carmen	125	shoemaker	53	"
	R	LoConte Louis	125	laborer	20	"
	S	*Pellegriti Maria—†	125	housewife	37	"
	T	Pellegriti Peter	125	shoemaker	38	"
	U	*Sicuranza Angela—†	125	housewife	69	"
	V	Sicuranza Anthony	125	laborer	68	
	X	Nazzaro Catherine—†	127	operator	20	
	Y	Nazzaro Jennie—†	127	"	22	
	Z	Nazzaro Mary—†	127	housewife	52	"
1532						
	A	Nazzaro Phyllis—†	127	laborer	26	
	B	Nazzaro Anna—†	127	operator	24	
	C	Nazzaro Josephine—†	127	"	22	
	D	Nazzaro Susan—†	127	housewife	47	"
	E	Valletta Michael	129	barber	40	
	F	Valletta Rose—†	129	housewife	37	"
	G	Gaeta Anna—†	129	"	33	
	H	*Gaeta Dante	129	blacksmith	42	"

Page.	Letter.	Full Name.	Residence, Jan. 1, 1938.	Occupation.	Supposed Age.	Reported Residence, Jan. 1, 1937. Street and Number.

Cottage Street—Continued

	K	*Fusco Martha—†	129	housekeeper	49	here
	L	*Saia Gennaro	129	laborer	38	"
	M	*Saia Julia—†	129	housewife	34	"
	N	*Lessa Antonetta—†	129	"	45	
	O	Lessa Joseph	129	laborer	21	
	P	Checo Mary—†	131	housewife	40	"
	R	Checo Ralph	131	laborer	46	
	S	Scopa Frank	131	"	38	
	T	*Rauseo Angelo	131	"	54	
	U	Rauseo Domenic	131	operator	24	"
	V	Rauseo John	131	machinist	23	"
	W	*Rauseo Michelina—†	131	housewife	47	"
	X	Rauseo Rocco	131	printer	26	
	Y	Rauseo Vito	131	laborer	21	"
	Z	Spinazzola Marie—†	131	housewife	21	133 Orleans
1533						
	A	Spinazzola Pasquale	131	shoemaker	23	133 "
	B	Stagliola Antonette—†	131	housewife	26	here
	C	*Stagliola Domenic	131	longshoreman	30	"
	D	Inglese Grace—†	133	housewife	38	"
	E	Inglese Joseph	133	chauffeur	44	"
	F	*Inglese Mary G—†	133	housewife	82	"
	G	Centofante Edward	133	musician	23	"
	H	Centofante Samuel	133	contractor	54	"
	K	Gardini Eleanor—†	133	housewife	23	57 Lubec
	L	*Gardini Joseph	133	laborer	25	57 "
	M	Sacco Albert J	133	upholsterer	30	146 Gove
	N	Sacco Antonio J	133	laborer	22	146 "
	O	Sacco Esther—†	133	operator	24	146 "
	P	Sacco John	133	laborer	31	146 '
	R	Sacco Pasquale	133	"	33	146 "
	S	Sasso Joseph	135	operator	37	here
	T	*Sasso Mary G—†	135	at home	63	"
	U	Sasso Theresa—†	135	housewife	36	"
	V	Beatrice Filomena—†	135	"	45	119 Cottage
	W	Beatrice Lucy—†	135	floorwoman	20	119 "
	X	Beatrice Marsilio	135	laborer	52	119 "
	Y	DiRocco Louise—†	135	operator	34	119 "
	Z	*Schettino Frank	135	"	40	here
1534						
	A	*Schettino Susan—†	135	housewife	33	"

Page.	Letter.	Full Name.	Residence, Jan. 1, 1938.	Occupation.	Supposed Age.	Reported Residence, Jan. 1, 1937. Street and Number.

Cottage Street—Continued

Page.	Letter.	Full Name.	Residence, Jan. 1, 1938.	Occupation.	Supposed Age.	Reported Residence, Jan. 1, 1937. Street and Number.
	B	Maniante Enrico	135	teacher	25	here
	C	*Maniante Vincenzo	135	retired	65	"
	D	*DeFronzo Mary—†	137	housewife	70	"
	E	Recupero Angelo	137	pedler	24	
	F	Recupero Rosalie—†	137	housewife	23	"
	G	Mazzone Assunta—†	137	"	30	
	H	Mazzone Pasquale	137	molder	37	
	K	Mucci Antonetta—†	137	at home	21	
	L	*Mucci Lucy—†	137	housewife	51	"
	M	Ferullo John	137	operator	31	10 Antrim
	N	Ferullo Mildred—†	137	housewife	28	10 "
	O	*Polcari Caroline—†	137	"	37	here
	P	*Polcari Pasquale	137	barber	41	"
	R	Molinaro Albert	139	operator	27	"
	S	Molinaro Elvira—†	139	housewife	21	"
	T	Cirame Charles	139	teacher	27	
	U	Cirame Jacqueline—†	139	"	32	
	V	Cirame Joseph	139	laborer	39	
	W	Cirame Mary—†	139	clerk	34	
	X	Rubino Josephine—†	139	housewife	35	"
	Y	Rubino Louis	139	machinist	45	"
	Z	*Casto Joseph	139	laborer	45	
1535						
	A	*Casto Rosaria—†	139	housewife	36	"
	B	Pirio Elvira—†	139	dressmaker	24	"
	C	Pirio Jeremiah	139	cutter	25	
	D	Griecci Angelo	141	guard	32	
	E	*Griecci Mary—†	141	housewife	29	"
	F	Siciliano Joseph	141	clerk	26	
	G	Siciliano Josephine—†	141	housewife	22	"
	H	Perdichizzi Frank	141	manufacturer	28	6 Greenough lane
	K	Perdichizzi Josephine—†	141	operator	23	414 Commerc'l
	L	Interbartolo Joseph	141	hatter	26	251 Marion
	M	Interbartolo Rose—†	141	housewife	23	217 Chelsea
	N	Barrese Jeremiah	141	timekeeper	28	here
	O	Barrese Marie—†	141	housewife	21	"
	P	Giangregorio Attilio	143	laborer	21	"
	R	*Giangregorio Carmella—†	143	operator	43	"
	S	*Giangregorio Lawrence	143	laborer	57	
	T	Giangregorio Raffaela—†	143	at home	23	
	U	DeLuca Anthony L	143	operator	27	

Page.	Letter.	Full Name.	Residence, Jan. 1, 1938.	Occupation.	Supposed Age.	Reported Residence, Jan. 1, 1937. Street and Number.

Cottage Street—Continued

Page.	Letter.	Full Name.	Residence, Jan. 1, 1938.	Occupation.	Supposed Age.	Reported Residence, Jan. 1, 1937. Street and Number.
	v	DeLuca Grace—†	143	housewife	25	here
	w	*Dalia Joseph	143	laborer	64	"
	x	*Dalia Maria—†	143	housewife	48	"
	y	Langone Mary—†	143	"	24	Lynn
	z	Langone Michael	143	laborer	26	118 Bremen
1536						
	A	Coviello Bernardino	143	"	41	here
	B	*Coviello Mathilda—†	143	housewife	39	"
	C	Colarusso Antonio	145	bottler	59	"
	D	Colarusso Elizabeth—†	145	housewife	42	"
	E	Colarusso Angelina—†	145	"	49	
	F	Colarusso Domenic	145	operator	25	"
	G	Colarusso Enrico	145	laborer	28	
	H	Colarusso Philip	145	"	53	
	K	Molinaro Anna—†	145	operator	24	"
	L	Molinaro Pasqualina—†	145	housewife	56	"
	M	Molinaro Thomas	145	laborer	58	
	N	Molinaro Yolanda—†	145	operator	23	"
	O	Lochiatto Joseph	147	"	32	
	P	Lochiatto Rose—†	147	"	29	"
	R	*Falanga Frank	147	"	34	24 Brooks
	S	*Falanga Louise—†	147	housewife	29	24 "
	T	Molinaro Edith—†	147	"	32	here
	U	Molinaro Peter	147	mechanic	35	"
	V	Ciullo Filomena—†	147	housewife	24	"
	W	Ciullo Michael	147	laborer	29	
	X	*Giangregorio Josephine-†	147	housewife	54	"
	Y	Giangregorio Louis A	147	laborer	63	
	Z	Coviello Antonio	149	"	34	
1537						
	A	*Coviello Ida—†	149	housewife	27	"
	B	Montalto Mary—†	149	operator	33	160 Cottage
	C	Bavaro Dominic	149	"	26	here
	D	Bavaro Virginia—†	149	housewife	25	"
	E	*DiGenova Palmina—†	149	at home	35	"
	F	Cogliani Jennie—†	149	housewife	22	62 Haynes
	G	Cogliani Louis	149	operator	24	170 Paris
	H	Coviello Alexander	149	cutter	20	here
	K	*Coviello Rose—†	149	housewife	66	"
	L	*Coviello Sebastiano	149	laborer	66	"
	M	*Manzi Sophia—†	151	housewife	52	"

Page.	Letter.	FULL NAME.	Residence, Jan. 1, 1938.	Occupation.	Supposed Age.	Reported Residence, Jan. 1, 1937. Street and Number.

Cottage Street—Continued

	N	Colito Anthony	151	laborer	39	here
	O	Colito Mary—†	151	housewife	31	"
	P	Ippolito Louis	151	laborer	43	"
	R	Ippolito Theresa—†	151	housewife	38	"
	S	*Modugno Salvatore	151	laborer	50	
	T	Manzi Anthony	151	timekeeper	30	"
	U	Manzi Marion—†	151	housewife	28	"
	V	*Masiello Giovannina—†	151	"	44	
	W	Masiello Joseph	151	laborer	45	
	X	Ciampa Ernest L	151	"	20	
	Y	Ciampa Marie T—†	151	housewife	38	"
	Z	*DiStasio Anita—†	152	"	21	
1538						
	A	*DiStasio Nicholas	152	laborer	50	"
	B	DiStasio Santo	152	clerk	22	
	C	*Uva Nunziata—†	152	housewife	42	"
	D	Uva Rocco	152	storekeeper	46	"
	E	Uva Stanley	152	laborer	20	"
	F	*Bernabei Giovanni	152	"	54	
	G	*Bernabei Josephine—†	152	housewife	43	"
	H	*DiBenedetto Eleanor—†	152	"	37	
	K	DiBenedetto Thomas	152	tailor	47	"
	L	Salerna Vincenza—†	153	housewife	80	"
	M	Umana Antonetta—†	153	storekeeper	49	"
	N	Umana Mario	153	baker	23	"
	P	Griecci Mildred—†	154	housewife	32	"
	R	Griecci Patrick	154	laborer	32	"
	S	Tramonte Lena—†	154	housewife	23	156 Cottage
	T	Tramonte Oreste	154	operator	41	156 "
	U	*Mercurio Angelina—†	154	housewife	39	87 Everett
	V	Mercurio Domenico	154	laborer	39	87 Cottage
	W	Antonioli Anthony	154	salesman	32	here
	X	Antonioli Louise—†	154	housewife	28	"
	Y	D'Alto Domenic	154	hatter	25	"
	Z	*D'Alto Louisa—†	154	housewife	54	"
1539						
	A	D'Alto Michael	154	laborer	21	
	B	D'Alto Pasquale	154	"	59	
	C	D'Alto Sabino	154	"	23	"
	D	Vernarelli Alfred	154	chauffeur	26	236 Maverick
	E	*Vernarelli Grace—†	154	housewife	23	236 "

Page.	Letter.	Full Name.	Residence, Jan. 1, 1938.	Occupation.	Supposed Age.	Reported Residence, Jan. 1, 1937. Street and Number.
		Cottage Street—Continued				
	F	Ruggiero Anthony	154	operator	35	here
	G	Ruggiero Eva—†	154	housewife	33	“
	H	DiMarco Antoinette—†	155	“	21	161 Cottage
	K	DiMarco Vincent	155	laborer	23	85 London
	L	*Peppino Frances—†	155	operator	29	here
	M	*Peppino Mary—†	155	housewife	54	“
	N	*Peppino Sadie—†	155	operator	31	“
	O	*Peppino Salvatore	155	laborer	64	
	P	Guzzardi Daniel	155	operator	44	“
	R	*Guzzardi Gina—†	155	housewife	43	“
	T	Buontempo Michael	155	laborer	42	358 Sumner
	S	Buontempo Rose—†	155	housewife	37	358 “
	U	Caporale Carmella—†	155	“	33	here
	V	Caporale Peter	155	operator	34	“
	W	DeFurio Grace—†	155	housewife	34	“
	X	DeFurio Nicholas	155	laborer	43	
	Y	*DeMaio Lena—†	156	housekeeper	64	“
	Z	*Tramonte Carmello	156	retired	86	“
1540						
	A	*Lenarduzzi Fermino	156	laborer	35	
	B	*Lenarduzzi Mary—†	156	housewife	30	“
	C	Fitzgerald Antoinette—†	156	“	29	
	D	Fitzgerald Lawrence	156	machinist	28	“
	E	Albaro Josephine—†	156	housewife	27	158 Cottage
	F	Albaro Samuel	156	laborer	29	158 “
	G	Gatto Antonio	156	inspector	50	here
	H	Gatto Natale	156	operator	24	“
	K	Gatto Vincenzo	156	laborer	60	“
	L	Tramonte Ernest	156	“	47	
	M	Tramonte Rose—†	156	housewife	37	“
	N	Gatto Natalie—†	156	housekeeper	27	“
	O	Gatto Rose—†	156	operator	30	“
	P	Fleury Jeannette F—†	156	housewife	22	Maine
	R	Gatto Carmen	156	operator	24	153 Gladstone
	S	Gatto Mildred—†	156	housewife	22	153 “
	T	Cioto Dominic	157	cleanser	22	here
	U	*Cioto Frank	157	laborer	56	“
	V	Cioto Gilda—†	157	operator	24	“
	W	*Cioto Marion—†	157	housewife	50	“
	X	DiFranza Frances—†	157	“	32	
	Y	DiFranza Paul	157	engineer	38	

Page.	Letter.	Full Name.	Residence, Jan. 1, 1938.	Occupation.	Supposed Age.	Reported Residence, Jan. 1, 1937. Street and Number.

Cottage Street—Continued

Page.	Letter.	Full Name.	Residence, Jan. 1, 1938.	Occupation.	Supposed Age.	Reported Residence, Jan. 1, 1937. Street and Number.
	z	Annese Catello	157	oiler	59	here
1541						
	A	Annese Rose—†	157	housewife	62	"
	B	Paolini Enrico	157	laborer	28	
	C	*Paolini Marietta—†	157	housewife	67	"
	D	Conti Paul	157	laborer	40	
	E	Salvi Dominic	157	"	43	
	F	Salvi Rosina—†	157	housewife	37	"
	H	*Capuana Giuseppe	158	storekeeper	51	"
	K	*Capuana Ida—†	158	housewife	47	"
	L	Capuana Josephine—†	158	dressmaker	23	"
	N	Cerullo Carmella—†	158	housewife	32	"
	O	Cerullo Luigi	158	operator	40	"
	P	Barbaro Eugene	158	laborer	27	
	R	Barbaro Serafina—†	158	housewife	21	"
	S	*Castagnozzi Maria—†	158	"	44	
	T	Castagnozzi Maria—†	158	clerk	22	
	U	*Castagnozzi Sebastian	158	laborer	49	
	V	Ferranto Benjamin	158	chauffeur	29	"
	W	Ferranto Frances—†	158	housewife	23	"
	X	Piscioneri Domenic	158	cutter	33	
	Y	*Piscioneri Jennie—†	158	housewife	27	"
	Z	DelGreco John	159	laborer	32	
1542						
	A	*DelGreco Mary—†	159	housewife	28	"
	B	Constantino Antonio	159	laborer	44	
	C	*Constantino Theodore	159	"	61	
	D	*Petuzzi Amelia—†	159	housewife	62	"
	E	Petuzzi Vico	159	laborer	22	
	F	Mucci Alfred	159	"	33	
	G	*Mucci Gemma—†	159	housewife	27	"
	H	Girolamo Frank	159	laborer	32	
	K	*Girolamo Philomena—†	159	housewife	29	"
	L	Ciulla Fanny—†	159	"	36	
	M	Ciulla James	159	laborer	44	
	N	*Cocca Maria—†	159	housewife	32	"
	O	*Recchia Alphonse	159	laborer	48	
	P	*Recchia Antoinetta—†	159	housewife	40	"
	R	Recchia Marietta—†	159	clerk	20	
	S	*Villani Antonetta—†	160	housewife	46	"
	T	*Villani Joseph	160	laundryman	48	"

Page.	Letter.	Full Name.	Residence, Jan. 1, 1938.	Occupation.	Supposed Age.	Reported Residence, Jan. 1, 1937. Street and Number.

Cottage Street—Continued

Page.	Letter.	Full Name.	Residence, Jan. 1, 1938.	Occupation.	Supposed Age.	Reported Residence, Jan. 1, 1937. Street and Number.
	U	Villani Pellegrino	160	chauffeur	21	here
	V	*Barbarisi Sophie—†	160	housekeeper	73	"
	W	*Aiello Elvira—†	160	housewife	44	"
	X	Aiello Joseph	160	tailor	49	
	Y	DeGloria Marie—†	160	housewife	28	"
	Z	DeGloria Rosario	160	laborer	31	
1543						
	A	*Collorone Mary—†	160	housewife	29	"
	B	Collorone Michael	160	laborer	31	"
	C	Guarino Marie—†	160	housewife	23	5 Havre
	D	Guarino Ralph	160	laborer	30	5 "
	E	Giggi Armand	160	"	28	here
	F	Giggi Esther—†	160	at home	29	"
	G	Giggi Lucy—†	160	operator	32	"
	H	Giggi Michael	160	retired	65	
	K	*Davolio Angelina—†	161	housewife	34	"
	L	Davolio Dominic	161	laborer	37	"
	M	*Paolini Donato	161	"	56	"
	N	Paolini Pasquale	161	carpenter	36	"
	O	*Paolini Ursula—†	161	housewife	55	"
	P	Paolini Amedeo	161	laborer	49	
	R	Paolini Desolina—†	161	housewife	53	"
	S	Forlizzi Carolina—†	161	"	21	
	T	Forlizzi Daniel	161	chauffeur	22	"
	U	Capecci Nicholas	161	laborer	48	
	V	*Capecci Nina—†	161	housewife	38	"
	W	D'Amico Reginald	161	laborer	26	"
	X	D'Amico Rose—†	161	housewife	27	"
	Y	DiZio Angelo	161	laborer	22	
	Z	DiZio Joseph	161	"	54	
1544						
	A	*DiZio Marion—†	161	housewife	46	"
	B	*Lanna Michael	162	shoemaker	39	"
	C	*LaCorte Lucy—†	162	housewife	40	"
	D	*LaCorte Michael	162	operator	51	"
	E	*Nobillo Vincenza—†	162	housekeeper	72	"
	F	Sulprizio Bernardino	162	laborer	68	"
	G	Sulprizio Theresa—†	162	housewife	60	"
	H	*Annese Amelia—†	162	"	30	
	K	Annese Joseph	162	laborer	30	
	L	Sulprizio Carmella—†	162	housewife	42	"

Page.	Letter.	Full Name.	Residence, Jan. 1, 1938.	Occupation.	Supposed Age.	Reported Residence, Jan. 1, 1937. Street and Number.

Cottage Street—Continued

Page.	Letter.	Full Name.	Residence, Jan. 1, 1938.	Occupation.	Supposed Age.	Reported Residence, Jan. 1, 1937. Street and Number.
	M	Sulprizio Concetta—†	162	dressmaker	21	here
	N	Sulprizio Joseph	162	laborer	49	"
	O	Bondenza Guy	162	"	30	"
	P	Bondenza Virginia—†	162	housewife	21	"
	R	Scannelli Edith—†	162	"	28	
	S	Scannelli Robert	162	chauffeur	26	"
	T	LaCorte James	163	laborer	36	
	U	LaCorte Jennie—†	163	housewife	24	"
	V	*LaCorte John B	163	chauffeur	35	"
	W	LaCorte Leona—†	163	housewife	30	"
	X	*LaCorte Angelina—†	163	"	47	
	Y	LaCorte Felice	163	tailor	54	
	Z	LaCorte Pasquale	163	operator	20	"
1545						
	A	LaCorte Gaetano	163	laborer	48	
	B	*LaCorte Italia—†	163	housewife	41	"
	C	LaCorte John	163	laborer	26	
	D	LaCorte Mary—†	163	operator	26	"
	E	*Giusto Francesco	163	laborer	41	
	F	*Giusto Theresa—†	163	housewife	41	"
	G	*Calzoni Joseph	164	laborer	52	
	K	*DiBenedetto Francesca-†	164	housekeeper	65	"
	L	*Luongo Amaria—†	164	housewife	45	"
	M	Luongo Antonette—†	164	dressmaker	20	"
	N	Luongo Marino	164	laborer	48	"
	O	*Morelli Filomena—†	164	housewife	36	"
	P	Morelli Luigi	164	laborer	42	
	R	*Meoli Ernest	164	"	41	
	S	*Meoli Mary—†	164	housewife	32	"
	T	*Luongo Assunta—†	164	"	49	
	U	*Luongo Giacomo	164	laborer	57	"
	V	Diecidue Lucy—†	164	housewife	28	188 Cottage
	W	*Diecidue Rosario	164	fisherman	31	188 "
	X	*Rossetti Josephine—†	165	floorwoman	48	here
	Y	Rossetti Rocco	165	operator	53	"
	Z	*Maiona Anthony	165	cook	44	"
1546						
	A	Maiona Catherine—†	165	housewife	36	"
	B	DiBenedetto Enrico	165	dealer	41	
	C	*DiBenedetto Laura—†	165	housewife	38	"
	D	*Palmerini Guarino	165	laborer	56	
	E	*Palmerini Santa—†	165	housewife	54	"

Page.	Letter.	Full Name.	Residence, Jan. 1, 1938.	Occupation.	Supposed Age.	Reported Residence, Jan. 1, 1937. Street and Number.

Cottage Street—Continued

Page.	Letter.	Full Name.	Residence, Jan. 1, 1938.	Occupation.	Supposed Age.	Reported Residence, Jan. 1, 1937. Street and Number.
	F	Cella Eva—†	165	floorwoman	20	71 Lubec
	G	*Cella Ferdinand	165	laborer	61	71 "
	H	Cella Joseph	165	"	25	71 "
	K	*Monaco Angelo	165	"	47	here
	L	*Monaco Grace—†	165	housewife	43	"
	M	*Peppino Gaetano	166	retired	73	"
	N	*Peppino Giuseppina—†	166	housewife	66	"
	P	*Peppino Annie—†	166	operator	26	"
	O	*Peppino Ralph	166	"	23	"
	R	Opitto Ernest	166	machinist	28	58 Frankfort
	S	Opitto Josephine—†	166	housewife	26	58 "
	T	Guerra James	166	laborer	27	58 "
	U	Guerra Jennie—†	166	housewife	28	58 "
	V	Carangelo Domenic G	166	foreman	24	59 Lubec
	W	Carangelo Louise—†	166	housewife	23	59 "
	X	Salucco Carmen	166	operator	37	here
	Y	*Salucco Josephine—†	166	housewife	32	"
1547						
	A	*Cameratta Albert	166	pedler	43	"
	B	*Cameratta Josephine—†	166	housewife	32	"
	C	Ravagno Louise—†	167	"	20	"
	D	Ravagno Santo	167	orderly	22	"
	E	Morello Agostino	167	clerk	28	"
	F	*Morello Concetta—†	167	housewife	57	"
	G	Morello Dominic	167	laborer	24	"
	H	Morello Flora—†	167	at home	20	"
	K	Morello Francesco	167	longshoreman	29	"
	L	Morello Gaetano	167	laborer	71	"
	M	Morello Gennaro	167	"	32	"
	O	Bolognese Ottavio	167	operator	35	"
	N	*DeProfio Mary—†	167	housewife	69	"
	P	DeProfio Sabatino	167	retired	69	"
	R	Memmolo Dante	167	machinist	20	"
	S	Memmolo Louis	167	laborer	50	"
	T	*D'Amico Adelina—†	167	housewife	59	"
	U	D'Amico Alphonso	167	laborer	24	"
	V	D'Amico George	167	"	22	"
	Y	Fasciano Joseph	168	storekeeper	57	"
	Z	*Fasciano Josephine—†	168	housewife	44	"
1548						
	A	Palmerini Luigi	168	laborer	26	"
	B	Palmerini Mary—†	168	housewife	28	"

Page.	Letter.	Full Name.	Residence, Jan. 1, 1938.	Occupation.	Supposed Age.	Reported Residence, Jan. 1, 1937. Street and Number.
		Cottage Street—Continued				
	C	*Amaru Elvira—†	168	housewife	35	123 Cottage
	D	Amaru Salvatore	168	laborer	40	123 “
	E	Cefaioli Calisto	168	“	57	here
	F	Cefaioli Elena—†	168	clerk	23	“
	G	*Leone Achille	168	laborer	42	“
	H	*Leone Filomena—†	168	housewife	33	“
	K	Grallo Joseph	168	laborer	22	98 Webster
	L	Grallo Mary—†	168	housewife	21	98 “
	M	*Zaffino Antonette—†	168	“	32	95 Maverick
	N	*Zaffino Gennaro	168	laborer	43	95 “
	O	*Debole Pasquale	169	“	26	here
	P	Debole Salvina—†	169	housewife	23	“
	R	Salini Leo	169	laborer	21	“
	S	*Salini Vincenza—†	169	housewife	57	“
	T	*Salini Vincenzo	169	retired	64	
	U	Maggiore Carmen	169	baker	26	“
	V	Maggiore Victoria—†	169	housewife	23	“
	W	*D'Alessandro Fontilla—†	169	“	34	562 E Eighth
	X	D'Alessandro Joseph	169	laborer	45	562 “
	Y	*Bernabei Dominic	169	operator	57	here
	Z	Bernabei John	169	laborer	23	“
1549						
	A	*Bernabei Josephine—†	169	housewife	50	“
	B	Bernabei Michael	169	laborer	27	
	C	*Salini Americo	169	chauffeur	27	“
	D	Salini Palmina—†	169	housewife	24	“
	F	*Paolino Anna—†	170	“	42	
	G	Paolino Umberto	170	laborer	46	
	H	Bolognese Domenic	170	“	47	
	K	*Bolognese Lettie—†	170	housewife	37	“
	L	*LaMarca Josephine—†	170	“	31	64 Bremen
	M	LaMarca Stephen	170	operator	32	64 “
	N	Cieri Adrienne—†	170	“	20	here
	O	*Cieri Elvira—†	170	housewife	45	“
	P	Cieri Filomena—†	170	operator	23	“
	R	Cieri Frank	170	laborer	50	
	S	Cieri Pasqualina—†	170	saleswoman	22	“
	T	*DoGiovanni Adeline—†	170	housewife	48	“
	U	DiGiovanni Joseph	170	cutter	47	
	V	DiGiovanni Dora—†	170	dressmaker	23	“
	W	*DiGiovanni Nicholas	170	retired	73	

Page.	Letter.	FULL NAME.	Residence, Jan. 1, 1938.	Occupation.	Supposed Age.	Reported Residence, Jan. 1, 1937. Street and Number.

Cottage Street—Continued

	X	DiGiovanni Nicholas	170	cutter	21	here
	Y	Carbone Carmine	171	laborer	33	"
	Z	Carbone Caroline—†	171	housewife	31	"
1550						
	A	Carbone Ralph	171	operator	23	
	B	Meneguzzi Anna—†	171	inspector	23	"
	C	Meneguzzi Louisa—†	171	operator	21	
	D	*Meneguzzi Regina—†	171	housewife	59	"
	E	Meneguzzi Rinalda—†	171	operator	20	
	F	*Ferrara Mary—†	171	housewife	42	"
	G	*Ferrara Theodore	171	storekeeper	45	"
	H	Carbone Ciriaco	171	retired	71	"
	K	Carbone Ciriaco, jr	171	chauffeur	25	"
	L	Carbone Rose—†	171	housewife	24	"
	M	Iacovello Carmella—†	171	"	35	
	N	Iacovello Vito A	171	operator	44	
	O	Grasso Angelo	171	laborer	58	
	P	Grasso Consolino	171	mechanic	22	"
	R	*Grasso Josephine—†	171	housewife	59	"
	S	*DeLucca Henry	172	laborer	54	
	T	Sisto Antonio	172	"	49	
	U	Sisto Lucy—†	172	housewife	40	"
	V	*Zitano Antonio	172	laborer	73	"
	W	*Catino Carmella—†	172	housewife	32	72 Frankfort
	X	Catino Crescenzo	172	laborer	42	72 "
	Y	*Pirra Theresa—†	172	housekeeper	62	72 "
	Z	*LaCresta Jennie—†	172	housewife	44	here
1551						
	A	LaCresta Sabatino	172	laborer	45	
	B	DiFronzo Alphonso	172	operator	22	
	C	*DiFronzo Constantino	172	tailor	55	
	D	DiFronzo Domenic	172	laborer	24	
	E	*Odardi Vincent	172	"	39	
	F	Genari James	172	"	48	
	G	Genari Vincenza—†	172	housewife	40	"
	H	*Putingano Domenic	172	tailor	53	Brockton
	K	*Putingano Lucia—†	172	housewife	43	"
	L	Iannillo Antonio	173	foreman	54	here
	M	Iannillo Generoso	173	timekeeper	25	"
	N	Iannillo Ida—†	173	operator	20	"
	O	Iannillo Maria—†	173	housewife	55	"

Page.	Letter.	Full Name.	Residence, Jan. 1, 1938.	Occupation.	Supposed Age.	Reported Residence, Jan. 1, 1937. Street and Number.

Cottage Street—Continued

	P	D'Alessandro Michael	173	laborer	37	here
	R	*D'Alessandro Sarah—†	173	housewife	33	"
	S	Zarrella Florence—†	173	"	29	"
	T	Zarrella Louis	173	laborer	33	
	U	*Agostinelli Lucia—†	173	housewife	43	"
	V	*Agostinelli Rinaldo	173	laborer	50	
	W	Mea Alda—†	173	operator	23	
	X	*Mea Anna—†	173	housewife	43	"
	Y	*Mea Enrico	173	laborer	51	
	Z	*Caiani Elena—†	174	housekeeper	66	"
1552						
	A	Galiazzo Domenic	174	laborer	20	
	B	Galiazzo Nicholas	174	operator	54	"
	C	Caiani Ella—†	174	housewife	32	"
	D	Caiani Ovidio	174	laborer	38	
	E	Moscone Henry	174	"	32	
	F	Moscone Mary—†	174	housewife	26	"
	G	*Forcellese Bice—†	174	"	38	
	H	*Forcellese Peter	174	tailor	40	
	K	*D'Amico Frances—†	174	housewife	45	"
	L	D'Amico Luigi	174	laborer	21	
	M	D'Amico Mary—†	174	operator	24	
	N	D'Amico Sabatino	174	laborer	47	
	O	Giggi Charles C	174	"	36	
	P	Giggi Yolanda—†	174	housewife	33	"
	R	DiGianvittori Gino	174	musician	20	"
	S	DiGianvittori Ralph	174	laborer	48	
	T	Uva Pasquale	175	"	24	
	U	Uva Rose—†	175	housewife	22	"
	V	Testa Emma—†	175	"	25	18 Bremen
	W	Testa Guy	175	operator	24	18 "
	X	*Mucci Anna—†	175	housewife	35	here
	Y	Mucci Frank	175	operator	37	"
	Z	Mucci Dominic	175	"	31	"
1553						
	A	*Mucci Mary—†	175	housewife	60	96 Everett
	B	*Mucci Pasquale	175	laborer	63	here
	C	Mucci Umberto	175	"	29	"
	D	DiNardo Flaviano	175	"	49	"
	E	*DiNardo Joseph	175	"	23	"
	F	*DiNardo Pasquale	175	housewife	47	"
	G	Grasso Constantino	175	laborer	22	

Page.	Letter.	Full Name.	Residence, Jan. 1, 1938.	Occupation.	Supposed Age.	Reported Residence, Jan. 1, 1937. Street and Number.

Cottage Street—Continued

Page.	Letter.	Full Name.	Residence, Jan. 1, 1938.	Occupation.	Supposed Age.	Reported Residence, Jan. 1, 1937. Street and Number.
	H	Grasso Liziario	175	laborer	46	here
	K	*Grasso Rose—†	175	housewife	48	"
	L	*Cieri Alfonzo	177	laborer	50	"
	M	*Cieri Belmina—†	177	housewife	47	"
	N	Rulli Antonio	177	laborer	47	
	O	*Rulli Domenica—†	177	housewife	38	"
	P	Cermone Antonio	177	laborer	52	
	R	*Cermone Frances—†	177	housewife	51	"
	S	Cermone Joseph	177	mechanic	22	"
	T	Cermone Mary—†	177	operator	20	
	U	Cermone Prudence—†	177	housewife	24	"
	V	*Paolini Elvira—†	177	"	44	
	W	*Paolini Vincenzo	177	laborer	44	
	X	Sinibaldi Angelina—†	177	housewife	56	"
	Y	Sinibaldi Albert	177	chauffeur	22	"
	Z	Sinibaldi Frank	177	laborer	58	
1554						
	A	Sinibaldi Italina—†	177	typist	20	
	B	Sinibaldi Nicholas	177	clerk	25	
	C	*Recchia Alfred	177	laborer	48	
	D	*Recchia Tobia—†	177	housewife	38	"
	E	Marmiani Eda—†	179	"	26	
	F	Marmiani John	179	repairman	29	"
	G	*Ventresca Carmella—†	179	housewife	51	"
	H	Ventresca Charles	179	laborer	54	
	K	Flammini Ernest	179	"	42	
	L	*Flammini Florinda—†	179	housewife	40	"
	M	Capone Joseph	179	laborer	50	
	N	*Capone Pauline—†	179	housewife	49	"
	O	Capone Pellegrino	179	laborer	21	
	P	*Molino Faustino	179	carpenter	32	"
	R	Molino Raffaela—†	179	housewife	24	"
	S	Cordone Angelina—†	179	"	40	
	T	Cordone Loretto	179	janitor	41	
	V	*Bataglia Carmella—†	181	housewife	64	"
	W	Bataglia Carmen	181	laborer	59	
	X	Bataglia Carmen, jr	181	butcher	31	
	Y	Bataglia Frederick	181	barber	28	
	Z	Bataglia Lena—†	181	housewife	26	"
1555						
	A	Lauter Antonetta—†	181	"	26	
	B	Lauter Robert	181	clerk	34	

Page.	Letter.	Full Name.	Residence, Jan. 1, 1938.	Occupation.	Supposed Age.	Reported Residence, Jan. 1, 1937. Street and Number.

Cottage Street—Continued

Page.	Letter.	Full Name.	Residence, Jan. 1, 1938.	Occupation.	Supposed Age.	Reported Residence, Jan. 1, 1937. Street and Number.
	C	Fiorillo Giuseppe	181	laborer	50	here
	D	Fiorillo Louise—†	181	housewife	39	"
	E	Marotta Anthony	181	upholsterer	22	"
	F	Marotta Charles	181	laborer	50	
	G	*Marotta Lucia—†	181	housewife	49	"
	K	Muccio Lena—†	182	"	56	
	L	Muccio Salvatore	182	storekeeper	61	"
	M	Gaglini Maria—†	182	housekeeper	57	"
	N	Mucci Carmello	182	laborer	37	"
	O	Mucci Laura—†	182	housewife	27	"
	P	DiDomenico Anthony	182	shoemaker	38	"
	R	*DiDomenico Liberata—†	182	housewife	39	"
	S	*Mercuri Carmella—†	182	"	31	
	T	Mercuri George	182	tailor	38	
	U	*DiCalogero Catherine—†	182	housewife	33	"
	V	*DiCalogero Paul	182	baker	37	
	W	*Grande Concetta—†	182	housewife	43	"
	X	Grande Stephen	182	laborer	45	
	Y	*Ciambiello Francesca—†	182	housewife	41	"
	Z	*Ciambiello Frank	182	laborer	55	
1556						
	C	Cerase Charles	184	"	30	
	D	Cerase Pauline—†	184	housewife	26	"
	E	Gianbartolomei Elvira-†	184	"	37	
	F	Giambartolomei John	184	laborer	37	
	G	DeSousa Abello	184	"	27	
	H	*Spagnoli Julia—†	184	housewife	35	"
	K	Spagnoli Luigi	184	laborer	44	
	L	*Pelosi Julia—†	184	housewife	37	"
	M	Pelosi Vito A	184	operator	41	
	O	Ventura Virginia—†	186	housewife	29	"
	P	*Griecci Attilio	186	laborer	28	
	R	*Griecci Filomena—†	186	housewife	59	"
	S	Ippolito Salvatore	186	musician	47	"
	T	*Ippolito Vincenza—†	186	housewife	78	"
	U	*Fiantata Grace—†	186	"	50	
	V	*Fiantata Philip	186	laborer	62	
	W	Fiantata Philip, jr	186	musician	22	"
	X	Fiantata Rose—†	186	dressmaker	24	"
	Y	*DiGiampaolo Concetta-†	186	housewife	46	"
	Z	DiGiampaolo Luigi	186	laborer	51	

Page.	Letter.	FULL NAME.	Residence, Jan. 1, 1938.	Occupation.	Supposed Age.	Reported Residence, Jan. 1, 1937. Street and Number.

1557
Cottage Street—Continued

	A	Iritano Anna—†	186	housewife	32	here
	B	Iritano Joseph	186	laborer	44	"
	C	Guarino Domenico	186	retired	67	"
	D	*Guarino Rose—†	186	housewife	61	"
	E	Ciulla Joseph	186	fisherman	46	"
	F	Ciulla Lena—†	186	housewife	39	"
	G	*Billardi Concetta—†	188	housekeeper	74	306 Maverick
	H	Palumbo John	188	laborer	39	306 "
	L	*Naples Giacomo	188	"	44	here
	M	Naples Mary—†	188	housewife	34	"
	O	*Natalucci Lucy—†	188	"	59	"
	P	Natalucci Maria—†	188	tailoress	21	
	R	Natalucci Philip	188	operator	28	"
	T	Albano Anthony	188	laborer	21	
	U	*Albano Carmine	188	"	46	
	V	Albano Joseph	188	"	24	
	W	Beatrice Alexander	188	"	20	
	X	Beatrice Marie—†	188	operator	22	"
	Y	Beatrice Pasquale	188	laborer	52	"
	Z	*Fusco Rocco	190	"	21	148 Everett
1558						
	B	Marmiano Alexander	190	"	20	here
	C	Marmiano Angelina—†	190	housewife	22	"
	D	Marmiano Anthony	190	laborer	25	"
	E	*Marmiano Rose—†	190	housewife	52	"
	H	*Amato Marietta—†	190	"	39	
	K	*Amato Pasquale	190	salesman	48	"
	G	Moni Germano	190	laborer	46	
	L	*Giangregorio Carolina—†	190	housewife	47	"
	M	Giangregorio Mary—†	190	seamstress	22	"
	N	*Giangregorio Pasquale	190	laborer	50	
	O	Febo Frank	190	"	42	
	P	*Febo Vincenza—†	190	housewife	32	"
	S	Nocilla Anna—†	190	"	32	
	R	Nocilla Salvatore	190	clerk	35	
	T	*Barbarese Constantino	192	retired	72	"
	U	Luciano Augostino	192	laborer	44	190 Cottage
	V	*Sturniolo Carmen	192	chauffeur	34	549 Sumner
	W	*Sturniolo Jennie—†	192	housewife	42	549 "
	X	*Margerone Mary—†	192	"	47	here

Page.	Letter.	Full Name.	Residence, Jan. 1, 1938.	Occupation.	Supposed Age.	Reported Residence, Jan. 1, 1937. Street and Number.

Cottage Street—Continued

Page.	Letter.	Full Name.	Residence, Jan. 1, 1938.	Occupation.	Supposed Age.	Reported Residence, Jan. 1, 1937. Street and Number.
	Y	Margerone Paul	192	laborer	51	here
	Z	Mosco Sulprimo	192	"	23	"
1559						
	A	*Corlito Jessie—†	192	housewife	29	89 Orleans
	B	*Corlito Michael	192	laborer	33	89 "
	C	Whitcomb Eugene	192	"	27	89 "
	D	*Leone Anna—†	192	housewife	38	here
	E	Leone Salvatore	192	laborer	36	"
	F	*Fulco Carmella—†	192	housewife	42	"
	G	*Fulco Charles	192	laborer	43	
	H	DiNocco Antonio	192	"	60	
	K	DiNocco Ermino	192	chauffeur	26	"
	L	DiNocco Romeo	192	operator	28	
	M	DiNocco Sabatino	192	clerk	22	
	N	*DiNocco Vincenza—†	192	housewife	50	"
	O	Dana James	192	laborer	22	
	P	*Dana Joseph	192	"	54	
	R	*Dana Josephine—†	192	housewife	40	"
	S	Cianci Natalie—†	194	"	41	
	T	Cianci Pauline—†	194	seamstress	21	"
	U	Cianci Sebastian	194	laborer	49	"
	V	Montanini Domenic	194	"	26	
	W	Montanini Josephine—†	194	housewife	24	"
	X	*Cannelli Alphonso	194	laborer	55	
	Y	*Cannelli Anna—†	194	housewife	52	"
	Z	*Vespa Angelo	194	laborer	40	
1560						
	A	Vespa Eva—†	194	housewife	34	"
	B	Forlizzi Antonette—†	194	operator	21	"
	C	*Forlizzi Erminia—†	194	housewife	51	"
	D	Forlizzi Pasquale	194	laborer	52	
	E	*Pirrotti Fiore	194	"	41	

Everett Street

Page.	Letter.	Full Name.	Residence, Jan. 1, 1938.	Occupation.	Supposed Age.	Reported Residence, Jan. 1, 1937. Street and Number.
	F	Dragoni Angela—†	72	housewife	33	18 Frankfort
	G	Dragoni Nicholas	72	mechanic	39	18 "
	H	*Fannara Anna—†	72	housewife	53	here
	K	Fannara Anthony	72	laborer	21	"
	L	Fannara James	72	"	22	"
	R	Simonelli Carmen	75	barber	24	

Page.	Letter.	FULL NAME.	Residence, Jan. 1, 1938.	Occupation.	Supposed Age.	Reported Residence, Jan. 1, 1937. Street and Number.

Everett Street—Continued

	S	Simonelli Catherine—†	75	housewife	24	here
	T	Pulicari Angelina—†	75	"	39	"
	U	Pulicari Joseph	75	storekeeper	41	"
	V	Nobilio Egrena—†	75	housewife	40	"
	W	Nobilio Joseph	75	tailor	40	
	X	Romani Adeline—†	76	operator	24	"
	Y	*Romani Ermengildo	76	laborer	59	
	Z	Romani Louis	76	"	22	
1561						
	A	Pantalone Antonio	76	"	42	
	B	Pantalone Santa—†	76	housewife	40	"
	C	Morrow Alexander	76	laborer	22	
	D	Morrow Amelia—†	76	housewife	49	"
	E	Morrow William	76	laborer	56	"
	G	Simonelli Ida—†	78	at home	28	
	H	Simonelli John	78	barber	58	
	K	Giacabella Charles	78	laborer	33	
	L	*Giacabella Marie—†	78	housewife	28	"
	N	DellaRusso Catherine—†	80	"	34	
	O	DellaRusso Harry	80	laborer	44	
	P	*Sersante Concetta—†	80	housewife	61	"
	R	*Sersante Gervasio	80	retired	68	
	S	Sersante Joseph	80	laborer	28	
	V	Marino Gino	83	"	30	
	W	Marino Turina—†	83	housewife	30	"
	X	DiMichele Angelina—†	83	"	33	
	Y	DiMichele Crescenzo	83	baker	33	
	Z	Zuffante Mary—†	83	housewife	32	"
1562						
	A	Zuffante Salvatore	83	chauffeur	33	"
	B	Ferro Carmella—†	84	housewife	36	"
	C	Ferro John	84	musician	43	"
	E	McVey Elizabeth—†	85	housewife	23	"
	F	McVey Joseph	85	laborer	24	"
	G	Bagarozza Alberta—†	85	housewife	24	87 Everett
	H	Bagarozza Joseph	85	clerk	32	87 "
	K	Guazzerotti Joseph	85	tinsmith	34	here
	L	Guazzerotti Susan—†	85	housewife	32	"
	M	DiRosa Anna—†	87	"	30	"
	N	DiRosa Carmen	87	laborer	28	"
	O	Spano Ralph	87	"	30	56 Everett

Page.	Letter.	Full Name.	Residence, Jan. 1, 1938.	Occupation.	Supposed Age.	Reported Residence, Jan. 1, 1937. Street and Number.

Everett Street—Continued

Page	Letter	Full Name	Residence, Jan. 1, 1938	Occupation	Supposed Age	Reported Residence, Jan. 1, 1937
	P	Spano Rose—†	87	housewife	26	56 Everett
	R	Villani Angelina—†	87	clerk	21	here
	S	Villani Dominic	87	chauffeur	30	“
	T	Villani Ernest	87	bartender	23	“
	V	Villani Guarino	87	laborer	54	
	U	Villani Marie—†	87	housewife	50	“
	W	Villani William	87	painter	26	
	X	Marroni Alice—†	88	clerk	22	
	Y	Marroni Amos	88	laborer	27	
	Z	Marroni Eliza—†	88	housewife	51	“
1563						
	A	Marroni Primo	88	laborer	56	
	B	Marcucci Margaret—†	89	housewife	42	“
	C	Marcucci Michael	89	cutter	36	
	D	Forgone Angelina—†	89	housewife	77	“
	E	Forgone Antonio	89	cutter	34	
	F	Forgone Gennaro	89	retired	82	“
	H	*Caridnale Augustina—†	90	housewife	71	164 Gove
	K	*Cardinale Michael	90	retired	64	164 “
	L	Guerra Amelia—†	90	housewife	21	here
	M	*Guerra Catherine—†	90	“	47	“
	N	Guerra James	90	laborer	53	“
	O	Lerra Fay—†	91	clerk	21	
	P	Lerra Mary—†	91	housewife	24	“
	R	Lerra Thomas	91	laborer	25	
	S	DiDonato Antonetta—†	91	housewife	38	“
	T	DiDonato Florenzo	91	operator	44	“
	U	Petricca Carmella—†	91	housewife	30	“
	V	Petricca Dominic	91	laborer	33	“
	W	*Armata Mary—†	92	housewife	25	76 Sumner
	X	Armata William	92	laborer	32	76 “
	Y	DiGuilio Assunta—†	92	housewife	36	here
	Z	DiGiulio James	92	laborer	41	“
1564						
	A	Stella Charles, jr	92	electrician	37	“
	B	Stella Ruth—†	92	housewife	36	“
	C	Arciero Mary—†	93	“	32	
	D	Arciero Michael	93	operator	34	“
	E	Polino Antonetta—†	93	housewife	35	“
	F	Polino John	93	bartender	41	“
	G	Sinacola Anthony	93	laborer	65	

Page.	Letter.	Full Name.	Residence, Jan. 1, 1938.	Occupation.	Supposed Age.	Reported Residence, Jan. 1, 1937. Street and Number.

Everett Street—Continued

Page.	Letter.	Full Name.	Residence, Jan. 1, 1938.	Occupation.	Supposed Age.	Reported Residence, Jan. 1, 1937. Street and Number.
	H	Arciero Peter	93	operator	40	here
	K	DeAngelis Joseph	93	laborer	64	"
	L	DeAngelis Marie—†	93	housewife	73	"
	M	DiGiulio Angelina—†	94	at home	39	
	N	Marrotta Frank	94	laborer	39	
	O	Marrotta Mary—†	94	housewife	32	"
	P	DeFillippis Louis	94	operator	34	"
	R	DeFillippis Lucy—†	94	housewife	28	"
	S	*DiGregorio Frank	94	laborer	63	190 Cottage
	T	*DiGregorio Phyllis—†	94	housewife	42	190 "
	U	*Viccaro Rocco	94	laborer	56	here
	V	*Viccaro Victoria—†	94	housewife	50	"
	W	Sharffa Mary—†	94	housekeeper	32	16 Foster
	X	Ippolito Cosmo	94	laborer	51	here
	Y	*DeGloria Jennie—†	94	housewife	38	"
	Z	DeGloria Joseph	94	laborer	24	"
1565						
	A	DeGloria Philip	94		53	
	B	DiNicolantonio Concezio	96	"	58	
	C	DiNicolantonio Frank	96	"	30	
	D	DiNicolantonio Ralph	96	dealer	23	"
	E	Vaccaro Anna—†	96	at home	23	16 Foster
	G	*Pace Lucy—†	96	housewife	32	here
	H	Pace Philipo	96	laborer	39	"
	K	*Ficarra Elizabeth—†	96	housewife	52	"
	L	Ficarra Jennie—†	96	operator	20	
	M	Ficarra Joseph	96	laborer	24	
	N	*Ficarra Nicholas	96	"	26	
	O	Ficarra Vincenzo	96	"	63	
	P	Minichiello Josephine—†	96	housewife	21	"
	R	Minichiello Zachary	96	barber	28	
	T	*Brunetta Antonia—†	96	housewife	53	"
	U	*Brunetta Antonio	96	laborer	53	
	V	*Bertolino Louis	97	"	48	
	W	*Bertolino Ramona—†	97	housewife	45	"
	X	Aramando Daniel	97	clerk	21	
	Y	Aramando Matteo	97	laborer	57	
	Z	Solamini John	97	musician	47	"
1566						
	A	Bertolino Christe	97	baker	26	
	B	Bertolino Theresa—†	97	housewife	23	"

Page.	Letter.	Full Name.	Residence, Jan. 1, 1938.	Occupation.	Supposed Age.	Reported Residence, Jan. 1, 1937. Street and Number.

Everett Street—Continued

	c	Potenza Antonetta—†	98	housewife	34	here
	d	Potenza Peter	98	laborer	43	"
	e	*Serino Antonio	98	"	42	"
	f	Serino Victoria—†	98	housewife	37	"
	g	*Crescenzio Angelina—†	98	"	36	
	h	Crescenzio Carmen	98	laborer	39	"
	k	Del Sette Frances—†	99	housewife	24	20 Bremen
	l	DelSette Peter	99	laborer	29	20 "
	m	*Draga Frank	99	"	52	76 Webster
	n	*Draga Theresa—†	99	housewife	52	76 "
	o	Mattarossa Emilio	99	laborer	37	here
	p	Mattarossa Giuseppe	99	retired	78	"
	r	*Andracchio Marie—†	100	at home	67	"
	s	Andracchio Frank	100	cutter	30	
	t	Andracchio Mary—†	100	housewife	26	"
	u	Andracchio Marie—†	100	"	27	
	v	*Andracchio Salvatore	100	cutter	32	
	w	*D'Alleva Dominic	102	laborer	34	
	x	D'Alleva Nellie—†	102	housewife	22	"
	y	*Dausilio Jennie—†	102	"	57	
	z	Dausilio Salvatore	102	janitor	58	
1567						
	a	Messina Carmella—†	102	housewife	27	"
	b	Messina Vincent	102	operator	36	"
	c	Mercurio Louis	103	retired	70	
	d	*Mercurio Nicolina—†	103	housewife	67	"
	e	Vaccaro Annie—†	103	"	37	
	f	Vaccaro Philip	103	laborer	46	
	g	Gucciardi Concetta—†	103	housewife	40	"
	h	Gucciardi Settino	103	laborer	40	
	k	Rapallo Stefano	103	"	40	
	l	Carcerano Antonetta—†	105	housewife	21	"
	m	Carcerano Salvatore	105	laborer	26	
	n	Musto Louis	105	operator	23	"
	o	Musto Sophie—†	105	housewife	22	"
	p	Musto Angelo	105	tailor	53	
	r	Musto Julia—†	105	housewife	52	"
	s	*Ingo Farbona—†	106	at home	88	
	t	Trapasso Antonetta—†	106	housewife	47	"
	u	Trapasso Frank	106	chauffeur	22	"
	v	Trapasso Mary—†	106	at home	21	

Page.	Letter.	FULL NAME.	Residence, Jan. 1, 1938.	Occupation.	Supposed Age.	Reported Residence, Jan. 1, 1937. Street and Number.

Everett Street—Continued

	W	Trapasso Salvatore	106	engineer	51	here
	X	*Condrillo Julia—†	106	at home	79	"
	Y	Bottaro Anthony	106	laborer	21	"
	Z	Bottaro Frank	106	"	46	
1568						
	A	Bottaro Theresa—†	106	housewife	39	"
	B	*Argenio Carmella—†	107	"	48	
	C	*Argenio Joseph	107	laborer	47	
	D	D'Enrico Savino	107	"	52	
	E	D'Enrico Vincenza—†	107	housewife	44	"
	F	D'Enrico Vincenzo	107	laborer	22	
	H	*Giasullo Anthony	110	mechanic	35	"
	K	Giasullo Josephine—†	110	housewife	33	"
	L	*Melito Marie—†	110	at home	56	
	M	*Melito Palmina—†	110	housewife	33	"
	N	Melito Vito	110	laborer	34	"
	O	*D'Amelio Fiorando	110	"	34	Italy
	P	D'Amelio Frank	110	"	37	here
	R	*D'Amelio Ida—†	110	housewife	34	"
	S	Dionisi Amadio	111	baker	42	"
	T	Dionisi Mary—†	111	housewife	38	"
	U	Salini Julia—†	111	"	30	
	V	Salini Philip	111	baker	32	
	X	Perna Raymond	114	shoemaker	32	"
	Y	Perna Ruth—†	114	housewife	27	"
	Z	*Angelo Joseph	114	laborer	42	
1569						
	A	Angelo Josephine—†	114	housewife	33	"
	B	D'Italia Angelo	114	operator	45	"
	C	D'Italia Anna—†	114	stitcher	20	
	D	D'Italia Pauline—†	114	housewife	38	"
	E	*Guerra Frank	115	laborer	40	100 Marginal
	F	Guerra Josephine—†	115	housewife	22	100 "
	G	Capoccia Eleanor—†	115	at home	47	here
	H	*Cipriano John	115	laborer	55	"
	K	Rizzo Nazzaro	115	"	67	"
	L	Sasso Angelo	115	"	48	
	M	Sasso Josephine—†	115	housewife	45	"
	O	*Delcora Carmen	rear 115	retired	76	6 Sumner pl
	P	*Chiampa Louis	" 115	"	83	here
	R	*Dambola George	" 115	laborer	43	"

Page.	Letter.	Full Name.	Residence, Jan. 1, 1938.	Occupation.	Supposed Age.	Reported Residence, Jan. 1, 1937. Street and Number.

Everett Street—Continued

	S	Gulla Antonio	rear 115	laborer	52	Cohasset
	T	Gulla Vincenza—†	" 115	housewife	42	"
	U	Gulla William F	" 115	laborer	24	"
	V	*DeFuria Lorenzo	" 115	baker	40	here
	W	*Solamine Edward	" 115	laborer	50	"
	X	Buono Angelo	116	cutter	26	"
	Y	Buono Stella—†	116	housewife	26	"
	Z	Guarino Alfred	116	operator	22	"
1570						
	A	Guarino Jennie—†	116	at home	25	
	B	Guarino Joseph	116	laborer	58	
	C	DiGiorgio Camille—†	116	operator	21	"
	D	*DiGiorgio John	116	tailor	56	
	E	*DiGiorgio Lucy—†	116	housewife	50	"
	F	DiGiorgio Marie—†	116	tailoress	27	
	G	DiGiorgio Mildred—†	116	"	29	"
	H	Pelrine Agnes—†	120	housewife	37	"
	K	Pelrine Edward	120	laborer	52	
	L	*Collins Catherine—†	120	housewife	56	"
	M	Collins Catherine—†	120	clerk	24	
	N	*Collins James	120	retired	70	
	O	Collins Margaret—†	120	operator	20	"
	P	Dionne Ethel—†	120	housewife	28	"
	R	Dionne Henry	120	U S A	34	"
	S	*Grant Frank	120	retired	79	
	T	Grant James	120	laborer	39	
	U	*Grant Mary—†	120	housewife	65	"
	V	Penta Frances—†	122	"	27	"
	W	Penta Salvatore	122	watchman	34	98 Chelsea
	X	Vitale Felix	122	barber	37	here
	Y	*Vitale Jennie—†	122	housewife	31	"
	Z	Mastrangello Amelia—†	122	"	23	"
1571						
	A	Mastrangello Severio	122	chauffeur	24	"
	B	Pagliarulo Carmen	124	clerk	20	
	C	Pagliarulo Donata—†	124	operator	23	
	D	*Pagliarulo Raffaela—†	124	housewife	58	"
	E	Pagliarulo Vito	124	laborer	54	
	F	Buono Carlo	126	mechanic	21	"
	G	*Buono Concetta—†	126	housewife	52	"
	H	Buono Eleanor—†	126	"	21	

Page.	Letter.	Full Name.	Residence, Jan. 1, 1938.	Occupation.	Supposed Age.	Reported Residence, Jan. 1, 1937. Street and Number.

Everett Street—Continued

	K	D'Andria Pauline—†	126	operator	36	here
	L	*Salerno Antonio	128	laborer	65	"
	M	*Salerno Marie—†	128	housewife	63	"
	N	Doyle Lucy—†	128	"	28	
	O	Doyle Martin L	128	longshoreman	32	"
	P	Fabiano Angelina—†	128	housewife	27	"
	R	*Fabiano Nicholas	128	chauffeur	33	"
	T	D'Amato Henry	131	"	29	
	U	D'Amato Mary—†	131	housewife	58	"
	V	*Calvino Gaetano	131	laborer	53	
	W	*Calvino Lucy—†	131	housewife	43	"
	X	Calvino Philip	131	laborer	26	
	Y	Bruno Carmella—†	131	housewife	44	"
	Z	Bruno Giuseppe	131	laborer	54	
1572						
	A	Morrelli Claire—†	133	clerk	21	
	B	Morrelli Eugene	133	mechanic	24	"
	C	Morrelli Ralph	133	laborer	25	
	D	Morrelli Virginia—†	133	housewife	58	"
	E	Maglio Frank	134	laborer	26	
	F	Maglio Julia—†	134	housewife	24	"
	G	*Screti John	134	laborer	40	
	H	*Screti Mary—†	134	housewife	36	"
	K	Leon John	134	laborer	43	
	L	*Leon Maria—†	134	housewife	33	"
	N	*Melito Philomena—†	136	"	30	
	O	Melito Vincent	136	chauffeur	35	"
	P	*LaPorta Stella—†	136	housewife	40	"
	R	*LaPorta Vincenzo	136	laborer	42	
	S	Mancusi Charles	136	timekeeper	31	"
	T	Mancusi Joseph	136	retired	71	"
	W	Murphy Cornelius	139	"	62	
	X	Murphy Mary F—†	139	housewife	50	"
	Z	DeNunzio Evelyn—†	140	"	28	417 Meridian
1573						
	A	DeNunzio Joseph	140	mechanic	33	417 "
	B	*Laiacona Frances—†	140	housewife	54	here
	C	Laiacona Frank	140	tailor	24	"
	D	*Laiacona Salvatore	140	laborer	59	"
	E	DiGloria Florence—†	140	housewife	34	"
	F	DiGloria Samuel	140	laborer	41	

Everett Street—Continued

Page.	Letter.	Full Name.	Residence, Jan. 1, 1938.	Occupation.	Supposed Age.	Reported Residence, Jan. 1, 1937. Street and Number.
	G	Alexanderson Margaret-†	141	housewife	34	N Hampshire
	H	Alexanderson Robert	141	seaman	39	"
	K	Olivera Salvatore	141	shoemaker	50	here
	L	Francis Antonette—†	142	housewife	21	"
	M	Francis Joseph	142	laborer	24	"
	N	Luongo Nicholas	142	"	41	
	O	*Luongo Raffaela—†	142	housewife	40	"
	P	Buonopane Michael	142	laborer	43	
	R	*Buonopane Prisca—†	142	housewife	44	"
	S	Maglio Michael	143	operator	34	"
	T	Maglio Rose—†	143	housewife	28	"
	U	*Oliva Alphonso	143	laborer	58	
	V	Puopolo Carmina—†	143	at home	21	
	W	*Puopolo Michael	143	laborer	54	
	X	*Puopolo Raffaele	143	"	57	
	Y	*Rozzo Sabatino	143	"	71	"
	Z	Coscia Amy—†	144	housewife	39	148 Everett
1574						
	A	Coscia Louise—†	144	dressmaker	20	148 "
	B	Coscia Ralph	144	clerk	21	148 "
	C	*Coscia William	144	laborer	45	148 "
	D	*Famularo Achiello	144	"	53	170 "
	E	*Famularo Elizabeth—†	144	housewife	47	170 "
	F	Spinazzola Gaetano	144	laborer	26	170 "
	G	Spinazzola Leonard	144	"	29	170 "
	H	*Buttera Jean—†	144	housewife	38	here
	K	*Buttera Vincent	144	clerk	39	"
	M	Mangone Pearl—†	146	housewife	31	"
	N	Mangone Thomas	146	operator	36	
	O	Consalvi Emilio	146	laborer	29	
	P	Consalvi Rose—†	146	housewife	23	"
	R	Petruccelli Frances—†	146	operator	44	"
	S	Calvino Caroline—†	146	housewife	20	20 Brooks
	T	Calvino James	146	operator	24	133 Everett
	U	Montiscenti Dominic	147	shoeworker	55	here
	V	Montiscenti Mary—†	147	housewife	37	"
	W	Montiscenti Rose—†	147	at home	24	"
	Y	Montesanti Elizabeth—†	148	housewife	27	"
	Z	Montesanti Frank	148	clerk	27	
1575						
	A	*Briganti Esther—†	148	housewife	50	"

Page.	Letter.	Full Name.	Residence, Jan. 1, 1938.	Occupation.	Supposed Age.	Reported Residence, Jan. 1, 1937. Street and Number.

Everett Street—Continued

Page.	Letter.	Full Name.	Residence, Jan. 1, 1938.	Occupation.	Supposed Age.	Reported Residence, Jan. 1, 1937. Street and Number.
	B	Briganti Samuel	148	laborer	56	92 Bremen
	C	DeSisto Jeremiah	148	"	43	here
	E	*Rauseo Antonio	150	"	50	"
	F	*Rauseo Catherine—†	150	housewife	51	"
	G	Rauseo Frank	150	chauffeur	24	"
	H	Rauseo Michael	150	clerk	22	
	L	*Ballerini Dominic	150	machinist	41	"
	K	Ballerini Philomena—†	150	housewife	29	"
	N	Murphy Mary—†	153	at home	40	"
	O	*Defeo Anna—†	153	housewife	26	166 Cottage
	P	Defeo Brenno	153	laborer	37	166 "
	R	Sgobbo Antonio	153	"	41	here
	S	Sgobbo Nicolina—†	153	housewife	68	"
	U	Rausco Anna—†	155	"	25	"
	V	Rausco Rocco	155	laborer	25	
	W	Salamone Josephine—†	155	housewife	24	"
	X	Salamone Peter	155	foreman	26	
	Y	Zeoli Clara—†	155	housewife	45	"
	Z	Zeoli Dominic	155	tailor	57	
1576						
	A	Zeoli Nicholas	155	laborer	22	
	B	Fagone Angelina—†	156	housewife	21	"
	C	Fagone Michael	156	clerk	23	
	D	*Vitale Filomena—†	156	housewife	37	"
	E	Vitale Paul	156	shoemaker	36	"
	G	Capodilupo Aldino	158	salesman	26	Revere
	H	*Capodilupo Marie—†	158	housewife	61	here
	K	*Santosuosso Rose—†	158	at home	25	"
	L	Cerbone Amelia—†	159	hairdresser	25	"
	M	*Cerbone Josephine—†	159	housewife	53	"
	N	*Cerbone Peter	159	laborer	58	
	O	*Frusciante Angelina—†	160	housewife	48	"
	P	*Frusciante Anthony	160	laborer	53	
	R	Frusciante Ralph	160	"	21	
	S	Turco Alphonse	160	"	53	
	T	*Turco Filomena—†	160	housewife	79	"
	U	Turco John	160	laborer	40	
	V	Pierro Annie—†	160	housewife	55	"
	W	Pierro Anthony	160	printer	22	"
	X	Lascolla Mary—†	164	housewife	25	131 Cottage
	Y	Lascolla Peter	164	laborer	39	131 "

Page.	Letter.	Full Name.	Residence, Jan. 1, 1938.	Occupation.	Supposed Age.	Reported Residence, Jan. 1, 1937. Street and Number.
		Everett Street—Continued				
	z	*Lascolla Antonetta—†	164	housewife	38	here
1577						
	A	*Lascolla Orazio	164	laborer	41	"
	C	Carforio Antonio	165	"	62	"
	D	*Carforio Bridget—†	165	housewife	62	"
	E	Salamone Angelina—†	165	at home	22	"
	F	Salamone Josephine—†	165	"	44	"
	G	Penta George	165	laborer	30	"
	H	Penta Viola—†	165	housewife	28	"
	L	*Festa Josephine—†	166	"	54	"
	M	Festa Louis	166	laborer	24	"
	N	Festa Marie—†	166	clerk	22	"
	O	*Derrico Carmella—†	166	housewife	44	"
	P	Derrico Michael	166	operator	25	"
	R	Derrico Vincenza—†	166	at home	24	"
	T	Sarro Angelina—†	170	housewife	71	"
	U	Sarro Carmene	170	retired	69	"
	W	Santilli Angelina—†	170	housewife	28	222 Everett
	X	Santilli Pasquale	170	laborer	24	222 "
	Y	Antillio Albert	171	"	25	381 Maverick
	Z	Correale James	171	"	34	381 "
1578						
	A	Correale Rose—†	171	housewife	30	381 "
	C	Correale Carmen	172	chauffeur	41	here
	D	Correale Mary—†	172	housewife	30	"
	E	St George Albert	174	longshoreman	42	"
	F	St George Patrick	174	laborer	20	"
	G	*Favuzza Frank	176	operator	38	"
	H	*Favuzza Josephine—†	176	housewife	62	"
	K	Rossetti Ernest	176	shoemaker	25	219 Marion
	L	Rossetti Vera—†	176	housewife	24	219 "
	M	*Faricella Antonetta—†	176	at home	43	here
	N	Ravagno Alice—†	176	housewife	30	"
	O	Ravagno Salvatore	176	operator	32	"
	P	Stella Charles	176	laborer	27	"
	R	*Stella Joseph	176	retired	78	"
	S	Stella Rose—†	176	housewife	32	"
	U	O'Connell Annie—†	177	at home	47	"
	V	O'Connell Hilary J	177	B F D	38	"
	W	O'Connell Mary—†	177	housewife	35	"

Page.	Letter.	Full Name.	Residence, Jan. 1, 1938.	Occupation.	Supposed Age.	Reported Residence, Jan. 1, 1937. Street and Number.
1579						
		Gove Street				
	C	D'Amico Jean C—†	142	entertainer	31	here
	D	Capone Antonetta—†	142	housewife	23	46 Maverick
	E	*Capone Benjamin	142	laborer	40	46 "
	F	Corsano Dora—†	142	housewife	27	here
	G	Corsano Edmund	142	engineer	30	"
	H	Langone Angeline—†	142	operator	24	"
	K	Langone John	142	painter	27	
	L	*Puorro Antonetta—†	142	housewife	44	"
	M	Puorro Julia—†	142	stitcher	21	
	N	Puorro Natalina—†	142	"	23	
	O	Cappucci Carmella—†	142	operator	27	
	P	Cappucci Catherine—†	142	housewife	60	"
	R	Cappucci Virginia—†	142	operator	29	"
	S	*Caloia Charles	142	laborer	45	
	T	*Liberatore Linda—†	142	housewife	50	"
	U	Liberatore Margaret—†	142	operator	20	"
	V	Liberatore Rocco	142	blacksmith	53	"
	W	Ciampa Alphonse	142	laborer	23	3 Hooten ct
	X	Ciampa Lucille—†	142	housewife	21	here
	Y	Pascone Carmella—†	146	operator	22	"
	Z	Pascone Eustachio	146	laborer	57	"
1580						
	A	Pascone Theresa—†	146	housewife	57	"
	B	Pascone Vito	146	chauffeur	29	"
	C	Porfido Giacomo	146	tailor	38	
	D	Porfido Margaret—†	146	housewife	33	"
	E	Petrillo Columbia—†	146	"	32	"
	F	Petrillo Henry	146	janitor	31	48 Brooks
	G	Corsano Annie—†	146	housewife	55	here
	H	Corsano Nicholas D	146	engineer	32	142 Gove
	K	Pelosi Achille	146	tailor	42	131 Orleans
	L	*Pelosi Maria—†	146	housewife	35	131 "
	M	Scrima Catherine—†	146	"	41	here
	N	Scrima Raymond	146	operator	41	"
	O	Lopilato Catherine—†	164	housewife	59	"
	P	Lopilato Michael	164	laborer	66	
	R	Scalfani Frances—†	164	housewife	20	"
	S	Scalfani Frank	164	cutter	25	187 North
	U	Tartoloni Anthony	164	packer	24	here
	V	Tartoloni Lucy—†	164	housewife	23	"

Page.	Letter.	Full Name.	Residence, Jan. 1, 1938.	Occupation.	Supposed Age.	Reported Residence, Jan. 1, 1937. Street and Number.

Gove Street—Continued

	W	*Tediscucci Lucia—†	164	housekeeper	46	155 Cottage
	X	*Gambale Bertha—†	164	housewife	40	here
	Y	D'Agresto Antonette—†	164	typist	25	"
	Z	D'Agresto Caroline—†	164	seamstress	27	"
1581						
	A	D'Agresto James	164	laborer	21	
	B	*D'Agresto Mary—†	164	housewife	50	"
	C	*Napolitano Maria—†	165	housekeeper	70	"
	D	*LaVecchio Angelina—†	165	housewife	58	"
	E	*LaVecchio Antonio	165	laborer	61	
	F	LaVecchio Joseph	165	draftsman	21	"
	G	LaVecchio Mildred—†	165	inspector	27	"
	H	LaVecchio Sarah—†	165	operator	23	
	K	Lunetta Eva—†	165	housewife	30	"
	L	Lunetta Stephen	165	operator	33	
	M	DiFranza Bernardo	165	laborer	40	
	N	*DiFranza Maria—†	165	housewife	35	"
	O	Pepicelli Antonetta—†	165	"	31	
	P	Pepicelli Antonio	165	laborer	34	
	R	*D'Agresta Angelina—†	165	housewife	39	"
	S	D'Agresta Gaetano	165	laborer	47	
	T	*Pucillo Carmine	165	"	31	
	U	*Pucillo Maria—†	165	housewife	23	"
	V	Naples Domenic	165	operator	40	"
	W	Naples Mary—†	165	housewife	31	"
	X	Iannicconi Achille	166	laborer	22	
	Y	Iannicconi Charles	166	"	52	
	Z	Iannicconi Eugene	166	clerk	20	
1582						
	A	*Iannicconi Josephine—†	166	housewife	47	"
	B	Iannicconi Louis	166	barber	25	
	C	*D'Anorfio Mary—†	166	housewife	37	"
	D	Catania Jennie—†	166	"	32	
	E	Catania Joseph	166	painter	36	
	F	*Masiello Rose—†	166	housewife	32	"
	G	Masiello Tiberio	166	laborer	38	
	H	Mori Filomena—†	166	operator	22	
	K	Mori Frances—†	166	stitcher	29	
	L	*Mori Maria—†	166	housewife	61	"
	M	*Masiello Filomena—†	166	"	37	"
	N	Masiello Pellegrino	166	laborer	42	

Page.	Letter.	Full Name.	Residence, Jan. 1, 1938.	Occupation.	Supposed Age.	Reported Residence, Jan. 1, 1937. Street and Number.

Gove Street—Continued

	o	*Mercurio Edgar	166	laborer	37	here
	p	Mercurio Pasqualina—†	166	housewife	30	"
	r	DeRosa Angelo	168	operator	24	"
	s	Romano Anna—†	168	housewife	45	"
	t	Romano Frank	168	laborer	56	
	u	Romano Vincent	168	operator	23	"
	v	*Cappozzo Assunta—†	168	housewife	78	"
	w	*Cappozzo Crescenzo	168	retired	78	
	x	DeRosa Crescenzo	168	laborer	28	
	y	DeGianvittorio Adelaide—†	168	dressmaker	60	"
	z	*DeGianvittorio Concetta—†	168	housewife	39	"
1583						
	a	*DeGianvittorio Giovanni	168	shoemaker	42	"
	b	*DeMarco Antonio	168	operator	33	"
	c	DeMarco Leonora—†	168	housewife	25	"
	d	*Selvitella Antonio	168	pedler	60	
	e	*Selvitella Michael	168	machinist	41	"
	f	*Selvitella Pasqualina—†	168	housewife	62	"
	g	*Savino Giovanni	168	blacksmith	44	"
	h	*Savino Regina—†	168	housewife	42	"
	k	DeLucia Alfredo	168	operator	47	"
	l	*DeLucia Maria—†	168	housewife	47	"
	m	Dragani Ruggiero	168	operator	51	Connecticut
	n	*Sica Bruno	174	mattressmaker	45	140 Marginal
	o	*Sica Leonard J	174	tinsmith	46	140 "
	p	*Sica Marian—†	174	housewife	77	140 "
	r	DiLorenzo Edward	174	tailor	64	here
	s	DiLorenzo Edward	174	mechanic	26	"
	t	*DiLorenzo Giuseppina—†	174	housewife	60	"
	u	*Antionioli Carlo	174	tailor	41	
	v	*Antionioli Eleanora—†	174	housewife	37	"
	w	*Antionioli Louise—†	174	dressmaker	29	"
	x	Antionioli Mary—†	174	housewife	67	"
	y	Sinibaldi Giuseppe	174	laborer	55	
	z	*Sinibaldi Maria—†	174	housewife	54	"
1584						
	a	Barrasso Angelina—†	176	operator	22	"
	b	Lanza Angelo	176	laborer	34	
	c	Lanza Pamlina—†	176	housewife	29	"
	d	Prisco Joseph	176	laborer	33	152 Prince
	e	Prisco Quinta—†	176	housewife	27	152 "

Page.	Letter.	Full Name.	Residence, Jan. 1, 1938.	Occupation.	Supposed Age.	Reported Residence, Jan. 1, 1937. Street and Number.

Gove Street—Continued

	F	*Florio Ercilia—†	176	housewife	70	here
	G	*Florio Frank	176	laborer	66	"
	H	*Savini Antonio	176	chauffeur	33	"
	K	Savini Mary—†	176	housewife	34	"
	L	*DiGianvittorio Adele—†	176	"	50	
	M	*DiGianvittorio Egidio	176	musician	54	..
	N	*Stringi Nellie—†	176	housekeeper	36	"

Hooten Court

	O	Simonelli Alphonso	1	laborer	51	171 Everett
	P	*Simonelli Josephine—†	1	housewife	50	171 "
	R	Simonelli Pasquale	1	laborer	26	171 "
	S	Simonelli Ralph	1	"	22	171 "
	T	Martone Joseph	1	"	44	here
	U	Martone Mary—†	1	housewife	36	"
	V	*Ferreira Manuel	2	longshorman	45	11 Havre
	W	Ferreira Mary—†	2	housewife	30	11 "
	X	*Vigliotta Francisco	2	laborer	50	here
	Y	Cerbone Eugene	2	upholsterer	23	159 Everett
	Z	Cerbone Hilda—†	2	housewife	20	38 Lamson
1585						
	A	Chiampa Angelo	3	laborer	20	here
	B	*Chiampa Caroline—†	3	housewife	46	"
	C	*Rozzi Antonio	5	laborer	44	"
	D	Rozzi James	5	"	22	
	E	*Rozzi Theresa—†	5	housewife	44	"
	G	Pero Catherine—†	6	"	65	
	H	Pero Charles W	6	machinist	46	"
	K	Salamone Benedict	6	barber	22	
	L	Salamone Biagio	6	clerk	20	
	M	*Salamone Josephine—†	6	housewife	52	"
	N	*Donovan James	8	longshoreman	64	"
	O	Donovan Nora—†	8	housewife	66	"
	P	Laracy Harold	8	longshoreman	26	"
	R	Laracy Margaret—†	8	clerk	24	
	S	Driscoll John H	11	longshoreman	45	"
	U	Soldano Antonio	12	laborer	37	
	V	*Soldano Ida—†	12	housewife	32	"

Page.	Letter.	Full Name.	Residence, Jan. 1, 1938.	Occupation.	Supposed Age.	Reported Residence, Jan. 1, 1937. Street and Number.

Lamson Court

	X	Cummings Hannah B—†		housewife	80	here
	Y	Cummings John		longshoreman	47	"
	Z	Cummings Richard	3	"	42	"
1586						
	A	Bellizia Antonio	4	retired	73	
	D	Johnson Carl A	5	laborer	62	
	E	Johnson Sophie—†	5	housewife	61	"
	F	Iaconelli Biagio	7	laborer	50	
	G	Iaconelli Carmella—†	7	housewife	51	"
	H	*Iaconelli Domenic	7	laborer	56	"
	K	Iaconelli Nicholas	9	"	26	Rhode Island
	L	Rossi Carl	9	"	34	here
	M	*Rossi Filomena—†	9	housewife	31	"
	N	*Delguardio Carmella—†	10	"	45	"
	O	Delguardio Giuseppe	10	laborer	50	
	P	*Lessia Frank	10	"	52	"
	R	*Brunette Angelo	10	"	60	4 Liverpool av
	S	*Lentini James	10	chauffeur	30	4 Everett
	T	*Lentini Lena—†	10	housewife	29	4 "
	V	St John Edmund	11	operator	22	here
	W	St John Edward J	11	longshoreman	50	"
	X	St John Loretta—†	11	operator	25	"
	Y	St John Mary—†	11	housewife	52	"
	Z	St John Paul J	11	longshoreman	27	"
1587						
	A	*Manganiello Raffaele	12	laborer	49	"
	B	*DeParolese Loreto	15	"	55	115 Everett
	C	Marcantonio Andrew	17	"	21	here
	D	*Marcantonio Gaetano	17	"	50	"
	E	Marcantonio Gaetano	17	"	20	"
	F	*Marcantonio Jennie—†	17	housewife	50	"
	G	Marcantonio Josephine—†	17	operator	23	

Lamson Street

	H	Maguire Thomas A	16	clerk	50	here
	K	Maramaldi Fred	19	laborer	45	"
	L	Maramaldi Jacinto	19	operator	20	"
	M	Maramaldi Theresa—†	19	housewife	38	"
	N	Cacchiotti Annette—†	19	"	37	
	O	Cacchiotti Francesco	19	laborer	42	

Page.	Letter.	Full Name.	Residence, Jan. 1, 1938.	Occupation.	Supposed Age.	Reported Residence, Jan. 1, 1937. Street and Number.

Lamson Street—Continued

	P	Guarino Annette—†	19	housewife	31	here
	R	Guarino Michael	19	clerk	32	"
	S	Festa James	21	laborer	24	"
	T	Festa Sylvia—†	21	housewife	23	"
	U	Clark Arthur S	21	attendant	59	"
	V	Clark Lottie G—†	21	stenographer	33	"
	W	Clark Margaret M—†	21	housewife	53	"
	X	Clark Richard J	21	operator	25	"
	Y	Mingobelli Josephine—†	21	housewife	46	"
	Z	Mingobelli Lena—†	21	at home	24	
1588						
	A	Mingobelli Pasquale	21	laborer	48	
	B	Calamito Michael	rear 21	retired	57	
	C	Soldano Antonetta—†	" 21	housewife	31	"
	D	Soldano Francisco	" 21	laborer	33	
	G	Manning Mary J—†	24	at home	63	
	H	*Pellegrine Mary R—†	26	storekeeper	82	"
	K	Pellegrine Margaret M—†	26	housewife	36	"
	L	Pellegrine Thomas S	26	B F D	40	
	M	Bossi Charles	35	laborer	26	
	N	*Bossi Clara—†	35	housewife	26	"
	O	*Porzio Carmella—†	35	housekeeper	66	"
	P	Mirabello Antonio	35	bellboy	25	"
	R	Mirabello Frank	35	machinist	49	"
	S	*Mirabello Rose—†	35	housewife	44	"
	T	Mirabello William	35	laborer	24	
	U	Mirabello Ralph	35	"	22	"
	V	Mirabello Theresa—†	35	housewife	23	5 Sumner pl
	W	Tozza Anthony	36	laborer	20	here
	X	*Tozza Rose—†	36	housewife	54	"
	Y	*Sarpi Ambrose	36	laborer	44	"
	Z	Sarpi Anita—†	36	nurse	20	
1589						
	A	*Sarpi Josephine—†	36	housewife	42	"
	B	Sarpi Marie—†	36	saleswoman	21	"
	C	Bandanza Clara—†	38	housewife	30	"
	D	Bandanza Joseph	38	operator	35	"
	E	*Surette Emaline—†	38	housewife	42	"
	F	*Surette Martin	38	laborer	47	
	G	Puorro Jeremiah	39	storekeeper	44	"
	H	*Conti Anthony	39	laborer	53	"

Lamson Street—Continued

Page.	Letter.	Full Name.	Residence, Jan. 1, 1938.	Occupation.	Supposed Age.	Reported Residence, Jan. 1, 1937. Street and Number.
	K	*Conti Biaggia—†	39	housewife	47	here
	L	Conti Rose—†	39	operator	20	"
	M	D'Argenio Christine—†	39	stitcher	21	"
	N	D'Argenio Mary—†	39	housewife	41	"
	O	Benson Margaret—†	41	"	68	
	P	Benson Margaret—†	41	clerk	37	
	R	Caughey Catherine—†	41	housewife	35	"
	S	Caughey Martin T	41	chauffeur	36	"
	T	Caughey Michael	41	teamster	40	"
	U	Callan Nora E—†	43	housekeeper	55	"
	V	Nelson Mary T—†	43	"	46	"
	W	Reppucci Ethel M—†	45	housewife	34	371 Sumner
	X	Reppucci Michael A	45	electrician	43	371 "
	Y	Parziale Emilio	45	laborer	40	here
	Z	*Parziale Viola—†	45	housewife	38	"
1590	A	Parziale Frank	47	operator	28	
	B	Parziale James	47	laborer	22	
	C	*Parziale Joseph	47	"	53	
	D	*Parziale Susan—†	47	housewife	58	"
	E	Cieri Domenic	47	laborer	29	
	F	*Cieri Mary—†	47	housewife	50	"
	G	Cieri Susan—†	47	stitcher	24	
	H	Cieri Thomas	47	tailor	22	

Lowland Place

Page.	Letter.	Full Name.	Residence, Jan. 1, 1938.	Occupation.	Supposed Age.	Reported Residence, Jan. 1, 1937. Street and Number.
	K	Mario Filomena—†	1	housewife	24	here
	L	*Mario Lewis	1	baker	29	"

Lubec Street

Page.	Letter.	Full Name.	Residence, Jan. 1, 1938.	Occupation.	Supposed Age.	Reported Residence, Jan. 1, 1937. Street and Number.
	M	Corsano Annie—†	55	housewife	53	here
	N	Corsano Vincent	55	contractor	67	"
	O	*Scaduto Angeline—†	55	housewife	38	"
	P	Scaduto Joseph	55	laborer	45	172 Cottage
	R	Scaduto Joseph	55	clerk	20	172 "
	S	Riccio Dominic	55	laborer	46	here
	T	*Riccio Lena—†	55	housewife	42	"
	U	*Campanti James	57	laborer	48	"
	V	*Campanti Mary—†	57	housewife	38	"

Page.	Letter.	Full Name.	Residence, Jan. 1, 1938.	Occupation.	Supposed Age.	Reported Residence, Jan. 1, 1937. Street and Number.

Lubec Street—Continued

	W	Ventre Lillian—†	57	housewife	26	here
	X	*Savatto Annie—†	57	"	34	"
	Y	*Savatto Salvatore	57	laborer	40	"
	Z	*Madalena Alfonsena—†	57	housewife	52	"
1591						
	A	Madalena Angelo	57	retired	60	
	B	Madalena George	57	janitor	21	
	C	Madalena Joseph	57	"	25	
	D	Madalena Lucy—†	57	clerk	24	"
	E	*Ricci May—†	57	housewife	43	"
	F	Ricci Theodore	57	laborer	41	
	G	*Scrima Mary—†	57	housewife	44	"
	H	*Scrima Patrick	57	shoemaker	46	"
	K	Scrima Rose—†	57	clerk	20	"
	L	*Castaldo Michael	59	laborer	48	133 Cottage
	M	*Castaldo Ralph	59	student	26	here
	N	*Castaldo Rose—†	59	housewife	45	133 Cottage
	O	Muscate Angelo	59	laborer	30	here
	P	Muscate Rose—†	59	housewife	26	"
	R	*Corangelo Carmella—†	59	"	47	"
	S	*Carangelo Nicholas	59	laborer	47	
	T	Naglieri Antonio	59	"	60	
	U	*Naglieri Jennie—†	59	housewife	40	"
	V	Miranda Carmella—†	59	"	20	
	W	Miranda Peter	59	barber	23	
	X	DiFranza Assunta—†	59	housewife	48	"
	Y	DiFranza Carmella—†	59	at home	25	
	Z	DiFranza Leonardo	59	cutter	48	"
1592						
	A	DiFranza Mary—†	59	stenographer	23	"
	B	Zichittella Anna—†	61	packer	22	"
	C	*Zichittella John	61	painter	45	
	D	*Zichittella Mary—†	61	housewife	45	"
	F	*Carbott Albert	61	cook	55	
	G	*Carbott Anna—†	61	housewife	44	"
	H	Carbott Antonio	61	student	21	
	K	*Serino Amedio	61	laborer	43	
	L	*Serino Theresa—†	61	housewife	41	"
	M	*Castellarin Anthony	61	laborer	32	
	N	Castellarin Elda—†	61	housewife	25	"
	O	*Barrese Erminia—†	61	"	57	

Page.	Letter.	Full Name.	Residence, Jan. 1, 1938.	Occupation.	Supposed Age.	Reported Residence, Jan. 1, 1937. Street and Number.

Lubec Street—Continued

	P	*Barrese Gerardo	61	tailor	60	here
	R	*Leto Gandolfo	63	laborer	34	"
	S	Leto Jennie—†	63	housewife	24	"
	T	Rizzo Giuseppe	63	laborer	55	
	U	*Rizzo Josephine—†	63	housewife	61	"
	V	*Imbrici Raffaela—†	63	"	60	
	W	Imbrici Ralph	63	laborer	23	
	X	*Imbrici Rose—†	63	stitcher	26	
	Y	*Imbrici Sabino	63	laborer	62	
	Z	DePari Amelia—†	63	housewife	24	"
1593						
	A	DePari Frank	63	laborer	26	
	B	*Mussuto Mary—†	63	housewife	37	"
	C	Mussuto Nicholas	63	laborer	41	
	D	Scanzillo Angelo	63	"	33	
	E	*Scanzillo Louise—†	63	housewife	30	"
	F	*DiBenedetto Adeline—†	65	"	45	
	G	*DiBenedetto John	65	laborer	49	
	H	Pardo Angelo	65	chauffeur	28	"
	K	Pardo Annetta—†	65	operator	28	
	L	Cucugliato Raymond	65	storekeeper	48	"
	M	Pardo Joseph	65	laborer	62	"
	N	Pardo Joseph L	65	inspector	20	"
	O	*Pardo Mary—†	65	operator	48	"
	P	Marinelli Amelia—†	69	housewife	31	"
	R	Marinelli Joseph	69	mechanic	31	"
	S	*Giunta Ida—†	69	housewife	36	"
	T	*Giunta Philip	69	laborer	42	
	U	*Giordano Angelina—†	69	housewife	59	"
	V	Giordano Antonette—†	69	clerk	26	
	W	Giordano Caroline—†	69	packer	35	
	X	Giordano Eleanor—†	69	operator	23	
	Y	Giordano Emma—†	69	"	21	
	Z	Giordano Henry	69	laborer	35	
1594						
	A	Giordano Jennie—†	69	clerk	38	
	B	Giordano Susan—†	69	operator	28	
	C	*Riccio Angelina—†	69	housewife	52	"
	D	Riccio Francisco	69	laborer	60	
	E	Riccio Helen—†	69	dressmaker	22	"
	F	Riccio Rosina—†	69	"	25	

Page.	Letter.	Full Name.	Residence, Jan. 1, 1938.	Occupation.	Supposed Age.	Reported Residence, Jan. 1, 1937. Street and Number.

Lubec Street—Continued

	G	*DiRenzo Anna F—†	69	housewife	63	here
	H	DiRenzo Gaetano	69	retired	65	112 Webster
	K	Parziale John	71	laborer	31	30 Decatur
	L	Parziale Mary—†	71	housewife	25	30 "
	N	Cericola Alfred	71	checker	20	here
	O	Cericola Thomas	71	tailor	63	"
	P	Lacedra Michael	71	"	40	222 Lexington
	R	Lacedra Nancy—†	71	housewife	41	222 "
	S	Serra Christine—†	71	seamstress	20	here
	T	Serra Joseph	71	laborer	42	"
	U	*Serra Rose—†	71	housewife	42	"
	V	DiLibero Alexandro	71	laborer	36	59 Lubec
	W	*DiLibero Rose—†	71	housewife	37	59 "
	X	Marinelli Antonetta—†	73	"	24	972 Benningt'n
	Y	Marinelli Dominic	73	chauffeur	27	972 "
	Z	*Marinelli Gaetano	73	"	53	972 "
1595						
	A	Froco Mary—†	73	housewife	30	20 Lincoln
	B	Froco Salvatore	73	laborer	37	20 "
	D	*Matarazzo Armando	73	"	42	here
	C	*Matarazzo Margaret—†	73	housewife	33	"
	E	Nazzaro Ciro	73	laborer	42	"
	F	*Nazzaro Raffaela—†	73	housewife	42	"
	G	*D'Amico Antonette—†	73	"	48	
	K	*Parelli Annie—†	73	"	43	
	L	Parelli Modestino	73	laborer	51	"
	M	Armata Frank	73	"	54	55 Lubec
	N	*Armata Mary—†	73	housewife	52	55 "
	O	Danna Anna—†	75	operator	27	here
	P	*Danna Grace—†	75	housewife	46	"
	R	Danna James	75	operator	25	"
	S	Danna Minnie—†	75	"	21	"
	T	*Danna Salvatore	75	laborer	56	
	U	Danna Sebastian	75	salesman	24	"
	X	Colarusso Alvita—†	75	housewife	41	"
	Y	Colarusso Belagrino	75	laborer	48	
	Z	Fuccillo Anthony	75	operator	23	
1596						
	A	Fuccillo Esther—†	75	inspector	26	"
	B	*Fuccillo Michael	75	laborer	57	
	C	*Fuccillo Nunzia—†	75	housewife	56	"

Page.	Letter.	Full Name.	Residence, Jan. 1, 1938.	Occupation.	Supposed Age.	Reported Residence, Jan. 1, 1937. Street and Number.

Lubec Street—Continued

	D	Polito Bartolo	75	laborer	41	here
	E	Polito Grace—†	75	housewife	36	"
	F	*Bucheni Carmella—†	75	"	40	"
	G	*Bucheni Malindo	75	laborer	51	
	H	Zuffanti Celia—†	75	housewife	31	"
	K	Zuffanti Louis	75	operator	36	"
	L	Straccia Joseph	77	laborer	34	67 Frankfort
	M	*Straccia Palmera—†	77	housewife	32	67 "
	N	*Rosetta Mary—†	77	"	49	here
	O	*Rosetta Michael	77	laborer	60	"
	P	*Vigliotta Anthony	77	"	44	"
	R	Vigliotta Dominic	77	"	22	
	S	Vigliotta Helen—†	77	homeworker	26	"
	T	*Vigliotta Mary—†	77	housewife	42	"
	U	*Memmello Marciano	77	laborer	48	
	V	*Memmello Michelena—†	77	housewife	48	"
	W	*Paradesa Anna—†	77	"	74	
	X	*Paulicelli Grace—†	77	"	27	
	Y	Paulicelli Michael	77	laborer	27	
	Z	*DeFlumeri Mary—†	77	housewife	34	"
1597						
	A	*DeFlumeri Vincent	77	laborer	49	
	B	Caldarelli Clara—†	77	clerk	24	
	C	*Caldarelli Faustino	77	laborer	53	
	D	*Caldarelli Laura—†	77	housewife	53	"
	E	Caldarelli Natale	77	printer	22	
	F	*DiFilippo Angelo	77	laborer	42	
	G	*DiFilippo Antoinette—†	77	housewife	45	"
	H	DiTomasso Frances—†	79	clerk	22	
	K	*DiTomasso Gustino	79	laborer	43	
	L	*DiTomasso Santo	79	"	24	
	M	*Diotalevi Alexandro	79	"	51	
	N	*Diotalevi Amelia—†	79	housewife	45	"
	O	Arcadipani Andrew	79	laborer	38	"
	P	*Arcadipani Grace—†	79	housewife	36	"
	R	*Piscitelli Angelina—†	79	"	38	
	S	Piscitelli Joseph	79	laborer	38	
	T	Galante Joseph	79	operator	41	
	U	*Galante Lena—†	79	"	38	
	V	Lionetto Grace—†	79	housewife	36	"
	W	Lionetto John	79	laborer	49	

Page.	Letter.	Full Name.	Residence, Jan. 1, 1938.	Occupation.	Supposed Age.	Reported Residence, Jan. 1, 1937. Street and Number.

Lubec Street—Continued

Page.	Letter.	Full Name.	Residence, Jan. 1, 1938.	Occupation.	Supposed Age.	Reported Residence, Jan. 1, 1937. Street and Number.
	X	DiFlumeri John	79	laborer	34	here
	Y	DiFlumeri Rose—†	79	housewife	31	"
	Z	Tuttanilla Dora—†	79	"	33	"
1598						
	A	Tuttanilla Michael	79	laborer	47	"
	B	Caso Louis	81	painter	38	
	C	Caso Theresa—†	81	housewife	31	"
	D	*Drainoni Gaetano	81	musician	34	"
	E	Drainoni Mary—†	81	housewife	29	"
	F	*Caso Concordia—†	81	"	76	
	G	Caso Frank	81	manufacturer	33	"
	H	Castaldo Christina—†	81	housewife	33	"
	K	*Castaldo Ralph	81	laborer	37	
	L	DiIeso Daniel	81	"	53	
	M	DiIeso Josephine—†	81	housewife	21	"
	N	*DiIeso Mary—†	81	"	43	
	O	DiIeso Paul	81	laborer	22	
	P	DellaFanno Lee—†	81	housewife	27	"
	R	DellaFanno Patrick	81	longshoreman	29	"
	S	*DiFranza Filomena—†	81	housewife	45	"
	T	*Pelosi Annie—†	81	"	37	133 Cottage
	U	Pelosi Michael	81	shoemaker	44	here
	V	Cioto Lucy—†	83	housewife	21	"
	W	Cioto Mario	83	chauffeur	21	"
	X	Polsonetti Joseph	83	laborer	50	
	Y	*Polsonetti Michelena—†	83	housewife	36	"
	Z	*Gallo Generosa—†	83	"	51	
1599						
	A	Gallo John	83	laborer	53	
	B	Montanino Joseph	83	operator	27	"
	C	*Montanino Louise—†	83	housewife	60	"
	D	Montanino Mary—†	83	clerk	21	
	E	Montanino Michael	83	laborer	57	
	F	Montanino Sadie—†	83	laundress	23	"
	G	Casciolo Emily—†	83	housewife	32	"
	H	Casciolo Joseph	83	shoemaker	35	"
	K	Pellecchia Carlo	83	laborer	24	
	L	Pellecchia Dominica—†	83	clerk	20	"
	M	Pellecchia Josephine—†	83	housewife	55	"
	N	Colannino Anthony	85	clerk	23	
	O	Colannino Frank	85	student	20	

Page.	Letter.	Full Name.	Residence, Jan. 1, 1938.	Occupation.	Supposed Age.	Reported Residence, Jan. 1, 1937. Street and Number.
		Lubec Street—Continued				
	P	Colannino Joseph	85	student	21	here
	R	Colannino Raffaele	85	laborer	54	"
	S	DeMarco Angelo	85	butcher	26	"
	T	DeMarco Mary—†	85	housewife	28	"
	U	*Sullo Antonio	85	laborer	52	
	V	Sullo Lucy—†	85	student	20	
	W	*Sullo Mary—†	85	housewife	47	"
	Y	DeFreitas Louis	85	clerk	37	
	X	DeFreitas Phyllis—†	85	housewife	28	"
	Z	Rossi Dominic	85	laborer	47	
1600		**Maverick Street**				
	B	Caton Frances—†	226	housewife	35	here
	C	Caton Joseph	226	manufacturer	36	"
	D	Scandone Joseph	226	laborer	38	"
	E	Campiglia Catherine—†	226	milliner	35	
	F	DiStasio Louis	226	operator	35	
	G	DiStasio Pauline—†	226	housewife	28	"
	H	Lamanno Salvatore	226	operator	36	217 Maverick
	K	McGaffigan Albert A	228	salesman	28	here
	L	McGaffigan Cassie—†	228	housewife	27	"
	M	DeMayo Charles	228	machinist	52	"
	N	DeMayo Edward	228	clerk	24	
	O	DeMayo Elizabeth—†	228	housewife	47	"
	P	DeMayo George	228	clerk	21	
	R	Zenkin Mary—†	230	housewife	27	"
	S	Zenkin Walter	230	upholsterer	37	"
	T	Costa Andrew	230	student	21	
	U	Costa Anthony	230	printer	25	
	V	Costa Jennie—†	230	clerk	22	"
	W	Costa Joseph	230	laborer	31	
	X	*Costa Rose—†	230	housewife	58	"
	Y	LaRaia Frances—†	230	"	35	"
	Z	*Leonardo Angeline—†	230	"	51	219 Maverick
1601						
	A	Leonardo Flora—†	230	operator	22	here
	B	Leonardo Nicholas	230	laborer	62	219 Maverick
	D	Pinto Antonio	236	"	33	150 Bremen
	E	Pinto Nancy—†	236	cook	21	150 "
	F	Pinto Rose—†	236	housewife	61	150 "

Page.	Letter.	Full Name.	Residence, Jan. 1, 1938.	Occupation.	Supposed Age.	Reported Residence, Jan. 1, 1937. Street and Number.
		Maverick Street—Continued				
	G	Nappi Americo	236	operator	27	here
	H	Nappi Anna—†	236	"	20	"
	K	Nappi John	236	"	61	"
	L	*Nappi Julia—†	236	housewife	55	"
	N	*Castronovo Anthony	236	operator	29	
	O	*Castronovo Lena—†	236	housewife	23	"
	P	Vernarelli Giacomo	236	tailor	60	
	R	Costanza Pasquale A	238	retired	76	
	S	Costanza Catherine—†	238	housewife	40	"
	T	Costanza Pasquale	238	physician	38	"
	U	Costanza Linda—†	238	operator	27	"
	V	*Costanza Mary—†	238	housewife	62	"
	W	Costanza Rose—†	238	at home	30	
	Z	Santarpio Eva—†	244	housewife	31	"
1602						
	A	Santarpio Joseph	244	bartender	27	"
	B	Santarpio Michael	244	salesman	30	"
	C	*Schifino Dinato	244	retired	60	
	D	Schifino John	244	operator	20	
	E	Schifino Josephine—†	244	"	28	
	F	*Schifino Nicolina—†	244	housewife	60	"
	G	Schifino Pasqualina—†	244	operator	26	
	H	*Bisciotte Mary—†	246	housewife	60	"
	K	Bisciotte Rose—†	246	stitcher	21	
	L	Messina Edward	246	merchant	47	"
	M	Messina Edward, jr	246	salesman	22	"
	N	Messina Frances—†	246	housewife	40	"
	O	Bevilacqua Anthony	246	cutter	24	
	P	*Bevilacqua Ralph	246	operator	50	
	R	*Bevilacqua Victoria—†	246	housewife	47	"
	S	Iritano Frank	247	repairman	42	"
	T	Iritano Louise—†	247	housewife	38	"
	U	Camuso Amelia—†	247	student	24	
	V	Camuso John	247	pharmacist	32	"
	W	DeMinico Adele—†	247	housewife	55	"
	X	DeMinico Robert	247	operator	62	"
	Y	DeBellis Benjamin	247	"	46	135 Cottage
	Z	DeBellis Louise—†	247	housewife	37	135 "
1603						
	A	*Avelino Pasquale	248	laborer	51	here
	B	Altri John	248	longshoreman	27	"

Page.	Letter.	Full Name.	Residence, Jan. 1, 1938.	Occupation.	Supposed Age.	Reported Residence, Jan. 1, 1937. Street and Number.

Maverick Street—Continued

Page.	Letter.	Full Name.	Residence, Jan. 1, 1938.	Occupation.	Supposed Age.	Reported Residence, Jan. 1, 1937. Street and Number.
	C	Altri Laura—†	248	housewife	26	here
	D	Warner Laura—†	248	"	65	"
	E	Whiting Joseph	248	chauffeur	35	"
	F	*Santilli Anthony	248	laborer	60	
	G	*Santilli Julia—†	248	housewife	48	"
	K	*Leone Dominic	249	laborer	53	
	L	Leone Lucy—†	249	operator	22	"
	M	*Leone Victoria—†	249	housewife	46	"
	N	*Procaccini Joseph	249	laborer	36	
	O	*Procaccini Mary—†	249.	housewife	29	"
	P	Connolly John	249	clerk	23	
	R	Connolly Lucy—†	249	housewife	23	"
	S	Palange Joseph	249	operator	63	"
	T	Palange Michelina—†	249	housewife	60	"
	U	Scharffa Pasquale	249	laborer	63	
	V	*Anazalone Josephine—†	249	housewife	44	"
	W	Anazalone Pasquale	249	shoemaker	56	"
	X	Melchiondo Mary—†	249	inspector	27	"
	Y	Marani Frances—†	249	stitcher	20	
	Z	Marani John	249	dealer	61	
1604						
	A	Marani Mary—†	249	operator	21	"
	B	*Marani Rachael—†	249	housewife	50	"
	C	Hamel Alphonse	249	fireman	38	
	D	Hamel Antonette—†	249	housewife	25	"
	E	*Graziano Jeanne—†	249	"	45	
	F	*Graziano Ralph	249	laborer	43	"
	H	*Falviano Vetere	249	"	34	171 Brooks
	G	Russo Angelo	249	"	34	here
	K	Ferullo Anna—†	249	housewife	22	"
	L	Ferullo Michael	249	laborer	29	"
	M	*Guarracino Bambina—†	249	houseworker	52	"
	N	Leone Fiorino	249	electrician	24	"
	R	Zuccarro Edna—†	250	housewife	50	"
	S	Griffin Catherine—†	250	stitcher	37	
	T	Walsh Mary—†	250	housewife	66	"
	U	Simpson David	250	longshoreman	50	"
	V	Simpson Margaret—†	250	housewife	48	"
	W	Simpson Mary—†	250	clerk	25	
	Y	Morrione Peter	252	laborer	30	
	Z	*Morrione Santa—†	252	saleswoman	25	"

Page.	Letter.	Full Name.	Residence, Jan. 1, 1938.	Occupation.	Supposed Age.	Reported Residence, Jan. 1, 1937. Street and Number.
1605		**Maverick Street**—Continued				
	A	Madalena Gilda—†	252	housewife	26	296 Maverick
	B	Madalena Theodore	252	machinist	28	57 Lubec
	C	Grillo Baldassare	252	laborer	45	127 Saratoga
	D	Grillo Caroline—†	252	housewife	56	127 "
	E	LaMarca Jennie—†	254	"	22	here
	F	*LaMarca Joseph	254	operator	29	"
	G	Mastascusa Attilio	254	cutter	28	"
	H	Mastascusa Clementina–†	254	housewife	67	"
	K	Mastascusa America—†	254	"	29	"
	L	Mastascusa Ralph	254	tailor	31	"
	M	Pingaro Mildred—†	260	housewife	40	74 Everett
	N	Viscomi Eleanor—†	260	clerk	21	74 "
	O	Viscomi Irene—†	260	operator	23	74 "
	P	Serino Anna—†	260	housewife	34	here
	R	Serino Umberto	260	chauffeur	38	"
	S	Liberti Angelo	260	physician	47	"
	T	*Liberti Vincenzo	260	teacher	50	
	U	DiNardo Dominic	262	laborer	45	
	V	*DiNardo Mary—†	262	housewife	41	"
	W	Felzani Anna—†	262	"	60	
	X	Felzani Joseph	262	tailor	63	
	Y	*Ficcaglia Antonette—†	262	housewife	45	"
	Z	Ficcaglia Vincent	262	laborer	23	
1606						
	A	Rossetti Benjamin	262	salesman	24	77 Lubec
	B	Rossetti Mary—†	262	housewife	21	here
	C	*Pollastrone Mary—†	264	"	32	"
	D	Pollastrone Pietro	264	operator	40	"
	E	DiBello Catherine—†	264	housewife	48	"
	F	DiBello Edward	264	letter carrier	20	"
	G	DiBello Michael	264	tailor	51	"
	H	Fifun Gerardo	264	clerk	32	
	K	Stella Armand	264	laborer	25	
	L	*Stella Carmella—†	264	housewife	56	"
	M	Stella Helen—†	264	tailoress	24	
	N	*Stella Joseph	264	laborer	57	"
	O	Stella Louis	264	"	27	
	R	Cuozzo Carl	266	chauffeur	25	"
	S	Cuozzo Grace—†	266	housewife	24	"
	T	DiNush Joseph	266	operator	33	"

Page.	Letter.	Full Name.	Residence, Jan. 1, 1938.	Occupation.	Supposed Age.	Reported Residence, Jan. 1, 1937. Street and Number.

Maverick Street—Continued

	U	DiNush Mary—†	266	housewife	32	here
	V	Tarzio Dominic	266	laborer	50	"
	W	Tarzio Palmera—†	266	housewife	60	"
	X	Tarzio William	266	laborer	20	
	Y	Picardi Jennie—†	268	housewife	30	"
	Z	Picardi Lawrence	268	clerk	33	
1607						
	A	Cataldo Generoso	268	inspector	62	"
	B	Cataldo John	268	seaman	32	
	C	Cataldo Lucy—†	268	housewife	60	"
	D	Cataldo Mary—†	268	forewoman	28	"
	E	Cataldo Victor	268	laborer	26	
	F	Recchia Adeline—†	268	housewife	30	"
	G	Recchia Vincenzo	268	tailor	37	
	H	Sullivan Elizabeth A—†	270	housewife	42	"
	K	Sullivan Thomas A	270	inspector	59	"
	L	*Hovde Nils	270	mechanic	70	"
	M	*Hovde Olivia—†	270	housewife	63	"
	N	*Myklbust Oleif—†	270	domestic	59	81 Com av
	O	O'Keefe Anna—†	270	bookbinder	52	here
	P	O'Keefe Daniel J	270	guard	40	"
	R	O'Keefe Margaret—†	270	bookbinder	48	"
	S	*Valerio Mary—†	273	housewife	32	Framingham
	T	Valerio Peter	273	laborer	36	"
	U	Woodford Anna—†	273	housewife	24	here
	V	Woodford Frederick	273	cutter	26	"
	W	Lepore Adeline—†	273	operator	26	"
	X	Lepore Anthony	273	bootblack	22	"
	Y	Lepore Mary—†	273	houseworker	28	"
	Z	Lepore Patricia—†	273	operator	23	"
1608						
	A	Valerio Antonio	273	laborer	40	N Newton
	B	Ventre Anthony	273	retired	75	here
	C	*Ruggiero Gaetano	273	laborer	47	2 Cottage pl
	D	Ruggiero Michael	273	salesman	22	2 "
	E	Ruggiero Salvatore	273	operator	24	2 "
	F	*Marcello Anna—†	273	housewife	36	here
	G	Marcello Charles	273	clerk	40	"
	H	Giordano Frank	276	plumber	44	"
	K	Giordano Josephine—†	276	housewife	38	"
	L	Sammartino Anthony	276	seaman	25	

Page.	Letter.	FULL NAME.	Residence, Jan. 1, 1938.	Occupation.	Supposed Age.	Reported Residence, Jan. 1, 1937. Street and Number.

Maverick Street—Continued

Page.	Letter.	FULL NAME.	Residence, Jan. 1, 1938.	Occupation.	Supposed Age.	Reported Residence, Jan. 1, 1937. Street and Number.
	M	Sammartino Maria—†	276	housewife	68	here
	N	D'Amato Nicholas	276	chauffeur	25	131 Everett
	O	D'Amato Rose—†	276	housewife	24	here
	P	*LaRaia Dominic	276	tailor	64	"
	R	*LaRaia Frances—†	276	housewife	47	"
	S	LaRaia Isabel—†	276	clerk	20	
	T	Grillo Americo	278	barber	33	
	U	Grillo Linda—†	278	housewife	32	"
	V	Drago Mary—†	278	"	30	
	W	Drago Robert	278	tailor	34	
	X	Grillo Arthur	278	laborer	21	
	Y	Grillo Frank C	278	counterman	36	"
	Z	*Grillo Jeremiah	278	laborer	68	
1609						
	A	*Grillo Josephine—†	278	housewife	55	"
	B	Messina Emma—†	278	"	25	Malden
	C	Aguda Mary—†	280	"	25	here
	D	Aguda Pasquale	280	baker	29	"
	E	Latanno Louis	280	laborer	55	"
	F	Latanno Michael	280	baker	22	
	G	*Latanno Rose—†	280	housewife	46	"
	H	Intoni Angelina—†	280	clerk	26	
	K	Intoni Ciriaco	280	laborer	55	
	L	*Intoni Lauretta—†	280	housewife	54	"
	M	Arricale Anthony	282	shoemaker	31	"
	N	Arricale Louise—†	282	housewife	28	"
	O	Vitale Jenny—†	282	"	49	122 Everett
	P	Vitale Joseph	282	barber	51	122 "
	R	Vitale Marie—†	282	clerk	20	122 "
	S	Schittino Anthony	282	operator	23	here
	T	*Schittino Nellie—†	282	housewife	45	"
	U	*Previte Nicolena—†	284	"	37	"
	V	Previte Peter	284	laborer	42	
	W	Terrizzi Carmella—†	284	clerk	26	
	X	Ingelson John A	284	laborer	77	
	Y	Nyberg Mabel F—†	284	housewife	40	"
	Z	Nyberg Sven	284	salesman	46	"
1610						
	A	Assenzo Benjamin	284	mechanic	29	"
	B	Assenzo Phyllis—†	284	housewife	29	"
	D	Palmieri Antonetta—†	286	"	32	

Page.	Letter.	Full Name.	Residence, Jan. 1, 1938.	Occupation.	Supposed Age.	Reported Residence, Jan. 1, 1937. Street and Number.

Maverick Street—Continued

	E	Palmieri Frank	286	barber	41	here
	F	Palmieri Catherine—†	286	clerk	32	“
	G	*Palmieri Joseph	286	barber	77	“
	H	Delpo Anthony	286	operator	50	“
	K	*Delpo Carolina—†	286	housewife	44	“
	L	Delpo Michael	286	laborer	45	
	M	Delpo Theresa—†	286	clerk	20	
	P	Knowles Bridget—†	296	housewife	74	“
	R	Knowles Mary—†	296	clerk	33	
	S	Knowles Peter	296	retired	80	
	T	Knowles Thomas	296	laborer	30	“
	U	Covino Samuel	296	clerk	29	193 Maverick
	V	Maruzzi Lena—†	296	housewife	37	193 “
	W	Maruzzi Michael	296	bartender	37	193 “
	X	*Maruzzi Pellegrino	296	laborer	80	193 “
	Y	*DiSilvio Carmello	296	“	58	here
	Z	DiSilvio Dominic	296	clerk	30	“
1611						
	A	DiSilvio John	296	laborer	29	Revere
	B	DiSilvio Nina—†	296	domestic	28	here
	C	Matarazza Alfred	297	operator	26	“
	D	Matarazza Susan—†	297	housewife	27	“
	E	*Porzio Henrietta—†	297	“	44	
	F	Porzio John	297	barber	49	
	G	Porzio Louis	297	salesman	22	“
	H	*Palmieri Louis	297	operator	37	
	K	Palmieri Rose—†	297	housewife	33	“
	L	Fiandoco Adeline—†	298	“	24	
	M	Fiandoco Pasquale	298	tailor	26	
	N	Fera Carolina—†	298	clerk	22	
	O	*Fera Frank	298	laborer	63	
	P	Fera John	298	“	27	
	R	*Fera Marie—†	298	housewife	56	“
	S	Porzio Nicholas	298	barber	40	
	T	Porzio Nora—†	298	housewife	36	“
	U	*DeLuca Jennie—†	299	“	49	
	V	DeLuca Salvatore	299	painter	22	“
	W	*Cerrone Nicholas	299	laborer	55	296 Maverick
	X	*Cerrone Raffaela—†	299	housewife	54	296 “
	Y	Cerrone Susan—†	299	operator	20	296 “
	Z	Yolanda Antoinette—†	299	housewife	22	296 “

Page.	Letter.	Full Name.	Residence, Jan. 1, 1938.	Occupation.	Supposed Age.	Reported Residence, Jan. 1, 1937. Street and Number.
1612		**Maverick Street**—Continued				
	A	Rivoire Concetta—†	299	housewife	51	here
	B	Rivoire Lanni	299	printer	52	"
	C	*Cellozi Dora—†	300	housewife	36	"
	D	Cellozi Michael	300	laborer	38	
	E	Russo Joseph	300	baker	59	
	F	Russo Josephine—†	300	clerk	23	
	G	Russo Mary F—†	300	"	26	"
	H	Russo Rose—†	300	"	22	
	K	Russo Susan—†	300	housewife	53	"
	L	D'Agostino Benjamin	300	clerk	20	
	M	D'Agostino Joseph	300	"	45	
	N	*D'Agostino Mary—†	300	housewife	60	"
	O	Filippone Andrew	301	operator	24	73 Maverick
	P	Filippone Frances—†	301	housewife	24	73 "
	R	Dearie James	301	retired	78	here
	S	Rowan Mary—†	301	housewife	40	"
	T	Lombardi Ralph	301	superintendent	28	"
	U	Lombardi Rose—†	301	housewife	24	"
	V	Marasca Ferdinand	302	operator	32	
	W	Marasca Lucy—†	302	housewife	27	"
	X	*Marasca Alfred	302	tailor	60	
	Y	Marasca Edith—†	302	stitcher	20	
	Z	Marasca Helen—†	302	clerk	25	
1613						
	A	Marasca Jennie—†	302	housewife	55	"
	B	Marasca Vincent	302	shoemaker	21	"
	C	Coviello Carmella—†	302	housewife	45	"
	D	Coviello Nicholas	302	laborer	60	
	E	Hale Joseph	303	clerk	29	
	F	Hale Madeline—†	303	operator	22	"
	G	Hale Mary—†	303	forewoman	49	"
	H	McCarthy James J	303	teamster	54	"
	K	McCarthy Johanna—†	303	housewife	55	"
	L	McCarthy Mary G—†	303	saleswoman	25	"
	M	McCarthy William J	303	salesman	28	"
	N	Jansen Hilda S—†	303	housewife	57	"
	O	*Matson Eric	303	supervisor	42	"
	P	Parilla Anthony	304	laborer	32	
	R	Parilla Emily—†	304	housewife	29	"
	S	*Garofalo Amelia—†	304	"	43	700 Benningt'n

Maverick Street—Continued

Page.	Letter.	Full Name.	Residence, Jan. 1, 1938.	Occupation.	Supposed Age.	Reported Residence, Jan. 1, 1937. Street and Number.
	T	*Garofalo Pasquale	304	laborer	46	700 Benningt'n
	U	Murdocca Jennie—†	304	clerk	23	here
	V	Murdocca Joseph	304	laborer	21	"
	W	*Murdocca Mary—†	304	housewife	50	"
	X	*Murdocca Vincent	304	laborer	60	
	Y	*Savino Angelina—†	306	housewife	63	"
	Z	Savino Helen—†	306	dressmaker	26	"
1614						
	A	*Savino Liberato	306	welder	33	"
	B	Savino Richard	306	operator	22	127 Dresser
	C	Savino Yolanda—†	306	housewife	24	here
	D	Manuele Alfred	306	clerk	24	"
	E	*Manuele John	306	tailor	49	"
	F	Manuele Mario	306	operator	20	
	G	*Manuele Mary—†	306	housewife	53	"
	H	Doyle Margaret—†	307	"	30	
	K	Doyle Thomas	307	timekeeper	32	"
	L	Nelson Bridget—†	307	housewife	65	"
	M	Nelson Florence—†	307	clerk	43	
	N	Nelson James	307	retired	70	"
	O	Gambale Michelina—†	315	housewife	29	r 220 Havre
	P	*Gambale Nicholas	315	laborer	50	r 220 "
	R	Rotundo Angelina—†	315	housewife	45	here
	S	Rotundo Antonio	315	laborer	52	"
	T	Rotundo Samuel	315	barber	20	"
	U	*Aledda Carmella—†	315	housewife	46	247 Maverick
	V	Aledda Mario	315	laborer	49	247 "
	W	Cresceane Agrippino	315	operator	54	247 "
	Y	Picardi Albert	317	clerk	23	here
	Z	Picardi Charles	317	photographer	30	"
1615						
	A	Picardi Louis	317	chauffeur	21	"
	B	Picardi Margaret—†	317	operator	27	"
	C	Picardi Mary—†	317	housewife	28	"
	D	*Picardi Ralph	317	laborer	54	
	E	*Nicolosi Charles	319	"	46	
	F	*Godfrey Richard	321	painter	62	
	G	*Godfrey Sarah—†	321	housewife	60	"
	H	DeDomico Concetta—†	321	"	42	
	K	DeDomico Frank	321	laborer	47	
	L	Cook Doris A—†	321	housewife	34	"

Page.	Letter.	Full Name.	Residence, Jan. 1, 1938.	Occupation.	Supposed Age.	Reported Residence, Jan. 1, 1937. Street and Number.
		Maverick Street—Continued				
	M	Cook Harold H	321	laborer	37	here
	N	Velardo Anthony	323	"	49	"
	O	Velardo Jennie—†	323	stitcher	20	"
	P	Velardo Joseph	323	laborer	26	
	R*	Velardo Mary—†	323	housewife	49	"
		McKay Place				
	S*	Messini Antonetta—†	9	housewife	70	here
	T	Messini Eleanor—†	9	clerk	34	"
	U	Glasso Florence—†	9	housewife	27	118 Lubec
	V	Glasso Joseph	9	laborer	29	118 "
	W	Kenneally Anna—†	9	housewife	30	here
	X	Kenneally James	9	laborer	32	"
	Y*	Cerio Giulio	9	barber	70	"
	Z	Cerio Modestina—†	9	housewife	65	"
1616						
	A	Zicconi Grace—†	9	"	23	
	B	Zicconi James	9	laborer	27	
		Porter Street				
	C	DeAngelis Angelina—†	191	operator	27	here
	D*	DeAngelis Carmella—†	191	housewife	60	"
	E*	DeAngelis Domenic	191	retired	67	"
	F	DeAngelis Filomena—†	191	operator	26	"
	G	DeAngelis Helen—†	191	at home	22	
	H	DeAngelis Michael	191	cutter	20	
	K*	Gardina Biagio	191	laborer	56	
	L*	Gardina Salvatore	191	upholsterer	24	"
	M	Lanzilli Irene L—†	191	housewife	30	"
	N	Lanzilli Nicholas	191	chauffeur	30	"
	O*	Antonioli Elizabeth—†	191	housewife	28	"
	P*	Antonioli James	191	laborer	36	
	R	Pisani Antonio	191	"	55	
	S	Pisani Michael A	191	"	21	
	T	Pisani Virginia—†	191	housewife	51	"
	U	Gerolamo Antonio	191	laborer	45	
	V	Gerolamo Assunta—†	191	housewife	38	"

Page.	Letter.	Full Name.	Residence, Jan. 1, 1938.	Occupation.	Supposed Age.	Reported Residence, Jan. 1, 1937. Street and Number.

Sumner Street

Page.	Letter.	Full Name.	Residence, Jan. 1, 1938.	Occupation.	Supposed Age.	Reported Residence, Jan. 1, 1937. Street and Number.
	W	Corso Florence—†	344	housewife	23	146 Webster
	X	Corso Frank	344	chauffeur	29	146 "
	Y	Scorziello Pasquale	344	butcher	22	here
	Z	Federico Mary—†	346	housewife	29	"
1617						
	A	Federico William R	346	tailor	27	
	B	Capone Ida—†	346	housewife	44	"
	C	Capone Inez M—†	346	at home	20	
	D	Capone John A	346	operator	21	"
	E	Capone Pasquale	346	merchant	49	"
	F	Capone Viga—†	346	operator	22	"
	K	*Gulinello Josephine—†	348	housewife	54	"
	L	*Gulinello Salvatore	348	laborer	59	
	M	*Yebba Mary—†	348	housewife	42	"
	N	Yebba Nicholas	348	laborer	47	
	O	*Yebba Tillie—†	348	at home	21	
	P	Delligato Jeremiah	348	laborer	29	
	R	Delligato Mary—†	348	housewife	23	"
	S	*Cuozzo Antonio	350	laborer	54	
	T	Cuozzo Geno	350	machinist	27	"
	U	Picardi Filomena—†	350	housewife	24	Lexington
	V	Picardi Louis	350	laundryman	24	here
	W	*Picardi Amato	350	laborer	50	"
	X	*Picardi Sophia—†	350	housewife	48	"
	Y	*Magliano Josephine—†	352	"	48	
	Z	Magliano Pasquale	352	salesman	57	"
1618						
	A	Magliano Rose—†	352	at home	29	"
	B	Scrima Adele—†	352	housewife	27	108 Webster
	C	Scrima John	352	chauffeur	27	108 "
	D	Manzoni Leonardi	354	laborer	63	here
	E	*Manzoni Vincenza—†	354	housewife	55	"
	F	*Iarocci Carmella—†	354	"	55	"
	G	Iarocci Michael	354	laborer	50	"
	K	Griecco Carmella—†	356	housewife	30	Chelsea
	L	Griecco Salvatore	356	dealer	41	"
	M	*Cecca Carmella—†	358	housewife	41	here
	N	Cecca Enrico	358	laborer	44	"
	P	*Colarusso Joseph	362	"	59	"
	R	Colarusso Patrick J	362	"	24	
	S	Colarusso Ralph	362	chauffeur	22	"

Page.	Letter.	Full Name.	Residence, Jan. 1, 1938.	Occupation.	Supposed Age.	Reported Residence, Jan. 1, 1937. Street and Number.

Sumner Street—Continued

Page.	Letter.	Full Name.	Residence, Jan. 1, 1938.	Occupation.	Supposed Age.	Reported Residence, Jan. 1, 1937. Street and Number.
	T	*DeFlumeri Elizabeth—†	364	housewife	47	15 Lamson ct
	U	DeFlumeri Jeremiah	364	laborer	47	15 "
	W	*DeNapoli Enrico	366	storekeeper	64	here
	X	Maratta Louis	366	clerk	30	Winthrop
	Z	*Moraes Antonio	368	seaman	43	here
1619						
	A	*Rose Domingo	368	"	37	New York
	B	Corsano Marie E—†	368	housewife	24	142 Gove
	C	Corsano Walter A	368	engineer	28	142 "
	E	DiFronzo Biagio	368	operator	29	here
	F	DiFronzo Nicolena—†	368	housewife	27	"
	G	Grella Alfred A	368	printer	24	"
	H	*Grella Carmella—†	368	housewife	53	"
	K	Grella Edmund J	368	engineer	28	
	L	Grella Esther—†	368	at home	22	"
	M	Marotta Lillian—†	368	bookkeeper	33	Winthrop
	N	Marotta Milenda—†	368	stitcher	28	"
	O	Amabile John	368	laborer	29	here
	P	Amabile Josephine—†	368	housewife	28	"
	R	Piro John	368	laborer	38	New York
	S	Piro Josephine—†	368	housewife	35	"
	T	Bradley Laura A—†	368	"	28	45 Maverick
	U	Bradley Roger W	368	laborer	22	18 Paris
	V	*Morelli Andrina—†	368	housewife	44	here
	W	Morelli Ubaldo	368	mechanic	44	"
	X	Cullen Anna—†	370	housewife	45	"
	Y	Cullen John E	370	fireman	33	
	Z	Hetorella Elizabeth M—†	370	housewife	22	"
1620						
	A	Addivinola Rose—†	370	at home	26	166 Cottage
	B	*Cretara Anthony	370	busboy	34	166 "
	C	Cretara Carmella—†	370	housewife	30	166 "
	D	Trunfio Corrina—†	372	"	44	here
	E	Trunfio Pasquale	372	barber	48	"
	F	Trunfio Paul	372	"	22	"
	G	Russo John	372	chauffeur	25	"
	H	Russo Rose—†	372	housewife	25	"
	K	DiFilippo Florence—†	372	"	30	"
	L	DiFilippo James	372	clerk	32	"
	M	Walsh Margaret M—†	376	housewife	58	33 Eutaw
	N	Walsh Patrick T	376	laborer	64	33 "

Page.	Letter.	Full Name.	Residence, Jan. 1, 1938.	Occupation.	Supposed Age.	Reported Residence, Jan. 1, 1937. Street and Number.

Sumner Street—Continued

	O	Giglio Antonio	376	engineer	50	here
	P	*Giglio Pompilia—†	376	housewife	46	"
	R	*Zirpolo Angelo	rear 376	operator	49	"
	S	Zirpolo Elizabeth—†	" 376	housewife	42	"
	T	Seminelli Madeline-†	" 376	"	40	N Saugus
	U	Seminelli Samuel	" 376	shoemaker	39	"
	V	*Sartori Adeline—†	" 376	housewife	60	350 Sumner
	W	Sartori John	" 376	laborer	34	350 "
	X	Sartori Joseph	" 376	longshoreman	30	350 "
	Y	Scopa Domenic	" 376	laborer	26	here
	Z	Scopa Louise—†	" 376	housewife	27	"
1621						
	A	Para Andrew	" 376	engineer	41	
	B	*Para Caroline—†	" 376	housewife	68	"
	C	*Para Gaetano	" 376	retired	76	
	D	Para Louis	" 376	fireman	45	
	E	Tamburrino Edith—†	" 376	housewife	24	"
	F	Tamburrino John	" 376	laborer	25	"
	G	Small Annie M—†	378	housewife	52	153 Everett
	H	Small Dorothea L—†	378	stenographer	20	153 "
	K	Marino Angelina—†	378	housewife	27	here
	L	Marino Salvatore	378	fisherman	29	"
	N	Blackburn Ella L—†	380	matron	60	"
	O	O'Neil Annie M—†	382	housewife	70	"
	P	O'Neil Grace M—†	382	at home	52	
	R	Walsh Josephine—†	382	housewife	38	"
	S	Walsh Richard	382	longshoreman	45	"
	U	Blanchard Harriet B—†	406	housewife	27	"
	V	Blanchard Wendell C	406	laborer	29	"
	W	Woodside Dudley A	406	"	24	504 Sumner
	X	Covalucci Alberta K—†	406	housewife	28	here
	Y	Covalucci Mario T	406	laborer	30	"
	Z	Casey Gerard J	408	engineer	23	"
1622						
	A	Casey Helen B—†	408	housewife	53	"
	B	Casey Jeremiah P	408	engineer	57	
	C	Collotta Catherine—†	410	housewife	47	"
	D	Collotta Orazio	410	painter	25	
	E	Collotta Rosario	410	barber	22	"
	F	Clemente Louis	410	laborer	23	41 Cottage
	G	Clemente Martha—†	410	housewife	25	41 "

Page.	Letter.	Full Name.	Residence, Jan. 1, 1938.	Occupation.	Supposed Age.	Reported Residence, Jan. 1, 1937. Street and Number.

Sumner Street—Continued

	H	Lewis Edith I—†	412	housewife	29	here
	K	Lewis John G	412	laborer	29	"
	L	Grasso Alfred	412	shoemaker	29	"
	M	Grasso Armando	412	clerk	22	
	N	Iannore Alfred	412	shoemaker	54	"
	O	Bolino Anthony	412	laborer	31	
	P	Bolino Vera—†	412	housewife	29	"
	R	Cassetina Alfred	414	clerk	28	
	S	Cassetina Rose—†	414	housewife	23	"
	T	*Milo Lena—†	414	"	32	
	U	Milo Leo	414	barber	37	
	V	Bibo Ida—†	414	operator	20	"
	W	Bibo John	414	laborer	58	
	X	Ahern Bridget—†	418	housewife	78	"
	Y	Ahern Daniel P	418	operator	37	"
	Z	Ahern James H	418	laborer	43	
1623						
	A	Ahern Joseph B	418	clerk	33	
	B	Ahern Nora C—†	418	housewife	47	"
	C	Ahern Theresa A—†	418	clerk	39	
	D	Nee Anna E—†	420	housewife	46	"
	E	Nee Thomas	420	laborer	47	
	F	Brophy Caroline—†	420	clerk	36	
	G	Brophy Mary V—†	420	"	38	
	H	Kelley John	420	"	66	
	K	Cassley Arthur	422	retired	67	
	L	Gillespie Catherine E—†	422	housewife	78	"
	M	Gillespie Frederick J	422	electrician	48	"
	N	Griffin Clara—†	422	at home	49	
	O	Curran Bridget—†	442	housekeeper	45	"
	P	Morgan Anna—†	442	at home	47	40 Falcon
	R	Staff Gertrude—†	442	housewife	31	40 "
	S	Staff John	442	chauffeur	32	40 "
	T	Jenkins Charles J	442	laborer	55	here
	U	Jenkins Elizabeth—†	442	housewife	49	"
	V	Jenkins John S	442	laborer	41	"
	W	Jenkins Mary—†	442	operator	52	"
	X	Welsh Charles	444	laborer	44	
	Y	Welsh John	444	"	42	

Page.	Letter.	FULL NAME.	Residence, Jan. 1, 1938.	Occupation.	Supposed Age.	Reported Residence, Jan. 1, 1937. Street and Number.
		Sumner Street—Continued				
	z	Hearn Annie—†	444	housewife	58	here
1624						
	A	Hearn William H	444	secretary	42	"
		Venice Street				
	c	*Verderico Anna—†	1	housewife	55	here
	D	Verderico George	1	laborer	23	"
	E	Verderico Theresa—†	1	housewife	23	"
	F	Miller Richard	2	mechanic	61	"

Ward 1—Precinct 21

CITY OF BOSTON

LIST OF RESIDENTS
20 YEARS OF AGE AND OVER

(NON-CITIZENS INDICATED BY ASTERISK)
(FEMALES INDICATED BY DAGGER)

AS OF

JANUARY 1, 1938

JOSEPH F. TIMILTY, } Listing
FREDERIC E. DOWLING, } Board.

CITY OF BOSTON PRINTING DEPARTMENT

Page.	Letter.	Full Name.	Residence, Jan. 1, 1938.	Occupation.	Supposed Age.	Reported Residence, Jan. 1, 1937. Street and Number.
1632		**Bremen Street**				
	A	Margiotti Anthony	100	retired	70	249 Maverick
	B	Rizzo Joseph	100	laborer	34	here
	C	Flodin Anna—†	101	at home	70	13 Emmons
	D	Flodin Carl	102	machinist	50	13 "
	E	Iavicoli George	102	musician	28	here
	F	Iavicoli Rose—†	102	housewife	22	"
	G	Ferrera Anna—†	102	"	38	"
	H	Ferrera Louis	102	roofer	40	
	K	*Tunnera Angelo	104	laborer	40	
	L	*Tunnera Jennie—†	104	housewife	40	"
	M	Cogliano Jerry	104	retired	60	
	N	Cogliano Rita—†	104	housewife	48	"
	O	*Iasonna Antoinette—†	104	"	62	
	P	*Iasonna Charles	104	laborer	30	
	R	*Iasonna Salvatore	104	painter	38	"
	S	Ricupero Alphonso	106	clerk	21	202 Paris
	T	Ricupero Henry	106	pipefitter	32	202 "
	U	*Ricupero Leonilda—†	106	housewfie	45	202 "
	V	Ricupero Angelo	106	barber	35	34 Frankfort
	W	Ricupero Barbara—†	106	housewife	34	34 "
	X	Ricupero Armand	106	attorney	28	here
	Y	Ricupero Catherine—†	106	housewife	25	"
	Z	*Sepe Carmella—†	108	"	65	"
1633						
	A	Sepe Pasquale	108	laborer	70	"
	B	*Maratia Elizabeth—†	108	housewife	44	110 Bremen
	C	*Maratia Giocomo	108	laborer	45	110 "
	D	Maratia Vincenzo	108	candymaker	21	110 "
	E	Arone Angelina—†	108	housewife	46	here
	F	Arone Joseph	108	laborer	21	"
	G	Arone Lawrence	108	"	48	"
	H	Fradau Christopher	110	oiler	52	
	K	Stella Charles	110	laborer	55	
	L	Stella John	110	chauffeur	25	"
	M	Stella Mary—†	110	housewife	57	"
	N	Stella Mary—†	110	at home	21	"
	O	Guinea Dolores—†	110	"	26	49 River
	P	Aleo Anna—†	112	housewife	21	here
	R	Aleo Salvatore	112	cabinetmaker	23	"
	S	Moreno Andrew	112	carpenter	38	257 Chelsea

Page.	Letter.	FULL NAME.	Residence, Jan. 1, 1938.	Occupation.	Supposed Age.	Reported Residence, Jan. 1, 1937. Street and Number.

Bremen Street—Continued

Page.	Letter.	FULL NAME.	Residence, Jan. 1, 1938.	Occupation.	Supposed Age.	Reported Residence, Jan. 1, 1937. Street and Number.
	T	Moreno Mary—†	112	housewife	33	257 Chelsea
	U	Mede Angelina—†	112	waitress	35	here
	V	Braccia Alfred	114	laborer	27	"
	W	Braccia Josephine—†	114	housewife	23	"
	X	Martinello Edith—†	114	"	32	
	Y	Martinello James	114	chauffeur	34	"
	Z	Grillo Angela—†	114	housewife	50	"
1634						
	A	Grillo Angelina—†	114	packer	22	
	B	Grillo Frank	114	laborer	54	
	C	Nigro Donato	116	candymaker	42	"
	D	Nigro Mary—†	116	housewife	45	"
	E	Inotte Nicola	116	retired	74	
	F	Inotte Pasqualina—†	116	housewife	64	"
	G	Mede Louis	116	bartender	34	"
	H	Capozzi Alphonso	116	laborer	42	
	K	Capozzi Rose—†	116	housewife	40	"
	L	Cicatelli Joseph	118	laborer	53	
	M	Cicatelli Rose—†	118	housewife	50	"
	N	Cicatelli Louise—†	118	at home	21	
	O	Cicatelli Rosario	118	laborer	61	
	P	*Langone Antonetta—†	118	housewife	72	"
	R	Langone Joseph	118	laborer	24	
	S	Langone Michael	118	"	26	
	T	*Langone Stephen	118	"	63	
	U	Mainiero Alice—†	120	housewife	28	"
	V	Mainiero Fred	120	painter	31	
	W	Mainiero Arthur	120	waiter	22	
	X	Mainiero Frank	120	retired	60	
	Y	Mainiero Netta—†	120	at home	24	
	Z	Mainiero Marion—†	120	housewife	35	"
1635						
	A	Mainiero Phillip	120	salesman	37	"
	C	Brogna Amelia—†	122	housewife	22	82 Bremen
	D	Brogna Joseph	122	laborer	24	82 "
	E	Caruso Saverio	122	"	49	184 Marginal
	G	Reggiona Antonette—†	124	tailoress	35	here
	H	Reggiona Domenic	124	barber	37	"
	K	DelGrosso Pasquale	124	chauffeur	39	"
	L	DelGrosso Pasqualina—†	124	housewife	33	"
	M	Pecorella Frances—†	124	"	43	

Page.	Letter.	Full Name.	Residence, Jan. 1, 1938.	Occupation.	Supposed Age.	Reported Residence, Jan. 1, 1937. Street and Number.

Bremen Street—Continued

	N	Pecorella Gaspara	124	chauffeur	47	here
	O	Aleo Joseph	126	barber	43	"
	P	Aleo Joseph, jr	126	laborer	20	"
	R	*Aleo Josephine—†	126	housewife	43	"
	S	*Lamborghini Adeline—†	126	"	51	
	T	Lamborghini Andrew	126	operator	21	
	U	Lamborghini Flavio	126	merchant	56	"
	V	*Pauletti Adeline—†	126	housewife	46	"
	W	Pauletti Amelia—†	126	at home	20	
	X	*Pauletti Antonio	126	mason	48	
	Y	DiPasquale Angelo	128	tailor	25	
	Z	DiPasquale Rosalie—†	128	housewife	26	"
1636						
	A	DeBlasio Catherine—†	128	"	41	
	B	DeBlasio Michael	128	laborer	41	
	C	*Fiore Antonio	128	"	43	
	D	*Fiore Lena—†	128	housewife	35	"
	E	Ciampi Armando	130	coppersmith	26	"
	F	Ciampi Bonifaci	130	"	22	
	G	Ciampi Ersilia—†	130	clerk	28	
	H	Ciampi Patrick	130	laborer	24	
	K	DePaulo Anna—†	130	housewife	26	"
	L	DePaulo Louis	130	presser	30	
	M	Popolo Helen—†	130	ar home	20	
	K	Popolo Joseph	130	laborer	52	
	O	*Popolo Marie—†	130	housewife	52	"
	P	*Leone Emily—†	132	"	55	"
	R	*Scimone James	132	musician	28	198 Chelsea
	S	*Scimone Mary—†	132	housewife	28	198 "
	T	Cerere Antonio	132	laborer	53	here
	U	*Cerere Elizabeth—†	132	housewife	58	"
	V	Cerere Florence—†	132	at home	22	"
	W	Cerere Sarah—†	132	"	20	
	X	Aiello Concetta—†	136	housewife	31	"
	Y	Aiello Joseph	136	laborer	33	
	Z	*Gionsiracusa Anna—†	136	housewife	46	"
1637						
	A	Gionsiracusa Nelson	136	tinsmith	24	"
	B	Gionsiracusa Paul	136	mason	44	"
	C	Gionsiracusa Frank	136	"	27	"
	D	Gionsiracusa Mary—†	136	housewife	27	"

Page.	Letter.	Full Name.	Residence, Jan. 1, 1938.	Occupation.	Supposed Age.	Reported Residence, Jan. 1, 1937. Street and Number.

Bremen Street—Continued

	E	Petrillo Anna—†	138	at home	21	here
	F	*Petrillo Rosie—†	138	housewife	44	"
	G	*Petrillo Samuel	138	operator	44	"
	H	Malta Lawrence, jr	140	carpenter	27	"
	K	Malta Mary—†	140	housewife	30	"
	L	Nocito Pauline—†	140	"	26	
	M	Nocito Vincent	140	laborer	24	
	N	Colucci Ralph	140	"	33	
	O	Colucci Theresa—†	140	housewife	34	"
	P	Spelladora John	140	shoemaker	35	"
	R	*Testa Antoinetta—†	142	housewife	55	"
	S	*Testa Constantino	142	laborer	55	
	T	Testa Gabriel	142	mechanic	30	"
	U	Testa Rose—†	142	at home	21	
	V	Testa Violet—†	142	stitcher	22	
	W	Trinchitella Alfred	144	laborer	38	
	X	*DeStefano Theresa—†	144	candymaker	42	"
	Z	Reo Filomena—†	146	housewife	22	"
1638						
	A	Reo Samuel	146	laborer	25	
	B	*Tracia Louise—†	146	housewife	54	"
	C	Conte Paul	146	laborer	33	
	D	Conte Rose—†	146	housewife	29	"
	E	*Seracusa Anthony	146	laborer	43	106 Bremen
	F	*Seracusa Joseph	146	packer	24	106 "
	G	*Seracusa Josephine—†	146	housewife	41	106 "
	H	*Brangiforte Filippa—†	148	"	25	here
	K	*Brangiforte Phillip	148	laborer	37	"
	L	Mortorana Antonetta—†	148	housewife	42	"
	M	Martorana Gaetano	148	operator	20	"
	N	Martorana Joseph	148	laborer	48	
	O	Martorana Mary—†	148	at home	23	
	P	DeLare Gaetano	148	laborer	48	
	R	DeLare Josephine—†	148	housewife	40	"
	S	Vetrano Dominic	150	shoemaker	29	"
	T	*Vetrano Gasper	150	retired	71	"
	U	Privite Antonio	150	laborer	48	198 Bremen
	V	*Privite Sarah—†	150	housewife	42	198 "
	W	Grimaldi Joseph	150	laborer	47	here
	X	*Grimaldi Mary—†	150	housewife	46	"
	Y	Grimaldi Vito	150	operator	21	"

Page.	Letter.	Full Name.	Residence, Jan. 1, 1938.	Occupation.	Supposed Age.	Reported Residence, Jan. 1, 1937. Street and Number.

Bremen Street—Continued

	z	*Rossi Armonda	152	chef	32	here
1639						
	A	Rossi Carmelinda—†	152	housewife	29	"
	B	*Carabes Antonetta—†	152	"	42	
	C	Carabes Carmen	152	laborer	42	
	D	Minechello Rocco	152	"	26	
	E	Storella Alfonso	152	shoemaker	41	"
	F	*Storella Tomisina—†	152	housewife	35	"
	G	Filadoro Louis	154	fireman	29	
	H	Filadoro Rose—†	154	housewife	29	"
	K	Votta Louis	154	laborer	23	
	L	*Votta Luigi	154	retired	65	
	M	Votta Michael	154	laborer	20	
	N	*Votta Theresa—†	154	housewife	62	"
	O	Albanese Josephine—†	156	"	24	"
	P	Albanese Louis	156	shoeworker	25	"
	R	*Ialuna Josephine—†	156	housewife	51	"
	S	Ialuna Nazareno	156	laborer	51	"
	T	*Malta Joseph	156	retired	63	"
	U	Mairtino Anna—†	158	housekeeper	42	315 Sumner
	V	Mairtino Paul	158	retired	77	315 "
	W	*Stella Anna—†	158	housewife	27	here
	X	Stella Joseph	158	laborer	32	"
	Y	Scarpa Frank	158	wrestler	21	185 Paris
	Z	Scarpa Lillian—†	158	housewife	20	58 Saratoga
1640						
	A	Lunetta Martina—†	160	"	24	here
	B	Lunetta Stephen	160	salesman	31	"
	C	Rizzari Nicholas	160	laborer	40	"
	D	*Rizzari Nora—†	160	housewife	35	"
	E	*Brunacci Placido	160	laborer	53	"
	F	*Iorio Anna—†	162	housewife	71	72 Franklin
	G	*Iorio Antonio	162	retired	72	72 "
	H	DeFronzo Anna—†	162	housewife	30	here
	K	DeFronzo Sanerio	162	laborer	28	"
	L	*Recupero Joseph	162	"	42	"
	O	Maguire Andrew	174	laundryman	27	"
	P	*Maguire Delphina—†	174	housewife	24	"
	R	Bordanaro Lena—†	174	candymaker	23	326 Bremen
	S	*Bordanaro Phillip	174	laborer	54	326 "
	T	*Bordanaro Rose—†	174	housewife	54	326 "

Page.	Letter.	Full Name.	Residence, Jan. 1, 1938.	Occupation.	Supposed Age.	Reported Residence, Jan. 1, 1937. Street and Number.

Bremen Street—Continued

	U	*Federico Esther—†	174	housewife	30	here
	V	*Federico Joseph	174	painter	28	"
	X	Guardabassio John	190	laborer	26	"
	Y	Guardabassio Joseph	190	printer	23	
	Z	*Nutaro Concetta—†	190	housekeeper	54	"
1641						
	A	*Menegucci Louis	190	laborer	30	
	B	Menegucci Marion—†	190	housewife	27	"
	C	*Riccio Alberta—†	190	"	36	
	D	Riccio Frank	190	laborer	45	
	E	Casaletto Augustino	192	"	23	
	F	Palermo Aggrippino	192	finisher	26	
	G	Palermo Santina—†	192	housewife	26	"
	H	Lepore John P	192	laborer	21	179 Marion
	K	Lepore Viola—†	192	housewife	20	179 "
	L	Cianciarulo Anthony	194	tailor	52	here
	M	Cianciarulo Elizabeth—†	194	tailoress	23	"
	N	Cianciarulo Gabriella—†	194	housewife	50	"
	O	Cianaiarulo Helen—†	194	tailoress	21	
	P	Cianciarulo Mary—†	194	"	24	
	R	Carco Constantino	194	laborer	40	
	S	Carco Francisco	194	shoemaker	37	"
	T	Carco Mary—†	194	housewife	31	"
	U	Fucillo Angelo	194	shipper	22	
	V	Fucillo Henry	194	chauffeur	44	"
	W	Fucillo Nancy—†	194	housewife	40	"
	X	Fucillo Vincent	194	laborer	20	
	Y	Pascucci Anthony	196	operator	28	
	Z	Pascucci Frances—†	196	housekeeper	62	"
1642						
	A	Pascucci Matilda—†	196	housewife	21	359 Princeton
	B	*Margarone Mary—†	196	"	42	here
	C	*Margarone Peter	196	candymaker	40	"
	D	*Margarone Rita—†	196	housekeeper	64	"
	E	*Palermo Antonetta—†	196	housewife	48	"
	F	Palermo John	196	foreman	52	
	G	Ciaburri Elizabeth—†	198	housewife	33	"
	H	Ciaburri Joseph	198	butcher	43	"
	K	*Bozzi Adeline—†	198	housewife	46	179 Princeton
	L	*Bozzi Louis	198	tailor	49	179 "
	M	Giannasoli Andrew	198	laborer	47	here

Page.	Letter.	Full Name.	Residence, Jan. 1, 1938.	Occupation.	Supposed Age.	Reported Residence, Jan. 1, 1937. Street and Number.

Bremen Street—Continued

	N	Giannasoli Lena—†	198	presser	23	here
	O	*Giannasoli Lucy—†	198	housewife	45	"
	P	Palermo Carmella—†	200	"	27	"
	R	Palermo Ignazio	200	tinsmith	24	
	S	Argenzio Amelia—†	200	housewife	63	"
	T	Argenzio Carmella M—†	200	"	30	
	U	Argenzio Joseph N	200	shoeworker	33	"
	V	Argenzio Louis	200	retired	76	
	W	LaCava Angelo	200	laborer	21	
	X	*LaCava Domenic	200	"	42	
	Y	LaCava Marion—†	200	at home	20	
	Z	*LaCava Mary—†	200	housewife	44	"
1643						
	A	*Faragia Agatina—†	202	housekeeper	67	"
	B	Abisso Agatina—†	202	seamstress	21	"
	C	*Abisso Croceffisso—†	202	housewife	45	"
	D	Abisso Salvatore	202	laborer	53	
	E	Peterson Albert E	202	clerk	32	
	F	Peterson Ruth—†	202	housewife	30	"
	H	Correale Esther—†	204	"	26	
	K	Correale James	204	laborer	28	"
	L	Campochiaro Charles	204	"	27	196 Chelsea
	M	*Campochiaro Croceffisso—†	204	housewife	53	196 "
	N	Campochiaro Guy	204	shoeworker	25	196 "
	O	*Campochiaro Joseph	204	laborer	56	196 "
	P	DiArcangelis Anna—†	204	housewife	47	here
	R	DiArcangelis Joseph	204	tailor	53	"
	S	*Anastasio Salvatore	206	merchant	61	"
	T	Palermo Frank	206	painter	24	328 Meridian
	U	Palermo Mildred—†	206	housewife	22	41 Saratoga
	V	Matera James	208	engineer	25	here
	W	Matera Mario	208	superintendent	21	"
	X	Matera Antonio	208	tailor	54	"
	Y	Matera Beatrice—†	208	housewife	60	"
	Z	Matera Francis	208	engineer	24	
1644						
	A	Lamborghini Dorothy—†	208	housewife	27	"
	B	Lamborghini Frank	208	clerk	27	
	C	Maccia John	210	cabinetmaker	26	"
	D	Rotigliano Lucy—†	210	housewife	29	"

Page.	Letter.	Full Name.	Residence, Jan. 1, 1938.	Occupation.	Supposed Age.	Reported Residence, Jan. 1, 1937. Street and Number.

Bremen Street—Continued

Page.	Letter.	Full Name.	Residence, Jan. 1, 1938.	Occupation.	Supposed Age.	Reported Residence, Jan. 1, 1937. Street and Number.
	E	Rotigliano Pasquale	210	upholsterer	36	here
	F	Ciampa Frank	210	chauffeur	42	"
	G	Ciampa Mary—†	210	housewife	42	"
	H	Guarino Joseph	210	laborer	45	
	K	Guarino Mary—†	210	housewife	34	"
	L	*Calvano Antoinette—†	212	at home	50	
	M	Calvano Thomas	212	laborer	43	
	N	*DeMarino Antonetta—†	212	housewife	37	"
	O	*DeMarino Antonio	212	laborer	49	
	P	*Ortolano Anna—†	212	housewife	41	"
	R	Ortolano Peter	212	baker	42	"
	S	*Cimmion Antonetta—†	214	housewife	61	224 Chelsea
	T	Cimmion Caroline—†	214	stitcher	22	224 "
	U	*Cimmion Samuel	214	mason	53	224 "
	V	Lasofsky Bronislaus	214	fireman	25	here
	W	Lasofsky Margaret P—†	214	housewife	24	"
	X	*Lasofsky Melvina—†	214	"	53	"
	Y	*Lasofsky Michael	214	laborer	55	
	Z	Mazzariello Joseph	216	merchant	48	"
1645						
	A	Mazzariello Mary—†	216	housewife	48	"
	B	Cutrone Jennie—†	216	"	27	
	C	Cutrone Peter	216	candymaker	32	"
	D	*Miniscalco Amelia—†	216	housewife	48	"
	E	Miniscalco Bruno	216	laborer	21	
	F	Miniscalco Joseph	216	carpenter	53	"
	G	Aloise Catherine—†	218	housewife	28	"
	H	Aloise Frank	218	laborer	28	
	K	*Lauria Concetta—†	218	housewife	64	"
	L	Lauria Joseph	218	chauffeur	26	"
	M	*Lauria Vincenzo	218	laborer	62	
	N	Domasco Celia—†	218	housewife	43	"
	O	Domasco Nicola	218	laborer	52	
	P	Campagna Edith—†	220	housewife	33	"
	R	Campagna Napoleon	220	painter	36	
	S	*Powers Anastasia—†	220	housewife	45	"
	T	Powers Ann—†	220	at home	21	
	U	*Powers Benjamin	220	laborer	55	
	V	Powers George R	220	clerk	53	
	W	Powers William H	220	inspector	50	"

Page.	Letter.	Full Name.	Residence, Jan. 1, 1938.	Occupation.	Supposed Age.	Reported Residence, Jan. 1, 1937. Street and Number.

Chelsea Street

Page.	Letter.	Full Name.	Residence, Jan. 1, 1938.	Occupation.	Supposed Age.	Reported Residence, Jan. 1, 1937. Street and Number.
	Y	Barbaro Salvatore	55	laborer	35	50 Chelsea
	Z	Maragioglio Baldassaro	55	merchant	40	50 "
1646						
	A	Maragioglio Josephine—†	55	housewife	35	50 "
	B	*DeVincenzo Diana—†	55	"	49	42 Cottage
	C	*DeVincenzo Thomas	55	laborer	49	42 "
	D	Turieri Angelo	57	"	42	63 Gove
	E	Turieri Mary—†	57	housewife	41	63 "
	F	Bell George	57	merchant	24	78 Paris
	G	*DiFranzio Otino	57	laborer	47	78 "
	H	DiFranzio Theresa—†	57	housewife	54	78 "
	K	*Leto Biagia—†	57	"	57	150 Bremen
	L	Leto Vincent	57	laborer	20	150 "
	M	*Singal James	57	retired	60	150 "
	N	Russo Charles	59	laborer	30	294 Sumner
	O	Russo Mary—†	59	housewife	28	here
	P	Tary Anthony	59	laborer	37	"
	R	*Tary Mary—†	59	housewife	33	"
	S	Macaluso Joseph	59	laborer	35	"
	T	*Macaluso Rosario	59	carpenter	45	"
	U	*Macaluso Salvatore	59	retired	80	"
	V	*Macaluso Tina—†	59	housewife	75	"
	W	DiRosa Angelina—†	61	"	28	112 Webster
	X	*DiRosa Dominic	61	laborer	29	112 "
	Y	Tassinari Edna A—†	61	packer	25	here
	Z	Tassinari Elizabeth—†	61	housewife	54	"
1647						
	A	Tassinari Mary L—†	61	stenographer	29	"
	B	Testa Vincent D	61	laborer	61	"
	C	Boitano Loretta—†	63	clerk	42	"
	D	Boitano Robert	63	merchant	42	"
	E	*Brambilla Andrew	63	retired	71	"
	F	Brambilla George	63	policeman	36	"
	G	Brambilla Gladys—†	63	housewife	31	Lynn
	H	Petrillo Concetta—†	65	"	51	here
	K	Petrillo Gaetano	65	barber	33	"
	L	Petrillo Grace—†	65	operator	21	"
	M	Petrillo Palmerino	65	retired	62	"
	N	Petrillo Palmerino, jr	65	timekeeper	24	"
	O	Maffeo Anna C—†	65	operator	31	"
	P	*Maffeo Marion —†	65	housewife	60	"

Page.	Letter.	Full Name.	Residence, Jan. 1, 1938.	Occupation.	Supposed Age.	Reported Residence, Jan. 1, 1937. Street and Number.

Chelsea Street—Continued

Page.	Letter.	Full Name.	Residence, Jan. 1, 1938.	Occupation.	Supposed Age.	Reported Residence, Jan. 1, 1937. Street and Number.
	R	Maffeo Pietro A	65	laborer	61	here
	S	Langiano Caroline—†	65	packer	29	"
	T	*Langiano Pasquale	65	candymaker	62	"
	U	Langiano Rose—†	65	operator	28	"
	V	*Langiano Thomasina—†	65	housewife	53	"
	X	Ragusa Anthony	67	shoemaker	55	"
	Y	Ragusa Gabriel	67	laborer	21	
	Z	Iannuzzi John	67	"	41	
1648						
	A	*Iannuzzi Mary—†	67	housewife	30	"
	B	Euchiello Donato	67	laborer	52	
	C	Euchiello Filomena—†	67	housewife	32	"
	E	Attiliana Julia—†	69	stitcher	20	
	F	*Attiliana Peter	69	laborer	52	"
	G	Mustone Christy	69	"	40	102 Bremen
	H	*Sorendino Carmella—†	69	housewife	56	102 "
	K	Sorendino Joseph	69	laborer	23	102 "
	L	*Sorendino Leonardo	69	"	54	102 "
	M	Sorendino Pasquale	69	clerk	21	102 "
	N	Aiello Carmella—†	69	housewife	42	here
	O	Aiello Ignazio	69	pressman	43	"
	P	Mandarano Frank	71	laborer	36	75 Lubec
	R	Mandarano Susan—†	71	housewife	27	75 "
	S	*George Ralph	71	retired	65	here
	T	*Mustone Mary—†	71	housewife	56	"
	U	*Mustone Vincent	71	laborer	58	"
	V	Accomando Gaetano	71	shoeworker	41	"
	W	*Accomando Lucy—†	71	housewife	39	"
	Y	*Todaro Lucy—†	73	"	27	
	Z	Todaro Philip	73	laborer	35	
1649						
	A	Blangiari Agrippino	73	"	41	23 Fleet
	B	*Blangiari Grace—†	73	housewife	36	23 "
	C	*DeFrancisco Eugene	73	clerk	29	here
	D	DeFrancisco Joseph	73	laborer	56	"
	E	*DeFrancisco Theresa—†	73	housewife	49	"
	F	Iorio Frances—†	75	"	38	207 Chelsea
	G	Iorio Luciano	75	barber	43	207 "
	H	*Defeo Dominic	75	laborer	54	here
	K	Martinello Francisco S	75	"	43	"
	L	*Martinello Josephine—†	75	housewife	39	"

Page.	Letter.	Full Name.	Residence, Jan. 1, 1938.	Occupation.	Supposed Age.	Reported Residence, Jan. 1, 1937. Street and Number.

Chelsea Street—Continued

	M	Ranelli Antonetta—†	75	packer	24	here
	N	*Ranelli Eliza—†	75	housewife	52	"
	O	Ranello Enrico	75	molder	56	"
	P	*Lucca Ida—†	77	housewife	53	"
	R	*Lucca Mario	77	baker	52	
	S	*Lucca Samuel	77	"	24	
	T	*Simione Anna—†	77	housewife	25	"
	U	Simione Louis	77	packer	26	"
	V	*Groce Dominic	79	merchant	46	"
	W	*Philip Frank	79	laborer	43	
	X	*Philip Mary—†	79	housewife	40	"
	Y	Ciriello Leonard	81	plumber	22	
	Z	*Ciriello Michael	81	retired	59	
1650						
	A	Ciriello Sadie—†	81	housewife	28	"
	B	Gioreani Leo	81	pipefitter	29	"
	C	Gioreani Mary—†	81	housewife	24	"
	D	*Tacelli Sue—†	83	"	39	
	E	Tacelli Vincent	83	shoeworker	41	"
	F	Zito Antoinette—†	83	beautician	21	"
	G	Zito Emily—†	83	housewife	43	"
	H	Zito Enis—†	83	beautician	22	"
	K	Zito Marie—†	83	"	25	
	L	Zito Vincent	83	contractor	46	"
	M	Zito Angelo	83	chauffeur	43	"
	N	Zito Carmella—†	83	housewife	45	"
	O	Zito Paul	83	chauffeur	21	"
	P	Magnificio Jerome W	85	pharmacist	28	"
	R	Magnificio Leonara—†	85	housewife	26	"
	S	*Valla Joseph	85	retired	67	
	T	Valla Joseph	85	repairman	28	"
	U	*Valla Josephine—†	85	housewife	52	"
	V	Valla Louis	85	chauffeur	26	"
	W	Valla Salvatore	85	clerk	22	
	X	Magnificio Anna—†	85	housewife	50	"
	Y	Magnificio John	85	barber	55	
	Z	Magnificio Joseph	85	jeweler	28	
1651						
	A	DeChristoforo Susie—†	87	housewife	62	"
	B	Pesaturo Margaret—†	87	"	25	
	C	Pesaturo Vincenzo	87	laborer	44	

Page.	Letter.	Full Name.	Residence, Jan. 1, 1938.	Occupation.	Supposed Age.	Reported Residence, Jan. 1, 1937. Street and Number.

Chelsea Street—Continued

	D	Calicchio Constantina—†	87	housewife	41	here
	E	Calicchio Cosmo	87	barber	44	"
	F	Calicchio Elvira—†	87	typist	20	"
	G	DePiero Joseph	87	laborer	37	
	H	DePiero Margaret—†	87	housewife	30	"
	K	Ferrera Jennie—†	89	"	49	6 Chelsea
	L	Ferrera Vincent	89	laborer	50	6 "
	M	*Ferrera Anna—†	89	housewife	25	here
	N	Ferrera Arthur	89	electrician	26	"
	O	Nigro Gilda—†	89	housewife	20	63 Lubec
	P	Nigro Jerry	89	salesman	22	134 Meridian
	R	Cobiello Prisco	91	shoeworker	35	here
	S	Gassiraro Baldasaro	91	laborer	47	"
	T	Gassiraro Mary—†	91	housewife	39	"
	U	*Costanzo Giacomina—†	91	"	39	
	V	Costanzo Placido	91	laborer	40	
	W	*Berlergrio Thomas	rear 91	retired	74	
	X	*DeLucca Anthony	" 91	"	69	
	Y	Grieco Carmella—†	" 91	housewife	29	"
	Z	Grieco Ercole	" 91	laborer	38	
1652						
	B	*Mazzola Concetta—†	95	housewife	26	"
	C	Mazzola Salvatore	95	tailor	33	"
	D	*Agri Lena—†	95	seamstress	25	111 Maverick
	E	Agri Lucio	95	tailor	27	111 "
	F	Mazzola Charles	95	"	40	here
	G	Mazzola Lucia—†	95	packer	21	"
	H	*Mazzola Mary—†	95	housewife	33	"
	K	*Smith Anna—†	97	"	52	
	L	Smith Benjamin	97	merchant	58	"
	M	Smith Florence—†	97	student	26	
	N	Arnesarno Alfred	97	barber	42	
	O	Arnesarno Fannie—†	97	housewife	40	"
	R	Cohen Jacob D	99	merchant	39	"
	S	*Cohen Jennie—†	99	housewife	38	"
	T	*Ferreta Dominic	99	laborer	56	
	U	*Ferreta Josephine—†	99	housewife	48	"
	V	Ferreta Salvatore	99	laborer	20	
	W	Barbaro Frederico	101	watchman	55	"
	X	Barbaro Rachael—†	101	housewife	58	"
	Y	Riccardi James	101	mechanic	29	"

Page.	Letter.	FULL NAME.	Residence, Jan. 1, 1938.	Occupation.	Supposed Age.	Reported Residence, Jan. 1, 1937. Street and Number.
		Chelsea Street—Continued				
	Z	Riccardi Palma—†	101	housewife	20	here
1653						
	A	Rock Helen—†	101	"	30	"
	B	Rock Timothy	101	chauffeur	32	"
	C	Rose Dorothy—†	101	clerk	21	"
	D	Rose Elizabeth—†	101	housewife	59	"
	E	Rose Patrick	101	seaman	59	"
	F	Rose William	101	wrapper	28	"
	H	Orlando Curcio	103	operator	22	"
	K	*Orlando Mary—†	103	housewife	45	"
	L	*Orlando Peter	103	operator	26	"
	M	*Orlando Simone	103	laborer	54	"
	N	*Misiano John	103	"	45	"
	O	Misiano Mary—†	103	housewife	41	"
	R	DeSteffano Anthony	105	student	20	"
	S	DeSteffano Frank	105	merchant	45	"
	T	*DeSteffano Jennie—†	105	housewife	45	"
	U	Trocano James	107	shoeworker	35	"
	V	Trocano Virginia—†	107	housewife	32	"
	W	Gelormini Costantino	107	machinist	40	"
	X	Gelormini Raphaela—†	107	housewife	39	"
	Y	*Smaldone Mary—†	107	"	60	"
	Z	*Smaldone Rosario	107	retired	64	"
1654						
	A	*Grasso Adelina—†	109	housewife	47	"
	B	*Grasso Pasquale	109	molder	57	"
	C	Grasso Vincenzo	109	merchant	38	"
	D	Bonuro Angelo	109	shoeworker	52	"
	E	Bonuro Rosa—†	109	housewife	41	"
	F	Faldetta Edward	109	laborer	53	28 Chelsea
	G	*Faldetta Mary—†	109	housewife	43	28 "
	H	Faldetta Mary—†	109	operator	21	here
	L	Suarez Antonetta—†	111	housewife	28	"
	M	Suarez Jose	111	fireman	33	"
	N	Lamattina Mary—†	111	housewife	30	"
	O	Lamattina Salvatore	111	stitcher	44	"
	P	*Palumbo John	113	laborer	55	"
	R	*Palumbo Rose—†	113	housewife	52	"
	S	*Falzone Lillie—†	113	"	43	324 Saratoga
	T	Falzone Salvatore	113	musician	23	324 "
	U	Falzone Vincent	113	laborer	50	324 "

Page.	Letter.	Full Name.	Residence, Jan. 1, 1938.	Occupation.	Supposed Age.	Reported Residence, Jan. 1, 1937. Street and Number.

Chelsea Street—Continued

	v	Falzone Vincent	113	musician	20	324 Saratoga
	Y	Parziale Archangelo	123	merchant	54	here
	z	Parziale Filomena—†	123	housewife	44	"
1655						
	A	Brosco Antonio	123	laborer	42	
	B	*Brosco Mary—†	123	housewife	40	"
	C	Ferrullo Joseph	123	laborer	35	
	D	Ferrullo Rita—†	123	housewife	32	"
	E	Masciullo Nicholas	123	laborer	56	
	G	Infantino Joseph	125	salesman	35	"
	H	Infantino Mary E—†	125	housewife	37	"
	K	Sciarappa John	125	operator	35	74 Chelsea
	L	*Sciarappa Martha—†	125	housewife	30	74 "
	M	*Raia Mary—†	125	"	39	15 Morris
	N	Raia Matteo	125	laborer	20	15 "
	P	Natali Gaetano	127	shoemaker	54	here
	R	Magaletta Anthony	127	cutter	25	"
	S	*Magaletta Mary—†	127	housewife	67	"
	T	Capolupo Concetta—†	127	stitcher	23	
	V	*Pagliuso Lucy—†	127	housewife	53	"
	U	Pagliuso Simone	127	laborer	62	
	W	*Molino Joseph	129	retired	67	"
	X	*Cambria Joseph	129	painter	50	201 Havre
	Y	Cambria Josephine—†	129	clerk	25	201 "
	Z	*Cambria Lillian—†	129	housewife	40	201 "
1656						
	A	*Trovato Anthony	129	laborer	20	201 "
	B	*Badollato Nicholas	129	painter	42	29 Maverick
	C	*Nicosia Angelo	129	retired	69	here
	D	*Nicosia Jennie—†	129	housewife	50	"
	F	*Albizer Ignazio	131	laborer	42	"
	G	*Albizer Theresa—†	131	housewife	49	"
	H	Faraci Charles	131	candymaker	38	"
	K	*Faraci Sarah—†	131	housewife	32	"
	L	*Aaronson Annie—†	131	"	50	
	M	*Aaronson Solomon	131	teacher	50	
	N	Guineiso Benjamin	133	cutter	23	
	O	Guineiso Jean—†	133	housewife	21	"
	P	*DeChristoforo Antonette—†	133	"	50	
	R	DeChristoforo Mary—†	133	packer	25	
	S	*DeChristoforo Nunzio	133	laborer	53	

Page.	Letter.	Full Name.	Residence, Jan. 1, 1938.	Occupation.	Supposed Age.	Reported Residence, Jan. 1, 1937. Street and Number.

Chelsea Street—Continued

	T	*Panarelli Fannie—†	133	housewife	41	here
	U	*Panarelli Joseph	133	laborer	54	"
	V	Alabiso Tina—†	135	at home	34	"
	W	*Yudelman Annie—†	135	housewife	80	"
	X	*Yudelman Morris	135	merchant	80	"
	Y	Capuano Lena—†	135	housewife	33	"
	Z	*Capuano Lewis	135	shoeworker	38	"
1657						
	A	Botte Ernest	137	operator	21	
	B	Botte Frank	137	chauffeur	50	"
	C	Botte Matilda—†	137	stitcher	22	
	D	*Botte Rachael—†	137	housewife	49	"
	E	Botte Josephine—†	137	operator	23	
	F	Botte Michael	137	laborer	25	
	G	*Brogna Albert	137	foreman	65	
	H	Brogna Gussie—†	137	housewife	29	"
	K	Brogna Joseph	137	salesman	28	"
	M	*Sebastiano Attardo	139	laborer	46	
	N	*Sebastiano Josephine—†	139	housewife	44	"
	O	*DeCristoforo Antonio	139	laborer	30	128 Havre
	P	*DeCristoforo Lucy—†	139	housewife	33	128 "
	R	Guttel John	141	student	20	here
	S	*Guttel Lena—†	141	housewife	41	"
	T	*Guttel Lewis	141	plumber	48	"
	U	*Rosa Grace—†	141	at home	44	
	V	Trocano Dominick	141	laborer	40	
	W	Mari Carmella—†	141	saleswoman	25	"
	X	Mari Frank	141	clerk	46	
	Y	Mari Lillian—†	141	housewife	47	"
	Z	Dawm Celia—†	143	at home	78	
1658						
	A	Siegel Molly—†	143	housewife	42	"
	B	Siegel Philip	143	salesman	43	"
	C	DiGregorio Carmella—†	143	housewife	31	"
	D	DiGregorio Giuseppe	143	laborer	46	"
	E	Amoroso Bernice—†	145	housewife	26	2 Savage ct
	F	Amoroso Joseph	145	laborer	44	6 Liverpool
	G	Spolsino Angeline—†	145	stitcher	24	here
	H	Spolsino Anthony	145	barber	21	"
	K	*Spolsino Filomena—†	145	housewife	43	"
	L	Spolsino Frank	145	barber	48	

Page.	Letter.	Full Name.	Residence, Jan. 1, 1938.	Occupation.	Supposed Age.	Reported Residence, Jan. 1, 1937. Street and Number.

Chelsea Street—Continued

	M	Levine Eva—†	145	at home	68	322 Blue Hill av
	N	Potchercoff Hyman	145	chauffeur	62	here
	O	*Potchercoff Jennie—†	145	housewife	65	"
	P	Saperia Jacob	145	retired	68	193 London
	R	*Stassano Leonora—†	147	housewife	24	here
	S	*Stassano Vito	147	plumber	26	"
	T	*DeGregorio Angelo	147	rubberworker	26	"
	U	DeGregorio Concetta—†	147	candymaker	20	"
	V	*DeGregorio Mario	147	rubberworker	49	"
	W	DeGregorio Mario, jr	147	"	22	
	X	*DeGregorio Mary—†	147	housewife	44	"
	Y	Stassano Anthony	147	laborer	52	
	Z	Stassano Joseph	147	clerk	24	
1659						
	A	Stassano Michael	147	"	21	
	B	*Consalvo Dora—†	149	housewife	25	"
	C	Consalvo Vito	149	leatherworker	30	"
	D	Esposito Loretta—†	149	housewife	35	New York
	E	*Esposito Salvatore	149	furrier	45	"
	F	Milano Josephine—†	149	housewife	24	here
	G	Milano Pasquale	149	tailor	26	"
	H	Gayhart Harry	151	laborer	22	"
	K	Gayhart James A	151	"	50	
	L	Gayhart Joseph	151	"	23	
	M	Gayhart Mary—†	151	housewife	40	"
	N	*Caccaviello Esther—†	151	"	50	
	O	*Caccaviello Michael	151	retired	60	"
	P	Lopilato Joseph	151	laborer	25	496 Sumner
	R	Lopilato Victoria—†	151	housewife	23	496 "
	S	Letteriello Adolph	153	pipelayer	28	113 Havre
	T	Letteriello Isabella—†	153	housewife	24	195 Marion
	U	Letteriello Louise—†	153	"	29	113 Havre
	V	Letteriello Mary—†	153	"	23	195 Marion
	W	Letteriello Nicholas	153	plumber	24	195 "
	X	Letteriello Ralph	153	gardener	29	195 "
	Y	*Farretra Jennie—†	155	at home	52	here
	Z	Sicuranzo Angelo	155	merchant	28	"
1660						
	A	Sicuranzo Carmella—†	155	housewife	27	"
	B	Costa Angelina—†	155	"	40	
	C	Costa Salvatore	155	laborer	46	

Page.	Letter.	Full Name.	Residence, Jan. 1, 1938.	Occupation.	Supposed Age.	Reported Residence, Jan. 1, 1937. Street and Number.

Chelsea Street—Continued

	D	Durante Marco	155	laborer	46	here
	E	Durante Theresa—†	155	housewife	39	"
	F	*Cassara Joseph	157	laborer	24	"
	G	*Cassara Mary—†	157	housewife	60	"
	H	Cassara Thomaso	157	merchant	68	"
	K	*Indingaro Caroline—†	157	at home	67	
	L	Indingaro Charles	157	fishcutter	44	"
	M	Indingaro James	157	laborer	32	"
	N	Indingaro Prisco	157	fishcutter	38	"
	O	DiGiulio Anthony	157	laborer	20	
	P	DiGiulio Michael	157	"	53	
	R	*DiGiulio Rose—†	157	housewife	43	"
	S	*Twersky Naomi—†	159	"	23	14 W J Kelly sq
	T	Twersky Samuel	159	clergyman	27	14 "
	U	*Kaplan Abraham	159	plumber	24	here
	V	*Kaplan Ethel—†	159	housewife	40	"
	W	*Kaplan Max	159	chauffeur	58	"
	X	*Klayman Henry	159	retired	66	
	Y	*Klayman Jennie—†	159	housewife	50	"
	Z	*Slotnick Harry	161	merchant	65	"
1661						
	A	*Slotnick Joseph	161	"	34	
	B	Slotnick Sylvia—†	161	at home	23	
	C	*Goldberg Ida—†	161	"	68	
	D	*Mandel Minnie—†	161	"	52	
	E	Lochiatto Alphonso	161	laborer	32	
	F	Lochiatto Philena—†	161	housewife	27	"
	H	Boncore Angelo	163	retired	77	
	K	*Boncore Cantina—†	163	housewife	66	"
	L	Boncore Joseph	163	tailor	24	
	O	Manuel Eva—†	165	housewife	27	"
	P	Manuel Frank	165	pharmacist	32	"
	R	*Gambardella Carmella–†	165	at home	44	122 Sumner
	S	*Gambardella Lewis	165	steward	21	122 "
	U	Yorks Abraham	167	plumber	62	here
	V	Yorks Ida—†	167	bookkeeper	28	"
	W	Yorks Rose—†	167	housewife	56	"
	X	Segal Minnie—†	167	at home	66	
	Y	Anzalone Antonio	169	baker	23	
	Z	*Anzalone Pasqualina—†	169	housewife	40	"

Page.	Letter.	Full Name.	Residence, Jan. 1, 1938.	Occupation.	Supposed Age.	Reported Residence, Jan. 1, 1937. Street and Number.

1662

Chelsea Street—Continued

	A	Caruso Angelo	169	rubberworker	58	here
	B	*Caruso Margaret—†	169	housewife	50	"
	C	Caruso Mario T	169	clerk	25	"
	D	Cammarta Antonetta—†	169	housewife	24	"
	E	Cammarta Charles	169	baker	29	
	H	*Gulino Joseph	171	laborer	48	
	K	*Gulino Josephine—†	171	housewife	38	"
	L	*Pitari Catherine—†	171	"	53	365 North
	M	Pitari Gabriel	171	laborer	61	365 "
	N	Jordan John W	173	retired	76	here
	O	Jordan Mabel H—†	173	at home	37	"
	P	Jordan Mary E—†	173	housewife	76	"
	R	Ormond Elizabeth A—†	173	at home	61	
	T	*Shulman Fannie—†	175	housewife	62	"
	U	*Shulman Max	175	tailor	65	
	V	Shulman Esther—†	175	operator	25	
	W	Shulman George	175	salesman	22	"
	X	Shulman Perry	175	cutter	22	
	Y	Shulman Samuel	175	manager	25	"
1663						
	A	*Sing Lee	177	laundryman	56	"
	B	*Eremka Catherine—†	177	housewife	42	"
	C	Eremka John	177	laborer	47	
	D	Marquard Matilda—†	177	housewife	29	"
	E	Marquard Michael	177	shoecutter	30	"
	G	Reese Lillian—†	179	houseworker	28	"
	H	Wood Margaret—†	179	at home	75	"
	K	*Eruzzione Concetta—†	179	housewife	52	149 Chelsea
	L	Eruzzione Filomena—†	179	clerk	22	149 "
	M	*Eruzzione Michael	179	ironworker	54	149 "
	N	Eruzzione Vincent	179	laborer	21	149 "
	O	*Cohen Bessie—†	181	housewife	57	here
	P	Cohen Dorothy—†	181	operator	27	"
	R	Cohen Celia—†	181	housewife	25	"
	S	Cohen Jack	181	printer	29	
	T	Cooper Israel	181	seaman	28	
	U	*Cooper Jacob	181	laborer	50	
	V	Cooper Joseph	181	"	21	
	W	Cooper Morris	181	"	24	

Page.	Letter.	Full Name.	Residence, Jan. 1, 1938.	Occupation.	Supposed Age.	Reported Residence, Jan. 1, 1937. Street and Number.

Chelsea Street—Continued

	X	*Cooper Sarah—†	181	housewife	54	here
	Z	Memmolo Catherine—†	183	"	21	"
1664						
	A	*Memmolo Michael	183	laborer	66	
	B	Memmolo Michael, jr	183	candymaker	24	"
	C	Memmolo Pasquale	183	laborer	21	138 Bremen
	D	*Zelenuk Alexander	185	"	45	here
	E	*Zelenuk Andrew	185	"	43	"
	F	*DiPerri Phillipa—†	185	housewife	83	"
	G	*DiPerri Salvatore	185	laborer	43	"
	H	Hanlon Jeremiah	185	chauffeur	40	908 Harris'n av
	K	Hanlon Sadie—†	185	housewife	40	908 "
	L	*Ganick Dora—†	187	at home	56	here
	N	Cardinale Carmine	187	laborer	45	"
	O	*Cardinale Filomena—†	187	housewife	47	"
	P	Cardinale John	187	operator	20	"
	R	*Cambria Giuseppe	189	retired	83	180 Sumner
	S	Tripodi John D	189	student	29	here
	T	*Tripodi Joseph	189	realtor	62	"
	U	*Tripodi Theresa—†	189	housewife	49	"
	V	*DeSilvia Manuel	189	longshoreman	52	"
	W	DeSilvia Mary—†	189	housewife	50	"
	X	Nelson Charlotte—†	191	"	40	229 Chelsea
	Y	Nelson Harry	191	laborer	52	229 "
	Z	*Menzinsky Martin	191	"	66	here
1665						
	A	*Pietwich Wojciech	191	boilermaker	55	"
	C	*Forte Irene—†	193	housewife	51	"
	D	*Forte Samuel	193	laborer	48	"
	E	Guarante Annie—†	193	housewife	22	"
	F	Guarante Olando	193	laborer	23	
	G	*Piazza Alphonso	193	"	49	"
	H	*Piazza Stella—†	193	housewife	38	"
	K	Cohen Isadore A	195	merchant	47	"
	L	Cohen Tillie—†	195	housewife	45	"

Cottage Street

	M	*Cogliandro Michaelena—†	68	housewife	43	here
	N	Cogliandro Severio	68	merchant	51	"
	P	*Donatello Alvera—†	70	housewife	47	"

Page.	Letter.	Full Name.	Residence, Jan. 1, 1938.	Occupation.	Supposed Age.	Reported Residence, Jan. 1, 1937. Street and Number.

Cottage Street—Continued

	R	Donatello Annette—†	70	hairdresser	21	here
	O	Donatello Benjamin	70	laborer	47	"
	T	Mastrantonio Maria—†	72	housekeeper	72	"
	U	Bonnello Antonetta—†	72	housewife	71	"
	V	Bonnello Carmine	72	retired	71	
	X	Gravellese Louisa—†	76	housewife	60	"
	Y	Gravellese Michael	76	merchant	64	"
	Z	LaScaleia Antonio	76	laborer	43	
1666						
	A	LaScaleia Armedeo	76	clerk	21	
	C*	Ruo Frances—†	78	housewife	23	"
	D*	Ruo Michael, jr	78	chauffeur	35	"
	E	Galuna James	78	merchant	37	"
	F	Galuna Jeannette—†	78	housewife	23	"
	H	Stella Esther—†	80	"	29	
	K	Stella Otis	80	bricklayer	30	"
	L	Vigliotte Pasquale	80	shoeworker	38	"
	M	Vigliotte Rose—†	80	housewife	35	"
	P	Vazza Americo	88	embalmer	33	"
	R	Vazza Clara—†	88	housewife	25	"
	S*	Vazza Emanuela—†	88	housekeeper	70	"
	T	Cancian Charles	88	laborer	35	"
	U	Cancian Edith—†	88	housewife	28	"
	V	Raffaele Angelo	88	laborer	30	
	W	Raffaele Jennie—†	88	housewife	27	"
	Y	Cusinotto Lillian—†	90	housekeeper	57	3 Paris pl
	Z*	Laurino Michael	90	expressman	56	here
1667						
	A	Manzione Sarah—†	90	housewife	23	"
	B	Manzione Severino	90	foreman	26	
	C	Pastore John	90	barber	47	
	D	Pastore Mary—†	90	housewife	43	"
	F*	Tromba Christina—†	92	"	49	
	G*	Tromba Pasquale	92	laborer	54	
	H	Lombardi Antonetta—†	92	housewife	32	"
	K	Lombardi Humbert	92	laborer	35	
	L	Evangelista Margaret—†	92	housewife	29	"
	M	Evangelista Nicola	92	laborer	30	
	O	Pastore Michael	94	salesman	28	"
	P	Spinelli Daniel	94	merchant	22	"
	R*	Spinelli Jennie—†	94	housewife	64	"

Page.	Letter.	FULL NAME.	Residence, Jan. 1, 1938.	Occupation.	Supposed Age.	Reported Residence, Jan. 1, 1937. Street and Number.

Cottage Street—Continued

Page.	Letter.	FULL NAME.	Residence, Jan. 1, 1938.	Occupation.	Supposed Age.	Reported Residence, Jan. 1, 1937. Street and Number.
	T	*Camiolo Antonio	96	laborer	48	here
	U	*Camiolo Concetta—†	96	housewife	39	"
	V	Camiolo Nunzio	96	laborer	21	"
	Z	Gregorio Antonio	98	"	29	
1668						
	A	Gregorio Jennie—†	98	housewife	28	"
	B	*Selvitella Carmine	98	laborer	72	
	C	*Selvitella Mary—†	98	housewife	68	"
	D	Selvitella Helen—†	98	"	28	
	E	Selvitella Joseph	98	candymaker	33	"
	G	DiMattia Domenic	100	carpenter	35	"
	H	*DiMattia Florence—†	100	housewife	30	"
	K	*DiMattia Nunzia—†	100	"	64	
	M	Vaccaro Luigi	102	laborer	47	
	N	*Vaccaro Michaelena—†	102	housewife	45	"
	O	Percardo Aurello	102	merchant	49	"
	P	Percardo Lucia—†	102	housewife	39	"

Emmet Place

Page.	Letter.	FULL NAME.	Residence, Jan. 1, 1938.	Occupation.	Supposed Age.	Reported Residence, Jan. 1, 1937. Street and Number.
	R	*Bisceiotti Peter	1	laborer	63	62 Bremen
	S	*Luongo Gennaro	1	"	68	here
	T	Evangelista Carmen	1	shoeworker	23	"
	U	Evangelista Giuseppe	1	laborer	36	"
	V	Ricco Eugene	1	"	25	
	W	*Bomba Vincenzio	2	retired	60	"
	X	*Prizio Anthony	2	laborer	69	Long Island
	Y	Maraio Giuseppe	2	"	42	here
	Z	*Maraio Mary—†	2	housewife	46	"
1669						
	A	*Colucci Pasquale	3	laborer	74	

Everett Street

Page.	Letter.	FULL NAME.	Residence, Jan. 1, 1938.	Occupation.	Supposed Age.	Reported Residence, Jan. 1, 1937. Street and Number.
	C	Wilkins Helen—†	6	housekeeper	21	111 Orleans
	D	*Camuso Elizabeth—†	6	housewife	47	here
	E	*Camuso Louis	6	laborer	48	"
	F	Matira Josephine—†	6	housekeeper	36	"
	G	Elacqua Antonina—†	8	"	24	149 Maverick
	H	Liazza John	8	laborer	35	here
	K	*Liazza Victoria—†	8	housewife	24	"

Page.	Letter.	Full Name.	Residence, Jan. 1, 1938.	Occupation.	Supposed Age.	Reported Residence, Jan. 1, 1937. Street and Number.

Everett Street—Continued

	L	Denaro Joseph J	8	fireman	35	here
	M	Scaramella Dora C—†	8	housewife	32	"
	N	Scaramella John C	8	clerk	43	"
	P	Frangello Anna—†	11	housewife	40	"
	R	Frangello Gaetano	11	carpenter	43	"
	S	Presutti Gaetano	11	laborer	23	
	T	Zichittella Mildred—†	11	housewife	33	"
	U	Zichittella Vincent	11	painter	37	
	W	Picillo Achille	13	laborer	50	
	X	Picillo Henry	13	"	24	
	Y	Picillo Michael	13	chauffeur	21	"
	Z	*Picillo Sarah—†	13	housewife	47	"
1670						
	A	Barrasso Adeline—†	15	operator	23	"
	B	Barrasso Caroline—†	15	housewife	51	"
	C	Barrasso Christy	15	watchman	57	"
	D	Barrasso Emilio	15	barber	25	
	E	Barrasso Ernest	15	student	20	
	F	*Falcucci Marion—†	17	housewife	27	"
	G	*Falcucci Rocco	17	painter	37	"
	H	*Faretra Felicia—†	18	housewife	50	1 Emmet pl
	K	Faretra Nicola	18	laborer	62	1 "
	L	Vitale Elizabeth—†	18	housewife	22	here
	M	Vitale Vincent	18	laborer	20	"
	T	Small Eleanor—†	21	cook	22	Somerville
	U	Small Samuel	21	seaman	21	"
	V	Driscoll Florence—†	21	baker	25	here
	W	Driscoll Helen—†	21	operator	21	"
	X	Driscoll John L	21	shipper	45	"
	Y	Driscoll Margaret—†	21	housewife	45	"
	Z	DeSimone Concetta—†	21	"	20	
1671						
	A	DeSimone Philip	21	laborer	26	
	C	Butler Agnes D—†	23	housewife	34	"
	D	Murphy Arthur T	23	foreman	40	
	E	O'Donnell Eugene F	23	laborer	29	
	F	Stevens Josephine—†	25	housewife	21	"
	G	Stevens Theodore L	25	janitor	20	
	H	*DiZio Anna—†	25	housewife	32	"
	K	DiZio Guarino	25	tailor	42	
	L	Giunto Angela—†	27	stitcher	45	

Page.	Letter.	Full Name.	Residence, Jan. 1, 1938.	Occupation.	Supposed Age.	Reported Residence, Jan. 1, 1937. Street and Number.

Everett Street—Continued

Page.	Letter.	Full Name.	Residence, Jan. 1, 1938.	Occupation.	Supposed Age.	Reported Residence, Jan. 1, 1937. Street and Number.
	M	*Giunto Cologera—†	27	housewife	63	here
	N	*Giunto Gandolfo	27	laborer	66	"
	O	Giunto Josephine—†	27	candyworker	33	"
	P	*DiZio Evelyn—†	29	housewife	46	"
	R	DiZio Vincenzo	29	laborer	50	"
	S	Testa Antonio	31	"	46	165 Cottage
	T	*Testa Mary—†	31	housewife	40	165 "
	U	Maninno Gaetano	33	merchant	50	here
	V	*Raso Philomena—†	33	housewife	41	"
	W	*Raso Rocco	33	laborer	41	"
	X	DeRose Mary—†	35	housewife	32	"
	Y	DeRose Rocco	35	foreman	36	
	Z	Terrazano Concetta—†	37	housewife	34	"
1672						
	A	Terrazano Pasquale	37	laborer	38	"
	B	Briana Joseph	39	"	22	27 Decatur
	C	Briana Mary A—†	39	housewife	21	27 "
	D	*Camplese Hugo	39	laborer	23	31 Everett
	E	*Camplese John	39	shoeworker	21	here
	F	*Camplese Theresa—†	39	housewife	46	31 Everett
	G	Guarino Anthony	39	candymaker	26	here
	H	*Guarino Carmen	39	laborer	52	"
	K	Baptista Carmella—†	42	housewife	30	"
	L	Baptista Ralph	42	candyworker	32	"
	M	*Caputo Angelina—†	42	housewife	44	"
	N	Caputo Frank	42	shipper	23	
	O	*Caputo Nicholas	42	laborer	47	
	P	Baptista Mario	42	shoeworker	26	"
	R	*Baptista Samuel	42	candyworker	63	"
	S	*Baptista Theresa—†	42	housewife	63	"
	T	Larkin Delia—†	44	"	60	
	U	Larkin Helen R—†	44	"	21	
	V	Larkin John P	44	clerk	29	
	W	Barrett James	44	retired	75	
	X	Barrett John	44	laborer	33	
	Y	Barrett Mary—†	44	housekeeper	40	"
	Z	Kelley Daniel	44	longshoreman	42	"
1673						
	A	Kelley Mary—†	44	domestic	65	"
	C	DiPietro Alfred	45	laborer	20	
	B	DiPietro Anna—†	45	housewife	53	"

Page.	Letter.	Full Name.	Residence, Jan. 1, 1938.	Occupation.	Supposed Age.	Reported Residence, Jan. 1, 1937. Street and Number.

Everett Street—Continued

	D	DiPietro Anthony	45	clerk	22	here
	E	DiPietro Josephine—†	45	packer	29	"
	F	DiPietro Margaret—†	45	at home	28	"
	G	DiPietro William	45	carpenter	60	"
	H	DiPietro Helen—†	45	packer	30	
	K	DiPietro William, jr	45	clerk	23	
	L	Cardello Joseph	45	laborer	37	
	M	Cardello Rose—†	45	housewife	29	"
	N	Tango Mildred—†	46	"	28	
	O	Tango Victor	46	laborer	35	"
	P	Colli Gasper	46	painter	27	147 Havre
	R	Colli Josephine—†	46	housewife	22	147 "
	S	Capozzi Mario—†	46	mechanic	26	17 Eaton
	T	*Capozzi Mary—†	46	housewife	26	17 "
	U	*Vandanza Santo	46	laborer	63	here
	V	Coppola Gabriel	48	laundryman	26	"
	W	*Coppola Rose—†	48	housewife	21	"
	X	Matarazzo Domenic	48	tailor	21	
	Y	*Matarazzo Isabelle—†	48	housewife	57	"
	Z	Matarazzo Pellegrino	48	laborer	61	
1674						
	A	*Ferrara Eliza—†	48	housewife	46	"
	B	Ferrara Nicola P	48	laborer	57	
	C	Driscoll John M	49	"	29	
	D	Driscoll Nellie—†	49	housewife	23	"
	E	Morello James P	49	salesman	32	"
	F	Morello Peter	49	retired	78	
	G	Morello John	49	coppersmith	36	"
	H	Morello Susan—†	49	housewife	33	"
	K	Trevisani Anibale	50	tileworker	54	"
	L	Trevisani Anibale	50	laborer	22	
	M	*Trevisani Mary—†	50	housewife	50	"
	N	Fratelli Adolph	50	laborer	44	
	O	*Fratelli Julia—†	50	housewife	43	"
	P	*Santini Angelina—†	50	housekeeper	57	"
	R	DiPietro Amelia—†	51	packer	26	"
	S	Famiglietti Antonio	51	laborer	21	
	T	*Famiglietti Joseph	51	"	46	"
	U	*Famiglietti Mary—†	51	housewife	49	"
	V	DiPietro Anthony	51	tinsmith	28	
	W	Ivone Concetta—†	52	housewife	35	"

Page.	Letter.	Full Name.	Residence, Jan. 1, 1938.	Occupation.	Supposed Age.	Reported Residence, Jan. 1, 1937. Street and Number.

Everett Street—Continued

	X	Ivone Frank	52	operator	42	here
	Y	*Cozzo Felicia—†	52	housekeeper	75	"
	Z	Germano Charles	52	laborer	25	140 Everett
1675						
	A	Germano Josephine—†	52	housewife	23	140 "
	C	*Spano Clementina—†	54	"	55	here
	D	Spano Frank	54	shoeworker	25	"
	E	Spano Pasquale	54	laborer	59	"
	F	*Leone Antonette—†	54	housewife	29	"
	G	*Leone Raffaelo	54	laborer	40	
	H	*Candella Maria—†	56	housewife	49	"
	K	*Canedlla Salvatore	56	laborer	49	"
	L	Palumbo Frank	56	"	24	Revere
	M	*Palumbo Vivian—†	56	housewife	21	51 Morris
	N	Corzzo Anna—†	56	"	31	421 Saratoga
	O	Corzzo Fred	56	woodcarver	41	Medford
	P	*Vinciguerra Eleanor—†	58	housewife	25	17 London
	R	*Vinciguerra Vincent	58	toolmaker	27	17 "
	S	Rindoni Santo	58	laborer	31	here
	T	Rindoni Cincenzia—†	58	housewife	26	"
	U	Palazzuolo Antonio	58	laborer	40	"
	V	*Palazzuolo Constantina—†	58	housewife	42	"
	W	*Mastrolia Alphonso	60	bartender	40	"
	X	Mastrolia Emilio	60	laborer	20	
	Y	*Mastrolia Lena—†	60	housewife	40	"
1676						
	A	Inperato Philip	60	chef	58	
	B	*Principato Joseph	60	laborer	31	
	C	*Principato Mary—†	60	housewife	30	"
	D	Polcari Domenic	62	mechanic	36	56 Everett
	E	Polcari Lillian—†	62	housewife	28	56 "
	F	*Beatrice Amelia—†	62	"	54	here
	G	Beatrice Antoñio	62	laborer	31	"
	H	*Beatrice Martin	62	"	65	"
	K	Beatrice Michael	62	"	20	
	L	Beatrice Pasquale	62	"	23	
	M	Veader Angelina—†	62	housewife	29	"
	N	Veader Francis A	62	chauffeur	31	"
	O	Sarro Joseph	64	painter	35	
	P	Sarro Mary—†	64	housewife	34	"
	R	Cinciolo Antonio	64	laborer	25	

Everett Street—Continued

Page.	Letter.	Full Name.	Residence, Jan. 1, 1938.	Occupation.	Supposed Age.	Reported Residence, Jan. 1, 1937. Street and Number.
	s	*Cinicolo Grace—†	64	housewife	64	here
	T	*Cinicolo Raffael	64	laborer	66	"
	U	Cinicolo Rose—†	64	stitcher	21	"
	V	*DelPrato Luigi	64	laborer	50	
	W	*DelPrato Michelina—†	64	housewife	49	"

Frankfort Street

Page.	Letter.	Full Name.	Residence, Jan. 1, 1938.	Occupation.	Supposed Age.	Reported Residence, Jan. 1, 1937. Street and Number.
	Z	Pace Leo	12	laborer	44	here
1677						
	A	*DeMario Angelina—†	12	housewife	48	"
	B	DeMario Angelo	12	laborer	47	
	C	DeMario Joseph	12	"	21	"
	D	*Stellato Eleanor	14	housewife	34	New York
	E	*D'Amico Betty—†	14	"	34	here
	F	D'Amico Gaetano	14	shoeworker	37	"
	G	Narda Anna—†	15	housewife	50	"
	H	Narda Frank	15	janitor	69	
	K	Narda Marie—†	15	packer	28	
	L	DeSousa Joseph	15	painter	36	
	M	DeSousa Mary—†	15	housewife	28	"
	N	Bartoli Edith—†	15	"	22	
	O	Bartoli Joseph G, jr	15	salesman	24	"
	P	Jiachetti Jennie—†	15	housewife	28	"
	R	*Teza Jiacomina—†	15	"	46	"
	S	Teza Sebastiano	15	laborer	53	7 Chelsea pl
	T	Morano Leonard	16	"	27	here
	U	*Morano Mary—†	16	housewife	23	"
	V	Scifo Joseph	16	laborer	35	"
	W	Scifo Mary—†	16	housewife	30	"
	X	Scifo Antonio	16	laborer	27	9 McKay pl
	Y	*Scifo Florence—†	16	at home	65	here
	Z	*Scifo Josephine—†	16	housewife	27	9 McKay pl
1678						
	B	*Liberatore Lodovico	16	cobbler	55	here
	A	Liberatore Mary—†	16	typist	21	"
	C	*Liberatore Restituta—†	16	housewife	48	"
	D	Albo Christoforo	16	tailor	60	
	E	Giambrone Anthony	17	shoeworker	25	"
	F	Giambrone Jennie—†	17	housewife	24	"
	G	Durante Eugene	17	laborer	46	

Page.	Letter.	FULL NAME.	Residence, Jan. 1, 1938.	Occupation.	Supposed Age.	Reported Residence, Jan. 1, 1937. Street and Number.

Frankfort Street—Continued

Page.	Letter.	FULL NAME.	Residence, Jan. 1, 1938.	Occupation.	Supposed Age.	Reported Residence, Jan. 1, 1937. Street and Number.
	H	Durante John	17	merchant	22	here
	K	*Durante Teresa—†	17	housewife	54	"
	L	*Guardabascio Assunta—†	17	"	66	"
	M	*Venuti Louise—†	17	at home	38	
	N	*Cocchi Aldo	18	longshoreman	27	"
	O	Cocchi Alice—†	18	housewife	25	"
	P	Wolinsky Ethel—†	18	packer	27	"
	R	*Cianci Michaelina—†	18	housewife	37	164 Gove
	S	*Cianci Santo	18	laborer	54	164 "
	T	*Milano Catherine—†	18	housewife	38	here
	U	Milano Philip	18	carpenter	42	"
	V	Pettine Amilcare	19	retired	77	"
	W	Pettine Frank	19	agent	47	122 London
	X	Pettine Martha—†	19	housewife	40	here
	Y	*DeFlumeri Amelia—†	19	"	36	"
	Z	DeFlumeri Joseph	19	contractor	38	"
1679						
	A	DeFlumeri Anna—†	19	housewife	39	"
	B	DeFlumeri Anthony	19	lineman	44	
	C	*Ranieri Antoinetta—†	20	at home	89	
	D	*Muratore Savina—†	20	housewife	24	"
	E	Muratore William	20	machinist	26	"
	F	Stergios James M	20	waiter	36	
	G	Stergios Rose—†	20	housewife	27	"
	H	*D'Amico Madeline—†	20	"	41	
	K	*D'Amico Vincenzo	20	candymaker	46	"
	L	LoCalzo Antonio	20	laborer	45	137 Cottage
	M	*LoCalzo Carmella—†	20	housewife	35	137 "
	N	Marino Angelina—†	20	packer	31	here
	O	Marino Joseph	20	oiler	29	"
	P	DiLorenzo Josephine—†	24	tailoress	44	"
	R	Marini Anna—†	24	at home	74	
	S	Giustina Margaret—†	24	housewife	30	"
	T	Giustina Victor	24	foreman	33	
	U	*Zicconi Frances—†	24	housewife	52	"
	V	Zicconi John	24	foreman	65	
	W	Conti Jennie—†	24	housewife	38	"
	X	Conti Joseph	24	laborer	42	
	Y	*Zona Anthony	24	retired	78	
	Z	Marini Emilio	24	laborer	42	

Page.	Letter.	Full Name.	Residence, Jan. 1, 1938.	Occupation.	Supposed Age.	Reported Residence, Jan. 1, 1937. Street and Number.

1680
Frankfort Street—Continued

	A	Marini Susie—†	24	housewife	42	here
	C	Mattaroccia Cecil	24	laborer	28	"
	B	*Mattaroccia Celia—†	24	housewife	51	"
	D	Mattaroccia Nancy—†	24	stitcher	26	
	E	Pariso Joseph	26	assembler	30	"
	F	Pariso Rocco	26	mechanic	25	"
	G	Sollitto Margaret—†	26	at home	65	
	H	Bettano Anthony	26	bartender	35	"
	K	Bettano Eleanor—†	26	packer	35	
	L	*Bettano Victoria—†	26	housewife	68	"
	M	DiTroia Bruno	26	laborer	31	
	N	*DiTroia Pia—†	26	housewife	32	"
	O	*Perro Frances—†	26	"	28	
	P	Perro John	26	merchant	34	"
	S	DiBerto Antoinetta—†	32	seamstress	24	"
	T	*DiBerto Concetta—†	32	at home	29	
	U	*DiBerto Emma—†	32	housewife	55	"
	V	DiBerto Gilda—†	32	storekeeper	22	"
	W	*DiBerto Romeo	32	retired	60	"
	Y	DiStaula Louis	32	shoeworker	25	"
	Z	DiStaula Margaret—†	32	housewife	25	"
1681						
	A	D'Alesaandro Americo	32	laborer	30	
	B	D'Alessandro Iva—†	32	housewife	23	"
	C	Merluzzo Anthony	32	mechanic	46	"
	D	*Merluzzo Marina—†	32	housewife	27	"
	E	Vaccari Amedeo	34	mechanic	43	"
	F	Vaccari Columbia—†	34	packer	31	"
	G	Vaccari Eliza—†	34	housewife	62	"
	H	Vaccari Lena—†	24	packer	25	
	M	*Rainone Andrea	34	retired	70	"
	K	Velardo Clementine B—†	34	housewife	34	110 Benningt'n
	L	Velardo Domenic C	34	mechanic	36	110 "
	N	*D'Alessandro Angelina—†	34	housewife	50	here
	O	D'Alessandro Rico	34	laborer	23	"
	P	Iacono Eleanor—†	34	housewife	27	"
	R	Iacono Stanley A	34	laborer	33	
	S	Gigante Gabriel	36	"	35	
	T	*Gigante Rita—†	36	housewife	39	"

Page.	Letter.	Full Name.	Residence, Jan. 1, 1938.	Occupation.	Supposed Age.	Reported Residence, Jan. 1, 1937. Street and Number.

Frankfort Street—Continued

Page.	Letter.	Full Name.	Residence, Jan. 1, 1938.	Occupation.	Supposed Age.	Reported Residence, Jan. 1, 1937. Street and Number.
	U	*Troiani Anna—†	36	housewife	63	10 Corey Hill rd
	V	Troiani Seraphino	36	tailor	67	10 "
	W	*Ciullo Angelina—†	36	housewife	53	here
	X	*Ciullo Gennaro	36	retired	57	"
	Y	Ciullo George	36	laborer	23	"
	Z	Catanzariti Clara—†	36	housewife	25	"
1682						
	A	Catanzariti Onofrio J	36	laborer	30	
	B	Sestito Buonoventura	36	baker	41	
	C	*Sestito Mary—†	36	housewife	45	"
	D	Maragioglio Mary—†	36	"	28	67 Lexington
	E	*Filippone Antonio	38	laborer	55	here
	F	*Filippone Teresa—†	38	housewife	39	"
	G	Dello Russo Mary—†	38	at home	30	"
	H	*Buonanno Anna—†	38	housewife	58	"
	K	*Buonanno Nicola	38	laborer	59	
	L	Mele Domenic	38	janitor	41	"
	M	Mele Marietta—†	38	operator	21	
	N	*Mele Teresa—†	38	housewife	43	"
	O	*Fiorino Philip	38	retired	75	94 Chelsea
	P	*Fiorino Vincenza—†	38	housewife	68	94 "
	R	*Colangelo Carmella—†	40	"	36	here
	S	Colangelo Leonardo	40	blacksmith	44	"
	T	Colangelo Nicola	40	student	20	"
	U	Tontodonato John	40	laborer	65	
	V	*Tontodonato Maria—†	40	housewife	64	"
	W	*Tangusso Lillian—†	40	"	35	
	X	Tangusso Michael	40	shoeworker	43	"
	Y	*Mazzotta Antonio	40	laborer	46	
	Z	*Mazzotta Catherine—†	40	housewife	42	"
1683						
	A	Mazzotta Domenic	40	laborer	23	
	B	Mazzotta Stephen	40	"	21	
	C	*Storneillo Maria—†	40	housewife	59	"
	D	Dente Cristoforo	42	laborer	22	
	E	Dente Joseph	42	"	45	
	F	*Dente Mary—†	42	operator	40	"
	H	DiGiacomandrea Carmen	42	laborer	38	"
	K	DiGiacomandrea Elvira–†	42	housewife	28	67 Frankfort
	L	Laronia Marcellina	42	laborer	46	here
	M	Laronia Mary—†	42	housewife	50	"

Page.	Letter.	Full Name.	Residence, Jan. 1, 1938.	Occupation.	Supposed Age.	Reported Residence, Jan. 1, 1937. Street and Number.

Frankfort Street—Continued

Page.	Letter.	Full Name.	Residence, Jan. 1, 1938.	Occupation.	Supposed Age.	Reported Residence, Jan. 1, 1937. Street and Number.
	N	Piro Rosina—†	42	at home	63	here
	O	Ranieri Celestino	44	chauffeur	22	"
	P	Ranieri Concetta—†	44	housewife	47	"
	R	Ranieri Oscar	44	boxmaker	24	"
	S	Ranieri Tito	44	laborer	52	
	T	D'Amico Anna—†	44	seamstress	24	"
	U	*D'Amico Rose—†	44	housewife	50	"
	V	D'Amico Sabina—†	44	seamstress	23	"
	W	Ranieri Angelo	44	laborer	47	
	X	*Ranieri Carmella—†	44	housewife	47	"
	Y	*Cavotti Mary—†	44	packer	46	
	Z	DiBerto Amelia—†	44	seamstress	40	"
1684						
	A	*DiBerto Edward	44	tailor	46	"
	C	Giuffrida Anna—†	54	packer	24	170 Cottage
	D	*Giuffrida Antoinetta—†	54	housewife	56	170 "
	E	Giuffrida Joseph	54	shoeworker	29	170 "
	F	*Giuffrida Mario	54	merchant	64	170 "
	G	Luongo Carmella—†	54	housewife	30	here
	H	Luongo Charles	54	salesman	37	"
	K	D'Ambrosia Samuel	54	retired	72	"
	L	Zarella Mary—†	54	clerk	35	
	M	*Zarella Michael	54	baker	36	
	N	Piscitelli Lucia—†	54	housewife	31	"
	O	Piscitelli Salvatore	54	laborer	42	
	P	*Salvato Amedeo	54	tailor	45	
	R	*Salvato Josephine—†	54	housewife	43	"
	S	Salvato Lily—†	54	operator	21	"
	U	Santoro Lena—†	54	housewife	44	"
	T	Santoro Sabino	54	cobbler	50	
	V	*Francessa Maria—†	58	housewife	55	"
	W	*Abruzzese Adele—†	58	"	30	
	X	*Abruzzese Generoso	58	tailor	33	"
	Y	*Natale Maria—†	58	at home	65	11 New
	Z	Russo Antonio	58	laborer	34	11 "
1685						
	A	*Russo Julia—†	58	housewife	29	11 "
	B	*Catalfamo Carmella—†	58	"	55	63 Gove
	C	Catalfamo Filippo	58	laborer	56	63 "
	D	*Napolitano Antoinetta—†	58	housewife	40	here
	E	*Napolitano Frank	58	laborer	40	"

Page.	Letter.	Full Name.	Residence, Jan. 1, 1938.	Occupation.	Supposed Age.	Reported Residence, Jan. 1, 1937. Street and Number.

Frankfort Street—Continued

	F	*Laudanno Genevieve—†	60	housewife	51	here
	G	Laudanno Luigi	60	musician	51	"
	H	Laudanno Theresa—†	60	stitcher	21	"
	K	Gasparini Amedeo	60	carpenter	56	169 Cottage
	L	Catena Frank	60	laborer	33	here
	M	Catena Rose—†	60	housewife	29	"
	N	*Mercantonio Carmen	60	laborer	47	"
	O	*Marcantonio Margaret—†	60	housewife	42	"
	P	Todisco Achille	60	tailor	47	
	R	*Todisco Fannie—†	60	housewife	45	"
	S	Iannuzzi Mary—†	62	"	26	4 Eagle sq
	T	Iannuzzi Vito	62	shoeworker	29	160 Bremen
	U	Poto Antonette—†	62	housewife	22	here
	V	Poto Vito	62	laborer	22	"
	X	*Parcella Constance—†	62	housewife	49	"
	Y	*Parcella James	62	laborer	52	
	Z	Parcella Peter	62	mechanic	20	"
1686						
	A	Villani Carmella—†	62	housewife	38	"
	B	Villani Fiorento	62	shoeworker	48	"
	C	Mangini Giovanni	62	rubberworker	47	"
	D	*Mangini Maria—†	62	housewife	42	"
	E	*Marchetti Marco	62	retired	77	
	F	Alterio Eliza—†	63	housewife	54	"
	G	Alterio Michael	63	laborer	24	
	H	Alterio Pasquale	63	"	50	
	K	Ciampa Mary—†	63	housewife	28	"
	L	Ciampa Raffaele	63	painter	38	
	M	Alterio Natale	63	shipper	27	
	N	Alterio Rose—†	63	housewife	28	"
	O	Grillo Anna—†	63	"	25	
	P	Grillo John	63	cutter	34	
	R	*Zirella Paul	63	laborer	60	
	S	*Zirella Raffaela—†	63	housewife	41	"
	U	Bruno Girdo	64	student	23	
	V	*Bruno Maria—†	64	housewife	48	"
	W	Bruno Michael	64	barber	47	
	X	Bruno Orga—†	64	saleswoman	20	"
	T	Bruno Osvalda—†	64	clerk	25	
	Y	*Ruggiero Nicola	64	retired	78	
	Z	*Grafone Filomena—†	64	housewife	34	"

Frankfort Street—Continued

Page.	Letter.	Full Name.	Residence, Jan. 1, 1938.	Occupation.	Supposed Age.	Reported Residence, Jan. 1, 1937. Street and Number.
1687	A	Grafone Michael	64	shoemaker	38	here
	B	*Cafazzo Antonio	64	laborer	46	"
	C	*Cafazzo Maria—†	64	housewife	33	"
	D	Gulla Pantaleone	64	laborer	42	
	E	*Gulla Rosina—†	64	housewife	38	"
	F	Gangi John	65	cabinetmaker	44	"
	G	*Gangi Phyllis—†	65	housewife	34	"
	H	*Aulino Salvatore	65	operator	31	
	K	Aulino Theresa—†	65	packer	29	
	L	Aulino Alfonso	65	"	24	
	M	Aulino Antoinetta—†	65	tailoress	25	
	N	*Aulino Theresa—†	65	housewife	52	"
	O	Bartolo Anna—†	65	operator	35	
	P	Bartolo Joseph	65	painter	39	"
	R	Blundo Angelo	65	laborer	43	58 Everett
	S	*Blundo Maria—†	65	housewife	42	58 "
	T	Minichiello Pasquale	66	laborer	48	here
	U	Minichiello Rose—†	66	housewife	47	"
	V	*Ricotti Jennie—†	66	packer	24	"
	W	*Ricotti Lucia—†	66	housewife	63	"
	X	*Dichio Antonetta—†	66	housekeeper	39	"
	Z	Peluso Fred	66	laborer	47	"
	Y	*Peluso Raffaela—†	66	housewife	43	"
1688	A	*Giorgione Ralph	66	salesman	33	"
	B	*LoConte Angelina—†	66	housewife	31	"
	C	LoConte Frederico	66	pressman	32	"
	D	LoConte Rafaele	66	laborer	40	"
	E	Ferullo Alfred	67	"	28	142 Gove
	F	Ferullo Elizabeth—†	67	housewife	25	142 "
	G	Fiore Charles	67	printer	24	394 K
	H	*Fiore Rose—†	67	housewife	22	119½ Orleans
	K	Marasca Elda—†	67	"	27	here
	L	Marasca Joseph	67	machinist	29	"
	M	*Amore Assunta—†	67	housewife	55	"
	N	*Amore Matteo	67	laborer	55	"
	O	Gulinello Frank	67	chauffeur	27	N Hampshire
	P	Gulinello Jennie—†	67	housewife	23	17 Minot
	R	Salerno Alberto	68	timekeeper	34	here
	S	*Salerno Francesco	68	retired	73	"

Page.	Letter.	Full Name.	Residence, Jan. 1, 1938.	Occupation.	Supposed Age.	Reported Residence, Jan. 1, 1937. Street and Number.

Frankfort Street—Continued

Page.	Letter.	Full Name.	Residence, Jan. 1, 1938.	Occupation.	Supposed Age.	Reported Residence, Jan. 1, 1937. Street and Number.
	T	Salerno Genovefa—†	68	at home	25	here
	U	*Salerno Maria—†	68	housewife	67	"
	V	*Metta Carmella—†	68	"	52	70 Frankfort
	W	Metta Nichola	68	laborer	22	70 "
	X	Metta Sabino	68	"	53	70 "
	Y	Dichiara Josephine—†	68	housewife	32	here
	Z	Dichiara Thomas	68	laborer	34	"
1689						
	A	*Bucci Antonio	68	shoeworker	50	"
	B	*Bucci Maria—†	68	housewife	50	"
	C	Bucci Pietro	68	boilermaker	21	"
	D	Cappluzzo Augostino	68	laborer	40	
	E	*Cappluzzo Rafaela—†	68	housewife	41	"
	F	Monterisi Frank	68	stitcher	27	
	G	*Montarisi Madelena—†	68	housewife	51	"
	H	Monterisi Peter	68	chauffeur	25	"
	K	Lauria Agrippino	69	chemist	33	
	L	Lauria Laura—†	69	housewife	31	"
	M	Rizza Jennie—†	69	"	29	
	N	Rizza Joseph	69	chauffeur	31	"
	O	Morra Albert	69	printer	21	99A Prince
	P	*Morra Anthony	69	retired	72	Medford
	S	*Stracia Ferdinando	69	laborer	62	here
	T	*Stracia Theresa—†	69	housewife	61	"
	U	Tambarini Gino	69	shipper	23	"
	V	Tamborini Sue—†	69	housewife	21	"
	W	*DeLauretis Maria—†	70	"	76	
	X	*DeLauretis Pasquale	70	laborer	40	
	Y	Gasbarro Vincent	70	machinist	38	"
	Z	*Leandro Immaculate—†	70	housewife	33	"
1690						
	A	Leandro Joseph	70	laborer	45	"
	B	*Annese Antonetta—†	70	housewife	33	62 Frankfort
	C	Annese Antonio	70	painter	42	62 "
	D	Schena Antonio	70	laborer	40	here
	E	*Schena Rosie—†	70	housewife	37	"
	F	Gasbarro Domenico	70	laborer	50	"
	G	Gasbarro Rubina—†	70	housewife	45	"
	H	*Petrillo Frank	70	laborer	53	
	K	*Petrillo Rose—†	70	housewife	52	"

Page.	Letter.	Full Name.	Residence, Jan. 1, 1938.	Occupation.	Supposed Age.	Reported Residence, Jan. 1, 1937. Street and Number.

Frankfort Street—Continued

	L	Mootrey Angelina—†	71	packer	27	here
	M	Mootrey James N	71	presser	31	"
	N	Simonelli Angelo	71	shoeworker	25	"
	O	Simonelli Angelo A	71	laborer	57	
	P	Simonelli Raffaela—†	71	housewife	52	"
	R*	Terrino Clementina—†	72	at home	75	
	S*	Voltolini Joseph	72	shoeworker	59	"
	T	Dunn James	72	laborer	24	10 Breed
	U	Dunn Rose—†	72	housewife	22	10 "
	V	DellaCroce Amaria—†	72	"	44	141 Cottage
	W	DellaCroce Generoso	72	shoeworker	46	141 "
	X	Picardo Domenic	72	presser	25	141 "
	Y*	Picardo Phyllis—†	72	housewife	24	141 "
	Z	Picardo Angelo	72	laborer	50	here
1691						
	A*	Picardo Felizia—†	72	housewife	51	"
	B*	Gagliardi Mary—†	72	"	43	
	C	Gagliardi Michael	72	laborer	43	
	D*	Ruggero Francesca—†	74	housewife	57	"
	E	Ruggero Guiseppe	74	laborer	67	
	F	Ruggero Lucy—†	74	operator	24	
	G	Ruggero Eleanor—†	74	housewife	24	"
	H	Ruggero Fred	74	operator	31	
	K*	Datello Bella—†	74	housewife	38	"
	L*	Datello John	74	laborer	41	
	M	Ruggero Carmen	74	laundryworker	28	"
	N	Ruggero Josephine—†	74	housewife	26	"
	O*	Aloisi Mary—†	74	"	30	
	P*	Aloisi Samuel	74	operator	39	
	R	Scialabba Anna—†	76	housewife	64	"
	S	Scialabba Joseph	76	laborer	22	
	T	Piscitelli Angelina—†	76	housewife	23	"
	U	Piscitelli Michael	76	laborer	30	
	V*	Dattoli Bella—†	76	housewife	38	"
	W	Dattoli John	76	laborer	43	"
	X	Giglio Benjamin	76	machinist	25	376 Sumner
	Y	Giglio Eleanor—†	76	housewife	20	172 Cottage
	Z	Esposito Anna—†	76	"	20	49 Jeffries
1692						
	A	Esposito Thomas	76	painter	24	152 Chelsea

Page.	Letter.	FULL NAME.	Residence, Jan. 1, 1938.	Occupation.	Supposed Age.	Reported Residence, Jan. 1, 1937. Street and Number.
		Frankfort Street—Continued				
	B	DiGianni Michael	76	merchant	42	here
	C	*DiGianni Rosalie—†	76	housewife	42	"
	D	Stella Anna—†	78	"	28	"
	E	*Stella Gaetano	78	laborer	39	
	F	Cafano Cosmo	78	chauffeur	22	"
	G	Cafano Mary—†	78	housewife	40	"
	H	DeLuca Sophie—†	78	"	20	109 Wordsworth
	K	Deluca Vito	78	laborer	23	109 "
	L	Basilesco Poteuza	78	tailor	40	Everett
	M	Panduosco Palmino—†	78	housewife	64	here
	N	Panduosco Peter	78	retired	67	"
	O	Scialabba Anthony	78	engineer	26	60 Frankfort
	P	Scialabba Josephine—†	78	housewife	20	60 "
	R	*Catana Angelina—†	78	"	59	here
	S	Catana Michael	78	laborer	62	"
	T	Forti Natale	80	mechanic	32	"
	U	Forti Rose—†	80	housewife	31	"
	V	Nigro Frank	80	machinist	31	"
	W	Nigro Philomena—†	80	housewife	23	"
	X	*Farinola Jennie—†	80	"	45	
	Y	Farinola Salvatore	80	laborer	53	
	Z	Murano Andrew	80	carpenter	55	"
1693						
	A	Murano Raymond	80	mechanic	22	"
	B	*Murano Susan—†	80	housewife	52	"
	C	Lucibello Andrew	80	baker	36	
	D	Lucibello Philomena—†	80	housewife	30	"
	E	*Caiazza Antonio	80	leathercutter	53	"
	F	*Caiazza Mary—†	80	housewife	44	"
	G	Caiazza Thomas	80	salesman	25	"
	H	*Pupa Christina—†	80	at home	72	
		Gould's Court				
	K	Lespasio Domenic		laborer	22	here
	L	Lespasio Margaret—†		seamstress	23	"
	M	Lespasio Michael		laborer	20	"
	N	*Lespasio Rose—†		housewife	53	"
	O	Thornton Alice M—†		housekeeper	45	"
	P	Thornton Thomas A	5	boilermaker	62	"

Page.	Letter.	Full Name.	Residence, Jan. 1, 1938.	Occupation.	Supposed Age.	Reported Residence, Jan. 1, 1937. Street and Number.

Gove Street

Page.	Letter.	Full Name.	Residence, Jan. 1, 1938.	Occupation.	Supposed Age.	Reported Residence, Jan. 1, 1937. Street and Number.
	R	*Lanzi Domenic	60	carpenter	56	here
	S	*Lanzi Govina—†	60	housewife	62	"
	V	Doull John	62	operator	32	"
	W	Doull Mary—†	62	housewife	29	"
	X	Grosso Domenic	62	laborer	55	
	Y	*Grosso Susan—†	62	seamstress	55	"
	Z	Bisignani Richard	62	attorney	26	"
1694						
	A	*Bisignani Rose—†	62	housewife	65	"
	B	*Cipriani Francesca—†	64	"	74	
	C	Cipriani Salvatore	64	retired	77	
	D	*Mauro Amelia—†	64	housewife	44	"
	E	Mauro Pelegrino	64	tailor	48	
	F	Lalicata Joseph	64	painter	20	
	G	Lalicata Josephine—†	64	stitcher	22	
	H	Lalicata Mario	64	chauffeur	24	"
	K	*Lalicata Paul	64	laborer	52	
	L	*Lalicata Rose—†	64	housewife	44	"
	M	Ligiero Mary—†	66	"	23	
	N	Ligiero Orlando	66	laborer	26	
	O	*DelMuto Filomena—†	66	housewife	41	"
	P	*DelMuto Frank	66	carpenter	44	"
	R	DiFazio Antonio	66	longshoreman	52	"
	S	DiFazio Peter	66	plumber	22	"
	T	*Agnelli Alfonso	128	clergyman	50	Canada
	U	Andreotti Edward	128	janitor	27	here
	V	Barrelli Henry	128	clergyman	25	"
	W	Brambilla Sixtus	128	"	38	14 N Bennet
	X	Checchia Domenic	128	"	32	New York
	Y	Nix Christopher	128	"	45	here
	Z	*Nuti Giuseppe	128	chef	61	"
1695						
	A	Tricomi Jennie—†	132	housewife	43	"
	B	Tricomi Joseph	132	mechanic	21	"
	C	Tricomi Josephine—†	132	operator	26	"
	D	Tricomi Peter	132	barber	54	
	E	Schittino Angelo	132	cleanser	26	
	F	*Degnio Savino	132	laborer	60	
	G	*Degnio Vincenza—†	132	housewife	58	"
	H	*Caso Frances—†	132	"	42	
	K	Caso Nicholas	132	trainman	45	"

Page.	Letter.	Full Name.	Residence, Jan. 1, 1938.	Occupation.	Supposed Age.	Reported Residence, Jan. 1, 1937. Street and Number.
		Gove Street—Continued				
	L	*Maniglia Agatina—†	132	housewife	24	here
	M	*Maniglia Leo	132	barber	34	“
	N	*Dattoli Ciriaco	134	retired	72	“
	O	*Dattoli Rosina—†	134	housewife	74	“
	P	*DelFraino Antonio	134	laborer	33	184 Chelsea
	R	DelFraino Margaret—†	134	housewife	26	184 “
	S	Plagenza Frank	134	laborer	53	here
	T	*Plagenza Mary—†	134	housewife	45	“
	U	*Sollazzo Angelina—†	134	“	43	“
	V	Sollazzo Frank	134	clerk	20	
	W	Gallo Madelena—†	134	housekeeper	44	“
	X	*Tucone Maria—†	134	at home	74	“
	Y	Letendre Margaret—†	134	housewife	30	48 Chelsea
	Z	Letendre Wilfred	134	clerk	43	48 “
1696		**Lubec Street**				
	A	*DelloRusso Angelina—†	58	housewife	43	here
	B	DelloRusso Gaetano	58	merchant	45	“
	C	*DeLisi Adeline—†	58	housewife	44	“
	D	DeLisi Felix	58	laborer	46	
	E	*Dattoli Grace—†	58	housewife	26	“
	F	Dattoli Vincent	58	barber	40	
	G	Lobarusso Helen—†	58	housewife	27	“
	H	Lobarusso John	58	laborer	31	
	K	Errico Edith—†	58	houseworker	28	“
	L	Errico Edward	58	laborer	62	
	M	*Errico Maria—†	58	housewife	66	“
	N	Miranda Americo	58	operator	29	
	O	Miranda Antonio	58	barber	24	
	P	Miranda Edith—†	58	clerk	20	“
	R	Miranda Nicholas	58	barber	59	“
	S	Miranda Rose—†	58	housewife	59	“
	T	DeRosa James	60	merchant	21	19 Lowell
	U	DeRosa Susan—†	60	housewife	22	7 Drake pl
	V	*Lazzara Carmella—†	60	“	55	here
	W	Lazzara Joseph	60	laborer	63	“
	X	*Lamusico Donatella—†	60	housewife	37	“
	Y	Lamusico Giuseppe	60	laborer	45	
	Z	*Coppola Carmen	60	“	45	

Page.	Letter.	Full Name.	Residence, Jan. 1, 1938.	Occupation.	Supposed Age.	Reported Residence, Jan. 1, 1937. Street and Number.

1697

Lubec Street—Continued

	A	*Mussi Anthony	60	laborer	52	here
	B	*Mussi Susan—†	60	housewife	54	"
	C	Diminico Antonio	60	laborer	26	"
	D	Diminico Felix	60	shoeworker	26	"
	F	*DellAria Concetta—†	62	housewife	47	"
	G	DellAria Grace—†	62	candyworker	23	"
	H	DellAria Jennie—†	62	"	21	
	K	*DellAria Vito	62	laborer	59	
	L	LaRosa Vendetto	62	shoeworker	49	"
	M	LaRosa Salvatore	62	student	20	
	N	LaRosa Santa—†	62	houseworker	21	"
	O	*Gambino Annie—†	62	housewife	60	"
	P	Gambino Catherine—†	62	candyworker	27	"
	R	Martin Joseph	62	laborer	45	
	S	Martin Mary—†	62	housewife	44	"
	T	Luongo George	62	laborer	35	
	U	Luongo Jennie—†	62	housewife	28	"
	V	*Minerva Caroline—†	64	"	39	
	W	*Minerva Nunzio	64	laborer	47	
	X	Cali Phyllis—†	64	housewife	24	"
	Y	Cali Rocco	64	waiter	30	
	Z	*Nocillo Frank	64	laborer	66	
1698						
	A	*Nocillo Josephine—†	64	housewife	46	"
	B	Nocillo Margaret—†	64	packer	22	
	C	Nocillo Vincent	64	laborer	29	
	D	*Cibene Annie—†	64	housewife	46	"
	E	Cibene Anthony	64	operator	26	
	F	Cibene Silvino	64	laborer	48	
	G	Degregorio Clementine—†	64	housewife	38	"
	H	Degregorio Vincent	64	glassworker	42	"

Marion Street

	K	Napolitano Michael	247	laborer	41	here
	L	*Tassone Grace—†	247	housewife	29	"
	M	*Tassone Rose—†	247	at home	75	"
	N	Tassone Ventura	247	salesman	41	"
	O	*Papasodoro Catherine—†	247	housewife	57	"
	P	*Papasodoro Giuseppe	247	laborer	59	"

Page.	Letter.	Full Name.	Residence, Jan. 1, 1938.	Occupation.	Supposed Age.	Reported Residence, Jan. 1, 1937. Street and Number.

Marion Street—Continued

	R	Papasodoro Michael	247	laborer	23	here
	S	Cardinale Joseph E	249	"	22	187 Chelsea
	T	Cardinale Josephine—†	249	housewife	22	198 Putnam
	U	Carnabuci Carmello	249	barber	64	here
	V	*Carnabuci Dominica—†	249	housewife	55	"
	W	Carnabuci Margaret—†	249	operator	23	"
	X	Carnabuci Mary—†	249	stitcher	26	
	Y	Carnabuci Caroline—†	249	at home	26	
	Z	Carnabuci Jennie—†	249	operator	29	
1699						
	A	Carnabuci Peter	249	tailor	59	"
	B	Duchi Anthony	251	butcher	27	225 Lexington
	C	Duchi Josephine—†	251	housewife	23	222 E Eagle
	D	Schepici Anthony	251	laborer	21	here
	E	*Schepici Concetta—†	251	housewife	55	"
	F	Schepici Joseph	251	laborer	27	"
	G	*Schepici Stelario	251	"	52	
	H	Interbartolo Florence—†	251	operator	22	
	K	*Interbartolo Joseph	251	"	63	
	L	Interbartolo Margaret—†	251	"	25	
	M	*Interbartolo Rose—†	251	housewife	58	"
	N	*Montecalvo Angelina—†	253	"	59	
	O	*Montecalvo Nicholas	253	laborer	66	
	P	Montecalvo Rose—†	253	candymaker	23	"
	R	*Dicrescenzio Mary—†	253	housewife	39	"
	S	*Dicrescenzio Saverio	253	laborer	53	69 Chelsea
	T	Montecalvo Angela—†	253	housewife	35	here
	U	Montecalvo Marciano	253	candymaker	38	"
	V	Paventi Antonetta—†	255	housewife	21	"
	W	Paventi Saverio	255	broker	26	
	X	Colagiovanni Donato	255	shoemaker	46	"
	Y	Colagiovanni Josephine-†	255	stitcher	21	
	Z	*Colagiovanni Louise—†	255	housewife	42	"
1700						
	A	Lunetta Joseph	255	laborer	65	203 London
	B	*Lunetta Rose—†	255	housewife	55	here
	C	Lunetta Salvatore	255	boxmaker	20	"

Maverick Street

	H	*Yocca Patrick	169	locksmith	46	here
	K	*Durante Frank	169	retired	65	"

Page.	Letter.	Full Name.	Residence, Jan. 1, 1938.	Occupation.	Supposed Age.	Reported Residence, Jan. 1, 1937. Street and Number.

Maverick Street—Continued

Page.	Letter.	Full Name.	Residence, Jan. 1, 1938.	Occupation.	Supposed Age.	Reported Residence, Jan. 1, 1937. Street and Number.
	L	*Durante Sarah—†	169	housewife	72	here
	M	Trocano Angelina—†	169	packer	32	"
	N	*Trocano Joseph	169	retired	74	"
	O	Trocano Joseph	169	clerk	36	
	P	*Trocano Mary—†	169	housewife	71	"
	R	Trocano Rose—†	169	packer	29	
	T	*Ranieri Antonio	171	shoemaker	43	"
	U	Loguidice Antonio	171	carpenter	52	"
	V	Loguidice Mary—†	171	housewife	42	"
	W	Indorato James	171	laborer	22	
	X	*Indorato Josephine—†	171	housewife	43	"
	Y	Indorato Ottavio	171	clerk	21	
	Z	Indorato Salvatore	171	laborer	53	
1701						
	A	*Bruno Mary—†	172	at home	76	
	B	Fagone Josephine—†	172	housewife	41	"
	C	Fagone Mary—†	172	tailoress	20	
	D	Guarino Louis	172	carpenter	42	"
	E	*Guarino Rose—†	172	housewife	38	"
	F	Aiello Domenic	173	operator	21	"
	G	Aiello Frank	173	candymaker	32	"
	H	*Aiello John	173	laborer	38	
	K	Aiello Joseph	173	shipper	27	
	L	DeAngelis Joseph	173	baker	35	
	M	DeAngelis Sadie—†	173	housewife	34	"
	N	Campagna Napoleon	173	laborer	25	
	O	*Campagna Philomena—†	173	housewife	60	"
	R	Graziano Nellie—†	174	clerk	22	
	S	Graziano Paul	174	operator	24	"
	T	*Vilella Theresa—†	174	housewife	52	"
	U	*Vilella Thomas	174	tailor	56	
	V	Bartuccio Alfred	174	laborer	23	
	W	Bartuccio Anna—†	174	clerk	21	
	X	Bartuccio Concetta—†	174	housewife	53	"
	Y	Bartuccio Olympia	174	candymaker	22	"
1702						
	A	*DeAngelis Angelo	175	baker	63	
	B	*DeAngelis Anna—†	175	housewife	62	"
	C	DeAngelis Dominic	175	baker	21	
	D	*DeAngelis Angelina—†	175	housewife	33	"
	E	DeAngelis Frank	175	baker	34	
	F	Raimo Anthony	177	printer	50	

Page.	Letter.	Full Name.	Residence, Jan. 1, 1938.	Occupation.	Supposed Age.	Reported Residence, Jan. 1, 1937. Street and Number.

Maverick Street—Continued

Page.	Letter.	Full Name.	Residence, Jan. 1, 1938.	Occupation.	Supposed Age.	Reported Residence, Jan. 1, 1937. Street and Number.
	G	*Raimo Mary—†	177	housewife	47	here
	M	Cadelo Catherine—†	178	"	59	"
	N	Cadelo John	178	agent	54	"
	O	Falardo Carmen	178	barber	37	
	P	*Falardo Mary—†	178	housewife	33	"
	S	Wright Mary L—†	180	stitcher	29	
	T	Wright Robert H	180	laborer	25	
	U	Zarba Elveria—†	180	housewife	37	"
	V	Zarba Joseph	180	manager	40	"
	Y	*DiRinzo Antonio	183	laborer	38	
	Z	*DiRinzo Concetta—†	183	housewife	36	"
1703						
	A	Scalafani Antonio	183	laborer	26	
	B	Scalafani Stella—†	183	housewife	22	"
	C	Amato Martin	183	manager	37	"
	D	*Tarallo Mary—†	183	housewife	37	"
	E	Tarallo Romano	183	candymaker	43	"
	F	*Lewis Charles	185	laundryman	66	"
	G	Blundo Ignazio	185	laborer	25	
	H	Blundo Vincenza—†	185	housewife	52	"
	K	Tamburo Anthony	185	tailor	36	
	L	*Tamburo Julia—†	185	housewife	62	"
	N	Poto James	186	laborer	39	
	O	DiNuccio Alphonsus	186	"	33	
	P	DiNuccio Eleanor—†	186	housewife	29	"
	R	Alberti Geramano	186	laborer	30	
	S	Alberti Mary—†	186	housewife	27	"
	U	D'Agostino Madeline—†	187	"	28	
	V	D'Agostino Salvatore	187	salesman	30	"
	W	Tesla Americo	187	printer	28	
	X	Tesla Palmina—†	187	housewife	29	"
	Z	*Rumley Joseph	188	lineman	36	Cambridge
1704						
	A	Rumley Rose—†	188	housewife	35	"
	B	*Ferrante Josephine—†	188	"	47	here
	C	*Ferrante Sebastino	188	laborer	63	"
	D	Justo Joseph	188	"	26	"
	G	Rinaldi Anna E—†	190	tailoress	25	
	H	Rinaldi Anthony	190	laborer	38	
	K	Rinaldi Florence—†	190	housewife	35	"
	L	Rinaldi Lucy—†	190	clerk	22	

Page.	Letter.	Full Name.	Residence, Jan. 1, 1938.	Occupation.	Supposed Age.	Reported Residence, Jan. 1, 1937. Street and Number.

Maverick Street—Continued

Page.	Letter.	Full Name.	Residence, Jan. 1, 1938.	Occupation.	Supposed Age.	Reported Residence, Jan. 1, 1937. Street and Number.
	M	Rinaldi Antonetta—†	190	housewife	39	here
	N	Rinaldi Dominick A	190	custodian	48	"
	P	LaRosa Emma—†	191	housewife	31	"
	R	LaRosa John	191	chauffeur	39	"
	T	Bozzi Henrietta—†	191	housewife	20	122 Saratoga
	S	Bozzi Louis, jr	191	manager	23	122 "
	U	DiCicco Irene—†	191	housewife	39	here
	V	DiCicco John	191	clerk	40	"
	W	Bettano Catherine—†	191	housewife	30	"
	X	Bettano John	191	bartender	31	"
	Y	*Cardella John	191	laundryworker	46	"
1705						
	B	Piccelli Luigi	192	laborer	24	
	C	Piccelli Mildred—†	192	housewife	23	"
	D	Turco Anthony	192	laborer	45	
	E	Turco Elvena—†	192	housewife	42	"
	F	Siciliano Raffaela—†	193	"	52	
	G	Siciliano William	193	ironworker	57	"
	H	*Maglio Angelo	193	candymaker	46	"
	K	Maglio Anthony	193	salesman	21	"
	L	*Maglio Concetta—†	193	housewife	44	"
	M	Maglio Louis	193	clerk	20	"
	N	Guglielmi Catherine—†	193	housewife	51	72 Chelsea
	O	Guglielmi Mario	193	laborer	20	here
	P	Fuccillo Catherine—†	194	housewife	28	"
	R	Fuccillo Frank	194	painter	28	"
	S	Daddario Matthew	194	candymaker	28	"
	T	Daddario Rose—†	194	housewife	26	"
	U	Argenzio Angela—†	194	"	33	"
	V	Argenzio Louis	194	painter	39	
	W	*Argenzio Rose—†	194	housewife	75	"
	X	*Reuti Joseph	rear 194	laborer	46	127 Maverick
	Y	*Reuti Susan—†	" 194	housewife	37	127 "
	Z	Luti Anna—†	195	"	30	here
1706						
	A	Luti James	195	butcher	35	"
	B	*Testa Mary—†	195	housewife	57	"
	C	Testa Vincenzo	195	operator	57	"
	D	Testa Anthony J	195	manager	33	"
	E	Testa Nancy—†	195	housewife	32	"
	F	Cheffro Mary—†	196	saleswoman	27	"

Page.	Letter.	Full Name.	Residence, Jan. 1, 1938.	Occupation.	Supposed Age.	Reported Residence, Jan. 1, 1937. Street and Number.

Maverick Street—Continued

Page.	Letter.	Full Name.	Residence, Jan. 1, 1938.	Occupation.	Supposed Age.	Reported Residence, Jan. 1, 1937. Street and Number.
	G	Cheffro Silverio	196	laborer	23	here
	H	Cheffro Sylvester	196	operator	26	“
	K	*Melchionda Carmella—†	196	housewife	49	“
	L	Bettano Doris—†	196	“	33	
	M	Bettano Joseph	196	skipper	39	
	N	*Sardeletti Geneva—†	196	housewife	45	“
	O	Sardeletti Joseph	196	laborer	21	
	P	Sardeletti Louise—†	196	clerk	26	
	T	Ciccarelli Gennaro	198	shoeworker	39	“
	U	Ciccarelli Guglielma—†	198	housewife	28	“
	V	*Piccorella Andrew	198	laborer	56	286 Sumner
	W	Piccorella Anthony	198	“	24	286 “
	X	Piccorella Bernardo	198	“	29	286 “
	Y	Piccorella Margaret—†	198	clerk	22	286 ‘
	Z	*Piccorella Mary—†	198	housewife	51	286 “
1707						
	A	*DeStefano Angelina—†	200	“	45	12 Chelsea
	B	*DeStefano John	200	laborer	45	12 “
	C	Domenico Josephine—†	200	housewife	42	here
	D	Domenico Thomas D	200	laborer	44	“
	G	DiPietro Clancy	204	undertaker	53	“
	H	DiPietro Lydia—†	204	clerk	22	
	K	DiPietro Ralph	204	undertaker	20	“
	L	DiPietro Rose—†	204	housewife	51	“
	M	DiPietro Silvio	204	student	23	
	P	Bonfiglio Emma—†	206	clerk	21	
	R	*Bonfiglio Santo	206	laborer	53	
	S	Bonfiglio Vincenza—†	206	housewife	52	“
	T	Bonfiglio William	206	laborer	26	“
	U	Eason George	206	seaman	27	406 Sumner
	V	Eason Marie—†	206	housewife	25	406 “
	W	Schena Rocco	206	laborer	40	406 “
	X	Schena Sadie—†	206	housewife	38	406 “
	Y	D'Agostino Angelo	208	laborer	56	here
	Z	D'Agostino Anthony	208	electrician	24	“
1708						
	A	D'Agostino Edith—†	208	clerk	22	
	B	D'Agostino Helen—†	208	“	21	
	C	D'Agostino Josephine—†	208	housewife	72	“
	D	*D'Agostino Nancy—†	208	“	50	
	E	Pellecchia Jean—†	208	“	30	

Page.	Letter.	FULL NAME.	Residence, Jan. 1, 1938.	Occupation.	Supposed Age.	Reported Residence, Jan. 1, 1937. Street and Number.

Maverick Street—Continued

	F	Pellecchia Joseph	208	shoeworker	31	here
	G	*Commaroto Anthony	208	barber	24	"
	H	Commaroto Margaret—†	208	housewife	23	"
	K	Malchanoff Josephine—†	208	"	27	
	L	Romano Anthony	208	instructor	27	"
	M	Romano Margaret—†	208	housewife	27	"
	N	Lawford Frederick A	210	chauffeur	41	"
	O	Lawford Lillian M—†	210	physician	44	"
	P	Gerome Frank	210	shoemaker	30	"
	R	Gerome Josephine—†	210	housewife	29	"
	S	Russo Frank	210	laborer	26	
	T	Russo Stella—†	210	housewife	22	"
	U	*Chicariello Anthony	210	laborer	72	
	V	Chicariello John	210	"	23	
	W	*Chicariello Martara—†	210	housewife	50	"
	X	Amato Emilio	210	laborer	40	
	Y	Paterno Angelina—†	210	housewife	42	"
	Z	*Paterno Stephen	210	laborer	47	
1709						
	A	Baptista Angelina—†	211	housewife	24	"
	B	Baptista William	211	operator	27	"
	C	Imbriano Louis	211	chef	25	
	D	Imbriano Yolanda—†	211	housewife	25	"
	E	Buancucci Domenica—†	211	"	50	
	F	*Cerulli Nina—†	212	"	35	
	G	Cerulli Victor	212	laborer	57	
	H	*Conte Jennie—†	212	housewife	60	"
	K	*Conte Joseph	212	laborer	57	
	L	*Turco Antonetta—†	212	housewife	40	"
	M	Turco John	212	laborer	41	
	N	*Petrolio Celestina—†	212	housewife	51	"
	O	*Petrolio Louise—†	212	candymaker	52	"
	P	*Finocchio Anna—†	212	housewife	41	"
	R	*Finocchio Frank	212	laborer	57	
	S	Armanti Fortunato	213	retired	71	
	T	Watts Irene—†	213	candy packer	53	"
	U	Guerra Anthony	213	shipper	27	
	V	*Guerra Catherine—†	213	housewife	63	"
	W	Guerra Salvatore	213	packer	22	
	X	Guerra Theresa—†	213	seamstress	25	"
	Y	*Salvo Sarah—†	213	housewife	47	"

Page.	Letter.	Full Name.	Residence, Jan. 1, 1938.	Occupation.	Supposed Age.	Reported Residence, Jan. 1, 1937. Street and Number.

Maverick Street—Continued

Page.	Letter.	Full Name.	Residence, Jan. 1, 1938.	Occupation.	Supposed Age.	Reported Residence, Jan. 1, 1937. Street and Number.
	z	Salvo Vita—†	213	at home	20	here
1710						
	A	Siracusa Nicholas	215	barber	30	
	B	Siracusa Theresa—†	215	housewife	29	"
	C	DeSimone Jennie—†	215	at home	23	"
	D	*DeSimone Mary—†	215	housewife	48	"
	E	DeSimone Peter	215	manager	50	"
	F	Bagnera Anthony	215	laborer	49	
	G	Bagnera Beatrice—†	215	packer	24	
	H	Bagnera Helen—†	215	"	23	
	K	Bagnera Joseph	215	laborer	27	
	L	*Bagnera Lena—†	215	housewife	47	"
	M	Fiorette Michael	217	painter	33	
	N	Fiorette Nellie—†	217	housewife	25	"
	O	*Mercurio Elizabeth—†	217	"	49	215 Maverick
	P	*Mercurio Joseph	217	metalworker	53	215 "
	R	Mercurio William	217	"	23	215 "
	S	*Trodella Antonio	217	retired	55	here
	T	*Trodella Mary—†	217	housewife	47	"
	U	DeNietoles Anthony	219	laborer	33	"
	V	DeNietoles Mary—†	219	housewife	29	"
	W	DeNietoles Catherine—†	219	"	61	
	X	DeNietoles Vincent	219	tailor	68	"
	Y	Ramuno Angelina—†	219	operator	22	89 Chelsea
	Z	*Ramuno Joseph	219	expressman	50	89 "
1711						
	A	Ramuno Rose—†	219	housekeeper	21	89 "
	B	Marino Accurcio	223	packer	29	here
	C	Marino Rose—†	223	housewife	27	"
	D	*Ciello Frances—†	223	"	54	"
	E	Ciello Nicholas	223	laborer	54	
	F	Constanza Jennie—†	223	housewife	43	"
	G	Constanza Louis	223	molder	45	
	H	Battaglia Louis	225	agent	32	
	K	Battaglia Marie—†	225	housewife	32	"
	L	Gravellese Anthony	225	merchant	33	"
	M	Gravellese Josephine—†	225	housewife	34	"
	N	Dente Alessio	225	retired	55	
	O	Dente Concetta—†	225	housewife	53	"
	P	Dente Virginia—†	225	seamstress	22	"

Page.	Letter.	Full Name.	Residence, Jan. 1, 1938.	Occupation.	Supposed Age.	Reported Residence, Jan. 1, 1937. Street and Number.

Maverick Street—Continued

Page.	Letter.	Full Name.	Residence, Jan. 1, 1938.	Occupation.	Supposed Age.	Reported Residence, Jan. 1, 1937. Street and Number.
	R	Briano Angelo	227	laborer	27	here
	S	Briano Bessie—†	227	housewife	27	"
	T	*Pirone Josephine—†	227	"	44	"
	U	*Pirone Patrick	227	shoeworker	45	"
	V	*Pirone Filomena—†	227	housewife	34	"
	W	*Pirone Gennaro	227	shoeworker	41	"
	Y	Maddalone Frank	229	laborer	23	
	Z	*Maddalone Rose—†	229	housewife	62	"
1712						
	A	*Mastaro Nunzio	229	laborer	58	
	B	DelPrete Antonetta—†	229	housewife	24	"
	C	DelPrete Gennaro	229	laborer	28	
	D	Brena Filomena—†	231	waitress	31	
	E	DeAngelis Anthony	231	manager	54	
	F	Sabia Anthony	231	"	33	
	H	Sabia Dora—†	231	housewife	28	"
	K	Sabia Joseph	231	manager	60	"
	G	Sabia Theodora—†	231	housewife	60	"
	L	Collarone Angelo	233	laborer	22	
	M	*Collarone Josephine—†	233	housewife	52	"
	N	*Collorone Richard	233	laborer	58	
	O	Gioiosa Charles	237	plumber	38	
	R	Sabia Marion—†	241	physician	28	"
	S	Sabia Michael	241	manager	35	"
	T	Corleto Benjamin	241	retired	66	
	U	Corleto Marion—†	241	housewife	62	"

McKay Place

Page.	Letter.	Full Name.	Residence, Jan. 1, 1938.	Occupation.	Supposed Age.	Reported Residence, Jan. 1, 1937. Street and Number.
	V	*Pasto Alba—†	2	housewife	42	here
	W	Pasto James	2	laborer	47	"
	X	*Pilige Catherine—†	2	housewife	75	"
	Y	Magaletta Frank	2	laborer	47	
	Z	Magaletta Josephine—†	2	housewife	40	"
1713						
	A	Prestanzio Philomena—†	2	"	77	
	B	*Tonaglia Alphonsus	2	laborer	53	
	C	DeFlorio Blanche—†	2	housewife	34	"
	D	DeFlorio Joseph	2	laborer	34	
	E	*Ferrulo Amelia—†	2	housewife	75	"

Page.	Letter.	Full Name.	Residence, Jan. 1, 1938.	Occupation.	Supposed Age.	Reported Residence, Jan. 1, 1937. Street and Number.

Orleans Street

Page.	Letter.	Full Name.	Residence, Jan. 1, 1938.	Occupation.	Supposed Age.	Reported Residence, Jan. 1, 1937. Street and Number.
	G	Somma John	80	laborer	22	here
	H	*Somma Ralph	80	"	53	"
	K	*Somma Rose—†	80	housewife	53	"
	L	*Cencini Gasparo	80	plasterer	55	"
	M	Bonasoro John	80	mechanic	22	"
	N	*Bonasoro Josephine—†	80	housewife	42	"
	O	Bonasoro Vincent	80	laborer	54	
	P	*Armato Jasper	80	"	54	
	R	*Armato Jennie—†	80	housewife	54	"
	S	Armato John	80	laborer	22	
	T	Juliano John	80	"	40	
	U	Juliano Philomena—†	80	housewife	37	"
	V	Armato Domenic	80	shoeworker	42	"
	W	*Armato Maria—†	80	housewife	42	"
	X	Barasi Bessie—†	80	"	25	
	Y	*Barasi Spaso	80	laborer	42	
	Z	*Morano Imacolata—†	80	at home	45	
1714						
	A	Simpson Charles	80	laborer	26	
	B	Simpson Philomena—†	80	housewife	25	"
	C	DeMatteo Domateo	80	operator	49	"
	D	DeMatteo Gaetana—†	80	housewife	40	"
	E	DeMatteo George	80	clerk	21	"
	F	Gulla Anthony	80	bartender	54	"
	G	Gulla Anthony, jr	80	packer	24	
	H	Gulla Grace—†	80	housewife	44	"
	K	Gulla Gregorio	80	barber	26	
	L	Gulla Rose—†	80	operator	20	"
	M	Emmett Mary—†	83	housewife	38	"
	N	Emmett Oliver	83	ironworker	41	"
	O	Leary Catherine—†	83	milliner	50	
	P	Fallon Catherine—†	83	at home	90	
	R	*Matorelle Michael	85	laborer	21	
	S	*Miano Eugene	85	"	50	
	T	*Miano Stella—†	85	housewife	50	"
	U	*Malafronte Theresa—†	85	at home	42	174 Chelsea
	V	Mastrangelo Rocco	85	laborer	40	here
	W	Amore Josephine—†	87	housekeeper	37	Wilmington
	X	Ciampa Anthony	87	chauffeur	34	here
	Y	Ciampa Mary—†	87	housewife	23	"
	Z	*Guarnero Carmello	87	retired	72	"

Orleans Street—Continued

Page.	Letter.	Full Name.	Residence, Jan. 1, 1938.	Occupation.	Supposed Age.	Reported Residence, Jan. 1, 1937. Street and Number.
1715						
	A	*Guarnero Maria—†	87	housewife	68	here
	B	Avola Alexander	89	shoeworker	24	90 Lexington
	C	Avola Edith—†	89	housewife	24	90 "
	D	*Contrado Adeline—†	89	"	38	here
	E	Contrado Pasquale	89	painter	44	"
	F	Muccaldi Joseph	89	shoemaker	50	S Braintree
	G	Muccaldi Rose—†	89	housewife	47	"
	K	Grandolfi Alfred	93	musician	21	here
	L	*Grandolfi George	93	shoeworker	65	"
	M	*Grandolfi Jennie—†	93	housewife	60	"
	N	*Grandolfi Angelina—†	93	"	42	
	O	*Grandolfi Antonio	93	merchant	44	"
	P	Grandolfi Jennie—†	93	saleswoman	21	"
	R	Poto George	101	laborer	38	
	S	Poto Yolande—†	101	housewife	35	"
	T	Capozzi Angelina—†	101	stitcher	20	
	U	*Capozzi Josephine—†	101	operator	26	
	V	Capozzi Michaelina—†	101	packer	21	
	W	*Capozzi Nicolatta—†	101	housewife	50	"
	X	*Falanga Joseph	101	laborer	57	
	Y	Falanga Leo	101	shoeworker	22	"
	Z	Falanga Lillian—†	101	candymaker	20	"
1716						
	A	Falanga Mary—†	101	housewife	56	"
	B	Falanga Andrew	102	shoeworker	32	34 Shelby
	C	Falanga Mary—†	102	housewife	29	34 "
	D	Irvin Edmund J	102	seaman	34	here
	E	Irvin Mary E—†	102	housewife	62	"
	F	Saunders Albert N	102	timekeeper	30	"
	G	Saunders Alice G—†	102	housewife	28	"
	H	Almeida Anthony	102	laborer	36	
	K	Almeida Mary—† —†	102	housewife	31	"
	L	McFarland Margaret—†	102	clerk	21	"
	M	*Toft Henry	103	fishcutter	34	216 E Eagle
	N	Toft Irene—†	103	housewife	26	216 "
	P	Santoro Bernardino	103	presser	22	here
	R	Santoro Madeline—†	103	housewife	43	"
	S	*Santoro Nicholas	103	laborer	49	"
	U	*Santangelo Bambina—†	104	housewife	42	"
	V	*Santangelo Michael	104	laborer	52	

Page.	Letter.	Full Name.	Residence, Jan. 1, 1938.	Occupation.	Supposed Age.	Reported Residence. Jan. 1, 1937. Street and Number.

Orleans Street—Continued

Page.	Letter.	Full Name.	Residence, Jan. 1, 1938.	Occupation.	Supposed Age.	Reported Residence. Jan. 1, 1937. Street and Number.
	x	*Giugunto Maria—†	106	housewife	60	here
	y	*Giugunto Vincenzo	106	retired	65	"
	z	*Ventulli Rose—†	106	at home	85	"
1717						
	A	Bracci Matteo	106	laborer	23	3 Percival pl
	B	*Bracci Michael	106	"	59	3 "
	C	*Bracci Philomena—†	106	housewife	49	3 "
	D	Fedesco Antonio	107	laborer	24	here
	E	*Fedesco Lena—†	107	stitcher	55	"
	F	DiFilippo Joseph	107	salesman	57	104 Chelsea
	G	*LaValle Concetta—†	107	housewife	52	115 Orleans
	H	LaValle Frederick	107	candymaker	48	115 "
	K	Minotti Arthur	107	merchant	31	here
	L	Minotti Edward	107	"	58	"
	M	*Barbacano Lucy—†	107	housewife	36	"
	N	*Barbacano Sabino	107	laborer	46	"
	O	Brogna Mary—†	107	housewife	57	2 Percival pl
	P	Brogna Virginia—†	107	typist	21	2 "
	R	Malacaso Rose—†	107	at home	22	here
	S	Amerena Anna—†	107	housewife	27	"
	T	Amerena Frank	107	laborer	30	"
	U	Amoroso Louise—†	107	housewife	31	"
	V	Amoroso Rosario	107	painter	40	
	W	DiMatteo Noah	107	laborer	31	
	X	DiMatteo Rose—†	107	housewife	26	"
	Y	Indrisano Emilio	107	painter	25	
	Z	Indrisano Mildred—†	107	housewife	25	"
1718						
	B	Altri Julia—†	108A	"	30	"
	C	Christina Lillian—†	108A	"	20	1 Percival pl
	D	Christina Louis	108A	laborer	22	1 "
	E	Terramagra Frank	108A	"	24	here
	F	Terramagra Sylvia—†	108A	housewife	23	"
	G	Anzalone Antonio	108A	chauffeur	24	"
	H	Anzalone Josephine—†	108A	housewife	27	"
	K	Harris Edith—†	108A	packer	26	"
	M	Casaburri Antonio	109	laborer	26	200 Maverick
	N	Casaburri Florence—†	109	housewife	24	200 "
	L	*Casaburri Addolorata—†	109	"	53	200 "
	O	Casaburri Nicola	109	laborer	54	200 "
	P	Cottone Ignazio	109	"	46	here

Page.	Letter.	FULL NAME.	Residence, Jan. 1, 1938.	Occupation.	Supposed Age.	Reported Residence, Jan. 1, 1937. Street and Number.

Orleans Street—Continued

	R	*Cottone Marguerita—†	109	housewife	42	here
	S	Altri Joseph	111	laborer	23	54 Cottage
	T	Altri Mary—†	111	housewife	40	54 "
	U	Brown John	111	steamfitter	38	28 Havre
	V	Ceruolo Anthony	111	plasterer	57	here
	W	Ceruolo John	111	entertainer	30	"
	X	Ceruolo Josephine—†	111	at home	24	"
	Y	Ceruolo Louis	111	laborer	20	
	Z	Ceruolo Marie—†	111	housewife	54	"
1719						
	A	Ceruolo Emilio	111	chauffeur	28	"
	B	Ceruolo Susan—†	111	assembler	30	"
	C	Monica Josephine—†	113	housewife	33	"
	D	Monica Sabino	113	laborer	34	
	E	Senese Michael	113	"	26	
	F	Senese Phyllis—†	113	housewife	28	"
	G	Sallese Carmella—†	113	"	28	
	H	Sallese Pasquale	113	salesman	30	"
	K	Iannacone Eugenio	115	laborer	40	
	L	*Maggio Vita—†	115	at home	64	
	M	Tripoli Anna—†	115	housewife	40	"
	N	Tripoli Frank	115	merchant	51	"
	O	Tripoli Mary—†	115	stenographer	21	"
	P	*Tripoli Salvatore	115	candymaker	48	"
	R	DiBerto Mary—†	115	stitcher	23	221 London
	S	DiBerto Romeo	115	butcher	26	30 Frankfort
	T	Mechenzi Jennie V—†	115	clerk	21	here
	U	*Romano Santa—†	115	housewife	39	"
	V	Romano Santo	115	laborer	50	"
	W	*Durante Elizabeth—†	115	housewife	33	"
	X	*Durante Joseph	115	shoeworker	40	"
	Y	Sotera Salvatore	115	operator	37	"
	Z	Sotera Vita—†	115	housewife	29	"
1720						
	A	*Giorgione Camella—†	115	"	53	
	B	Giorgione Edith—†	115	shoeworker	26	"
	C	Giorgione James	115	mechanic	24	"
	D	Giorgione Mario	115	clerk	20	
	E	Giorgione Sylvio—†	115	timekeeper	22	"
	F	Bertolino Frank	115	cutter	42	
	G	*Bertolino Ina—†	115	housewife	39	"

Page.	Letter.	Full Name.	Residence, Jan. 1, 1938.	Occupation.	Supposed Age.	Reported Residence, Jan. 1, 1937. Street and Number.
		Orleans Street—Continued				
	H	*Mancuso Frank	117	retired	68	here
	K	*Mancuso Grace—†	117	housewife	52	"
	L	*Marotta Joseph	117	laborer	51	"
	M	Marotta Libby	117	"	23	
	N	*Marotta Rose—†	117	housewife	43	"
	O	Marotta Salvatore	117	laborer	21	
	P	Capone Agnes—†	117	housewife	25	"
	R	Capone Alfred	117	merchant	48	"
	S	Fartaglini Andrew	117	baker	32	
	T	Fartaglini Mildred—†	117	candymaker	28	"
	U	Iacuzio Mary—†	117	housewife	25	"
	V	Iacuzio Nicholas	117	baker	25	
	W	Lunetta Frances—†	117	housewife	53	"
	X	Lunetta Nicholas	117	painter	22	
	Y	Lunetta Salvatore	117	carpenter	54	"
	Z	Celata Alphonso	117	pipefitter	34	"
1721						
	A	*Celata Esther—†	117	housewife	35	"
	B	*Plunder Gerald	117	painter	52	
	C	Plunder Lena—†	117	operator	24	
	D	*Plunder Pasqualina—†	117	housewife	60	"
	E	Plunder Robert	117	clerk	22	
	G	Prusutti Mario	118	tailor	48	
	H	D'Alesandro Antonio	118	laborer	34	
	K	D'Alesandro Camella—†	118	housewife	33	"
	L	Ferraro Angelo	119	laborer	23	
	M	*Spinazzola Carmine	119	retired	63	
	N	*Spinazzola Marie—†	119	housewife	48	"
	O	Ciampa Antonio	119	laborer	52	
	P	*Ciampa Joseph	119	baker	22	
	R	*Ciampa Michael	119	salesman	25	"
	S	*Ciampa Rosaria—†	119	housewife	43	"
	W	Magnasco Gesimondo	129	blacksmith	21	"
	X	Magnasco John	129	laborer	63	
	Y	Magnasco Nicholas	129	buyer	29	
	Z	*Magnasco Rose—†	129	housewife	52	"
1722						
	A	Magnasco Emilio	129	laborer	25	
	B	Magnasco Josephine—†	129	seamstress	27	"
	C	Magnasco Mary—†	129	at home	21	
	D	*DeLuca Anna—†	129	housewife	32	"

Page.	Letter.	Full Name.	Residence, Jan. 1, 1938.	Occupation.	Supposed Age.	Reported Residence, Jan. 1, 1937. Street and Number.

Orleans Street—Continued

Page.	Letter.	Full Name.	Residence, Jan. 1, 1938.	Occupation.	Supposed Age.	Reported Residence, Jan. 1, 1937. Street and Number.
	E	DeLuca Carmine	129	janitor	47	here
	F	*Magnasco Florence—†	129	housewife	49	"
	G	Magnasco James	129	laborer	22	"
	H	Magnasco Jennie—†	129	at home	20	
	K	*Magnasco Rosildo	129	laborer	57	
	L	Rossetti Angie—†	129	housewife	28	"
	M	Rossetti Stephen	129	baker	28	
	N	*Chiulli Mary—†	129	housewife	39	"
	O	Chiulli Sabatino	129	laborer	47	"
	R	Gerosa Carlo	130	baker	49	
	S	*Gerosa Frances—†	130	housewife	37	"
	T	Maragioglio Anna—†	130	"	29	
	U	Maragioglio William	130	electrician	40	"
	V	Barry Florence—†	131	at home	38	
	W	Puzzo Mary—†	131	candyworker	41	"
	X	Puzzo Michael	131	laborer	51	
	Y	*Pisano Rose—†	131	at home	38	
	Z	*DeSciscio Angelo	131	shoeworker	33	"
1723						
	A	DeSciscio Yolanda—†	131	housewife	31	"
	B	Mori Catherine—†	131	"	26	166 Gove
	C	Mori Joseph	131	laborer	27	166 "
	D	Ferri John	131	"	45	here
	E	Ferri Santa—†	131	housewife	37	"
	F	*Bellone Amelia—†	132	"	34	121 Cottage
	G	*Bellone Ciro	132	shoeworker	47	121 "
	H	*Zona Angelina—†	132	housewife	40	here
	K	Zona Philip	132	barber	45	"
	L	*Leone Maria—†	132	housewife	49	"
	M	Leone Romolo	132	musician	47	"
	N	Freni Louis	133	pressman	21	"
	O	Freni Mary—†	133	housewife	22	"
	P	*DeMartini Gaspara—†	133	"	57	134 Gove
	R	*DeMartini Joseph	133	laborer	57	134 "
	S	Blandini Frank	133	"	47	here
	T	Blandini Phyllis—†	133	housewife	43	"
	V	*Spinnazzola Louis	133	shoeworker	27	"
	W	*Spinnazzola Mary—†	133	housewife	49	"
	X	Martinoli Ida—†	135	"	56	240½ Leyden
	Y	Martinoli Joseph	135	laborer	61	240½ "
	Z	Martinoli Emil	135	clerk	32	240½ "

Page.	Letter.	Full Name.	Residence, Jan. 1, 1938.	Occupation.	Supposed Age.	Reported Residence, Jan. 1, 1937. Street and Number.
1724						

Orleans Street—Continued

Page.	Letter.	Full Name.	Residence, Jan. 1, 1938.	Occupation.	Supposed Age.	Reported Residence, Jan. 1, 1937. Street and Number.
	A	Martinoli Mary—†	135	housewife	23	240½ Leyden
	B	Marando Pasquale	135	laborer	43	here
	C	*Sambrone Frank	135	"	49	"
	D	*Sambrone Katherine—†	135	housewife	38	"
	E	Cardinale Florence—†	135	saleswoman	23	"
	F	Cardinale Michael	135	laborer	25	
	G	Faielli Joseph	135	"	42	
	H	*Faielli Mary C—†	135	housewife	39	"
	K	*Cozzo John	137	mason	68	
	L	*Cozzo Lena—†	137	housewife	60	"
	M	Cozzo Frank	137	mason	31	
	N	Cozzo Jennie—†	137	packer	34	
	O	Banino Dorothy—†	137	housewife	27	"
	P	Banino Robert	137	laborer	30	"
	R	Moore George	137	retired	75	Woburn
	T	*Schipani Frank	137	shoemaker	31	here
	S	*Schipani Mary—†	137	housewife	26	"
	U	Lanzo Constance—†	137	packer	24	"
	V	Lanzo Joseph	137	candymaker	28	Chelsea
	W	Speziale Angelo	137	laborer	52	here
	X	*Speziale Grace—†	137	housewife	41	"
	Y	*Falcone Attilio	140	laborer	64	"
	Z	Lally Anna—†	140	housewife	40	"
1725						
	A	*Lally Constantino	140	bootblack	48	"
	B	*Lespasio Grace—†	140	housewife	42	2 Percival pl

Percival Place

Page.	Letter.	Full Name.	Residence, Jan. 1, 1938.	Occupation.	Supposed Age.	Reported Residence, Jan. 1, 1937. Street and Number.
	C	Biancucci Vincenzo	1	laborer	60	here
	D	*Monteccano Concetta—†	1	matron	45	40 Chelsea
	E	Migliore Anna—†	1	housewife	44	85 Everett
	F	Migliore Carmen	1	shoeworker	44	85 "
	G	*Pettinichio Luigi	1	laborer	53	Milford
	H	*Ricciardi Marie—†	1	housewife	75	here
	K	*Tango Angelina—†	1	"	75	"
	L	Colarusso Frank	2	laborer	29	"
	M	Colarusso Mary—†	2	housewife	29	"
	N	*Lorenzo Domenic	2	mechanic	51	73 Lubec
	O	Lorenzo Victoria—†	2	housewife	34	73 "

Page.	Letter.	Full Name.	Residence, Jan. 1, 1938.	Occupation.	Supposed Age.	Reported Residence, Jan. 1, 1937. Street and Number.

Percival Place—Continued

	P	Vadalla Joseph	2	shoeworker	28	here
	R	Vadalla Lena—†	2	housewife	24	"
	S	*Rizzuti Domenic	3	laborer	24	14 Bremen
	T	Rizzuti Sarah—†	3	housewife	27	14 "
	U	*DiMattia Alphonse	3	retired	83	here
	V	Chiardi Valentino	3	laborer	36	"

Porter Street

	X	Venuti Frances—†	119	housewife	29	here
	Y	Venuti Frank	119	laborer	31	"
	Z	*Santinello Amelia—†	119	housewife	46	"
1726						
	A	Accomando Felix	130	operator	21	"
	B	Accomando Felix	130	bartender	55	"
	C	*Accomando Mary—†	130	housewife	50	"
	D	Accomando Nora—†	130	operator	22	"
	E	Pisano Anna—†	134	stitcher	34	
	F	Pisano Pasquale	134	shoeworker	34	"
	G	Arnesani Frances—†	136	housewife	34	"
	H	*Arnesani Joseph	136	barber	39	
	K	Staiti Joseph	136	shoeworker	55	"
	L	*Staiti Mary—†	136	housewife	54	"
	M	Staiti Salvio	136	laborer	23	"
	N	Palermo Albert	138	foreman	26	140 Porter
	O	Palermo Constance—†	138	housewife	26	140 "
	P	Nigro Concetta—†	138	at home	25	here
	R	Nigro Gilda—†	138	floorwoman	20	"
	S	*Nigro Margaret—†	138	housewife	45	"
	T	Nigro Rosario	138	laborer	52	"
	U	Luise Pasquale	140	watchman	63	110 Paris
	V	*Luise Theresa—†	140	at home	72	110 "
	W	Ciacciarelli Vincent	142	merchant	48	here
	X	Pasquariello Gabriel	142	laborer	48	"
	Y	Pasquariello Margaret—†	142	stitcher	20	"
	Z	*Pasquariello Theresa—†	142	housewife	46	"
1727						
	A	Rosello Mario	142	merchant	42	"
	B	*Pastore Pasqualina—†	142	housewife	49	"
	C	Pastore Vincenzo	142	laborer	52	"

Page.	Letter.	Full Name.	Residence, Jan. 1, 1938.	Occupation.	Supposed Age.	Reported Residence, Jan. 1, 1937. Street and Number.

Rockingham Court

Page.	Letter.	Full Name.	Residence, Jan. 1, 1938.	Occupation.	Supposed Age.	Reported Residence, Jan. 1, 1937. Street and Number.
	E	*Conti Caroline—†	2	housewife	79	108 Orleans
	F	*Conti John	2	merchant	73	108 "
	G	D'Errico Christina—†	2	housewife	24	95 London
	H	D'Errico Michael	2	laborer	24	95 "

Sumner Street

Page.	Letter.	Full Name.	Residence, Jan. 1, 1938.	Occupation.	Supposed Age.	Reported Residence, Jan. 1, 1937. Street and Number.
	O	Darcy Matthew	254	manager	52	here
	P	Hayes Harold	254	laborer	37	"
	R	Hayes Susan A—†	254	housewife	62	"
	S	Hogan Anna S—†	254	"	70	
	T	Hogan Christopher F	254	retired	74	
	V	*Ferrullo Fortuna—†	256	housewife	42	"
	W	*Ferrullo Joseph	256	laborer	43	
	X	*Cipriano Nina—†	256	housewife	35	"
	Y	Cipriano Peter A	256	laborer	40	
1728						
	B	Lombardo Anthony	264	"	22	
	C	*Lombardo Concetta—†	264	housewife	46	"
	D	*Lombardo Joseph	264	laborer	48	
	E	Mattera Caesar	264	"	52	
	F	Mattera Jennie—†	264	clerk	21	
	G	Mattera Josephine—†	264	housewife	50	"
	H	Mattera Mary—†	264	packer	28	
	K	Mattera Michael	264	laborer	25	
	L	Mattera Salvatore	264	"	24	
	O	Culkeen Edward	268	"	40	
	P	Culkeen Mildred—†	268	housewife	24	"
	R	Cutrone James	268	clerk	26	
	S	*Cutrone Jennie—†	268	housewife	48	"
	T	*Cutrone Joseph	268	shoemaker	52	"
	V	Bottaro Anthony	270	candymaker	21	"
	W	Bottaro Joseph	270	laborer	55	"
	X	Bottaro Lena—†	270	housewife	46	"
	Y	*Mangiaratti Ida—†	270	"	47	
	Z	Mangiaratti Joseph	270	laborer	28	
1729						
	A	Mangiaratti Sabastiano	270	"	54	
	C	Martucci Carmella—†	272	housewife	45	"
	D	Martucci Joseph	272	laborer	53	
	E	Cipriano Rose—†	272	at home	62	"

Page.	Letter.	Full Name.	Residence, Jan. 1, 1938.	Occupation.	Supposed Age.	Reported Residence, Jan. 1, 1937. Street and Number.

Sumner Street—Continued

	F	Armedi Anthony	274	pressman	25	here
	G	Armedi Hilda—†	274	housewife	23	"
	H	Nuzzo Americo	274	chauffeur	36	"
	K	Nuzzo Virginia—†	274	housewife	33	"
	L	Travalini Fred	274	foreman	26	
	M	Travalini Josephine—†	274	housewife	25	"
	N	Pignato Josephine—†	276	"	30	
	O	Pignato Michael	276	laborer	39	
	P	Graziano Antonio	276	electrician	26	"
	R	Graziano Mary—†	276	housewife	23	"
	S	Ciccarelli Bessie—†	276	"	40	
	T	Ciccarelli Philip	276	tailor	46	
	U	Bimber George	278	laborer	59	
	V	*Vertuccio Phyllis—†	278	at home	70	
	W	DiAngelo Anna—†	278	stitcher	23	
	X	*DiAngelo James	278	retired	65	
	Y	DiAngelo Rose—†	278	stitcher	21	
	Z	*DiAngelo Sarah—†	278	housewife	55	"
1730						
	A	Cabral Anthony	278	laborer	45	
	B	Cabral Manuel	278	retired	84	
	D	Cervizzi Bernardo	282	storekeeper	57	"
	E	Cervizzi Domenic	282	clerk	29	"
	F	Cervizzi Maria—†	282	housewife	50	"
	G	Cervizzi Vincenzo	282	clerk	26	
	H	Paladino Louis	282	laborer	40	
	K	Paladino Mary—†	282	housewife	40	"
	N	Melchiondo Edward	284	shoeworker	25	"
	O	Melchiondo William	284	laborer	23	
	S	DiPietro Angelo	286	guard	43	
	T	DiPietro Blanche—†	286	housewife	41	"
	U	DiPietro Joseph	286	bartender	40	"
	V	Pelosi Agnes—†	286	housewife	37	"
	W	Pelosi Michael	286	laborer	43	"
	X	Sardella Joseph	288	"	38	47 Chelsea
	Y	Sardella Mary—†	288	housewife	33	47 "
	Z	*Rigano Jennie—†	288	"	68	here
1731						
	A	*Rigano Joseph	288	retired	72	
	B	Martiangelo Frank	288	laborer	63	
	C	Martiangelo Josephine—†	288	housewife	54	"

Page.	Letter.	Full Name.	Residence, Jan. 1, 1938.	Occupation.	Supposed Age.	Reported Residence, Jan. 1, 1937. Street and Number.
		Sumner Street—Continued				
	D	Pollack Bertha H—†	290	at home	40	here
	E	*Macrena Joseph	292	retired	60	"
	G	Russo Catherine—†	294	tailoress	24	"
	H	Russo Sarah—†	294	at home	69	"
	K	Fiore Josephine—†	294	housewife	47	"
	L	Fiore Louise—†	294	packer	21	"
	M	Fiore Vincent	294	laborer	50	"
	N	Pisiello Mary—†	294	clerk	23	"
	O	Rubano Frank A	300	salesman	32	"
	P	Rubano Helen—†	300	housewife	26	"
	R	Rubano Frances—†	300	operator	22	"
	S	*Rubano Frank	300	laborer	47	"
	T	Rubano Rose—†	300	housewife	43	"
	U	Lettieri Samuel	300	bootblack	26	"
	V	Rubano Barbato	300	"	53	"
	W	Rubano Josephine—†	300	housewife	50	"
	X	Liberatore Carolina—†	302	"	55	"
	Y	Liberatore Pasquale	302	laborer	58	"
	Z	Salerno Joseph	302	"	29	"
1732						
	A	Salerno Olga—†	302	housewife	27	"
	B	Salerno Frank	302	laborer	27	"
	C	*Salerno Josephine—†	302	housewife	50	"
	D	Salerno Josephine—†	302	packer	23	"
	E	Salerno Mary—†	302	"	25	"
	F	*Salerno Paul	302	laborer	59	"
	L	Pirroni Frances—†	306	housewife	40	"
	M	Pirroni John	306	shoemaker	54	"
	K	Pirroni Hamilcar Y	306	salesman	22	"
	N	Pirroni Mary R—†	306	dressmaker	21	"
	O	Belmonte Alesandro	306	laborer	40	"
	P	Belmonte Angelina—†	306	housewife	40	"
	R	Duane Joseph D	308	clerk	60	"
	S	Duane Mary E—†	308	teacher	30	"
	T	Houghton Mary L—†	308	at home	58	"
	U	Casey Catherine—†	312	housewife	57	"
	V	Casey Dennis	312	clerk	59	"
	W	Hock Emma C—†	312	typist	24	"
	X	Hock Margaret M—†	312	housewife	53	"
	Y	Hock William H	312	baker	53	"
	Z	Day Sidney F	314	lineman	54	"

Page.	Letter.	FULL NAME.	Residence, Jan. 1, 1938.	Occupation.	Supposed Age.	Reported Residence, Jan. 1, 1937. Street and Number.

1733

Sumner Street—Continued

Page.	Letter.	FULL NAME.	Residence, Jan. 1, 1938.	Occupation.	Supposed Age.	Reported Residence, Jan. 1, 1937. Street and Number.
1733	A	Quinn Mary G—†	314	housewife	49	here
	B	Quinn William J	314	laborer	45	"
	C	Quinn William R	314	mechanic	24	"
	D	Rieley Ethel—†	314	packer	36	
	E	Grasso Luigi	318	retired	80	
	F	Grasso Marie—†	318	housewife	72	"
	G	Grasso Linda—†	318	"	37	
	H	Grasso Thomas O	318	machinist	40	"
	K	Caprio Adeline—†	318	housewife	40	"
	L	Caprio John	318	laborer	42	
	M	Figliolino Joseph	320	storekeeper	62	"
	N	Meola Antonio	320	laborer	30	"
	O	*Meola Jennie—†	320	housewife	28	"
	P	Scopa Emma—†	320	"	43	
	R	Scopa John	320	laborer	47	
	T	Grecco Adeline—†	324	dressmaker	23	"
	U	Grecco Flaminio	324	shoemaker	59	"
	V	Grecco Frances—†	324	housewife	54	"
	W	Grecco Jennie—†	324	dressmaker	22	"
	Y	Soldani Grace—†	328	housewife	55	"
	Z	Soldani Josephine—†	328	clerk	34	
1734	A	Soldani Louis	328	laborer	36	
	B	Soldani Michael	328	retired	57	
	C	Soldani Vincenza—†	328	housewife	36	"
	E	Kelleher Helen—†	334	salesman	39	"
	F	Kelleher Mary—†	334	at home	74	"
	G	Kelleher Mary—†	334	bookkeeper	47	"
	H	Kelleher William	334	laborer	43	"
	K	Goldenberg Abraham	334	chemist	44	
	L	Goldenberg Frances—†	334	housewife	40	"

Ward 1—Precinct 22

CITY OF BOSTON

LIST OF RESIDENTS
20 YEARS OF AGE AND OVER

(NON-CITIZENS INDICATED BY ASTERISK)
(FEMALES INDICATED BY DAGGER)

AS OF

JANUARY 1, 1938

JOSEPH F. TIMILTY, } Listing
FREDERIC E. DOWLING, } Board.

CITY OF BOSTON PRINTING DEPARTMENT

Page.	Letter.	FULL NAME.	Residence, Jan. 1, 1938.	Occupation.	Supposed Age.	Reported Residence, Jan. 1, 1937. Street and Number.
1744						
		Antrim Street				
	A	*Colleary James W	2	manager	41	here
	B	Colleary Jessie—†	2	housewife	35	"
	C	Pennall Amelia—†	2	at home	41	"
	D	Pennall Aurelia—†	2	housewife	72	"
	F	*Gagliardi George	5	retired	71	
	G	*Gagliardi Josephine—†	5	housewife	69	"
	H	Gagliardi Joseph	5	machinist	21	"
	K	*Gagliardi Mary—†	5	housewife	42	"
	L	Gagliardi Salvatore	5	laborer	47	
	M	Scopa Mary—†	5	housewife	22	"
	N	Scopa Roland	5	laborer	29	
	O	Halpin Charlotte G—†	7	housewife	32	"
	P	Halpin Thomas P	7	fireman	41	
	R	Martorana Elizabeth—†	7	housewife	52	"
	S	Martorana Ernest	7	plumber	31	
	T	Martorana Julia—†	7	operator	24	
	U	Martorana Michael	7	laborer	66	
	V	Martorana Sylvia—†	7	operator	22	
	W	Maglio Domenic	7	laborer	40	
	X	Maglio Ida—†	7	housewife	34	"
	Y	O'Shea Annie—†	8	"	53	
	Z	O'Shea Irene M—†	8	clerk	25	
1745						
	A	O'Shea James C	8		53	
	B	Bouchie Frank	8	"	33	
	C	*Bouchie Maria—†	8	housewife	72	"
	D	*Weber Barbara—†	8	"	41	
	E	Weber Karl	8	machinist	52	"
	F	Caprio Agnes M—†	9	housewife	31	"
	G	Caprio Charles J	9	laborer	38	
	H	Donahue David J	9	clerk	37	
	K	Graham John J	9	foreman	48	
	L	Graham Theresa A—†	9	housewife	48	"
	M	Beatrice Maria—†	9	"	35	
	N	Beatrice Peter	9	proprietor	38	"
	O	Celona Frank	10	polisher	49	86 Havre
	P	Celona Frank, jr	10	teacher	25	86 "
	R	*Celona Sarah—†	10	housewife	46	86 "
	S	*Catapano Anna—†	10	"	37	here
	T	Catapano Frank	10	tailor	41	"

Page.	Letter.	Full Name.	Residence, Jan. 1, 1938.	Occupation.	Supposed Age.	Reported Residence, Jan. 1, 1937. Street and Number.
		Antrim Street—Continued				
	U	Gaglini Angelina—†	10	housewife	27	here
	V	Gaglini George	10	printer	31	"
	W	Calicchio Albert	11	carpenter	46	"
	X	Calicchio Diamante—†	11	seamstress	20	"
	Y	*Calicchio Lucretia—†	11	housewife	46	"
	Z	*Spagnola Anibal	11	shoeworker	41	"
1746						
	A	*Spagnola Dorothy—†	11	operator	36	
	B	Powers Anna M—†	12	housewife	70	"
	C	Powers Dorothy M—†	12	clerk	31	
	D	Powers Edward B	12	electrician	43	"
	E	Frazer Alfred	12	attendant	75	"
	F	Frazer Edmund	12	bookkeeper	38	"
	G	Frazer George	12	electrician	33	"
	H	Frazer Sarah—†	12	housewife	70	"
	K	Campanella Anna—†	12	"	29	
	L	*Campanella John	12	dealer	32	
	M	Maniglia Diego	14	barber	31	
	N	Maniglia Rose—†	14	housewife	30	"
	O	McLaughlin George H	14	printer	61	
	P	McLaughlin Margaret H–†	14	housewife	61	"
	R	McLaughlin Mary E—†	14	clerk	23	
	S	Blasi Arthur	14	operator	50	"
	T	*Blasi Nora—†	14	"	47	
		Ashley Street				
	U	DeLaurie Amelia—†	12	housekeeper	35	here
	V	DeRocco Caroline—†	12	housewife	33	"
	W	DeRocco Domenic	12	operator	38	"
	X	Perrier Eleanor D—†	18	housewife	27	Revere
	Y	Perrier Leo A	18	meatcutter	30	"
	Z	Pucillo Antonio	18	laborer	39	here
1747						
	A	*Pucillo Assunta—†	18	housekeeper	67	"
	B	*Pucillo Vertina—†	18	housewife	36	"
	C	Minichiello A Albert	18	engineer	29	
	D	Minichiello Anna—†	18	milliner	27	"
	E	Minichiello Anthony J	18	clerk	25	29 Lourdes av
	F	Minichiello Elsie L—†	18	housewife	27	Medford
	G	Minichiello Emilio	18	clerk	20	here

Page.	Letter.	Full Name.	Residence, Jan. 1, 1938.	Occupation.	Supposed Age.	Reported Residence, Jan. 1, 1937. Street and Number.

Ashley Street—Continued

	H	*Minichiello Felix	18	laborer	68	here
	K	Minichiello Phyllis—†	18	stenographer	23	"
	L	Staffier Anthony	22	auditor	28	"
	M	Staffier Jennie—†	22	housewife	26	"
	N	Blasi Louis	22	tailor	50	
	O	DiLorenzo Alda—†	22	at home	21	
	P	DiLorenzo Gennaro	22	laborer	23	
	R	DiLorenzo Rose—†	22	stitcher	25	
	S	DiLorenzo Thomas	22	tailor	52	
	T	Kelly Mary R—†	22	housewife	39	"
	U	Kelly William T	22	clerk	41	"
	V	DiFronzo Angelo	26	"	28	72 St Andrew rd
	W	DiFronzo Camille—†	26	housewife	24	83 Chelsea
	X	Savasta Frank I	26	manager	54	here
	Y	Savasta Lillian M—†	26	housewife	54	"
	Z	Savasta Samuel J	26	musician	31	"
1748						
	A	Magaletta Paul	26	machinist	34	"
	B	Magaletta Rose—†	26	housewife	28	"
	C	Velardo John L	32	laborer	25	
	D	Velardo Nicoletta—†	32	housewife	21	"
	E	Mandra Joseph	32	chauffeur	50	"
	E1	Mandra Mary—†	32	housewife	40	"
	F	*Mosarra Anna—†	32	dressmaker	60	"
	G	*Scalata Angelina—†	32	housewife	32	"
	H	Scalata Joseph	32	barber	40	
	K	DiLorenzo Domenic	32	operator	28	
	L	DiLorenzo Mary—†	32	housewife	59	"
	M	Zitano Mary—†	32	"	32	
	N	Zitano Peter	32	foreman	35	
	O	Morelli Chester	36	mechanic	37	"
	P	Morelli Vermondia—†	36	housewife	34	"
	R	*LoCoute Concetta—†	36	"	33	
	S	LoCoute Frank	36	salesman	41	"
	T	*Acker Helen—†	36	housewife	29	"
	U	*Acker William	36	cook	34	
	V	Ciampa Anthony	36	laborer	36	
	W	Ciampa George	36	chauffeur	27	"
	X	Franzese Jennie—†	36	housewife	32	"
	Y	Franzese William F	36	tailor	35	"
	Z	Capillo Anna—†	40	housewife	31	24 White

Page.	Letter.	Full Name.	Residence, Jan. 1, 1938.	Occupation.	Supposed Age.	Reported Residence, Jan. 1, 1937. Street and Number.
1749						
		Ashley Street—Continued				
	A	Capillo Rosario	40	chauffeur	31	24 White
	B	Capillo Carl	40	timekeeper	27	911 Saratoga
	C	Capillo Domenic	40	laborer	24	911 "
	D	*Capillo Pauline—†	40	housekeeper	55	911 "
	E	Burton Charles	40	engineer	50	here
	F	*Burton Margaret—†	40	housewife	43	"
	G	Noonan Margaret—†	40	at home	74	"
	H	Staffieri Angelo	44	tailor	38	
	K	Staffieri Olympia—†	44	housewife	30	"
	L	Coranello Joseph	44	letter carrier	33	"
	M	Coranello Mary—†	44	housewife	33	"
	N	Giuffre Carmello	44	operator	34	
	O	Giuffre Josephine—†	44	housewife	34	"
	P	*Statuti John	49	storekeeper	66	"
	R	*Statuti Louise—†	49	housewife	60	"
	S	Maffei Eleanor—†	49	"	25	"
	T	Maffei Vincent	49	attorney	25	125 Faywood av
	U	Siragusa James J	52	physician	41	here
	V	Siragusa Katherine P—†	52	housewife	37	"
	W	Sweeney Mary A—†	52	at home	65	"
	Z	Donahue Ethel M—†	91	housewife	35	"
1750						
	A	Donahue Thomas A	91	laborer	35	
	B	Donahue William	91	retired	78	
	C	Damiano Anna—†	91	teacher	20	
	D	Damiano Mary—†	91	housewife	43	"
	E	Damiano Peter	91	operator	47	"
	F	Connell Agnes—†	135	clerk	21	
	G	Connell Lewis	135	chauffeur	52	"
	H	Connell Rose—†	135	housewife	48	"
	K	Bertucelli George	135	baker	30	
	L	Bertucelli Jessie—†	135	stitcher	28	
	M	Bertucelli Placido	135	laborer	61	
	N	*Bertucelli Virginia—†	135	housewife	57	"
		Bennington Street				
	O	*Lombardo Bridget—†	728	housewife	28	here
	P	Lombardo Rocco	728	laborer	47	"
	R	Vaccaro Rose—†	728	seamstress	26	"
	S	Vaccaro Salvatore	728	operator	34	

Page.	Letter.	Full Name.	Residence, Jan. 1, 1938.	Occupation.	Supposed Age.	Reported Residence, Jan. 1, 1937. Street and Number.

Bennington Street—Continued

Page.	Letter.	Full Name.	Residence, Jan. 1, 1938.	Occupation.	Supposed Age.	Reported Residence, Jan. 1, 1937. Street and Number.
	T	Balduzzi Frank	728	designer	26	here
	U	Balduzzi Mario	728	mechanic	41	"
	V	Balduzzi Natalie—†	728	housewife	38	"
	W	*Balduzzi Rachel—†	728	housekeeper	61	"
	X	Dallenotti Frank	728	operator	58	"
	Z	Anzalone Charles	732	retired	65	
1751						
	A	*Anzalone Mary—†	732	housewife	62	"
	B	*Anzalone Fannie—†	732	"	42	
	C	Anzalone Placido	732	storekeeper	49	"
	D	*Anzalone Carmella—†	732	housewife	40	"
	E	Anzalone Francesco	732	storekeeper	52	"
	F	Anzalone Josephine—†	732	teacher	21	"
	G	Feeley Edward J	734	B F D	42	"
	H	Feeley Edward J, jr	734	usher	22	
	K	Feeley Mary F—†	734	housewife	42	"
	L	Sheehan Paul	734	B F D	43	"
	M	Hollander Helen—†	734	housewife	46	20 Neptune rd
	N	Hollander Helen P—†	734	secretary	27	20 "
	O	Hollander William	734	timekeeper	21	20 "
	P	Bell Annie—†	734	housewife	62	Winthrop
	R	Cadigan Catherine F—†	734	"	67	here
	S	Cadigan James T	734	laborer	43	"
	T	Cadigan John R	734	foreman	34	"
	U	Lazzarino John J	736	manager	34	"
	V	Lazzarino Louise—†	736	housewife	26	"
	W	Landry Joseph P	736	laborer	38	
	X	Landry Mary A—†	736	housewife	35	"
	Y	Celentano James	736	cutter	42	
	Z	Celentano Josephine—†	736	housewife	35	"
1752						
	A	Mitchell Albion E	738	operator	58	"
	B	Mitchell Ida L—†	738	housewife	54	"
	C	Doyle Catherine—†	738	"	60	
	D	Doyle Cecelia—†	738	clerk	37	
	E	Doyle Eleanor—†	738	stenographer	35	"
	F	McGowan Sarah—†	738	waitress	54	"
	G	Stewart John J	738	clerk	26	
	H	Stewart John P	738	engineer	57	
	K	Stewart Mary—†	738	housewife	56	"
	L	Delaney Katherine—†	740	"	40	

Page.	Letter.	FULL NAME.	Residence, Jan. 1, 1938.	Occupation.	Supposed Age.	Reported Residence, Jan. 1, 1937. Street and Number.

Bennington Street—Continued

	M	Delaney Thomas M	740	foreman	40	here
	N	Lawton Annie—†	740	housewife	65	"
	O	Lawton Thomas	740	bookkeeper	30	"
	P	Curran Edith C—†	740	housewife	36	"
	R	Curran Patrick J	740	inspector	37	"
	S	McLaughlin Ann—†	740	nurse	23	577 Benningt'n
	T	McLaughlin Catherine R—†	740	"	26	577 "
	U	McLaughlin Charles C	740	bartender	27	577 "
	V	Mack John F	742	clerk	41	here
	W	Thornton Annie—†	742	housewife	42	"
	X	Thornton Frank A	742	mechanic	40	"
	Y	Thornton William H	742	"	39	"
	Z	Searle Mary—†	742	operator	20	23 Neptune rd
1753						
	A	Smith Mary—†	742	housewife	70	23 "
	B	Smith Ruth—†	742	packer	27	23 "
	C	Smith William P	742	laborer	44	23 "
	D	Cooke Cecil	742	"	34	here
	E	Cooke Katherine—†	742	housewife	30	"
	F	Barker Harry	744	chauffeur	47	63 Wordsworth
	G	Barker Margaret—†	744	housewife	46	63 "
	H	Clogston Abbie L—†	744	"	63	here
	K	Clogston Frank A	744	clerk	60	"
	L	Pigeon George W	744	mechanic	67	"
	M	Monahan Bridget—†	744	housewife	70	"
	N	Monahan John J	744	mechanic	38	"
	O	Monahan Richard J	744	clerk	39	
	P	Roskelly Catherine B—†	746	housewife	45	"
	R	Roskelly Josiah	746	laborer	55	
	S	Beale Benjamin T	746	retired	73	
	T	Beale Benjamin T	746	clerk	36	
	U	Beale Ellen—†	746	housewife	65	"
	V	Beale Gertrude—†	746	operator	38	
	W	Beale John	746	laborer	34	
	X	Driscoll John	746	"	50	
	Y	Musto Armand	746	machinist	24	"
	Z	Musto Clara—†	746	at home	22	
1754						
	A	Musto Fortuna—†	746	housewife	54	"
	B	Musto Joseph	746	machinist	56	"
	C	Musto Nancy—†	746	dressmaker	26	"

Page.	Letter.	FULL NAME.	Residence, Jan. 1, 1938.	Occupation.	Supposed Age.	Reported Residence, Jan. 1, 1937. Street and Number.

Bennington Street—Continued

	D	Arena Salvatore	960	salesman	28	here
	E	Arena Theresa—†	960	housewife	28	"
	F	Merola Ascanio	960	operator	52	"
	G	Merola Augustine	960	"	26	
	H	Merola Corrina—†	960	at home	20	
	K	Merola Elvira—†	960	housewife	48	"
	L	Juliano Joseph	960	salesman	37	"
	M	Juliano Louise—†	960	housewife	31	"
	N	Juliano Orazio	960	retired	76	
	O	Dacey Concetta—†	962	housewife	27	"
	P	Dacey Timothy	962	laborer	27	"
	R	Spinale Charles	962	operator	29	15 Hale
	S	*Albanese Josephine—†	962	housewife	34	here
	T	Albanese Samuel	962	shoemaker	37	"
	U	*Polsonetti Agostino	964	operator	27	"
	V	Polsonetti Ethel—†	964	housewife	26	"
	W	Polsonetti Enocenzo	964	tailor	34	
	X	*Polsonetti Leonora—†	964	housewife	75	"
	Y	Polsonetti Croceffissa—†	964	"	30	
	Z	*Polsonetti Filomena—†	964	tailoress	45	
1755						
	A	Polsonetti Frank	964	tailor	49	
	B	Polsonetti Louis	964	"	53	
	C	Polsonetti Louisa—†	964	at home	20	
	D	*Polsonetti Olympia—†	964	housewife	54	"
	E	Burke Catherine C—†	966	"	44	
	F	Burke George F	966	mechanic	57	"
	G	Perkins Cecelia—†	966	housewife	30	"
	H	Perkins William H	966	contractor	31	"
	K	Napier Helen—†	966	housewife	49	"
	L	Napier Stephen	966	inspector	51	"
	M	Mersolini Robert	968	student	20	50 St Andrew rd
	N	Massa Ida—†	968	housewife	38	50 "
	O	Massa Rose—†	968	housekeeper	36	50 "
	P	Ciccolo James	968	barber	67	here
	R	Ciccolo Joseph	968	musician	29	"
	S	Ciccolo Mary—†	968	clerk	31	"
	T	Ciccolo Providence—†	968	secretary	26	"
	U	Ciccolo Sadie—†	968	housewife	62	"
	V	Ciccolo Sophie—†	968	at home	24	"
	W	Salemme Pasquale	968	clerk	23	103 Leyden

Page.	Letter.	FULL NAME.	Residence, Jan. 1, 1938.	Occupation.	Supposed Age.	Reported Residence, Jan. 1, 1937. Street and Number.

Bennington Street—Continued

Page.	Letter.	FULL NAME.	Residence, Jan. 1, 1938.	Occupation.	Supposed Age.	Reported Residence, Jan. 1, 1937. Street and Number.
	X	Strati Joseph	968	tailor	55	103 Leyden
	Y	*Strati Mary—†	968	housewife	49	103 "
	Z	*Arena Florence—†	970	"	43	here
1756						
	A	*Arena Gaetano	970	painter	50	
	B	Arena John	970	laborer	20	
	C	Arena Paulina—†	970	operator	21	"
	D	Cogliandro Antonetta—†	970	housewife	21	"
	E	Cogliandro Antonio	970	barber	24	
	F	Cogliandro Carmelo	970	operator	60	"
	G	Cogliandro Florence—†	970	housewife	21	"
	H	DiFrancesco Francesco	970	barber	48	
	K	DiFrancesco Frank	970	operator	23	"
	L	*DiFrancesco Grace—†	970	housewife	46	"
	M	Colacey Albert	972	engineer	29	1008 Bennington
	N	Colacey Edith—†	972	housewife	26	1008 "
	O	*Borsa Bridget—†	972	"	44	here
	P	Borsa Frank	972	laborer	21	"
	R	Borsa Frederick	972	tailor	45	"
	S	DeMarco Josephine—†	972	housewife	31	"
	T	DeMarco Sabino	972	barber	34	
	V	Famolare Celia—†	976	housewife	28	"
	W	Famolare Manuel	976	laborer	30	
	X	Petrillo Carmen	976	"	28	
	Y	Petrillo George	976	"	21	
	Z	Petrillo Nancy—†	976	housewife	20	"
1757						
	A	Petrillo Theresa—†	976	tailoress	47	
	B	Barretta Theresa—†	976	at home	70	
	C	Blanciardo Mariano	976	laborer	27	
	D	DiLorenzo Dorothy—†	976	packer	25	
	E	DiLorenzo Louise—†	976	domestic	45	"
	L	Bouchie Gilbert	1004	retired	80	
	M	Bouchie Henry E	1004	laborer	49	
		Bouchie Victoria—†	1004	housewife	71	"
		McLaughlin Charles R	1004	B F D	55	
	N T	Goulston Irma—†	1008	housewife	34	"
	U	Goulston Louis	1008	dentist	38	
	V	Bersocola Dina—†	1008	housewife	50	"
	W	Bersocola Theresa—†	1008	stitcher	22	
	X	Guarino Henry	1008	chauffeur	24	"

Page.	Letter.	Full Name.	Residence, Jan. 1, 1938.	Occupation.	Supposed Age.	Reported Residence, Jan. 1, 1937. Street and Number.

Bennington Street—Continued

Page.	Letter.	Full Name.	Residence, Jan. 1, 1938.	Occupation.	Supposed Age.	Reported Residence, Jan. 1, 1937. Street and Number.
	Y	Perrone Ida—†	1008	housewife	24	11 Boardman
	Z	Perrone John	1008	laundryman	31	11 "
1758						
	A	Santarpio Elizabeth—†	1008	housewife	25	here
	B	Santarpio Vincent	1008	chauffeur	26	"
	C	Ruggiero Catherine—†	1008	housewife	33	"
	D	Ruggiero Gaetano	1008	contractor	46	"
	E	Gundersen Marie—†	1008	cook	53	
	F	Sardina Esther—†	1008	housewife	27	"
	G	Sardina Humbert	1008	dealer	26	"
	H	Murray James H	1008	chauffeur	23	537 Benningt'n
	K	Murray Jennie—†	1008	stitcher	23	537 "
	L	Colarino Aldo	1008	clerk	23	here
	M	*Colarino Catrina—†	1008	housewife	58	"
	N	Frongillo Adeline—†	1008	"	27	"
	O	Frongillo John	1008	chauffeur	28	"
	P	Sacco Vincent J	1008	"	42	21 Ashley
	R	Sinatra Eleanor M—†	1008	operator	24	here
	S	Sinatra Salvatore J	1008	chauffeur	26	"
	X	Gilbrook Ida M—†	1022	housewife	57	"
	Y	Gilbrook Joseph W	1022	mechanic	54	"
	Z	*Lotti Eugenia—†	1022	housewife	44	"
1759						
	A	*Lotti John	1022	cook	44	
	D	Hicks Mamie—†	1024	housewife	48	"
	E	Hicks Wilfred	1024	operator	58	
	F	Hogan William J	1024	policeman	27	"
	G	Ramsell Harry E	1024	fireman	52	Medford
	H	Vozzella Albert	1024	laborer	29	here
	K	Vozzella Mildred—†	1024	housewife	29	"
	L	Ashton Daisy—†	1024	"	48	"
	M	Ashton James	1024	operator	45	"
	N	Dorgan Lawrence	1024	agent	40	417 Frankfort
	O	Leslie Charles	1024	retired	65	143 Poplar
	P	McGrath Michael	1024	fireman	41	here
	R	O'Neil Ellen—†	1024	at home	59	"
	S	Sweeney Edward	1024	cutter	28	"
	T	Thompson Walter	1024	policeman	54	"
	U	Winston Bernard	1024	janitor	43	
	Z	DiNunno Maria F—†	1046	housewife	26	"

Page.	Letter.	Full Name.	Residence, Jan. 1, 1938.	Occupation.	Supposed Age.	Reported Residence, Jan. 1, 1937. Street and Number.

1760

Bennington Street—Continued

Page.	Letter.	Full Name.	Residence, Jan. 1, 1938.	Occupation.	Supposed Age.	Reported Residence, Jan. 1, 1937. Street and Number.
	A	DiNunno Vincent	1046	secretary	32	here
	B	Fasano Philip	1046	laborer	45	"
	C	Grieci Assunta—†	1048	seamstress	29	"
	D	*Grieci Christina—†	1048	housewife	56	"
	E	*Grieci Pasquale	1048	guard	65	
	F	McGlinchey Edith L—†	1050	housewife	51	"
	G	Fagan Daniel	1052	laborer	22	
	H	Fagan Daniel F	1052	foreman	66	
	K	Fagan Douglas C	1052	clerk	40	
	L	Fagan Nellie—†	1052	housewife	60	"
	M	Kerrigan Patrick	1052	laborer	68	
	N	Kerrigan William	1052	cutter	57	
	O	Gunn Francis A	1052	laborer	27	
	P	Gunn Joseph F	1052	"	21	
	R	Gunn Mary A—†	1052	housewife	49	"
	S	Gunn Mary B—†	1052	operator	25	
	T	Pinkham Dorothy B—†	1052	waitress	24	
	U	Pinkham Ella B—†	1052	housewife	46	"
	V	DeAngelis Flora—†	1054	"	37	
	W	DeAngelis Michael	1054	operator	39	"
	X	Ballerini Edmund	1054	shoemaker	23	"
	Y	Ballerini Felice	1054	"	60	
	Z	Ballerini Gaetano	1054	operator	29	"
1761						
	A	Ballerini Lena—†	1054	dressmaker	30	"
	B	Ballerini Michael	1054	operator	22	"
	C	Ferrante Ida—†	1054	housewife	34	"
	D	Ferrante John	1054	tailor	42	
	E	Giarla Alberto	1056	machinist	38	"
	F	Giarla Josephine—†	1056	housewife	36	"
	G	Giarla Louis	1056	clerk	21	
	H	Addresi Alice—†	1056	cutter	24	
	K	Addresi Anthony	1056	cook	32	
	L	Addresi Frank	1056	machinist	57	"
	M	Addresi Lena—†	1056	at home	22	
	N	Addresi Nicoletta—†	1056	housewife	50	"
	O	Addresi Peter	1056	machinist	25	"
	P	Hesenius Annie—†	1056	housewife	50	125 Wordsworth
	R	Hesenius Francis	1056	laborer	30	125 "
	S	Hesenius Helen—†	1056	clerk	25	125 "

Page.	Letter.	Full Name.	Residence, Jan. 1, 1938.	Occupation.	Supposed Age.	Reported Residence, Jan. 1, 1937. Street and Number.

Bennington Street—Continued

	T	Hesenius Laurence	1056	laborer	21	125 Wordsworth
	U	Lawlor John J	1056	oiler	42	125 "
	V	Forgeron Lula—†	1058	housewife	41	here
	W	Forgeron Theodore	1058	mechanic	41	"
	X	Tosney Christopher J	1058	teacher	27	"
	Y	Tosney John J	1058	letter carrier	57	"
	Z	Tosney John J, jr	1058	student	24	
1762						
	A	Tosney Mary A—†	1058	housewife	54	"
	B	Tosney Rita M—†	1058	operator	21	"
	C	*Campanella Bartoloni	1058	storekeeper	58	"
	D	Campanella Frances—†	1058	bookkeeper	23	"
	E	*Campanella Jennie—†	1058	clerk	48	
	F	Campanella Joseph	1058	salesman	20	"
	G	Wynters John W	1062	laborer	35	"
	H	Wynters Matilda A—†	1062	housewife	35	"
	K	Anzolone Adolph	1062	agent	43	
	L	*Anzolone Anna—†	1062	housewife	51	"
	M	Day Albert W	1062	retired	60	
	N	Day Elizabeth A—†	1062	nurse	34	
	O	Famolare Caroline—†	1064	housewife	64	"
	P	Famolare Domenic	1064	retired	70	
	R	Famolare John	1064	barber	45	
	S	Famolare Josephine—†	1064	operator	38	"
	T	Famolare Paul	1064	clerk	31	
	U	Scally Campbell	1064	baker	54	
	V	Scally Veronica—†	1064	housewife	48	"
	W	*Fasolino Elvira—†	1064	"	43	"
	X	*Fasolino Michael	1064	actor	56	
	Y	Lynn Edward J	1066	student	23	
	Z	Lynn John	1066	cutter	50	
1763						
	A	Lynn Rose—†	1066	at home	20	
	B	Ciarfella Diego	1066	laborer	37	
	C	Ciarfella Mary—†	1066	housewife	36	"
	D	*Polsonetti Anthony	1066	tailor	41	
	E	*Polsonetti Pauline—†	1066	housewife	33	"
	F	Steele Katherine—†	1070	operator	32	"
	G	Cadigan William J	1072	machinist	44	"
	H	Driscoll Lillian—†	1072	housekeeper	27	"
	K	*Roche Alice—†	1072	matron	45	57 Wordsworth

Page.	Letter.	FULL NAME.	Residence, Jan. 1, 1938.	Occupation.	Supposed Age.	Reported Residence, Jan. 1, 1937. Street and Number.

Bennington Street—Continued

Page.	Letter.	FULL NAME.	Residence, Jan. 1, 1938.	Occupation.	Supposed Age.	Reported Residence, Jan. 1, 1937. Street and Number.
	L	Roche Jean—†	1072	waitress	24	57 Wordsworth
	M	Cuneo Emma M—†	1072	housewife	54	here
	N	Cuneo John B	1072	retired	63	"
	O	Cuneo John J	1072	musician	24	"
	P	Cuneo Mabel L—†	1072	assembler	34	"

Boardman Street

Page.	Letter.	FULL NAME.	Residence, Jan. 1, 1938.	Occupation.	Supposed Age.	Reported Residence, Jan. 1, 1937. Street and Number.
	V	Cataldo Alice—†	7	clerk	21	here
	W	Cataldo Anthony	7	laborer	27	"
	X	*Cataldo Charles	7	contractor	54	"
	Y	*Cataldo Theresa—†	7	housewife	47	"
	Z	Maggioli Agnes—†	7	"	36	
1764						
	A	Maggioli Eugene	7	chauffeur	41	"
	B	Maggioli Leo	7	"	39	
	C	Nastasia John	9	laborer	32	
	D	Nastasia Mary—†	9	housewife	30	"
	E	Langone Lena—†	9	"	24	
	F	Langone Patrick	9	optician	26	
	G	DiLorenzo Carmine	9	student	23	
	H	*DiLorenzo Gaetano	9	barber	50	
	K	*DiLorenzo Madeline—†	9	housewife	48	"
	L	*Cataldo Clorinda—†	9	"	37	
	M	Cataldo Louis	9	operator	43	"
	N	Bianco Nicholas	11	clerk	22	60 Leyden
	O	Fortunate Ella—†	11	operator	34	21 Whitby
	P	*Spagnolo Elizabeth—†	11	housewife	34	here
	R	*Spagnolo Vincent	11	operator	39	"
	S	Famulari Anthony	11	"	26	"
	T	*Famulari Domenic	11	pedler	67	
	U	*Famulari Flora—†	11	housewife	55	"
	V	Famulari Ignacio	11	operator	23	
	W	Cappillo Annette—†	15	clerk	44	
	X	Forest Mary—†	15	operator	63	"
	Y	Pennell Leon	15	mechanic	45	"
	Z	Pennell Marie—†	15	housewife	37	"
1765						
	A	Vitale Frank	15	operator	23	"
	B	Vitale Madeline—†	15	housewife	22	"
	C	Lopez John A	16	counterman	34	"

Page.	Letter.	FULL NAME.	Residence, Jan. 1, 1938.	Occupation.	Supposed Age.	Reported Residence, Jan. 1, 1937. Street and Number.

Boardman Street—Continued

	D	Lopez Mildred S—†	16	housewife	34	here
	E	Sacco Albert	16	assembler	31	"
	F	Sacco George M	16	optician	23	"
	G	Sacco Henry E	16	"	24	
	H	Sacco John M	16	chauffeur	26	"
	K	Sacco Orlando D	16	electrician	32	"
	L	Guarino Ercolino	19	laborer	34	
	M	Sacco Joseph	19	salesman	39	"
	N	Sacco Leontica—†	19	housewife	35	"
	O	Young Marie—†	19	nurse	28	
	P	Centracchio Anthony A	19	attorney	31	"
	R	Centracchio Lillian—†	19	housewife	25	"
	S	Cicco Mary—†	19	"	34	
	T	Cicco Michael	19	laborer	39	
	U	Morse Andrew	23	longshoreman	36	"
	V	Morse Eva—†	23	housewife	36	"
	W	Patti Mary—†	23	"	25	
	X	Patti Salvatore	23	machinist	37	"
	Y	Raffo George	23	laborer	36	
	Z	Raffo John	23	laundryman	37	"
1766						
	A	Raffo Margaret—†	23	operator	22	
	B	*Raffo Marie—†	23	housewife	64	"
	C	Raffo Rose—†	23	operator	39	
	E	Whalen Henry J	29	chauffeur	37	"
	F	Whalen Louise B—†	29	housewife	36	"
	G	Casale Gertrude—†	31	"	36	
	H	Casale Herbert	31	architect	38	"
	K	Dente Alphonse	31	pharmacist	25	"
	L	Dente Ida—†	31	housewife	21	"
	M	Mulone Catherine—†	33	"	27	
	N	Mulone Giacomo	33	longshoreman	27	"
	O	Cerullo Antonia—†	33	housekeeper	49	"
	P	Sofrine Blanche V—†	33	housewife	34	"
	R	Sofrine Manuel B	33	laborer	37	
	S	*Sparaco Concetta—†	35	housewife	58	"
	T	Sparaco Emilio	35	operator	29	
	U	Sparaco Frank	35	optician	20	
	V	Sparaco Mary—†	35	assembler	23	"
	W	*Sparaco Samuel	35	retired	63	
	X	Sparaco John	35	laborer	39	

Page.	Letter.	Full Name.	Residence, Jan. 1, 1938.	Occupation.	Supposed Age.	Reported Residence, Jan. 1, 1937. Street and Number.

Boardman Street—Continued

Page.	Letter.	Full Name.	Residence, Jan. 1, 1938.	Occupation.	Supposed Age.	Reported Residence, Jan. 1, 1937.
	Y	*Sparaco Lillian—†	35	housewife	39	here
	Z	*Cimmino Carmella—†	41	"	58	"
1767						
	A	Cimmino Guilda—†	41	saleswoman	25	"
	B	Cimmino Rose—†	41	"	23	
	C	*DeSimone Anna—†	41	housewife	46	"
	D	DeSimone Vincenzo	41	laborer	45	
	E	LaVita Eleanor—†	41	saleswoman	23	"
	F	LaVita Leonora—†	41	at home	20	"
	G	Ahern Florence E—†	47	housewife	34	691 Benningt'n
	H	Ahern Frank J	47	paymaster	35	691 "
	K	Grant Florence E—†	47	saleswoman	53	691 "
	L	Cucchiarella Giacomo	49	laborer	68	here
	M	O'Brien Edith M—†	49	housewife	22	"
	N	O'Brien Thomas W	49	laborer	26	"
	P	Boudrow Alice—†	53	housewife	31	"
	R	Boudrow Philip	53	mechanic	34	"
	S	Higgins Mary—†	53	housekeeper	36	"
	V	Vecchio Domenic	111	laborer	32	"
	W	Vecchio Margaret—†	111	housewife	34	"
	X	Murray Walter T	111	laborer	23	705 Benningt'n
	Y	DeLeo Anna—†	111	housewife	24	here
	Z	DeLeo Joseph	111	operator	24	"
1768						
	A	*Visconti Anna—†	148	housewife	72	"
	B	*Visconti Joseph	148	retired	78	
	C	Abramo Florence—†	148	housewife	26	"
	D	Abramo John	148	laborer	30	
	E	Abbott Antonette—†	148	housewife	33	"
	F	Abbott Dennis	148	longshoreman	38	"
	G	*Vecchio Joseph	162	laborer	67	
	H	*Vecchio Maria—†	162	housewife	56	"
	K	Vecchio Vito	162	chauffeur	29	"
	L	Puligiesi Jennie—† rear	162	housewife	25	"
	M	Puligiesi Vincent "	162	guard	26	

Breed Street

Page.	Letter.	Full Name.	Residence, Jan. 1, 1938.	Occupation.	Supposed Age.	Reported Residence, Jan. 1, 1937.
	S	*Penner Elizabeth—†	rear 5	housekeeper	58	152 Everett
	T	Badgley Mabel—†	5A	"	23	174 Brooks
	U	McDonald Edward	7	chauffeur	34	here

Page.	Letter.	Full Name.	Residence, Jan. 1, 1938.	Occupation.	Supposed Age.	Reported Residence, Jan. 1, 1937. Street and Number.

Breed Street—Continued

Page.	Letter.	Full Name.	Residence, Jan. 1, 1938.	Occupation.	Supposed Age.	Reported Residence, Jan. 1, 1937. Street and Number.
	V	McDonald Jeannette—†	7	housewife	30	here
	W	Cavagnaro Mario J	7	retired	72	"
	X	*Cavagnaro Mary L—†	7	housewife	66	"
	Y	Cavagnaro Robert V	7	laborer	36	"
	Z	Carey Helen M—†	7	housewife	33	1004 Bennington
1769						
	A	Carey William H	7	clerk	34	1004 "
	B	O'Connell Margaret M—†	7	housewife	59	1004 "
	C	O'Connell Paul C	7	laborer	20	1004 "
	D	O'Connell Peter H	7	"	60	1004 "
	E	Taft Harold	9	chauffeur	29	225 Leyden
	F	Taft Marie—†	9	housewife	24	225 "
	G	Benincuore Angelina—†	9	"	47	here
	H	Benincuore Nicholas	9	barber	54	"
	L	Hames Ella—†	10	housewife	38	"
	M	Hames Joseph	10	laborer	40	
	N	Sardina Angelina—†	10	housewife	22	"
	O	*Sardina Carmella—†	10	"	56	
	P	*Sardina Joseph	10	retired	60	
	R	Sardina Stephen	10	laborer	24	
	Z	*DeSimone Joseph	17	"	57	
1770						
	A	DeSimone Josephine—†	17	bookkeeper	27	"
	B	DeSimone Lena—†	17	stenographer	26	"
	C	DeSimone Leonora—†	17	housewife	52	"
	D	Traina Anna—†	17	"	39	
	E	Traina Leo	17	dealer	45	
	F	Traina Salvatore	17	student	20	
	G	Giuffre Joseph	17	dealer	39	
	H	Giuffre Josephine—†	17	housewife	35	"
	K	*London Anna—†	17	"	59	
	L	London Dominic	17	clerk	22	
	M	London John	17	laborer	37	"
	O	Leighton John	20	clerk	37	278 K
	P	Vitale Nicholas	20	barber	64	here
	R	Vitale Rose—†	20	housewife	54	"
	S	Patti Anthony, jr	20	bookkeeper	26	"
	T	Patti Antonio	20	machinist	62	"
	U	Patti Josephine—†	20	housewife	62	"
	V	Patti Mary—†	20	saleswoman	22	"
	W	Patti Sebastian	20	clerk	24	

Page.	Letter.	Full Name.	Residence, Jan. 1, 1938.	Occupation.	Supposed Age.	Reported Residence, Jan. 1, 1937. Street and Number.

Breed Street—Continued

Page.	Letter.	Full Name.	Residence, Jan. 1, 1938.	Occupation.	Supposed Age.	Reported Residence, Jan. 1, 1937. Street and Number.
	Y	*Morrelli Pedro	23	retired	71	here
	Z	*Morrelli Rosa—†	23	housewife	69	"
1771						
	A	Pitman Lucy—†	23	"	60	
	B	Pitman Mary E—†	23	stenographer	22	"
	C	Pitman Rita—†	23	dressmaker	20	"
	D	Pitman William A	23	painter	56	
	E	Malatesta Isadore	23	bartender	26	"
	F	Mangini Albert L	23	"	30	
	G	Mangini Alma—†	23	housewife	28	"
	H	*Mangini Angela—†	23	housekeeper	61	"
	K	Porcello Diore	23	operator	40	"
	L	Porcello Florence—†	23	housewife	47	"
	M	Porcello Helen—†	23	"	36	
	N	Porcello Jeremiah	23	operator	51	
	O	Culkeen Elizabeth L—†	25	housewife	47	"
	P	Culkeen John J	25	realtor	52	
	R	Culkeen Joseph L	25	clerk	21	
	S	Culkeen Virginia—†	25	"	23	
	T	Moltedo Aurelia—†	25	housewife	45	"
	U	Moltedo Henry R	25	electrician	36	"
	V	Moltedo Mildred B—†	25	clerk	49	
	W	Moltedo Virginia—†	25	housewife	70	"
	X	Merritt Arthur R	25	constable	31	263 Princeton
	Y	Merritt Edward F	25	painter	34	263 "
	Z	Merritt William J	25	policeman	37	263 "
1772						
	A	Viglione Anna M—†	25	housewife	38	here
	B	Viglione Patrick	25	proprietor	36	"
	C	Buckley Edmund	26	clergyman	27	Lake st
	D	Cahill Mary—†	26	housekeeper	64	here
	E	Cronin Francis	26	clergyman	65	"
	F	Talbot Celanie—†	26	housekeeper	59	"
	G	Walsh Edward A	26	clergyman	35	"
	H	Giordano Ciro	40	manager	43	"
	K	Giordano Judith—†	40	housewife	39	"
	L	Giannotti Aldo	40	cook	29	1059 Saratoga
	M	Giannotti Alice—†	40	housewife	30	1059 "
	N	*Giannotti Anna—†	40	"	56	1059 "
	O	*Giannotti Egidio	40	cook	60	1059 "
	P	Mandia Mary—†	40	secretary	28	here

Page.	Letter.	Full Name.	Residence, Jan. 1, 1938.	Occupation.	Supposed Age.	Reported Residence, Jan. 1, 1937. Street and Number.
		Breed Street—Continued				
	R	Mandia Winifred—†	40	housewife	49	here
	S	Calledare Alfred	42	bellboy	22	15 Neptune rd
	T	Calledare Antonio	42	stonecutter	26	15 "
	U	*Calledare Michael	42	"	54	15 "
	V	*Calledare Virginia—†	42	housewife	44	15 "
	W	Firorillo Anna—†	42	clerk	25	70 Chelsea
	X	Firorillo Josephine—†	42	operator	37	70 "
	Y	Fischer Joseph F	42	policeman	39	here
	Z	Fischer Mary C—†	42	housewife	33	"
1773						
	A	*Saggese Assunta—†	42	"	68	"
	B	*Saggese John	42	retired	74	"
	D	Dicenzo Arthur	46	laborer	28	"
	E	Dicenzo Iola—†	46	operator	20	"
	F	Dicenzo Joseph	46	storekeeper	58	"
	G	Dicenzo Louise—†	46	seamstress	22	"
	H	*Dicenzo Margaret—†	46	housewife	51	"
	K	*Meoli Antonetta—†	46	"	33	"
	L	Meoli Marino	46	operator	43	"
	M	Celia Carmella—†	46	housewife	26	"
	N	*Celia Joseph	46	baker	32	"
	O	Forey Victoria—†	56	housekeeper	39	"
	P	Amerena Joseph	56	machinist	56	"
	R	Amerena Joseph E, jr	56	storekeeper	30	"
	S	Wood Alice—†	82	housewife	28	"
	T	Wood Waymon	82	superintendent	35	"
	U	Testa Carmine	82	machinist	32	"
	V	Testa Mary—†	82	housewife	31	"
	W	*Berando Angela—†	82	"	54	"
	X	Berando Anna—†	82	at home	25	"
	Y	*Berando Julius	82	machinist	58	"
	Z	Berando Katherine—†	82	operator	28	"
1774		**Ford Street**				
	D	Lento Ida—†	4	housewife	30	here
	E	Lento Samuel	4	shoemaker	36	"
	F	Sinopli Jeremiah	4	laborer	41	"
	G	*DiMinico Christopher	4	"	50	"
	H	*DiMinico Vincenza—†	4	housewife	50	"
	K	Margarici Antonio	6	laborer	49	40 Orient av

Page.	Letter.	Full Name.	Residence, Jan. 1, 1938.	Occupation.	Supposed Age.	Reported Residence, Jan. 1, 1937. Street and Number.
		Ford Street—Continued				
	L	Margarici Lillian—†	6	housewife	42	here
	M	Famolare John	6	chauffeur	39	"
	N	Famolare Ruth—†	6	housewife	34	"
	O	Bartello Josephine—†	6	"	34	
	P	Bartello Leo	6	chauffeur	37	"
	R	Suozzo Angelina—†	7	housewife	34	"
	S	Suozzo Pasquale	7	chauffeur	38	"
	T	Sullivan Emma L—†	7	housewife	40	"
	U	Sullivan James A	7	salesman	43	"
	V	Vicceitto Louis	7	retired	67	
	W	*Vicceitto Santa—†	7	housewife	63	"
	X	*Carresi Pasquale	7	retired	81	
	Y	Carresi Salvatore	7	laborer	33	
	Z	Lombardi Sebastian	8	"	25	
1775						
	A	Lombardi Yolande—†	8	housewife	21	"
	C	Famolare Angelina—†	8	"	40	
	D	Famolare Philip	8	chauffeur	40	"
	E	*Sarro Manuela—†	11	housewife	58	"
	F	Sarro Peter	11	laborer	58	
	G	Vatalaro Anthony	11	"	30	
	H	Vatalaro Mary—†	11	housewife	26	"
	K	*Guarino Carlo	21	laborer	43	
	L	*Guarino Lucy—†	21	housewife	45	"
	M	McGlinchey John J	21	timekeeper	31	"
	N	McGlinchey Virginia—†	21	housewife	30	"
	O	Sacco Edward G	21	architect	29	"
	P	Sacco Mary A—†	21	housewife	29	"
		Gladstone Street				
	R	Lecorn Bertram	136	janitor	43	here
	S	Lecorn Margaret—†	136	housewife	44	"
	T	*Marino Genevieve—†	140	"	50	"
	U	Marino Joseph	140	painter	29	
	V	*Marino Philip	140	storekeeper	54	"
	W	McDonald Jerome N	153	laborer	48	"
	X	McDonald Margaret—†	153	housewife	47	"
	Y	McDonald Margaret M—†	153	clerk	20	
	Z	Bomarsi Felix	153	laborer	46	

Gladstone Street—Continued

Page.	Letter.	Full Name.	Residence, Jan. 1, 1938.	Occupation.	Supposed Age.	Reported Residence, Jan. 1, 1937. Street and Number.
1776						
	A	Bomarsi Rita—†	153	housewife	36	here
	B	Spinney Anna—†	165	"	28	"
	C	Spinney Leland	165	clerk	30	"
	D	Casale Agnes A—†	165	musician	40	"
	E	Casale Annie M—†	165	housewife	62	"
	F	Roberts John	165	manager	34	"
	G	Roberts Mildred—†	165	housewife	32	"
	H	Kelly John C	175	mortician	47	216 Orient av
	K	Kelly Rose V—†	175	housewife	45	216 "
	L	*Zani Ardella—†	175	"	48	here
	M	Zani Carolina—†	175	clerk	27	"
	N	Zani Johanna—†	175	"	25	"
	O	Zani John	175	contractor	55	"
	P	Zani Joseph	175	student	21	
	R	Zani Leo	175	laborer	23	
	S	Massuco Rita—†	176	housewife	33	"
	T	Massuco Robert	176	laborer	35	
	U	Casassa Alfred	176	operator	22	"
	W	Casassa Emma—†	176	housewife	44	"
	V	Casassa Evelyn—†	176	clerk	20	
	X	Casassa John	176	printer	24	
	Y	Casassa Stephen	176	manager	59	"
	Z	Meehan Edward J	176	laborer	52	"
1777						
	A	Meehan Eleanor—†	176	secretary	22	"
	B	Meehan Elizabeth F—†	176	housekeeper	52	"
	C	Zambrogno Celso V	176	clerk	20	"
	D	Zambrogno Louise—†	176	housewife	40	"
	E	Zambrogno Natale A	176	backsmith	44	"
	F	Barry Helene—†	183	housewife	37	"
	G	Barry Thomas E	183	teacher	38	
	M	Pecci Peter	185	artist	27	
	N	Pecci Rose—†	185	housewife	25	"
	O	Benvissuto Mary—†	185	"	50	
	P	Benvissuto Paul	185	laborer	62	
	R	*Ascolese Anthony	187	manager	37	"
	S	Ascolese Josephine—†	187	housewife	31	"
	U	McDonald Bessie—†	189	"	33	
	V	McDonald Melvin M	189	typist	44	
	W	McKay Catherine E—†	189	housewife	57	"

Page.	Letter.	FULL NAME.	Residence, Jan. 1, 1938.	Occupation.	Supposed Age.	Reported Residence, Jan. 1, 1937. Street and Number.

Gladstone Street—Continued

	K	McKay Duncan A	189	bookkeeper	60	here
	Y	Roy Walter	189	porter	50	"
	Z	Gross Levina—†	189	housekeeper	36	"
1778						
	A	Barbante Joseph	191	laborer	33	
	B	Barbante Rose—†	191	housewife	30	"
	C	Sykes Angela—†	191	"	28	
	D	Sykes Water	191	clerk	35	
	E	*Bienchi Carlo	192	laborer	58	
	F	*Bienchi Rose—†	192	housewife	58	"
	G	Roccia Florence—†	192	"	33	
	H	Roccia Nicholas	192	manager	35	"
	K	Abramo Joseph	195	operator	36	
	L	Abramo Mary—†	195	housewife	29	"
	M	*Ferri Fortunato	195	dealer	49	"
	N	*Ferri Marcella—†	195	housewife	47	"
	O	*Uguccione Attillio	196	laborer	45	
	P	Uguccione Marcella—†	196	housewife	42	"
	R	Morris Margaret—†	196	"	40	
	S	Morris Patrick	196	fireman	41	
	T	Morris Catherine—†	196	housewife	40	"
	U	Morris William	196	druggist	36	"
	V	DiCenzo Dena—†	199	housewife	28	"
	W	DiCenzo William	199	manager	30	
	X	Battaini Ambrose	199	artist	24	
	Y	*Battaini Teresa—†	199	housewife	52	"
	Z	Clark John	199	laborer	42	
1779						
	A	Colombo Joseph	199	"	48	
	B	Collins Alice F—†	203	housewife	48	"
	C	Collins James J	203	chauffeur	23	"
	D	Collins John J	203	contractor	49	"
	E	Collins Lawrence F	203	chauffeur	21	"
	F	Collins Mary A—†	203	at home	25	
	G	Capinella Blanche—†	203	housewife	38	"
	H	Capinella Domenic	203	operator	43	"
	K	Crovo Herman F	204	counterman	33	"
	L	Crovo Mary—†	204	housewife	29	"
	M	Bottini Eleanor—†	204	"	40	
	N	Bottini Sebastian	204	laborer	41	
	O	Miller Edward	204	electrician	54	"

Page.	Letter.	Full Name.	Residence, Jan. 1, 1938.	Occupation.	Supposed Age.	Reported Residence, Jan. 1, 1937. Street and Number.
		Gladstone Street—Continued				
	P	Miller Mary—†	204	housewife	50	here
	R	Solari Fred	204	contractor	50	“
	S	Marino Alfonso	207	operator	43	“
	T	Marino Antonetta—†	207	housewife	41	“
	U	Solari Edmund J	207	manager	31	“
	V	Solari Nellie—†	207	housewife	25	“
	W	Watson John	208	secretary	70	“
	X	Watson John A	208	electrician	39	“
	Y	Watson Martha S—†	208	housewife	71	“
	Z	Nasta Alfonso	211	repairman	36	“
1780						
	A	Nasta Josephine—†	211	housewife	28	“
	B	Nasta Rose—†	211	“	41	
	C*	Nasta Salvatore	211	repairman	43	“
	D	Strangie Augustino	215	salesman	24	“
	E*	Strangie Carmella—†	215	housewife	47	“
	F	Gardella Lawrence	215	operator	36	
	G	Solari Andrew	215	chauffeur	38	“
	H	Solari Mary—†	215	housewife	38	“
	K	Doyle James	219	fisherman	56	1059 Saratoga
	L	Doyle Josephine—†	219	housewife	50	1059 “
	M	Doyle Ralph T	219	fisherman	24	here
	N	Sanchioni Adolph	223	superintendent	49	“
	O	Sanchioni Vilma—†	223	housewife	47	“
		Leyden Street				
	P	Ricci Anna—†	15	housewife	29	here
	R	Ricci Sylvio	15	laborer	30	“
	S	Canevaro Louisa—†	23	housekeeper	77	“
	T	Oberti Annie—†	23	“	78	"
	U*	Salotti Mary—†	29	housewife	42	“
	V*	Salotti Paul	29	laborer	45	
	W	Bernardi Angeline—†	29	operator	27	“
	X	Bernardi August	29	“	23	
	Y	Bernardi Clara—†	29	clerk	24	
	Z*	Bernardi Deno	29	dealer	56	
1781						
	A*	Bernardi Edith—†	29	housewife	56	“
	B	Bernardi Louis	29	operator	28	
	C	Bernardi Rinaldo	29	laborer	20	

Page.	Letter.	Full Name.	Residence, Jan. 1, 1938.	Occupation.	Supposed Age.	Reported Residence, Jan. 1, 1937. Street and Number.

Leyden Street—Continued

Page.	Letter.	Full Name.	Residence, Jan. 1, 1938.	Occupation.	Supposed Age.	Reported Residence, Jan. 1, 1937. Street and Number.
	D	Bacigalupo Louis M	29	operator	23	here
	E	Bacigalupo Louise—†	29	bookkeeper	21	"
	F	Bacigalupo Mary A—†	29	housewife	50	"
	G	Bacigalupo Walter A	29	designer	53	
	H	Bacigalupo Walter L	29	laborer	25	
	K	Bonugli Arline—†	33	clerk	20	
	L	Bonugli Domenic	33	manager	49	"
	M	Bonugli Jessie—†	33	housewife	49	"
	N	Catriale Guy	35	chauffeur	38	"
	O	Catriale Olympia—†	35	housewife	34	"
	P	DeMarchi Anna—†	35	"	43	
	R	DeMarchi Frank E	35	mechanic	54	"
	S	Sacco Briscoe	35	laborer	51	
	T	Sacco Louise M—†	35	clerk	20	
	U	Sacco Mary—†	35	housewife	49	"
	V	Barker Horace	35	laborer	35	
	W	Barker Madeline—†	35	housewife	33	"
	X	Evans Grover	35	laborer	35	
	Y	Evans Jennie—†	35	housewife	36	"
	Z	Simonini Casimiro	35	butcher	40	
1782						
	A	Simonini Escola—†	35	housewife	38	"
	B	DeLeo Antonio	47	laborer	22	
	C	DeLeo Raffeale	47	shoemaker	64	"
	D	Solari Eva—†	49	secretary	45	"
	E	Solari Mary—†	49	at home	87	
	F	Martinelli Carlo	53	laborer	38	
	G	Martinelli Lucy—†	53	housewife	34	"
	H	Lucca Jennie—†	55	"	32	
	K	Lucca Rocco	55	laborer	38	
	L	*Strange Frank	57	salesman	49	"
	M	Strange Josephine—†	57	housewife	38	"
	N	Censabella Mildred—†	59	housekeeper	29	687 Saratoga
	O	Sarro Antonio	59	laborer	45	here
	R	Bianco Josephine—†	60	clerk	25	"
	S	*Bianco Mary—†	60	housewife	53	"
	T	Bianco Salvatore	60	laborer	30	
	U	Labardini Frank	60	operator	49	
	V	Labardini Rose—†	60	housewife	49	"
	W	Pedone Anna—†	61	"	24	
	X	Pedone Samuel	61	attendant	24	"

Page.	Letter.	Full Name.	Residence, Jan. 1, 1938.	Occupation.	Supposed Age.	Reported Residence, Jan. 1, 1937. Street and Number.

Leyden Street—Continued

Page.	Letter.	Full Name.	Residence, Jan. 1, 1938.	Occupation.	Supposed Age.	Reported Residence, Jan. 1, 1937. Street and Number.
	Y	McCarthy John	61	laundryman	35	here
	Z	McCarthy Mary—†	61	housewife	35	"
1783						
	A	McCarthy Mary—†	61	"	35	
	B	Colantuone Jennie—†	61	"	54	"
	C	Colantuone Paul	61	laborer	57	"
	D	Bonapane Amedeo	63	operator	35	"
	E	Bonapane Palmenia—†	63	housewife	33	"
	F	Ciampa Adeline—†	63	"	48	
	G	Ciampa Angelo	63	laborer	54	
	H	Colantuone Joseph	65	chauffeur	30	"
	K	Colantuone Rose M—†	65	housewife	28	"
	L	Amoroso Albert	67	laborer	21	"
	M	Amoroso Aniello	67	operator	58	
	N	Amoroso Elizabeth—†	67	at home	20	
	O	Amoroso John	67	chauffeur	27	"
	P	Amoroso Rose—†	67	housewife	49	"
	R	Christopher Charles	68	operator	29	
	S	Christopher Frank	68	"	25	
	T	*Christopher Jeremiah	68	"	55	
	U	Christopher John	68		46	
	V	Christopher Joseph	68	"	25	
	W	Christopher Mary—†	68	clerk	22	
	X	*Christopher Rose—†	68	housewife	80	"
	Y	Christopher Domenic	68	operator	34	
	Z	Christopher Mary—†	68	housewife	28	"
1784						
	B	Femia Joseph	70	laborer	43	"
	C	Femia Victoria—†	70	housewife	38	"
	D	DeStefano Frank	71	laborer	26	
	E	DeStefano Josephine—†	71	housewife	43	"
	K	Massa Amelia—†	71	"	67	
	L	Massa Amelia F—†	71	operator	44	
	F	Massa Andrew L	71	laborer	33	
	G	Massa Catherine L—†	71	stenographer	29	"
	H	Massa Charles	71	clerk	37	"
	M	Lemos Anna—†	71	operator	35	
	N	Lemos Joseph	71	cook	47	
	O	Lemos Lucinda—†	71	operator	33	
	P	Femia Nicholas	72	baker	21	
	R	Russo Anthony	72	laborer	51	

Page.	Letter.	Full Name.	Residence, Jan. 1, 1938.	Occupation.	Supposed Age.	Reported Residence, Jan. 1, 1937. Street and Number.

Leyden Street—Continued

Page.	Letter.	Full Name.	Residence, Jan. 1, 1938.	Occupation.	Supposed Age.	Reported Residence, Jan. 1, 1937. Street and Number.
	S	Russo Catherine—†	72	housewife	50	here
	T	*Casenza Salvatore	72	retired	76	"
	U	*Lagamosino Andrew	74	"	82	"
	V	Lagamosino Anthony	74	manager	44	"
	W	Lagamosino Rose—†	74	dressmaker	42	"
	X	Lagamosino Victoria—†	74	housewife	70	"
	Z	Delaney James F	78	painter	41	
1785						
	A	Delaney Virginia—†	78	housewife	39	"
	B	Lagamosina Louis	78	laborer	49	
	C	Lagamosina Mary—†	78	housewife	49	"
	D	Dappolonio Elizabeth—†	79	stitcher	21	
	E	Dappolonio Frank	79	tinsmith	49	
	F	Dappolonio Rose—†	79	housewife	44	"
	G	Deloia Carmine	79	janitor	27	
	H	Deloia Nellie—†	79	stitcher	23	
	K	*Avolio Margaret—†	79	housewife	51	"
	L	Bernardi Isadore	80	inspector	33	"
	M	Massa Gerardo	80	fireman	47	
	N	Massa Ida—†	80	housewife	48	"
	O	Massa Ralph	80	clerk	23	
	P	Duggan John A	80	manufacturer	49	"
	R	Duggan Sophia B—†	80	housewife	44	"
	S	DiCicco Catherine—†	82	"	24	
	T	DiCicco John	82	laborer	31	
	U	DiCicco Albert	82	"	26	
	V	DiCicco James	82	retired	77	
	W	DiCicco Lena—†	82	housewife	23	"
	X	Bergamasco Mary—†	82	"	40	
	Y	Bergamasco Michael	82	butcher	46	
1786						
	A	*Zozzi Lena—†	83	housewife	48	"
	B	Zozzi Mary—†	83	operator	25	"
	C	*Zozzi Nicholas	83	butcher	50	
	D	Zozzi Nicholina—†	83	operator	20	
	E	*Rossi Natalina—†	83	housewife	47	"
	F	*Rossi Ottavio	83	butcher	48	
	G	Rossi Alfred	83	counterman	22	"
	H	Rossi Americo	83	laborer	26	
	K	*Rossi Andrew	83	butcher	60	
	L	*Rossi Della—†	83	housewife	66	"

Page.	Letter.	Full Name.	Residence, Jan. 1, 1938.	Occupation.	Supposed Age.	Reported Residence, Jan. 1, 1937. Street and Number.

Leyden Street—Continued

Page.	Letter.	Full Name.	Residence, Jan. 1, 1938.	Occupation.	Supposed Age.	Reported Residence, Jan. 1, 1937. Street and Number.
	M	Rossi Nello	83	butcher	30	here
	N	Caradonna Mary—†	87	housewife	33	"
	O	Caradonna Peter	87	clerk	34	"
	P	Puzo Adeline—†	87	operator	30	
	R	*Puzo Frank	87	attendant	65	"
	S	*Puzo Mary—†	87	housewife	65	"
	T	Puzo Theresa—†	87	clerk	21	
	U	Alessandroni Aldo	87	operator	22	"
	V	Alessandroni Maria—†	87	housewife	49	"
	W	Alessandroni Nora—†	87	operator	23	"
	X	Alessandroni Salvatore	87	shoemaker	49	"
	Y	*Fiorentino Giuseppe	88	retired	77	
	Z	Fiorentino Grace—†	88	housewife	70	"
1787	A	*Saisi Ella—†	88	"	28	136 Leyden
	B	*Saisi Orlando	88	manager	30	136 "
	C	*Morganti Georgia—†	88	housewife	51	53 "
	D	Morganti Raffaello	88	salesman	53	53 "
	E	*Morganti Vincenzina—†	88	at home	26	53 "
	F	Murphy Caroline G—†	91	housewife	45	here
	G	Murphy James H	91	electrician	50	"
	H	Murphy Pauline—†	91	dressmaker	21	"
	K	Bourque Edmund F	91	machinist	33	"
	L	Bourque Yvette—†	91	housewife	24	"
	M	*LoConte Elvira—†	96	"	43	
	N	*LoConte Joseph	96	storekeeper	43	"
	O	Carideo Carmella M—†	96	at home	28	"
	P	Carideo Theresa—†	96	housewife	69	"
	R	Gaetini Frank	96	barber	37	
	S	Gaetini Margaret—†	96	housewife	35	"
	T	Massucco Alma—†	100	seamstress	22	"
	U	Massucco Domenic	100	retired	64	
	V	Massucco Susan—†	100	housewife	57	"
	W	Pochini Albert	100	clerk	23	
	X	Pochini Michael	100	waiter	63	
	Y	Martuccio Anthony	101	laborer	25	
	Z	*Martuccio John	101	"	56	
1788	A	*Martuccio Mary—†	101	housewife	52	"
	B	Martuccio William	101	salesman	22	"
	C	Mazzarella Albert	101	laborer	20	

Page.	Letter.	Full Name.	Residence, Jan. 1, 1938.	Occupation.	Supposed Age.	Reported Residence, Jan. 1, 1937. Street and Number.

Leyden Street—Continued

	D	Mazzarella Ernest	101	laborer	22	here
	E	Mazzarella Leonard	101	"	34	"
	F	Mazzarella Mary—†	101	stitcher	26	"
	G	Mazzarella Philomena—†	101	housewife	58	"
	H	Marotta Anthony	101	counterman	34	"
	K	Marotta Lena—†	101	housewife	31	"
	L	Mazzarella Margaret—†	101	"	26	
	M	Mazzarella Orlando	101	counterman	32	"
	N	Faiella Jennie—†	103	housewife	23	88 Faywood av
	O	Faiella Joseph	103	salesman	26	88 "
	P	Gilardi Adeline—†	103	housewife	23	here
	R	Gilardi Frank	103	fisherman	26	"
	S	Cipoletta Palmina—†	105	housewife	24	"
	T	Cipoletta William	105	chauffeur	26	"
	U	*Sozio Angelo	105	retired	61	
	V	Sozio Guy	105	printer	25	
	W	*Sozio Josephine—†	105	housewife	55	"
	X	Sozio Mario	105	operator	29	"
	Y	Sozio Pasquale	105	chauffeur	27	"
	Z	Rosatto Frank	115	machinist	21	"
1789						
	A	Rosatto John	115	operator	22	
	B	Rosatto Luigi	115	fireman	54	
	C	*Rosatto Maria—†	115	housewife	41	"
	D	Church Agnes—†	115	clerk	27	
	E	Church Mary—†	115	saleswoman	52	"
	F	Fatta Deogratis	125	clergyman	61	"
	G	Toma Louis	125	"	53	
	H	Maestri Edmund	126	operator	26	"
	K	Maestri Faust P	126	upholsterer	27	"
	L	*Maestri Luigi	126	tailor	62	
	M	Maestri Max	126	mechanic	31	"
	N	Maestri Rose—†	126	operator	23	"
	O	Maestri Samuel	126	"	29	
	P	*Maestri Vita—†	126	housewife	58	"
	R	*Filippini Emily—†	126	"	35	
	S	*Filippini Pasquale	126	laborer	46	"
	T	*Frederick Rita—†	128	housewife	65	"
	U	Frederick Vito	128	tailor	75	
	V	*Nonni Carmella—†	129	housewife	43	"
	W	Nonni Jeremiah	129	janitor	25	

Page.	Letter.	Full Name.	Residence, Jan. 1, 1938.	Occupation.	Supposed Age.	Reported Residence, Jan. 1, 1937. Street and Number.
		Leyden Street—Continued				
	X	LaRosa Esther—†	129	housewife	25	here
	Y	LaRosa John	129	laborer	29	"
	Z	DeMarco Antonio	131	"	40	"
1790						
	A	DeMarco Elizabeth—†	131	housewife	38	"
	B	Garroni Charles	131	laborer	21	
	C	*Garroni Pasquale	131	waiter	55	
	D	Garroni Rose—†	131	clerk	24	
	E	*Garroni Victoria—†	131	housewife	42	"
	F	Gaeta Anna—†	131	"	22	
	G	Gaeta Jeremiah	131	machinist	28	"
	H	Curti Constantino	135	painter	58	
	K	Curti Edward	135	laborer	25	
	L	Curti Marion—†	135	housewife	60	"
	M	Curti Victor	135	at home	20	"
	N	Velardo John B	135	laborer	27	130 Princeton
	O	Velardo Mae—†	135	housewife	26	130 "
	P	Colantuoni Alfredo	136	laborer	42	here
	R	*Colantuoni Jennie—†	136	housewife	40	"
	S	Cariani Eleanor—†	136	"	45	150 Leyden
	T	Cariani Walter	136	bartender	44	150 "
	U	Merola Anna—†	136	housewife	34	here
	V	Merola Gerardo	136	laborer	44	"
	W	Baldassaro Bernard	137	"	30	"
	X	Baldassaro Esther—†	137	housewife	28	"
	Y	Gleason Walter	137	laborer	36	
	Z	Pallazo Margaret—†	137	stitcher	25	
1791						
	A	Allegra Joseph	137	barber	37	
	B	Allegra Josephine—†	137	housewife	33	"
	C	*Allegra Madeline—†	137	"	58	
	D	Allegra Stephen	137	mechanic	34	"
	E	Ferrara John	139	chauffeur	26	"
	F	Ferrara Mildred—†	139	housewife	23	"
	G	DiGregorio Joseph	139	chauffeur	39	"
	H	DiGregorio Theresa—†	139	housewife	34	"
	K	Sullivan Emily—†	140	"	30	
	L	Sullivan James	140	laborer	30	
	M	Ciampa Eugene	140	salesman	27	"
	N	*Ciampa Felix	140	laborer	70	

Page.	Letter.	FULL NAME.	Residence, Jan. 1, 1938.	Occupation.	Supposed Age.	Reported Residence, Jan. 1, 1937. Street and Number.

Leyden Street—Continued

	O	Ciampa Bella—†	142	housewife	27	13 Willard
	P	Ciampa Frank A	142	artist	29	13 "

Montmorenci Avenue

	S	DiSessa Peter A	2	policeman	40	189 Wordsworth
	T	DiSessa Theresa—†	2	housewife	37	here
	U	Turpin Mabel F—†	4	"	25	"
	V	Turpin Richard J	4	engineer	27	"
	X	Foster Martha K—†	12	housekeeper	60	"
	Y	Paterson Julia O—†	16	housewife	33	"
	Z	Paterson Thomas C	16	manager	37	"
1792						
	A	Bonner Catherine—†	24	housewife	71	"
	B	Bonner Joseph H	24	retired	75	
	C	Carroll Catherine A—†	32	housewife	27	"
	D	Carroll William J, jr	32	chauffeur	27	"
	E	Rawson Anna M—†	32	housewife	51	"
	E[1]	Rawson Robert J	32	clerk	22	
	F	Rawson Thomas R	32	teacher	55	
	G	Rawson Thomas R, jr	32	clerk	29	
	H	Kelly Josephine D—†	43	housewife	39	"
	K	Kelly William J	43	B F D	41	
	L	Mahoney Alice J—†	51	stenographer	30	"
	M	Mahoney Catherine L—†	51	housewife	58	"
	N	Mahoney G Frank	51	retired	60	
	O	Mahoney Helen V—†	51	teacher	25	
	P	Bradley Annette F—†	63	stenographer	21	"
	R	Bradley Hugh H	63	salesman	42	"
	S	Bradley John P	63	clerk	20	
	T	Bradley Mildred C—†	63	housewife	42	"

Orient Avenue

	U	Donatelli Jennie—†	162	housewife	38	here
	V	Donatelli Joseph	162	repairman	42	"
	W	*Donatelli Assunta—†	164	housewife	40	"
	X	*Donatelli Augusto	164	tailor	39	
	Y	Addison Catherine—†	166	at home	85	
	Z	Watson Mary G—†	166	housewife	61	"

Page.	Letter.	Full Name.	Residence, Jan. 1, 1938.	Occupation.	Supposed Age.	Reported Residence, Jan. 1, 1937. Street and Number.

1793

Orient Avenue—Continued

	A	Watson Rudolph F	166	retired	62	here
	B	*Viscione Annie—†	169	housewife	46	"
	C	Viscione Charles	169	operator	21	"
	D	Viscione Frank	169	"	21	
	E	Viscione Ralph	169	"	49	
	F	Paterson Charles E	170	manufacturer	68	"
	G	Paterson Ella—†	170	housewife	73	"
	H	Walters Dorothy D—†	170	housekeeper	56	Needham
	K	DiSessa Louis	176	policeman	44	here
	L	DiSessa Mary F—†	176	housewife	42	"
	M	DiSessa Peter E	176	laborer	21	"
	N	Lagna Joseph	176	"	24	14 St Edward rd
	O	Lagna Mary—†	176	housewife	24	here
	P	DeStefano Anthony	190	contractor	38	"
	R	DeStefano Catherine—†	190	housewife	38	"
	S	MacLeod Alexander	191	janitor	30	"
	T	MacLeod Rosalie—†	191	housewife	28	"
	U	Walsh Ella M—†	191	"	60	
	V	Walsh Peter S	191	laundryman	60	"
	W	Angelucci Assunto	198	laborer	43	
	X	Angelucci Mary—†	198	housewife	38	"
	Y	Sonego Elmira—†	198	"	31	9 Breed
	Z	Sonego Sante	198	laborer	34	9 "
1794						
	A	*Belli Angelina—†	205	housewife	45	here
	B	Belli Gino	205	machinist	21	"
	C	Belli Luigi	205	engineer	51	"
	D	Carbone Dora—†	216	agent	25	40 Gladstone
	E	*Carbone Judith—†	216	housewife	54	40 "
	F	Carbone Olga—†	216	agent	25	40 "
	G	Carbone Vito	216	superintendent	54	40 "
	H	Palladino Frederick	216	druggist	44	40 "
	K	*Palladino Louise—†	232	housewife	32	here
	L	Palladino Rocco	232	restaurateur	32	"
	M	McNeill Beatrice M—†	236	housewife	46	"
	N	McNeill Charles M	236	policeman	52	"
	O	McNeill Harriet H—†	236	housewife	79	"
	P	McNeill Hazel W—†	236	nurse	24	
	R	Federico Angelina—†	240	housewife	39	"
	S	Federico Paul	240	laborer	47	

Page.	Letter.	FULL NAME.	Residence, Jan. 1, 1938.	Occupation.	Supposed Age.	Reported Residence, Jan. 1, 1937. Street and Number.

Orient Avenue—Continued

	T	Bumpus Sarah A—†	244	housewife	32	here
	U	Bumpus Warren E	244	teacher	37	"
	V	Hochmuth Eva A—†	248	housewife	44	"
	W	Hochmuth Francis W	248	student	22	
	X	Hochmuth William W	248	superintendent	46	"
	Y	Carresi John	251	salesman	37	"
	Z	Carresi Rose—†	251	housewife	36	"
1795						
	A	Caponigro Margaret—†	252	housekeeper	20	"
	B	Tobia Elvira—†	252	housewife	28	"
	C	Tobia Fred	252	salesman	35	"
	D	Shafer Edward	255	operator	28	"
	E	Shafer Henry W	255	retired	80	
	F	Shafer Henry W, jr	255	B F D	47	
	G	Shafer Ruth—†	255	housewife	29	"

Saratoga Street

	H	Jackson Gaynell M—†	865	at home	50	here
	K	Spano Pasquale	865	laborer	42	"
	L	*Santangelo Anna—†	869	housewife	48	"
	M	Santangelo Charles	869	laborer	25	
	N	*Santangelo Joseph	869	"	49	
	O	Santangelo Lucy—†	869	operator	21	"
	P	Sacco Florence—†	871	stitcher	22	
	R	Sacco John	871	manufacturer	23	"
	S	*Sacco Louise—†	871	housewife	47	"
	T	*Sacco Sabato	871	foreman	48	
	U	DeSimone Carlo	871	engineer	37	"
	V	Pastore Marciano	871	laborer	46	
	W	*Pastore Rose—†	871	housewife	44	"
	X	Durante Armand	873	laborer	26	
	Y	*Durante Pasqualina—†	873	housewife	54	"
	Z	*Durante Vegiano	873	shoemaker	56	"
1796						
	A	Kinnear Beatrice—†	873	housewife	20	247 Lexington
	B	Kinnear George	873	laborer	26	247 "
	C	White George A	873	chauffeur	23	247 "
	D	Nucci Enis—†	875	packer	25	here
	E	*Nucci Eva—†	875	housewife	53	"
	F	*Nucci Lazzaro	875	laborer	61	"

Page.	Letter.	FULL NAME.	Residence, Jan. 1, 1938.	Occupation.	Supposed Age.	Reported Residence, Jan. 1, 1937. Street and Number.

Saratoga Street—Continued

	G	Nucci Margaret—†	875	at home	21	here
	H	McDonald John	875	painter	38	160 Falcon
	K	*McDonald Margaret—†	875	housewife	37	160 "
	L	Tranchina Ida—†	877	"	31	1 Anthony pl
	M	Tranchina Joseph	877	laborer	35	1 "
	N	Conigliaro Anthony	877	"	51	here
	O	Conigliaro Concetta—†	877	housewife	48	"
	P	Mastronarino Carolina–†	879	"	42	"
	R	Mastronarino Daniel	879	operator	49	"
	S	Mastronarino Mary—†	879	at home	21	
	T	McCormack Catherine—†	879A	housewife	48	"
	U	McCormack Herbert	879A	laborer	50	
	V	Joy James J	897	"	54	
	W	Joy John	897	"	26	
	X	Joy Mary—†	897	operator	23	
	Y	Joy Sarah—†	897	housewife	53	"
	Z	Joy Walter	897	clerk	21	
1797						
	A	Caruso Anthony	898	laborer	25	
	B	Caruso Louise—†	898	operator	26	
	C	Caruso Mary—†	898	housewife	23	"
	D	*Caruso Peter	898	laborer	57	
	E	Fahey Hannah—†	901	housewife	61	"
	F	Fahey Mary C—†	901	operator	28	"
	G	Fahey Thomas M	901	bartender	32	"
	H	Crosby Ann C—†	901	forewoman	43	"
	K	Crosby Catherine F—†	901	clerk	44	
	L	Crosby Martin J	901	chauffeur	35	"
	M	Crosby Mary I—†	901	clerk	39	
	N	Crosby Rose A—†	901	housewife	73	"
	O	Young Anna I—†	901	"	35	
	P	Young Joseph P	901	clerk	40	
	R	Connelly Mary L—†	901	inspector	37	"
	S	Nealon Harold	903	clerk	23	
	T	Nealon Hazel—†	903	housewife	22	"
	U	Thornton George J	903	mechanic	37	"
	V	Thornton Mary M—†	903	housewife	36	"
	W	*DeCicco Alice—†	903	at home	90	409 Chelsea
	X	Pellegrino Frank	903	watchman	50	here
	Y	Pellegrino Joseph	903	clerk	24	"
	Z	Pellegrino Philomena—†	903	housewife	45	"

Page.	Letter.	Full Name.	Residence, Jan. 1, 1938.	Occupation.	Supposed Age.	Reported Residence, Jan. 1, 1937. Street and Number.

1798
Saratoga Street—Continued

	A	Faulkner Grace V—†	905	housewife	28	here
	B	Faulkner Joseph R	905	salesman	37	"
	C	Wessling Helen—†	905	housewife	32	"
	D	Wessling William	905	machinist	36	"
	E	Faulkner George	905	"	65	"
	F	Faulkner George J	905	salesman	41	36 Lenoxdale
	G	Faulkner Mary M—†	905	stenographer	35	here
	H	Osborne Mary—†	907	stitcher	33	"
	K	Osborne William	907	laborer	39	"
	L	Iarusso Mary—†	907	at home	38	
	M	Anderson Arthur	907	electrician	27	"
	N	Anderson Oscar	907	carpenter	47	"
	O	Anderson Victoria—†	907	housewife	47	"
	P	Lagorio Andrew A	911	operator	40	"
	R	Lagorio Margaret—†	911	housewife	35	"
	S	Arrigo Marie—†	911	"	39	
	T	Arrigo Philip M	911	musician	39	"
	U	Morrison Herbert L	911	policeman	47	95 Trenton
	V	Morrison Mildred E—†	911	housewife	37	95 "
	Z	Maggiore Imprimo	951	retired	74	here
1799						
	A	*Maggiore Josephine—†	951	housewife	56	"
	B	Maggiore Mary—†	951	hairdresser	21	"
	C	Cecero Mary—†	951	housewife	30	"
	D	Cecero Nicholas	951	draftsman	32	"
	E	Fronduto Jane—†	951	housewife	25	83 Lubec
	F	Fronduto Vincent	951	serviceman	30	Winthrop
	G	D'Anni John	953	laborer	32	here
	H	D'Anni Mary—†	953	housewife	29	"
	K	Corrado Mark	953	cutter	49	"
	L	Corrado Phyllis—†	953	housewife	43	"
	M	Scaramozzino Angelo	953	operator	28	"
	N	Scaramozzino Celia—†	953	housewife	27	"
	O	Carino George	955	clerk	27	531 Benningt'n
	P	Carino Goldie—†	955	housewife	20	531 "
	R	Crucioli Domenic	955	laborer	45	here
	S	Crucioli Pasqualina—†	955	housewife	35	"
	T	Ginta Joseph	955	barber	43	"
	U	*Ginta Margaret—†	955	housewife	41	"
	V	Margareci Placido	955	operator	44	"

Page.	Letter.	Full Name.	Residence, Jan. 1, 1938.	Occupation.	Supposed Age.	Reported Residence, Jan. 1, 1937. Street and Number.

Saratoga Street—Continued

	W	Tannozzini Ido	957	laborer	52	here
	X	Tannozzini Joseph	957	"	20	"
	Y	*Tannozzini Mabel—†	957	housewife	42	"
	Z	Pennacchini Francis	957	barber	53	"
1800						
	A	Pennacchini Rose—†	957	housewife	45	"
	B	*Iannetti Mary—†	957	"	44	
	C	Iannetti Raymond	957	machinist	21	"
	D	Iannetti Venturino	957	laborer	52	"
	E	McNeil Albert	958	painter	30	245 Everett
	F	McNeil Beatrice—†	958	operator	28	245 "
	G	McNeil Bridget—†	958	housewife	68	245 "
	H	McNeil John A	958	retired	69	245 "
	K	McNeil John E	958	laborer	35	245 "
	L	Kendrick Ellen—†	958	forewoman	37	245 "
	N	Campanaro Anna—†	959	dressmaker	27	here
	O	Campanaro Florence—†	959	"	22	"
	P	Campanaro Gabriel	959	operator	38	"
	R	*Campanaro Pasqualina-†	959	housewife	62	"
	S	Anzalone Mary J—†	959	"	25	
	T	Anzalone Thomas	959	mechanic	35	"
	U	Saverino Anthony	959	chauffeur	29	"
	V	Saverino Margaret—†	959	housewife	24	"
	W	Merghotti John	960	baker	39	
	X	Merghotti Sadie—†	960	housewife	34	"
	Y	*Cosato Mary—†	960	"	41	"
	Z	Cosato Virgino	960	tailor	49	"
1801						
	A	Forlani Frank	961	clerk	22	
	B	*Forlani Mary—†	961	housewife	39	"
	C	*Pino Guy	961	laborer	42	
	D	Pino Mary—†	961	housewife	35	"
	E	*Arena Anthony	961	retired	75	
	F	Arena Concetta—†	961	clerk	25	
	G	*Pino Mary—†	961	housewife	45	"
	H	*Pino Orazio	961	laborer	51	"
	K	Gerstenheim Frances—†	962	stitcher	28	116 Gladstone
	L	Gerstenheim Henry	962	salesman	25	116 "
	M	Iannaccone Louise—†	963	housewife	24	here
	N	Iannaccone Pellegrino	963	operator	24	"
	O	Alessi Josephine—†	963	housewife	25	"

Page.	Letter.	FULL NAME.	Residence, Jan. 1, 1938.	Occupation.	Supposed Age.	Reported Residence, Jan. 1, 1937. Street and Number.

Saratoga Street—Continued

	P	Alessi Vico	963	laborer	34	here
	R	Panaro Concenzio	963	"	55	"
	S	Panaro Edith—†	963	clerk	21	"
	T	Panaro Olga—†	963	"	23	
	U	Panaro Olivia—†	963	housewife	56	"
	V	Ciampa Eleanor—†	965	"	24	108 Orleans
	W	Ciampa Joseph	965	laborer	27	108 "
	X	DiLegani John	965	barber	45	here
	Y	Sgroi Joseph	965	salesman	45	42 Breed
	Z	Sgroi Josephine—†	965	housewife	63	42 "
1802						
	A	Mazzapica Annie—†	965	"	42	here
	B	Mazzapica Charles	965	barber	45	"
	C	Mazzapica Phyllis—†	965	at home	20	"
	D	*Fiorentino Michael	967	baker	55	
	E	Sacco Carmella—†	967	stenographer	24	"
	F	Sacco John	967	barber	50	"
	G	Sacco John, jr	967	student	23	
	H	Sacco Raffaella—†	967	housewife	42	"
	K	Mazzarella Constance—†	967	"	25	79 Webster
	L	Mazzarella Frank	967	operator	30	79 "
	M	McGeney Alfred J	968	laborer	55	here
	N	McGeney Mary S—†	968	housewife	54	"
	O	Covitz Hyman	968	contractor	25	"
	P	Fooks Abraham	968	"	48	
	R	Fooks Gertrude—†	968	housewife	49	"
	S	McGrath Catherine—†	968	"	53	653 Saratoga
	T	McGrath James	968	laborer	22	653 "
	U	McGrath John	968	"	26	653 "
	V	McGrath Nicholas	968	usher	20	653 "
	X	Magee Francis J	971	student	24	142 St Andrew rd
	Y	Magee Paul C	971	brewer	21	142 "
	Z	Caggiano Ernest	971	embalmer	39	here
1803						
	A	Caggiano Grace—†	971	housewife	36	"
	B	*Velardi Guiseppe	971	retired	87	
	E	Vesce Anthony D	974	treasurer	46	"
	F	Vesce Clara C—†	974	housewife	36	563 Saratoga
	G	Vesce Frank	974	retired	77	here
	H	Cianci Dorothy—†	974	housewife	36	"
	K	Cianci William	974	musician	37	"

Page.	Letter.	Full Name.	Residence, Jan. 1, 1938.	Occupation.	Supposed Age.	Reported Residence, Jan. 1, 1937. Street and Number.

Saratoga Street—Continued

Page.	Letter.	Full Name.	Residence, Jan. 1, 1938.	Occupation.	Supposed Age.	Reported Residence, Jan. 1, 1937. Street and Number.
	L	Maniglia Alphonse	974	barber	25	here
	M	Maniglia Diega—†	974	housewife	21	"
	N	DeStefano Etta A—†	974	stenographer	28	"
	O	*DeStefano Josephine—†	974	housewife	65	"
	P	DeStefano Lillian M—†	974	at home	30	
	R	Wightman Grace—†	974	"	31	..
	S	Berry Carmella—†	974	housewife	27	"
	T	*Berry Lawrence	974	chauffeur	31	"
	U	Delano Alice B—†	974	housewife	49	"
	V	Delano William L	974	bartender	50	"
1804						
	C	Cavagnaro Rose—†	980	housekeeper	55	"
	D	Niutta Peter	980	barber	49	..
	E	DePino Grace—†	980	housewife	62	"
	F	DePino Leo	980	chauffeur	24	"
	G	DePino Mary—†	980	at home	20	
	H	DePino Nicholas	980	upholsterer	26	"
	L	*Cergua Angelina—†	984	housewife	34	"
	M	Cergua Anthony	984	laborer	49	
	N	DePalma Mary—†	984	packer	22	
	O	*DePalma Nancy—†	984	housewife	50	"
	P	DePalma Nicholas	984	laborer	25	..
	R	*Cassello Frank	984	coppersmith	60	"
	S	*DeAngelis Catherine—†	984	housewife	67	Everett
	T	DeAngelis Eleanor—†	984	at home	26	"
	U	DeAngelis Nafaldo	984	laborer	24	"
	V	*DeAngelis Sabino	984	retired	79	"
	W	*Ferri Creside—†	986	housewife	46	here
	X	Ferri Myra—†	986	clerk	25	"
	Y	Capillo Charles	986	laborer	49	"
	Z	Capillo Esther—†	986	at home	27	
1805						
	A	Capillo Ethel—†	986	housewife	47	"
	B	Coelho Ruth M—†	986	"	37	
	C	Collins Joseph	986	laborer	41	
	D	Stewart James	986	retired	77	

Tower Street

Page.	Letter.	Full Name.	Residence, Jan. 1, 1938.	Occupation.	Supposed Age.	Reported Residence, Jan. 1, 1937. Street and Number.
	E	Cotter Margaret M—†	20	housewife	42	here
	F	Cotter William J	20	porter	48	"

Trident Street

Page.	Letter.	Full Name.	Residence, Jan. 1, 1938.	Occupation.	Supposed Age.	Reported Residence, Jan. 1, 1937. Street and Number.
	G	Giordano Lucy—†	16	housewife	39	here
	H	Giordano Pasquale	16	chauffeur	47	"

Whitby Street

Page.	Letter.	Full Name.	Residence, Jan. 1, 1938.	Occupation.	Supposed Age.	Reported Residence, Jan. 1, 1937. Street and Number.
	K	Famolare Charles I	9	chauffeur	37	here
	L	Famolare James	9	"	28	"
	M	Famolare Joseph	9	retired	66	"
	N	Famolare Josephine—†	9	housewife	63	"
	O	Famolare Salvatore	9	chauffeur	24	"
	P	Famolare Stephen	9	"	30	
	R	Famolare Domenic	9	watchman	36	"
	S	*Famolare Elena—†	9	housewife	38	"
	T	DiMella Angelina—†	9	"	44	
	U	DiMella Domenic	9	tailor	48	
	V	DiMella Louise—†	9	clerk	23	
	X	DeFrancesco Andrew	10	salesman	20	"
	Y	DeFrancesco Angelina—†	10	housewife	43	"
	Z	DeFrancesco John	10	operator	49	
1806						
	A	DeFrancesco Rose—†	10	"	22	
	B	Covino Carmello	10	chauffeur	20	"
	C	Covino Sarah—†	10	housewife	41	"
	D	Schipelliti Jennie—†	12	"	27	"
	E	Schipelliti Vincent	12	operator	31	Cambridge
	F	Bartolo Lena—†	12	housewife	38	here
	G	Bartolo Louis	12	barber	40	"
	H	Famolare Angelina—†	12	housewife	53	"
	K	Famolare John	12	storekeeper	57	"
	L	Famolare Louis	12	laborer	28	"
	M	Bonugli Mary—†	16	housekeeper	43	"
	N	Bonugli Rose—†	16	at home	80	"
	O	Ratto Emma—†	16	housewife	39	12 Whitby
	P	Ratto Joseph	16	clerk	43	12 "
	R	*Luti Alexander	16	dealer	54	here
	S	*Luti Annie—†	16	housewife	50	"
	T	Luti Charles	16	laborer	29	"
	U	Luti Christina—†	16	stitcher	30	
	V	Luti Frank	16	operator	22	
	W	*Carrideo Carmen	21	brakeman	60	"
	X	*Carrideo Carolina—†	21	housewife	54	"

Page.	Letter.	Full Name.	Residence, Jan. 1, 1938.	Occupation.	Supposed Age.	Reported Residence, Jan. 1, 1937. Street and Number.

Whitby Street—Continued

	Y	Carrideo Frank	21	laborer	25	here
	Z	Carrideo John	21	"	28	"
1807						
	A	Carrideo Josephine—†	21	cleaner	20	"
	B	Carrideo Lillian—†	21	operator	23	"
	C	Carrideo Irene—†	21	housewife	35	"
	D	Carrideo Patrick	21	bookkeeper	36	"

Lightning Source UK Ltd.
Milton Keynes UK
UKHW012222210119
335963UK00009B/262/P